11. Format for Bank Reconciliation:

Cash balance according to bank statement		$xxx
Add: Additions by depositor not on bank statement	$xx	
Bank errors	xx	xx
		$xxx
Deduct: Deductions by depositor not on bank statement	$xx	
Bank errors	xx	xx
Adjusted balance..		$xxx
Cash balance according to depositor's records		$xxx
Add: Additions by bank not recorded by depositor..	$xx	
Depositor errors.....................................	xx	xx
		$xxx
Deduct: Deductions by bank not recorded by depositor	$xx	
Depositor errors.....................................	xx	xx
Adjusted balance..		$xxx

12. Inventory Costing Methods:

1. First-in, First-out (fifo)
2. Last-in, First-out (lifo)
3. Average Cost

13. Interest Computations:

$$\text{Interest} = \text{Face Amount (or Principal)} \times \text{Rate} \times \text{Time}$$

14. Methods of Determining Annual Depreciation:

STRAIGHT-LINE: $\dfrac{\text{Cost} - \text{Estimated Residual Value}}{\text{Estimated Life}}$

DECLINING-BALANCE: Rate* × Book Value at Beginning of Period

*Rate is commonly twice the straight-line rate (1 ÷ Estimated Life).

15. Cash Provided by Operations on Statement of Cash Flows (indirect method):

Net income, per income statement		$xx
Add: Depreciation of fixed assets	$xx	
Amortization of bond payable discount and intangible assets	xx	
Decreases in current assets (receivables, inventories, prepaid expenses)................	xx	
Increases in current liabilities (accounts and notes payable, accrued liabilities)	xx	
Losses on disposal of assets and retirement of debt	xx	xx
Deduct: Amortization of bond payable premium......	$xx	
Increases in current assets (receivables, inventories, prepaid expenses)................	xx	
Decreases in current liabilities (accounts and notes payable, accrued liabilities)	xx	
Gains on disposal of assets and retirement of debt	xx	xx
Net cash flow from operating activities...................		$xx

16. Contribution Margin Ratio = $\dfrac{\text{Sales} - \text{Variable Costs}}{\text{Sales}}$

17. Break-Even Sales (Units) = $\dfrac{\text{Fixed Costs}}{\text{Unit Contribution Margin}}$

18. Sales (Units) = $\dfrac{\text{Fixed Costs} + \text{Target Profit}}{\text{Unit Contribution Margin}}$

19. Margin of Safety = $\dfrac{\text{Sales} - \text{Sales at Break-Even Point}}{\text{Sales}}$

20. Operating Leverage = $\dfrac{\text{Contribution Margin}}{\text{Income from Operations}}$

21. Variances

$$\text{Direct Materials Price Variance} = \frac{\text{Actual Price per Unit} - }{\text{Standard Price}} \times \frac{\text{Actual Quantity}}{\text{Used}}$$

$$\text{Direct Materials Quantity Variance} = \frac{\text{Actual Quantity Used} - }{\text{Standard Quantity}} \times \frac{\text{Standard Price}}{\text{per Unit}}$$

$$\text{Direct Labor Rate Variance} = \frac{\text{Actual Rate per Hour} - }{\text{Standard Rate}} \times \frac{\text{Actual Hours}}{\text{Worked}}$$

$$\text{Direct Labor Time Variance} = \frac{\text{Actual Hours Worked} - }{\text{Standard Hours}} \times \frac{\text{Standard Rate}}{\text{per Hour}}$$

$$\text{Variable Factory Overhead Controllable Variance} = \frac{\text{Actual Variable Factory Overhead}}{} - \frac{\text{Budgeted Variable Factory Overhead for Actual Amount Produced}}{}$$

$$\text{Fixed Factory Overhead Volume Variance} = \frac{\text{100\% of Normal Capacity} - \text{Std. Capacity for Amount Produced}}{} \times \frac{\text{Std. Fixed Factory Overhead Rate}}{}$$

22. Rate of Return on Investment (ROI) = $\dfrac{\text{Income from Operations}}{\text{Invested Assets}}$

Alternative ROI Computation:

$$\text{ROI} = \frac{\text{Income from Operations}}{\text{Sales}} \times \frac{\text{Sales}}{\text{Invested Assets}}$$

23. Capital Investment Analysis Methods:

1. Methods That Ignore Present Values:
   A. Average Rate of Return Method
   B. Cash Payback Method
2. Methods That Use Present Values:
   A. Net Present Value Method
   B. Internal Rate of Return Method

24. Average Rate of Return = $\dfrac{\text{Estimated Average Annual Income}}{\text{Average Investment}}$

25. Present Value Index = $\dfrac{\text{Total Present Value of Net Cash Flow}}{\text{Amount to Be Invested}}$

26. Present Value Factor for an Annuity of $1 = $\dfrac{\text{Amount to Be Invested}}{\text{Equal Annual Net Cash Flows}}$

11,000,000 successful results. This edition appears nearly 75 years after the first edition of the text from which it is derived, *Accounting*, was published in 1929. Yet this is the text that takes accounting into the 21st century – and not in spite of tradition, but *because* of it. For if *Financial Accounting* and *Accounting* have a tradition, it can be summarized as innovation that produces results. Over 11 million students have been introduced to accounting via this family of texts. And that's a tradition you can build on.

Starting Fresh

Preparing a new edition of a classic text takes an army of colleagues. A simple acknowledgments section alone is not enough – so we salute the people who continue to make this family of texts the most widely used textbooks for accounting principles.

Users of the 7th edition provided valuable classroom feedback. Focus groups and questionnaire respondents shared their personal insights. And dozens of reviewers kept us on track during the revision of this edition. We took these comments very seriously, and the text is stronger because of them.

But that's only part of the reason that this is the text of choice. The companies we profile have grown and changed over time, and so has *Financial Accounting*. This evolution has been organized by a long list of distinguished authors, editors, and reviewers, all making unique and invaluable contributions whose echoes can still be heard today.

Looking Forward

Back in 1929, author James McKinsey could not have imagined the success and influence this family of texts has enjoyed, or that his original vision would remain intact. As the current authors, we appreciate the responsibility of protecting this vision, while continuing to shape it to meet the needs of students and instructors. We sincerely thank our many colleagues who have helped to make it happen.

> *"The teaching of accounting is no longer designed to train professional accountants only. With the growing complexity of business and the constantly increasing difficulty of the problems of management, it has become essential that everyone who aspires to a position of responsibility should have a knowledge of the fundamental principles of accounting."*
>
> – James O. McKinsey,
> author, first edition, 1929

The Business of Business is Accounting

Financial Accounting 8e focuses squarely on the business of business – how accounting contributes to effective management while emphasizing the most important accounting procedures. Why? Because it's a simple fact that 80% of accounting courses are filled with non-accounting majors. So we've designed *Financial Accounting 8e* to speak to *anyone* who takes an introductory accounting course:

■ **Ch 1 Introduction to Accounting and Business.** This chapter begins with a section that defines business and describes common types of businesses, forms of organization, and the diverse interests of a business's stakeholders.

Type of Adjustment	Adjusting Entry	Effect of Omitting Adjusting Entry on the Balance Sheet and Income Statement
Deferred expense	Dr. Expense	Expenses Understated and Net Income Overstated
	Cr. Asset	Assets Overstated and Owner's Equity Overstated
Deferred revenue	Dr. Liability	Liabilities Overstated and Owner's Equity Understated
	Cr. Revenue	Revenues Understated and Net Income Understated
Accrued expense	Dr. Expense	Expenses Understated and Net Income Overstated
	Cr. Liability	Liabilities Understated and Owner's Equity Overstated
Accrued revenue	Dr. Asset	Assets Understated and Owner's Equity Understated
	Cr. Revenue	Revenues Understated and Net Income Understated
Fixed assets	Dr. Expense	Expenses Understated and Net Income Overstated
	Cr. Contra Asset	Assets Overstated and Owner's Equity Overstated

■ **Ch 3 The Matching Concept and the Adjusting Process.** A table summarizes each type of adjustment, adjusting entry, and the financial statement effect of omitting an adjusting entry. The discussion of adjustments ends with the adjusted trial balance.

■ **Ch 4 Completing the Accounting Cycle.** The work sheet is introduced in this chapter. Lines on the work sheet illustrations are numbered to assist you in your classroom presentation.

■ **Ch 5 Accounting Systems and Internal Controls.** An illustration of the revenue and collection cycle in a computerized accounting system, using QuickBooks®, is included.

■ **Ch 6 Accounting for Merchandising Businesses.** The discussion of perpetual inventory systems gives students a clear understanding of inventory accounting by drawing connections to buying groceries or fast food meals.

■ **Ch 8 Receivables.** The discussion of discounting notes receivable is in a chapter appendix.

■ **Ch 9 Inventories.** The concept of inventory cost flows is introduced without reference to the perpetual or periodic systems. The journal entries in a perpetual system are presented alongside the inventory subsidiary ledger to illustrate the FIFO and LIFO flow of costs.

■ **Ch 10 Fixed Assets and Intangible Assets.** Gains and losses on exchanges of fixed assets are discussed only from a GAAP viewpoint.

■ **Ch 13 Corporations: Income and Taxes, Stockholders' Equity, and Investments in Stocks.** A section on reporting stockholders' equity is included. A section covering short-term investments in stocks is included at the end of the chapter.

■ **Appendixes** on **Foreign Currency Transactions** and **Partnerships** are at the end of the text.

Features That Speak to Students

The design is as colorful and dynamic as the text, which is broken into conceptual segments designed to help students make the connection between accounting and business:

Setting the Stage. The beginning of each chapter connects the student's own experiences to the chapter's topic. This tangible link is a great motivator.

Business on Stage. This brief presentation of a business concept introduces accounting functions in a business context.

Encore. Did it work? Each chapter ends with a quick, fascinating story about a real business that succeeded or failed because it chose to observe or ignore the chapter's principle.

Other features that keep students on track and motivated:

Questions & Answers in the margin of the text help students check whether they understand what they've just read.

 Points of Interest. These margin notes offer insight into subjects of special interest to students, such as careers and current events.

Summaries within each chapter bring special attention to important points.

Business Transactions. In Chapters 1 and 2, students are introduced to business transactions through non-business events that help them better understand the nature of transactions.

Real World Notes. J.C. Penney Co. and General Electric are just a couple of the familiar examples that provide a close-up look at how accounting operates in the marketplace.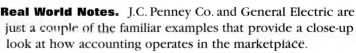
These examples are highlighted in the margin of the text:

AT&T	*Gillette*
Campbell Soup Company	*Hewlett Packard*
Coca-Cola Enterprises Inc.	*Mercedes-Benz*
Delta Air Lines	*UPS*
Ford Motor Co.	

Financial Analysis and Interpretation. At the end of each chapter, a section describes an important element of financial analysis to help students understand the information in financial statements and how that information is used.

Taking Lessons Into Life

Procedures are important, but it takes much more to make a successful transition into the business world. This edition gives students the special tools they will need to thrive in the real world:

- **Critical-Thinking and Decision-Making Activities.** Students need to develop analytical abilities, not just memorize rules. These activities focus on understanding and solving issues. Some are presented as dialogues – a conversation in which students can "observe" and "participate" when they respond to the issue being discussed.

  - **Group Learning Activities** let students learn accounting and business concepts while building teamwork skills.

  - **Internet Activities** launch students into accounting-related areas of the Worldwide Web's ever-expanding universe.

  - **"What Do You Think?"** These exercises and activities let students speculate about the real-world effects of newly learned material.

  - **"What's Wrong With This?"** These innovative exercises challenge students to analyze and discover what is wrong with a financial statement, a report, or a management decision.

- **Communications Items.** These activities help students develop communication skills that will be essential on the job, regardless of the fields they pursue.

Accounting must be practiced to be understood and retained. The quantity and quality of these end-of-chapter resources have always been distinguishing characteristics of *Financial Accounting*:

- **Continuing Problem in Chs. 1-4.** Here's a great opportunity for students to practice what they've learned – and now they can use the General Ledger Software with this problem. As they study each step of the accounting cycle, students can follow a single company – *Dancin Music* – from its transactions to the effect of those transactions on its financial statements.

- **Illustrative Problem and Solution.** A solved problem models one or more of a chapter's assignment problems, helping students make the most of the chapter and end-of-chapter materials.

- **Self-Examination Questions** include a matching activity to help students review and retain terms and definitions.

- **Exercises.** An average of 20 exercises at the end of each chapter – more than any other text on the market – can be assigned or used as examples in the classroom. Most of these exercises focus on only one specific chapter objective.

- **Problems.** Each chapter includes two full sets of problems for use as classroom illustrations, for assignments, for alternate assignments, or for independent studying. This edition features shortened problems to provide better focus on key chapter topics.

■ **Comprehensive Problems.** At the end of Chs. 4, 6, 11, and 14, cumulative learning applications integrate and summarize the concepts of several chapters to test students' comprehension.

New Tools to Get the Job Done Right

We've designed our entire supplement package around the comments instructors have provided about their courses and teaching needs. These comments have made this supplement package the best in the business.

Available to Students – Because each student has different needs, *Financial Accounting 8e* offers a broad range of supplements. Both print material and easy-to-use, affordable technologies help students succeed in the course and in the business world. Some of these supplements are:

■ **Working Papers.** The traditional Working Papers are available both with and without problem-specific forms for preparing solutions for all exercises and problems.

■ **Working Papers Plus**, prepared by John Wanlass of DeAnza College. This alternative to traditional working papers integrates the exercises and selected problems from the text with forms for preparing their solutions.

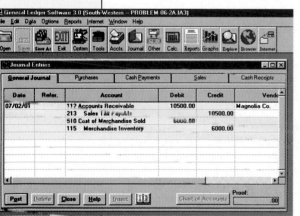

■ **General Ledger Software**, prepared by Dale Klooster and Warren Allen. This best-selling educational general ledger package is enhanced with a problem checker that enables students to determine if their entries are correct. Solving end-of-chapter problems, the continuing problem, and comprehensive problems as well as practice sets is as easy as clicking icons with a mouse.

■ **Spreadsheet Applications Software.** This completely revised software gives students the opportunity to solve dozens of problems by using Excel®.

■ **Study Guide**, prepared by Carl Warren and Jim Reeve. The Study Guide includes quiz and test tips and multiple choice, fill-in-the-blank, and true-false questions with solutions.

■ **PROFIT in the Classroom.** Using this award-winning software to solve specific problems in the textbook helps students get a firm grasp of debits and credits and the principles related to basic transactions for accounts receivable and payable, inventory, and payroll.

■ **WebTutor Advantage on WebCT** and **WebTutor Advantage on Blackboard** give students access to study resources and interactive experiences beyond the classroom. Special resources for instructors include powerful communication and other course management tools.

■ **Personal WebTutor Advantage.** This product includes a wealth of content, including PowerPoint, review problems with audio, automatically-scored quizzes, exercises, and terminology reinforcement.

■ **Personal Trainer.** This innovative Internet-based tutorial gives students hints as they solve exercises from the text and allows them to track their progress.

■ **WebTutor on WebCT** and **WebTutor on Blackboard** provide interactive reinforcement to help students grasp complex concepts.

■ **Product Web Site.** At the text's Web site, students have free access to additional quizzes, drills, e-lectures, Excel application templates, review problems, and many other study resources.

Available to Instructors – South-Western Publishing continues to lead the field in supplements for instructors, from traditional printed materials to the latest integrated classroom technology. Among these support tools are:

■ **Product Support Site** – A variety of instructor resources are now available through South-Western's password-protected Web site. Text-specific and other related resources are organized by chapter and topic. Many of these resources are also available on CD-ROM.

■ **An Instructor's Guide to Making the Most of Online Resources** is an imaginative resource to help you connect your classroom with *Financial Accounting 8e* and its dynamic spectrum of digital teaching and learning resources.

■ **Videos.** A complete video course is available for distance learning and to help complete a student's onsite classroom experience. A collection of brief **Business in Focus** videos highlight how accounting impacts people and processes in the business world.

■ **PowerPoint™ Presentation**, prepared by Doug Cloud of Pepperdine University. The PowerPoint Presentation enhances lectures and simplifies class preparation. You can also add your own custom slides, using this popular software package.

■ **Instructor's CD-ROM** is a convenient source for the PowerPoint Presentation, Instructor's Manual, Test Bank, ExamView®, and Excel Application Templates and Solutions.

**Warren
Reeve
Fess**

■ **Traditional Ancillaries.** The Solutions Manual and Instructor's Manual are available on South-Western's password-protected Web site, on the instructor's CD-ROM, as well as in separate bound volumes. The Test Bank is also included in the ExamView® Pro Testing Software on the instructor's CD-ROM, as well as in separate bound volumes.

■ The **Instructor's Manual** contains a wide range of writing exercises, group learning activities, demonstration problems, and accounting scenarios.

■ The **Test Bank** includes more than 2,800 true/false questions, multiple choice questions, and problems, plus chapter and multi-chapter achievement tests.

■ **ExamView Pro Testing Software** is easy-to-use software that allows you to customize exams, practice tests, and tutorials and deliver them over a network, on the Web, or in printed form.

Warren
Reeve
Fess

Acknowledging the Team of Leaders

A student's first impression of a course is the leader of the classroom – the instructor. Because the textbook plays an important supporting role in the teaching/learning environment, our collaboration with instructors is invaluable. We thank them for their contribution to making *Financial Accounting 8e* a text unsurpassed in quality.

Sheila Ammons
Austin Community College

Tom Badley
Pete Karsten
Nick Kondyles
Bob Vandellan
Baker College

Sheryl Alley
Ball State University

Richard Green
Bay State College

Ken Gustafson
Christopher Mayer
Florence McGovern
Bergen Community College

Laura Altomonte
Frank Paliotta
Berkeley College

Preston Wilks
Big Bend Community College

Bob Holman
Blue River Community College

Stanley Chu
Stanley Solomon
Borough of Manhattan Community College

Randy Glover
Brevard Community College

Clarice McCoy
Dave Weaver
Brookhaven College

Lois Slutsky
Broward Community College

Laurel Berry
Sam Lanzafame
Bryant & Stratton

Ann Rowell
Beverly Terry
Brad Zorn
Central Piedmont Community College

Michael Farina
Cerritos College

Joan Ryan
Clackamas Community College

James Halstead
Clatsop Community College

Bonnie Goodwin
Corinthian Colleges, Inc.

Jerry Holtke
Crafton Hills College

Larry Bender
James Burke
Alan Vogel
Vicki Vorell
Cuyahoga Community College

James Donovan
Deb Kiss
David Medved
Davenport University

Patricia H. Holmes
Cindy Tomes
Des Moines Area Community College

Joyce Barden
Richard Monbrod
Kathy Perdue
Karen Stewart
Devry Institutes

Ron L. Hulstein
Dickinson State University

Terry Mullins
Dyersburg State Community College

Aurora P. Delores
James L. Haydon
East Los Angeles College

Donnie Kristof-Nelson
Edmonds Community College

Shirley Aoto
Phil Knypstra
El Camino College

Rose Garvey
Elizabethtown Community College

W. T. Hall
Fayetteville Technical Community College

Michael Prockton
Finger Lakes Community College

Lynn Clements
Florida Southern College

Joe Chandler
Alice Sineath
Forsyth Technical Community College

Karen Brayden
Front Range Community College

Allen Wash
Gaston College

Christy Kloezeman
Glendale Community College

Leo Chow
Gaspare DiLorenzo
Gloucester County College

Thomas Welsch
Harold Washington College

Robert Held
Harper College

Joni Onishi
Hawaii Community College

Bob Hardin
Bill Harvey
Henry Ford Community College

Irving Mason
Herkimer County Community College

Tesfaye Bireda
Earl McMillan
Linda Overstreet
Margo Rock
Joe Teston
Allen Wright
Hillsborough Community College

Audra Kimble
Holmes Community College

Eugene Cardamone
Hudson Valley Community College

Todd Hansink
Imperial Valley College

John Klett
James Reap
Indian River Community College

Dawn Humburg
Iowa Central Community College

Gene Hale
Iowa Western Community College

Robert Urell
Irvine Valley College

Vicki Greshik
Jamestown College

Kelly Cranford
Jeanette Rogers
Jefferson State Community College

David Moore
Kankakee Community College

Tim Holmeyer
Keller Graduate School

Chuck Cunningham
Jim Crowther
Mary Tharp
Jack Zeller
Kirkwood Community College

Ronald L. Werley
Tom Grant
Kutztown University

Stephen Ahrens
Al Partington
Terry Thomsen
L.A. Pierce College

Douglas Clouse
Janice Ivansek
Ted Latz
Lakeland Community College

Luke Waller
Lindenwood University

Jim Kahl
Lower Columbia College

Sam Dean
David Keys
Macon State College

Georgia Buckles
Patricia Cook
Alexandria Tomany
Manchester Community College

Deborah Bowsher
Marion Technical College

Joe Goodro
Robert Gronstal
David K. Ho
Peg Johnson
Ed Napravnik
Idalene Williams
Eileen Zuerlein
Metro Community College

Ana Cruz
Maria Mari
Ben Sadler
Miami-Dade Community College

Cathy Larson
Middlesex Community College

Eddie Evans
Jean Killey
Janice Stoudemire
Bruce Tallant
Barbara Wagers
Midlands Technical College

Rex Bruington
Elaine Evans
Mississippi University for Women

Naomi Karolinski
Susan Murphy
Renee Rigoni
Jim Rolfe
Mike Ruff
Chris Sardone
Edward Vaneske
Monroe Community College

Gloria M. Halpren
William Johnstone
Richard Lenet
Robert Laycock
Hank Stupi
Montgomery College

Carl Essig
*Montgomery County
Community College*

Tom Barrett
Jim Lentz
*Moraine Valley
Community College*

Fran Haldar
*Northcentral
Technical College*

David Morris
*North Georgia College & State
University*

Stephen Carter
Karen Russom
North Harris College

Joe Carthey
*Northeast Iowa
Community College*

Linda Hischke
*Northeast Wisconsin
Technical College*

Ellen Goldberg
Judy Grant
B. Kheradmand
Marsha Murphy
L. D. Pape
*Northern Virginia
Community College*

Dawn Stevens
*Northwest Mississippi
Community College*

Michael Milstein
Oakton Community College

Christopher Kwak
Carolyn Strickler
Ohlone College

Myra Decker
Connie Nieser
*Oklahoma City
Community College*

Pat Garran
Orlando College North

Phil Reffitt
Orlando College South

Joan Holloway
Patrick McMahon
John Murphy
Joanne Nikides
Gracelyn Stuart
*Palm Beach
Community College*

Tom Joyce
Gary Woods
Pasadena City College

Richard Irvine
Carla Rich
Pensacola Junior College

Charles McCord
Portland Community College

Betty Habershon
*Prince George's
Community College*

Dan Luna
*Raritan Valley
Community College*

Walt DeAguero
Saddleback College

Robert Dan
Hector Martinez
Cathy Sanders
San Antonio College

Janet Courts
San Bernardino Valley College

Jeff Jackson
Bob Perkins
Roy Sanchez
Dan Straut
Randall Whitmore
San Jacinto College

Ken Couvillion
Richard Ghio
Nick Walker
Jack Wiehler
San Joaquin Delta College

Susan Crosson
Santa Fe Community College

Pat Halliday
Teri Bernstein
Santa Monica College

Carol Chiarella
*Schenectady County
Community College*

Donna Chadwick
Mary Beth Govan
Bill Hoover
Jim Putoff
James Shimko
Sinclair Communtiy College

Dianne Bridges
South Plains College

Nap Lucchini
*South Puget Sound
Community College*

David Laurel
*South Texas
Community College*

John Davis
Southern Wesleyan University

Steve Hester
Gloria Worthy
*Southwest Tennessee
Community College*

Don Brunner
Bernie Hill
Jeff Waybright
*Spokane Falls
Community College*

Carlo Muzio
St. John's University

Carolyn Byrd
St. Petersburg Junior College

Charles Heck
Henri Leclerc
Thomas Lohmann
Alphonse Reggiero
Robert Rovegno
*Suffolk County
Community College*

Elliott Kamlet
SUNY - Binghamton

Bill Rose
Tampa College-Brandon

Marilyn Fisher
Tampa College-Lakeland

Jon Baskins
Tampa College-Pinellas

Charles Zaruba
Tampa College-Tampa

Steve Fabian
Technical Careers Institute

Sherry Lenhart
*Terra State Community
College*

Paul Cameron
Texas A & M - Corpus Christi

George Otto
Truman College

Susan Pope
University of Akron

Yvonne Brown
Jill Burnett
Constance Cooper
Tracey Hawkins
Sanford Kahn
University of Cincinnati

Carol Shaver
*University of Louisiana
at Monroe*

Barry Farber
University of Maine

Richard Campbell
University of Rio Grande

Ruby Brogan
James Poythress
Woody Wimmer
*Virginia Western
Community College*

Brenda Hester
*Volunteer State
Community College*

J. Thomas Love
*Walters State
Community College*

David R. Konrath
*Washington State
Community College*

Lana Bone
Randy Castello
Clo Hampton
West Valley College

Debbie Goorbin
*Westchester
Community College*

Jim Cassidy
Kurt Schindler
George Trent
*Wilbur Wright
Community College*

**We also thank the
following students
who participated
in focus groups:**

Sinclair Community College
Mark Dues
Adriana Goldenberg
Lise Pizza
Shinoosh Shafie
Roseann Tracy
Jason Wells

Ball State University
Zach Michler
Corey Mills
Lucinda Nicklay
Sue Ellen Philpot
Nathan VanNatter

Brief Contents

Appendices:

EIGHTH EDITION

Financial Accounting

CARL S. WARREN
Professor of Accounting
University of Georgia, Athens

JAMES M. REEVE
Professor of Accounting
University of Tennessee, Knoxville

PHILIP E. FESS
Professor Emeritus of Accounting
University of Illinois, Champaign-Urbana

SOUTH-WESTERN
™
THOMSON LEARNING

Australia · Canada · Mexico · Singapore · Spain · United Kingdom · United States

FINANCIAL ACCOUNTING, 8e,
by Warren, Reeve, and Fess

Team Director: David L. Shaut
Senior Acquisitions Editor: Sharon Oblinger
Senior Developmental Editor: Ken Martin
Senior Marketing Manager: Dan Silverburg
Production Editor: Mark Sears
Editorial Assistant: Heather Mann
Manufacturing Coordinator: Doug Wilke
Internal Design: Lou Ann Thesing
Cover Design: Paul Neff Design
Cover Illustration: ©2000/Lou Beach
Internal Illustrations: Rob Schuster and GGS Information Services
Photo Research: Feldman & Associates, Inc.
Photo Manager: Cary Benbow
Media Technology Editor: Diane Van Bakel
Media Developmental Editors: Christine Wittmer and Sally Nieman
Media Production Editor: Lora Craver
Production House: Litten Editing and Production, Inc.
Compositor: GGS Information Services, Inc.
Printer: Quebecor World

Printed in the United States of America
2 3 4 5   03 02 01

For more information contact South-Western College Publishing, 5101 Madison Road, Cincinnati, Ohio,
45227 or find us on the Internet at http://www.swcollege.com

For permission to use material from this text or product, contact us by
- **telephone: 1-800-730-2214**
- **fax: 1-800-730-2215**
- **web: http://www.thomsonrights.com**

Library of Congress Cataloging-in-Publication Data
The complete version of the text is catalogued as follows:

Warren, Carl S.
    Accounting / Carl S. Warren, James M. Reeve, Philip E. Fess. —20th ed.
        p. cm.
    Includes index.
    ISBN 0-324-02542-4 (alk. paper)
        1. Accounting.   I. Reeve, James M., 1953-   II. Fess, Philip E.   III. Title.
    HF5635.W266   2001
    657—dc21   00-053141

ISBN: 0-324-02539-4

CARL S. WARREN

Dr. Carl S. Warren is the Arthur Andersen & Co. Alumni Professor of Accounting at the J.M. Tull School of Accounting at the University of Georgia, Athens. Professor Warren received his Ph.D. from Michigan State University in 1973. Dr. Warren's experience in listening to users of his texts sharpens his keen focus on helping students learn. When he is not teaching classes or writing text-books, Dr. Warren enjoys golf, racquetball, and fishing.

JAMES M. REEVE

Dr. James M. Reeve is Professor of Accounting at the University of Tennessee, Knoxville. He received his Ph.D. from Oklahoma State University in 1980. Dr. Reeve is founder of the Cost Management Institute and a member of the Institute for Productivity Through Quality faculty at the University of Tennessee. In addition to his teaching experience, Dr. Reeve brings to this text a wealth of experience consulting on managerial accounting issues with numerous companies, including Procter & Gamble, AMOCO, Rockwell International, Harris Corporation, and Freddie Mac. Dr. Reeve's interests outside the classroom and the business world include golf, skiing, reading, and travel.

PHILIP E. FESS

Dr. Philip E. Fess is the Arthur Andersen & Co. Alumni Professor of Accountancy Emeritus at the University of Illinois, Champaign-Urbana. He received his Ph.D. from the University of Illinois. Dr. Fess has been involved in writing text-books for over twenty-five years, and his knowledge of how to make texts user-friendly is reflected on the pages of this edition. Dr. Fess plays golf and tennis, and he has represented the United States in international tennis competition.

Contents

Photo Credits

Introduction to Accounting and Business

objectives

After studying this chapter, you should be able to:

1 Describe the nature of a business.

2 Describe the role of accounting in business.

3 Describe the importance of business ethics and the basic principles of proper ethical conduct.

4 Describe the profession of accounting.

5 Summarize the development of accounting principles and relate them to practice.

6 State the accounting equation and define each element of the equation.

7 Explain how business transactions can be stated in terms of the resulting changes in the basic elements of the accounting equation.

8 Describe the financial statements of a proprietorship and explain how they interrelate.

9 Use the ratio of liabilities to owner's equity to analyze the ability of a business to withstand poor business conditions.

o you use accounting? Yes, we all use accounting information in one form or another. For example, when you think about buying a car, you use accounting-type information to determine whether you can afford it and whether to lease or buy. Similarly, when you decided to attend college, you considered the costs (the tuition, textbooks, and so on). Most likely, you also considered the benefits (the ability to obtain a higher-paying job or a more desirable job).

Is accounting important to you? Yes, accounting is important in your personal life as well as your career, even though you may not become an accountant. For example, assume that you are the owner/manager of a small Mexican restaurant and are considering opening another restaurant in a neighboring town. Accounting information about the restaurant will be a major factor in your deciding whether to open the new restaurant and the bank's deciding whether to finance the expansion.

Our primary objective in this text is to illustrate basic accounting concepts that will help you to make good personal and business decisions. We begin by discussing what a business is, how it operates, and the role that accounting plays.

Nature of a Business

objective 1

Describe the nature of a business.

You can probably list some examples of companies with which you have recently done business. Your examples might be large companies, such as **Coca-Cola**, **Dell Computer**, or **Amazon.com**. They might be local companies, such as gas stations or grocery stores, or perhaps employers. They might be restaurants, law firms, or medical offices. What do all these examples have in common that identify them as businesses?

In general, a business is an organization in which basic resources (inputs), such as materials and labor, are assembled and processed to provide goods or services (outputs) to customers.[1] Businesses come in all sizes, from a local coffee house to a **DaimlerChrysler**, which sells several billion dollars worth of cars and trucks each year. A business's customers are individuals or other businesses who purchase goods or services in exchange for money or other items of value. In contrast, a church is not a business because those who receive its services are not obligated to pay for them.

The objective of most businesses is to maximize profits. **Profit** is the difference between the amounts received from customers for goods or services provided and the amounts paid for the inputs used to provide the goods or services. Some businesses operate with an objective other than to maximize profits. The objective of such nonprofit businesses is to provide some benefit to society, such as medical research or conservation of natural resources. In other cases, governmental units such as cities operate water works or sewage treatment plants on a nonprofit basis. We will focus in this text on businesses operating to earn a profit. Keep in mind, though, that many of the same concepts and principles apply to nonprofit businesses as well.

Types of Businesses

There are three different types of businesses that are operated for profit: manufacturing, merchandising, and service businesses. Each type of business has unique characteristics.

---

[1] A complete glossary of terms appears at the end of the text.

Manufacturing businesses change basic inputs into products that are sold to individual customers. Examples of manufacturing businesses and some of their products are shown below.

Manufacturing Business	Product
General Motors	Cars, trucks, vans
Intel	Computer chips
Boeing	Jet aircraft
Nike	Athletic shoes and apparel
Coca-Cola	Beverages
Sony	Stereos and televisions

Merchandising businesses also sell products to customers. However, rather than making the products, they purchase them from other businesses (such as manufacturers). In this sense, merchandisers bring products and customers together. Examples of merchandising businesses and some of the products they sell are shown below.

Merchandising Business	Product
Wal-Mart	General merchandise
Toys "R" Us	Toys
Circuit City	Consumer electronics
Lands' End	Apparel
Amazon.com	Internet books, music, video retailer

Service businesses provide services rather than products to customers. Examples of service businesses and the types of services they offer are shown below.

Service Business	Service
Disney	Entertainment
Delta Air Lines	Transportation
Marriott Hotels	Hospitality and lodging
Merrill Lynch	Financial advice
Andersen Consulting	Management consulting

Roughly eight out of every ten workers in the United States are service providers. In the past twenty years, 90% of the new jobs created in the United States have been in service businesses.

Source: Walter Kiechel III, "How We Will Work in the Year 2000," *Fortune* (May 17, 1993), p 46.

BUSINESS ON STAGE

The Factors of Production

Businesses convert basic inputs into goods and services for customers. These inputs are called *factors of production*. The factors of production common to all businesses are natural resources, labor, capital, and entrepreneurs. Natural resources are the basic raw materials, including farmland, forests, and mineral deposits. Labor is the employees who contribute their intellectual and physical efforts to a business. Capital represents the financial resources (money) invested in the business to purchase such items as machinery and buildings. Entrepreneurs are the people who combine natural resources, labor, and capital to produce goods and services.

Let's examine a small pizza restaurant as an example of a business. The pizza ingredients of dough, tomato sauce, sausage, pepperoni, and cheese represent the natural resources that are derived from farming the land. The employees (labor) are the servers, the delivery person, the cash register clerk, and the baker. The money required to purchase the land, building, and equipment is the capital. The owner/manager who began the business and operates it on a daily basis is the entrepreneur. ■

Types of Business Organizations

A business is normally organized as one of three different forms: proprietorship, partnership, or corporation. In the following paragraphs, we briefly describe each form and discuss its advantages and disadvantages.

A proprietorship is owned by one individual. More than 70% of the businesses in the United States are organized as proprietorships. The popularity of this form is due to the ease and the low cost of organizing. The primary disadvantage of proprietorships is that the financial resources available to the business are limited to the individual owner's resources. Small local businesses such as hardware stores, repair shops, laundries, restaurants, and maid services are often organized as proprietorships.

As a business grows and more financial and managerial resources are needed, it may become a partnership. A partnership is owned by two or more individuals. Like proprietorships, small local businesses such as automotive repair shops, music stores, beauty salons, and clothing stores may be organized as partnerships. Currently, about 10% of the businesses in the United States are organized as partnerships.

A corporation is organized under state or federal statutes as a separate legal entity. The ownership of a corporation is divided into shares of stock. A corporation issues the stock to individuals or other businesses, who then become owners or stockholders of the corporation.

A primary advantage of the corporate form is the ability to obtain large amounts of resources by issuing stock. For this reason, most companies that require large investments in equipment and facilities are organized as corporations. For example, **Toys "R" Us** has raised over $800 million by issuing shares of common stock to finance its operations. Other examples of corporations include **General Motors**, **Ford**, **International Business Machines (IBM)**, **Coca-Cola**, and **General Electric**.

> Manufacturing, merchandising, and service businesses are commonly organized as either proprietorships, partnerships, or corporations.

About 20% of the businesses in the United States are organized as corporations. Given that most large companies are organized as corporations, over 90% of the total dollars of business receipts are received by corporations. Thus, corporations have a major influence on the economy.

The three types of businesses we discussed earlier—manufacturing, merchandising, and service—may be either proprietorships, partnerships, or corporations. However, because of the large amount of resources required to operate a manufacturing business, most manufacturing businesses are corporations. Likewise, most large retailers such as **Wal-Mart**, **Sears**, and **JCPenney** are corporations.

Business Stakeholders

A business stakeholder is a person or entity having an interest in the economic performance of the business. These stakeholders normally include the owners, managers, employees, customers, creditors, and the government.

The **owners** who have invested resources in the business clearly have an interest in how well the business performs. Most owners want to get the most economic value for their investments. To the extent that the business is profitable, owners will expect to share in the business profits. Since owners may eventually decide to sell their business, they also have an interest in the total economic worth of the business. This economic worth may reflect results of past profits as well as prospects for future profits.

The **managers** are those individuals who the owners have authorized to operate the business. Managers are primarily evaluated on the economic performance of the business. The managers of poor-performing businesses are often fired by the owners. Thus, managers have an incentive to maximize the economic value of the business. Owners may offer managers salary contracts that are tied directly to how well the business performs. For example, a manager might receive a percent of the profits or a percent of the increase in profits. Such contracts are often referred to as profit-sharing plans.

The **employees** provide services to the business in exchange for a paycheck. The employees have an interest in the economic performance of the business because their jobs depend upon it. During business downturns, it is not unusual for a business to lay off workers for extended periods of time. Whenever a business fails, the employees lose their jobs permanently. Employee labor unions often use the good economic performance of a business to argue for wage increases. In contrast, businesses often cite poor economic performance as a reason for decreasing wages or denying raises.

The **customers** may also have an interest in the continued success of a business. For example, if **Apple Computer** were to fail, customers might not be able to get hardware and software for their computers. Likewise, customers who purchase advance tickets on **Southwest Airlines** have an interest in whether Southwest will continue in business. Frequent flyers on **Eastern Airlines** lost their accumulated frequent-flyer points when Eastern went out of business.

Like the owners, the **creditors** invest resources in the business by extending credit, such as a loan. They, too, have an interest in how well the business performs. In order for the creditors to recover their investment, the business must generate enough cash to pay them back. In addition, creditors view the business as their customer and thus have a stake in the continued success of the business.

Various **governments** have an interest in the economic performance of businesses. City, county, state, and federal governments collect taxes from businesses within their jurisdictions. The better a business does, the more taxes the government can collect. In addition, workers are taxed on their wages. In contrast, workers who are laid off and are unemployed can file claims for unemployment compensation, which results in a financial burden for the government. City and state governments often provide incentives for businesses to locate in their jurisdictions.

The state of Alabama offered **Daimler-Chrysler** millions of dollars in incentives to locate a Mercedes plant in Alabama.

BUSINESS ON STAGE
Successful Entrepreneurs

What are the characteristics of entrepreneurs who successfully start and manage a new business?

It goes without saying that an entrepreneur must have a thorough technical knowledge of the business. For example, a successful computer consultant must have a thorough knowledge of computers. Entrepreneurs must also have basic management skills, such as the ability to organize and interact with others. Terms that are often used to describe entrepreneurs and examples of some well-known entrepreneurs and their companies are listed below.

Terms
Vision
Perseverance
Independent
Self-confident
Risk taker
High energy level
Motivated
Personal drive
Spirit of adventure
Need for achievement
Self-starter
Sense of commitment
Willingness to make personal sacrifices
Communication skills

Entrepreneur	Company
Jeffrey Yang	Yahoo!
Henry Ford	Ford Motor Company
George Eastman	Kodak
King C. Gillette	Gillette Company
Steven Jobs	Apple Computer
Bill Gates	Microsoft
Frederick Smith	Federal Express
Sam Walton	Wal-Mart

Examples of entrepreneurs also include the owners of many small businesses in your community, from local restaurants to video rental stores. ∎

The Role of Accounting in Business

What is the role of accounting in business? The simplest answer to this question is that accounting provides information for managers to use in operating the business. In addition, accounting provides information to other stakeholders to use in assessing the economic performance and condition of the business.

In a general sense, **accounting** can be defined as an information system that provides reports to stakeholders about the economic activities and condition of a business. As we indicated earlier in this chapter, we will focus our discussions on accounting and its role in business. However, many of the concepts in this text apply also to individuals, governments, and other types of organizations. For example, individuals must account for activities such as hours worked, checks written, and bills due. Stakeholders for individuals include creditors, dependents, and the government. A main interest of the government is making sure that individuals pay the proper taxes.

> **Accounting is an information system that provides reports to stakeholders about the economic activities and condition of a business.**

You may think of accounting as the "language of business." This is because accounting is the means by which business information is communicated to the stakeholders. For example, accounting reports summarizing the profitability of a new product help **Coca-Cola's** management decide whether to continue selling the product. Likewise, financial analysts use accounting reports in deciding whether to recommend the purchase of Coca-Cola's stock. Banks use accounting reports in determining the amount of credit to extend to Coca-Cola. Suppliers use accounting reports in deciding whether to offer credit for Coca-Cola's purchases of supplies and raw materials. State and federal governments use accounting reports as a basis for assessing taxes on Coca-Cola.

The process by which accounting provides information to business stakeholders is illustrated in Exhibit 1. A business must first identify its stakeholders. It must then

Exhibit 1 Accounting Information and the Stakeholders of a Business assess the various informational needs of those stakeholders and design its accounting system to meet those needs. Finally, the accounting system records the economic data about business activities and events, which the business reports to the stakeholders according to their informational needs.

Stakeholders use accounting reports as a primary source of information on which they base their decisions. They use other information as well. For example, in deciding whether to extend credit to an appliance store, a banker might use economic forecasts to assess the future demand for the store's products. During periods of economic downturn, the demand for consumer appliances normally declines. The banker might inquire about the ability and reputation of the managers of the business. For small corporations, bankers may require major stockholders to personally guarantee the loans of the business. Finally, bankers might consult industry publications that rank similar businesses as to their quality of products, customer satisfaction, and future prospects for growth.

Business Ethics

objective 3

Describe the importance of business ethics and the basic principles of proper ethical conduct.

Stanley James Cardiges, the former top U.S. sales representative for **American Honda**, admitted to receiving $2 million to $5 million in illegal kickbacks from dealers. After being sentenced to five years in prison, he admitted to "falling into a pattern [of unethical behavior] early in my career . . . and went along with the crowd."

Source: "Ex-Honda Executive Handed 5-Year Sentence," The Associated Press, *Knoxville News Sentinel*, August 26, 1995.

Individuals may have different views about what is "right" and "wrong" in a given situation. For example, you may believe it is wrong to copy another student's homework and hand it in as your own. Other students may feel that it is acceptable to copy homework if the instructor has no stated rule against it. Unfortunately, business managers sometimes find themselves in situations where they feel pressure to violate personal ethics. For example, managers of **Sears** automotive service departments were accused of recommending unnecessary repairs and overcharging customers for actual repairs in order to meet company goals and earn bonuses.

The moral principles that guide the conduct of individuals are called **ethics**. Regardless of differences among individuals, proper ethical conduct implies a behavior that considers the impact of one's actions on society and others. In other words, proper ethical conduct implies that you not only consider what's in your best interest, but also what's in the best interests of others.

Ethical conduct is good business. For example, an automobile manufacturer that fails to correct a safety defect to save costs may later lose sales due to lack of consumer confidence. Likewise, a business that pollutes the environment may find itself the target of lawsuits and customer boycotts.

Businesspeople should work within an ethical framework.[2] Although an ethical framework is based on individual experiences and training, there are a number of sound principles that form the foundation for ethical behavior:

1. *Avoid small ethical lapses.* Small ethical lapses may appear harmless in and of themselves. Unfortunately, such lapses can compromise your work. Small ethical lapses can build up and lead to larger consequences later.

Point of Interest
Most colleges and universities publish a Student Code of Conduct that sets forth the ethical conduct expected of students.

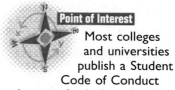
A survey of top managers by the accounting firm of **Deloitte & Touche** reported that "an enterprise actually strengthens its competitive position by maintaining high ethical standards." *Ethics in Business*, Deloitte & Touche (January 1988).

---

[2] An ethics discussion case is provided at the end of each chapter to focus attention on meaningful ethical situations that accountants often face in practice.

2. *Focus on your long-term reputation.* One characteristic of an ethical dilemma is that it places you under severe short-term pressure. The ethical dilemma is created by the stated or unstated threat that failure to "go along" may result in undesirable consequences. You should respond to ethical dilemmas by minimizing the short-term pressures and focusing on long-term reputation instead. Your reputation is very valuable. You will lose your effectiveness if your reputation becomes tarnished.

3. *Expect to suffer adverse personal consequences for holding to an ethical position.* In some unethical organizations, managers have endured career setbacks for not budging from their ethical positions. Some managers have resigned because they were unable to support management in what they perceived as unethical behavior. Thus, in the short term, ethical behavior can sometimes adversely affect your career.

Profession of Accounting

objective 4

Describe the profession of accounting.

Accountants engage in either private accounting or public accounting. Accountants employed by a business firm or a not-for-profit organization are said to be engaged in **private accounting**. Accountants and their staff who provide services on a fee basis are said to be employed in **public accounting**.

Because all functions within a business use accounting information, experience in private or public accounting provides a solid foundation for a career. Many positions in industry and in government agencies are held by individuals with accounting backgrounds. For example, in a Special Bonus Issue on "The Corporate Elite," *Business Week* reported the career paths for the chief executives of the 1,000 largest public corporations. These career paths are shown in Exhibit 2.

Exhibit 2 Career Paths of Corporate Executives

A career in accounting can be financially rewarding. Warren Jensen, a Certified Public Accountant, recently accepted a position with Amazon.com as its Chief Financial Officer (CFO). Mr. Jensen, the former CFO of Delta Air Lines, received stock options in Amazon.com that are potentially worth $745 million.

Source: Sara Nathan, *USA Today*, "Amazon Lured President with $1.3B in Options," March 17, 2000.

Private Accounting

The scope of activities and duties of private accountants varies widely. Private accountants are frequently called management accountants. If they are employed by a manufacturer, they may be referred to as *industrial* or *cost accountants*. The chief accountant in a business may be called the **controller**. Various state and federal agencies and other not-for-profit agencies also employ accountants.

The Institute of Certified Management Accountants, an affiliate of the Institute of Management Accountants (IMA), sponsors the **Certified Management Accountant (CMA)** program. The CMA certificate is evidence of competence in management accounting. Becoming a CMA requires a college degree, two years of experience, and successful completion of a two-day examination. Continuing professional education is required for renewal of the CMA certificate. In addition, members of the IMA must adhere to standards of ethical conduct.

The Institute of Internal Auditors sponsors a similar program for internal auditors. Internal auditors are accountants who review the accounting and operating procedures prescribed by their firms. Accountants who specialize in internal auditing may be granted the **Certified Internal Auditor (CIA)** certificate.

Public Accounting

In public accounting, an accountant may practice as an individual or as a member of a public accounting firm. Public accountants who have met a state's education, experience, and examination requirements may become **Certified Public Accountants (CPAs)**.

The requirements for obtaining a CPA certificate differ among the various states. All states require a college education in accounting, and most states require 150 semester hours of college credit. In addition, a candidate must pass a two-day examination prepared by the American Institute of Certified Public Accountants (AICPA).

Most states do not permit individuals to practice as CPAs until they have had from one to three years' experience in public accounting. Some states, however, accept similar employment in private accounting as equivalent experience. All states require continuing professional education and adherence to standards of ethical conduct.[3]

Specialized Accounting Fields

You may think that all accounting is the same. However, you will find several specialized fields of accounting in practice. The two most common are financial accounting and managerial accounting. Other fields include cost accounting, environmental accounting, tax accounting, accounting systems, international accounting, not-for-profit accounting, and social accounting.

Financial accounting is primarily concerned with the recording and reporting of economic data and activities for a business. Although such reports provide useful information for managers, they are the primary reports for owners, creditors, governmental agencies, and the public. For example, if you wanted to buy some stock in **PepsiCo**, **American Airlines**, or **McDonald's**, how would you know in which company to invest? One way is to review financial reports and compare the financial performance and condition of each company. The purpose of financial accounting is to provide such reports.

Managerial accounting, or **management accounting**, uses both financial accounting and estimated data to aid management in running day-to-day operations and in planning future operations. Management accountants gather and report information that is relevant and timely to the decision-making needs of management. For example, management might need information on alternative ways to finance

[3] The text of the *Code of Professional Conduct* of the American Institute of Certified Public Accountants is reproduced in Appendix B.

the construction of a new building. Alternatively, management might need information on whether to expand its operations into a new product line. Thus, reports to management can differ widely in form and content.

Generally Accepted Accounting Principles

objective 5

Summarize the development of accounting principles and relate them to practice.

 The FASB is also developing a broad conceptual framework for financial accounting. Seven *Statements of Financial Accounting Concepts* have been published to date.

If the management of a company could record and report financial data as it saw fit, comparisons among companies would be difficult, if not impossible. Thus, financial accountants follow **generally accepted accounting principles (GAAP)** in preparing reports. These reports allow investors and other stakeholders to compare one company to another.

To illustrate the importance of generally accepted accounting principles, assume that each sports conference in college football used different rules for counting touchdowns. For example, assume that the Pacific Athletic Conference (PAC 10) counted a touchdown as six points and the Atlantic Coast Conference (ACC) counted a touchdown as two points. It would be difficult to evaluate the teams under such different scoring systems. A standard set of rules and a standard scoring system help fans compare teams across conferences. Likewise, a standard set of generally accepted accounting principles allows for the comparison of financial performance and condition across companies.

Accounting principles and concepts develop from research, accepted accounting practices, and pronouncements of authoritative bodies. Currently, the **Financial Accounting Standards Board (FASB)** is the authoritative body having the primary responsibility for developing accounting principles. The FASB publishes *Statements of Financial Accounting Standards* and *Interpretations* to these Standards.

Because generally accepted accounting principles impact how companies report and what they report, all stakeholders are interested in the setting of these principles. For example, the FASB proposed a standard on how to account for options granted employees and managers to purchase shares of ownership in the company. The proposal was opposed by managers because it would negatively impact the financial results of many companies. Managers and others, including the United States Senate, urged the FASB to revise or drop the proposal.[4] In response to these comments, the FASB significantly revised the proposed standard.

In this chapter and throughout this text, we emphasize accounting principles and concepts. It is through this emphasis on the "why" of accounting as well as the "how" that you will gain an understanding of the full significance of accounting. In the following paragraphs, we discuss the business entity concept and the cost concept.

Business Entity Concept

The individual business unit is the business entity for which economic data are needed. This entity could be an automobile dealer, a department store, or a grocery store. The business entity must be identified, so that the accountant can determine which economic data should be analyzed, recorded, and summarized in reports.

The **business entity concept** is important because it limits the economic data in the accounting system to data related directly to the activities of the business. In other words, the business is viewed as an entity separate from its owners, creditors, or other stakeholders. For example, the accountant for a business with one owner (a proprietorship) would record the activities of the business only, not the personal activities, property, or debts of the owner.

Under the business entity concept, the activities of a business are recorded separately from the activities of the stakeholders.

[4] Glenn Alan Cheney, "Senate Rips FASB on Stock Options," *Accounting Today* (May 23, 1994).

The Cost Concept

If a building is bought for $150,000, that amount should be entered into the buyer's accounting records. The seller may have been asking $170,000 for the building up to the time of the sale. The buyer may have initially offered $130,000 for the building. The building may have been assessed at $125,000 for property tax purposes. The buyer may have received an offer of $175,000 for the building the day after it was acquired. These latter amounts have no effect on the accounting records because they did not result in an exchange of the building from the seller to the buyer. The **cost concept** is the basis for entering the *exchange price, or cost, of $150,000* into the accounting records for the building.

Continuing the illustration, the $175,000 offer received by the buyer the day after the building was acquired indicates that it was a bargain purchase at $150,000. To use $175,000 in the accounting records, however, would record an illusory or unrealized profit. If, after buying the building, the buyer accepts the offer and sells the building for $175,000, a profit of $25,000 is then realized and recorded. The new owner would record $175,000 as the cost of the building.

Using the cost concept involves two other important accounting concepts—objectivity and the unit of measure. The **objectivity concept** requires that the accounting records and reports be based upon objective evidence. In exchanges between a buyer and a seller, both try to get the best price. Only the final agreed-upon amount is objective enough for accounting purposes. If the amounts at which properties were recorded were constantly being revised upward and downward based on offers, appraisals, and opinions, accounting reports would soon become unstable and unreliable.

The **unit of measure concept** requires that economic data be recorded in dollars. Money is a common unit of measurement for reporting uniform financial data and reports.

Assets, Liabilities, and Owner's Equity

objective 6

State the accounting equation and define each element of the equation.

The resources owned by a business are its **assets**. Examples of assets include cash, land, buildings, and equipment. The rights or claims to the properties are normally divided into two principal types: (1) the rights of creditors and (2) the rights of owners. The rights of creditors represent debts of the business and are called **liabilities**. The rights of the owners are called **owner's equity**. The relationship between the two may be stated in the form of an equation, as follows:

$$\text{Assets} = \text{Liabilities} + \text{Owner's Equity}$$

This equation is known as the **accounting equation**. It is usual to place liabilities before owner's equity in the accounting equation because creditors have first rights to the assets. The claim of the owners is sometimes given greater emphasis by transposing liabilities to the other side of the equation, which yields:

Assets − Liabilities = Owner's Equity

To illustrate, if the assets owned by a business amount to $100,000 and the liabilities amount to $30,000, the owner's equity is equal to $70,000, as shown below.

If a company's assets increase by $20,000 and its liabilities decrease by $5,000, how much did the owner's equity increase or decrease?

Change in Assets	=	Change in Liabilities	+	Change in Owner's Equity
+$20,000	=	−$5,000	+	X
+$25,000	=			X

Assets	−	Liabilities	=	Owner's Equity
$100,000	−	$30,000	=	$70,000

Business Transactions and the Accounting Equation

objective 7

Explain how business transactions can be stated in
terms of the resulting
changes in the basic ele-
ments of the accounting
equation.

Paying a monthly telephone bill of $168 affects a business's financial condition be-
cause it now has less cash on hand. Such an economic event or condition that directly changes an entity's financial condition or directly affects its results of operations is a **business transaction**. For example, purchasing land for $50,000 is a
business transaction. In contrast, a change in a business's credit rating does not directly affect cash or any other element of its financial condition.

All business transactions can be stated in terms of changes in the elements of
the accounting equation. You will see how business transactions affect the accounting
equation by studying some typical transactions. As a basis for illustration, we will
use a business organized by Chris Clark.

Assume that on November 1, 2002, Chris Clark begins a business that will be known
as NetSolutions. The first phase of Chris' business plan is to operate NetSolutions
as a service business that provides assistance to individuals and small businesses in
developing web pages and in configuring and installing application software. Chris
expects this initial phase of the business to last one to two years. During this period,
Chris will gather information on the soft-
ware and hardware needs of customers.
During the second phase of the business
plan, Chris plans to expand NetSolutions
into an Internet-based retailer of software
and hardware for individuals and small
businesses.

Each transaction or group of similar
transactions during NetSolutions' first month
of operations is described in the following
paragraphs. The effect of each transaction
on the accounting equation is then shown.

> **All business transactions
> can be stated in terms of
> changes in the elements of
> the accounting equation.**

Transaction a.   Chris Clark deposits $25,000 in a bank account in the name of
NetSolutions. The effect of this transaction is to increase the asset cash (on the left
side of the equation) by $25,000. To balance the equation, the owner's equity (on
the right side of the equation) is increased by the same amount. The equity of the
owner is referred to by using the owner's name and "Capital," such as "Chris Clark,
Capital." The effect of this transaction on NetSolutions' accounting equation is shown
below.

	Assets	=	**Owner's Equity**
	Cash	=	Chris Clark, Capital
a.	25,000		25,000 Investment
			by Chris Clark

Note that since Chris Clark is the sole owner, NetSolutions is a proprietorship.
Note, too, that the accounting equation shown above relates only to the business,
NetSolutions. Under the business entity concept, Chris Clark's personal assets, such
as a home or personal bank account, and personal liabilities are excluded from the
equation.

Transaction b.   If you purchased this textbook by paying cash, you entered into
a transaction in which you exchanged one asset for another. That is, you exchanged
cash for the textbook. Businesses often enter into similar transactions. NetSolutions,
for example, exchanged $20,000 cash for land. The land is located in a new busi-
ness park with convenient access to transportation facilities. Chris Clark plans to rent

office space and equipment during the first phase of the business plan. During the second phase, Chris plans to build an office and warehouse on the land.

The purchase of the land changes the makeup of the assets but does not change the total assets. The items in the equation prior to this transaction and the effect of the transaction are shown next, as well as the new amounts, or *balances*, of the items.

Q & A

If NetSolutions had purchased a van for $28,000, paying $8,000 cash and signing a loan agreement (note payable) for $20,000, how would the transaction be recorded using the accounting equation?

Cash	+	Van	=	Notes Payable
−8,000	+	28,000		+20,000

	Assets			=	Owner's Equity
	Cash	+	Land	=	Chris Clark, Capital
Bal.	25,000			=	25,000
b.	−20,000		+20,000		
Bal.	5,000		20,000		25,000

Transaction c. You have probably used a credit card at one time or another to buy clothing or other merchandise. In this type of transaction, you received clothing for a promise to pay your credit card bill in the future. That is, you received an asset and incurred a liability to pay a future bill. During the month, NetSolutions entered into a similar transaction, buying supplies for $1,350 and agreeing to pay the supplier in the near future. This type of transaction is called a purchase *on account*. The liability created is called an **account payable**. Items such as supplies that will be used in the business in the future are called **prepaid expenses**, which are assets. The effect of this transaction is to increase assets and liabilities by $1,350, as follows:

Real World

Other examples of common prepaid expenses include insurance and rent. Businesses usually report these assets together as a single item, prepaid expenses.

	Assets					=	Liabilities	+	Owner's Equity
							Accounts		Chris Clark,
	Cash	+	Supplies	+	Land	=	Payable	+	Capital
Bal.	5,000				20,000				25,000
c.			+1,350				+1,350		
Bal.	5,000		1,350		20,000		1,350		25,000

Transaction d. You may have earned money by painting houses. If so, you received money for rendering services to a customer. Likewise, a business earns money by selling goods or services to its customers. This amount is called **revenue**.

During its first month of operations, NetSolutions provided services to customers, earning fees of $7,500 and receiving the amount in cash. The receipt of cash increases NetSolutions' assets and also increases Chris Clark's equity in the business. Thus, this transaction increased cash and the owner's equity by $7,500, as shown here.

	Assets					=	Liabilities	+	Owner's Equity
							Accounts		Chris Clark,
	Cash	+	Supplies	+	Land	=	Payable	+	Capital
Bal.	5,000		1,350		20,000		1,350		25,000
d.	+ 7,500								+ 7,500 Fees earned
Bal.	12,500		1,350		20,000		1,350		32,500

Special terms may be used to describe certain kinds of revenue, such as **sales** for the sale of merchandise. Revenue from providing services is called **fees earned**. For example, a physician would record fees earned for services to patients. Other examples include **rent revenue** (money received for rent) and **interest revenue** (money received for interest).

Instead of requiring the payment of cash at the time services are provided or goods are sold, a business may accept payment at a later date. Such revenues are called *fees on account* or *sales on account*. In such cases, the firm has an **account receivable**, which is a claim against the customer. An account receivable is an asset, and the revenue is earned as if cash had been received. When customers pay their accounts, there is an exchange of one asset for another. Cash increases, while accounts receivable decreases.

Transaction e. If you painted houses to earn money, you probably used your own ladders and brushes. NetSolutions also spent cash or used up other assets in earning revenue. The amounts used in this process of earning revenue are called **expenses**. Expenses include supplies used, wages of employees, and other assets and services used in operating the business.

For NetSolutions, the expenses paid during the month were as follows: wages, $2,125; rent, $800; utilities, $450; and miscellaneous, $275. Miscellaneous expenses include small amounts paid for such items as postage, coffee, and magazine subscriptions. The effect of this group of transactions is the opposite of the effect of revenues. These transactions reduce cash and owner's equity, as shown here.

		Assets			=	Liabilities	+	Owner's Equity	
	Cash	+	Supplies	+	Land	Accounts Payable	+	Chris Clark, Capital	
Bal.	12,500		1,350		20,000	1,350		32,500	
e.	−3,650							−2,125	Wages expense
								− 800	Rent expense
								− 450	Utilities expense
								− 275	Misc. expense
	8,850		1,350		20,000	1,350		28,850	

Businesses usually record each revenue and expense transaction separately as it occurs. However, to simplify this illustration, we have summarized NetSolutions' revenues and expenses for the month in transactions (d) and (e).

Transaction f. When you pay your monthly credit card bill, you decrease the cash in your checking account and also decrease the amount you owe to the credit card company. Likewise, when NetSolutions pays $950 to creditors during the month, it reduces both assets and liabilities, as shown below.

		Assets			=	Liabilities	+	Owner's Equity	
	Cash	+	Supplies	+	Land	Accounts Payable	+	Chris Clark, Capital	
Bal.	8,850		1,350		20,000	1,350		28,850	
f.	−950					−950			
Bal.	7,900		1,350		20,000	400		28,850	

You should note that paying an amount on account is different from paying an amount for an expense. The payment of an expense reduces owner's equity, as illustrated in transaction (e). Paying an amount on account reduces the amount owed on a liability.

Transaction g. At the end of the month, the cost of the supplies on hand (not yet used) is $550. The remainder of the supplies ($1,350 − $550) was used in the operations of the business and is treated as an expense. This decrease of $800 in supplies and owner's equity is shown as follows:

	Assets			=	Liabilities	+	Owner's Equity	
	Cash	+ Supplies	+ Land	=	Accounts Payable	+	Chris Clark, Capital	
Bal.	7,900	1,350	20,000		400		28,850	
g.		−800					− 800	Supplies expense
Bal.	7,900	550	20,000		400		28,050	

Transaction h. At the end of the month, Chris Clark withdraws $2,000 in cash from the business for personal use. This transaction is the exact opposite of an investment in the business by the owner. Cash and owner's equity are decreased. The cash payment is not a business expense but a withdrawal of a part of the owner's equity. The effect of the $2,000 withdrawal is shown as follows:

	Assets			=	Liabilities	+	Owner's Equity	
	Cash	+ Supplies	+ Land	=	Accounts Payable	+	Chris Clark, Capital	
Bal.	7,900	550	20,000		400		28,050	
h.	−2,000						−2,000	Withdrawal
Bal.	5,900	550	20,000		400		26,050	

You should be careful not to confuse withdrawals by the owner with expenses. Withdrawals *do not* represent assets or services used in the process of earning revenues. The owner's equity decrease from the withdrawals is listed in the equation under Capital. This is because withdrawals are considered a distribution of capital to the owner.

Summary. The transactions of NetSolutions are summarized as follows. They are identified by letter, and the balance of each item is shown after each transaction.

	Assets			=	Liabilities	+	Owner's Equity	
	Cash	+ Supplies	+ Land	=	Accounts Payable	+	Chris Clark, Capital	
a.	+25,000						+25,000	Investment by Chris Clark
b.	−20,000		+20,000					
Bal.	5,000		20,000				25,000	
c.		+1,350			+1,350			
Bal.	5,000	1,350	20,000		1,350		25,000	
d.	+ 7,500						+ 7,500	Fees earned
Bal.	12,500	1,350	20,000		1,350		32,500	
e.	− 3,650						− 2,125	Wages expense
							− 800	Rent expense
							− 450	Utilities expense
							− 275	Misc. expense
Bal.	8,850	1,350	20,000		1,350		28,850	
f.	− 950				− 950			
Bal.	7,900	1,350	20,000		400		28,850	
g.		− 800					− 800	Supplies expense
Bal.	7,900	550	20,000		400		28,050	
h.	− 2,000						− 2,000	Withdrawal
Bal.	5,900	550	20,000		400		26,050	

In reviewing the preceding summary, you should note the following, which apply to all types of businesses:

1. The effect of every transaction is *an increase or a decrease in one or more of the accounting equation elements.*
2. The two sides of the accounting equation are *always equal.*
3. The owner's equity is *increased by amounts invested by the owner* and is *decreased by withdrawals by the owner.* In addition, the owner's equity is *increased by revenues* and is *decreased by expenses.* The effects of these four types of transactions on owner's equity are illustrated in Exhibit 3.

Exhibit 3 Effects of Transactions on Owner's Equity

Financial Statements

objective 8

Describe the financial statements of a proprietorship and explain how they interrelate.

After transactions have been recorded and summarized, reports are prepared for users. The accounting reports that provide this information are called **financial statements**. The principal financial statements of a proprietorship are the income statement, the statement of owner's equity, the balance sheet, and the statement of cash flows. The order in which the statements are normally prepared and the nature of the data presented in each statement are as follows:

*   **Income statement**—A summary of the revenue and expenses *for a specific period of time*, such as a month or a year.
*   **Statement of owner's equity**—A summary of the changes in the owner's equity that have occurred *during a specific period of time*, such as a month or a year.
*   **Balance sheet**—A list of the assets, liabilities, and owner's equity *as of a specific date*, usually at the close of the last day of a month or a year.
*   **Statement of cash flows**—A summary of the cash receipts and cash payments *for a specific period of time*, such as a month or a year.

The basic features of the four statements and their interrelationships are illustrated in Exhibit 4. The data for the statements were taken from the summary of transactions of NetSolutions.

All financial statements should be identified by the name of the business, the title of the statement, and the *date* or *period of time*. The data presented in the income statement, the statement of owner's equity, and the statement of cash flows are for a period of time. The data presented in the balance sheet are for a specific date.

Exhibit 4 Financial
Statements

NetSolutions
Income Statement
For the Month Ended November 30, 2002

Fees earned						$7	5	0 0	00
Operating expenses:									
Wages expense	$2	1	2 5	00					
Rent expense		8	0 0	00					
Supplies expense		8	0 0	00					
Utilities expense		4	5 0	00					
Miscellaneous expense		2	7 5	00					
Total operating expenses							4	4 5 0	00
Net income						$3	0	5 0	00

NetSolutions
Statement of Owner's Equity
For the Month Ended November 30, 2002

Chris Clark, capital, November 1, 2002						$			0
Investment on November 1, 2002	$25	0	0 0	00					
Net income for November		3	0 5	0 00					
	$28	0	5 0	00					
Less withdrawals		2	0 0	0 00					
Increase in owner's equity						26	0	5 0	00
Chris Clark, capital, November 30, 2002						$26	0	5 0	00

NetSolutions
Balance Sheet
November 30, 2002

Assets					Liabilities				
Cash	$ 5	9	0 0	00	Accounts payable	$		4 0 0	00
Supplies		5	5 0	00	**Owner's Equity**				
Land	20	0	0 0	00	Chris Clark, capital	26	0	5 0	00
					Total liabilities and				
Total assets	$26	4	5 0	00	owner's equity	$26	4	5 0	00

NetSolutions
Statement of Cash Flows
For the Month Ended November 30, 2002

Cash flows from operating activities:									
Cash received from customers	$ 7	5	0 0	00					
Deduct cash payments for expenses and									
payments to creditors	4	6	0 0	00					
Net cash flow from operating activities						$ 2	9	0 0	00
Cash flows from investing activities:									
Cash payments for acquisition of land						(20	0	0 0	00)
Cash flows from financing activities:									
Cash received as owner's investment	$25	0	0 0	00					
Deduct cash withdrawal by owner	2	0	0 0	00					
Net cash flow from financing activities						23	0	0 0	00
Net cash flow and November 30, 2002 cash balance						$ 5	9	0 0	00

You should note the use of indents, captions, dollar signs, and rulings in the financial statements. They aid the reader by emphasizing the sections of the statements.

Income Statement

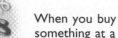

The income statement reports the revenues and expenses for a period of time, based on the **matching concept.** This concept is applied by *matching* the expenses with the revenue generated during a period by those expenses. The income statement also reports the excess of the revenue over the expenses incurred. This excess of the revenue over the expenses is called **net income** or **net profit**. If the expenses exceed the revenue, the excess is a **net loss.**

The effects of revenue earned and expenses incurred during the month for Net-Solutions were shown in the equation as increases and decreases in owner's equity (capital). Net income for a period has the effect of increasing owner's equity (capital) for the period, whereas a net loss has the effect of decreasing owner's equity (capital) for the period.

Net income—the excess of revenue over expenses—increases owner's equity.

The revenue, expenses, and the net income of $3,050 for NetSolutions are reported in the income statement in Exhibit 4. The order in which the expenses are listed in the income statement varies among businesses. One method is to list them in order of size, beginning with the larger items. Miscellaneous expense is usually shown as the last item, regardless of the amount.

Statement of Owner's Equity

The statement of owner's equity reports the changes in the owner's equity for a period of time. It is prepared *after* the income statement because the net income or net loss for the period must be reported in this statement. Similarly, it is prepared *before* the balance sheet, since the amount of owner's equity at the end of the period must be reported on the balance sheet. Because of this, the statement of owner's equity is often viewed as the connecting link between the income statement and balance sheet.

Three types of transactions affected owner's equity for NetSolutions during November: (1) the original investment of $25,000, (2) the revenue and expenses that resulted in net income of $3,050 for the month, and (3) a withdrawal of $2,000 by the owner. This information is summarized in the statement of owner's equity in Exhibit 4.

Balance Sheet

The balance sheet in Exhibit 4 reports the amounts of NetSolutions' assets, liabilities, and owner's equity at the end of November. These amounts are taken from the last line of the summary of transactions presented earlier. The form of balance sheet shown in Exhibit 4 is called the **account form** because it resembles the basic format of the accounting equation, with assets on the left side and the liabilities and owner's equity sections on the right side. We illustrate an alternative form of balance sheet called the **report form** in a later chapter. It presents the liabilities and owner's equity sections below the assets section.

The assets section of the balance sheet normally presents assets in the order that they will be converted into cash or used in operations. Cash is presented first, followed by receivables, supplies, prepaid insurance, and other assets. The assets of a more permanent nature are shown next, such as land, buildings, and equipment.

In the liabilities section of the balance sheet in Exhibit 4, accounts payable is the only liability. When there are two or more categories of liabilities, each should be listed and the total amount of liabilities presented as follows.

Liabilities

Accounts payable	$12,900	
Wages payable	2,570	
Total liabilities		$15,470

Statement of Cash Flows

The statement of cash flows consists of three sections, as we see in Exhibit 4: (1) operating activities, (2) investing activities, and (3) financing activities. Each of these sections is briefly described below.

Cash Flows from Operating Activities. This section reports a summary of cash receipts and cash payments from operations. The net cash flow from operating activities ($2,900 in Exhibit 4) will normally differ from the amount of net income for the period ($3,050 in Exhibit 4). This difference occurs because revenues and expenses may not be recorded at the same time that cash is received from customers or paid to creditors.

Cash Flows from Investing Activities. This section reports the cash transactions for the acquisition and sale of relatively permanent assets.

Cash Flows from Financing Activities. This section reports the cash transactions related to cash investments by the owner, borrowings, and cash withdrawals by the owner.

Preparing the statement of cash flows requires an understanding of concepts that we have not discussed in this chapter. Therefore, we will illustrate the preparation of the statement of cash flows in a later chapter.

FINANCIAL ANALYSIS AND INTERPRETATION

objective 9

Use the ratio of liabilities to owner's equity to analyze the ability of a business to withstand poor business conditions.

As we discussed earlier in this chapter, financial statements are useful to bankers, creditors, owners, and other stakeholders in analyzing and interpreting the financial performance and condition of a business. Throughout this text, we will discuss various tools that are often used in practice to analyze and interpret the financial performance and condition of a business. The first such tool we will introduce is especially useful in analyzing the ability of a business to pay its creditors.

The relationship between liabilities and owner's equity, expressed as a ratio, is calculated as follows:

$$\text{Ratio of liabilities to owner's equity} = \frac{\text{Total liabilities}}{\text{Total owner's equity (or Total stockholders' equity)}}$$

To illustrate, NetSolutions' ratio of liabilities to owner's equity at the end of November is 0.015, as calculated below.

NET SOLUTIONS

$$\text{Ratio of liabilities to owner's equity} = \frac{\$400}{\$26,050} = 0.015$$

Corporations normally refer to total owner's equity as total stockholders' equity. Thus, you should substitute total stockholders' equity for total owner's equity when computing this ratio for a corporation.

The rights of creditors to a business's assets take precedence over the rights of the owners or stockholders. Thus, the lower the ratio of liabilities to owner's equity, the better able the business is to withstand poor business conditions and still fully meet its obligations to creditors.

To illustrate, a ratio of 1 indicates that the liabilities and owner's equity are equal. In other words, if the business suffers a loss equal to the total liabilities, the amount of total assets available to creditors will not drop below their claims on the assets. If this were to happen, the creditors could collect their claims and the owner would be left with nothing.

ENCORE

Home Depot

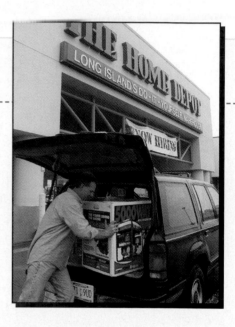

Businesses begin in many ways. The beginning of Home Depot took place in the spring of 1978, with two words: "You're fired!"

At the time of their firing, Bernie Marcus was chief executive officer and Arthur Blank was chief financial officer of Handy Dan Stores, a subsidiary of Daylin Corporation. Under their leadership, Handy Dan had grown to 66 stores and almost $155 million in sales. Handy Dan was earning more ($7.8 million) than the corporation as a whole, which earned only $7 million. Bernie and Arthur's success, however, wasn't sufficient to shield them from the forces of corporate politics.

Bernie and Arthur used their firings to create a golden opportunity to develop their vision for a chain of home improvement stores that would challenge the industry's conventional wisdom. Unfortunately, not only were they out of work, but they had little

capital with which to start a new venture. Bernie and Arthur courted potential investors, including H. Ross Perot, who at that time was relatively unknown. If Perot would invest $2 million in the venture, he would receive 70 percent of the then unnamed company. The negotiations broke down, however, when Perot would not agree to let Bernie keep his used Cadillac as a company car. Instead, he suggested that Bernie purchase a new, more expensive Chevrolet. "My people don't drive Cadillacs," Perot insisted.

Though Bernie and Arthur had to plead with vendors, banks, and investors for financing and credit in the early years, they were able to scrape up enough financing to open three Home Depot stores in Atlanta in 1979 and a fourth in 1980.

In 1999, Home Depot celebrated its 20th anniversary, with over 800 stores throughout the United

States and South America. Sales have grown from $7 million in 1979 to over $30 billion today. Bernie and Arthur have become two of the richest men in America. As for Ross Perot, the investment that he backed out of would currently be worth approximately $60 billion!

Source: Adapted from *Built from Scratch*, by Bernie Marcus and Arthur Blank, with Bob Andelman (Times Business-Random House, 1999). ■

KEY POINTS

1 Describe the nature of a business.

A business is an organization in which basic resources (inputs), such as materials and labor, are assembled and processed to provide goods or services (outputs) to customers. The objective of most businesses is to maximize profits.

There are three different types of businesses that are operated for profit: manufacturing, merchandising, and service businesses. A business is normally organized in one of three different forms: proprietorship, partnership, or corporation. A business stakeholder is a person or entity (such as an owner, manager,

employee, customer, creditor, or the government) who has an interest in the economic performance of the business.

2 Describe the role of accounting in business.

Accounting is an information system that provides reports to stakeholders about the economic activities and condition of a business. Accounting is the "language of business."

3 Describe the importance of business ethics and the basic principles of proper ethical conduct.

Ethics are moral principles that guide the conduct of individuals. Proper ethical conduct implies a behavior that considers the impact of one's actions on society and others. Sound ethical principles include (1) avoiding small ethical lapses, (2) focusing on your long-term reputation, and (3) being willing to suffer adverse personal consequences for holding to an ethical position.

4 Describe the profession of accounting.

Accountants are engaged in either private accounting or public accounting. The two most common specialized fields of accounting are financial accounting and managerial accounting. Other fields include cost accounting, environmental accounting, tax accounting, accounting systems, international accounting, not-for-profit accounting, and social accounting.

5 Summarize the development of accounting principles and relate them to practice.

Financial accountants follow generally accepted accounting principles (GAAP) in preparing reports so that stakeholders can compare one company to another. Accounting principles and concepts

develop from research, accepted accounting practices, and pronouncements of authoritative bodies. Currently, the Financial Accounting Standards Board (FASB) is the authoritative body having the primary responsibility for developing accounting principles.

The business entity concept views the business as an entity separate from its owners, creditors, or other stakeholders. The business entity limits the economic data in the accounting system to that related directly to the activities of the business. The cost concept requires that properties and services bought by a business be recorded in terms of actual cost. The objectivity concept requires that the accounting records and reports be based upon objective evidence. The unit of measure concept requires that economic data be recorded in dollars.

6 State the accounting equation and define each element of the equation.

The resources owned by a business and the rights or claims to these resources may be stated in the form of an equation, as follows:

Assets =
Liabilities + Owner's Equity

7 Explain how business transactions can be stated in terms of the resulting changes in the basic elements of the accounting equation.

All business transactions can be stated in terms of the change in one or more of the three elements of the accounting equation. That is, the effect of every transaction can be stated in terms of increases or decreases in one or more of these elements, while maintaining the equality between the two sides of the equation.

8 Describe the financial statements of a proprietorship and explain how they interrelate.

The principal financial statements of a proprietorship are the income statement, the statement of owner's equity, the balance sheet, and the statement of cash flows. The income statement reports a period's net income or net loss, which also appears on the statement of owner's equity. The ending owner's capital reported on the statement of owner's equity is also reported on the balance sheet. The ending cash balance is reported on the balance sheet and the statement of cash flows.

9 Use the ratio of liabilities to owner's equity to analyze the ability of a business to withstand poor business conditions.

The ratio of liabilities to owner's equity is useful in analyzing the ability of a business to pay its creditors. The lower the ratio, the better able the business is to withstand poor business conditions and still fully meet its obligations to creditors.

ILLUSTRATIVE PROBLEM

Cecil Jameson, Attorney-at-Law, is a proprietorship owned and operated by Cecil Jameson. On July 1 of the current year, Cecil Jameson, Attorney-at-Law, has the following assets and liabilities: cash, $1,000; accounts receivable, $3,200; supplies, $850; land, $10,000; accounts payable, $1,530. Office space and office equipment are currently being rented, pending the construction of an office complex on land purchased last year. Business transactions during July are summarized as follows:

a. Received cash from clients for services, $3,928.
b. Paid creditors on account, $1,055.
c. Received cash from Cecil Jameson as an additional investment, $3,700.

d. Paid office rent for the month, $1,200.
e. Charged clients for legal services on account, $2,025.
f. Purchased office supplies on account, $245.
g. Received cash from clients on account, $3,000.
h. Received invoice for paralegal services from Legal Aid Inc. for July (to be paid on August 10), $1,635.
i. Paid the following: wages expense, $850; answering service expense, $250; utilities expense, $325; and miscellaneous expense, $75.
j. Determined that the cost of office supplies on hand was $980; therefore, the cost of supplies used during the month was $115.
k. Jameson withdrew $1,000 in cash from the business for personal use.

Instructions

1. Determine the amount of owner's equity (Cecil Jameson's capital) as of July 1 of the current year.
2. State the assets, liabilities, and owner's equity as of July 1 in equation form similar to that shown in this chapter. In tabular form below the equation, indicate the increases and decreases resulting from each transaction and the new balances after each transaction. Explain the nature of each increase and decrease in owner's equity by an appropriate notation at the right of the amount.
3. Prepare an income statement for July, a statement of owner's equity for July, and a balance sheet as of July 31.

Solution

1. Assets − Liabilities = Owner's Equity (Cecil Jameson, capital)
$15,050 − $1,530 = Owner's Equity (Cecil Jameson, capital)
$13,520 = Owner's Equity (Cecil Jameson, capital)

2.

	Cash	+	Accounts Receivable	+	Supplies	+	Land	=	Accounts Payable	+	Cecil Jameson, Capital	
Bal.	1,000		3,200		850		10,000		1,530		13,520	
a.	+3,928										+ 3,928	Fees earned
Bal.	4,928		3,200		850		10,000		1,530		17,448	
b.	−1,055								−1,055			
Bal.	3,873		3,200		850		10,000		475		17,448	
c.	+3,700										+ 3,700	Investment
Bal.	7,573		3,200		850		10,000		475		21,148	
d.	−1,200										− 1,200	Rent expense
Bal.	6,373		3,200		850		10,000		475		19,948	
e.			+2,025								+ 2,025	Fees earned
Bal.	6,373		5,225		850		10,000		475		21,973	
f.					+ 245				+ 245			
Bal.	6,373		5,225		1,095		10,000		720		21,973	
g.	+3,000		−3,000									
Bal.	9,373		2,225		1,095		10,000		720		21,973	
h.									+1,635		− 1,635	Paralegal exp.
Bal.	9,373		2,225		1,095		10,000		2,355		20,338	
i.	−1,500										− 850	Wages exp.
											− 250	Answ. svc. exp.
											− 325	Utilities exp.
											− 75	Misc. exp.
Bal.	7,873		2,225		1,095		10,000		2,355		18,838	
j.					− 115						− 115	Supplies exp.
Bal.	7,873		2,225		980		10,000		2,355		18,723	
k.	−1,000										− 1,000	Withdrawal
	6,873		2,225		980		10,000		2,355		17,723	

3.

Cecil Jameson, Attorney-at-Law
Income Statement
For the Month Ended July 31, 20—

Fees earned						$5	9	5	3	00
Operating expenses:									
Paralegal expense	$1	6	3	5	00				
Rent expense	1	2	0	0	00				
Wages expense		8	5	0	00				
Utilities expense		3	2	5	00				
Answering service expense		2	5	0	00				
Supplies expense		1	1	5	00				
Miscellaneous expense			7	5	00				
Total operating expenses							4	4	5	0	00
Net income						$1	5	0	3	00

Cecil Jameson, Attorney-at-Law
Statement of Owner's Equity
For the Month Ended July 31, 20—

Cecil Jameson, capital, July 1, 20—						$13	5	2	0	00
Additional investment by owner	$3	7	0	0	00				
Net income for the month	1	5	0	3	00				
	$5	2	0	3	00				
Less withdrawals	1	0	0	0	00				
Increase in owner's equity							4	2	0	3	00
Cecil Jameson, capital, July 31, 20—						$17	7	2	3	00

Cecil Jameson, Attorney-at-Law
Balance Sheet
July 31, 20—

Assets						Liabilities					
Cash	$ 6	8	7	3	00	Accounts payable	$ 2	3	5	5	00
Accounts receivable	2	2	2	5	00	**Owner's Equity**					
Supplies		9	8	0	00	Cecil Jameson, capital	17	7	2	3	00
Land	10	0	0	0	00	Total liabilities and					
Total assets	$20	0	7	8	00	owner's equity	$20	0	7	8	00

SELF-EXAMINATION QUESTIONS   Answers at End of Chapter

Matching

Match each of the following statements with its proper term. Some terms may not be used.

A.	**Account form**	___ 1.	An organization in which basic resources (inputs), such as materials and labor, are assembled and processed to provide goods or services (outputs) to customers.
B.	**Account payable**		

C. Account receivable

D. Accounting

E. Accounting equation

F. Assets

G. Balance sheet

H. Business

I. Business entity concept

J. Business stakeholder

K. Business transaction

L. Corporation

M. Cost concept

N. Ethics

O. Expenses

P. Financial accounting

Q. Financial Accounting Standards Board (FASB)

R. Generally accepted accounting principles (GAAP)

S. Income statement

T. Liabilities

U. Managerial accounting

V. Managers

W. Manufacturing

X. Matching concept

Y. Merchandising

Z. Net income

AA. Net loss

BB. Objectivity concept

CC. Owner's equity

DD. Partnership

EE. Prepaid expenses

FF. Proprietorship

GG. Report form

HH. Revenue

II. Service

JJ. Statement of cash flows

KK. Statement of owner's equity

LL. Unit of measure concept

____ 2. A type of business that changes basic inputs into products that are sold to individual customers.

____ 3. A type of business that purchases products from other businesses and sells them to customers.

____ 4. A business owned by one individual.

____ 5. A business owned by two or more individuals

____ 6. A business organized under state or federal statutes as a separate legal entity.

____ 7. A person or entity who has an interest in the economic performance of a business.

____ 8. Individuals authorized by the owners to operate the business.

____ 9. An information system that provides reports to stakeholders about the economic activities and condition of a business.

____ 10. Moral principles that guide the conduct of individuals.

____ 11. A specialized field of accounting concerned primarily with the recording and reporting of economic data and activities to stakeholders outside the business.

____ 12. A specialized field of accounting that uses estimated data to aid management in running day-to-day operations and in planning future operations.

____ 13. The authoritative body that has the primary responsibility for developing accounting principles.

____ 14. A concept of accounting that limits the economic data in the accounting system to data related directly to the activities of the business.

____ 15. A concept of accounting requiring that economic data be recorded in dollars.

____ 16. The resources owned by a business.

____ 17. The rights of creditors that represent debts of the business.

____ 18. The rights of the owners.

____ 19. Assets = Liabilities + Owner's Equity

____ 20. An economic event or condition that directly changes an entity's financial condition or directly affects its results of operations.

____ 21. The liability created by a purchase on account.

____ 22. Items such as supplies that will be used in the business in the future.

____ 23. A claim against the customer.

____ 24. The amounts used in the process of earning revenue.

____ 25. The amount a business earns by selling goods or services to its customers.

____ 26. A summary of the revenue and expenses *for a specific period of time*, such as a month or a year.

____ 27. A summary of the changes in owner's equity that have occurred *during a specific period of time*, such as a month or a year.

____ 28. A list of the assets, liabilities, and owner's equity *as of a specific date*, usually at the close of the last day of a month or a year.

____ 29. A summary of the cash receipts and cash payments *for a specific period of time*, such as a month or a year.

____ 30. A concept of accounting in which expenses are matched with the revenue generated during a period by those expenses.

____ 31. The form of balance sheet that resembles the basic format of the accounting equation, with assets on the left side and the liabilities and owner's equity sections on the right side.

Multiple Choice

1. A profit-making business operating as a separate legal entity and in which ownership is divided into shares of stock is known as a:
   A. proprietorship.   C. partnership.
   B. service business.   D. corporation.

2. The resources owned by a business are called:
   A. assets.
   B. liabilities.
   C. the accounting equation.
   D. owner's equity.

3. A listing of a business entity's assets, liabilities, and owner's equity as of a specific date is:
   A. a balance sheet.
   B. an income statement.
   C. a statement of owner's equity.
   D. a statement of cash flows.

4. If total assets increased $20,000 during a period and total liabilities increased $12,000 during the same period, the amount and direction (increase or decrease) of the change in owner's equity for that period is:
   A. a $32,000 increase.   C. an $8,000 increase.
   B. a $32,000 decrease.   D. an $8,000 decrease.

5. If revenue was $45,000, expenses were $37,500, and the owner's withdrawals were $10,000, the amount of net income or net loss would be:
   A. $45,000 net income.   C. $37,500 net loss.
   B. $7,500 net income.   D. $2,500 net loss.

CLASS DISCUSSION QUESTIONS

1. What is the objective of most businesses?
2. Who are normally included as the stakeholders of a business?
3. What is the role of accounting in business?
4. What three sound principles form the foundation for ethical behavior?
5. Distinguish between private accounting and public accounting.
6. Identify what the abbreviation FASB stands for and describe how the FASB sets generally accepted accounting principles.
7. Lynda Lyons is the owner of Fast Delivery Service. Recently, Lynda paid interest of $3,500 on a personal loan of $60,000 that she used to begin the business. Should Fast Delivery Service record the interest payment? Explain.
8. On April 18, Neece Repair Service extended an offer of $95,000 for land that had been priced for sale at $100,000. On April 25, Neece Repair Service accepted the seller's counteroffer of $97,500. Describe how Neece Repair Service should record the land.
9. a. Land with an assessed value of $200,000 for property tax purposes is acquired by a business for $350,000. Seven years later, the plot of land has an assessed value of $240,000 and the business receives an offer of $400,000 for it. Should the monetary amount assigned to the land in the business records now be increased?
   b. Assuming that the land acquired in (a) was sold for $400,000, how would the various elements of the accounting equation be affected?
10. What are the two principal rights to the properties of a business?
11. Name the three elements of the accounting equation.
12. Describe the difference between an account receivable and an account payable.
13. A business had revenues of $130,000 and operating expenses of $145,000. Did the business (a) incur a net loss or (b) realize net income?
14. A business had revenues of $280,000 and operating expenses of $270,000. Did the business (a) incur a net loss or (b) realize net income?
15. What two types of transactions increase the owner's equity of a proprietorship?
16. Briefly describe the nature of the information provided by each of the following financial statements: the income statement, the statement of owner's equity, the balance sheet, and the statement of cash flows.
17. Indicate whether each of the financial statements in Question 16 covers a period of time or is for a specific date.
18. What particular item of financial or operating data appears on both the income statement and the statement of owner's equity? What item appears on both the balance sheet and the statement of owner's equity?
19. What are the three types of activities reported in the statement of cash flows?

A TRADITION OF EXCELLENCE

Tradition. Inspiration. Results.

Thank you for following in the tradition of 11 million students who have achieved outstanding results using this very text. To help you even further, we have developed incredible resources to make learning accounting even easier. You can purchase these supplements by visiting

http://warren.swcollege.com.

Here are numerous resources to help you get the results you want:

Personal WebTutor Advantage

GO TO THIS URL TO PURCHASE THIS PRODUCT:
pwt.swcollege.com

- Automatic and immediate feedback from quizzes and exams.
- Interactive, multimedia rich explanation of concepts.
- Online exercises that reinforce what you've learned.
- Flashcards that include audio support.
- Greater interaction and involvement through online discussion forums.

General Ledger Software
0-324-05199-9

- This software package teaches you the basics of a computerized accounting system in an easy-to-use environment.
- You will get hints and tips completing end-of-chapter problems.
- You will get immediate feedback to determine if you have done the problems correctly.

Personal Trainer
ACCOUNTING,
Chs. 1-24 0-324-07050-0
FINANCIAL ACCOUNTING,
Chs. 1-16 0-324-12376-0

- This online tutorial will help you complete the end-of-chapter exercises from the textbook, with hints.
- You will get immediate feedback to determine if you have done the exercises correctly.
- This product will not only save you time on your homework but will help you learn the concepts.

Spreadsheet Applications Software
Chs. 1-16 0-324-05195-6
Chs. 12-24 0-324-05196-4

- You will learn how Excel is used in accounting situations.

Study Guide
Chs. 1-16 0-324-05193-X
Chs. 12-24 0-324-05194-8

- This guide will give you quiz and test hints.
- You can practice the concepts you learn through numerous multiple choice, fill-in-the-blank, true-false questions, and exercises, all with solutions.

Working Papers
Chs. 1-16 0-324-05187-5
Chs. 12-24 0-324-05197-2

- This supplement contains forms that help you organize your solutions.

Working Papers Plus
Chs. 1-16 0-324-05189-1
Chs. 12-24 0-324-05190-5

- This special edition of Working Papers integrates the Working Papers forms with exercises and selected problems from the text.

INTACCT
(Internet Accounting Tutor)
FINANCIAL 0-324-01592-5
MANAGERIAL 0-324-01613-1
rama.swcollege.com

- This product, designed to be used with any introductory accounting textbook, will give you reinforcement of key accounting concepts in an interactive format.
- You can see how to apply the concepts with practice problems and demonstration problems.
- You can email your INTACCT homework problems to your instructor to grade.

⊙ Save on these products by purchasing online at

EXERCISES

Exercise 1–1
Professional ethics
Objective 3

A fertilizer manufacturing company wants to relocate to Collier County. A 13-year-old report from a fired researcher at the company says the company's product is releasing toxic by-products. The company has suppressed that report. A second report commissioned by the company shows there is no problem with the fertilizer.

➤ Should the company's chief executive officer reveal the context of the unfavorable report in discussions with Collier County representatives? Discuss.

Source: "Business Leaders Ponder Ethical Questions," *Naples Daily News*, May 12, 1991, p. 1E.

Exercise 1–2
Business entity concept
Objective 5

Bag-One Sports sells hunting and fishing equipment and provides guided hunting and fishing trips. Bag-One Sports is owned and operated by Marc Trailer, a well-known sports enthusiast and hunter. Marc's wife, Robin, owns and operates Red Bird Boutique, a women's clothing store. Marc and Robin have established a trust fund to finance their children's college education. The trust fund is maintained by First Wyoming Bank in the name of the children, Sparrow and Trout.

For each of the following transactions, identify which of the entities listed should record the transaction in its records.

Entities

B	Bag-One Sports
F	First Wyoming Bank
R	Red Bird Boutique
X	None of the above

1. Marc received a cash advance from customers for a guided hunting trip.
2. Robin deposited a $5,000 personal check in the trust fund at First Wyoming Bank.
3. Robin purchased three dozen spring dresses from a Denver designer for a special spring sale.
4. Marc paid a local doctor for his annual physical, which was required by the workmen's compensation insurance policy carried by Bag-One Sports.
5. Marc paid for an advertisement in a hunters' magazine.
6. Robin purchased mutual fund shares as an investment for the children's trust.
7. Marc paid for dinner and a movie to celebrate their tenth wedding anniversary.
8. Robin donated several dresses from inventory for a local charity auction for the benefit of a women's abuse shelter.
9. Marc paid a breeder's fee for an English springer spaniel to be used as a hunting guide dog.
10. Robin paid her dues to the Optimist Club.

Exercise 1–3
Accounting equation
Objective 6

The total assets and total liabilities of **Coca-Cola** and **PepsiCo** at the end of their 1999 fiscal years are shown below.

	Coca-Cola (in millions)	PepsiCo (in millions)
Assets	$21,623	$17,551
Liabilities	12,110	10,670

Determine the owner's equity of each company.

Exercise 1–4
Accounting equation
Objective 6

✓ a. $51,500

Determine the missing amount for each of the following:

	Assets	=	Liabilities	+	Owner's Equity
a.	X	=	$20,000	+	$31,500
b.	$62,750	=	X	+	10,000
c.	57,000	=	38,000	+	X

Exercise 1–5
Accounting equation

Objectives 6, 8

SPREADSHEET

✓ b. $230,000

Jason Seagle is the owner and operator of Go-For-It, a motivational consulting business. At the end of its accounting period, December 31, 2002, Go-For-It has assets of $325,000 and liabilities of $142,000. Using the accounting equation and considering each case independently, determine the following amounts:

a. Jason Seagle, capital, as of December 31, 2002.
b. Jason Seagle, capital, as of December 31, 2003, assuming that assets increased by $84,000 and liabilities increased by $37,000 during 2003.
c. Jason Seagle, capital, as of December 31, 2003, assuming that assets decreased by $8,000 and liabilities increased by $17,000 during 2003.
d. Jason Seagle, capital, as of December 31, 2003, assuming that assets increased by $75,000 and liabilities decreased by $17,500 during 2003.
e. Net income (or net loss) during 2003, assuming that as of December 31, 2003, assets were $425,000, liabilities were $105,000, and there were no additional investments or withdrawals.

Exercise 1–6
Asset, liability, owner's equity items

Objective 7

Indicate whether each of the following is identified with (1) an asset, (2) a liability, or (3) owner's equity:

a. fees earned
b. supplies
c. wages expense
d. land
e. accounts payable
f. cash

Exercise 1–7
Effect of transactions on accounting equation

Objective 7

Describe how the following business transactions affect the three elements of the accounting equation.

a. Invested cash in business.
b. Received cash for services performed.
c. Purchased supplies for cash.
d. Paid for utilities used in the business.
e. Purchased supplies on account.

Exercise 1–8
Effect of transactions on accounting equation

Objective 7

✓ (a)(1) increase $50,000

a. A vacant lot acquired for $65,000 is sold for $115,000 in cash. What is the effect of the sale on the total amount of the seller's (1) assets, (2) liabilities, and (3) owner's equity?
b. Assume that the seller owes $28,000 on a loan for the land. After receiving the $115,000 cash in (a), the seller pays the $28,000 owed. What is the effect of the payment on the total amount of the seller's (1) assets, (2) liabilities, and (3) owner's equity?

Exercise 1–9
Effect of transactions on owner's equity

Objective 7

Indicate whether each of the following types of transactions will (a) increase owner's equity or (b) decrease owner's equity:

1. owner's investments
2. revenues
3. expenses
4. owner's withdrawals

Exercise 1–10
Transactions

Objective 7

The following selected transactions were completed by Next Day Delivery Service during October:

1. Received cash for providing delivery services, $12,150.
2. Paid creditors on account, $2,500.
3. Received cash from owner as additional investment, $75,000.
4. Paid advertising expense, $625.
5. Billed customers for delivery services on account, $6,900.
6. Purchased supplies for cash, $750.
7. Paid rent for October, $2,500.
8. Received cash from customers on account, $3,180.

9. Determined that the cost of supplies on hand was $180; therefore, $570 of supplies had been used during the month.
10. Paid cash to owner for personal use, $2,500.

Indicate the effect of each transaction on the accounting equation by listing the numbers identifying the transactions, (1) through (10), in a vertical column, and inserting at the right of each number the appropriate letter from the following list:

a. Increase in an asset, decrease in another asset.
b. Increase in an asset, increase in a liability.
c. Increase in an asset, increase in owner's equity.
d. Decrease in an asset, decrease in a liability.
e. Decrease in an asset, decrease in owner's equity.

Exercise 1–11
Nature of transactions
Objective 7

✓ d. $2,950

Joe Black operates his own catering service. Summary financial data for July are presented in equation form as follows. Each line designated by a number indicates the effect of a transaction on the equation. Each increase and decrease in owner's equity, except transaction (5), affects net income.

	Cash	+	Supplies	+	Land	=	Liabilities	+	Owner's Equity
Bal.	6,000		750		30,000		7,500		29,250
1.	+15,000								+15,000
2.	− 2,000				+ 2,000				
3.	−11,250								−11,250
4.			+500				+ 500		
5.	− 1,500								− 1,500
6.	− 5,300						−5,300		
7.			−800						− 800
Bal.	950		450		32,000		2,700		30,700

a. Describe each transaction.
b. What is the amount of net decrease in cash during the month?
c. What is the amount of net increase in owner's equity during the month?
d. What is the amount of the net income for the month?
e. How much of the net income for the month was retained in the business?

Exercise 1–12
Net income and owner's withdrawals
Objective 8

The income statement of a proprietorship for the month of January indicates a net income of $52,750. During the same period, the owner withdrew $60,000 in cash from the business for personal use.

Would it be correct to say that the business incurred a net loss of $7,250 during the month? Discuss.

Exercise 1–13
Net income and owner's equity for four businesses
Objective 8

✓ Company Y: Net loss, ($25,000)

Four different proprietorships, W, X, Y, and Z, show the same balance sheet data at the beginning and end of a year. These data, exclusive of the amount of owner's equity, are summarized as follows:

	Total Assets	Total Liabilities
Beginning of the year	$375,000	$150,000
End of the year	$600,000	$325,000

On the basis of the above data and the following additional information for the year, determine the net income (or loss) of each company for the year. (*Hint:* First determine the amount of increase or decrease in owner's equity during the year.)

Company W: The owner had made no additional investments in the business and had made no withdrawals from the business.

Company X: The owner had made no additional investments in the business but had withdrawn $30,000.

Company Y: The owner had made an additional investment of $75,000 but had made no withdrawals.

Company Z: The owner had made an additional investment of $75,000 and had withdrawn $30,000.

Exercise 1–14
Balance sheet items
Objective 8

From the following list of selected items taken from the records of Kagy Appliance Service as of a specific date, identify those that would appear on the balance sheet:

1. Utilities Expense
2. Fees Earned
3. Supplies
4. Wages Expense
5. Accounts Payable
6. Cash
7. Supplies Expense
8. Land
9. Dale Schuber, Capital
10. Wages Payable

Exercise 1–15
Income statement items
Objective 8

Based on the data presented in Exercise 1–14, identify those items that would appear on the income statement.

Exercise 1–16
Statement of owner's equity
Objective 8

✓ Meg Douma, capital June 30, 2003: $393,750

Financial information related to Douma Company, a proprietorship, for the month ended June 30, 2003, is as follows:

Net income for June	$ 91,250
Meg Douma's withdrawals during June	15,000
Meg Douma, capital, June 1, 2003	317,500

Prepare a statement of owner's equity for the month ended June 30, 2003.

Exercise 1–17
Income statement
Objective 8

✓ Net income: $63,800

Surgery Services was organized on April 1, 2003. A summary of the revenue and expense transactions for April follows:

Fees earned	$165,800
Wages expense	71,500
Miscellaneous expense	2,250
Rent expense	25,000
Supplies expense	3,250

Prepare an income statement for the month ended April 30.

Exercise 1–18
Missing amounts from balance sheet and income statement data
Objective 8

✓ (a) $130,250

One item is omitted in each of the following summaries of balance sheet and income statement data for four different proprietorships, I, II, III, and IV.

	I	II	III	IV
Beginning of the year:				
Assets	$600,000	$125,000	$100,000	(d)
Liabilities	360,000	65,000	76,000	$150,000
End of the year:				
Assets	745,000	175,000	90,000	310,000
Liabilities	325,000	55,000	80,000	170,000
During the year:				
Additional investment in the business	(a)	25,000	10,000	50,000
Withdrawals from the business	40,000	8,000	(c)	75,000
Revenue	197,750	(b)	115,000	140,000
Expenses	108,000	32,000	122,500	160,000

Determine the missing amounts, identifying them by letter. (*Hint:* First determine the amount of increase or decrease in owner's equity during the year.)

Exercise 1–19
Balance sheets, net income

Objective 8

✓ b. $11,330

Financial information related to the proprietorship of Revival Interiors for August and September of the current year is as follows:

	August 31, 20—	**September 30, 20—**
Accounts payable	$ 3,850	$ 4,150
Accounts receivable	8,500	9,780
Laura Fedro, capital	?	?
Cash	15,000	25,500
Supplies	750	600

a. Prepare balance sheets for Revival Interiors as of August 31 and as of September 30 of the current year.
b. Determine the amount of net income for September, assuming that the owner made no additional investments or withdrawals during the month.
c. Determine the amount of net income for September, assuming that the owner made no additional investments but withdrew $7,500 during the month.

Exercise 1–20
Financial statements

Objective 8

Each of the following items is shown in the financial statements of **Exxon Mobil Corporation**. Identify the financial statement (balance sheet or income statement) in which each item would appear.

a. Operating expenses
b. Crude oil inventory
c. Income taxes payable
d. Sales
e. Investments
f. Marketable securities
g. Exploration expenses
h. Notes and loans payable
i. Cash equivalents
j. Long-term debt
k. Selling expenses
l. Notes receivable
m. Equipment
n. Accounts payable
o. Prepaid taxes

Exercise 1–21
Statement of cash flows

Objective 8

Indicate whether each of the following activities would be reported on the statement of cash flows as (a) an operating activity, (b) an investing activity, or (c) a financing activity:

1. Cash received as owner's investment
2. Cash paid for land
3. Cash received from fees earned
4. Cash paid for expenses

Exercise 1–22
Financial statements

Objective 8

✓ Correct Amount of Total Assets is $13,875

Aspen Realty, organized February 1, 2003, is owned and operated by Lynn Soby. How many errors can you find in the following financial statements for Aspen Realty, prepared after its second month of operations?

Aspen Realty
Income Statement
March 31, 2003

Sales commissions		$37,100
Operating expenses:		
Office salaries expense	$23,150	
Rent expense	7,800	
Automobile expense	1,750	
Miscellaneous expense	550	
Supplies expense	225	
Total operating expenses		33,475
Net income		$13,625

Lynn Soby
Statement of Owner's Equity
March 31, 2002

Lynn Soby, capital, March 1, 2003	$ 7,450
Less withdrawals during March	1,000
	$ 6,450
Additional investment during March	1,500
	$ 7,950
Net income for the month	13,625
Lynn Soby, capital, March 31, 2003	$21,575

Balance Sheet
For the Month Ended March 31, 2003

Assets			Liabilities		
Cash	$2,350		Accounts receivable	$10,200
Accounts payable	2,300		Supplies	1,325
			Owner's Equity	
			Lynn Soby, capital	21,575
Total assets	$4,650		Total liabilities and owner's equity	$33,100

Exercise 1–23
Ratio of liabilities to stockholders' equity

Objective 9

The financial statements for **Cisco Systems, Inc.** are presented in Appendix G at the end of the text.

Cisco Systems is the worldwide leader in networking for the Internet. Cisco Systems provides both hardware and software to enable its customers to create Internet solutions that provide seamless access to information. You can learn more about Cisco Systems by visiting its web site at **www.cisco.com**.

a. Determine the ratio of liabilities to stockholders' equity for Cisco Systems at the end of 2000 and 1999. Use only current liabilities in the numerator.
b. What conclusions regarding the margin of protection to the creditors can you draw from your analysis?

PROBLEMS SERIES A

Problem 1–1A
Transactions

Objective 7

✓ Cash Bal. at End of Feb.: $7,070

On February 1 of the current year, Linda Neece established a business to manage rental property. She completed the following transactions during February:

a. Opened a business bank account with a deposit of $10,000 from personal funds.
b. Purchased supplies (pens, file folders, and copy paper) on account, $1,150.
c. Received cash from fees earned for managing rental property, $4,500.
d. Paid rent on office and equipment for the month, $2,500.
e. Paid creditors on account, $675.
f. Billed customers for fees earned for managing rental property, $3,250.
g. Paid automobile expenses (including rental charges) for month, $980, and miscellaneous expenses, $775.
h. Paid office salaries, $1,500.
i. Determined that the cost of supplies on hand was $215; therefore, the cost of supplies used was $935.
j. Withdrew cash for personal use, $1,000.

Instructions

1. Indicate the effect of each transaction and the balances after each transaction, using the following tabular headings:

	Assets	**=**	**Liabilities**	**+**	**Owner's Equity**
Cash + Accounts Receivable + Supplies		=	Accounts Payable	+	Linda Neece, Capital

Explain the nature of each increase and decrease in owner's equity by an appropriate notation at the right of the amount.

2. ✏️ ➤ Briefly explain why the owner's investment and revenues increased owner's equity, while withdrawals and expenses decreased owner's equity.

Problem 1–2A
Financial statements

Objective 8

SPREADSHEET

✓ Net income: $40,865

Following are the amounts of the assets and liabilities of Fly Away Travel Agency at December 31, 2003, the end of the current year, and its revenue and expenses for the year. The capital of Ryan Stecker, owner, was $14,500 on January 1, 2003, the beginning of the current year. During the current year, Stecker withdrew $30,000.

Accounts payable	$ 3,200
Accounts receivable	19,500
Cash	7,200
Fees earned	117,480
Miscellaneous expense	1,750
Rent expense	27,000
Supplies	1,865
Supplies expense	2,125
Utilities expense	10,240
Wages expense	35,500

Instructions

1. Prepare an income statement for the current year ended December 31, 2003.
2. Prepare a statement of owner's equity for the current year ended December 31, 2003.
3. Prepare a balance sheet as of December 31, 2003.

Problem 1–3A
Financial statements

Objective 8

✓ Net income: $5,950

Loren Thurlow established Eagle Financial Services on January 1, 2003. Eagle Financial Services offers financial planning advice to its clients. The effect of each transaction and the balances after each transaction for January are as follows:

	Assets					**=**	**Liabilities**	**+**	**Owner's Equity**	
	Cash	+	Accounts Receivable	+	Supplies	=	Accounts Payable	+	Loren Thurlow, Capital	
a.	+12,500								+12,500	Investment
b.					+1,325		+1,325			
Bal.	12,500				1,325		1,325		12,500	
c.	− 900						− 900			
Bal.	11,600				1,325		425		12,500	
d.	+ 8,750								+ 8,750	Fees earned
Bal.	20,350				1,325		425		21,250	
e.	− 2,500								− 2,500	Rent expense
Bal.	17,850				1,325		425		18,750	
f.	− 1,600								− 1,250	Auto expense
									− 350	Misc. expense
Bal.	16,250				1,325		425		17,150	
g.	− 2,000								− 2,000	Salaries expense
Bal.	14,250				1,325		425		15,150	
h.					−1,050				− 1,050	Supplies expense
Bal.	14,250				275		425		14,100	
i.			+4,350						+ 4,350	Fees earned
Bal.	14,250		4,350		275		425		18,450	
j.	− 3,000								− 3,000	Withdrawal
Bal.	11,250		4,350		275		425		15,450	

Instructions

1. Prepare an income statement for the month ended January 31, 2003.
2. Prepare a statement of owner's equity for the month ended January 31, 2003.
3. Prepare a balance sheet as of January 31, 2003.

Problem 1–4A

Transactions; financial statements

Objectives 7, 8

✓ Net income: $7,050

On March 1 of the current year, Dori French established Deal Realty. French completed the following transactions during the month of March:

a. Opened a business bank account with a deposit of $5,000 from personal funds.
b. Purchased supplies (pens, file folders, fax paper, etc.) on account, $1,250.
c. Paid creditor on account, $850.
d. Earned sales commissions, receiving cash, $16,200.
e. Paid rent on office and equipment for the month, $2,000.
f. Withdrew cash for personal use, $4,500.
g. Paid automobile expenses (including rental charge) for month, $1,900, and miscellaneous expenses, $350.
h. Paid office salaries, $4,250.
i. Determined that the cost of supplies on hand was $600; therefore, the cost of supplies used was $650.

Instructions

1. Indicate the effect of each transaction and the balances after each transaction, using the following tabular headings:

Assets	=	Liabilities	+	Owner's Equity
Cash + Supplies	=	Accounts Payable	+	Dori French, Capital

Explain the nature of each increase and decrease in owner's equity by an appropriate notation at the right of the amount.
2. Prepare an income statement for March, a statement of owner's equity for March, and a balance sheet as of March 31.

Problem 1–5A

Transactions; financial statements

Objectives 7, 8

GENERAL LEDGER

✓ Net income: $9,250

Persnickety Cleaners is owned and operated by Bea Cheever. A building and equipment are currently being rented, pending expansion to new facilities. The actual work of dry cleaning is done by another company at wholesale rates. The assets and the liabilities of the business on July 1 of the current year are as follows: Cash, $6,250; Accounts Receivable, $18,100; Supplies, $2,200; Land, $40,000; Accounts Payable, $7,800. Business transactions during July are summarized as follows:

a. Received cash from cash customers for dry cleaning sales, $15,750.
b. Paid rent for the month, $2,500.
c. Purchased supplies on account, $1,650.
d. Paid creditors on account, $5,100.
e. Charged customers for dry cleaning sales on account, $8,920.
f. Received monthly invoice for dry cleaning expense for July (to be paid on August 10), $6,000.
g. Paid the following: wages expense, $2,400; truck expense, $1,580; utilities expense, $960; miscellaneous expense, $630.
h. Received cash from customers on account, $12,100.
i. Determined that the cost of supplies on hand was $2,500; therefore, the cost of supplies used during the month was $1,350.
j. Withdrew $7,500 cash for personal use.

Instructions

1. Determine the amount of Bea Cheever's capital as of July 1 of the current year.
2. State the assets, liabilities, and owner's equity as of July 1 in equation form similar to that shown in this chapter. In tabular form below the equation, indicate increases and decreases resulting from each transaction and the new balances after each transaction.

Explain the nature of each increase and decrease in owner's equity by an appropriate notation at the right of the amount.
3. Prepare an income statement for July, a statement of owner's equity for July, and a balance sheet as of July 31.

Problem 1–6A
Missing amount from financial statements

Objective 8

SPREADSHEET

✓ k. $15,000

The financial statements at the end of Magic Realty's first month of operations are shown below.

Instructions

By analyzing the interrelationships among the four financial statements, determine the proper amounts for (a) through (q).

Magic Realty
Income Statement
For the Month Ended April 30, 2003

Fees earned		$	(a)
Operating expenses:			
Wages expense	$4 2 5 0 00		
Rent expense	1 6 0 0 00		
Supplies expense	(b)		
Utilities expense	9 0 0 00		
Miscellaneous expense	5 5 0 00		
Total operating expenses		8 8 0 0 00	
Net income		$6 2 0 0 00	

Magic Realty
Statement of Owner's Equity
For the Month Ended April 30, 2003

Ray Conway, capital, April 1, 2003		$	(c)
Investment on April 1, 2003	$20 0 0 0 00		
Net income for April		(d)	
		(e)	
Less withdrawals	7 0 0 0 00		
Increase in owner's equity			(f)
Ray Conway, capital, April 30, 2003			(g)

Magic Realty
Balance Sheet
April 30, 2003

Assets			Liabilities		
Cash	$ 2 9 0 0 00		Accounts payable	$ 8 0 0 00	
Supplies	1 1 0 0 00		**Owner's Equity**		
Land	20 0 0 0 00		Ray Conway, capital		(i)
			Total liabilities and		
Total assets	(h)		owner's equity		(j)

Magic Realty
Statement of Cash Flows
For the Month Ended April 30, 2003

Cash flows from operating activities:															
Cash received from customers	$			(k)										
Deduct cash payments for expenses and															
payments to creditors	9	1	0	0	00									
Net cash flow from operating activities							$			(l)			
Cash flows from investing activities:															
Cash payments for acquisition of land										(m)			
Cash flows from financing activities:															
Cash received as owner's investment				(n)										
Deduct cash withdrawal by owner				(o)										
Net cash flow from financing activities										(p)			
Net cash flow and April 30, 2003 cash balance										(q)			

PROBLEMS SERIES B

Problem 1–1B
Transactions

Objective 7

✓ Cash Bal. at End of March:
$14,695

Fran Cowles established an insurance agency on March 1 of the current year and completed the following transactions during March:

a. Opened a business bank account with a deposit of $15,000 from personal funds.
b. Purchased supplies on account, $750.
c. Paid creditors on account, $625.
d. Received cash from fees earned on insurance commissions, $5,250.
e. Paid rent on office and equipment for the month, $1,000.
f. Paid automobile expenses for month, $880, and miscellaneous expenses, $350.
g. Paid office salaries, $1,200.
h. Determined that the cost of supplies on hand was $175; therefore, the cost of supplies used was $575.
i. Billed insurance companies for sales commissions earned, $7,350.
j. Withdrew cash for personal use, $1,500.

Instructions

1. Indicate the effect of each transaction and the balances after each transaction, using the following tabular headings:

Assets	=	Liabilities	+	Owner's Equity
Cash + Accounts Receivable + Supplies	=	Accounts Payable	+	Fran Cowles, Capital

Explain the nature of each increase and decrease in owner's equity by an appropriate notation at the right of the amount.

2. Briefly explain why the owner's investment and revenues increased owner's equity, while withdrawals and expenses decreased owner's equity.

Problem 1–2B
Financial statements

Objective 8

SPREADSHEET

At the top of the next page are the amounts of the assets and liabilities of Hiawatha Travel Service at April 30, 2003, the end of the current year, and its revenue and expenses for the year. The capital of Rob Graybill, owner, was $25,000 at May 1, 2002, the beginning of the current year, and the owner withdrew $15,000 during the current year.

Instructions

1. Prepare an income statement for the current year ended April 30, 2003.
2. Prepare a statement of owner's equity for the current year ended April 30, 2003.
3. Prepare a balance sheet as of April 30, 2003.

Accounts payable	$ 6,100
Accounts receivable	15,675
Cash	26,525
Fees earned	131,600
Miscellaneous expense	1,475
Rent expense	18,900
Supplies	1,675
Supplies expense	3,550
Taxes expense	2,800
Utilities expense	11,250
Wages expense	65,850

Problem 1–3B
Financial statements

Objective 8

✓ Net income: $2,970

Chester Hoche established Infinet Computer Services on October 1, 2003. The effect of each transaction and the balances after each transaction for October are as follows:

		Assets			=	Liabilities	+	Owner's Equity	
			Accounts			Accounts		Chester Hoche,	
	Cash	+	Receivable	+ Supplies	=	Payable	+	Capital	
a.	+ 5,000							+ 5,000	Investment
b.				+720		+720			
Bal.	5,000			720		720		5,000	
c.	+ 4,500							+ 4,500	Fees earned
Bal.	9,500			720		720		9,500	
d.	− 1,800							− 1,800	Rent expense
Bal.	7,700			720		720		7,700	
e.	− 250					−250			
Bal.	7,450			720		470		7,700	
f.			+3,750					+ 3,750	Fees earned
Bal.	7,450		3,750	720		470		11,450	
g.	− 1,155							− 780	Auto expense
								− 375	Misc. expense
Bal.	6,295		3,750	720		470		10,295	
h.	− 2,000							− 2,000	Salaries expense
Bal.	4,295		3,750	720		470		8,295	
i.				−325				− 325	Supplies expense
Bal.	4,295		3,750	395		470		7,970	
j.	− 1,000							− 1,000	Withdrawal
Bal.	3,295		3,750	395		470		6,970	

Instructions

1. Prepare an income statement for the month ended October 31, 2003.
2. Prepare a statement of owner's equity for the month ended October 31, 2003.
3. Prepare a balance sheet as of Ocotber 31, 2003.

Problem 1–4B
Transactions; financial statements

Objectives 7, 8

✓ Net income: $8,975

On August 1, 2003, of the current year, Angie Tate established Vogue Realty. Tate completed the following transactions during the month of August:

a. Opened a business bank account with a deposit of $10,000 from personal funds.
b. Paid rent on office and equipment for the month, $3,600.
c. Paid automobile expenses (including rental charge) for month, $900, and miscellaneous expenses, $550.
d. Purchased supplies (pens, file folders, and copy paper) on account, $1,325.
e. Earned sales commissions, receiving cash, $18,750.

(continued)

f.   Paid creditor on account, $690.
g.   Paid office salaries, $4,000.
h.   Withdrew cash for personal use, $3,000.
i.   Determined that the cost of supplies on hand was $600; therefore, the cost of supplies used was $725.

Instructions

1.   Indicate the effect of each transaction and the balances after each transaction, using the following tabular headings:

Assets	=	Liabilities	+	Owner's Equity
Cash + Supplies	=	Accounts Payable	+	Angie Tate, Capital

Explain the nature of each increase and decrease in owner's equity by an appropriate notation at the right of the amount.
2.   Prepare an income statement for August, a statement of owner's equity for August, and a balance sheet as of August 31.

Problem 1–5B
Transactions; financial statements

Objectives 7, 8

GENERAL LEDGER

✓ Net income: $8,075

Swan Dry Cleaners is owned and operated by Merritt Paisley. A building and equipment are currently being rented, pending expansion to new facilities. The actual work of dry cleaning is done by another company at wholesale rates. The assets and the liabilities of the business on November 1 of the current year are as follows: Cash, $7,400; Accounts Receivable, $13,750; Supplies, $1,560; Land, $25,000; Accounts Payable, $3,880. Business transactions during November are summarized as follows:

a.   Paid rent for the month, $3,000.
b.   Charged customers for dry cleaning sales on account, $6,150.
c.   Paid creditors on account, $1,680.
d.   Purchased supplies on account, $840.
e.   Received cash from cash customers for dry cleaning sales, $14,600.
f.   Received cash from customers on account, $11,750.
g.   Received monthly invoice for dry cleaning expense for November (to be paid on December 10), $5,400.
h.   Paid the following: wages expense, $1,800; truck expense, $725; utilities expense, $510; miscellaneous expense, $190.
i.   Determined that the cost of supplies on hand was $1,350; therefore, the cost of supplies used during the month was $1,050.
j.   Withdrew $5,000 for personal use.

Instructions

1.   Determine the amount of Merritt Paisley's capital as of November 1 of the current year.
2.   State the assets, liabilities, and owner's equity as of November 1 in equation form similar to that shown in this chapter. In tabular form below the equation, indicate increases and decreases resulting from each transaction and the new balances after each transaction. Explain the nature of each increase and decrease in owner's equity by an appropriate notation at the right of the amount.
3.   Prepare an income statement for November, a statement of owner's equity for November, and a balance sheet as of November 30.

Problem 1–6B
Missing amount from financial statements

Objective 8

✓ i. $50,550

The financial statements at the end of Ruby River Realty's first month of operations are shown below.

Instructions
By analyzing the interrelationships among the four financial statements, determine the proper amounts for (a) through (q).

SPREADSHEET

Ruby River Realty
Income Statement
For the Month Ended June 30, 2003

Fees earned			$23 5 0 0 00
Operating expenses:			
Wages expense	$ (a)		
Rent expense	2 4 0 0 00		
Supplies expense	2 0 0 0 00		
Utilities expense	1 3 5 0 00		
Miscellaneous expense	8 2 5 00		
Total operating expenses			11 9 5 0 00
Net income			(b)

Ruby River Realty
Statement of Owner's Equity
For the Month Ended June 30, 2003

R.J. Cain, capital, June 1, 2003		$ (c)
Investment on June 1, 2003	$ (d)	
Net income for June	(e)	
	(f)	
Less withdrawals	(g)	
Increase in owner's equity		(h)
R.J. Cain, capital, June 30, 2003		(i)

Ruby River Realty
Balance Sheet
June 30, 2003

Assets		Liabilities	
Cash	$14 7 5 0 00	Accounts payable	$ 1 2 0 0 00
Supplies	1 0 0 0 00	**Owner's Equity**	
Land	(j)	R.J. Cain, capital	(l)
		Total liabilities and	
Total assets	(k)	owner's equity	(m)

Ruby River Realty
Statement of Cash Flows
For the Month Ended June 30, 2003

Cash flows from operating activities:		
Cash received from customers	$ (n)	
Deduct cash payments for expenses and		
payments to creditors	11 7 5 0 00	
Net cash flow from operating activities		$ (o)
Cash flows from investing activities:		
Cash payments for acquisition of land		(36 0 0 0 00)
Cash flows from financing activities:		
Cash received as owner's investment	$45 0 0 0 00	
Deduct cash withdrawal by owner	6 0 0 0 00	
Net cash flow from financing activities		(p)
Net cash flow and June 30, 2003 cash balance		(q)

CONTINUING PROBLEM

GENERAL LEDGER

✓ 2. Net income: $265

Lynn Kwan enjoys listening to all types of music and owns countless CDs and tapes. Over the years, Lynn has gained a local reputation for knowledge of music from classical to rap and the ability to put together sets of recordings that appeal to all ages.

During the last several months, Lynn served as a guest disc jockey on a local radio station. In addition, Lynn has entertained at several friends' parties as the host deejay.

On November 1, 2002, Lynn established a proprietorship known as Dancin Music. Using an extensive collection of CDs and tapes, Lynn will serve as a disc jockey on a fee basis for weddings, college parties, and other events. During November, Lynn entered into the following transactions:

Nov. 1. Deposited $3,500 in a checking account in the name of Dancin Music.
  2. Received $1,000 from a local radio station for serving as the guest disc jockey for November.
  2. Agreed to share office space with a local real estate agency, Golino Realty. Dancin Music will pay one-fourth of the rent. In addition, Dancin Music agreed to pay a portion of the salary of the receptionist and to pay one-fourth of the utilities. Paid $500 for the rent of the office.
  4. Purchased supplies (blank cassette tapes, poster board, extension cords, etc.) from Bruce Office Supply Co. for $175. Agreed to pay $50 within 10 days and the remainder by December 3, 2002.
  6. Paid $300 to a local radio station to advertise the services of Dancin Music twice daily for two weeks.
  8. Paid $325 to a local electronics store for rent on two CD players, two cassette players, and eight speakers.
  12. Paid $100 (music expense) to Dynamic Music for the use of its current demo CDs and tapes to make cassette tapes of various music sets.
  13. Paid Bruce Office Supply Co. $50 on account.
  16. Received $75 from a dentist for providing two music sets for the dentist to play for her patients.
  22. Served as disc jockey for a wedding party. The father of the bride agreed to pay $600 the 1st of December.
  25. Received $250 from a friend for serving as the disc jockey for a cancer charity ball hosted by the local hospital.
  29. Paid $120 (music expense) to Score Music for the use of its library of demo CDs and tapes.
  30. Received $450 for serving as disc jockey for a local club's monthly dance.
  30. Paid Golino Realty $200 for Dancin Music's share of the receptionist's salary for November.
  30. Paid Golino Realty $150 for Dancin Music's share of the utilities for November.
  30. Determined that the cost of supplies on hand is $85. Therefore, the cost of supplies used during the month was $90.
  30. Paid for miscellaneous expenses, $75.
  30. Paid $250 royalties (music expense) to Federated Clearing for use of various artists' music during the month.
  30. Withdrew $125 of cash from Dancin Music for personal use.

Instructions

1. Indicate the effect of each transaction and the balances after each transaction, using the following tabular headings:

Assets			=	Liabilities	+	Owner's Equity
Cash + Accounts Receivable + Supplies			=	Accounts Payable	+	Lynn Kwan, Capital

Explain the nature of each increase and decrease in owner's equity by an appropriate notation at the right of the amount.
2. Prepare an income statement for Dancin Music for the month ended November 30, 2002.
3. Prepare a statement of owner's equity for Dancin Music for the month ended November 30, 2002.
4. Prepare a balance sheet for Dancin Music as of November 30, 2002.

SPECIAL ACTIVITIES

Activity 1–1
Phinney Enterprises
Ethics and professional conduct in business

Joel Phinney, president of Phinney Enterprises, applied for a $150,000 loan from Bridger National Bank. The bank requested financial statements from Phinney Enterprises as a basis for granting the loan. Joel has told his accountant to provide the bank with a balance sheet. Joel has decided to omit the other financial statements because there was a net loss during the past year.

In groups of three or four, discuss the following questions:

1. Is Joel behaving in a professional manner by omitting some of the financial statements?
2. a. What types of information about their businesses would owners be willing to provide bankers? What types of information would owners not be willing to provide?
   b. What types of information about a business would bankers want before extending a loan?
   c. What common interests are shared by bankers and business owners?

Activity 1–2
Expert Opinion
Net income

On January 3, 2002, Dr. Brittany North established Expert Opinion, a medical practice organized as a proprietorship. The following conversation occurred the following August between Dr. North and a former medical school classmate, Dr. Charles Ryder, at an American Medical Association convention in Bermuda.

Dr. Ryder: Brittany, good to see you again. Why didn't you call when you were in Las Vegas? We could have had dinner together.
Dr. North: Actually, I never made it to Las Vegas this year. My husband and kids went up to our Lake Tahoe condo twice, but I got stuck in New York. I opened a new consulting practice this January and haven't had any time for myself since.
Dr. Ryder: I heard about it . . . Expert . . . something . . . right?
Dr. North: Yes, Expert Opinion. My husband chose the name.
Dr. Ryder: I've thought about doing something like that. Are you making any money? I mean, is it worth your time?
Dr. North: You wouldn't believe it. I started by opening a bank account with $30,000, and my July bank statement has a balance of $180,000. Not bad for seven months—all pure profit.
Dr. Ryder: Maybe I'll try it in Las Vegas. Let's have breakfast together tomorrow and you can fill me in on the details.

Comment on Dr. North's statement that the difference between the opening bank balance ($30,000) and the July statement balance ($180,000) is pure profit.

Activity 1–3
Forty-Love
Transactions and financial statements

Yvonne Tobin, a junior in college, has been seeking ways to earn extra spending money. As an active sports enthusiast, Yvonne plays tennis regularly at the Racquet Club, where her family has a membership. The president of the club recently approached Yvonne with the proposal that she manage the club's tennis courts on weekends. Yvonne's primary duty would be to supervise the operation of the club's four indoor and six outdoor courts, including court reservations.

In return for her services, the club would pay Yvonne $75 per weekend, plus Yvonne could keep whatever she earned from lessons and the fees from the use of the ball machine. The club and Yvonne agreed to a one-month trial, after which both would consider an arrangement for the remaining two years of Yvonne's college career. On this basis, Yvonne organized Forty-Love. During September, Yvonne managed the tennis courts and entered into the following transactions:

a. Opened a business account by depositing $500.
b. Paid $160 for tennis supplies (practice tennis balls, etc.).
c. Paid $80 for the rental of videotape equipment to be used in offering lessons during September.
d. Arranged for the rental of two ball machines during September for $100. Paid $70 in advance, with the remaining $30 due October 1.

e.   Received $800 for lessons given during September.
f.   Received $150 in fees from the use of the ball machines during September.
g.   Paid $300 for salaries of part-time employees who answered the telephone and took reservations while Yvonne was giving lessons.
h.   Paid $75 for miscellaneous expenses.
i.   Received $300 from the club for managing the tennis courts during September.
j.   Determined that the cost of supplies on hand at the end of the month totaled $75; therefore, the cost of supplies used was $85.
k.   Withdrew $400 for personal use on September 30.

As a friend and accounting student, you have been asked by Yvonne to aid her in assessing the venture.

1.   Indicate the effect of each transaction and the balances after each transaction, using the following tabular headings:

Assets	=	Liabilities	+	Owner's Equity
Cash + Supplies	=	Accounts Payable	+	Yvonne Tobin, Capital

Explain the nature of each increase and decrease in owner's equity by an appropriate notation at the right of the amount.
2.   Prepare an income statement for September.
3.   Prepare a statement of owner's equity for September.
4.   Prepare a balance sheet as of September 30.
5.   a.   Assume that Yvonne Tobin could earn $7 per hour working 20 hours each of the four weekends as a waitress. Evaluate which of the two alternatives, working as a waitress or operating Forty-Love, would provide Yvonne with the most income per month.
     b.   Discuss any other factors that you believe Yvonne should consider before discussing a long-term arrangement with the Racquet Club.

Activity 1–4
Into the Real World
Certification requirements for accountants

By satisfying certain specific requirements, accountants may become certified as public accountants (CPAs), management accountants (CMAs), or internal auditors (CIAs). Find the certification requirements for one of these accounting groups by accessing the appropriate Internet site listed below.

Site	Description
www.ais-cpa.com	This site lists the address and/or Internet link for each state's board of accountancy. Find your state's requirements.
www.imanet.org	This site lists the requirements for becoming a CMA.
www.theiia.org	This site lists the requirements for becoming a CIA.

Activity 1–5
Amazon.com
Cash flows

Amazon.com, an Internet retailer, was incorporated in July 1994, and opened its virtual doors on the web in July 1995. On the statement of cash flows, would you expect Amazon.com's net cash flows from operating, investing, and financing activities to be positive or negative for each year, 1996, 1997, and 1998? Use the following format for your answers, and briefly explain your logic.

	1998	1997	1996
Net cash flows from operating activities	positive		
Net cash flows from investing activities			
Net cash flows from financing activities			

ANSWERS TO SELF-EXAMINATION QUESTIONS

Matching

1.	H	5.	DD	9.	D	13.	Q	17.	T	21.	B	25.	HH	29.	JJ
2.	W	6.	L	10.	N	14.	I	18.	CC	22.	EE	26.	S	30.	X
3.	Y	7.	J	11.	P	15.	LL	19.	E	23.	C	27.	KK	31.	A
4.	FF	8.	V	12.	U	16.	F	20.	K	24.	O	28.	G		

Multiple Choice

1. **D** A corporation, organized in accordance with state or federal statutes, is a separate legal entity in which ownership is divided into shares of stock (answer D). A proprietorship (answer A) is an unincorporated business owned by one individual. A service business (answer B) provides services to its customers. It can be organized as a proprietorship, partnership, or corporation. A partnership (answer C) is an unincorporated business owned by two or more individuals.

2. **A** The resources owned by a business are called assets (answer A). The debts of the business are called liabilities (answer B), and the equity of the owners is called owner's equity (answer D). The relationship between assets, liabilities, and owner's equity is expressed as the accounting equation (answer C).

3. **A** The balance sheet is a listing of the assets, liabilities, and owner's equity of a business at a specific date (answer A). The income statement (answer B) is a summary of the revenue and expenses of a business for a specific period of time. The statement of owner's equity (answer C) summarizes the changes in owner's equity for a proprietorship or partnership during a specific period of time. The statement of cash flows (answer D) summarizes the cash receipts and cash payments for a specific period of time.

4. **C** The accounting equation is:

   Assets = Liabilities + Owner's Equity

   Therefore, if assets increased by $20,000 and liabilities increased by $12,000, owner's equity must have increased by $8,000 (answer C), as indicated in the following computation:

Assets	=	Liabilities + Owner's Equity
+$20,000	=	+$12,000 + Owner's Equity
+$20,000 − $12,000	=	Owner's Equity
+$8,000	=	Owner's Equity

5. **B** Net income is the excess of revenue over expenses, or $7,500 (answer B). If expenses exceed revenue, the difference is a net loss. Withdrawals by the owner are the opposite of the owner's investing in the business and do not affect the amount of net income or net loss.

Analyzing Transactions

2

objectives

After studying this chapter, you should be able to:

1. Explain why accounts are used to record and summarize the effects of transactions on financial statements.

2. Describe the characteristics of an account.

3. List the rules of debit and credit and the normal balances of accounts.

4. Analyze and summarize the financial statement effects of transactions.

5. Prepare a trial balance and explain how it can be used to discover errors.

6. Discover errors in recording transactions and correct them.

7. Use horizontal analysis to compare financial statements from different periods.

A ssume that you have been hired by a pizza restaurant to deliver pizzas, using your own car. You will be paid $6.00 per hour plus $0.30 per mile plus tips. What is the best way for you to determine how many miles you have driven each day in delivering pizzas?

One method would be to record the odometer mileage before work and then at quitting time. The difference would be the miles driven. For example, if the odometer read 56,743 at the start of work and 56,889 at the end of work, you would have driven 146 miles. This method is subject to error, however, if you copy down the wrong reading or make a math error.

In the same way, business managers need information about the status of the business at different points in time. Such information is useful for analyzing the effects of transactions on the business and for making decisions. For example, the manager of your neighborhood dry cleaners needs to know how much cash is available, how much has been spent, and what services have been provided.

In Chapter 1, we analyzed and recorded this kind of information by using the accounting equation, Assets = Liabilities + Owner's Equity. Since such a format is not practical for most businesses, in Chapter 2 we will study more efficient methods of recording transactions. We will conclude this chapter by discussing how accounting errors may occur and how they may be detected by the accounting process.

Usefulness of an Account

objective 1

Explain why accounts are used to record and summarize the effects of transactions on financial statements.

The increases and decreases in each financial statement item are shown in an account.

Before making a major cash purchase, such as buying a CD player, you need to know the balance of your bank account. Likewise, managers need timely, useful information in order to make good decisions about their businesses.

How are accounting systems designed to provide this information? We illustrated a very simple design in Chapter 1, where transactions were recorded and summarized in the accounting equation format. However, this format is difficult to use when thousands of transactions must be recorded daily. Thus, accounting systems are designed to show the increases and decreases in each financial statement item in a separate record. This record is called an account. For example, since cash appears on the balance sheet, a separate record is kept of the increases and decreases in cash. Likewise, a separate record is kept of the increases and decreases for supplies, land, accounts payable, and the other balance sheet items. Similar records would be kept for income statement items, such as fees earned, wages expense, and rent expense.

A group of accounts for a business entity is called a ledger. A list of the accounts in the ledger is called a chart of accounts. The accounts are normally listed in the order in which they appear in the financial statements. The balance sheet accounts are usually listed first, in the order of assets, liabilities, and owner's equity. The income statement accounts are then listed in the order of revenues and expenses. Each of these major account classifications is briefly described below.

Assets are resources owned by the business entity. These resources can be physical items, such as cash and supplies, or intangibles that have value, such as patent rights. Some other examples of assets include accounts receivable, prepaid expenses (such as insurance), buildings, equipment, and land.

Liabilities are debts owed to outsiders (creditors). Liabilities are often identified on the balance sheet by titles that include the word *payable*. Examples of liabilities include accounts payable, notes payable, and wages payable. Cash received before services are delivered creates a liability to perform the services. These future service commitments are often called *unearned revenues*. Examples of unearned revenues are magazine subscriptions received by a publisher and tuition received by a college at the beginning of a term.

Owner's equity is the owner's right to the assets of the business. For a proprietorship, the owner's equity on the balance sheet is represented by the balance of the owner's *capital* account. A **drawing** account represents the amount of withdrawals made by the owner.

Revenues are increases in owner's equity as a result of selling services or products to customers. Examples of revenues include fees earned, fares earned, commissions revenue, and rent revenue.

The using up of assets or consuming services in the process of generating revenues results in **expenses**. Examples of typical expenses include wages expense, rent expense, utilities expense, supplies expense, and miscellaneous expense.

A chart of accounts is designed to meet the information needs of a company's managers and other users of its financial statements. The accounts within the chart of accounts are numbered for use as references. A flexible numbering system is normally used, so that new accounts can be added without affecting other account numbers.

Exhibit 1 is NetSolutions' chart of accounts that we will be using in this chapter. Additional accounts will be introduced in later chapters. In Exhibit 1, each account number has two digits. The first digit indicates the major classification of the ledger in which the account is located. Accounts beginning with 1 represent assets; 2, liabilities; 3, owner's equity; 4, revenue; and 5, expenses. The second digit indicates the location of the account within its class.

Procter & Gamble's account numbers have over 30 digits to reflect P&G's many different operations and regions.

BUSINESS ON STAGE

The Telltale Chart of Accounts

What does a chart of accounts reveal about a business's operations? Look at the following revenue and expense accounts taken from the chart of accounts for a newspaper:

- Revenue accounts:
  - Circulation—carriers
  - Circulation—vending machines
  - Circulation—mail subscriptions
  - Advertising—commercial
  - Advertising—classified

- Expense accounts:
  - Newsprint
  - News ink
  - Wire services
  - Correspondent fees
  - Photography
  - Telephone
  - Postage
  - Delivery
  - Wages

These accounts reveal that the newspaper receives its primary revenues from circulation and advertising.

In addition, the accounts reflect some of the decision-making needs of management. For example, matching the revenues from commercial and classified advertising with the related expenses helps management determine whether these services are profitable. This might lead management to consider expanding the paper's advertising space to take advantage of this profitability. ■

Exhibit 1 Chart of Accounts for NetSolutions

Balance Sheet Accounts		Income Statement Accounts	
I. Assets		**4. Revenue**	
11	Cash	41	Fees Earned
12	Accounts Receivable		**5. Expenses**
14	Supplies	51	Wages Expense
15	Prepaid Insurance	52	Rent Expense
17	Land	54	Utilities Expense
18	Office Equipment	55	Supplies Expense
	2. Liabilities	59	Miscellaneous Expense
21	Accounts Payable		
23	Unearned Rent		
	3. Owner's Equity		
31	Chris Clark, Capital		
32	Chris Clark, Drawing		

Characteristics of an Account

objective 2

Describe the characteristics of an account.

An account, in its simplest form, has three parts. First, each account has a title, which is the name of the item recorded in the account. Second, each account has a space for recording increases in the amount of the item. Third, each account has a space for recording decreases in the amount of the item. The account form presented below is called a **T account** because it resembles the letter T. The left side of the account is called the *debit* side, and the right side is called the *credit* side.[1]

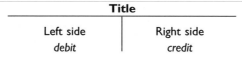

Point of Interest
Many times when accountants analyze complex transactions, they use T accounts to simplify the thought process. In the same way, you will find T accounts a useful device in this and later accounting courses.

Amounts entered on the left side of an account, regardless of the account title, are called **debits** to the account. When debits are entered in an account, the account is said to be *debited* (or charged). Amounts entered on the right side of an account are called **credits**, and the account is said to be *credited*. Debits and credits are sometimes abbreviated as *Dr.* and *Cr.*

In the cash account that follows, transactions involving receipts of cash are listed on the debit side of the account. The transactions involving cash payments are listed on the credit side. If at any time the total of the cash receipts is needed, the entries on the debit side of the account may be added and the total ($10,950) inserted below the last debit.[2] The total of the cash payments, $6,850 in the example, may be inserted on the credit side in a similar manner. Subtracting the smaller sum from the

> **Amounts entered on the left side of an account are debits, and amounts entered on the right side of an account are credits.**

---

[1] The terms *debit* and *credit* are derived from the Latin *debere* and *credere*.
[2] This amount, called a *memorandum balance*, should be written in small figures or identified in some other way to avoid mistaking the amount for an additional debit.

larger, \$10,950 − \$6,850, identifies the amount of cash on hand, \$4,100. This amount is called the **balance of the account**. It may be inserted in the account, next to the total of the debit column. In this way, the balance is identified as a **debit balance**. If a balance sheet were to be prepared at this time, cash of \$4,100 would be reported.

	Cash		
Debit side of account	3,750 4,300 2,900	850 1,400 700	Credit side of account
4,100	10,950	2,900 1,000	
	Total debits	6,850	
Balance of account (Total debits − Total credits)		Total credits	

Analyzing and Summarizing Transactions in Accounts

objective 3

List the rules of debit and credit and the normal balances of accounts.

NET SOLUTIONS

Every business transaction affects at least two accounts. To illustrate how transactions are analyzed and summarized in accounts, we will use the NetSolutions transactions from Chapter 1, with dates added. First, we illustrate how transactions (a), (b), (c), and (f) are analyzed and summarized in balance sheet accounts (assets, liabilities, and owner's equity). Next, we illustrate how transactions (d), (e), and (g) are analyzed and summarized in income statement accounts (revenues and expenses). Finally, we illustrate how the withdrawal of cash by Chris Clark, transaction (h), is analyzed and summarized in the accounts.

> **Every transaction affects at least two accounts.**

Transactions and Balance Sheet Accounts

Chris Clark's first transaction, (a), was to deposit \$25,000 in a bank account in the name of NetSolutions. The effect of this November 1 transaction on the balance sheet is to increase cash and owner's equity, as shown below.

NetSolutions **Balance Sheet** **November 1, 2002**																		
Assets						**Owner's Equity**						
Cash	\$25	0	0	0	00	Chris Clark, capital	\$25	0	0	0	00	

Point of Interest
A journal can be thought of as being similar to an individual's diary.

This transaction is initially entered in a record called a **journal**. The title of the account to be debited is listed first, followed by the amount to be debited. The title of the account to be credited is listed below and to the right of the debit, followed by the amount to be credited. This process of recording a transaction in the journal is called **journalizing**. This form of recording a transaction is called a **journal entry**. The journal entry for transaction (a) is shown below.

Entry A

	JOURNAL				Page 1	
Date	**Description**	**Post. Ref.**	**Debit**		**Credit**	
2002 Nov 1	Cash		25 0 0 0 00			1
	Chris Clark, Capital				25 0 0 0 00	2
	Invested cash in NetSolutions.					3

The increase in the asset (Cash), which is reported on the left side of the balance sheet, is debited to the cash account. The increase in owner's equity, which is reported on the right side of the balance sheet, is credited to the Chris Clark, capital account. As other assets are acquired, the increases are also recorded as debits to asset accounts. Likewise, other increases in owner's equity will be recorded as credits to owner's equity accounts.

The effects of this transaction are shown in the accounts by transferring the amount and date of the journal entry to the left (debit) side of Cash and to the right (credit) side of Chris Clark, Capital, as follows:

Cash		Chris Clark, Capital	
Nov. 1 25,000			Nov. 1 25,000

On November 5 (transaction b), NetSolutions bought land for $20,000, paying cash. This transaction increases one asset account and decreases another. It is entered in the journal as a $20,000 increase (debit) to Land and a $20,000 decrease (credit) to Cash, as shown below.

Entry B

						4
	5 Land		20 0 0 0 00			5
	Cash				20 0 0 0 00	6
	Purchased land for building site.					7

The effect of this entry is shown in the accounts of NetSolutions as follows:

Cash		Land		Chris Clark, Capital	
Nov. 1 25,000	Nov. 5 20,000	Nov. 5 20,000			Nov. 1 25,000

On November 10 (transaction c), NetSolutions purchased supplies on account for $1,350. This transaction increases an asset account and increases a liability account. It is entered in the journal as a $1,350 increase (debit) to Supplies and a $1,350 increase (credit) to Accounts Payable, as shown below. To simplify the illustration, the effect of entry (c) and the remaining journal entries for NetSolutions will be shown in the accounts later.

Entry C

						8
	10 Supplies		1 3 5 0 00			9
	Accounts Payable				1 3 5 0 00	10
	Purchased supplies on account.					11

On November 30 (transaction f), NetSolutions paid creditors on account, $950. This transaction decreases a liability account and decreases an asset account. It is entered in the journal as a $950 decrease (debit) to Accounts Payable and a $950 decrease (credit) to Cash, as shown below.

Entry F

23					23
24	30	Accounts Payable	9 5 0 00		24
25		Cash		9 5 0 00	25
26		Paid creditors on account.			26

In the preceding examples, you should observe that the left side of asset accounts is used for recording increases and the right side is used for recording decreases. Also, the right side of liability and owner's equity accounts is used to record increases, and the left side of such accounts is used to record decreases. The left side of all accounts, whether asset, liability, or owner's equity, is the debit side, and the right side is the credit side. Thus, a debit may be either an increase or a decrease, depending on the account affected. Likewise, a credit may be either an increase or a decrease, depending on the account. The general rules of debit and credit for balance sheet accounts may be thus stated as follows:

> The left side of all accounts is the debit side, and the right side is the credit side.

	Debit	Credit
Asset accounts	Increase (+)	Decrease (−)
Liability accounts	Decrease (−)	Increase (+)
Owner's equity (capital) accounts	Decrease (−)	Increase (+)

The rules of debit and credit may also be stated in relationship to the accounting equation, as shown below.

Balance Sheet Accounts

ASSETS		LIABILITIES	
Asset Accounts		Liability Accounts	
Debit	Credit	Debit	Credit
for	for	for	for
increases	decreases	decreases	increases
(+)	(−)	(−)	(+)

OWNER'S EQUITY	
Owner's Equity Accounts	
Debit	Credit
for	for
decreases	increases
(−)	(+)

Income Statement Accounts

The analysis of revenue and expense transactions focuses on how each transaction affects owner's equity. Transactions that increase revenue will increase owner's equity. Just as increases in owner's equity are recorded as credits, so, too, are increases in revenue accounts. Transactions that increase expense will decrease owner's equity. Just as decreases in owner's equity are recorded as debits, increases in expense accounts are recorded as debits.

We will use NetSolutions' transactions (d), (e), and (g) to illustrate the analysis of transactions and the rules of debit and credit for revenue and expense accounts. On November 18 (transaction d), NetSolutions received fees of $7,500 from customers for services provided. This transaction increases an asset account and increases a revenue account. It is entered in the journal as a $7,500 increase (debit) to Cash and a $7,500 increase (credit) to Fees Earned, as shown below.

Entry D

12					12
13	18	Cash	7 5 0 0 00		13
14		Fees Earned		7 5 0 0 00	14
15		Received fees from customers.			15

Throughout the month, NetSolutions incurred the following expenses: wages, $2,125; rent, $800; utilities, $450; and miscellaneous, $275. To simplify the illustration, the entry to journalize the payment of these expenses is recorded on November 30 (transaction e), as shown below. This transaction increases various expense accounts and decreases an asset account.

Entry E

17	30	Wages Expense	2 1 2 5 00		17
18		Rent Expense	8 0 0 00		18
19		Utilities Expense	4 5 0 00		19
20		Miscellaneous Expense	2 7 5 00		20
21		Cash		3 6 5 0 00	21
22		Paid expenses.			22

Regardless of the number of accounts, the sum of the debits is always equal to the sum of the credits in a journal entry. This equality of debits and credits for each transaction is built into the accounting equation: Assets = Liabilities + Owner's Equity. It is also because of this double equality that the system is known as **double-entry accounting**.

> **The sum of the debits must always equal the sum of the credits.**

On November 30, NetSolutions recorded the amount of supplies used in the operations during the month (transaction g). This transaction increases an expense account and decreases an asset account. The journal entry for transaction (g) is shown below.

Entry G

28	30	Supplies Expense	8 0 0 00		28
29		Supplies		8 0 0 00	29
30		Recorded supplies used during			30
31		November.			31

The general rules of debit and credit for analyzing transactions affecting income statement accounts are stated as follows:

	Debit	Credit
Revenue accounts	Decrease (−)	Increase (+)
Expense accounts	Increase (+)	Decrease (−)

The rules of debit and credit for income statement accounts may also be summarized in relationship to the owner's equity in the accounting equation, as shown below.

Income Statement Accounts

Expense Accounts		Revenue Accounts	
Debit for increases (+)	Credit for decreases (−)	Debit for decreases (−)	Credit for increases (+)

Withdrawals by the Owner

The owner of a proprietorship may withdraw cash from the business for personal use. This is common practice for owners devoting full time to the business, since the business may be the owner's main source of income. Such withdrawals have the effect of decreasing owner's equity. Just as decreases in owner's equity are recorded as debits, increases in withdrawals are recorded as debits. Withdrawals are debited to an account with the owner's name followed by *Drawing* or *Personal*.

In transaction (h), Chris Clark withdrew $2,000 in cash from NetSolutions for personal use. The effect of this transaction is to increase the drawing account and decrease the cash account. The journal entry for transaction (h) is shown below.

Entry H

	2002				
1	Nov.	30	Chris Clark, Drawing	2 0 0 0 00		1
2			Cash		2 0 0 0 00	2
3			Chris Clark withdrew cash for			3
4			personal use.			4

BUSINESS ON STAGE

Good Communication

Most managers would probably agree that they spend a majority of their time communicating with peers, employees, suppliers, stockholders, customers, and various others. To be successful in business, you must be a good communicator. Some helpful rules of good communication include the following:

- Have a clear idea of what you hope to accomplish from the communication and know what you want to say before you say it.
- Remember that oral communication is more than just words. Your tone of voice, facial expressions, and gestures can say more than your words.
- Keep your audience in mind by considering their needs and interests.
- Always follow up to see that your message was understood.

- Be a good listener by not interrupting, avoiding hasty judgments, asking questions, and paying attention. ■

Source: Adapted from *The World of Business* by L. Gitman and C. McDaniel (2d Edition), p. 262.

Normal Balances of Accounts

The sum of the increases recorded in an account is usually equal to or greater than the sum of the decreases recorded in the account. For this reason, the normal balances of all accounts are positive rather than negative. For example, the total debits (increases) in an asset account will ordinarily be greater than the total credits (decreases). Thus, asset accounts normally have debit balances.

The rules of debit and credit and the normal balances of the various types of accounts are summarized as follows:

	Increase (Normal Balance)	Decrease
Balance sheet accounts:		
Asset	Debit	Credit
Liability	Credit	Debit
Owner's Equity:		
Capital	Credit	Debit
Drawing	Debit	Credit
Income statement accounts:		
Revenue	Credit	Debit
Expense	Debit	Credit

A debit balance in which of the following accounts—Cash, Drawing, Wages Expense, Supplies, Fees Earned—would indicate that an error has occurred?

Fees Earned

When an account normally having a debit balance actually has a credit balance, or vice versa, an error may have occurred or an unusual situation may exist. For example, a credit balance in the office equipment account could result only from an error. On the other hand, a debit balance in an accounts payable account could result from an overpayment.

Illustration of Analyzing and Summarizing Transactions

Analyze and summarize the financial statement effects of transactions.

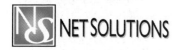

How does a transaction take place in a business? First, a manager or other employee authorizes the transaction. The transaction then takes place. The businesses involved in the transaction usually prepare documents that give details of the transaction. These documents then become the basis for analyzing and recording the transaction. For example, Chris Clark might authorize the purchase of supplies for NetSolutions by telling an employee to buy computer paper at the local office supply store. The employee purchases the supplies for cash and receives a sales slip from the office supply store listing the supplies bought. The employee then gives the sales slip to Chris Clark, who verifies and records the transaction.

Point of Interest In computerized accounting systems, some transactions may be automatically authorized and recorded when certain events occur. For example, the salaries of managers may be paid automatically at the end of each pay period.

As we discussed in the preceding section, a transaction is first recorded in a journal. Thus, the journal is a history of transactions by date. Periodically, the journal entries are transferred to the accounts in the ledger. The ledger is a history of transactions by account. The process of transferring the debits and credits from the journal entries to the accounts is called posting. The flow of a transaction from its authorization to its posting in the accounts is shown in Exhibit 2.

Exhibit 2 Flow of Business Transactions

1. Transaction authorized

2. Transaction takes place

3. Business document prepared

4. Entry recorded in journal

5. Entry posted to ledger

The double-entry accounting system is a very powerful tool in analyzing the effects of transactions. Using this system to analyze transactions is summarized as follows:

1. Determine whether an asset, a liability, owner's equity, revenue, or expense account is affected by the transaction.
2. For each account affected by the transaction, determine whether the account increases or decreases.
3. Determine whether each increase or decrease should be recorded as a debit or a credit.

In practice, businesses use a variety of formats for recording journal entries. A business may use one all-purpose journal, sometimes called a **two-column journal**, or it may use several journals. In the latter case, each journal is used to record different types of transactions, such as cash receipts or cash payments. The journals may be part of either a manual accounting system or a computerized accounting system.[3]

To illustrate recording a transaction in an all-purpose journal and posting in a manual accounting system, we will use the December transactions of NetSolutions. The first transaction in December occurred on December 1.

Dec. 1. NetSolutions paid a premium of $2,400 for a comprehensive insurance policy covering liability, theft, and fire. The policy covers a two-year period.

Analysis: When you purchased insurance for your automobile, you may have been required to pay the insurance premium in advance. In this case, your transaction was similar to NetSolutions. Advance payments of expenses such as insurance are prepaid expenses, which are assets. For NetSolutions, the asset acquired for the

[3] The use of special journals and computerized accounting systems is discussed in later chapters, after the basics of accounting systems have been covered.

cash payment is insurance protection for 24 months. The asset Prepaid Insurance increases and is debited for $2,400. The asset Cash decreases and is credited for $2,400.

The recording and posting of this transaction is shown in Exhibit 3.

Exhibit 3 Diagram of the Recording and Posting of a Debit and a Credit

Note where the date of the transaction is recorded in the journal. Also note that the entry is explained as the payment of an insurance premium. Such explanations should be brief. For unusual and complex transactions, such as a long-term rental arrangement, the journal entry explanation may include a reference to the rental agreement or other business document.

You will note that the T account form is not used in this illustration. Although the T account clearly separates debit and credit entries, it is inefficient for summarizing a large quantity of transactions. In practice, the T account is usually replaced with the standard form shown in Exhibit 3.

The debits and credits for each journal entry are posted to the accounts in the order in which they occur in the journal. In posting to the standard account, (1) the date is entered, and (2) the amount of the entry is entered. For future reference, (3) the journal page number is inserted in the Posting Reference column of the account, and (4) the account number is inserted in the Posting Reference column of the journal.

The remaining December transactions for NetSolutions are analyzed in the following paragraphs. These transactions are posted to the ledger in Exhibit 4, shown later. To simplify and reduce repetition, some of the December transactions are stated in summary form. For example, cash received for services is normally recorded on a daily basis. In this example, however, only summary totals are recorded at the middle and end of the month. Likewise, all fees earned on account during December are recorded at the middle and end of the month. In practice, each fee earned is recorded separately.

Dec. 1. NetSolutions paid rent for December, $800. The company from which NetSolutions is renting its store space now requires the payment of rent on the 1st of each month, rather than at the end of the month.

Analysis: You may pay monthly rent on an apartment on the first of each month. Your rent transaction is similar to NetSolutions. The advance payment of rent is an asset, much like the advance payment of the insurance premium in the preceding transaction. However, unlike the insurance premium, this prepaid rent will expire in one month. When an asset that is purchased will be used up in a short period of time, such as a month, it is normal to debit an expense account initially. This avoids having to transfer the balance from an asset account (Prepaid Rent) to an expense account (Rent Expense) at the end of the month. Thus, when the rent for December is prepaid at the beginning of the month, Rent Expense is debited for $800 and Cash is credited for $800.

Q&A *What would likely cause the cash account to have a credit balance?*

An error or an overdrawn cash account.

10		1	Rent Expense	52	8 0 0 00		10
11			Cash	11		8 0 0 00	11
12			Paid rent for December.				12

Dec. 1. NetSolutions received an offer from a local retailer to rent the land purchased on November 5. The retailer plans to use the land as a parking lot for its employees and customers. NetSolutions agreed to rent the land to the retailer for three months, with the rent payable in advance. NetSolutions received $360 for three months' rent beginning December 1.

Analysis: By agreeing to rent the land and accepting the $360, NetSolutions has incurred an obligation (liability) to the retailer. This obligation is to make the land available for use for three months and not to interfere with its use. The liability created by receiving the cash in advance of providing the service is called **unearned revenue**. Thus, the $360 received is an increase in an asset and is debited to Cash. The liability account Unearned Rent increases and is credited for $360. As time passes, the unearned rent liability will decrease and will become revenue.

14		1	Cash	11	3 6 0 00		14
15			Unearned Rent	23		3 6 0 00	15
16			Received advance payment for				16
17			three months' rent on land.				17

Real World Magazines that receive subscriptions in advance must record the receipts as unearned revenues. Likewise, airlines that receive ticket payments in advance must record the receipts as unearned revenues until the passengers use the tickets.

Dec. 4. NetSolutions purchased office equipment on account from Executive Supply Co. for $1,800.

Analysis: The asset account Office Equipment increases and is therefore debited for $1,800. The liability account Accounts Payable increases and is credited for $1,800.

19		4	Office Equipment	18	1 8 0 0 00		19
20			Accounts Payable	21		1 8 0 0 00	20
21			Purchased office equipment				21
22			on account.				22

Dec. 6. NetSolutions paid $180 for a newspaper advertisement.

Analysis: An expense increases and is debited for $180. The asset Cash decreases and is credited for $180. Expense items that are expected to be minor in amount are normally included as part of the miscellaneous expense. Thus, Miscellaneous Expense is debited for $180.

24		6	Miscellaneous Expense	59	1 8 0 00		24
25			Cash	11		1 8 0 00	25
26			Paid for newspaper ad.				26

Dec. 11. NetSolutions paid creditors $400.

Analysis: This payment decreases the liability account Accounts Payable, which is debited for $400. Cash also decreases and is credited for $400.

28		11	Accounts Payable	21	4 0 0 00		28
29			Cash	11		4 0 0 00	29
30			Paid creditors on account.				30

Dec. 13. NetSolutions paid a receptionist and a part-time assistant $950 for two weeks' wages.

Analysis: This transaction is similar to the December 6 transaction, where an expense account is increased and Cash is decreased. Thus, Wages Expense is debited for $950, and Cash is credited for $950.

			JOURNAL			Page 3	
	Date		Description	Post. Ref.	Debit	Credit	
1	2002 Dec.	13	Wages Expense	51	9 5 0 00		1
2			Cash	11		9 5 0 00	2
3			Paid two weeks' wages.				3

Dec. 16. NetSolutions received $3,100 from fees earned for the first half of December.

Analysis: Cash increases and is debited for $3,100. The revenue account Fees Earned increases and is credited for $3,100.

5		16	Cash	11	3 1 0 0 00			5
6			Fees Earned	41		3 1 0 0 00		6
7			Received fees from customers.					7

Dec. 16. Fees earned on account totaled $1,750 for the first half of December.

Analysis: Assume that you have agreed to take care of a neighbor's dog for a week for $100. At the end of the week, you agree to wait until the first of the next month to receive the $100. Like NetSolutions, you have provided services on account and thus have a right to receive the payment from your neighbor. When a business agrees that payment for services provided or goods sold can be accepted at a later date, the firm has an **account receivable**, which is a claim against the customer. The account receivable is an asset, and the revenue is earned even though no cash has been received. Thus, Accounts Receivable increases and is debited for $1,750. The revenue account Fees Earned increases and is credited for $1,750.

9		16	Accounts Receivable	12	1 7 5 0 00			9
10			Fees Earned	41		1 7 5 0 00		10
11			Recorded fees earned on account.					11

Dec. 20. NetSolutions paid $900 to Executive Supply Co. on the $1,800 debt owed from the December 4 transaction.

Analysis: This is similar to the transaction of December 11.

13		20	Accounts Payable	21	9 0 0 00			13
14			Cash	11		9 0 0 00		14
15			Paid part of amount owed to					15
16			Executive Supply Co.					16

Dec. 21. NetSolutions received $650 from customers in payment of their accounts.

Analysis: When customers pay amounts owed for services they have previously received, one asset increases and another asset decreases. Thus, Cash is debited for $650, and Accounts Receivable is credited for $650.

18		21	Cash	11	6 5 0 00			18
19			Accounts Receivable	12		6 5 0 00		19
20			Received cash from customers					20
21			on account.					21

Dec. 23. NetSolutions paid $1,450 for supplies.

Analysis: The asset account Supplies increases and is debited for $1,450. The asset account Cash decreases and is credited for $1,450.

		23	Supplies	14	1 4 5 0 00		
23							23
24			Cash	11		1 4 5 0 00	24
25			Purchased supplies.				25

Dec. 27. NetSolutions paid the receptionist and the part-time assistant $1,200 for two weeks' wages.

Analysis: This is similar to the transaction of December 13.

		27	Wages Expense	51	1 2 0 0 00		
27							27
28			Cash	11		1 2 0 0 00	28
29			Paid two weeks' wages.				29

Dec. 31. NetSolutions paid its $310 telephone bill for the month.

Analysis: You pay a telephone bill each month. Businesses, such as NetSolutions, also must pay monthly utility bills. Such transactions are similar to the transaction of December 6. The expense account Utilities Expense is debited for $310, and Cash is credited for $310.

		31	Utilities Expense	54	3 1 0 00		
31							31
32			Cash	11		3 1 0 00	32
33			Paid telephone bill.				33

Dec. 31. NetSolutions paid its $225 electric bill for the month.

Analysis: This is similar to the preceding transaction.

			JOURNAL			Page 4	
	Date		**Description**	**Post. Ref.**	**Debit**	**Credit**	
1	2002 Dec.	31	Utilities Expense	54	2 2 5 00		1
2			Cash	11		2 2 5 00	2
3			Paid electric bill.				3

Dec. 31. NetSolutions received $2,870 from fees earned for the second half of December.

Analysis: This is similar to the transaction of December 16.

		31	Cash	11	2 8 7 0 00		
5							5
6			Fees Earned	41		2 8 7 0 00	6
7			Received fees from customers.				7

Dec. 31. Fees earned on account totaled $1,120 for the second half of December.

Analysis: This is similar to the transaction of December 16.

	31	Accounts Receivable	12	1 1 2 0 00		9
10		Fees Earned	41		1 1 2 0 00	10
11		Recorded fees earned on account.				11

Dec. 31. Chris Clark withdrew $2,000 for personal use.

Analysis: This transaction resulted in an increase in the amount of withdrawals and is recorded by a $2,000 debit to Chris Clark, Drawing. The decrease in business cash is recorded by a $2,000 credit to Cash.

13	31	Chris Clark, Drawing	32	2 0 0 0 00		13
14		Cash	11		2 0 0 0 00	14
15		Chris Clark withdrew cash for				15
16		personal use.				16

The journal for NetSolutions since it was organized on November 1 is shown in Exhibit 4. Exhibit 4 also shows the ledger after the transactions for both November and December have been posted.

Exhibit 4 Journal and Ledger—NetSolutions

		JOURNAL			Page 1	
	Date	**Description**	**Post. Ref.**	**Debit**	**Credit**	
1	2002 Nov. 1	Cash	11	25 0 0 0 00		1
2		Chris Clark, Capital	31		25 0 0 0 00	2
3		Invested cash in NetSolutions.				3
4						4
5	5	Land	17	20 0 0 0 00		5
6		Cash	11		20 0 0 0 00	6
7		Purchased land for building site.				7
8						8
9	10	Supplies	14	1 3 5 0 00		9
10		Accounts Payable	21		1 3 5 0 00	10
11		Purchased supplies on account.				11
12						12
13	18	Cash	11	7 5 0 0 00		13
14		Fees Earned	41		7 5 0 0 00	14
15		Received fees from customers.				15
16						16
17	30	Wages Expense	51	2 1 2 5 00		17
18		Rent Expense	52	8 0 0 00		18
19		Utilities Expense	54	4 5 0 00		19
20		Miscellaneous Expense	59	2 7 5 00		20
21		Cash	11		3 6 5 0 00	21
22		Paid expenses.				22
23						23
24	30	Accounts Payable	21	9 5 0 00		24
25		Cash	11		9 5 0 00	25
26		Paid creditors on account.				26
27						27
28	30	Supplies Expense	55	8 0 0 00		28
29		Supplies	14		8 0 0 00	29
30		Supplies used during November.				30

Exhibit 4 (continued)

	Date		Description	Post. Ref.	Debit	Credit	
1	2002 Nov.	30	Chris Clark, Drawing	32	2 0 0 0 00		1
2			Cash	11		2 0 0 0 00	2
3			Chris Clark withdrew cash for				3
4			personal use.				4
5							5
6	Dec.	1	Prepaid Insurance	15	2 4 0 0 00		6
7			Cash	11		2 4 0 0 00	7
8			Paid premium on two-year policy.				8
9							9
10		1	Rent Expense	52	8 0 0 00		10
11			Cash	11		8 0 0 00	11
12			Paid rent for December.				12
13							13
14		1	Cash	11	3 6 0 00		14
15			Unearned Rent	23		3 6 0 00	15
16			Received advance payment for				16
17			three months' rent on land.				17
18							18
19		4	Office Equipment	18	1 8 0 0 00		19
20			Accounts Payable	21		1 8 0 0 00	20
21			Purchased office equipment				21
22			on account.				22
23							23
24		6	Miscellaneous Expense	59	1 8 0 00		24
25			Cash	11		1 8 0 00	25
26			Paid for newspaper ad.				26
27							27
28		11	Accounts Payable	21	4 0 0 00		28
29			Cash	11		4 0 0 00	29
30			Paid creditors on account.				30

JOURNAL   Page 2

JOURNAL   Page 3

	Date		Description	Post. Ref.	Debit	Credit	
1	2002 Dec.	13	Wages Expense	51	9 5 0 00		1
2			Cash	11		9 5 0 00	2
3			Paid two weeks' wages.				3
4							4
5		16	Cash	11	3 1 0 0 00		5
6			Fees Earned	41		3 1 0 0 00	6
7			Received fees from customers.				7
8							8
9		16	Accounts Receivable	12	1 7 5 0 00		9
10			Fees Earned	41		1 7 5 0 00	10
11			Recorded fees earned on account.				11

Exhibit 4 (continued)

	Date		Description	Post. Ref.	Debit	Credit	
13		20	Accounts Payable	21	9 0 0 00		13
14			Cash	11		9 0 0 00	14
15			Paid part of amount owed to				15
16			Executive Supply Co.				16
17							17
18		21	Cash	11	6 5 0 00		18
19			Accounts Receivable	12		6 5 0 00	19
20			Received cash from customers				20
21			on account.				21
22							22
23		23	Supplies	14	1 4 5 0 00		23
24			Cash	11		1 4 5 0 00	24
25			Purchased supplies.				25
26							26
27		27	Wages Expense	51	1 2 0 0 00		27
28			Cash	11		1 2 0 0 00	28
29			Paid two weeks' wages.				29
30							30
31		31	Utilities Expense	54	3 1 0 00		31
32			Cash	11		3 1 0 00	32
33			Paid telephone bill.				33

JOURNAL — Page 3

JOURNAL — Page 4

	Date		Description	Post. Ref.	Debit	Credit	
1	2002 Dec.	31	Utilities Expense	54	2 2 5 00		1
2			Cash	11		2 2 5 00	2
3			Paid electric bill.				3
4							4
5		31	Cash	11	2 8 7 0 00		5
6			Fees Earned	41		2 8 7 0 00	6
7			Received fees from customers.				7
8							8
9		31	Accounts Receivable	12	1 1 2 0 00		9
10			Fees Earned	41		1 1 2 0 00	10
11			Recorded fees earned on account.				11
12							12
13		31	Chris Clark, Drawing	32	2 0 0 0 00		13
14			Cash	11		2 0 0 0 00	14
15			Chris Clark withdrew cash for				15
16			personal use.				16
17							17
18							18
19							19

Exhibit 4 (continued)

LEDGER

ACCOUNT *Cash*   **ACCOUNT NO.** *11*

Date		Item	Post. Ref.	Debit	Credit	Balance Debit	Balance Credit
2002 Nov.	1		1	25 0 0 0 00		25 0 0 0 00	
	5		1		20 0 0 0 00	5 0 0 0 00	
	18		1	7 5 0 0 00		12 5 0 0 00	
	30		1		3 6 5 0 00	8 8 5 0 00	
	30		1		9 5 0 00	7 9 0 0 00	
	30		2		2 0 0 0 00	5 9 0 0 00	
Dec.	1		2		2 4 0 0 00	3 5 0 0 00	
	1		2		8 0 0 00	2 7 0 0 00	
	1		2	3 6 0 00		3 0 6 0 00	
	6		2		1 8 0 00	2 8 8 0 00	
	11		2		4 0 0 00	2 4 8 0 00	
	13		3		9 5 0 00	1 5 3 0 00	
	16		3	3 1 0 0 00		4 6 3 0 00	
	20		3		9 0 0 00	3 7 3 0 00	
	21		3	6 5 0 00		4 3 8 0 00	
	23		3		1 4 5 0 00	2 9 3 0 00	
	27		3		1 2 0 0 00	1 7 3 0 00	
	31		3		3 1 0 00	1 4 2 0 00	
	31		4		2 2 5 00	1 1 9 5 00	
	31		4	2 8 7 0 00		4 0 6 5 00	
	31		4		2 0 0 0 00	2 0 6 5 00	

ACCOUNT *Accounts Receivable*   **ACCOUNT NO.** *12*

Date		Item	Post. Ref.	Debit	Credit	Balance Debit	Balance Credit
2002 Dec.	16		3	1 7 5 0 00		1 7 5 0 00	
	21		3		6 5 0 00	1 1 0 0 00	
	31		4	1 1 2 0 00		2 2 2 0 00	

ACCOUNT *Supplies*   **ACCOUNT NO.** *14*

Date		Item	Post. Ref.	Debit	Credit	Balance Debit	Balance Credit
2002 Nov.	10		1	1 3 5 0 00		1 3 5 0 00	
	30		1		8 0 0 00	5 5 0 00	
Dec.	23		3	1 4 5 0 00		2 0 0 0 00	

Exhibit 4 *(continued)*

ACCOUNT Prepaid Insurance   ACCOUNT NO. 15

Date	Item	Post. Ref.	Debit	Credit	Balance Debit	Balance Credit
2002 Dec. 1		2	2 4 0 0 00		2 4 0 0 00	

ACCOUNT Land   ACCOUNT NO. 17

Date	Item	Post. Ref.	Debit	Credit	Balance Debit	Balance Credit
2002 Nov. 5		1	20 0 0 0 00		20 0 0 0 00	

ACCOUNT Office Equipment   ACCOUNT NO. 18

Date	Item	Post. Ref.	Debit	Credit	Balance Debit	Balance Credit
2002 Dec. 4		2	1 8 0 0 00		1 8 0 0 00	

ACCOUNT Accounts Payable   ACCOUNT NO. 21

Date	Item	Post. Ref.	Debit	Credit	Balance Debit	Balance Credit
2002 Nov. 10		1		1 3 5 0 00		1 3 5 0 00
30		1	9 5 0 00			4 0 0 00
Dec. 4		2		1 8 0 0 00		2 2 0 0 00
11		2	4 0 0 00			1 8 0 0 00
20		3	9 0 0 00			9 0 0 00

ACCOUNT Unearned Rent   ACCOUNT NO. 23

Date	Item	Post. Ref.	Debit	Credit	Balance Debit	Balance Credit
2002 Dec. 1		2		3 6 0 00		3 6 0 00

ACCOUNT Chris Clark, Capital   ACCOUNT NO. 31

Date	Item	Post. Ref.	Debit	Credit	Balance Debit	Balance Credit
2002 Nov. 1		1		25 0 0 0 00		25 0 0 0 00

Exhibit 4 (continued)

ACCOUNT Chris Clark, Drawing   ACCOUNT NO. 32

Date	Item	Post. Ref.	Debit	Credit	Balance Debit	Balance Credit
2002 Nov. 30		2	2 0 0 0 00		2 0 0 0 00	
Dec. 31		4	2 0 0 0 00		4 0 0 0 00	

ACCOUNT Fees Earned   ACCOUNT NO. 41

Date	Item	Post. Ref.	Debit	Credit	Balance Debit	Balance Credit
2002 Nov. 18		1		7 5 0 0 00		7 5 0 0 00
Dec. 16		3		3 1 0 0 00		10 6 0 0 00
16		3		1 7 5 0 00		12 3 5 0 00
31		4		2 8 7 0 00		15 2 2 0 00
31		4		1 1 2 0 00		16 3 4 0 00

ACCOUNT Wages Expense   ACCOUNT NO. 51

Date	Item	Post. Ref.	Debit	Credit	Balance Debit	Balance Credit
2002 Nov. 30		1	2 1 2 5 00		2 1 2 5 00	
Dec. 13		3	9 5 0 00		3 0 7 5 00	
27		3	1 2 0 0 00		4 2 7 5 00	

ACCOUNT Rent Expense   ACCOUNT NO. 52

Date	Item	Post. Ref.	Debit	Credit	Balance Debit	Balance Credit
2002 Nov. 30		1	8 0 0 00		8 0 0 00	
Dec. 1		2	8 0 0 00		1 6 0 0 00	

ACCOUNT Utilities Expense   ACCOUNT NO. 54

Date	Item	Post. Ref.	Debit	Credit	Balance Debit	Balance Credit
2002 Nov. 30		1	4 5 0 00		4 5 0 00	
Dec. 31		3	3 1 0 00		7 6 0 00	
31		4	2 2 5 00		9 8 5 00	

Exhibit 4 *(concluded)*

ACCOUNT *Supplies Expense*					ACCOUNT NO. 55	
Date	Item	Post. Ref.	Debit	Credit	Balance Debit	Balance Credit
2002 Nov. 30		1	8 0 0 00		8 0 0 00	

ACCOUNT *Miscellaneous Expense*					ACCOUNT NO. 59	
Date	Item	Post. Ref.	Debit	Credit	Balance Debit	Balance Credit
2002 Nov. 30		1	2 7 5 00		2 7 5 00	
Dec. 6		2	1 8 0 00		4 5 5 00	

Trial Balance

objective 5

Prepare a trial balance and explain how it can be used to discover errors.

How can you be sure that you have not made an error in posting the debits and credits to the ledger? One way is to determine the equality of the debits and credits in the ledger. This equality should be proved at the end of each accounting period, if not more often. Such a proof, called a **trial balance**, may be in the form of a computer printout or in the form shown in Exhibit 5.

Point of Interest
The proof of the equality of the debit and credit balances is called a trial balance because a "trial" is a process of proving or testing.

Exhibit 5 Trial Balance

NetSolutions Trial Balance December 31, 2002		
Cash	2 0 6 5 00	
Accounts Receivable	2 2 2 0 00	
Supplies	2 0 0 0 00	
Prepaid Insurance	2 4 0 0 00	
Land	20 0 0 0 00	
Office Equipment	1 8 0 0 00	
Accounts Payable		9 0 0 00
Unearned Rent		3 6 0 00
Chris Clark, Capital		25 0 0 0 00
Chris Clark, Drawing	4 0 0 0 00	
Fees Earned		16 3 4 0 00
Wages Expense	4 2 7 5 00	
Rent Expense	1 6 0 0 00	
Utilities Expense	9 8 5 00	
Supplies Expense	8 0 0 00	
Miscellaneous Expense	4 5 5 00	
	42 6 0 0 00	42 6 0 0 00

The first step in preparing the trial balance is to determine the balance of each account in the ledger. When the standard account form is used, the balance of each account appears in the balance column on the same line as the last posting to the account.

The trial balance does not provide complete proof of the accuracy of the ledger. It indicates only that the debits and the credits are equal. This proof is of value, however, because errors often affect the equality of debits and credits. If the two totals of a trial balance are not equal, an error has occurred. In the remainder of this chapter, we will discuss procedures for discovering and correcting errors.

Discovery and Correction of Errors

objective 6

Discover errors in recording transactions and correct them.

Errors will sometimes occur in journalizing and posting transactions. In the following paragraphs, we describe and illustrate how errors may be discovered and corrected. In some cases, however, an error might not be significant enough to affect the decisions of management or others. In such cases, the materiality concept implies that the error may be treated in the easiest possible way. For example, an error of a few dollars in recording an asset as an expense for a business with millions of dollars in assets would be considered immaterial, and a correction would not be necessary. In the remaining paragraphs, we assume that errors discovered are material and should be corrected.

Many large corporations such as **Microsoft** and **Quaker Oats** round the figures in their financial statements to millions of dollars.

Discovery of Errors

As mentioned previously, preparing the trial balance is one of the primary ways to discover errors in the ledger. However, it indicates only that the debits and credits are equal. If the two totals of the trial balance are not equal, it is probably due to one or more of the errors described in Exhibit 6.

Among the types of errors that will *not* cause the trial balance totals to be unequal are the following:

1. Failure to record a transaction or to post a transaction.
2. Recording the same erroneous amount for both the debit and the credit parts of a transaction.
3. Recording the same transaction more than once.
4. Posting a part of a transaction correctly as a debit or credit but to the wrong account.

It is obvious that care should be used in recording transactions in the journal and in posting to the accounts. The need for accuracy in determining account balances and reporting them on the trial balance is also evident.

Errors in the accounts may be discovered in various ways: (1) through audit procedures, (2) by looking at the trial balance or (3) by chance. If the two trial balance totals are not equal, the amount of the difference between the totals should be determined before searching for the error.

The amount of the difference between the two totals of a trial balance sometimes gives a clue as to the nature of the error or where it occurred. For example, a difference of 10, 100, or 1,000 between two totals is often the result of an error in addition. A difference between totals can also be due to omitting a debit or a

Exhibit 6 Errors Causing
Unequal Trial Balance

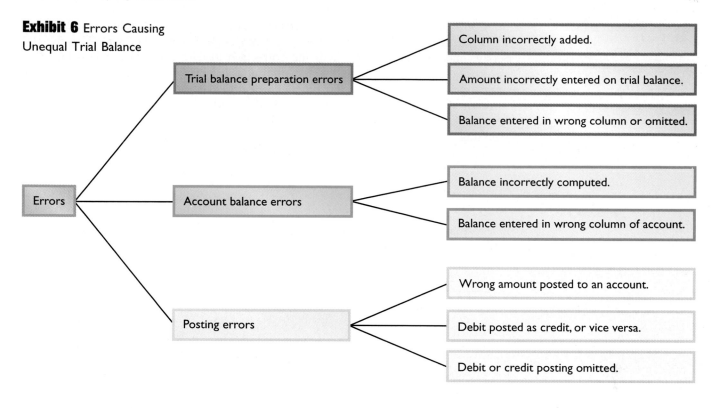

credit posting. If the difference can be evenly divided by 2, the error may be due to the posting of a debit as a credit, or vice versa. For example, if the debit total is $20,640 and the credit total is $20,236, the difference of $404 may indicate that a credit posting of $404 was omitted or that a credit of $202 was incorrectly posted as a debit.

Two other common types of errors are known as transpositions and slides. A *transposition* occurs when the order of the digits is changed mistakenly, such as writing $542 as $452 or $524. In a *slide*, the entire number is mistakenly moved one or more spaces to the right or the left, such as writing $542.00 as $54.20 or $5,420.00. If an error of either type has occurred and there are no other errors, the difference between the two trial balance totals can be evenly divided by 9.

If an error is not revealed by the trial balance, the steps in the accounting process must be retraced, beginning with the last step and working back to the entries in the journal. Usually, errors causing the trial balance totals to be unequal will be discovered before all of the steps are retraced.

Q&A *What type of error occurs when $14,500 is recorded as $15,400?*

A transposition.

Correction of Errors

The procedures used to correct an error in journalizing or posting vary according to the nature of the error and when the error is discovered. These procedures are summarized in Exhibit 7.

Exhibit 7 Procedures for Correcting Errors

Error	Correction Procedure
1. Journal entry is incorrect but not posted.	Draw a line through the error and insert correct title or amount.
2. Journal entry is correct but posted incorrectly.	Draw a line through the error and post correctly.
3. Journal entry is incorrect and posted.	Journalize and post a correcting entry.

Correcting the first two types of errors shown in Exhibit 7 involves simply drawing a line through the error and inserting the correct title or amount. Usually, the person making corrections initials the correction in case questions arise later.

Correcting the third type of error in Exhibit 7 is more complex. To illustrate, assume that on May 5 a $12,500 purchase of office equipment on account was incorrectly journalized and posted as a debit to Supplies and a credit to Accounts Payable for $12,500. This posting of the incorrect entry is shown in the following T accounts.

	Supplies		Accounts Payable	
Incorrect:	12,500			12,500

Before making a correcting entry, it is best to determine the debit(s) and credit(s) that should have been recorded. These are shown in the following T accounts.

	Office Equipment		Accounts Payable	
Correct:	12,500			12,500

Comparing the two sets of T accounts shows that the incorrect debit to Supplies may be corrected by debiting Office Equipment for $12,500 and crediting Supplies for $12,500. The following correcting entry is then journalized and posted:

Entry to Correct Error:

18	May	31	Office Equipment	18	12 50 0 00		18
19			Supplies	14		12 5 0 0 00	19
20			To correct erroneous debit				20
21			to Supplies on May 5. See invoice				21
22			from Bell Office Equipment Co.				22

FINANCIAL ANALYSIS AND INTERPRETATION

objective 7

Use horizontal analysis to compare financial statements from different periods.

A single item appearing in a financial statement is often useful in interpreting the financial results of a business. However, comparing this item in a current statement with the same item in prior statements often makes the financial information more useful. Horizontal analysis is the term used to describe such comparisons.

In horizontal analysis, the amount of each item on the current financial statements is compared with the same item on one or more earlier statements. The increase or decrease in the *amount* of the item is computed, together with the *percent* of increase or decrease. When two statements are being compared, the earlier statement is used as the base for computing the amount and the percent of change.

To illustrate, the horizontal analysis of two income statements for J. Holmes, Attorney-at-Law, is shown in Exhibit 8. Exhibit 8 indicates both favorable and unfavorable trends affecting the income statement of J. Holmes, Attorney-at-Law. The increase in fees earned is a favorable trend, as is the decrease in supplies expense. Unfavorable trends include the increase in wages expense, utilities expense, and miscellaneous expense. These expenses increased faster than the increase in revenues, with total operating expenses increasing by 30.6%. Overall, net income increased by $15,800, or 19.9%, a favorable trend.

The significance of the various increases and decreases in the revenue and expense items in Exhibit 8 should be investigated to see if operations could be further

Exhibit 8 Horizontal Analysis of Income Statement

			Increase (Decrease)	
J. Holmes, Attorney-at-Law Income Statement For the Years Ended December 31, 2002 and 2003				
	2003	2002	Amount	Percent
Fees earned	$187,500	$150,000	$37,500	25.0%
Operating expenses:				
Wages expense	$ 60,000	$ 45,000	$15,000	33.3%
Rent expense	15,000	12,000	3,000	25.0%
Utilities expense	12,500	9,000	3,500	38.9%
Supplies expense	2,700	3,000	(300)	(10.0)%
Miscellaneous expense	2,300	1,800	500	27.8%
Total operating expenses	$ 92,500	$ 70,800	$21,700	30.6%
Net income	$ 95,000	$ 79,200	$15,800	19.9%

improved. For example, the increase in utilities expense of 38.9% was the result of renting additional office space for use by a part-time law student in performing paralegal services. This explains the increase in rent expense of 25% and the increase in wages expense of 33.3%. The increase in revenues of 25% reflects the fees generated by the new paralegal.

The preceding example illustrates how horizontal analysis can be useful in interpreting and analyzing financial statements. Horizontal analyses similar to that shown in Exhibit 8 can also be performed for the balance sheet, the statement of owner's equity, and the statement of cash flows.

ENCORE

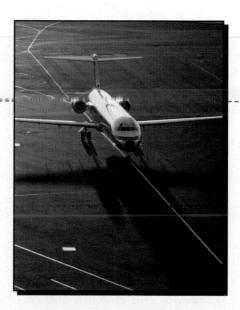

The Hijacking Receivable

A company's chart of accounts should reflect the basic nature of its operations. Occasionally, however, transactions take place that give rise to unusual accounts. The following is a story of one such account.

During the early 1970s, before strict airport security was implemented across the United States, several airlines experienced hijacking incidents. One such incident occurred on November 10, 1972, when a Southern Airways DC-9 en route from Memphis to Miami was hijacked during a stopover in Birmingham, Alabama. The

three hijackers boarded the plane in Birmingham armed with handguns and hand grenades. At gunpoint, the hijackers took the plane, the plane's crew of four, and 27 passengers to nine American cities, Toronto, and eventually to Havana, Cuba.

During the long flight, the hijackers threatened to crash the plane into the Oak Ridge, Tennessee, nuclear facilities, insisted on talking with President Nixon, and demanded a ransom of $10 million. Southern Airways, however, was only able to come up with $2 million. Eventually, the pilot

talked the hijackers into settling for the $2 million when the plane landed in Chattanooga for refueling.

Upon landing in Havana, the Cuban authorities arrested the hijackers and, after a brief delay, sent the plane, passengers, and crew back to the United States. The hijackers and $2 million stayed in Cuba.

How did Southern Airways account for and report the hijacking payment in its subsequent financial statements? As you might have analyzed, the initial entry credited Cash for $2 million. The debit was to an account entitled "Hijacking Payment." This account was reported as a type of receivable under "other assets" on Southern's balance sheet. The company maintained that it would be able to collect the cash from the Cuban government and that, therefore, a receivable existed. In fact, in August 1975, Southern Airways was repaid $2 million by the Cuban government, which was, at that time, attempting to improve relations with the United States. ■

KEY POINTS

1 Explain why accounts are used to record and summarize the effects of transactions on financial statements.

The record used for recording individual transactions is an account. A group of accounts is called a ledger. The system of accounts that make up a ledger is called a chart of accounts. The accounts are numbered and listed in the order in which they appear in the balance sheet and the income statement.

2 Describe the characteristics of an account.

The simplest form of an account, a T account, has three parts: (1) a title, which is the name of the item recorded in the account; (2) a left side, called the debit side; (3) a right side, called the credit side. Amounts entered on the left side of an account, regardless of the account title, are called debits to the account. Amounts entered on the right side of an account are called credits. Periodically, the debits in an account are added, the credits in the account are added, and the balance of the account is determined.

3 List the rules of debit and credit and the normal balances of accounts.

General rules of debit and credit have been established for recording increases or decreases in asset, liability, owner's equity, revenue, expense, and drawing accounts. Each transaction is recorded so that the sum of the debits is always equal to the sum of the credits. Transactions are initially entered in a record called a journal.

The sum of the increases recorded in an account is usually equal to or greater than the sum of the decreases recorded in the account. For this reason, the normal balance of an account is indicated by the side of the account (debit or credit) that receives the increases.

The rules of debit and credit and normal account balances are summarized in the following table:

	Increase (Normal Balance)	Decrease
Balance sheet accounts:		
Asset	Debit	Credit
Liability	Credit	Debit
Owner's Equity:		
Capital	Credit	Debit
Drawing	Debit	Credit
Income statement accounts:		
Revenue	Credit	Debit
Expense	Debit	Credit

4 Analyze and summarize the financial statement effects of transactions.

Transactions are analyzed by determining whether: (1) an asset, liability, owner's equity, revenue, or expense account is affected, (2) each account affected increases or decreases, and (3) each increase or decrease is recorded as a debit or a credit. A journal is used for recording the transaction initially. The journal entries are periodically posted to the accounts.

5 Prepare a trial balance and explain how it can be used to discover errors.

A trial balance is prepared by listing the accounts from the ledger and their balances. If the two totals of the trial balance are not equal, an error has occurred.

6 Discover errors in recording transactions and correct them.

Errors may be discovered (1) by audit procedures, (2) by looking at the trial balance or (3) by chance. The procedures for correcting errors are summarized in Exhibit 7.

7 Use horizontal analysis to compare financial statements from different periods.

In horizontal analysis, the amount of each item on the current financial statements is compared with the same item on one or more earlier statements. The increase or decrease in the *amount* of the item is computed, together with the *percent* of increase or decrease.

ILLUSTRATIVE PROBLEM

J. F. Outz, M.D., has been practicing as a cardiologist for three years. During April, 2002, Outz completed the following transactions in her practice of cardiology.

April 1. Paid office rent for April, $800.
    3. Purchased equipment on account, $2,100.
    5. Received cash on account from patients, $3,150.
    8. Purchased X-ray film and other supplies on account, $245.
    9. One of the items of equipment purchased on April 3 was defective. It was returned with the permission of the supplier, who agreed to reduce the account for the amount charged for the item, $325.
    12. Paid cash to creditors on account, $1,250.
    17. Paid cash for renewal of a six-month property insurance policy, $370.
    20. Discovered that the balances of the cash account and the accounts payable account as of April 1 were overstated by $200. A payment of that amount to a creditor in March had not been recorded. Journalize the $200 payment as of April 20.
    24. Paid cash for laboratory analysis, $545.
    27. Paid cash from business bank account for personal and family expenses, $1,250.
    30. Recorded the cash received in payment of services (on a cash basis) to patients during April, $1,720.
    30. Paid salaries of receptionist and nurses, $1,725.
    30. Paid various utility expenses, $360.
    30. Recorded fees charged to patients on account for services performed in April, $5,145.
    30. Paid miscellaneous expenses, $132.

Outz's account titles, numbers, and balances as of April 1 (all normal balances) are listed as follows: Cash, 11, $4,123; Accounts Receivable, 12, $6,725; Supplies, 13, $290; Prepaid Insurance, 14, $465; Equipment, 18, $19,745; Accounts Payable, 22, $765; J. F. Outz, Capital, 31, $30,583; J. F. Outz, Drawing, 32; Professional Fees, 41; Salary Expense, 51; Rent Expense, 53; Laboratory Expense, 55; Utilities Expense, 56; Miscellaneous Expense, 59.

Instructions

1. Open a ledger of standard four-column accounts for Dr. Outz as of April 1. Enter the balances in the appropriate balance columns and place a check mark (✓) in the posting reference column. (*Hint:* Verify the equality of the debit and credit balances in the ledger before proceeding with the next instruction.)
2. Journalize each transaction in a two-column journal.
3. Post the journal to the ledger, extending the month-end balances to the appropriate balance columns after each posting.
4. Prepare a trial balance as of April 30.

Solution

2. and **3.**

	Date		Description	Post. Ref.	Debit	Credit	
1	2002 April	1	Rent Expense	53	8 0 0 00		1
2			Cash	11		8 0 0 00	2
3			Paid office rent for April.				3
4							4
5		3	Equipment	18	2 1 0 0 00		5
6			Accounts Payable	22		2 1 0 0 00	6
7			Purchased equipment on account.				7

JOURNAL   **Page 27**

	Date	Description	Post. Ref.	Debit	Credit	
8						8
9	5	Cash	11	3 1 5 0 00		9
10		Accounts Receivable	12		3 1 5 0 00	10
11		Received cash on account.				11
12						12
13	8	Supplies	13	2 4 5 00		13
14		Accounts payable	22		2 4 5 00	14
15		Purchased supplies.				15
16						16
17	9	Accounts Payable	22	3 2 5 00		17
18		Equipment	18		3 2 5 00	18
19		Returned defective equipment.				19
20						20
21	12	Accounts Payable	22	1 2 5 0 00		21
22		Cash	11		1 2 5 0 00	22
23		Paid creditors on account.				23
24						24
25	17	Prepaid Insurance	14	3 7 0 00		25
26		Cash	11		3 7 0 00	26
27		Renewed 6-month property policy.				27
28						28
29	20	Accounts Payable	22	2 0 0 00		29
30		Cash	11		2 0 0 00	30
31		Recorded March payment				31
32		to creditor.				32

JOURNAL — Page 27

	Date	Description	Post. Ref.	Debit	Credit	
1	2002 April 24	Laboratory Expense	55	5 4 5 00		1
2		Cash	11		5 4 5 00	2
3		Paid for laboratory analysis.				3
4						4
5	27	J. F. Outz, Drawing	32	1 2 5 0 00		5
6		Cash	11		1 2 5 0 00	6
7		J. F. Outz withdrew cash for				7
8		personal use.				8
9						9
10	30	Cash	11	1 7 2 0 00		10
11		Professional Fees	41		1 7 2 0 00	11
12		Received fees from patients.				12
13						13
14	30	Salary Expense	51	1 7 2 5 00		14
15		Cash	11		1 7 2 5 00	15
16		Paid salaries.				16

JOURNAL — Page 28

		JOURNAL			Page 28	
	Date	Description	Post. Ref.	Debit	Credit	
17						17
18	30	Utilities Expense	56	3 6 0 00		18
19		Cash	11		3 6 0 00	19
20		Paid utilities.				20
21						21
22	30	Accounts Receivable	12	5 1 4 5 00		22
23		Professional Fees	41		5 1 4 5 00	23
24		Recorded fees earned on account.				24
25						25
26	30	Miscellaneous Expense	59	1 3 2 00		26
27		Cash	11		1 3 2 00	27
28		Paid expenses.				28

1. and **3.**

ACCOUNT Cash					ACCOUNT NO. 11	
					Balance	
Date	Item	Post. Ref.	Debit	Credit	Debit	Credit
2002 April 1	Balance	✓			4 1 2 3 00	
1		27		8 0 0 00	3 3 2 3 00	
5		27	3 1 5 0 00		6 4 7 3 00	
12		27		1 2 5 0 00	5 2 2 3 00	
17		27		3 7 0 00	4 8 5 3 00	
20		27		2 0 0 00	4 6 5 3 00	
24		28		5 4 5 00	4 1 0 8 00	
27		28		1 2 5 0 00	2 8 5 8 00	
30		28	1 7 2 0 00		4 5 7 8 00	
30		28		1 7 2 5 00	2 8 5 3 00	
30		28		3 6 0 00	2 4 9 3 00	
30		28		1 3 2 00	2 3 6 1 00	

ACCOUNT Accounts Receivable					ACCOUNT NO. 12	
					Balance	
Date	Item	Post. Ref.	Debit	Credit	Debit	Credit
2002 April 1	Balance	✓			6 7 2 5 00	
5		27		3 1 5 0 00	3 5 7 5 00	
30		28	5 1 4 5 00		8 7 2 0 00	

ACCOUNT Supplies					ACCOUNT NO. 13	
					Balance	
Date	Item	Post. Ref.	Debit	Credit	Debit	Credit
2002 April 1	Balance	✓			2 9 0 00	
8		27	2 4 5 00		5 3 5 00	

ACCOUNT *Prepaid Insurance*   **ACCOUNT NO. 14**

Date	Item	Post. Ref.	Debit	Credit	Balance Debit	Balance Credit
2002 April 1	Balance	✓			4 6 5 00	
17		27	3 7 0 00		8 3 5 00	

ACCOUNT *Equipment*   **ACCOUNT NO. 18**

Date	Item	Post. Ref.	Debit	Credit	Balance Debit	Balance Credit
2002 April 1	Balance	✓			19 7 4 5 00	
3		27	2 1 0 0 00		21 8 4 5 00	
9		27		3 2 5 00	21 5 2 0 00	

ACCOUNT *Accounts Payable*   **ACCOUNT NO. 22**

Date	Item	Post. Ref.	Debit	Credit	Balance Debit	Balance Credit
2002 April 1	Balance	✓				7 6 5 00
3		27		2 1 0 0 00		2 8 6 5 00
8		27		2 4 5 00		3 1 1 0 00
9		27	3 2 5 00			2 7 8 5 00
12		27	1 2 5 0 00			1 5 3 5 00
20		27	2 0 0 00			1 3 3 5 00

ACCOUNT *J. F. Outz, Capital*   **ACCOUNT NO. 31**

Date	Item	Post. Ref.	Debit	Credit	Balance Debit	Balance Credit
2002 April 1	Balance	✓				30 5 8 3 00

ACCOUNT *J. F. Outz, Drawing*   **ACCOUNT NO. 32**

Date	Item	Post. Ref.	Debit	Credit	Balance Debit	Balance Credit
2002 April 27		28	1 2 5 0 00		1 2 5 0 00	

ACCOUNT Professional Fees						ACCOUNT NO. 41	
		Post.				Balance	
Date	Item	Ref.	Debit	Credit		Debit	Credit
2002 April 30		28		1 7 2 0 00			1 7 2 0 00
30		28		5 1 4 5 00			6 8 6 5 00

ACCOUNT Salary Expense						ACCOUNT NO. 51	
		Post.				Balance	
Date	Item	Ref.	Debit	Credit		Debit	Credit
2002 April 30		28	1 7 2 5 00			1 7 2 5 00	

ACCOUNT Rent Expense						ACCOUNT NO. 53	
		Post.				Balance	
Date	Item	Ref.	Debit	Credit		Debit	Credit
2002 April 1		27	8 0 0 00			8 0 0 00	

ACCOUNT Laboratory Expense						ACCOUNT NO. 55	
		Post.				Balance	
Date	Item	Ref.	Debit	Credit		Debit	Credit
2002 April 24		28	5 4 5 00			5 4 5 00	

ACCOUNT Utilities Expense						ACCOUNT NO. 56	
		Post.				Balance	
Date	Item	Ref.	Debit	Credit		Debit	Credit
2002 April 30		28	3 6 0 00			3 6 0 00	

ACCOUNT Miscellaneous Expense						ACCOUNT NO. 59	
		Post.				Balance	
Date	Item	Ref.	Debit	Credit		Debit	Credit
2002 April 30		28	1 3 2 00			1 3 2 00	

4.

J. F. Outz, M.D. Trial Balance April 30, 2002					
Cash	2 3 6 1 00				
Accounts Receivable	8 7 2 0 00				
Supplies	5 3 5 00				
Prepaid Insurance	8 3 5 00				
Equipment	21 5 2 0 00				
Accounts Payable			1 3 3 5 00		
J. F. Outz, Capital			30 5 8 3 00		
J. F. Outz, Drawing	1 2 5 0 00				
Professional Fees			6 8 6 5 00		
Salary Expense	1 7 2 5 00				
Rent Expense	8 0 0 00				
Laboratory Expense	5 4 5 00				
Utilities Expense	3 6 0 00				
Miscellaneous Expense	1 3 2 00				
	38 7 8 3 00		38 7 8 3 00		

SELF-EXAMINATION QUESTIONS   Answers at End of Chapter

Matching

Match each of the following statements with its proper term. Some terms may not be used.

A.	account
B.	assets
C.	balance of the account
D.	chart of accounts
E.	credits
F.	debits
G.	double-entry accounting
H.	drawing
I.	expenses
J.	horizontal analysis
K.	journal
L.	journal entry
M.	journalizing
N.	ledger
O.	liabilities
P.	materiality concept
Q.	objectivity concept
R.	owner's equity
S.	posting

___ 1. An accounting form that is used to record the increases and decreases in each financial statement item.

___ 2. A group of accounts for a business.

___ 3. A list of the accounts in the ledger.

___ 4. Resources that are owned by the business.

___ 5. Debts owed to outsiders (creditors).

___ 6. The owner's right to the assets of the business.

___ 7. Increases in owner's equity as a result of selling services or products to customers.

___ 8. Assets used up or services consumed in the process of generating revenues.

___ 9. The simplest form of an account.

___ 10. Amounts entered on the left side of an account.

___ 11. Amounts entered on the right side of an account.

___ 12. The amount of the difference between the debits and the credits that have been entered into an account.

___ 13. The initial record in which the effects of a transaction are recorded.

___ 14. The process of recording a transaction in the journal.

___ 15. The form of recording a transaction in a journal.

___ 16. A system of accounting for recording transactions, based on recording increases and decreases in accounts so that debits equal credits.

___ 17. The account used to record amounts withdrawn by an owner of a proprietorship.

T.	**revenues**
U.	**slide**
V.	**T account**
W.	**transposition**
X.	**trial balance**
Y.	**two-column journal**
Z.	**unearned revenue**
AA.	**vertical analysis**

___ 18. The process of transferring the debits and credits from the journal entries to the accounts.

___ 19. An all-purpose journal.

___ 20. The liability created by receiving revenue in advance.

___ 21. A summary listing of the titles and balances of accounts in the ledger.

___ 22. A concept of accounting that implies that an error may be treated in the easiest possible way.

___ 23. An error in which the order of the digits is changed, such as writing $542 as $452 or $524.

___ 24. An error in which the entire number is moved one or more spaces to the right or the left, such as writing $542.00 as $54.20 or $5,420.00.

___ 25. Financial analysis that compares an item in a current statement with the same item in prior statements.

Multiple Choice

1. A debit may signify:
   A. an increase in an asset account.
   B. a decrease in an asset account.
   C. an increase in a liability account.
   D. an increase in the owner's capital account.

2. The type of account with a normal credit balance is:
   A. an asset.   C. a revenue.
   B. drawing.   D. an expense.

3. A debit balance in which of the following accounts would indicate a likely error?
   A. Accounts Receivable
   B. Cash
   C. Fees Earned
   D. Miscellaneous Expense

4. The receipt of cash from customers in payment of their accounts would be recorded by a:
   A. debit to Cash; credit to Accounts Receivable.
   B. debit to Accounts Receivable; credit to Cash.
   C. debit to Cash; credit to Accounts Payable.
   D. debit to Accounts Payable; credit to Cash.

5. The form listing the titles and balances of the accounts in the ledger on a given date is the:
   A. income statement.
   B. balance sheet.
   C. statement of owner's equity.
   D. trial balance.

CLASS DISCUSSION QUESTIONS

1. What is the difference between an account and a ledger?
2. Describe in general terms the sequence of accounts in the ledger.
3. Do the terms *debit* and *credit* signify increase or decrease or can they signify either? Explain.
4. Explain why the rules of debit and credit are the same for liability accounts and owner's equity accounts.
5. What is the effect (increase or decrease) of a debit to an expense account (a) in terms of owner's equity and (b) in terms of expense?
6. What is the effect (increase or decrease) of a credit to a revenue account (a) in terms of owner's equity and (b) in terms of revenue?
7. Meadows Company adheres to a policy of depositing all cash receipts in a bank account and making all payments by check. The cash account as of July 31 has a credit balance of $900, and there is no undeposited cash on hand. (a) Assuming no errors occurred during journalizing or posting, what caused this unusual balance? (b) Is the $900 credit balance in the cash account an asset, a liability, owner's equity, a revenue, or an expense?
8. Rearrange the following in proper sequence: (a) entry is posted to ledger, (b) business transaction occurs, (c) entry is recorded in journal, (d) business document is prepared, (e) business transaction is authorized.
9. Describe the three procedures required to post the credit portion of the following journal entry (Fees Earned is account no. 41):

JOURNAL					Page 19	
Date	Description	Post. Ref.	Debit		Credit	
2003 Nov. 23	Accounts Receivable	12	3 0 2 0 00			1
	Fees Earned				3 0 2 0 00	2

10. In the journal, what indicates that an entry has been posted to the accounts?

11. Shaw Company performed services in October for a specific customer, for a fee of $4,230. Payment was received the following November. (a) Was the revenue earned in October or November? (b) What accounts should be debited and credited in (1) October and (2) November?

12. What proof is provided by a trial balance?

13. If the two totals of a trial balance are equal, does it mean that there are no errors in the accounting records? Explain.

14. Assume that a trial balance is prepared with an account balance of $21,750 listed as $21,570 and an account balance of $6,100 listed as $610. Identify the transposition and the slide.

15. Assume that when a purchase of supplies of $1,050 for cash was recorded, both the debit and the credit were journalized and posted as $1,500. (a) Would this error cause the trial balance to be out of balance? (b) Would the trial balance be out of balance if the $1,050 entry had been journalized correctly but the credit to Cash had been posted as $1,500?

16. How is a correction made when an error in an account title or amount in the journal is discovered before the entry is posted?

17. In journalizing and posting the entry to record the purchase of supplies on account, the accounts receivable account was credited in error. What is the preferred procedure to correct this error?

18. Banks rely heavily upon customers' deposits as a source of funds. Demand deposits normally pay interest to the customer, who is entitled to withdraw at any time without prior notice to the bank. Checking and NOW (negotiable order of withdrawal) accounts are the most common form of demand deposits for banks. Assume that ABC Storage has a checking account at American Savings Bank. What type of account (asset, liability, owner's equity, revenue, expense, drawing) does the account balance of $13,850 represent from the viewpoint of (a) ABC Storage and (b) American Savings Bank?

Real World

RESOURCES FOR YOUR SUCCESS ONLINE AT

http://warren.swcollege.com

Remember! If you need additional help, visit South-Western's Web site.
See page 26 for a description of the online and printed materials that are available.

Warren
Reeve
Fess

EXERCISES

Exercise 2–1
Chart of accounts
Objective 1

The following accounts appeared in recent financial statements of **Continental Airlines**:

Accounts Payable	Flight Equipment
Aircraft Fuel Expense	Landing Fees
Air Traffic Liability	Passenger Revenue
Cargo and Mail Revenue	Purchase Deposits for Flight Equipment
Commissions	Spare Parts and Supplies

Identify each account as either a balance sheet account or an income statement account. For each balance sheet account, identify it as an asset, a liability, or owner's equity. For each income statement account, identify it as a revenue or an expense.

Exercise 2–2
Chart of accounts
Objective 1

Cameron Interiors is owned and operated by Kim Walks, an interior decorator. In the ledger of Cameron Interiors, the first digit of the account number indicates its major account classification (1—assets, 2—liabilities, 3—owner's equity, 4—revenues, 5—expenses). The second digit of the account number indicates the specific account within each of the preceding major account classifications.

Match each account number with its most likely account in the list below. The account numbers are 11, 12, 13, 21, 31, 32, 41, 51, 52, and 53.

Accounts:

Accounts Payable	Kim Walks, Drawing
Accounts Receivable	Land
Cash	Miscellaneous Expense
Fees Earned	Supplies Expense
Kim Walks, Capital	Wages Expense

Exercise 2–3
Chart of accounts
Objective 1

The Charisma School is a newly organized business that teaches people how to inspire and influence others. The list of accounts to be opened in the general ledger is as follows:

Accounts Payable	Gerald Emerson, Capital	Supplies
Accounts Receivable	Gerald Emerson, Drawing	Supplies Expense
Cash	Miscellaneous Expense	Unearned Rent
Equipment	Prepaid Insurance	Wages Expense
Fees Earned	Rent Expense	

List the accounts in the order in which they should appear in the ledger of The Charisma School and assign account numbers. Each account number is to have two digits: the first digit is to indicate the major classification (*1* for assets, etc.), and the second digit is to identify the specific account within each major classification (*11* for Cash, etc.).

Exercise 2–4
Identifying transactions
Objectives 2, 3

World Co. is a travel agency. The nine transactions recorded by World during April, its first month of operations, are indicated in the following T accounts:

Cash			
(1) 30,000	(2)	1,500	
(7) 9,500	(3)	10,000	
	(4)	4,050	
	(6)	7,500	
	(8)	3,000	

Equipment	
(3) 30,000	

Emmer Liu, Drawing	
(8) 3,000	

Accounts Receivable	
(5) 13,000	(7) 9,500

Accounts Payable	
(6) 7,500	(3) 20,000

Service Revenue	
	(5) 13,000

Supplies	
(2) 1,500	(9) 1,050

Emmer Liu, Capital	
	(1) 30,000

Operating Expenses	
(4) 4,050	
(9) 1,050	

Indicate for each debit and each credit: (a) whether an asset, liability, owner's equity, drawing, revenue, or expense account was affected and (b) whether the account was increased (+) or decreased (−). Present your answers in the following form, with transaction (1) given as an example:

	Account Debited		**Account Credited**	
Transaction	**Type**	**Effect**	**Type**	**Effect**
(1)	asset	+	owner's equity	+

Exercise 2–5
Journal entries
Objectives 3, 4

Based upon the T accounts in Exercise 2–4, prepare the nine journal entries from which the postings were made. Journal entry explanations may be omitted.

Exercise 2–6
Trial balance
Objective 5

Based upon the data presented in Exercise 2–4, prepare a trial balance, listing the accounts in their proper order.

✓ Total Debit Column: $55,500

Exercise 2–7
Normal entries for accounts
Objective 3

During the month, Quark Labs Co. has a substantial number of transactions affecting each of the following accounts. State for each account whether it is likely to have (a) debit entries only, (b) credit entries only, or (c) both debit and credit entries.

1. Accounts Payable
2. Accounts Receivable
3. Cash
4. Fees Earned

5. Lindsey Perkins, Drawing
6. Miscellaneous Expense
7. Supplies Expense

Exercise 2–8
Normal balances of accounts
Objective 3

Identify each of the following accounts of Century Services Co. as asset, liability, owner's equity, revenue, or expense, and state in each case whether the normal balance is a debit or a credit.

a. Accounts Payable
b. Accounts Receivable
c. Cash
d. Craig Arant, Capital
e. Craig Arant, Drawing

f. Equipment
g. Fees Earned
h. Rent Expense
i. Salary Expense
j. Supplies

Exercise 2–9
Rules of debit and credit
Objective 3

The following table summarizes the rules of debit and credit. For each of the items (a) through (l), indicate whether the proper answer is a debit or a credit.

	Increase	**Decrease**	**Normal Balance**
Balance sheet accounts:			
Asset	Debit	Credit	(a)
Liability	(b)	(c)	(d)
Owner's Equity:			
Capital	(e)	(f)	Credit
Drawing	(g)	Credit	(h)
Income statement accounts:			
Revenue	(i)	Debit	(j)
Expense	(k)	Credit	(l)

Exercise 2–10
Capital account balance
Objectives 2, 3

As of January 1, Kristi Toohey, Capital, had a credit balance of $7,500. During the year, withdrawals totaled $5,000 and the business incurred a net loss of $6,000.

a. Calculate the balance of Kristi Toohey, Capital, as of the end of the year.
b. Assuming that there have been no recording errors, will the balance sheet prepared at December 31 balance? Explain.

Exercise 2–11
Cash account balance

Objectives 2, 3

During the month, Kapok Co. received $312,800 in cash and paid out $295,000 in cash.

a. Do the data indicate that Kapok Co. earned $17,800 during the month? Explain.

b. If the balance of the cash account is $26,300 at the end of the month, what was the cash balance at the beginning of the month?

Exercise 2–12
Account balances

Objectives 2, 3

✓ c. $13,800

a. On June 1, the cash account balance was $3,850. During June, cash receipts totaled $11,850 and the June 30 balance was $4,150. Determine the cash payments made during June.

b. On May 1, the accounts receivable account balance was $18,500. During May, $21,000 was collected from customers on account. Assuming the May 31 balance was $27,500, determine the fees billed to customers on account during May.

c. During January, $60,500 was paid to creditors on account and purchases on account were $77,700. Assuming the January 31 balance of Accounts Payable was $31,000, determine the account balance on January 1.

Exercise 2–13
Transactions

Objectives 3, 4

The Wildcat Co. has the following accounts in its ledger: Cash; Accounts Receivable; Supplies; Office Equipment; Accounts Payable; Bob Lyons, Capital; Bob Lyons, Drawing; Fees Earned; Rent Expense; Advertising Expense; Utilities Expense; Miscellaneous Expense.

Journalize the following selected transactions in a two-column journal. Journal entry explanations may be omitted.

March 1. Paid rent for the month, $2,500.
     2. Paid advertising expense, $600.
     4. Paid cash for supplies, $1,050.
     6. Purchased office equipment on account, $4,500.
     8. Received cash from customers on account, $3,600.
    12. Paid creditor on account, $2,150.
    20. Withdrew cash for personal use, $1,000.
    25. Paid cash for repairs to office equipment, $120.
    30. Paid telephone bill for the month, $195.
    31. Fees earned and billed to customers for the month, $11,150.
    31. Paid electricity bill for the month, $280.

Exercise 2–14
Journalizing and posting

Objectives 3, 4

On November 12, 2003, Trux Co. purchased $1,720 of supplies on account. In Trux Co.'s chart of accounts, the supplies account is No. 15 and the accounts payable account is No. 21.

a. Journalize the November 12, 2003 transaction on page 29 of Trux Co.'s two-column journal. Include an explanation of the entry.

b. Prepare a four-column account for Supplies. Enter a debit balance of $390 as of November 1, 2003. Place a check mark (✓) in the posting reference column.

c. Prepare a four-column account for Accounts Payable. Enter a credit balance of $9,681 as of November 1, 2003. Place a check mark (✓) in the posting reference column.

d. Post the November 12, 2003 transaction to the accounts.

Exercise 2–15
Transactions and T accounts

Objectives 2, 3, 4

SPREADSHEET

The following selected transactions were completed during September of the current year:

1. Billed customers for fees earned, $8,210.
2. Purchased supplies on account, $1,070.
3. Received cash from customers on account, $6,150.
4. Paid creditors on account, $750.

a. Journalize the above transactions in a two-column journal, using the appropriate number to identify the transactions. Journal entry explanations may be omitted.

b. Post the entries prepared in (a) to the following T accounts: Cash, Supplies, Accounts Receivable, Accounts Payable, Fees Earned. To the left of each amount posted in the accounts, place the appropriate number to identify the transactions.

Exercise 2–16
Trial balance

Objective 5

✓ Total Credit Column: $503,500

The accounts in the ledger of Bogart Park Co. as of August 31 of the current year are listed in alphabetical order as follows. All accounts have normal balances. The balance of the cash account has been intentionally omitted.

Accounts Payable	$ 13,710
Accounts Receivable	27,500
Cash	?
Don Cline, Capital	110,290
Don Cline, Drawing	25,000
Fees Earned	333,500
Insurance Expense	5,000
Land	125,000
Miscellaneous Expense	9,900
Notes Payable	40,000
Prepaid Insurance	3,150
Rent Expense	58,000
Supplies	4,100
Supplies Expense	5,900
Unearned Rent	6,000
Utilities Expense	41,500
Wages Expense	175,000

Prepare a trial balance, listing the accounts in their proper order and inserting the missing figure for cash.

Exercise 2–17
Effect of errors on trial balance

Objective 5

Indicate which of the following errors, each considered individually, would cause the trial balance totals to be unequal:

a. Payment of a cash withdrawal of $3,500 was journalized and posted as a debit of $5,300 to Salary Expense and a credit of $3,500 to Cash.
b. A payment of $6,100 for equipment purchased was posted as a debit of $1,600 to Equipment and a credit of $1,600 to Cash.
c. A fee of $1,850 earned and due from a client was not debited to Accounts Receivable or credited to a revenue account, because the cash had not been received.
d. A receipt of $325 from an account receivable was journalized and posted as a debit of $325 to Cash and a credit of $325 to Fees Earned.
e. A payment of $1,075 to a creditor was posted as a debit of $1,075 to Accounts Payable and a debit of $1,075 to Cash.

Exercise 2–18
Errors in trial balance

Objective 5

✓ Total of Credit Column: $167,255

The following preliminary trial balance of Entrée Co., a sports ticket agency, does not balance:

Entrée Co.
Trial Balance
December 31, 20—

Cash	75,350	
Accounts Receivable	23,600	
Prepaid Insurance		3,300
Equipment	86,000	
Accounts Payable		9,450
Unearned Rent		2,570
Byron Reynolds, Capital	91,615	
Byron Reynolds, Drawing	10,000	
Service Revenue		64,940
Wages Expense		33,400
Advertising Expense	5,200	
Miscellaneous Expense		1,380
	291,765	115,040

When the ledger and other records are reviewed, you discover the following: (1) the debits and credits in the cash account total $75,350 and $53,975, respectively; (2) a billing of $1,000 to a customer on account was not posted to the accounts receivable account; (3) a payment of $1,500 made to a creditor on account was not posted to the accounts payable account; (4) the balance of the unearned rent account is $2,750; (5) the correct balance of the equipment account is $68,000; and (6) each account has a normal balance.

Prepare a corrected trial balance.

Exercise 2–19
Effect of errors on trial balance

Objective 5

The following errors occurred in posting from a two-column journal:

1. A debit of $750 to Accounts Payable was posted as a credit.
2. A credit of $350 to Cash was posted as $530.
3. A debit of $800 to Cash was posted to Miscellaneous Expense.
4. A debit of $1,050 to Supplies was posted twice.
5. A debit of $1,575 to Wages Expense was posted as $5,175.
6. A credit of $3,175 to Accounts Payable was not posted.
7. An entry debiting Accounts Receivable and crediting Fees Earned for $4,500 was not posted.

Considering each case individually (i.e., assuming that no other errors had occurred), indicate: (a) by "yes" or "no" whether the trial balance would be out of balance; (b) if answer to (a) is "yes," the amount by which the trial balance totals would differ; and (c) whether the debit or credit column of the trial balance would have the larger total. Answers should be presented in the following form, with error (1) given as an example:

Error	(a) Out of Balance	(b) Difference	(c) Larger Total
1.	yes	$1,500	credit

Exercise 2–20
Errors in trial balance

Objective 5

How many errors can you find in the following trial balance? All accounts have normal balances.

What's Wrong With This?

✔ Total of Credit Column: $120,900

Goulet Co.
Trial Balance
For the Month Ending January 31, 2003

Cash	8,010	
Accounts Receivable		16,400
Prepaid Insurance	2,400	
Equipment	52,000	
Accounts Payable	1,850	
Salaries Payable		750
Pug Myslik, Capital		39,600
Pug Myslik, Drawing		5,000
Service Revenue		78,700
Salary Expense	28,400	
Advertising Expense		7,200
Miscellaneous Expense	1,190	
	94,150	94,150

Exercise 2–21
Entries to correct errors

Objective 6

The following errors took place in journalizing and posting transactions:

a. A withdrawal of $20,000 by Julie Snyder, owner of the business, was recorded as a debit to Salary Expense and a credit to Cash.
b. Rent of $3,000 paid for the current month was recorded as a debit to Rent Expense and a credit to Accounts Payable.

Journalize the entries to correct the errors. Omit explanations.

Exercise 2–22
Entries to correct errors

Objective 6

The following errors took place in journalizing and posting transactions:

a. A $750 purchase of supplies on account was recorded as a debit to Miscellaneous Expense and a credit to Cash.
b. Cash of $2,700 received on account was recorded as a debit to Accounts Payable and a credit to Cash.

Journalize the entries to correct the errors. Omit explanations.

Exercise 2–23
Horizontal analysis of income statement

Objective 7

The financial statements for **Cisco Systems, Inc.**, are presented in Appendix G at the end of the text.

a. For Cisco Systems, comparing 2000 with 1999, determine the amount of change and the percent of change for
   1. net sales (revenues) and
   2. sales and marketing expenses.
b. ✏ ➝ What conclusions can you draw from your analysis of the net sales and the selling, marketing, and administrative expenses?

PROBLEMS SERIES A

Problem 2–1A
Entries into T accounts and trial balance

Objectives 2, 3, 4, 5

✓ 3. Total of Debit Column: $33,925

Sherry Lundin, an architect, opened an office on March 1 of the current year. During the month, she completed the following transactions connected with her professional practice:

a. Transferred cash from a personal bank account to an account to be used for the business, $15,000.
b. Paid March rent for office and workroom, $2,000.
c. Purchased used automobile for $11,500, paying $2,500 cash and giving a note payable for the remainder.
d. Purchased office and computer equipment on account, $5,500.
e. Paid cash for supplies, $750.
f. Paid cash for annual insurance policies, $1,050.
g. Received cash from client for plans delivered, $3,100.
h. Paid cash for miscellaneous expenses, $75.
i. Paid cash to creditors on account, $2,950.
j. Paid installment due on note payable, $400.
k. Received invoice for blueprint service, due in April, $525.
l. Recorded fee earned on plans delivered, payment to be received in April, $4,150.
m. Paid salary of assistant, $1,200.
n. Paid gas, oil, and repairs on automobile for March, $150.

Instructions

1. Record the foregoing transactions directly in the following T accounts, without journalizing: Cash; Accounts Receivable; Supplies; Prepaid Insurance; Automobiles; Equipment; Notes Payable; Accounts Payable; Sherry Lundin, Capital; Professional Fees; Rent Expense; Salary Expense; Automobile Expense; Blueprint Expense; Miscellaneous Expense. To the left of the amount entered in the accounts, place the appropriate letter to identify the transaction.
2. Determine the balances of the T accounts having two or more debits or credits. A memorandum balance should be inserted in accounts having both debits and credits, in the manner illustrated in the chapter. For accounts with entries on one side only (such as Professional Fees), there is no need to insert the memorandum balance in the item column. For accounts containing only a single debit and a single credit (such as Notes Payable), the memorandum balance should be inserted in the appropriate item column. Accounts containing a single entry only (such as Prepaid Insurance) do not need a memorandum balance.
3. Prepare a trial balance for Sherry Lundin, Architect, as of March 31 of the current year.

Problem 2–2A
Journal entries and trial balance

Objectives 2, 3, 4, 5

GENERAL LEDGER

✓ 4. c. $4,225

On May 1, 2003, Jim Lindley established Homestead Realty, which completed the following transactions during the month:

a. Jim Lindley transferred cash from a personal bank account to an account to be used for the business, $7,500.
b. Paid rent on office and equipment for the month, $2,500.
c. Purchased supplies on account, $1,200.
d. Paid creditor on account, $900.
e. Earned sales commissions, receiving cash, $15,750.
f. Paid automobile expenses (including rental charge) for month, $2,400, and miscellaneous expenses, $1,250.
g. Paid office salaries, $4,500.
h. Determined that the cost of supplies used was $875.
i. Withdrew cash for personal use, $2,500.

Instructions

1. Journalize entries for transactions (a) through (i), using the following account titles: Cash; Supplies; Accounts Payable; Jim Lindley, Capital; Jim Lindley, Drawing; Sales Commissions; Office Salaries Expense; Rent Expense; Automobile Expense; Supplies Expense; Miscellaneous Expense. Explanations may be omitted.
2. Prepare T accounts, using the account titles in (1). Post the journal entries to these accounts, placing the appropriate letter to the left of each amount to identify the transactions. Determine the account balances, after all posting is complete, for all accounts having two or more debits or credits. A memorandum balance should also be inserted in accounts having both debits and credits, in the manner illustrated in the chapter. For accounts with entries on one side only, there is no need to insert a memorandum balance in the item column. For accounts containing only a single debit and a single credit, the memorandum balance should be inserted in the appropriate item column.
3. Prepare a trial balance as of May 31, 2003.
4. Determine the following:
   a. Amount of total revenue recorded in the ledger.
   b. Amount of total expenses recorded in the ledger.
   c. Amount of net income for May.

Problem 2–3A
Journal entries and trial balance

Objectives 2, 3, 4, 5

GENERAL LEDGER

✓ 3. Total of Credit Column: $47,400

On April 5 of the current year, John Bike established an interior decorating business, Tucson Designs. During the remainder of the month, John completed the following transactions related to the business:

April 5. John transferred cash from a personal bank account to an account to be used for the business, $18,000.
6. Paid rent for period of April 6 to end of month, $2,000.
7. Purchased office equipment on account, $10,500.
8. Purchased a used truck for $18,000, paying $10,000 cash and giving a note payable for the remainder.
10. Purchased supplies for cash, $1,315.
12. Received cash for job completed, $7,300.
20. Paid annual premiums on property and casualty insurance, $1,200.
23. Recorded jobs completed on account and sent invoices to customers, $4,950.
24. Received an invoice for truck expenses, to be paid in July, $450.
29. Paid utilities expense, $750.
29. Paid miscellaneous expenses, $210.
30. Received cash from customers on account, $2,200.
30. Paid wages of employees, $3,000.
30. Paid creditor a portion of the amount owed for equipment purchased on April 7, $1,800.
30. Withdrew cash for personal use, $3,500.

Instructions

1. Journalize each transaction in a two-column journal, referring to the following chart of accounts in selecting the accounts to be debited and credited. (Do not insert the account numbers in the journal at this time.) Explanations may be omitted.

11	Cash	31	John Bike, Capital
12	Accounts Receivable	32	John Bike, Drawing
13	Supplies	41	Fees Earned
14	Prepaid Insurance	51	Wages Expense
16	Equipment	53	Rent Expense
18	Truck	54	Utilities Expense
21	Notes Payable	55	Truck Expense
22	Accounts Payable	59	Miscellaneous Expense

2. Post the journal to a ledger of four-column accounts, inserting appropriate posting references as each item is posted. Extend the balances to the appropriate balance columns after each transaction is posted.

3. Prepare a trial balance for Tucson Designs as of April 30.

Problem 2–4A

Journal entries and trial balance

Objectives 2, 3, 4, 5

GENERAL LEDGER

✓ 4. Total of Debit Column:

$265,200

Eastside Realty acts as an agent in buying, selling, renting, and managing real estate. The account balances at the end of March of the current year are as follows:

11	Cash	18,150	
12	Accounts Receivable	48,750	
13	Prepaid Insurance	1,100	
14	Office Supplies	1,050	
16	Land	0	
21	Accounts Payable		11,510
22	Notes Payable		0
31	Reba Heflin, Capital		34,340
32	Reba Heflin, Drawing	1,000	
41	Fees Earned		126,500
51	Salary and Commission Expense	74,100	
52	Rent Expense	15,000	
53	Advertising Expense	8,900	
54	Automobile Expense	2,750	
59	Miscellaneous Expense	1,550	
		172,350	172,350

The following business transactions were completed by Eastside Realty during April of the current year:

April 1. Paid rent on office for month, $5,000.
   2. Purchased office supplies on account, $1,375.
   5. Paid annual insurance premiums, $1,650.
   8. Received cash from clients on account, $20,200.
   15. Purchased land for a future building site for $75,000, paying $7,500 in cash and giving a note payable for the remainder.
   17. Paid creditors on account, $4,150.
   20. Returned a portion of the office supplies purchased on April 2, receiving full credit for their cost, $275.
   24. Paid advertising expense, $1,050.
   27. Discovered an error in computing a commission; received cash from the salesperson for the overpayment, $350.
   28. Paid automobile expense (including rental charges for an automobile), $715.
   29. Paid miscellaneous expenses, $215.
   30. Recorded revenue earned and billed to clients during the month, $28,400.
   30. Paid salaries and commissions for the month, $11,500.
   30. Withdrew cash for personal use, $2,000.

Instructions

1. Record the April 1 balance of each account in the appropriate balance column of a four-column account, write *Balance* in the item section, and place a check mark (✓) in the posting reference column.

2. Journalize the transactions for April in a two-column journal. Journal entry explanations may be omitted.
3. Post to the ledger, extending the account balance to the appropriate balance column after each posting.
4. Prepare a trial balance of the ledger as of April 30.

If the working papers correlating with this textbook are not used, omit Problem 2–5A.

Problem 2–5A
Errors in trial balance
Objectives 5, 6

✓ 7. Total of Debit Column:
$33,338.10

The following records of Reliable TV Repair are presented in the working papers:

- Journal containing entries for the period March 1–31.
- Ledger to which the March entries have been posted.
- Preliminary trial balance as of March 31, which does not balance.

Locate the errors, supply the information requested, and prepare a corrected trial balance according to the following instructions. The balances recorded in the accounts as of March 1 and the entries in the journal are correctly stated. If it is necessary to correct any posted amounts in the ledger, a line should be drawn through the erroneous figure and the correct amount inserted above. Corrections or notations may be inserted on the preliminary trial balance in any manner desired. It is not necessary to complete all of the instructions if equal trial balance totals can be obtained earlier. However, the requirements of instructions (6) and (7) should be completed in any event.

Instructions

1. Verify the totals of the preliminary trial balance, inserting the correct amounts in the schedule provided in the working papers.
2. Compute the difference between the trial balance totals.
3. Compare the listings in the trial balance with the balances appearing in the ledger, and list the errors in the space provided in the working papers.
4. Verify the accuracy of the balance of each account in the ledger, and list the errors in the space provided in the working papers.
5. Trace the postings in the ledger back to the journal, using small check marks to identify items traced. Correct any amounts in the ledger that may be necessitated by errors in posting, and list the errors in the space provided in the working papers.
6. Journalize as of March 31 the payment of $100 for advertising expense. The bill had been paid on March 31 but was inadvertently omitted from the journal. Post to the ledger. (Revise any amounts necessitated by posting this entry.)
7. Prepare a new trial balance.

Problem 2–6A
Corrected trial balance
Objectives 5, 6

SPREADSHEET

✓ 1. Total of Debit Column: $90,000

Persian Carpet has the following trial balance as of March 31 of the current year:

Cash	7,315	
Accounts Receivable	5,545	
Supplies	1,010	
Prepaid Insurance	250	
Equipment	25,000	
Notes Payable		20,000
Accounts Payable		4,960
Serena Nodvin, Capital		18,800
Serena Nodvin, Drawing	5,500	
Fees Earned		54,790
Wages Expense	31,100	
Rent Expense	7,455	
Advertising Expense	320	
Miscellaneous Expense	1,505	
	85,000	98,550

The debit and credit totals are not equal as a result of the following errors:

a. The balance of cash was understated by $900.
b. A cash receipt of $1,750 was posted as a debit to Cash of $7,150.

c. A debit of $2,500 for a withdrawal by the owner was posted as a credit to Serena Nodvin, Capital.
d. The balance of $3,200 in Advertising Expense was entered as $320 in the trial balance.
e. A debit of $580 to Accounts Receivable was not posted.
f. A return of $125 of defective supplies was erroneously posted as a $215 credit to Supplies.
g. The balance of Notes Payable was overstated by $5,000.
h. An insurance policy acquired at a cost of $150 was posted as a credit to Prepaid Insurance.
i. Gas, Electricity, and Water Expense, with a balance of $3,150, was omitted from the trial balance.
j. A debit of $1,050 in Accounts Payable was overlooked when determining the balance of the account.

Instructions

1. Prepare a corrected trial balance as of March 31 of the current year.
2. Does the fact that the trial balance in (1) is balanced mean that there are no errors in the accounts? Explain.

PROBLEMS SERIES B

Problem 2–1B
Entries into T accounts and trial balance

Objectives 2, 3, 4, 5

✓ 3. Total of Debit Column: $48,175

James Bitnar, an architect, opened an office on September 1 of the current year. During the month, he completed the following transactions connected with his professional practice:

a. Transferred cash from a personal bank account to an account to be used for the business, $25,000.
b. Purchased used automobile for $18,300, paying $6,000 cash and giving a note payable for the remainder.
c. Paid September rent for office and workroom, $2,500.
d. Paid cash for supplies, $300.
e. Purchased office and computer equipment on account, $6,200.
f. Paid cash for annual insurance policies on automobile and equipment, $1,200.
g. Received cash from a client for plans delivered, $3,725.
h. Paid cash to creditors on account, $2,100.
i. Paid cash for miscellaneous expenses, $120.
j. Received invoice for blueprint service, due in following month, $350.
k. Recorded fee earned on plans delivered, payment to be received in October, $3,500.
l. Paid salary of assistant, $1,500.
m. Paid cash for miscellaneous expenses, $105.
n. Paid installment due on note payable, $800.
o. Paid gas, oil, and repairs on automobile for September, $145.

Instructions

1. Record the foregoing transactions directly in the following T accounts, without journalizing: Cash; Accounts Receivable; Supplies; Prepaid Insurance; Automobiles; Equipment; Notes Payable; Accounts Payable; James Bitnar, Capital; Professional Fees; Rent Expense; Salary Expense; Blueprint Expense; Automobile Expense; Miscellaneous Expense. To the left of each amount entered in the accounts, place the appropriate letter to identify the transaction.
2. Determine the balances of the T accounts having two or more debits or credits. A memorandum balance should be inserted in accounts having both debits and credits, in the manner illustrated in the chapter. For accounts with entries on one side only (such as Professional Fees), there is no need to insert the memorandum balance in the item column. For accounts containing only a single debit and a single credit (such as Notes Payable), the memorandum balance should be inserted in the appropriate item column. Accounts containing a single entry only (such as Prepaid Insurance) do not need a memorandum balance.
3. Prepare a trial balance for James Bitnar, Architect, as of September 30 of the current year.

Problem 2–2B

Journal entries and trial balance

Objectives 2, 3, 4, 5

GENERAL LEDGER

✓ 4. c. $10,245

On December 1, 2003, Mary Jo Croy established Preferred Realty, which completed the following transactions during the month:

a.   Mary Jo Croy transferred cash from a personal bank account to an account to be used for the business, $10,000.
b.   Purchased supplies on account, $1,900.
c.   Earned sales commissions, receiving cash, $22,600.
d.   Paid rent on office and equipment for the month, $4,500.
e.   Paid creditor on account, $1,000.
f.   Withdrew cash for personal use, $3,000.
g.   Paid automobile expenses (including rental charge) for month, $1,900, and miscellaneous expenses, $1,050.
h.   Paid office salaries, $4,000.
i.   Determined that the cost of supplies used was $905.

Instructions

1.   Journalize entries for transactions (a) through (i), using the following account titles: Cash; Supplies; Accounts Payable; Mary Jo Croy, Capital; Mary Jo Croy, Drawing; Sales Commissions; Rent Expense; Office Salaries Expense; Automobile Expense; Supplies Expense; Miscellaneous Expense. Journal entry explanations may be omitted.
2.   Prepare T accounts, using the account titles in (1). Post the journal entries to these accounts, placing the appropriate letter to the left of each amount to identify the transactions. Determine the account balances, after all posting is complete, for all accounts having two or more debits or credits. A memorandum balance should be inserted in accounts having both debits and credits, in the manner illustrated in the chapter. For accounts with entries on one side only, there is no need to insert a memorandum balance in the item column. For accounts containing only a single debit and a single credit, the memorandum balance should be inserted in the appropriate item column.
3.   Prepare a trial balance as of December 31, 2003.
4.   Determine the following:
  a.   Amount of total revenue recorded in the ledger.
  b.   Amount of total expenses recorded in the ledger.
  c.   Amount of net income for December.

Problem 2–3B

Journal entries and trial balance

Objectives 2, 3, 4, 5

GENERAL LEDGER

✓ 3. Total of Credit Column: $33,480

On October 10 of the current year, Kirk Hurwitz established an interior decorating business, Marquis Designs. During the remainder of the month, Kirk Hurwitz completed the following transactions related to the business:

Oct. 10.   Kirk transferred cash from a personal bank account to an account to be used for the business, $15,000.
   10.   Paid rent for period of October 10 to end of month, $1,600.
   11.   Purchased a truck for $15,000, paying $5,000 cash and giving a note payable for the remainder.
   13.   Purchased equipment on account, $3,500.
   14.   Purchased supplies for cash, $1,050.
   14.   Paid annual premiums on property and casualty insurance, $750.
   15.   Received cash for job completed, $3,100.
   21.   Paid creditor for equipment purchased on October 13, $3,500.
   24.   Recorded jobs completed on account and sent invoices to customers, $5,100.
   26.   Received an invoice for truck expenses, to be paid in November, $280.
   27.   Paid utilities expense, $1,205.
   27.   Paid miscellaneous expenses, $180.
   29.   Received cash from customers on account, $2,420.
   30.   Paid wages of employees, $2,500.
   31.   Withdrew cash for personal use, $1,000.

Instructions

1.   Journalize each transaction in a two-column journal, referring to the following chart of accounts in selecting the accounts to be debited and credited. (Do not insert the account numbers in the journal at this time.) Journal entry explanations may be omitted.

11	Cash	31	Kirk Hurwitz, Capital

11 Cash   31 Kirk Hurwitz, Capital
12 Accounts Receivable   32 Kirk Hurwitz, Drawing
13 Supplies   41 Fees Earned
14 Prepaid Insurance   51 Wages Expense
16 Equipment   53 Rent Expense
18 Truck   54 Utilities Expense
21 Notes Payable   55 Truck Expense
22 Accounts Payable   59 Miscellaneous Expense

2. Post the journal to a ledger of four-column accounts, inserting appropriate posting references as each item is posted. Extend the balances to the appropriate balance columns after each transaction is posted.
3. Prepare a trial balance for Marquis Designs as of October 31.

Problem 2–4B
Journal entries and trial balance

Objectives 2, 3, 4, 5

GENERAL LEDGER

✓ 4. Total of Debit Column: $240,100

Gallatin Realty acts as an agent in buying, selling, renting, and managing real estate. The account balances at the end of November of the current year are as follows:

11	Cash	19,500	
12	Accounts Receivable	28,600	
13	Prepaid Insurance	1,750	
14	Office Supplies	625	
16	Land	0	
21	Accounts Payable		3,250
22	Notes Payable		0
31	Katie Chaney, Capital		12,625
32	Katie Chaney, Drawing	10,000	
41	Fees Earned		158,725
51	Salary and Commission Expense	83,075	
52	Rent Expense	16,000	
53	Advertising Expense	10,500	
54	Automobile Expense	3,950	
59	Miscellaneous Expense	600	
		174,600	174,600

The following business transactions were completed by Gallatin Realty during December of the current year:

Dec. 1. Purchased office supplies on account, $1,100.
     2. Paid rent on office for month, $1,600.
     3. Received cash from clients on account, $24,200.
     8. Paid annual insurance premiums, $1,925.
    10. Returned a portion of the office supplies purchased on December 1, receiving full credit for their cost, $150.
    14. Paid advertising expense, $2,150.
    23. Paid creditors on account, $1,650.
    29. Paid miscellaneous expenses, $215.
    30. Paid automobile expense (including rental charges for an automobile), $850.
    31. Discovered an error in computing a commission; received cash from the salesperson for the overpayment, $500.
    31. Paid salaries and commissions for the month, $10,850.
    31. Recorded revenue earned and billed to clients during the month, $26,200.
    31. Purchased land for a future building site for $50,000, paying $10,000 in cash and giving a note payable for the remainder.
    31. Withdrew cash for personal use, $2,500.

Instructions

1. Record the December 1 balance of each account in the appropriate balance column of a four-column account, write *Balance* in the item section, and place a check mark (✓) in the posting reference column.

2. Journalize the transactions for December in a two-column journal. Journal entry explanations may be omitted.
3. Post to the ledger, extending the account balance to the appropriate balance column after each posting.
4. Prepare a trial balance of the ledger as of December 31.

If the working papers correlating with this textbook are not used, omit Problem 2–5B.

Problem 2–5B
Errors in trial balance

Objectives 5, 6

✓ 7. Total of Credit Column:

$33,338.10

The following records of Reliable TV Repair are presented in the working papers:

- Journal containing entries for the period March 1–31.
- Ledger to which the March entries have been posted.
- Preliminary trial balance as of March 31, which does not balance.

Locate the errors, supply the information requested, and prepare a corrected trial balance according to the following instructions. The balances recorded in the accounts as of March 1 and the entries in the journal are correctly stated. If it is necessary to correct any posted amounts in the ledger, a line should be drawn through the erroneous figure and the correct amount inserted above. Corrections or notations may be inserted on the preliminary trial balance in any manner desired. It is not necessary to complete all of the instructions if equal trial balance totals can be obtained earlier. However, the requirements of instructions (6) and (7) should be completed in any event.

Instructions

1. Verify the totals of the preliminary trial balance, inserting the correct amounts in the schedule provided in the working papers.
2. Compute the difference between the trial balance totals.
3. Compare the listings in the trial balance with the balances appearing in the ledger, and list the errors in the space provided in the working papers.
4. Verify the accuracy of the balance of each account in the ledger, and list the errors in the space provided in the working papers.
5. Trace the postings in the ledger back to the journal, using small check marks to identify items traced. Correct any amounts in the ledger that may be necessitated by errors in posting, and list the errors in the space provided in the working papers.
6. Journalize as of March 31 the payment of $163.40 for gas and electricity. The bill had been paid on March 31 but was inadvertently omitted from the journal. Post to the ledger. (Revise any amounts necessitated by posting this entry.)
7. Prepare a new trial balance.

Problem 2–6B
Corrected trial balance

Objectives 5, 6

SPREADSHEET

✓ I. Total of Debit Column:

$130,000

Patel Videography has the following trial balance as of December 31 of the current year:

Cash	1,865	
Accounts Receivable	7,250	
Supplies	1,232	
Prepaid Insurance	330	
Equipment	30,000	
Notes Payable		11,500
Accounts Payable		3,025
Ramesh Patel, Capital		21,000
Ramesh Patel, Drawing	4,500	
Fees Earned		98,900
Wages Expense	56,730	
Rent Expense	11,585	
Advertising Expense	525	
Gas, Electricity, and Water Expense	3,150	
	117,167	134,425

The debit and credit totals are not equal as a result of the following errors:

a. The balance of cash was overstated by $2,500.
b. A cash receipt of $3,100 was posted as a credit to Cash of $1,300.

c. A debit of $1,250 to Accounts Receivable was not posted.

d. A return of $168 of defective supplies was erroneously posted as a $186 credit to Supplies.

e. An insurance policy acquired at a cost of $310 was posted as a credit to Prepaid Insurance.

f. The balance of Notes Payable was overstated by $1,500.

g. A credit of $75 in Accounts Payable was overlooked when the balance of the account was determined.

h. A debit of $3,000 for a withdrawal by the owner was posted as a credit to Ramesh Patel, Capital.

i. The balance of $5,250 in Advertising Expense was entered as $525 in the trial balance.

j. Miscellaneous Expense, with a balance of $1,320, was omitted from the trial balance.

Instructions

1. Prepare a corrected trial balance as of December 31 of the current year.
2. ✏️▶ Does the fact that the trial balance in (1) is balanced mean that there are no errors in the accounts? Explain.

CONTINUING PROBLEM

GENERAL LEDGER

✓ 4. Total of Debit Column: $15,880

The transactions completed by Dancin Music during November 2002 were described at the end of Chapter 1. The following transactions were completed during December, the second month of the business's operations:

Dec. 1. Lynn Kwan made an additional investment in Dancin Music by depositing $1,500 in Dancin Music's checking account.

1. Instead of continuing to share office space with a local real estate agency, Lynn decided to rent office space near a local music store. Paid rent for December, $800.

1. Paid a premium of $1,680 for a comprehensive insurance policy covering liability, theft, and fire. The policy covers a two-year period.

2. Received $600 on account.

3. On behalf of Dancin Music, Lynn signed a contract with a local radio station, KPRG, to provide guest spots for the next three months. The contract requires Dancin Music to provide a guest disc jockey for 80 hours per month for a monthly fee of $1,200. Any additional hours beyond 80 will be billed to KPRG at $20 per hour. In accordance with the contract, Lynn received $2,400 from KPRG as an advance payment for the first two months.

3. Paid $125 on account.

4. Paid an attorney $75 for reviewing the December 3rd contract with KPRG. (Record as Miscellaneous Expense.)

5. Purchased office equipment on account from One-Stop Office Mart, $2,500.

8. Paid for a newspaper advertisement, $100.

11. Received $300 for serving as a disc jockey for a college fraternity party.

13. Paid $250 to a local audio electronics store for rental of various equipment (speakers, CD players, etc.).

14. Paid wages of $600 to receptionist and part-time assistant.

16. Received $550 for serving as a disc jockey for a wedding reception.

18. Purchased supplies on account, $375.

21. Paid $120 to Dynamic Music for use of its current demo CDs and tapes in making cassettes of various music sets.

22. Paid $250 to a local radio station to advertise the services of Dancin Music twice daily for the remainder of December.

23. Served as disc jockey for an annual holiday party for $780. Received $200, with the remainder due January 6, 2003.

27. Paid electric bill, $280.

28. Paid wages of $600 to receptionist and part-time assistant.

29. Paid miscellaneous expenses, $85.

30. Served as a disc jockey for a pre-New Year's Eve charity ball for $600. Received $300, with the remainder due on January 10, 2003.

Dec. 31. Received $1,000 for serving as a disc jockey for a New Year's Eve party.
    31. Paid $300 royalties (music expense) to Federated Clearing for use of various artists' music during December.
    31. Withdrew $1,000 cash from Dancin Music for personal use.

Dancin Music's chart of accounts and the balance of accounts as of December 1, 2002 (all normal balances), are as follows:

11	Cash	$3,080
12	Accounts Receivable	600
14	Supplies	85
15	Prepaid Insurance	—
17	Office Equipment	—
21	Accounts Payable	125
23	Unearned Revenue	—
31	Lynn Kwan, Capital	3,500
32	Lynn Kwan, Drawing	125
41	Fees Earned	2,375
50	Wages Expense	200
51	Office Rent Expense	500
52	Equipment Rent Expense	325
53	Utilities Expense	150
54	Music Expense	470
55	Advertising Expense	300
56	Supplies Expense	90
59	Miscellaneous Expense	75

Instructions

1. Enter the December 1, 2002 account balances in the appropriate balance column of a four-column account. Write *Balance* in the Item column, and place a check mark (✔) in the Posting Reference column. (*Hint:* Verify the equality of the debit and credit balances in the ledger before proceeding with the next instruction.)
2. Analyze and journalize each transaction in a two-column journal, omitting journal entry explanations.
3. Post the journal to the ledger, extending the account balance to the appropriate balance column after each posting.
4. Prepare a trial balance as of December 31, 2002.

SPECIAL ACTIVITIES

Activity 2–1
City Motors Co.
Ethics and professional conduct in business

At the end of the current month, Dana Fossum prepared a trial balance for City Motors Co. The credit side of the trial balance exceeds the debit side by a significant amount. Dana has decided to add the difference to the balance of the miscellaneous expense account in order to complete the preparation of the current month's financial statements by a 5 o'clock deadline. Dana will look for the difference next week when she has more time.

➤ Discuss whether Dana is behaving in a professional manner.

Activity 2–2
State College
Account for revenue

State College requires students to pay tuition each term before classes begin. Students who have not paid their tuition are not allowed to enroll or to attend classes.

What journal entry do you think State College would use to record the receipt of the students' tuition payments? Describe the nature of each account in the entry.

Activity 2–3
Landmark Data Company
Record transactions

The following discussion took place between Marc Bolli, the office manager of Landmark Data Company, and a new accountant, Kelly Holt.

Kelly: I've been thinking about our method of recording entries. It seems that it's inefficient.
Marc: In what way?
Kelly: Well—correct me if I'm wrong—it seems like we have unnecessary steps in the process. We could easily develop a trial balance by posting our transactions directly into the ledger and bypassing the journal altogether. In this way we could combine the recording and posting process into one step and save ourselves a lot of time. What do you think?
Marc: We need to have a talk.

➤ What should Marc say to Kelly?

Activity 2–4
Lodge Construction Co.
Debits and credits

The following excerpt is from a conversation between Jill Rhyne, the president and chief operating officer of Lodge Construction Co., and her neighbor, Sean Resnik.

Sean: Jill, I'm taking a course in night school, "Intro to Accounting." I was wondering—could you answer a couple of questions for me?
Jill: Well, I will if I can.
Sean: Okay, our instructor says that it's critical we understand the basic concepts of accounting, or we'll never get beyond the first test. My problem is with those rules of debit and credit . . . you know, assets increase with debits, decrease with credits, etc.
Jill: Yes, pretty basic stuff. You just have to memorize the rules. It shouldn't be too difficult.
Sean: Sure, I can memorize the rules, but my problem is I want to be sure I understand the basic concepts behind the rules.

For example, why can't assets be increased with credits and decreased with debits like revenue? As long as everyone did it that way, why not? It would seem easier if we had the same rules for all increases and decreases in accounts.

Also, why is the left side of an account called the debit side? Why couldn't it be called something simple . . . like the "LE" for Left Entry? The right side could be called just "RE" for Right Entry.

Finally, why are there just two sides to an entry? Why can't there be three or four sides to an entry?

In a group of four or five, select one person to play the role of Jill and one person to play the role of Sean.

1. After listening to the conversation between Jill and Sean, help Jill answer Sean's questions.
2. What information (other than just debit and credit journal entries) could the accounting system gather that might be useful to Jill in managing Lodge Construction Co.?

Activity 2–5
Fairway Caddy Service
Transactions and income statement

Shelley Dolvin is planning to manage and operate Fairway Caddy Service at Livingston Golf and Country Club during June through August. Shelley will rent a small maintenance building from the country club for $200 per month and will offer caddy services, including cart rentals, to golfers. Shelley has had no formal training in record keeping.

Shelley keeps notes of all receipts and expenses in a shoe box. An examination of Shelley's shoe box records for June revealed the following:

June 1. Withdrew $1,500 from personal bank account to be used to operate the caddy service.
1. Paid rent to Livingston Golf and Country Club, $200.
2. Paid for golf supplies (practice balls, etc.), $150.
3. Arranged for the rental of forty regular (pulling) golf carts and ten gasoline-driven carts for $1,000 per month. Paid $750 in advance, with the remaining $250 due June 20.
7. Purchased supplies, including gasoline, for the golf carts on account, $180. Livingston Golf and Country Club has agreed to allow Shelley to store the gasoline in one of its fuel tanks at no cost.

June 15. Received cash for services from June 1–15, $1,120.
17. Paid cash to creditors on account, $180.
20. Paid remaining rental on golf carts, $250.
22. Purchased supplies, including gasoline, on account, $170.
25. Accepted IOUs from customers on account, $380.
28. Paid miscellaneous expenses, $125.
30. Received cash for services from June 16-30, $1,475.
30. Paid telephone and electricity (utilities) expenses, $105.
30. Paid wages of part-time employees, $260.
30. Received cash in payment of IOUs on account, $175.
30. Determined the amount of supplies on hand at the end of June, $98.

Shelley has asked you several questions concerning her financial affairs to date, and she has asked you to assist with her record keeping and reporting of financial data.

a. To assist Shelley with her record keeping, prepare a chart of accounts that would be appropriate for Fairway Caddy Service.
b. Prepare an income statement for June in order to help Shelley assess the profitability of Fairway Caddy Service. For this purpose, the use of T accounts may be helpful in analyzing the effects of each June transaction.
c. Based on Shelley's records of receipts and payments, calculate the amount of cash on hand on June 30. For this purpose, a T account for cash may be useful.
d. ✏️➤ A count of the cash on hand on June 30 totaled $2,120. Briefly discuss the possible causes of the difference between the amount of cash computed in (c) and the actual amount of cash on hand.

Activity 2–6
Into the Real World
Opportunities for accountants

The increasing complexity of the current business and regulatory environment has created an increased demand for accountants who can analyze business transactions and interpret their effects on the financial statements. In addition, a basic ability to analyze the effects of transactions is necessary to be successful in all fields of business as well as in other disciplines, such as law. To better understand the importance of accounting in today's environment, search the Internet or your local newspaper for job opportunities. One possible Internet site is **www.jobweb.com**. Then do one of the following:

1. Print a listing of at least two ads for accounting jobs. Alternatively, bring to class at least two newspaper ads for accounting jobs.
2. Print a listing of at least two ads for nonaccounting jobs for which some knowledge of accounting is preferred or necessary. Alternatively, bring to class at least two newspaper ads for such jobs.

ANSWERS TO SELF-EXAMINATION QUESTIONS

Matching

1. A	6. R	11. E	16. G	21. X
2. N	7. T	12. C	17. H	22. P
3. D	8. I	13. K	18 S	23. W
4. B	9. V	14. M	19. Y	24. U
5. O	10. F	15. L	20. Z	25. J

Multiple Choice

1. **A** A debit may signify an increase in an asset account (answer A) or a decrease in a liability or owner's capital account. A credit may signify a decrease in an asset account (answer B) or an increase in a liability or owner's capital account (answers C and D).

2. **C** Liability, capital, and revenue (answer C) accounts have normal credit balances. Asset (answer A), drawing (answer B), and expense (answer D) accounts have normal debit balances.

3. **C** Accounts Receivable (answer A), Cash (answer B), and Miscellaneous Expense (answer D) would all normally have debit balances. Fees Earned should normally have a credit balance. Hence, a debit balance in Fees Earned (answer C) would indicate a likely error in the recording process.

4. **A** The receipt of cash from customers on account increases the asset Cash and decreases the asset Accounts Receivable, as indicated by answer A. Answer B has the debit and credit reversed, and answers C and D involve transactions with creditors (accounts payable) and not customers (accounts receivable).

5. **D** The trial balance (answer D) is a listing of the balances and the titles of the accounts in the ledger on a given date, so that the equality of the debits and credits in the ledger can be verified. The income statement (answer A) is a summary of revenue and expenses for a period of time. The balance sheet (answer B) is a presentation of the assets, liabilities, and owner's equity on a given date. The statement of owner's equity (answer C) is a summary of the changes in owner's equity for a period of time.

The Matching Concept and the Adjusting Process

3

o b j e c t i v e s

After studying this chapter, you should be able to:

1 Explain how the matching concept relates to the accrual basis of accounting.

2 Explain why adjustments are necessary and list the characteristics of adjusting entries.

3 Journalize entries for accounts requiring adjustment.

4 Summarize the adjustment process and prepare an adjusted trial balance.

5 Use vertical analysis to compare financial statement items with each other and with industry averages.

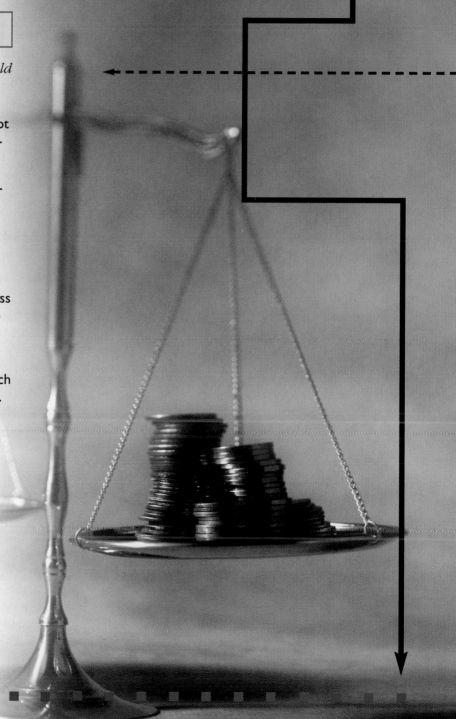

A ssume that you rented an apartment last month and signed a nine-month lease. When you signed the lease agreement, you were required to pay the final month's rent of $500. This amount is not returnable to you.

You are now applying for a student loan at a local bank. The loan application requires a listing of all your assets. Should you list the $500 deposit as an asset?

The answer to this question is "yes." The deposit is an asset to you until you receive the use of the apartment in the ninth month.

A business faces similar accounting problems at the end of a period. A business must determine what assets, liabilities, and owner's equity should be reported on its balance sheet. It must also determine what revenues and expenses should be reported on its income statement.

As we illustrated in previous chapters, transactions are normally recorded as they take place. Periodically, financial statements are prepared, summarizing the effects of the transactions on the financial position and operations of the business.

At any one point in time, however, the accounting records may not reflect all transactions. For example, most businesses do not record the daily use of supplies. Likewise, revenue may have been earned from providing services to customers, yet the customers have not been billed by the time the accounting period ends. Thus, at the end of the period, the revenue and receivable accounts must be updated.

In this chapter, we describe and illustrate this updating process. We will focus on accounts that normally require updating and the journal entries that update them.

The Matching Concept

objective 1

Explain how the matching concept relates to the accrual basis of accounting.

American Airlines uses the accrual basis of accounting. Revenues are recognized when passengers take flights, not when the passenger makes the reservation or pays for the ticket.

When accountants prepare financial statements, they assume that the economic life of the business can be divided into time periods. Using this **accounting period concept**, accountants must determine in which period the revenues and expenses of the business should be reported. To determine the appropriate period, accountants will use either (1) the cash basis of accounting or (2) the accrual basis of accounting.

Under the **cash basis**, revenues and expenses are reported in the income statement in the period in which cash is received or paid. For example, fees are recorded when cash is received from clients, and wages are recorded when cash is paid to employees. The net income (or net loss) is the difference between the cash receipts (revenues) and the cash payments (expenses).

Under the **accrual basis**, revenues are reported in the income statement in the period in which they are earned. For example, revenue is reported when the services are provided to customers. Cash may or may not be received from customers during this period. The concept that supports this reporting of revenues is called the **revenue recognition concept**.

A bank loan officer requires an individual, who normally keeps records on a cash basis, to list assets (automobiles, homes, investments, etc.) on an application for a loan or a line of credit. In addition, the application often asks for an estimate of the individual's liabilities, such as outstanding credit card amounts and automobile loan balances. In a sense, the loan application converts the individual's cash-basis accounting system to an estimated accrual basis. The loan officer uses this information to assess the individual's ability to repay the loan.

Under the accrual basis, expenses are reported in the same period as the revenues to which they relate. For example, employee wages are reported as an expense in the

> The matching concept supports reporting revenues and related expenses in the same period.

period in which the employees provided services to customers, and not necessarily when the wages are paid.

The accounting concept that supports reporting revenues and related expenses in the same period is called the **matching concept**, or **matching principle**. Under this concept, an income statement will report the resulting income or loss for the period.

Generally accepted accounting principles require the use of the accrual basis. However, small service businesses may use the cash basis because they have few receivables and payables. For example, attorneys, physicians, and real estate agents often use the cash basis. For them, the cash basis will yield financial statements similar to those prepared under the accrual basis.

For most large businesses, the cash basis will not provide accurate financial statements for user needs. For this reason, we will emphasize the accrual basis in the remainder of this text. The accrual basis and its related matching concept require an analysis and updating of some accounts when financial statements are prepared. In the following paragraphs, we will describe and illustrate this process, called the **adjusting process**.

Nature of the Adjusting Process

objective 2

Explain why adjustments are necessary and list the characteristics of adjusting entries.

At the end of an accounting period, many of the balances of accounts in the ledger can be reported, without change, in the financial statements. For example, the balance of the cash account is normally the amount reported on the balance sheet.

Some accounts in the ledger, however, require updating. For example, the balances listed for prepaid expenses are normally overstated because the use of these assets is not recorded on a day-to-day basis. The balance of the supplies account usually represents the cost of supplies at the beginning of the period plus the cost of supplies acquired during the period. To record the daily use of supplies would require many entries with small amounts. In addition, the total amount of supplies is small relative to other assets, and managers usually do not require day-to-day information about supplies.

> All adjusting entries affect at least one income statement account and one balance sheet account.

The journal entries that bring the accounts up to date at the end of the accounting period are called **adjusting entries**. All adjusting entries affect at least one income statement account and one balance sheet account. Thus, an adjusting entry will *always* involve a revenue or an expense account *and* an asset or a liability account.

Is there an easy way to know when an adjusting entry is needed? Yes, four basic items require adjusting entries. The first two items are **deferrals**. Deferrals are created by recording a transaction in a way that *delays* or *defers* the recognition of an expense or a revenue, as described below.

- **Deferred expenses**, or **prepaid expenses**, are items that have been initially recorded as assets but are expected to become expenses over time or through the normal operations of the business. Supplies and prepaid insurance are two examples of prepaid expenses that may require adjustment at the end of an accounting period. Other examples include prepaid advertising and prepaid interest.
- **Deferred revenues**, or **unearned revenues**, are items that have been initially recorded as liabilities but are expected to become revenues over time or through the normal operations of the business. An example of deferred revenue is unearned rent. Other examples include tuition received in advance by a school, an annual retainer fee received by an attorney, premiums received in advance by an insurance company, and magazine subscriptions received in advance by a publisher.

The second two items that require adjusting entries are accruals. **Accruals** are created by an unrecorded expense that has been incurred or an unrecorded revenue that has been earned, as described below.

- **Accrued expenses**, or **accrued liabilities**, are expenses that have been incurred *but have not been recorded* in the accounts. An example of an accrued expense is accrued wages owed to employees at the end of a period. Other examples include accrued interest on notes payable and accrued taxes.
- **Accrued revenues**, or **accrued assets**, are revenues that have been earned *but have not been recorded* in the accounts. An example of an accrued revenue is fees for services that an attorney has provided but hasn't billed to the client at the end of the period. Other examples include unbilled commissions by a travel agent, accrued interest on notes receivable, and accrued rent on property rented to others.

How do you tell the difference between deferrals and accruals? Determine when cash is received or paid, as shown in Exhibit 1. If cash is received (for revenue) or paid (for expense) in the *current* period, but the revenue or expense relates to a future period, the revenue or expense is a deferred item. If cash will not be received or paid until a *future* period, but the revenue or expense relates to the current period, the revenue or expense is an accrued item.

Exhibit 1 Deferrals and Accruals

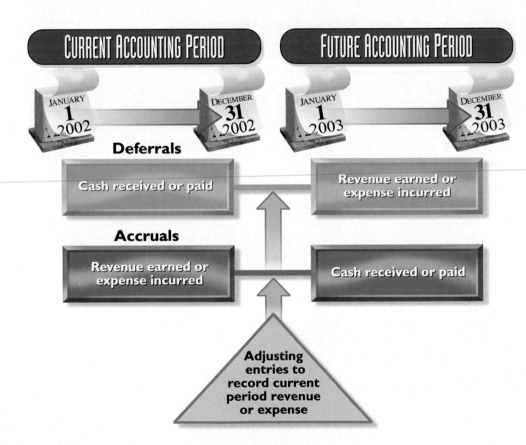

Recording Adjusting Entries

Journalize entries for accounts requiring adjustment.

The examples of adjusting entries in the following paragraphs are based on the ledger of NetSolutions as reported in the December 31, 2002 trial balance in Exhibit 2. To simplify the examples, T accounts are used. The adjusting entries are shown in color in the accounts to separate them from other transactions.

Exhibit 2 Unadjusted Trial
Balance for NetSolutions

NetSolutions Trial Balance December 31, 2002												
Cash		2	0	6	5	00						
Accounts Receivable		2	2	2	0	00						
Supplies		2	0	0	0	00						
Prepaid Insurance		2	4	0	0	00						
Land	20	0	0	0	0	00						
Office Equipment	1	8	0	0	0	00						
Accounts Payable									9	0	0	00
Unearned Rent									3	6	0	00
Chris Clark, Capital								25	0	0	0	00
Chris Clark, Drawing		4	0	0	0	00						
Fees Earned								16	3	4	0	00
Wages Expense		4	2	7	5	00						
Rent Expense		1	6	0	0	00						
Utilities Expense			9	8	5	00						
Supplies Expense			8	0	0	00						
Miscellaneous Expense			4	5	5	00						
	42	6	0	0	0	00	42	6	0	0	0	00

An expanded chart of accounts for NetSolutions is shown in Exhibit 3. The additional accounts that will be used in this chapter are shown in color.

Exhibit 3 Expanded Chart
of Accounts for NetSolutions

Balance Sheet Accounts	Income Statement Accounts
1. Assets	**4. Revenue**
11 Cash	41 Fees Earned
12 Accounts Receivable	42 Rent Revenue
14 Supplies	**5. Expenses**
15 Prepaid Insurance	51 Wages Expense
17 Land	52 Rent Expense
18 Office Equipment	53 Depreciation Expense
19 Accumulated Depreciation	54 Utilities Expense
2. Liabilities	55 Supplies Expense
21 Accounts Payable	56 Insurance Expense
22 Wages Payable	59 Miscellaneous Expense
23 Unearned Rent	
3. Owner's Equity	
31 Chris Clark, Capital	
32 Chris Clark, Drawing	

Deferred Expenses (Prepaid Expenses)

The concept of adjusting the accounting records was introduced in Chapters 1 and 2 in the illustration for NetSolutions. In that illustration, supplies were purchased on November 10 (transaction c). The supplies used during November were recorded on November 30 (transaction g).

The balance in NetSolutions' **supplies** account on December 31 is $2,000. Some of these supplies (computer diskettes, paper, envelopes, etc.) were used during December, and some are still on hand (not used). If either amount is known, the other can be determined. It is normally easier to determine the cost of the supplies on hand at the end of the month than it is to keep a daily record of those used. Assuming that on December 31 the amount of supplies on hand is $760, the amount to be transferred from the asset account to the expense account is $1,240, computed as follows:

Supplies available during December (balance of account)	$2,000
Supplies on hand, December 31	760
Supplies used (amount of adjustment)	$1,240

As we discussed in Chapter 2, increases in expense accounts are recorded as debits and decreases in asset accounts are recorded as credits. Hence, at the end of December, the supplies expense account should be debited for $1,240, and the supplies account should be credited for $1,240 to record the supplies used during December. The adjusting journal entry and T accounts for Supplies and Supplies Expense are as follows:

2	2002 Dec.	31	Supplies Expense	55	1 2 4 0 00		2
3			Supplies	14		1 2 4 0 00	3

Supplies

Bal.	2,000	Dec. 31	1,240
760			

Supplies Expense

Bal.	800		
Dec. 31	1,240		
	2,040		

After the adjustment has been recorded and posted, the supplies account has a debit balance of $760. This balance represents an asset that will become an expense in a future period.

> **The balance of a prepaid (deferred) expense is an asset that will become an expense in a future period.**

The debit balance of $2,400 in NetSolutions' **prepaid insurance** account represents a December 1 prepayment of insurance for 24 months. At the end of December, the insurance expense account should be increased (debited), and the prepaid insurance account should be decreased (credited) by $100, the insurance for one month. The adjusting journal entry and T accounts for Prepaid Insurance and Insurance Expense are as follows:

5		31	Insurance Expense	56	1 0 0 00		5
6			Prepaid Insurance	15		1 0 0 00	6

Prepaid Insurance

Bal.	2,400	Dec. 31	100
2,300			

Insurance Expense

Dec. 31	100

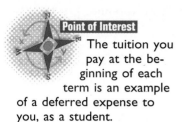

After the adjustment has been recorded and posted, the prepaid insurance account has a debit balance of $2,300. This balance represents an asset that will become an expense in future periods. The insurance expense account has a debit balance of $100, which is an expense of the current period.

What is the effect of omitting adjusting entries? If the preceding adjustments for supplies ($1,240) and insurance ($100) are not recorded, the financial statements prepared as of December 31 will be misstated. On the income statement, Supplies Expense and Insurance Expense will be understated by a total of $1,340, and net income will be overstated by $1,340. On the balance sheet, Supplies and Prepaid Insurance will be overstated by a total of $1,340. Since net income increases owner's equity, Chris Clark, Capital will also be overstated by $1,340 on the balance sheet. The effects of omitting these adjusting entries on the income statement and balance sheet are shown below.

	Amount of Misstatement	
Income Statement		
Revenues correctly stated	$XXX	
Expenses understated by	(1,340)	
Net income overstated by　(1)	$1,340	
Balance Sheet		
Assets overstated by	$1,340	(2)
Liabilities correctly stated	$XXX	
Owner's equity overstated by	1,340	
Total liabilities and owner's equity overstated by	$1,340	

Arrow (1) indicates the effect of the understated expenses on assets. Arrow (2) indicates the effect of the overstated net income on owner's equity.

Prepayments of expenses are sometimes made at the beginning of the period in which they will be *entirely consumed*. On December 1, for example, NetSolutions paid rent of $800 for the month. On December 1, the rent payment represents the asset prepaid rent. The prepaid rent expires daily, and at the end of December, the entire amount has become an expense (rent expense). In cases such as this, the initial payment is recorded as an expense rather than as an asset. Thus, if the payment is recorded as a debit to Rent Expense, no adjusting entry is needed at the end of the period.[1]

Q & A
Supplies of $1,250 were on hand at the beginning of the period, supplies of $3,800 were purchased during the period, and supplies of $1,000 were on hand at the end of the period. What is the supplies expense for the period?

$4,050 ($1,250 + $3,800 − $1,000)

Deferred Revenue (Unearned Revenue)

According to NetSolutions' trial balance on December 31, the balance in the **unearned rent** account is $360. This balance represents the receipt of three months' rent on December 1 for December, January, and February. At the end of December, the unearned rent account should be decreased (debited) by $120, and the rent revenue account should be increased (credited) by $120. The $120 represents the rental revenue for one month ($360/3). The adjusting journal entry and T accounts are shown below.

8		31	Unearned Rent	23	1 2 0 00		8
9			Rent Revenue	42		1 2 0 00	9

[1] This alternative treatment of recording the cost of supplies, rent, and other prepayments of expenses is discussed in Appendix C.

Unearned Rent				Rent Revenue	
Dec. 31	120	Bal.	360	Dec. 31	120
		240			

Sears, Roebuck and Co. sells extended warranty contracts with terms between 12 and 36 months. The receipts from sales of these contracts are reported as unearned revenue (deferred revenue) on Sears' balance sheet. Revenue is recorded as the contracts expire.

If NetSolutions' adjustment for unearned rent had incorrectly been made for $180 instead of $120, what would have been the effect on the financial statements?

- -

Revenues would have been overstated by $60; net income would have been overstated by $60; liabilities would have been understated by $60; and owner's equity would have been overstated by $60.

After the adjustment has been recorded and posted, the unearned rent account, which is a liability, has a credit balance of $240. This amount represents a deferral that will become revenue in a future period. The rent revenue account has a balance of $120, which is revenue of the current period.[2]

If the preceding adjustment of unearned rent and rent revenue is not recorded, the financial statements prepared on December 31 will be misstated. On the income statement, Rent Revenue and the net income will be understated by $120. On the balance sheet, Unearned Rent will be overstated by $120, and Chris Clark, Capital will be understated by $120. The effects of omitting this adjusting entry are shown below.

	Amount of Misstatement
Income Statement	
Revenues understated by	$ (120)
Expenses correctly stated	XXX
Net income understated by	$ (120)
Balance Sheet	
Assets correctly stated	$ XXX
Liabilities overstated by	$ 120
Owner's equity understated by	(120)
Total liabilities and	
owner's equity correctly stated	$ XXX

[2] An alternative treatment of recording revenues received in advance of their being earned is discussed in Appendix C.

BUSINESS ON STAGE

Technology and Business

The business environment is a dynamic one in which there is constant change, with challenges and opportunities. The current technology revolution affects all businesses.

Computer and telecommunication technologies affect the production, storage, and use of information by businesses. Many businesses have developed web sites for use in marketing products and services, and for communicating with stakeholders. New software applications range from accounting software that provides updated accounting information to business simulation software capable of gauging the impact of alternative business decisions on operations.

The technological revolution challenges businesses to adapt quickly to software and hardware improvements. Such improvements offer opportunities for businesses to develop new products, reach more customers, develop new channels of product distribution, lower operating costs, improve product quality, obtain immediate customer feedback, and react quickly to market changes. Businesses unable to adapt quickly to the technological revolution may find themselves at a competitive disadvantage.

Technology also provides you with new and exciting opportunities. To the extent that you develop your computer and technological skills and talents, you will improve your chances of finding a job and advancing rapidly in your career. ■

Callaway Golf Company, a manufacturer of such innovative golf clubs as the "Big Bertha" driver, reports accrued warranty expense on its balance sheet.

Accrued Expenses (Accrued Liabilities)

Some types of services, such as insurance, are normally paid for *before* they are used. These prepayments are deferrals. Other types of services are paid for *after* the service has been performed. For example, wages expense accumulates or *accrues* hour by hour and day by day, but payment may be made only weekly, biweekly, or monthly. The amount of such an accrued but unpaid item at the end of the accounting period is both an expense and a liability. In the case of wages expense, if the last day of a pay period is not the last day of the accounting period, the accrued wages expense and the related liability must be recorded in the accounts by an adjusting entry. This adjusting entry is necessary so that expenses are properly matched to the period in which they were incurred.

At the end of December, accrued wages for NetSolutions were $250. This amount is an additional expense of December and is debited to the **wages expense** account. It is also a liability as of December 31 and is credited to Wages Payable. The adjusting journal entry and T accounts are shown below.

11	31	Wages Expense	51	2 5 0 00		11
12		Wages Payable	22		2 5 0 00	12

	Wages Expense			**Wages Payable**	
Bal.	4,275			Dec. 31	250
Dec. 31	250				
	4,525				

After the adjustment has been recorded and posted, the debit balance of the wages expense account is $4,525, which is the wages expense for the two months, November and December. The credit balance of $250 in Wages Payable is the amount of the liability for wages owed as of December 31.

The accrual of the wages expense for NetSolutions is summarized in Exhibit 4. Note that NetSolutions paid wages of $950 on December 13 and $1,200 on December 27. These payments covered the biweekly pay periods that ended on those days. The wages of $250 incurred for Monday and Tuesday, December 30 and 31, are accrued at December 31. The wages paid on January 10 totaled $1,275, which included the $250 accrued wages of December 31.

What would be the effect on the financial statements if the adjustment for wages ($250) is not recorded? On the income statement, Wages Expense will be understated by $250, and the net income will be overstated by $250. On the balance sheet, Wages Payable will be understated by $250, and Chris Clark, Capital will be overstated by $250. The effects of omitting this adjusting entry are shown below.

Assume that weekly wages of $1,500 are paid on Fridays. If wages are incurred evenly throughout the week, what is the accrued wages payable if the accounting period ends on a Tuesday?

$600 ($1,500/5 × 2 days)

	Amount of Misstatement
Income Statement	
Revenues correctly stated	$ XXX
Expenses understated by	(250)
Net income overstated by	$ 250
Balance Sheet	
Assets correctly stated	$ XXX
Liabilities understated by	$ (250)
Owner's equity overstated by	250
Total liabilities and owner's equity correctly stated	$ XXX

Exhibit 4 Accrued Wages

1. Wages are paid on the second and fourth Fridays for the two-week periods ending on those Fridays. The payments were $950 on December 13 and $1,200 on December 27.

2. The wages accrued for Monday and Tuesday, December 30 and 31, are $250.

3. Wages paid on Friday, January 10, total $1,275.

December

S	M	T	W	T	F	S
1	2	3	4	5	6	7
8	9	10	11	12	13	14
15	16	17	18	19	20	21
22	23	24	25	26	27	28
29	30	31				

Wages expense (paid), $950

Wages expense (paid), $1,200

Wages expense (accrued), $250

January

				1	2	3	4
5	6	7	8	9	10	11	

Wages expense (paid), $1,275

Accrued Revenues (Accrued Assets)

Tandy Corporation and Subsidiaries is engaged in consumer electronics retailing and owns **Radio Shack** and **Incredible Universe**. Tandy accrues revenue (accrued receivables) for finance charges, late charges, and returned check fees related to its credit operations.

During an accounting period, some revenues are recorded only when cash is received. Thus, at the end of an accounting period, there may be items of revenue that have been earned *but have not been recorded*. In such cases, the amount of the revenue should be recorded by debiting an asset account and crediting a revenue account.

To illustrate, assume that NetSolutions signed an agreement with Dankner Co. on December 15. The agreement provides that NetSolutions will be on call to answer computer questions and render assistance to Dankner Co.'s employees. The services provided will be billed to Dankner Co. on the fifteenth of each month at a rate of $20 per hour. As of December 31, NetSolutions had provided 25 hours of assistance to Dankner Co. Although the revenue of $500 (25 hours × $20) will be billed and collected in January, NetSolutions earned the revenue in December. The adjusting journal entry and T accounts to record the claim against the customer (an account receivable) and the **fees earned** in December are shown below.

14	31	Accounts Receivable	12	5 0 0 00	14
15		Fees Earned	41		5 0 0 00 15

Accounts Receivable				**Fees Earned**		
Bal.	2,220				Bal.	16,340
Dec. 31	500	←	→		Dec. 31	500
	2,720					16,840

If the adjustment for the accrued asset ($500) is not recorded, Fees Earned and the net income will be understated by $500 on the income statement. On the balance sheet, Accounts Receivable and Chris Clark, Capital will be understated by $500. The effects of omitting this adjusting entry are shown below.

	Amount of Misstatement
Income Statement	
Revenues **understated by**	$ (500)
Expenses **correctly stated**	XXX
Net income **understated by**	$ (500)
Balance Sheet	
Assets **understated by**	$ (500)
Liabilities **correctly stated**	$ XXX
Owner's equity **understated by**	(500)
Total liabilities and owner's equity understated by	$ (500)

Fixed Assets

Physical resources that are owned and used by a business and are permanent or have a long life are called **fixed assets**, or **plant assets**. In a sense, fixed assets are a type of long-term deferred expense. However, because of their nature and long life, they are discussed separately from other deferred expenses, such as supplies and prepaid insurance.

NetSolutions' fixed assets include office equipment that is used much like supplies are used to generate revenue. Unlike supplies, however, there is no visible reduction in the quantity of the equipment. Instead, as time passes, the equipment loses its ability to provide useful services. This decrease in usefulness is called **depreciation**.

All fixed assets, except land, lose their usefulness. Decreases in the usefulness of assets that are used in generating revenue are recorded as expenses. However, such decreases for fixed assets are difficult to measure. For this reason, a portion of the cost of a fixed asset is recorded as an expense each year of its useful life. This periodic expense is called **depreciation expense**. Methods of computing depreciation expense are discussed and illustrated in a later chapter.

The adjusting entry to record depreciation is similar to the adjusting entry for supplies used. The account debited is a depreciation expense account. However, the asset account Office Equipment is not credited because both the original cost of a fixed asset and the amount of depreciation recorded since its purchase are normally reported on the balance sheet. The account credited is an **accumulated depreciation** account. Accumulated depreciation accounts are called **contra accounts**, or **contra asset accounts** because they are deducted from the related asset accounts on the balance sheet.

Normal titles for fixed asset accounts and their related contra asset accounts are as follows:

Lowe's Companies, Inc. and Subsidiaries reported land, buildings, and store equipment at a cost of over $2.3 billion and accumulated depreciation of over $460 million.

Fixed Asset	Contra Asset
Land	None—Land is not depreciated.
Buildings	Accumulated Depreciation—Buildings
Store Equipment	Accumulated Depreciation—Store Equipment
Office Equipment	Accumulated Depreciation—Office Equipment

The adjusting entry to record depreciation for December for NetSolutions is illustrated in the following journal entry and T accounts. The estimated amount of depreciation for the month is assumed to be $50.

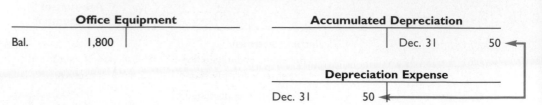

	31	Depreciation Expense	53	5 0 00		17
18		Accumulated Depreciation—				18
19		Office Equipment	19		5 0 00	19

Office Equipment		**Accumulated Depreciation**	
Bal.	1,800	Dec. 31	50

	Depreciation Expense	
Dec. 31	50	

If equipment cost $5,000 and the related accumulated depreciation is $3,000, what is the book value?

$2,000 ($5,000 − $3,000)

The $50 increase in the accumulated depreciation account is subtracted from the $1,800 cost recorded in the related fixed asset account. The difference between the two balances is the $1,750 cost that has not yet been depreciated. This amount ($1,750) is called the **book value of the asset** (or **net value**), which may be presented on the balance sheet in the following manner:

Office equipment	$1,800	
Less accumulated depreciation	50	$1,750

You should note that the market value of a fixed asset usually differs from its book value. This is because depreciation is an *allocation* method, not a *valuation* method. That is, depreciation allocates the cost of a fixed asset to expense over its estimated life. Depreciation does not attempt to measure changes in market values, which may vary significantly from year to year.

If the previous adjustment for depreciation ($50) is not recorded, Depreciation Expense on the income statement will be understated by $50, and the net income will be overstated by $50. On the balance sheet, the book value of Office Equipment and Chris Clark, Capital will be overstated by $50. The effects of omitting the adjustment for depreciation are shown below.

	Amount of Misstatement
Income Statement	
Revenues correctly stated	$XX
Expenses understated by	(50)
Net income overstated by	$ 50
Balance Sheet	
Assets overstated by	$ 50
Liabilities correctly stated	$XX
Owner's equity overstated by	50
Total liabilities and owner's equity overstated by	$ 50

Summary of Adjustment Process

objective 4

Summarize the adjustment process and prepare an adjusted trial balance.

We have described and illustrated the basic types of adjusting entries in the preceding section. A summary of these basic adjustments, including the type of adjustment, the adjusting entry, and the effect of omitting an adjustment on the financial statements, is shown in Exhibit 5.

Exhibit 5 Summary of Basic Adjustments

Type of Adjustment	Adjusting Entry	Effect of Omitting Adjusting Entry on the Balance Sheet and Income Statement
Deferred expense	Dr. Expense	Expenses Understated and Net Income Overstated
	Cr. Asset	Assets Overstated and Owner's Equity Overstated
Deferred revenue	Dr. Liability	Liabilities Overstated and Owner's Equity Understated
	Cr. Revenue	Revenues Understated and Net Income Understated
Accrued expense	Dr. Expense	Expenses Understated and Net Income Overstated
	Cr. Liability	Liabilities Understated and Owner's Equity Overstated
Accrued revenue	Dr. Asset	Assets Understated and Owner's Equity Understated
	Cr. Revenue	Revenues Understated and Net Income Understated
Fixed assets	Dr. Expense	Expenses Understated and Net Income Overstated
	Cr. Contra Asset	Assets Overstated and Owner's Equity Overstated

Q&A

Which of the accounts—Fees Earned, Miscellaneous Expense, Cash, Wages Expense, Supplies, Accounts Receivable, Drawing, Equipment, Accumulated Depreciation— would normally require an adjusting entry?

Fees Earned; Wages Expense; Supplies; Accounts Receivable; Accumulated Depreciation.

The adjusting entries for NetSolutions that we illustrated in this chapter are shown in Exhibit 6. The adjusting entries are dated as of the last day of the period. However, because some time may be needed for collecting the adjustment information, the entries are usually recorded at a later date. Each entry may be supported by an explanation, but a caption above the first adjusting entry is acceptable.

These adjusting entries have been posted to the ledger for NetSolutions, and are shown in color in Exhibit 7. You should note that in the posting process the Post. Ref. column of the journal indicates the account number to which the entry was posted. The corresponding Post. Ref. column of the account indicates the journal page from which the entry was posted.

Exhibit 6 Adjusting Entries
—NetSolutions

	JOURNAL				PAGE 5
Date	Description	Post. Ref.	Debit	Credit	
	Adjusting Entries				1
2002 Dec. 31	Supplies Expense	55	1 2 4 0 00		2
	Supplies	14		1 2 4 0 00	3
					4
31	Insurance Expense	56	1 0 0 00		5
	Prepaid Insurance	15		1 0 0 00	6
					7
31	Unearned Rent	23	1 2 0 00		8
	Rent Revenue	12		1 2 0 00	9
					10
31	Wages Expense	51	2 5 0 00		11
	Wages Payable	22		2 5 0 00	12
					13
31	Accounts Receivable	12	5 0 0 00		14
	Fees Earned	41		5 0 0 00	15
					16
31	Depreciation Expense	53	5 0 00		17
	Accumulated Depreciation—				18
	Office Equipment	19		5 0 00	19

Exhibit 7 Ledger with Adjusting Entries—NetSolutions

ACCOUNT Cash ACCOUNT NO. 11

Date	Item	Post. Ref.	Debit	Credit	Balance Debit	Balance Credit
2002 Nov. 1		1	25,000		25,000	
5		1		20,000	5,000	
18		1	7,500		12,500	
30		1		3,650	8,850	
30		1		950	7,900	
30		2		2,000	5,900	
Dec. 1		2		2,400	3,500	
1		2		800	2,700	
1		2	360		3,060	
6		2		180	2,880	
11		2		400	2,480	
13		3		950	1,530	
16		3	3,100		4,630	
20		3		900	3,730	
21		3	650		4,380	
23		3		1,450	2,930	
27		3		1,200	1,730	
31		3		310	1,420	
31		4		225	1,195	
31		4	2,870		4,065	
31		4		2,000	2,065	

ACCOUNT Accounts Receivable ACCOUNT NO. 12

Date	Item	Post. Ref.	Debit	Credit	Balance Debit	Balance Credit
2002 Dec. 16		3	1,750		1,750	
21		3		650	1,100	
31		4	1,120		2,220	
31	Adjusting	5	500		2,720	

ACCOUNT Supplies ACCOUNT NO. 14

Date	Item	Post. Ref.	Debit	Credit	Balance Debit	Balance Credit
2002 Nov. 10		1	1,350		1,350	
30		1		800	550	
Dec. 23		3	1,450		2,000	
31	Adjusting	5		1,240	760	

ACCOUNT Prepaid Insurance ACCOUNT NO. 15

Date	Item	Post. Ref.	Debit	Credit	Balance Debit	Balance Credit
2002 Dec. 1		2	2,400		2,400	
31	Adjusting	5		100	2,300	

ACCOUNT Land ACCOUNT NO. 17

Date	Item	Post. Ref.	Debit	Credit	Balance Debit	Balance Credit
2002 Nov. 5		1	20,000		20,000	

ACCOUNT Office Equipment ACCOUNT NO. 18

Date	Item	Post. Ref.	Debit	Credit	Balance Debit	Balance Credit
2002 Dec. 4		2	1,800		1,800	

ACCOUNT Accumulated Depreciation ACCOUNT NO. 19

Date	Item	Post. Ref.	Debit	Credit	Balance Debit	Balance Credit
2002 Dec. 31	Adjusting	5		50		50

ACCOUNT Accounts Payable ACCOUNT NO. 21

Date	Item	Post. Ref.	Debit	Credit	Balance Debit	Balance Credit
2002 Nov. 10		1		1,350		1,350
30		1	950			400
Dec. 4		2		1,800		2,200
11		2	400			1,800
20		3	900			900

ACCOUNT Wages Payable ACCOUNT NO. 22

Date	Item	Post. Ref.	Debit	Credit	Balance Debit	Balance Credit
2002 Dec. 31	Adjusting	5		250		250

ACCOUNT Unearned Rent ACCOUNT NO. 23

Date	Item	Post. Ref.	Debit	Credit	Balance Debit	Balance Credit
2002 Dec. 1		2		360		360
31	Adjusting	5	120			240

ACCOUNT Chris Clark, Capital ACCOUNT NO. 31

Date	Item	Post. Ref.	Debit	Credit	Balance Debit	Balance Credit
2002 Nov. 1		1		25,000		25,000

Exhibit 7 (concluded)

ACCOUNT Chris Clark, Drawing — **ACCOUNT NO. 32**

Date	Item	Post. Ref.	Debit	Credit	Balance Debit	Balance Credit
2002 Nov. 30		2	2,000		2,000	
Dec. 31		4	2,000		4,000	

ACCOUNT Fees Earned — **ACCOUNT NO. 41**

Date	Item	Post. Ref.	Debit	Credit	Balance Debit	Balance Credit
2002 Nov. 18		1		7,500		7,500
Dec. 16		3		3,100		10,600
16		3		1,750		12,350
31		4		2,870		15,220
31		4		1,120		16,340
31	Adjusting	5		500		16,840

ACCOUNT Rent Revenue — **ACCOUNT NO. 42**

Date	Item	Post. Ref.	Debit	Credit	Balance Debit	Balance Credit
2002 Dec. 31	Adjusting	5		120		120

ACCOUNT Wages Expense — **ACCOUNT NO. 51**

Date	Item	Post. Ref.	Debit	Credit	Balance Debit	Balance Credit
2002 Nov. 30		1	2,125		2,125	
Dec. 13		3	950		3,075	
27		3	1,200		4,275	
31	Adjusting	5	250		4,525	

ACCOUNT Rent Expense — **ACCOUNT NO. 52**

Date	Item	Post. Ref.	Debit	Credit	Balance Debit	Balance Credit
2002 Nov. 30		1	800		800	
Dec. 1		2	800		1,600	

ACCOUNT Depreciation Expense — **ACCOUNT NO. 53**

Date	Item	Post. Ref.	Debit	Credit	Balance Debit	Balance Credit
2002 Dec. 31	Adjusting	5	50		50	

ACCOUNT Utilities Expense — **ACCOUNT NO. 54**

Date	Item	Post. Ref.	Debit	Credit	Balance Debit	Balance Credit
2002 Nov. 30		1	450		450	
Dec. 31		3	310		760	
31		4	225		985	

ACCOUNT Supplies Expense — **ACCOUNT NO. 55**

Date	Item	Post. Ref.	Debit	Credit	Balance Debit	Balance Credit
2002 Nov. 30		1	800		800	
Dec. 31	Adjusting	5	1,240		2,040	

ACCOUNT Insurance Expense — **ACCOUNT NO. 56**

Date	Item	Post. Ref.	Debit	Credit	Balance Debit	Balance Credit
2002 Dec. 31	Adjusting	5	100		100	

ACCOUNT Miscellaneous Expense — **ACCOUNT NO. 59**

Date	Item	Post. Ref.	Debit	Credit	Balance Debit	Balance Credit
2002 Nov. 30		1	275		275	
Dec. 6		2	180		455	

After all the adjusting entries have been posted, another trial balance, called the **adjusted trial balance**, is prepared. The purpose of the adjusted trial balance is to verify the equality of the total debit balances and total credit balances before we prepare the financial statements. If the adjusted trial balance does not balance, an error has occurred. However, as we discussed in Chapter 2, errors may have occurred even though the adjusted trial balance totals agree. For example, the adjusted trial balance totals would agree if an adjusting entry has been omitted.

To highlight the effect of the adjustments on the accounts, Exhibit 8 shows the unadjusted trial balance, the accounts affected by the adjustments, and the adjusted

Exhibit 8 Trial Balances

	NetSolutions Unadjusted Trial Balance December 31, 2002				Effect of Adjusting Entry			NetSolutions Adjusted Trial Balance December 31, 2002		
1	Cash	2,065		1		1	Cash	2,065		1
2	Accounts Receivable	2,220		2	+ 500	2	Accounts Receivable	2,720		2
3	Supplies	2,000		3	−1,240	3	Supplies	760		3
1	Prepaid Insurance	2,100		4	100	4	Prepaid Insurance	2,300		4
5	Land	20,000		5		5	Land	20,000		5
6	Office Equipment	1,800		6		6	Office Equipment	1,800		6
7	Accumulated Depreciation			7	+ 50	7	Accumulated Depreciation		50	7
8	Accounts Payable		900	8		8	Accounts Payable		900	8
9	Wages Payable			9	+ 250	9	Wages Payable		250	9
10	Unearned Rent		360	10	− 120	10	Unearned Rent		240	10
11	Chris Clark, Capital		25,000	11		11	Chris Clark, Capital		25,000	11
12	Chris Clark, Drawing	4,000		12		12	Chris Clark, Drawing	4,000		12
13	Fees Earned		16,340	13	+ 500	13	Fees Earned		16,840	13
14	Rent Revenue			14	+ 120	14	Rent Revenue		120	14
15	Wages Expense	4,275		15	+ 250	15	Wages Expense	4,525		15
16	Rent Expense	1,600		16		16	Rent Expense	1,600		16
17	Depreciation Expense			17	+ 50	17	Depreciation Expense	50		17
18	Utilities Expense	985		18		18	Utilities Expense	985		18
19	Supplies Expense	800		19	+1,240	19	Supplies Expense	2,040		19
20	Insurance Expense			20	+ 100	20	Insurance Expense	100		20
21	Miscellaneous Expense	455		21		21	Miscellaneous Expense	455		21
22		42,600	42,600	22		22		43,400	43,400	22

trial balance. In Chapter 4, we discuss how financial statements, including a classified balance sheet, can be prepared from an adjusted trial balance. We also discuss the use of a work sheet as an aid to summarize the data for preparing adjusting entries and financial statements.

FINANCIAL ANALYSIS AND INTERPRETATION

objective 5

Use vertical analysis to compare financial statement items with each other and with industry averages.

Comparing each item in a current statement with a total amount within that same statement can be useful in highlighting significant relationships within a financial statement. **Vertical analysis** is the term used to describe such comparisons.

In vertical analysis of a balance sheet, each asset item is stated as a percent of the total assets. Each liability and owner's equity item is stated as a percent of the total liabilities and owner's equity. In vertical analysis of an income statement, each item is stated as a percent of revenues or fees earned.

Vertical analysis may also be prepared for several periods to highlight changes in relationships over time. Vertical analysis of two years of income statements for J. Holmes, Attorney-at-Law, is shown in Exhibit 9.

Exhibit 9 indicates both favorable and unfavorable trends affecting the income statement of J. Holmes, Attorney-at-Law. The increase in wages expense of 2% (32% − 30%) is an unfavorable trend, as is the increase in utilities expense of 0.7% (6.7% − 6.0%). A favorable trend is the decrease in supplies expense of 0.6% (2.0% − 1.4%). Rent expense and miscellaneous expense as a percent of fees earned were

Exhibit 9 Vertical Analysis of Income Statements

	2003		2002	
	Amount	**Percent**	**Amount**	**Percent**
J. Holmes, Attorney-at-Law **Income Statements** **For the Years Ended December 31, 2002 and 2003**				
Fees earned	$187,500	100.0%	$150,000	100.0%
Operating expenses:				
Wages expense	$60,000	32.0%	$45,000	30.0%
Rent expense	15,000	8.0%	12,000	8.0%
Utilities expense	12,500	6.7%	9,000	6.0%
Supplies expense	2,700	1.4%	3,000	2.0%
Miscellaneous expense	2,300	1.2%	1,800	1.2%
Total operating expenses	$92,500	49.3%	$70,800	47.2%
Net income	$95,000	50.7%	$79,200	52.8%

constant. The net result of these trends was that net income decreased as a percent of fees earned from 52.8% to 50.7%.

The analysis of the various percentages shown for J. Holmes, Attorney-at-Law, can be enhanced by comparisons with industry averages published by trade associations and financial information services. Any major differences between industry averages should be investigated.

ENCORE

"Intel Inside"

Intel Corporation develops and produces microprocessors for personal computers. Intel's earnings have grown from a $195 million loss in 1986 to over $7 billion of operating income in 1999. Intel's success has been driven by its ability to design, develop, and produce newer and faster microprocessors. This ability has been a result of a strong research and development effort in which spending has increased at an annual rate of 21% over the past ten years. Intel's current microprocessor is so tiny that it would take 500 of them placed end to end to be as large as a human hair!

Intel's microprocessors have become well-known, beginning with the 8086 processor and continuing with the 286, 386, and 486 processors. Rather than name its next generation of microprocessor the 586, Intel named its new chip the "Pentium" and registered it as a trademark. This prevented Intel's competitors from selling their products as "Pentiums," which they had been able to do with the numbers 386 and 486. In addition, Intel began a promotional campaign to identify its microprocessor as unique. Intel did this by entering into a cooperative program with computer manufacturers and distributors to label personal computers with the slogan "Intel Inside" or "Pentium Inside."

Intel has been highly successful. However, technology companies such as Intel are subject to significant risks that their products will become outdated as technology changes. This is why Intel has invested so heavily in research and development over the years. In addition, Intel has the potential risk for faulty product designs or production of faulty processors due to poor quality control. For example, Intel discovered an error related to the divide function in the floating point unit of one of its Pentium micro-

processors. This error required an adjusting entry for replacement processors and inventory write-downs, which cost Intel approximately $475

million. More recently, Intel has had to recall its Pentium III chip. ∎

KEY POINTS

1 Explain how the matching concept relates to the accrual basis of accounting.
The accrual basis of accounting requires the use of an adjusting process at the end of the accounting period to match revenues and expenses properly. Revenues are reported in the period in which they are earned, and expenses are matched with the revenues they generate.

2 Explain why adjustments are necessary and list the characteristics of adjusting entries.
At the end of an accounting period, some of the amounts listed on the trial balance are not necessarily current balances. For example, amounts listed for prepaid expenses are normally overstated because the use of these assets has not been recorded on a daily basis. A delay in recognizing an expense already paid or a revenue already received is called a deferral.

Some revenues and expenses related to a period may not be recorded at the end of the period, since these items are normally recorded only when cash has

been received or paid. A revenue or expense that has not been paid or recorded is called an accrual.

The entries required at the end of an accounting period to bring accounts up to date and to ensure the proper matching of revenues and expenses are called adjusting entries. Adjusting entries require a debit or a credit to a revenue or an expense account and an offsetting debit or credit to an asset or a liability account.

Adjusting entries affect amounts reported in the income statement and the balance sheet. Thus, if an adjusting entry is not recorded, these financial statements will be incorrect (misstated).

3 Journalize entries for accounts requiring adjustment.
Adjusting entries illustrated in this chapter include deferred (prepaid) expenses, deferred (unearned) revenues, accrued expenses (accrued liabilities), and accrued revenues (accrued assets). In addition, the adjusting entry necessary to record depreciation on fixed assets was illustrated.

4 Summarize the adjustment process and prepare an adjusted trial balance.
A summary of adjustments, including the type of adjustment, the adjusting entry, and the effect of omitting an adjustment on the financial statements, is shown in Exhibit 5. After all the adjusting entries have been posted, the equality of the total debit balances and total credit balances is verified by an adjusted trial balance.

5 Use vertical analysis to compare financial statement items with each other and with industry averages.
Comparing each item in a current statement with a total amount within the same statement is called vertical analysis. In vertical analysis of a balance sheet, each asset item is stated as a percent of the total assets. Each liability and owner's equity item is stated as a percent of the total liabilities and owner's equity. In vertical analysis of an income statement, each item is stated as a percent of revenues or fees earned.

ILLUSTRATIVE PROBLEM

Three years ago, T. Roderick organized Harbor Realty. At July 31, 2003, the end of the current year, the unadjusted trial balance of Harbor Realty appears as shown at the top of the following page. The data needed to determine year-end adjustments are as follows:

a. Supplies on hand at July 31, 2003, $380.
b. Insurance premiums expired during the year, $315.
c. Depreciation of equipment during the year, $4,950.
d. Wages accrued but not paid at July 31, 2003, $440.
e. Accrued fees earned but not recorded at July 31, 2003, $1,000.
f. Unearned fees on July 31, 2003, $750.

Harbor Realty
Trial Balance
July 31, 2003

	Debit	Credit
Cash	3 4 2 5 00	
Accounts Receivable	7 0 0 0 00	
Supplies	1 2 7 0 00	
Prepaid Insurance	6 2 0 00	
Office Equipment	51 6 5 0 00	
Accumulated Depreciation		9 7 0 0 00
Accounts Payable		9 2 5 00
Wages Payable		0 00
Unearned Fees		1 2 5 0 00
T. Roderick, Capital		29 0 0 0 00
T. Roderick, Drawing	5 2 0 0 00	
Fees Earned		59 1 2 5 00
Wages Expense	22 4 1 5 00	
Depreciation Expense	0 00	
Rent Expense	4 2 0 0 00	
Utilities Expense	2 7 1 5 00	
Supplies Expense	0 00	
Insurance Expense	0 00	
Miscellaneous Expense	1 5 0 5 00	
	100 0 0 0 00	100 0 0 0 00

Instructions

1. Prepare the necessary adjusting journal entries.
2. Determine the balance of the accounts affected by the adjusting entries and prepare an adjusted trial balance.

Solution

1.

JOURNAL

	Date		Description	Post. Ref.	Debit	Credit	
1	2003 July	31	Supplies Expense		8 9 0 00		1
2			Supplies			8 9 0 00	2
3							3
4		31	Insurance Expense		3 1 5 00		4
5			Prepaid Insurance			3 1 5 00	5
6							6
7		31	Depreciation Expense		4 9 5 0 00		7
8			Accumulated Depreciation			4 9 5 0 00	8
9							9
10		31	Wages Expense		4 4 0 00		10
11			Wages Payable			4 4 0 00	11
12							12
13		31	Accounts Receivable		1 0 0 0 00		13
14			Fees Earned			1 0 0 0 00	14
15							15
16		31	Unearned Fees		5 0 0 00		16
17			Fees Earned			5 0 0 00	17

2.

Harbor Realty Adjusted Trial Balance July 31, 2003											
Cash	3	4	2	5	00						
Accounts Receivable	8	0	0	0	00						
Supplies		3	8	0	00						
Prepaid Insurance		3	0	5	00						
Office Equipment	51	6	5	0	00						
Accumulated Depreciation						14	6	5	0	00	
Accounts Payable							9	2	5	00	
Wages Payable							4	4	0	00	
Unearned Fees							7	5	0	00	
T. Roderick, Capital						29	0	0	0	00	
T. Roderick, Drawing	5	2	0	0	00						
Fees Earned						60	6	2	5	00	
Wages Expense	22	8	5	5	00						
Depreciation Expense	4	9	5	0	00						
Rent Expense	4	2	0	0	00						
Utilities Expense	2	7	1	5	00						
Supplies Expense		8	9	0	00						
Insurance Expense		3	1	5	00						
Miscellaneous Expense	1	5	0	5	00						
	106	3	9	0	00	106	3	9	0	00	

SELF-EXAMINATION QUESTIONS   Answers at End of Chapter

Matching
Match each of the following statements with its proper term. Some terms may not be used.

A. **accounting period concept**

B. **accrual basis**

C. **accrued expenses**

D. **accrued revenues**

E. **accumulated depreciation**

F. **adjusted trial balance**

G. **adjusting entries**

H. **adjusting process**

I. **book value of the asset**

J. **cash basis**

K. **closing entries**

L. **contra account**

M. **deferred expenses**

N. **deferred revenues**

O. **depreciation**

____ 1. The accounting concept that assumes that the economic life of the business can be divided into time periods.

____ 2. Under this basis of accounting, revenues and expenses are reported in the income statement in the period in which cash is received or paid.

____ 3. Under this basis of accounting, revenues are reported in the income statement in the period in which they are earned.

____ 4. The accounting concept that supports reporting revenues when the services are provided to customers.

____ 5. The accounting concept that supports reporting revenues and the related expenses in the same period.

____ 6. An analysis and updating of the accounts when financial statements are prepared.

____ 7. The journal entries that bring the accounts up to date at the end of the accounting period.

____ 8. Items that have been initially recorded as assets but are expected to become expenses over time or through the normal operations of the business.

____ 9. Items that have been initially recorded as liabilities but are expected to become revenues over time or through the normal operations of the business.

____10. Expenses that have been incurred *but not recorded* in the accounts.

____11. Revenues that have been earned *but not recorded* in the accounts.

P. depreciation expense

Q. final trial balance

R. fixed assets

S. horizontal analysis

T. matching concept

U. objectivity concept

V. post-closing trial balance

W. revenue recognition concept

X. vertical analysis

___ 12. Physical resources that are owned and used by a business and are permanent or have a long life.

___ 13. The decrease in the ability of a fixed asset to provide useful services.

___ 14. The portion of the cost of a fixed asset that is recorded as an expense each year of its useful life.

___ 15. The asset account credited when recording the depreciation of a fixed asset.

___ 16. The difference between the cost of a fixed asset and its accumulated depreciation.

___ 17. The trial balance prepared after all the adjusting entries have been posted.

___ 18. An analysis that compares each item in a current statement with a total amount within the same statement.

___ 19. An account offset against another account.

Multiple Choice

1. Which of the following items represents a deferral?
   A. Prepaid insurance
   B. Wages payable
   C. Fees earned
   D. Accumulated depreciation

2. If the supplies account, before adjustment on May 31, indicated a balance of $2,250, and supplies on hand at May 31 totaled $950, the adjusting entry would be:
   A. debit Supplies, $950; credit Supplies Expense, $950.
   B. debit Supplies, $1,300; credit Supplies Expense, $1,300.
   C. debit Supplies Expense, $950; credit Supplies, $950.
   D. debit Supplies Expense, $1,300; credit Supplies, $1,300.

3. The balance in the unearned rent account for Jones Co. as of December 31 is $1,200. If Jones Co. failed to record the adjusting entry for $600 of rent earned during December, the effect on the balance sheet and income statement for December is:
   A. assets understated $600; net income overstated $600.

   B. liabilities understated $600; net income understated $600.
   C. liabilities overstated $600; net income understated $600.
   D. liabilities overstated $600; net income overstated $600.

4. If the estimated amount of depreciation on equipment for a period is $2,000, the adjusting entry to record depreciation would be:
   A. debit Depreciation Expense, $2,000; credit Equipment, $2,000.
   B. debit Equipment, $2,000; credit Depreciation Expense, $2,000.
   C. debit Depreciation Expense, $2,000; credit Accumulated Depreciation, $2,000.
   D. debit Accumulated Depreciation, $2,000; credit Depreciation Expense, $2,000.

5. If the equipment account has a balance of $22,500 and its accumulated depreciation account has a balance of $14,000, the book value of the equipment is:
   A. $36,500.   C. $14,000.
   B. $22,500   D. $8,500.

CLASS DISCUSSION QUESTIONS

1. How are revenues and expenses reported on the income statement under (a) the cash basis of accounting and (b) the accrual basis of accounting?

2. Fees for services provided are billed to a customer during 2002. The customer remits the amount owed in 2003. During which year would the revenues be reported on the income statement under (a) the cash basis? (b) the accrual basis?

3. Employees performed services in 2002, but the wages were not paid until 2003. During which year would the wages expense be reported on the income statement under (a) the cash basis? (b) the accrual basis?

4. Is the matching concept related to (a) the cash basis of accounting or (b) the accrual basis of accounting?

5. Is the balance listed for cash on the trial balance, before the accounts have been adjusted, the amount that should normally be reported on the balance sheet? Explain.

6. Is the balance listed for supplies on the trial balance, before the accounts have been adjusted, the amount that should normally be reported on the balance sheet? Explain.

7. Why are adjusting entries needed at the end of an accounting period?

8. Are adjusting entries in the journal dated as of the last day of the fiscal period or as of the day the entries are actually made? Explain.

9. What is the difference between *adjusting entries* and *correcting entries?*

10. Identify the five different categories of adjusting entries frequently required at the end of an accounting period.

11. If the effect of the credit portion of an adjusting entry is to increase the balance of a liability account, which of the following statements describes the effect of the debit portion of the entry?
    a. Increases the balance of a revenue account.
    b. Increases the balance of an expense account.
    c. Increases the balance of an asset account.

12. Does every adjusting entry have an effect on determining the amount of net income for a period? Explain.

13. What is the nature of the balance in the prepaid insurance account at the end of the accounting period (a) before adjustment? (b) after adjustment?

14. On November 1 of the current year, a business paid the November rent on the building that it occupies. (a) Do the rights acquired at November 1 represent an asset or an expense? (b) What is the justification for debiting Rent Expense at the time of payment?

15. In accounting for depreciation on equipment, what is the name of the contra asset account?

16. (a) Explain the purpose of the two accounts: Depreciation Expense and Accumulated Depreciation. (b) What is the normal balance of each account? (c) Is it customary for the balances of the two accounts to be equal in amount? (d) In what financial statements, if any, will each account appear?

RESOURCES FOR YOUR SUCCESS ONLINE AT

http://warren.swcollege.com

Remember! If you need additional help, visit South-Western's Web site.
See page 26 for a description of the online and printed materials that are available.

EXERCISES

Exercise 3–1
Classify accruals and deferrals

Objectives 2, 3

Classify the following items as (a) deferred expense (prepaid expense), (b) deferred revenue (unearned revenue), (c) accrued expense (accrued liability), or (d) accrued revenue (accrued asset).

1. Fees earned but not yet received.
2. Taxes owed but payable in the following period.
3. Salary owed but not yet paid.
4. Supplies on hand.
5. Fees received but not yet earned.
6. Utilities owed but not yet paid.
7. A two-year premium paid on a fire insurance policy.
8. Subscriptions received in advance by a magazine publisher.

Exercise 3–2
Classify adjusting entries

Objectives 2, 3

The following accounts were taken from the unadjusted trial balance of O'Neil Co., a congressional lobbying firm. Indicate whether or not each account would normally require an adjusting entry. If the account normally requires an adjusting entry, use the following notation to indicate the type of adjustment:

AE—Accrued Expense
AR—Accrued Revenue
DR—Deferred Revenue
DE—Deferred Expense

To illustrate, the answers for the first two accounts are shown below.

Account	Answer
Tip Perkey, Drawing	Does not normally require adjustment.
Accounts Receivable	Normally requires adjustment (AR).
Accumulated Depreciation	
Cash	
Interest Payable	
Interest Receivable	
Land	
Office Equipment	
Prepaid Insurance	
Supplies Expense	
Unearned Fees	
Wages Expense	

Exercise 3–3
Adjusting entry for supplies
Objective 3

The balance in the supplies account, before adjustment at the end of the year, is $1,475. Journalize the adjusting entry required if the amount of supplies on hand at the end of the year is $241.

Exercise 3–4
Determine supplies purchased
Objective 3

The supplies and supplies expense accounts at December 31, after adjusting entries have been posted at the end of the first year of operations, are shown in the following T accounts:

Supplies			Supplies Expense	
Bal.	418		Bal.	1,943

Determine the amount of supplies purchased during the year.

Exercise 3–5
Effect of omitting adjusting entry
Objective 3

At December 31, the end of the first month of operations, the usual adjusting entry transferring supplies used to an expense account is omitted. Which items will be incorrectly stated, because of the error, on (a) the income statement for December and (b) the balance sheet as of December 31? Also indicate whether the items in error will be overstated or understated.

Exercise 3–6
Adjusting entries for prepaid insurance
Objective 3

The balance in the prepaid insurance account, before adjustment at the end of the year, is $4,280. Journalize the adjusting entry required under each of the following *alternatives* for determining the amount of the adjustment: (a) the amount of insurance expired during the year is $1,020; (b) the amount of unexpired insurance applicable to future periods is $3,260.

Exercise 3–7
Adjusting entries for prepaid insurance
Objective 3

The prepaid insurance account had a balance of $3,600 at the beginning of the year. The account was debited for $1,200 for premiums on policies purchased during the year. Journalize the adjusting entry required at the end of the year for each of the following situations: (a) the amount of unexpired insurance applicable to future periods is $3,450; (b) the amount of insurance expired during the year is $1,875.

Exercise 3–8
Adjusting entries for unearned fees
Objective 3

✓ Amount of entry: $3,950

The balance in the unearned fees account, before adjustment at the end of the year, is $6,750. Journalize the adjusting entry required if the amount of unearned fees at the end of the year is $2,800.

Exercise 3–9
Effect of omitting adjusting entry
Objective 3

At the end of March, the first month of the business year, the usual adjusting entry transferring rent earned to a revenue account from the unearned rent account was omitted. Indicate which items will be incorrectly stated, because of the error, on (a) the income statement for March and (b) the balance sheet as of March 31. Also indicate whether the items in error will be overstated or understated.

Exercise 3–10
Adjusting entries for accrued salaries
Objective 3

✓ a. Amount of entry: $5,500

Taylor Fork Realty Co. pays weekly salaries of $13,750 on Friday for a five-day week ending on that day. Journalize the necessary adjusting entry at the end of the accounting period, assuming that the period ends (a) on Tuesday, (b) on Wednesday.

Exercise 3–11
Determine wages paid
Objective 3

The wages payable and wages expense accounts at December 31, after adjusting entries have been posted at the end of the first year of operations, are shown in the following T accounts:

Wages Payable		**Wages Expense**	
Bal.	1,960	Bal.	87,430

Determine the amount of wages paid during the year.

Exercise 3–12
Effect of omitting adjusting entry
Objective 3

Accrued salaries of $3,100 owed to employees for December 30 and 31 are not considered in preparing the financial statements for the year ended December 31. Indicate which items will be erroneously stated, because of the error, on (a) the income statement for the year and (b) the balance sheet as of December 31. Also indicate whether the items in error will be overstated or understated.

Exercise 3–13
Effect of omitting adjusting entry
Objective 3

Assume that the error in Exercise 3–12 was not corrected and that the $3,100 of accrued salaries was included in the first salary payment in January. Indicate which items will be erroneously stated, because of failure to correct the initial error, on (a) the income statement for the month of January and (b) the balance sheet as of January 31.

Exercise 3–14
Adjusting entries for prepaid and accrued taxes
Objective 3

✓ b. $10,975

Millennium Financial Services was organized on April 1 of the current year. On April 2, Millennium prepaid $1,020 to the city for taxes (license fees) for the *next* 12 months and debited the prepaid taxes account. Millennium is also required to pay in January an annual tax (on property) for the *previous* calendar year. The estimated amount of the property tax for the current year (April 1 to December 31) is $10,210. (a) Journalize the two adjusting entries required to bring the accounts affected by the two taxes up to date as of December 31, the end of the current year. (b) What is the amount of tax expense for the current year?

Exercise 3–15
Effects of errors on financial statements
Objective 3

For a recent period, **Circuit City Stores** reported accrued expenses and other current liabilities of $204,561,000. For the same period, Circuit City reported earnings of $528,758,000 before income taxes. If accrued expenses and other current liabilities had not been recorded, what would have been the earnings (loss) before income taxes?

Real World

Exercise 3–16
Effects of errors on financial statements

Objective 3

✓ b. 85.7%

The balance sheet for **The Quaker Oats Company** as of December 31, 1999, includes the following accrued expenses as liabilities:

Accrued payroll, benefits and bonus	$139,100,000
Accrued advertising and merchandising	138,700,000
Other accrued liabilities	252,300,000

The income before taxes for The Quaker Oats Company for the year ended December 31, 1999, was $618,300,000. (a) If the accruals had not been recorded at December 31, 1999, by how much would income before taxes have been misstated for the fiscal year ended December 31, 1999? (b) What is the percentage of the misstatement in (a) to the reported income of $618,300,000?

Exercise 3–17
Effects of errors on financial statements

Objective 3

✓ I. a. Revenue understated, $10,390

The accountant for Maxim Medical Co., a medical services consulting firm, mistakenly omitted adjusting entries for (a) unearned revenue ($10,390) and (b) accrued wages ($2,440). Indicate the effect of each error, considered individually, on the income statement for the current year ended December 31. Also indicate the effect of each error on the December 31 balance sheet. Set up a table similar to the following, and record your answers by inserting the dollar amount in the appropriate spaces. Insert a zero if the error does not affect the item.

	Error (a)		Error (b)	
	Over-stated	Under-stated	Over-stated	Under-stated
1. Revenue for the year would be	$	$	$	$
2. Expenses for the year would be	$	$	$	$
3. Net income for the year would be	$	$	$	$
4. Assets at December 31 would be	$	$	$	$
5. Liabilities at December 31 would be	$	$	$	$
6. Owner's equity at December 31 would be	$	$	$	$

Exercise 3–18
Effects of errors on financial statements

Objective 3

If the net income for the current year had been $437,720 in Exercise 3–17, what would be the correct net income if the proper adjusting entries had been made?

Exercise 3–19
Adjusting entry for accrued fees

Objective 3

At the end of the current year, $7,260 of fees have been earned but have not been billed to clients.

a. Journalize the adjusting entry to record the accrued fees.
b. If the cash basis rather than the accrual basis had been used, would an adjusting entry have been necessary? Explain.

Exercise 3–20
Adjusting entries for unearned and accrued fees

Objective 3

The balance in the unearned fees account, before adjustment at the end of the year, is $48,000. Of these fees, $16,000 have been earned. In addition, $7,500 of fees have been earned but have not been billed. Journalize the adjusting entries (a) to adjust the unearned fees account and (b) to record the accrued fees.

Exercise 3–21
Effect on financial statements of omitting adjusting entry

Objective 3

The adjusting entry for accrued fees was omitted at December 31, the end of the current year. Indicate which items will be in error, because of the omission, on (a) the income statement for the current year and (b) the balance sheet as of December 31. Also indicate whether the items in error will be overstated or understated.

Exercise 3–22
Adjustment for depreciation
Objective 3

The estimated amount of depreciation on equipment for the current year is $3,000. Journalize the adjusting entry to record the depreciation.

Exercise 3–23
Determine fixed asset's book value
Objective 3

The balance in the equipment account is $518,500, and the balance in the accumulated depreciation—equipment account is $120,750.

a. What is the book value of the equipment?
b. Does the balance in the accumulated depreciation account mean that the equipment's loss of value is $120,750? Explain.

Exercise 3–24
Book value of fixed assets
Objective 3

Microsoft Corporation reported *Property, Plant, and Equipment* of $3,321 million and *Accumulated Depreciation* of $1,418 million at June 30, 2000.

a. What was the book value of the fixed assets at June 30, 2000?
b. Would the book value of Microsoft Corporation's fixed assets normally approximate their fair market values?

Exercise 3–25
Adjusting entries for depreciation; effect of error
Objective 3

On December 31, a business estimates depreciation on equipment used during the first year of operations to be $8,500. (a) Journalize the adjusting entry required as of December 31. (b) If the adjusting entry in (a) were omitted, which items would be erroneously stated on (1) the income statement for the year and (2) the balance sheet as of December 31?

Exercise 3–26
Adjusting entries from trial balances
Objectives 3, 4

The unadjusted and adjusted trial balances for Medico Services Co. on December 31, 2003, are shown below.

Medico Services Co.
Trial Balance
December 31, 2003

	Unadjusted		Adjusted	
Cash	8		8	
Accounts Receivable	19		21	
Supplies	6		2	
Prepaid Insurance	10		6	
Land	13		13	
Equipment	20		20	
Accumulated Depr.—Equip.		4		5
Accounts Payable		13		13
Wages Payable		0		1
Brian Stuart, Capital		46		46
Brian Stuart, Drawing	4		4	
Fees Earned		37		39
Wages Expense	12		13	
Rent Expense	4		4	
Insurance Expense	0		4	
Utilities Expense	2		2	
Depreciation Expense	0		1	
Supplies Expense	0		4	
Miscellaneous Expense	2		2	
Totals	100	100	104	104

Journalize the five entries that adjusted the accounts at December 31, 2003. None of the accounts were affected by more than one adjusting entry.

Exercise 3–27
Adjusting entries from trial balances

Objectives 3, 4

✓ Corrected trial balance totals, $171,520

The accountant for St. Elmo Laundry prepared the following unadjusted and adjusted trial balances. Assume that all balances in the unadjusted trial balance and the amounts of the adjustments are correct. How many errors can you find in the accountant's adjusting entries?

St. Elmo Laundry
Trial Balance
October 31, 2003

	Unadjusted		Adjusted	
Cash	3,790		3,790	
Accounts Receivable	8,000		12,500	
Laundry Supplies	3,750		5,660	
Prepaid Insurance*	2,825		1,325	
Laundry Equipment	85,600		80,880	
Accumulated Depreciation		55,700		55,700
Accounts Payable		4,950		4,950
Wages Payable				850
Nicole Chun, Capital		23,900		23,900
Nicole Chun, Drawing	8,000		8,000	
Laundry Revenue		76,900		76,900
Wages Expense	24,500		24,500	
Rent Expense	15,575		15,575	
Utilities Expense	8,500		8,500	
Depreciation Expense			4,720	
Laundry Supplies Expense			1,910	
Insurance Expense			500	
Miscellaneous Expense	910		910	
	161,450	161,450	168,770	162,300

*$1,500 of insurance expired during the year.

Exercise 3–28
Vertical analysis of income statement

Objective 5

The financial statements for **Cisco Systems, Inc.** are presented in Appendix G at the end of the text.

a. Determine for Cisco Systems:
   1. The amount of the change and percent of change in net income for the year ended July 29, 2000.
   2. The percentage relationship between net income and net sales (net income divided by net sales) for the years ended July 29, 2000 and July 31, 1999.
b. What conclusions can you draw from your analysis?

PROBLEMS SERIES A

Problem 3–1A
Adjusting entries

Objective 3

On December 31, the end of the current year, the following data were accumulated to assist the accountant in preparing the adjusting entries for Epoch Realty:

a. The supplies account balance on December 31 is $1,750. The supplies on hand on December 31 are $245.
b. The unearned rent account balance on December 31 is $6,750, representing the receipt of an advance payment on December 1 of three months' rent from tenants.
c. Wages accrued but not paid at December 31 are $1,800.
d. Fees accrued but unbilled at December 31 are $10,600.
e. Depreciation of office equipment for the year is $3,100.

Instructions

1. Journalize the adjusting entries required at December 31.
2. Briefly explain the difference between adjusting entries and entries that would be made to correct errors.

Problem 3–2A
Adjusting entries
Objective 3

Selected account balances before adjustment for Gibraltar Realty at December 31, the end of the current year, are as follows:

	Debits	Credits		Debits	Credits
Accounts Receivable	$ 9,250		Unearned Fees		$ 7,000
Supplies	2,750		Fees Earned		97,950
Prepaid Rent	30,000		Wages Expense	$39,400	
Equipment	52,500		Rent Expense	—	
Accumulated Depreciation		$8,900	Depreciation Expense	—	
Wages Payable		—	Supplies Expense	—	

Data needed for year-end adjustments are as follows:

a. Unbilled fees at December 31, $3,150.
b. Supplies on hand at December 31, $555.
c. Rent expired during year, $18,000.
d. Depreciation of equipment during year, $1,575.
e. Unearned fees at December 31, $2,700.
f. Wages accrued but not paid at December 31, $875.

Instructions

Journalize the six adjusting entries required at December 31, based upon the data presented.

Problem 3–3A
Adjusting entries
Objective 3

Jupiter Company, an electronics repair store, prepared the following trial balance at the end of its first year of operations:

GENERAL LEDGER

Jupiter Company
Trial Balance
November 30, 2003

Cash	1,150	
Accounts Receivable	7,500	
Supplies	1,800	
Equipment	37,900	
Accounts Payable		1,750
Unearned Fees		2,000
Melanie Cochran, Capital		26,000
Melanie Cochran, Drawing	1,500	
Fees Earned		45,250
Wages Expense	10,500	
Rent Expense	8,000	
Utilities Expense	5,750	
Miscellaneous Expense	900	
	75,000	75,000

For preparing the adjusting entries, the following data were assembled:

a. Fees earned but unbilled on November 30 were $1,100.
b. Supplies on hand on November 30 were $380.
c. Depreciation of equipment was estimated to be $2,200 for the year.
d. The balance in unearned fees represented the November 1 receipt in advance for services to be provided. Only $800 of the services was provided between November 1 and November 30.
e. Unpaid wages accrued on November 30 were $400.

Instructions

Journalize the adjusting entries necessary on November 30.

Problem 3–4A

Adjusting entries

Objectives 3, 4

SPREADSHEET

GENERAL
LEDGER

Oriole Company specializes in the repair of music equipment and is owned and operated by Kaye Santora. On April 30, 2003, the end of the current year, the accountant for Oriole Company prepared the following trial balances:

Oriole Company
Trial Balance
April 30, 2003

	Unadjusted		Adjusted	
Cash	7,825		7,825	
Accounts Receivable	30,500		30,500	
Supplies	3,950		800	
Prepaid Insurance	3,750		1,500	
Equipment	92,150		92,150	
Accumulated Depreciation—Equipment		33,480		42,500
Automobiles	36,500		36,500	
Accumulated Depreciation—Automobiles		18,250		22,900
Accounts Payable		8,310		9,390
Salaries Payable		—		1,800
Unearned Service Fees		5,000		3,000
Kaye Santora, Capital		69,470		69,470
Kaye Santora, Drawing	5,000		5,000	
Service Fees Earned		244,600		246,600
Salary Expense	172,300		174,100	
Rent Expense	18,000		18,000	
Supplies Expense	—		3,150	
Depreciation Expense—Equipment	—		9,020	
Depreciation Expense—Automobiles	—		4,650	
Utilities Expense	4,700		5,780	
Taxes Expense	2,725		2,725	
Insurance Expense	—		2,250	
Miscellaneous Expense	1,710		1,710	
	379,110	379,110	395,660	395,660

Instructions

Journalize the seven entries that adjusted the accounts at April 30. None of the accounts were affected by more than one adjusting entry.

Problem 3–5A

Adjusting entries and adjusted trial balances

Objectives 3, 4

SPREADSHEET

GENERAL
LEDGER

✓ 2. Total of Debit Column:
$538,320

Guantanamo Company is a small editorial services company owned and operated by Ronaldo Manuel. On December 31, 2003, the end of the current year, Guantanamo Company's accounting clerk prepared the trial balance shown at the top of the next page.

The data needed to determine year-end adjustments are as follows:

a. Unexpired insurance at December 31, $1,900.
b. Supplies on hand at December 31, $475.
c. Depreciation of building for the year, $1,620.
d. Depreciation of equipment for the year, $5,500.
e. Rent unearned at December 31, $1,500.
f. Accrued salaries and wages at December 31, $2,050.
g. Fees earned but unbilled on December 31, $4,150.

Instructions

1. Journalize the adjusting entries. Add additional accounts as needed.
2. Determine the balances of the accounts affected by the adjusting entries and prepare an adjusted trial balance.

Guantanamo Company
Trial Balance
December 31, 2003

Cash	5,700	
Accounts Receivable	21,900	
Prepaid Insurance	4,500	
Supplies	1,720	
Land	75,000	
Building	141,500	
Accumulated Depreciation—Building		91,700
Equipment	90,100	
Accumulated Depreciation—Equipment		65,300
Accounts Payable		8,100
Unearned Rent		7,500
Ronaldo Manuel, Capital		134,000
Ronaldo Manuel, Drawing	10,000	
Fees Earned		218,400
Salaries and Wages Expense	110,580	
Utilities Expense	28,250	
Advertising Expense	20,200	
Repairs Expense	11,500	
Miscellaneous Expense	4,050	
	525,000	525,000

Problem 3–6A

Adjusting entries and errors

Objective 3

✓ Corrected Net Income:
$135,300

At the end of April, the first month of operations, the following selected data were taken from the financial statements of Jay Harriman, an attorney:

Net income for April	$129,575
Total assets at April 30	275,600
Total liabilities at April 30	18,575
Total owner's equity at April 30	257,025

In preparing the financial statements, adjustments for the following data were overlooked:

a. Supplies used during April, $1,125.
b. Unbilled fees earned at April 30, $10,200.
c. Depreciation of equipment for April, $2,500.
d. Accrued wages at April 30, $850.

Instructions

1. Journalize the entries to record the omitted adjustments.
2. Determine the correct amount of net income for April and the total assets, liabilities, and owner's equity at April 30. In addition to indicating the corrected amounts, indicate the effect of each omitted adjustment by setting up and completing a columnar table similar to the following. Adjustment (a) is presented as an example.

	Net Income	Total Assets	Total Liabilities	Total Owner's Equity
Reported amounts	$129,575	$275,600	$18,575	$257,025
Corrections:				
Adjustment (a)	−1,125	−1,125	0	−1,125
Adjustment (b)				
Adjustment (c)				
Adjustment (d)				
Corrected amounts				

PROBLEMS SERIES B

Problem 3–1B
Adjusting entries
Objective 3

On December 31, the end of the current year, the following data were accumulated to assist the accountant in preparing the adjusting entries for Bravo Realty:

a. Fees accrued but unbilled at December 31 are $6,300.
b. The supplies account balance on December 31 is $2,100. The supplies on hand at December 31 are $310.
c. Wages accrued but not paid at December 31 are $1,500.
d. The unearned rent account balance at December 31 is $5,200, representing the receipt of an advance payment on December 1 of four months' rent from tenants.
e. Depreciation of office equipment for the year is $3,500.

Instructions
1. Journalize the adjusting entries required at December 31.
2. Briefly explain the difference between adjusting entries and entries that would be made to correct errors.

Problem 3–2B
Adjusting entries
Objective 3

Selected account balances before adjustment for Lambada Realty at July 31, the end of the current year, are as follows:

	Debits	Credits		Debits	Credits
Accounts Receivable	$10,250		Unearned Fees		$ 6,500
Supplies	1,970		Fees Earned		100,850
Prepaid Rent	18,000		Wages Expense	$39,750	
Equipment	70,500		Rent Expense	—	
Accumulated Depreciation		$26,900	Depreciation Expense	—	
Wages Payable		—	Supplies Expense	—	

Data needed for year-end adjustments are as follows:

a. Supplies on hand at July 31, $600.
b. Depreciation of equipment during year, $2,000.
c. Rent expired during year, $12,000.
d. Wages accrued but not paid at July 31, $1,060.
e. Unearned fees at July 31, $3,000.
f. Unbilled fees at July 31, $7,180.

Instructions
Journalize the six adjusting entries required at July 31, based upon the data presented.

Problem 3–3B
Adjusting entries
Objective 3

GENERAL LEDGER

Brown Trout Co., an outfitter store for fishing treks, prepared the following trial balance at the end of its first year of operations:

Brown Trout Co.
Trial Balance
June 30, 2003

Cash	1,150	
Accounts Receivable	8,500	
Supplies	1,300	
Equipment	19,900	
Accounts Payable		750
Unearned Fees		2,000
Courtney Yarber, Capital		27,000
Courtney Yarber, Drawing	1,000	
Fees Earned		36,750
Wages Expense	20,150	
Rent Expense	9,850	
Utilities Expense	3,750	
Miscellaneous Expense	900	
	66,500	66,500

For preparing the adjusting entries, the following data were assembled:

a. Supplies on hand on June 30 were $280.
b. Fees earned but unbilled on June 30 were $2,750.
c. Depreciation of equipment was estimated to be $1,500 for the year.
d. Unpaid wages accrued on June 30 were $450.
e. The balance in unearned fees represented the June 1 receipt in advance for services to be provided. Only $900 of the services were provided between June 1 and June 30.

Instructions

Journalize the adjusting entries necessary on June 30.

Problem 3–4B
Adjusting entries
Objectives 3, 4

SPREADSHEET
GENERAL
LEDGER

Tinker Company specializes in the maintenance and repair of signs, such as billboards. On October 31, 2003, the accountant for Tinker Company prepared the following trial balances:

Tinker Company
Trial Balance
October 31, 2003

	Unadjusted		Adjusted	
Cash	6,750		6,750	
Accounts Receivable	18,400		18,400	
Supplies	5,880		1,030	
Prepaid Insurance	2,700		1,100	
Land	47,500		47,500	
Buildings	107,480		107,480	
Accumulated Depreciation—Buildings		79,600		85,100
Trucks	72,000		72,000	
Accumulated Depreciation—Trucks		22,800		31,900
Accounts Payable		8,920		9,595
Salaries Payable		—		960
Unearned Service Fees		7,500		3,500
Jordan Holbrook, Capital		93,890		93,890
Jordan Holbrook, Drawing	5,000		5,000	
Service Fees Earned		152,680		156,680
Salary Expense	81,200		82,160	
Depreciation Expense—Trucks	—		9,100	
Rent Expense	9,600		9,600	
Supplies Expense	—		4,850	
Utilities Expense	6,200		6,875	
Depreciation Expense—Buildings	—		5,500	
Taxes Expense	1,720		1,720	
Insurance Expense	—		1,600	
Miscellaneous Expense	960		960	
	365,390	365,390	381,625	381,625

Instructions

Journalize the seven entries that adjusted the accounts at October 31. None of the accounts were affected by more than one adjusting entry.

Problem 3–5B
Adjusting entries and adjusted trial balances
Objectives 3, 4

Humvee Service Co., which specializes in appliance repair services, is owned and operated by Jon Grabowski. Humvee Service Co.'s accounting clerk prepared the following trial balance at December 31, 2003:

SPREADSHEET

GENERAL LEDGER

✓ 2. Total of Debit Column:

$535,620

Humvee Service Co.
Trial Balance
December 31, 2003

Cash	5,200	
Accounts Receivable	16,200	
Prepaid Insurance	4,000	
Supplies	2,450	
Land	100,000	
Building	141,500	
Accumulated Depreciation—Building		95,700
Equipment	90,100	
Accumulated Depreciation—Equipment		65,300
Accounts Payable		7,500
Unearned Rent		6,000
Jon Grabowski, Capital		127,100
Jon Grabowski, Drawing	5,000	
Fees Earned		218,400
Salaries and Wages Expense	90,800	
Utilities Expense	28,200	
Advertising Expense	19,000	
Repairs Expense	13,500	
Miscellaneous Expense	4,050	
	520,000	520,000

The data needed to determine year-end adjustments are as follows:

a. Depreciation of building for the year, $2,100.
b. Depreciation of equipment for the year, $4,000.
c. Accrued salaries and wages at December 31, $3,170.
d. Unexpired insurance at December 31, $1,900.
e. Fees earned but unbilled on December 31, $6,350.
f. Supplies on hand at December 31, $675.
g. Rent unearned at December 31, $3,500.

Instructions

1. Journalize the adjusting entries. Add additional accounts as needed.
2. Determine the balances of the accounts affected by the adjusting entries and prepare an adjusted trial balance.

Problem 3–6B

Adjusting entries and errors

Objective 3

✓ Corrected Net Income:

$422,345

At the end of August, the first month of operations, the following selected data were taken from the financial statements of Toreka Bowen, an attorney:

Net income for August	$417,950
Total assets at August 31	771,500
Total liabilities at August 31	210,350
Total owner's equity at August 31	561,150

In preparing the financial statements, adjustments for the following data were overlooked:

a. Unbilled fees earned at August 31, $13,800.
b. Depreciation of equipment for August, $5,000.
c. Accrued wages at August 31, $1,300.
d. Supplies used during August, $3,105.

Instructions

1. Journalize the entries to record the omitted adjustments. *(continued)*

2. Determine the correct amount of net income for August and the total assets, liabilities, and owner's equity at August 31. In addition to indicating the corrected amounts, indicate the effect of each omitted adjustment by setting up and completing a columnar table similar to the following. Adjustment (a) is presented as an example.

	Net Income	Total Assets	Total Liabilities	Total Owner's Equity
Reported amounts	$417,950	$771,500	$210,350	$561,150
Corrections:				
Adjustment (a)	+13,800	+13,800	0	+13,800
Adjustment (b)	_____	_____	_____	_____
Adjustment (c)	_____	_____	_____	_____
Adjustment (d)	_____	_____	_____	_____
Corrected amounts	_____	_____	_____	_____

CONTINUING PROBLEM

The trial balance that you prepared for Dancin Music at the end of Chapter 2 should appear as follows:

GENERAL LEDGER

✓ 3. Total of Debit Column: $16,595

Dancin Music
Trial Balance
December 31, 2002

Cash	3,665	
Accounts Receivable	880	
Supplies	460	
Prepaid Insurance	1,680	
Office Equipment	2,500	
Accounts Payable		2,875
Unearned Revenue		2,400
Lynn Kwan, Capital		5,000
Lynn Kwan, Drawing	1,125	
Fees Earned		5,605
Wages Expense	1,400	
Office Rent Expense	1,300	
Equipment Rent Expense	575	
Utilities Expense	430	
Music Expense	890	
Advertising Expense	650	
Supplies Expense	90	
Miscellaneous Expense	235	
	15,880	15,880

The data needed to determine adjustments for the two-month period ending December 31, 2002, are as follows:

a. During December, Dancin Music provided guest disc jockeys for KPRG for a total of 110 hours. For information on the amount of the accrued revenue to be billed to KPRG, see the contract described in the December 3, 2002 transaction at the end of Chapter 2.
b. Supplies on hand at December 31, $85.
c. The balance of the prepaid insurance account relates to the December 1, 2002 transaction at the end of Chapter 2.
d. Depreciation of the office equipment is $50.

e. The balance of the unearned revenue account relates to the contract between Dancin Music and KPRG, described in the December 3, 2002 transaction at the end of Chapter 2.

f. Accrued wages as of December 31, 2002, were $65.

Instructions

1. Prepare adjusting journal entries. You will need the following additional accounts:

    18 Accumulated Depreciation—Office Equipment
    22 Wages Payable
    57 Insurance Expense
    58 Depreciation Expense

2. Post the adjusting entries, inserting balances in the accounts affected.
3. Prepare an adjusted trial balance.

SPECIAL ACTIVITIES

Activity 3–1
Nadu Real Estate Co.
*Ethics and professional
conduct in business*

Stacey Nairn opened Nadu Real Estate Co. on January 1, 2002. At the end of the first year, the business needed additional capital. On behalf of Nadu Real Estate, Stacey applied to American City Bank for a loan of $75,000. Based on Nadu Real Estate's financial statements, which had been prepared on a cash basis, the American City Bank loan officer rejected the loan as too risky.

After receiving the rejection notice, Stacey instructed her accountant to prepare the financial statements on an accrual basis. These statements included $31,500 in accounts receivable and $11,200 in accounts payable. Stacey then instructed her accountant to record an additional $18,000 of accounts receivable for commissions on property for which a contract had been signed on December 27, 2002, but which would not be formally "closed" and the title transferred until January 20, 2003.

Stacey then applied for a $75,000 loan from First National Bank, using the revised financial statements. On this application, Stacey indicated that she had not previously been rejected for credit.

Discuss the ethical and professional conduct of Stacey Nairn in applying for the loan from First National Bank.

Activity 3–2
Ford Motor Co.
Accrued expense

On December 30, 2003, you buy a Ford Expedition. It comes with a three-year, 36,000-mile warranty. On January 21, 2004, you return the Expedition to the dealership for some basic repairs covered under the warranty. The cost of the repairs to the dealership is $610. In what year, 2003 or 2004, should Ford Motor Co. recognize the cost of the warranty repairs as an expense?

Activity 3–3
United Airlines
Accrued revenue

The following is an excerpt from a conversation between Dawn Abrams and Kala Wiggins just before they boarded a flight to Paris on United Airlines. They are going to Paris to attend their company's annual sales conference.

Dawn: Kala, aren't you taking an introductory accounting course at State College?
Kala: Yes, I decided it's about time I learned something about accounting. You know, our annual bonuses are based upon the sales figures that come from the accounting department.
Dawn: I guess I never really thought about it.
Kala: You should think about it! Last year, I placed a $200,000 order on December 26. But when I got my bonus, the $200,000 sale wasn't included. They said it hadn't been shipped until January 6, so it would have to count in next year's bonus.
Dawn: A real bummer!

Kala: Right! I was counting on that bonus including the $200,000 sale.

Dawn: Did you complain?

Kala: Yes, but it didn't do any good. Ed, the head accountant, said something about matching revenues and expenses. Also, something about not recording revenues until the sale is final. I figure I'd take the accounting course and find out whether he's just jerking me around.

Dawn: I never really thought about it. When do you think United Airlines will record its revenues from this flight?

Kala: Mmm . . . I guess it could record the revenue when it sells the ticket . . . or . . . when the boarding passes are taken at the door . . . or . . . when we get off the plane . . . or when our company pays for the tickets . . . or . . . I don't know. I'll ask my accounting instructor.

Discuss when United Airlines should recognize the revenue from ticket sales to properly match revenues and expenses.

Activity 3–4
Eminent Television Repair
Adjustments and financial statements

Several years ago, your father opened Eminent Television Repair. He made a small initial investment and added money from his personal bank account as needed. He withdrew money for living expenses at irregular intervals. As the business grew, he hired an assistant. He is now considering adding more employees, purchasing additional service trucks, and purchasing the building he now rents. To secure funds for the expansion, your father submitted a loan application to the bank and included the most recent financial statements (shown below) prepared from accounts maintained by a part-time bookkeeper.

Eminent Television Repair
Income Statement
For the Year Ended December 31, 2003

Service revenue		$51,750
Less: Rent paid	$18,000	
Wages paid	12,300	
Supplies paid	5,100	
Utilities paid	4,175	
Insurance paid	2,400	
Miscellaneous payments	2,150	44,125
Net income		$ 7,625

Eminent Television Repair
Balance Sheet
December 31, 2003

Assets

Cash	$ 8,600
Amounts due from customers	3,100
Truck	30,000
Total assets	$41,700

Equities

Owner's capital	$41,700

After reviewing the financial statements, the loan officer at the bank asked your father if he used the accrual basis of accounting for revenues and expenses. Your father responded that he did and that is why he included an account for "Amounts Due from Customers." The loan officer then asked whether or not the accounts were adjusted prior to the preparation of the statements. Your father answered that they had not been adjusted.

a. Why do you think the loan officer suspected that the accounts had not been adjusted prior to the preparation of the statements?

b. Indicate possible accounts that might need to be adjusted before an accurate set of financial statements could be prepared.

Activity 3–5
Into the Real World
Codes of ethics

Obtain a copy of your college or university's student code of conduct. In groups of three or four, answer the following questions.

1. Compare this code of conduct with the accountant's Codes of Professional Conduct in Appendix B at the end of this text. What are the similarities and differences between the two codes of conduct?
2. One of your classmates asks you for permission to copy your homework, which your instructor will be collecting and grading for part of your overall term grade. Although your instructor has not stated whether one student may or may not copy another student's homework, is it ethical for you to allow your classmate to copy your homework? Is it ethical for your classmate to copy your homework?

ANSWERS TO SELF-EXAMINATION QUESTIONS

Matching

1. A	5. T	9. N	13. O	17. F
2. J	6. H	10. C	14. P	18. X
3. B	7. G	11. D	15. E	19. L
4. W	8. M	12. R	16. I	

Multiple Choice

1. **A** A deferral is the delay in recording an expense already paid, such as prepaid insurance (answer A). Wages payable (answer B) is considered an accrued expense or accrued liability. Fees earned (answer C) is a revenue item. Accumulated depreciation (answer D) is a contra account to a fixed asset.

2. **D** The balance in the supplies account, before adjustment, represents the amount of supplies available. From this amount ($2,250) is subtracted the amount of supplies on hand ($950) to determine the supplies used ($1,300). Since increases in expense accounts are recorded by debits and decreases in asset accounts are recorded by credits, answer D is the correct entry.

3. **C** The failure to record the adjusting entry debiting unearned rent, $600, and crediting rent revenue, $600, would have the effect of overstating liabilities by $600 and understating net income by $600 (answer C).

4. **C** Since increases in expense accounts (such as depreciation expense) are recorded by debits and it is customary to record the decreases in usefulness of fixed assets as credits to accumulated depreciation accounts, answer C is the correct entry.

5. **D** The book value of a fixed asset is the difference between the balance in the asset account and the balance in the related accumulated depreciation account, or $22,500 − $14,000, as indicated by answer D ($8,500).

Completing the Accounting Cycle

4

objectives

After studying this chapter, you should be able to:

1   Prepare a work sheet.

2   Prepare financial statements from a work sheet.

3   Prepare the adjusting and closing entries from a work sheet.

4   Review the seven basic steps of the accounting cycle.

5   Explain what is meant by the fiscal year and the natural business year.

6   Analyze and interpret the financial solvency of a business by computing working capital and the current ratio.

Most of us have had to file a personal tax return. At the beginning of the year, you estimate your upcoming income and decide whether you need to increase your payroll tax withholdings or perhaps pay estimated taxes. During the year, you earn income, make investments, and enter into other tax-related transactions, such as making charitable contributions. At the end of the year, your employer sends you a tax withholding information form (W-2 form), and you collect the tax records needed for completing your yearly tax forms. If any tax is owed, you pay it; if you overpaid your taxes, you file for a refund. As the next year begins, you start the cycle all over again.

Businesses also go through a cycle of activities. At the beginning of the cycle, management plans where it wants the business to go and begins the necessary actions to achieve its operating goals. Throughout the cycle, which is normally one year, the accountant records the operating activities (transactions) of the business. At the end of the cycle, the accountant prepares financial statements that summarize the operating activities for the year. The accountant then prepares the accounts for recording the operating activities in the next cycle.

As we saw in Chapter 1, the initial cycle for NetSolutions began with Chris Clark's investment in the business on November 1, 2002. The cycle continued with recording NetSolutions' transactions for November and December, as we discussed in Chapters 1 and 2. In Chapter 3, the cycle continued and we recorded the adjusting entries for the two months ending December 31, 2002. Now, in this chapter, we discuss the flow of the adjustment data into the accounts and into the financial statements. We show this process by using a work sheet. We conclude this chapter by discussing how the accounting records are prepared for the next period.

Work Sheet

objective 1

Prepare a work sheet.

> The work sheet is a useful device for understanding the flow of the accounting data from the unadjusted trial balance to the financial statements.

Accountants often use **working papers** for collecting and summarizing data they need for preparing various analyses and reports. Such working papers are useful tools, but they are not considered a part of the formal accounting records. This is in contrast to the chart of accounts, the journal, and the ledger, which are essential parts of the accounting system.

Real World Common spreadsheet programs used in business include Microsoft Excel® and Lotus 1-2-3®.

Working papers are usually prepared by using a spreadsheet program on a computer.

The **work sheet** is a working paper that accountants can use to summarize adjusting entries and the account balances for the financial statements. In small companies with few accounts and adjustments, a work sheet may not be necessary. For example, the financial statements for NetSolutions can be prepared directly from the adjusted trial balance illustrated in Chapter 3. In a computerized accounting system, a work sheet may not be necessary because the software program automatically posts entries to the accounts and prepares financial statements.

The work sheet (Exhibits 1 through 4) is a useful device for understanding the flow of the accounting data from the unadjusted trial balance to the financial statements (Exhibit 5). This flow of data is the same in either a manual or a computerized accounting system.

Unadjusted Trial Balance Columns

To begin the work sheet, list at the top the name of the business, the type of working paper (work sheet), and the period of time, as shown in Exhibit 1. Next, enter the unadjusted trial balance directly on the work sheet. The work sheet in Exhibit 1 shows the unadjusted trial balance for NetSolutions at December 31, 2002.

Adjustments Columns

The adjustments that we explained and illustrated for NetSolutions in Chapter 3 are entered in the Adjustments columns, as shown in Exhibit 2. Cross-referencing (by letters) the debit and credit of each adjustment is useful in reviewing the work sheet. It is also helpful for identifying the adjusting entries that need to be recorded in the journal.

The order in which the adjustments are entered on the work sheet is not important. Most accountants enter the adjustments in the order in which the data are assembled. If the titles of some of the accounts to be adjusted do not appear in the trial balance, they should be inserted in the Account Title column, below the trial balance totals, as needed.

To review, the entries in the Adjustments columns of the work sheet are:

(a) **Supplies.** The supplies account has a debit balance of $2,000. The cost of the supplies on hand at the end of the period is $760. Therefore, the supplies expense for December is the difference between the two amounts, or $1,240. Enter the adjustment by writing (1) $1,240 in the Adjustments Debit column on the same line as Supplies Expense and (2) $1,240 in the Adjustments Credit column on the same line as Supplies.

(b) **Prepaid Insurance.** The prepaid insurance account has a debit balance of $2,400, which represents the prepayment of insurance for 24 months beginning December 1. Thus, the insurance expense for December is $100 ($2,400/24). Enter the adjustment by writing (1) $100 in the Adjustments Debit column on the same line as Insurance Expense and (2) $100 in the Adjustments Credit column on the same line as Prepaid Insurance.

(c) **Unearned Rent.** The unearned rent account has a credit balance of $360, which represents the receipt of three months' rent, beginning with December. Thus, the rent revenue for December is $120. Enter the adjustment by writing (1) $120 in the Adjustments Debit column on the same line as Unearned Rent and (2) $120 in the Adjustments Credit column on the same line as Rent Revenue.

(d) **Wages.** Wages accrued but not paid at the end of December total $250. This amount is an increase in expenses and an increase in liabilities. Enter the adjustment by writing (1) $250 in the Adjustments Debit column on the same line as Wages Expense and (2) $250 in the Adjustments Credit column on the same line as Wages Payable.

(e) **Accrued Fees.** Fees accrued at the end of December but not recorded total $500. This amount is an increase in an asset and an increase in revenue. Enter the adjustment by writing (1) $500 in the Adjustments Debit column on the same line as Accounts Receivable and (2) $500 in the Adjustments Credit column on the same line as Fees Earned.

(f) **Depreciation.** Depreciation of the office equipment is $50 for December. Enter the adjustment by writing (1) $50 in the Adjustments Debit column on the same line as Depreciation Expense and (2) $50 in the Adjustments Credit column on the same line as Accumulated Depreciation.

Total the Adjustments columns to verify the mathematical accuracy of the adjustment data. The total of the Debit column must equal the total of the Credit column.

Exhibit 1 Work Sheet with Unadjusted Trial Balance Entered

NetSolutions
Work Sheet
For the Two Months Ended December 31, 2002

	Account Title	Trial Balance Dr.	Trial Balance Cr.	Adjustments Dr.	Adjustments Cr.	Adjusted Trial Balance Dr.	Adjusted Trial Balance Cr.	Income Statement Dr.	Income Statement Cr.	Balance Sheet Dr.	Balance Sheet Cr.	
1	Cash	2,065										1
2	Accounts Receivable	2,220										2
3	Supplies	2,000										3
4	Prepaid Insurance	2,400										4
5	Land	20,000										5
6	Office Equipment	1,800										6
7	Accounts Payable		900									7
8	Unearned Rent		360									8
9	Chris Clark, Capital		25,000									9
10	Chris Clark, Drawing	4,000										10
11	Fees Earned		16,340									11
12	Wages Expense	4,275										12
13	Rent Expense	1,600										13
14	Utilities Expense	985										14
15	Supplies Expense	800										15
16	Miscellaneous Expense	455										16
17		42,600	42,600									17
18												18
19												19
20												20
21												21
22												22
23												23
24												24
25												25

The work sheet is used for summarizing the effects of adjusting entries. It also aids in preparing financial statements.

Exhibit 5 Financial Statements Prepared from Work Sheet

NetSolutions
Income Statement
For the Two Months Ended December 31, 2002

Fees earned	$16 8 4 0 00	
Rent revenue	1 2 0 00	
Total revenues		$16 9 6 0 00
Expenses:		
Wages expense	$ 4 5 2 5 00	
Supplies expense	2 0 4 0 00	
Rent expense	1 6 0 0 00	
Utilities expense	9 8 5 00	
Insurance expense	1 0 0 00	
Depreciation expense	5 0 00	
Miscellaneous expense	4 5 5 00	
Total expenses		9 7 5 5 00
Net income		$ 7 2 0 5 00

NetSolutions
Statement of Owner's Equity
For the Two Months Ended December 31, 2002

Chris Clark, capital, November 1, 2002		$ 0
Investment on November 1, 2002	$25 0 0 0 00	
Net income for November and December	7 2 0 5 00	
	$32 2 0 5 00	
Less withdrawals	4 0 0 0 00	
Increase in owner's equity		28 2 0 5 00
Chris Clark, capital, December 31, 2002		$28 2 0 5 00

NetSolutions
Balance Sheet
December 31, 2002

Assets			Liabilities		
Current assets:			Current liabilities:		
Cash	$ 2 0 6 5 00		Accounts payable	$ 9 0 0 00	
Accounts receivable	2 7 2 0 00		Wages payable	2 5 0 00	
Supplies	7 6 0 00		Unearned rent	2 4 0 00	
Prepaid insurance	2 3 0 0 00		Total liabilities		$ 1 3 9 0 00
Total current assets		$ 7 8 4 5 00			
Property, plant, and equipment:					
Land	$20 0 0 0 00				
Office equipment $1,800					
Less accum. depr. 50	1 7 5 0 00		**Owner's Equity**		
Total property, plant,			Chris Clark, capital		28 2 0 5 00
and equipment		21 7 5 0 00	Total liabilities and		
Total assets		$29 5 9 5 00	owner's equity		$29 5 9 5 00

Adjusted Trial Balance Columns

The adjustment data are added to or subtracted from the amounts in the unadjusted Trial Balance columns. The adjusted amounts are then extended to (placed in) the Adjusted Trial Balance columns, as shown in Exhibit 2. For example, the cash amount of $2,065 is extended to the Adjusted Trial Balance Debit column, since no adjustments affected Cash. Accounts Receivable has an initial balance of $2,220 and a debit adjustment (increase) of $500. The amount to write in the Adjusted Trial Balance Debit column is the debit balance of $2,720. The same procedure continues until all account balances are extended to the Adjusted Trial Balance columns. Total the columns of the Adjusted Trial Balance to verify the equality of debits and credits.

Income Statement and Balance Sheet Columns

The work sheet is completed by extending the adjusted trial balance amounts to the Income Statement and Balance Sheet columns. The amounts for revenues and expenses are extended to the Income Statement columns. The amounts for assets, liabilities, owner's capital, and drawing are extended to the Balance Sheet columns.[1]

In the NetSolutions work sheet, the first account listed is Cash, and the balance appearing in the Adjusted Trial Balance Debit column is $2,065. Cash is an asset, is listed on the balance sheet, and has a debit balance. Therefore, $2,065 is extended to the Balance Sheet Debit column. The Fees Earned balance of $16,840 is extended to the Income Statement Credit column. The same procedure continues until all account balances have been extended to the proper columns, as shown in Exhibit 3.

After all of the balances have been extended to the four statement columns, total each of these columns, as shown in Exhibit 4. The difference between the two Income Statement column totals is the amount of the net income or the net loss for the period. Likewise, the difference between the two Balance Sheet column totals is also the amount of the net income or net loss for the period.

If the Income Statement Credit column total (representing total revenue) is greater than the Income Statement Debit column total (representing total expenses), the difference is the net income. If the Income Statement Debit column total is greater than the Income Statement Credit column total, the difference is a net loss. For NetSolutions, the computation of net income is as follows:

Total of Credit column (revenues)	$16,960
Total of Debit column (expenses)	9,755
Net income (excess of revenues over expenses)	$ 7,205

Q&A

If the total of the Balance Sheet Debit column of the work sheet is $350,000 and the total of the Balance Sheet Credit column is $400,000, what is the net income or net loss?

- - - - - - - - - - - - - - - - - - - -

$50,000 net loss ($350,000 − $400,000)

As shown in Exhibit 4, write the amount of the net income, $7,205, in the Income Statement Debit column and the Balance Sheet Credit column. Write the term *Net income* in the Account Title column. If there was a net loss instead of net income, you would write the amount in the Income Statement Credit column and the Balance Sheet Debit column and the term *Net loss* in the Account Title column. Inserting the net income or net loss in the statement columns on the work sheet shows the effect of transferring the net balance of the revenue and expense accounts to the owner's capital account. Later in this chapter, we explain how to journalize this transfer.

After the net income or net loss has been entered on the work sheet, again total each of the four statement columns. The totals of the two Income Statement columns must now be equal. The totals of the two Balance Sheet columns must also be equal.

---

[1] The balances of the capital and drawing accounts are also extended to the Balance Sheet columns because this work sheet does not provide for separate Statement of Owner's Equity columns.

Financial Statements

objective 2

Prepare financial statements from a work sheet.

The work sheet is an aid in preparing the income statement, the statement of owner's equity, and the balance sheet, which are presented in Exhibit 5. In the following paragraphs, we discuss these financial statements for NetSolutions, prepared from the completed work sheet in Exhibit 4. The statements are similar in form to those presented in Chapter 1.

Income Statement

The income statement is normally prepared directly from the work sheet. However, the order of the expenses may be changed. As we did in Chapter 1, we list the expenses in the income statement in Exhibit 5 in order of size, beginning with the larger items. Miscellaneous expense is the last item, regardless of its amount.

Statement of Owner's Equity

The first item normally presented on the statement of owner's equity is the balance of the proprietor's capital account at the beginning of the period. On the work sheet, however, the amount listed as capital is not always the account balance at the beginning of the period. The proprietor may have invested additional assets in the business during the period. Hence, for the beginning balance and any additional investments, it is necessary to refer to the capital account in the ledger. These amounts, along with the net income (or net loss) and the drawing amount shown in the work sheet, are used to determine the ending capital account balance.

The basic form of the statement of owner's equity is shown in Exhibit 5. For NetSolutions, the amount of drawings by the owner was less than the net income. If the owner's withdrawals had exceeded the net income, the order of the net income and the withdrawals would have been reversed. The difference between the two items would then be deducted from the beginning capital account balance. Other factors, such as additional investments or a net loss, also require some change in the form, as shown in the following example:

Allan Johnson, capital, January 1, 2002	$39,000	
Additional investment during the year	6,000	
Total		$45,000
Net loss for the year	$ 5,600	
Withdrawals	9,500	
Decrease in owner's equity		15,100
Allan Johnson, capital, December 31, 2002		$29,900

Balance Sheet

The balance sheet in Exhibit 5 was expanded by adding subsections for current assets; property, plant, and equipment; and current liabilities. Such a balance sheet is a *classified* balance sheet. In the following paragraphs, we describe some of the sections and subsections that may be used in a balance sheet. We will introduce additional sections in later chapters.

Assets

Assets are commonly divided into classes for presentation on the balance sheet. Two of these classes are (1) current assets and (2) property, plant, and equipment.

> **Two common classes of assets are current assets and property, plant, and equipment.**

Current Assets. Cash and other assets that are expected to be converted to cash or sold or used up usually within one year or less, through the normal operations of the business, are called current assets. In addition to cash, the current assets usually owned by a service business are notes receivable, accounts receivable, supplies, and other prepaid expenses.

Notes receivable are amounts customers owe. They are written promises to pay the amount of the note and possibly interest at an agreed rate. Accounts receivable are also amounts customers owe, but they are less formal than notes and do not provide for interest. Accounts receivable normally result from providing services or selling merchandise on account. Notes receivable and accounts receivable are current assets because they will usually be converted to cash within one year or less.

Property, Plant, and Equipment. The property, plant, and equipment section may also be described as **fixed assets** or **plant assets**. These assets include equipment, machinery, buildings, and land. With the exception of land, as we discussed in Chapter 3, fixed assets depreciate over a period of time. The cost, accumulated depreciation, and book value of each major type of fixed asset is normally reported on the balance sheet or in accompanying notes.

BUSINESS ON STAGE

The Operating Cycle

The operations of a manufacturing business involve the purchase of raw materials (purchasing activity), the conversion of the raw materials into a product through the use of labor and machinery (production activity), the sale and distribution of the products to customers (sales activity), and the receipt of cash from customers (collection activity). This overall process is referred to as the *operating cycle*. Thus, the operating cycle begins with spending cash and it ends with receiving cash from customers. The operating cycle for a manufacturing business is shown below.

Operating cycles differ, depending upon the nature of the business and its operations. For example, the operating cycles for tobacco, distillery, and lumber industries are much longer than the operating cycles of the auto-mobile, consumer electronics, and home furnishings industries. Likewise, the operating cycles for retailers are usually shorter than for manufacturers because retailers purchase goods in a form ready for sale to the customer. Of course, some retailers will have shorter operating cycles than others because of the nature of their products. For example, a jewelry store or an automobile dealer normally has a longer operating cycle than a consumer electronics store or a grocery store.

Businesses with longer operating cycles normally have higher profit margins on their products than businesses with shorter operating cycles. For example, it is not unusual for jewelry stores to price their jewelry at 30%–50% above cost. In contrast, grocery stores operate on very small profit margins, often below 5%. Grocery stores make up the difference by selling their products more quickly. ■

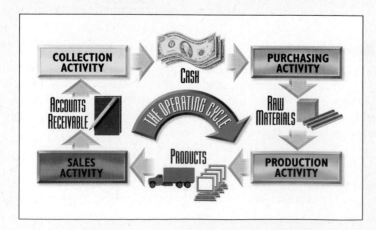

Liabilities

Two common classes of liabilities are current liabilities and long-term liabilities.

Liabilities are the amounts the business owes to creditors. The two most common classes of liabilities are (1) current liabilities and (2) long-term liabilities.

Current Liabilities. Liabilities that will be due within a short time (usually one year or less) and that are to be paid out of current assets are called **current liabilities**. The most common liabilities in this group are notes payable and accounts payable. Other current liability accounts commonly found in the ledger are Wages Payable, Interest Payable, Taxes Payable, and Unearned Fees.

Long-Term Liabilities. Liabilities that will not be due for a long time (usually more than one year) are called **long-term liabilities**. If NetSolutions had long-term liabilities, they would be reported below the current liabilities. As long-term liabilities come due and are to be paid within one year, they are classified as current liabilities. If they are to be renewed rather than paid, they would continue to be classified as long-term. When an asset is pledged as security for a liability, the obligation may be called a *mortgage note payable* or a *mortgage payable*.

Owner's Equity

The owner's right to the assets of the business is presented on the balance sheet below the liabilities section. The owner's equity is added to the total liabilities, and this total must be equal to the total assets.

Adjusting and Closing Entries

objective 3

Prepare the adjusting and closing entries from a work sheet.

As we discussed in Chapter 3, the adjusting entries are recorded in the journal at the end of the accounting period. If a work sheet has been prepared, the data for these entries are in the Adjustments columns. For NetSolutions, the adjusting entries prepared from the work sheet are shown in Exhibit 6.

After the adjusting entries have been posted to NetSolutions' ledger, shown in Exhibit 10, the ledger is in agreement with the data reported on the financial statements. The balances of the accounts reported on the balance sheet are carried forward from year to year. Because they are relatively permanent, these accounts are called **real accounts**. The balances of the accounts reported on the income statement are *not* carried forward from year to year. Likewise, the balance of the owner's withdrawal account, which is reported on the statement of owner's equity, is not carried forward. Because these accounts report amounts for only one period, they are called **temporary accounts** or **nominal accounts**.

To report amounts for only one period, temporary accounts should have zero balances at the beginning of a period. How are these balances converted to zero? The revenue and expense account balances are transferred to an account called **Income Summary**. The balance of Income Summary is then transferred to the owner's capital account. The balance of the owner's drawing account is also transferred to the owner's capital account. The entries that transfer these balances are called **closing entries**. The transfer process is called the **closing process**. Exhibit 7 is a diagram of this process.

Closing entries transfer the balances of temporary accounts to the owner's capital account.

Exhibit 6 Adjusting Entries for NetSolutions

	Date		Description	Post. Ref.	Debit	Credit	
			JOURNAL			PAGE 5	
1			Adjusting Entries				1
2	2002 Dec.	31	Supplies Expense	55	1 2 4 0 00		2
3			Supplies	14		1 2 4 0 00	3
4							4
5		31	Insurance Expense	56	1 0 0 00		5
6			Prepaid Insurance	15		1 0 0 00	6
7							7
8		31	Unearned Rent	23	1 2 0 00		8
9			Rent Revenue	42		1 2 0 00	9
10							10
11		31	Wages Expense	51	2 5 0 00		11
12			Wages Payable	22		2 5 0 00	12
13							13
14		31	Accounts Receivable	12	5 0 0 00		14
15			Fees Earned	41		5 0 0 00	15
16							16
17		31	Depreciation Expense	53	5 0 00		17
18			Accumulated Depreciation—				18
19			Office Equipment	19		5 0 00	19

Exhibit 7 The Closing Process

THE CLOSING PROCESS

2 Expenses are transferred to Income Summary

INCOME SUMMARY

1 Revenues are transferred to Income Summary

3 Net Income or Net Loss is transferred to Owner's Capital

OWNER'S CAPITAL

4 Drawings are transferred to Owner's Capital

The income summary account does not appear on the financial statements.

You should note that Income Summary is used only at the end of the period. At the beginning of the closing process, Income Summary has no balance. During the closing process, Income Summary will be debited and credited for various amounts. At the end of the closing process, Income Summary will again have no balance. Because Income Summary has the effect of clearing the revenue and expense accounts of their balances, it is sometimes called a **clearing account**. Other titles used for this account include Revenue and Expense Summary, Profit and Loss Summary, and Income and Expense Summary.

It is possible to close the temporary revenue and expense accounts without using a clearing account such as Income Summary. In this case, the balances of the revenue and expense accounts are closed directly to the owner's capital account. This process is automatic in a computerized accounting system. In a manual system, the use of an income summary account aids in detecting and correcting errors.

Journalizing and Posting Closing Entries

Four closing entries are required at the end of an accounting period, as outlined in Exhibit 7. The account titles and balances needed in preparing these entries may be obtained from the work sheet, the income statement and the statement of owner's equity, or the ledger. If a work sheet is used, the data for the first two entries appear in the Income Statement columns. The amount for the third entry is the net income or net loss appearing at the bottom of the work sheet. The amount for the fourth entry is the drawing account balance that appears in the Balance Sheet Debit column of the work sheet.

A flowchart of the closing entries for NetSolutions is shown in Exhibit 8. The balances in the accounts are those shown in the Adjusted Trial Balance columns of the work sheet in Exhibit 2.

Exhibit 8 Flowchart of Closing Entries for NetSolutions

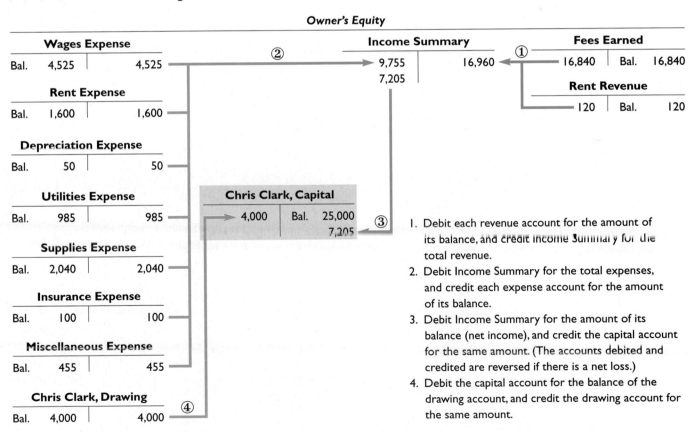

The closing entries for NetSolutions are shown in Exhibit 9. After the closing entries have been posted to the ledger, as shown in Exhibit 10, the balance in the capital account will agree with the amount reported on the statement of owner's equity and the balance sheet. In addition, the revenue, expense, and drawing accounts will have zero balances.

Exhibit 9 Closing Entries for NetSolutions

	Date		Description	Post. Ref.	Debit	Credit	
1			Closing Entries				1
2	2002 Dec.	31	Fees Earned	41	16 8 4 0 00		2
3			Rent Revenue	42	1 2 0 00		3
4			Income Summary	33		16 9 6 0 00	4
5							5
6		31	Income Summary	33	9 7 5 5 00		6
7			Wages Expense	51		4 5 2 5 00	7
8			Rent Expense	52		1 6 0 0 00	8
9			Depreciation Expense	53		5 0 00	9
10			Utilities Expense	54		9 8 5 00	10
11			Supplies Expense	55		2 0 4 0 00	11
12			Insurance Expense	56		1 0 0 00	12
13			Miscellaneous Expense	59		4 5 5 00	13
14							14
15		31	Income Summary	33	7 2 0 5 00		15
16			Chris Clark, Capital	31		7 2 0 5 00	16
17							17
18		31	Chris Clark, Capital	31	4 0 0 0 00		18
19			Chris Clark, Drawing	32		4 0 0 0 00	19

JOURNAL   **PAGE 6**

Exhibit 10 Ledger for NetSolutions

LEDGER

ACCOUNT *Cash*   **ACCOUNT NO. 11**

Date	Item	Post. Ref.	Debit	Credit	Balance Debit	Balance Credit
2002 Nov. 1		1	25 0 0 0 00		25 0 0 0 00	
5		1		20 0 0 0 00	5 0 0 0 00	
18		1	7 5 0 0 00		12 5 0 0 00	
30		1		3 6 5 0 00	8 8 5 0 00	
30		1		9 5 0 00	7 9 0 0 00	
30		2		2 0 0 0 00	5 9 0 0 00	
Dec. 1		2		2 4 0 0 00	3 5 0 0 00	
1		2		8 0 0 00	2 7 0 0 00	
1		2	3 6 0 00		3 0 6 0 00	
6		2		1 8 0 00	2 8 8 0 00	
11		2		4 0 0 00	2 4 8 0 00	
13		3		9 5 0 00	1 5 3 0 00	
16		3	3 1 0 0 00		4 6 3 0 00	
20		3		9 0 0 00	3 7 3 0 00	
21		3	6 5 0 00		4 3 8 0 00	
23		3		1 4 5 0 00	2 9 3 0 00	
27		3		1 2 0 0 00	1 7 3 0 00	
31		3		3 1 0 00	1 4 2 0 00	
31		4		2 2 5 00	1 1 9 5 00	
31		4	2 8 7 0 00		4 0 6 5 00	
31		4		2 0 0 0 00	2 0 6 5 00	

Exhibit 10 (continued)

ACCOUNT *Accounts Receivable*   **ACCOUNT NO.** *12*

Date		Item	Post. Ref.	Debit	Credit	Balance Debit	Balance Credit
2002 Dec.	16		3	1 7 5 0 00		1 7 5 0 00	
	21		3		6 5 0 00	1 1 0 0 00	
	31		4	1 1 2 0 00		2 2 2 0 00	
	31	Adjusting	5	5 0 0 00		2 7 2 0 00	

ACCOUNT *Supplies*   **ACCOUNT NO.** *14*

Date		Item	Post. Ref.	Debit	Credit	Balance Debit	Balance Credit
2002 Nov.	10		1	1 3 5 0 00		1 3 5 0 00	
	30		1		8 0 0 00	5 5 0 00	
Dec.	23		3	1 4 5 0 00		2 0 0 0 00	
	31	Adjusting	5		1 2 4 0 00	7 6 0 00	

ACCOUNT *Prepaid Insurance*   **ACCOUNT NO.** *15*

Date		Item	Post. Ref.	Debit	Credit	Balance Debit	Balance Credit
2002 Dec.	1		2	2 4 0 0 00		2 4 0 0 00	
	31	Adjusting	5		1 0 0 00	2 3 0 0 00	

ACCOUNT *Land*   **ACCOUNT NO.** *17*

Date		Item	Post. Ref.	Debit	Credit	Balance Debit	Balance Credit
2002 Nov.	5		1	20 0 0 0 00		20 0 0 0 00	

ACCOUNT *Office Equipment*   **ACCOUNT NO.** *18*

Date		Item	Post. Ref.	Debit	Credit	Balance Debit	Balance Credit
2002 Dec.	4		2	1 8 0 0 00		1 8 0 0 00	

ACCOUNT *Accumulated Depreciation*   **ACCOUNT NO.** *19*

Date		Item	Post. Ref.	Debit	Credit	Balance Debit	Balance Credit
2002 Dec.	31	Adjusting	5		5 0 00		5 0 00

Exhibit 10 *(continued)*

ACCOUNT *Accounts Payable*   **ACCOUNT NO. 21**

Date		Item	Post. Ref.	Debit	Credit	Balance Debit	Balance Credit
2002 Nov.	10		1		1 3 5 0 00		1 3 5 0 00
	30		1	9 5 0 00			4 0 0 00
Dec.	4		2		1 8 0 0 00		2 2 0 0 00
	11		2	4 0 0 00			1 8 0 0 00
	20		3	9 0 0 00			9 0 0 00

ACCOUNT *Wages Payable*   **ACCOUNT NO. 22**

Date		Item	Post. Ref.	Debit	Credit	Balance Debit	Balance Credit
2002 Dec.	31	Adjusting	5		2 5 0 00		2 5 0 00

ACCOUNT *Unearned Rent*   **ACCOUNT NO. 23**

Date		Item	Post. Ref.	Debit	Credit	Balance Debit	Balance Credit
2002 Dec.	1		2		3 6 0 00		3 6 0 00
	31	Adjusting	5	1 2 0 00			2 4 0 00

ACCOUNT *Chris Clark, Capital*   **ACCOUNT NO. 31**

Date		Item	Post. Ref.	Debit	Credit	Balance Debit	Balance Credit
2002 Nov.	1		1		25 0 0 0 00		25 0 0 0 00
Dec.	31	Closing	6		7 2 0 5 00		32 2 0 5 00
	31	Closing	6	4 0 0 0 00			28 2 0 5 00

ACCOUNT *Chris Clark, Drawing*   **ACCOUNT NO. 32**

Date		Item	Post. Ref.	Debit	Credit	Balance Debit	Balance Credit
2002 Nov.	30		2	2 0 0 0 00		2 0 0 0 00	
Dec.	31		4	2 0 0 0 00		4 0 0 0 00	
	31	Closing	6		4 0 0 0 00	—	—

ACCOUNT *Income Summary*   **ACCOUNT NO. 33**

Date		Item	Post. Ref.	Debit	Credit	Balance Debit	Balance Credit
2002 Dec.	31	Closing	6		16 9 6 0 00		16 9 6 0 00
	31	Closing	6	9 7 5 5 00			7 2 0 5 00
	31	Closing	6	7 2 0 5 00		—	—

Exhibit 10 (continued)

ACCOUNT Fees Earned   ACCOUNT NO. 41

Date		Item	Post. Ref.	Debit	Credit	Balance Debit	Balance Credit
2002 Nov.	18		1		7 5 0 0 00		7 5 0 0 00
Dec.	16		3		3 1 0 0 00		10 6 0 0 00
	16		3		1 7 5 0 00		12 3 5 0 00
	31		4		2 8 7 0 00		15 2 2 0 00
	31		4		1 1 2 0 00		16 3 4 0 00
	31	Adjusting	5		5 0 0 00		16 8 4 0 00
	31	Closing	6	16 8 4 0 00		—	—

ACCOUNT Rent Revenue   ACCOUNT NO. 42

Date		Item	Post. Ref.	Debit	Credit	Balance Debit	Balance Credit
2002 Dec.	31	Adjusting	5		1 2 0 00		1 2 0 00
	31	Closing	6	1 2 0 00		—	—

ACCOUNT Wages Expense   ACCOUNT NO. 51

Date		Item	Post. Ref.	Debit	Credit	Balance Debit	Balance Credit
2002 Nov.	30		1	2 1 2 5 00		2 1 2 5 00	
Dec.	13		3	9 5 0 00		3 0 7 5 00	
	27		3	1 2 0 0 00		4 2 7 5 00	
	31	Adjusting	5	2 5 0 00		4 5 2 5 00	
	31	Closing	6		4 5 2 5 00	—	—

ACCOUNT Rent Expense   ACCOUNT NO. 52

Date		Item	Post. Ref.	Debit	Credit	Balance Debit	Balance Credit
2002 Nov.	30		1	8 0 0 00		8 0 0 00	
Dec.	1		2	8 0 0 00		1 6 0 0 00	
	31	Closing	6		1 6 0 0 00	—	—

ACCOUNT Depreciation Expense   ACCOUNT NO. 53

Date		Item	Post. Ref.	Debit	Credit	Balance Debit	Balance Credit
2002 Dec.	31	Adjusting	5	5 0 00		5 0 00	
	31	Closing	6		5 0 00	—	—

Exhibit 10 (concluded)

ACCOUNT Utilities Expense — ACCOUNT NO. 54

Date	Item	Post. Ref.	Debit	Credit	Balance Debit	Balance Credit
2002 Nov. 30		1	4 5 0 00		4 5 0 00	
Dec. 31		3	3 1 0 00		7 6 0 00	
31		4	2 2 5 00		9 8 5 00	
31	Closing	6		9 8 5 00	—	—

ACCOUNT Supplies Expense — ACCOUNT NO. 55

Date	Item	Post. Ref.	Debit	Credit	Balance Debit	Balance Credit
2002 Nov. 30		1	8 0 0 00		8 0 0 00	
Dec. 31	Adjusting	5	1 2 4 0 00		2 0 4 0 00	
31	Closing	6		2 0 4 0 00	—	—

ACCOUNT Insurance Expense — ACCOUNT NO. 56

Date	Item	Post. Ref.	Debit	Credit	Balance Debit	Balance Credit
2002 Dec. 31	Adjusting	5	1 0 0 00		1 0 0 00	
31	Closing	6		1 0 0 00	—	—

ACCOUNT Miscellaneous Expense — ACCOUNT NO. 59

Date	Item	Post. Ref.	Debit	Credit	Balance Debit	Balance Credit
2002 Nov. 30		1	2 7 5 00		2 7 5 00	
Dec. 6		2	1 8 0 00		4 5 5 00	
31	Closing	6		4 5 5 00	—	—

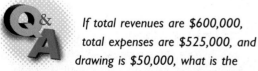

If total revenues are $600,000, total expenses are $525,000, and drawing is $50,000, what is the balance of the income summary account that is closed to the owner's capital?

$75,000 ($600,000 − $525,000). The drawing account balance is closed directly to the owner's capital, rather than to Income Summary.

After the entry to close an account has been posted, a line should be inserted in both balance columns opposite the final entry. The next period's transactions for the revenue, expense, and drawing accounts will be posted directly below the closing entry.

Post-Closing Trial Balance

The last accounting procedure for a period is to prepare a trial balance after the closing entries have been posted. The purpose of the **post-closing** (after closing) **trial balance** is to make sure that the ledger is in balance at the beginning of the next period. The accounts and amounts should agree exactly with the accounts and amounts listed on the balance sheet at the end of the period. The post-closing trial balance for NetSolutions is shown in Exhibit 11.

Instead of preparing a formal post-closing trial balance, it is possible to list the accounts directly from the ledger, using a computer. The computer printout, in effect, becomes the post-closing trial balance. Without such a printout, there is no efficient means of determining the cause of unequal trial balance totals.

Exhibit 11 Post-Closing Trial Balance

NetSolutions Post-Closing Trial Balance December 31, 2002		
Cash	2 0 6 5 00	
Accounts Receivable	2 7 2 0 00	
Supplies	7 6 0 00	
Prepaid Insurance	2 3 0 0 00	
Land	20 0 0 0 00	
Office Equipment	1 8 0 0 00	
Accumulated Depreciation		5 0 00
Accounts Payable		9 0 0 00
Wages Payable		2 5 0 00
Unearned Rent		2 4 0 00
Chris Clark, Capital		28 2 0 5 00
	29 6 4 5 00	29 6 4 5 00

Accounting Cycle

objective 4

Review the seven basic steps of the accounting cycle.

The process that begins with analyzing and journalizing transactions and ends with the post-closing trial balance is called the **accounting cycle**. The most important output of the accounting cycle is the financial statements.

Understanding the steps of the accounting cycle is essential for further study of accounting. The basic steps of the cycle are shown, by number, in the flowchart in Exhibit 12.

Real World In a computerized accounting system, the software automatically records and posts transactions. The ledger and supporting records are maintained in computerized master files. In addition, a work sheet is normally not prepared.

Fiscal Year

objective 5

Explain what is meant by the fiscal year and the natural business year.

In the NetSolutions illustration, operations began on November 1 and the accounting period was for two months, November and December. A proprietorship is required by the federal income tax law, except in rare cases, to maintain the same accounting period as its owner. Since Chris Clark maintains a calendar-year accounting period for tax purposes, NetSolutions must also close its accounts on December 31, 2002. In future years, the financial statements for Net-Solutions will be prepared for twelve months ending on December 31 each year.

NET SOLUTIONS

The annual accounting period adopted by a business is known as its **fiscal year**. Fiscal years begin with the first day of the month selected and end on the last day of the following twelfth month. The period most commonly used is the calendar year. Other periods are not unusual, especially for businesses organized as corporations. For example, a corporation may adopt a fiscal year that ends when business activities have reached the lowest point in its annual operating cycle. Such a fiscal year is called the **natural business year**. At the low point in its operating cycle, a business has more time to analyze the results of operations and to prepare financial statements.

Exhibit 12 Accounting Cycle

① Transactions are analyzed and recorded in the journal.
② Transactions are posted to the ledger.
③ A trial balance is prepared, adjustment data are assembled, and the work sheet is completed.
④ Financial statements are prepared.
⑤ Adjusting entries are journalized and posted to the ledger.
⑥ Closing entries are journalized and posted to the ledger.
⑦ A post-closing trial balance is prepared.

Because companies with fiscal years often have highly seasonal operations, investors and others should be careful in interpreting partial-year reports for such companies. That is, you should expect the results of operations for these companies to vary significantly throughout the fiscal year.

The financial history of a business may be shown by a series of balance sheets and income statements for several fiscal years. If the life of a business is expressed by a line moving from left to right, the series of balance sheets and income statements may be graphed as follows:

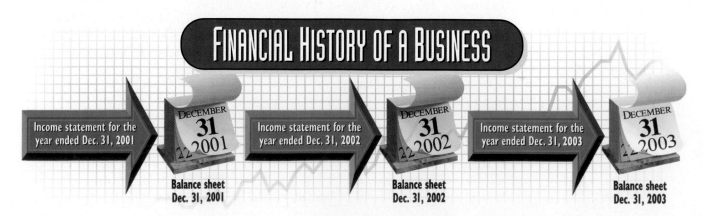

You may think of the income statements, balance sheets, and financial history of a business as similar to the record of a college football team. The final score of each football game is similar to the net income reported on the income statement of a business. The team's season record after each game is similar to the balance sheet. At the end of the season, the final record of the team measures its success or failure. Likewise, at the end of a life of a business, its final balance sheet is a measure of its financial success or failure.

Accounting Trends & Techniques, published by the American Institute of Certified Public Accountants, reported the following results of a survey concerning the month of the fiscal year-end of 600 industrial and merchandising companies:

Percentage of Companies with Fiscal Years Ending in the Month of:

January	4%	July	1%
February	2	August	2
March	2	September	6
April	2	October	4
May	2	November	3
June	9	December	63

FINANCIAL ANALYSIS AND INTERPRETATION

objective 6

Analyze and interpret the financial solvency of a business by computing working capital and the current ratio.

The ability of a business to pays its debts is called **solvency**. Two financial measures for evaluating a business's short-term solvency are working capital and the current ratio. **Working capital** is the excess of the current assets of a business over its current liabilities, as shown below.

Working capital = Current assets − Current liabilities

An excess of the current assets over the current liabilities implies that the business is able to pay its current liabilities. If the current liabilities are greater than the current assets, the business may not be able to pay its debts and continue in business.

To illustrate, NetSolutions' working capital at the end of 2002 is $6,455, as computed below. This amount of working capital implies that NetSolutions can pay its current liabilities.

Working capital = Current assets − Current liabilities
Working capital = $7,845 − $1,390
Working capital = $6,455

The **current ratio** is another means of expressing the relationship between current assets and current liabilities. The current ratio is computed by dividing current assets by current liabilities, as shown below.

Current ratio = Current assets/Current liabilities

To illustrate, the current ratio for NetSolutions at the end of 2002 is 5.6, computed as follows:

Current ratio = Current assets/Current liabilities
Current ratio = $7,845/$1,390 = 5.6

The current ratio is useful in making comparisons across companies and with industry averages. To illustrate, assume that as of December 31, 2002, the working capital of a company that competes with NetSolutions is much greater than $6,455, but its current ratio is only 1.3. Considering these facts alone, NetSolutions is in a more favorable position to obtain short-term credit, even though the competing company has a greater amount of working capital.

ENCORE

BMW

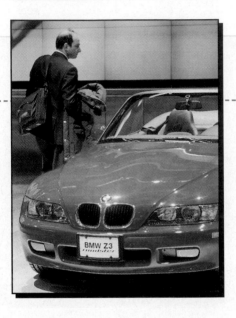

Financial statements prepared under accounting practices in other countries often differ from those prepared under generally accepted accounting principles found in the United States. This is to be expected, since cultures and market structures differ from country to country.

To illustrate, **BMW Group** prepares its financial statements under German law and German accounting principles. In doing so, BMW's balance sheet reports fixed assets first, followed by current assets. It also reports owner's equity before the liabilities. In contrast, balance sheets prepared under U.S. accounting principles report current assets followed by fixed assets and current liabilities followed by long-term liabilities and owner's equity. The U.S. form of balance sheet is organized to emphasize creditor interpretation and analysis. For example, current assets and current liabilities are presented first, so that working capital and the current ratio can be easily computed. Likewise, to emphasize their importance, liabilities are reported before owner's equity.

Regardless of these differences, the basic principles underlying the accounting equation and the double-entry accounting system are the same in Germany and the United States.

Even though differences in recording and reporting exist, the accounting equation holds true: the total assets still equal the total liabilities and owner's equity. ∎

APPENDIX: REVERSING ENTRIES

Some of the adjusting entries recorded at the end of an accounting period have an important effect on otherwise routine transactions that occur in the following period. A typical example is accrued wages owed to employees at the end of a period. If there has been an adjusting entry for accrued wages expense, the first payment of wages in the following period will include the accrual. In the absence of some special provision, Wages Payable must be debited for the amount owed for the earlier period, and Wages Expense must be debited for the portion of the payroll that represents expense for the later period. However, an *optional* entry—the reversing entry—may be used to simplify the analysis and recording of this first payroll entry in a period. As the term implies, a **reversing entry** is the exact opposite of the adjusting entry to which it relates. The amounts and accounts are the same as the adjusting entry; the debits and credits are reversed.

We will illustrate the use of reversing entries by using the data for NetSolutions' accrued wages, which were presented in Chapter 3. These data are summarized in Exhibit 13.

NET SOLUTIONS

Exhibit 13 Accrued Wages

1. Wages are paid on the second and fourth Fridays for the two-week periods ending on those Fridays.

2. The wages accrued for Monday and Tuesday, December 30 and 31, are $250.

3. Wages paid on Friday, January 10, total $1,275.

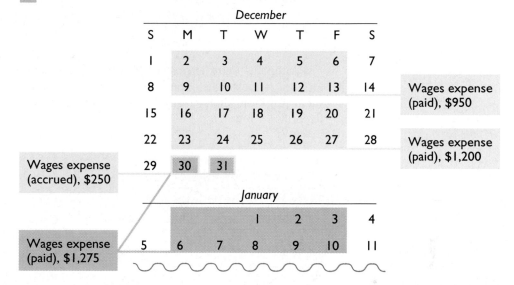

The adjusting entry for the accrued wages of December 30 and 31 is as follows:

Dec.	31	Wages Expense	51	2 5 0 00	
		Wages Payable	22		2 5 0 00

After the adjusting entry has been posted, Wages Expense will have a debit balance of $4,525 ($4,275 + $250), and Wages Payable will have a credit balance of $250. After the closing process is completed, Wages Expense will have a zero balance and will be ready for entries in the next period. Wages Payable, on the other hand, has a balance of $250. Without a reversing entry, it is necessary to record the $1,275 payroll on January 10 as follows.

2003 Jan.	10	Wages Payable	22	2 5 0 00	
		Wages Expense	51	1 0 2 5 00	
		Cash	11		1 2 7 5 00

The employee who records the January 10th entry must refer to the prior period's adjusting entry to determine the amount of the debits to Wages Payable and Wages Expense. Because the January 10th payroll is not recorded in the usual manner, there is a greater chance that an error may occur. This chance of error is reduced by recording a reversing entry as of the first day of the fiscal period. For example, the reversing entry for the accrued wages expense is as follows:

2003 Jan.	1	Wages Payable	22	2 5 0 00	
		Wages Expense	51		2 5 0 00

The reversing entry transfers the $250 liability from Wages Payable to the credit side of Wages Expense. The nature of the $250 is unchanged—it is still a liability. When the payroll is paid on January 10, the following entry is recorded:

				Debit	Credit
Jan.	10	Wages Expense	51	1 2 7 5 00	
		Cash	11		1 2 7 5 00

After this entry is posted, Wages Expense has a debit balance of $1,025. This amount is the wages expense for the period January 1–10. The sequence of entries, including adjusting, closing, and reversing entries, is illustrated in the following accounts:

ACCOUNT *Wages Payable*   **ACCOUNT NO. 22**

Date		Item	Post. Ref.	Debit	Credit	Balance Debit	Balance Credit
2002 Dec.	31	Adjusting	5		2 5 0 00		2 5 0 00
2003 Jan.	1	Reversing	7	2 5 0 00		—	—

ACCOUNT *Wages Expense*   **ACCOUNT NO. 51**

Date		Item	Post. Ref.	Debit	Credit	Balance Debit	Balance Credit
2002 Nov.	30		1	2 1 2 5 00		2 1 2 5 00	
Dec.	13		3	9 5 0 00		3 0 7 5 00	
	27		3	1 2 0 0 00		4 2 7 5 00	
	31	Adjusting	5	2 5 0 00		4 5 2 5 00	
	31	Closing	6		4 5 2 5 00	—	—
2003 Jan.	1	Reversing	7		2 5 0 00		2 5 0 00
	10		7	1 2 7 5 00		1 0 2 5 00	

In addition to accrued expenses (accrued liabilities), reversing entries may be journalized for accrued revenues (accrued assets). For example, the following reversing entry could be recorded for NetSolutions' accrued fees earned:

				Debit	Credit
Jan.	1	Fees Earned	41	5 0 0 00	
		Accounts Receivable	12		5 0 0 00

Reversing entries may also be journalized for prepaid expenses that are initially recorded as expenses and unearned revenues that are initially recorded as revenues. These situations are described and illustrated in Appendix C.

As we mentioned, the use of reversing entries is optional. However, with the increased use of computerized accounting systems, data entry personnel may be inputting routine accounting entries. In such an environment, reversing entries may be useful, since these individuals may not recognize the impact of adjusting entries on the related transactions in the following period.

KEY POINTS

1 Prepare a work sheet.

The work sheet is prepared by first entering a trial balance in the Trial Balance columns. The adjustments are then entered in the Adjustments Debit and Credit columns. The Trial Balance amounts plus or minus the adjustments are extended to the Adjusted Trial Balance columns. The work sheet is completed by extending the Adjusted Trial Balance amounts of assets, liabilities, owner's capital, and drawing to the Balance Sheet columns. The Adjusted Trial Balance amounts of revenues and expenses are extended to the Income Statement columns. The net income (or net loss) for the period is entered on the work sheet in the Income Statement Debit (or Credit) column and the Balance Sheet Credit (or Debit) column. Each of the four statement columns is then totaled.

2 Prepare financial statements from a work sheet.

The income statement is normally prepared directly from the work sheet. On the income statement, the expenses are normally presented in the order of size, from largest to smallest.

The basic form of the statement of owner's equity is prepared by listing the beginning balance of owner's equity, adding investments in the business and net income during the period, and deducting the owner's withdrawals. The amount listed on the work sheet as capital does not always represent the account balance at the beginning of the accounting period. The proprietor may have invested additional assets in the business during the period. Hence, for the beginning

balance and any additional investments, it is necessary to refer to the capital account.

Various sections and subsections are often used in preparing a balance sheet. Two common classes of assets are current assets and fixed assets. Cash and other assets that are normally expected to be converted to cash or sold or used up within one year or less are called current assets. Property, plant, and equipment may also be called fixed assets or plant assets. The cost, accumulated depreciation, and book value of each major type of fixed asset are normally reported on the balance sheet.

Two common classes of liabilities are current liabilities and long-term liabilities. Liabilities that will be due within a short time (usually one year or less) and that are to be paid out of current assets are called current liabilities. Liabilities that will not be due for a long time (usually more than one year) are called long-term liabilities.

The owner's claim against the assets is presented below the liabilities section and added to the total liabilities. The total liabilities and total owner's equity must equal the total assets.

3 Prepare the adjusting and closing entries from a work sheet.

The data for journalizing the adjusting entries are in the Adjustments columns of the work sheet. The four entries required in closing the temporary accounts are:

1. Debit each revenue account for the amount of its balance, and credit Income Summary for the total revenue.

2. Debit Income Summary for the total expenses, and credit each expense account for the amount of its balance.
3. Debit Income Summary for the amount of its balance (net income), and credit the capital account for the same amount. (Debit and credit are reversed if there is a net loss.)
4. Debit the capital account for the balance of the drawing account, and credit the drawing account for the same amount.

After the closing entries have been posted to the ledger, the balance in the capital account will agree with the amount reported on the statement of owner's equity and balance sheet. In addition, the revenue, expense, and drawing accounts will have zero balances.

The last step of the accounting cycle is to prepare a post-closing trial balance. The purpose of the post-closing trial balance is to make sure that the ledger is in balance at the beginning of the next period.

4 Review the seven basic steps of the accounting cycle.

The basic steps of the accounting cycle are:

1. Transactions are analyzed and recorded in a journal.
2. Transactions are posted to the ledger.
3. A trial balance is prepared, adjustment data are assembled, and the work sheet is completed.
4. Financial statements are prepared.
5. Adjusting entries are journalized and posted to the ledger.

6. Closing entries are journalized and posted to the ledger.
7. A post-closing trial balance is prepared.

5 Explain what is meant by the fiscal year and the natural business year.

The annual accounting period adopted by a business is known as its fiscal year. A corporation may adopt a fiscal year that ends when business activities have reached the lowest point in its annual operating cycle. Such a fiscal year is called the natural business year.

6 Analyze and interpret the financial solvency of a business by computing working capital and the current ratio.

The ability of a business to pay its debts is called solvency. Two financial measures for evaluating a business's short-term solvency are working capital and the current ratio. Working capital is the excess of the current assets of a business over its current liabilities. The current ratio is computed by dividing current assets by current liabilities.

ILLUSTRATIVE PROBLEM

Three years ago, T. Roderick organized Harbor Realty. At July 31, 2003, the end of the current fiscal year, the trial balance of Harbor Realty is as follows:

Harbor Realty
Trial Balance
July 31, 2003

Cash	3 4 2 5 00	
Accounts Receivable	7 0 0 0 00	
Supplies	1 2 7 0 00	
Prepaid Insurance	6 2 0 00	
Office Equipment	51 6 5 0 00	
Accumulated Depreciation		9 7 0 0 00
Accounts Payable		9 2 5 00
Unearned Fees		1 2 5 0 00
T. Roderick, Capital		29 0 0 0 00
T. Roderick, Drawing	5 2 0 0 00	
Fees Earned		59 1 2 5 00
Wages Expense	22 4 1 5 00	
Rent Expense	4 2 0 0 00	
Utilities Expense	2 7 1 5 00	
Miscellaneous Expense	1 5 0 5 00	
	100 0 0 0 00	100 0 0 0 00

The data needed to determine year-end adjustments are as follows:

a. Supplies on hand at July 31, 2003, are $380.
b. Insurance premiums expired during the year are $315.
c. Depreciation of equipment during the year is $4,950.
d. Wages accrued but not paid at July 31, 2003, are $440.
e. Accrued fees earned but not recorded at July 31, 2003, are $1,000.
f. Unearned fees on July 31, 2003, are $750.

Instructions
1. Enter the trial balance on a ten-column work sheet and complete the work sheet.
2. Prepare an income statement, a statement of owner's equity (no additional investments were made during the year), and a balance sheet.
3. On the basis of the data in the work sheet, journalize the closing entries.

Solution

1.

Harbor Realty
Work Sheet
For the Year Ended July 31, 2003

Account Title	Trial Balance Dr.	Trial Balance Cr.	Adjustments Dr.	Adjustments Cr.	Adjusted Trial Balance Dr.	Adjusted Trial Balance Cr.	Income Statement Dr.	Income Statement Cr.	Balance Sheet Dr.	Balance Sheet Cr.	
Cash	3 4 2 5				3 4 2 5				3 4 2 5		1
Accounts Receivable	7 0 0 0		(e)1 0 0 0		8 0 0 0				8 0 0 0		2
Supplies	1 2 7 0			(a) 8 9 0	3 8 0				3 8 0		3
Prepaid Insurance	6 2 0			(b) 3 1 5	3 0 5				3 0 5		4
Office Equipment	51 6 5 0				51 6 5 0				51 6 5 0		5
Accum. Depreciation		9 7 0 0		(c)4 9 5 0		14 6 5 0				14 6 5 0	6
Accounts Payable		9 2 5				9 2 5				9 2 5	7
Unearned Fees		1 2 5 0	(f) 5 0 0			7 5 0				7 5 0	8
T. Roderick, Capital		29 0 0 0				29 0 0 0				29 0 0 0	9
T. Roderick, Drawing	5 2 0 0				5 2 0 0				5 2 0 0		10
Fees Earned		59 1 2 5		(e)1 0 0 0		60 6 2 5		60 6 2 5			11
				(f) 5 0 0							12
Wages Expense	22 4 1 5		(d) 4 4 0		22 8 5 5		22 8 5 5				13
Rent Expense	4 2 0 0				4 2 0 0		4 2 0 0				14
Utilities Expense	2 7 1 5				2 7 1 5		2 7 1 5				15
Miscellaneous Expense	1 5 0 5				1 5 0 5		1 5 0 5				16
	100 0 0 0	100 0 0 0									17
Supplies Expense			(a) 8 9 0		8 9 0		8 9 0				18
Insurance Expense			(b) 3 1 5		3 1 5		3 1 5				19
Depreciation Expense			(c)4 9 5 0		4 9 5 0		4 9 5 0				20
Wages Payable				(d) 4 4 0		4 4 0				4 4 0	21
			8 0 9 5	8 0 9 5	106 3 9 0	106 3 9 0	37 4 3 0	60 6 2 5	68 9 6 0	45 7 6 5	22
Net Income							23 1 9 5			23 1 9 5	23
							60 6 2 5	60 6 2 5	68 9 6 0	68 9 6 0	24

2.

Harbor Realty
Income Statement
For the Year Ended July 31, 2003

Fees earned			$60 6 2 5 00
Operating expenses:			
Wages expense	$22 8 5 5 00		
Depreciation expense	4 9 5 0 00		
Rent expense	4 2 0 0 00		
Utilities expense	2 7 1 5 00		
Supplies expense	8 9 0 00		
Insurance expense	3 1 5 00		
Miscellaneous expense	1 5 0 5 00		
Total operating expenses		37 4 3 0 00	
Net income		$23 1 9 5 00	

Harbor Realty
Statement of Owner's Equity
For the Year Ended July 31, 2003

T. Roderick, capital, August 1, 2002			$29 0 0 0 00
Net income for the year	$23 1 9 5 00		
Less withdrawals	5 2 0 0 00		
Increase in owner's equity			17 9 9 5 00
T. Roderick, capital, July 31, 2003			$46 9 9 5 00

Harbor Realty
Balance Sheet
July 31, 2003

Assets				Liabilities			
Current assets:				Current liabilities:			
Cash	$ 3 4 2 5 00			Accounts payable	$ 9 2 5 00		
Accounts receivable	8 0 0 0 00			Unearned fees	7 5 0 00		
Supplies	3 8 0 00			Wages payable	4 4 0 00		
Prepaid insurance	3 0 5 00			Total liabilities			$ 2 1 1 5 00
Total current assets		$12 1 1 0 00					
Property, plant, and equipment:				**Owner's Equity**			
Office equipment	$51 6 5 0 00			T. Roderick, capital			46 9 9 5 00
Less accumulated depr.	14 6 5 0 00	37 0 0 0 00		Total liabilities and			
Total assets		$49 1 1 0 00		owner's equity			$49 1 1 0 00

3.

	JOURNAL				PAGE	
	Date	**Description**	**Post. Ref.**	**Debit**	**Credit**	
1		Closing Entries				1
2	2003 July 31	Fees Earned		60 6 2 5 00		2
3		Income Summary			60 6 2 5 00	3
4						4
5	31	Income Summary		37 4 3 0 00		5
6		Wages Expense			22 8 5 5 00	6
7		Rent Expense			4 2 0 0 00	7
8		Utilities Expense			2 7 1 5 00	8
9		Miscellaneous Expense			1 5 0 5 00	9
10		Supplies Expense			8 9 0 00	10
11		Insurance Expense			3 1 5 00	11
12		Depreciation Expense			4 9 5 0 00	12
13						13
14	31	Income Summary		23 1 9 5 00		14
15		T. Roderick, Capital			23 1 9 5 00	15
16						16
17	31	T. Roderick, Capital		5 2 0 0 00		17
18		T. Roderick, Drawing			5 2 0 0 00	18

Matching

Match each of the following statements with its proper term. Some terms may not be used.

A.	accounting cycle
B.	adjusted trial balance
C.	adjusting entries
D.	closing entries
E.	current assets
F.	current liabilities
G.	current ratio
H.	fiscal year
I.	Income Summary
J.	long-term liabilities
K.	natural business year
L.	note receivable
M.	owner's equity
N.	permanent assets
O.	post-closing trial balance
P.	property, plant, and equipment
Q.	real accounts
R.	solvency
S.	temporary accounts
T.	work sheet
U.	working capital

___ 1. A working paper that accountants may use to summarize adjusting entries and the account balances for the financial statements.

___ 2. Cash and other assets that are expected to be converted to cash or sold or used up, usually within one year or less, through the normal operations of the business.

___ 3. A customer's written promise to pay an amount and possibly interest at an agreed-upon rate.

___ 4. Liabilities that will be due within a short time (usually one year or less) and that are to be paid out of current assets.

___ 5. Liabilities that usually will not be due for more than one year.

___ 6. An account to which the revenue and expense account balances are transferred at the end of a period.

___ 7. The trial balance prepared after the closing entries have been posted.

___ 8. The annual accounting period adopted by a business.

___ 9. A fiscal year that ends when business activities have reached the lowest point in an annual operating cycle.

___ 10. The process that begins with analyzing and journalizing transactions and ends with the post-closing trial balance.

___ 11. The ability of a business to pays its debts.

___ 12. The excess of the current assets of a business over its current liabilities.

___ 13. A financial ratio that is computed by dividing current assets by current liabilities.

___ 14. The entries that transfer the balances of the revenue, expense, and drawing accounts to the owner's capital account.

___ 15. The section of the balance sheet that includes equipment, machinery, buildings, and land.

___ 16. Accounts that report amounts for only one period.

Multiple Choice

1. Which of the following accounts in the Adjusted Trial Balance columns of the work sheet would be extended to the Balance Sheet columns?
   A. Utilities Expense   C. M. E. Jones, Drawing
   B. Rent Revenue   D. Miscellaneous Expense

2. Which of the following accounts would be classified as a current asset on the balance sheet?
   A. Office Equipment
   B. Land
   C. Accumulated Depreciation
   D. Accounts Receivable

3. Which of the following entries closes the owner's drawing account at the end of the period?
   A. Debit the drawing account, credit the income summary account.
   B. Debit the owner's capital account, credit the drawing account.

   C. Debit the income summary account, credit the drawing account.
   D. Debit the drawing account, credit the owner's capital account.

4. Which of the following accounts would not be closed to the income summary account at the end of a period?
   A. Fees Earned
   B. Wages Expense
   C. Rent Expense
   D. Accumulated Depreciation

5. Which of the following accounts would not be included in a post-closing trial balance?
   A. Cash
   B. Fees Earned
   C. Accumulated Depreciation
   D. J. C. Smith, Capital

CLASS DISCUSSION QUESTIONS

1. Is the work sheet a substitute for the financial statements? Discuss.
2. In the Income Statement columns of the work sheet, the Debit column total is greater than the Credit column total before the amount for the net income or net loss has been included. Would the income statement report a net income or a net loss? Explain.
3. In the Balance Sheet columns of the work sheet for Teton Co. for the current year, the Debit column total is $68,500 greater than the Credit column total before the amount for net income or net loss has been included. Would the income statement report a net income or a net loss? Explain.
4. Describe the nature of the assets that compose the following sections of a balance sheet: (a) current assets, (b) property, plant, and equipment.
5. What is the difference between a current liability and a long-term liability?
6. What types of accounts are referred to as temporary accounts?
7. Why are closing entries required at the end of an accounting period?
8. What is the difference between adjusting entries and closing entries?
9. Describe the four entries that close the temporary accounts.
10. What type of accounts are closed by transferring their balances (a) as a debit to Income Summary, (b) as a credit to Income Summary?
11. To what account is the income summary account closed?
12. To what account is the owner's drawing account closed?
13. What is the purpose of the post-closing trial balance?
14. What is the natural business year?
15. Why might a department store select a fiscal year ending January 31, rather than a fiscal year ending December 31?
16. The fiscal years for several well-known companies were as follows:

Company	Fiscal Year Ending
Kmart	January 30
JCPenney	January 26
Zayre Corp.	January 26
Toys "R" Us, Inc.	February 3
Federated Department Stores	February 3
The Limited, Inc.	February 2

What general characteristic shared by these companies explains why they do not have fiscal years ending December 31?

EXERCISES

Exercise 4–1
Place account balances in a work sheet

Objective 1

The balances for the accounts listed below appear in the Adjusted Trial Balance columns of the work sheet. Indicate whether each balance should be extended to (a) an Income Statement column or (b) a Balance Sheet column.

1. Accounts Payable
2. Accounts Receivable
3. Fees Earned
4. Jamie Baggett, Drawing
5. Jamie Baggett, Capital
6. Supplies
7. Unearned Fees
8. Utilities Expense
9. Wages Expense
10. Wages Payable

Exercise 4–2
Classify accounts

Objective 1

Balances for each of the following accounts appear in the Adjusted Trial Balance columns of the work sheet. Identify each as (a) asset, (b) liability, (c) revenue, or (d) expense.

1. Accounts Receivable
2. Fees Earned
3. Insurance Expense
4. Land
5. Prepaid Advertising
6. Prepaid Insurance
7. Rent Revenue
8. Salary Expense
9. Salary Payable
10. Supplies
11. Supplies Expense
12. Unearned Rent

Exercise 4–3
Steps in completing a work sheet

Objective 1

The steps performed in completing a work sheet are listed below in random order.

a. Enter the amount of net income or net loss for the period in the proper Income Statement column and Balance Sheet column.
b. Add the Debit and Credit columns of the Balance Sheet and Income Statement columns of the work sheet to verify that the totals are equal.
c. Enter the unadjusted account balances from the general ledger into the unadjusted Trial Balance columns of the work sheet.
d. Add the Debit and Credit columns of the Balance Sheet and Income Statement columns of the work sheet to determine the amount of net income or net loss for the period.
e. Extend the adjusted trial balance amounts to the Income Statement columns and the Balance Sheet columns.
f. Add the Debit and Credit columns of the Adjusted Trial Balance columns of the work sheet to verify that the totals are equal.
g. Add or deduct adjusting entry data to trial balance amounts and extend amounts to the Adjusted Trial Balance columns.
h. Add the Debit and Credit columns of the Adjustments columns of the work sheet to verify that the totals are equal.
i. Add the Debit and Credit columns of the unadjusted Trial Balance columns of the work sheet to verify that the totals are equal.
j. Enter the adjusting entries into the work sheet, based upon the adjustment data.

Indicate the order in which the preceding steps would be performed in preparing and completing a work sheet.

Exercise 4–4
Adjustment data on work sheet

Objective 1

SPREADSHEET

✓ Total debits of Adjustments column: $14

Francesca Services Co. offers cleaning services to business clients. The trial balance for Francesca Services Co. has been prepared on the work sheet for the year ended December 31, 2003, shown at the top of the following page.

The data for year-end adjustments are as follows:

a. Fees earned, but not yet billed, $3.
b. Supplies on hand, $1.
c. Insurance premiums expired, $5.
d. Depreciation expense, $2.
e. Wages accrued, but not paid, $1.

Enter the adjustment data, and place the balances in the Adjusted Trial Balance columns.

Francesca Services Co.
Work Sheet
For the Year Ended December 31, 2003

Account Title	Trial Balance Dr.	Trial Balance Cr.	Adjustments Dr.	Adjustments Cr.	Adjusted Trial Balance Dr.	Adjusted Trial Balance Cr.
Cash	4					
Accounts Receivable	25					
Supplies	4					
Prepaid Insurance	6					
Land	25					
Equipment	16					
Accumulated Depr.—Equip.		1				
Accounts Payable		13				
Wages Payable		0				
Pamela Latham, Capital		56				
Pamela Latham, Drawing	4					
Fees Earned		30				
Wages Expense	8					
Rent Expense	4					
Insurance Expense	0					
Utilities Expense	2					
Depreciation Expense	0					
Supplies Expense	0					
Miscellaneous Expense	2					
Totals	100	100				

Exercise 4–5

Complete a work sheet

Objective 1

✓ Net income: $6

Francesca Services Co. offers cleaning services to business clients. Complete the following work sheet for Francesca Services Co.

Francesca Services Co.
Work Sheet
For the Year Ended December 31, 2003

Account Title	Adjusted Trial Balance Dr.	Adjusted Trial Balance Cr.	Income Statement Dr.	Income Statement Cr.	Balance Sheet Dr.	Balance Sheet Cr.
Cash	4					
Accounts Receivable	28					
Supplies	1					
Prepaid Insurance	1					
Land	25					
Equipment	16					
Accumulated Depr.—Equip.		3				
Accounts Payable		13				
Wages Payable		1				
Pamela Latham, Capital		56				
Pamela Latham, Drawing	4					
Fees Earned		33				
Wages Expense	9					
Rent Expense	4					
Insurance Expense	5					
Utilities Expense	2					
Depreciation Expense	2					
Supplies Expense	3					
Miscellaneous Expense	2					
Totals	106	106				
Net income (loss)						

Exercise 4–6
Financial statements

Objective 2

✓ Pamela Latham, capital, Dec. 31, 2003; $58

Based upon the data in Exercise 4–5, prepare an income statement, statement of owner's equity, and balance sheet for Francesca Services Co.

Exercise 4–7
Adjusting entries

Objective 3

Based upon the data in Exercise 4–4, prepare the adjusting entries for Francesca Services Co.

Exercise 4–8
Closing entries

Objective 3

Based upon the data in Exercise 4–5, prepare the closing entries for Francesca Services Co.

Exercise 4–9
Income statement

Objective 2

The following account balances were taken from the Adjusted Trial Balance columns of the work sheet for Speedy Messenger Service, a delivery service firm, for the current fiscal year ended April 30, 2003:

Fees Earned	$173,700
Salaries Expense	37,100
Rent Expense	12,500
Utilities Expense	7,500
Supplies Expense	2,750
Miscellaneous Expense	1,350
Insurance Expense	1,500
Depreciation Expense	4,200

Prepare an income statement.

Exercise 4–10
Income statement; net loss

Objective 2

The following revenue and expense account balances were taken from the ledger of Panda Services Co. after the accounts had been adjusted on January 31, 2003, the end of the current fiscal year:

Depreciation Expense	$ 7,500
Insurance Expense	3,500
Miscellaneous Expense	2,250
Rent Expense	31,270
Service Revenue	101,123
Supplies Expense	3,100
Utilities Expense	8,500
Wages Expense	46,800

Prepare an income statement.

Exercise 4–11
Income statement

Objective 2

✓ a. Net income: $631,263

FedEx Corporation had the following revenue and expense account balances (in thousands) at its fiscal year-end of May 31, 1999:

Rentals and Landing Fees	$ 1,396,694
Maintenance and Repairs	958,873
Purchased Transportation	1,537,785
Fuel	604,929
Salaries and Employee Benefits	7,087,728
Other Operating Expenses	2,989,257
Depreciation and Amortization	1,035,118
Interest Expense	98,191
Revenues	16,773,400
Provision for Income Taxes	429,731
Other Expenses	3,831

a.   Prepare an income statement.

b.   ━━► Compare your income statement with the 1999 income statement that is available at the FedEx Corporation web site, which is linked to the text's web site at **warren.swcollege.com**. What similarities and differences do you see?

Exercise 4–12
Statement of owner's equity

Objective 2

Greenhorn Services Co. offers its services to new arrivals in the Belgrade area. Selected accounts from the ledger of Greenhorn Services Co. for the current fiscal year ended July 31, 2003, are as follows:

John Bozeman, Capital				John Bozeman, Drawing			
July 31	11,000	Aug. 1	183,750	Oct. 30	2,000	July 31	11,000
		July 31	44,250	Jan. 31	2,000		
				Apr. 30	2,000		
				July 31	5,000		

Income Summary			
July 31	577,150	July 31	621,400
31	44,250		

Prepare a statement of owner's equity for the year.

Exercise 4–13
Statement of owner's equity; net loss

Objective 2

✓ Tori Jeter, capital, Oct. 31, 2003; $256,150

Selected accounts from the ledger of Yankee Sports for the current fiscal year ended October 31, 2003, are as follows:

Tori Jeter, Capital				Tori Jeter, Drawing			
Oct. 31	6,000	Nov. 1	310,300	Jan. 31	2,000	Oct. 31	6,000
31	48,150			Apr. 30	2,000		
				July 31	1,000		
				Oct. 31	1,000		

Income Summary			
Oct. 31	523,400	Oct. 31	475,250
		31	48,150

Prepare a statement of owner's equity for the year.

Exercise 4–14
Classify assets

Objective 2

Identify each of the following as (a) a current asset or (b) property, plant, and equipment:

1. Accounts receivable   3. Cash   5. Prepaid insurance
2. Building   4. Equipment   6. Supplies

Exercise 4–15
Balance sheet classification

Objective 2

At the balance sheet date, a business owes a mortgage note payable of $375,000, the terms of which provide for monthly payments of $12,500.

━━► Explain how the liability should be classified on the balance sheet.

Exercise 4–16
Balance sheet

Objective 2

✓ Total assets: $96,550

Shoshone Co. offers personal weight reduction consulting services to individuals. After all the accounts have been closed on June 30, 2003, the end of the current fiscal year, the balances of selected accounts from the ledger of Shoshone Co. are as follows:

Accounts Payable	$ 8,750	Prepaid Insurance	$3,100
Accounts Receivable	18,725	Prepaid Rent	2,400
Accumulated Depreciation—Equipment	21,100	Salaries Payable	1,750
Cash	2,150	Supplies	675
Equipment	90,600	Unearned Fees	1,200
Keith Ferris, Capital	84,850		

Prepare a classified balance sheet.

Exercise 4–17
Balance sheet

Objective 2

✓ Corrected balance sheet, total assets: $158,660

List the errors you find in the following balance sheet. Prepare a corrected balance sheet.

ZigZag Services Co.
Balance Sheet
For the Year Ended March 31, 2003

Assets			Liabilities		
Current assets:			Current liabilities:		
Cash	$ 3,170		Accounts receivable		$ 8,390
Accounts payable	4,390		Accum. depr.—building		23,000
Supplies	750		Accum. depr.—equipment		16,000
Prepaid insurance	1,600		Net loss		10,000
Land	100,000		Total liabilities		$ 57,390
Total current assets		$109,910			
Property, plant, and equipment:			Owner's Equity		
Building	$ 55,500		Wages payable		$ 975
Equipment	28,250		Danielle Adcock, capital		153,295
Total property, plant, and equipment		$101,750	Total owner's equity		$154,270
Total assets		$211,660	Total liabilities and owner's equity		$211,660

Exercise 4–18
Adjusting entries from work sheet

Objective 3

The Purification Co. is a consulting firm specializing in pollution control. The entries in the Adjustments columns of the work sheet for The Purification Co. are shown below.

	Adjustments	
	Dr.	**Cr.**
Accounts Receivable	5,100	
Supplies		1,225
Prepaid Insurance		1,000
Accumulated Depreciation—Equipment		1,800
Wages Payable		900
Unearned Rent	2,500	
Fees Earned		5,100
Wages Expense	900	
Supplies Expense	1,225	
Rent Revenue		2,500
Insurance Expense	1,000	
Depreciation Expense	1,800	

Prepare the adjusting journal entries.

Exercise 4–19
Identify accounts to be closed

Objective 3

From the following list, identify the accounts that should be closed to Income Summary at the end of the fiscal year:

a. Accounts Payable
b. Accumulated Depreciation— Buildings
c. Depreciation Expense—Buildings
d. Drew Meehan, Capital
e. Drew Meehan, Drawing
f. Equipment

g. Fees Earned
h. Land
i. Salaries Expense
j. Salaries Payable
k. Supplies
l. Supplies Expense

Exercise 4–20
Closing entries

Objective 3

Prior to its closing, Income Summary had total debits of $631,335 and total credits of $812,575.

➤ Briefly explain the purpose served by the income summary account and the nature of the entries that resulted in the $631,335 and the $812,575.

Exercise 4–21
Closing entries
Objective 3

✓ b. $582,150

After all revenue and expense accounts have been closed at the end of the fiscal year, Income Summary has a debit of $512,900 and a credit of $729,350. At the same date, Brenda Paxton, Capital has a credit balance of $405,700, and Brenda Paxton, Drawing has a balance of $40,000. (a) Journalize the entries required to complete the closing of the accounts. (b) Determine the amount of Brenda Paxton, Capital at the end of the period.

Exercise 4–22
Closing entries
Objective 3

Image Services Co. offers its services to individuals desiring to improve their personal images. After the accounts have been adjusted at January 31, the end of the fiscal year, the following balances were taken from the ledger of Image Services Co.

Adam Pastore, Capital	$325,750	Rent Expense	$74,000
Adam Pastore, Drawing	45,000	Supplies Expense	15,500
Fees Earned	380,700	Miscellaneous Expense	4,500
Wages Expense	205,300		

Journalize the four entries required to close the accounts.

Exercise 4–23
Identify permanent accounts
Objective 3

Which of the following accounts will usually appear in the post-closing trial balance?

a. Accounts Receivable
b. Accumulated Depreciation
c. Cash
d. Depreciation Expense
e. Equipment
f. Ernest Byrd, Capital
g. Ernest Byrd, Drawing
h. Fees Earned
i. Supplies
j. Wages Expense
k. Wages Payable

Exercise 4–24
Post-closing trial balance
Objective 3

✓ Correct column totals, $59,725

An accountant prepared the following post-closing trial balance:

Buchanan Repairs Co.
Post-Closing Trial Balance
July 31, 2003

Cash	5,125	
Accounts Receivable	18,500	
Supplies		1,100
Equipment		35,000
Accumulated Depreciation—Equipment	11,100	
Accounts Payable	6,250	
Salaries Payable		1,500
Unearned Rent	3,000	
Sydney Buchanan, Capital	37,875	
	81,850	37,600

Prepare a corrected post-closing trial balance. Assume that all accounts have normal balances and that the amounts shown are correct.

Exercise 4–25
Steps in the accounting cycle
Objective 4

Rearrange the following steps in the accounting cycle in proper sequence:

a. Financial statements are prepared.
b. Closing entries are journalized and posted to the ledger.
c. Adjusting entries are journalized and posted to the ledger.
d. A post-closing trial balance is prepared.
e. Transactions are analyzed and recorded in the journal.
f. Transactions are posted to the ledger.
g. A trial balance is prepared, adjustment data are assembled, and the work sheet is completed.

Exercise 4–26
Working capital and current ratio

Objective 6

The financial statements for **Cisco Systems, Inc.** are presented in Appendix G at the end of the text.

a. Determine the working capital and the current ratio for Cisco Systems as of July 29, 2000 and July 31, 1999.
b. ✏ What conclusions concerning the company's ability to meets its financial obligations can you draw from these data?

Appendix Exercise 4–27
Adjusting and reversing entries

On the basis of the following data, (a) journalize the adjusting entries at December 31, 2003, the end of the current fiscal year, and (b) journalize the reversing entries on January 1, 2004, the first day of the following year.

1. Sales salaries are uniformly $13,500 for a five-day workweek, ending on Friday. The last payday of the year was Friday, December 28.
2. Accrued fees earned but not recorded at December 31, $8,175.

Appendix Exercise 4–28
Entries posted to the wages expense account

Portions of the wages expense account of a business are as follows:

ACCOUNT	*Wages Expense*					ACCOUNT NO. 53	
						Balance	
Date	Item	Post. Ref.	Dr.	Cr.		Dr.	Cr.
2003							
Dec. 26	(1)	81	25,000			1,275,000	
31	(2)	82	15,000			1,290,000	
31	(3)	83		1,290,000		—	—
2004							
Jan. 1	(4)	84		15,000			15,000
2	(5)	85	25,000			10,000	

a. Indicate the nature of the entry (payment, adjusting, closing, reversing) from which each numbered posting was made.
b. Journalize the complete entry from which each numbered posting was made.

PROBLEMS SERIES A

Problem 4–1A
Work sheet and related items

Objectives 1, 2, 3

SPREADSHEET
GENERAL LEDGER

✓ 2. Net income: $14,980

The trial balance of The Pickerel Laundromat at July 31, 2003, the end of the current fiscal year, is shown at the top of the next page. The data needed to determine year-end adjustments are as follows:

a. Laundry supplies on hand at July 31 are $1,140.
b. Insurance premiums expired during the year are $1,500.
c. Depreciation of equipment during the year is $6,000.
d. Wages accrued but not paid at July 31 are $1,100.

Instructions

1. Enter the trial balance on a ten-column work sheet and complete the work sheet. Add accounts as needed.
2. Prepare an income statement, a statement of owner's equity (no additional investments were made during the year), and a balance sheet.
3. On the basis of the adjustment data in the work sheet, journalize the adjusting entries.
4. On the basis of the data in the work sheet, journalize the closing entries.

The Pickerel Laundromat
Trial Balance
July 31, 2003

Cash	3,290	
Laundry Supplies	5,850	
Prepaid Insurance	3,000	
Laundry Equipment	109,750	
Accumulated Depreciation		52,700
Accounts Payable		4,950
Shane Pond, Capital		39,450
Shane Pond, Drawing	3,500	
Laundry Revenue		77,900
Wages Expense	23,400	
Rent Expense	16,400	
Utilities Expense	8,500	
Miscellaneous Expense	1,310	
	175,000	175,000

Problem 4–2A

Adjusting and closing entries; statement of owner's equity

Objectives 2, 3

SPREADSHEET

✓ 2. Chandra Domir, capital, April 30: $71,230

The Breakthrough Company is an investigative services firm that is owned and operated by Chandra Domir. On April 30, 2003, the end of the current fiscal year, the accountant for The Breakthrough Company prepared a work sheet, a part of which is shown here.

The Breakthrough Company
Work Sheet (Partial)
April 30, 2003

	Income Statement		Balance Sheet	
Cash			4,325	
Accounts Receivable			18,600	
Supplies			1,610	
Prepaid Insurance			1,350	
Equipment			80,750	
Accumulated Depreciation—Equipment				23,995
Accounts Payable				6,230
Salaries Payable				2,480
Taxes Payable				1,200
Unearned Rent				1,500
Chandra Domir, Capital				64,715
Chandra Domir, Drawing			7,500	
Service Fees Earned		175,900		
Rent Revenue		3,000		
Salary Expense	129,865			
Rent Expense	16,000			
Supplies Expense	4,310			
Depreciation Expense—Equipment	3,500			
Utilities Expense	3,460			
Taxes Expense	3,115			
Insurance Expense	2,925			
Miscellaneous Expense	1,710			
	164,885	178,900	114,135	100,120
Net income	14,015			14,015
	178,900	178,900	114,135	114,135

Instructions

1. Journalize the entries that were required to close the accounts at April 30.
2. Prepare a statement of owner's equity for the fiscal year ended April 30, 2003. There were no additional investments during the year.
3. If Chandra Domir, Capital decreased $20,000 after the closing entries were posted, what was the amount of net income or net loss?

If the working papers correlating with this textbook are not used, omit Problem 4–3A.

Problem 4–3A

Ledger accounts, work sheet, and related items

Objectives 1, 2, 3

✓ 2. Net income: $18,703

The ledger and trial balance of Idiom.com as of January 31, 2003, the end of the first month of its current fiscal year, are presented in the working papers.

Instructions

1. Complete the ten-column work sheet. Data needed to determine the necessary adjusting entries are as follows:
    a. Service revenue accrued at January 31 is $1,750.
    b. Supplies on hand at January 31 are $350.
    c. Insurance premiums expired during January are $100.
    d. Depreciation of the building during January is $500.
    e. Depreciation of equipment during January is $150.
    f. Unearned rent at January 31 is $2,040.
    g. Wages accrued at January 31 are $400.
2. Prepare an income statement, a statement of owner's equity, and a balance sheet. (*Note:* The owner made an additional investment during the period.)
3. Journalize and post the adjusting entries, inserting balances in the accounts affected.
4. Journalize and post the closing entries. Indicate closed accounts by inserting a line in both Balance columns opposite the closing entry.
5. Prepare a post-closing trial balance.

Problem 4–4A

Work sheet and financial statements

Objectives 1, 2, 3

GENERAL LEDGER

✓ 2. Net income: $58,270

Figure-Eight Company maintains and repairs warning lights, such as those found on radio towers and lighthouses. Figure-Eight Company prepared the following trial balance at October 31, 2003, the end of the current fiscal year:

Figure-Eight Company
Trial Balance
October 31, 2003

Cash	5,500	
Accounts Receivable	16,500	
Prepaid Insurance	3,000	
Supplies	1,950	
Land	70,000	
Building	100,500	
Accumulated Depreciation—Building		81,700
Equipment	72,400	
Accumulated Depreciation—Equipment		63,800
Accounts Payable		4,100
Unearned Rent		1,500
Tina Stroud, Capital		57,700
Tina Stroud, Drawing	4,000	
Fees Revenue		171,200
Salaries and Wages Expense	60,200	
Advertising Expense	18,500	
Utilities Expense	15,100	
Repairs Expense	9,300	
Miscellaneous Expense	3,050	
	380,000	380,000

The data needed to determine year-end adjustments are as follows:

a. Fees revenue accrued at October 31 is $2,500.
b. Insurance expired during the year is $2,000.
c. Supplies on hand at October 31 are $450.
d. Depreciation of building for the year is $1,620.
e. Depreciation of equipment for the year is $3,160.
f. Accrued salaries and wages at October 31 are $2,000.
g. Unearned rent at October 31 is $500.

Instructions

1. Enter the trial balance on a ten-column work sheet and complete the work sheet. Add accounts as needed.
2. Prepare an income statement for the year ended October 31.
3. Prepare a statement of owner's equity for the year ended October 31. No additional investments were made during the year.
4. Prepare a balance sheet as of October 31.
5. Compute the percent of net income to total revenue for the year.

Problem 4–5A
Ledger accounts, work sheet, and related items

Objectives 1, 2, 3

GENERAL LEDGER

✓ 3. Net income: $33,655

The trial balance of Parachute Repairs at March 31, 2003, the end of the current year, and the data needed to determine year-end adjustments are as follows:

Parachute Repairs
Trial Balance
March 31, 2003

11	Cash	2,950	
13	Supplies	4,295	
14	Prepaid Insurance	2,735	
16	Equipment	40,650	
17	Accumulated Depreciation—Equipment		9,209
18	Trucks	36,300	
19	Accumulated Depreciation—Trucks		6,400
21	Accounts Payable		2,015
31	Jesse Yoder, Capital		26,426
32	Jesse Yoder, Drawing	5,000	
41	Service Revenue		91,950
51	Wages Expense	23,925	
53	Rent Expense	10,600	
55	Truck Expense	7,350	
59	Miscellaneous Expense	2,195	
		136,000	136,000

a. Supplies on hand at March 31 are $750.
b. Insurance premiums expired during year are $2,000.
c. Depreciation of equipment during year is $3,380.
d. Depreciation of trucks during year is $4,400.
e. Wages accrued but not paid at March 31 are $900.

Instructions

1. For each account listed in the trial balance, enter the balance in the appropriate Balance column of a four-column account and place a check mark (✓) in the Posting Reference column.
2. Enter the trial balance on a ten-column work sheet and complete the work sheet. Add accounts as needed.
3. Prepare an income statement, a statement of owner's equity (no additional investments were made during the year), and a balance sheet.

4. Journalize and post the adjusting entries, inserting balances in the accounts affected. The following additional accounts from Parachute's chart of accounts should be used: Wages Payable, 22; Supplies Expense, 52; Depreciation Expense—Equipment, 54; Depreciation Expense—Trucks, 56; Insurance Expense, 57.
5. Journalize and post the closing entries. (Income Summary is account #33 in the chart of accounts.) Indicate closed accounts by inserting a line in both Balance columns opposite the closing entry.
6. Prepare a post-closing trial balance.

PROBLEMS SERIES B

Problem 4–1B
Work sheet and related items

Objectives 1, 2, 3

SPREADSHEET
GENERAL LEDGER

✓ 2. Net income: $21,690

The trial balance of Ford's Laundry at October 31, 2003, the end of the current fiscal year, and the data needed to determine year-end adjustments are as follows:

Ford's Laundry
Trial Balance
October 31, 2003

Cash	3,100	
Laundry Supplies	6,560	
Prepaid Insurance	4,490	
Laundry Equipment	105,100	
Accumulated Depreciation		40,200
Accounts Payable		6,100
Ralph Edsel, Capital		37,800
Ralph Edsel, Drawing	2,000	
Laundry Revenue		150,900
Wages Expense	61,400	
Rent Expense	36,000	
Utilities Expense	13,650	
Miscellaneous Expense	2,700	
	235,000	235,000

a. Wages accrued but not paid at October 31 are $1,150.
b. Depreciation of equipment during the year is $7,000.
c. Laundry supplies on hand at October 31 are $1,750.
d. Insurance premiums expired during the year are $2,500.

Instructions

1. Enter the trial balance on a ten-column work sheet and complete the work sheet. Add accounts as needed.
2. Prepare an income statement, a statement of owner's equity (no additional investments were made during the year), and a balance sheet.
3. On the basis of the adjustment data in the work sheet, journalize the adjusting entries.
4. On the basis of the data in the work sheet, journalize the closing entries.

Problem 4–2B
Adjusting and closing entries; statement of owner's equity

Objectives 2, 3

The Epitome Company is a financial planning services firm owned and operated by Kerri Latimer. As of December 31, 2003, the end of the current fiscal year, the accountant for The Epitome Company prepared a work sheet, part of which is shown on the following page.

Instructions

1. Journalize the entries that were required to close the accounts at December 31.
2. Prepare a statement of owner's equity for the fiscal year ended December 31. There were no additional investments during the year.
3. If the balance of Kerri Latimer, Capital decreased $18,000 after the closing entries were posted, what was the amount of net income or net loss?

SPREADSHEET

The Epitome Company
Trial Balance
December 31, 2003

	Income Statement		Balance Sheet	
Cash			5,650	
Accounts Receivable			18,960	
Supplies			2,790	
Prepaid Insurance			2,500	
Land			55,000	
Buildings			120,000	
Accumulated Depreciation—Buildings				72,400
Equipment			82,000	
Accumulated Depreciation—Equipment				40,900
Accounts Payable				7,870
Salaries Payable				1,150
Taxes Payable				4,000
Unearned Rent				500
Kerri Latimer, Capital				111,750
Kerri Latimer, Drawing			10,000	
Service Fees Earned		174,260		
Rent Revenue		1,500		
Salary Expense	72,650			
Depreciation Expense—Equipment	11,100			
Rent Expense	9,000			
Supplies Expense	7,970			
Utilities Expense	5,300			
Depreciation Expense—Buildings	5,200			
Taxes Expense	4,150			
Insurance Expense	1,000			
Miscellaneous Expense	1,060			
	117,430	175,760	296,900	238,570
Net income	58,330			58,330
	175,760	175,760	296,900	296,900

If the working papers correlating with this textbook are not used, omit Problem 4–3B.

Problem 4–3B
Ledger accounts and work sheet, and related items

Objectives 1, 2, 3

The ledger and trial balance of Idiom.com as of January 31, 2003, the end of the first month of its current fiscal year, are presented in the working papers.

Instructions

1. Complete the ten-column work sheet. Data needed to determine the necessary adjusting entries are as follows:
   a. Service revenue accrued at January 31 is $2,750.
   b. Supplies on hand at January 31 are $500.
   c. Insurance premiums expired during January are $150.
   d. Depreciation of the building during January is $625.
   e. Depreciation of equipment during January is $200.
   f. Unearned rent at January 31 is $2,020.
   g. Wages accrued but not paid at January 31 are $600.
2. Prepare an income statement, a statement of owner's equity, and a balance sheet. (*Note:* The owner made an additional investment during the period.)
3. Journalize and post the adjusting entries, inserting balances in the accounts affected.
4. Journalize and post the closing entries. Indicate closed accounts by inserting a line in both Balance columns opposite the closing entry. Insert the new balance of the capital account.
5. Prepare a post-closing trial balance.

Problem 4–4B
Work sheet and financial statements

Objectives 1, 2, 3

GENERAL LEDGER

✓ 2. Net loss: $9,470

Sanguine Company offers legal consulting advice to death-row inmates. Sanguine Company prepared the following trial balance at June 30, 2003, the end of the current fiscal year:

Sanguine Company
Trial Balance
June 30, 2003

Cash	2,200	
Accounts Receivable	7,500	
Prepaid Insurance	1,800	
Supplies	1,350	
Land	50,000	
Building	137,500	
Accumulated Depreciation—Building		51,700
Equipment	90,100	
Accumulated Depreciation—Equipment		35,300
Accounts Payable		3,500
Unearned Rent		3,000
Sebrena Marsh, Capital		212,500
Sebrena Marsh, Drawing	10,000	
Fees Revenue		188,400
Salaries and Wages Expense	101,200	
Advertising Expense	58,200	
Utilities Expense	19,000	
Repairs Expense	11,500	
Miscellaneous Expense	4,050	
	494,400	494,400

The data needed to determine year-end adjustments are as follows:

a. Accrued fees revenue at June 30 are $1,750.
b. Insurance expired during the year is $800.
c. Supplies on hand at June 30 are $650.
d. Depreciation of building for the year is $1,620.
e. Depreciation of equipment for the year is $3,500.
f. Accrued salaries and wages at June 30 are $1,050.
g. Unearned rent at June 30 is $1,000.

Instructions

1. Enter the trial balance on a ten-column work sheet and complete the work sheet. Add accounts as needed.
2. Prepare an income statement for the year ended June 30.
3. Prepare a statement of owner's equity for the year ended June 30. No additional investments were made during the year.
4. Prepare a balance sheet as of June 30.
5. Compute the percent of total revenue to total assets for the year.

Problem 4–5B
Ledger accounts, work sheet, and related items

Objectives 1, 2, 3

The trial balance of Dagwood Repairs at December 31, 2003, the end of the current year, is shown at the top of the following page. The data needed to determine year-end adjustments are as follows:

a. Supplies on hand at December 31 are $800.
b. Insurance premiums expired during year are $1,500.
c. Depreciation of equipment during year is $6,080.
d. Depreciation of trucks during year is $5,500.
e. Wages accrued but not paid at December 31 are $500.

✓ 2. Net income: $18,695

Dagwood Repairs
Trial Balance
December 31, 2003

11	Cash	1,825	
13	Supplies	3,820	
14	Prepaid Insurance	2,500	
16	Equipment	44,200	
17	Accumulated Depreciation—Equipment		9,050
18	Trucks	15,000	
19	Accumulated Depreciation—Trucks		27,100
21	Accounts Payable		4,015
31	Scott Waters, Capital		24,885
32	Scott Waters, Drawing	3,000	
41	Service Revenue		79,950
51	Wages Expense	22,010	
53	Rent Expense	10,100	
55	Truck Expense	9,350	
59	Miscellaneous Expense	3,195	
		145,000	145,000

Instructions

1. For each account listed in the trial balance, enter the balance in the appropriate Balance column of a four-column account and place a check mark (✓) in the Posting Reference column.
2. Enter the trial balance on a ten-column work sheet and complete the work sheet. Add accounts as needed.
3. Prepare an income statement, a statement of owner's equity (no additional investments were made during the year), and a balance sheet.
4. Journalize and post the adjusting entries, inserting balances in the accounts affected. The following additional accounts from Dagwood's chart of accounts should be used: Wages Payable, 22; Supplies Expense, 52; Depreciation Expense—Equipment, 54; Depreciation Expense—Trucks, 56; Insurance Expense, 57.
5. Journalize and post the closing entries. (Income Summary is account #33 in the chart of accounts.) Indicate closed accounts by inserting a line in both Balance columns opposite the closing entry.
6. Prepare a post-closing trial balance.

CONTINUING PROBLEM

✓ 2. Net income: $1,275

The unadjusted trial balance of Dancin Music as of December 31, 2002, along with the adjustment data for the two months ended December 31, 2002, are shown in Chapter 3.

Instructions
1. Prepare a ten-column work sheet.
2. Prepare an income statement, a statement of owner's equity, and a balance sheet. (*Note:* Lynn Kwan made investments in Dancin Music on November 1 and December 1, 2002.)
3. Journalize and post the closing entries. The income summary account is #33 in the ledger of Dancin Music. Indicate closed accounts by inserting a line in both Balance columns opposite the closing entry.
4. Prepare a post-closing trial balance.

COMPREHENSIVE PROBLEM 1

GENERAL
LEDGER

✓ 4. Net income: $7,925

For the past several years, Dustin Larkin has operated a part-time consulting business from his home. As of June 1, 2003, Dustin decided to move to rented quarters and to operate the business, which was to be known as Quixote Consulting, on a full-time basis. Quixote Consulting entered into the following transactions during June:

June 1. The following assets were received from Dustin Larkin: cash, $10,000; accounts receivable, $1,500; supplies, $1,250; and office equipment, $7,500. There were no liabilities received.
  1. Paid three months' rent on a lease rental contract, $4,500.
  2. Paid the premiums on property and casualty insurance policies, $1,800.
  4. Received cash from clients as an advance payment for services to be provided and recorded it as unearned fees, $3,000.
  5. Purchased additional office equipment on account from Crawford Company, $1,800.
  6. Received cash from clients on account, $800.
  10. Paid cash for a newspaper advertisement, $120.
  12. Paid Crawford Company for part of the debt incurred on June 5, $800.
  12. Recorded services provided on account for the period June 1–12, $2,250.
  14. Paid part-time receptionist for two weeks' salary, $400.
  17. Recorded cash from cash clients for fees earned during the period June 1–16, $3,175.
  18. Paid cash for supplies, $750.
  20. Recorded services provided on account for the period June 13–20, $1,100.
  24. Recorded cash from cash clients for fees earned for the period June 17–24, $1,850.
  26. Received cash from clients on account, $1,600.
  27. Paid part-time receptionist for two weeks' salary, $400.
  29. Paid telephone bill for June, $130.
  30. Paid electricity bill for June, $200.
  30. Recorded cash from cash clients for fees earned for the period June 25–30, $2,050.
  30. Recorded services provided on account for the remainder of June, $1,000.
  30. Dustin withdrew $4,500 for personal use.

Instructions

1. Journalize each transaction in a two-column journal, referring to the following chart of accounts in selecting the accounts to be debited and credited. (Do not insert the account numbers in the journal at this time.)

11	Cash	31	Dustin Larkin, Capital
12	Accounts Receivable	32	Dustin Larkin, Drawing
14	Supplies	41	Fees Earned
15	Prepaid Rent	51	Salary Expense
16	Prepaid Insurance	52	Rent Expense
18	Office Equipment	53	Supplies Expense
19	Accumulated Depreciation	54	Depreciation Expense
21	Accounts Payable	55	Insurance Expense
22	Salaries Payable	59	Miscellaneous Expense
23	Unearned Fees		

2. Post the journal to a ledger of four-column accounts.
3. Prepare a trial balance as of June 30, 2003, on a ten-column work sheet, listing all the accounts in the order given in the ledger. Complete the work sheet, using the following adjustment data:
  a. Insurance expired during June is $150.
  b. Supplies on hand on June 30 are $1,020.
  c. Depreciation of office equipment for June is $500.
  d. Accrued receptionist salary on June 30 is $120.
  e. Rent expired during June is $1,500.
  f. Unearned fees on June 30 are $2,000.
4. Prepare an income statement, a statement of owner's equity, and a balance sheet.

(continued)

5. Journalize and post the adjusting entries.
6. Journalize and post the closing entries. (Income Summary is account #33 in the chart of accounts.) Indicate closed accounts by inserting a line in both Balance columns opposite the closing entry.
7. Prepare a post-closing trial balance.

SPECIAL ACTIVITIES

Activity 4–1
Van Dyck Co.
Ethics and professional conduct in business

Van Dyck Co. is a graphics arts design consulting firm. Chadwick Joiner, its treasurer and vice president of finance, has prepared a classified balance sheet as of October 31, 2003, the end of its fiscal year. This balance sheet will be submitted with Van Dyck's loan application to Western Trust & Savings Bank.

In the Current Assets section of the balance sheet, Chadwick reported a $50,000 receivable from Christie Shariff, the president of Van Dyck, as a trade account receivable. Christie borrowed the money from Van Dyck in February 2002 for a down payment on a new home. She has orally assured Chadwick that she will pay off the account receivable within the next year. Chadwick reported the $50,000 in the same manner on the preceding year's balance sheet.

Evaluate whether it is acceptable for Chadwick Joiner to prepare the October 31, 2003 balance sheet in the manner indicated above.

Activity 4–2
Flanders Supplies Co.
Financial statements

The following is an excerpt from a telephone conversation between Gail Richie, president of Flanders Supplies Co., and Gary Weir, owner of On-Time Employment Co.

Gail: Gary, you're going to have to do a better job of finding me a new computer programmer. That last guy was great at programming, but he didn't have any common sense.
Gary: What do you mean? The guy had a master's degree with straight A's.
Gail: Yes, well, last month he developed a new financial reporting system. He said we could do away with manually preparing a work sheet and financial statements. The computer would automatically generate our financial statements with "a push of a button."
Gary: So what's the big deal? Sounds to me like it would save you time and effort.
Gail: Right! The balance sheet showed a minus for supplies!
Gary: Minus supplies? How can that be?
Gail: That's what I asked.
Gary: So, what did he say?
Gail: Well, after he checked the program, he said that it must be right. The minuses were greater than the pluses . . .
Gary: Didn't he know that supplies can't have a credit balance—it must have a debit balance?
Gail: He asked me what a debit and credit were.
Gary: I see your point.

1. Comment on (a) the desirability of computerizing Flanders Supplies Co.'s financial reporting system, (b) the elimination of the work sheet in a computerized accounting system, and (c) the computer programmer's lack of accounting knowledge.
2. Explain to the programmer why supplies could not have a credit balance.

Activity 4–3
Megabit.com
Financial statements

Assume that you recently accepted a position with the Big Timber National Bank as an assistant loan officer. As one of your first duties, you have been assigned the responsibility of evaluating a loan request for $50,000 from Megabit.com, a small proprietorship. In support of the loan application, Erica Salley, owner, submitted a "Statement of Accounts" (trial balance) for the first year of operations ended December 31, 2003.

1. Explain to Erica Salley why a set of financial statements (income statement, statement of owner's equity, and balance sheet) would be useful to you in evaluating the loan request.

2. In discussing the "Statement of Accounts" with Erica Salley, you discovered that the accounts had not been adjusted at December 31. Analyze the "Statement of Accounts" (shown below) and indicate possible adjusting entries that might be necessary before an accurate set of financial statements could be prepared.

Megabit.com
Statement of Accounts
December 31, 2003

Cash	3,120	
Billings Due from Others	10,150	
Supplies (chemicals, etc.)	14,950	
Trucks	32,750	
Equipment	26,150	
Amounts Owed to Others		6,700
Investment in Business		57,260
Service Revenue		117,300
Wages Expense	70,100	
Utilities Expense	16,900	
Rent Expense	4,800	
Insurance Expense	1,400	
Other Expenses	940	
	181,260	181,260

3. ◖▬▬▶ Assuming that an accurate set of financial statements will be submitted by Erica Salley in a few days, what other considerations or information would you require before making a decision on the loan request?

Activity 4–4
Into the Real World
Compare balance sheets

In groups of three or four, compare the balance sheets of two different companies, and present to the class a summary of the similarities and differences of the two companies. You may obtain the balance sheets you need from one of the following sources:

1. Your school or local library.
2. The investor relations department of each company.
3. The company's web site on the Internet.
4. EDGAR (Electronic Data Gathering, Analysis, and Retrieval), the electronic archives of financial statements filed with the Securities and Exchange Commission.

SEC documents can be retrieved using the EdgarScan™ service from Pricewaterhouse-Coopers at **edgarscan.pwcglobal.com**. To obtain annual report information, key in a company name in the appropriate space. EdgarScan will list the reports available to you for the company you've selected. Select the most recent annual report filing, identified as a 10-K or 10-K405. EdgarScan provides an outline of the report, including the separate financial statements, which can also be selected in an Excel spreadsheet.

ANSWERS TO SELF-EXAMINATION QUESTIONS

Matching

1.	T	3.	L	5.	J	7.	O	9.	K	11.	R	13.	G	15.	P
2.	E	4.	F	6.	I	8.	H	10.	A	12.	U	14.	D	16.	S

Multiple Choice

1. **C** The drawing account, M. E. Jones, Drawing (answer C), would be extended to the Balance Sheet columns of the work sheet. Utilities Expense (answer A), Rent Revenue (answer B), and Miscellaneous Expense (answer D) would all be extended to the Income Statement columns of the work sheet.

2. **D** Cash or other assets that are expected to be converted to cash or sold or used up within one year or less, through the normal operations of the business, are classified as current assets on the balance sheet. Accounts Receivable (answer D) is a current asset, since it will normally be converted to cash within one

year. Office Equipment (answer A), Land (answer B), and Accumulated Depreciation (answer C) are all reported in the property, plant, and equipment section of the balance sheet.

3. **B** The entry to close the owner's drawing account is to debit the owner's capital account and credit the drawing account (answer B).

4. **D** Since all revenue and expense accounts are closed at the end of the period, Fees Earned (answer A), Wages Expense (answer B), and Rent Expense (answer C) would all be closed to Income Summary. Accumulated

Depreciation (answer D) is a contra asset account that is not closed.

5. **B** Since the post-closing trial balance includes only balance sheet accounts (all of the revenue, expense, and drawing accounts are closed), Cash (answer A), Accumulated Depreciation (answer C), and J. C. Smith, Capital (answer D) would appear on the post-closing trial balance. Fees Earned (answer B) is a temporary account that is closed prior to preparing the post-closing trial balance.

Accounting Systems and Internal Controls

5

o b j e c t i v e s

After studying this chapter, you should be able to:

1 Define an accounting system and describe its implementation.

2 List the three objectives of internal control, and define and give examples of the five elements of internal control.

3 Journalize and post transactions in a manual accounting system that uses subsidiary ledgers and special journals.

4 Describe and give examples of additional subsidiary ledgers and modified special journals.

5 Apply computerized accounting to the revenue and collection cycle.

ontrols are a part of your everyday life. At one extreme, laws are used to govern your behavior. For example, the speed limit is a control on your driving, designed for traffic safety. In addition, you are also affected by many nonlegal controls. For example, you can keep credit card receipts in order to compare your transactions to the monthly credit card statement. Comparing receipts to the monthly statement is a control designed to catch mistakes made by the credit card company. Likewise, recording checks in your checkbook is a control that you can use at the end of the month to verify the accuracy of your bank statement. In addition, banks give you a personal identification number (PIN) as a control against unauthorized access to your cash if you lose your automated teller machine (ATM) card. Dairies use freshness dating on their milk containers as a control to prevent the purchase or sale of soured milk. As you can see, you use and encounter controls every day.

Just as there are many examples of controls throughout society, businesses must also implement controls to help guide the behavior of their employees toward business objectives. For example, some businesses require you to punch a time card when you enter and leave the workplace. This is a control used to verify that you get paid for the actual hours you worked.

In this chapter, we will discuss controls that can be included in accounting systems to provide reasonable assurance that the financial statements are reliable. We will apply the principles of accounting systems design to manual systems as well as computerized accounting systems.

Basic Accounting Systems

objective 1

Define an accounting system and describe its implementation.

In the four previous chapters, we developed an accounting system for NetSolutions. An **accounting system** is the methods and procedures for collecting, classsifying, summarizing, and reporting a business's financial and operating information. The accounting system for most businesses, however, is more complex than NetSolutions'. Accounting systems for large businesses must be able to collect, accumulate, and report many types of transactions. For example, **United Airlines'** accounting system collects and maintains information on ticket reservations, credit card collections, aircraft maintenance, employee hours, frequent-flier mileage balances, fuel consumption, and travel agent commissions, just to name a few. As you might expect, United Airlines' accounting system has evolved as the company has grown.

Accounting systems evolve through a three-step process as a business grows and changes. The first step in this process is **analysis**, which consists of (1) identifying the needs of those who use the business's financial information and (2) determining how the system should provide this information. For NetSolutions, we determined that Chris Clark would need financial statements for the new business. In the second step, the system is **designed** so that it will meet the users' needs. For NetSolutions, a very basic manual system was designed. This system included a chart of accounts, a two-column journal, and a general ledger. Finally, the system is **implemented** and used. For NetSolutions, the system was used to record transactions and prepare financial statements.

Once a system has been implemented, **feedback**, or input, from the users of the information can be used to analyze and improve the system. For example, in

Hershey Foods learned the hard way about the importance of careful analysis and design prior to implementing a complex information system. Hershey implemented a $112 million computer system by using a "big-bang" start-up, rather than using a gradual implementation strategy. When the switch was thrown, the company ran into immediate problems shipping orders to customers. As a result, profits were cut by 20%, and product shipments during the all-important Halloween selling season were delayed.

later chapters we will see that Net-Solutions will expand its chart of accounts as it becomes a more complex business.

Internal controls and information processing methods are essential in an accounting system. **Internal controls** are the policies and procedures that protect assets from misuse, ensure that business information is accurate, and ensure that laws and regulations are being followed. **Processing methods** are the means by which the system collects, summarizes, and reports accounting information. These methods may be either *manual* or *computerized*. In the following sections, we will discuss internal controls, manual accounting systems that use special journals, and computerized accounting systems.

Internal Control

objective 2

List the three objectives of internal control, and define and give examples of the five elements of internal control.

Businesses use internal controls to guide their operations and prevent abuses of their systems. For example, assume that you own and manage a lawn care service. Your business uses several employee teams, and you provide each team with a vehicle and lawn equipment. What are some of the issues you would face as a manager in controlling the operations of this business? Below are some examples.

- Lawn care must be provided on time.
- The quality of lawn care services must meet customer expectations.
- Employees must provide work for the hours they are paid.
- Lawn care equipment should be used for business purposes only.
- Vehicles should be used for business purposes only.
- Customers must be billed and bills collected for services rendered.

Internal controls protect assets, ensure that business information is accurate, and ensure that regulations are being followed.

How would you address these issues? You could, for example, develop a schedule at the beginning of each day and then inspect the work at the end of the day to verify that it was completed according to quality standards. You could have "surprise" inspections by arriving on site at random times to verify that the teams are working according to schedule. You could require employees to "clock in" at the beginning of the day and "clock out" at the end of the day to make sure that they are paid for hours worked. You could require the work teams to return the vehicles and equipment to a central location to prevent unauthorized use. You could keep a log of odometer readings at the end of each day to verify that the vehicle has not been used for "joy riding." You could bill customers after you have inspected the work and then monitor the collection of all receivables. All of these are examples of internal control.

Objectives of Internal Control

The objectives of internal control are to provide reasonable assurance that:

1. assets are safeguarded and used for business purposes.
2. business information is accurate.
3. employees comply with laws and regulations.

Internal control can safeguard assets by preventing theft, fraud, misuse, or misplacement. One of the most serious breaches of internal control is employee fraud. **Employee fraud** is the intentional act of deceiving an employer for personal gain. Such deception may range from purposely overstating expenses on a travel expense report in order to receive a higher reimbursement to embezzling millions of dollars through complex schemes.

Accurate business information is necessary for operating a business successfully. The safeguarding of assets and accurate information often go hand-in-hand. The reason is that employees attempting to defraud a business will also need to adjust the accounting records in order to hide the fraud.

Businesses must comply with applicable laws, regulations, and financial reporting standards. Examples of such standards and laws include environmental regulations, contract terms, safety regulations, and generally accepted accounting principles (GAAP).

Elements of Internal Control

How does management achieve its internal control objectives? Management is responsible for designing and applying five **elements of internal control** to meet the three internal control objectives. These elements are:[1]

1. the control environment
2. risk assessment
3. control procedures
4. monitoring
5. information and communication

The elements of internal control are illustrated in Exhibit 1. In this exhibit, the elements of internal control form an umbrella over the business to protect it from control threats. The business's control environment is represented by the size of the umbrella. Risk assessment, control procedures, and monitoring are the fabric that keeps the umbrella from leaking. Information and communication links the umbrella to management. In the following paragraphs, we discuss each of these elements.

Control Environment

A business's control environment is the overall attitude of management and employees about the importance of controls. One of the factors that influences the control environment is *management's philosophy and operating style.* A management that overemphasizes operating goals and deviates from control policies may indirectly encourage employees to ignore controls. For example, the pressure to achieve revenue targets may encourage employees to fraudulently record sham sales. On the other hand, a management that emphasizes the importance of controls and encourages adherence to control policies will create an effective control environment.

The business's *organizational structure,* which is the framework for planning and controlling operations, also influences the control environment. For example, a department store chain might organize each of its stores as separate business units. Each store manager has full authority over pricing and other operating activities. In such a structure, each store manager has the responsibility for establishing an effective control environment.

---

[1] *Internal Control—Integrated Framework by the Committee of Sponsoring Organizations* of the Treadway Commission (COSO), pp. 12–14. This document provides a professionally sponsored framework for internal control.

Exhibit 1 Elements of Internal Control

Personnel policies also affect the control environment. Personnel policies involve the hiring, training, evaluation, compensation, and promotion of employees. In addition, job descriptions, employee codes of ethics, and conflict-of-interest policies are part of the personnel policies. Such policies and procedures can enhance the internal control environment if they provide reasonable assurance that only competent, honest employees are hired and retained.

Risk Assessment

All organizations face risks. Examples of risk include changes in customer requirements, competitive threats, regulatory changes, changes in economic factors such as interest rates, and employee violations of company policies and procedures. Management should assess these risks and take necessary actions to control them, so that the objectives of internal control can be achieved.

Once risks are identified, they can be analyzed to estimate their significance, to assess their likelihood of occurring, and to determine actions that will minimize them. For example, the manager of a warehouse operation may analyze the risk of employee back injuries, which might give rise to lawsuits. If the manager determines that the risk is significant, the company may take action by purchasing back support braces for its warehouse employees and requiring them to wear the braces.

Control Procedures

Control procedures are established to provide reasonable assurance that business goals will be achieved, including the prevention of fraud. In the following paragraphs, we will briefly discuss control procedures that can be integrated throughout the accounting system. These procedures are listed in Exhibit 2.

 An accounting clerk for the Grant County (Washington) Alcoholism Program was in charge of collecting money, making deposits, and keeping the records. While the clerk was away on maternity leave, the replacement clerk discovered a fraud: $17,800 in fees had been collected but had been hidden for personal gain.

Competent Personnel, Rotating Duties, and Mandatory Vacations. The successful operation of an accounting system requires procedures to ensure that people are able to perform the duties to which they are assigned. Hence, it is necessary that all accounting employees be adequately trained and supervised in performing their jobs. It may also be advisable to rotate duties of clerical personnel and mandate vacations for nonclerical personnel. These policies encourage employees to adhere to prescribed procedures. In addition, existing errors or fraud may be detected.

Separating Responsibilities for Related Operations. To decrease the possibility of inefficiency, errors, and fraud, the responsibility for related operations should be divided among two or more persons. For example, the responsibilities

Exhibit 2 Internal Control
Procedures

for purchasing, receiving, and paying for computer supplies should be divided among three persons or departments. If the same person orders supplies, verifies the receipt of the supplies, and pays the supplier, the following abuses are possible:

1. Orders may be placed on the basis of friendship with a supplier, rather than on price, quality, and other objective factors.
2. The quantity and quality of supplies received may not be verified, thus causing payment for supplies not received or poor-quality supplies.
3. Supplies may be stolen by the employee.
4. The validity and accuracy of invoices may be verified carelessly, thus causing the payment of false or inaccurate invoices.

The "checks and balances" provided by dividing responsibilities among various departments requires no duplication of effort. The business documents prepared by one department are designed to coordinate with and support those prepared by other departments.

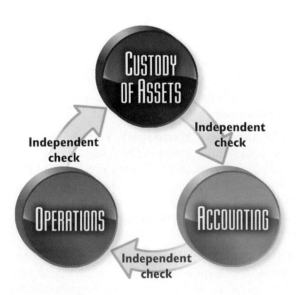

Separating Operations, Custody of Assets, and Accounting. Control policies should establish the responsibilities for various business activities. To reduce the possibility of errors and fraud, the responsibilities for operations, custody of assets, and accounting should be separated. The accounting records then serve as an independent check on the individuals who have custody of the assets and who engage in the business operations. For example, the employees entrusted with handling cash receipts from credit customers should not record cash receipts in the accounting records. To do so would allow employees to borrow or steal cash and hide the theft in the records. Likewise, if those engaged in operating activities also record the results of operations, they could distort the accounting reports to show favorable results. For example, a store manager whose year-end bonus is based upon operating profits might be tempted to record fictitious sales in order to receive a larger bonus.

Over $700,000 of child support money disappeared over seven years due to the alleged falsification of checks by an accountant in Indiana's Family and Social Services Administration. The fraud could have been discovered, according to the State Examiner, if the agency reconciled its books, controlled access to blank checks, and used receipts.

Why is separation of duties considered a control procedure?

Internal control is enhanced by separating the control of a transaction from the record-keeping function. Fraud is more easily committed when a single individual controls both the transaction and the accounting for the transaction.

Proofs and Security Measures. Proofs and security measures should be used to safeguard assets and ensure reliable accounting data. This control procedure applies to many different techniques, such as authorization, approval, and reconciliation procedures. For example, employees who travel on company business may be required to obtain a department manager's approval on a travel request form.

Other examples of control procedures include the use of bank accounts and other measures to ensure the safety of cash and valuable documents. A cash register that displays the amount recorded for each sale and provides the customer a printed receipt can be an effective part of the internal control structure. An all-night convenience store could use the following security measures to deter robberies:

1. Locate the cash register near the door, so that it is fully visible from outside the store; have two employees work late hours; employ a security guard.
2. Deposit cash in the bank daily, before 5 p.m.
3. Keep only small amounts of cash on hand after 5 p.m. by depositing excess cash in a store safe that can't be opened by employees on duty.
4. Install cameras and alarm systems.

Monitoring

Monitoring the internal control system locates weaknesses and improves control effectiveness. The internal control system can be monitored through either ongoing efforts by management or by separate evaluations. Ongoing monitoring efforts may include observing both employee behavior and warning signs from the accounting system. The indicators shown in Exhibit 3 may be clues to internal control problems.[2]

Exhibit 3 Indicators of Internal Control Problems

CLUES TO POTENTIAL PROBLEMS

Warning signs with regard to people

Warning signs from the accounting system

Warning signs with regard to people	Warning signs from the accounting system
1. Abrupt change in lifestyle (without winning the lottery).	1. Missing documents or gaps in transaction numbers (could mean documents are being used for fraudulent transactions).
2. Close social relationships with suppliers.	2. An unusual increase in customer refunds (refunds may be phony).
3. Refusing to take a vacation.	3. Differences between daily cash receipts and bank deposits (could mean receipts are pocketed before being deposited).
4. Frequent borrowing from other employees.	4. Sudden increase in slow payments (employee may be pocketing the payment).
5. Excessive use of alcohol or drugs.	5. Backlog in recording transactions (possibly an attempt to delay detection of fraud).

[2] Edwin C. Bliss, "Employee Theft," *Boardroom Reports*, July 15, 1994, pp. 5–6.

In one of the largest frauds ever committed against a university, a former financial aid officer for **New York University** was charged with stealing $4.1 million from the state of New York. The aid officer allegedly falsified over a thousand tuition assistance checks to students who were not entitled to receive aid and who did not know about the checks. The aid officer deposited the bogus checks for personal use. The initial evidence of the fraud was the officer's spending of $785,000 on expensive jewelry.

Separate monitoring evaluations are generally performed when there are major changes in strategy, senior management, business structure, or operations. In large businesses, internal auditors who are independent of operations normally are responsible for monitoring the internal control system. Internal auditors can report issues and concerns to an audit committee of the board of directors, who are independent of management. In addition, external auditors also evaluate internal control as a normal part of their annual financial statement audit.

Information and Communication

Information and communication are essential elements of internal control. Information about the control environment, risk assessment, control procedures, and monitoring are needed by management to guide operations and ensure compliance with reporting, legal, and regulatory requirements.

Management can also use external information to assess events and conditions that impact decision making and external reporting. For example, management uses information from the Financial Accounting Standards Board (FASB) to assess the impact of possible changes in reporting standards.

BUSINESS ON STAGE

Accounting Systems and Profit Measurement

A Greek restaurant owner in Canada had his own system of accounting. He kept his accounts payable in a cigar box on the left-hand side of his cash register, his daily cash returns in the cash register, and his receipts for paid bills in another cigar box on the right. A truly "manual" system.

When his youngest son graduated as an accountant, he was appalled by his father's primitive methods. "I don't know how you can run a business that way," he said. "How do you know what your profits are?"

"Well, son," the father replied, "when I got off the boat from Greece, I had nothing but the pants I was wearing. Today, your brother is a doctor. You are an accountant. Your sister is a speech therapist. Your

mother and I have a nice car, a city house, and a country home. We have a good business, and everything is paid for...."

"So, you add all that together, subtract the pants, and there's your profit!" ∎

Manual Accounting Systems

o b j e c t i v e 3

Journalize and post transactions in a manual accounting system that uses subsidiary ledgers and special journals.

After the internal control procedures have been developed, the basic processing method must be selected. Accounting systems may be either manual or computerized. Since an understanding of manual accounting systems assists managers in recognizing the relationships that exist between accounting data and accounting reports, we illustrate manual systems first.

In preceding chapters, all transactions for NetSolutions were manually recorded in an all-purpose (two-column) journal. The journal entries were then posted individually to the accounts in the ledger. Such manual accounting systems are simple to use and easy to understand. Manually kept records may serve a business reasonably well when the amount of data collected, stored, and used is relatively small. For a large business with a large database, however, such manual processing is too costly and time-consuming. For example, a large company such as **AT&T** has millions of long-distance telephone fees earned on account with millions of customers daily. Each telephone fee on account requires an entry debiting Accounts Receivable and crediting Fees Earned. In addition, a record of each customer's receivable must be kept. Clearly, a simple manual system would not serve the business needs of AT&T.

When a business has a large number of similar transactions, using an all-purpose journal is inefficient and impractical. In such cases, subsidiary ledgers and special journals are useful. In addition, the manual system can be supplemented or replaced by a computerized system. Although we will illustrate the manual use of subsidiary ledgers and special journals, the basic principles described in the following paragraphs also apply to a computerized accounting system.

Subsidiary Ledgers

An accounting system should be designed to provide information on the amounts due from various customers (accounts receivable) and amounts owed to various creditors (accounts payable). A separate account for each customer and creditor could be added to the ledger. However, as the number of customers and creditors increases, the ledger becomes awkward to use when it includes many customers and creditors.

A large number of individual accounts with a common characteristic can be grouped together in a separate ledger called a **subsidiary ledger**. The primary ledger, which contains all of the balance sheet and income statement accounts, is then called the **general ledger**. Each subsidiary ledger is represented in the general ledger by a summarizing account, called a **controlling account**. The sum of the balances of the accounts in a subsidiary ledger must equal the balance of the related controlling account. Thus, you may think of a subsidiary ledger as a secondary ledger that supports a controlling account in the general ledger.

> **The sum of the balances of the subsidiary ledger accounts must equal the balance of the related controlling account.**

The individual accounts with customers are arranged in alphabetical order in a subsidiary ledger called the **accounts receivable subsidiary ledger**, or **customers ledger**. The controlling account in the general ledger that summarizes the debits and credits to the individual customer accounts is *Accounts Receivable*. The individual accounts with creditors are arranged in alphabetical order in a subsidiary ledger called the **accounts payable subsidiary ledger**, or **creditors ledger**. The related controlling account in the general ledger is *Accounts Payable*. The relationship between the general ledger and these subsidiary ledgers is illustrated in Exhibit 4.

Special Journals

One method of processing data more efficiently in a manual accounting system is to expand the all-purpose two-column journal to a multicolumn journal. Each column in a multicolumn journal is used only for recording transactions that affect a certain account. For example, a special column could be used only for recording debits to the cash account, and another special column could be used only for recording credits to the cash account. The addition of the two special columns would eliminate the writing of *Cash* in the journal for every receipt and every payment of cash. Also, there would be no need to post each individual debit and credit to the cash account. Instead, the *Cash Dr.* and *Cash Cr.* columns could be totaled periodically and only the totals posted. In a similar way, special columns could be added for recording credits to Fees Earned, debits and credits to Accounts Receivable and Accounts Payable, and for other entries that are often repeated.

An all-purpose multicolumn journal may be adequate for a small business that has many transactions of a similar nature. However, a journal that has many columns for recording many different types of transactions is impractical for larger businesses.

Exhibit 4 General Ledger and Subsidiary Ledgers

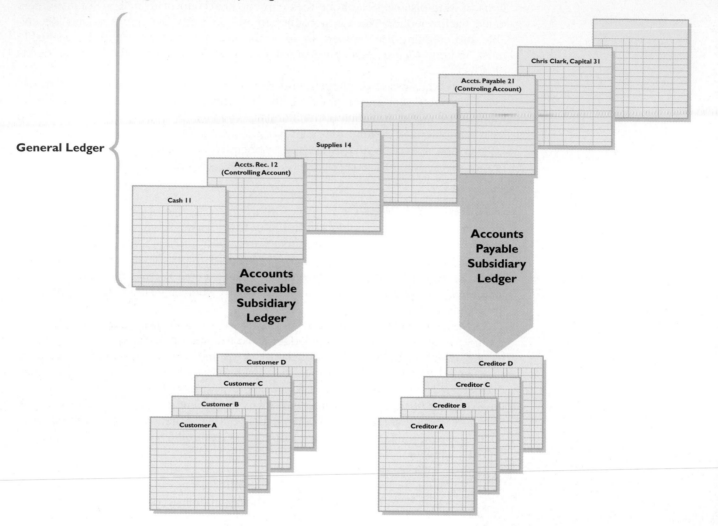

The next logical extension of the accounting system is to replace the single multicolumn journal with several **special journals**. Each special journal is designed to be used for recording a single kind of transaction that occurs frequently. For example, since most businesses have many transactions in which cash is paid out, they will likely use a special journal for recording cash payments. Likewise, they will use another special journal for recording cash receipts. Special journals are a method of summarizing transactions, which is a basic feature of any accounting system.

The format and number of special journals that a business uses depends upon the nature of the business. A business that gives credit might use a special journal designed for recording only revenue from services provided on credit. On the other hand, a business that does not give credit would have no need for such a journal. In other cases, record-keeping costs may be reduced by using supporting documents as special journals.

The transactions that occur most often in a small- to medium-size service business and the special journals in which they are recorded are as follows:

> **Special journals are a method of summarizing transactions.**

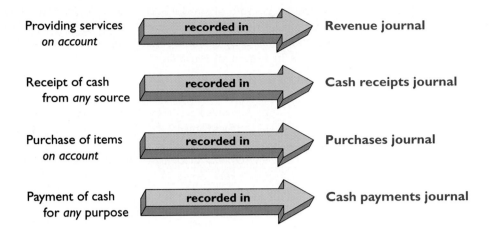

Providing services on account	recorded in →	Revenue journal
Receipt of cash from *any* source	recorded in →	Cash receipts journal
Purchase of items on account	recorded in →	Purchases journal
Payment of cash for *any* purpose	recorded in →	Cash payments journal

The all-purpose two-column journal, called the general journal or simply the **journal**, can be used for entries that do not fit into any of the special journals. For example, adjusting and closing entries are recorded in the general journal.

In the following paragraphs, we illustrate special journals and subsidiary ledgers in a manual accounting system for NetSolutions. To simplify the illustration, we will use a minimum number of transactions. We will focus our discussion on two common operating cycles: (1) the revenue and collection cycle and (2) the purchase and payment cycle. We will assume that NetSolutions had the following selected general ledger balances on March 1, 2003:

Account Number	Account	Balance
11	Cash	$6,200
12	Accounts Receivable	3,400
14	Supplies	2,500
18	Office Equipment	2,500
21	Accounts Payable	1,230

Manual Accounting System: The Revenue and Collection Cycle

The **revenue and collection cycle** for NetSolutions consists of providing services on account and collecting cash from customers. Revenues earned on account create a customer receivable and will be recorded in a revenue journal. Customers' accounts receivable are collected and will be recorded in a cash receipts journal.

Internal control is enhanced by separating the function of recording revenue transactions in the revenue journal from recording cash collections in the cash receipts journal. For example, if these duties are separated, it is more difficult for one person to embezzle cash collections and manipulate the accounting records.

Revenue Journal

The revenue journal is used only for recording **fees earned on account**. *Cash fees earned would be recorded in the cash receipts* *journal*. The sale of products is recorded in a **sales journal**, which is similar to the revenue journal. We will compare the efficiency of using a revenue journal with a general journal by assuming that NetSolutions recorded the following revenue transactions in a general journal:

2003 Mar.	2	Accounts Receivable—MyMusicClub.com	12/✔	2 2 0 0 00	
		Fees Earned	41		2 2 0 0 00
	6	Accounts Receivable—RapZone.com	12/✔	1 7 5 0 00	
		Fees Earned	41		1 7 5 0 00
	18	Accounts Receivable—Web Cantina	12/✔	2 6 5 0 00	
		Fees Earned	41		2 6 5 0 00
	27	Accounts Receivable—MyMusicClub.com	12/✔	3 0 0 0 00	
		Fees Earned	41		3 0 0 0 00

> The general journal entry on March 2 is posted as a $2,200 debit to Accounts Receivable in the general ledger, a $2,200 debit to MyMusicClub.com in the accounts receivable subsidiary ledger, and a $2,200 credit to Fees Earned in the general ledger.

For these four transactions, NetSolutions recorded eight account titles and eight amounts. In addition, NetSolutions made 12 postings to the ledgers—four to Accounts Receivable in the general ledger, four to the accounts receivable subsidiary ledger (indicated by each check mark), and four to Fees Earned in the general ledger. These transactions could be recorded more efficiently in a revenue journal, as shown in Exhibit 5. In each revenue transaction, the amount of the debit to Accounts Receivable is the same as the amount of the credit to Fees Earned. Therefore, only a single amount column is necessary. The date, invoice number, customer name, and amount are entered separately for each transaction.

Exhibit 5 Revenue Journal

				REVENUE JOURNAL		PAGE 35
	Date	Invoice No.		Account Debited	Post. Ref.	Accts. Rec. Dr. Fees Earned Cr.
1	2003 Mar. 2	615		MyMusicClub.com		2 2 0 0 00
2	6	616		RapZone.com		1 7 5 0 00
3	18	617		Web Cantina		2 6 5 0 00
4	27	618		MyMusicClub.com		3 0 0 0 00
5	31					9 6 0 0 00

The basic procedure of posting from a revenue journal is shown in Exhibit 6. A single monthly total is posted to Accounts Receivable and Fees Earned in the general ledger. Each transaction, such as the $2,200 debit to MyMusicClub.com, must also be posted individually to a customer account in the accounts receivable subsidiary ledger. These postings to customer accounts should be made frequently. In this way, management has information on the current balance of each customer's account. Since the balances in the customer accounts are usually debit balances, the three-column account form shown in the exhibit is often used.

Exhibit 6 Revenue Journal
Postings to Ledgers

REVENUE JOURNAL   **PAGE 35**

	Date	Invoice No.	Account Debited	Post. Ref.	Accts. Rec. Dr. Fees Earned Cr.	
	2003					
1	March 2	615	MyMusicClub.com	✔	2,200	1
2	6	616	RapZone.com	✔	1,750	2
3	18	617	Web Cantina	✔	2,650	3
4	27	618	MyMusicClub.com	✔	3,000	4
5	31				9,600	5
6					(12) (41)	6

GENERAL LEDGER

ACCOUNT   Accounts Receivable   **Account No. 12**

Date	Item	Post. Ref.	Dr.	Cr.	Balance Dr.	Balance Cr.
2003						
March 1	Balance	✔			3,400	
31		R35	9,600		13,000	

ACCOUNT   Fees Earned   **Account No. 41**

Date	Item	Post. Ref.	Dr.	Cr.	Balance Dr.	Balance Cr.
2003						
March 31		R35		9,600		9,600

ACCOUNTS RECEIVABLE SUBSIDIARY LEDGER

NAME: MyMusicClub.com

Date	Item	Post. Ref.	Dr.	Cr.	Balance
2003					
March 2		R35	2,200		2,200
27		R35	3,000		5,200

NAME: RapZone.com

Date	Item	Post. Ref.	Dr.	Cr.	Balance
2003					
March 6		R35	1,750		1,750

NAME: Web Cantina

Date	Item	Post. Ref.	Dr.	Cr.	Balance
2003					
March 1	Balance	✔			3,400
18		R35	2,650		6,050

What is the relationship between the revenue journal and the ledger accounts?

Revenue transactions are recorded and summarized in the revenue journal. Thus, the revenue journal is the source of postings to the subsidiary and general ledger accounts. The fees earned from services provided on account to individual customers are posted from the revenue journal to the customer subsidiary ledger accounts. At the end of the period, the total of the revenue journal column is then posted as a debit to the accounts receivable controlling account and a credit to the revenue account.

To provide a trail of the entries posted to the subsidiary ledger, the source of these entries is indicated in the *Posting Reference* column of each account by inserting the letter *R* (for revenue journal) and the page number of the revenue journal. A check mark (✔) instead of a number is then inserted in the *Posting Reference* column of the revenue journal, as shown in Exhibit 6.

If a customer's account has a credit balance, that fact should be indicated by an asterisk or parentheses in the *Balance* column. When an account's balance is zero, a line may be drawn in the *Balance* column.

At the end of each month, the amount column of the revenue journal is totaled. This total is equal to the sum of the month's debits to the individual accounts in the subsidiary ledger. It is posted in the general ledger as a debit to Accounts Receivable and a credit to Fees Earned, as shown in Exhibit 6. The respective account numbers (12 and 41) are then inserted below the total in the revenue journal to indicate that the posting is completed, as shown in Exhibit 6. In this way, all of the transactions for fees earned during the month are posted to the general ledger only once—at the end of the month—greatly simplifying the posting process.

Cash Receipts Journal

All transactions that involve the receipt of cash are recorded in a **cash receipts journal**. Thus, the cash receipts journal has a column entitled *Cash Dr.*, as shown in Exhibit 7. All transactions recorded in the cash receipts journal will involve an entry in the *Cash Dr.* column. For example, on March 28 NetSolutions received cash of $2,200 from MyMusicClub.com and entered that amount in the *Cash Dr.* column.

The kinds of transactions in which cash is received and how often they occur determine the titles of the other columns. For NetSolutions, the most frequent source of cash is collections from customers. Thus, the cash receipts journal in Exhibit 7 has an *Accounts Receivable Cr.* column. On March 28, when MyMusicClub.com made a payment on its account, NetSolutions entered *MyMusicClub.com* in the *Account Credited* column and entered *2,200* in the *Accounts Receivable Cr.* column.

The *Other Accounts Cr.* column in Exhibit 7 is used for recording credits to any account for which there is no special credit column. For example, NetSolutions received cash on March 1 for rent. Since no special column exists for Rent Revenue, NetSolutions entered *Rent Revenue* in the *Account Credited* column and entered *400* in the *Other Accounts Cr.* column.

Postings from the cash receipts journal to the ledgers of NetSolutions are also shown in Exhibit 7. This posting process is similar to that of the revenue journal. At regular intervals, each amount in the *Other Accounts Cr.* column is posted to the proper account in the general ledger. The posting is indicated by inserting the account number in the *Posting Reference* column of the cash receipts journal. The posting reference *CR* (for cash receipts journal) and the proper page number are inserted in the *Posting Reference* columns of the accounts.

The amounts in the *Accounts Receivable Cr.* column are posted individually to the customer accounts in the accounts receivable subsidiary ledger. These postings should be made frequently. The posting reference *CR* and the proper page number are inserted in the *Posting Reference* column of each customer's account. A check mark is placed in the *Posting Reference* column of the cash receipts journal to show that each amount has been posted. None of the individual amounts in the *Cash Dr.* column is posted separately.

At the end of the month, all of the amount columns are totaled. The debits should equal the credits. Because each amount in the *Other Accounts Cr.* column has been posted individually to a general ledger account, a check mark is inserted below the column total to indicate that no further action is needed. The totals of the *Accounts Receivable Cr.* and *Cash Dr.* columns are posted to the proper accounts in the general ledger, and their account numbers are inserted below the totals to show that the postings have been completed.

Accounts Receivable Control and Subsidiary Ledger

After all posting has been completed for the month, the sum of the balances in the accounts receivable subsidiary ledger should be compared with the balance of the accounts receivable controlling account in the general ledger. If the controlling account and the subsidiary ledger do not agree, the error or errors must be located and corrected. The balances of the individual customer accounts may be summarized in a schedule of accounts receivable. The total of NetSolutions' schedule of accounts receivable, $5,650, agrees with the balance of its accounts receivable controlling account on March 31, 2003, as shown below.

Accounts Receivable— (Controlling)		NetSolutions Schedule of Accounts Receivable March 31, 2003	
Balance, March 31, 2003	$5,650	MyMusicClub.com	$3,000
		RapZone.com	0
		Web Cantina	2,650
		Total accounts receivable	$5,650

Exhibit 7 Cash Receipts
Journal and Postings

CASH RECEIPTS JOURNAL — PAGE 14

	Date	Account Credited	Post. Ref.	Other Accounts Cr.	Accounts Receivable Cr.	Cash Dr.	
1	2003 March 1	Rent Revenue	42	400		400	1
2	19	Web Cantina	✔		3,400	3,400	2
3	28	MyMusicClub.com	✔		2,200	2,200	3
4	30	RapZone.com	✔		1,750	1,750	4
5	31			400	7,350	7,750	5
6				(✔)	(12)	(11)	6

GENERAL LEDGER

ACCOUNT Rent Revenue — Account No. 42

Date	Item	Post. Ref.	Dr.	Cr.	Balance Dr.	Balance Cr.
2003 March 1		CR14		400		400

ACCOUNT Accounts Receivable — Account No. 12

Date	Item	Post. Ref.	Dr.	Cr.	Balance Dr.	Balance Cr.
2003 March 1	Balance	✔			3,400	
31		R35	9,600		13,000	
31		CR14		7,350	5,650	

ACCOUNT Cash — Account No. 11

Date	Item	Post. Ref.	Dr.	Cr.	Balance Dr.	Balance Cr.
2003 March 1	Balance	✔			6,200	
31		CR14	7,750		13,950	

ACCOUNTS RECEIVABLE SUBSIDIARY LEDGER

NAME: MyMusicClub.com

Date	Item	Post. Ref.	Dr.	Cr.	Balance
2003 March 2		R35	2,200		2,200
27		R35	3,000		5,200
28		CR14		2,200	3,000

NAME: RapZone.com

Date	Item	Post. Ref.	Dr.	Cr.	Balance
2003 March 6		R35	1,750		1,750
30		CR14		1,750	—

NAME: Web Cantina

Date	Item	Post. Ref.	Dr.	Cr.	Balance
2003 March 1	Balance	✔			3,400
18		R35	2,650		6,050
19		CR14		3,400	2,650

PURCHASES ON ACCOUNT

SUPPLIER

NET-SOLUTIONS

PAYMENTS OF CASH

Manual Accounting System: The Purchase and Payment Cycle

The **purchase and payment cycle** for NetSolutions consists of purchases on account and payments of cash to suppliers. To make purchases of supplies and other items on account requires establishing a supplier account payable. These transactions will be recorded in a purchases journal. The payments of suppliers' accounts payable will be recorded in the cash payments journal.

Internal control is enhanced by separating the function of recording purchases in the purchases journal from recording cash payments in the cash payments journal. Separating duties in this way prevents an individual from establishing a fictitious supplier and then collecting payments for fictitious purchases from this supplier.

Purchases Journal

The **purchases journal** is designed for recording all **purchases on account**. *Cash purchases would be recorded in the cash payments* *journal*. The purchases journal has a column entitled *Accounts Payable Cr.* The purchases journal also has special columns for recording debits to the accounts most often affected. Since NetSolutions makes frequent debits to its supplies account, a *Supplies Dr.* column is included for these transactions. For example, as shown in Exhibit 8, NetSolutions recorded the purchase of supplies on March 3 by entering *600* in the *Supplies Dr.* column, *600* in the *Accounts Payable Cr.* column, and *Howard Supplies* in the *Account Credited* column.

The *Other Accounts Dr.* column in Exhibit 8 is used to record purchases, on account, of any item for which there is no special debit column. The title of the account to be debited is entered in the *Other Accounts* column, and the amount is entered in the *Amount* column. For example, NetSolutions recorded the purchase

Exhibit 8 Purchases Journal and Postings

PURCHASES JOURNAL — PAGE 11

	Date	Account Credited	Post. Ref.	Accounts Payable Cr.	Supplies Dr.	Other Accounts Dr.	Post. Ref.	Amount	
1	2003 March 3	Howard Supplies	✔	600	600				1
2	7	Donnelly Supplies	✔	420	420				2
3	12	Jewett Business Systems	✔	2,800		Office Equipment	18	2,800	3
4	19	Donnelly Supplies	✔	1,450	1,450				4
5	27	Howard Supplies	✔	960	960				5
6	31			6,230	3,430			2,800	6
7				(21)	(14)			(✔)	7

GENERAL LEDGER

ACCOUNT Accounts Payable — Account No. 21

Date	Item	Post. Ref.	Dr.	Cr.	Balance
2003					
March 1	Balance	✔			1,230
31		P11		6,230	7,460

ACCOUNT Supplies — Account No. 14

Date	Item	Post. Ref.	Dr.	Cr.	Balance
2003					
March 1	Balance	✔			2,500
31		P11	3,430		5,930

ACCOUNT Office Equipment — Account No. 18

Date	Item	Post. Ref.	Dr.	Cr.	Balance
2003					
March 1	Balance	✔			2,500
12		P11	2,800		5,300

ACCOUNTS PAYABLE SUBSIDIARY LEDGER

NAME: Donnelly Supplies

Date	Item	Post. Ref.	Dr.	Cr.	Balance
2003					
March 7		P11		420	420
19		P11		1,450	1,870

NAME: Grayco Supplies

Date	Item	Post. Ref.	Dr.	Cr.	Balance
2003					
March 1	Balance	✔			1,230

NAME: Howard Supplies

Date	Item	Post. Ref.	Dr.	Cr.	Balance
2003					
March 3		P11		600	600
27		P11		960	1,560

NAME: Jewett Business Systems

Date	Item	Post. Ref.	Dr.	Cr.	Balance
2003					
March 12		P11		2,800	2,800

of office equipment on account on March 12 by entering *Office Equipment* in the *Other Accounts Dr.* column, *2,800* in the *Amount* column, *2,800* in the *Accounts Payable Cr.* column, and *Jewett Business Systems* in the *Account Credited* column.

Postings from the purchases journal to the ledgers of NetSolutions are also shown in Exhibit 8. The principles used in posting the purchases journal are similar to those used in posting the revenue and cash receipts journals. The source of the entries posted to the subsidiary and general ledgers is indicated in the *Posting Reference* column of each account by inserting the letter *P* (for purchases journal) and the page number of the purchases journal. A check mark (✓) is inserted in the *Posting Reference* column of the purchases journal after each credit is posted to a creditor's account in the accounts payable subsidiary ledger.

At regular intervals, the amounts in the *Other Accounts Dr.* column are posted to the accounts in the general ledger. As each amount is posted, the related general ledger account number is inserted in the *Posting Reference* column of the *Other Accounts* section.

At the end of each month, the amount columns in the purchases journal are totaled. The sum of the two debit column totals should equal the sum of the credit column.

The totals of the *Accounts Payable Cr.* and *Supplies Dr.* columns are posted to the appropriate general ledger accounts in the usual manner, with the related account numbers inserted below the column totals. Because each amount in the *Other Accounts Dr.* column was posted individually, a check mark is placed below the $2,800 total to show that no further action is needed.

Cash Payments Journal

The special columns for the **cash payments journal** are determined in the same manner as for the revenue, cash receipts, and purchases journals. The determining factors are the kinds of transactions to be recorded and how often they occur.

The cash payments journal has a *Cash Cr.* column, as shown in Exhibit 9. All transactions recorded in the cash payments journal will involve an entry in this column. Payments to creditors on account happen often enough to require an *Accounts Payable Dr.* column. Debits to creditor accounts for invoices paid are recorded in the *Accounts Payable Dr.* column. For example, on March 15 NetSolutions paid $1,230 on its account with Grayco Supplies. NetSolutions recorded this transaction by entering *1,230* in the *Accounts Payable Dr.* column, *1,230* in the *Cash Cr.* column, and *Grayco Supplies* in the *Account Debited* column.

NetSolutions makes all payments by check. As each transaction is recorded in the cash payments journal, the related check number is entered in the column at the right of the *Date* column. The check numbers are helpful in controlling cash payments, and they provide a useful cross-reference.

The *Other Accounts Dr.* column is used for recording debits to any account for which there is no special column. For example, NetSolutions paid $1,600 on March 2 for rent. The transaction was recorded by entering *Rent Expense* in the space provided and *1,600* in the *Other Accounts Dr.* and *Cash Cr.* columns.

Postings from the cash payments journal to the ledgers of NetSolutions are also shown in Exhibit 9. The amounts entered in the *Accounts Payable Dr.* column are posted to the individual creditor accounts in the accounts payable subsidiary ledger. These postings should be made frequently. After each posting, *CP* (for cash payments journal) and the page number of the journal are inserted in the *Posting Reference* column of the account. A check mark is placed in the *Posting Reference* column of the cash payments journal to indicate that each amount has been posted.

At regular intervals, each item in the *Other Accounts Dr.* column is also posted individually to an account in the general ledger. The posting is indicated by writing the account number in the *Posting Reference* column of the cash payments journal.

At the end of the month, each of the amount columns in the cash payments journal is totaled. The sum of the two debit totals is compared with the credit total

Exhibit 9 Cash Payments Journal and Postings

CASH PAYMENTS JOURNAL PAGE 7

	Date	Ck. No.	Account Debited	Post. Ref.	Other Accounts Dr.	Accounts Payable Dr.	Cash Cr.	
	2003							
1	March 2	150	Rent Expense	52	1,600		1,600	1
2	15	151	Grayco Supplies	✔		1,230	1,230	2
3	21	152	Jewett Business Systems	✔		2,800	2,800	3
4	22	153	Donnelly Supplies	✔		420	420	4
5	30	154	Utilities Expense	54	1,050		1,050	5
6	31	155	Howard Supplies	✔		600	600	6
7	31				2,650	5,050	7,700	7
8					(✔)	(21)	(11)	8

GENERAL LEDGER

ACCOUNT Accounts Payable   Account No. 21

Date	Item	Post. Ref.	Dr.	Cr.	Balance
2003					
March 1	Balance	✔			1,230
31		P11		6,230	7,460
31		CP7	5,050		2,410

ACCOUNT Cash   Account No. 11

Date	Item	Post. Ref.	Dr.	Cr.	Balance
2003					
March 1	Balance	✔			6,200
31		CR14	7,750		13,950
31		CP7		7,700	6,250

ACCOUNT Rent Expense   Account No. 52

Date	Item	Post. Ref.	Dr.	Cr.	Balance
2003					
March 2		CP7	1,600		1,600

ACCOUNT Utilities Expense   Account No. 54

Date	Item	Post. Ref.	Dr.	Cr.	Balance
2003					
March 30		CP7	1,050		1,050

ACCOUNTS PAYABLE SUBSIDIARY LEDGER

NAME: Donnelly Supplies

Date	Item	Post. Ref.	Dr.	Cr.	Balance
2003					
March 7		P11		420	420
19		P11		1,450	1,870
22		CP7	420		1,450

NAME: Grayco Supplies

Date	Item	Post. Ref.	Dr.	Cr.	Balance
2003					
March 1	Balance	✔			1,230
15		CP7	1,230		—

NAME: Howard Supplies

Date	Item	Post. Ref.	Dr.	Cr.	Balance
2003					
March 3		P11		600	600
27		P11		960	1,560
31		CP7	600		960

NAME: Jewett Business Systems

Date	Item	Post. Ref.	Dr.	Cr.	Balance
2003					
March 12		P11		2,800	2,800
21		CP7	2,800		—

to determine their equality. A check mark is placed below the total of the *Other Accounts Dr.* column to indicate that no further action is needed. When each of the totals of the other two columns is posted to the general ledger, an account number is inserted below each column total.

Accounts Payable Control and Subsidiary Ledger

After all posting has been completed for the month, the sum of the balances in the accounts payable subsidiary ledger should be compared with the balance of the accounts payable controlling account in the general ledger. If the controlling account and the subsidiary ledger do not agree, the error or errors must be located and corrected. The balances of the individual supplier accounts may be summarized in a schedule of accounts payable. The total of NetSolutions' schedule of accounts payable, $2,410, agrees with the balance of the accounts payable controlling account on March 31, 2003, as shown below.

Accounts Payable— (Controlling)		NetSolutions Schedule of Accounts Payable March 31, 2003	
Balance, March 31, 2003	$2,410	Donnelly Supplies	$1,450
		Grayco Supplies	0
		Howard Supplies	960
		Jewett Business Systems	0
		Total	$2,410

Adapting Manual Accounting Systems

objective 4

Describe and give examples of additional subsidiary ledgers and modified special journals.

The preceding sections of this chapter illustrate subsidiary ledgers and special journals that are common for a medium-size business. Many businesses use subsidiary ledgers for other accounts, in addition to Accounts Receivable and Accounts Payable. Also, special journals are often adapted or modified in practice to meet the specific needs of a business. In the following paragraphs, we describe other subsidiary ledgers and modified special journals.

Additional Subsidiary Ledgers

Generally, subsidiary ledgers are used for accounts that consist of a large number of individual items, each of which has unique characteristics. For example, businesses may use a subsidiary equipment ledger to keep track of each item of equipment purchased, its cost, location, and other data. Such ledgers are similar to the accounts receivable and accounts payable subsidiary ledgers that we illustrated in this chapter.

Modified Special Journals

A business may modify its special journals by adding one or more columns for recording transactions that occur frequently. For example, a business may collect sales taxes that must be remitted periodically to the taxing authorities. Thus, the business may add a special column for *Sales Taxes Payable* in its revenue journal, as shown below.

					REVENUE JOURNAL			PAGE 40	
	Date	Invoice No.	Account Debited	Post. Ref.	Accts. Rec. Dr.	Fees Earned Cr.	Sales Taxes Payable Cr.	
1	2003 Nov. 2	842	Litten Co.	✔	4 7 7 0 00	4 5 0 0 00	2 7 0 00	1
2	3	843	Kauffman Supply Co.	✔	1 1 6 6 00	1 1 0 0 00	6 6 00	2

Some other examples of how special journals may be modified for a variety of different types of businesses are:

- **Farm**—The purchases journal may be modified to include columns for various types of seeds (corn, wheat), livestock (cows, hogs, sheep), fertilizer, and fuel.
- **Automobile Repair Shop**—The revenue journal may be modified to include columns for each major type of repair service. In addition, columns for warranty repairs, credit card charges, and sales taxes may be added.
- **Hospital**—The cash receipts journal may be modified to include columns for receipts from patients on account, from Blue Cross/Blue Shield or other major insurance reimbursers, and Medicare.
- **Movie Theater**—The cash receipts journal may be modified to include columns for revenues from admissions, gift certificates, and concession sales.
- **Restaurant**—The purchases journal may be modified to include columns for food, linen, silverware and glassware, and kitchen supplies.

Regardless of how a special journal is modified, the basic principles and procedures discussed in this chapter apply. For example, the columns in special journals are normally totaled at periodic intervals. The totals of the debit and credit columns are then compared to verify their equality before the totals are posted to the general ledger accounts.

BUSINESS ON STAGE

The E-commerce Revolution

The speed at which on-line commerce has gripped the United States has been nothing short of spectacular. The force of e-commerce can be felt in two major arenas: business to consumer, termed *B2C e-commerce*, and business to business, termed *B2B e-commerce*. B2C e-commerce uses the Internet to connect manufacturers or retailers with ultimate consumers. One of the best examples of the B2C business is **Amazon.com**, which connects book publishers with book buyers. The B2C business adds value by saving the consumer time in physically going to a store for an item.

On the other hand, the B2B e-commerce companies use the Internet to connect businesses with other businesses. The B2B business can be designed around either a *vertical* or *horizontal* hub. A vertical hub connects business buyers with business sellers within a particular industry. Examples include **SciQuest**, which provides an electronic market for biomedical and pharmaceutical products for the health care industry, and **Chemdex**, which provides a similar Internet marketplace for the chemical industry. The horizontal B2B hub provides the same function, or business process,

across different industries. For example, **iMark.com** provides a service of buying and selling used capital equipment across many industries. **Commerce One** provides procurement auctions for a broad array of industrial products, serving such customers as **General Motors**. The B2B hub creates value by providing an electronic market where one did not exist previously. Such a market benefits suppliers by providing more customers and benefits customers by providing more choices and more competitive prices. ∎

Computerized Accounting Systems

objective 5

Apply computerized accounting to the revenue and collection cycle.

Computerized accounting systems have become more widely used as the cost of hardware and software has declined. In addition, computerized accounting systems have three main advantages over manual systems. First, computerized systems simplify the record-keeping process. Transactions are recorded in electronic forms and, at the same time, posted electronically to general and subsidiary ledger accounts.

Second, computerized systems are generally more accurate than manual systems. Third, computerized systems provide management current account balance information to support decision making, since account balances are posted as the transactions occur.

QuickBooks®, as does most accounting software, uses electronic forms. An electronic form is a window that appears like a paper form. The form has spaces, or fields, in which to input information about a particular type of transaction. Many of the information spaces have pull-down lists for easy data entry.

How do computerized accounting systems work? We will illustrate the revenue and collection cycle of NetSolutions by using a popular accounting application called QuickBooks®.

As shown in Exhibit 10, the first step is to enter information onto an electronic invoice form, as illustrated for the March 2 MyMusicClub .com invoice (No. 615). When the form is completed, it may be printed out and mailed to the customer. In addition, upon completing the invoice form the software automatically records the fees earned and posts the $2,200 to the MyMusicClub.com account receivable.

In step two, the collection from the customer is received. Upon collection, the "receive payment" electronic form is opened and completed. In Exhibit 10, this form indicates that a $2,200 payment was collected from MyMusicClub.com on March 28. This amount was applied to invoice 615, as shown by the check mark next to the March 2 date at the bottom of the form. The March 27 invoice of $3,000 remains uncollected, as shown at the bottom of the form. When this screen is completed, the cash account is automatically updated to reflect the increase in cash, and the MyMusicClub.com accounts receivable balance is automatically reduced from $5,200 to $3,000.

At any time, managers may request reports from the software. In step three, three such reports are illustrated in Exhibit 10: (1) the customer balance summary, (2) the income by customer summary, and (3) the check register. The reports are shown for March 31, 2003. Notice that the customer balance summary lists the outstanding accounts receivable balances by customer. This is essentially a report providing the details of the accounts receivable subsidiary ledger. It shows essentially the same information as NetSolutions' Schedule of Accounts Receivable on p. 192. The income by customer summary provides a listing of revenue by customer, which is similar to information provided by the revenue journal in a manual system. This listing is created from the electronic invoice form used in the first step of the cycle. The check register (First National Bank) lists the explanations for changes in the cash balance due to receipts and payments. Since receipts are only illustrated in this example, this report is similar to the cash receipts journal under the manual system. This listing is created from the "receive payment form" used in Step 2.

At the end of the month, the manual system posted revenue journal and cash collection totals to the accounts receivable controlling account. In a computerized system, special journals typically are not used. Instead, transactions are recorded in electronic forms, which are automatically posted to affected accounts at the time the form is completed. In a manual system, the controlling account balance can be reconciled to the sum of the individual customer account balances to identify any posting and mathematical errors. The computer, however, does not make posting and mathematical errors. Thus, there are no month-end postings to controlling accounts. Controlling accounts are simply the sum of the balances of any individual subsidiary account balances.

A new type of computerized accounting system is now available using just a Web browser. Web-based accounting systems, such as those offered by **NetLedger**, reside on the provider's server and can be accessed from anywhere in the world. Smaller businesses can set up their general ledger, accounts receivable, and accounts payable on Web pages and then use the service for their accounting system.

We have illustrated the revenue and collection cycle to help you understand how a portion of a computerized accounting system works. A similar description could be provided for the purchases and payments cycle. A description of a complete computerized accounting system is beyond our scope. However, a thorough understanding of this chapter provides a solid foundation for applying the accounting system concepts in either a manual or a computerized system.

Exhibit 10 The Revenue and Collection Cycle in QuickBooks®

1. **Record fee by filling out an electronic invoice form.**

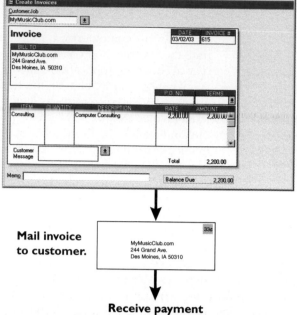

Automatic Postings
Dr. Accounts Receivable—
MyMusicClub.com
    Cr. Revenue

Mail invoice to customer.

Receive payment

2. **Record collection of payment by filling out "receive payment" form.**

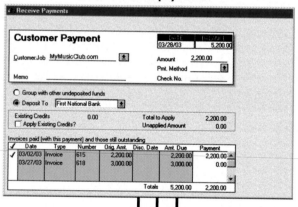

Dr. Cash
    Cr. Accounts Receivable—
    MyMusicClub.com

3. **Prepare reports.**

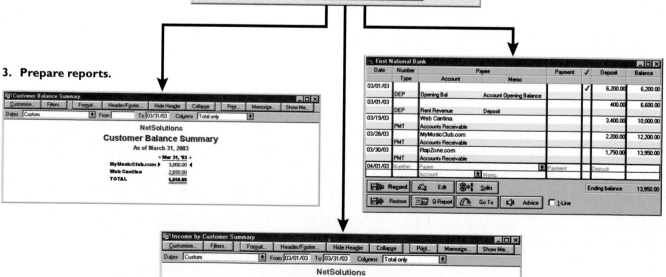

ENCORE

Fraud and Redemption

At the age of 16, Barry Minkow began a carpet cleaning company out of his parents' garage. Minkow aggressively promoted his company to Wall Street and attracted many outside investors. During this time, Minkow was considered a teenage tycoon. The story of his company, called **ZZZZ Best**, ended abruptly when Minkow, at the age of 21, was sentenced to 25 years for defrauding investors out of $26 million by falsely claiming his company was profitable and successful. Seven years later, upon his release from prison, Minkow claimed to be a changed man.

Minkow said his experience taught him the symptoms of personal corruption and the lack of business controls.

- **Small compromises may lead to larger ones.** Minkow says for him it started with a $200 money order theft from a local liquor store. This escalated to overcharging customers' credit cards, and then eventually to investor fraud. Minkow says the fraudulent behavior becomes easy

to rationalize: "If I can get away with it the first time, I can probably do it again with the same result."

- **An unhealthy obsession with what others think about you.** Minkow states that he felt insecure because he lived in an area where classmates were driven to school in Mercedes, and this led to an obsession for personal wealth and prestige.
- **Taking shortcuts, or the easy way out.** Minkow tells the story of completing a carpet cleaning job and selling the customer an additional $100 Scotchguard application. When returning to his truck, he found that there was no Scotchguard left. Minkow sprayed the customer's carpet with water, rather than going back to the shop and picking up more Scotchguard.
- **Pride.** Minkow says his mother came to his office during the height of his fame and asked whether he knew God. Minkow responded, "God. How much is He? I'll buy Him."

The reformed Minkow has now written a book, is conducting Bible studies, has earned degrees in theology, is a radio talk-show host, and is providing lectures on his experiences. He states that any money from these efforts will go toward paying back the investors who lost their savings in ZZZZ Best. To those that say it's just another scam, his response is that "authenticity is confirmed by consistency." Minkow's defrauded investors will wait and see. ■

Sources: Los Angeles Times staff interview, March 31, 1995; Barry Minkow, "My Million-Dollar Lesson About Compromise," *New Man* (January–February 1996), pp. 34–37.

KEY POINTS

1 Define an accounting system and describe its implementation.

An accounting system is the methods and procedures for collecting, classifying, summarizing, and reporting a business's financial information. The three steps through which an accounting system evolves are (1) analysis of information needs, (2) design of the system, and (3) implementation of the system's design.

2 List the three objectives of internal control, and define and give examples of the five elements of internal control.

Internal control provides reasonable assurance that (1) assets are safeguarded and used for business purposes, (2) business information is accurate, and (3) laws and regulations are complied with. The five elements of internal

control are the control environment, risk assessment, control procedures, monitoring, and information and communication.

3 Journalize and post transactions in a manual accounting system that uses subsidiary ledgers and special journals.

Subsidiary ledgers may be used to maintain separate records for each customer (the accounts receivable subsidiary ledger) and creditor (the accounts payable subsidiary ledger). Each subsidiary ledger is represented in the general ledger by a summarizing account, called a controlling account. The sum of the balances of the accounts in a subsidiary ledger must agree with the balance of the related controlling account.

Special journals may be used to reduce the processing time and expense of recording a large number of similar transactions. The revenue journal is used to record the sale of services on account. The cash receipts journal is used to record all receipts of cash. The purchases journal is used to record purchases on ac-

count. The cash payments journal is used to record all payments of cash. The general journal is used for recording transactions that do not fit in any of the special journals. The use of each special journal and the accounts receivable and accounts payable subsidiary ledgers is illustrated in the chapter.

4 Describe and give examples of additional subsidiary ledgers and modified special journals.

Subsidiary ledgers may be maintained for a variety of accounts, such as fixed assets, as well as accounts receivable and accounts payable. Special journals may be modified by adding columns in

which to record frequently occurring transactions. For example, an additional column is often added to the revenue journal for recording the collection of sales taxes payable.

5 Apply computerized accounting to the revenue and collection cycle.

Computerized accounting systems are similar to manual accounting systems. The main advantages of a computerized accounting system are the simultaneous recording and posting of transactions, the high degree of accuracy, and the timeliness of reporting. An example of the revenue and collection cycle using QuickBooks® is provided in the chapter.

ILLUSTRATIVE PROBLEM

Selected transactions of O'Malley Co. for the month of May are as follows:

a.	May	1	Issued Check No. 1001 in payment of rent for May, $1,200.
b.		2	Purchased office supplies on account from McMillan Co., $3,600.
c.		4	Issued Check No. 1003 in payment of transportation charges on the supplies purchased on May 2, $320.
d.		8	Provided services on account to Waller Co., Invoice No. 51, $4,500.
e.		9	Issued Check No. 1005 for office supplies purchased, $450.
f.		10	Received cash for office supplies sold to employees at cost, $120.
g.		11	Purchased office equipment on account from Fender Office Products, $15,000.
h.		12	Issued Check No. 1010 in payment of the supplies purchased from McMillan Co. on May 2, $3,600.
i.		16	Provided services on account to Riese Co., Invoice No. 58, $8,000.
j.		18	Received $4,500 from Waller Co. in payment of May 8 invoice.
k.		20	Invested additional cash in the business, $10,000.
l.		25	Provided services for cash, $15,900.
m.		30	Issued Check No. 1040 for withdrawal of cash for personal use, $1,000.
n.		30	Issued Check No. 1041 in payment of electricity and water bills, $690.
o.		30	Issued Check No. 1042 in payment of office and sales salaries for May, $15,800.
p.		31	Journalized adjusting entries from the work sheet prepared for the fiscal year ended May 31.

O'Malley Co. maintains a revenue journal, a cash receipts journal, a purchases journal, a cash payments journal, and a general journal. In addition, accounts receivable and accounts payable subsidiary ledgers are used.

Instructions

1. Indicate the journal in which each of the preceding transactions, (a) through (p), would be recorded.
2. Indicate whether an account in the accounts receivable or accounts payable subsidiary ledgers would be affected for each of the preceding transactions.
3. Journalize transactions (b), (c), (d), (h), and (j) in the appropriate journals.

Solution

1.	Journal	2.	Subsidiary Ledger
a.	Cash payments journal		
b.	Purchases journal		Accounts payable ledger
c.	Cash payments journal		
d.	Revenue journal		Accounts receivable ledger
e.	Cash payments journal		
f.	Cash receipts journal		
g.	Purchases journal		Accounts payable ledger
h.	Cash payments journal		Accounts payable ledger
i.	Revenue journal		Accounts receivable ledger
j.	Cash receipts journal		Accounts receivable ledger
k.	Cash receipts journal		
l.	Cash receipts journal		
m.	Cash payments journal		
n.	Cash payments journal		
o.	Cash payments journal		
p.	General journal		

3.

Transaction (b):

PURCHASES JOURNAL

Date	Account Credited	Post. Ref.	Accounts Payable Cr.	Office Supplies Dr.	Other Accounts Dr.	Post. Ref.	Amount
May 2	McMillan Co.		3 6 0 0 00	3 6 0 0 00			

Transactions (c) and (h):

CASH PAYMENTS JOURNAL

Date	Ck. No.	Account Debited	Post. Ref.	Other Accounts Dr.	Accounts Payable Dr.	Cash Cr.
May 4	1003	Transportation In		3 2 0 00		3 2 0 00
12	1010	McMillan Co.			3 6 0 0 00	3 6 0 0 00

Transaction (d):

			REVENUE JOURNAL		
Date	Invoice No.	Account Debited	Post. Ref.	Accts. Rec. Dr. Fees Earned Cr.	
May 8	51	Waller Co.		4 5 0 0 00	

Transaction (j):

		CASH RECEIPTS JOURNAL				
Date	Account Credited	Post. Ref.	Other Accounts Cr.	Accounts Receivable Cr.	Cash Dr.	
May 18	Waller Co.			4 5 0 0 00	4 5 0 0 00	

Matching

Match each of the following statements with its proper term. Some terms may not be used.

A. accounting system
B. accounts payable subsidiary ledger
C. accounts receivable subsidiary ledger
D. application
E. cash payments journal
F. cash receipts journal
G. controlling account
H. elements of internal control
I. employee fraud
J. general journal
K. general ledger
L. internal controls

___ 1. The journal in which all cash payments are recorded.

___ 2. The journal in which all cash receipts are recorded.

___ 3. The intentional act of deceiving an employer for personal gain.

___ 4. The subsidiary ledger containing the individual accounts with customers (debtors).

___ 5. Journals designed to be used for recording a single type of transaction.

___ 6. The methods and procedures used by a business to collect, classify, summarize, and report financial data for use by management and external users.

___ 7. The policies and procedures used to safeguard assets, ensure accurate business information, and ensure compliance with laws and regulations.

___ 8. The subsidiary ledger containing the individual accounts with suppliers (creditors).

___ 9. The control environment, risk assessment, control activities, information and communication, and monitoring.

___10. The journal in which all sales of services on account are recorded.

___11. The account in the general ledger that summarizes the balances of the accounts in a subsidiary ledger.

M.	**purchases journal**
N.	**revenue journal**
O.	**special journals**
P.	**subsidiary ledger**

___ 12. The journal in which all items purchased on account are recorded.

___ 13. The two-column form used for entries that do not "fit" in any of the special journals.

___ 14. The primary ledger, when used in conjunction with subsidiary ledgers, that contains all of the balance sheet and income statement accounts.

___ 15. A ledger containing individual accounts with a common characteristic.

Multiple Choice

1. The initial step in the process of developing an accounting system is called:
   A. analysis
   B. design
   C. implementation
   D. feedback

2. The policies and procedures used by management to protect assets from misuse, ensure accurate business information, and ensure compliance with laws and regulations are called:
   A. internal controls
   B. systems analysis
   C. systems design
   D. systems implementation

3. A payment of cash for the purchase of services should be recorded in the:
   A. purchases journal
   B. cash payments journal
   C. revenue journal
   D. cash receipts journal

4. When there are a large number of individual accounts with a common characteristic, it is common to place them in a separate ledger called:
   A. a subsidiary ledger
   B. a creditors ledger
   C. an accounts payable ledger
   D. an accounts receivable ledger

5. Which of the following would be used in a computerized accounting system?
   A. Revenue journal
   B. Cash receipts journal
   C. Electronic invoice form
   D. Month-end postings to the general ledger

CLASS DISCUSSION QUESTIONS

1. Why is the accounting system of a business an information system?
2. What is the three-step process of systems evolution?
3. What are the three objectives of internal control?
4. Name and describe the five elements of internal control.
5. How does a policy of rotating clerical employees from job to job aid in strengthening the control procedures within the control environment?
6. Why should the responsibility for a sequence of related operations be divided among different persons?
7. Why should the employee who handles cash receipts not have the responsibility for maintaining the accounts receivable records?
8. In an attempt to improve operating efficiency, one employee was made responsible for all purchasing, receiving, and storing of supplies. Is this organizational change wise from an internal control standpoint? Explain.
9. The ticket seller at a movie theater doubles as a ticket taker for a few minutes each day while the ticket taker is on a break. Which control procedure of a business's system of internal control is violated in this situation?
10. Why should the responsibility for maintaining the accounting records be separated from the responsibility for operations?
11. What is the term applied (a) to the ledger containing the individual customer accounts and (b) to the single account summarizing accounts receivable?
12. What are the major advantages of the use of special journals?
13. Environmental Services Co. uses the special journals described in this chapter. Which journal will be used to record fees earned (a) for cash, (b) on account?
14. In recording 250 fees earned on account during a single month, how many times will it be necessary to write Fees Earned (a) if each transaction, including fees earned,

is recorded individually in a two-column general journal; (b) if each transaction for fees earned is recorded in a revenue journal?

15. How many individual postings to Fees Earned for the month would be needed in Question 14 if the procedure described in (a) had been used; if the procedure described in (b) had been used?

16. During the current month, the following errors occurred in recording transactions in the purchases journal or in posting from it.
    a. An invoice for $900 of supplies from Hoffman Co. was recorded as having been received from Hoffer Co., another supplier.
    b. A credit of $840 to JPC Company was posted as $480 in the subsidiary ledger.
    c. An invoice for equipment of $6,500 was recorded as $5,500.
    d. The Accounts Payable column of the purchases journal was overstated by $2,000. How will each error come to the bookkeeper's attention, other than by chance discovery?

17. The Accounts Payable and Cash columns in the cash payments journal were unknowingly overstated by $100 at the end of the month. (a) Assuming no other errors in recording or posting, will the error cause the trial balance totals to be unequal? (b) Will the creditors ledger agree with the accounts payable controlling account?

18. Assuming the use of a two-column general journal, a purchases journal, and a cash payments journal as illustrated in this chapter, indicate the journal in which each of the following transactions should be recorded:
    a. Purchase of supplies for cash.
    b. Purchase of office supplies on account.
    c. Payment of cash on account to creditor.
    d. Purchase of store equipment on account.
    e. Payment of cash for office supplies.

19. What is an electronic form and how is it used in a computerized accounting system?

RESOURCES FOR YOUR SUCCESS ONLINE AT

http://warren.swcollege.com

Remember! If you need additional help, visit South-Western's Web site.
See page 26 for a description of the online and printed materials that are available.

EXERCISES

Exercise 5–1
Internal controls

Objective 2

Connie Stevens has recently been hired as the manager of Big Apple Deli. Big Apple Deli is a national chain of franchised delicatessens. During her first month as store manager, Connie encountered the following internal control situations:

a. Big Apple Deli has one cash register. Prior to Connie's joining the deli, each employee working on a shift would take a customer order, accept payment, and then prepare the order. Connie made one employee on each shift responsible for taking orders and accepting the customer's payment. Other employees prepare the orders.

b. Since only one employee uses the cash register, that employee is responsible for counting the cash at the end of the shift and verifying that the cash in the drawer matches the amount of cash sales recorded by the cash register. Connie expects each cashier to balance the drawer to the penny *every* time—no exceptions.

c. Connie caught an employee putting a box of 100 single-serving bags of potato chips in his car. Not wanting to create a scene, Connie smiled and said, "I don't think you're putting those chips on the right shelf. Don't they belong inside the deli?" The employee returned the chips to the stockroom.

✏ ► State whether you agree or disagree with Connie's method of handling each situation and explain your answer.

Exercise 5–2

Internal controls

Objective 2

Summer Breeze is a retail store specializing in women's clothing. The store has established a liberal return policy for the holiday season in order to encourage gift purchases. Any item purchased during November and December may be returned through January 31, with a receipt, for cash or exchange. If the customer does not have a receipt, cash will still be refunded for any item under $25. If the item is more than $25, a check is mailed to the customer.

Whenever an item is returned, a store clerk completes a return slip, which the customer signs. The return slip is placed in a special box. The store manager visits the return counter approximately once every two hours to authorize the return slips. Clerks are instructed to place the returned merchandise on the proper rack on the selling floor as soon as possible.

This year, returns at Summer Breeze have reached an all-time high. There are a large number of returns under $25 without receipts.

a. ✏ ► How can sales clerks employed at Summer Breeze use the store's return policy to steal money from the cash register?

b. 1. ✏ ► What internal control weaknesses do you see in the return policy that make cash thefts easier?

2. Would issuing a store credit in place of a cash refund for all merchandise returned without a receipt reduce the possibility of theft? List some advantages and disadvantages of issuing a store credit in place of a cash refund.

3. Assume that Summer Breeze is committed to the current policy of issuing cash refunds without a receipt. What changes could be made in the store's procedures regarding customer refunds in order to improve internal control?

Exercise 5–3

Internal controls for bank lending

Objective 2

United Savings Bank provides loans to businesses in the community through its Commercial Lending Department. Small loans (less than $100,000) may be approved by an individual loan officer, while larger loans (greater than $100,000) must be approved by a board of loan officers. Once a loan is approved, the funds are made available to the loan applicant under agreed upon terms. The president of United Savings Bank has instituted a policy whereby she has the individual authority to approve loans up to $5,000,000. The president believes that this policy will allow flexibility to approve loans to valued clients much quicker than under the previous policy.

✏ ► As an internal auditor of United Savings Bank, how would you respond to this change in policy?

Exercise 5–4

Internal controls

Objective 2

One of the largest fraud losses in history involved a securities trader for the Singapore office of **Barings Bank**, a British merchant bank. The trader established an unauthorized account number that was used to hide $1.4 billion in losses. Even after Barings' internal auditors noted that the trader both executed trades and recorded them, management did not take action. As a result, a lone individual in a remote office bankrupted an internationally recognized firm overnight.

✏ ► What general weaknesses in Barings' internal controls contributed to the occurrence and size of the fraud?

Exercise 5–5

Internal controls

Objective 2

In the **Equity Funding** fraud, approximately $2 billion of insurance policies that were claimed to have been sold by the company were bogus. The bogus policies, which were supported by falsified policy applications, were listed along with real policies on Equity Funding's computer files (records). Equity Funding personnel, including the computer programmers, kept these files in a separate room where they were easily accessible. In addition, computer programmers and other company personnel had access to the computer.

✏ ► What general weaknesses in Equity Funding's internal controls contributed to the occurrence and size of the fraud?

Exercise 5–6
Financial statement fraud

Objective 2

The former chairman, the CFO, and the controller of **Donnkenny**, an apparel company that makes sportswear for Pierre Cardin and Victoria Jones, pleaded guilty to financial statement fraud. These managers used false journal entries to record fictitious sales, hid inventory in public warehouses so that it could be recorded as "sold," and required sales orders to be backdated so that the sale could be moved back to an earlier period. The combined effect of these actions caused $25 million out of $40 million in quarterly sales to be phony.

a. Why might control procedures listed in this chapter be insufficient in stopping this type of fraud?

b. How could this type of fraud be stopped?

Exercise 5–7
Identify postings from revenue journal

Objective 3

Using the following revenue journal for Capstone Consulting Co., identify each of the posting references, indicated by a letter, as representing (1) posting to general ledger accounts, or (2) posting to subsidiary ledger accounts.

REVENUE JOURNAL

Date	Invoice No.	Account Debited	Post. Ref.	Accounts Receivable Dr. Fees Earned Cr.
Nov. 1	772	Environmental Safety Co.	(a)	$3,125
10	773	Greenberg Co.	(b)	1,050
20	774	Smith and Smith	(c)	1,520
27	775	Envirolab	(d)	965
30				$6,660
				(e)

Exercise 5–8
Accounts receivable ledger

Objective 3

SPREADSHEET

Based upon the data presented in Exercise 5–7, assume that the beginning balances for the customer accounts were zero, except for Envirolab, which had a $570 beginning balance. In addition, there were no collections during the period.

a. Set up a T account for Accounts Receivable and T accounts for the four accounts needed in the customer ledger.

b. Post to the T accounts.

c. Determine the balance in the accounts.

d. Prepare a schedule of accounts receivable at November 30.

✓ d. Total accounts receivable, $7,230

Exercise 5–9
Identify journals

Objective 3

Assuming the use of a two-column (all-purpose) general journal, a revenue journal, and a cash receipts journal as illustrated in this chapter, indicate the journal in which each of the following transactions should be recorded:

a. Adjustment to record accrued salaries at the end of the year.

b. Receipt of cash on account from a customer.

c. Providing services on account.

d. Investment of additional cash in the business by the owner.

e. Receipt of cash for rent.

f. Receipt of cash refund from overpayment of taxes.

g. Closing of drawing account at the end of the year.

h. Sale of office supplies on account, at cost, to a neighboring business.

i. Receipt of cash from sale of office equipment.

j. Providing services for cash.

Exercise 5–10
Identify journals

Objective 3

Assuming the use of a two-column (all-purpose) general journal, a purchases journal, and a cash payments journal as illustrated in this chapter, indicate the journal in which each of the following transactions should be recorded:

a. Purchase of services on account.

b. Adjustment to record depreciation at the end of the month.

c. Adjustment to record accrued salaries at the end of the period.
d. Advance payment of a one-year fire insurance policy on the office.
e. Purchase of an office computer on account.
f. Purchase of office equipment for cash.
g. Adjustment to prepaid insurance at the end of the month.
h. Adjustment to prepaid rent at the end of the month.
i. Purchase of office supplies for cash.
j. Purchase of office supplies on account.
k. Payment of six months' rent in advance.

Exercise 5–11
Identify transactions in accounts receivable ledger

Objective 3

The debits and credits from three related transactions are presented in the following customer's account taken from the accounts receivable subsidiary ledger.

NAME   *Good Times Catering*
ADDRESS   *1319 Maple Street*

Date	Item	Post. Ref.	Debit	Credit	Balance
2003					
Sep. 3		R50	570		570
9		J9		80	490
13		CR38		490	—

Describe each transaction, and identify the source of each posting.

Exercise 5–12
Schedule of accounts receivable

Objective 3

✓ Accounts Receivable balance, April 30, $6,665

The revenue and cash receipts journal for Adrian Co. are shown below. The accounts receivable control account has an April 1, 2003 balance of $4,670.

		REVENUE JOURNAL		PAGE 16	
Date	Invoice No.	Account Debited	Post. Ref.	Accounts Rec. Dr. Fees Earned Cr.	
2003					
April 6	1	Danforth Co.	✓	1,500	
14	2	Vivid Media Inc.	✓	7,300	
22	3	Danforth Co.	✓	2,250	
27	4	Korvette Co.	✓	975	
28	5	Trask Co.	✓	3,440	
31				15,465	
				(12) (41)	

	CASH RECEIPTS JOURNAL				PAGE 36
Date	Account Credited	Post. Ref.	Fees Earned Cr.	Accts. Rec. Cr.	Cash Dr.
2003					
April 6	Trask Co.	✓	—	4,670	4,670
11	Fees Earned		3,400		3,400
18	Danforth Co.	✓	—	1,500	1,500
28	Vivid Media Inc.	✓	—	7,300	7,300
30			3,400	13,470	16,870
			(41)	(12)	(11)

Prepare the schedule of accounts receivable and determine that the total agrees with the ending balance of the Accounts Receivable controlling account.

Exercise 5–13
Revenue and cash receipts journals

Objective 3

Transactions related to revenue and cash receipts completed by Connections.com during the month of October 2003 are as follows:

Oct. 2. Issued Invoice No. 512 to Conrad Co., $730.
    4. Received cash from CMI, Inc. for $240.
    8. Issued Invoice No. 513 to Orlando Co., $310.
  12. Issued Invoice No. 514 to Drake Inc., $870.
  19. Received cash from Drake Inc., $530.
  22. Issued Invoice No. 515 to Electronic Central, Inc., $250.
  27. Received cash from Higgins, Inc. for services provided, $70.
  29. Received cash from Conrad Co. for invoice of Oct. 2.
  31. Received cash from McCleary Co. for services provided, $50.

Prepare a single-column revenue journal and a cash receipts journal to record these transactions. Use the following column headings for the cash receipts journal: Fees Earned, Accounts Receivable, and Cash. Place a check mark (✓) in the Post. Ref. Column, as appropriate.

Exercise 5–14
Identify postings from purchases journal

Objective 3

Using the following purchases journal, identify each of the posting references, indicated by a letter, as representing (1) a posting to a general ledger account, (2) a posting to a subsidiary ledger account, or (3) that no posting is required.

PURCHASES JOURNAL   PAGE 49

						Other Accounts Dr.		
Date	Account Credited	Post. Ref.	Accounts Payable Cr.	Store Supplies Dr.	Office Supplies Dr.	Account	Post. Ref.	Amount
2003								
June 4	Corter Supply Co.	(a)	4,200		4,200			
6	Coastal Insurance Co.	(b)	5,325			Prepaid Insurance	(c)	5,325
11	Keller Bros.	(d)	2,000			Office Equipment	(e)	2,000
13	Taylor Products	(f)	1,675	1,400	275			
20	Keller Bros.	(g)	5,500			Store Equipment	(h)	5,500
27	Miller Supply Co.	(i)	2,740	2,740				
30			21,440	4,140	4,475			12,825
			(j)	(k)	(l)			(m)

Exercise 5–15
Identify postings from cash payments journal

Objective 3

Using the following cash payments journal, identify each of the posting references, indicated by a letter, as representing (1) a posting to a general ledger account, (2) a posting to a subsidiary ledger account, or (3) that no posting is required.

CASH PAYMENTS JOURNAL   PAGE 46

Date	Ck. No.	Account Debited	Post. Ref.	Other Accounts Dr.	Accounts Payable Dr.	Cash Cr.
2003						
July 3	611	Aquatic Systems Co.	(a)		4,000	4,000
5	612	Utilities Expense	(b)	325		325
10	613	Prepaid Rent	(c)	3,200		3,200
17	614	Advertising Expense	(d)	640		640
20	615	Derby Co.	(e)		1,450	1,450
22	616	Office Equipment	(f)	3,900		3,900
25	617	Office Supplies	(g)	250		250
27	618	Evans Co.	(h)		5,500	5,500
31	619	Salaries Expense	(i)	1,750		1,750
31				10,065	10,950	21,015
				(j)	(k)	(l)

Exercise 5–16

Identify transactions in accounts payable ledger account

Objective 3

The debits and credits from three related transactions are presented in the following creditor's account taken from the accounts payable ledger.

NAME *Echo Co.*
ADDRESS *1717 Kirby Street*

Date	Item	Post. Ref.	Debit	Credit	Balance
2003					
July 6		P34		12,200	12,200
10		J10	400		11,800
16		CP37	11,800		—

Describe each transaction, and identify the source of each posting.

Exercise 5–17

Schedule of accounts payable

Objective 3

SPREADSHEET

✓ Accts. Pay., 6/30, $7,020

The cash payment and purchases journals for Landry Landscaping are shown below. The accounts payable control account has a June 1, 2004 balance of $1,390.

		CASH PAYMENTS JOURNAL					PAGE 31
Date	Ck. No.	Account Debited	Post. Ref.	Other Accounts Dr.	Accounts Payable Dr.	Cash Cr.	
2004							
June 4	203	Augusta Sod Co.	✓		1,390	1,390	
5	204	Utilities Expense	54	325		325	
15	205	Mayfield Lumber Co.	✓		4,350	4,350	
27	206	Owens Fertilizer	✓		1,450	1,450	
30				325	7,190	7,515	
				(✓)	(21)	(11)	

		PURCHASES JOURNAL					PAGE 22
					Other Accounts Dr.		
Date	Account Credited	Post. Ref.	Accounts Payable Cr.	Landscaping Supplies Dr.	Account	Post Ref.	Amount
2004							
June 3	Mayfield Lumber Co.	✓	4,350	4,350			
7	Gibraltar Insurance Co.	✓	1,100		Prepaid Insurance	17	1,100
14	Owens Fertilizer	✓	1,450	1,450			
24	Augusta Sod Co.	✓	2,780	2,780			
29	Mayfield Lumber Co.	✓	3,140	3,140			
30			12,820	11,720			1,100
			(21)	(14)			(✓)

Prepare the schedule of accounts payable and determine that the total agrees with the ending balance of the Accounts Payable controlling account.

Exercise 5–18

Purchases and cash payments journals

Objective 3

Transactions related to purchases and cash payments completed by Sanitary Cleaners during the month of May 2004 are as follows:

May 1. Issued Check No. 57 to Liquid Klean Supplies, Inc., in payment of account, $125.
   3. Purchased cleaning supplies on account from Industrial Products, Inc., $85.

May 8. Issued Check No. 58 to purchase equipment from Hamilton Equipment Sales, $450.
    12. Purchased cleaning supplies on account from Carver Paper Products, Inc., $190.
    15. Issued Check No. 59 to Fountain Laundry Service in payment of account, $80.
    17. Purchased supplies on account from Liquid Klean Supplies, $110.
    20. Purchased laundry services from Fountain Laundry Service on account, $70.
    25. Issued Check No. 60 to Industrial Products, Inc. in payment of May 3rd invoice.
    31. Issued Check No. 61 in payment of salaries, $2,900.

Prepare a purchases journal and a cash payments journal to record these transactions. The forms of the journals are similar to those illustrated in the text. Place a check mark (✓) in the Post. Ref. Column, as appropriate. Sanitary Cleaners uses the following accounts:

Equipment	18
Salary Expense	51
Laundry Service Expense	53

Exercise 5–19

Error in accounts payable ledger and schedule of accounts payable

Objective 3

✓ b. Total accounts payable, $36,950

After Green Earth Environmental Services had completed all postings for October in the current year (2003), the sum of the balances in the following accounts payable ledger did not agree with the $36,950 balance of the controlling account in the general ledger.

NAME   *Martinez Mining Co.*
ADDRESS   *1240 W. Main Street*

Date	Item	Post. Ref.	Debit	Credit	Balance
2003					
Oct. 1	Balance	✓			4,750
10		CP22	4,750		—
17		P30		3,900	3,900
25		J7	350		2,550

NAME   *Cutler and Powell*
ADDRESS   *717 Elm Street*

Date	Item	Post. Ref.	Debit	Credit	Balance
2003					
Oct. 1	Balance	✓			6,100
18		CP23	6,100		—
29		P31		9,100	9,100

NAME   *C. D. Greer and Son*
ADDRESS   *972 S. Tenth Street*

Date	Item	Post. Ref.	Debit	Credit	Balance
2003					
Oct. 17		P30		3,750	3,750
27		P31		10,000	13,750

NAME   *Donnelly Minerals Inc.*
ADDRESS   *1170 Mattis Avenue*

Date	Item	Post. Ref.	Debit	Credit	Balance
2003					
Oct. 1	Balance	✓			8,300
7		P30		4,900	13,300
12		J7	300		13,000
20		CP23	5,500		7,500

NAME   *Valley Power*
ADDRESS   *915 E. Walnut Street*

Date	Item	Post. Ref.	Debit	Credit	Balance
2003					
Oct. 5		P30		3,150	3,150

Assuming that the controlling account balance of $36,950 has been verified as correct, (a) determine the error(s) in the preceding accounts and (b) prepare a schedule of accounts payable from the corrected accounts payable subsidiary ledger.

Exercise 5–20
Identify postings from special journals

Objective 3

Delta Consulting Company makes most of its sales and purchases on credit. It uses the five journals described in this chapter (revenue, cash receipts, purchases, cash payments, and general journals). Identify the journal most likely used in recording the postings for selected transactions indicated by letter in the following T accounts:

Cash				
a.	11,190	b.	9,280	

Prepaid Rent			
		c.	400

Accounts Receivable				
d.	12,410	e.	10,500	

Accounts Payable				
f.	7,600	g.	6,500	

Office Supplies	
h.	6,500

Fees Earned		
	i.	12,410

Rent Expense	
j.	400

Exercise 5–21
Cash receipts journal

Objective 3

The following cash receipts journal headings have been suggested for a small service firm. How many errors can you find in the headings?

CASH RECEIPTS JOURNAL   PAGE 12

Date	Account Credited	Post. Ref.	Fees Earned Cr.	Accounts Rec. Cr.	Cash Cr.	Other Accounts Dr.

Exercise 5–22
Modified special journals

Objectives 3, 4

✓ c. 2. $819

Wellguard Health Clinic was established on June 15, 2003. The clients for whom Wellguard provided health services during the remainder of June are listed below. These clients pay Wellguard the amount indicated plus a 5% sales tax.

June 16. A. Sommerfeld on account, Invoice No. 1, $200 plus tax.
  19. K. Lee, Invoice No. 2, $120 plus tax.
  21. J. Koss, Invoice No. 3, $60 plus tax.
  22. D. Jeffries, Invoice No. 4, $100 plus tax.
  24. K. Sallinger, in exchange for medical supplies having a value of $160, plus tax.
  26. J. Koss, Invoice No. 5, $260 plus tax.
  28. K. Lee, Invoice No. 6, $40 plus tax.

a. Journalize the transactions for June, using a three-column revenue journal and a two-column general journal. Post the customer accounts in the accounts receivable subsidiary ledger and insert the balance immediately after recording each entry.
b. Post the general journal and the revenue journal to the following general ledger accounts, inserting account balances only after the last postings:

(continued)

12   Accounts Receivable
14   Medical Supplies
22   Sales Tax Payable
41   Fees Earned

c. 1. What is the sum of the balances in the accounts receivable subsidiary ledger at
        June 30?
    2. What is the balance of the controlling account at June 30?

Exercise 5–23
Computerized accounting systems

Objective 5

Most computerized accounting systems use electronic forms to record transaction information, such as the invoice form illustrated in Exhibit 10.

a. Identify the key input fields (spaces) in an electronic invoice form.
b. What accounts are posted from an electronic invoice form?
c. Why aren't special journal totals posted to control accounts at the end of the month in an electronic accounting system?

PROBLEMS SERIES A

Problem 5–1A
Revenue journal; accounts receivable and general ledgers

Objective 3

SPREADSHEET

✓ 1. Revenue journal, total fees
earned, $815

Three R's Co. was established on January 20, 2003, to provide educational services. The services provided during the remainder of the month are as follows:

Jan. 21. J. Dunlop, Invoice No. 1, $70 on account.
     22. L. Summers, Invoice No. 2, $180 on account.
     24. T. Morris, Invoice No. 3, $65 on account.
     25. L. Summers, $130 in exchange for educational supplies.
     27. F. Mintz, Invoice No. 4, $165 on account.
     28. D. Bennett, Invoice No. 5, $120 on account.
     30. L. Summers, Invoice No. 6, $105 on account.
     31. T. Morris, Invoice No. 7, $110 on account.

Instructions

1. Journalize the transactions for January, using a single-column revenue journal and a two-column general journal. Post to the following customer accounts in the accounts receivable ledger, and insert the balance immediately after recording each entry: D. Bennett; J. Dunlop; F. Mintz; T. Morris; L. Summers.
2. Post the revenue journal and the general journal to the following accounts in the general ledger, inserting the account balances only after the last postings:

    12   Accounts Receivable
    13   Supplies
    41   Fees Earned

3. a. What is the sum of the balances of the accounts in the subsidiary ledger at January 31?
    b. What is the balance of the controlling account at January 31?
4. Assume that on February 1, the state in which Three R's Co. operates begins requiring that sales tax be collected on educational services. Briefly explain how the revenue journal may be modified to accommodate sales of services on account that require the collection of a state sales tax.

Problem 5–2A
Revenue and cash receipts journals; accounts receivable and general ledgers

Objective 3

Transactions related to revenue and cash receipts completed by Pyramid Architects Co. during the period June 2–30, 2003, are as follows:

June 2. Issued Invoice No. 793 to Morton Co., $7,900.
      5. Received cash from Mendez Co. for the balance owed on its account.
      6. Issued Invoice No. 794 to Quest Co., $2,360.
     13. Issued Invoice No. 795 to Ping Co., $5,790.
         Post revenue and collections to the accounts receivable subsidiary ledger.
     15. Received cash from Quest Co. for the balance owed on June 1.

**GENERAL
LEDGER**

✓ 3. Total cash receipts, $43,030

June 16. Issued Invoice No. 796 to Quest Co., $4,600.
   Post revenue and collections to the accounts receivable subsidiary ledger.
19. Received cash from Morton Co. for the balance due on invoice of June 2.
20. Received cash from Quest Co. for invoice of June 6.
22. Issued Invoice No. 797 to Mendez Co., $7,810.
25. Received $4,400 note receivable in partial settlement of the balance due on the Ping Co. account.
30. Recorded cash fees earned, $11,450.
   Post revenue and collections to the accounts receivable subsidiary ledger.

Instructions

1. Insert the following balances in the general ledger as of June 1:

11	Cash	$12,150
12	Accounts Receivable	21,320
14	Notes Receivable	5,000
41	Fees Earned	—

2. Insert the following balances in the accounts receivable subsidiary ledger as of June 1:

Mendez Co.	$11,560
Morton Co.	—
Ping Co.	—
Quest Co.	9,760

3. Prepare a single-column revenue journal and a cash receipts journal. Use the following column headings for the cash receipts journal: Fees Earned, Accounts Receivable, and Cash. The Fees Earned column is used to record cash fees. Insert a check mark (✓) in the Post. Ref. Column.
4. Using the two special journals and the two-column general journal, journalize the transactions for June. Post to the accounts receivable subsidiary ledger, and insert the balances at the points indicated in the narrative of transactions. Determine the balance in the customer's account before recording a cash receipt.
5. Total each of the columns of the special journals, and post the individual entries and totals to the general ledger. Insert account balances after the last posting.
6. Determine that the subsidiary ledger agrees with the controlling account in the general ledger.

Problem 5–3A

Purchases, accounts payable account, and accounts payable ledger

Objective 3

**GENERAL
LEDGER**

✓ 3. Total accounts payable credit, $14,845

Elegant Estate Landscaping designs and installs landscaping. The landscape designers and office staff use office supplies, while field supplies (rock, bark, etc.) are used in the actual landscaping. Purchases on account completed by Elegant Estate Landscaping during July 2003 are as follows:

July 2. Purchased office supplies on account from Lapp Co., $890.
   5. Purchased office equipment on account from Peach Computers Co., $3,400.
   9. Purchased office supplies on account from Executive Office Supply Co., $420.
  13. Purchased field supplies on account from Yin Co., $980.
  14. Purchased field supplies on account from Nelson Co., $3,200.
  17. Purchased field supplies on account from Yin Co., $1,680.
  24. Purchased field supplies on account from Nelson Co., $2,680.
  29. Purchased office supplies on account from Executive Office Supply Co., $355.
  31. Purchased field supplies on account from Nelson Co., $1,240.

Instructions

1. Insert the following balances in the general ledger as of July 1:

14	Field Supplies	$ 5,820
15	Office Supplies	830
18	Office Equipment	14,300
21	Accounts Payable	655

(continued)

2. Insert the following balances in the accounts payable subsidiary ledger as of July 1:

      Executive Office Supply $400
      Lapp Co.   255
      Nelson Co.   —
      Peach Computers Co.   —
      Yin Co.   —

3. Journalize the transactions for July, using a purchases journal similar to the one illustrated in this chapter. Prepare the purchases journal with columns for Accounts Payable, Field Supplies, Office Supplies, and Other Accounts. Post to the creditor accounts in the accounts payable subsidiary ledger immediately after each entry.
4. Post the purchases journal to the accounts in the general ledger.
5. a. What is the sum of the balances in the subsidiary ledger at July 31?
    b. What is the balance of the controlling account at July 31?

Problem 5–4A
Purchases and cash payments journals; accounts payable and general ledgers

Objective 3

GENERAL LEDGER

✓ 1. Total cash payments, $56,665

Purity Water Testing Service was established on June 16, 2003. Purity uses field equipment and field supplies (chemicals and other supplies) to analyze water for unsafe contaminants in streams, lakes, and ponds. Transactions related to purchases and cash payments during the remainder of June are as follows:

June 16. Issued Check No. 1 in payment of rent for the remainder of June, $1,200.
      16. Purchased field supplies on account from Heath Supply Co., $3,650.
      16. Purchased field equipment on account from Juan Equipment Co., $9,500.
      17. Purchased office supplies on account from Aztec Supply Co., $415.
      19. Issued Check No. 2 in payment of field supplies, $1,850, and office supplies, $250.
          Post the journals to the accounts payable subsidiary ledger.
      23. Purchased office supplies on account from Aztec Supply Co., $325.
      23. Issued Check No. 3 to purchase land from the owner, $25,000.
      24. Issued Check No. 4 to Heath Supply Co. in payment of invoice, $3,650.
      26. Issued Check No. 5 to Juan Equipment Co. in payment of invoice, $9,500.
          Post the journals to the accounts payable subsidiary ledger.
      30. Acquired land in exchange for field equipment having a cost of $6,700.
      30. Purchased field supplies on account from Heath Supply Co., $5,300.
      30. Issued Check No. 6 to Aztec Supply Co. in payment of invoice, $415.
      30. Purchased the following from Juan Equipment Co. on account: field supplies, $1,200, and field equipment, $2,900.
      30. Issued Check No. 7 in payment of salaries, $14,800.
          Post the journals to the accounts payable subsidiary ledger.

Instructions

1. Journalize the transactions for June. Use a purchases journal and a cash payments journal, similar to those illustrated in this chapter, and a two-column general journal. Refer to the following partial chart of accounts:

    11   Cash   19   Land
    14   Field Supplies   21   Accounts Payable
    15   Office Supplies   61   Salary Expense
    17   Field Equipment   71   Rent Expense

At the points indicated in the narrative of transactions, post to the following accounts in the accounts payable subsidiary ledger:

Aztec Supply Co.
Heath Supply Co.
Juan Equipment Co.

2. Post the individual entries (Other Accounts columns of the purchases journal and the cash payments journal and both columns of the general journal) to the appropriate general ledger accounts.

3. Total each of the columns of the purchases journal and the cash payments journal and post the appropriate totals to the general ledger. (Because the problem does not include transactions related to cash receipts, the cash account in the ledger will have a credit balance.)
4. Prepare a schedule of accounts payable.

Problem 5–5A

All journals and general ledger; trial balance

Objective 3

GENERAL LEDGER

✓ 2. Total cash receipts, $41,080

The transactions completed by Mercury Delivery Company during July 2003, the first month of the fiscal year, were as follows:

July 1. Issued Check No. 610 for July rent, $2,400.
  2. Issued Invoice No. 940 to Capps Co., $3,500.
  3. Received check for $5,400 from Pease Co. in payment of account.
  5. Purchased a vehicle on account from Browning Transportation, $24,600.
  6. Purchased office equipment on account from Bell Computer Co., $3,600.
  6. Issued Invoice No. 941 to Collins Co., $6,210.
  9. Issued Check No. 611 for fuel expense, $850.
  10. Received check from Sokol Co. in payment of $7,800 invoice.
  10. Issued Check No. 612 for $5,100 to Office To Go, Inc., in payment of invoice.
  10. Issued Invoice No. 942 to Joy Co., $3,230.
  11. Issued Check No. 613 for $3,050 to Crowne Supply Co. in payment of account.
  11. Issued Check No. 614 for $960 to Porter Co. in payment of account.
  12. Received check from Capps Co. in payment of $3,500 invoice.
  13. Issued Check No. 615 to Browning Transportation in payment of $24,600 balance.
  16. Issued Check No. 616 for $18,500 for cash purchase of a vehicle.
  16. Cash fees earned for July 1–16, $12,400.
  17. Issued Check No. 617 for miscellaneous administrative expense, $430.
  18. Purchased maintenance supplies on account from Crowne Supply Co., $1,420.
  19. Purchased the following on account from McClain Co.: maintenance supplies, $2,020; office supplies, $440.
  20. Issued Check No. 618 in payment of advertising expense, $2,300.
  20. Used $4,000 maintenance supplies to repair delivery vehicles.
  23. Purchased office supplies on account from Office To Go, Inc., $750.
  24. Issued Invoice No. 943 to Sokol Co., $4,440.
  24. Issued Check No. 619 to K. Huss as a personal withdrawal, $5,000.
  25. Issued Invoice No. 944 to Collins Co., $5,000.
  25. Received check for $3,560 from Pease Co. in payment of balance.
  26. Issued Check No. 620 to Bell Computer Co. in payment of $3,600 invoice of July 6.
  30. Issued Check No. 621 for monthly salaries as follows: driver salaries, $15,400; office salaries, $7,500.
  31. Cash fees earned for July 17–31, $8,420.
  31. Issued Check No. 622 in payment for office supplies, $900.

Instructions

1. Enter the following account balances in the general ledger as of July 1:

11	Cash	$ 56,800	32	K. Huss, Drawing	—
12	Accounts Receivable	16,760	41	Fees Earned	—
14	Maintenance Supplies	9,300	51	Driver Salaries Expense	—
15	Office Supplies	4,500	52	Maintenance Supplies	
16	Office Equipment	24,300		Expense	—
17	Accumulated Depreciation		53	Fuel Expense	—
	—Office Equipment	4,500	61	Office Salaries Expense	—
18	Vehicles	84,600	62	Rent Expense	—
19	Accumulated Depreciation		63	Advertising Expense	—
	—Vehicles	12,300	64	Miscellaneous Adminis-	
21	Accounts Payable	9,110		trative Expense	—
31	K. Huss, Capital	170,350			

(continued)

2. Journalize the transactions for July 2003, using the following journals similar to those illustrated in this chapter: cash receipts journal, purchases journal (with columns for Accounts Payable, Maintenance Supplies, Office Supplies, and Other Accounts), single-column revenue journal, cash payments journal, and two-column general journal. You do not need to make daily postings to the individual accounts in the accounts payable ledger and the accounts receivable ledger.
3. Post the appropriate individual entries to the general ledger.
4. Total each of the columns of the special journals and post the appropriate totals to the general ledger; insert the account balances.
5. Prepare a trial balance.
6. Verify the agreement of each subsidiary ledger with its controlling account. The sum of the balances of the accounts in the subsidiary ledgers as of July 31 are:

Accounts receivable $18,880
Accounts payable   4,630

PROBLEMS SERIES B

Problem 5–1B
Revenue journal; accounts receivable and general ledgers

Objective 3

SPREADSHEET

✓ 1. Revenue journal, total fees earned, $11,135

Accu-Tax Accounting Services was established on August 15, 2003, to provide accounting and income tax preparation services. The services provided during the remainder of the month are listed below.

Aug. 18. Jacob Co., Invoice No. 1, $840 on account.
     20. Ro-Gain Co., Invoice No. 2, $650 on account.
     22. Franklin Co., Invoice No. 3, $2,150 on account.
     27. Carson Co., Invoice No. 4, $1,870 on account.
     28. Bower Co., Invoice No. 5, $1,200 on account.
     28. Ro-Gain Co., $490 in exchange for supplies.
     30. Ro-Gain Co., Invoice No. 6, $3,440 on account.
     31. Franklin Co., Invoice No. 7, $985 on account.

Instructions

1. Journalize the transactions for August, using a single-column revenue journal and a two-column general journal. Post to the following customer accounts in the accounts receivable ledger, and insert the balance immediately after recording each entry: Bower Co.; Carson Co.; Franklin Co.; Jacob Co.; Ro-Gain Co.
2. Post the revenue journal to the following accounts in the general ledger, inserting the account balances only after the last postings:

    12   Accounts Receivable
    14   Supplies
    41   Fees Earned

3. a.   What is the sum of the balances of the accounts in the subsidiary ledger at August 31?
    b.   What is the balance of the controlling account at August 31?
4. Assume that on September 1, the state in which Accu-Tax operates begins requiring that sales tax be collected on accounting services. Briefly explain how the revenue journal may be modified to accommodate sales of services on account requiring the collection of a state sales tax.

Problem 5–2B
Revenue and cash receipts journals; accounts receivable and general ledgers

Objective 3

Transactions related to revenue and cash receipts completed by Highland Engineering Services during the period November 2–30, 2003, are as follows:

Nov. 2. Issued Invoice No. 717 to Yamura Co., $5,790.
     3. Received cash from AGI Co. for the balance owed on its account.
     7. Issued Invoice No. 718 to Hardy Co., $4,120.
     10. Issued Invoice No. 719 to Ross and Son, $12,360.
     Post revenue and collections to the accounts receivable subsidiary ledger.

GENERAL LEDGER

✓ 3. Total cash receipts, $30,470

Nov. 14. Received cash from Hardy Co. for the balance owed on November 1.
16. Issued Invoice No. 720 to Hardy Co., $8,320.
   Post revenue and collections to the accounts receivable subsidiary ledger.
19. Received cash from Yamura Co. for the balance due on invoice of November 2.
20. Received cash from Hardy Co. for invoice of November 7.
23. Issued Invoice No. 721 to AGI Co., $7,040.
30. Recorded cash fees earned, $4,550.
30. Received office equipment of $10,000 in partial settlement of balance due on the Ross and Son account.
   Post revenue and collections to the accounts receivable subsidiary ledger.

Instructions

1. Insert the following balances in the general ledger as of November 1:

11	Cash	$18,940
12	Accounts Receivable	16,010
18	Office Equipment	32,600
41	Fees Earned	—

2. Insert the following balances in the accounts receivable subsidiary ledger as of November 1:

AGI Co.	$12,340
Hardy Co.	3,670
Ross and Son	—
Yamura Co.	—

3. Prepare a single-column revenue journal and a cash receipts journal. Use the following column headings for the cash receipts journal: Fees Earned, Accounts Receivable, and Cash. The Fees Earned column is used to record cash fees. Insert a check mark (✓) in the Post. Ref. Column.
4. Using the two special journals and the two-column general journal, journalize the transactions for November. Post to the accounts receivable subsidiary ledger, and insert the balances at the points indicated in the narrative of transactions. Determine the balance in the customer's account before recording a cash receipt.
5. Total each of the columns of the special journals, and post the individual entries and totals to the general ledger. Insert account balances after the last posting.
6. Determine that the subsidiary ledger agrees with the controlling account in the general ledger.

Problem 5–3B

Purchases, accounts payable account, and accounts payable ledger

Objective 3

GENERAL LEDGER

✓ 3. Total accounts payable credit, $21,800

G. Washington Surveyors provides survey work for construction projects. The office staff use office supplies, while surveying crews use field supplies. Purchases on account completed by G. Washington Surveyors during May 2003 are as follows:

May 1. Purchased field supplies on account from Wendell Co., $3,540.
3. Purchased office supplies on account from Lassiter Co., $320.
8. Purchased field supplies on account from Trent Supply, $1,890.
12. Purchased field supplies on account from Wendell Co., $2,000.
15. Purchased office supplies on account from J-Mart Co., $485.
19. Purchased office equipment on account from Eskew Co., $5,100.
23. Purchased field supplies on account from Trent Supply, $2,450.
26. Purchased office supplies on account from J-Mart Co., $415.
30. Purchased field supplies on account from Trent Supply, $5,600.

Instructions

1. Insert the following balances in the general ledger as of May 1:

14	Field Supplies	$ 5,300
15	Office Supplies	1,230
18	Office Equipment	18,400
21	Accounts Payable	4,240

(continued)

2. Insert the following balances in the accounts payable subsidiary ledger as of May 1:

Eskew Co.	$3,200
J-Mart Co.	620
Lassiter Co.	420
Trent Supply	—
Wendell Co.	—

3. Journalize the transactions for May, using a purchases journal similar to the one illustrated in this chapter. Prepare the purchases journal with columns for Accounts Payable, Field Supplies, Office Supplies, and Other Accounts. Post to the creditor accounts in the accounts payable ledger immediately after each entry.
4. Post the purchases journal to the accounts in the general ledger.
5. a. What is the sum of the balances in the subsidiary ledger at May 31?
   b. What is the balance of the controlling account at May 31?

Problem 5–4B
Purchases and cash payments journals; accounts payable and general ledgers

Objective 3

GENERAL LEDGER

✓ 1. Total cash payments, $97,290

Texas Tea Exploration Co. was established on March 15, 2003, to provide oil-drilling services. Texas Tea uses field equipment (rigs and pipe) and field supplies (drill bits and lubricants) in its operations. Transactions related to purchases and cash payments during the remainder of March are as follows:

Mar. 16. Issued Check No. 1 in payment of rent for the remainder of March, $2,400.
16. Purchased field equipment on account from PMI Sales, Inc., $24,500.
17. Purchased field supplies on account from Culver Supply Co., $12,300.
18. Issued Check No. 2 in payment of field supplies, $1,400, and office supplies, $440.
20. Purchased office supplies on account from Ange Supply Co., $2,450.
   Post the journals to the accounts payable subsidiary ledger.
24. Issued Check No. 3 to PMI Sales, Inc., in payment of March 16 invoice.
26. Issued Check No. 4 to Culver Supply Co. in payment of March 17 invoice.
28. Issued Check No. 5 to purchase land from the owner, $38,000.
28. Purchased office supplies on account from Ange Supply Co., $3,600.
   Post the journals to the accounts payable subsidiary ledger.
30. Purchased the following from PMI Sales, Inc. on account: field supplies, $18,500, and office equipment, $17,900.
30. Issued Check No. 6 to Ange Supply Co. in payment of March 20 invoice.
30. Purchased field supplies on account from Culver Supply Co., $8,400.
31. Issued Check No. 7 in payment of salaries, $15,800.
31. Acquired land in exchange for field equipment having a cost of $9,500.
   Post the journals to the accounts payable subsidiary ledger.

Instructions

1. Journalize the transactions for March. Use a purchases journal and a cash payments journal, similar to those illustrated in this chapter, and a two-column general journal. Refer to the following partial chart of accounts:

11	Cash		19	Land
14	Field Supplies		21	Accounts Payable
15	Office Supplies		61	Salary Expense
17	Field Equipment		71	Rent Expense
18	Office Equipment			

At the points indicated in the narrative of transactions, post to the following accounts in the accounts payable ledger:

Ange Supply Co.
Culver Supply Co.
PMI Sales, Inc.

2. Post the individual entries (Other Accounts columns of the purchases journal and the cash payments journal; both columns of the general journal) to the appropriate general ledger accounts.
3. Total each of the columns of the purchases journal and the cash payments journal, and post the appropriate totals to the general ledger. (Because the problem does not include transactions related to cash receipts, the cash account in the ledger will have a credit balance.)
4. Prepare a schedule of accounts payable.

Problem 5–5B

All journals and general ledger; trial balance

Objective 3

GENERAL
LEDGER

✓ 2. Total cash receipts, $71,245

The transactions completed by Direct Express Courier Company during May 2003, the first month of the fiscal year, were as follows:

May 1. Issued Check No. 205 for May rent, $900.
 2. Purchased a vehicle on account from McIntyre Sales Co., $19,700.
 3. Purchased office equipment on account from Office Mate, Inc., $3,970.
 5. Issued Invoice No. 91 to Martin Co., $7,230.
 6. Received check for $6,245 from Baker Co. in payment of invoice.
 7. Issued Invoice No. 92 to Trent Co., $3,620.
 9. Issued Check No. 206 for fuel expense, $680.
 10. Received check for $9,480 from Sing Co. in payment of invoice.
 10. Issued Check No. 207 to Office City in payment of $510 invoice.
 10. Issued Check No. 208 to Bastille Co. in payment of $1,470 invoice.
 11. Issued Invoice No. 93 to Joy Co., $5,200.
 11. Issued Check No. 209 to Porter Co. in payment of $270 invoice.
 12. Received check for $7,230 from Martin Co. in payment of invoice.
 13. Issued Check No. 210 to McIntyre Sales Co. in payment of $19,700 invoice.
 16. Cash fees earned for May 1–16, $14,450.
 16. Issued Check No. 211 for purchase of a vehicle, $21,300.
 17. Issued Check No. 212 for miscellaneous administrative expenses, $280.
 18. Purchased maintenance supplies on account from Bastille Co., $1,480.
 18. Received check for rent revenue on office space, $1,400.
 19. Purchased the following on account from Master Supply Co.: maintenance supplies, $1,950, and office supplies, $550.
 20. Issued Check No. 213 in payment of advertising expense, $6,800.
 20. Used maintenance supplies with a cost of $3,500 to overhaul vehicle engines.
 21. Purchased office supplies on account from Office City, $490.
 24. Issued Invoice No. 94 to Sing Co., $9,230.
 25. Received check for $13,240 from Baker Co. in payment of invoice.
 25. Issued Invoice No. 95 to Trent Co., $5,900.
 26. Issued Check No. 214 to Office Mate, Inc. in payment of $3,970 invoice.
 27. Issued Check No. 215 to F. Martinez as a personal withdrawal, $4,000.
 30. Issued Check No. 216 in payment of driver salaries, $23,500.
 31. Issued Check No. 217 in payment of office salaries, $15,250.
 31. Issued Check No. 218 for office supplies, $230.
 31. Cash fees earned for May 17–31, $19,200.

Instructions

1. Enter the following account balances in the general ledger as of May 1:

11	Cash	$ 37,900	32	F. Martinez, Drawing	—
12	Accounts Receivable	28,965	41	Fees Earned	—
14	Maintenance Supplies	6,150	42	Rent Revenue	—
15	Office Supplies	2,580	51	Driver Salaries Expense	—
16	Office Equipment	14,370	52	Maintenance Supplies	
17	Accumulated Depreciation			Expense	—
	—Office Equipment	3,000	53	Fuel Expense	—
18	Vehicles	48,000	61	Office Salaries Expense	—
19	Accumulated Depreciation		62	Rent Expense	—
	—Vehicles	13,590	63	Advertising Expense	—
21	Accounts Payable	2,250	64	Miscellaneous Adminis-	
31	F. Martinez, Capital	119,125		trative Expense	—

(continued)

2. Journalize the transactions for May 2003, using the following journals similar to those illustrated in this chapter: single-column revenue journal, cash receipts journal, purchases journal (with columns for Accounts Payable, Maintenance Supplies, Office Supplies, and Other Accounts), cash payments journal, and two-column general journal. You do not need to make daily postings to the individual accounts in the accounts payable ledger and the accounts receivable ledger.
3. Post the appropriate individual entries to the general ledger.
4. Total each of the columns of the special journals, and post the appropriate totals to the general ledger; insert the account balances.
5. Prepare a trial balance.
6. Verify the agreement of each subsidiary ledger with its controlling account. The sum of the balances of the accounts in the subsidiary ledgers as of May 31 are as follows:

Accounts receivable	$23,950
Accounts payable	4,470

SPECIAL ACTIVITIES

Activity 5–1
Armor Security Co.
Ethics and professional conduct in business

Lee Baskin sells security systems for Armor Security Co. Baskin has a monthly sales quota of $40,000. If Baskin exceeds this quota, he is awarded a bonus. In measuring the quota, a sale is credited to the salesperson when a customer signs a contract for installation of a security system. Through the 25th of the current month, Baskin has sold $30,000 in security systems.

Vortex Co., a business rumored to be on the verge of bankruptcy, contacted Baskin on the 26th of the month about having a security system installed. Baskin estimates that the contract would yield about $14,000 worth of business for Armor Security Co. In addition, this contract would be large enough to put Baskin "over the top" for a bonus in the current month. However, Baskin is concerned that Vortex Co. will not be able to make the contract payment after the security system is installed. In fact, Baskin has heard rumors that a competing security services company refused to install a system for Vortex Co. because of these concerns.

Upon further consideration, Baskin concluded that his job is to sell security systems and that it's someone else's problem to collect the resulting accounts receivable. Thus, Baskin wrote the contract with Vortex Co. and received a bonus for the month.

Discuss whether Lee Baskin was acting in an ethical manner. How might Armor Security Co. use internal controls to prevent this scenario from occurring?

Activity 5–2
Blacktop Pavement Co.
Manual vs. computerized accounting systems

The following conversation took place between Blacktop Pavement Co.'s bookkeeper, Gerry Monroe, and the accounting supervisor, Lyn Hargrove.

Lyn: Gerry, I'm thinking about bringing in a new computerized accounting system to replace our manual system. I guess this will mean that you will need to learn how to do computerized accounting.

Gerry: What does computerized accounting mean?

Lyn: I'm not sure, but you'll need to prepare for this new way of doing business.

Gerry: I'm not so sure we need a computerized system. I've been looking at some of the sample reports from the software vendor. It looks to me as if the computer will not add much to what we are already doing.

Lyn: What do you mean?

Gerry: Well, look at these reports. This Sales by Customer Report looks like our revenue journal, and the Deposit Detail Report looks like our cash receipts journal. Granted, the computer types them, so they look much neater than my special journals, but I don't see that we're gaining much from this change.

Lyn: Well, surely there's more to it than nice-looking reports. I've got to believe that a computerized system will save us time and effort someplace.

Gerry: I don't see how. We still need to key in transactions into the computer. If anything, there may be more work when it's all said and done.

━━▶ Do you agree with Gerry? Why might a computerized environment be preferred over the manual system?

Activity 5–3
Windsor Company
Internal controls

Like most businesses, when Windsor Company renders services to another business, it is typical that the service is rendered "on account," rather than as a cash transaction. As a result, Windsor Company has an account receivable for the service provided. Likewise, the company receiving the service has an account payable for the amount owed for services received. At a later date, Windsor Company will receive cash from the customer to satisfy the accounts receivable balance. However, when individuals conduct transactions with each other, it is common for the transaction to be for cash. For example, when you buy a pizza, you often pay with cash.

━━▶ Why is it unusual for businesses such as Windsor Company to engage in cash transactions, while for individuals it is more common?

Activity 5–4
Cisco Systems, Inc.
Accounting system performance

Corporations can take up to several weeks to close their books after an accounting period ends (often quarterly). During this time, adjusting entries are made, mistakes are corrected, and various journal entries are posted. As a result, management must wait until the books are closed before it can use the financial accounting information for decision making.

━━▶ What does the annual report for **Cisco Systems, Inc.**, in Appendix G (page G-4) indicate about how Cisco Systems closes its books, and how does this impact the decision-making ability of Cisco's management?

Activity 5–5
Ragsdale Medical Group
Design of accounting systems

For the past few years, your client, Ragsdale Medical Group (RMG), has operated a small medical practice. RMG's current annual revenues are $420,000. Because the accountant has been spending more and more time each month recording all transactions in a two-column journal and preparing the financial statements, RMG is considering improving the accounting system by adding special journals and subsidiary ledgers. RMG has asked you to help with this project and has compiled the following information:

Type of Transaction	Estimated Frequency per Month
Fees earned on account	240
Purchase of medical supplies on account	190
Cash receipts from patients on account	175
Cash payments on account	160
Cash receipts from patients at time services provided	120
Purchase of office supplies on account	35
Purchase of magazine subscriptions on account	5
Purchase of medical equipment on account	4
Cash payments for office salaries	3
Cash payments for utilities expense	3

A local sales tax is collected on all patient bills, and monthly financial statements are prepared.

1. ━━▶ Briefly discuss the circumstances under which special journals would be used in place of a two-column (all-purpose) journal. Include in your answer your recommendations for RMG's medical practice.
2. Assume that RMG has decided to use a revenue journal and a purchases journal. Design the format for each journal, giving special consideration to the needs of the medical practice.
3. Which subsidiary ledgers would you recommend for the medical practice?

Activity 5–6
Into the Real World
Web-based accounting systems

Web-based application software is one of the newest trends in business computing. Major software firms such as **Oracle**, **SAP**, and **Seibel Systems** are running their core products on the web. **NetLedger** is one of the first small business web-based accounting systems.

➤ Go to the text's Web site at **warren.swcollege.com** and click on the link to the NetLedger site. Read about the product from the site, and prepare a memo to management, defining web based accounting. Also, outline the advantages and disadvantages of web-based accounting compared to running software on a company's internal computer network.

ANSWERS TO SELF-EXAMINATION QUESTIONS

Matching

1. E	3. I	5. O	7. L	9. H	11. G	13. J	15. P
2. F	4. C	6. A	8. B	10. N	12. M	14. K	

Multiple Choice

1. **A** Analysis (answer A) is the initial step of determining the informational needs and how the system provides this information. Design (answer B) is the step in which proposals for changes are developed. Implementation (answer C) is the final step involving carrying out or implementing the proposals for changes. Feedback (answer D) is not a separate step but is considered part of the systems implementation.

2. **A** The policies and procedures that are established to safeguard assets, ensure accurate business information, and ensure compliance with laws and regulations are called internal controls (answer A). The three steps in setting up an accounting system are (1) analysis (answer B), (2) design (answer C), and (3) implementation (answer D).

3. **B** All payments of cash for any purpose are recorded in the cash payments journal (answer B). Only purchases of services or other items on account are recorded in the purchases journal (answer A). All sales of services on account are recorded in the revenue journal (answer C), and all receipts of cash are recorded in the cash receipts journal (answer D).

4. **A** The general term used to describe the type of separate ledger that contains a large number of individual accounts with a common characteristic is a subsidiary ledger (answer A). The creditors ledger (answer B), sometimes called the accounts payable ledger (answer C), is a specific subsidiary ledger containing only individual accounts with creditors. Likewise, the accounts receivable ledger (answer D), also called the customers ledger, is a specific subsidiary ledger containing only individual accounts with customers.

5. **C** Both the revenue journal (answer A) and the cash receipts journal (answer B) are generally not used in a computerized accounting system. Rather, electronic forms, such as an electronic invoice form (answer C), are used to record original transactions. The computer automatically posts transactions from electronic forms to the general ledger and individual accounts at the time the transactions are recorded. Therefore, month-end postings to the general ledger (answer D) are not necessary in a computerized accounting system.

Accounting for Merchandising Businesses

6

objectives

After studying this chapter, you should be able to:

1 Distinguish the activities of a service business from those of a merchandising business.

2 Journalize the entries for merchandise transactions, including:
   a. Merchandise purchases
   b. Merchandise sales
   c. Merchandise transportation costs
   d. Transactions for both the buyer and the seller

3 Prepare a chart of accounts for a merchandising business.

4 Prepare an income statement for a merchandising business.

5 Describe the accounting cycle for a merchandising business.

6 Compute the ratio of net sales to assets as a measure of how effectively a business is using its assets.

A ssume that you bought groceries at a store and received the receipt shown here. This receipt indicates that you purchased three items totaling $5.28, the sales tax was $0.32 (6%), the total due was $5.60, you gave the clerk $10.00, and you received change of $4.40. The receipt also indicates that the sale was made by Store #426 of the Ingles chain, located in Athens, Georgia. The date and time of the sale and other data used internally by the store are also indicated.

When you buy groceries, textbooks, school supplies, or an automobile, you are doing business with a retail or merchandising business. The accounting for a merchandising business is more complex than for a service business. For example, the accounting system for a merchandiser must be designed to record the receipt of goods for resale, keep track of the goods available for sale, and record the sale and cost of the merchandise sold.

In this chapter, we will focus on the accounting principles and concepts for merchandising businesses. We begin our discussion by highlighting the basic differences between the activities of merchandise and service businesses. We then describe and illustrate purchases and sales transactions and financial statements for merchandising businesses.

```
INGLES #426
ATHENS GA

                            10/02/02
GROCERY                       2.99L
GROCERY                       1.00L
FZ FOOD                       1.29L
SUBTOTAL                      5.28
TAX                            .32
TOTAL                         5.60

CASH                         10.00

CHANGE                        4.40

# ITEMS     3


    THANK YOU C123 R03 T12:38
```

Nature of Merchandising Businesses

objective 1

Distinguish the activities of a service business from those of a merchandising business.

How do the activities of NetSolutions, an attorney, and an architect, which are service businesses, differ from those of **Wal-Mart** or **Kmart**, which are merchandising businesses? These differences are best illustrated by focusing on the revenues and expenses in the following condensed income statements:

Service Business		Merchandising Business	
Fees earned	$XXX	Sales	$XXX
Operating expenses	−XXX	Cost of merchandise sold	−XXX
Net income	$XXX	Gross profit	$XXX
		Operating expenses	−XXX
		Net income	$XXX

 NETSOLUTIONS

The revenue activities of a service business involve providing services to customers. On the income statement for a service business, the revenues from services are reported as *fees earned*. The operating expenses incurred in providing the services are subtracted from the fees earned to arrive at *net income*.

In contrast, the revenue activities of a merchandising business involve the buying and selling of merchandise. A merchandising business must first purchase merchandise to sell to its customers. When this merchandise is sold, the revenue is reported as sales, and its cost is recognized as an expense called the **cost of merchandise sold**. The cost of merchandise sold is subtracted from sales to arrive at gross profit. This amount is called **gross profit** because it is the profit *before* deducting operating expenses.

Merchandise on hand (not sold) at the end of an accounting period is called **merchandise inventory**. Merchandise inventory is reported as a current asset on the balance sheet.

In the remainder of this chapter, we illustrate transactions that affect the income statement (sales, cost of merchandise sold, and gross profit) and the balance sheet (merchandise inventory). We will assume that NetSolutions implemented the second phase of its business plan in January 2004. During the fall of 2003, NetSolutions notified its customers that it would terminate its consulting services on December 31, 2003. Beginning on January 1, 2004, NetSolutions began operations as an Internet-based retailer of software and hardware for individuals and small businesses.

> For many merchandising businesses, the cost of merchandise sold is usually the largest expense. For example, the approximate percentage of cost of merchandise sold to sales is 70% for **JC Penney Company** and 72% for **The Home Depot**.

Merchandise transactions are recorded in the accounts, using the rules of debit and credit that we described and illustrated in earlier chapters. Special journals may be used, or transactions may be entered, recorded, and posted to the accounts electronically. Although journal entries may not be manually prepared, we will use a two-column general journal format in this chapter in order to simplify the discussion.[1]

$$\text{Sales} - \text{Cost of Merchandise Sold} = \text{Gross Profit}$$

$$\text{Gross Profit} - \text{Operating Expenses} = \text{Net Income}$$

Accounting for Purchases

objective 2a

Journalize the entries for merchandise purchases.

There are two systems for accounting for merchandise: perpetual and periodic. In the **perpetual inventory system**, each purchase and sale of merchandise is recorded in an inventory account. As a result, the amount of merchandise available for sale and the amount sold are continuously (perpetually) disclosed in the inventory records. In the **periodic inventory system**, the inventory records do not show the amount available for sale or sold during the period. Instead, a detailed listing of the merchandise for sale (called a **physical inventory**) at the end of the accounting period is prepared. This physical inventory is used to determine the cost of the merchandise on hand at the end of the period and the cost of the merchandise sold during the period.

Large retailers and many small merchandising businesses use computerized perpetual inventory systems. Such systems

> In a perpetual inventory system, each purchase and the cost of each sale are recorded in Merchandise Inventory.

---

[1] Special journals and computerized accounting systems for merchandising businesses are described in Appendix 1 at the end of this chapter.

normally use bar codes, such as the one on the back of this textbook. An optical scanner reads the bar code to record merchandise purchased and sold.

Because the perpetual inventory system is widely used, we illustrate it in this chapter. We describe and illustrate the periodic inventory system in a later chapter and in an appendix at the end of the text.

Under the perpetual inventory system, cash purchases of merchandise are recorded as follows:

Retailers, such as **Best Buy**, **Kmart**, **Sears**, and **Wal-Mart**, and grocery store chains, such as **Winn-Dixie** and **Kroger**, use bar codes and optical scanners as part of their computerized inventory systems.

	Date		Description	Post. Ref.	Debit	Credit	
JOURNAL						**PAGE 24**	
1	20— Jan.	3	Merchandise Inventory		2 5 1 0 00		1
2			Cash			2 5 1 0 00	2
3			Purchased inventory from Bowen Co.				3

Purchases of merchandise on account are recorded as follows:

	Date		Description	Post. Ref.	Debit	Credit	
5	Jan.	4	Merchandise Inventory		9 2 5 0 00		5
6			Accounts Payable—Thomas Corporation			9 2 5 0 00	6
7			Purchased inventory on account.				7

Purchases Discounts

The terms of a purchase are normally indicated on the **invoice** or bill that the seller sends to the buyer. An example of such an invoice is shown in Exhibit 1.

Exhibit 1 Invoice

Omega Technologies	1000 Matrix Blvd. San Jose, CA. 95116-1000		
			Made in U.S.A.
SOLD TO NetSolutions 5101 Washington Ave. Cincinnati, OH 45227-5101		**CUSTOMER'S ORDER NO. & DATE** 412 Jan. 10, 2004 **REFER TO INVOICE NO.** 106-8	
DATE SHIPPED Jan. 12, 2004	**HOW SHIPPED AND ROUTE** US Express Trucking Co.	**TERMS** 2/10, n/30	**INVOICE DATE** Jan. 12, 2004
FROM San Francisco	**F.O.B.** Cincinnati	**PREPAID OR COLLECT?** Prepaid	
QUANTITY 10	**DESCRIPTION** 3COM Megahertz 10/100 Lan PC Card	**UNIT PRICE** 150.00	**AMOUNT** 1,500.00

The terms for when payments for merchandise are to be made, agreed on by the buyer and the seller, are called the **credit terms**. If payment is required on delivery, the terms are *cash* or *net cash*. Otherwise, the buyer is allowed an amount of time, known as the **credit period**, in which to pay.

The credit period usually begins with the date of the sale as shown on the invoice. If payment is due within a stated number of days after the date of the invoice, such as 30 days, the terms are *net 30 days*. These terms may be written as *n/30*.[2] If payment is due by the end of the month in which the sale was made, the terms are written as *n/eom*.

As a means of encouraging the buyer to pay before the end of the credit period, the seller may offer a discount. For example, a seller may offer a 2% discount if the buyer pays within 10 days of the invoice date. If the buyer does not take the discount, the total amount is due within 30 days. These terms are expressed as *2/10, n/30* and are read as *2% discount if paid within 10 days, net amount due within 30 days*. The credit terms of 2/10, n/30 are summarized in Exhibit 2, using the information from the invoice in Exhibit 1.

Exhibit 2 Credit Terms

Discounts taken by the buyer for early payment of an invoice are called **purchases discounts**. These discounts reduce the cost of the merchandise purchased. Most businesses design their accounting systems so that all available discounts are taken. Even if the buyer has to borrow to make the payment within a discount period, it is normally to the buyer's advantage to do so. To illustrate, assume that NetSolutions borrows money to pay the invoice for $1,500, shown in Exhibit 1. The last day of the discount period in which the $30 discount can be taken is January 22, 2004. The money is borrowed for the remaining 20 days of the credit period. If we assume an annual interest rate of 12% and a 360-day year, the interest on the loan of $1,470 ($1,500 − $30) is $9.80 ($1,470 × 12% × 20/360). The net savings to NetSolutions is $20.20, computed as follows:

Discount of 2% on $1,500	$30.00
Interest for 20 days at rate of 12% on $1,470	− 9.80
Savings from borrowing	$20.20

The savings can also be seen by comparing the interest rate on the money saved by taking the discount and the interest rate on the money borrowed to take

-----

[2] The word *net* as used here does not have the usual meaning of a number after deductions have been subtracted, as in *net income*.

the discount. For NetSolutions, the interest rate on the money saved in this example is estimated by converting 2% for 20 days to a yearly rate, as follows:

$$2\% \times \frac{360 \text{ days}}{20 \text{ days}} = 2\% \times 18 = 36\%$$

If NetSolutions borrows the money to take the discount, it *pays* interest of 12%. If NetSolutions does not take the discount, it *pays* estimated interest of 36% for using the $30 for an additional 20 days.

Under the perpetual inventory system, the buyer initially debits the merchandise inventory account for the amount of the invoice. When paying the invoice, the buyer credits the merchandise inventory account for the amount of the discount. In this way, the merchandise inventory shows the *net* cost to the buyer. For example, NetSolutions would record the invoice in Exhibit 1 and its payment at the end of the discount period as follows:

Jan.	12	Merchandise Inventory	1 5 0 0 00	
		Accounts Payable—Omega Technologies		1 5 0 0 00
		Invoice 106-8.		
	22	Accounts Payable—Omega Technologies	1 5 0 0 00	
		Cash		1 4 7 0 00
		Merchandise Inventory		3 0 00
		Paid Invoice 106-8.		

If NetSolutions does not take the discount because it does not pay Invoice 106-8 until February 11, it would record the payment as follows:

Feb.	11	Accounts Payable—Omega Technologies	1 5 0 0 00	
		Cash		1 5 0 0 00
		Paid Invoice 106-8 after discount		
		period.		

Purchases Returns and Allowances

When merchandise is returned (**purchases return**) or a price adjustment is requested (**purchases allowance**), the buyer (debtor) usually sends the seller a letter or a debit memorandum. A **debit memorandum**, shown in Exhibit 3, informs the seller of the amount the buyer proposes to *debit* to the account payable due the seller. It also states the reasons for the return or the request for a price reduction.

The buyer may use a copy of the debit memorandum as the basis for recording the return or allowance or wait for approval from the seller (creditor). In either case, the buyer must debit Accounts Payable and credit Merchandise Inventory. To illustrate, NetSolutions records the return of the merchandise indicated in the debit memo in Exhibit 3 as follows:

Mar.	7	Accounts Payable—Maxim Systems	9 0 0 00	
		Merchandise Inventory		9 0 0 00
		Debit Memo No. 18.		

Exhibit 3 Debit
Memorandum

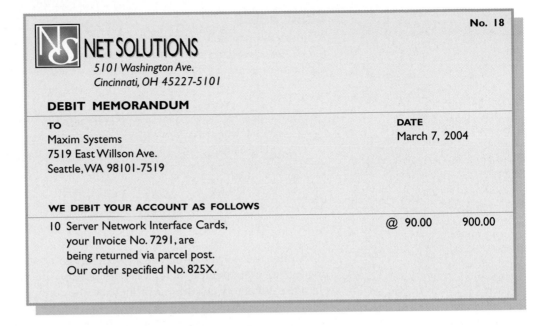

No. 18

NET SOLUTIONS

5101 Washington Ave.
Cincinnati, OH 45227-5101

DEBIT MEMORANDUM

TO	DATE
Maxim Systems	March 7, 2004
7519 East Willson Ave.	
Seattle, WA 98101-7519	

WE DEBIT YOUR ACCOUNT AS FOLLOWS

10 Server Network Interface Cards, your Invoice No. 7291, are being returned via parcel post. Our order specified No. 825X.	@ 90.00	900.00

When a buyer returns merchandise or has been granted an allowance prior to paying the invoice, the amount of the debit memorandum is deducted from the invoice amount. The amount is deducted before the purchase discount is computed. For example, assume that on May 2, NetSolutions purchases $5,000 of merchandise from Alpha Data Link, subject to terms 2/10, n/30. On May 4, NetSolutions returns $3,000 of the merchandise, and on May 12, NetSolutions pays the original invoice less the return. NetSolutions would record these transactions as follows:

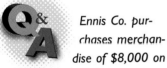

Ennis Co. purchases merchandise of $8,000 on terms 2/10, n/30. Ennis pays the original invoice, less a return of $2,500, within the discount period. How much did Ennis Co. pay?

$5,390 [($8,000 − $2,500) × 2% = $110 discount; $8,000 − $2,500 − $110 = $5,390]

May	2	Merchandise Inventory		5 0 0 0 00	
		Accounts Payable—Alpha Data Link			5 0 0 0 00
		Purchased merchandise.			
	4	Accounts Payable—Alpha Data Link		3 0 0 0 00	
		Merchandise Inventory			3 0 0 0 00
		Returned portion of merchandise			
		purchased.			
	12	Accounts Payable—Alpha Data Link		2 0 0 0 00	
		Cash			1 9 6 0 00
		Merchandise Inventory			4 0 00
		Paid invoice [($5,000 − $3,000) × 2%			
		= $40; $2,000 − $40 = $1,960].			

Accounting for Sales

Journalize the entries for merchandise sales.

Revenue from merchandise sales is usually identified in the ledger as *Sales*. Sometimes a business will use a more exact title, such as *Sales of Merchandise*.

Cash Sales

A business may sell merchandise for cash. Cash sales are normally rung up (entered) on a cash register and recorded in the accounts. To illustrate, if cash sales for January 3 are $1,800, they can be recorded as follows:

	Date		Description	Post. Ref.	Debit	Credit	
1	20— Jan.	3	Cash		1 8 0 0 00		1
2			Sales			1 8 0 0 00	2
3			To record cash sales.				3

JOURNAL — PAGE 25

Under the perpetual inventory system, the cost of merchandise sold and the reduction in merchandise inventory should also be recorded. In this way, the merchandise inventory account will indicate the amount of merchandise on hand (not sold). On the income statement at the end of the period, the balance of the cost of merchandise sold account is subtracted from the related sales for the period in order to determine the gross profit. To illustrate, assume that the cost of merchandise sold on January 3 was $1,200. The entry to record the cost of merchandise sold and the reduction in the merchandise inventory is as follows:

Jan.	3	Cost of Merchandise Sold		1 2 0 0 00		
		Merchandise Inventory			1 2 0 0 00	
		To record the cost of merchandise				
		sold.				

How do retailers record sales made with the use of credit cards? Sales made to customers using credit cards issued by banks, such as **MasterCard** or **VISA**, are recorded as *cash sales*. The seller deposits the credit card receipts for these sales directly into its bank account.

Normally, banks charge service fees for handling credit card sales. The seller debits these service fees to an expense account. An entry at the end of a month to record the payment of service charges on bank credit card sales is shown below.

Jan.	31	Credit Card Expense		4 8 00		
		Cash			4 8 00	
		To record service charges on credit				
		card sales for the month.				

Sales on Account

A business may sell merchandise on account. The seller records such sales as a debit to Accounts Receivable and a credit to Sales. An example of an entry for a sale on account of $510 follows. The cost of merchandise sold was $280.

Jan.	12	Accounts Receivable—Sims Co.		5 1 0 00		
		Sales			5 1 0 00	
		Invoice No. 7172.				

Jan.	12	Cost of Merchandise Sold	2 8 0 00		
		Merchandise Inventory		2 8 0 00	
		Cost of merchandise sold on Invoice			
		No. 7172.			

A retailer may accept **MasterCard** or **VISA** but not **American Express.** Why? The service fees that credit card companies charge retailers are the primary reason that some businesses do not accept all credit cards. For example, American Express Co.'s service fees are normally higher than MasterCard's or VISA's. As a result, some retailers choose not to accept American Express cards. The disadvantage of this practice is that the retailer may lose customers to competitors who do accept American Express cards.

Sales may also be made to customers using nonbank credit cards. An example of a nonbank credit card is the **American Express** card. Nonbank credit card sales must first be reported to the card company before cash is received. Therefore, such sales create a *receivable* with the card company. Before the card company pays cash, it normally deducts a service fee. For example, assume that American Express card sales of $1,000 are made and reported to the card company on January 20. The cost of the merchandise sold was $550. On January 27, the card company deducts a service fee of $50 and sends $950 to the seller. These transactions are recorded by the seller as follows:

Jan.	20	Accounts Receivable—American Express	1 0 0 0 00		
		Sales		1 0 0 0 00	
		American Express (nonbank) credit card			
		sales.			
	20	Cost of Merchandise Sold	5 5 0 00		
		Merchandise Inventory		5 5 0 00	
		Cost of merchandise sold on American			
		Express credit card sales.			
	27	Cash	9 5 0 00		
		Credit Card Expense	5 0 00		
		Accounts Receivable—American Express		1 0 0 0 00	
		Received cash from American Express for			
		sales reported on January 20.			

Sales Discounts

As we mentioned in our discussion of purchase transactions, a seller may offer the buyer credit terms that include a discount for early payment. The seller refers to such discounts as **sales discounts**, which reduce sales revenue.

To reduce sales, the sales account could be debited. However, managers may want to know the amount of the sales discounts for a period in deciding whether to change credit terms. For this reason, the seller records the sales discounts in a separate account. The sales discounts account is a *contra* (or *offsetting*) account to Sales. To illustrate, assume that cash is received within the discount period (10 days) from the credit sale of $1,500, shown on the invoice in Exhibit 1. Omega Technologies would record the receipt of the cash as follows:

Jan.	22	Cash	1 4 7 0 00		
		Sales Discounts	3 0 00		
		Accounts Receivable—NetSolutions		1 5 0 0 00	
		Collection on Invoice No. 106-8, less			
		2% discount.			

Sales Returns and Allowances

Merchandise sold may be returned to the seller (**sales return**). In addition, because of defects or for other reasons, the seller may reduce the initial price at which the goods were sold (**sales allowance**). If the return or allowance is for a sale on account, the seller usually issues the buyer a **credit memorandum**. This memorandum shows the amount of and the reason for the seller's credit to an account receivable. A credit memorandum is illustrated in Exhibit 4.

Exhibit 4 Credit Memorandum

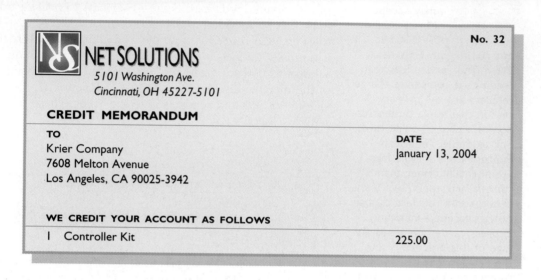

Like sales discounts, sales returns and allowances reduce sales revenue. They also result in additional shipping and other expenses. Since managers often want to know the amount of returns and allowances for a period, the seller records sales returns and allowances in a separate account. Sales Returns and Allowances is a *contra* (or *offsetting*) account to Sales.

The seller debits Sales Returns and Allowances for the amount of the return or allowance. If the original sale was on account, the seller credits Accounts Receivable. Since the merchandise inventory is kept up to date in a perpetual system, the seller adds the cost of the returned merchandise to the merchandise inventory account. The seller must also credit the cost of returned merchandise to the cost of merchandise sold account, since this account was debited when the original sale was recorded. To illustrate, assume that the cost of the merchandise returned in Exhibit 4 was $140. NetSolutions records the credit memo in Exhibit 4 as follows:

Jan.	13	Sales Returns and Allowances		2 2 5 00		
		Accounts Receivable—Krier Company				2 2 5 00
		Credit Memo No. 32.				
	13	Merchandise Inventory		1 4 0 00		
		Cost of Merchandise Sold				1 4 0 00
		Cost of merchandise returned, Credit				
		Memo No. 32.				

What if the buyer pays for the merchandise and the merchandise is later returned? In this case, the seller may issue a credit and apply it against other accounts receivable owed by the buyer, or the cash may be refunded. If the credit is applied against the buyer's other receivables, the seller records entries similar to those preceding. If cash is refunded for merchandise returned or for an allowance, the seller debits Sales Returns and Allowances and credits Cash.

Sales Taxes

The five states with the highest sales tax are Illinois, Minnesota, Nevada, Texas, and Washington. Some states have no sales tax, including Alaska, Delaware, Montana, New Hampshire, and Oregon.

Almost all states and many other taxing units levy a tax on sales of merchandise.[3] The liability for the sales tax is incurred when the sale is made.

At the time of a cash sale, the seller collects the sales tax. When a sale is made on account, the seller charges the tax to the buyer by debiting Accounts Receivable. The seller credits the sales account for the amount of the sale and credits the tax to Sales Tax Payable. For example, the seller would record a sale of $100 on account, subject to a tax of 6%, as follows:

Business collects sales tax from customers

Business remits sales tax to state

Aug.	12	Accounts Receivable—Lemon Co.	1 0 6 00		
		Sales		1 0 0 00	
		Sales Tax Payable			6 00
		Invoice No. 339.			

Normally on a regular basis, the seller pays to the taxing unit the amount of the sales tax collected. The seller records such a payment as follows:

Sept.	15	Sales Tax Payable	2 9 0 0 00	
		Cash		2 9 0 0 00
		Payment for sales taxes collected		
		during August.		

Trade Discounts

Wholesalers are businesses that sell merchandise to other businesses rather than to the general public. Many wholesalers publish catalogs. Rather than updating their catalogs frequently, wholesalers often publish price updates, which may involve large discounts from the list prices in their catalogs. In addition, wholesalers may offer special discounts to certain classes of buyers, such as government agencies or businesses that order large quantities. Such discounts are called **trade discounts**.

Sellers and buyers do not normally record the list prices of merchandise and the related trade discounts in their accounts. For example, assume that an item has a list price of $1,000 and a 40% trade discount. The seller records the sale of the item at $600 [$1,000 less the trade discount of $400 ($1,000 × 40%)]. Likewise, the buyer records the purchase at $600.

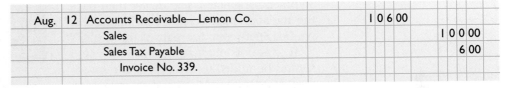

Q&A *A seller offered a 30% trade discount on an item listed in its catalog for $2,400. At what amount would the buyer record the purchase?*

$1,680 [$2,400 − ($2,400 × 30%), or $2,400 × 70%]

---

[3] Businesses that purchase merchandise for resale to others are normally exempt from paying sales taxes on their purchases. Only final buyers of merchandise normally pay sales taxes.

Transportation Costs

objective 2c

Journalize the entries for merchandise transportation costs.

The terms of a sale should indicate when the ownership (title) of the merchandise passes to the buyer. This point determines which party, the buyer or the seller, must pay the transportation costs.[4]

The ownership of the merchandise may pass to the buyer when the seller delivers the merchandise to the transportation company or freight carrier. For example, **DaimlerChrysler** records the sale and the transfer of ownership of its vehicles to dealers when the vehicles are shipped. In this case, the terms are said to be **FOB (free on board) shipping point.** This term means that DaimlerChrysler is responsible for the transportation charges to the shipping point, which is where the shipment originates. The dealer then pays the transportation costs to the final destination. Such costs are part of the dealer's total cost of purchasing inventory and should be added to the cost of the inventory by debiting Merchandise Inventory.

> The buyer bears the transportation costs if the shipping terms are FOB shipping point.

To illustrate, assume that on June 10, NetSolutions buys merchandise from Magna Data on account, $900, terms FOB shipping point, and pays the transportation cost of $50. NetSolutions records these two transactions as follows:

June	10	Merchandise Inventory		9 0 0 00	
		Accounts Payable—Magna Data			9 0 0 00
		Purchased merchandise, terms FOB			
		shipping point.			
	10	Merchandise Inventory		5 0 00	
		Cash			5 0 00
		Paid shipping cost on merchandise			
		purchased.			

> The seller bears the transportation costs if the shipping terms are FOB destination.

The ownership of the merchandise may pass to the buyer when the buyer receives the merchandise. In this case, the terms are said to be **FOB (free on board) destination.** This term means that the seller delivers the merchandise to the buyer's final destination, free of transportation charges to the buyer. The seller thus pays the transportation costs to the final destination. The seller debits Transportation Out or Delivery Expense, which is reported on the seller's income statement as an expense.

To illustrate, assume that on June 15, NetSolutions sells merchandise to Kranz Company on account, $700, terms FOB destination. The cost of the merchandise sold is $480, and NetSolutions pays the transportation cost of $40. NetSolutions records the sale, the cost of the sale, and the transportation cost as follows:

---

[4] The passage of title also determines whether the buyer or seller must pay other costs, such as the cost of insurance, while the merchandise is in transit.

Sometimes FOB shipping point and FOB destination are expressed in terms of the location at which the title to the merchandise passes to the buyer. For example, if **Toyota Motor Co.'s** assembly plant in Osaka, Japan, sells automobiles to a dealer in Chicago, FOB shipping point could be expressed as FOB Osaka. Likewise, FOB destination could be expressed as FOB Chicago.

June	15	Accounts Receivable—Kranz Company	7 0 0 00	
		Sales		7 0 0 00
		Sold merchandise, terms FOB		
		destination.		
	15	Cost of Merchandise Sold	4 8 0 00	
		Merchandise Inventory		4 8 0 00
		Recorded cost of merchandise sold to		
		Kranz Company.		
	15	Transportation Out	4 0 00	
		Cash		4 0 00
		Paid shipping cost on merchandise sold.		

Shipping terms, the passage of title, and whether the buyer or seller is to pay the transportation costs are summarized in Exhibit 5.

Exhibit 5 Transportation Terms

Martin Co. sells $4,000 of merchandise to Oblinger Co. on account on terms 2/10, n/30, FOB shipping point. As a convenience to Oblinger, Martin Co. pays transportation costs of $250 and adds those costs to the invoice. (a) How much will Martin Co. bill Oblinger? (b) If Oblinger Co. pays within the discount period, what amount will Oblinger pay Martin?

(a) $4,250 ($4,000 + $250); (b) $4,170 [$4,000 − ($4,000 × 2%) + $250]

As a convenience to the buyer, the seller may prepay the transportation costs, even though the terms are FOB shipping point. The seller will then add the transportation costs to the invoice. The buyer will debit Merchandise Inventory for the total amount of the invoice, including the transportation costs.

To illustrate, assume that on June 20, NetSolutions sells merchandise to Planter Company on account, $800, terms FOB shipping point. NetSolutions pays the transportation cost of $45 and adds it to the invoice.

The cost of the merchandise sold is $360. NetSolutions records these transactions as follows:

June 20	Accounts Receivable—Planter Company		800 00	
	Sales			800 00
	Sold merchandise, terms FOB shipping point.			
20	Cost of Merchandise Sold		360 00	
	Merchandise Inventory			360 00
	Recorded cost of merchandise sold to Planter Company.			
20	Accounts Receivable—Planter Company		45 00	
	Cash			45 00
	Prepaid shipping cost on merchandise sold.			

Illustration of Accounting for Merchandise Transactions

objective 2d

Journalize the entries for merchandise transactions for both the buyer and the seller.

Each merchandising transaction affects a buyer and a seller. In the following illustration, we show how the same transactions would be recorded by both the seller and the buyer. In this example, the seller is Scully Company and the buyer is Burton Co.

Transaction	Scully Company (Seller)		Burton Co. (Buyer)	
July 1. Scully Company sold merchandise on account to Burton Co., $7,500, terms FOB shipping point, n/45. The cost of the merchandise sold was $4,500.	Accounts Receivable—Burton Co. Sales Cost of Merchandise Sold Merchandise Inventory	7,500 4,500	 7,500 4,500	Merchandise Inventory Accounts Payable—Scully Co.	7,500 7,500
July 2. Burton Co. paid transportation charges of $150 on July 1 purchase from Scully Company.	No entry.		Merchandise Inventory Cash	150 150
July 5. Scully Company sold merchandise on account to Burton Co., $5,000, terms FOB destination, n/30. The cost of the merchandise sold was $3,500.	Accounts Receivable—Burton Co. Sales Cost of Merchandise Sold Merchandise Inventory	5,000 3,500	 5,000 3,500	Merchandise Inventory Accounts Payable—Scully Co.	5,000 5,000

Transaction	Scully Company (Seller)		Burton Co. (Buyer)	

July 7. Scully Company paid transportation costs of $250 for delivery of merchandise sold to Burton Co. on July 5.	Transportation Out
	   Cash
		250
		   250
			No entry.	

July 13. Scully Company issued Burton Co. a credit memorandum for merchandise returned, $1,000. The merchandise had been purchased by Burton Co. on account on July 5. The cost of the merchandise returned was $700.	Sales Returns & Allowances
	   Accounts Receivable—Burton Co.
	
	Merchandise Inventory
	   Cost of Merchandise Sold
		1,000
		   1,000
		
		700
		   700
			Accounts Payable—Scully Co.
			   Merchandise Inventory
				1,000
				   1,000

July 15. Scully Company received payment from Burton Co. for purchase of July 5.	Cash
	   Accounts Receivable—Burton Co.
		4,000
		   4,000
			Accounts Payable—Scully Co.
			   Cash
				4,000
				   4,000

July 18. Scully Company sold merchandise on account to Burton Co., $12,000, terms FOB shipping point, 2/10, n/eom. Scully Company prepaid transportation costs of $500, which were added to the invoice. The cost of the merchandise sold was $7,200.	Accounts Receivable—Burton Co.
	   Sales
	
	Accounts Receivable—Burton Co.
	   Cash
	
	Cost of Merchandise Sold
	   Merchandise Inventory
		12,000
		   12,000
		
		500
		   500
		
		7,200
		   7,200
			Merchandise Inventory
			   Accounts Payable—Scully Co.
				12,500
				   12,500

July 28. Scully Company received payment from Burton Co. for purchase of July 18, less discount (2% × $12,000).	Cash
	Sales Discounts
	   Accounts Receivable—Burton Co.
		12,260
		240
		   12,500
			Accounts Payable—Scully Co.
			   Merchandise Inventory
			   Cash
				12,500
				   240
				   12,260

Chart of Accounts for a Merchandising Business

objective 3

Prepare a chart of accounts for a merchandising business.

The chart of accounts for a merchandising business should reflect the types of merchandising transactions we have described in this chapter. As a basis for illustration, we use NetSolutions.

On January 1, 2004, when NetSolutions began its operations as an Internet-based retailer of software and hardware, it stopped providing consulting services. As a result, NetSolutions' chart of accounts changed from that of a service business to that of a merchandiser. A new chart of accounts for NetSolutions is shown in Exhibit 6. The accounts related to merchandising transactions are shown in color.

NetSolutions is now using three-digit account numbers, which permits it to add new accounts as they are needed. The first digit indicates the major financial statement classification (1 for assets, 2 for liabilities, and so on). The second digit indicates the subclassification (e.g., 11 for current assets, 12 for noncurrent assets).

Exhibit 6 Chart of Accounts for NetSolutions, Merchandising Business

Balance Sheet Accounts		Income Statement Accounts	
	100 Assets		400 Revenues
110	Cash	410	Sales
111	Notes Receivable	411	Sales Returns and Allowances
112	Accounts Receivable	412	Sales Discounts
113	Interest Receivable		500 Costs and Expenses
115	Merchandise Inventory	510	Cost of Merchandise Sold
116	Office supplies	520	Sales Salaries Expense
117	Prepaid Insurance	521	Advertising Expense
120	Land	522	Depreciation Expense—Store Equipment
123	Store Equipment	523	Transportation Out
124	Accumulated Depreciation— Store Equipment	529	Miscellaneous Selling Expense
125	Office Equipment	530	Office Salaries Expense
126	Accumulated Depreciation— Office Equipment	531	Rent Expense
	200 Liabilities	532	Depreciation Expense—Office Equipment
210	Accounts Payable	533	Insurance Expense
211	Salaries Payable	534	Office Supplies Expense
212	Unearned Rent	539	Misc. Administrative Expense
215	Notes Payable		600 Other Income
	300 Owner's Equity	610	Rent Revenue
310	Chris Clark, Capital	611	Interest Revenue
311	Chris Clark, Drawing		700 Other Expense
312	Income Summary	710	Interest Expense

The third digit identifies the specific account (e.g., 110 for Cash, 123 for Store Equipment).

NetSolutions is using a more complex numbering system because it has a greater variety of transactions. In addition, its growth creates a need for more detailed information for use in managing it. For example, a wages expense account was adequate for NetSolutions when it was a small service business with few employees. However, as a merchandising business, NetSolutions now uses two payroll accounts, one for Sales Salaries Expense and one for Office Salaries Expense.

Income Statement for a Merchandising Business

objective 4

Prepare an income statement for a merchandising business.

Although merchandising transactions affect the balance sheet in reporting inventory, they primarily affect the income statement. There are two widely used formats for preparing an income statement for a merchandising business: multiple step and single step.

Multiple-Step Form

The **multiple-step income statement** contains several sections, subsections, and subtotals. We use NetSolutions' income statement, shown in Exhibit 7, as a basis for illustrating this form of statement.

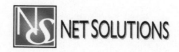

Exhibit 7 Multiple-Step Income Statement

The multiple-step form is used more often than the single-step form, as shown here.

Companies using the single-step form **26%**

Companies using the multiple-step form **74%**

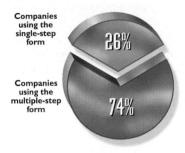

Source: 1999 edition of *Accounting Trends & Techniques.*

NetSolutions Income Statement For the Year Ended December 31, 2004				
Revenue from sales:				
Sales		$720 1 8 5 00		
Less: Sales returns and allowances	$ 6 1 4 0 00			
Sales discounts	5 7 9 0 00	1 1 9 3 0 00		
Net sales			$708 2 5 5 00	
Cost of merchandise sold			525 3 0 5 00	
Gross profit			$182 9 5 0 00	
Operating expenses:				
Selling expenses:				
Sales salaries expense	$60 0 3 0 00			
Advertising expense	10 8 6 0 00			
Depr. expense—store equipment	3 1 0 0 00			
Miscellaneous selling expense	6 3 0 00			
Total selling expense		$ 74 6 2 0 00		
Administrative expenses:				
Office salaries expense	$21 0 2 0 00			
Rent expense	8 1 0 0 00			
Depr. expense—office equipment	2 4 9 0 00			
Insurance expense	1 9 1 0 00			
Office supplies expense	6 1 0 00			
Misc. administrative expense	7 6 0 00			
Total administrative expenses		34 8 9 0 00		
Total operating expenses			109 5 1 0 00	
Income from operations			$ 73 4 4 0 00	
Other income:				
Interest revenue	$ 3 8 0 0 00			
Rent revenue	6 0 0 00			
Total other income		$ 4 4 0 0 00		
Other expense:				
Interest expense		2 4 4 0 00	1 9 6 0 00	
Net income			$ 75 4 0 0 00	

The amount of detail presented in the various sections varies from company to company. For example, instead of reporting gross sales, sales returns and allowances, and sales discounts, some companies just report net sales.

Revenue from Sales

The total amount charged customers for merchandise sold, for cash and on account, is reported in this section. Sales returns and allowances and sales discounts are deducted from this total to yield *net sales*.

Cost of Merchandise Sold

The cost of merchandise sold during the period may also be called the **cost of goods sold** or the **cost of sales**.

If net sales is $500,000 and gross profit is $180,000, what is the cost of merchandise sold?

$320,000

Gross Profit

The excess of net sales over the cost of merchandise sold is called the **gross profit**. It is sometimes called **gross profit on sales** or **gross margin**.

Operating Expenses

Most merchandising businesses classify operating expenses as either selling expenses or administrative expenses. Expenses that are incurred directly in the selling of merchandise are **selling expenses**. They include such expenses as salespersons' salaries, store supplies used, depreciation of store equipment, and advertising. Expenses incurred in the administration or general operations of the business are **administrative expenses** or **general expenses**. Examples of these expenses are office salaries, depreciation of office equipment, and office supplies used. Credit card expense is also normally classified as an administrative expense.

Expenses that are related to both selling and administration may be divided between the two classifications. In small businesses, however, such expenses as rent,

BUSINESS ON STAGE

Retailing

Retail operations can be classified as either (1) in-store retailing or (2) non-store retailing. There are ten general types of in-store retailing and four general types of nonstore retailing. Each type is briefly described below.

In-Store Retailing	Description	Examples
Department	Offers a variety of merchandise in many departments under one roof; each department is a separate buying and selling center	Sears, Rich's, JCPenney, Bloomingdale's
Specialty store	Offers a specific type of merchandise and carries a complete assortment	Toys R Us, Radio Shack, Zales Jewelers, Circuit City
Variety store	Offers a variety of inexpensive goods	Dollar General, Ben Franklin
Convenience store	Offers convenience goods, with long store hours	Circle K, 7 Eleven
Supermarket	Offers a wide variety of food, with self-service	Safeway, Kroger, Publix
Discount store	Offers low prices and high turnover of merchandise	Target, Kmart, Wal-Mart
Off-price retailer	Offers merchandise at prices 25% or more below normal prices, with low service	T.J. Maxx, Ross
Factory outlet store	Offers close-outs and factory seconds; usually owned by the manufacturer	Levi Strauss, Bass, Polo, Lenox
Wholesale club	Offers food and general merchandise at deeply discounted prices to members	Sam's, Costco
Catalog store	Offers merchandise in showrooms where customers order from catalogs	Sears, Cabela's

Nonstore Retailing	Description	Examples
Vending machine	Offers merchandise for sale from machines	Canteen
Direct selling	Salesperson sells merchandise in customer's home	Avon, Amway
Direct response marketing	Offers merchandise for sale through catalogs, direct mail, and advertising	Lands' End, J. Crew, L.L. Bean
Internet selling	Offers merchandise for sale through the Internet	Amazon.com CDNOW

insurance, and taxes are commonly reported as administrative expenses. Transactions for small, infrequent expenses are often reported as Miscellaneous Selling Expense or Miscellaneous Administrative Expense.

Income from Operations

The excess of gross profit over total operating expenses is called **income from operations** or **operating income**. The relationships of income from operations to total assets and to net sales are important factors in judging the efficiency and profitability of operations. If operating expenses are greater than the gross profit, the excess is called a **loss from operations**.

Other Income and Other Expense

Revenue from sources other than the primary operating activity of a business is classified as **other income**. In a merchandising business, these items include income from interest, rent, and gains resulting from the sale of fixed assets.

Expenses that cannot be traced directly to operations are identified as **other expense**. Interest expense that results from financing activities and losses incurred in the disposal of fixed assets are examples of these items.

Other income and other expense are offset against each other on the income statement. If the total of other income exceeds the total of other expense, the difference is added to income from operations. If the reverse is true, the difference is subtracted from income from operations.

Net Income

The final figure on the income statement is called **net income** (or **net loss**). It is the net increase (or net decrease) in the owner's equity as a result of the period's profit-making activities.

Single-Step Form

In the **single-step income statement**, the total of all expenses is deducted *in one step* from the total of all revenues. Such a statement is shown in Exhibit 8 for NetSolutions. The statement has been condensed to focus on its primary features.

The single-step form emphasizes total revenues and total expenses as the factors that determine net income. A criticism of the single-step form is that such amounts as gross profit and income from operations are not readily available for analysis.

Intel Corporation recently reported over $2 billion in other income from gains on the sale of investments in **Micron Technology Inc.** and other investment income.

Exhibit 8 Single-Step Income Statement

NetSolutions Income Statement For the Year Ended December 31, 2004			
Revenues:			
Net sales			$708 255 00
Interest revenue			3 800 00
Rent revenue			600 00
Total revenues			$712 655 00
Expenses:			
Cost of merchandise sold	$525 305 00		
Selling expenses	74 620 00		
Administrative expenses	34 890 00		
Interest expense	2 440 00		
Total expenses			637 255 00
Net income			$ 75 400 00

The Accounting Cycle for a Merchandising Business

objective 5

Describe the accounting cycle for a merchandising business.

Earlier in this chapter, we described and illustrated the chart of accounts and the analysis and recording of transactions for a merchandising business. We also illustrated the preparation of an income statement for a merchandiser, NetSolutions, at the end of an accounting cycle. In the remainder of this chapter, we describe the other elements of the accounting cycle for a merchandising business. In this discussion, we will focus primarily on the elements of this cycle that are likely to differ from those of a service business.

Merchandise Inventory Shrinkage

In 2000, retailers lost an estimated $28 billion to inventory shrinkage. The primary causes of the shrinkage were employee theft (44.2%), shoplifting (33.5%), and errors (17.2%).

"Crooked Workers Cost Stores," Renee DeGross, *The Atlanta Journal Constitution*, September 21, 2000.

Under the perpetual inventory system, a separate merchandise inventory account is maintained in the ledger. During the accounting period, this account shows the amount of merchandise for sale at any time. However, merchandising businesses may experience some loss of inventory due to shoplifting, employee theft, or errors in recording or counting inventory. As a result, the physical inventory taken at the end of the accounting period may differ from the amount of inventory shown in the inventory records. Normally, the amount of merchandise for sale, as indicated by the balance of the merchandise inventory account, is larger than the total amount of merchandise counted during the physical inventory. For this reason, the difference is often called inventory shrinkage or **inventory shortage**.

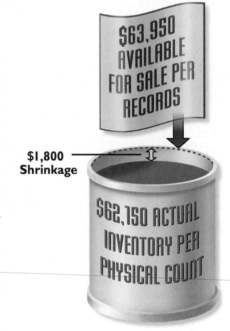

To illustrate, NetSolutions' inventory records indicate that $63,950 of merchandise should be available for sale on December 31, 2004. The physical inventory taken on December 31, 2004, however, indicates that only $62,150 of merchandise is actually available. Thus, the inventory shrinkage for the year ending December 31, 2004, is $1,800 ($63,950 − $62,150), as shown at the right. This amount is recorded by the following adjusting entry:

		Adjusting Entry										
Dec.	31	Cost of Merchandise Sold			1	8	0	0	00			
		Merchandise Inventory								1	8 0 0	00

If the inventory account has a balance of $280,000 and the physical inventory indicates merchandise on hand of $265,000, what is the amount of inventory shrinkage?

- -

$15,000 ($280,000 − $265,000)

After this entry has been recorded, the accounting records agree with the actual physical inventory at the end of the period. Since no system of procedures and safeguards can totally eliminate it, inventory shrinkage is often considered a normal cost of operations. If the amount of the shrinkage is abnormally large, it may be disclosed separately on the income statement. In such cases, the shrinkage may be recorded in a separate account, such as Loss from Merchandise Inventory Shrinkage.

Work Sheet

Merchandising businesses that use a perpetual inventory system are also likely to use a computerized accounting system. In a computerized system, the adjusting entries are recorded and financial statements prepared without using a work sheet. For this reason, we illustrate the work sheet and the adjusting entries for NetSolutions in the appendix at the end of this chapter.

Statement of Owner's Equity

The statement of owner's equity for NetSolutions is shown in Exhibit 9. This statement is prepared in the same manner that we described previously for a service business.

Exhibit 9 Statement of Owner's Equity for Merchandising Business

NetSolutions Statement of Owner's Equity For the Year Ended December 31, 2004		
Chris Clark, capital, January 1, 2004		$153 800 00
Net income for year	$75 400 00	
Less withdrawals	18 000 00	
Increase in owner's equity		57 400 00
Chris Clark, capital, December 31, 2004		$211 200 00

Balance Sheet

As we discussed and illustrated in previous chapters, the balance sheet may be presented with assets on the left-hand side and the liabilities and owner's equity on the right-hand side. This form of the balance sheet is called the **account form**. The balance sheet may also be presented in a downward sequence in three sections. This form of balance sheet is called the **report form**. The report form of balance sheet for NetSolutions is shown in Exhibit 10. In this balance sheet, note that merchandise inventory at the end of the period is reported as a current asset and that the current portion of the note payable is $5,000.

Closing Entries

The closing entries for a merchandising business are similar to those for a service business. The first entry closes the temporary accounts with credit balances, such as Sales, to the income summary account. The second entry closes the temporary accounts with debit balances, including Sales Returns and Allowances, Sales Discounts, and Cost of Merchandise Sold, to the income summary account. The third entry closes the balance of the income summary account to the owner's capital account. The fourth entry closes the owner's drawing account to the owner's capital account.

In a computerized accounting system, the closing entries are prepared automatically. For this reason, we illustrate the closing entries for NetSolutions in the appendix at the end of this chapter.

Exhibit 10 Report Form of
Balance Sheet

NetSolutions Balance Sheet December 31, 2004				
Assets				
Current assets:				
Cash		$52 9 5 0 00		
Notes receivable		35 0 0 0 00		
Accounts receivable		55 8 8 0 00		
Interest receivable		2 0 0 00		
Merchandise inventory		62 1 5 0 00		
Office supplies		4 8 0 00		
Prepaid insurance		2 6 5 0 00		
Total current assets			$209 3 1 0 00	
Property, plant, and equipment:				
Land		$20 0 0 0 00		
Store equipment	$27 1 0 0 00			
Less accumulated depreciation	5 7 0 0 00	21 4 0 0 00		
Office equipment	$15 5 7 0 00			
Less accumulated depreciation	4 7 2 0 00	10 8 5 0 00		
Total property, plant, and equipment			52 2 5 0 00	
Total assets			$261 5 6 0 00	
Liabilities				
Current liabilities:				
Accounts payable		$22 4 2 0 00		
Note payable (current portion)		5 0 0 0 00		
Salaries payable		1 1 4 0 00		
Unearned rent		1 8 0 0 00		
Total current liabilities			$ 30 3 6 0 00	
Long-term liabilities:				
Note payable (final payment due 2014)			20 0 0 0 00	
Total liabilities			$ 50 3 6 0 00	
Owner's Equity				
Chris Clark, capital			211 2 0 0 00	
Total liabilities and owner's equity			$261 5 6 0 00	

FINANCIAL ANALYSIS AND INTERPRETATION

objective 6

Compute the ratio of net sales to assets as a measure of how effectively a business is using its assets.

The ratio of net sales to assets measures how effectively a business is using its assets to generate sales. A high ratio indicates an effective use of assets. The assets used in computing the ratio may be the total assets at the end of the year, the average of the total assets at the beginning and end of the year, or the average of the monthly assets. For our purposes, we will use the average of the total assets at the beginning and end of the year. The ratio is computed as follows:

$$\text{Ratio of net sales to assets} = \frac{\text{Net sales}}{\text{Average total assets}}$$

To illustrate the use of this ratio, the following data are taken from annual reports of **Sears** and **JCPenney**:

	Sears	JCPenney
Net sales (in millions)	$41,071	$30,678
Total assets (in millions):		
Beginning of year	37,675	23,638
End of year	36,954	23,493

The ratio of net sales to assets for each company is as follows:

	Sears	JCPenney
Ratio of net sales to assets:	1.10*	1.30**

*$41,071/[($37,675 + $36,954)/2]
**$30,678/[($23,638 + $23,493)/2]

Based on these ratios, JCPenney appears better than Sears in utilizing its assets to generate sales. Comparing this ratio over time for both Sears and JCPenney, as well as comparing it with industry averages, would provide a better basis for interpreting the financial performance of each company.

ENCORE

Wal-Mart

As a young man just out of the Army, Sam Walton wanted to go into retailing and operate his own business. With $5,000 of his own money and a loan of $20,000 from his father-in-law, he opened his first store in Newport, Arkansas, on September 1, 1945. This first store was a Ben Franklin variety store. Within five years, this store was the No. 1 Ben Franklin store—for sales and profit—not only in Arkansas, but in a six-state region. Unfortunately, Sam forgot to include a renewal clause in the lease for his store building. His landlord decided not to renew Sam's lease, but instead offered to buy the business, including fixtures and inventory. The landlord wanted to purchase the profitable store for his son to own and operate. Without any other suitable location in town, Sam had to sell.

Unwilling to quit, Sam purchased a new store in Bentonville, Arkansas, and opened Walton's Five and Dime on August 1, 1951. By 1960, Sam had opened fifteen variety stores, with revenues of $1.4 million. Sam realized the potential of discounting when a regional discounter moved into Arkansas. So Sam opened his first Wal-Mart on July 2, 1962, choosing the name Wal-Mart because it didn't have many letters, which would make it cheaper to build and maintain the store signs. To avoid competing with Kmart, Sam initially expanded into small towns of less than 10,000 people.

The rest of the story is history. Wal-Mart grew from 32 stores and $31 million in sales in 1970 to 276 stores and $1.2 billion in sales in 1980.

Sam Walton

Today it has over 2,000 stores and $95 billion in sales. During that time, Wal-Mart issued stock, opened Sam's Clubs, and Sam Walton became one of the richest men in America. ■

APPENDIX 1: ACCOUNTING SYSTEMS FOR MERCHANDISERS

Merchandising companies may use either manual or computerized accounting systems, similar to those used by service businesses. In this appendix, we describe and illustrate special journals and electronic forms that merchandise businesses may use in these systems.

Manual Accounting System

In a manual accounting system, a merchandise business normally uses four special journals: sales journal (for sales on account), purchases journal (for purchases on account), cash receipts journal, and cash payments journal. These journals can be adapted from the special journals that we illustrated earlier for a service business.

Exhibit 11 illustrates NetSolutions' sales journal, which is modified from a revenue journal. In a sales journal, each transaction is recorded by entering the sales amount in the *Accounts Receivable Dr./Sales Cr.* column and entering the cost of the merchandise sold amount in the *Cost of Merchandise Sold Dr./Merchandise Inventory Cr.* column. The totals of the two columns would be posted to the four general ledger accounts. The inventory and accounts receivable subsidiary ledgers would be updated when each transaction is recorded.

Exhibit 11 Sales Journal for a Merchandising Business

	Date		Invoice No.	Account Debited	Post. Ref.	Accts. Rec. Dr. Sales Cr.	Cost of Merchandise Sold Dr. Merchandise Inventory Cr.	
1	2004 Mar.	2	810	Berry Co.	✔	2 7 5 0 00	2 0 0 0 00	1
2		14	811	Handler Co.	✔	4 2 6 0 00	3 4 7 0 00	2
3		19	812	Jordan Co.	✔	5 8 0 0 00	4 6 5 0 00	3
4		26	813	Kenner Co.	✔	4 5 0 0 00	3 8 4 0 00	4
5						17 3 1 0 00	13 9 6 0 00	5
6						(112) (410)	(510) (115)	6

SALES JOURNAL — PAGE 35

Exhibit 12 illustrates a purchases journal for NetSolutions' merchandising business. This journal is similar to the purchases journal for NetSolutions' service business that we illustrated previously. It includes an *Accounts Payable Cr.* column and a *Merchandise Inventory Dr.* column, rather than a *Supplies Dr.* column. At the end of the month, these two column totals would be posted to the general ledger controlling accounts, Accounts Payable and Merchandise Inventory. The amounts in *Other Accounts Dr.* would be posted individually. The inventory and accounts payable subsidiary ledgers would be updated when each transaction is recorded.

Exhibit 13 illustrates a portion of NetSolutions' cash receipts journal. In this journal, cash sales are recorded in a *Sales Cr.* column rather than a *Fees Earned Cr.* column. In addition, the cost of merchandise sold for cash is recorded in a *Cost of*

Exhibit 12 Purchases Journal for a Merchandising Business

	Date		Account Credited	Post. Ref.	Accounts Payable Cr.	Merchandise Inventory Dr.	Other Accounts Dr.	Post. Ref.	Amount	
	PURCHASES JOURNAL								**PAGE 11**	
1	2004 Mar.	4	Compu-Tek	✔	13 88 0 00	13 88 0 00				1
2		7	Omega Technologies	✔	4 65 0 00	4 65 0 00				2
3		15	Dale Furniture Co.	✔	5 70 0 00		Store Equipment	123	5 70 0 00	3
4		22	Alpha Data Link	✔	3 84 0 00	3 84 0 00				4
5		29	Power Electronics	✔	3 20 0 00	3 20 0 00				5
6					31 27 0 00	25 57 0 00			5 70 0 00	6
7					(210)	(115)			(✔)	7

Exhibit 13 Cash Receipts Journal for Merchandising Business

	Date	Account Credited	Post. Ref.	Other Accounts Cr.	Cost of Merchandise Sold Dr. Merchandise Inventory Cr.	Sales Cr.	Accounts Receivable Cr.	Sales Discounts Dr.	Cash Dr.
	CASH RECEIPTS JOURNAL								**PAGE 14**
	2004 Mar. 3	Sales	✔		4 00 00	6 00 00			6 00 00
	12	Berry Co.	✔				2 75 0 00	5 5 00	2 69 5 00

Merchandise Sold Dr./Merchandise Inventory Cr. column. Each entry in this column is posted to the inventory subsidiary ledger at the time the transaction is recorded. Sales discounts are recorded in a *Sales Discounts Dr.* column. At the end of the month, all the column totals except for *Other Accounts Cr.* are posted to the general ledger.

Exhibit 14 illustrates a portion of the cash payments journal for NetSolutions. This journal is modified for a merchandising business by adding a *Merchandise Inventory Cr.* column for recording discounts on purchases paid within the discount period. Each entry in this column is posted to the inventory subsidiary ledger at the time the transaction is recorded. At the end of the month, all the column totals except for *Other Accounts Dr.* are posted to the general ledger.

Exhibit 14 Cash Payments Journal for Merchandising Business

	Date		Ck. No.	Account Debited	Post. Ref.	Other Accounts Dr.	Accounts Payable Dr.	Merchandise Inventory Cr.	Cash Cr.	
	CASH PAYMENTS JOURNAL								**PAGE 7**	
1	2004 Mar.	14	210	Compu-Tek	✔		13 88 0 00		13 88 0 00	1
2		17	211	Omega Technologies	✔		4 65 0 00	9 3 00	4 55 7 00	2

Computerized Accounting Systems

In computerized accounting systems, special journals may be replaced by electronic forms that capture the necessary information. The software then uses this information as the basis for making entries automatically. In QuickBooks, for example, the inventory items to be purchased and sold must first be identified, using an "Edit Item" form. The software will later record each item's purchase or sale, using information from this form. The Edit Item form in Exhibit 15 shows this information for NetSolutions' purchase of LT-1000 network servers from Compu-Tek. Each server cost $3,470 per unit and will be sold for $4,260 per unit.

Exhibit 15 Edit Item Form

After inventory items have been described inside QuickBooks, transaction data can be entered. We will begin with NetSolutions' March 4, 2004 purchase from Compu-Tek, which we illustrated previously in the purchases journal in Exhibit 12. We will use the "Enter Bills" form, shown in Exhibit 16, to record the purchase of four LT-1000s from Compu-Tek.

Exhibit 16 Enter Bills Form

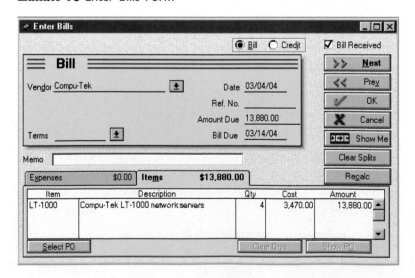

Automatic Postings

Dr. Merch. Inv.—LT-1000	13,880	
Cr. Accounts Payable—Compu-Tek		13,880

After the Enter Bills form has been completed, the software adds the cost of four LT-1000s to NetSolutions' inventory. At the same time, it establishes an account payable to Compu-Tek for $13,880.

Now, assume that on March 14 NetSolutions bills Handler Co. for one of these network servers, as illustrated in the sales journal in Exhibit 11. Using the "Create Invoices" form in QuickBooks, as shown in Exhibit 17, we enter the sale and the software establishes an account receivable for Handler Co. In addition, the software reduces the inventory stock level of the LT-1000 by $3,470 and records the cost of goods sold. This latter transaction is recorded automatically and is not shown on the Create Invoices form.

Exhibit 17 Create Invoices Form

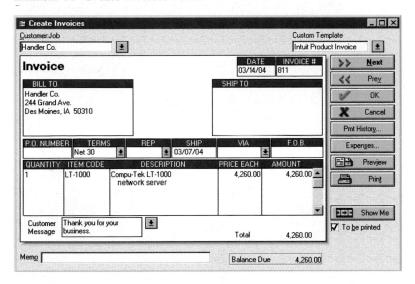

Automatic Postings

Dr. Accts. Rec.—Handler Co.	4,260	
Cr. Sales		4,260
Dr. Cost of Merch. Sold	3,470	
Cr. Merch. Inv.—LT-1000		3,470

An income statement prepared after these forms have been completed would show sales of $4,260, cost of goods sold of $3,470, and gross profit of $790. A balance sheet would show accounts receivable of $4,260, inventory of $10,410 (3 × $3,470), and accounts payable of $13,880.

APPENDIX 2: WORK SHEET AND ADJUSTING AND CLOSING ENTRIES FOR A MERCHANDISING BUSINESS

A merchandising business that does not use a computerized accounting system may use a work sheet in assembling the data for preparing financial statements and adjusting and closing entries. In this appendix, we illustrate such a work sheet, along with the adjusting and closing entries for a merchandising business.

The work sheet in Exhibit 18 is for NetSolutions on December 31, 2004, the end of its first year of operations as a merchandiser. In this work sheet, we list all of the accounts, including the accounts that have no balances, in the order that they appear in NetSolutions' ledger.

The data needed for adjusting the accounts of NetSolutions are as follows:

Interest accrued on notes receivable on December 31, 2004		$ 200
Physical merchandise inventory on December 31, 2004		62,150
Office supplies on hand on December 31, 2004		480
Insurance expired during 2004		1,910
Depreciation during 2004 on: Store equipment		3,100
Office equipment		2,490
Salaries accrued on December 31, 2004: Sales salaries	$780	
Office salaries	360	1,140
Rent earned during 2004		600

Exhibit 18 Work Sheet for Merchandising Business

NetSolutions
Work Sheet
For the Year Ended December 31, 2004

	Account Title	Trial Balance Dr.	Trial Balance Cr.	Adjustments Dr.	Adjustments Cr.	Adjusted Trial Balance Dr.	Adjusted Trial Balance Cr.	Income Statement Dr.	Income Statement Cr.	Balance Sheet Dr.	Balance Sheet Cr.	
1	Cash	52,950				52,950				52,950		1
2	Notes Receivable	35,000				35,000				35,000		2
3	Accounts Receivable	55,880				55,880				55,880		3
4	Interest Receivable			(a) 200		200				200		4
5	Merchandise Inventory	63,950			(b)1,800	62,150				62,150		5
6	Office Supplies	1,090			(c) 610	480				480		6
7	Prepaid Insurance	4,560			(d)1,910	2,650				2,650		7
8	Land	20,000				20,000				20,000		8
9	Store Equipment	27,100				27,100				27,100		9
10	Accum. Depr.—Store Equip.		2,600		(e)3,100		5,700				5,700	10
11	Office Equipment	15,570				15,570				15,570		11
12	Accum. Depr.—Office Equip.		2,230		(f) 2,490		4,720				4,720	12
13	Accounts Payable		22,420				22,420				22,420	13
14	Salaries Payable				(g)1,140		1,140				1,140	14
15	Unearned Rent		2,400	(h) 600			1,800				1,800	15
16	Notes Payable											16
17	(final payment due 2014)		25,000				25,000				25,000	17
18	Chris Clark, Capital		153,800				153,800				153,800	18
19	Chris Clark, Drawing	18,000				18,000				18,000		19
20	Sales		720,185				720,185		720,185			20
21	Sales Returns and Allowances	6,140				6,140		6,140				21
22	Sales Discounts	5,790				5,790		5,790				22
23	Cost of Merchandise Sold	523,505		(b)1,800		525,305		525,305				23
24	Sales Salaries Expense	59,250		(g) 780		60,030		60,030				24
25	Advertising Expense	10,860				10,860		10,860				25
26	Depr. Exp.—Store Equip.			(e)3,100		3,100		3,100				26
27	Miscellaneous Selling Expense	630				630		630				27
28	Office Salaries Expense	20,660		(g) 360		21,020		21,020				28
29	Rent Expense	8,100				8,100		8,100				29
30	Depr. Exp.—Office Equip.			(f)2,490		2,490		2,490				30
31	Insurance Expense			(d)1,910		1,910		1,910				31
32	Office Supplies Expense			(c) 610		610		610				32
33	Misc. Administrative Expense	760				760		760				33
34	Rent Revenue				(h) 600		600		600			34
35	Interest Revenue		3,600		(a) 200		3,800		3,800			35
36	Interest Expense	2,440				2,440		2,440				36
37		932,235	932,235	11,850	11,850	939,165	939,165	649,185	724,585	289,980	214,580	37
38	Net income							75,400			75,400	38
39								724,585	724,585	289,980	289,980	39

(a) Interest earned but not received on notes receivable, $200.

(b) Merchandise inventory shrinkage for period, $1,800 ($63,950 − $62,150).

(c) Office supplies used, $610 ($1,090 − $480).

(d) Insurance expired, $1,910.

(e) Depreciation of store equipment, $3,100.

(f) Depreciation of office equipment, $2,490.

(g) Salaries accrued but not paid
(sales salaries, $780; office salaries, $360), $1,140.

(h) Rent earned from amount received in advance, $600.

There is no specific order in which to analyze the accounts in the work sheet, assemble the adjustment data, and make the adjusting entries. However, you can normally save time by selecting the accounts in the order in which they appear on the trial balance. Using this approach, the adjustment for accrued interest is listed first {entry (a) on the work sheet}, followed by the adjustment for merchandise inventory shrinkage {entry (b) on the work sheet}, and so on.

After all the adjustments have been entered on the work sheet, the Adjustments columns are totaled to prove the equality of debits and credits. As we illustrated in previous chapters, the adjusted amounts of the balances in the Trial Balance columns are extended to the Adjusted Trial Balance columns.[5] The Adjusted Trial Balance columns are then totaled to prove the equality of debits and credits.

The balances, as adjusted, are then extended to the statement columns. The four statement columns are totaled, and the net income or net loss is determined. For NetSolutions, the difference between the credit and debit columns of the Income Statement section is $75,400, the amount of the net income. The difference between the debit and credit columns of the Balance Sheet section is also $75,400, which is the increase in owner's equity as a result of the net income. Agreement between the two balancing amounts is evidence of debit-credit equality and mathematical accuracy.

The income statement, statement of owner's equity, and balance sheet are prepared from the work sheet in a manner similar to that of a service business. The Adjustments columns in the work sheet provide the data for journalizing the adjusting entries. NetSolutions' adjusting entries at the end of 2004 are as follows:

	Date		Description	Post. Ref.	Debit	Credit	
1	2004		Adjusting Entries				1
2	Dec.	31	Interest Receivable	113	2 0 0 00		2
3			Interest Revenue	611		2 0 0 00	3
4							4
5		31	Cost of Merchandise Sold	510	1 8 0 0 00		5
6			Merchandise Inventory	115		1 8 0 0 00	6
7							7
8		31	Office Supplies Expense	534	6 1 0 00		8
9			Office Supplies	116		6 1 0 00	9
10							10
11		31	Insurance Expense	533	1 9 1 0 00		11
12			Prepaid Insurance	117		1 9 1 0 00	12
13							13
14		31	Depreciation Expense—				14
15			Store Equipment	522	3 1 0 0 00		15
16			Accumulated Depreciation—				16
17			Store Equipment	124		3 1 0 0 00	17
18							18
19		31	Depreciation Expense—				19
20			Office Equipment	532	2 4 9 0 00		20
21			Accumulated Depreciation—				21
22			Office Equipment	126		2 4 9 0 00	22

JOURNAL — **PAGE 28**

[5] Some accountants prefer to eliminate the Adjusted Trial Balance columns and to extend the adjusted balances directly to the statement columns. Such a work sheet is often used if there are only a few adjustment items.

		JOURNAL			PAGE 28	
	Date	Description	Post. Ref.	Debit	Credit	
24	31	Sales Salaries Expense	520	7 8 0 0 00		24
25		Office Salaries Expense	530	3 6 0 00		25
26		Salaries Payable	211		1 1 4 0 00	26
27						27
28	31	Unearned Rent	212	6 0 0 00		28
29		Rent Revenue	610		6 0 0 00	29

The Income Statement columns of the work sheet provide the data for preparing the closing entries. The closing entries for NetSolutions at the end of 2004 are as follows:

			JOURNAL			PAGE 29	
	Date		Description	Post. Ref.	Debit	Credit	
1	2004		Closing Entries				1
2	Dec.	31	Sales	410	720 1 8 5 00		2
3			Rent Revenue	610	6 0 0 00		3
4			Interest Revenue	611	3 8 0 0 00		4
5			Income Summary	312		724 5 8 5 00	5
6							6
7		31	Income Summary	312	649 1 8 5 00		7
8			Sales Returns and Allowances	411		6 1 4 0 00	8
9			Sales Discounts	412		5 7 9 0 00	9
10			Cost of Merchandise Sold	510		525 3 0 5 00	10
11			Sales Salaries Expense	520		60 0 3 0 00	11
12			Advertising Expense	521		10 8 6 0 00	12
13			Depr. Expense—Store Equipment	522		3 1 0 0 00	13
14			Miscellaneous Selling Expense	529		6 3 0 00	14
15			Office Salaries Expense	530		21 0 2 0 00	15
16			Rent Expense	531		8 1 0 0 00	16
17			Depr. Expense—Office Equipment	532		2 4 9 0 00	17
18			Insurance Expense	533		1 9 1 0 00	18
19			Office Supplies Expense	534		6 1 0 00	19
20			Misc. Administrative Expense	539		7 6 0 00	20
21			Interest Expense	710		2 4 4 0 00	21
22							22
23		31	Income Summary	312	75 4 0 0 00		23
24			Chris Clark, Capital	310		75 4 0 0 00	24
25							25
26		31	Chris Clark, Capital	310	18 0 0 0 00		26
27			Chris Clark, Drawing	311		18 0 0 0 00	27

The balance of Income Summary, after the first two closing entries have been posted, is the net income or net loss for the period. The third closing entry transfers this balance to the owner's capital account. NetSolutions' income summary account after the closing entries have been posted is as follows:

ACCOUNT *Income Summary*					ACCOUNT NO. *312*	
		Post.			Balance	
Date	Item	Ref.	Debit	Credit	Debit	Credit
2004 Dec. 31	Revenues	29		724 585 00		724 585 00
31	Expenses	29	649 185 00			75 400 00
31	Net income	29	75 400 00		—	—

After the closing entries have been prepared and posted to the accounts, a post-closing trial balance may be prepared to verify the debit-credit equality. The only accounts that should appear on the post-closing trial balance are the asset, contra asset, liability, and owner's capital accounts with balances. These are the same accounts that appear on the end-of-period balance sheet.

KEY POINTS

1 Distinguish the activities of a service business from those of a merchandising business.

The primary differences between a service business and a merchandising business relate to revenue activities. Merchandising businesses purchase merchandise for selling to customers.

On a merchandising business's income statement, revenue from selling merchandise is reported as sales. The cost of the merchandise sold is subtracted from sales to arrive at gross profit. The operating expenses are subtracted from gross profit to arrive at net income.

Merchandise inventory, which is merchandise not sold, is reported as a current asset on the balance sheet.

2a Journalize the entries for merchandise purchases.

Purchases of merchandise for cash or on account are recorded by debiting Merchandise Inventory. For purchases of merchan-

dise on account, the credit terms may allow cash discounts for early payment. Such purchases discounts are viewed as a reduction in the cost of the merchandise purchased. When merchandise is returned or a price adjustment is granted, the buyer credits Merchandise Inventory.

2b Journalize the entries for merchandise sales.

Sales of merchandise for cash or on account are recorded by crediting Sales. The cost of merchandise sold and the reduction in merchandise inventory are also recorded for the sale.

For sales of merchandise on account, the credit terms may allow sales discounts for early payment. Such discounts are recorded by the seller as a debit to Sales Discounts. Sales discounts are reported as a deduction from the amount initially recorded in Sales. Likewise, when merchandise is returned or a price adjustment is granted, the seller debits Sales Returns and Allowances.

The liability for sales tax is incurred when the sale is made and is recorded by the seller as a credit to the sales tax payable account. When the amount of the sales tax is paid to the taxing unit, Sales Tax Payable is debited and Cash is credited.

Many wholesalers offer trade discounts, which are discounts off the list prices of merchandise. Normally, neither the seller or the buyer records the list price and the related trade discount in the accounts.

2c Journalize the entries for merchandise transportation costs.

When merchandise is shipped FOB shipping point, the buyer pays the transportation costs and debits Merchandise Inventory. When merchandise is shipped FOB destination, the seller pays the transportation costs and debits Transportation Out or Delivery Expense. If the seller prepays transportation costs as a convenience to the buyer, the seller debits Accounts Receivable for the costs.

2d Journalize the entries for merchandise transactions for both the buyer and the seller.

The illustration in this chapter summarizes the entries that the seller and the buyer of merchandise would record.

3 Prepare a chart of accounts for a merchandising business.

The chart of accounts for a merchandising business is more complex than that for a service business and normally includes accounts such as Sales, Sales Discounts, Sales Returns and Allowances, Cost of Merchandise Sold, and Merchandise Inventory.

4 Prepare an income statement for a merchandising business.

The income statement for a merchandising business reports sales, cost of merchandise sold, and gross profit. The income statement can be prepared in either the multiple-step form or the single-step form.

5 Describe the accounting cycle for a merchandising business.

The accounting cycle for a merchandising business is similar to that of a service business. However, a merchandiser is likely to experience inventory shrinkage, which must be recorded. The normal adjusting entry is to debit Cost of Merchandise Sold and credit Merchandise Inventory for the amount of the shrinkage.

The balance sheet may be prepared in either the account form or the report form. Merchandise inventory should be reported as a current asset.

6 Compute the ratio of net sales to assets as a measure of how effectively a business is using its assets.

The assets used in computing the ratio of net sales to assets may be total assets at the end of the year, the average of the total assets at the beginning and end of the year, or the average of the monthly assets. A high ratio of net sales to assets indicates an effective use of assets.

ILLUSTRATIVE PROBLEM

The following transactions were completed by Montrose Company during May of the current year. Montrose Company uses a perpetual inventory system.

May 3. Purchased merchandise on account from Floyd Co., $4,000, terms FOB shipping point, 2/10, n/30, with prepaid transportation costs of $120 added to the invoice.

5. Purchased merchandise on account from Kramer Co., $8,500, terms FOB destination, 1/10, n/30.

6. Sold merchandise on account to C. F. Howell Co., list price $4,000, trade discount 30%, terms 2/10, n/30. The cost of the merchandise sold was $1,125.

8. Purchased office supplies for cash, $150.

10. Returned merchandise purchased on May 5 from Kramer Co., $1,300.

13. Paid Floyd Co. on account for purchase of May 3, less discount.

14. Purchased merchandise for cash, $10,500.

15. Paid Kramer Co. on account for purchase of May 5, less return of May 10 and discount.

16. Received cash on account from sale of May 6 to C. F. Howell Co., less discount.

19. Sold merchandise on nonbank credit cards and reported accounts to the card company, American Express, $2,450. The cost of the merchandise sold was $980.

22. Sold merchandise on account to Comer Co., $3,480, terms 2/10, n/30. The cost of the merchandise sold was $1,400.

24. Sold merchandise for cash, $4,350. The cost of the merchandise sold was $1,750.

25. Received merchandise returned by Comer Co. from sale on May 22, $1,480. The cost of the returned merchandise was $600.

31. Received cash from card company for nonbank credit card sales of May 19, less $140 service fee.

Instructions

1. Journalize the preceding transactions.
2. Journalize the adjusting entry for merchandise inventory shrinkage, $3,750.

Solution

1.

May	3	Merchandise Inventory	4,120	
		Accounts Payable—Floyd Co.		4,120
	5	Merchandise Inventory	8,500	
		Accounts Payable—Kramer Co.		8,500
	6	Accounts Receivable—C. F. Howell Co.	2,800	
		Sales		2,800
		[$4,000 − (30% × $4,000)]		
	6	Cost of Merchandise Sold	1,125	
		Merchandise Inventory		1,125
	8	Office Supplies	150	
		Cash		150
	10	Accounts Payable—Kramer Co.	1,300	
		Merchandise Inventory		1,300
	13	Accounts Payable—Floyd Co.	4,120	
		Merchandise Inventory		80
		Cash		4,040
		[$4,000 − (2% × $4,000) + $120]		
	14	Merchandise Inventory	10,500	
		Cash		10,500
	15	Accounts Payable—Kramer Co.	7,200	
		Merchandise Inventory		72
		Cash		7,128
		[($8,500 − $1,300) × 1% = $72;		
		$8,500 − $1,300 − $72 = $7,128]		
	16	Cash	2,744	
		Sales Discounts	56	
		Accounts Receivable—C. F. Howell Co.		2,800
	19	Accounts Receivable—American Express	2,450	
		Sales		2,450
	19	Cost of Merchandise Sold	980	
		Merchandise Inventory		980
	22	Accounts Receivable—Comer Co.	3,480	
		Sales		3,480
	22	Cost of Merchandise Sold	1,400	
		Merchandise Inventory		1,400
	24	Cash	4,350	
		Sales		4,350
	24	Cost of Merchandise Sold	1,750	
		Merchandise Inventory		1,750
	25	Sales Returns and Allowances	1,480	
		Accounts Receivable—Comer Co.		1,480
	25	Merchandise Inventory	600	
		Cost of Merchandise Sold		600
	31	Cash	2,310	
		Credit Card Expense	140	
		Accounts Receivable—American Express		2,450

2.

May	31	Cost of Merchandise Sold	3,750	
		Merchandise Inventory		3,750

SELF-EXAMINATION QUESTIONS   Answers at End of Chapter

Matching

Match each of the following statements with its proper term. Some terms may not be used.

A. account form

B. administrative expenses (general expenses)

C. cost of merchandise sold

D. credit memorandum

E. debit memorandum

F. FOB (free on board) destination

G. FOB (free on board) shipping point

H. gross profit

I. income from operations (operating income)

J. inventory shrinkage

K. invoice

L. loss from operations

M. merchandise inventory

N. multiple-step income statement

O. other expense

P. other income

Q. periodic inventory system

R. perpetual inventory system

S. physical inventory

T. purchases return or allowance

U. purchases discounts

V. report form

W. sales discounts

X. sales return or allowance

Y. selling expenses

Z. single-step income statement

AA. trade discounts

___ 1. The cost that is reported as an expense when merchandise is sold.

___ 2. Sales minus the cost of merchandise sold.

___ 3. Merchandise on hand (not sold) at the end of an accounting period.

___ 4. The inventory system in which each purchase and sale of merchandise is recorded in an inventory account.

___ 5. The inventory system in which the inventory records do not show the amount available for sale or sold during the period.

___ 6. A detailed listing of the merchandise for sale at the end of an accounting period.

___ 7. The bill that the seller sends to the buyer.

___ 8. Discounts taken by the buyer for early payment of an invoice.

___ 9. From the buyer's perspective, returned merchandise or an adjustment for defective merchandise.

___ 10. A form used by a buyer to inform the seller of the amount the buyer proposes to debit to the account payable due the seller.

___ 11. From the seller's perspective, discounts that a seller may offer the buyer for early payment.

___ 12. From the seller's perspective, returned merchandise or an adjustment for defective merchandise.

___ 13. A form used by a seller to inform the buyer of the amount the seller proposes to credit to the account receivable due from the buyer.

___ 14. Discounts from the list prices in published catalogs or special discounts offered to certain classes of buyers.

___ 15. Freight terms in which the buyer pays the transportation costs from the shipping point to the final destination.

___ 16. Freight terms in which the seller pays the transportation costs from the shipping point to the final destination.

___ 17. A form of income statement that contains several sections, subsections, and subtotals.

___ 18. Expenses that are incurred directly in the selling of merchandise.

___ 19. Expenses incurred in the administration or general operations of the business.

___ 20. The excess of gross profit over total operating expenses.

___ 21. The excess of operating expenses over gross profit.

___ 22. Revenue from sources other than the primary operating activity of a business.

___ 23. Expenses that cannot be traced directly to operations.

___ 24. A form of income statement in which the total of all expenses is deducted from the total of all revenues.

___ 25. The amount by which the merchandise for sale, as indicated by the balance of the merchandise inventory account, is larger than the total amount of merchandise counted during the physical inventory.

___ 26. The form of balance sheet in which assets are reported on the left-hand side and the liabilities and owner's equity on the right-hand side.

___ 27. The form of balance sheet in which assets, liabilities, and owner's equity are reported in a downward sequence.

Multiple Choice

1. If merchandise purchased on account is returned, the buyer may inform the seller of the details by issuing:
   A. a debit memorandum
   B. a credit memorandum
   C. an invoice
   D. a bill

2. If merchandise is sold on account to a customer for $1,000, terms FOB shipping point, 1/10, n/30, and the seller prepays $50 in transportation costs, the amount of the discount for early payment would be:
   A. $0
   B. $5.00
   C. $10.00
   D. $10.50

3. The income statement in which the total of all expenses is deducted from the total of all revenues is termed:
   A. multiple-step form
   B. single-step form
   C. account form
   D. report form

4. On a multiple-step income statement, the excess of net sales over the cost of merchandise sold is called:
   A. operating income
   B. income from operations
   C. gross profit
   D. net income

5. Which of the following expenses would normally be classified as Other expense on a multiple-step income statement?
   A. Depreciation expense—office equipment
   B. Sales salaries expense
   C. Insurance expense
   D. Interest expense

CLASS DISCUSSION QUESTIONS

1. What distinguishes a merchandising business from a service business?
2. Can a business earn a gross profit but incur a net loss? Explain.
3. What is the name of the account in which purchases of merchandise are recorded in a perpetual inventory system?
4. What is the name of the account in which sales of merchandise are recorded?
5. How does the accounting for sales to customers using bank credit cards, such as MasterCard and VISA, differ from accounting for sales to customers using nonbank credit cards, such as American Express?
6. The credit period during which the buyer of merchandise is allowed to pay usually begins with what date?
7. What is the meaning of (a) 1/10, n/60; (b) n/30; (c) n/eom?
8. It is not unusual for a customer to drive into some **Texaco**, **Chevron**, or **Conoco** gasoline stations and discover that the cash price per gallon is 3 or 4 cents less than the credit price per gallon. As a result, many customers pay cash rather than use their credit cards. Why would a gasoline station owner establish such a policy?
9. What is the nature of (a) a credit memorandum issued by the seller of merchandise, (b) a debit memorandum issued by the buyer of merchandise?
10. Who bears the transportation costs when the terms of sale are (a) FOB shipping point, (b) FOB destination?
11. Name at least three accounts that would normally appear in the chart of accounts of a merchandising business but would not appear in the chart of accounts of a service business.
12. Differentiate between the multiple-step and the single-step forms of the income statement.
13. What are the major advantages and disadvantages of the single-step form of income statement compared to the multiple-step statement?
14. What type of revenue is reported in the Other income section of the multiple-step income statement?
15. The Hansen Office Equipment, which uses a perpetual inventory system, experienced a normal inventory shrinkage of $12,860. What accounts would be debited and credited to record the adjustment for the inventory shrinkage at the end of the accounting period?
16. Assume that Hansen Office Equipment in Question 15 experienced an abnormal inventory shrinkage of $210,500. Hansen Office Equipment has decided to record the abnormal inventory shrinkage so that it would be separately disclosed on the income statement. What account would be debited for the abnormal inventory shrinkage?

EXERCISES

Exercise 6–1
Determining gross profit

Objective 1

During the current year, merchandise is sold for $170,000 cash and for $620,000 on account. The cost of the merchandise sold is $474,000.

a. What is the amount of the gross profit?
b. Compute the gross profit percentage (gross profit divided by sales).
c. ✏️➤ Will the income statement necessarily report a net income? Explain.

Exercise 6–2
Determining cost of merchandise sold

Objective 1

In 1999, **Walgreen Co.** reported net sales of $17,838.8 million. Its gross profit was $4,860.2 million. What was the amount of Walgreen's cost of merchandise sold?

Exercise 6–3
Purchase-related transaction

Objective 2

Degas Company purchased merchandise on account from a supplier for $3,500, terms 2/10, n/30. Degas Company returned $750 of the merchandise and received full credit.

a. If Degas Company pays the invoice within the discount period, what is the amount of cash required for the payment?
b. Under a perpetual inventory system, what account is credited by Degas Company to record the return?

Exercise 6–4
Determining amounts to be paid on invoices

Objective 2

✓ a. $2,772

Determine the amount to be paid in full settlement of each of the following invoices, assuming that credit for returns and allowances was received prior to payment and that all invoices were paid within the discount period.

	Merchandise	Transportation Paid by Seller		Returns and Allowances
a.	$4,000	—	FOB shipping point, 1/10, n/30	$1,200
b.	1,500	$50	FOB shipping point, 2/10, n/30	700
c.	9,500	—	FOB destination, n/30	400
d.	2,500	75	FOB shipping point, 1/10, n/30	600
e.	5,000	—	FOB destination, 2/10, n/30	—

Exercise 6–5
Purchase-related transactions
Objective 2

✓ B: $5,049

A retailer is considering the purchase of ten units of a specific item from either of two suppliers. Their offers are as follows:

A: $500 a unit, total of $5,000, 2/10, n/30, plus transportation costs of $175.
B: $510 a unit, total of $5,100, 1/10, n/30, no charge for transportation.

Which of the two offers, A or B, yields the lower price?

Exercise 6–6
Purchase-related transactions
Objective 2

The debits and credits from four related transactions are presented in the following T accounts. Describe each transaction.

Cash		
(2)	75	
(4)	3,920	

Accounts Payable		
(3)	1,000	(1) 5,000
(4)	4,000	

Merchandise Inventory		
(1)	5,000	(3) 1,000
(2)	75	(4) 80

Exercise 6–7
Purchase-related transactions
Objective 2

✓ (c) Cash, cr. $8,330

Citron Co., a women's clothing store, purchased $12,000 of merchandise from a supplier on account, terms FOB destination, 2/10, n/30. Citron Co. returned $3,500 of the merchandise, receiving a credit memorandum, and then paid the amount due within the discount period. Journalize Citron Co.'s entries to record (a) the purchase, (b) the merchandise return, and (c) the payment.

Exercise 6–8
Purchase-related transactions
Objective 2

✓ (e) Cash, dr. $960

Journalize entries for the following related transactions of Aloha Company:

a. Purchased $9,000 of merchandise from Green Co. on account, terms 2/10, n/30.
b. Paid the amount owed on the invoice within the discount period.
c. Discovered that $2,000 of the merchandise was defective and returned items, receiving credit.
d. Purchased $1,000 of merchandise from Green Co. on account, terms n/30.
e. Received a check for the balance owed from the return in (c), after deducting for the purchase in (d).

Exercise 6–9
Sales-related transactions, including the use of credit cards
Objective 2

Journalize the entries for the following transactions:

a. Sold merchandise for cash, $15,000. The cost of the merchandise sold was $8,500.
b. Sold merchandise on account, $7,500. The cost of the merchandise sold was $4,000.
c. Sold merchandise to customers who used MasterCard and VISA, $7,750. The cost of the merchandise sold was $3,850.
d. Sold merchandise to customers who used American Express, $8,100. The cost of the merchandise sold was $5,860.
e. Paid an invoice from First National Bank for $350, representing a service fee for processing MasterCard and VISA sales.
f. Received $7,776 from American Express Company after a $324 collection fee had been deducted.

Exercise 6–10
Sales returns and allowances
Objective 2

During the year, sales returns and allowances totaled $112,150. The cost of the merchandise returned was $67,300. The accountant recorded all the returns and allowances by debiting the sales account and crediting Cost of Merchandise Sold for $112,150.
➤ Was the accountant's method of recording returns acceptable? Explain. In your explanation, include the advantages of using a sales returns and allowances account.

Exercise 6–11
Sales-related transactions
Objective 2

After the amount due on a sale of $5,500, terms 2/10, n/eom, is received from a customer within the discount period, the seller consents to the return of the entire shipment. The cost of the merchandise returned was $3,380. (a) What is the amount of the refund owed to the customer? (b) Journalize the entries made by the seller to record the return and the refund.

Exercise 6–12
Sales-related transactions
Objective 2

The debits and credits for three related transactions are presented in the following T accounts. Describe each transaction.

Cash				Sales		
(5)	7,425				(1)	10,000

Accounts Receivable				Sales Discounts		
(1)	10,000	(3)	2,500	(5)	75	
		(5)	7,500			

Merchandise Inventory				Sales Returns and Allowances		
(4)	1,500	(2)	6,000	(3)	2,500	

				Cost of Merchandise Sold		
				(2)	6,000	(4)	1,500

Exercise 6–13
Sales-related transactions
Objective 2

✓ d. $15,175

Merchandise is sold on account to a customer for $15,000, terms FOB shipping point, 3/10, n/30. The seller paid the transportation costs of $625. Determine the following: (a) amount of the sale, (b) amount debited to Accounts Receivable, (c) amount of the discount for early payment, and (d) amount due within the discount period.

Exercise 6–14
Sales tax
Objective 2

✓ c. $3,180

A sale of merchandise on account for $3,000 is subject to a 6% sales tax. (a) Should the sales tax be recorded at the time of sale or when payment is received? (b) What is the amount of the sale? (c) What is the amount debited to Accounts Receivable? (d) What is the title of the account to which the $180 is credited?

Exercise 6–15
Sales tax transactions
Objective 2

Journalize the entries to record the following selected transactions:

a.   Sold $6,000 of merchandise on account, subject to a sales tax of 5%. The cost of the merchandise sold was $3,600.
b.   Paid $4,380 to the state sales tax department for taxes collected.

Exercise 6–16
Sales-related transactions
Objective 2

Sterile Co., a furniture wholesaler, sells merchandise to Bawd Co. on account, $8,000, terms 2/15, n/30. The cost of the merchandise sold is $4,800. Sterile Co. issues a credit memorandum for $500 for merchandise returned and subsequently receives the amount due within the discount period. The cost of the merchandise returned is $300. Journalize Sterile Co.'s entries for (a) the sale, including the cost of the merchandise sold, (b) the credit memorandum, including the cost of the returned merchandise, and (c) the receipt of the check for the amount due from Bawd Co.

Exercise 6–17
Purchase-related transactions
Objective 2

Based on the data presented in Exercise 6–16, journalize Bawd Co.'s entries for (a) the purchase, (b) the return of the merchandise for credit, and (c) the payment of the invoice within the discount period.

Exercise 6–18
Normal balances of merchandise accounts

Objective 2

What is the normal balance of the following accounts: (a) Cost of Merchandise Sold, (b) Merchandise Inventory, (c) Sales, (d) Sales Discounts, (e) Sales Returns and Allowances, (f) Transportation Out?

Exercise 6–19
Chart of accounts

Objective 3

Chime Co. is a newly organized business with the following list of accounts, arranged in alphabetical order:

Accounts Payable
Accounts Receivable
Accumulated Depreciation—Office Equipment
Accumulated Depreciation—Store Equipment
Advertising Expense
Cash
Cost of Merchandise Sold
Depreciation Expense—Office Equipment
Depreciation Expense—Store Equipment
Income Summary
Insurance Expense
Interest Expense
Interest Receivable
Interest Revenue
Kimberly Skilling, Capital
Kimberly Skilling, Drawing
Land
Merchandise Inventory
Miscellaneous Administrative Expense

Miscellaneous Selling Expense
Notes Payable (short-term)
Notes Receivable (short-term)
Office Equipment
Office Salaries Expense
Office Supplies
Office Supplies Expense
Prepaid Insurance
Rent Expense
Salaries Payable
Sales
Sales Discounts
Sales Returns and Allowances
Sales Salaries Expense
Store Equipment
Store Supplies
Store Supplies Expense
Transportation Out

Construct a chart of accounts, assigning account numbers and arranging the accounts in balance sheet and income statement order, as illustrated in Exhibit 6. Each account number is three digits: the first digit is to indicate the major classification ("1" for assets, and so on); the second digit is to indicate the subclassification ("11" for current assets, and so on); and the third digit is to identify the specific account ("110" for Cash, and so on).

Exercise 6–20
Income statement for merchandiser

Objective 4

For the fiscal year, sales were $7,230,000, sales discounts were $320,000, sales returns and allowances were $580,000, and the cost of merchandise sold was $4,338,000. What was the amount of net sales and gross profit?

Exercise 6–21
Income statement for merchandiser

Objective 4

The following expenses were incurred by a merchandising business during the year. In which expense section of the income statement should each be reported: (a) selling, (b) administrative, or (c) other?

1. Advertising expense.
2. Depreciation expense on office equipment.
3. Insurance expense on store equipment.
4. Interest expense on notes payable.
5. Office supplies used.
6. Rent expense on office building.
7. Salaries of office personnel.
8. Salary of sales manager.

Exercise 6–22
Single-step income statement

Objective 4

Summary operating data for The Lifeboat Company during the current year ended April 30, 2003, are as follows: cost of merchandise sold, $1,460,000; administrative expenses, $225,000; interest expense, $37,500; rent revenue, $30,000; net sales, $3,600,000; and selling expenses, $375,000. Prepare a single-step income statement.

✓ Net income: $1,532,500

Exercise 6–23
Determining amounts for items omitted from income statement

Objective 4

✓ a. $10,000
✓ h. $690,000

Two items are omitted in each of the following four lists of income statement data. Determine the amounts of the missing items, identifying them by letter.

Sales	$298,000	$500,000	$700,000	$ (g)
Sales returns and allowances	(a)	15,000	(e)	30,500
Sales discounts	8,000	8,000	10,000	37,000
Net sales	280,000	(c)	665,000	(h)
Cost of merchandise sold	(b)	285,000	(f)	540,000
Gross profit	130,000	(d)	200,000	150,000

Exercise 6–24
Multiple-step income statement

Objective 4

How many errors can you find in the following income statement?

The Functor Company
Income Statement
For the Year Ended July 31, 2003

Revenue from sales:			
Sales		$3,000,000	
Add: Sales returns and allowances	$58,000		
Sales discounts	14,500	72,500	
Gross sales			$3,072,500
Cost of merchandise sold			1,495,000
Income from operations			$1,577,500
Operating expenses:			
Selling expenses		$ 145,000	
Transportation out		5,300	
Administrative expenses		87,200	
Total operating expenses			237,500
			$1,340,000
Other expense:			
Interest revenue			47,500
Gross profit			$1,292,500

Exercise 6–25
Multiple-step income statement

Objective 4

✓ Net income: $97,500

On August 31, 2003, the balances of the accounts appearing in the ledger of Noble Company, a furniture wholesaler, are as follows:

Administrative Expenses	$ 60,000	Salaries Payable	$ 3,220
Building	512,500	Sales	775,000
Cash	48,500	Sales Discounts	20,000
Cost of Merchandise Sold	450,000	Sales Returns and Allowances	45,000
Interest Expense	7,500	Selling Expenses	95,000
Merchandise Inventory	130,000	Shawn Vaughn, Capital	608,580
Notes Payable	25,000	Shawn Vaughn, Drawing	25,000
Office Supplies	10,600	Store Supplies	7,700

a. Prepare a multiple-step income statement for the year ended August 31, 2003.
b. Compare the major advantages and disadvantages of the multiple-step and single-step forms of income statements.

Exercise 6–26
Adjusting entry for merchandise inventory shrinkage

Objective 5

Nocturnal Inc.'s perpetual inventory records indicate that $417,200 of merchandise should be on hand on October 31, 2003. The physical inventory indicates that $400,680 of merchandise is actually on hand. Journalize the adjusting entry for the inventory shrinkage for Nocturnal Inc. for the year ended October 31, 2003.

Exercise 6–27
Closing the accounts of a merchandiser
Objective 5

From the following list, identify the accounts that should be closed to Income Summary at the end of the fiscal year: (a) Accounts Receivable, (b) Cost of Merchandise Sold, (c) Merchandise Inventory, (d) Sales, (e) Sales Discounts, (f) Sales Returns and Allowances, (g) Salaries Expense, (h) Salaries Payable, (i) Supplies, (j) Supplies Expense.

Exercise 6–28
Ratio of net sales to total assets
Objective 6

The financial statements for **Cisco Systems, Inc.,** are presented in Appendix G at the end of the text.

a. Determine the ratio of net sales to average total assets for Cisco Systems for the years ended July 29, 2000 and July 31, 1999.
b. What conclusions can be drawn from these ratios concerning the trend in the ability of Cisco Systems to effectively use its assets to generate sales?

Note: Cisco Systems' total assets on July 25, 1998 were $8,972,000,000.

Exercise 6–29
Ratio of net sales to total assets
Objective 6

Winn-Dixie Stores reported the following data in its financial statements for 1999:

Net sales and revenues	$14,136,503,000
Total assets at end of 1999	3,149,147,000
Total assets at end of 1998	3,068,714,000

a. Compute the ratio of net sales to assets for 1999. Round to two decimal places.
b. Would you expect the ratio of net sales to assets for Winn-Dixie to be similar to or different from that of **Zales Jewelers**? Why?

Appendix 1
Exercise 6–30
Merchandising special journals

✓ d. $27,000

Holiday Rug Company had the following credit sales transactions during July 2003:

Date	Customer	Quantity	Rug Style	Sales
July 3	Ricky Craig	1	10 by 6 Chinese	$ 8,000
8	K. Thomas	1	8 by 10 Persian	8,000
19	L. Lao	1	8 by 10 Indian	9,000
26	Joel Jarnicki	1	10 by 12 Persian	12,000

The July 1 inventory was $13,000, consisting of:

Quantity	Style	Cost per Rug	Total Cost
2	10 by 6 Chinese	$3,000	$6,000
2	8 by 10 Persian	3,500	7,000

During July, Holiday Rug Company purchased the following rugs from Hunan Rug Importers:

Date	Quantity	Rug Style	Cost per Rug	Amount
July 10	2	8 by 10 Indian	$4,000	$ 8,000
12	1	10 by 6 Chinese	3,500	3,500
21	3	10 by 12 Persian	6,500	19,500

The general ledger includes the following accounts:

Account Number	Account
11	Accounts Receivable
12	Merchandise Inventory
21	Accounts Payable
41	Sales
51	Cost of Merchandise Sold

a. Record the sales in a two-column sales journal. Use the sales journal form shown in the appendix at the end of this chapter. Begin with Invoice Number 80.
b. Record the purchases in a purchases journal. Use the purchases journal form shown in the appendix at the end of this chapter.
c. Assume that you have posted the journal entries to the appropriate ledgers. Insert the correct posting references in the sales and purchases journals.
d. Determine the July 31 balance of Merchandise Inventory.

Appendix 2
Exercise 6–31
Closing entries

Based on the data presented in Exercise 6–25, journalize the closing entries.

PROBLEMS SERIES A

Problem 6–1A
Purchase-related transactions

Objective 2

GENERAL
LEDGER

The following selected transactions were completed by Bushwhack Company during October of the current year:

Oct. 1. Purchased merchandise from Riverhill Co., $10,500, terms FOB destination, n/30.
   3. Purchased merchandise from Windsor Co., $8,000, terms FOB shipping point, 2/10, n/eom. Prepaid transportation costs of $150 were added to the invoice.
   4. Purchased merchandise from Picadilly Co., $7,500, terms FOB destination, 2/10, n/30.
   6. Issued debit memorandum to Picadilly Co. for $1,000 of merchandise returned from purchase on October 4.
  13. Paid Windsor Co. for invoice of October 3, less discount.
  15. Paid Picadilly Co. for invoice of October 4, less debit memorandum of October 6 and discount.
  19. Purchased merchandise from Ivy Co., $5,000, terms FOB shipping point, n/eom.
  19. Paid transportation charges of $120 on October 19 purchase from Ivy Co.
  20. Purchased merchandise from Hatcher Co., $8,000, terms FOB destination, 1/10, n/30.
  30. Paid Hatcher Co. for invoice of October 20, less discount.
  31. Paid Riverhill Co. for invoice of October 1.
  31. Paid Ivy Co. for invoice of October 19.

Instructions
Journalize the entries to record the transactions of Bushwhack Company for October.

Problem 6–2A
Sales-related transactions

Objective 2

GENERAL
LEDGER
SPREADSHEET

The following selected transactions were completed by Fastball Supply Co., which sells office supplies primarily to wholesalers and occasionally to retail customers.

July 2. Sold merchandise on account to Magnolia Co., $10,500, terms FOB destination, 2/10, n/30. The cost of the merchandise sold was $6,000.
   3. Sold merchandise for $2,000 plus 5% sales tax to cash customers. The cost of merchandise sold was $1,100.
   4. Sold merchandise on account to McNutt Co., $2,800, terms FOB shipping point, n/eom. The cost of merchandise sold was $1,800.
   5. Sold merchandise for $1,400 plus 5% sales tax to customers who used Master-Card. Deposited credit card receipts into the bank. The cost of merchandise sold was $750.
  12. Received check for amount due from Magnolia Co. for sale on July 2.
  14. Sold merchandise to customers who used American Express cards, $8,600. The cost of merchandise sold was $6,200.
  16. Sold merchandise on account to Westpark Co., $12,000, terms FOB shipping point, 1/10, n/30. The cost of merchandise sold was $7,200.
  18. Issued credit memorandum for $3,000 to Westpark Co. for merchandise returned from sale on July 16. The cost of the merchandise returned was $1,800.
  19. Sold merchandise on account to Hempel Co., $7,500, terms FOB shipping point, 1/10, n/30. Added $85 to the invoice for transportation costs prepaid. The cost of merchandise sold was $4,500.

July 26. Received check for amount due from Westpark Co. for sale on July 16 less credit memorandum of July 18 and discount.

27. Received $9,410 from American Express for $10,000 of sales reported July 1–12.

28. Received check for amount due from Hempel Co. for sale of July 19.

31. Received check for amount due from McNutt Co. for sale of July 4.

31. Paid Fast Delivery Service $1,050 for merchandise delivered during July to customers under shipping terms of FOB destination.

Aug. 3. Paid First National Bank $690 for service fees for handling MasterCard sales during July.

15. Paid $3,100 to state sales tax division for taxes owed on July sales.

Instructions

Journalize the entries to record the transactions of Fastball Supply Co.

Problem 6–3A

Sales-related and purchase-related transactions

Objective 2

GENERAL
LEDGER

The following were selected from among the transactions completed by The Knapsack Company during April of the current year:

Apr. 3. Purchased merchandise on account from Velcro Co., list price $30,000, trade discount 20%, terms FOB destination, 2/10, n/30.

4. Sold merchandise for cash, $5,100. The cost of the merchandise sold was $3,000.

5. Purchased merchandise on account from Summit Co., $7,500, terms FOB shipping point, 2/10, n/30, with prepaid transportation costs of $200 added to the invoice.

6. Returned $4,000 of merchandise purchased on April 3 from Velcro Co.

11. Sold merchandise on account to Bowles Co., list price $2,250, trade discount 20%, terms 1/10, n/30. The cost of the merchandise sold was $1,050.

13. Paid Velcro Co. on account for purchase of April 3, less return of April 6 and discount.

14. Sold merchandise on nonbank credit cards and reported accounts to the card company, American Express, $7,850. The cost of the merchandise sold was $3,900.

15. Paid Summit Co. on account for purchase of April 5, less discount.

21. Received cash on account from sale of April 11 to Bowles Co., less discount.

24. Sold merchandise on account to Hardigree Co., $4,200, terms 1/10, n/30. The cost of the merchandise sold was $1,850.

28. Received cash from American Express for nonbank credit card sales of April 14, less $314 service fee.

30. Received merchandise returned by Hardigree Co. from sale on April 24, $1,100. The cost of the returned merchandise was $600.

Instructions

Journalize the transactions.

Problem 6–4A

Sales-related and purchase-related transactions for seller and buyer

Objective 2

The following selected transactions were completed during July between Snap Company and Buckle Co.:

July 1. Snap Company sold merchandise on account to Buckle Co., $11,750, terms FOB destination, 2/15, n/eom. The cost of the merchandise sold was $7,000.

2. Snap Company paid transportation costs of $350 for delivery of merchandise sold to Buckle Co. on July 1

5. Snap Company sold merchandise on account to Buckle Co., $17,500, terms FOB shipping point, n/eom. The cost of the merchandise sold was $10,000.

6. Buckle Co. returned $2,000 of merchandise purchased on account on July 1 from Snap Company. The cost of the merchandise returned was $1,200.

9. Buckle Co. paid transportation charges of $200 on July 5 purchase from Snap Company.

15. Snap Company sold merchandise on account to Buckle Co., $20,000, terms FOB shipping point, 1/10, n/30. Snap Company paid transportation costs of $1,750, which were added to the invoice. The cost of the merchandise sold was $12,000.

16. Buckle Co. paid Snap Company for purchase of July 1, less discount and less return of July 6.

25. Buckle Co. paid Snap Company on account for purchase of July 15, less discount.

31. Buckle Co. paid Snap Company on account for purchase of July 5.

Instructions

Journalize the July transactions for (1) Snap Company and (2) Buckle Co.

Problem 6–5A

Multiple-step income statement and report form of balance sheet

Objectives 4, 5

GENERAL LEDGER

✓ 1. Net income: $100,000

The following selected accounts and their current balances appear in the ledger of Mandolin Co. for the fiscal year ended March 31, 2003:

Cash	$ 33,750	Sales Returns and Allowances	$ 23,100
Notes Receivable	120,000	Sales Discounts	21,900
Accounts Receivable	121,000	Cost of Merchandise Sold	775,000
Merchandise Inventory	175,000	Sales Salaries Expense	173,200
Office Supplies	5,600	Advertising Expense	43,800
Prepaid Insurance	3,400	Depreciation Expense—	
Office Equipment	85,000	Store Equipment	6,400
Accumulated Depreciation—		Miscellaneous Selling Expense	1,600
Office Equipment	12,800	Office Salaries Expense	84,150
Store Equipment	153,000	Rent Expense	31,350
Accumulated Depreciation—		Depreciation Expense—	
Store Equipment	34,200	Office Equipment	12,700
Accounts Payable	55,600	Insurance Expense	3,900
Salaries Payable	2,400	Office Supplies Expense	1,300
Note Payable		Miscellaneous Administrative	
(final payment due 2013)	56,000	Expense	1,600
Teresa Pryor, Capital	470,750	Interest Revenue	11,000
Teresa Pryor, Drawing	35,000	Interest Expense	6,000
Sales	1,275,000		

Instructions

1. Prepare a multiple-step income statement.
2. Prepare a statement of owner's equity.
3. Prepare a report form of balance sheet, assuming that the current portion of the note payable is $7,500.
4. Briefly explain (a) how multiple-step and single-step income statements differ and (b) how report-form and account-form balance sheets differ.

Problem 6–6A

Single-step income statement and account form of balance sheet

Objectives 4, 5

SPREADSHEET

✓ 3. Total assets: $649,750

Selected accounts and related amounts for Mandolin Co. for the fiscal year ended March 31, 2003, are presented in Problem 6–5A.

Instructions

1. Prepare a single-step income statement in the format shown in Exhibit 8.
2. Prepare a statement of owner's equity.
3. Prepare an account form of balance sheet, assuming that the current portion of the note payable is $7,500.

Appendix 2
Problem 6–7A

Work sheet, financial statements, and adjusting and closing entries

✓ 2. Net income: $126,750

The accounts and their balances in the ledger of Thorax Co. on December 31, 2003, are as follows:

Cash	$ 28,000	Office Equipment	$ 50,000
Accounts Receivable	132,500	Accumulated Depreciation—	
Merchandise Inventory	195,000	Office Equipment	17,200
Prepaid Insurance	9,700	Accounts Payable	66,700
Store Supplies	4,250	Salaries Payable	—
Office Supplies	2,100	Unearned Rent	1,200
Store Equipment	157,000	Note Payable	
Accumulated Depreciation—		(final payment due 2013)	105,000
Store Equipment	40,300	Ethan Faust, Capital	224,600

Ethan Faust, Drawing	$ 30,000	Miscellaneous Selling Expense	$ 1,600
Income Summary	—	Office Salaries Expense	34,000
Sales	915,000	Rent Expense	16,000
Sales Returns and Allowances	11,900	Insurance Expense	—
Sales Discounts	7,100	Depreciation Expense—	
Cost of Merchandise Sold	576,200	Office Equipment	—
Sales Salaries Expense	76,400	Office Supplies Expense	—
Advertising Expense	25,000	Miscellaneous Administrative	
Depreciation Expense—		Expense	1,650
Store Equipment	—	Rent Revenue	—
Store Supplies Expense	—	Interest Expense	11,600

The data needed for year-end adjustments on December 31 are as follows:

Physical merchandise inventory on December 31		$189,000
Insurance expired during the year		5,000
Supplies on hand on December 31:		
Store supplies		1,300
Office supplies		750
Depreciation for the year:		
Store equipment		4,500
Office equipment		2,800
Salaries payable on December 31:		
Sales salaries	$3,850	
Office salaries	1,150	5,000
Unearned rent on December 31		400

Instructions

1. Prepare a work sheet for the fiscal year ended December 31, 2003. List all accounts in the order given.
2. Prepare a multiple-step income statement.
3. Prepare a statement of owner's equity.
4. Prepare a report form of balance sheet, assuming that the current portion of the note payable is $20,000.
5. Journalize the adjusting entries.
6. Journalize the closing entries.

PROBLEMS SERIES B

Problem 6–1B
Purchase-related transactions

Objective 2

GENERAL LEDGER

The following selected transactions were completed by Beagley Co. during March of the current year:

Mar. 1. Purchased merchandise from Lumpkin Co., $9,000, terms FOB shipping point, 2/10, n/eom. Prepaid transportation costs of $350 were added to the invoice.
  5. Purchased merchandise from Guthrie Co., $9,200, terms FOB destination, n/30.
  10. Paid Lumpkin Co. for invoice of March 1, less discount.
  13. Purchased merchandise from Mickle Co., $7,500, terms FOB destination, 1/10, n/30.
  14. Issued debit memorandum to Mickle Co. for $2,500 of merchandise returned from purchase on March 13.
  18. Purchased merchandise from Aschor Company, $11,500, terms FOB shipping point, n/eom.
  18. Paid transportation charges of $200 on March 18 purchase from Aschor Company.
  19. Purchased merchandise from Hatcher Co., $7,500, terms FOB destination, 2/10, n/30.
  23. Paid Mickle Co. for invoice of March 13, less debit memorandum of March 14 and discount.
  29. Paid Hatcher Co. for invoice of March 19, less discount.

Mar. 31. Paid Aschor Company for invoice of March 18.
     31. Paid Guthrie Co. for invoice of March 5.

Instructions
Journalize the entries to record the transactions of Beagley Co. for March.

Problem 6–2B
Sales-related transactions

Objective 2

GENERAL
LEDGER

SPREADSHEET

The following selected transactions were completed by Sprinkle Supplies Co., which sells irrigation supplies primarily to wholesalers and occasionally to retail customers.

May 1. Sold merchandise on account to Lynlex Co., $4,500, terms FOB shipping point, n/eom. The cost of merchandise sold was $2,300.
   2. Sold merchandise for $5,000 plus 6% sales tax to cash customers. The cost of merchandise sold was $3,750.
   5. Sold merchandise on account to Maple Company, $11,500, terms FOB destination, 1/10, n/30. The cost of merchandise sold was $7,000.
   8. Sold merchandise for $4,150 plus 6% sales tax to customers who used VISA cards. Deposited credit card receipts into the bank. The cost of merchandise sold was $2,800.
  13. Sold merchandise to customers who used American Express cards, $4,500. The cost of merchandise sold was $2,600.
  14. Sold merchandise on account to Blech Co., $7,500, terms FOB shipping point, 1/10, n/30. The cost of merchandise sold was $4,000.
  15. Received check for amount due from Maple Company for sale on May 5.
  16. Issued credit memorandum for $800 to Blech Co. for merchandise returned from sale on May 14. The cost of the merchandise returned was $360.
  18. Sold merchandise on account to Fortson Company, $6,850, terms FOB shipping point, 2/10, n/30. Paid $210 for transportation costs and added them to the invoice. The cost of merchandise sold was $4,100.
  24. Received check for amount due from Blech Co. for sale on May 14 less credit memorandum of May 16 and discount.
  27. Received $7,680 from American Express for $8,000 of sales reported during the week of May 1–12.
  28. Received check for amount due from Fortson Company for sale of May 18.
  31. Paid Anywhere Delivery Service $1,500 for merchandise delivered during May to customers under shipping terms of FOB destination.
  31. Received check for amount due from Lynlex Co. for sale of May 1.
June 3. Paid First National Bank $525 for service fees for handling MasterCard sales during May.
  10. Paid $1,100 to state sales tax division for taxes owed on May sales.

Instructions
Journalize the entries to record the transactions of Sprinkle Supplies Co.

Problem 6–3B
Sales-related and purchase-related transactions

Objective 2

GENERAL
LEDGER

The following were selected from among the transactions completed by Pelops Company during March of the current year:

Mar. 3. Purchased merchandise on account from Spruce Co., list price $18,000, trade discount 35%, terms FOB shipping point, 2/10, n/30, with prepaid transportation costs of $620 added to the invoice.
   5. Purchased merchandise on account from Blake Co., $10,000, terms FOB destination, 1/10, n/30.
   6. Sold merchandise on account to Howell Co., list price $7,500, trade discount 40%, terms 2/10, n/30. The cost of the merchandise sold was $1,850.
   7. Returned $1,800 of merchandise purchased on March 5 from Blake Co.
  13. Paid Spruce Co. on account for purchase of March 3, less discount.
  15. Paid Blake Co. on account for purchase of March 5, less return of March 7 and discount.
  16. Received cash on account from sale of March 6 to Howell Co., less discount.
  19. Sold merchandise on nonbank credit cards and reported accounts to the card company, American Express, $4,450. The cost of the merchandise sold was $2,950.
  22. Sold merchandise on account to Morton Co., $3,480, terms 2/10, n/30. The cost of the merchandise sold was $1,400.

Mar. 23. Sold merchandise for cash, $7,350. The cost of the merchandise sold was $3,750.
25. Received merchandise returned by Morton Co. from sale on March 22, $1,480. The cost of the returned merchandise was $600.
31. Received cash from American Express for nonbank credit card sales of March 19, less $290 service fee.

Instructions
Journalize the transactions.

Problem 6–4B
Sales-related and purchase-related transactions for seller and buyer
Objective 2

The following selected transactions were completed during November between Subliminal Company and Bungee Company:

Nov. 2. Subliminal Company sold merchandise on account to Bungee Company, $12,000, terms FOB shipping point, 2/10, n/30. Subliminal Company paid transportation costs of $500, which were added to the invoice. The cost of the merchandise sold was $7,500.
8. Subliminal Company sold merchandise on account to Bungee Company, $13,500, terms FOB destination, 1/15, n/eom. The cost of the merchandise sold was $9,500.
8. Subliminal Company paid transportation costs of $750 for delivery of merchandise sold to Bungee Company on November 8.
12. Bungee Company returned $3,000 of merchandise purchased on account on November 8 from Subliminal Company. The cost of the merchandise returned was $1,600.
12. Bungee Company paid Subliminal Company for purchase of November 2, less discount.
23. Bungee Company paid Subliminal Company for purchase of November 8, less discount and less return of November 12.
24. Subliminal Company sold merchandise on account to Bungee Company, $9,000, terms FOB shipping point, n/eom. The cost of the merchandise sold was $5,400.
26. Bungee Company paid transportation charges of $250 on November 24 purchase from Subliminal Company.
30. Bungee Company paid Subliminal Company on account for purchase of November 24.

Instructions
Journalize the November transactions for (1) Subliminal Company and (2) Bungee Company.

Problem 6–5B
Multiple-step income statement and report form of balance sheet
Objectives 4, 5

GENERAL LEDGER

✓ 1. Net income: $68,000

The following selected accounts and their current balances appear in the ledger of Cypress Co. for the fiscal year ended June 30, 2003:

Cash	$ 26,500	Sales Returns and Allowances	$ 21,000
Notes Receivable	50,000	Sales Discounts	11,000
Accounts Receivable	62,000	Cost of Merchandise Sold	1,070,000
Merchandise Inventory	100,000	Sales Salaries Expense	210,000
Office Supplies	2,600	Advertising Expense	28,300
Prepaid Insurance	6,800	Depreciation Expense—	
Office Equipment	64,000	Store Equipment	4,600
Accumulated Depreciation—		Miscellaneous Selling Expense	1,100
Office Equipment	10,800	Office Salaries Expense	41,000
Store Equipment	117,500	Rent Expense	22,150
Accumulated Depreciation—		Insurance Expense	12,750
Store Equipment	48,600	Depreciation Expense—	
Accounts Payable	27,000	Office Equipment	9,000
Salaries Payable	2,000	Office Supplies Expense	900
Note Payable		Miscellaneous Administrative	
(final payment due 2013)	30,000	Expense	1,200
Reid York, Capital	268,000	Interest Revenue	5,000
Reid York, Drawing	25,000	Interest Expense	4,000
Sales	1,500,000		

Instructions

1. Prepare a multiple-step income statement.
2. Prepare a statement of owner's equity.
3. Prepare a report form of balance sheet, assuming that the current portion of the note payable is $2,500.
4. Briefly explain (a) how multiple-step and single-step income statements differ and (b) how report-form and account-form balance sheets differ.

Problem 6–6B
Single-step income statement and account form of balance sheet

Objectives 4, 5

SPREADSHEET

✓ 3. Total assets: $370,000

Selected accounts and related amounts for Cypress Co. for the fiscal year ended June 30, 2003, are presented in Problem 6–5B.

Instructions

1. Prepare a single-step income statement in the format shown in Exhibit 8.
2. Prepare a statement of owner's equity.
3. Prepare an account form of balance sheet, assuming that the current portion of the note payable is $2,500.

Appendix 2
Problem 6–7B
Work sheet, financial statements, and adjusting and closing entries

✓ 2. Net income: $258,865

The accounts and their balances in the ledger of Zirconium Co. on December 31, 2003, are as follows:

Cash	$ 31,165	Sales	$1,147,500
Accounts Receivable	126,100	Sales Returns and Allowances	15,500
Merchandise Inventory	435,000	Sales Discounts	6,000
Prepaid Insurance	10,600	Cost of Merchandise Sold	601,200
Store Supplies	3,750	Sales Salaries Expense	86,400
Office Supplies	1,700	Advertising Expense	29,450
Store Equipment	225,000	Depreciation Expense—	
Accumulated Depreciation—		Store Equipment	—
Store Equipment	40,300	Store Supplies Expense	—
Office Equipment	72,000	Miscellaneous Selling Expense	1,885
Accumulated Depreciation—		Office Salaries Expense	60,000
Office Equipment	17,200	Rent Expense	30,000
Accounts Payable	66,700	Insurance Expense	—
Salaries Payable	—	Depreciation Expense—	
Unearned Rent	1,200	Office Equipment	—
Note Payable		Office Supplies Expense	—
(final payment due 2013)	195,000	Miscellaneous Administrative	
Haley Gaffney, Capital	332,100	Expense	1,650
Haley Gaffney, Drawing	50,000	Rent Revenue	—
Income Summary	—	Interest Expense	12,600

The data needed for year-end adjustments on December 31 are as follows:

Physical merchandise inventory on December 31		$418,500
Insurance expired during the year		6,000
Supplies on hand on December 31:		
Store supplies		1,500
Office supplies		700
Depreciation for the year:		
Store equipment		8,500
Office equipment		4,500
Salaries payable on December 31:		
Sales salaries	$3,450	
Office salaries	2,550	6,000
Unearned rent on December 31		400

Instructions

1. Prepare a work sheet for the fiscal year ended December 31, 2003. List all accounts in the order given.
2. Prepare a multiple-step income statement.
3. Prepare a statement of owner's equity.
4. Prepare a report form of balance sheet, assuming that the current portion of the note payable is $35,000.
5. Journalize the adjusting entries.
6. Journalize the closing entries.

COMPREHENSIVE PROBLEM 2

GENERAL LEDGER

✓ 5. Net income: $184,440

Fluorescent Co. is a merchandising business. The account balances for Fluorescent Co. as of May 1, 2003 (unless otherwise indicated), are as follows:

110	Cash	$ 19,160
111	Notes Receivable	5,000
112	Accounts Receivable	31,220
115	Merchandise Inventory	153,900
116	Prepaid Insurance	3,750
117	Store Supplies	2,550
123	Store Equipment	104,300
124	Accumulated Depreciation—Store Equipment	12,600
210	Accounts Payable	18,450
211	Salaries Payable	—
310	Brittany Rose, Capital, June 1, 2002	113,280
311	Brittany Rose, Drawing	10,000
312	Income Summary	—
410	Sales	815,750
411	Sales Returns and Allowances	20,600
412	Sales Discounts	13,200
510	Cost of Merchandise Sold	460,500
520	Sales Salaries Expense	64,400
521	Advertising Expense	18,000
522	Depreciation Expense	—
523	Store Supplies Expense	—
529	Miscellaneous Selling Expense	2,800
530	Office Salaries Expense	30,500
531	Rent Expense	18,600
532	Insurance Expense	—
539	Miscellaneous Administrative Expense	1,650
611	Interest Revenue	50

During May, the last month of the fiscal year, the following transactions were completed:

May 1. Paid rent for May, $2,000.
  3. Purchased merchandise on account from Tredwell Co., terms 2/10, n/30, FOB shipping point, $10,000.
  4. Paid transportation charges on purchase of May 3, $375.
  6. Sold merchandise on account to Parish Co., terms 2/10, n/30, FOB shipping point, $8,500. The cost of the merchandise sold was $5,000.

May 7. Received $6,500 cash from Oxford Co. on account, no discount.
10. Sold merchandise for cash, $15,300. The cost of the merchandise sold was $9,000.
13. Paid for merchandise purchased on May 3, less discount.
14. Received merchandise returned on sale of May 6, $1,500. The cost of the merchandise returned was $900.
15. Paid advertising expense for last half of May, $1,500.
16. Received cash from sale of May 6, less return of May 14 and discount.
19. Purchased merchandise for cash, $7,400.
19. Paid $5,950 to Lipham Co. on account, no discount.
20. Sold merchandise on account to Petroski Co., terms 1/10, n/30, FOB shipping point, $16,000. The cost of the merchandise sold was $9,600.
21. For the convenience of the customer, paid shipping charges on sale of May 20, $600.
21. Received $11,750 cash from Gant Co. on account, no discount.
21. Purchased merchandise on account from Walden Co., terms 1/10, n/30, FOB destination, $15,000.
24. Returned $3,500 of damaged merchandise purchased on May 21, receiving credit from the seller.
26. Refunded cash on sales made for cash, $600. The cost of the merchandise returned was $360.
28. Paid sales salaries of $2,750 and office salaries of $1,220.
29. Purchased store supplies for cash, $350.
30. Sold merchandise on account to Hartel Co., terms 2/10, n/30, FOB shipping point, $23,100. The cost of the merchandise sold was $13,200.
30. Received cash from sale of May 20, less discount, plus transportation paid on May 21.
31. Paid for purchase of May 21, less return of May 24 and discount.

Instructions

(*Note:* If the work sheet described in the appendix is used, follow the alternative instructions.)

1. Enter the balances of each of the accounts in the appropriate balance column of a four-column account. Write *Balance* in the item section, and place a check mark (✓) in the Posting Reference column.
2. Journalize the transactions for May.
3. Post the journal to the general ledger, extending the month-end balances to the appropriate balance columns after all posting is completed. In this problem, you are not required to update or post to the accounts receivable and accounts payable subsidiary ledgers.
4. Journalize and post the adjusting entries, using the following adjustment data:

a.	Merchandise inventory on May 31		$139,750
b.	Insurance expired during the year		1,250
c.	Store supplies on hand on May 31		1,050
d.	Depreciation for the current year		7,400
e.	Accrued salaries on May 31:		
	Sales salaries	$350	
	Office salaries	180	530

5. Prepare a multiple-step income statement, a statement of owner's equity, and a report form of balance sheet.
6. Journalize and post the closing entries. Indicate closed accounts by inserting a line in both balance columns opposite the closing entry. Insert the new balance in the owner's capital account.
7. Prepare a post-closing trial balance.

Alternative Instructions

1. Enter the balances of each of the accounts in the appropriate balance column of a four-column account. Write *Balance* in the item section, and place a check mark (✓) in the Posting Reference column.
2. Journalize the transactions for May.
3. Post the journal to the general ledger, extending the month-end balances to the appropriate balance columns after all posting is completed. In this problem, you are not required to update or post to the accounts receivable and accounts payable subsidiary ledgers.
4. Prepare a trial balance as of May 31 on a ten-column work sheet, listing all accounts in the order given in the ledger. Complete the work sheet for the fiscal year ended May 31, using the following adjustment data:

a.	Merchandise inventory on May 31		$139,750
b.	Insurance expired during the year		1,250
c.	Store supplies on hand on May 31		1,050
d.	Depreciation for the current year		7,400
e.	Accrued salaries on May 31:		
	Sales salaries	$350	
	Office salaries	180	530

5. Prepare a multiple-step income statement, a statement of owner's equity, and a report form of balance sheet.
6. Journalize and post the adjusting entries.
7. Journalize and post the closing entries. Indicate closed accounts by inserting a line in both balance columns opposite the closing entry. Insert the new balance in the owner's capital account.
8. Prepare a post-closing trial balance.

SPECIAL ACTIVITIES

Activity 6–1
Couperin Company
Ethics and professional conduct in business

On October 1, 2003, Couperin Company, a garden retailer, purchased $15,000 of corn seed, terms 2/10, n/30, from Kernel Co. Even though the discount period had expired, Bryant Harness subtracted the discount of $300 when he processed the documents for payment on October 15, 2003.

Discuss whether Bryant Harness behaved in a professional manner by subtracting the discount, even though the discount period had expired.

Activity 6–2
The Movie Store Co.
Purchases discounts and accounts payable

The Movie Store Co. is owned and operated by Amy Lell. The following is an excerpt from a conversation between Amy Lell and Tammi Beach, the chief accountant for The Movie Store.

Amy: Tammi, I've got a question about this recent balance sheet.
Tammi: Sure, what's your question?
Amy: Well, as you know, I'm applying for a bank loan to finance our new store in Three Forks, and I noticed that the accounts payable are listed as $130,000.
Tammi: That's right. Approximately $100,000 of that represents amounts due our suppliers, and the remainder is miscellaneous payables to creditors for utilities, office equipment, supplies, etc.
Amy: That's what I thought. But as you know, we normally receive a 2% discount from our suppliers for earlier payment, and we always try to take the discount.
Tammi: That's right. I can't remember the last time we missed a discount.

Amy: Well, in that case, it seems to me the accounts payable should be listed minus the 2% discount. Let's list the accounts payable due suppliers as $98,000, rather than $100,000. Every little bit helps. You never know. It might make the difference between getting the loan and not.

➤ How would you respond to Amy Lell's request?

Activity 6–3
Mega Sound versus
Decibel Electronics
Determining cost of purchase

The following is an excerpt from a conversation between Gina Bellamy and Kim Craft. Gina is debating whether to buy a stereo system from Mega Sound, a locally owned electronics store, or Decibel Electronics, a mail order electronics company.

Gina: Kim, I don't know what to do about buying my new stereo.
Kim: What's the problem?
Gina: Well, I can buy it locally at Mega Sound for $495.00. However, Decibel Electronics has the same system listed for $499.99.
Kim: So what's the big deal? Buy it from Mega Sound.
Gina: It's not quite that simple. Decibel said something about not having to pay sales tax, since I was out-of-state.
Kim: Yes, that's a good point. If you buy it at Mega Sound, they'll charge you 5% sales tax.
Gina: But Decibel Electronics charges $12.50 for shipping and handling. If I have them send it next-day air, it'll cost $25 for shipping and handling.
Kim: I guess it is a little confusing.
Gina: That's not all. Mega Sound will give an additional 1% discount if I pay cash. Otherwise, they will let me use my MasterCard, or I can pay it off in three monthly installments.
Kim: Anything else???
Gina: Well . . . Decibel says I have to charge it on my MasterCard. They don't accept checks.
Kim: I am not surprised. Many mail-order houses don't accept checks.
Gina: I give up. What would you do?

1. Assuming that Decibel Electronics doesn't charge sales tax on the sale to Gina, which company is offering the best buy?
2. ➤ What might be some considerations other than price that might influence Gina's decision on where to buy the stereo system?

Activity 6–4
Hercules Parts
Company
Sales discounts

Your sister operates Hercules Parts Company, a mail-order boat parts distributorship that is in its third year of operation. The following income statement was recently prepared for the year ended July 31, 2003:

Hercules Parts Company
Income Statement
For the Year Ended July 31, 2003

Revenues:		
Net sales		$600,000
Interest revenue		5,000
Total revenues		$605,000
Expenses:		
Cost of merchandise sold	$420,000	
Selling expenses	66,000	
Administrative expenses	34,000	
Interest expense	10,000	
Total expenses		530,000
Net income		$ 75,000

Your sister is considering a proposal to increase net income by offering sales discounts of 2/15, n/30, and by shipping all merchandise FOB shipping point. Currently, no sales discounts are allowed and merchandise is shipped FOB destination. It is estimated that these credit terms will increase net sales by 10%. The ratio of the cost of merchandise sold to net sales is expected to be 70%. All selling and administrative expenses are expected to remain unchanged, except for store supplies, miscellaneous selling, office supplies, and miscellaneous administrative expenses, which are expected to increase proportionately with increased net sales. The amounts of these preceding items for the year ended July 31, 2003, were as follows:

Store supplies expense	$5,000
Miscellaneous selling expense	2,000
Office supplies expense	1,000
Miscellaneous administrative expense	1,800

The other income and other expense items will remain unchanged. The shipment of all merchandise FOB shipping point will eliminate all transportation-out expenses, which for the year ended July 31, 2003, were $20,150.

1. Prepare a projected single-step income statement for the year ending July 31, 2004, based on the proposal.
2. a. ✏️ Based on the projected income statement in (1), would you recommend the implementation of the proposed changes?
   b. Describe any possible concerns you may have related to the proposed changes described in (1).

Activity 6–5
Into the Real World
Shopping for a television

Assume that you are planning to purchase a 50-inch Sony television. In groups of three or four, determine the lowest cost for the television, considering the available alternatives and the advantages and disadvantages of each alternative. For example, you could purchase locally, through mail order, or through an Internet shopping service. Consider such factors as delivery charges, interest-free financing, discounts, coupons, and availability of warranty services. Prepare a report for presentation to the class.

ANSWERS TO SELF-EXAMINATION QUESTIONS

Matching

1.	C	5.	Q	9.	T	13.	D	17.	N	21.	L	25.	J
2.	H	6.	S	10.	E	14.	AA	18.	Y	22.	P	26.	A
3.	M	7.	K	11.	W	15.	G	19.	B	23.	O	27.	V
4.	R	8.	U	12.	X	16.	F	20.	I	24.	Z		

Multiple Choice

1. **A** A debit memorandum (answer A), issued by the buyer, indicates the amount the buyer proposes to debit to the accounts payable account. A credit memorandum (answer B), issued by the seller, indicates the amount the seller proposes to credit to the accounts receivable account. An invoice (answer C) or a bill (answer D), issued by the seller, indicates the amount and terms of the sale.

2. **C** The amount of discount for early payment is $10 (answer C), or 1% of $1,000. Although the $50 of transportation costs paid by the seller is debited to the cus-

tomer's account, the customer is not entitled to a discount on that amount.

3. **B** The single-step form of income statement (answer B) is so named because the total of all expenses is deducted in one step from the total of all revenues. The multiple-step form (answer A) includes numerous sections and subsections with several subtotals. The account form (answer C) and the report form (answer D) are two common forms of the balance sheet.

4. **C** Gross profit (answer C) is the excess of net sales over the cost of merchandise sold. Operating income

(answer A) or income from operations (answer B) is the excess of gross profit over operating expenses. Net income (answer D) is the final figure on the income statement after all revenues and expenses have been reported.

5. **D** Expenses such as interest expense (answer D) that cannot be associated directly with operations are identified as *Other expense* or *Nonoperating expense.* De-preciation expense—office equipment (answer A) is an administrative expense. Sales salaries expense (answer B) is a selling expense. Insurance expense (answer C) is a mixed expense with elements of both selling expense and administrative expense. For small businesses, insurance expense is usually reported as an administrative expense.

Cash

objectives

After studying this chapter, you should be able to:

1 Describe the nature of cash and the importance of internal control over cash.

2 Summarize basic procedures for achieving internal control over cash receipts.

3 Summarize basic procedures for achieving internal control over cash payments, including the use of a voucher system.

4 Describe the nature of a bank account and its use in controlling cash.

5 Prepare a bank reconciliation and journalize any necessary entries.

6 Account for small cash transactions using a petty cash fund.

7 Summarize how cash is presented on the balance sheet.

8 Compute and interpret the ratio of cash to current liabilities.

f your bank returns checks it has paid from your account, along with your monthly bank statement, you may have noticed a magnetic coding in the bottom right-hand corner of each check. This coding indicates the amount of the check. In the past, you may have accepted this coding, as well as the bank statement, as correct. However, a clerk may have entered the magnetic coding incorrectly, which causes the check to be processed for the wrong amount. For example, the following check written for $25 was incorrectly processed as $250:

Ed Smith 1026 3rd Ave., So. Lansing, Wisconsin 58241	7406 7/23/20 03 64-7088/2611

PAY TO THE ORDER OF *Jones Co.* $ *25 $\frac{00}{100}$*

Twenty-Five Dollars and $\frac{no}{100}$ DOLLARS

FIRST FEDERAL SAVINGS BANK OF WISCONSIN
LANSING, WISCONSIN

FOR   *Ed Smith*

⑆261170889⑆ 04 33 503662⑈ 7406 ⑈00000 25000⑈

We are all concerned about our cash. Likewise, businesses are concerned about safeguarding and controlling cash. Inadequate controls can and often do lead to theft, misuse of funds, or otherwise embarrassing situations. For example, in one of the biggest errors in banking history, **Chemical Bank** incorrectly deducted customer automated teller machine (ATM) withdrawals twice from each customer's account. For instance, if a customer withdrew $100 from an account, the customer actually had $200 deducted from the account balance. Before the error was discovered, Chemical Bank mistakenly deducted about $15 million from more than 100,000 customer accounts. The error was caused by inadequate controls over the changing of the bank's computer programs.[1]

To detect errors, control procedures should be used by both you and the bank. In this chapter, we will apply basic internal control concepts and procedures to the control of cash.

Nature of Cash and the Importance of Controls Over Cash

objective 1

Describe the nature of cash and the importance of internal control over cash.

Cash includes coins, currency (paper money), checks, money orders, and money on deposit that is available for unrestricted withdrawal from banks and other financial institutions. Normally, you can think of cash as anything that a bank would accept for deposit in your account. For example, a check made payable to you could normally be deposited in a bank and thus is considered cash.

We will assume in this chapter that a business maintains only *one* bank account, represented in the ledger as *Cash*. In practice, however, a business may have several bank accounts, such as one for general cash payments and another for payroll. For each of its bank accounts, the business will maintain a ledger account, one of which may be called *Cash in Bank—First Bank*, for example. It will also maintain

---

[1] Saul Hansell, "Cash Machines Getting Greedy at a Big Bank," *The Wall Street Journal*, February 18, 1994.

Point of Interest
The Internet has given rise to a form of cash called "cybercash."

separate ledger accounts for cash that it does not keep in the bank, such as cash for small payments, and cash used for special purposes, such as travel reimbursements. We will introduce some of these other cash accounts in the chapter.

Because of the ease with which money can be transferred, cash is the asset most likely to be diverted and used improperly by employees. In addition, many transactions either directly or indirectly affect the receipt or the payment of cash. Businesses must therefore design and use controls that safeguard cash and control the authorization of cash transactions. In the following paragraphs, we will discuss these controls.

Control of Cash Receipts

objective 2

Summarize basic procedures for achieving internal control over cash receipts.

To protect cash from theft and misuse, a business must control cash from the time it is received until it is deposited in a bank. Such procedures are called **preventive controls**. Procedures that are designed to detect theft or misuse of cash are called **detective controls**. In a sense, detective controls are also preventive in nature, since employees are less likely to steal or misuse cash if they know there is a good chance they will be discovered.

Retail businesses normally receive cash from two main sources: (1) cash receipts from customers and (2) mail receipts from customers making payments on account. These two sources of cash are shown in Exhibit 1.

Exhibit 1 Retailers' Sources of Cash

Fast-food restaurants, such as **McDonald's, Wendy's,** and **Burger King,** receive cash primarily from over-the-counter sales to customers. Mail-order and Internet retailers, such as **Lands' End, Orvis, L.L. Bean,** and **Amazon.com,** receive cash primarily through the mail and from credit card companies.

Controlling Cash Received from Cash Sales

Regardless of the source of cash receipts, every business must properly safeguard and record its cash receipts. One of the most important controls to protect cash received in over-the-counter sales is a cash register. You may have noticed that when a clerk (cashier) enters the amount of a sale, the cash register normally displays the amount. This is a control to ensure that the clerk has charged you the correct amount. You also receive a receipt to verify the accuracy of the amount.

At the beginning of a work shift, each cash register clerk is given a cash drawer that contains a predetermined amount of cash for making change for customers. The amount in each drawer is sometimes called a **change fund**. At the end of the work shift, each clerk and the supervisor count the cash in the clerk's cash drawer. The amount of cash in each drawer should equal the beginning amount of cash plus the cash sales for the day. However, errors in recording cash sales or errors in making change cause the amount of actual cash on hand to differ from this amount. Such differences are recorded in a cash short and over account. For example, the following entry records a clerk's cash sales of $3,150 when the actual cash on hand is $3,142:

		Cash	3 1 4 2 00	
		Cash Short and Over	8 00	
		Sales		3 1 5 0 00
		To record cash sales and actual cash		
		on hand.		

At the end of the accounting period, a debit balance in the cash short and over account is included in Miscellaneous Administrative Expense in the income statement. A credit balance is included in the Other Income section. If a clerk consistently has significant cash short and over amounts, the supervisor may require the clerk to take additional training.

After a cash register clerk's cash has been counted and recorded on a memorandum form, the cash is then placed in a store safe in the Cashier's Department until it can be deposited in the bank. The supervisor forwards the clerk's cash register tapes to the Accounting Department, where they become the basis for recording the transactions for the day.

Controlling Cash Received in the Mail

Cash is received in the mail when customers pay their bills. This cash is usually in the form of checks and money orders. Most companies' invoices are designed so that customers return a portion of the invoice, called a **remittance advice**, with their payment. The employee who opens the incoming mail should initially compare the amount of cash received with the amount shown on the remittance advice. If a customer does not return a remittance advice, an employee prepares one. Like the cash register, the remittance advice serves as a record of cash initially received. It also helps ensure that the posting to the customer's account is accurate. Finally, as a preventive control, the employee opening the mail normally also stamps checks and money orders "For Deposit Only" in the bank account of the business.

Some retail companies use debit card systems to transfer and record the receipt of cash. In a debit card system, a customer pays for goods at the time of purchase by presenting a plastic card. The card authorizes the electronic transfer of cash from the customer's checking account to the retailer's bank account at the time of the sale.

All cash received in the mail is sent to the Cashier's Department. An employee there combines it with the receipts from cash sales and prepares a bank deposit ticket. The remittance advices and their summary totals are delivered to the Accounting Department. An accounting clerk then prepares the records of the transactions and posts them to the customer accounts.

When cash is deposited in the bank, the bank normally stamps a duplicate copy of the deposit ticket with the amount received. This bank receipt is returned to the Accounting Department, where a clerk then compares the receipt with the total amount that should have been deposited. This control helps ensure that all the cash is deposited and that no cash is lost or stolen on the way to the bank. Any shortages are thus promptly detected.

The separation of the duties of the Cashier's Department, which handles cash, and the Accounting Department, which records cash, is a preventive control. If Accounting Department employees both handled and recorded cash, an employee could steal cash and change the accounting records to hide the theft.

Internal Control of Cash Payments

objective 3

Summarize basic procedures for achieving internal control over cash payments, including the use of a voucher system.

Internal control of cash payments should provide reasonable assurance that payments are made for only authorized transactions. In addition, controls should ensure that cash is used efficiently. For example, controls should ensure that all available discounts, such as purchase and trade discounts, are taken.

In a small business, an owner/manager may sign all checks, based upon personal knowledge of goods and services purchased. In a large business, however, checks are often prepared by employees who do not have such a complete knowledge of the transactions. In a large business, for example, the duties of purchasing goods, inspecting the goods received, and verifying the invoices are usually performed by different employees. These duties must be coordinated to ensure that checks for proper amounts are issued to creditors. One system used for this purpose is the voucher system.

Howard Schultz & Associates (HS&A) specializes in reviewing cash payments for its clients. HS&A searches for errors, such as duplicate payments, failures to take discounts, and inaccurate computations. The typical amount recovered for a client is about one-tenth of 1 percent (0.1%) of the total payments reviewed. This averages to about $300,000 per client. In one case, HS&A recovered over $4.5 million for a client.

Source: Thomas Buell, Jr., "Demand Grows for Auditor," *The Naples Daily News*, January 12, 1992, p. 14E.

Basic Features of the Voucher System

A **voucher system** is a set of procedures for authorizing and recording liabilities and cash payments. A voucher system normally uses (1) vouchers, (2) a file for unpaid vouchers, and (3) a file for paid vouchers. Generally, a voucher is any document that serves as proof of authority to pay cash. For example, an invoice properly approved for payment could be considered a voucher. In many businesses, however, a **voucher** is a special form for recording relevant data about a liability and the details of its payment. An example of such a form is shown in Exhibit 2.

Each voucher includes the creditor's invoice number and the amount and terms of the invoice. The accounts used in recording the purchase (or transaction) are listed in the *account distribution*.

A voucher is normally prepared in the Accounting Department, after all necessary supporting documents have been received. For example, when a voucher is prepared for the purchase of goods, the voucher should be supported by the supplier's invoice, a purchase order, and a receiving report. In preparing the voucher, an accounts payable clerk verifies the quantity, price, and mathematical accuracy of the supporting documents. This provides assurance that the payment is for goods that were properly ordered and received.

Exhibit 2 Voucher

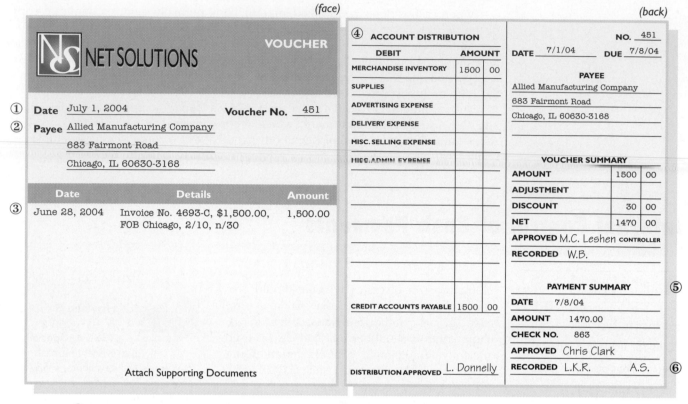

(face)   (back)

NET SOLUTIONS   **VOUCHER**

④ **ACCOUNT DISTRIBUTION**   **NO.** 451

DEBIT	AMOUNT
MERCHANDISE INVENTORY	1500 00
SUPPLIES	
ADVERTISING EXPENSE	
DELIVERY EXPENSE	
MISC. SELLING EXPENSE	
MISC. ADMIN. EXPENSE	

DATE 7/1/04   **DUE** 7/8/04

PAYEE
Allied Manufacturing Company
683 Fairmont Road
Chicago, IL 60630-3168

① **Date** July 1, 2004   **Voucher No.** 451
② **Payee** Allied Manufacturing Company
683 Fairmont Road
Chicago, IL 60630-3168

VOUCHER SUMMARY

AMOUNT	1500	00
ADJUSTMENT		
DISCOUNT	30	00
NET	1470	00

APPROVED M.C. Leshen **CONTROLLER**
RECORDED W.B.

Date	Details	Amount
③ June 28, 2004	Invoice No. 4693-C, $1,500.00, FOB Chicago, 2/10, n/30	1,500.00

PAYMENT SUMMARY ⑤

DATE	7/8/04
AMOUNT	1470.00
CHECK NO.	863

APPROVED Chris Clark

CREDIT ACCOUNTS PAYABLE	1500	00

Attach Supporting Documents

DISTRIBUTION APPROVED L. Donnelly

RECORDED L.K.R.   A.S. ⑥

① Date the voucher was prepared
② Name and address of the creditor
③ Description of the supporting documents

④ Accounts used to record the purchase or transaction
⑤ Details of payment
⑥ Spaces for signature or initials of approving employees

After a voucher is prepared, the voucher and its supporting documents are given to the proper official for approval. After it has been approved, the voucher is returned to the Accounting Department, where it is recorded in the accounts. It is then filed in an unpaid voucher file by its due date so that all available purchase discounts are taken.[2]

On its due date, the voucher is removed from the unpaid voucher file. The date, the number, and the amount of the check written in payment are listed on the back of the voucher. The payment of the voucher is recorded in the same manner as the payment of an account payable.

After payment, vouchers are marked "Paid" and are usually filed in numerical order in a paid voucher file. They are then readily available for examination by employees needing information about past payments.

A voucher system may be either manual or computerized. In a computerized system, properly approved supporting documents (such as purchase orders and receiving reports) would be entered directly into computer files. At the due date, the checks would be automatically generated and mailed to creditors. At that time, the voucher would be automatically transferred to a paid voucher file. In some cases, payments may be made electronically rather than by check.

---

[2] Occasionally, a purchase discount is missed. Some companies record the amounts of missed discounts in an account titled *Discounts Lost*. Doing so allows managers to monitor the significance of discounts lost. Since most companies design controls to take all purchase discounts, we do not illustrate the use of a discounts lost account.

BUSINESS ON STAGE

The Federal Reserve System

One of the most powerful financial institutions in the United States is the *Federal Reserve System*, often referred to as the *Fed*. The Federal Reserve System consists of twelve district banks located in the following cities: Boston, New York, Philadelphia, Cleveland, Charlotte, Atlanta, St. Louis, Chicago, Minneapolis, Kansas City, Dallas, and San Francisco. The Fed's overall operations are coordinated by a seven-member Board of Governors headquartered in Washington, D.C. Four key activities of the Fed are (1) carrying out monetary policy, (2) setting rules on credit, (3) distributing currency, and (4) clearing checks.

The Fed carries out monetary policy in three ways. First, the Fed's open-market operations involve the purchase and sale of government se-

curities. For example, when the Fed buys U.S. securities in the open market, it puts money into the economy. Second, the Fed sets the requirements for reserves that member banks must maintain on deposit. These reserves are unavailable for loans or other investments. Current reserve requirements range from 3% to 10% of a bank's deposits. Third, the Fed sets the discount rate. This rate is the interest rate that the Fed charges member banks for loans. The discount rate is often quoted in the financial press. It indirectly affects the interest rates that member banks charge customers on credit card balances, home mortgages, and other types of loans.

The Fed sets rules on credit in various ways. For example, the Fed sets minimum down payments and maximum repayment periods on con-

sumer loans of member banks. The Fed also sets margin requirements for purchasing securities such as stocks. For example, if the margin requirement is 40%, then an investor who purchases stocks worth $20,000 must pay at least $8,000. The remaining $12,000 can be financed.

The Fed distributes to member banks the coins minted and the paper money printed by the U.S. Treasury. Almost all paper money is in the form of Federal Reserve Notes. For example, if you look at a dollar bill, you will see the words *Federal Reserve Note* above the picture of George Washington.

Finally, the Fed helps banks clear checks. The Fed's check-clearing system lets banks quickly convert checks drawn on other banks into cash. ■

Electronic Funds Transfer

TeleCheck Services, Inc., the world's leading check acceptance company, is offering an online real-time check payment option for purchases made over the Internet. "It is apparent from the rapid growth of online sales that many consumers are as comfortable writing checks for Internet purchases as they are at their local brick-and-mortar store," explains Steve Shaper, chief executive officer of TeleCheck.

With rapidly changing technology, new systems are being devised to more efficiently record and transfer cash among companies. Such systems often use **electronic funds transfer (EFT)**. In an EFT system, computers rather than paper (money, checks, etc.) are used to effect cash transactions. For example, a business may pay its employees by means of EFT. Under such a system, employees may authorize the deposit of their payroll checks directly into checking accounts. Each pay period, the business electronically transfers the employees' net pay to their checking accounts through the use of computer systems and telephone lines. Likewise, many companies are using EFT systems to pay their suppliers and other vendors.

Bank Accounts: Their Nature and Use as a Control Over Cash

objective 4

Describe the nature of a bank account and its use in controlling cash.

Most of you are already familiar with bank accounts. You have a checking account at a local bank, credit union, savings and loan association, or other financial institution. In this section, we discuss the nature of a bank account used by a business. The features of such accounts will be similar to your own bank account. We then discuss the use of bank accounts as an additional control over cash.

Business Bank Accounts

A business often maintains several bank accounts. The forms used with each bank account are a signature card, deposit ticket, check, and record of checks drawn.

When you open a checking account, you sign a **signature card**. This card is used by the bank to verify the signature on checks that are submitted for payment. Also, when you open an account, the bank assigns an identifying number to the account.

The details of a deposit are listed by the depositor on a printed **deposit ticket** supplied by the bank. These forms are often prepared in duplicate. The bank teller stamps or initials a copy of the deposit ticket and gives it to the depositor as a receipt. Other types of receipts may also be used to give the depositor written proof of the date and the total amount of the deposit.

A **check** is a written document signed by the depositor, ordering the bank to pay a sum of money to an individual or entity. There are three parties to a check—the drawer, the drawee, and the payee. The **drawer** is the one who signs the check, ordering payment by the bank. The **drawee** is the bank on which the check is drawn. The **payee** is the party to whom payment is to be made.

The name and address of the depositor are usually printed on each check. In addition, checks are prenumbered, so that they can easily be kept track of by both the issuer and the bank. Banks encode their identification number and the depositor's account number in magnetic ink on each check. These numbers make it possible for the bank to sort and post checks automatically. When a check is presented for payment, the amount for which it is drawn is inserted, next to the account number, in magnetic ink. The processed check shown at the beginning of this chapter illustrated these features.

A record of each check should be prepared at the time a check is written. A small booklet called a **transactions register** is often used by both businesses and individuals for this purpose.

The purpose of a check may be written in space provided on the check or on an attachment to the check. Normally, checks issued to a creditor on account are sent with a form that identifies the specific invoice that is being paid. The purpose of this **remittance advice** is to make sure that proper credit is recorded in the accounts of the creditor. In this way, mistakes are less likely to occur. A check and remittance advice is shown in Exhibit 3.

Before depositing the check, the payee removes the remittance advice. The payee may then use the remittance advice as written proof of the details of the cash receipt.

Bank Statement

Banks usually maintain a record of all checking account transactions. A summary of all transactions, called a **statement of account**, is mailed to the depositor, usually each month. Like any account with a customer or a creditor, the bank statement

Exhibit 3 Check and Remittance Advice

POWER NETWORKING				363

POWER NETWORKING   363

1000 Belkin   Los Angeles, CA 90014-1000   July 07 20 03   9-42/720

Pay to the Order of   Interface Data Systems $ 921.20

Nine hundred twenty-one 20/100 -------------------------------- **Dollars**

VALLEY NATIONAL BANK OF LOS ANGELES
LOS ANGELES, CA 90020-4283   (310) 851-5151   MEMBER FDIC

K.R. Simons   **Treasurer**
Earl M. Hartman   **Vice President**

⑃072000423⑃   1627042   363‖

DETACH THIS PORTION BEFORE CASHING

Date	Description	Gross Amount	Deductions	Net Amount
07/07/03	Invoice No. 529482	940.00	18.80	921.20

POWER NETWORKING

shows the beginning balance, additions, deductions, and the balance at the end of the period. A typical bank statement is shown in Exhibit 4.

The depositor's checks received by the bank during the period may accompany the bank statement, arranged in the order of payment. The paid checks are stamped "Paid," together with the date of payment. Other entries that the bank has made in the depositor's account may be described in debit or credit memorandums enclosed with the statement.

You should note that a depositor's checking account balance *in the bank's records* is a liability with a credit balance. Debit memorandums issued by the bank on a depositor's account therefore decrease the depositor's balance. Likewise, credit memorandums increase the depositor's balance. A bank issues a debit memorandum to charge (decrease) a depositor's account for service charges or for deposited checks returned because of insufficient funds. Likewise, a bank issues a credit memorandum when it increases the depositor's account for collecting a note receivable for the depositor, making a loan to the depositor, receiving a wire deposit, or adding interest to the depositor's account.[3]

Bank Accounts as a Control Over Cash

A bank account is one of the primary tools a business uses to control cash. For example, businesses often require that all cash receipts be initially deposited in a bank account. Likewise, businesses usually

> A bank account and a business's records provide a double record of cash transactions.

[3] Although interest-bearing checking accounts are common for individuals, Federal Reserve Regulation Q prohibits the paying of interest on corporate checking accounts.

Exhibit 4 Bank Statement

MEMBER FDIC   PAGE   1

VALLEY NATIONAL BANK
OF LOS ANGELES

LOS ANGELES, CA 90020-4253   (310)851-5151

ACCOUNT NUMBER	1627042	
FROM 6/30/03	TO 7/31/03	
BALANCE	4,218.60	

POWER NETWORKING
1000 Belkin Street
Los Angeles, CA 90014-1000

22 DEPOSITS	13,749.75
52 WITHDRAWALS	14,698.57
3 OTHER DEBITS AND CREDITS	90.00CR
NEW BALANCE	3,359.78

* – – CHECKS AND OTHER DEBITS – – –		* – – – DEPOSITS – –	* – – DATE – –	* – – BALANCE – – *
819.40	122.54	585.75	07/01	3,862.41
369.50	732.26	20.15	421.53	07/02	3,162.03
600.00	190.70	52.50	781.30	07/03	3,100.13
25.93	160.00	662.50	07/05	3,576.70
921.20	NSF 300.00	503.18	07/07	2,858.68

32.26	535.09	932.00	07/29	3,404.40
21.10	126.20	705.21	07/30	3,962.31
	SC 18.00	MS 408.00	07/30	4,352.31
26.12	1,615.13	648.72	07/31	3,359.78

EC — ERROR CORRECTION	OD — OVERDRAFT
MS — MISCELLANEOUS	PS — PAYMENT STOPPED
NSF — NOT SUFFICIENT FUNDS	SC — SERVICE CHARGE

* * *   * * *   * * *

THE RECONCILEMENT OF THIS STATEMENT WITH YOUR RECORDS IS ESSENTIAL.
ANY ERROR OR EXCEPTION SHOULD BE REPORTED IMMEDIATELY.

use checks to make all cash payments, except for very small amounts. When such a system is used, there is a double record of cash transactions—one by the business and the other by the bank.

A business can use a bank statement to compare the cash transactions recorded in its accounting records to those recorded by the bank. The cash balance shown by a bank statement is usually different from the cash balance shown in the accounting records of the business, as shown in Exhibit 5.

This difference may be the result of a delay by either party in recording transactions. For example, there is a time lag of one day or more between the date a check is written and the date that it is presented to the bank for payment. If the depositor mails deposits to the bank or uses the night depository, a time lag between the date of the deposit and the date that it is recorded by the bank is also probable. The bank may also debit or credit the depositor's account for transactions about which the depositor will not be informed until later.

The difference may be the result of errors made by either the business or the bank in recording transactions. For example, the business may incorrectly post to Cash a check written for $4,500 as $450. Likewise, a bank may incorrectly record the amount of a check, as we illustrated at the beginning of this chapter.

Exhibit 5 Power Networking's Records and Bank Statement

Bank Statement				Power Networking Records	
Beginning Balance		$ 4,218.60		Beginning Balance	$ 4,227.60
Additions:					
Deposits		13,749.75		Deposits	14,565.95
Miscellaneous		408.00			
Deductions:					
Checks		14,698.57		Checks	16,243.56
NSF Check	$300				
Service Charge	18	318.00			
Ending Balance		$ 3,359.78		Ending Balance	$ 2,549.99

Power Networking should determine the reason for the difference in these two amounts.

Bank Reconciliation

For effective control, the reasons for the difference between the cash balance on the bank statement and the cash balance in the accounting records should be determined by preparing a bank reconciliation. A **bank reconciliation** is a listing of the items and amounts that cause the cash balance reported in the bank statement to differ from the balance of the cash account in the ledger.

A bank reconciliation is usually divided into two sections. The first section begins with the cash balance according to the bank statement and ends with the adjusted balance. The second section begins with the cash balance according to the depositor's records and ends with the adjusted balance. The two amounts designated as the adjusted balance must be equal. The content of the bank reconciliation is shown below.

Cash balance according to bank statement		$XXX	Cash balance according to depositor's records . .		$XXX
Add: Additions by depositor not on			Add: Additions by bank not recorded by		
bank statement	$XX		depositor	$XX	
Bank errors	XX	XX	Depositor errors	XX	XX
		$XXX			$XXX
Deduct: Deductions by depositor not on			Deduct: Deductions by bank not recorded		
bank statement	$XX		by depositor	$XX	
Bank errors	XX	XX	Depositor errors	XX	XX
Adjusted balance		$XXX	Adjusted balance		$XXX

must be equal

The following steps are useful in finding the reconciling items and determining the adjusted balance of Cash:

1. Compare each deposit listed on the bank statement with unrecorded deposits appearing in the preceding period's reconciliation and with deposit receipts or other records of deposits. *Add deposits not recorded by the bank to the balance according to the bank statement.*
2. Compare paid checks with outstanding checks appearing on the preceding period's reconciliation and with recorded checks. *Deduct checks outstanding that have not been paid by the bank from the balance according to the bank statement.*

3. Compare bank credit memorandums to entries in the journal. For example, a bank would issue a credit memorandum for a note receivable and interest that it collected for a depositor. *Add credit memorandums that have not been recorded to the balance according to the depositor's records.*

4. Compare bank debit memorandums to entries recording cash payments. For example, a bank normally issues debit memorandums for service charges and check printing charges. A bank also issues debit memorandums for not-sufficient-funds checks. A *not-sufficient-funds (NSF) check* is a customer's check that was recorded and deposited but was not paid when it was presented to the customer's bank for payment. NSF checks are normally charged back to the customer as an account receivable. *Deduct debit memorandums that have not been recorded from the balance according to the depositor's records.*

5. List any errors discovered during the preceding steps. For example, if an amount has been recorded incorrectly by the depositor, the amount of the error should be added to or deducted from the cash balance according to the depositor's records. Similarly, errors by the bank should be added to or deducted from the cash balance according to the bank statement.

To illustrate a bank reconciliation, we will use the bank statement for Power Networking in Exhibit 4. This bank statement shows a balance of $3,359.78 as of July 31. The cash balance in Power Networking's ledger as of the same date is $2,549.99. The following reconciling items are revealed by using the steps outlined above:

Deposit of July 31, not recorded on bank statement . . . . $ 816.20
Checks outstanding: No. 812, $1,061.00; No. 878, $435.39; No. 883, $48.60 . . . . . . 1,544.99
Note plus interest of $8 collected by bank (credit memorandum), not recorded
  in the journal 408.00
Check from customer (Thomas Ivey) returned by bank because of insufficient
  funds (NSF) 300.00
Bank service charges (debit memorandum), not recorded in the journal 18.00
Check No. 879 for $732.26 to Taylor Co. on account, recorded in the journal
  as $723.26 . . . . 9.00

The bank reconciliation based on the bank statement and the reconciling items is shown in Exhibit 6.

Exhibit 6 Bank Reconciliation for Power Networking

Power Networking
Bank Reconciliation
July 31, 2003

Cash balance according to bank statement		$3,359 78	Cash balance according to depositor's records	$2,549 99
Add deposit of July 31, not recorded by bank		816 20	Add note and interest collected by bank	408 00
		$4,175 98		$2,957 99
Deduct outstanding checks:			Deduct: Check returned because of insufficient funds	$ 300 00
No. 812	$1,061 00		Bank service charges	18 00
No. 878	435 39		Error in recording	
No. 883	48 60	1,544 99	Check No. 879	9 00	327 00
Adjusted balance		$2,630 99	Adjusted balance	$2,630 99

Entries must be made in the depositor's accounts for any items that affect the business's record of cash.

No entries are necessary on the depositor's records as a result of the information included in the first section of the bank reconciliation. This section begins with the cash balance according to the bank statement. However, the bank should be notified of any errors that need to be corrected on its records.

Any items in the second section of the bank reconciliation must be recorded in the depositor's accounts. This section begins with the cash balance according to the depositor's records. For example, journal entries should be made for any unrecorded bank memorandums and any depositor's errors.

The journal entries for Power Networking, based on the preceding bank reconciliation, are as follows:

1	July	31	Cash	4 0 8 00			1
2			Notes Receivable		4 0 0 00		2
3			Interest Revenue		8 00		3
4			Note collected by bank.				4
5							5
6		31	Accounts Receivable—Thomas Ivey	3 0 0 00			6
7			Miscellaneous Administrative Expense	1 8 00			7
8			Accounts Payable—Taylor Co.	9 00			8
9			Cash		3 2 7 00		9
10			NSF check, bank service charges, and error				10
11			in recording Check No. 879.				11

Q&A *Assume that the bank recorded a deposit of $4,100 as $1,400. How would this bank error be shown on the bank reconciliation?*

The error of $2,700 would be added to the cash balance according to the bank statement.

After these entries have been posted, the cash account will have a debit balance of $2,630.99. This balance agrees with the adjusted cash balance shown on the bank reconciliation. This is the amount of cash available as of July 31 and the amount that would be reported on Power Networking's July 31 balance sheet.

Although businesses may reconcile their bank accounts in a slightly different format from what we described above, the objective is the same: to control cash by reconciling the company's records to the records of an independent outside source, the bank. In doing so, any errors or misuse of cash may be detected.

For effective control, the bank reconciliation should be prepared by an employee who does not take part in or record cash transactions. When these duties are not properly separated, mistakes are likely to occur, and it is more likely that cash will be stolen or otherwise misapplied. For example, an employee who takes part in all of these duties could prepare and cash an unauthorized check, omit it from the accounts, and omit it from the reconciliation.

Point of Interest

If you reconcile your bank account each month, you first scan your bank statement for any bank entries that you have not yet recorded. Examples of such entries include service charges (a debit entry) and interest earned (a credit entry). You then enter these amounts in your checkbook (register) and determine the balance of your account. If you stop at this point, you are assuming that the bank hasn't made any errors.

If you fully reconcile your account, you should also scan your checkbook for items that the bank has not yet recorded: (1) deposits in transit and (2) outstanding checks. Deposits in transit should be added to the bank balance, and outstanding checks should be subtracted from the bank balance. The result is an adjusted bank balance, which should agree with the balance of your checkbook. If the two are not equal, either you or the bank has made an error.

Petty Cash

objective 6

Account for small cash transactions using a petty cash fund.

As in your own day-to-day life, it is usually not practical for a business to write checks to pay small amounts, such as postage. Yet, these small payments may occur often enough to add up to a significant total amount. Thus, it is desirable to control such payments. For this purpose, a special cash fund, called a **petty cash fund**, is used.

A petty cash fund is established by first estimating the amount of cash needed for payments from the fund during a period, such as a week or a month. After necessary approvals, a check is written and cashed for this amount. The money obtained from cashing the check is then given to an employee, called the petty cash custodian, who is authorized to disburse monies from the fund. For control purposes, the company may place restrictions on the maximum amount and the types of payments that can be made from the fund.

 Businesses often use other cash funds to meet their special needs, such as travel expenses for salespersons. For example, each salesperson might be given $200 for travel-related expenses. Periodically, the salesperson submits a detailed expense report and the travel funds are replenished.

Each time monies are paid from petty cash, the custodian records the details of the payment on a petty cash receipt form. A typical petty cash receipt is illustrated in Exhibit 7.

Exhibit 7 Petty Cash Receipt

PETTY CASH RECEIPT

No. _____121_____   Date ___August 1, 2003___

Paid to _____Metropolitan Times_____   **Amount**

For _____Daily newspaper_____ | 3 | 00 |

Charge to ____Miscellaneous Administrative Expense____

Payment received:

_____S.O. Hall_____   **Approved by** _____N.E.R._____

The petty cash fund is normally replenished at periodic intervals, or when it is depleted or reaches a minimum amount. When a petty cash fund is replenished, the accounts debited are determined by summarizing the petty cash receipts. A check is then written for this amount, payable to the petty cash custodian.

To illustrate normal petty cash fund entries, assume that a petty cash fund of $100 is established on August 1. The entry to record this transaction is as follows:

13	Aug.	1	Petty Cash		1 0 0 00		13
14			Cash			1 0 0 00	14
15			Established petty cash fund.				15

At the end of August, the petty cash receipts indicate expenditures for the following items: office supplies, $28; postage (office supplies), $22; store supplies, $35; and daily newspapers (miscellaneous administrative expense), $3. The entry to replenish the petty cash fund on August 31 is as follows:

17	Aug.	31	Office Supplies	5 0 00		17
18			Store Supplies	3 5 00		18
19			Miscellaneous Administrative Expense	3 00		19
20			Cash		8 8 00	20
21			Replenished petty cash fund.			21

Replenishing the petty cash fund restores it to its original amount of $100. You should note that there is no entry in Petty Cash when the fund is replenished. Petty Cash is debited only when the fund is initially set up or when the amount of the fund is increased at a later time. Petty Cash is credited if it is being decreased.

Petty Cash is debited only when the fund is set up or the amount of the fund is increased.

Presentation of Cash on the Balance Sheet

objective 7

Summarize how cash is presented on the balance sheet.

Cash is the most liquid asset, and therefore it is listed as the first asset in the Current Assets section of the balance sheet. Most companies present only a single cash amount on the balance sheet by combining all their bank and cash fund accounts.

A company may have cash in excess of its operating needs. In such cases, the company normally invests in highly liquid investments in order to earn interest. These investments are called **cash equivalents**.[4] Examples of cash equivalents include U.S. Treasury Bills, notes issued by major corporations (referred to as commercial paper), and money market funds. Companies that have invested excess cash in cash equivalents usually report *Cash and cash equivalents* as one amount on the balance sheet.

Banks may require depositors to maintain minimum cash balances in their bank accounts. Such a balance is called a **compensating balance**. This requirement is often imposed by the bank as a part of a loan agreement or line of credit. A *line of credit* is a preapproved amount the bank is willing to lend to a customer upon request. Compensating balance requirements should be disclosed in notes to the financial statements.

Real World

The following note discloses compensating balance requirements for **Kmart Corporation**: ... *In support of lines of credit, it is expected that compensating balances will be maintained on deposit with the banks, which will average 10% of the line to the extent that it is not in use and an additional 10% on the portion in use. ...*

---

[4] To be classified as a cash equivalent, according to *FASB Statement 95*, the investment is expected to be converted to cash within 90 days.

FINANCIAL ANALYSIS AND INTERPRETATION

objective 8

Compute and interpret the ratio of cash to current liabilities.

In an earlier chapter, we discussed the use of working capital and the current ratio in evaluating a company's ability to pay its current liabilities (short-term solvency). Both of these measures assume that the noncash current assets will be converted to cash in time to pay the current liabilities. For most companies, these measures are useful for assessing short-term solvency. However, a company that is in financial distress may have difficulty converting its receivables, inventory, and prepaid assets to cash on a timely basis. In these cases, the ratio of cash to current liabilities may be useful in assessing the ability of creditors to collect what they are owed. Because this ratio is most relevant for companies in financial distress, it is called the **doomsday ratio**.[5] Its name comes from the worst case assumption that the business ceases to exist and only the cash on hand is available to meet creditor obligations.

In computing the ratio of cash to current liabilities, cash and cash equivalents are used in the numerator, as shown below.

$$\text{Doomsday ratio} = \frac{\textbf{Cash and cash equivalents}}{\textbf{Current liabilities}}$$

To illustrate, assume the following data for Laettner Co. and Oakley Co. for the current year:

	Laettner Co.	**Oakley Co.**
Cash and cash equivalents	$100,000	$ 120,000
Current liabilities	400,000	1,500,000

The doomsday ratio for each company is computed as follows. In this case, Oakley Co. is more risky to creditors than is Laettner.

	Doomsday Ratio	
Laettner Co.	0.25	($100,000/$400,000)
Oakley Co.	0.08	($120,000/$1,500,000)

Because most businesses maintain cash and cash equivalents at amounts substantially less than their current liabilities, the doomsday ratio is almost always less than one. For example, the doomsday ratio for **Tandy Corporation** is 0.18. For **La-Z-Boy Chair Company**, it is 0.25.

Differences among companies will occur because of differences in management philosophy and operating styles. Nevertheless, a comparison over time that indicates a decreasing ratio generally indicates more risk for creditors.

[5] This ratio is discussed more fully in *101 Business Ratios* by Sheldon Gates, McLane Publications, Scottsdale, Arizona, 1993.

ENCORE

The Theft at Perini Corporation

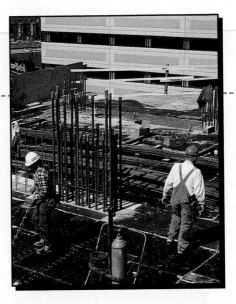

The financial vice-president of **Perini Corporation** received a disturbing call from one of the company's banks. The bank reported that Perini's bank account was substantially overdrawn. Perini, a large construction company based near Boston, had never overdrawn any of its bank accounts in over twenty-five years. Shortly thereafter, another of Perini's banks called and reported that its Perini account was also overdrawn. A review of the recent bank statements, which had been lying around unreconciled for two weeks, revealed canceled checks of more than $1.1 million that had not been recorded.

Perini kept its unused checks in an unlocked room. Perini also kept its supply of coffee cups in the same room, where every clerk and secretary had access to them. A quick review revealed two missing boxes of checks.

Perini used a checkwriting machine that automatically signed the vice-president's name. Unfortunately, Perini didn't implement the controls suggested by its auditor. Instead, the machine-processed checks were placed in an unlocked box, there was no reconciliation of the counter on the machine with the number of checks that should have been written, and the keys to lock the machine were not carefully safeguarded. The vice-president said that such controls were "too much trouble."

The rest of the story involves a possible suspect who is killed in a lovers' feud involving a neurosurgeon; a bizarre arson in Perini's financial offices; a hit-and-run accident involving a boat; and a quiet accountant who purchased a new Continental, moved to Las Vegas, bought an expensive house, and began running sex shows in casinos. Even though the FBI assigned one of its best agents to the case, the money was never recovered and the perpetrator of the theft remains a mystery. ∎

KEY POINTS

1 Describe the nature of cash and the importance of internal control over cash.
Cash includes coins, currency (paper money), checks, money orders, and money on deposit that is available for unrestricted withdrawal from banks and other financial institutions. Because of the ease with which money can be transferred, businesses should design and use controls that safeguard cash and authorize cash transactions.

2 Summarize basic procedures for achieving internal control over cash receipts.
One of the most important controls to protect cash received in over-the-counter sales is a cash register. A remittance advice is a preventive control for cash received through the mail. Separating the duties of handling cash and recording cash is also a preventive control.

3 Summarize basic procedures for achieving internal control over cash payments, including the use of a voucher system.
A voucher system is a set of procedures for authorizing and recording liabilities and cash payments. A voucher system uses vouchers, a file for unpaid vouchers, and a file for paid vouchers.

4 Describe the nature of a bank account and its use in controlling cash.
The forms used with bank accounts are a signature card, deposit ticket, check, and record of checks drawn. Each month, the bank usually sends a bank statement to the depositor, summarizing all of the transactions for the month. The bank statement allows a business to compare the cash transactions recorded in the accounting records to those recorded by the bank.

5 Prepare a bank reconciliation and journalize any necessary entries.

The first section of the bank reconciliation begins with the cash balance according to the bank statement. This balance is adjusted for the depositor's changes in cash that do not appear on the bank statement and for any bank errors. The second section begins with the cash balance according to the depositor's records. This balance is adjusted for the bank's changes in cash that do not appear on the depositor's records and for any depositor errors. The adjusted balances for the two sections must be equal.

No entries are necessary on the depositor's records as a result of the information included in the first section of the bank reconciliation. However, the items in the second section must be journalized on the depositor's records.

6 Account for small cash transactions using a petty cash fund.

A petty cash fund may be used by a business to make small payments that occur frequently. The money in a petty cash fund is placed in the custody of a specific employee, who authorizes payments from the fund. Periodically or when the amount of money in the fund is depleted or reduced to a minimum amount, the fund is replenished.

7 Summarize how cash is presented on the balance sheet.

Cash is listed as the first asset in the Current Assets section of the balance sheet. Companies that have invested excess cash in highly liquid investments usually report *Cash and cash equivalents* on the balance sheet.

8 Compute and interpret the ratio of cash to current liabilities.

A company that is in financial distress may have difficulty converting its receivables, inventory, and prepaid assets to cash on a timely basis. In these cases, the ratio of cash to current liabilities, called the doomsday ratio, may be useful in assessing the ability of creditors to collect what they are owed.

ILLUSTRATIVE PROBLEM

The bank statement for Urethane Company for June 30, 2003, indicates a balance of $9,143.11. All cash receipts are deposited each evening in a night depository, after banking hours. The accounting records indicate the following summary data for cash receipts and payments for June:

Cash balance as of June 1	$ 3,943.50
Total cash receipts for June	28,971.60
Total amount of checks issued in June	28,388.85

Comparing the bank statement and the accompanying canceled checks and memorandums with the records reveals the following reconciling items:

a. The bank had collected for Urethane Company $1,030 on a note left for collection. The face of the note was $1,000.
b. A deposit of $1,852.21, representing receipts of June 30, had been made too late to appear on the bank statement.
c. Checks outstanding totaled $5,265.27.
d. A check drawn for $139 had been incorrectly charged by the bank as $157.
e. A check for $30 returned with the statement had been recorded in the depositor's records as $240. The check was for the payment of an obligation to Avery Equipment Company for the purchase of office supplies on account.
f. Bank service charges for June amounted to $18.20.

Instructions

1. Prepare a bank reconciliation for June.
2. Journalize the entries that should be made by Urethane Company.

Solution

1.

Urethane Company
Bank Reconciliation
June 30, 2003

Cash balance according to bank statement		$ 9,143.11
Add: Deposit of June 30 not recorded by bank	$1,852.21	
Bank error in charging check as $157 instead of $139	18.00	1,870.21
		$11,013.32
Deduct: Outstanding checks		5,265.27
Adjusted balance		$ 5,748.05
Cash balance according to depositor's records		$ 4,526.25*
Add: Proceeds of note collected by bank, including $30 interest	$1,030.00	
Error in recording check	210.00	1,240.00
		$ 5,766.25
Deduct: Bank service charges		18.20
Adjusted balance		$ 5,748.05

*$3,943.50 + $28,971.60 − $28,388.85

2.

Cash	1,240.00	
Notes Receivable		1,000.00
Interest Revenue		30.00
Accounts Payable—Avery Equipment		210.00
Miscellaneous Administrative Expense	18.20	
Cash		18.20

SELF-EXAMINATION QUESTIONS
Answers at End of Chapter

Matching
Match each of the following statements with its proper term. Some terms may not be used.

A. bank reconciliation
B. bank statement
C. cash
D. cash equivalents
E. cash receipts journal
F. cash short and over account
G. doomsday ratio
H. electronic funds transfer (EFT)
I. notes receivable
J. petty cash fund
K. voucher
L. voucher system
M. working capital ratio

___ 1. Coins, currency (paper money), checks, money orders, and money on deposit that is available for unrestricted withdrawal from banks and other financial institutions.

___ 2. A set of procedures for authorizing and recording liabilities and cash payments.

___ 3. A special form for recording relevant data about a liability and the details of its payment.

___ 4. A system in which computers rather than paper (money, checks, etc.) are used to effect cash transactions.

___ 5. A special cash fund to pay relatively small amounts.

___ 6. The analysis that details the items responsible for the difference between the cash balance reported in the bank statement and the balance of the cash account in the ledger.

___ 7. Highly liquid investments that are usually reported with cash on the balance sheet.

___ 8. The ratio of cash and cash equivalents to current liabilities.

Multiple Choice

1. The bank erroneously charged Tropical Services' account for $450.50 for a check that was correctly written and recorded by Tropical Services as $540.50. To reconcile the bank account of Tropical Services at the end of the month, you would:
   A. add $90 to the cash balance according to the bank statement.
   B. add $90 to the cash balance according to Tropical Services' records.
   C. deduct $90 from the cash balance according to the bank statement.
   D. deduct $90 from the cash balance according to Tropical Services' records.

2. In preparing a bank reconciliation, the amount of checks outstanding would be:
   A. added to the cash balance according to the bank statement.
   B. deducted from the cash balance according to the bank statement.
   C. added to the cash balance according to the depositor's records.
   D. deducted from the cash balance according to the depositor's records.

3. Journal entries based on the bank reconciliation are required for:
   A. additions to the cash balance according to the depositor's records.
   B. deductions from the cash balance according to the depositor's records.
   C. both A and B.
   D. neither A nor B.

4. A petty cash fund is:
   A. used to pay relatively small amounts.
   B. established by estimating the amount of cash needed for disbursements of relatively small amounts during a specified period.
   C. reimbursed when the amount of money in the fund is reduced to a predetermined minimum amount.
   D. all of the above.

5. Which of the following is the correct entry to replenish a petty cash fund?
   A. Debit Petty Cash; credit Cash
   B. Debit various expense accounts; credit Petty Cash
   C. Debit various expense accounts; credit Cash
   D. Debit Cash; credit Petty Cash

CLASS DISCUSSION QUESTIONS

1. Why is cash the asset that often warrants the most attention in the design of an effective internal control structure?
2. The combined cash count of all cash registers at the close of business is $110 less than the cash sales indicated by the cash register tapes. (a) In what account is the cash shortage recorded? (b) Are cash shortages debited or credited to this account?
3. In which section of the income statement would a credit balance in Cash Short and Over be reported?
4. Before a voucher for the purchase of merchandise is approved for payment, supporting documents should be compared to verify the accuracy of the liability. Name an example of a supporting document for the purchase of merchandise.
5. When is a voucher recorded?
6. The accounting clerk pays all obligations by prenumbered checks. What are the strengths and weaknesses in the internal control over cash payments in this situation?
7. In what order are vouchers ordinarily filed (a) in the unpaid voucher file and (b) in the paid voucher file? Give reasons for the answers.
8. The balance of Cash is likely to differ from the bank statement balance. What two factors are likely to be responsible for the difference?
9. What is the purpose of preparing a bank reconciliation?
10. Do items reported on the bank statement as credits represent (a) additions made by the bank to the depositor's balance, or (b) deductions made by the bank from the depositor's balance?
11. What entry should be made if a check received from a customer and deposited is returned by the bank for lack of sufficient funds (an NSF check)?
12. Explain why some cash payments are made in coins and currency from a petty cash fund.
13. What account or accounts are debited when (a) establishing a petty cash fund and (b) replenishing a petty cash fund?
14. The petty cash account has a debit balance of $750. At the end of the accounting period, there is $112 in the petty cash fund, along with petty cash receipts totaling $638. Should the fund be replenished as of the last day of the period? Discuss.
15. How are cash equivalents reported in the financial statements?
16. How is a compensating balance reported in the financial statements?

EXERCISES

Exercise 7–1
Internal control of cash receipts
Objective 2

The procedures used for over-the-counter receipts are as follows. At the close of each day's business, the sales clerks count the cash in their respective cash drawers, after which they determine the amount recorded by the cash register and prepare the memorandum cash form, noting any discrepancies. An employee from the cashier's office counts the cash, compares the total with the memorandum, and takes the cash to the cashier's office.

a. Indicate the weak link in internal control.
b. How can the weakness be corrected?

Exercise 7–2
Internal control of cash receipts
Objective 2

Kathy Beal works at the drive-through window of Fletch's Burgers. Occasionally, when a drive-through customer orders, Kathy fills the order and pockets the customer's money. She does not ring up the order on the cash register.
Identify the internal control weaknesses that exist at Fletch's Burgers, and discuss what can be done to prevent this theft.

Exercise 7–3
Internal control of cash receipts
Objective 2

The mailroom employees send all remittances and remittance advices to the cashier. The cashier deposits the cash in the bank and forwards the remittance advices and duplicate deposit slips to the Accounting Department.

a. Indicate the weak link in internal control in the handling of cash receipts.
b. How can the weakness be corrected?

Exercise 7–4
Entry for cash sales; cash short
Objective 2

The actual cash received from cash sales was $18,153.79, and the amount indicated by the cash register total was $18,178.31. Journalize the entry to record the cash receipts and cash sales.

Exercise 7–5
Entry for cash sales; cash over

The actual cash received from cash sales was $9,357.69, and the amount indicated by the cash register total was $9,346.22. Journalize the entry to record the cash receipts and cash sales.

Exercise 7–6
Internal control of cash payments
Objective 3

Fiedler Co. is a medium-size merchandising company. An investigation revealed that in spite of a sufficient bank balance, a significant amount of available cash discounts had been lost because of failure to make timely payments. In addition, it was discovered that several purchases invoices had been paid twice.
Outline procedures for the payment of vendors' invoices, so that the possibilities of losing available cash discounts and of paying an invoice a second time will be minimized.

Exercise 7–7
Internal control of cash payments
Objective 3

Herringbone Company, a communications equipment manufacturer, recently fell victim to an embezzlement scheme masterminded by one of its employees. To understand the scheme, it is necessary to review Herringbone's procedures for the purchase of services.
The purchasing agent is responsible for ordering services (such as repairs to a photocopy machine or office cleaning) after receiving a service requisition from an autho-

rized manager. However, since no tangible goods are delivered, a receiving report is not prepared. When the Accounting Department receives an invoice billing Herringbone for a service call, the accounts payable clerk calls the manager who requested the service in order to verify that it was performed.

The embezzlement scheme involves Kellie Barth, the manager of plant and facilities. Kellie arranged for her uncle's company, Barth Industrial Supply and Service, to be placed on Herringbone's approved vendor list. Kellie did not disclose the family relationship.

On several occasions, Kellie would submit a requisition for services to be provided by Barth Industrial Supply and Service. However, the service requested was really not needed, and it was never performed. Barth would bill Herringbone for the service and then split the cash payment with Kellie.

➤ Explain what changes should be made to Herringbone's procedures for ordering and paying for services in order to prevent such occurrences in the future.

Exercise 7–8
Bank reconciliation
Objective 5

Identify each of the following reconciling items as: (a) an addition to the cash balance according to the bank statement, (b) a deduction from the cash balance according to the bank statement, (c) an addition to the cash balance according to the depositor's records, or (d) a deduction from the cash balance according to the depositor's records. (None of the transactions reported by bank debit and credit memorandums have been recorded by the depositor.)

1. Outstanding checks, $3,512.30.
2. Deposit in transit, $10,000.
3. Note collected by bank, $8,000.
4. Check for $89 incorrectly charged by bank as $98.
5. Check drawn by depositor for $200 but incorrectly recorded as $2,000.
6. Check of a customer returned by bank to depositor because of insufficient funds, $775.
7. Bank service charges, $25.

Exercise 7–9
Entries based on bank reconciliation
Objective 5

Which of the reconciling items listed in Exercise 7–8 require an entry in the depositor's accounts?

Exercise 7–10
Bank reconciliation
Objective 5

✓ Adjusted balance: $8,961.45

The following data were accumulated for use in reconciling the bank account of Juno Co. for July:

a. Cash balance according to the depositor's records at July 31, $8,530.20.
b. Cash balance according to the bank statement at July 31, $3,457.25.
c. Checks outstanding, $1,276.20.
d. Deposit in transit, not recorded by bank, $6,780.40.
e. A check for $270 in payment of an account was erroneously recorded in the check register as $720.
f. Bank debit memorandum for service charges, $18.75.

Prepare a bank reconciliation, using the format shown in Exhibit 6.

Exercise 7–11
Entries for bank reconciliation
Objective 5

Using the data presented in Exercise 7–10, journalize the entry or entries that should be made by the depositor.

Exercise 7–12
Entries for note collected by bank
Objective 5

Accompanying a bank statement for Lyric Company is a credit memorandum for $12,500, representing the principal ($12,000) and interest ($500) on a note that had been collected by the bank. The depositor had been notified by the bank at the time of the collection, but had made no entries. Journalize the entry that should be made by the depositor to bring the accounting records up to date.

Exercise 7–13
Bank reconciliation
Objective 5

An accounting clerk for Noxious Co. prepared the following bank reconciliation:

✓ Adjusted balance: $13,445.00

Noxious Co.
Bank Reconciliation
March 31, 2003

Cash balance according to depositor's records		$10,100.75
Add: Outstanding checks	$7,557.12	
Error by Noxious Co. in recording Check		
No. 1621 as $2,510 instead of $2,150	360.00	
Note for $2,500 collected by bank, including interest	3,000.00	10,917.12
		$21,017.87
Deduct: Deposit in transit on March 31	$6,150.00	
Bank service charges	15.75	6,165.75
Cash balance according to bank statement		$14,852.12

a. From the data in the above bank reconciliation, prepare a new bank reconciliation for Noxious Co., using the format shown in the illustrative problem.

b. If a balance sheet were prepared for Noxious Co. on March 31, 2003, what amount should be reported for cash?

Exercise 7–14

Bank reconciliation

Objective 5

✓ Corrected adjusted balance: $9,998.02

How many errors can you find in the following bank reconciliation?

Protractor Co.
Bank Reconciliation
For the Month Ended November 30, 2003

Cash balance according to bank statement			$ 9,767.76
Add outstanding checks:			
No. 721		$ 545.95	
739		172.75	
743		459.60	
744		601.50	1,779.80
			$11,547.56
Deduct deposit of November 30, not recorded by bank			2,010.06
Adjusted balance			$10,537.50
Cash balance according to depositor's records			$ 4,363.62
Add: Proceeds of note collected by bank:			
Principal	$5,000.00		
Interest	750.00	$5,750.00	
Service charges		20.00	5,770.00
			$10,133.62
Deduct: Check returned because of			
insufficient funds		$ 635.60	
Error in recording November 10			
deposit of $3,718 as $3,178		540.00	1,175.60
Adjusted balance			$ 8,958.02

Exercise 7–15

Using bank reconciliation to determine cash receipts stolen

Objective 5

Ovation Co. records all cash receipts on the basis of its cash register tapes. Ovation Co. discovered during November 2003 that one of its sales clerks had stolen an undetermined amount of cash receipts when he took the daily deposits to the bank. The following data have been gathered for November:

Cash in bank according to the general ledger	$11,573.22
Cash according to the November 30, 2003 bank statement	14,271.14
Outstanding checks as of November 30, 2003	2,901.38
Bank service charge for November	25.10
Note receivable, including interest collected by bank in November	3,060.00

No deposits were in transit on November 30, which fell on a Sunday.

a. Determine the amount of cash receipts stolen by the sales clerk.
b. What accounting controls would have prevented or detected this theft?

Exercise 7–16
Petty cash fund entries

Objective 6

Journalize the entries to record the following:

a. Check No. 3910 is issued to establish a petty cash fund of $600.
b. The amount of cash in the petty cash fund is now $69.98. Check No. 4183 is issued to replenish the fund, based on the following summary of petty cash receipts: office supplies, $315.83; miscellaneous selling expense, $112.60; miscellaneous administrative expense, $88.10. (Since the amount of the check to replenish the fund plus the balance in the fund do not equal $600, record the discrepancy in the cash short and over account.)

Exercise 7–17
Variation in cash balances

Objective 7

For a recent fiscal year, **Kmart's** quarterly balances of cash and cash equivalents were as follows:

End of January	$498 million
End of April	$733 million
End of July	$556 million
End of October	$350 million

 What would you expect would be the cause of the variation in Kmart's balances of cash and cash equivalents?

Exercise 7–18
Doomsday ratio

Objective 8

The financial statements for **Cisco Systems, Inc.**, are presented in Appendix G at the end of the text.

a. Compute the doomsday ratio for Cisco Systems, Inc. for 2000 and 1999.
b. What conclusions can be drawn from comparing the ratios for 2000 and 1999?

PROBLEMS SERIES A

Problem 7–1A
Evaluating internal control of cash

Objectives 1, 2, 3

The following procedures were recently installed by Gambrel Company:

a. Along with petty cash expense receipts for postage, office supplies, etc., several post-dated employee checks are in the petty cash fund.
b. The accounts payable clerk prepares a voucher for each disbursement. The voucher along with the supporting documentation is forwarded to the treasurer's office for approval.
c. At the end of each day, an accounting clerk compares the duplicate copy of the daily cash deposit slip with the deposit receipt obtained from the bank.
d. The bank reconciliation is prepared by the cashier, who works under the supervision of the treasurer.
e. At the end of the day, cash register clerks are required to use their own funds to make up any cash shortages in their registers.
f. All mail is opened by the mail clerk, who forwards all cash remittances to the cashier. The cashier prepares a listing of the cash receipts and forwards a copy of the list to the accounts receivable clerk for recording in the accounts.

g. After necessary approvals have been obtained for the payment of a voucher, the treasurer signs and mails the check. The treasurer then stamps the voucher and supporting documentation as paid and returns the voucher and supporting documentation to the accounts payable clerk for filing.

h. At the end of each day, any deposited cash receipts are placed in the bank's night depository.

Instructions

Indicate whether each of the procedures of internal control over cash represents (1) a strength or (2) a weakness. For each weakness, indicate why it exists.

Problem 7–2A

Transactions for petty cash; cash short and over

Objectives 2, 6

SPREADSHEET

Towaway Company completed the following selected transactions during January of the current year:

Jan. 3. Established a petty cash fund of $750.

10. The cash sales for the day, according to the cash register tapes, totaled $5,970.60. The actual cash received from cash sales was $6,001.75.

28. Petty cash on hand was $145.18. Replenished the petty cash fund for the following disbursements, each evidenced by a petty cash receipt:

Jan. 4. Store supplies, $181.50.

5. Express charges on merchandise sold, $80 (Transportation Out).

8. Office supplies, $12.75.

15. Office supplies, $39.30.

17. Postage stamps, $66 (Office Supplies).

20. Repair to office calculator, $37.50 (Miscellaneous Administrative Expense).

22. Postage due on special delivery letter, $15.00 (Miscellaneous Administrative Expense).

24. Express charges on merchandise sold, $125 (Transportation Out).

27. Office supplies, $41.15.

30. The cash sales for the day, according to the cash register tapes, totaled $5,055.50. The actual cash received from cash sales was $5,010.25.

31. Increased the petty cash fund by $50.

Instructions
Journalize the transactions.

Problem 7–3A

Bank reconciliation and entries

Objective 5

SPREADSHEET

GENERAL LEDGER

✓ 1. Adjusted balance: $20,395.95

The cash account for Wok Co. at November 30, 2003, indicated a balance of $16,190.95. The bank statement indicated a balance of $21,016.30 on November 30, 2003. Comparing the bank statement and the accompanying canceled checks and memorandums with the records revealed the following reconciling items:

a. Checks outstanding totaled $5,169.75.

b. A deposit of $4,189.40, representing receipts of November 30, had been made too late to appear on the bank statement.

c. The bank had collected $4,500 on a note left for collection. The face of the note was $4,000.

d. A check for $2,850 returned with the statement had been incorrectly recorded by Wok Co. as $2,580. The check was for the payment of an obligation to Kiser Co. for the purchase of office equipment on account.

e. A check drawn for $1,375 had been erroneously charged by the bank as $1,735.

f. Bank service charges for November amounted to $25.00.

Instructions

1. Prepare a bank reconciliation.

2. Journalize the necessary entries. The accounts have not been closed.

Problem 7–4A
Bank reconciliation and entries

Objective 5

GENERAL
LEDGER

✓ 1. Adjusted balance: $3,599.87

The cash account for Magneto Co. at August 1 of the current year indicated a balance of $2,705.37. During August, the total cash deposited was $21,077.75, and checks written totaled $21,770.25. The bank statement indicated a balance of $3,465.50 on August 31. Comparing the bank statement, the canceled checks, and the accompanying memorandums with the records revealed the following reconciling items:

a. Checks outstanding totaled $2,003.84.
b. A deposit of $1,148.21, representing receipts of August 31, had been made too late to appear on the bank statement.
c. The bank had collected for Magneto Co. $1,620 on a note left for collection. The face of the note was $1,500.
d. A check for $110 returned with the statement had been incorrectly charged by the bank as $1,100.
e. A check for $86 returned with the statement had been recorded by Magneto Co. as $68. The check was for the payment of an obligation to Adgate Co. on account.
f. Bank service charges for August amounted to $15.

Instructions

1. Prepare a bank reconciliation as of August 31.
2. Journalize the necessary entries. The accounts have not been closed.

Problem 7–5A
Bank reconciliation and entries

Objective 5

✓ 1. Adjusted balance: $10,622.02

Kudzu Company deposits all cash receipts each Wednesday and Friday in a night depository, after banking hours. The data required to reconcile the bank statement as of June 30 have been taken from various documents and records and are reproduced as follows. The sources of the data are printed in capital letters. All checks were written for payments on account.

CASH ACCOUNT:
Balance as of June 1 $7,317.40

CASH RECEIPTS FOR MONTH OF JUNE $8,451.58

DUPLICATE DEPOSIT TICKETS:
Date and amount of each deposit in June:

Date	Amount	Date	Amount	Date	Amount
June 1	$1,080.50	June 10	$ 896.61	June 22	$897.34
3	854.17	15	882.95	24	942.71
8	840.50	17	1,246.74	29	810.06

CHECKS WRITTEN:
Number and amount of each check issued in June:

Check No.	Amount	Check No.	Amount	Check No.	Amount
740	$237.50	747	Void	754	$249.75
741	495.15	748	$450.90	755	272.75
742	501.90	749	640.13	756	113.95
743	671.30	750	276.77	757	407.95
744	506.88	751	299.37	758	159.60
745	117.25	752	537.01	759	501.50
746	298.66	753	380.95	760	486.39

Total amount of checks issued in June $7,605.66

JUNE BANK STATEMENT:

		MEMBER FDIC			PAGE	1

AMERICAN NATIONAL BANK OF DETROIT

DETROIT, MI 48201-2500 (313)933-8547

KUDZU COMPANY

ACCOUNT NUMBER

FROM 6/01/20–   TO 6/30/20–

BALANCE   7,447.20

9 DEPOSITS   8,691.77

20 WITHDRAWALS   7,345.91

4 OTHER DEBITS AND CREDITS   2,298.70CR

NEW BALANCE   11,091.76

* – – – – CHECKS AND OTHER DEBITS – – – – – *				– – DEPOSITS – – *	– DATE – *	– – BALANCE – – *
No. 731	162.15	No. 738	251.40	690.25	06/01	7,723.90
No. 739	60.55	No. 740	237.50	1,080.50	06/02	8,506.35
No. 741	495.15	No. 742	501.90	854.17	06/04	8,363.47
No. 743	671.30	No. 744	506.88	840.50	06/09	8,025.79
No. 745	117.25	No. 746	298.66	MS 2,500.00	06/09	10,109.88
No. 748	450.90	No. 749	640.13	MS 125.00	06/09	9,143.85
No. 750	276.77	No. 751	299.37	896.61	06/11	9,464.32
No. 752	537.01	No. 753	380.95	882.95	06/16	9,429.31
No. 754	449.75	No. 756	113.95	1,606.74	06/18	10,472.35
No. 757	407.95	No. 760	486.39	897.34	06/23	10,475.35
				942.71	06/25	11,418.06
		NSF	291.90		06/28	11,126.16
		SC	34.40		06/30	11,091.76

EC — ERROR CORRECTION   OD — OVERDRAFT

MS — MISCELLANEOUS   PS — PAYMENT STOPPED

NSF — NOT SUFFICIENT FUNDS   SC — SERVICE CHARGE

   * * *   * * *   * * *

THE RECONCILEMENT OF THIS STATEMENT WITH YOUR RECORDS IS ESSENTIAL.
ANY ERROR OR EXCEPTION SHOULD BE REPORTED IMMEDIATELY.

BANK RECONCILIATION FOR PRECEDING MONTH

Kudzu Company
Bank Reconciliation
May 31, 20—

Cash balance according to bank statement		$7,447.20
Add deposit for May 31, not recorded by bank		690.25
		$8,137.45
Deduct outstanding checks:		
No. 731	$162.15	
736	345.95	
738	251.40	
739	60.55	820.05
Adjusted balance		$7,317.40
Cash balance according to depositor's records		$7,352.50
Deduct service charges		35.10
Adjusted balance		$7,317.40

Instructions

1. Prepare a bank reconciliation as of June 30. If errors in recording deposits or checks are discovered, assume that the errors were made by the company. Assume that all deposits are from cash sales. All checks are written to satisfy accounts payable.
2. Journalize the necessary entries. The accounts have not been closed.
3. What is the amount of Cash that should appear on the balance sheet as of June 30?
4. If in preparing the bank reconciliation you note that a canceled check for $270 has been incorrectly recorded by the bank as $720, briefly explain how the error would be included in the bank reconciliation and how it should be corrected.

PROBLEMS SERIES B

Problem 7–1B

Evaluate internal control of cash

Objectives 1, 2, 3

The following procedures were recently installed by The Recipe Company:

a. The bank reconciliation is prepared by the accountant.
b. Disbursements are made from the petty cash fund only after a petty cash receipt has been completed and signed by the payee.
c. Checks received through the mail are given daily to the accounts receivable clerk for recording collections on account and for depositing in the bank.
d. At the end of a shift, each cashier counts the cash in his or her cash register, unlocks the tape, and compares the amount of cash with the amount on the tape to determine cash shortages and overages.
e. Each cashier is assigned a separate cash register drawer to which no other cashier has access.
f. All sales are rung up on the cash register, and a receipt is given to the customer. All sales are recorded on a tape locked inside the cash register.
g. Vouchers and all supporting documents are perforated with a PAID designation after being paid by the treasurer.

Instructions

 Indicate whether each of the procedures of internal control over cash represents (1) a strength or (2) a weakness. For each weakness, indicate why it exists.

Problem 7–2B

Transactions for petty cash, cash short and over

Objectives 2, 6

SPREADSHEET

Spandex Company completed the following selected transactions during September of the current year:

Sept. 1. Established a petty cash fund of $800.
    8. The cash sales for the day, according to the cash register tapes, totaled $8,995.60. The actual cash received from cash sales was $9,008.15.
   29. Petty cash on hand was $100.50. Replenished the petty cash fund for the following disbursements, each evidenced by a petty cash receipt:
      Sept. 3. Store supplies, $110.75.
          7. Express charges on merchandise purchased, $180.75 (Merchandise Inventory).
         10. Office supplies, $74.30.
         11. Office supplies, $35.20.
         12. Postage stamps, $52.00 (Office Supplies).
         16. Repair to adding machine, $69.50 (Miscellaneous Administrative Expense).
         21. Repair to typewriter, $51.50 (Miscellaneous Administrative Expense).
         22. Postage due on special delivery letter, $10.00 (Miscellaneous Administrative Expense).
         27. Express charges on merchandise purchased, $105.60 (Merchandise Inventory).
   30. The cash sales for the day, according to the cash register tapes, totaled $10,009.50. The actual cash received from cash sales was $9,999.90.
   30. Decreased the petty cash fund by $200.

Instructions

Journalize the transactions.

Problem 7–3B
Bank reconciliation and entries

Objective 5

SPREADSHEET
GENERAL LEDGER

✓ I. Adjusted balance: $21,506.10

The cash account for Viaduct Systems at March 31, 2003, indicated a balance of $17,474.35. The bank statement indicated a balance of $23,391.40 on March 31, 2003. Comparing the bank statement and the accompanying canceled checks and memorandums with the records reveals the following reconciling items:

a. Checks outstanding totaled $5,010.80.
b. A deposit of $3,215.50, representing receipts of March 31, had been made too late to appear on the bank statement.
c. The bank had collected $3,600 on a note left for collection. The face of the note was $3,000.
d. A check for $1,050 returned with the statement had been incorrectly recorded by Viaduct Systems as $1,500. The check was for the payment of an obligation to Bates Co. for the purchase of office supplies on account.
e. A check drawn for $878 had been incorrectly charged by the bank as $788.
f. Bank service charges for March amounted to $18.25.

Instructions

1. Prepare a bank reconciliation.
2. Journalize the necessary entries. The accounts have not been closed.

Problem 7–4B
Bank reconciliation and entries

Objective 5

GENERAL LEDGER

✓ I. Adjusted balance: $12,001.88

The cash account for Actuator Co. on June 1, 2003, indicated a balance of $6,911.95. During June, the total cash deposited was $70,500.40, and checks written totaled $67,568.47. The bank statement indicated a balance of $13,880.45 on June 30, 2003. Comparing the bank statement, the canceled checks, and the accompanying memorandums with the records revealed the following reconciling items:

a. Checks outstanding totaled $6,180.27.
b. A deposit of $4,481.70, representing receipts of June 30, had been made too late to appear on the bank statement.
c. A check for $310 had been incorrectly charged by the bank as $130.
d. A check for $257.25 returned with the statement had been recorded by Actuator Co. as $527.25. The check was for the payment of an obligation to Sylvester & Son on account.
e. The bank had collected for Actuator Co. $1,908 on a note left for collection. The face of the note was $1,800.
f. Bank service charges for June amounted to $20.

Instructions

1. Prepare a bank reconciliation as of June 30.
2. Journalize the necessary entries. The accounts have not been closed.

Problem 7–5B
Bank reconciliation and entries

Objective 5

✓ I. Adjusted balance: $14,219.09

Mademoiselle Interiors deposits all cash receipts each Wednesday and Friday in a night depository, after banking hours. The data required to reconcile the bank statement as of August 31 have been taken from various documents and records and are reproduced as follows. The sources of the data are printed in capital letters. All checks were written for payments on account.

CASH ACCOUNT:
Balance as of August 1 $10,578.00

CASH RECEIPTS FOR MONTH OF AUGUST   6,305.60

DUPLICATE DEPOSIT TICKETS:
Date and amount of each deposit in August:

Date	Amount	Date	Amount	Date	Amount
Aug. 2	$569.50	Aug. 12	$580.70	Aug. 23	$ 731.45
5	701.80	16	600.10	26	601.50
9	819.24	19	701.26	31	1,000.05

CHECKS WRITTEN:
Number and amount of each check issued in August:

Check No.	Amount	Check No.	Amount	Check No.	Amount
614	$243.50	621	$309.50	628	$ 737.70
615	350.10	622	Void	629	329.90
616	279.90	623	Void	630	882.80
617	395.50	624	770.01	631	1,081.56
618	135.10	625	158.63	632	62.40
619	320.10	626	550.03	633	310.08
620	238.87	627	318.73	634	103.30

Total amount of checks issued in August $7,878.01

AUGUST BANK STATEMENT:

		MEMBER FDIC		PAGE 1

A
NB
AMERICAN NATIONAL BANK OF DETROIT
DETROIT, MI 48201-2500   (313)933-8547

ACCOUNT NUMBER

FROM 8/01/20–   TO 8/31/20–

BALANCE   10,422.80

9 DEPOSITS   6,086.35

20 WITHDRAWALS   7,514.11

MADEMOISELLE INTERIORS

4 OTHER DEBITS
AND CREDITS   5,150.50CR

NEW BALANCE   14,145.54

* - - - - - CHECKS AND OTHER DEBITS - - - - - - - * - DEPOSITS - * - DATE - * - BALANCE - *

No.580	310.10	No.612	92.50			780.80	08/01	10,801.00
No.613	137.50	No.614	243.50			569.50	08/03	10,989.50
No.615	350.10	No.616	279.90			701.80	08/06	11,061.30
No.617	395.50	No.618	435.40			819.24	08/11	11,049.64
No.619	320.10	No.620	238.87			580.70	08/13	11,071.37
No.621	309.50	No.624	707.01		MS 5,000.00		08/14	15,054.86
No.625	158.63	No.626	550.03		MS 400.00		08/14	14,746.20
No.627	318.73	No.629	329.90			600.10	08/17	14,697.67
No.630	882.80	No.631	1,081.56	NSF 225.40			08/20	12,507.91
No.632	62.40	No.633	310.08			701.26	08/21	12,836.69
						731.45	08/24	13,568.14
						601.50	08/28	14,169.64
		SC	24.10				08/31	14,145.54

EC — ERROR CORRECTION   OD — OVERDRAFT
MS — MISCELLANEOUS   PS — PAYMENT STOPPED
NSF — NOT SUFFICIENT FUNDS   SC — SERVICE CHARGE

* * *   * * *   * * *

THE RECONCILEMENT OF THIS STATEMENT WITH YOUR RECORDS IS ESSENTIAL.
ANY ERROR OR EXCEPTION SHOULD BE REPORTED IMMEDIATELY.

Instructions

1. Prepare a bank reconciliation as of August 31. If errors in recording deposits or checks are discovered, assume that the errors were made by the company. Assume that all deposits are from cash sales. All checks are written to satisfy accounts payable.
2. Journalize the necessary entries. The accounts have not been closed.
3. What is the amount of Cash that should appear on the balance sheet as of August 31?

4. ◀━━▶ If in preparing the bank reconciliation you note that a canceled check for $275 has been incorrectly recorded by the bank as $725, briefly explain how the error would be included in the bank reconciliation and how it should be corrected.

BANK RECONCILIATION FOR PRECEDING MONTH:

Mademoiselle Interiors
Bank Reconciliation
July 31, 20—

Cash balance according to bank statement		$10,422.80
Add deposit of July 31, not recorded by bank		780.80
		$11,203.60
Deduct outstanding checks:		
No. 580	$310.10	
No. 602	85.50	
No. 612	92.50	
No. 613	137.50	625.60
Adjusted balance		$10,578.00
Cash balance according to depositor's records		$10,605.70
Deduct service charges		27.70
Adjusted balance		$10,578.00

SPECIAL ACTIVITIES

Activity 7–1
The Breadbasket Co.
Ethics and professional conduct in business

During the preparation of the bank reconciliation for The Breadbasket Co., Lee Roberts, the assistant controller, discovered that City National Bank incorrectly recorded a $718 check written by The Breadbasket Co. as $178. Lee has decided not to notify the bank but wait for the bank to detect the error. Lee plans to record the $540 error as Other Income if the bank fails to detect the error within the next three months.

◀━━▶ Discuss whether Lee is behaving in a professional manner.

Activity 7–2
Zoom Electronics
Internal controls

The following is an excerpt from a conversation between two sales clerks, Karol Bolton and Bill Hall. Both Karol and Bill are employed by Zoom Electronics, a locally owned and operated computer retail store.

Karol: Did you hear the news?
Bill: What news?
Karol: Melanie and Richard were both arrested this morning.
Bill: What? Arrested? You're putting me on!
Karol: No, really! The police arrested them first thing this morning. Put them in handcuffs, read them their rights—the whole works. It was unreal!
Bill: What did they do?
Karol: Well, apparently they were filling out merchandise refund forms for fictitious customers and then taking the cash.
Bill: I guess I never thought of that. How did they catch them?
Karol: The store manager noticed that returns were twice that of last year and seemed to be increasing. When he confronted Melanie, she became flustered and admitted to taking the cash, apparently over $1,800 in just three months. They're going over the last six months' transactions to try to determine how much Richard stole. He apparently started stealing first.

◀━━▶ Suggest appropriate control procedures that would have prevented or detected the theft of cash.

Activity 7–3
Ethnic Grocery Stores
Internal controls

The following is an excerpt from a conversation between the store manager of Ethnic Grocery Stores, Jill Allen, and Gary Malone, president of Ethnic Grocery Stores.

Gary: Jill, I'm concerned about this new scanning system.

Jill: What's the problem?

Gary: Well, how do we know the clerks are ringing up all the merchandise?

Jill: That's one of the strong points about the system. The scanner automatically rings up each item, based on its bar code. We update the prices daily, so we're sure that the sale is rung up for the right price.

Gary: That's not my concern. What keeps a clerk from pretending to scan items and then simply not charging his friends? If his friends were buying 10–15 items, it would be easy for the clerk to pass through several items with his finger over the bar code or just pass the merchandise through the scanner with the wrong side showing. It would look normal for anyone observing. In the old days, we at least could hear the cash register ringing up each sale.

Jill: I see your point.

Suggest ways that Ethnic Grocery Stores could prevent or detect the theft of merchandise as described.

Activity 7–4
Mammoth Markets
Ethics and professional conduct in business

Devon Payne and Meredith Sibley are both cash register clerks for Mammoth Markets. Kelley Russell is the store manager for Mammoth Markets. The following is an excerpt of a conversation between Devon and Meredith:

Devon: Meredith, how long have you been working for Mammoth Markets?

Meredith: Almost five years this October. You just started two weeks ago . . . right?

Devon: Yes. Do you mind if I ask you a question?

Meredith: No, go ahead.

Devon: What I want to know is, have they always had this rule that if your cash register is short at the end of the day, you have to make up the shortage out of your own pocket?

Meredith: Yes, as long as I've been working here.

Devon: Well, it's the pits. Last week I had to pay in almost $30.

Meredith: It's not that big a deal. I just make sure that I'm not short at the end of the day.

Devon: How do you do that?

Meredith: I just short-change a few customers early in the day. There are a few jerks that deserve it anyway. Most of the time, their attention is elsewhere and they don't think to check their change.

Devon: What happens if you're over at the end of the day?

Meredith: Kelley lets me keep it as long as it doesn't get to be too large. I've not been short in over a year. I usually clear about $10 to $20 extra per day.

Discuss this case from the viewpoint of proper controls and professional behavior.

Activity 7–5
Pegasus Company
Bank reconciliation and internal control

The records of Pegasus Company indicate a March 31 cash balance of $9,806.05, which includes undeposited receipts for March 30 and 31. The cash balance on the bank statement as of March 31 is $8,004.95. This balance includes a note of $2,500 plus $200 interest collected by the bank but not recorded in the journal. Checks outstanding on March 31 were as follows: No. 670, $481.20; No. 679, $510; No. 690, $616.50; No. 1996, $127.40; No. 1997, $520; and No. 1999, $851.50.

On March 3, the cashier resigned, effective at the end of the month. Before leaving on March 31, the cashier prepared the following bank reconciliation:

Cash balance per books, March 31		$ 9,806.05
Add outstanding checks:		
No. 1996	$127.40	
1997	520.00	
1999	851.50	1,198.90
		$11,004.95
Less undeposited receipts		3,000.00
Cash balance per bank, March 31		$ 8,004.95
Deduct unrecorded note with interest		2,700.00
True cash, March 31		$ 5,304.95

```
Calculator Tape of Outstanding Checks:
            0.00 *
          127.40 +
          520.00 +
          851.50 +
        1,198.90 *
```

Subsequently, the owner of Pegasus Company discovered that the cashier had stolen all undeposited receipts in excess of the $3,000 on hand on March 31. The owner, a close family friend, has asked your help in determining the amount that the former cashier has stolen.

1. Determine the amount the cashier stole from Pegasus Company. Show your computations in good form.
2. How did the cashier attempt to conceal the theft?
3. a. Identify two major weaknesses in internal controls, which allowed the cashier to steal the undeposited cash receipts.
   b. Recommend improvements in internal controls, so that similar types of thefts of undeposited cash receipts can be prevented.

Activity 7–6
Into the Real World
Observe internal controls over cash

Select a business in your community and observe its internal controls over cash receipts and cash payments. The business could be a bank or a bookstore, restaurant, department store, or other retailer. In groups of three or four, identify and discuss the similarities and differences in each business's cash internal controls.

Activity 7–7
Into the Real World
Invest excess cash

You have $50,000 cash. Go to the Web site of (or visit) a local bank and collect information about the savings and checking options that are available. Identify the option that is best for you and why it is best.

ANSWERS TO SELF-EXAMINATION QUESTIONS

Matching
1. C   2. L   3. K   4. H   5. J   6. A   7. D   8. G

Multiple Choice

1. **C** The error was made by the bank, so the cash balance according to the bank statement needs to be adjusted. Since the bank deducted $90 ($540.50 − $450.50) too little, the error of $90 should be deducted from the cash balance according to the bank statement (answer C).

2. **B** On any specific date, the cash account in a depositor's ledger may not agree with the account in the bank's ledger because of delays and/or errors by either party in recording transactions. The purpose of a bank reconciliation, therefore, is to determine the reasons for any differences between the two account balances.

All errors should then be corrected by the depositor or the bank, as appropriate. In arriving at the adjusted (correct) cash balance according to the bank statement, outstanding checks must be deducted (answer B) to adjust for checks that have been written by the depositor but that have not yet been presented to the bank for payment.

3. **C** All reconciling items that are added to and deducted from the cash balance according to the depositor's records on the bank reconciliation (answer C) require that journal entries be made by the depositor to correct errors made in recording transactions or to bring the cash account up to date for delays in recording transactions.

4. **D** To avoid the delay, annoyance, and expense that is associated with paying all obligations by check, rel-

atively small amounts (answer A) are paid from a petty cash fund. The fund is established by estimating the amount of cash needed to pay these small amounts during a specified period (answer B), and it is then reimbursed when the amount of money in the fund is reduced to a predetermined minimum amount (answer C).

5. **C** The journal entry to replenish the petty cash account debits the various expense accounts for which funds were disbursed and credits Cash (answer C). A petty cash account is established or increased by debiting Petty Cash and crediting Cash (answer A). A petty cash account is decreased or done away with by debiting Cash and crediting Petty Cash (answer D). Entry B is not a normal entry involving petty cash.

Receivables

8

objectives

After studying this chapter, you should be able to:

1 List the common classifications of receivables.

2 Summarize and provide examples of internal control procedures that apply to receivables.

3 Describe the nature of and the accounting for uncollectible receivables.

4 Journalize the entries for the allowance method of accounting for uncollectibles, and estimate uncollectible receivables based on sales and on an analysis of receivables.

5 Journalize the entries for the direct write off of uncollectible receivables.

6 Describe the nature and characteristics of promissory notes.

7 Journalize the entries for notes receivable transactions.

8 Prepare the Current Assets presentation of receivables on the balance sheet.

9 Compute and interpret the accounts receivable turnover and the number of days' sales in receivables.

Assume that you have decided to sell your car to a neighbor for $7,500. Your neighbor agrees to pay you $1,500 immediately and the remaining $6,000 in a year. How much should you charge your neighbor for interest?

You could determine an appropriate interest rate by asking some financial institutions what they currently charge their customers. Using this information as a starting point, you could then negotiate with your neighbor and agree upon a rate. Assuming that the agreed-upon rate is 8%, you will receive interest totaling $480 for the one-year loan.

In this chapter, we will describe and illustrate how interest is computed. In addition, we will discuss the accounting for receivables, including uncollectible receivables. Most of these receivables result from a business providing services or selling merchandise on account.

Classification of Receivables

objective 1

List the common classifications of receivables.

Many companies sell on credit in order to sell more services or products. The receivables that result from such sales are normally classified as accounts receivable or notes receivable. The term **receivables** includes all money claims against other entities, including people, business firms, and other organizations. These receivables are usually a significant portion of the total current assets.

An annual report of La-Z-Boy Chair Company reported that receivables made up over 60% of La-Z-Boy's current assets.

Accounts Receivable

The most common transaction creating a receivable is selling merchandise or services on credit. The receivable is recorded as a debit to the accounts receivable account. Such **accounts receivable** are normally expected to be collected within a relatively short period, such as 30 or 60 days. They are classified on the balance sheet as a current asset.

Notes Receivable

Notes receivable are amounts that customers owe, for which a formal, written instrument of credit has been issued. As long as notes receivable are expected to be collected within a year, they are normally classified on the balance sheet as a current asset.

Notes are often used for credit periods of more than sixty days. For example, a dealer in automobiles or furniture may require a down payment at the time of sale and accept a note or a series of notes for the remainder. Such arrangements usually provide for monthly payments.

Notes may be used to settle a customer's account receivable. Notes and accounts receivable that result from sales transactions are sometimes called **trade receivables**. Unless we indicate otherwise, we will assume that all notes and accounts receivable in this chapter are from sales transactions.

Other Receivables

Other receivables are normally listed separately on the balance sheet. If they are expected to be collected within one year, they are classified as current assets. If

Point of Interest

If you have purchased an automobile on credit, you probably signed a note. From your viewpoint, the note is a note payable. From the creditor's viewpoint, the note is a note receivable.

collection is expected beyond one year, they are classified as noncurrent assets and reported under the caption *Investments*. **Other receivables** include interest receivable, taxes receivable, and receivables from officers or employees.

Internal Control of Receivables

The principles of internal control that we discussed in prior chapters can be used to establish controls to safeguard receivables. For example, the four functions of credit approval, sales, accounting, and collections should be separated, as shown in Exhibit 1.

The individuals responsible for sales should be separate from the individuals accounting for the receivables and approving credit. By doing so, the accounting and credit approval functions serve as independent checks on sales. The employee who handles the accounting for receivables should not be involved with collecting receivables. Separating these functions reduces the possibility of errors and misuse of funds.

Exhibit 1 Separating the Receivable Functions

To illustrate the need to separate functions, assume that the accounts receivable billing clerk has access to cash receipts from customer collections. The clerk can steal a customer's cash payment and then alter the customer's monthly statement to indicate that the payment was received. The customer would not complain and the theft could go undetected.

To further illustrate the need for internal control of receivables, assume that salespersons have authority to approve credit. If the salespersons are paid commissions, say 10% of sales, they can increase their commissions by approving poor credit risks. Thus, the credit approval function is normally assigned to individuals outside the sales area.

BUSINESS ON STAGE

The Five "Cs"

Credit standards are used by businesses to decide which customers should receive credit and how much credit they should receive. Setting credit standards requires businesses to assess the customer's "creditworthiness" or credit "quality." Traditionally, assessing creditworthiness involves considering the five Cs of credit. Each of these five Cs is briefly described below.

1. *Character* refers to the probability that the customer will honor an obligation. Many credit managers insist that this is the most important of the Cs. It reflects on the honesty of the customer and the customer's feeling of moral responsibility to honor debts.

Credit managers often seek information on a customer's character by making inquiries within the business community. Such inquiries may be made with local bankers, attorneys, other creditors, and even competitors.

2. *Capacity* refers to a customer's ability to pay. Credit managers assess this factor by reviewing the customer's past payment history, a general knowledge of the customer's business, and perhaps even a physical observation of the customer's operations.

3. *Capital* refers to the general condition of the customer's business as assessed from the financial statements. Credit managers usually place special emphasis on

solvency and liquidity measures and ratios such as working capital and the current ratio.

4. *Collateral* refers to assets that the customer may be willing to pledge as security for the credit. Financial institutions usually require collateral for major loans to businesses. The collateral may take the form of any asset, such as land, buildings, or inventory.

5. *Conditions* refers to the national and regional economic trends that may affect a customer's ability to pay. For example, during economic downturns credit managers usually tighten credit standards, with the anticipation that more customers will not be able to pay. ■

Uncollectible Receivables

objective 3

Describe the nature of and the accounting for uncollectible receivables.

In addition to their own credit departments, many businesses use external credit agencies, such as **Dun and Bradstreet**, to evaluate credit customers.

In prior chapters, we described and illustrated the accounting for transactions involving sales of merchandise or services on credit. A major issue that we have not yet discussed is uncollectible receivables from these transactions.

Businesses attempt to limit the number and amount of uncollectible receivables by using various controls. The primary controls in this area involve the credit-granting function. These controls normally involve investigating customer creditworthiness, using references and background checks. For example, most of us have completed credit application forms requiring such information. Companies may also impose credit limits on new customers. For example, you may have been limited to a maximum of $500 or $1,000 when your credit card was first issued to you.

Once a receivable is past due, companies should use procedures to maximize the collection of an account. After repeated attempts at collection, such procedures may include turning an account over to a collection agency.

Retail businesses often attempt to shift the risk of uncollectible receivables to other companies. For example, some retailers do not accept sales on account but will only accept cash or credit cards. Such policies effectively shift the risk to the credit card companies. Other retailers, however, such as **Macy's**, **Sears**, and **JCPenney's**, have issued their own credit cards.

Companies often sell their receivables to other companies. This transaction is called **factoring** the receivables, and the buyer of the receivables is called a **factor**. An advantage of factoring is that the company selling its receivables receives immediate cash for operating and other needs. In addition, depending upon the factoring agreement, some of the risk of uncollectible accounts may be shifted to the factor.[1]

Regardless of the care used in granting credit and the collection procedures used, a part of the credit sales will not be collectible. The operating expense incurred because of the failure to collect receivables is called **uncollectible accounts expense**, **bad debts expense**, or **doubtful accounts expense**.[2]

When does an account or a note become uncollectible? There is no general rule for determining when an account becomes uncollectible. The fact that a debtor fails to pay an account according to a sales contract or fails to pay a note on the due date does not necessarily mean that the account will be uncollectible. The debtor's bankruptcy is one of the most significant indications of partial or complete uncollectibility. Other indications include the closing of the customer's business and the failure of repeated attempts to collect.

There are two methods of accounting for receivables that appear to be uncollectible. The **allowance method** provides an expense for uncollectible receivables in advance of their write-off.[3] The other procedure, called the **direct write-off method**, recognizes the expense only when accounts are judged to be worthless. We will discuss each of these methods next.

Allowance Method of Accounting for Uncollectibles

objective 4

Journalize the entries for the allowance method of accounting for uncollectibles, and estimate uncollectible receivables based on sales and on an analysis of receivables.

Most large businesses use the allowance method to estimate the uncollectible portion of their trade receivables. To illustrate this method, we will use assumed data for Richards Company. This new business began in August and chose to use the calendar year as its fiscal year. The accounts receivable account has a balance of $105,000 at the end of December.

The customer accounts making up the $105,000 balance in Accounts Receivable include some that are past due. However, Richards doesn't know which specific accounts will be uncollectible at this time. It is likely that some accounts will be collected only in part and that others will become worthless. Based on a careful study, Richards estimates that a total of $4,000 will eventually be uncollectible. The following adjusting entry at the end of the fiscal period records this estimate:

		Adjusting Entry		
Dec.	31	Uncollectible Accounts Expense	4 0 0 0 00	
		Allowance for Doubtful Accounts		4 0 0 0 00

Because the $4,000 reduction in accounts receivable is an estimate, it cannot be credited to specific customer accounts or to the accounts receivable controlling account. Instead, a **contra asset** account entitled *Allowance for Doubtful Accounts* is credited.

As with all periodic adjustments, the entry above serves two purposes. First, it reduces the value of the receivables to the amount of cash expected to be realized in the future. This amount, which is $101,000 ($105,000 − $4,000), is called the **net**

---

[1] The accounting for the factoring of accounts receivable is discussed in advanced accounting texts.

[2] If both notes and accounts are involved, both may be included in the expense account title, as in Uncollectible Notes and Accounts Expense, or Uncollectible Receivables Expense.

[3] The allowance method is not acceptable for determining the federal income tax of most taxpayers.

realizable value of the receivables. Second, the adjusting entry matches the $4,000 expense of uncollectible accounts with the related revenues of the period.

After the adjusting entry has been posted, as shown in the following T accounts, Accounts Receivable still has a debit balance of $105,000. This balance is the amount of the total claims against customers on account. The credit balance of $4,000 in Allowance for Doubtful Accounts is the amount to be deducted from Accounts Receivable to determine the net realizable value. The balance of the Uncollectible Accounts Expense is reported in the current period income statement, normally as an administrative expense. This classification is used because the credit-granting and collection duties are the responsibilities of departments within the administrative area.

> The adjusting entry reduces receivables to their net realizable value and matches the uncollectible expense with revenues.

Q&A

If the balance of accounts receivable is $380,000 and the balance of the allowance for doubtful accounts is $56,000, what is the net realizable value of the receivables?

$324,000 ($380,000 − $56,000)

Accounts Receivable			
Aug. 31	20,000	Sept. 30	15,000
Sept. 30	25,000	Oct. 31	25,000
Oct. 31	40,000	Nov. 30	23,000
Nov. 30	38,000	Dec. 31	30,000
Dec. 31	75,000		
			93,000
Bal. 105,000	198,000		

Allowance for Doubtful Accounts	
	Dec. 31 Adj. 4,000

Uncollectible Accounts Expense	
Dec. 31 Adj. 4,000	

Write-Offs to the Allowance Account

When a customer's account is identified as uncollectible, it is written off against the allowance account as follows:

Jan.	21	Allowance for Doubtful Accounts			6 1 0 00				
		Accounts Receivable—John Parker					6 1 0 00		
		To write off the uncollectible							
		account.							

ADJUSTING ENTRY (Fills the bucket)

ALLOWANCE FOR UNCOLLECTIBLE ACCOUNTS

WRITE OFF ACCOUNTS (Empties the bucket)

The authorization to support this entry should come from a designated manager. It should normally be in writing.

The total amount written off against the allowance account during a period will rarely be equal to the amount in the account at the beginning of the period. The allowance account will have a credit balance at the end of the period if the write-offs during the period are less than the beginning balance. It will have a debit balance if the write-offs exceed the beginning balance. However, after the year-end adjusting entry is recorded, the allowance account should have a credit balance. The flow into and out of the allowance account can be shown as in the illustration at the left.

An account receivable that has been written off against the allowance account may later be collected. In such cases, the account should be reinstated by an entry that reverses the write-off entry. The cash received in payment should then be recorded as a receipt on account. For example, assume that the account of $610 written off in the preceding entry is later collected on June 10. The entry to reinstate the account and the entry to record its collection are as follows:

June	10	Accounts Receivable—John Parker	6 1 0 00	
		Allowance for Doubtful Accounts		6 1 0 00
		To reinstate account written off		
		earlier in the year.		
	10	Cash	6 1 0 00	
		Accounts Receivable—John Parker		6 1 0 00
		To record collection on account.		

The percentage of uncollectible accounts will vary across companies and industries. For example, in their annual reports, **JCPenney** reported 1.7% of its receivables as uncollectible, **Deere & Company** (manufacturer of John Deere tractors, etc.) reported only 1.0% of its dealer receivables as uncollectible, and **Columbia HCA Healthcare Corporation** reported 45.6% of its receivables as uncollectible.

The two preceding entries can be combined. However, recording two separate entries in the customer's account, with proper notation of the write-off and reinstatement, provides useful credit information.

Estimating Uncollectibles

How is the amount of uncollectible accounts estimated? The estimate of uncollectibles at the end of a fiscal period is based on past experience and forecasts of the future. When the general economy is doing well, the amount of uncollectible expense is normally less than it would be when the economy is doing poorly. The estimate of uncollectibles is usually based on either (1) the amount of sales, as shown on the income statement for the period, or (2) the amount of the receivables, as shown on the balance sheet at the end of the period, and the age of the receivable accounts.

Estimate Based on Sales

The estimate based on sales is _added_ to any balance in Allowance for Doubtful Accounts.

Accounts receivable are created by credit sales. The amount of credit sales during the period may therefore be used to estimate the amount of uncollectible accounts expense. The amount of this estimate is added to whatever balance exists in Allowance for Doubtful Accounts. For example, assume that the allowance account has a credit balance of $700 before adjustment. It is estimated from past experience that 1% of credit sales will be uncollectible. If credit sales for the period are $300,000, the adjusting entry for uncollectible accounts at the end of the period is as follows:

		Adjusting Entry		
Dec.	31	Uncollectible Accounts Expense	3 0 0 0 00	
		Allowance for Doubtful Accounts		3 0 0 0 00

Before the year-end adjustment, Allowance for Doubtful Accounts has a credit balance of $45,000. Uncollectible accounts are estimated as 2% of credit sales of $1,200,000. The accounts receivable balance before adjustment is $290,000. What are (1) the uncollectible expense for the period, (2) the balance of Allowance for Doubtful Accounts after adjustment, and (3) the net realizable value of the receivables after adjustment?

----

(1) $24,000 (2% × $1,200,000); (2) $69,000 ($24,000 + $45,000); and (3) $221,000 ($290,000 − $69,000)

After the adjusting entry has been posted, the balance of the allowance account is $3,700. If there had been a debit balance of $200 in the allowance account before the year-end adjustment, the amount of the adjustment would still have been $3,000. The balance in the allowance account would have been $2,800 ($3,000 − $200).

The estimate-based-on-sales method *emphasizes the matching of uncollectible accounts expense with the related sales of the period.* Thus, this method places more emphasis on the income statement than on the balance sheet.

The Commercial Collection Agency Section of the Commercial Law League of America reported the following collection rates by number of months past due:

Number of months past due

Estimate Based on Analysis of Receivables

The longer an account receivable remains outstanding, the less likely that it will be collected. Thus, we can base the estimate of uncollectible accounts on how long the accounts have been outstanding. For this purpose, we can use a process called **aging the receivables**.

In aging the receivables, an aging schedule is prepared by classifying each receivable by its due date. The number of days an account is past due is determined from the due date of the account to the date the aging schedule is prepared. To illustrate, assume that Rodriguez Company is preparing an aging schedule as of August 31. Its account receivable for Saxon Woods Company was due on May 29. As of August 31, Saxon's account is 94 days past due, as shown below.

Number of days past due in May	2 days (31–29)
Number of days past due in June	30 days
Number of days past due in July	31 days
Number of days past due in August	31 days
Total number of days past due	94 days

After the number of days past due has been determined for each account, an aging schedule is prepared similar to the one shown in Exhibit 2.

Exhibit 2 Aging of Accounts Receivable

Customer	Balance	Not Past Due	Days Past Due					
			1–30	31–60	61–90	91–180	181–365	over 365
Ashby & Co.	$ 150			$ 150				
B.T. Barr	610					$ 350	$260	
Brock Co.	470	$ 470						
Saxon Woods Co.	160					160		
Total	$86,300	$75,000	$4,000	$3,100	$1,900	$1,200	$800	$300

The aging schedule is completed by adding the columns to determine the total amount of receivables in each age class. A sliding scale of percentages, based on industry or company experience, is used to estimate the amount of uncollectibles in each age class, as shown in Exhibit 3.

Based on Exhibit 3, the desired balance for the Allowance for Doubtful Accounts is estimated as $3,390. Comparing this estimate with the unadjusted balance of the allowance account determines the amount

> The estimate based on receivables is compared to the balance in the allowance account to determine the amount of the adjusting entry.

Exhibit 3 Estimate of
Uncollectible Accounts

Age Interval	Balance	Estimated Uncollectible Accounts	
		Percent	Amount
Not past due	$75,000	2%	$1,500
1–30 days past due	4,000	5	200
31–60 days past due	3,100	10	310
61–90 days past due	1,900	20	380
91–180 days past due	1,200	30	360
181–365 days past due	800	50	400
Over 365 days past due	300	80	240
Total	$86,300		$3,390

of the adjusting entry for Uncollectible Accounts Expense. For example, assume that the unadjusted balance of the allowance account is a credit balance of $510. The amount to be added to this balance is therefore $2,880 ($3,390 − $510). The adjusting entry is as follows:

		Adjusting Entry		
Aug.	31	Uncollectible Accounts Expense	2 8 8 0 00	
		Allowance for Doubtful Accounts		2 8 8 0 00

Q&A Before the year-end adjustment, Allowance for Doubtful Accounts has a debit balance of $3,000. Using the aging-of-receivables method, the desired balance of the allowance for doubtful accounts is estimated as $55,000. The accounts receivable balance before adjustment is $290,000. What are (1) the uncollectible expense for the period, (2) the balance of Allowance for Doubtful Accounts after adjustment, and (3) the net realizable value of the receivables after adjustment?

(1) $58,000 ($3,000 + $55,000); (2) $55,000; and (3) $235,000 ($290,000 − $55,000)

After the adjusting entry has been posted, the credit balance in the allowance account is $3,390, the desired amount. The net realizable value of the receivables is $82,910 ($86,300 − $3,390). If the unadjusted balance of the allowance account had been a debit balance of $300, the amount of the adjustment would have been $3,690 ($3,390 + $300).

Estimates of the uncollectible accounts expense based on the analysis of receivables *emphasizes the current net realizable value of the receivables.* Thus, this method places more emphasis on the balance sheet than on the income statement.

Direct Write-Off Method of Accounting for Uncollectibles

objective 5

Journalize the entries for the direct write-off of uncollectible receivables.

The allowance method emphasizes reporting uncollectible accounts expense in the period in which the related sales occur. This emphasis on matching expenses with related revenue is the preferred method of accounting for uncollectible receivables.

There are situations, however, where it is impossible to estimate, with reasonable accuracy, the uncollectibles at the end of the period. Also, if a business sells most of its goods or services on a cash basis, the amount of its expense from uncollectible accounts is usually small. In such cases, the amount of receivables is also likely to represent a small part of the current assets. Examples of such a business are a restaurant, an attorney's office, and a small retail store such as a hardware store. In such cases, the direct write-off method of recording uncollectible expense may be used.

Under the direct write-off method, uncollectible accounts expense is not recorded until an account has been determined to be worthless. Thus, an allowance account and an adjusting entry are not needed at the end of the period. The entry to write off an account that has been determined to be uncollectible is as follows:

May	10	Uncollectible Accounts Expense	4 2 0 00	
		Accounts Receivable—D. L. Ross		4 2 0 00
		To write off uncollectible account.		

What if a customer later pays on an account that has been written off? If this happens, the account should be reinstated. The account is reinstated by reversing the earlier write-off entry. For example, assume that the account written off in the May 10 entry is collected in November of the same fiscal year.[4] The entry to reinstate the account is as follows:

Nov.	21	Accounts Receivable—D. L. Ross	4 2 0 00	
		Uncollectible Accounts Expense		4 2 0 00
		To reinstate account written off		
		earlier in the year.		

Cash received in payment of the reinstated amount is recorded in the usual manner. That is, Cash is debited and Accounts Receivable is credited for $420.

Characteristics of Notes Receivable

objective 6

Describe the nature and characteristics of promissory notes.

A claim supported by a note has some advantages over a claim in the form of an account receivable. By signing a note, the debtor recognizes the debt and agrees to pay it according to the terms listed. A note is therefore a stronger legal claim if there is a court action.

A **promissory note** is a written promise to pay a sum of money on demand or at a definite time. It is payable to the order of a person or firm or to the bearer or holder of the note. It is signed by the person or firm that makes the promise. The one to whose order the note is payable is called the **payee**, and the one making the promise is called the **maker**. In the example in Exhibit 4, Judson Company is the payee and Willard Company is the maker.

Notes have several characteristics that affect how they are recorded and reported in the financial statements. We describe these characteristics next.

---

[4] As a practical matter, the entries to record the collection on an account previously written off are the same, regardless of whether the collection occurs in the current period or in a later fiscal period.

Exhibit 4 Promissory Note

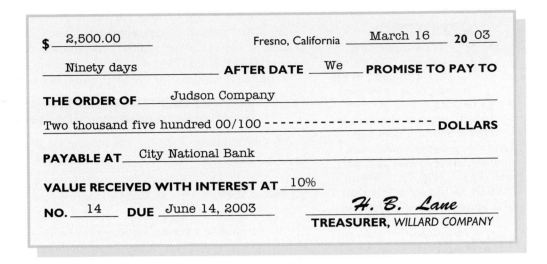

$ _2,500.00_   Fresno, California _March 16_ 20_03_

Ninety days   **AFTER DATE** _We_ **PROMISE TO PAY TO**

THE ORDER OF _Judson Company_

Two thousand five hundred 00/100 - **DOLLARS**

PAYABLE AT _City National Bank_

VALUE RECEIVED WITH INTEREST AT _10%_

NO. _14_ **DUE** _June 14, 2003_   *H. B. Lane*
                               TREASURER, *WILLARD COMPANY*

Due Date

The date a note is to be paid is called the **due date** or **maturity date**. The period of time between the issuance date and the due date of a short-term note may be stated in either days or months. When the term of a note is stated in days, the due date is the specified number of days after its issuance. To illustrate, the due date of the 90-day note in Exhibit 4 is determined as follows:

MARCH   APRIL   MAY   JUNE

16   31 | 30 | 31 | 14

15 + 30 + 31 + 14

Total of 90 days

What is the due date of a 120-day note receivable dated September 9?

January 7 [21 days in September (30 days − 9 days) + 31 days in October + 30 days in November + 31 days in December + 7 days in January = 120 days]

The term of a note may be stated as a certain number of months after the issuance date. In such cases, the due date is determined by counting the number of months from the issuance date. For example, a three-month note dated June 5 would be due on September 5. A two-month note dated July 31 would be due on September 30.

Interest

A note normally specifies that interest be paid for the period between the issuance date and the due date.[5] Notes covering a period of time longer than one year normally provide that the interest be paid semiannually, quarterly, or at some other stated interval. When the term of the note is less than one year, the interest is usually payable at the time the note is paid.

---

[5] You may occasionally see references to non-interest-bearing notes receivable. Such notes, which are not widely used, normally include an implicit interest rate.

What is the maturity value of a $15,000, 90-day, 12% note?

$15,450 [$15,000 + ($15,000 × 0.12 × 90/360)]

The interest rate on notes is normally stated in terms of a year, regardless of the actual period of time involved. Thus, the interest on $2,000 for one year at 12% is $240 (12% of $2,000). The interest on $2,000 for one-fourth of one year at 12% is $60 (1/4 of $240).

The basic formula for computing interest is as follows:

$$\text{Face Amount (or Principal)} \times \text{Rate} \times \text{Time} = \text{Interest}$$

To illustrate the formula, the interest on the note in Exhibit 4 is computed as follows:

$$\$2,500 \times 0.10 \times \frac{90}{360} = \$62.50 \text{ interest}$$

In computing interest for a period of less than one year, agencies of the federal government and many financial institutions use the actual number of days in the year, 365. In the preceding computation, for example, the time would have been stated as 90/365 of one year. To simplify computations, however, we will use 360 days.

Maturity Value

The amount that is due at the maturity or due date is called the **maturity value**. The maturity value of a note is the sum of the face amount and the interest. In the note in Exhibit 4, the maturity value is $2,562.50 ($2,500 face amount plus $62.50 interest).

Accounting for Notes Receivable

objective 7

Journalize the entries for notes receivable transactions.

As we mentioned earlier, a note may be received from a customer to replace an account receivable. To illustrate, assume that a 30-day, 12% note dated November 21, 2003, is accepted in settlement of the account of W. A. Bunn Co., which is past due and has a balance of $6,000. The entry to record the transaction is as follows:

Nov.	21	Notes Receivable		6 0 0 0 00	
		Accounts Receivable—W. A. Bunn Co.			6 0 0 0 00
		Received 30-day, 12% note dated			
		November 21, 2003.			

When the note matures, the entry to record the receipt of $6,060 ($6,000 principal plus $60 interest) is as follows:

Dec.	21	Cash		6 0 6 0 00	
		Notes Receivable			6 0 0 0 00
		Interest Revenue			6 0 00
		Received principal and interest on			
		matured note.			

If the maker of a note fails to pay the debt on the due date, the note is a **dishonored note receivable**. When a note is dishonored, the face value of the note plus any interest due is transferred to the accounts receivable account. For example, assume that the $6,000, 30-day, 12% note received from W. A. Bunn Co. and recorded on November 21 is dishonored at maturity. The entry to transfer the note and the interest back to the customer's account is as follows:

Dec.	21	Accounts Receivable—W. A. Bunn Co.	6 0 6 0 00		
		Notes Receivable		6 0 0 0 00	
		Interest Revenue		6 0 00	
		To record dishonored note and			
		interest.			

The interest of $60 has been earned, even though the note has been dishonored. If the account receivable is uncollectible, the amount of $6,060 will be written off against the Allowance for Doubtful Accounts.

If a note matures in a later fiscal period, the interest accrued in the period in which the note is received must be recorded by an adjusting entry. For example, assume that a 90-day, 12% note dated December 1, 2003, is received from Crawford Company to settle its account, which has a balance of $4,000. Assuming that the accounting period ends on December 31, the entries to record the receipt of the note, accrued interest, and payment of the note at maturity are shown below.

2003 Dec.	1	Notes Receivable	4 0 0 0 00		
		Accounts Receivable—Crawford			
		Company		4 0 0 0 00	
		Received note in settlement of			
		account.			
	31	Interest Receivable	4 0 00		
		Interest Revenue		4 0 00	
		Adjusting entry for accrued			
		interest, $4,000 × 0.12 × 30/360.			

2004 Mar.	1	Cash	4 1 2 0 00		
		Notes Receivable		4 0 0 0 00	
		Interest Receivable		4 0 00	
		Interest Revenue		8 0 00	
		Received payment of note and			
		interest; maturity value, $4,000 +			
		($4,000 × 0.12 × 90/360).			

The interest revenue account is closed at the end of each accounting period. The amount of interest revenue is normally reported in the Other Income section of the income statement.

BUSINESS ON STAGE

Interest and the Length of a Year

Whenever a business borrows money or enters into a credit agreement that requires the payment of interest, it is important that the business understand how the interest will be computed. For example, the difference in 180 days' interest computed on the basis of a 365-day year versus a 360-day year is shown below for a loan of $40,000 at an interest rate of 12%.

$40,000 × 0.12 × 180/365 = $2,367.12

$40,000 × 0.12 × 180/360 = $2,400.00

The difference of $32.88 may seem small, but for a business that might enter into thousands of such transactions for millions of dollars, the difference between computing interest on a 360-day year versus a 365-day year can be significant. ■

Receivables on the Balance Sheet

objective 8

Prepare the Current Assets presentation of receivables on the balance sheet.

All receivables that are expected to be realized in cash within a year are presented in the Current Assets section of the balance sheet. It is normal to list the assets in the order of their liquidity. This is the order in which they are expected to be converted to cash during normal operations. An example of the presentation of receivables is shown in the partial balance sheet for Crabtree Co. in Exhibit 5.

Exhibit 5 Receivables on Balance Sheet

The following credit risk disclosure appeared in the financial statements of **Deere & Company:**

Credit receivables have significant concentrations of credit risk in the agricultural, industrial, lawn and grounds care, and recreational (non-Deere equipment) business sectors. . . . The portion of credit receivables related to the agricultural equipment business was 60%; that related to the industrial equipment business was 12%; that related to the lawn and grounds care equipment business was 7%; and that related to the recreational equipment business was 21%. On a geographic basis, there is not a disproportionate concentration of credit risk in any area. . . .

Crabtree Co. Balance Sheet December 31, 2003					
Assets					
Current assets:					
Cash				$119 5 0 0 00	
Notes receivable				250 0 0 0 00	
Accounts receivable	$445 0 0 0 00				
Less allowance for doubtful accounts	15 0 0 0 00		430 0 0 0 00		
Interest receivable				14 5 0 0 00	

The balance of Crabtree's notes receivable, accounts receivable, and interest receivable accounts are reported in Exhibit 5. The allowance for doubtful accounts is subtracted from the accounts receivable. Alternatively, the accounts receivable may be listed on the balance sheet at its net realizable value of $430,000, with a note showing the amount of the allowance. If the allowance account includes provisions for doubtful notes as well as accounts, it should be deducted from the total of Notes Receivable and Accounts Receivable.

Other disclosures related to receivables are presented either on the face of the financial statements or in the accompanying notes. Such disclosures include the market (fair) value of the receivables.[6] In addition, if unusual credit risks exist within the receivables, the nature of the risks should be disclosed. For example, if the majority of the receivables are due from one customer or are due from customers located in one area of the country or one industry, these facts should be disclosed.[7]

FINANCIAL ANALYSIS AND INTERPRETATION

objective 9

Compute and interpret the accounts receivable turnover and the number of days' sales in receivables.

Businesses that grant long credit terms tend to have relatively greater amounts tied up in accounts receivable than those granting short credit terms. In either case, it is desirable to collect receivables as promptly as possible. The cash collected from receivables improves solvency and lessens the risk of loss from uncollectible accounts. Two financial measures that are especially useful in evaluating the efficiency in collecting receivables are (1) the accounts receivable turnover and (2) the number of days' sales in receivables.

The **accounts receivable turnover** measures how frequently during the year the accounts receivable are being converted to cash. For example, with credit terms of 2/10, n/30 days, the accounts receivable should turn over more than twelve times per year. The accounts receivable turnover is computed as follows:

$$\text{Accounts receivable turnover} = \frac{\textbf{Net sales on account}}{\textbf{Average accounts receivable}}$$

The average accounts receivable can be determined by using monthly data or by simply adding the beginning and ending accounts receivable balances and dividing by two. For example, assume that Sidner Company offers credit terms of 2/10, n/30 and has net sales on account of $36,000,000 and beginning and ending accounts receivable balances of $1,080,000 and $1,220,000. The accounts receivable turnover is 31.3, as shown below.

$$\text{Accounts receivable turnover} = \frac{\textbf{Net sales on account}}{\textbf{Average accounts receivable}}$$

$$= \frac{\$36,000,000}{(\$1,080,000 + \$1,220,000)/2} = 31.3$$

The **number of days' sales in receivables** is an estimate of the length of time the accounts receivable have been outstanding. With credit terms of 2/10, n/30 days, the number of days' sales in receivables should be less than 20 days. It is computed as follows:

$$\text{Number of days' sales in receivables} = \frac{\textbf{Accounts receivable, end of year}}{\textbf{Average daily sales on account}}$$

Average daily sales on account is determined by dividing net sales on account by 365 days. For example, using the preceding data for Sidner Company, the number of days' sales in receivables is 12.4, as shown on the following page.

---

[6] *Statement of Financial Accounting Standards, No. 107,* "Disclosures about Fair Value of Financial Instruments," Financial Accounting Standards Board, Norwalk, 1991, pars. 10 and 19.

[7] *Statement of Financial Accounting Standards, No. 105,* "Disclosure of Information about Financial Instruments with Off-Balance-Sheet Risk and Financial Instruments with Concentrations of Credit Risk," Financial Accounting Standards Board, Norwalk, 1990, par. 20, and *Statement of Financial Accounting Standards, No. 107, op.cit.,* par. 13.

$$\text{Number of days' sales in receivables} = \frac{\text{Accounts receivable, end of year}}{\text{Average daily sales on account}}$$

$$= \frac{\$1,220,000}{(\$36,000,000/365 \text{ days})} = 12.4$$

For these measures to be meaningful, a company should compare its current measures with those from prior periods and with industry figures. An improvement in the efficiency in collecting accounts receivable is indicated when the accounts receivable turnover increases and the number of days' sales in receivables decreases.

ENCORE

Need a Friendly Loan?

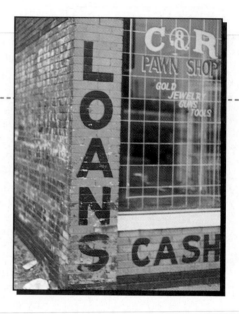

If you are approached by a stranger and offered a quick loan to help you out of a financial bind, you should probably think twice. A young police officer in Hong Kong wishes he had.

Sergeant Li Chi-lok went to a local casino on a Friday night to play pai kau (Chinese dominoes). By 4 a.m. Saturday, he had lost his $9,000 gambling stake. Tired and out of money, he watched other gamblers until a young man approached him. "Did you win or lose? If you need money, we have some," the loan shark said. Sergeant Li yielded to temptation and borrowed $10,000, but was only given $9,000—$1,000 was taken as a service charge. When he stopped gambling, he had borrowed $20,000 and owed $25,000.

The loan sharks took Sergeant Li to an apartment, where he was told to call relatives to pay off his debt. However, the interest accumulated

rapidly. By midday on Saturday, the amount owed had risen to $33,000. Twelve hours later, it rose to $44,000, and by lunchtime on Sunday it had risen to $60,000. Sergeant Li was allowed to go after his mother deposited $20,000 in a bank account and he signed an IOU for the remaining debt. During his ordeal, Sergeant Li was tied up and severely beaten. His injuries included a punctured lung and a broken leg, arm, and finger.

Loan sharks aren't confined to Hong Kong. In the United Kingdom, there are more than 27,000 legal moneylenders, who charge annual interest rates up to 500%. In the United States, most states have usury laws restricting the amount of interest that a creditor may charge. However, illegal loan sharking still exists. For example, a Boston loan shark and gambling bookie recently pleaded guilty to charging 100 customers

interest rates ranging from 100% to 500%. In New York, a restaurant owner testified that he had paid $60,000 on a $20,000 loan, but it was still not enough to satisfy a Buffalo loan shark. In another case, a woman embezzled more than $100,000 from a doctor she worked for in order to pay her husband's loan shark. She escaped prosecution by cooperating with the FBI's case against the loan shark. ■

APPENDIX: DISCOUNTING NOTES RECEIVABLE

Although it is not a common transaction, a company may endorse its notes receivable and transfer them to a bank. The bank transfers cash (the **proceeds**) to the company after deducting a **discount** (interest) that is computed on the maturity value of the note for the discount period. The discount period is the time that the bank must hold the note before it becomes due.

To illustrate, assume that a 90-day, 12%, $1,800 note receivable from Pryor & Co., dated April 8, is discounted at the payee's bank on May 3 at the rate of 14%. The data used in determining the effect of the transaction are as follows:

Face value of note dated April 8	$1,800.00
Interest on note (90 days at 12%)	54.00
Maturity value of note due July 7	$1,854.00
Discount on maturity value (65 days from May 3 to July 7, at 14%)	46.87
Proceeds	$1,807.13

The endorser records as interest revenue the excess of the proceeds from discounting the note, $1,807.13, over its face value, $1,800, as follows:

May	3	Cash		1 8 0 7 13	
		Notes Receivable			1 8 0 0 00
		Interest Revenue			7 13
		Discounted $1,800, 90-day, 12% note			
		at 14%.			

What if the proceeds from discounting a note receivable are less than the face value? When this situation occurs, the endorser records the excess of the face value over the proceeds as interest expense. The length of the discount period and the difference between the interest rate and the discount rate determine whether interest expense or interest revenue will result from discounting.

Without a statement limiting responsibility, the endorser of a note is committed to paying the note if the maker defaults. This potential liability is called a **contingent liability**. Thus, the endorser of a note that has been discounted has a contingent liability until the due date. If the maker pays the promised amount at maturity, the contingent liability is removed without any action on the part of the endorser. If, on the other hand, the maker dishonors the note and the endorser is notified according to legal requirements, the endorser's liability becomes an actual one.

When a discounted note receivable is dishonored, the bank notifies the endorser and asks for payment. In some cases, the bank may charge a **protest fee** for notifying the endorser that a note has been dishonored. The entire amount paid to the bank by the endorser, including the interest and protest fee, should be debited to the account receivable of the maker. For example, assume that the $1,800, 90-day, 12% note discounted on May 3 is dishonored at maturity by the maker, Pryor & Co. The bank charges a protest fee of $12. The endorser's entry to record the payment to the bank is as follows:

July	7	Accounts Receivable—Pryor & Co.		1 8 6 6 00	
		Cash			1 8 6 6 00
		Paid dishonored, discounted note			
		(maturity value of $1,854 plus protest			
		fee of $12).			

KEY POINTS

1 List the common classifications of receivables.

The term receivables includes all money claims against other entities, including people, business firms, and other organizations. They are normally classified as accounts receivable, notes receivable, or other receivables.

2 Summarize and provide examples of internal control procedures that apply to receivables.

The internal controls that apply to receivables include the separation of responsibilities for related functions. In this way, the work of one employee can serve as a check on the work of another employee.

3 Describe the nature of and the accounting for uncollectible receivables.

The two methods of accounting for uncollectible receivables are the allowance method and the direct write-off method. The allowance method provides in advance for uncollectible receivables. The direct write-off method recognizes the expense only when the account is judged to be uncollectible.

4 Journalize the entries for the allowance method of accounting for uncollectibles, and estimate uncollectible receivables based on sales and on an analysis of receivables.

A year-end adjusting entry provides for (1) the reduction of the value of the receivables to the amount of cash expected to be realized from them in the future and (2) the allocation to the current period of the expected expense resulting from such reduction. The adjusting entry debits Uncollectible Accounts Expense and credits Allowance for Doubtful Accounts. When an account is believed to be uncollectible, it is written off against the allowance account.

When the estimate of uncollectibles is based on the amount of sales for the fiscal period, the adjusting entry is made without regard to the balance of the allowance account. When the estimate of uncollectibles is based on the amount and the age of the receivable accounts at the end of the period, the adjusting entry is recorded so that the balance of the allowance account will equal the estimated uncollectibles at the end of the period.

The allowance account, which will have a credit balance after the adjusting entry has been posted, is a contra asset account. The uncollectible accounts expense is generally reported on the income statement as an administrative expense.

5 Journalize the entries for the direct write-off of uncollectible receivables.

Under the direct write-off method, the entry to write off an account debits Uncollectible Accounts Expense and credits Accounts Receivable. Neither an allowance account nor an adjusting entry is needed at the end of the period.

6 Describe the nature and characteristics of promissory notes.

A note is a written promise to pay a sum of money on demand or at a definite time. Characteristics of notes that affect how they are recorded and reported include the due date, interest rate, and maturity value. The basic formula for computing interest on a note is: Principal × Rate × Time = Interest. The due date is the date a note is to be paid, and the period of time between the issuance date and the due date is normally stated in either days or months. The maturity value of a note is the sum of the face amount and the interest.

7 Journalize the entries for notes receivable transactions.

A note received in settlement of an account receivable is recorded as a debit to Notes Receivable and a credit to Accounts Receivable. When a note matures, Cash is debited, Notes Receivable is credited, and Interest Revenue is credited. If the maker of a note fails to pay the debt on the due date, the note is said to be dishonored. When the holder of a dishonored note has been paid by the endorser, the amount of the endorser's claim against the maker of the note is debited to an accounts receivable account.

8 Prepare the Current Assets presentation of receivables on the balance sheet.

All receivables that are expected to be realized in cash within a year are presented in the Current Assets section of the balance sheet. It is normal to list the assets in the order of their liquidity, which is the order in which they can be converted to cash in normal operations.

9 Compute and interpret the accounts receivable turnover and the number of days' sales in receivables.

The accounts receivable turnover is net sales on account divided by average accounts receivable. It measures how frequently accounts receivable are being converted into cash. The number of days' sales in receivables is the end-of-year accounts receivable divided by the average daily sales on account. It measures the length of time the accounts receivable have been outstanding.

ILLUSTRATIVE PROBLEM

Ditzler Company, a construction supply company, uses the allowance method of accounting for uncollectible accounts receivable. Selected transactions completed by Ditzler Company are as follows:

Feb. 1. Sold merchandise on account to Ames Co., $8,000. The cost of the merchandise sold was $4,500.

Mar. 15. Accepted a 60-day, 12% note for $8,000 from Ames Co. on account.

Apr. 9. Wrote off a $2,500 account from Dorset Co. as uncollectible.

    21. Loaned $7,500 cash to Jill Klein, receiving a 90-day, 14% note.

May 14. Received the interest due from Ames Co. and a new 90-day, 14% note as a renewal of the loan. (Record both the debit and the credit to the notes receivable account.)

June 13. Reinstated the account of Dorset Co., written off on April 9, and received $2,500 in full payment.

July 20. Jill Klein dishonored her note.

Aug. 12. Received from Ames Co. the amount due on its note of May 14.

    19. Received from Jill Klein the amount owed on the dishonored note, plus interest for 30 days at 15%, computed on the maturity value of the note.

Dec. 16. Accepted a 60-day, 12% note for $12,000 from Global Company on account.

    31. It is estimated that 3% of the credit sales of $1,375,000 for the year ended December 31 will be uncollectible.

Instructions

1. Journalize the transactions. Omit explanations.
2. Journalize the adjusting entry to record the accrued interest on December 31 on the Global Company note.

Solution

1.

				Debit	Credit
Feb.	1	Accounts Receivable—Ames Co.		8 0 0 0 00	
		Sales			8 0 0 0 00
	1	Cost of Merchandise Sold		4 5 0 0 00	
		Merchandise Inventory			4 5 0 0 00
Mar.	15	Notes Receivable—Ames Co.		8 0 0 0 00	
		Accounts Receivable—Ames Co.			8 0 0 0 00
Apr.	9	Allowance for Doubtful Accounts		2 5 0 0 00	
		Accounts Receivable—Dorset Co.			2 5 0 0 00
	21	Notes Receivable—Jill Klein		7 5 0 0 00	
		Cash			7 5 0 0 00
May	14	Notes Receivable—Ames Co.		8 0 0 0 00	
		Cash		1 6 0 00	
		Notes Receivable—Ames Co.			8 0 0 0 00
		Interest Revenue			1 6 0 00
June	13	Accounts Receivable—Dorset Co.		2 5 0 0 00	
		Allowance for Doubtful Accounts			2 5 0 0 00
	13	Cash		2 5 0 0 00	
		Accounts Receivable—Dorset Co.			2 5 0 0 00

July	20	Accounts Receivable—Jill Klein	7 7 6 2 50			
		Notes Receivable—Jill Klein			7 5 0 0 00	
		Interest Revenue			2 6 2 50	
Aug.	12	Cash	8 2 8 0 00			
		Notes Receivable—Ames Co.			8 0 0 0 00	
		Interest Revenue			2 8 0 00	
	19	Cash	7 8 5 9 53			
		Accounts Receivable—Jill Klein			7 7 6 2 50	
		Interest Revenue			9 7 03	
		($7,762.50 × 15% × 30/360)				
Dec.	16	Notes Receivable—Global Company	12 0 0 0 00			
		Accounts Receivable—Global Company			12 0 0 0 00	
	31	Uncollectible Accounts Expense	41 2 5 0 00			
		Allowance for Doubtful Accounts			41 2 5 0 00	

2.

Dec.	31	Interest Receivable	6 0 00			
		Interest Revenue			6 0 00	
		($12,000 × 12% × 15/360)				

SELF-EXAMINATION QUESTIONS   Answers at End of Chapter

Matching

Match each of the following statements with its proper term. Some terms may not be used.

A. accounts receivable	___ 1. All money claims against other entities, including people, business firms, and other organizations.
B. accounts receivable turnover	___ 2. A receivable created by selling merchandise or services on credit.
C. aging the receivables	___ 3. Amounts customers owe, for which a formal, written instrument of credit has been issued.
D. allowance method	___ 4. The operating expense incurred because of the failure to collect receivables.
E. contra asset	___ 5. The method of accounting for uncollectible accounts that provides an expense for uncollectible receivables in advance of their write-off.
F. direct write-off method	___ 6. The method of accounting for uncollectible accounts that recognizes the expense only when accounts are judged to be worthless.
G. dishonored note receivable	___ 7. The process of analyzing the accounts receivable and classifying them according to various age groupings, with the due date being the base point for determining age.
H. maturity value	___ 8. The amount that is due at the maturity or due date of a note.
I. notes receivable	___ 9. A note that the maker fails to pay on the due date.
J. number of days' sales in receivables	___10. An estimate of the length of time the accounts receivable have been outstanding.
K. promissory note	___11. Measures how frequently during the year the accounts receivable are being converted to cash.
L. receivables	___12. A written promise to pay a sum of money on demand or at a definite time.
M. uncollectible accounts expense	

Multiple Choice

1. At the end of the fiscal year, before the accounts are adjusted, Accounts Receivable has a balance of $200,000 and Allowance for Doubtful Accounts has a credit balance of $2,500. If the estimate of uncollectible accounts determined by aging the receivables is $8,500, the amount of uncollectible accounts expense is:
   A. $2,500
   B. $6,000
   C. $8,500
   D. $11,000

2. At the end of the fiscal year, Accounts Receivable has a balance of $100,000 and Allowance for Doubtful Accounts has a balance of $7,000. The expected net realizable value of the accounts receivable is:
   A. $7,000
   B. $93,000
   C. $100,000
   D. $107,000

3. What is the maturity value of a 90-day, 12% note for $10,000?
   A. $8,800
   B. $10,000
   C. $10,300
   D. $11,200

4. What is the due date of a $12,000, 90-day, 8% note receivable dated August 5?
   A. October 31
   B. November 2
   C. November 3
   D. November 4

5. When a note receivable is dishonored, Accounts Receivable is debited for what amount?
   A. The face value of the note
   B. The maturity value of the note
   C. The maturity value of the note less accrued interest
   D. The maturity value of the note plus accrued interest

CLASS DISCUSSION QUESTIONS

1. What are the three classifications of receivables?
2. What types of transactions give rise to accounts receivable?
3. In what section of the balance sheet should a note receivable be listed if its term is (a) 120 days, (b) 6 years?
4. Give two examples of other receivables.
5. The accounts receivable clerk is also responsible for handling cash receipts. Which principle of internal control is violated in this situation?
6. Which of the two methods of accounting for uncollectible accounts provides for the recognition of the expense at the earlier date?
7. What kind of an account (asset, liability, etc.) is Allowance for Doubtful Accounts, and is its normal balance a debit or a credit?
8. After the accounts are adjusted and closed at the end of the fiscal year, Accounts Receivable has a balance of $783,150 and Allowance for Doubtful Accounts has a balance of $41,694. Describe how the accounts receivable and the allowance for doubtful accounts are reported on the balance sheet.
9. A firm has consistently adjusted its allowance account at the end of the fiscal year by adding a fixed percent of the period's net sales on account. After five years, the balance in Allowance for Doubtful Accounts has become very large in relationship to the balance in Accounts Receivable. Give two possible explanations.
10. Which of the two methods of estimating uncollectibles provides for the most accurate estimate of the current net realizable value of the receivables?
11. For a business, what are the advantages of a note receivable in comparison to an account receivable?
12. Fryer Company issued a promissory note to Corbett Company. (a) Who is the payee? (b) What is the title of the account used by Corbett Company in recording the note?
13. If a note provides for payment of principal of $75,000 and interest at the rate of 8%, will the interest amount to $6,000? Explain.
14. The maker of a $6,000, 10%, 120-day note receivable failed to pay the note on the due date of April 30. What accounts should be debited and credited by the payee to record the dishonored note receivable?
15. The note receivable dishonored in Question 14 is paid on May 30 by the maker, plus interest for 30 days, 9%. What entry should be made to record the receipt of the payment?
16. Under what caption should accounts receivable be reported on the balance sheet?

EXERCISES

Exercise 8–1

Internal control procedures

Objective 2

Lunar Company sells carpeting. Over 60% of all carpet sales are on credit. The following procedures are used by Lunar to process this large number of credit sales and the subsequent collections.

a. All credit sales to a first-time customer must be approved by the Credit Department. Salespersons will assist the customer in filling out a credit application, but an employee in the Credit Department is responsible for verifying employment and checking the customer's credit history before granting credit.

b. Lunar's standard credit period is 30 days. The Credit Department may approve an extension of this repayment period of up to one year. Whenever an extension is granted, the customer signs a promissory note. Up to 10% of the credit sales in any one year are for repayment periods exceeding 30 days.

c. A formal ledger is not maintained for customers who sign promissory notes. Lunar simply keeps a copy of each signed note in a file cabinet. These unpaid notes are filed by due date.

d. Lunar employs an accounts receivable clerk. The clerk is responsible for recording customer credit sales (based on sales tickets), receiving cash from customers, giving customers credit for their payments, and handling all customer billing complaints.

e. The general ledger control account for Accounts Receivable is maintained by the General Accounting Department at Lunar. This department records total credit sales, based on credit sale information from the store's electronic cash register, and total customer receipts, based on the bank deposit slip.

State whether each of these procedures is appropriate or inappropriate, considering the principles of internal control. If inappropriate, state which internal control procedure is violated.

Exercise 8–2

Nature of uncollectible accounts

Objective 3

✓ a. 4.3%

Hilton Hotels Corporation owns and operates casinos at several of its hotels, located primarily in Nevada. At the end of a recent fiscal year, the following accounts and notes receivable were reported (in thousands):

Hotel accounts and notes receivable	$75,796	
Less: Allowance for doubtful accounts	3,256	
		$72,540
Casino accounts receivable	$26,334	
Less: Allowance for doubtful accounts	6,654	
		19,680

a. Compute the percentage of allowance for doubtful accounts to the gross hotel accounts and notes receivable for the end of the fiscal year.

b. Compute the percentage of the allowance for doubtful accounts to the gross casino accounts receivable for the end of the fiscal year.

c. Discuss possible reasons for the difference in the two ratios computed in (a) and (b).

Exercise 8–3
Number of days past due

Objective 4

✓ The Body Shop, 58 days

Diamond Auto Supply distributes new and used automobile parts to local dealers throughout the Southeast. Diamond's credit terms are n/30. As of the end of business on July 31, the following accounts receivable were past due.

Account	Due Date	Amount
The Body Shop	June 3	$3,000
Custom Auto	July 1	2,500
Hometown Repair	March 22	500
Jake's Auto Repair	May 19	1,000
Like New	June 18	750
Sally's	April 12	1,800
Uptown Auto	May 8	500
Westside Repair & Tow	May 31	1,100

Determine the number of days each account is past due.

Exercise 8–4
Aging-of-receivables schedule

Objective 4

The accounts receivable clerk for Romance Mattress Company prepared the following partially completed aging-of-receivables schedule as of the end of business on November 30.

Customer	Balance	Not Past Due	Days Past Due			
			1–30	31–60	61–90	Over 90
Aaron Brothers Inc.	2,000	2,000				
Abell Company	1,500		1,500			
Zollo Company	5,000				5,000	
Subtotals	872,500	540,000	180,000	78,500	42,300	31,700

The following accounts were unintentionally omitted from the aging schedule.

Customer	Balance	Due Date
Tamika Industries	$25,000	August 24
Ruppert Company	8,500	September 3
Welborne Inc.	35,000	October 17
Kristi Company	6,500	November 5
Simrill Company	12,000	December 3

a. Determine the number of days past due for each of the preceding accounts.
b. Complete the aging-of-receivables schedule.

Exercise 8–5
Estimating allowance for doubtful accounts

Objective 4

✓ $62,690

Romance Mattress Company has a past history of uncollectible accounts, as shown below. Estimate the allowance for doubtful accounts, based on the aging-of-receivables schedule you completed in Exercise 8–4.

Age Class	Percentage Uncollectible
Not past due	2%
1–30 days past due	4
31–60 days past due	10
61–90 days past due	20
Over 90 days past due	40

Exercise 8–6
Adjustment for uncollectible accounts
Objective 4

Using the data in Exercise 8–5, assume that the allowance for doubtful accounts for Romance Mattress Company has a credit balance of $6,890 before adjustment on November 30. Journalize the adjusting entry for uncollectible accounts as of November 30.

Exercise 8–7
Estimating doubtful accounts
Objective 4

Phoenician Co. is a wholesaler of office supplies. An aging of the company's accounts receivable on December 31, 2003, and a historical analysis of the percentage of uncollectible accounts in each age category are as follows:

Age Interval	Balance	Percent Uncollectible
Not past due	$350,000	1%
1–30 days past due	90,000	3
31–60 days past due	17,000	6
61–90 days past due	13,000	10
91–180 days past due	9,400	60
Over 180 days past due	3,600	80
	$483,000	

Estimate what the proper balance of the allowance for doubtful accounts should be as of December 31, 2003.

Exercise 8–8
Entry for uncollectible accounts
Objective 4

Using the data in Exercise 8–7, assume that the allowance for doubtful accounts for Phoenician Co. had a debit balance of $1,891 as of December 31, 2003.
Journalize the adjusting entry for uncollectible accounts as of December 31, 2003.

Exercise 8–9
Providing for doubtful accounts
Objective 4

✓ a. $15,000
✓ b. $14,600

At the end of the current year, the accounts receivable account has a debit balance of $775,000, and net sales for the year total $6,000,000. Determine the amount of the adjusting entry to provide for doubtful accounts under each of the following assumptions:

a. The allowance account before adjustment has a credit balance of $4,750. Uncollectible accounts expense is estimated at 1/4 of 1% of net sales.
b. The allowance account before adjustment has a credit balance of $3,750. An aging of the accounts in the customer's ledger indicates estimated doubtful accounts of $18,350.
c. The allowance account before adjustment has a debit balance of $5,050. Uncollectible accounts expense is estimated at 1/2 of 1% of net sales.
d. The allowance account before adjustment has a debit balance of $5,050. An aging of the accounts in the customer's ledger indicates estimated doubtful accounts of $31,400.

Exercise 8–10
Entries to write off accounts receivable
Objectives 4, 5

SPREADSHEET

Query.com, a computer consulting firm, has decided to write off the $4,800 balance of an account owed by a customer. Journalize the entry to record the write-off, (a) assuming that the allowance method is used, and (b) assuming that the direct write-off method is used.

Exercise 8–11
Entries for uncollectible receivables, using allowance method
Objective 4

Journalize the following transactions in the accounts of Rhino Company, a restaurant supply company that uses the allowance method of accounting for uncollectible receivables:

Jan. 13. Sold merchandise on account to Renee Hart, $8,100. The cost of the merchandise sold was $4,750.

Feb. 12. Received $2,000 from Renee Hart and wrote off the remainder owed on the sale of January 13 as uncollectible.

July 3. Reinstated the account of Renee Hart that had been written off on February 12 and received $6,100 cash in full payment.

Exercise 8–12

Entries for uncollectible accounts, using direct write-off method

Objective 5

Journalize the following transactions in the accounts of Menthol Co., a hospital supply company that uses the direct write-off method of accounting for uncollectible receivables:

Aug. 8. Sold merchandise on account to Dr. Beth Mears, $10,500. The cost of the merchandise sold was $6,175.

Sept. 7. Received $8,000 from Dr. Beth Mears and wrote off the remainder owed on the sale of August 8 as uncollectible.

Dec. 20. Reinstated the account of Dr. Beth Mears that had been written off on September 7 and received $2,500 cash in full payment.

Exercise 8–13

Effect of doubtful accounts on net income

Objectives 4, 5

During its first year of operations, Yarmouth Automotive Supply Co. had net sales of $3,050,000, wrote off $52,800 of accounts as uncollectible using the direct write-off method, and reported net income of $112,800. If the allowance method of accounting for uncollectibles had been used, 2% of net sales would have been estimated as uncollectible. Determine what the net income would have been if the allowance method had been used.

Exercise 8–14

Effect of doubtful accounts on net income

Objectives 4, 5

Using the data in Exercise 8–13, assume that during the second year of operations Yarmouth Automotive Supply Co. had net sales of $3,800,000, wrote off $64,500 of accounts as uncollectible using the direct write-off method, and reported net income of $162,300.

a.   Determine what net income would have been in the second year if the allowance method (using 2% of net sales) had been used in both the first and second years.

b.   Determine what the balance of the allowance for doubtful accounts would have been at the end of the second year if the allowance method had been used in both the first and second years.

Exercise 8–15

Determine due date and interest on notes

Objective 6

✓ a. May 5; $150

Determine the due date and the amount of interest due at maturity on the following notes:

	Date of Note	Face Amount	Term of Note	Interest Rate
a.	March 6	$10,000	60 days	9%
b.	May 20	6,000	60 days	10%
c.	June 2	7,500	90 days	12%
d.	August 30	15,000	120 days	10%
e.	October 1	12,500	60 days	12%

Exercise 8–16

Entries for notes receivable

Objectives 6, 7

✓ b. $15,300

Funchal Interior Decorators issued a 90-day, 8% note for $15,000, dated April 6, to Maderia Furniture Company on account.

a.   Determine the due date of the note.

b.   Determine the maturity value of the note.

c.   Journalize the entries to record the following: (1) receipt of the note by the payee, and (2) receipt by the payee of payment of the note at maturity.

Exercise 8–17

Entries for notes receivable

Objective 7

The series of seven transactions recorded in the following T accounts were related to a sale to a customer on account and the receipt of the amount owed. Briefly describe each transaction.

Cash		Notes Receivable	
(7) 23,028		(5) 22,000	(6) 22,000

Page 338 — Chapter 8 · Receivables

T-accounts:

Accounts Receivable		Sales Returns and Allowances
(1) 25,000 / (3) 3,000		(3) 3,000
(6) 22,725 / (5) 22,000		
/ (7) 22,725		

Merchandise Inventory	Cost of Merchandise Sold
(4) 1,800 / (2) 15,000	(2) 15,000 / (4) 1,800

Sales	Interest Revenue
(1) 25,000	(6) 725 / (7) 303

Exercise 8–18 — Entries for notes receivable, including year-end entries. Objective 7

The following selected transactions were completed by Lupine Co., a supplier of elastic bands for clothing:

2002
Dec. 13. Received from Stout Co., on account, a $30,000, 120-day, 9% note dated December 13.
31. Recorded an adjusting entry for accrued interest on the note of December 13.
31. Closed the interest revenue account. The only entry in this account originated from the December 31 adjustment.
2003
Apr. 12. Received payment of note and interest from Stout Co.

Journalize the transactions.

Exercise 8–19 — Entries for receipt and dishonor of note receivable. Objective 7

Journalize the following transactions of Galaxy Theater Productions:

July 3. Received a $50,000, 90-day, 7% note dated July 3 from Hermes Company on account.
Oct. 1. The note is dishonored by Hermes Company.
31. Received the amount due on the dishonored note plus interest for 30 days at 9% on the total amount charged to Hermes Company on October 1.

Exercise 8–20 — Entries for receipt and dishonor of notes receivable. Objectives 4, 7

Journalize the following transactions in the accounts of Dimitrious Co., which operates a riverboat casino:

Apr. 1. Received a $10,000, 30-day, 6% note dated April 1 from Wilcox Co. on account.
18. Received a $12,000, 30-day, 9% note dated April 18 from Aaron Co. on account.
May 1. The note dated April 1 from Wilcox Co. is dishonored, and the customer's account is charged for the note, including interest.
June 17. The note dated April 18 from Aaron Co. is dishonored, and the customer's account is charged for the note, including interest.
July 30. Cash is received for the amount due on the dishonored note dated April 1 plus interest for 90 days at 8% on the total amount debited to Wilcox Co. on May 1.
Sept. 3. Wrote off against the allowance account the amount charged to Aaron Co. on June 17 for the dishonored note dated April 18.

Exercise 8–21 — Receivables in the balance sheet. Objective 8

List any errors you can find in the following partial balance sheet.

Dragonfly Company
Balance Sheet
December 31, 2003

Assets

Current assets:		
Cash		$ 63,750
Notes receivable	$200,000	
Less interest receivable	12,000	188,000
Accounts receivable	$376,180	
Plus allowance for doubtful accounts	30,500	406,680

Exercise 8–22
Accounts receivable turnover; number of days' sales in receivables

Objective 9

The financial statements for **Cisco Systems, Inc.**, are presented in Appendix G at the end of the text. Assume that all sales are credit sales and that the accounts receivable were $1,303,000,000 at July 25, 1998.

a. Compute the accounts receivable turnover for 1999 and 2000.
b. Compute the number of days' sales in receivables at July 31, 1999 and July 29, 2000.
c. ✏️ What conclusions can be drawn from these analyses regarding Cisco Systems' efficiency in collecting receivables?

Appendix Exercise 8–23
Discounting notes receivable

Dacca Co., a building construction company, holds a 90-day, 6% note for $40,000, dated May 15, which was received from a customer on account. On June 14, the note is discounted at the bank at the rate of 10%.

a. Determine the maturity value of the note.
b. Determine the number of days in the discount period.
c. Determine the amount of the discount. Round to the nearest dollar.
d. Determine the amount of the proceeds.
e. Journalize the entry to record the discounting of the note on June 14.

Appendix Exercise 8–24
Entries for receipt and discounting of note receivable and dishonored notes

Journalize the following transactions in the accounts of Shapiro Theater Productions:

April 1. Received a $75,000, 60-day, 8% note dated April 1 from Creswell Company on account.
May 1. Discounted the note at First City Bank at 9%.
    31. The note is dishonored by Creswell Company; paid the bank the amount due on the note, plus a protest fee of $500.
June 30. Received the amount due on the dishonored note plus interest for 30 days at 12% on the total amount charged to Creswell Company on May 31.

PROBLEMS SERIES A

Problem 8–1A
Entries related to uncollectible accounts

Objective 4

GENERAL LEDGER

✓ 3. $755,050

The following transactions, adjusting entries, and closing entries were completed by The AllStar Gallery during the current fiscal year ended December 31:

Feb. 21. Reinstated the account of Merryl Alber, which had been written off in the preceding year as uncollectible. Journalized the receipt of $2,025 cash in full payment of Alber's account.
Mar. 31. Wrote off the $5,500 balance owed by Amos Co., which is bankrupt.
July 7. Received 35% of the $8,000 balance owed by Morton Co., a bankrupt business, and wrote off the remainder as uncollectible.
Aug. 29. Reinstated the account of Louis Sabo, which had been written off two years earlier as uncollectible. Recorded the receipt of $1,200 cash in full payment.
Dec. 31. Wrote off the following accounts as uncollectible (compound entry): Dailey Co., $10,050; Sun Co., $7,260; Zheng Furniture, $3,775; Carey Wenzel, $2,820.
    31. Based on an analysis of the $787,550 of accounts receivable, it was estimated that $32,500 will be uncollectible. Journalized the adjusting entry.
    31. Journalized the entry to close the appropriate account to Income Summary.

Instructions

1. Record the January 1 credit balance of $30,000 in Allowance for Doubtful Accounts.
2. Journalize the transactions and the adjusting and closing entries. Post each entry that affects the following three selected accounts and determine the new balances:

115	Allowance for Doubtful Accounts
313	Income Summary
718	Uncollectible Accounts Expense

(continued)

3. Determine the expected net realizable value of the accounts receivable as of December 31.
4. Assuming that instead of basing the provision for uncollectible accounts on an analysis of receivables, the adjusting entry on December 31 had been based on an estimated expense of 1/2 of 1% of the net sales of $7,400,000 for the year, determine the following:
   a. Uncollectible accounts expense for the year.
   b. Balance in the allowance account after the adjustment of December 31.
   c. Expected net realizable value of the accounts receivable as of December 31.

Problem 8–2A
Aging of receivables; estimating allowance for doubtful accounts

Objective 4

SPREADSHEET

✓ 3. $57,283

Lipshy Wigs Company supplies wigs and hair care products to beauty salons throughout California and the Pacific Northwest. The accounts receivable clerk for Lipshy Wigs prepared the following partially completed aging-of-receivables schedule as of the end of business on December 31, 2003:

Customer	Balance	Not Past Due	1–30	31–60	61–90	91–120	Over 120
Austin Beauty	10,000	10,000					
Blount Wigs	5,500			5,500			
Zabka's	2,900		2,900				
Subtotals	780,000	398,600	197,250	98,750	33,300	29,950	22,150

The following accounts were unintentionally omitted from the aging schedule.

Customer	Due Date	Balance
Houseal Uniquely Yours	July 1, 2003	900
Country Designs	Aug. 2, 2003	4,000
Treat's	Sept. 9, 2003	1,200
Molina's Beauty Store	Sept. 29, 2003	1,100
Ginburg Supreme	Oct. 10, 2003	1,500
Steve's Hair Products	Oct. 17, 2003	600
Hairy's Hair Care	Oct. 31, 2003	2,000
VanDiver's Images	Nov. 18, 2003	700
Lopez's Blond Bombs	Nov. 28, 2003	1,800
Josset Ritz	Nov. 30, 2003	3,500
Cool Designs	Dec. 1, 2003	1,000
Buttram Images	Jan. 3, 2004	6,200

Lipshy Wigs has a past history of uncollectible accounts by age category, as follows:

Age Class	Percentage Uncollectible
Not past due	1%
1–30 days past due	4
31–60 days past due	8
61–90 days past due	15
91–120 days past due	30
Over 120 days past due	80

Instructions

1. Determine the number of days past due for each of the preceding accounts.
2. Complete the aging-of-receivables schedule.
3. Estimate the allowance for doubtful accounts, based on the aging-of-receivables schedule.
4. Assume that the allowance for doubtful accounts for Lipshy Wigs has a credit balance of $11,350 before adjustment on December 31, 2003. Illustrate the effect on the accounts and financial statements of the adjustment for uncollectible accounts.

Problem 8–3A

Compare two methods of accounting for uncollectible receivables

Objectives 4, 5

✓ 1. Year 4: Balance of allowance account, end of year, $6,750

Minaret Company, which operates a chain of 30 electronics supply stores, has just completed its fourth year of operations. The direct write-off method of recording uncollectible accounts expense has been used during the entire period. Because of substantial increases in sales volume and amount of uncollectible accounts, the firm is considering changing to the allowance method. Information is requested as to the effect that an annual provision of 1/2% of sales would have had on the amount of uncollectible accounts expense reported for each of the past four years. It is also considered desirable to know what the balance of Allowance for Doubtful Accounts would have been at the end of each year. The following data have been obtained from the accounts:

Year	Sales	Uncollectible Accounts Written Off	Year of Origin of Accounts Receivable Written Off as Uncollectible			
			1st	2nd	3rd	4th
1st	$ 750,000	$ 600	$ 600			
2nd	820,000	1,650	750	$ 900		
3rd	1,050,000	6,200	1,800	1,400	$3,000	
4th	2,250,000	9,150		1,900	2,950	$4,300

Instructions

1. Assemble the desired data, using the following column headings:

	Uncollectible Accounts Expense			Balance of Allowance Account, End of Year
Year	Expense Actually Reported	Expense Based on Estimate	Increase (Decrease) in Amount of Expense	

2. ✎ Experience during the first four years of operations indicated that the receivables were either collected within two years or had to be written off as uncollectible. Does the estimate of 1/2% of sales appear to be reasonably close to the actual experience with uncollectible accounts originating during the first two years? Explain.

Problem 8–4A

Details of notes receivable and related entries

Objectives 6, 7

SPREADSHEET

✓ 1. Note 2: Due date, Sept. 4; Interest due at maturity, $150

Diaz Co. produces advertising videos. During the last six months of the current fiscal year, Diaz Co. received the following notes.

	Date	Face Amount	Term	Interest Rate
1.	May 17	$12,000	45 days	8%
2.	July 6	10,000	60 days	9%
3.	Aug. 1	16,500	90 days	8%
4.	Sept. 1	20,000	90 days	7%
5.	Nov. 29	18,000	60 days	9%
6.	Dec. 18	36,000	60 days	12%

Instructions

1. Determine for each note (a) the due date and (b) the amount of interest due at maturity, identifying each note by number.
2. Journalize the entry to record the dishonor of Note (3) on its due date. *(continued)*

3. Journalize the adjusting entry to record the accrued interest on Notes (5) and (6) on December 31.
4. Journalize the entries to record the receipt of the amounts due on Notes (5) and (6) in January and February.

Problem 8–5A

Notes receivable entries

Objective 7

The following data relate to notes receivable and interest for Robbins Co., a financial services company. (All notes are dated as of the day they are received.)

Mar. 1. Received a $13,000, 9%, 60-day note on account.
      21. Received a $7,500, 8%, 90-day note on account.
Apr. 30. Received $13,195 on note of March 1.
May 16. Received a $40,000, 7%, 90-day note on account.
      31. Received a $6,000, 8%, 30-day note on account.
June 19. Received $7,650 on note of March 21.
      30. Received $6,040 on note of May 31.
July 1. Received a $5,000, 12%, 30-day note on account.
      31. Received $5,050 on note of July 1.
Aug. 14. Received $40,700 on note of May 16.

Instructions
Journalize the entries to record the transactions.

Problem 8–6A

Sales and notes receivable transactions

Objective 7

GENERAL LEDGER

The following were selected from among the transactions completed during the current year by Sonora Co., an appliance wholesale company:

Jan. 7. Sold merchandise on account to Thi Co., $7,500. The cost of merchandise sold was $3,800.
Mar. 8. Accepted a 60-day, 8% note for $7,500 from Thi Co. on account.
May   7. Received from Thi Co. the amount due on the note of March 8.
June 1. Sold merchandise on account to Kohl's for $5,000. The cost of merchandise sold was $3,500.
      5. Loaned $11,000 cash to Michele Duncan, receiving a 30-day, 6% note.
      11. Received from Kohl's the amount due on the invoice of June 1, less 2% discount.
July 5. Received the interest due from Michele Duncan and a new 60-day, 9% note as a renewal of the loan of June 5. (Record both the debit and the credit to the notes receivable account.)
Sept. 3. Received from Michele Duncan the amount due on her note of July 5.
      4. Sold merchandise on account to Stover Co., $8,000. The cost of merchandise sold was $5,500.
Oct. 4. Accepted a 60-day, 6% note for $8,000 from Stover Co. on account.
Dec. 3. Stover Co. dishonored the note dated October 4.
      29. Received from Stover Co. the amount owed on the dishonored note, plus interest for 26 days at 6% computed on the maturity value of the note.

Instructions
Journalize the transactions. Round to the nearest dollar.

PROBLEMS SERIES B

Problem 8–1B

Entries related to uncollectible accounts

Objective 4

GENERAL LEDGER

✓ 3. $623,050

The following transactions, adjusting entries, and closing entries were completed by Cascade Contractors Co. during the current fiscal year ended December 31:

Mar. 17. Received 80% of the $17,500 balance owed by Baxter Co., a bankrupt business, and wrote off the remainder as uncollectible.
Apr. 20. Reinstated the account of Susan Evans, which had been written off in the preceding year as uncollectible. Journalized the receipt of $3,782 cash in full payment of Evans' account.
July 29. Wrote off the $4,500 balance owed by Cofer Co., which has no assets.
Oct. 31. Reinstated the account of Mostafa Co., which had been written off in the preceding year as uncollectible. Journalized the receipt of $7,500 cash in full payment of the account.

Dec. 31. Wrote off the following accounts as uncollectible (compound entry): Grovner Co., $1,950; Nance Co., $2,600; Powell Distributors, $3,500; J. J. Levi, $5,200.

31. Based on an analysis of the $635,750 of accounts receivable, it was estimated that $12,700 will be uncollectible. Journalized the adjusting entry.

31. Journalized the entry to close the appropriate account to Income Summary.

Instructions

1. Record the January 1 credit balance of $10,050 in Allowance for Doubtful Accounts.
2. Journalize the transactions and the adjusting and closing entries. Post each entry that affects the following three selected accounts and determine the new balances:

    | 115 | Allowance for Doubtful Accounts |
    | 313 | Income Summary |
    | 718 | Uncollectible Accounts Expense |

3. Determine the expected net realizable value of the accounts receivable as of December 31.
4. Assuming that instead of basing the provision for uncollectible accounts on an analysis of receivables, the adjusting entry on December 31 had been based on an estimated expense of 1/4 of 1% of the net sales of $5,100,000 for the year, determine the following:
    a. Uncollectible accounts expense for the year.
    b. Balance in the allowance account after the adjustment of December 31.
    c. Expected net realizable value of the accounts receivable as of December 31.

Problem 8–2B

Aging of receivables; estimating allowance for doubtful accounts

Objective 4

SPREADSHEET

✓ 3. $69,810

Wickman Company supplies flies and fishing gear to sporting goods stores and outfitters throughout the western United States. The accounts receivable clerk for Wickman prepared the following partially completed aging-of-receivables schedule as of the end of business on December 31, 2003:

Customer	Balance	Not Past Due	Days Past Due				
			1–30	31–60	61–90	91–120	Over 120
Alexandra Fishery	15,000	15,000					
Cutthroat Sports	5,500			5,500			
Yellowstone Sports	2,900		2,900				
Subtotals	880,000	448,600	247,250	98,750	33,300	29,950	22,150

The following accounts were unintentionally omitted from the aging schedule.

Customer	Due Date	Balance
Adel Sports & Flies	June 21, 2003	1,500
Buzzer Sports	July 30, 2003	3,000
Marabou Flies	Sept. 9, 2003	2,500
Midge Co.	Sept. 30, 2003	1,100
Adventure Outfitters	Oct. 10, 2003	2,500
Pheasant Tail Sports	Oct. 17, 2003	600
Red Tag Sporting Goods	Oct. 30, 2003	2,000
Ross Sports	Nov. 18, 2003	500

Customer	Due Date	Balance
Sawyer's Pheasant Tail	Nov. 28, 2003	1,800
Tent Caddis Outfitters	Nov. 30, 2003	3,500
Wulff Company	Dec. 1, 2003	1,000
Zug Bug Sports	Jan. 6, 2004	6,200

Wickman Company has a past history of uncollectible accounts by age category, as follows:

Age Class	Percentage Uncollectible
Not past due	2%
1–30 days past due	4
31–60 days past due	8
61–90 days past due	20
91–120 days past due	40
Over 120 days past due	80

Instructions

1. Determine the number of days past due for each of the preceding accounts.
2. Complete the aging-of-receivables schedule.
3. Estimate the allowance for doubtful accounts, based on the aging-of-receivables schedule.
4. Assume that the allowance for doubtful accounts for Wickman Company has a debit balance of $1,800 before adjustment on December 31, 2003. Journalize the adjusting entry for uncollectible accounts.

Problem 8–3B

Compare two methods of accounting for uncollectible receivables

Objectives 4, 5

✓ 1. Year 4: Balance of allowance account, end of year, $12,250.

Interlink Company, a telephone service and supply company, has just completed its fourth year of operations. The direct write-off method of recording uncollectible accounts expense has been used during the entire period. Because of substantial increases in sales volume and amount of uncollectible accounts, the firm is considering changing to the allowance method. Information is requested as to the effect that an annual provision of 3/4% of sales would have had on the amount of uncollectible accounts expense reported for each of the past four years. It is also considered desirable to know what the balance of Allowance for Doubtful Accounts would have been at the end of each year. The following data have been obtained from the accounts:

Year	Sales	Uncollectible Accounts Written Off	Year of Origin of Accounts Receivable Written Off as Uncollectible			
			1st	2nd	3rd	4th
1st	$ 650,000	$2,500	$2,500			
2nd	760,000	2,950	1,900	$1,050		
3rd	950,000	5,700	700	4,000	$1,000	
4th	1,800,000	7,800		1,200	2,550	$4,050

Instructions

1. Assemble the desired data, using the following column headings:

	Uncollectible Accounts Expense			Balance of Allowance Account, End of Year
Year	Expense Actually Reported	Expense Based on Estimate	Increase (Decrease) in Amount of Expense	

2. Experience during the first four years of operations indicated that the receivables were either collected within two years or had to be written off as uncollectible. Does the estimate of 3/4% of sales appear to be reasonably close to the actual experience with uncollectible accounts originating during the first two years? Explain.

Problem 8–4B
Details of notes receivable and related entries

Objectives 6, 7

SPREADSHEET

✓ 1. Note 2: Due date, July 15; Interest due at maturity, $175.

Matrix Co. wholesales bathroom fixtures. During the current fiscal year, Matrix Co. received the following notes.

	Date	Face Amount	Term	Interest Rate
1.	March 3	$36,000	60 days	8%
2.	June 15	17,500	30 days	12%
3.	Aug. 20	9,200	120 days	6%
4.	Oct. 31	12,000	60 days	9%
5.	Nov. 23	15,000	60 days	6%
6.	Dec. 27	9,000	30 days	12%

Instructions

1. Determine for each note (a) the due date and (b) the amount of interest due at maturity, identifying each note by number.
2. Journalize the entry to record the dishonor of Note (3) on its due date.
3. Journalize the adjusting entry to record the accrued interest on Notes (5) and (6) on December 31.
4. Journalize the entries to record the receipt of the amounts due on Notes (5) and (6) in January.

Problem 8–5B
Notes receivable entries

Objective 7

The following data relate to notes receivable and interest for Teleport Optic Co., a cable manufacturer and supplier. (All notes are dated as of the day they are received.)

June 1. Received a $15,800, 9%, 60-day note on account.
July 16. Received a $30,000, 10%, 120-day note on account.
31. Received $16,037 on note of June 1.
Sept. 1. Received a $24,000, 9%, 60-day note on account.
Oct. 31. Received $24,360 on note of September 1.
Nov. 8. Received a $24,000, 7%, 30-day note on account.
13. Received $31,000 on note of July 16.
30. Received a $15,000, 10%, 30-day note on account.
Dec. 8. Received $24,140 on note of November 8.
30. Received $15,125 on note of November 30.

Instructions
Journalize entries to record the transactions.

Problem 8–6B
Sales and notes receivable transactions

Objective 7

GENERAL LEDGER

The following were selected from among the transactions completed by Greco Co. during the current year. Greco Co. sells and installs home and business security systems.

Jan. 8. Loaned $6,000 cash to Mark Tift, receiving a 90-day, 8% note.
Feb. 3. Sold merchandise on account to Messina and Son, $18,000. The cost of the merchandise sold was $10,000.
Feb. 12. Sold merchandise on account to Gwyn Co., $25,000. The cost of merchandise sold was $15,000.
Mar. 5. Accepted a 60-day, 6% note for $18,000 from Messina and Son on account.
14. Accepted a 60-day, 12% note for $25,000 from Gwyn Co. on account.
Apr. 8. Received the interest due from Mark Tift and a new 90-day, 9% note as a renewal of the loan of January 8. (Record both the debit and the credit to the notes receivable account.)
May 4. Received from Messina and Son the amount due on the note of March 5.
13. Gwyn Co. dishonored its note dated March 14.
June 12. Received from Gwyn Co. the amount owed on the dishonored note, plus interest for 30 days at 12% computed on the maturity value of the note.
July 7. Received from Mark Tift the amount due on his note of April 8.
Aug. 23. Sold merchandise on account to MacKenzie Co., $8,000. The cost of the merchandise sold was $5,000.
Sept. 2. Received from MacKenzie Co. the amount of the invoice of August 23, less 1% discount.

Instructions
Journalize the transactions.

SPECIAL ACTIVITIES

Activity 8–1
Billings National Bank
*Ethics and professional
conduct in business*

Tricia Fenton, vice-president of operations for Billings National Bank, has instructed the bank's computer programmer to use a 365-day year to compute interest on depository accounts (payables). Tricia also instructed the programmer to use a 360-day year to compute interest on loans (receivables).

➤ Discuss whether Tricia is behaving in a professional manner.

Activity 8–2
**Jefferson Construction
Supplies Co.**
*Collecting accounts
receivable*

The following is an excerpt from a conversation between the office manager, Jamie Luthi, and the president of Jefferson Construction Supplies Co., David King. Jefferson sells building supplies to local contractors.

Jamie: David, we're going to have to do something about these overdue accounts receivable. One-third of our accounts are over 60 days past due, and I've had accounts that have stayed open for almost a year!

David: I didn't realize it was that bad. Any ideas?

Jamie: Well, we could stop giving credit. Make everyone pay with cash or a credit card. We accept MasterCard and Visa already, but only the walk-in customers use them. Almost all of the contractors put purchases on their bills.

David: Yes, but we've been allowing credit for years. As far as I know, all of our competitors allow contractors credit. If we stopped giving credit, we'd lose many of our contractors. They'd just go elsewhere. You know, some of these guys run up bills as high as $40,000 or $60,000. There's no way they could put that kind of money on a credit card.

Jamie: That's a good point. But we've got to do something.

David: How many of the contractor accounts do you actually end up writing off as uncollectible?

Jamie: Not many. Almost all eventually pay. It's just that they take so long!

➤ Suggest one or more solutions to Jefferson Construction Supplies Co.'s problem concerning the collection of accounts receivable.

Activity 8–3
Retriever Wholesale Co.
Value of receivables

The following is an excerpt from a conversation between Kay Kinder, the president and owner of Retriever Wholesale Co., and Michele Stephens, Retriever's controller. The conversation took place on January 4, 2003, shortly after Michele began preparing the financial statements for the year ending December 31, 2002.

Michele: Kay, I've completed my analysis of the collectibility of our accounts receivable. My staff and I estimate that the allowance for doubtful accounts should be somewhere between $60,000 and $90,000. Right now, the balance of the allowance account is $18,000.

Kay: Oh, no! We are already below the estimated earnings projection I gave the bank last year. We used that as a basis for convincing the bank to loan us $100,000. They're going to be upset! Is there any way we can increase the allowance without the adjustment increasing expenses?

Michele: I'm afraid not. The allowance can only be increased by debiting the uncollectible accounts expense account.

Kay: Well, I guess we're stuck. The bank will just have to live with it. But let's increase the allowance by only $42,000. That gets us into our range of estimates with the minimum expense increase.

Michele: Kay, there is one more thing we need to discuss.

Kay: What now?

Michele: Jill, my staff accountant, noticed that you haven't made any payments on your receivable for over a year. Also, it has increased from $20,000 last year to $80,000. Jill thinks we ought to reclassify it as a noncurrent asset and report it as an "other receivable."

Kay: What's the problem? Didn't we just include it in accounts receivable last year?
Michele: Yes, but last year it was immaterial.
Kay: Look, I'll make a $60,000 payment next week. So let's report it as we did last year.

➤ If you were Michele, how would you address Kay's suggestions?

Activity 8–4
Sheepshank Co.
Estimate uncollectible accounts

For several years, sales have been on a "cash only" basis. On January 1, 2000, however, Sheepshank Co. began offering credit on terms of n/30. The amount of the adjusting entry to record the estimated uncollectible receivables at the end of each year has been 1/4 of 1% of credit sales, which is the rate reported as the average for the industry. Credit sales and the year-end credit balances in Allowance for Doubtful Accounts for the past four years are as follows:

Year	Credit Sales	Allowance for Doubtful Accounts
2000	$7,800,000	$ 5,100
2001	8,000,000	11,100
2002	8,100,000	16,850
2003	9,250,000	25,375

Carisa Parker, president of Sheepshank Co., is concerned that the method used to account for and write off uncollectible receivables is unsatisfactory. She has asked for your advice in the analysis of past operations in this area and for recommendations for change.

1. Determine the amount of (a) the addition to Allowance for Doubtful Accounts and (b) the accounts written off for each of the four years.
2. a. ➤ Advise Carisa Parker as to whether the estimate of 1/4 of 1% of credit sales appears reasonable.
   b. ➤ Assume that after discussing (a) with Carisa Parker, she asked you what action might be taken to determine what the balance of Allowance for Doubtful Accounts should be at December 31, 2003, and what possible changes, if any, you might recommend in accounting for uncollectible receivables. How would you respond?

Activity 8–5
Into the Real World
Granting credit

Group Activity

In groups of three or four, determine how credit is typically granted to customers. Interview an individual responsible for granting credit for a bank, a department store, an automobile dealer, or other business in your community. You should ask such questions as the following:

1. What procedures are used to decide whether to grant credit to a customer?
2. What procedures are used to try to collect from customers who are delinquent in their payments?
3. Approximately what percentage of customers' accounts are written off as uncollectible in a year?

➤ Summarize your findings in a report to the class.

Activity 8–6
Into the Real World
Collection of receivables

Go to the Web page of two department store chains, **Federated Department Stores Inc.** and **Dillard's Inc.** The Internet sites for these companies are:

www.federated-fds.com
www.dillards.com

Using the financial information provided at each site, calculate the most recent accounts receivable turnover for each company, and identify which company is collecting its receivables faster.

ANSWERS TO SELF-EXAMINATION QUESTIONS

Matching

1.	L	3.	I	5.	D	7.	C	9.	G	11. B
2.	A	4.	M	6.	F	8.	H	10.	J	12. K

Multiple Choice

1. **B** The estimate of uncollectible accounts, $8,500 (answer C), is the amount of the desired balance of Allowance for Doubtful Accounts after adjustment. The amount of the current provision to be made for uncollectible accounts expense is thus $6,000 (answer B), which is the amount that must be added to the Allowance for Doubtful Accounts credit balance of $2,500 (answer A) so that the account will have the desired balance of $8,500.

2. **B** The amount expected to be realized from accounts receivable is the balance of Accounts Receivable, $100,000, less the balance of Allowance for Doubtful Accounts, $7,000, or $93,000 (answer B).

3. **C** Maturity value is the amount that is due at the maturity or due date. The maturity value of $10,300 (answer C) is determined as follows:

Face amount of note	$10,000
Plus interest ($10,000 × 0.12 × 90/360)	300
Maturity value of note	$10,300

4. **C** November 3 is the due date of a $12,000, 90-day, 8% note receivable dated August 5 [26 days in August (31 days − 5 days) + 30 days in September + 31 days in October + 3 days in November].

5. **B** If a note is dishonored, Accounts Receivable is debited for the maturity value of the note (answer B). The maturity value of the note is its face value (answer A) plus the accrued interest. The maturity value of the note less accrued interest (answer C) is equal to the face value of the note. The maturity value of the note plus accrued interest (answer D) is incorrect, since the interest would be added twice.

Inventories

o b j e c t i v e s

After studying this chapter, you should be able to:

1 Summarize and provide examples of internal control procedures that apply to inventories.

2 Describe the effect of inventory errors on the financial statements.

3 Describe three inventory cost flow assumptions and how they impact the income statement and balance sheet.

4 Compute the cost of inventory under the perpetual inventory system, using the following costing methods:

First-in, first-out
Last-in, first-out
Average cost

5 Compute the cost of inventory under the periodic inventory system, using the following costing methods:

First-in, first-out
Last-in, first-out
Average cost

6 Compare and contrast the use of the three inventory costing methods.

7 Compute the proper valuation of inventory at other than cost, using the lower-of-cost-or-market and net realizable value concepts.

8 Prepare a balance sheet presentation of merchandise inventory.

9 Estimate the cost of inventory, using the retail method and the gross profit method.

10 Compute and interpret the inventory turnover ratio and the number of days' sales in inventory. ■ ■ ■

Assume that you purchased a Compact Disc (CD)/Receiver in June. You planned on attaching two pairs of speakers to the system. Initially, however, you could afford only one pair of speakers, which cost $160. In October, you purchased the second pair of speakers at a cost of $180.

Over the holidays, someone broke into your home and stole one pair of speakers. Luckily, your renters/homeowners insurance policy will cover the theft, but the insurance company needs to know the cost of the speakers that were stolen.

All of the speakers are identical. To respond to the insurance company, however, you will need to identify which pair of speakers was stolen. Was it the first pair, which cost $160? Or was it the second pair, which cost $180? Whichever assumption you make may determine the amount that you receive from the insurance company.

Merchandising businesses make similar assumptions when identical merchandise is purchased at different costs. At the end of a period, some of the merchandise will be in inventory and some will have been sold. But which costs relate to the sold merchandise and which costs relate to the merchandise in inventory? The company's assumption can involve large dollar amounts and thus can have a significant impact on the financial statements. For example, **The Home Depot, Inc.** has merchandise inventories that total almost $5.5 billion, while **Xerox Corporation's** inventories total almost $3 billion.

In this chapter, we will discuss such issues as how to determine the cost of merchandise in inventory and the cost of merchandise sold. However, we begin this chapter by discussing internal controls over merchandise inventory.

Internal Control of Inventories

The cost of inventory is a significant item in many businesses' financial statements. What do we mean by the term inventory? **Inventory** is used to indicate (1) merchandise held for sale in the normal course of business and (2) materials in the process of production or held for production. In this chapter, we focus primarily on inventory of merchandise purchased for resale.

What costs should be included in inventory? As we have illustrated in earlier chapters, the cost of merchandise is its purchase price, less any purchases discounts. These costs are usually the largest portion of the inventory cost. Merchandise inventory also includes other costs, such as transportation, import duties, and insurance against losses in transit.

Circuit City's inventory represents over 75% of its current assets and over 50% of its total assets. Circuit City's cost of merchandise sold represents over 70% of its net sales.

For companies such as **Circuit City**, good internal control over inventory must be maintained. Two primary objectives of internal control over inventory are safeguarding the inventory and properly reporting it in the financial statements. These internal controls can be either preventive or detective in nature. A preventive control is designed to prevent errors or misstatements from occurring. A detective control is designed to detect an error or misstatement after it has occurred.

Jewelry stores normally keep diamond rings, bracelets, and other items in a locked glass case. Is this a preventive or a detective control?

This is a preventive control to protect against theft (shoplifting).

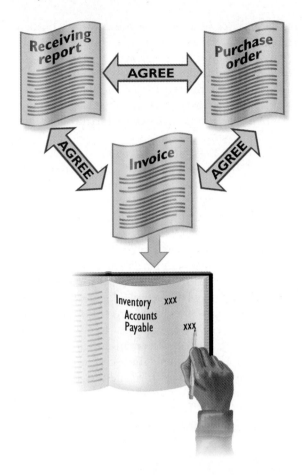

Control over inventory should begin as soon as the inventory is received. Prenumbered receiving reports should be completed by the company's receiving department in order to establish the initial accountability for the inventory. To make sure the inventory received is what was ordered, each receiving report should agree with the company's original purchase order for the merchandise. Likewise, the price at which the inventory was ordered, as shown on the purchase order, should be compared to the price at which the vendor billed the company, as shown on the vendor's invoice. After the receiving report, purchase order, and vendor's invoice have been reconciled, the company should record the inventory and related account payable in the accounting records.

Controls for safeguarding inventory include developing and using security measures to prevent inventory damage or employee theft. For example, inventory should be stored in a warehouse or other area to which access is restricted to authorized employees. The removal of merchandise from the warehouse should be controlled by using requisition forms, which should be properly authorized. The storage area should also be climate controlled to prevent damage from heat or cold. Further, when the business is not operating or is not open, the storage area should be locked.

When shopping, you may have noticed how retail stores protect inventory from customer theft. Retail stores often use such devices as two-way mirrors, cameras, and security guards. High-priced items are often displayed in locked cabinets. Retail clothing stores often place plastic alarm tags on valuable items such as leather coats. Sensors at the exit doors set off alarms if the tags have not been removed by the clerk. These controls are designed to prevent customers from shoplifting.

Using a perpetual inventory system for merchandise also provides an effective means of control over inventory. The amount of each type of merchandise is always readily available in a subsidiary **inventory ledger**. In addition, the subsidiary ledger can be an aid in maintaining inventory quantities at proper levels. Frequently comparing balances with predetermined maximum and minimum levels allows for the timely reordering of merchandise and prevents the ordering of excess inventory.

To ensure the accuracy of the amount of inventory reported in the financial statements, a merchandising business should take a **physical inventory** (i.e., count the merchandise). In a perpetual inventory system, the physical inventory is compared to the recorded inventory in order to determine the amount of shrinkage or shortage. If the inventory shrinkage is unusually large, management can investigate further and take any necessary corrective action. Knowledge that a physical inventory will be taken also helps prevent employee thefts or misuses of inventory.

How does a business "take" a physical inventory? The first step in this process is to determine the quantity of each kind of merchandise owned by the business. A common practice is to use teams of two persons. One person determines the quantity, and the other lists the quantity and description on inventory count sheets. Quantities of high-cost items are usually verified by supervisors or a second count team.

What merchandise should be included in inventory? All the merchandise *owned* by the business on the inventory date should

Sam's Club and Wal-Mart stores use a greeter at the entry of each store to welcome customers. The greeter also serves as a preventive control by asking customers not to bring in packages or other bags, which could be used for shoplifting.

Most companies take their physical inventories when their inventory levels are the lowest. For example, most retailers take their physical inventory in late January or early February, which is after the holiday selling season but before restocking for spring.

All merchandise <u>owned</u> by a business should be included in the business's inventory.

be included. For merchandise in transit, the party (the seller or the buyer) who has title to the merchandise on the inventory date is the owner. To determine who has title, it may be necessary to examine purchases and sales invoices of the last few days of the current period and the first few days of the following period.

As we discussed in an earlier chapter, shipping terms determine when title passes. When goods are purchased or sold **FOB shipping point**, title passes to the buyer when the goods are shipped. When the terms are **FOB destination**, title passes to the buyer when the goods are delivered.

To illustrate, assume that Roper Co. orders $25,000 of merchandise on December 28, 2003. The merchandise is shipped FOB shipping point by the seller on December 30 and arrives at Roper Co.'s warehouse on January 4, 2004. As a result, the merchandise is not counted by the inventory crew on December 31, the end of Roper Co.'s fiscal year. However, the $25,000 of merchandise should be included in Roper's inventory because title has passed. Roper Co. should record the merchandise in transit on December 31, debiting Merchandise Inventory and crediting Accounts Payable for $25,000.

Manufacturers sometimes ship merchandise to retailers who act as the manufacturer's agent when selling the merchandise. The manufacturer retains title until the goods are sold. Such merchandise is said to be shipped *on consignment* to the retailers. The unsold merchandise is a part of the manufacturer's (consignor's) inventory, even though the merchandise is in the hands of the retailers. The consigned merchandise should not be included in the retailer's (consignee's) inventory.

Effect of Inventory Errors on Financial Statements

objective 2

Describe the effect of inventory errors on the financial statements.

Any errors in the inventory count will affect both the balance sheet and the income statement. For example, an error in the physical inventory will misstate the ending inventory, current assets, and total assets on the balance sheet. This is because the physical inventory is the basis for recording the adjusting entry for inventory shrinkage. Also, an error in taking the physical inventory misstates the cost of goods sold, gross profit, and net income on the income statement. In addition, because net income is closed to the owner's equity at the end of the period, owner's equity will also be misstated on the balance sheet. This misstatement of owner's equity will equal the misstatement of the ending inventory, current assets, and total assets.

To illustrate, assume that in taking the physical inventory on December 31, 2003, Sapra Company incorrectly recorded its physical inventory as $115,000 instead of the correct amount of $125,000. As a result, the merchandise inventory, current assets, and total assets reported on the December 31, 2003 balance sheet would be understated by $10,000 ($125,000 − $115,000). Because the ending physical inventory is understated, the inventory shrinkage and the cost of merchandise sold will be overstated by $10,000. Thus, the gross profit and the net income for the year will be understated by $10,000. Since the net income is closed to owner's equity at the end of the period, the owner's equity on the December 31, 2003 balance sheet will also be understated by $10,000. The effects on Sapra Company's financial statements are summarized as follows:

One of the most famous inventory frauds was perpetrated by **Crazy Eddie Inc.**, which operated electronics stores. The company reported rapid gains in sales and earnings due to what the company said was store expansion, adept sales-floor techniques, and catchy commercials. However, Crazy Eddie had overstated inventory counts at one warehouse by $10 million, drafted phony inventory count sheets, and included in inventory $4 million of merchandise that, in fact, was being returned to suppliers. As a result, income was overstated. The apparent purpose of the scheme was to "artificially inflate the net worth of the company" and the value of stock owned by the store's founder, Eddie Antar, and others.

Source: Jeffrey A. Tannenbaum, "Filings by Crazy Eddie Suggest Founder Led Scheme to Inflate Company's Value," *The Wall Street Journal,* May 31, 1988, p. 28.

At the end of 2003, the physical ending inventory of Melchor Co. was overstated by $25,000. What is the effect of this error on the financial statements?

On the 2003 balance sheet, the merchandise inventory, current assets, total assets, and owner's equity are overstated by $25,000. On the income statement, the cost of merchandise sold is understated by $25,000, and the gross profit and net income are overstated by $25,000.

	Amount of Misstatement
Balance Sheet:	
Merchandise inventory understated	$(10,000)
Current assets understated	(10,000)
Total assets understated	(10,000)
Owner's equity understated	(10,000)
Income Statement:	
Cost of merchandise sold overstated	$ 10,000
Gross profit understated	(10,000)
Net income understated	(10,000)

Now assume that in the preceding example the physical inventory had been *overstated* on December 31, 2003, by $10,000. That is, Sapra Company erroneously recorded its inventory as $135,000. In this case, the effects on the balance sheet and income statement would be just the *opposite* of those indicated above.

Errors in the physical inventory are normally detected in the period after they occur. In such cases, the financial statements of the prior year must be corrected. We will discuss such corrections in a later chapter.

Inventory Cost Flow Assumptions

objective 3

Describe three inventory cost flow assumptions and how they impact the income statement and balance sheet.

A major accounting issue arises when identical units of merchandise are acquired at different unit costs during a period. In such cases, when an item is sold, it is necessary to determine its unit cost so that the proper accounting entry can be recorded. To illustrate, assume that three identical units of Item X are purchased during May, as shown below.

	Item X	Units	Cost
May 10	Purchase	1	$ 9
18	Purchase	1	13
24	Purchase	1	14
Total		3	$36
Average cost per unit			$12

Assume that one unit is sold on May 30 for $20. If this unit can be identified with a specific purchase, the **specific identification method** can be used to determine the cost of the unit sold. For example, if the unit sold was purchased on May 18, the cost assigned to the unit is $13 and the gross profit is $7 ($20 − $13). If, however, the unit sold was purchased on May 10, the cost assigned to the unit is $9 and the gross profit is $11 ($20 − $9).

The specific identification method is not practical unless each unit can be identified accurately. An automobile dealer, for example, may be able to use this method, since each automobile has a unique serial number. For many businesses, however, identical units cannot be separately identified, and a cost flow must be assumed. That is, which units have been sold and which units are still in inventory must be assumed.

The specific identification method is normally used by automobile dealerships, jewelry stores, and art galleries.

There are three common cost flow assumptions used in business. Each of these assumptions is identified with an inventory costing method, as shown below.

Cost Flow Assumption	1. Cost flow is in the order in which the costs were incurred.	2. Cost flow is in the reverse order in which the costs were incurred.	3. Cost flow is an average of the costs.
Inventory Costing Method	First-in, first-out (fifo)	Last-in, first-out (lifo)	Average cost

When the **first-in, first-out (fifo) method** is used, the ending inventory is made up of the most recent costs. When the **last-in, first-out (lifo) method** is used, the ending inventory is made up of the earliest costs. When the **average cost method** is used, the cost of the units in inventory is an average of the purchase costs.

To illustrate, we use the preceding example to prepare the income statement for May and the balance sheet as of May 31 for each of the cost flow methods. These financial statements are shown in Exhibit 1.

As you can see, the selection of an inventory costing method can have a significant impact on the financial statements. For this reason, the selection has important implications for managers and others in analyzing and interpreting the financial statements. The chart in Exhibit 2 shows the frequency with which fifo, lifo, and the average methods are used in practice.

Inventory Costing Methods Under a Perpetual Inventory System

objective 4

Compute the cost of inventory under the perpetual inventory system, using the following costing methods:

First-in, first-out

Last-in, first-out

Average cost

In a perpetual inventory system, all merchandise increases and decreases are recorded in a manner similar to the recording of increases and decreases in cash. The merchandise inventory account at the beginning of an accounting period indicates the merchandise in stock on that date. Purchases are recorded by debiting *Merchandise Inventory* and crediting *Cash* or *Accounts Payable*. On the date of each sale, the cost of the merchandise sold is recorded by debiting *Cost of Merchandise Sold* and crediting *Merchandise Inventory*.

As we illustrated in the preceding section, when identical units of an item are purchased at different unit costs during a period, a cost flow must be assumed. In such cases, the fifo, lifo, or average cost method is used. We illustrate each of these methods, using the data for Item 127B, shown at the top of page 356.

Exhibit 1 Effect of Inventory Costing Methods on Financial Statements

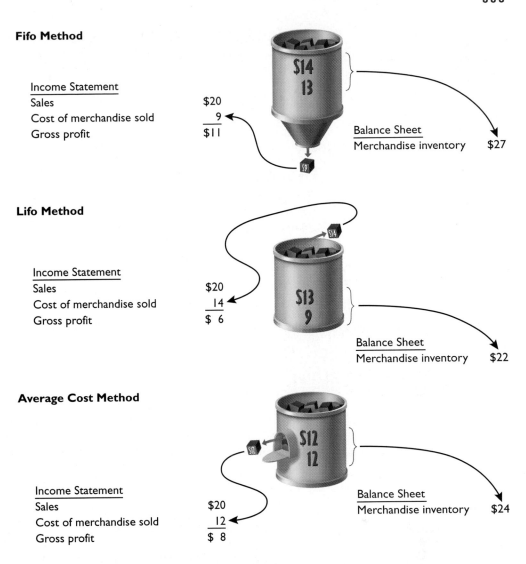

Fifo Method

Income Statement
Sales $20
Cost of merchandise sold   9
Gross profit $11

Balance Sheet
Merchandise inventory $27

Lifo Method

Income Statement
Sales $20
Cost of merchandise sold   14
Gross profit $ 6

Balance Sheet
Merchandise inventory $22

Average Cost Method

Income Statement
Sales $20
Cost of merchandise sold   12
Gross profit $ 8

Balance Sheet
Merchandise inventory $24

Exhibit 2 Inventory Costing Methods

INVENTORY COSTING METHODS

- Fifo 43%
- Lifo 34%
- Average 19%
- Other 4%

Source: *Accounting Trends & Techniques*, 53rd ed., American Institute of Certified Public Accountants, New York, 1999.

Item 127B		Units	Cost
Jan. 1	Inventory	10	$20
4	Sale	7	
10	Purchase	8	21
22	Sale	4	
28	Sale	2	
30	Purchase	10	22

Although e-tailers, such as **eToys**, **Amazon.com**, and **Furniture.com**, don't have retail stores, they still take possession of inventory in warehouses. Thus, they must account for inventory as we are illustrating in this chapter.

> Using fifo, costs are included in the merchandise sold in the order in which they were incurred.

First-In, First-Out Method

Most businesses dispose of goods in the order in which the goods are purchased. This would be especially true of perishables and goods whose styles or models often change. For example, grocery stores shelve their milk products by expiration dates. Likewise, men's and women's clothing stores display clothes by season. At the end of a season, they often have sales to clear their stores of off-season or out-of-style clothing. Thus, the fifo method is often consistent with the *physical flow* or movement of merchandise. To the extent that this is the case, the fifo method provides results that are about the same as those obtained by identifying the specific costs of each item sold and in inventory.

When the fifo method of costing inventory is used, costs are included in the cost of merchandise sold in the order in which they were incurred. To illustrate, Exhibit 3 shows the journal entries for purchases and sales and the inventory subsidiary ledger account for Item 127B. The number of units in inventory after each transaction, together with total costs and unit costs, are shown in the account. We assume that the units are sold for $30 each on account.

Exhibit 3 Entries and Perpetual Inventory Account (Fifo)

Jan. 4	Accounts Receivable	210	
	Sales		210
4	Cost of Merchandise Sold	140	
	Merchandise Inventory		140
10	Merchandise Inventory	168	
	Accounts Payable		168
22	Accounts Receivable	120	
	Sales		120
22	Cost of Merchandise Sold	81	
	Merchandise Inventory		81
28	Accounts Receivable	60	
	Sales		60
28	Cost of Merchandise Sold	42	
	Merchandise Inventory		42
30	Merchandise Inventory	220	
	Accounts Payable		220

Item 127B

	Purchases			Cost of Merchandise Sold			Inventory		
Date	Quantity	Unit Cost	Total Cost	Quantity	Unit Cost	Total Cost	Quantity	Unit Cost	Total Cost
Jan. 1							10	20	200
4				7	20	140	3	20	60
10	8	21	168				3	20	60
							8	21	168
22				3	20	60			
				1	21	21	7	21	147
28				2	21	42	5	21	105
30	10	22	220				5	21	105
							10	22	220

You should note that after the 7 units were sold on January 4, there was an inventory of 3 units at $20 each. The 8 units purchased on January 10 were acquired at a unit cost of $21, instead of $20. Therefore, the inventory after the January 10 purchase is reported on two lines, 3 units at $20 each and 8 units at $21 each. Next, note that the $81 cost of the 4 units sold on January 22 is made up of the remaining 3 units at $20 each and 1 unit at $21. At this point, 7 units are in inventory at a cost of $21 per unit. The remainder of the illustration is explained in a similar manner.

Last-In, First-Out Method

> **Using lifo, the cost of units sold is the cost of the most recent purchases.**

When the lifo method is used in a perpetual inventory system, the cost of the units sold is the cost of the most recent purchases. To illustrate, Exhibit 4 shows the journal entries for purchases and sales and the subsidiary ledger account for Item 127B, prepared on a lifo basis.

Exhibit 4 Entries and Perpetual Inventory Account (Lifo)

Jan. 4	Accounts Receivable	210	
	Sales		210
4	Cost of Merchandise Sold	140	
	Merchandise Inventory		140
10	Merchandise Inventory	168	
	Accounts Payable		168
22	Accounts Receivable	120	
	Sales		120
22	Cost of Merchandise Sold	84	
	Merchandise Inventory		84
28	Accounts Receivable	60	
	Sales		60
28	Cost of Merchandise Sold	42	
	Merchandise Inventory		42
30	Merchandise Inventory	220	
	Accounts Payable		220

Item 127B

	Purchases			Cost of Merchandise Sold			Inventory		
Date	Quantity	Unit Cost	Total Cost	Quantity	Unit Cost	Total Cost	Quantity	Unit Cost	Total Cost
Jan. 1							10	20	200
4				7	20	140	3	20	60
10	8	21	168				3	20	60
							8	21	168
22				4	21	84	3	20	60
							4	21	84
28				2	21	42	3	20	60
							2	21	42
30	10	22	220				3	20	60
							2	21	42
							10	22	220

If you compare the ledger accounts for the fifo perpetual system and the lifo perpetual system, you should discover that the accounts are the same through the January 10 purchase. Using lifo, however, the cost of the 4 units sold on January 22 is the cost of the units from the January 10 purchase ($21 per unit). The cost of the 7 units in inventory after the sale on January 22 is the cost of the 3 units remaining from the beginning inventory and the cost of the 4 units remaining from the January 10 purchase. The remainder of the lifo illustration is explained in a similar manner.

When the lifo method is used, the inventory ledger is sometimes maintained in units only. The units are converted to dollars when the financial statements are prepared at the end of the period.

The use of the lifo method was originally limited to rare situations in which the units sold were taken from the most recently acquired goods. For tax reasons, which we will discuss later, its use has greatly increased during the past few decades. Lifo is now often used even when it does not represent the physical flow of goods.

The fifo, lifo, and average **Real World** cost flow assumptions also apply to other areas of business. For example, individuals and businesses often purchase marketable securities at different costs per share. When such investments are sold, the investor must either specifically identify which shares are sold or use the fifo cost flow assumption. To illustrate, assume that a business purchased 100 shares of **Microsoft Corporation** at $85 and 100 shares at $95. If the business later sells 100 shares for $90, which shares did it sell? The business must determine the cost of the shares sold so that it can report either a gain or loss on the sale for tax purposes. In addition, it must report the gain or loss on its income statement.

Average Cost Method

When the average cost method is used in a perpetual inventory system, an average unit cost for each type of item is computed each time a purchase is made. This unit cost is then used to determine the cost of each sale until another purchase is made and a new average is computed. This averaging technique is called a *moving average*. Since the average cost method is rarely used in a perpetual inventory system, we do not illustrate it in this chapter.

Computerized Perpetual Inventory Systems

The records for a perpetual inventory system may be maintained manually. However, such a system is costly and time consuming for businesses with a large number of inventory items with many purchase and sales transactions. In most cases, the record keeping for perpetual inventory systems is computerized.

An example of using computers in maintaining perpetual inventory records for retail stores is described below.

1. The relevant details for each inventory item, such as a description, quantity, and unit size, are stored in an inventory record. The individual inventory records make up the computerized inventory file, the total of which agrees with the balance of the inventory ledger account.
2. Each time an item is purchased or returned by a customer, the inventory data are entered into the computer's inventory records and files.
3. Each time an item is sold, a salesclerk scans the item's bar code with an optical scanner. The scanner reads the magnetic code and rings up the sale on the cash register. The inventory records and files are then updated for the cost of goods sold.
4. After a physical inventory is taken, the inventory count data are entered into the computer. These data are compared with the current balances, and a listing of the overages and shortages is printed. The inventory balances are then adjusted to the quantities determined by the physical count.

Wal-Mart, Kmart, Sears, and **Real World** other retailers use bar code scanners as part of their perpetual inventory systems.

Such systems can be extended to aid managers in controlling and managing inventory quantities. For example, items that are selling fast can be reordered before the stock is depleted. Past sales patterns can be analyzed to determine when to mark down merchandise for sales and when to restock seasonal merchandise. In addition, such systems can provide managers with data for developing and fine-tuning their marketing strategies. For example, such data can be used to evaluate the effectiveness of advertising campaigns and sales promotions.

Inventory Costing Methods Under a Periodic Inventory System

objective 5

Compute the cost of inventory under the periodic inventory system, using the following costing methods:

First-in, first-out

Last-in, first-out

Average cost

When the periodic inventory system is used, only revenue is recorded each time a sale is made. No entry is made at the time of the sale to record the cost of the merchandise sold. At the end of the accounting period, a physical inventory is taken to determine the cost of the inventory and the cost of the merchandise sold.

For merchandising businesses that use the periodic system, the cost of merchandise sold during a period is reported in a separate section in the income statement. To illustrate, assume that NetSolutions opened a merchandising outlet selling personal computers and software. During 2004, NetSolutions purchased $340,000 of merchandise. If the inventory at December 31, 2004, the end of the year, is $59,700, the cost of merchandise sold during 2004 would be reported as follows:

Cost of merchandise sold:

Purchases	$340,000	
Less merchandise inventory, December 31, 2004	59,700	
Cost of merchandise sold		$280,300

To continue the illustration, assume that during 2005 NetSolutions purchased additional merchandise of $521,980. It received credit for purchases returns and allowances of $9,100, took purchases discounts of $2,525, and paid transportation costs of $17,400. The purchases returns and allowances and the purchases discounts are deducted from the total purchases to yield the *net purchases*. The transportation costs are added to the net purchases to yield the *cost of merchandise purchased*. These amounts would be reported in the cost of merchandise sold section of Net-Solutions' income statement for 2005 as follows:

Purchases			$521,980
Less: Purchases returns and allowances	$9,100		
Purchases discounts	2,525		11,625
Net purchases			$510,355
Add transportation in			17,400
Cost of merchandise purchased			$527,755

The ending inventory of NetSolutions on December 31, 2004, $59,700, becomes the beginning inventory for 2005. In the cost of merchandise sold section of the income statement for 2005, this beginning inventory is added to the cost of merchandise purchased to yield the *merchandise available for sale*. The ending inventory, which is assumed to be $62,150, is then subtracted from the merchandise available for sale to yield the cost of merchandise sold. The cost of merchandise sold during 2005 would be reported as follows:

Cost of merchandise sold:

Merchandise inventory, January 1, 2005			$ 59,700
Purchases		$521,980	
Less: Purchases returns and allowances	$9,100		
Purchases discounts	2,525	11,625	
Net purchases		$510,355	
Add transportation in		17,400	
Cost of merchandise purchased			527,755
Merchandise available for sale			$587,455
Less merchandise inventory, December 31, 2005			62,150
Cost of merchandise sold			$525,305

Like the perpetual inventory system, a cost flow assumption must be made when identical units are acquired at different unit costs during a period. In such cases, the fifo, lifo, or average cost method is used.

First-In, First-Out Method

To illustrate the use of the fifo method in a periodic inventory system, we assume the following data:

Jan. 1	Inventory:	200 units at	$ 9	$ 1,800
Mar. 10	Purchase:	300 units at	10	3,000
Sept. 21	Purchase:	400 units at	11	4,400
Nov. 18	Purchase:	100 units at	12	1,200
Available for sale during year		1,000		$10,400

What is the cost of merchandise sold if the beginning inventory is $50,000, the ending inventory is $65,000, the net purchases are $400,000, and the transportation in is $12,000?

$397,000 ($50,000 + $400,000 + $12,000 − $65,000)

The physical count on December 31 shows that 300 units have not been sold. Using the fifo method, the cost of the 700 units sold is determined as follows:

Earliest costs, Jan. 1:	200 units at	$ 9	$1,800
Next earliest costs, Mar. 10:	300 units at	10	3,000
Next earliest costs, Sept. 21:	200 units at	11	2,200
Cost of merchandise sold:	700		$7,000

Deducting the cost of merchandise sold of $7,000 from the $10,400 of merchandise available for sale yields $3,400 as the cost of the inventory at December 31. The $3,400 inventory is made up of the most recent costs incurred for this item. Exhibit 5 shows the relationship of the cost of merchandise sold during the year and the inventory at December 31.

Exhibit 5 First-In, First-Out Flow of Costs

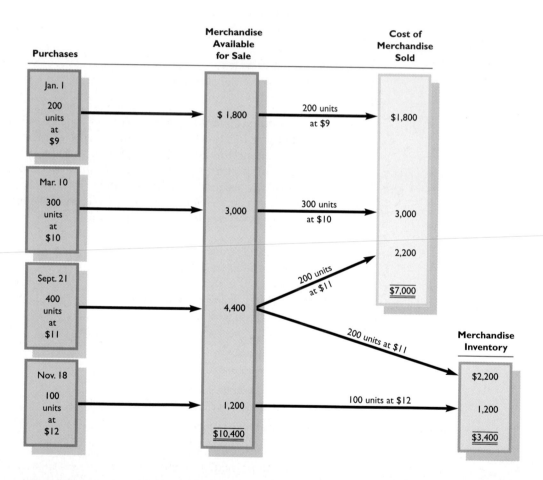

Last-In, First-Out Method

When the lifo method is used, the cost of merchandise sold is made up of the most recent costs. Based on the data in the fifo example, the cost of the 700 units of inventory is determined as follows:

Most recent costs, Nov. 18:	100 units at $12	$1,200
Next most recent costs, Sept. 21:	400 units at 11	4,400
Next most recent costs, Mar. 10:	200 units at 10	2,000
Cost of merchandise sold:	700	$7,600

Deducting the cost of merchandise sold of $7,600 from the $10,400 of merchandise available for sale yields $2,800 as the cost of the inventory at December 31. The $2,800 inventory is made up of the earliest costs incurred for this item. Exhibit 6 shows the relationship of the cost of merchandise sold during the year and the inventory at December 31.

Exhibit 6 Last-In, First-Out Flow of Costs

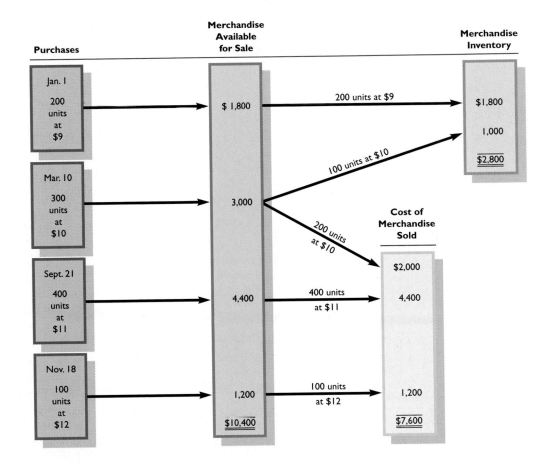

Average Cost Method

The average cost method is sometimes called the **weighted average method**. When this method is used, costs are matched against revenue according to an average of the unit costs of the goods sold. The same weighted average unit costs are used in determining the cost of the merchandise inventory at the end of the period. For businesses in which merchandise sales may be made up of various purchases of identical units, the average method approximates the physical flow of goods.

The weighted average unit cost is determined by dividing the total cost of the units of each item available for sale during the period by the related number of units of that item. Using the same cost data as in the fifo and lifo examples, the average cost of the 1,000 units, $10.40, and the cost of the 700 units, $7,280, are determined as follows:

Average unit cost: $10,400/1,000 units = $10.40
Cost of merchandise sold: 700 units at $10.40 = $7,280

Deducting the cost of merchandise sold of $7,280 from the $10,400 of merchandise available for sale yields $3,120 as the cost of the inventory at December 31.

Comparing Inventory Costing Methods

objective 6

Compare and contrast the use of the three inventory costing methods.

As we have illustrated, a different cost flow is assumed for each of the three alternative methods of costing inventories. You should note that if the cost of units had remained stable, all three methods would have yielded the same results. Since prices do change, however, the three methods will normally yield different amounts for (1) the cost of the merchandise sold for the period, (2) the gross profit (and net income) for the period, and (3) the ending inventory. Using the preceding examples for the periodic inventory system and assuming that net sales were $15,000, the following partial income statements indicate the effects of each method when prices are rising:[1]

Partial Income Statements

	First-In, First-Out	Average Cost	Last-In, First-Out
Net sales	$15,000	$15,000	$15,000
Cost of merchandise sold:			
Beginning inventory	$ 1,800	$ 1,800	$ 1,800
Purchases	8,600	8,600	8,600
Merchandise available for sale	$10,400	$10,400	$10,400
Less ending inventory	3,400	3,120	2,800
Cost of merchandise sold	7,000	7,280	7,600
Gross profit	$ 8,000	$ 7,720	$ 7,400

As shown above, the fifo method yielded the lowest amount for the cost of merchandise sold and the highest amount for gross profit (and net income). It also yielded the highest amount for the ending inventory. On the other hand, the lifo method yielded the highest amount for the cost of merchandise sold, the lowest amount for gross profit (and net income), and the lowest amount for ending inventory. The average cost method yielded results that were between those of fifo and lifo.

Use of the First-In, First-Out Method

When the fifo method is used during a period of inflation or rising prices, the earlier unit costs are lower than the more recent unit costs, as shown in the preceding fifo example. Much of the benefit of the larger amount of gross profit is lost, however, because the inventory must be replaced at ever higher prices. In fact, the balance sheet will report the ending merchandise inventory at an amount that is about the same as its current replacement cost. When the rate of inflation reaches double digits, as it did during the 1970s, the larger gross profits that result from the fifo method are often called *inventory profits* or *illusory profits*. You should note that in a period of deflation or declining prices, the effect is just the opposite.

Use of the Last-In, First-Out Method

When the lifo method is used during a period of inflation or rising prices, the results are opposite those of the other two methods. As shown in the preceding example, the lifo method will yield a higher amount of cost of merchandise sold, a lower amount of gross profit, and a lower amount of inventory at the end of the

Daimler-Chrysler's reason for changing from the fifo method to the lifo method was stated in the following footnote that accompanied its financial statements: *DaimlerChrysler changed its method of accounting from first-in, first-out (fifo) to last-in, first-out (lifo) for substantially all of its domestic productive inventories. The change to lifo was made to more accurately match current costs with current revenues.*

[1] Similar results would also occur when comparing inventory costing methods under a perpetual inventory system.

In the following note, **Sears, Roebuck and Co.** reported the difference in its inventory if fifo had been used instead of lifo: *Inventories would have been $730 million higher if valued on the first-in, first-out, or FIFO, method.*

period than the other two methods. The reason for these effects is that the cost of the most recently acquired units is about the same as the cost of their replacement. In a period of inflation, the more recent unit costs are higher than the earlier unit costs. Thus, it can be argued that the lifo method more nearly matches current costs with current revenues.

During periods of rising prices, using lifo offers an income tax savings. The income tax savings results because lifo reports the lowest amount of net income of the three methods. During the double-digit inflationary period of the 1970s, many businesses changed from fifo to lifo for the tax savings. However, the ending inventory on the balance sheet may be quite different from its current replacement cost. In such cases, the financial statements normally include a note that states the estimated difference between the lifo inventory and the inventory if fifo had been used. Again, you should note that in a period of deflation or falling price levels, the effects are just the opposite.

Use of the Average Cost Method

As you might have already reasoned, the average cost method of inventory costing is, in a sense, a compromise between fifo and lifo. The effect of price trends is averaged in determining the cost of merchandise sold and the ending inventory. For a series of purchases, the average cost will be the same, regardless of the direction of price trends. For example, a complete reversal of the sequence of unit costs presented in the preceding illustration would not affect the reported cost of merchandise sold, gross profit, or ending inventory.

BUSINESS ON STAGE

What Does It Cost to Have an Inventory?

Inventories are essential for merchandising and manufacturing businesses. Inventories are necessary in order to generate sales, and sales are necessary in order to generate profits.

The primary benefit of carrying inventory is that it provides protection against unexpected events and disruptions in business operations. For example, an unexpected strike by a supplier's employees can halt production for a manufacturer or cause lost sales for a merchandiser. Businesses that rely upon foreign suppliers are particularly affected by disruptions caused by international crises and events. Carrying inventory also allows a business to meet unexpected increases in the demand for its product. Thus, you can think of inventories as a buffer or cushion against the unexpected.

Inventory is not free, however. The costs of carrying inventory are classified as (1) holding costs, (2) ordering costs, and (3) stockout costs.

Holding costs include the costs of handling, storage, insurance, property taxes, and depreciation. In addition, holding costs for a merchandising business include losses that occur when customer preferences and tastes change unexpectedly and inventory is marked down. Finally, holding costs include the cost of funds that could be used for other purposes if they were not tied up in inventory. For example, if a business must borrow $100,000 at 10% to finance its inventories, then the interest of $10,000 per year is part of the cost of holding inventory.

Ordering costs are the costs of placing and processing orders with suppliers. Ordering costs also include the costs of investigating possible suppliers and negotiating contracts with suppliers.

Stockout costs include the costs of failing to meet customer demands— the cost of lost sales and lost profits, as well as lost customer goodwill. For a manufacturer, stockout costs include the costs of production delays and downtime, as well as the related costs of restarting production.

Inventory management involves the difficult task of balancing the benefits of carrying inventory against the related costs. In a merchandise business, inventory management is normally the responsibility of a merchandising manager or buyer. ∎

Valuation of Inventory at Other than Cost

objective 7

Compute the proper valuation of inventory at other than cost, using the lower-of-cost-or-market and net realizable value concepts.

As we indicated earlier, cost is the primary basis for valuing inventories. In some cases, however, inventory is valued at other than cost. Two such cases arise when (1) the cost of replacing items in inventory is below the recorded cost and (2) the inventory is not salable at normal sales prices. This latter case may be due to imperfections, shop wear, style changes, or other causes.

Valuation at Lower of Cost or Market

If the cost of replacing an item in inventory is lower than the original purchase cost, the **lower-of-cost-or-market (LCM) method** is used to value the inventory. *Market*, as used in *lower of cost or market*, is the cost to replace the merchandise on the inventory date. This market value is based on quantities normally purchased from the usual source of supply. In businesses where inflation is the norm, market prices rarely decline. In businesses where technology changes rapidly (e.g., microcomputers and televisions), market declines are common. The primary advantage of the lower-of-cost-or-market method is that gross profit (and net income) is reduced in the period in which the market decline occurred.

 If the cost of an item is $410, its current replacement cost is $400, and its selling price is $525, at what amount should the item be included in the inventory according to the LCM method?

$400

Dell Computer Company recorded over $39.3 million of charges (expenses) in writing down its inventory of notebook computers. The remaining inventories of computers were then sold at significantly reduced prices.

In applying the lower-of-cost-or-market method, the cost and replacement cost can be determined in one of three ways. Cost and replacement cost can be determined for (1) each item in the inventory, (2) major classes or categories of inventory, or (3) the inventory as a whole. In practice, the cost and replacement cost of each item are usually determined.

To illustrate, assume that there are 400 identical units of Item A in inventory, acquired at a unit cost of $10.25 each. If at the inventory date the item would cost $10.50 to replace, the cost price of $10.25 would be multiplied by 400 to determine the inventory value. On the other hand, if the item could be replaced at $9.50 a unit, the replacement cost of $9.50 would be used for valuation purposes.

Exhibit 7 illustrates a method of organizing inventory data and applying the lower-of-cost-or-market method to each inventory item. The amount of the market decline, $450 ($15,520 − $15,070), may be reported as a separate item on the income statement or included in the cost of merchandise sold. Regardless, net income will be reduced by the amount of the market decline.

Exhibit 7 Determining Inventory at Lower of Cost or Market

Commodity	Inventory Quantity	Unit Cost Price	Unit Market Price	Total Cost	Total Market	Total Lower of C or M
A	400	$10.25	$ 9.50	$ 4,100	$ 3,800	$ 3,800
B	120	22.50	24.10	2,700	2,892	2,700
C	600	8.00	7.75	4,800	4,650	4,650
D	280	14.00	14.75	3,920	4,130	3,920
Total				$15,520	$15,472	$15,070

Out-of-date merchandise is a major problem for many types of retailers. For example, you may have noticed the shelf-life dates of grocery products, such as milk, eggs, canned goods, and meat. Grocery stores often mark down the prices of products nearing the end of their shelf life to avoid having to dispose of the products as waste.

Valuation at Net Realizable Value

As you would expect, merchandise that is out of date, spoiled, or damaged or that can be sold only at prices below cost should be written down. Such merchandise should be valued at net realizable value. **Net realizable value** is the estimated selling price less any direct cost of disposal, such as sales commissions. For example, assume that damaged merchandise costing $1,000 can be sold for only $800, and direct selling expenses are estimated to be $150. This inventory should be valued at $650 ($800 − $150), which is its net realizable value.

Presentation of Merchandise Inventory on the Balance Sheet

objective 8

Prepare a balance sheet presentation of merchandise inventory.

Merchandise inventory is usually presented in the Current Assets section of the balance sheet, following receivables. Both the method of determining the cost of the inventory (fifo, lifo, or average) and the method of valuing the inventory (cost or the lower of cost or market) should be shown. It is not unusual for large businesses with varied activities to use different costing methods for different segments of their inventories. The details may be disclosed in parentheses on the balance sheet or in a footnote to the financial statements. Exhibit 8 shows how parentheses may be used.

General Motors Corporation uses the last-in, first-out (lifo) method to account for all U.S. inventories other than those of **Saturn Corporation** and **Hughes Electronics Corporation**. The cost of non-U.S., Saturn, and Hughes inventories is determined by using either first-in, first-out (fifo) or average cost.

Exhibit 8 Merchandise Inventory on the Balance Sheet

Afro-Arts
Balance Sheet
December 31, 2004

Assets		
Current assets:		
Cash		$ 19 4 0 0 00
Accounts receivable	$80 0 0 0 00	
Less allowance for doubtful accounts	3 0 0 0 00	77 0 0 0 00
Merchandise inventory—at lower of cost (first-in, first-out method) or market		216 3 0 0 00

A company may change its inventory costing methods for a valid reason. In such cases, the effect of the change and the reason for the change should be disclosed in the financial statements for the period in which the change occurred.

Estimating Inventory Cost

objective 9

Estimate the cost of inventory, using the retail method and the gross profit method.

It may be necessary for a business to know the amount of inventory when perpetual inventory records are not maintained and it is impractical to take a physical inventory. For example, a business that uses a periodic inventory system may need monthly income statements, but taking a physical inventory each month may be too costly. Moreover, when a disaster such as a fire has destroyed the inventory, the amount of the loss must be determined. In this case, taking a physical inventory is impossible, and even if perpetual inventory records have been kept, the accounting records may also have been destroyed. In such cases, the inventory cost can be estimated by using (1) the retail method or (2) the gross profit method.

Retail Method of Inventory Costing

The **retail inventory method** of estimating inventory cost is based on the relationship of the cost of merchandise available for sale to the retail price of the same merchandise. To use this method, the retail prices of all merchandise are maintained and totaled. Next, the inventory at retail is determined by deducting sales for the period from the retail price of the goods that were available for sale during the period. The estimated inventory cost is then computed by multiplying the inventory at retail by the ratio of cost to selling (retail) price for the merchandise available for sale, as illustrated in Exhibit 9.

Exhibit 9 Determining Inventory by the Retail Method

	Cost	Retail
Merchandise inventory, January 1	$ 19,400	$ 36,000
Purchases in January (net)	42,600	64,000
Merchandise available for sale	$ 62,000	$100,000
Ratio of cost to retail price: $\dfrac{\$62,000}{\$100,000} = 62\%$		
Sales for January (net)		70,000
Merchandise inventory, January 31, at retail		$ 30,000
Merchandise inventory, January 31, at estimated cost ($30,000 × 62%)		$ 18,600

When estimating the percent of cost to selling price, we assume that the mix of the items in the ending inventory is the same as the entire stock of merchandise available for sale. In Exhibit 9, for example, it is unlikely that the retail price of every item was made up of exactly 62% cost and 38% gross profit. We assume, however, that the weighted average of the cost percentages of the merchandise in the inventory ($30,000) is the same as in the merchandise available for sale ($100,000).

When the inventory is made up of different classes of merchandise with very different gross profit rates, the cost percentages and the inventory should be developed for each class of inventory.

One of the major advantages of the retail method is that it provides inventory figures for use in preparing monthly or quarterly statements when the periodic system is used. Department stores and similar merchandisers like to determine gross profit and operating income each month but may take a physical inventory only once a year. In addition, comparing the estimated ending inventory with the physical ending inventory, both at retail prices, will help identify inventory shortages resulting from shoplifting and other causes. Management can then take appropriate actions.

The retail method may also be used as an aid in taking a physical inventory. In this case, the items counted are recorded on the inventory sheets at their retail (selling) prices instead of their cost prices. The physical inventory at selling price is then converted to cost by applying the ratio of cost to selling (retail) price for the merchandise available for sale.

To illustrate, assume that the data in Exhibit 9 are for an entire fiscal year rather than for only January. If the physical inventory taken at the end of the year totaled $29,000, priced at retail, this amount rather than the $30,000 would be converted to cost. Thus, the inventory at cost would be $17,980 ($29,000 × 62%) instead of $18,600 ($30,000 × 62%). The $17,980 would be used for the year-end financial statements and for income tax purposes.

If the ratio of cost to retail is 70% and the ending inventory at retail is $100,000, what is the estimated ending inventory at cost?

$70,000 (70% × $100,000)

Gross Profit Method of Estimating Inventories

The **gross profit method** uses the estimated gross profit for the period to estimate the inventory at the end of the period. The gross profit is usually estimated from the actual rate for the preceding year, adjusted for any changes made in the cost and sales prices during the current period. By using the gross profit rate, the dollar amount of sales for a period can be divided into its two components: (1) gross profit and (2) cost of merchandise sold. The latter amount may then be deducted from the cost of merchandise available for sale to yield the estimated cost of the inventory.

Exhibit 10 illustrates the gross profit method for estimating a company's inventory on January 31. In this example, the inventory on January 1 is assumed to be $57,000, the net purchases during the month are $180,000, and the net sales during the month are $250,000. In addition, the historical gross profit was 30% of net sales.

Exhibit 10 Estimating Inventory by Gross Profit Method

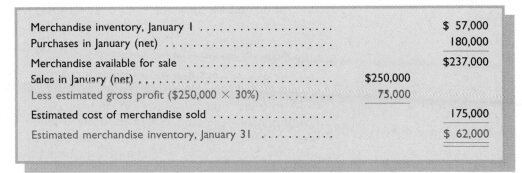

Merchandise inventory, January 1		$ 57,000
Purchases in January (net)		180,000
Merchandise available for sale		$237,000
Sales in January (net)	$250,000	
Less estimated gross profit ($250,000 × 30%)	75,000	
Estimated cost of merchandise sold		175,000
Estimated merchandise inventory, January 31		$ 62,000

What is the estimated cost of the ending inventory if the merchandise available for sale is $350,000, sales are $500,000, and the gross profit percentage is 40%?

$50,000 [$350,000 − (60% × $500,000)]

The gross profit method is useful for estimating inventories for monthly or quarterly financial statements in a periodic inventory system. It is also useful in estimating the cost of merchandise destroyed by fire or other disasters.

FINANCIAL ANALYSIS AND INTERPRETATION

objective 10

Compute and interpret the inventory turnover ratio and the number of days' sales in inventory.

A merchandising business should keep enough inventory on hand to meet the needs of its customers. A failure to do so may result in lost sales. At the same time, too much inventory reduces solvency by tying up funds that could be better used to expand or improve operations. In addition, excess inventory increases expenses such as storage, insurance, and property taxes. Finally, excess inventory increases the risk of losses due to price declines, damage, or changes in customers' buying patterns.

As with many types of financial analyses, it is possible to use more than one measure to analyze the efficiency and effectiveness by which a business manages its inventory. Two such measures are the inventory turnover and the number of days' sales in inventory.

Inventory turnover measures the relationship between the volume of goods (merchandise) sold and the amount of inventory carried during the period. It is computed as follows:

$$\text{Inventory turnover} = \frac{\text{Cost of merchandise sold}}{\text{Average inventory}}$$

The average inventory can be computed using weekly, monthly, or yearly figures. To simplify, we determine the average inventory by dividing the sum of the inventories at the beginning and end of the year by 2. As long as the amount of inventory carried throughout the year remains stable, this average will be accurate enough for our analysis.

To illustrate, the following data have been taken from recent annual reports for **SUPERVALU INC.** and **Zale Corporation**:

	SUPERVALU	Zale
Cost of merchandise sold	$15,620,127,000	$737,188,000
Inventories:		
Beginning of year	$1,115,529,000	$478,467,000
End of year	$1,067,837,000	$571,669,000
Average	$1,091,683,000	$525,068,000
Inventory turnover	14.3	1.4

The inventory turnover is 14.3 for SUPERVALU and 1.4 for Zale. Generally, the larger the inventory turnover, the more efficient and effective the management of inventory. However, differences in companies and industries are too great to allow specific statements as to what is a good inventory turnover. For example, SUPERVALU is a leading food distributor and the tenth largest food retailer in the United States. Because SUPERVALU's inventory is perishable, we would expect it to have a high inventory turnover. In contrast, Zale Corporation is the largest speciality retailer of fine jewelry in the United States. Thus, we would expect Zale to have a lower inventory turnover than SUPERVALU. As with other financial measures we have discussed, a comparison of a company's inventory turnover over time and with industry averages will provide useful insights into the management of its inventory.

The **number of days' sales in inventory** is a rough measure of the length of time it takes to acquire, sell, and replace the inventory. It is computed as follows:

$$\text{Number of days'} \atop \text{sales in inventory} = \frac{\text{Inventory, end of year}}{\text{Average daily cost of merchandise sold}}$$

The average daily cost of merchandise sold is determined by dividing the cost of merchandise sold by 365. The number of days' sales in inventory for SUPERVALU and Zale is computed as shown below.

	SUPERVALU	Zale
Average daily cost of merchandise sold:		
$15,620,127,000/365	$42,794,868	
$737,188,000/365		$2,019,693
Ending inventory	$1,067,837,000	$571,669,000
Number of days' sales in inventory	25 days	283 days

Generally, the lower the number of days' sales in inventory, the better. As with inventory turnover, we should expect differences among industries, such as those for SUPERVALU and Zale.

ENCORE

Unusual Inventories—The Strange but True

We usually think of inventory in terms of retail stores such as grocery stores, department stores, and convenience stores. In the following paragraphs, however, we describe what you might think of as unusual inventories.

- **Studio Props.** Theaters periodically have sales to clear out items from past shows. The **Studio Theatre** in Washington, D.C., included the following items in one of its sales: patio furniture from "Together, Teeth Apart"; restaurant equipment from the ultra-real diner in "The Wash"; "Goblin Market's" giant rocking horse, doll house, quilt, and toy chest; an evening gown from "Death and the Maiden"; and stuffed bunnies from "The Baltimore Waltz."

- **Movie Vehicles.** The mud-spattered 1930 Ford Model A pickup sat in a huge, heated garage. Although it looked like just an old truck, this Model A was a star of "The Untouchables." Pierre Laginess is the owner of **Antique and Classic Rental Service**, a Michigan-based business that provides used collector

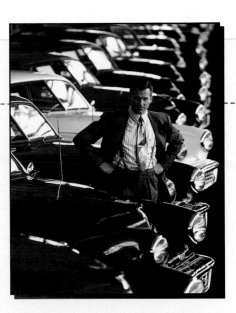

cars, trucks, and bicycles to film studios. The business began in the early 1970s when Laginess provided a stately, but menacing, 1928 Buick sedan for the original "Godfather." Since then, the business has provided vehicles for "Billy Bathgate," "Hoffa," "Lost in Yonkers," and the television series, "The Young Indiana Jones Chronicles." The business sells many of the cars that have been used in films. Laginess says producers shy away from a vehicle that has had too much exposure. Eagle-eyed fans recognize them, he said. So they go on sale.

- **Real Used Jeans.** While some jeans makers prewash, "stonewash," or even shotgun their garments to achieve the popular used look, at **Whiskey Dust** in New York City, you can get the sweaty cowboy finish the old-fashioned way: with real cowboy scent. Whiskey Dust's customers, which include rock stars Jon Bon Jovi and Eric Clapton, pay $65 for Montana Broke jeans that the store says were worn by genuine cowboys. Each well-used

pair comes with a guarantee of authenticity and a "Montana Broke Tracking Guide," explaining the origin of each rip, splotch, and frayed hem. The store's customers enthusiastically embrace its unusual inventory. "It's wonderful value. You get a lot of history." Several thousand miles away, Judy McFarlane, a 55-year-old Montana homemaker and a used jeans supplier, has little problem getting her inventory. "I don't even bother to advertise. People call me all the time." The cowboys "think it's a riot," says Ms. McFarlane.

- **Unwanted Ashes.** The merger of two funeral homes has caused an unusual inventory problem:

the unwanted, unclaimed ashes of 1,500 people who were cremated. The remains are those of eastern Washington residents who died between 1917 and 1972. A lot of remains come from the Great

Depression era of the 1930s and include doctors, lawyers, and people from all walks of life. For various reasons, relatives didn't claim the ashes. The state law provides that a funeral home can

dispose of unclaimed remains after a two-year holding period. The funeral home plans to pack the urns into caskets and bury them at a local cemetery. ■

KEY POINTS

1 Summarize and provide examples of internal control procedures that apply to inventories.

Internal control procedures for inventories include those developed to protect the inventories from damage, employee theft, and customer theft. In addition, a physical inventory count should be taken periodically to detect shortages as well as to deter employee thefts.

2 Describe the effect of inventory errors on the financial statements.

Any errors in reporting inventory based upon the physical inventory will misstate the ending inventory, current assets, total assets, and owner's equity on the balance sheet. In addition, the cost of goods sold, gross profit, and net income will be misstated on the income statement.

3 Describe three inventory cost flow assumptions and how they impact the income statement and balance sheet.

The three common cost flow assumptions used in business are the (1) first-in, first-out method, (2) last-in, first-out method, and (3) average cost method. Each method normally yields different amounts for the cost of merchandise sold and the ending merchandise inventory. Thus, the choice of a cost flow assumption directly affects the income statement and balance sheet.

4 Compute the cost of inventory under the perpetual inventory system, using the following costing methods:

First-in, first-out
Last-in, first-out
Average cost

In a perpetual inventory system, the number of units and the cost of each type of merchandise are recorded in a subsidiary inventory ledger, with a separate account for each type of merchandise. Inventory costs and the amounts charged against revenue are illustrated using the fifo and lifo methods.

5 Compute the cost of inventory under the periodic inventory system, using the following costing methods:

First-in, first-out
Last-in, first-out
Average cost

In a periodic inventory system, a physical inventory is taken to determine the cost of the inventory and the cost of merchandise sold. Inventory costs and the amounts charged against revenue are illustrated using fifo, lifo, and average cost methods.

6 Compare and contrast the use of the three inventory costing methods.

The three inventory costing methods will normally yield different amounts for (1) the ending inventory, (2) the cost of the

merchandise sold for the period, and (3) the gross profit (and net income) for the period. During periods of inflation, the fifo method yields the lowest amount for the cost of merchandise sold, the highest amount for gross profit (and net income), and the highest amount for the ending inventory. The lifo method yields the opposite results. During periods of deflation, the preceding effects are reversed. The average cost method yields results that are between those of fifo and lifo.

7 Compute the proper valuation of inventory at other than cost, using the lower-of-cost-or-market and net realizable value concepts.

If the market price of an item of inventory is lower than its cost, the lower market price is used to compute the value of the item. Market price is the cost to replace the merchandise on the inventory date. It is possible to apply the lower of cost or market to each item in the inventory, to major classes or categories, or to the inventory as a whole.

Merchandise that can be sold only at prices below cost should be valued at net realizable value, which is the estimated selling price less any direct cost of disposal.

8 Prepare a balance sheet presentation of merchandise inventory.

Merchandise inventory is usually presented in the Current Assets section of the balance sheet, following receivables. Both the method of determining the cost of the inventory (fifo, lifo, or average) and the method of valuing the inventory (cost or the lower of cost or market) should be shown.

9 Estimate the cost of inventory, using the retail method and the gross profit method.

In using the retail method to estimate inventory, the retail prices of all merchandise acquired are accumulated. The inventory at retail is determined by deducting

sales for the period from the retail price of the goods that were available for sale during the period. The inventory at retail is then converted to cost on the basis of the ratio of cost to selling (retail) price for the merchandise available for sale.

In using the gross profit method to estimate inventory, the estimated gross profit is deducted from the sales to determine the estimated cost of merchandise sold. This amount is then deducted from the cost of merchandise available for sale to determine the estimated ending inventory.

10 Compute and interpret the inventory turnover ratio and the number of days' sales in inventory.

The inventory turnover ratio, computed as the cost of merchandise sold divided by the average inventory, measures the relationship between the volume of goods (merchandise) sold and the amount of inventory carried during the period. The number of days' sales in inventory, computed as the ending inventory divided by the average daily cost of merchandise sold, measures the length of time it takes to acquire, sell, and replace the inventory.

ILLUSTRATIVE PROBLEM

Stewart Co.'s beginning inventory and purchases during the year ended December 31, 2004, were as follows:

		Units	Unit Cost	Total Cost
January 1	Inventory	1,000	$50.00	$ 50,000
March 10	Purchase	1,200	52.50	63,000
June 25	Sold 800 units			
August 30	Purchase	800	55.00	44,000
October 5	Sold 1,500 units			
November 26	Purchase	2,000	56.00	112,000
December 31	Sold 1,000 units			
Total		5,000		$269,000

Instructions

1. Determine the cost of inventory on December 31, 2004, using the perpetual inventory system and each of the following inventory costing methods:
   a. first-in, first-out
   b. last-in, first-out
2. Determine the cost of inventory on December 31, 2004, using the periodic inventory system and each of the following inventory costing methods:
   a. first-in, first-out
   b. last-in, first-out
   c. average cost
3. Assume that during the fiscal year ended December 31, 2004, sales were $290,000 and the estimated gross profit rate was 40%. Estimate the ending inventory at December 31, 2004, using the gross profit method.

Solution

1. a. First-in, first-out method: $95,200

Date	Purchases			Cost of Merchandise Sold			Inventory		
	Quantity	Unit Cost	Total Cost	Quantity	Unit Cost	Total Cost	Quantity	Unit Cost	Total Cost
Jan. 1 (2004)							1,000	50.00	50,000
Mar. 10	1,200	52.50	63,000				1,000	50.00	50,000
							1,200	52.50	63,000
June 25				800	50.00	40,000	200	50.00	10,000
							1,200	52.50	63,000
Aug. 30	800	55.00	44,000				200	50.00	10,000
							1,200	52.50	63,000
							800	55.00	44,000
Oct. 5				200	50.00	10,000	700	55.00	38,500
				1,200	52.50	63,000			
				100	55.00	5,500			
Nov. 26	2,000	56.00	112,000				700	55.00	38,500
							2,000	56.00	112,000
Dec. 31				700	55.00	38,500	1,700	56.00	95,200
				300	56.00	16,800			

b.   Last-in, first-out method: $91,000 ($35,000 + $56,000)

Date	Purchases			Cost of Merchandise Sold			Inventory		
	Quantity	Unit Cost	Total Cost	Quantity	Unit Cost	Total Cost	Quantity	Unit Cost	Total Cost
Jan. 1 (2004)							1,000	50.00	50,000
Mar. 10	1,200	52.50	63,000				1,000	50.00	50,000
							1,200	52.50	63,000
June 25				800	52.50	42,000	1,000	50.00	50,000
							400	52.50	21,000
Aug. 30	800	55.00	44,000				1,000	50.00	50,000
							400	52.50	21,000
							800	55.00	44,000
Oct. 5				800	55.00	44,000	700	50.00	35,000
				400	52.50	21,000			
				300	50.00	15,000			
Nov. 26	2,000	56.00	112,000				700	50.00	35,000
							2,000	56.00	112,000
Dec. 31				1,000	56.00	56,000	700	50.00	35,000
							1,000	56.00	56,000

2. a.   First-in, first-out method:
   1,700 units at $56 = $95,200

   b.   Last-in, first-out method:

1,000 units at $50.00	$50,000
700 units at $52.50	36,750
1,700 units	$86,750

   c.   Average cost method:

   Average cost per unit: $269,000 ÷ 5,000 units = $53.80
   Inventory, December 31, 2004:   1,700 units at $53.80 = $91,460

3.

Merchandise inventory, January 1, 2004		$ 50,000
Purchases (net)		219,000
Merchandise available for sale		$269,000
Sales (net)	$290,000	
Less estimated gross profit ($290,000 × 40%)	116,000	
Estimated cost of merchandise sold		174,000
Estimated merchandise inventory, December 31, 2004		$ 95,000

SELF-EXAMINATION QUESTIONS   Answers at End of Chapter

Matching
Match each of the following statements with its proper term. Some terms may not be used.

A. average cost method	__ 1. A detailed listing of merchandise on hand.
B. first-in, first-out (fifo) method	__ 2. A method of inventory costing based on the assumption that the costs of merchandise sold should be charged against revenue in the order in which the costs were incurred.
C. gross profit method	__ 3. A method of inventory costing based on the assumption that the most recent merchandise inventory costs should be charged against revenue.
D. inventory turnover	
E. last-in, first-out (lifo) method	__ 4. The method of inventory costing that is based upon the assumption that costs should be charged against revenue by using the weighted average unit cost of the items sold.
F. lower-of-cost-or-market (LCM) method	__ 5. A method of valuing inventory that reports the inventory at the lower of its cost or current market value (replacement cost).
G. net realizable value	__ 6. The estimated selling price of an item of inventory less any direct costs of disposal, such as sales commissions.
H. number of days' sales in inventory	__ 7. A method of estimating inventory cost that is based on the relationship of the cost of merchandise available for sale to the retail price of the same merchandise.
I. physical inventory	__ 8. A method of estimating inventory cost that is based on the relationship of gross profit to sales.
J. retail inventory method	__ 9. A ratio that measures the relationship between the volume of goods (merchandise) sold and the amount of inventory carried during the period.
	__ 10. A measure of the length of time it takes to acquire, sell, and replace the inventory.

Multiple Choice

1. If the inventory shrinkage at the end of the year is overstated by $7,500, the error will cause an:
   A. understatement of cost of merchandise sold for the year by $7,500.
   B. overstatement of gross profit for the year by $7,500.
   C. overstatement of merchandise inventory for the year by $7,500.
   D. understatement of net income for the year by $7,500.

2. The inventory costing method that is based on the assumption that costs should be charged against revenue in the order in which they were incurred is:
   A. fifo   C. average cost
   B. lifo   D. perpetual inventory

3. The following units of a particular item were purchased and sold during the period:

Beginning inventory	40 units at $20
First purchase	50 units at $21
Second purchase	50 units at $22
First sale	110 units
Third purchase	50 units at $23
Second sale	45 units

   What is the cost of the 35 units on hand at the end of the period as determined under the perpetual inventory system by the lifo costing method?
   A. $715   C. $700
   B. $705   D. $805

4. The following units of a particular item were available for sale during the period:

Beginning inventory	40 units at $20
First purchase	50 units at $21
Second purchase	50 units at $22
Third purchase	50 units at $23

What is the unit cost of the 35 units on hand at the end of the period as determined under the periodic inventory system by the fifo costing method?

A. $20 C. $22
B. $21 D. $23

5. If merchandise inventory is being valued at cost and the price level is steadily rising, the method of costing that will yield the highest net income is:

A. lifo C. average
B. fifo D. periodic

CLASS DISCUSSION QUESTIONS

1. What security measures may be used by retailers to protect merchandise inventory from customer theft?

2. Which inventory system provides the more effective means of controlling inventories (perpetual or periodic)? Why?

3. Before inventory purchases are recorded, the receiving report should be reconciled to what documents?

4. What document should be presented by an employee requesting inventory items to be released from the company's warehouse?

5. Why is it important to periodically take a physical inventory if the perpetual system is used?

6. The inventory shrinkage at the end of the year was understated by $15,000. (a) Did the error cause an overstatement or an understatement of the gross profit for the year? (b) Which items on the balance sheet at the end of the year were overstated or understated as a result of the error?

7. Bray Co. sold merchandise to Mansfield Company on December 31, FOB shipping point. If the merchandise is in transit on December 31, the end of the fiscal year, which company would report it in its financial statements? Explain.

8. A manufacturer shipped merchandise to a retailer on a consignment basis. If the merchandise is unsold at the end of the period, in whose inventory should the merchandise be included?

9. Do the terms *fifo* and *lifo* refer to techniques used in determining quantities of the various classes of merchandise on hand? Explain.

10. Does the term *last-in* in the lifo method mean that the items in the inventory are assumed to be the most recent (last) acquisitions? Explain.

11. If merchandise inventory is being valued at cost and the price level is steadily rising, which of the three methods of costing—fifo, lifo, or average cost—will yield (a) the highest inventory cost, (b) the lowest inventory cost, (c) the highest gross profit, (d) the lowest gross profit?

12. Which of the three methods of inventory costing—fifo, lifo, or average cost—will in general yield an inventory cost most nearly approximating current replacement cost?

13. If inventory is being valued at cost and the price level is steadily rising, which of the three methods of costing—fifo, lifo, or average cost—will yield the lowest annual income tax expense? Explain.

14. Can a company change its method of costing inventory? Explain.

15. Because of imperfections, an item of merchandise cannot be sold at its normal selling price. How should this item be valued for financial statement purposes?

16. How is the method of determining the cost of the inventory and the method of valuing it disclosed in the financial statements?

17. What uses can be made of the estimate of the cost of inventory determined by the gross profit method?

EXERCISES

Exercise 9–1
Internal control of inventories
Objective 1

Langley Hardware Store currently uses a periodic inventory system. Kevin White, the owner, is considering the purchase of a computer system that would make it feasible to switch to a perpetual inventory system.

Kevin is unhappy with the periodic inventory system because it does not provide timely information on inventory levels. Kevin has noticed on several occasions that the store runs out of good-selling items, while too many poor-selling items are on hand.

Kevin is also concerned about lost sales while a physical inventory is being taken. Langley Hardware currently takes a physical inventory twice a year. To minimize distractions, the store is closed on the day inventory is taken. Kevin believes that closing the store is the only way to get an accurate inventory count.

Will switching to a perpetual inventory system strengthen Langley Hardware's control over inventory items? Will switching to a perpetual inventory system eliminate the need for a physical inventory count? Explain.

Exercise 9–2
Internal control of inventories
Objective 1

Flyer's Luggage Shop is a small retail establishment located in a large shopping mall. This shop has implemented the following procedures regarding inventory items:

a. Since the display area of the store is limited, only a sample of each piece of luggage is kept on the selling floor. Whenever a customer selects a piece of luggage, the salesclerk gets the appropriate piece from the store's stockroom. Since all salesclerks need access to the stockroom, it is not locked. The stockroom is adjacent to the break room used by all mall employees.
b. Since the shop carries mostly high-quality, designer luggage, all inventory items are tagged with a control device that activates an alarm if a tagged item is removed from the store.
c. Whenever Flyer's receives a shipment of new inventory, the items are taken directly to the stockroom. Flyer's accountant uses the vendor's invoice to record the amount of inventory received.

State whether each of these procedures is appropriate or inappropriate, considering the principles of internal control. If it is inappropriate, state which internal control procedure is violated.

Exercise 9–3
Identifying items to be included in inventory
Objective 1

Mainstreet Co., which is located in Mason City, Iowa, has identified the following items for possible inclusion in its December 31, 2002 year-end inventory.

a. Mainstreet has segregated $6,570 of merchandise ordered by one of its customers for shipment on January 3, 2003.
b. Mainstreet has in its warehouse $30,500 of merchandise on consignment from Mahogany Co.
c. Merchandise Mainstreet shipped FOB shipping point on December 31, 2002, was picked up by the freight company at 11:50 p.m.
d. Merchandise Mainstreet shipped to a customer FOB shipping point was picked up by the freight company on December 26, 2002, but had still not arrived at its destination as of December 31, 2002.

e. Mainstreet has $15,750 of merchandise on hand, which was sold to customers earlier in the year, but which has been returned by customers to Mainstreet for various warranty repairs.
f. Mainstreet has sent $48,000 of merchandise to various retailers on a consignment basis.
g. On December 31, 2002, Mainstreet received $11,050 of merchandise that had been returned by customers because the wrong merchandise had been shipped. The replacement order is to be shipped overnight on January 3, 2003.
h. On December 27, 2002, Mainstreet ordered $18,000 of merchandise from a supplier in Des Moines. The merchandise was shipped FOB Des Moines on December 30, 2002, but had not been received by December 31, 2002.
i. On December 21, 2002, Mainstreet ordered $58,000 of merchandise, FOB Mason City. The merchandise was shipped from the supplier on December 28, 2002, but had not been received by December 31, 2002.

Indicate which items should be included (I) and which should be excluded (E) from the inventory.

Exercise 9–4
Effect of errors in physical inventory

Objective 2

Whitewater Co. sells canoes, kayaks, whitewater rafts, and other boating supplies. During the taking of its physical inventory on December 31, 2003, Whitewater incorrectly counted its inventory as $112,800 instead of the correct amount of $121,500.

a. State the effect of the error on the December 31, 2003 balance sheet of Whitewater.
b. State the effect of the error on the income statement of Whitewater for the year ended December 31, 2003.

Exercise 9–5
Effect of errors in physical inventory

Objective 2

Dean's Motorcycle Shop sells motorcycles, jet skis, and other related supplies and accessories. During the taking of its physical inventory on December 31, 2003, Dean's Motorcycle Shop incorrectly counted its inventory as $179,600 instead of the correct amount of $153,750.

a. State the effect of the error on the December 31, 2003 balance sheet of Dean's Motorcycle Shop.
b. State the effect of the error on the income statement of Dean's Motorcycle Shop for the year ended December 31, 2003.

Exercise 9–6
Error in inventory shrinkage

Objective 2

During 2003, the accountant discovered that the physical inventory at the end of 2002 had been understated by $20,500. Instead of correcting the error, however, the accountant assumed that a $20,500 overstatement of the physical inventory in 2003 would balance out the error.

➤ Are there any flaws in the accountant's assumption? Explain.

Exercise 9–7
Perpetual inventory using fifo

Objectives 3, 4

✓ Inventory balance, June 30, $806

Beginning inventory, purchases, and sales data for portable CD players are as follows:

June	1	Inventory	25 units at $41
	6	Sale	16 units
	13	Purchase	18 units at $42
	18	Sale	12 units
	22	Sale	4 units
	30	Purchase	8 units at $43

The business maintains a perpetual inventory system, costing by the first-in, first-out method. Determine the cost of the merchandise sold for each sale and the inventory balance after each sale, presenting the data in the form illustrated in Exhibit 3.

Exercise 9–8
Perpetual inventory using lifo
Objectives 3, 4

✓ Inventory balance, June 30, $797

Assume that the business in Exercise 9–7 maintains a perpetual inventory system, costing by the last-in, first-out method. Determine the cost of merchandise sold for each sale and the inventory balance after each sale, presenting the data in the form illustrated in Exhibit 4.

Exercise 9–9
Perpetual inventory using lifo
Objectives 3, 4

✓ Inventory balance, October 31, $1,680

Beginning inventory, purchases, and sales data for cell phones for October are as follows:

Inventory		Purchases		Sales	
Oct. 1	30 units at $110	Oct. 6	10 units at $120	Oct. 11	9 units
		21	15 units at $130	16	24 units
				31	8 units

Assuming that the perpetual inventory system is used, costing by the lifo method, determine the cost of the inventory balance at October 31, presenting data in the form illustrated in Exhibit 4.

Exercise 9–10
Perpetual inventory using fifo
Objectives 3, 4

✓ Inventory balance, October 31, $1,820

Assume that the business in Exercise 9–9 maintains a perpetual inventory system, costing by the first-in, first-out method. Determine the cost of the inventory balance at October 31, presenting the data in the form illustrated in Exhibit 3.

Exercise 9–11
Fifo, lifo costs under perpetual inventory system
Objectives 3, 4

✓ a. $800

The following units of a particular item were available for sale during the year:

Beginning inventory	19 units at $46
Sale	15 units at $90
First purchase	32 units at $48
Sale	25 units at $90
Second purchase	40 units at $50
Sale	35 units at $90

The firm uses the perpetual inventory system, and there are 16 units of the item on hand at the end of the year. What is the total cost of the ending inventory according to (a) fifo, (b) lifo?

Exercise 9–12
Identify items missing in determining cost of merchandise sold
Objective 5

For (a) through (d), identify the items designated by "X."

a. Purchases − (X + X) = Net purchases.
b. Net purchases + X = Cost of merchandise purchased.
c. Merchandise inventory (beginning) + Cost of merchandise purchased = X.
d. Merchandise available for sale − X = Cost of merchandise sold.

Exercise 9–13
Cost of merchandise sold and related items
Objective 5

SPREADSHEET

The following data were extracted from the accounting records of My Computers Company for the year ended November 30, 2003:

Merchandise Inventory, December 1, 2002	$ 75,750
Merchandise Inventory, November 30, 2003	88,200
Purchases	625,000
Purchases Returns and Allowances	14,500
Purchases Discounts	12,950
Sales	870,625
Transportation In	6,950

a. Prepare the cost of merchandise sold section of the income statement for the year ended November 30, 2003, using the periodic inventory method.

b. Determine the gross profit to be reported on the income statement for the year ended November 30, 2003.

Exercise 9–14
Cost of merchandise sold

Objective 5

How many errors can you find in the following schedule of cost of merchandise sold for the current year ended December 31, 2002?

Cost of merchandise sold:

Merchandise inventory, December 31, 2002			$ 75,000
Purchases		$500,000	
Plus: Purchases returns and allowances	$12,500		
Purchases discounts	6,500	19,000	
Gross purchases		$519,000	
Less transportation in		12,400	
Cost of merchandise purchased			506,600
Merchandise available for sale			$581,600
Less merchandise inventory, January 1, 2002			81,300
Cost of merchandise sold			$500,300

Exercise 9–15
Periodic inventory by three methods

Objectives 3, 5

The units of an item available for sale during the year were as follows:

Jan.	1	Inventory	25 units at $24
Feb.	4	Purchase	10 units at $25
July	20	Purchase	30 units at $28
Dec.	30	Purchase	35 units at $30

There are 40 units of the item in the physical inventory at December 31. The periodic inventory system is used. Determine the inventory cost by (a) the first-in, first-out method, (b) the last-in, first-out method, and (c) the average cost method.

Exercise 9–16
Periodic inventory by three methods; cost of merchandise sold

Objectives 3, 5

SPREADSHEET

The units of an item available for sale during the year were as follows:

Jan.	1	Inventory	21 units at $60
Mar.	4	Purchase	29 units at $65
Aug.	7	Purchase	10 units at $68
Nov.	15	Purchase	15 units at $70

There are 18 units of the item in the physical inventory at December 31. The periodic inventory system is used. Determine the inventory cost and the cost of merchandise sold by three methods, presenting your answers in the following form:

	Cost	
Inventory Method	**Merchandise Inventory**	**Merchandise Sold**
a. First-in, first-out	$	$
b. Last-in, first-out		
c. Average cost		

Exercise 9–17
Lower-of-cost-or-market inventory

Objective 7

On the basis of the following data, determine the value of the inventory at the lower of cost or market. Assemble the data in the form illustrated in Exhibit 7.

SPREADSHEET

Commodity	Inventory Quantity	Unit Cost Price	Unit Market Price
X3	9	$300	$320
Y10	16	110	115
A19	12	275	260
J2	15	51	45
J8	25	96	100

✓ LCM: $10,655

Exercise 9–18
Merchandise inventory on the balance sheet

Objective 8

Based on the data in Exercise 9–17 and assuming that cost was determined by the fifo method, show how the merchandise inventory would appear on the balance sheet.

Exercise 9–19
Retail inventory method

Objective 9

A business using the retail method of inventory costing determines that merchandise inventory at retail is $625,750. If the ratio of cost to retail price is 60%, what is the amount of inventory to be reported on the financial statements?

Exercise 9–20
Retail inventory method

Objective 9

SPREADSHEET

✓ Inventory, April 30: $214,210

On the basis of the following data, estimate the cost of the merchandise inventory at April 30 by the retail method:

		Cost	Retail
April 1	Merchandise inventory	$167,710	$ 270,500
April 1–30	Purchases (net)	651,000	1,050,000
April 1–30	Sales (net)		975,000

Exercise 9–21
Gross profit inventory method

Objective 9

The merchandise inventory was destroyed by fire on March 20. The following data were obtained from the accounting records:

Jan. 1	Merchandise inventory	$ 150,000
Jan. 1–Mar. 20	Purchases (net)	900,000
	Sales (net)	1,100,000
	Estimated gross profit rate	40%

a. Estimate the cost of the merchandise destroyed.
b. Briefly describe the situations in which the gross profit method is useful.

Exercise 9–22
Inventory turnover

Objective 10

Real World

The following data were taken from recent annual reports of **Gateway 2000 Inc.**, a vendor of personal computers and related products, and **American Greetings Corporation**, a manufacturer and distributor of greeting cards and related products:

	Gateway 2000	American Greetings
Cost of goods sold	$5,921,651,000	$757,080,000
Inventory, end of year	167,924,000	251,289,000
Inventory, beginning of the year	152,531,000	271,205,000

a. Determine the inventory turnover for Gateway 2000 and American Greetings.
b. Would you expect American Greetings' inventory turnover to be higher or lower than Gateway's? Why?

Exercise 9–23
Inventory turnover and number of days' sales in inventory

Objective 10

The financial statements for **Cisco Systems, Inc.,** are presented in Appendix G at the end of the text. Cisco Systems had inventories of $362,000,000 at July 25, 1998.

a. For the years ended July 29, 2000 and July 31, 1999, determine: (1) the inventory turnover, and (2) the number of days' sales in inventory.

b. ✏️━► What conclusions can be drawn from these analyses concerning Cisco Systems' efficiency in managing inventory?

PROBLEMS SERIES A

Problem 9–1A
Fifo perpetual inventory

Objectives 3, 4

SPREADSHEET

✓ 3. $7,480

The beginning inventory of floor mats at Eagle Office Supplies and data on purchases and sales for a three-month period are as follows:

Date		Transaction	Number of Units	Per Unit	Total
Sept.	1	Inventory	250	$ 6.10	$1,525
	8	Purchase	750	6.20	4,650
	20	Sale	450	9.00	4,050
	30	Sale	350	9.00	3,150
Oct.	8	Sale	50	9.10	455
	10	Purchase	500	6.10	3,050
	27	Sale	350	9.20	3,220
	31	Sale	200	9.15	1,830
Nov.	5	Purchase	750	6.00	4,500
	13	Sale	350	10.00	3,500
	23	Purchase	400	5.95	2,380
	30	Sale	500	10.00	5,000

Instructions

1. Record the inventory, purchases, and cost of merchandise sold data in a perpetual inventory record similar to the one illustrated in Exhibit 3, using the first-in, first-out method.
2. Determine the total sales and the total cost of floor mats sold for the period. Journalize the entries in the sales and cost of merchandise sold accounts. Assume that all sales were on account.
3. Determine the gross profit from sales for the period.
4. Determine the ending inventory cost.

Problem 9–2A
Lifo perpetual inventory

Objectives 3, 4

✓ 2. Gross profit, $7,510

The beginning inventory of floor mats at Eagle Office Supplies and data on purchases and sales for a three-month period are shown in Problem 9–1A.

Instructions

1. Record the inventory, purchases, and cost of merchandise sold data in a perpetual inventory record similar to the one illustrated in Exhibit 4, using the last-in, first-out method.
2. Determine the total sales, the total cost of floor mats sold, and the gross profit from sales for the period.
3. Determine the ending inventory cost.

Problem 9–3A
Periodic inventory by three methods

Objectives 3, 5

✓ 1. $7,875

Sixpack Appliances uses the periodic inventory system. Details regarding the inventory of appliances at July 1, 2002, purchases invoices during the year, and the inventory count at June 30, 2003, are summarized as follows:

Model	Inventory, July 1	Purchases Invoices			Inventory Count, June 30
		1st	2nd	3rd	
A103	7 at $242	6 at $250	5 at $260	10 at $259	9
C743	6 at 80	5 at 82	8 at 89	8 at 90	7
F1010	2 at 108	2 at 110	3 at 128	3 at 130	3
H142	8 at 88	4 at 79	3 at 85	6 at 92	8
P813	2 at 250	2 at 260	4 at 271	4 at 272	5
Q661	5 at 160	4 at 170	4 at 175	7 at 180	8
W490	—	4 at 150	4 at 200	4 at 202	5

Instructions

1. Determine the cost of the inventory on June 30, 2003, by the first-in, first-out method. Present data in columnar form, using the following headings:

Model	Quantity	Unit Cost	Total Cost

    If the inventory of a particular model comprises one entire purchase plus a portion of another purchase acquired at a different unit cost, use a separate line for each purchase.
2. Determine the cost of the inventory on June 30, 2003, by the last-in, first-out method, following the procedures indicated in (1).
3. Determine the cost of the inventory on June 30, 2003, by the average cost method, using the columnar headings indicated in (1).
4. ✏️➤ Discuss which method (fifo or lifo) would be preferred for income tax purposes in periods of (a) rising prices and (b) declining prices.

If the working papers correlating with this textbook are not used, omit Problem 9–4A.

Problem 9–4A
Lower-of-cost-or-market inventory

Objective 7

✓ Total LCM, $38,835

Data on the physical inventory of Minish Company as of December 31, 2003, are presented in the working papers. The quantity of each commodity on hand has been determined and recorded on the inventory sheet. Unit market prices have also been determined as of December 31 and recorded on the sheet. The inventory is to be determined at cost and also at the lower of cost or market, using the first-in, first-out method. Quantity and cost data from the last purchases invoice of the year and the next-to-the-last purchases invoice are summarized as follows:

Description	Last Purchases Invoice		Next-to-the-Last Purchases Invoice	
	Quantity Purchased	Unit Cost	Quantity Purchased	Unit Cost
A10	25	$ 60	30	$ 58
B23	30	208	20	205
D82	10	145	25	142
E34	150	25	100	24
F17	10	565	10	560
H99	100	15	100	14
K41	10	387	5	384
M21	500	6	500	6
R72	80	19	50	18
T15	5	255	4	260
BD1	100	20	75	19
MS3	7	701	6	699

Instructions

Record the appropriate unit costs on the inventory sheet, and complete the pricing of the inventory. When there are two different unit costs applicable to an item, proceed as follows:

1. Draw a line through the quantity, and insert the quantity and unit cost of the last purchase.
2. On the following line, insert the quantity and unit cost of the next-to-the-last purchase.
3. Total the cost and market columns and insert the lower of the two totals in the Lower of C or M column. The first item on the inventory sheet has been completed as an example.

Problem 9–5A

Retail method; gross profit method

Objective 9

✓ 1. $98,070

✓ 2. a. $163,750

Selected data on merchandise inventory, purchases, and sales for Typhoon Co. and Wheaton Co. are as follows:

	Cost	Retail
Typhoon Co.		
Merchandise inventory, August 1	$ 90,650	$ 129,500
Transactions during August:		
Purchases (net)	735,420	1,050,600
Sales		1,050,000
Sales returns and allowances		10,000
Wheaton Co.		
Merchandise inventory, April 1	$ 147,800	
Transactions during April and May:		
Purchases (net)	1,047,950	
Sales	1,750,000	
Sales returns and allowances	30,000	
Estimated gross profit rate	40%	

Instructions

1. Determine the estimated cost of the merchandise inventory of Typhoon Co. on August 31 by the retail method, presenting details of the computations.
2. a. Estimate the cost of the merchandise inventory of Wheaton Co. on May 31 by the gross profit method, presenting details of the computations.
   b. Assume that Wheaton Co. took a physical inventory on May 31 and discovered that $148,300 of merchandise was on hand. What was the estimated loss of inventory due to theft or damage during April and May?

PROBLEMS SERIES B

Problem 9–1B

Fifo perpetual inventory

Objectives 3, 4

SPREADSHEET

✓ 3. $239,800

The beginning inventory of drift boats at River's Edge Co. and data on purchases and sales for a three-month period are as follows:

Date		Transaction	Number of Units	Per Unit	Total
March	1	Inventory	15	$2,200	$ 33,000
	8	Purchase	25	2,250	56,250
	11	Sale	10	5,000	50,000
	22	Sale	13	5,000	65,000
April	3	Purchase	15	2,300	34,500
	10	Sale	10	5,100	51,000
	21	Sale	5	5,100	25,500
	30	Purchase	25	2,350	58,750
May	5	Sale	20	5,150	103,000
	13	Sale	12	5,150	61,800
	21	Purchase	20	2,400	48,000
	28	Sale	15	5,200	78,000

Instructions

1. Record the inventory, purchases, and cost of merchandise sold data in a perpetual inventory record similar to the one illustrated in Exhibit 3, using the first-in, first-out method.
2. Determine the total sales and the total cost of drift boats sold for the period. Journalize the entries in the sales and cost of merchandise sold accounts. Assume that all sales were on account.
3. Determine the gross profit from sales of drift boats for the period.
4. Determine the ending inventory cost.

Problem 9–2B

Lifo perpetual inventory

Objectives 3, 4

✓ 2. Gross profit, $237,800

The beginning inventory of drift boats and data on purchases and sales for a three-month period are shown in Problem 9–1B.

Instructions

1. Record the inventory, purchases, and cost of merchandise sold data in a perpetual inventory record similar to the one illustrated in Exhibit 4, using the last-in, first-out method.
2. Determine the total sales, the total cost of drift boats sold, and the gross profit from sales for the period.
3. Determine the ending inventory cost.

Problem 9–3B

Periodic inventory by three methods

Objectives 3, 5

✓ 1. $11,580

Yellowstone Appliances uses the periodic inventory system. Details regarding the inventory of appliances at January 1, 2003, purchases invoices during the year, and the inventory count at December 31, 2003, are summarized as follows:

Model	Inventory, January 1	Purchases Invoices 1st	2nd	3rd	Inventory Count, December 31
109A	4 at $140	6 at $144	8 at $148	7 at $156	5
110B	3 at 208	3 at 212	5 at 213	4 at 225	5
127X	2 at 520	2 at 527	2 at 530	2 at 535	3
143T	6 at 520	8 at 531	4 at 549	6 at 542	7
144Z	9 at 213	7 at 215	6 at 222	6 at 225	10
160M	6 at 305	3 at 310	3 at 316	4 at 317	5
180X	—	4 at 222	4 at 232	—	2

Instructions

1. Determine the cost of the inventory on December 31, 2003, by the first-in, first-out method. Present data in columnar form, using the following headings:

Model	Quantity	Unit Cost	Total Cost

If the inventory of a particular model comprises one entire purchase plus a portion of another purchase acquired at a different unit cost, use a separate line for each purchase.

2. Determine the cost of the inventory on December 31, 2003, by the last-in, first-out method, following the procedures indicated in (1).
3. Determine the cost of the inventory on December 31, 2003, by the average cost method, using the columnar headings indicated in (1).
4. ━━━▶ Discuss which method (fifo or lifo) would be preferred for income tax purposes in periods of (a) rising prices and (b) declining prices.

If the working papers correlating with this textbook are not used, omit Problem 9–4B.

Problem 9–4B

Lower-of-cost-or-market inventory

Objective 7

Data on the physical inventory of Trailblazer Co. as of December 31, 2003, are presented in the working papers. The quantity of each commodity on hand has been determined and recorded on the inventory sheet. Unit market prices have also been determined as of December 31 and recorded on the sheet. The inventory is to be determined at cost and also at the lower of cost or market, using the first-in, first-out method. Quantity and cost data from the last purchases invoice of the year and the next-to-the-last purchases invoice are summarized as follows:

	Last Purchases Invoice		Next-to-the-Last Purchases Invoice	
Description	**Quantity Purchased**	**Unit Cost**	**Quantity Purchased**	**Unit Cost**
A10	25	$ 60	40	$ 58
B23	25	190	15	191
D82	16	143	15	142
E34	150	25	100	27
F17	6	550	15	540
H99	75	14	100	13
K41	8	400	4	398
M21	500	6	500	7
R72	70	17	50	16
T15	5	250	4	260
BD1	120	19	115	17
MS3	8	701	7	699

Instructions

Record the appropriate unit costs on the inventory sheet, and complete the pricing of the inventory. When there are two different unit costs applicable to an item:

1. Draw a line through the quantity, and insert the quantity and unit cost of the last purchase.
2. On the following line, insert the quantity and unit cost of the next-to-the-last purchase.
3. Total the cost and market columns and insert the lower of the two totals in the Lower of C or M column. The first item on the inventory sheet has been completed as an example.

Problem 9–5B
Retail method; gross profit method

Objective 9

Selected data on merchandise inventory, purchases, and sales for Livingston Co. and Park Co. are as follows:

	Cost	Retail
Livingston Co.		
Merchandise inventory, February 1	$ 184,800	$ 280,000
Transactions during February:		
Purchases (net)	744,150	1,127,500
Sales		1,075,000
Sales returns and allowances		25,000
Park Co.		
Merchandise inventory, July 1	$ 217,500	
Transactions during July and August:		
Purchases (net)	1,491,100	
Sales	2,600,000	
Sales returns and allowances	150,000	
Estimated gross profit rate	42%	

Instructions

1. Determine the estimated cost of the merchandise inventory of Livingston Co. on February 28 by the retail method, presenting details of the computations.
2. a. Estimate the cost of the merchandise inventory of Park Co. on August 31 by the gross profit method, presenting details of the computations.
   b. Assume that Park Co. took a physical inventory on August 31 and discovered that $272,000 of merchandise was on hand. What was the estimated loss of inventory due to theft or damage during July and August?

SPECIAL ACTIVITIES

Activity 9–1
Xanadu Co.
Ethics and professional conduct in business

Xanadu Co. is experiencing a decrease in sales and operating income for the fiscal year ending December 31, 2003. Neil Whyte, controller of Xanadu Co., has suggested that all orders received before the end of the fiscal year be shipped by midnight, December 31, 2003, even if the shipping department must work overtime. Since Xanadu Co. ships all merchandise FOB shipping point, it would record all such shipments as sales for the year ending December 31, 2003, thereby offsetting some of the decreases in sales and operating income.

Discuss whether Neil Whyte is behaving in a professional manner.

Activity 9–2
Walgreen Co.
Fifo vs. lifo

The following footnote was taken from the 1999 financial statements of **Walgreen Co.**:

> *Inventories are valued on a . . . last-in, first-out (LIFO) cost . . . basis. At August 31, 1999 and 1998, inventories would have been greater by $536,000,000 and $490,800,000 respectively, if they had been valued on a lower of first-in, first-out (FIFO) cost or market basis.*

Additional data are as follows:

Earnings before income taxes, 1999	$1,027,300,000
Total lifo inventories, August 31, 1999	2,462,600,000

Based on the preceding data, determine (a) what the total inventories at August 31, 1999, would have been, using the fifo method, and (b) what the earnings before income taxes for the year ended August 31, 1999, would have been if fifo had been used instead of lifo.

Activity 9–3
Leconte Wholesale Co.
Lifo and inventory flow

The following is an excerpt from a conversation between John Lacy, the warehouse manager for Leconte Wholesale Co., and its accountant, Leanne Huskey. Leconte Wholesale operates a large regional warehouse that supplies produce and other grocery products to grocery stores in smaller communities.

John: Leanne, can you explain what's going on here with these monthly statements?
Leanne: Sure, John. How can I help you?
John: I don't understand this last-in, first-out inventory procedure. It just doesn't make sense.
Leanne: Well, what it means is that we assume that the last goods we receive are the first ones sold. So the inventory is made up of the items we purchased first.
John: Yes, but that's my problem. It doesn't work that way! We always distribute the oldest produce first. Some of that produce is perishable! We can't keep any of it very long or it'll spoil.
Leanne: John, you don't understand. We only *assume* that the products we distribute are the last ones received. We don't actually have to distribute the goods in this way.
John: I always thought that accounting was supposed to show what really happened. It all sounds like "make believe" to me! Why not report what really happens?

Respond to John's concerns.

Activity 9–4
Into the Real World
Observe internal controls over inventory

Select a business in your community and observe its internal controls over inventory. In groups of three or four, identify and discuss the similarities and differences in each business's inventory controls. Prepare a written summary of your findings.

Activity 9–5
Lectern Company
Costing inventory

Lectern Company began operations in 2002 by selling a single product. Data on purchases and sales for the year were as follows:

Purchases:

Date	Units Purchased	Unit Cost	Total Cost
April 8	3,875	$12.20	$ 47,275
May 10	4,125	13.00	53,625
June 4	5,000	13.20	66,000
July 10	5,000	14.00	70,000
August 3	3,400	14.25	48,450
October 5	1,600	14.50	23,200
November 1	1,000	14.95	14,950
December 10	1,000	16.00	16,000
	25,000		$339,500

Sales:

April	2,000 units
May	2,000
June	2,500
July	3,000
August	3,500
September	3,500
October	2,250
November	1,250
December	1,000
Total units	21,000
Total sales	$552,000

On January 3, 2003, the president of the company, Kevin Ivey, asked for your advice on costing the 4,000-unit physical inventory that was taken on December 31, 2002. Moreover, since the firm plans to expand its product line, he asked for your advice on the use of a perpetual inventory system in the future.

1. Determine the cost of the December 31, 2002 inventory under the periodic system, using the (a) first-in, first-out method, (b) last-in, first-out method, and (c) average cost method.
2. Determine the gross profit for the year under each of the three methods in (1).
3. a. Explain varying viewpoints why each of the three inventory costing methods may best reflect the results of operations for 2002.
   b. Which of the three inventory costing methods may best reflect the replacement cost of the inventory on the balance sheet as of December 31, 2002?
   c. Which inventory costing method would you choose to use for income tax purposes? Why?
   d. Discuss the advantages and disadvantages of using a perpetual inventory system. From the data presented in this case, is there any indication of the adequacy of inventory levels during the year?

Activity 9–6
Into the Real World
Compare inventory cost flow assumptions

In groups of three or four, examine the financial statements of a well-known retailing business. You may obtain the financial statements you need from one of the following sources:

1. Your school or local library.
2. The investor relations department of the company.
3. The company's Web site on the Internet.
4. EDGAR (Electronic Data Gathering, Analysis, and Retrieval), the electronic archives of financial statements filed with the Securities and Exchange Commission. SEC documents can be retrieved using the EdgarScan service from **PricewaterhouseCoopers** at

edgarscan.pwcglobal.com. To obtain annual report information, type in a company name in the appropriate space. EdgarScan will list the reports available to you for the company you've selected. Select the most recent annual report filing, identified as a 10-K or 10-K405. EdgarScan provides an outline of the report, including the separate financial statements. You can double-click the income statement and balance sheet for the selected company into an Excel spreadsheet for further analysis.

Determine the cost flow assumption(s) that the company is using for its inventory, and determine whether the company is using the lower-of-cost-or-market rule. Prepare a written summary of your findings.

ANSWERS TO SELF-EXAMINATION QUESTIONS

Matching

1. I
2. B
3. E
4. A
5. F
6. G
7. J
8. C
9. D
10. H

Multiple Choice

1. **D** The overstatement of inventory shrinkage by $7,500 at the end of the year will cause the cost of merchandise sold for the year to be overstated by $7,500, the gross profit for the year to be understated by $7,500, the merchandise inventory to be understated by $7,500, and the net income for the year to be understated by $7,500 (answer D).

2. **A** The fifo method (answer A) is based on the assumption that costs are charged against revenue in the order in which they were incurred. The lifo method (answer B) charges the most recent costs incurred against revenue, and the average cost method (answer C) charges a weighted average of unit costs of items sold against revenue. The perpetual inventory system (answer D) is a system and not a method of costing.

3. **A** The lifo method of costing is based on the assumption that costs should be charged against revenue in the reverse order in which costs were incurred. Thus, the oldest costs are assigned to inventory. Thirty of the 35 units would be assigned a unit cost of $20 (since 110 of the beginning inventory units were sold on the first sale), and the remaining 5 units would be assigned a cost of $23, for a total of $715 (answer A).

4. **D** The fifo method of costing is based on the assumption that costs should be charged against revenue in the order in which they were incurred (first-in, first-out). Thus, the most recent costs are assigned to inventory. The 35 units would be assigned a unit cost of $23 (answer D).

5. **B** When the price level is steadily rising, the earlier unit costs are lower than recent unit costs. Under the fifo method (answer B), these earlier costs are matched against revenue to yield the highest possible net income. The periodic inventory system (answer D) is a system and not a method of costing.

Fixed Assets and Intangible Assets

objectives

After studying this chapter, you should be able to:

1 Define fixed assets and describe the accounting for their cost.

2 Compute depreciation, using the following methods: straight-line method, units-of-production method, and declining-balance method.

3 Classify fixed asset costs as either capital expenditures or revenue expenditures.

4 Journalize entries for the disposal of fixed assets.

5 Define a lease and summarize the accounting rules related to the leasing of fixed assets.

6 Describe internal controls over fixed assets.

7 Compute depletion and journalize the entry for depletion.

8 Journalize the entries for acquiring and amortizing intangible assets, such as patents, copyrights, and goodwill.

9 Describe how depreciation expense is reported in an income statement, and prepare a balance sheet that includes fixed assets and intangible assets.

10 Compute and interpret the ratio of fixed assets to long-term liabilities.

A ssume that you are a certified flight instructor and you would like to earn a little extra money by teaching people how to fly. Since you don't own an airplane, one of the pilots at the local airport is willing to let you use her airplane for a fixed fee per year. You will also have to pay your share of the annual operating costs, based on hours flown. The owner will consider your request for upgrading the plane's equipment. At the end of the year, the owner has the right to cancel the agreement.

One of your friends is an airplane mechanic. He is familiar with the plane and has indicated that it needs its annual inspection. There is some structural damage on the right aileron. In addition to this repair, you would like to equip the plane with another radio and a better navigation system.

Since you will not have any ownership in the airplane, it is important for you to distinguish between normal operating costs and costs that add future value or worth to the airplane. These latter costs should be the responsibility of the owner. In this case, you should be willing to pay for part of the cost of the annual inspection. The cost of repairing the structural damage and upgrading the navigation system should be the responsibility of the owner.

Businesses also distinguish between the cost of a fixed asset and the cost of operating the asset. In this chapter, we discuss how to determine the portion of a fixed asset's cost that becomes an expense over a period of time. We also discuss accounting for the disposal of fixed assets and accounting for intangible assets, such as patents and copyrights.

Nature of Fixed Assets

objective 1

Define fixed assets and describe the accounting for their cost.

Businesses use a variety of fixed assets, such as equipment, furniture, tools, machinery, buildings, and land. **Fixed assets** are long-term or relatively permanent assets. They are **tangible assets** because they exist physically. They are owned and used by the business and are not offered for sale as part of normal operations. Other descriptive titles for these assets are **plant assets** or **property, plant, and equipment**.

There is no standard rule for the minimum length of life necessary for an asset to be classified as a fixed asset. Such assets must be capable of providing repeated use or benefit and are normally expected to last more than a year. However, an asset need not actually be used on an ongoing basis or even often. For example, standby equipment for use in the event of a breakdown of regular equipment or for use only during peak periods is included in fixed assets.

Long-term assets acquired for resale in the normal course of business are not classified as fixed assets, regardless of their permanent nature or the length of time they are held. For example, undeveloped land or other real estate acquired as an investment for resale should be listed on the balance sheet in the asset section entitled *Investments*.

The normal costs of using or operating a fixed asset are reported as expenses on a company's income statement. The costs of acquiring a fixed asset become expenses over a period of time. In the next section, we discuss these latter costs and their recognition as expenses.

Q & A

St. Mary's Hospital maintains an auxiliary generator for use in electrical outages. Such outages are rare, and the generator has not been used for the past two years. Should the generator be included as a fixed asset in St. Mary's ledger?

Yes. Even though the generator has not been used recently, it should be included as a fixed asset.

Glacier Co. is purchasing property (building and land) for use as a warehouse. In purchasing the land, Glacier has agreed to pay the prior owner's delinquent property taxes. Should the cost of paying the delinquent property taxes be included as part of the cost of the property?

Yes. All costs of acquiring the property, including the delinquent property taxes, should be included as part of the total cost of the property.

Costs of Acquiring Fixed Assets

The cost of acquiring a fixed asset includes all amounts spent to get it in place and ready for use. For example, freight costs and the costs of installing equipment are included as part of the asset's total cost. Exhibit 1 summarizes some of the common costs of acquiring fixed assets. These costs should be recorded by debiting the related fixed asset account, such as Land,[1] Building, Land Improvements, or Machinery and Equipment.

Costs *not necessary* for getting a fixed asset ready for use do not increase the asset's usefulness. Such costs should not be included as part of the asset's total cost. For example, the following costs should be debited to an expense account:

*   Vandalism
*   Mistakes in installation
*   Uninsured theft
*   Damage during unpacking and installing
*   Fines for not obtaining proper permits from government agencies

Nature of Depreciation

As we have discussed in earlier chapters, land has an unlimited life and therefore can provide unlimited services. On the other hand, other fixed assets such as equipment, buildings, and land improvements lose their ability, over time, to provide services. As a result, the costs of equipment, buildings, and land improvements should be transferred to expense accounts in a systematic manner during their expected useful lives. This periodic transfer of cost to expense is called **depreciation**.

The adjusting entry to record depreciation is usually made at the end of each month or at the end of the year. This entry debits *Depreciation Expense* and credits a *contra asset* account entitled *Accumulated Depreciation* or *Allowance for Depreciation*. The use of a contra asset account allows the original cost to remain unchanged in the fixed asset account.

Factors that cause a decline in the ability of a fixed asset to provide services may be identified as physical depreciation or functional depreciation. **Physical depreciation** occurs from wear and tear while in use and from the action of the weather. **Functional depreciation** occurs when a fixed asset is no longer able to provide services at the level for which it was intended. For example, a personal computer made in the 1980s would not be able to provide an Internet connection. Such advances in technology during this century have made functional depreciation an increasingly important cause of depreciation.

The term *depreciation* as used in accounting is often misunderstood because the same term is also used in business to mean a decline in the market value of an asset. However, the amount of a fixed asset's unexpired cost reported in the balance sheet usually does not agree with the amount that could be realized from its sale. Fixed assets are held for use in a business rather than for sale. It is assumed that the business will continue as a going concern. Thus, a decision to dispose of a fixed asset is based mainly on the usefulness of the asset to the business and not on its market value.

> The adjusting entry to record depreciation debits Depreciation Expense and credits Accumulated Depreciation.

Companies often use different useful lives for similar assets. For example, the primary useful life for buildings is 50 years for **JCPenney Co.**, while the useful life for buildings for **Tandy Corporation**, which operates **Radio Shack**, varies from 10 to 40 years.

----

[1] As discussed here, land is assumed to be used only as a location or site. Land acquired for its mineral deposits or other natural resources will be considered later in the chapter.

Exhibit 1 Costs of Acquiring
Fixed Assets

LAND

- Purchase price
- Sales taxes
- Permits from government agencies
- Broker's commissions
- Title fees
- Surveying fees
- Delinquent real estate taxes
- Razing or removing unwanted buildings, less any salvage
- Grading and leveling
- Paving a public street bordering the land

BUILDING

- Architects' fees
- Engineers' fees
- Insurance costs incurred during construction
- Interest on money borrowed to finance construction
- Walkways to and around the building
- Sales taxes
- Repairs (purchase of existing building)
- Reconditioning (purchase of existing building)
- Modifying for use
- Permits from government agencies

LAND IMPROVEMENTS

- Trees and shrubs
- Fences
- Outdoor lighting
- Paved parking areas

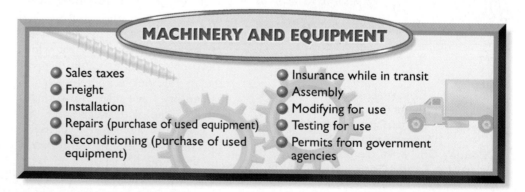

MACHINERY AND EQUIPMENT

- Sales taxes
- Freight
- Installation
- Repairs (purchase of used equipment)
- Reconditioning (purchase of used equipment)
- Insurance while in transit
- Assembly
- Modifying for use
- Testing for use
- Permits from government agencies

Point of Interest

Would you have more cash if you depreciated your car? The answer is no. Depreciation does not affect your cash flows. Likewise, depreciation does not affect the cash flows of a business. However, depreciation is subtracted in determining net income.

Another common misunderstanding is that accounting for depreciation provides cash needed to replace fixed assets as they wear out. This misunderstanding probably occurs because depreciation, unlike most expenses, does not require an outlay of cash in the period in which it is recorded. The cash account is neither increased nor decreased by the periodic entries that transfer the cost of fixed assets to depreciation expense accounts.

Accounting for Depreciation

objective 2

Compute depreciation, using the following methods: straight-line method, units-of-production method, and declining-balance method.

Three factors are considered in determining the amount of depreciation expense to be recognized each period. These three factors are (a) the fixed asset's initial cost, (b) its expected useful life, and (c) its estimated value at the end of its useful life. This third factor is called the **residual value**, **scrap value**, **salvage value**, or **trade-in value**. Exhibit 2 shows the relationship among the three factors and the periodic depreciation expense.

Exhibit 2 Factors that Determine Depreciation Expense

Periodic Depreciation Expense

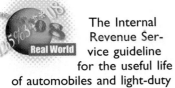

The Internal Revenue Service guideline for the useful life of automobiles and light-duty trucks is 5 years, while the designated life for most machinery and equipment is 7 years.

A fixed asset's **residual value** at the end of its expected useful life must be estimated at the time the asset is placed in service. If a fixed asset is expected to have little or no residual value when it is taken out of service, then its initial cost should be spread over its expected useful life as depreciation expense. If, however, a fixed asset is expected to have a significant residual value, the difference between its initial cost and its residual value, called the asset's **depreciable cost**, is the amount that is spread over the asset's useful life as depreciation expense.

A fixed asset's **expected useful life** must also be estimated at the time the asset is placed in service. Estimates of expected useful lives are available from various trade associations and other publications. For federal income tax purposes, the Internal Revenue Service has established guidelines for useful lives. These guidelines may also be helpful in determining depreciation for financial reporting purposes.

In practice, many businesses use the guideline that all assets placed in or taken out of service during the first half of a month are treated as if the event occurred on the first day of *that* month. That is, these businesses compute depreciation on these assets for the entire month. Likewise, all fixed asset additions and deductions during the second half of a month are treated as if the event occurred on the first day of the *next* month. We will follow this practice in this chapter.

It is not necessary that a business use a single method of computing depreciation for all its depreciable assets. The methods used in the accounts and financial statements may also differ from the methods used in determining income taxes and property taxes. The three methods used most often are (1) straight-line, (2) units-of-production, and (3) declining-balance.[2] Exhibit 3 shows the extent of the use of these methods in financial statements.

Exhibit 3 Use of Depreciation Methods

Source: Accounting Trends & Techniques, 53rd ed., American Institute of Certified Public Accountants, New York, 1999.

Straight-Line Method

The **straight-line method** provides for the same amount of depreciation expense for each year of the asset's useful life. For example, assume that the cost of a depreciable asset is $24,000, its estimated residual value is $2,000, and its estimated life is 5 years. The annual depreciation is computed as follows:

$$\frac{\$24{,}000 \text{ cost} - \$2{,}000 \text{ estimated residual value}}{5 \text{ years estimated life}} = \frac{\$4{,}400 \text{ annual}}{\text{depreciation}}$$

When an asset is used for only part of a year, the annual depreciation is pro-rated. For example, assume that the fiscal year ends on December 31 and that the asset in the above example is placed in service on October 1. The depreciation for the first fiscal year of use would be $1,100 ($4,400 × 3/12).

For ease in applying the straight-line method, the annual depreciation may be converted to a percentage of the depreciable cost. This percentage is determined by dividing 100% by the number of years of useful life. For example, a useful life of 20 years converts to a 5% rate (100%/20), 8 years converts to a 12.5% rate (100%/8), and so on.[3] In the above example, the annual depreciation of $4,400 can be computed by multiplying the depreciable cost of $22,000 by 20% (100%/5).

The straight-line method is simple and is widely used. It provides a reasonable transfer of costs to periodic expense when the asset's use and the related revenues from its use are about the same from period to period.

Q&A A truck that cost $35,000 has a residual value of $5,000 and a useful life of 12 years. What are (a) the depreciable cost, (b) the straight-line rate, and (c) the annual straight-line depreciation?

(a) $30,000 ($35,000 − $5,000), (b) 8⅓% (¹⁄₁₂), (c) $2,500 ($30,000 × 8⅓%).

[2] Another method not often used today, called the *sum-of-the-years-digits method*, is described and illustrated in the appendix at the end of this chapter.
[3] The depreciation rate may also be expressed as a fraction. For example, the annual straight-line rate for an asset with a 3-year useful life is 1/3.

Units-of-Production Method

How would you depreciate a fixed asset when its service is related to use rather than time? When the amount of use of a fixed asset varies from year to year, the units-of-production method is more appropriate than the straight-line method. In such cases, the units-of-production method better matches the depreciation expense with the related revenue.

The **units-of-production method** provides for the same amount of depreciation expense for each unit produced or each unit of capacity used by the asset. To apply this method, the useful life of the asset is expressed in terms of units of productive capacity such as hours or miles. The total depreciation expense for each accounting period is then determined by multiplying the unit depreciation by the number of units produced or used during the period. For example, assume that a machine with a cost of $24,000 and an estimated residual value of $2,000 is expected to have an estimated life of 10,000 operating hours. The depreciation for a unit of one hour is computed as follows:

$$\frac{\$24,000 \text{ cost} - \$2,000 \text{ estimated residual value}}{10,000 \text{ estimated hours}} = \frac{\$2.20 \text{ hourly}}{\text{depreciation}}$$

Assuming that the machine was in operation for 2,100 hours during a year, the depreciation for that year would be $4,620 ($2.20 × 2,100 hours).

Declining-Balance Method

The **declining-balance method** provides for a declining periodic expense over the estimated useful life of the asset. To apply this method, the annual straight-line depreciation rate is doubled. For example, the declining-balance rate for an asset with an estimated life of 5 years is 40%, which is double the straight-line rate of 20% (100%/5).

For the first year of use, the cost of the asset is multiplied by the declining-balance rate. After the first year, the declining **book value** (cost minus accumulated depreciation) of the asset is multiplied by this rate. To illustrate, the annual declining-balance depreciation for an asset with an estimated 5-year life and a cost of $24,000 is shown below.

Year	Cost	Accum. Depr. at Beginning of Year	Book Value at Beginning of Year	Rate	Depreciation for Year	Book Value at End of Year
1	$24,000		$24,000.00	40%	$9,600.00	$14,400.00
2	24,000	$ 9,600.00	14,400.00	40%	5,760.00	8,640.00
3	24,000	15,360.00	8,640.00	40%	3,456.00	5,184.00
4	24,000	18,816.00	5,184.00	40%	2,073.60	3,110.40
5	24,000	20,889.60	3,110.40	—	1,110.40	2,000.00

You should note that when the declining-balance method is used, the estimated residual value is *not* considered in determining the depreciation rate. It is also ignored in computing the periodic depreciation. However, the asset should not be depreciated below its estimated residual value. In the above example, the estimated residual value was $2,000. Therefore, the depreciation for the fifth year is $1,110.40 ($3,110.40 − $2,000.00) instead of $1,244.16 (40% × $3,110.40).

In the example above, we assumed that the first use of the asset occurred at the beginning of the fiscal year. This is normally not the case in practice, however, and depreciation for the first partial year of use must be computed. For example, assume that the asset above was in service at the end of the *third* month of the fiscal year. In this case, only a portion (9/12) of the first full year's depreciation of $9,600 is allocated to the first fiscal year. Thus, depreciation of $7,200 (9/12 × $9,600) is allocated to the first partial year of use. The depreciation for the second fiscal year would then be $6,720 [40% × ($24,000 − $7,200)].

Comparing Depreciation Methods

The straight-line method provides for the same periodic amounts of depreciation expense over the life of the asset. The units-of-production method provides for periodic amounts of depreciation expense that vary, depending upon the amount the asset is used.

The declining-balance method provides for a higher depreciation amount in the first year of the asset's use, followed by a gradually declining amount. For this reason, the declining-balance method is called an *accelerated depreciation method*. It is most appropriate when the decline in an asset's productivity or earning power is greater in the early years of its use than in later years. Further, using this method is often justified because repairs tend to increase with the age of an asset. The reduced amounts of depreciation in later years are thus offset to some extent by increased repair expenses.

The periodic depreciation amounts for the straight-line method and the declining-balance method are compared in Exhibit 4. This comparison is based on an asset cost of $24,000, an estimated life of 5 years, and an estimated residual value of $2,000.

Exhibit 4 Comparing Depreciation Methods

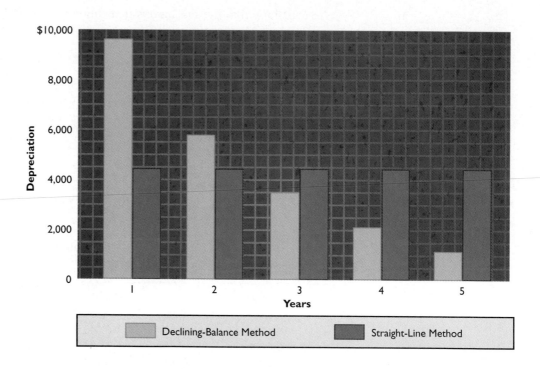

Depreciation for Federal Income Tax

The Internal Revenue Code specifies the *Modified Accelerated Cost Recovery System (MACRS)* for use by businesses in computing depreciation for tax purposes.[4] MACRS specifies eight classes of useful life and depreciation rates for each class. The two most common classes, other than real estate, are the 5-year class and the 7-year class.[5] The 5-year class includes automobiles and light-duty trucks, and the 7-year class includes most machinery and equipment. The depreciation deduction for these two classes is similar to that computed using the declining-balance method.

[4] Fixed assets that were acquired before 1987 are allowed to use depreciation methods other than MACRS. These are discussed in tax accounting texts.
[5] Real estate is in 27 1/2-year classes and 31 1/2-year classes and is depreciated by the straight-line method.

In using the MACRS rates, residual value is ignored, and all fixed assets are assumed to be put in and taken out of service in the middle of the year. For the 5-year-class assets, depreciation is spread over six years, as shown in the following MACRS schedule of depreciation rates:

Year	5-Year-Class Depreciation Rates
1	20.0%
2	32.0
3	19.2
4	11.5
5	11.5
6	5.8
	100.0%

What is the third year MACRS depreciation for an automobile that cost $26,000 and has a residual value of $6,500?

$4,992 ($26,000 × 19.2%)

To simplify its record keeping, a business will sometimes use the MACRS method for both financial statement and tax purposes. This is acceptable if MACRS does not result in significantly different amounts than would have been reported using one of the three depreciation methods discussed earlier in this chapter.

Using MACRS for both financial statement and tax purposes may, however, hurt a business. In one case, a business that had used MACRS depreciation for its financial statements lost a $1 million order because its fixed assets had low book values. The bank viewed these low book values as inadequate, so it would not loan the business the amount needed to produce the order.[6]

Revising Depreciation Estimates

Revising the estimates of the residual value and the useful life is normal. When these estimates are revised, they are used to determine the depreciation expense in future periods. They do not affect the amounts of depreciation expense recorded in earlier years.

To illustrate, assume that a fixed asset purchased for $130,000 was originally estimated to have a useful life of 30 years and a residual value of $10,000. The asset has been depreciated for 10 years by the straight-line method. At the end of ten years, the asset's book value (undepreciated cost) is $90,000, determined as follows:

Asset cost	$130,000
Less accumulated depreciation ($4,000 per year × 10 years)	40,000
Book value (undepreciated cost), end of tenth year	$ 90,000

For the $130,000 asset in the example on this page, assume that after 10 more years (20 years in total) its remaining useful life is estimated at 5 years with no residual value. What is the revised depreciation for the twenty-first year?

$11,200 ($130,000 − $40,000 depreciation for years 1–10 = $90,000; $90,000 − $34,000 depreciation for years 11–20 = $56,000; $56,000 divided by 5 years = $11,200)

During the eleventh year, it is estimated that the remaining useful life is 25 years (instead of 20) and that the residual value is $5,000 (instead of $10,000). The depreciation expense for each of the remaining 25 years is $3,400, computed as follows:

Book value (undepreciated cost), end of tenth year	$90,000
Less revised estimated residual value	5,000
Revised remaining depreciable cost	$85,000
Revised annual depreciation expense ($85,000/25)	$ 3,400

----

[6] Lee Berton, "Do's and Don'ts," *The Wall Street Journal*, June 10, 1988, p. 34R.

Composite-Rate Method

Assets may be grouped according to common traits, such as similar useful lives. For example, a group might include all delivery trucks with useful lives of less than 8 years. Likewise, a group might include all office equipment or all store fixtures. Depreciation may be determined for each group of assets, using a single *composite rate*, rather than a rate for each individual asset. The depreciation computations are similar for groups of assets as for individual assets.

Capital and Revenue Expenditures

objective 3

Classify fixed asset costs as either capital expenditures or revenue expenditures.

The costs of acquiring fixed assets, adding to a fixed asset, improving a fixed asset, or extending a fixed asset's useful life are called **capital expenditures**. Such expenditures are recorded by either debiting the asset account or its related accumulated depreciation account. Costs that benefit only the current period or costs incurred for normal maintenance and repairs are called **revenue expenditures**. Such expenditures are debited to expense accounts. For example, the cost of replacing spark plugs in an automobile or the cost of repainting a building should be debited to an expense account.

To properly match revenues and expenses, it is important to distinguish between capital and revenue expenditures. Capital expenditures will affect the depreciation expense of more than one period, while revenue expenditures will affect the expenses of only the current period.

Types of Capital Expenditures

We have discussed accounting for the initial costs of acquiring fixed assets. Capital expenditures on assets after they have been acquired may be either (a) additions, (b) betterments, or (c) extraordinary repairs.

Additions to Fixed Assets

The cost of an addition to a fixed asset should be debited to the related fixed asset account. For example, the cost of adding a new wing to a building should be debited to the building account. This cost should then be depreciated over its estimated useful life or the remaining useful life of the building, whichever is shorter.

Betterments

An expenditure that improves a fixed asset's operating efficiency or capacity for its remaining useful life is called a **betterment**. Such expenditures should be debited to the related fixed asset account. For example, if the power unit attached to a machine is replaced by one of greater capacity, its cost should be debited to the machine account. Also, the cost and the accumulated depreciation related to the old power unit should be removed from the accounts. The cost of the new power unit should then be depreciated over its estimated useful life or the remaining useful life of the machine, whichever is shorter.

Extraordinary Repairs

An expenditure that increases the useful life of an asset beyond its original estimate is called an **extraordinary repair**. Such expenditures should be debited to the related accumulated depreciation account. In such cases, the repairs are said to *restore* or *make good* a portion of the depreciation recorded in prior years. The depreciation for future periods should be computed on the basis of the revised book value of the asset and the revised estimate of the remaining useful life.

Identify each of the items related to a truck as an addition, a betterment, or an extraordinary repair: (a) a snowplow attachment that allows the truck to be used for snow removal, (b) a new transmission, (c) a hydraulic hitch to replace a manual hitch.

(a) addition, (b) extraordinary repair, (c) betterment.

To illustrate, assume that a machine costing $50,000 has no estimated residual value and an estimated useful life of 10 years. Assume also that the machine has been depreciated for 6 years by the straight-line method ($5,000 annual depreciation). At the beginning of the seventh year, an $11,500 extraordinary repair increases the remaining useful life of the machine to 7 years (instead of 4). The repair of $11,500 should be debited to Accumulated Depreciation. The annual depreciation for the remaining 7 years of use would be $4,500, computed as follows:

Cost of machine		$50,000
Less Accumulated Depreciation balance:		
Depreciation for first 6 years ($5,000 × 6)	$30,000	
Deduct debit for extraordinary repair	11,500	
Balance of Accumulated Depreciation		18,500
Revised book value of machine after extraordinary repair		$31,500
Annual depreciation ($31,500/7 years remaining useful life)		$ 4,500

Summary of Capital and Revenue Expenditures

Exhibit 5 summarizes the accounting for capital and revenue expenditures related to fixed assets.

Exhibit 5 Capital and Revenue Expenditures

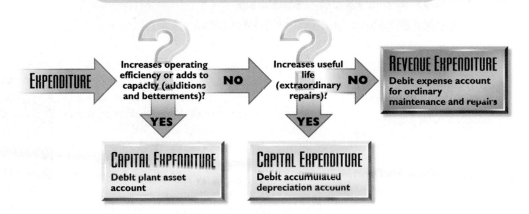

BUSINESS ON STAGE

Running Like a Top

Businesses that use equipment to provide goods or services must maintain that equipment. These businesses usually follow one of three maintenance philosophies: (1) corrective maintenance, (2) preventive maintenance, and (3) predictive maintenance.

• **Corrective maintenance.** Under this philosophy, equipment is repaired when the equipment breaks down. It would be similar to you replacing your car's engine every time it froze up because it needed an an oil change. Compa-

nies that use corrective maintenance don't want to waste time performing maintenance until there is an actual failure. Unfortunately, an unplanned machine failure can cause significant disruptions. Such disruptions include unplanned stops in production, delays in waiting for replacement parts, and additional repair due to broken machine components. Because of this, many consider corrective maintenance a poor philosophy.

• **Preventive maintenance.** Under this philosophy, equipment is repaired under a planned schedule. It would be similar to you changing your car's oil every 6,000 miles. Preventive maintenance is considered superior to corrective maintenance because the maintenance is planned. Therefore, employees can be trained, multiple machines can be repaired, or housekeeping can be performed during the scheduled maintenance. In addition,

replacement parts can be ordered ahead of time, minimizing delays caused by emergencies. Lastly, preventive maintenance may reduce the overall maintenance expenditures, because actual machine failures are minimized.

• **Predictive maintenance.** Under this new maintenance philosophy, equipment is repaired at the exact time it needs to be repaired prior to actual failure. It would be similar to you changing your car's oil when a sensor in the car indicated that the oil had reached a given level of impurity. Predictive maintenance is considered superior to preventive maintenance because maintenance is performed only when it is actually needed. This

may reduce the total amount of time that equipment spends in maintenance during its life, compared to preventive maintenance. At the same time, however, predictive maintenance may still be planned, once it is indicated—so it has the same advantages as preventive maintenance. New sensors and computers are being developed to support predictive maintenance. Vibration sensors are one example. These sensors are placed on machines to measure vibration, which indicates bearing wear. When the vibration levels reach a certain point, bearings are replaced, which is just prior to their failing. ∎

Disposal of Fixed Assets

objective 4

Journalize entries for the disposal of fixed assets.

Fixed assets that are no longer useful may be discarded, sold, or traded for other fixed assets. The details of the entry to record a disposal will vary. In all cases, however, the book value of the asset must be removed from the accounts. The entry for this purpose debits the asset's accumulated depreciation account for its balance on the date of disposal and credits the asset account for the cost of the asset.

A fixed asset should not be removed from the accounts only because it has been fully depreciated. If the asset is still used

> The entry to record the disposal of a fixed asset removes the cost of the asset and its accumulated depreciation from the accounts.

by the business, the cost and accumulated depreciation should remain in the ledger. This maintains accountability for the asset in the ledger. If the book value of the asset was removed from the ledger, the accounts would contain no evidence of the continued existence of the asset. In addition, the cost and the accumulated depreciation data on such assets are often needed for property tax and income tax reports.

Discarding Fixed Assets

When fixed assets are no longer useful to the business and have no residual or market value, they are discarded. To illustrate, assume that an item of equipment acquired at a cost of $25,000 is fully depreciated at December 31, the end of the preceding fiscal year. On February 14, the equipment is discarded. The entry to record this is as follows:

Feb.	14	Accumulated Depreciation—Equipment		25 0 0 0 00		
		Equipment				25 0 0 0 00
		To write off equipment discarded.				

If an asset has not been fully depreciated, depreciation should be recorded prior to removing it from service and from the accounting records. To illustrate, assume that equipment costing $6,000 is depreciated at an annual straight-line rate of 10%. In addition, assume that on December 31 of the preceding fiscal year, the accumulated depreciation balance, after adjusting entries, is $4,750. Finally, assume that the asset is removed from service on the following March 24. The entry to record the depreciation for the three months of the current period prior to the asset's removal from service is as follows:

Mar.	24	Depreciation Expense—Equipment		1 5 0 00		
		Accumulated Depreciation—Equipment				1 5 0 00
		To record current depreciation on				
		equipment discarded ($600 × $^{3}/_{12}$).				

The discarding of the equipment is then recorded by the following entry:

Mar.	24	Accumulated Depreciation—Equipment		4 9 0 0 00		
		Loss on Disposal of Fixed Assets		1 1 0 0 00		
		Equipment				6 0 0 0 00
		To write off equipment discarded.				

The loss of $1,100 is recorded because the balance of the accumulated depreciation account ($4,900) is less than the balance in the equipment account ($6,000). Losses on the discarding of fixed assets are nonoperating items and are normally reported in the Other Expense section of the income statement.

Selling Fixed Assets

The entry to record the sale of a fixed asset is similar to the entries illustrated above, except that the cash or other asset received must also be recorded. If the selling price is more than the book value of the asset, the transaction results in a gain. If the selling price is less than the book value, there is a loss.

To illustrate, assume that equipment is acquired at a cost of $10,000 and is depreciated at an annual straight-line rate of 10%. The equipment is sold for cash on October 12 of the eighth year of its use. The balance of the accumulated depreciation account as of the preceding December 31 is $7,000. The entry to update the depreciation for the nine months of the current year is as follows:

Oct.	12	Depreciation Expense—Equipment		7 5 0 00		
		Accumulated Depreciation—Equipment				7 5 0 00
		To record current depreciation on				
		equipment sold ($10,000 × $^{3}/_{4}$ × 10%).				

After the current depreciation is recorded, the book value of the asset is $2,250 ($10,000 − $7,750). The entries to record the sale, assuming three different selling prices, are as follows:

Sold at book value, for $2,250. No gain or loss.

Oct.	12	Cash	2 2 5 0 00		
		Accumulated Depreciation—Equipment	7 7 5 0 00		
		Equipment		10 0 0 0 00	

Sold below book value, for $1,000. Loss of $1,250.

Oct.	12	Cash	1 0 0 0 00		
		Accumulated Depreciation—Equipment	7 7 5 0 00		
		Loss on Disposal of Fixed Assets	1 2 5 0 00		
		Equipment		10 0 0 0 00	

Sold above book value, for $2,800. Gain of $550.

Oct.	12	Cash	2 8 0 0 00		
		Accumulated Depreciation—Equipment	7 7 5 0 00		
		Equipment		10 0 0 0 00	
		Gain on Disposal of Fixed Assets		5 5 0 00	

Exchanging Similar Fixed Assets

Old equipment is often traded in for new equipment having a similar use. In such cases, the seller allows the buyer an amount for the old equipment traded in. This amount, called the **trade-in allowance**, may be either greater or less than the book value of the old equipment. The remaining balance—the amount owed—is either paid in cash or recorded as a liability. It is normally called **boot**, which is its tax name.

Gains on Exchanges

Gains on exchanges of similar fixed assets are also not recognized for federal income tax purposes.

Gains on exchanges of similar fixed assets are not recognized for financial reporting purposes.[7] This is based on the theory that revenue occurs from the production and sale of goods produced by fixed assets and not from the exchange of similar fixed assets.

When the trade-in allowance exceeds the book value of an asset traded in and no gain is recognized, the cost recorded for the new asset can be determined in either of two ways:

> **1. Cost of new asset = List price of new asset − Unrecognized gain**
>
> *or*
>
> **2. Cost of new asset = Cash given (or liability assumed) + Book value of old asset**

[7] Gains on exchanges of similar fixed assets are recognized if cash (boot) is received. This topic is discussed in advanced accounting texts.

To illustrate, assume the following exchange:

Similar equipment acquired (new):

List price of new equipment	$5,000
Trade-in allowance on old equipment	1,100
Cash paid at June 19, date of exchange	$3,900

Equipment traded in (old):

Cost of old equipment	$4,000
Accumulated depreciation at date of exchange	3,200
Book value at June 19, date of exchange	$ 800

Recorded cost of new equipment:

Method One:

List price of new equipment		$5,000
Trade-in allowance	$1,100	
Book value of old equipment	800	
Unrecognized gain on exchange		(300)
Cost of new equipment		$4,700

Method Two:

Book value of old equipment	$ 800
Cash paid at date of exchange	3,900
Cost of new equipment	$4,700

Q&A *Equipment with a book value of $14,000 is traded in for similar equipment with a list price of $50,000. A trade-in allowance of $15,000 was allowed on the old equipment. What is the cost of the new equipment to be recorded in the accounts?*

$49,000 ($50,000 − $1,000 gain, or $14,000 + $35,000 boot)

The entry to record this exchange and the payment of cash is as follows:

June	19	Accumulated Depreciation—Equipment	3 2 0 0 00		
		Equipment (new equipment)	4 7 0 0 00		
		Equipment (old equipment)		4 0 0 0 00	
		Cash		3 9 0 0 00	
		To record exchange of equipment.			

Not recognizing the $300 gain ($1,100 trade-in allowance minus $800 book value) at the time of the exchange reduces future depreciation expense. That is, the depreciation expense for the new asset is based on a cost of $4,700 rather than on the list price of $5,000. In effect, the unrecognized gain of $300 reduces the total amount of depreciation taken during the life of the equipment by $300.

Losses on Exchanges

Real World *Losses on exchanges of similar fixed assets are not recognized for federal income tax purposes.*

For financial reporting purposes, losses are recognized on exchanges of similar fixed assets if the trade-in allowance is less than the book value of the old equipment. When there is a loss, the cost recorded for the new asset should be the market (list) price. To illustrate, assume the following exchange:

Similar equipment acquired (new):

List price of new equipment	$10,000
Trade-in allowance on old equipment	2,000
Cash paid at September 7, date of exchange	$ 8,000

Equipment traded in (old):

Cost of old equipment	$ 7,000
Accumulated depreciation at date of exchange	4,600
Book value at September 7, date of exchange	$ 2,400
Trade-in allowance on old equipment	2,000
Loss on exchange	$ 400

The entry to record the exchange is as follows:

Sept.	7	Accumulated Depreciation—Equipment	4 6 0 0 00		
		Equipment	10 0 0 0 00		
		Loss on Disposal of Fixed Assets	4 0 0 00		
		Equipment		7 0 0 0 00	
		Cash		8 0 0 0 00	
		To record exchange of equipment,			
		with loss.			

Review of Accounting for Exchanges of Similar Fixed Assets

Exhibit 6 reviews the accounting for exchanges of similar fixed assets, using the following data:

List price of new equipment acquired	$15,000
Cost of old equipment traded in	$12,500
Accumulated depreciation at date of exchange	10,100
Book value at date of exchange	$ 2,400

Leasing Fixed Assets

objective 5

Define a lease and summarize the accounting rules related to the leasing of fixed assets.

Of the companies surveyed in a recent edition of *Accounting Trends & Techniques*, 91% reported leases.

You are probably familiar with leases. A *lease* is a contract for the use of an asset for a stated period of time. Leases are frequently used in business. For example, automobiles, computers, medical equipment, buildings, and airplanes are often leased.

The two parties to a lease contract are the lessor and the lessee. The *lessor* is the party who owns the asset. The *lessee* is the party to whom the rights to use the asset are granted by the lessor. The lessee is obligated to make periodic rent payments for the lease term. All leases are classified by the lessee as either capital leases or operating leases.

A **capital lease** is accounted for as if the lessee has, in fact, purchased the asset. The lessee debits an asset account for the fair market value of the asset and credits a long-term lease liability account. The accounting for capital leases and the criteria that a capital lease must satisfy are discussed in more advanced accounting texts.

A lease that is not classified as a capital lease for accounting purposes is classified as an **operating lease**. The lessee records the payments under an operating lease by debiting *Rent Expense* and crediting *Cash*. Neither future lease obligations

Delta Air Lines had over $2.3 billion in lease commitments for the year ending June 30, 2000. Of 584 aircraft as of June 30, 1999, 256 were leased.

Exhibit 6 Summary Illustration—Accounting for Exchanges of Similar Fixed Assets

CASE ONE (GAIN): Trade-in allowance is more than book value of asset traded in.

Trade-in allowance, $3,000; cash paid, $12,000 ($15,000 − $3,000)

Cost of new asset	List price of new asset acquired, less unrecognized gain: $14,400 ($15,000 − $600) **or** Cash paid plus book value of asset traded in: $14,400 ($12,000 + $2,400)		
Gain recognized	None		
Entry	Equipment	14,400	
	Accumulated Depreciation	10,100	
	Equipment		12,500
	Cash		12,000

CASE TWO (LOSS): Trade-in allowance is less than book value of asset traded in.

Trade-in allowance, $2,000; cash paid, $13,000 ($15,000 − $2,000)

Cost of new asset	List price of new asset acquired: $15,000		
Loss recognized	$400		
Entry	Equipment	15,000	
	Accumulated Depreciation	10,100	
	Loss on Disposal of Fixed Assets	400	
	Equipment		12,500
	Cash		13,000

nor the future rights to use the leased asset are recognized in the accounts. However, the lessee must disclose future lease commitments in footnotes to the financial statements.

The asset rentals described in earlier chapters of this text were accounted for as operating leases. To simplify, we will continue to treat asset leases as operating leases.

Internal Control of Fixed Assets

objective 6

Describe internal controls over fixed assets.

Because of their dollar value and long-term nature, it is important to design and apply effective internal controls over fixed assets. Such controls should begin with authorization and approval procedures for the purchase of fixed assets. Controls should also exist to ensure that fixed assets are acquired at the lowest possible costs. One procedure to achieve this objective is to require competitive bids from preapproved vendors.

As soon as a fixed asset is received, it should be inspected and tagged for control purposes and recorded in a subsidiary ledger. This establishes the initial accountability for the asset. Subsidiary ledgers for fixed assets are also useful in determining depreciation expense and recording disposals. Operating data that may be recorded in the subsidiary ledger, such as number of breakdowns, length of time out of service, and cost of repairs, are useful in deciding whether to replace the asset. A company that maintains a computerized subsidiary ledger may use bar-coded tags, similar to the one on the back of this textbook, so that fixed asset data can be directly scanned into computer records.

Fixed assets should be insured against theft, fire, flooding, or other disasters. They should also be safeguarded from theft, misuse, or other damage. For example, fixed assets that are highly open to theft, such as computers, should be locked or otherwise protected when not in use. For computers, safeguarding also includes climate controls and special fire-extinguishing equipment. Procedures should also exist for training employees to properly operate fixed assets such as equipment and machinery.

A physical inventory of fixed assets should be taken periodically in order to verify the accuracy of the accounting records. Such an inventory would detect missing, obsolete, or idle fixed assets. In addition, fixed assets should be inspected periodically in order to determine their condition.

Careful control should also be exercised over the disposal of fixed assets. All disposals should be properly authorized and approved. Fully depreciated assets should be retained in the accounting records until disposal has been authorized and they are removed from service.

Natural Resources

objective 7

Compute depletion and journalize the entry for depletion.

The fixed assets of some businesses include timber, metal ores, minerals, or other natural resources. As these businesses harvest or mine and then sell these resources, a portion of the cost of acquiring them must be debited to an expense account. This process of transferring the cost of natural resources to an expense account is called **depletion**. The amount of depletion is determined by multiplying the quantity extracted during the period by the depletion rate. This rate is computed by dividing the cost of the mineral deposit by its estimated size.

Computing depletion is similar to computing units-of-production depreciation. To illustrate, assume that a business paid $400,000 for the mining rights to a mineral deposit estimated at 1,000,000 tons of ore. The depletion rate is $0.40 per ton ($400,000/1,000,000 tons). If 90,000 tons are mined during the year, the periodic depletion is $36,000 (90,000 tons × $0.40). The entry to record the depletion is shown below.

A business purchased mineral rights to 250,000 tons of ore for $1,500,000. If 35,000 tons of ore were mined in the first year, what are (a) the depletion rate per ton and (2) the depletion expense for the first year?

(a) **$6 per ton ($1,500,000/ 250,000 tons); (b) $210,000 (35,000 tons × $6)**

		Adjusting Entry			
Dec.	31	Depletion Expense	36 0 0 0 00		
		Accumulated Depletion		36 0 0 0 00	

Like the accumulated depreciation account, Accumulated Depletion is a *contra asset* account. It is reported on the balance sheet as a deduction from the cost of the mineral deposit.

Intangible Assets

objective 8

Journalize the entries for acquiring and amortizing intangible assets, such as patents, copyrights, and goodwill.

Patents, copyrights, trademarks, and goodwill are long-term assets that are useful in the operations of a business and are not held for sale. These assets are called **intangible assets** because they do not exist physically.

The basic principles of accounting for intangible assets are like those described earlier for fixed assets. The major concerns are determining (1) the initial cost and (2) the **amortization**—the amount of cost to transfer to expense. Amortization results from the passage of time or a decline in the usefulness of the intangible asset.

Patents

Manufacturers may acquire exclusive rights to produce and sell goods with one or more unique features. Such rights are granted by **patents**, which the federal government issues to inventors. These rights continue in effect for 20 years. A business may purchase patent rights from others, or it may obtain patents developed by its own research and development efforts.

The initial cost of a purchased patent, including any related legal fees, should be debited to an asset account. This cost should be written off, or amortized, over the years of the patent's expected usefulness. This period of time may be less than the remaining legal life of the patent. The estimated useful life of the patent may also change as technology or consumer tastes change.

The straight-line method is normally used to determine the periodic amortization. When the amortization is recorded, it is debited to an expense account and credited directly to the patents account. Not using a separate contra asset account is common for all intangible assets.

To illustrate, assume that at the beginning of its fiscal year a business acquires patent rights for $100,000. The patent had been granted 6 years earlier by the Federal Patent Office. Although the patent will not expire for 14 years, its remaining useful life is estimated as 5 years. The entry to amortize the patent at the end of the fiscal year is as follows:

		Adjusting Entry			
Dec.	31	Amortization Expense—Patents	20 0 0 0 00		
		Patents			20 0 0 0 00

Rather than purchase patent rights, a business may incur significant costs in developing patents through its own research and development efforts. Such **research and development costs** are usually accounted for as current operating expenses in the period in which they are incurred.

Expensing research and development costs in the period they are incurred is justified for two reasons. First, the future benefits from research and development efforts are highly uncertain. In fact, most research and development efforts do not result in patents. Second, even if a patent is granted, it may be difficult to objectively estimate its cost. If many research projects are in process at the same time, for example, it is difficult to separate the costs of one project from another.

Copyrights and Trademarks

The exclusive right to publish and sell a literary, artistic, or musical composition is granted by a **copyright**. Copyrights are issued by the federal government and extend for 70 years beyond the author's death. The costs of a copyright include all costs of creating the work plus any administrative or legal costs of obtaining the

The **RIAA (Recording Industry Association of America)** initiated a copyright infringement suit against **Napster.com**. The RIAA alledged that Napster promoted the piracy of MP3 music files through its file-sharing software.

Coke® is one of the world's most recogniz-able trademarks. As stated in *LIFE*, "Two-thirds of the earth is covered by water; the rest is covered by Coke. If the French are known for wine and the Germans for beer, America achieved global beverage dominance with fizzy water and caramel color."

copyright. A copyright that is purchased from another should be recorded at the price paid for it. Because of the uncertainty regarding the useful life of a copyright, it is normally amortized over a short period of time. For example, the copyright costs of this text are amortized over 3 years.

A **trademark** is a name, term, or symbol used to identify a business and its products. For example, the distinctive red-and-white Coca Cola logo is an example of a trademark. Most businesses identify their trademarks with ® in their advertise-ments and on their products. Under federal law, businesses can protect against others using their trademarks by registering them for 10 years and renewing the registra-tion for 10-year periods thereafter. Like a copyright, the legal costs of registering a trademark with the federal government should be recorded as an asset. Also, if a trademark is purchased from another business, the cost of its purchase would be recorded as an asset. The cost of a trademark should be amortized over its esti-mated useful life, but not more than 40 years.

In a recent annual report, **H.J. Heinz Company** reported that it amortizes goodwill, trademarks, and other intangibles over periods ranging from 3 to 40 years.

Goodwill

In business, **goodwill** refers to an intangible asset of a business that is created from such favorable factors as location, product quality, reputation, and managerial skill. Goodwill allows a business to earn a rate of return on its investment that is often in excess of the normal rate for other firms in the same business.

Generally accepted accounting principles permit the recording of goodwill in the accounts only if it is objectively determined by a transaction. An example of a transaction that may justify recording goodwill is the purchase or sale of a business. Goodwill must be amortized over its estimated useful life, which cannot exceed 40 years.

Financial Reporting for Fixed Assets and Intangible Assets

objective 9

Describe how depreciation expense is reported in an income statement, and pre-pare a balance sheet that includes fixed assets and intangible assets.

How should fixed assets and intangible assets be reported in the financial state-ments? The amount of depreciation and amortization expense of a period should be reported separately in the income statement or disclosed in a footnote. A general description of the method or methods used in computing depreciation should also be reported.

The amount of each major class of fixed assets should be disclosed in the bal-ance sheet or in footnotes. The related accumulated depreciation should also be disclosed, either by major class or in total. The fixed assets may be shown at their **book value** (cost less accumulated depreciation), which can also be described as their **net** amount. If there are too many classes of fixed assets, a single amount may be presented in the balance sheet, supported by a separate detailed listing. Fixed assets are normally presented under the more descriptive caption of **property, plant, and equipment**.

The cost of mineral rights or ore deposits is normally shown as part of the fixed assets section of the balance sheet. The related accumulated depletion should also be disclosed. In some cases, the mineral rights are shown net of depletion on the face of the balance sheet, accompanied by a footnote that discloses the amount of the accumulated depletion.

Intangible assets are usually reported in the balance sheet in a separate section immediately following fixed assets. The balance of each major class of intangible assets should be disclosed at an amount net of amortization taken to date. Exhibit 7 is a partial balance sheet that shows the reporting of fixed assets and intangible assets.

Exhibit 7 Fixed Assets and Intangible Assets in the Balance Sheet

Discovery Mining Co.
Balance Sheet
December 31, 20—

Assets

Total current assets				$ 462,500

Property, plant, and equipment:	Cost	Accum. Depr.	Book Value	
Land	$ 30,000	—	$ 30,000	
Buildings	110,000	$ 26,000	84,000	
Factory equipment	650,000	192,000	458,000	
Office equipment	120,000	13,000	107,000	
	$ 910,000	$ 231,000		$679,000

Mineral deposits:	Cost	Accum. Depl.	Book Value	
Alaska deposit	$1,200,000	$ 800,000	$ 400,000	
Wyoming deposit	750,000	200,000	550,000	
	$1,950,000	$1,000,000		950,000
Total property, plant, and equipment				1,629,000
Intangible assets:				
Patents			$ 75,000	
Goodwill			50,000	
Total intangible assets				125,000

FINANCIAL ANALYSIS AND INTERPRETATION

objective 10

Compute and interpret the ratio of fixed assets to long-term liabilities.

Long-term liabilities are often secured by fixed assets. The ratio of total fixed assets to long-term liabilities provides a solvency measure that indicates the margin of safety to creditors. It also gives an indication of the potential ability of the business to borrow additional funds on a long-term basis. The **ratio of fixed assets to long-term liabilities** is computed as follows:

$$\text{Ratio of fixed assets to long-term liabilities (debt)} = \frac{\text{Fixed assets (net)}}{\text{Long-term liabilities (debt)}}$$

To illustrate, the following data were taken from the 2000 and 1999 financial statements of **Procter & Gamble**:

	(in millions)	
	2000	**1999**
Property, plant, and equipment (net)	$13,692	$12,626
Long-term debt	8,916	6,231

The ratio of fixed assets to long-term liabilities (debt) is 1.5 ($13,692/$8,916) for 2000 and 2.0 ($12,626/$6,231) for 1999. The decrease in the ratio from 1999 to 2000 indicates less of a margin of safety for creditors. As with other financial measures, the interpretation and analysis is enhanced by comparisons over time and with industry averages.

ENCORE

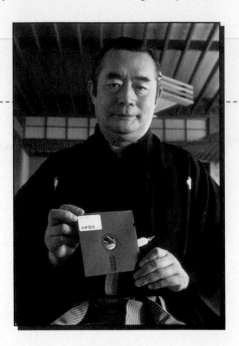

The Ultimate Inventor

Would you like to become an inventor and own patents worth millions? Yoshiro Nakamatsu, who bills himself as the Thomas Edison of Japan, hopes to open a school that will teach people how to create new products. Yoshiro Nakamatsu is the president of Tokyo's **Hi-Tech Innovation Institute** and claims to have 3,042 patents over his inventing career. Nakamatsu's net worth from royalties from his inventions is estimated at $75 million.

At the age of 5, with encouragement from his grandfather, Nakamatsu invented a stabilizer to make planes fly better. He was granted his first patent at age 14. Since then, he has licensed 16 patents to **IBM**, including one for his 1952 invention of the floppy disk for personal computers. Some of Nakamatsu's other inventions and what he claims they do include the following:

- **Yummy TV.** A snack food designed to relieve eye strain caused by watching too much TV.

- **Enerex.** An engine that produces energy from water.
- **Cerebrex Chair.** A chair that uses electronic impulses to both sharpen the mind and rest the body.
- **Nakamatsu Golf Putter.** A putter that has an oversized vibrating handle to make putting 93 percent accurate within 10 feet.
- **Anti-Gravity Floating Vibrating Three-Dimensional Sonic System.** A speaker system for stereo compact disc players and other electronic products.
- **Magnetic Eyeglasses.** Eyeglasses that have magnets attached to them for improving the blood circulation of the eyes.
- **Dr. Nakamatsu's Yummi Nutri Brain Biscuits.** Food for your brain.
- **Nakamatsu's Engine.** An engine that is far more efficient than gasoline or electric engines because it runs on "cosmic" power.

In his lectures, Nakamatsu offers the following advice on how to become a genius and excel at inventing: (1) swim, (2) lift weights, (3) sleep less than six hours a night, (4) work between the hours of midnight and 4 a.m., and (5) never have sex before the age of 24. ■

Source: Dean Takahashi, "Japanese Inventor Nearly Triples Edison's Output," *The Austin American-Statesman,* May 17, 1996.

APPENDIX: SUM-OF-THE-YEARS-DIGITS DEPRECIATION

At one time, the sum-of-the-years-digits method of depreciation was used by many businesses. However, the tax law changes of the 1980s limited its use for tax purposes.

Under the **sum-of-the-years-digits method**, depreciation expense is determined by multiplying the original cost of the asset less its estimated residual value by a smaller fraction each year. Thus, the sum-of-the-years-digits method is similar to the declining-balance method in that the depreciation expense declines each year.

A recent edition of *Accounting Trends & Techniques* reported that only 1%–2% of the surveyed companies now use this method for financial reporting purposes.

The denominator of the fraction used in determining the depreciation expense is the sum of the digits of the years of the asset's useful life. For example, an asset with a useful life of 5 years would have a denominator of 15 (5 + 4 + 3 + 2 +

1).[8] The numerator of the fraction is the number of years of useful life remaining at the beginning of each year for which depreciation is being computed. Thus, the numerator decreases each year by 1. For a useful life of 5 years, the numerator is 5 the first year, 4 the second year, 3 the third year, and so on.

The following depreciation schedule illustrates the sum-of-the-years-digits method for an asset with a cost of $24,000, an estimated residual value of $2,000, and an estimated useful life of 5 years:

Year	Cost Less Residual Value	Rate	Depreciation for Year	Accum. Depr. at End of Year	Book Value at End of Year
1	$22,000	5/15	$7,333.33	$ 7,333.33	$16,666.67
2	22,000	4/15	5,866.67	13,200.00	10,800.00
3	22,000	3/15	4,400.00	17,600.00	6,400.00
4	22,000	2/15	2,933.33	20,533.33	3,466.67
5	22,000	1/15	1,466.67	22,000.00	2,000.00

What if the fixed asset is not placed in service at the beginning of the year? When the date an asset is first put into service is not the beginning of a fiscal year, each full year's depreciation must be allocated between the two fiscal years benefited. To illustrate, assume that the asset in the above example was put into service at the beginning of the fourth month of the first fiscal year. The depreciation for that year would be $5,500 ($9/12 \times 5/15 \times$ $22,000). The depreciation for the second year would be $6,233.33, computed as follows:

$3/12 \times 5/15 \times$ $22,000	$1,833.33
$9/12 \times 4/15 \times$ $22,000	4,400.00
Total depreciation for second fiscal year	$6,233.33

KEY POINTS

1 Define fixed assets and describe the accounting for their cost.
Fixed assets are long-term tangible assets that are owned by the business and are used in the normal operations of the business. Examples of fixed assets are equipment, buildings, and land. The initial cost of a fixed asset includes all amounts spent to get the asset in place and ready for use. For example, sales tax, freight, insurance in transit, and installation costs are all included in the cost of a fixed asset. As time passes, all fixed assets except land lose their ability to provide services. As a result, the cost of a fixed asset should be transferred to an expense account, in a systematic manner, during the asset's expected useful life. This periodic transfer of cost to expense is called depreciation.

2 Compute depreciation, using the following methods: straight-line method, units-of-production method, and declining-balance method.
In computing depreciation, three factors need to be considered: (1) the fixed asset's initial cost, (2) the useful life of the asset, and (3) the residual value of the asset.
The straight-line method spreads the initial cost less the residual value equally over the useful life. The units-of-production method spreads the initial cost less the residual value equally over the units expected to be produced by the asset during its useful life. The declining-balance method is applied by multiplying the declining book value of the asset by twice the straight-line rate.

3 Classify fixed asset costs as either capital expenditures or revenue expenditures.
Costs for additions to fixed assets and other costs related to improving efficiency or capacity are classified as capital expenditures. Costs for additions to an asset and costs that add to the usefulness of the asset for more than one period (called betterments) are also classified as capital expenditures.

[8] The denominator can also be determined from the following formula: $S = N[(N + 1)/2]$, where S = sum of the digits and N = number of years of estimated life.

Costs that increase the useful life of an asset beyond the original estimate are capital expenditures and are called extraordinary repairs. Expenditures that benefit only the current period or that maintain normal operating efficiency are debited to expense accounts and are classified as revenue expenditures.

4 Journalize entries for the disposal of fixed assets.

The journal entries to record disposals of fixed assets will vary. In all cases, however, any depreciation for the current period should be recorded, and the book value of the asset is then removed from the accounts. The entry to remove the book value from the accounts is a debit to the asset's accumulated depreciation account and a credit to the asset account for the cost of the asset. For assets retired from service, a loss may be recorded for any remaining book value of the asset.

When a fixed asset is sold, the book value is removed and the cash or other asset received is also recorded. If the selling price is more than the book value of the asset, the transaction results in a gain. If the selling price is less than the book value, there is a loss.

When a fixed asset is exchanged for another of similar nature, no gain is recognized on the exchange. The acquired asset's cost is adjusted for any gains. A loss on an exchange of similar assets is recorded.

5 Define a lease and summarize the accounting rules

related to the leasing of fixed assets.

A lease is a contract for the use of an asset for a period of time. A capital lease is accounted for as if the lessee has purchased the asset. The lease payments under an operating lease are accounted for as rent expense for the lessee.

6 Describe internal controls over fixed assets.

Internal controls over fixed assets should include procedures for authorizing the purchase of assets. Once acquired, fixed assets should be safeguarded from theft, misuse, or damage. A physical inventory of fixed assets should be taken periodically.

7 Compute depletion and journalize the entry for depletion.

The amount of periodic depletion is computed by multiplying the quantity of minerals extracted during the period by a depletion rate. The depletion rate is computed by dividing the cost of the mineral deposit by its estimated size. The entry to record depletion debits a depletion expense account and credits an accumulated depletion account.

8 Journalize the entries for acquiring and amortizing intangible assets, such as patents, copyrights, and goodwill.

Long-term assets that are without physical attributes but are used in the business are classified as intangible assets. Examples of

intangible assets are patents, copyrights, trademarks, and goodwill. The initial cost of an intangible asset should be debited to an asset account. This cost should be written off, or amortized, over the years of the asset's expected usefulness by debiting an expense account and crediting the intangible asset account.

9 Describe how depreciation expense is reported in an income statement, and prepare a balance sheet that includes fixed assets and intangible assets.

The amount of depreciation expense and the method or methods used in computing depreciation should be disclosed in the financial statements. In addition, each major class of fixed assets should be disclosed, along with the related accumulated depreciation. Intangible assets are usually presented in the balance sheet in a separate section immediately following fixed assets. Each major class of intangible assets should be disclosed at an amount net of the amortization recorded to date.

10 Compute and interpret the ratio of fixed assets to long-term liabilities.

The ratio of fixed assets to long-term liabilities is a solvency measure that indicates the margin of safety to creditors. It also provides an indication of the ability of a company to borrow additional funds on a long-term basis.

ILLUSTRATIVE PROBLEM

McCollum Company, a furniture wholesaler, acquired new equipment at a cost of $150,000 at the beginning of the fiscal year. The equipment has an estimated life of 5 years and an estimated residual value of $12,000. Ellen McCollum, the president, has requested information regarding alternative depreciation methods.

Instructions

1. Determine the annual depreciation for each of the five years of estimated useful life of the equipment, the accumulated depreciation at the end of each year, and the

book value of the equipment at the end of each year by (a) the straight-line method and (b) the declining-balance method (at twice the straight-line rate).

2. Assume that the equipment was depreciated under the declining-balance method. In the first week of the fifth year, the equipment was traded in for similar equipment priced at $175,000. The trade-in allowance on the old equipment was $10,000, and cash was paid for the balance. Journalize the entry to record the exchange.

Solution

1.

	Year	Depreciation Expense	Accumulated Depreciation, End of Year	Book Value, End of Year
a.	1	$27,600*	$ 27,600	$122,400
	2	27,600	55,200	94,800
	3	27,600	82,800	67,200
	4	27,600	110,400	39,600
	5	27,600	138,000	12,000

*$27,600 = ($150,000 − $12,000) ÷ 5

	Year	Depreciation Expense	Accumulated Depreciation, End of Year	Book Value, End of Year
b.	1	$60,000**	$ 60,000	$ 90,000
	2	36,000	96,000	54,000
	3	21,600	117,600	32,400
	4	12,960	130,560	19,440
	5	7,440***	138,000	12,000

**$60,000 = $150,000 × 40%
***The asset is not depreciated below the estimated residual value of $12,000.

2.

Accumulated Depreciation—Equipment	130 5 6 0 00		
Equipment	175 0 0 0 00		
Loss on Disposal of Fixed Assets	9 4 4 0 00		
Equipment		150 0 0 0 00	
Cash		165 0 0 0 00	

SELF-EXAMINATION QUESTIONS

Answers at End of Chapter

Matching

Match each of the following statements with its proper term. Some terms may not be used.

A. accelerated depreciation method

B. amortization

C. betterment

D. book value

E. boot

F. capital expenditures

G. capital leases

H. copyright

I. declining-balance method

___ 1. Long-term or relatively permanent tangible assets that are used in the normal business operations.

___ 2. The systematic periodic transfer of the cost of a fixed asset to an expense account during its expected useful life.

___ 3. The estimated value of a fixed asset at the end of its useful life.

___ 4. A method of depreciation that provides for equal periodic depreciation expense over the estimated life of a fixed asset.

___ 5. A method of depreciation that provides for depreciation expense based on the expected productive capacity of a fixed asset.

___ 6. A method of depreciation that provides periodic depreciation expense based on the declining book value of a fixed asset over its estimated life.

___ 7. The cost of a fixed asset minus accumulated depreciation on the asset.

J.   depletion

K.   depreciation

L.   extraordinary repair

M.   fixed assets

N.   goodwill

O.   intangible assets

P.   operating leases

Q.   patents

R.   ratio of fixed assets to long-term liabilities

S.   ratio of fixed assets to total assets

T.   residual value

U.   revenue expenditures

V.   straight-line method

W.   trade-in allowance

X.   trademark

Y.   units-of-production method

____ 8. A depreciation method that provides for a higher depreciation amount in the first year of the asset's use, followed by a gradually declining amount of depreciation.

____ 9. The costs of acquiring fixed assets, adding to a fixed asset, improving a fixed asset, or extending a fixed asset's useful life.

____ 10. Costs that benefit only the current period or costs incurred for normal maintenance and repairs of fixed assets.

____ 11. An expenditure that improves a fixed asset's operating efficiency or capacity for its remaining useful life.

____ 12. An expenditure that increases the useful life of an asset beyond its original estimate.

____ 13. The amount a seller allows a buyer for a fixed asset that is traded in for a similar asset.

____ 14. The amount a buyer owes a seller when a fixed asset is traded in on a similar asset.

____ 15. Leases that include one or more provisions that result in treating the leased assets as purchased assets in the accounts.

____ 16. Leases that do not meet the criteria for capital leases and thus are accounted for as operating expenses.

____ 17. The process of transferring the cost of natural resources to an expense account.

____ 18. Long-term assets that are useful in the operations of a business, are not held for sale, and are without physical qualities.

____ 19. The periodic transfer of the cost of an intangible asset to expense.

____ 20. An intangible asset that is created from such favorable factors as location, product quality, reputation, and managerial skill.

____ 21. Exclusive rights to produce and sell goods with one or more unique features.

____ 22. An exclusive right to publish and sell a literary, artistic, or musical composition.

____ 23. A name, term, or symbol used to identify a business and its products.

____ 24. A financial ratio that provides a measure indicating the margin of safety to creditors.

Multiple Choice

1. Which of the following expenditures incurred in connection with acquiring machinery is a proper charge to the asset account?
   A. Freight
   B. Installation costs
   C. Both A and B
   D. Neither A nor B

2. What is the amount of depreciation, using the declining-balance method (twice the straight-line rate) for the second year of use for equipment costing $9,000, with an estimated residual value of $600 and an estimated life of 3 years?
   A. $6,000
   B. $3,000
   C. $2,000
   D. $400

3. An example of an accelerated depreciation method is:
   A. Straight-line
   B. Declining-balance
   C. Units-of-production
   D. Depletion

4. A fixed asset priced at $100,000 is acquired by trading in a similar asset that has a book value of $25,000. Assuming that the trade-in allowance is $30,000 and that $70,000 cash is paid for the new asset, what is the cost of the new asset for financial reporting purposes?
   A. $100,000
   B. $95,000
   C. $70,000
   D. $30,000

5. Which of the following is an example of an intangible asset?
   A. Patents
   B. Goodwill
   C. Copyrights
   D. All of the above

1. Which of the following qualities are characteristic of fixed assets? (a) tangible, (b) capable of repeated use in the operations of the business, (c) held for sale in the normal course of business, (d) used continuously in the operations of the business, (e) long-lived.

2. Penguin Office Equipment Co. has a fleet of automobiles and trucks for use by salespersons and for delivery of office supplies and equipment. Sioux City Auto Sales Co. has automobiles and trucks for sale. Under what caption would the automobiles and trucks be reported on the balance sheet of (a) Penguin Office Equipment Co., (b) Sioux City Auto Sales Co.?

3. Spiral Co. acquired an adjacent vacant lot with the hope of selling it in the future at a gain. The lot is not intended to be used in Spiral's business operations. Where should such real estate be listed in the balance sheet?

4. Tensile Company solicited bids from several contractors to construct an addition to its office building. The lowest bid received was for $340,000. Tensile Company decided to construct the addition itself at a cost of $325,000. What amount should be recorded in the building account?

5. Are the amounts at which fixed assets are reported in the balance sheet their approximate market values as of the balance sheet date? Discuss.

6. a. Does the recognition of depreciation in the accounts provide a special cash fund for the replacement of fixed assets? Explain.
   b. Describe the nature of depreciation as the term is used in accounting.

7. Name the three factors that need to be considered in determining the amount of periodic depreciation.

8. Trigger Company purchased a machine that has a manufacturer's suggested life of 15 years. The company plans to use the machine on a special project that will last 11 years. At the completion of the project, the machine will be sold. Over how many years should the machine be depreciated?

9. Is it necessary for a business to use the same method of computing depreciation (a) for all classes of its depreciable assets, (b) in the financial statements and in determining income taxes?

10. Of the three common depreciation methods, which is most widely used?

11. a. Under what conditions is the use of an accelerated depreciation method most appropriate?
    b. Why is an accelerated depreciation method often used for income tax purposes?
    c. What is the Modified Accelerated Cost Recovery System (MACRS), and under what conditions is it used?

12. A revision of depreciable fixed asset lives resulted in an increase in the remaining lives of certain fixed assets. The company would like to include, as income of the current period, the cumulative effect of the changes, which reduces the depreciation expense of past periods. Is this in accordance with generally accepted accounting principles? Discuss.

Source: "Q's and A's Technical Hotline," *Journal of Accountancy,* December 1991, p. 89.

13. Differentiate between the accounting for capital expenditures and revenue expenditures.

14. Immediately after a used truck is acquired, a new motor is installed and the tires are replaced at a total cost of $4,750. Is this a capital expenditure or a revenue expenditure?

15. For some of the fixed assets of a business, the balance in Accumulated Depreciation is exactly equal to the cost of the asset. (a) Is it permissible to record additional depreciation on the assets if they are still useful to the business? Explain. (b) When should an entry be made to remove the cost and the accumulated depreciation from the accounts?

16. In what sections of the income statement are gains and losses from the disposal of fixed assets presented?

17. Differentiate between a capital lease and an operating lease.

18. The financial statements of **La-Z-Boy Chair Company** contain the following footnote:

The Company has several long-term leases covering manufacturing facilities. The lease agreements require the Company to insure and maintain the facilities and provide for annual payments, which include interest. These leases give the Company the option to purchase the facilities for nominal amounts, or in some instances to renew the leases for extended periods at nominal annual rentals.

Would these leases be classified as operating or capital leases? Discuss.

19. Describe the internal controls for acquiring fixed assets.
20. Why is a physical count of fixed assets necessary?
21. What is the term applied to the periodic charge for (a) ore removed from a mine, (b) the use of an intangible asset?
22. a.   Over what period of time should the cost of a patent acquired by purchase be amortized?
    b.   In general, what is the required treatment for research and development costs?
23. How should (a) fixed assets and (b) intangible assets be reported in the balance sheet?

RESOURCES FOR YOUR SUCCESS ONLINE AT

http://warren.swcollege.com

Remember! If you need additional help, visit South-Western's Web site.
See page 26 for a description of the online and printed materials that are available.

EXERCISES

Exercise 10–1
Costs of acquiring fixed assets

Objective 1

Tracie Klein owns and operates Walcott Print Co. During July, Walcott Print Co. incurred the following costs in acquiring two printing presses. One printing press was new, and the other was used by a business that recently filed for bankruptcy.

Costs related to new printing press:

1. Sales tax on purchase price
2. Insurance while in transit
3. Freight
4. Special foundation
5. New parts to replace those damaged in unloading
6. Fee paid to factory representative for installation

Costs related to secondhand printing press:

7. Freight
8. Installation
9. Repair of vandalism during installation
10. Replacement of worn-out parts
11. Repair of damage incurred in reconditioning the press
12. Fees paid to attorney to review purchase agreement

a.   Indicate which costs incurred in acquiring the new printing press should be debited to the asset account.
b.   Indicate which costs incurred in acquiring the secondhand printing press should be debited to the asset account.

Exercise 10–2
Determine cost of land

Objective 1

A company has developed a tract of land into a ski resort. The company has cut the trees, cleared and graded the land and hills, and constructed ski lifts. (a) Should the tree cutting, land clearing, and grading costs of constructing the ski slopes be debited to the land account? (b) If such costs are debited to Land, should they be depreciated?

Source: "Technical Issues Feature," *Journal of Accountancy*, December 1987, p. 82.

Exercise 10–3
Determine cost of land

Objective 1

✓ $138,250

Birch Delivery Company acquired an adjacent lot to construct a new warehouse, paying $25,000 and giving a short-term note for $100,000. Legal fees paid were $1,750, delinquent taxes assumed were $7,500, and fees paid to remove an old building from the land were $5,500. Materials salvaged from the demolition of the building were sold for $1,500. A contractor was paid $412,500 to construct a new warehouse. Determine the cost of the land to be reported on the balance sheet.

Exercise 10–4
Nature of depreciation

Objective 1

Yarborough Metal Casting Co. reported $575,000 for equipment and $217,500 for accumulated depreciation—equipment on its balance sheet.
Does this mean (a) that the replacement cost of the equipment is $575,000 and (b) that $217,500 is set aside in a special fund for the replacement of the equipment? Explain.

Exercise 10–5
Straight-line depreciation rates

Objective 2

✓ a. 25%

Convert each of the following estimates of useful life to a straight-line depreciation rate, stated as a percentage, assuming that the residual value of the fixed asset is to be ignored: (a) 4 years, (b) 5 years, (c) 10 years, (d) 20 years, (e) 25 years, (f) 40 years, (g) 50 years.

Exercise 10–6
Straight-line depreciation

Objective 2

✓ $11,750

A refrigerator used by a meat processor has a cost of $112,000, an estimated residual value of $18,000, and an estimated useful life of 8 years. What is the amount of the annual depreciation computed by the straight-line method?

Exercise 10–7
Depreciation by units-of-production method

Objective 2

✓ $3,220

A diesel-powered generator with a cost of $375,000 and estimated residual value of $50,000 is expected to have a useful operating life of 75,000 hours. During November, the generator was operated 700 hours. Determine the depreciation for the month.

Exercise 10 8
Depreciation by units-of-production method

Objective 2

✓ a. Truck #1, credit Accumulated Depreciation, $8,400

Prior to adjustment at the end of the year, the balance in Trucks is $176,600 and the balance in Accumulated Depreciation—Trucks is $60,500. Details of the subsidiary ledger are as follows:

Truck No.	Cost	Estimated Residual Value	Estimated Useful Life	Accumulated Depreciation at Beginning of Year	Miles Operated During Year
1	$75,000	$5,000	250,000 miles	$21,000	30,000 miles
2	38,600	3,600	200,000	31,500	25,000
3	35,000	3,000	100,000	8,000	36,000
4	28,000	4,000	120,000	—	21,000

a. Determine the depreciation rates per mile and the amount to be credited to the accumulated depreciation section of each of the subsidiary accounts for the miles operated during the current year.
b. Journalize the entry to record depreciation for the year.

Exercise 10–9
Depreciation by two methods
Objective 2

✓ a. $15,400

A backhoe acquired on January 2 at a cost of $154,000 has an estimated useful life of 10 years. Assuming that it will have no residual value, determine the depreciation for each of the first two years (a) by the straight-line method and (b) by the declining-balance method, using twice the straight-line rate.

Exercise 10–10
Depreciation by two methods
Objective 2

✓ a. $8,100

A dairy storage tank acquired at the beginning of the fiscal year at a cost of $70,000 has an estimated residual value of $5,200 and an estimated useful life of 8 years. Determine the following: (a) the amount of annual depreciation by the straight-line method and (b) the amount of depreciation for the first and second year computed by the declining-balance method (at twice the straight-line rate).

Exercise 10–11
Partial-year depreciation
Objective 2

✓ a. First year, $7,350

Sandblasting equipment acquired at a cost of $64,000 has an estimated residual value of $5,200 and an estimated useful life of 6 years. It was placed in service on April 1 of the current fiscal year, which ends on December 31. Determine the depreciation for the current fiscal year and for the following fiscal year by (a) the straight-line method and (b) the declining-balance method, at twice the straight-line rate.

Exercise 10–12
Revision of depreciation
Objective 2

✓ a. $12,000

A warehouse with a cost of $500,000 has an estimated residual value of $20,000, an estimated useful life of 40 years, and is depreciated by the straight-line method. (a) What is the amount of the annual depreciation? (b) What is the book value at the end of the twentieth year of use? (c) If at the start of the twenty-first year it is estimated that the remaining life is 15 years and that the residual value is $5,000, what is the depreciation expense for each of the remaining 15 years?

Exercise 10–13
Book value of fixed assets
Objective 2

The following data were taken from recent annual reports of **Interstate Bakeries Corporation (IBC)**. Interstate Bakeries produces, distributes, and sells fresh bakery products nationwide through supermarkets, convenience stores, and its 67 bakeries and 1,500 thrift stores.

	Current Year	Preceding Year
Land and buildings	$388,618,000	$364,773,000
Machinery and equipment	953,625,000	894,533,000
Accumulated depreciation	447,797,000	364,791,000

a. Compute the book value of the fixed assets for the current year and the preceding year and explain the differences, if any.
b. Would you normally expect the book value of fixed assets to increase or decrease during the year?

Exercise 10–14
Capital and revenue expenditures
Objective 3

Yeats Co. incurred the following costs related to trucks and vans used in operating its delivery service:

1. Installed a hydraulic lift to a van.
2. Removed a two-way radio from one of the trucks and installed a new radio with a greater range of communication.
3. Overhauled the engine on one of the trucks that had been purchased four years ago.
4. Changed the oil and greased the joints of all the trucks and vans.
5. Replaced the brakes and alternator on a truck that had been in service for the past 5 years.
6. Installed security systems on three of the newer trucks.

7. Replaced two of the trucks' shock absorbers with new shock absorbers that allow for the delivery of heavier loads.
8. Repaired a flat tire on one of the vans.
9. Rebuilt the transmission on one of the vans that had been driven only 25,000 miles. The van was no longer under warranty.
10. Tinted the back and side windows of one of the vans to discourage theft of contents.

Classify each of the costs as a capital expenditure or a revenue expenditure. For those costs identified as capital expenditures, classify each as an addition, a betterment, or an extraordinary repair.

Exercise 10–15
Capital and revenue expenditures

Objective 3

Faith Inman owns and operates Yellow Ribbon Transport Co. During the past year, Faith incurred the following costs related to her 18-wheel truck.

1. Replaced the hydraulic brake system that had begun to fail during her latest trip through the Smoky Mountains.
2. Overhauled the engine.
3. Replaced a headlight that had burned out.
4. Removed the old CB radio and replaced it with a newer model with a greater range.
5. Replaced a shock absorber that had worn out.
6. Installed fog lights.
7. Installed a wind deflector on top of the cab to increase fuel mileage.
8. Modified the factory-installed turbo charger with a special-order kit designed to add 30 more horsepower to the engine performance.
9. Installed a television in the sleeping compartment of the truck.
10. Replaced the old radar detector with a newer model that detects the KA frequencies now used by many of the state patrol radar guns. The detector is wired directly into the cab, so that it is partially hidden. In addition, Faith fastened the detector to the truck with a locking device that prevents its removal.

Classify each of the costs as a capital expenditure or a revenue expenditure. For those costs identified as capital expenditures, classify each as an addition, a betterment, or an extraordinary repair.

Exercise 10–16
Major repair to fixed asset

Objective 3

✓ a. $22,000
✓ d. $15,000

A number of major structural repairs on a building were completed at the beginning of the current fiscal year at a cost of $50,000. The repairs are expected to extend the life of the building 8 years beyond the original estimate. The original cost of the building was $550,000, and it is being depreciated by the straight-line method for 25 years. The residual value is expected to be negligible and has been ignored. The balance of the related accumulated depreciation account after the depreciation adjustment at the end of the preceding year is $330,000.

a. What has the amount of annual depreciation been in past years?
b. To what account should the cost of repairs ($50,000) be debited?
c. What is the book value of the building after the repairs have been recorded?
d. What is the amount of depreciation for the current year, using the straight-line method (assuming that the repairs were completed at the very beginning of the year)?

Exercise 10–17
Entries for sale of fixed asset

Objective 4

Metal recycling equipment acquired on January 3, 2000, at a cost of $117,500, has an estimated useful life of 8 years, an estimated residual value of $7,500, and is depreciated by the straight-line method.

a. What was the book value of the equipment at December 31, 2003, the end of the fiscal year?
b. Assuming that the equipment was sold on July 1, 2004, for $53,500, journalize the entries to record (1) depreciation for the six months of the current year ending December 31, 2004, and (2) the sale of the equipment.

Exercise 10–18
Disposal of fixed asset

Objective 4

✓ b. $21,250

Equipment acquired on January 3, 2000, at a cost of $71,500, has an estimated useful life of 4 years and an estimated residual value of $4,500.

a. What was the annual amount of depreciation for the years 2000, 2001, and 2002, using the straight-line method of depreciation?
b. What was the book value of the equipment on January 1, 2003? *(continued)*

c. Assuming that the equipment was sold on January 2, 2003, for $18,000, journalize the entry to record the sale.

d. Assuming that the equipment had been sold on January 2, 2003, for $23,000 instead of $18,000, journalize the entry to record the sale.

Exercise 10–19
Asset traded for similar asset
Objective 4

A printing press priced at $220,000 is acquired by trading in a similar press and paying cash for the difference between the trade-in allowance and the price of the new press.

a. Assuming that the trade-in allowance is $35,000, what is the amount of cash given?

b. Assuming that the book value of the press traded in is $18,750, what is the cost of the new press for financial reporting purposes?

Exercise 10–20
Asset traded for similar asset
Objective 4

Assume the same facts as in Exercise 10–19, except that the book value of the press traded in is $41,700. (a) What is the amount of cash given? (b) What is the cost of the new press for financial reporting purposes?

Exercise 10–21
Entries for trade of fixed asset
Objective 4

On April 1, Cascade Co., a water distiller, acquired new bottling equipment with a list price of $285,000. Cascade received a trade-in allowance of $70,000 on the old equipment of a similar type, paid cash of $50,000, and gave a series of five notes payable for the remainder. The following information about the old equipment is obtained from the account in the equipment ledger: cost, $183,500; accumulated depreciation on December 31, the end of the preceding fiscal year, $96,000; annual depreciation, $12,000. Journalize the entries to record (a) the current depreciation of the old equipment to the date of trade-in and (b) the transaction on April 1 for financial reporting purposes.

Exercise 10–22
Entries for trade of fixed asset
Objective 4

On October 1, Rochne Co. acquired a new truck with a list price of $75,000. Rochne received a trade-in allowance of $15,000 on an old truck of similar type, paid cash of $10,000, and gave a series of five notes payable for the remainder. The following information about the old truck is obtained from the account in the equipment ledger: cost, $52,500; accumulated depreciation on December 31, the end of the preceding fiscal year, $36,000; annual depreciation, $4,500. Journalize the entries to record (a) the current depreciation of the old truck to the date of trade-in and (b) the transaction on October 1 for financial reporting purposes.

Exercise 10–23
Depreciable cost of asset acquired by exchange
Objective 4

On the first day of the fiscal year, a delivery truck with a list price of $45,000 was acquired in exchange for an old delivery truck and $28,000 cash. The old truck had a book value of $18,250 at the date of the exchange.

a. Determine the depreciable cost for financial reporting purposes.

b. Assuming that the book value of the old delivery truck was $14,000, determine the depreciable cost for financial reporting purposes.

Exercise 10–24
Internal control of fixed assets
Objective 6

DataNet Co. is a computer software company marketing products in the United States and Canada. While DataNet Co. has over 90 sales offices, all accounting is handled at the company's headquarters in Bozeman, Montana.

DataNet Co. keeps all its fixed asset records on a computerized system. The computer maintains a subsidiary ledger of all fixed assets owned by the company and calculates depreciation automatically. Whenever a manager at one of the ninety sales offices wants to purchase a fixed asset, a purchase request is submitted to headquarters for approval. Upon approval, the fixed asset is purchased and the invoice is sent back to headquarters so that the asset can be entered into the fixed asset system.

A manager who wants to dispose of a fixed asset simply sells or disposes of the asset and notifies headquarters to remove the asset from the system. Company cars and personal computers are frequently purchased by employees when they are disposed of. Most pieces of office equipment are traded in when new assets are acquired.

What internal control weakness exists in the procedures used to acquire and dispose of fixed assets at DataNet Co.?

Exercise 10–25

Depletion entries

Objective 7

Anaconda Co. acquired mineral rights for $30,000,000. The mineral deposit is estimated at 50,000,000 tons. During the current year, 7,500,000 tons were mined and sold for $6,500,000.

a. Determine the amount of depletion expense for the current year.
b. Journalize the adjusting entry to recognize the expense.

Exercise 10–26

Amortization entries

Objective 8

Langohr Company acquired patent rights on January 3, 2000, for $675,000. The patent has a useful life equal to its legal life of 18 years. On January 5, 2003, Langohr successfully defended the patent in a lawsuit at a cost of $45,000.

a. Determine the patent amortization expense for the current year ended December 31, 2003.
b. Journalize the adjusting entry to recognize the amortization.

Exercise 10–27

Balance sheet presentation

Objective 9

How many errors can you find in the following partial balance sheet?

Rosedale Company
Balance Sheet
December 31, 2003

Assets

Total current assets $397,500

	Replacement Cost	Accumulated Depreciation	Book Value
Property, plant, and equipment:			
Land	$ 75,000	$ 20,000	$ 55,000
Buildings	160,000	76,000	84,000
Factory equipment	350,000	192,000	158,000
Office equipment	120,000	77,000	43,000
Patents	80,000	—	80,000
Goodwill	45,000	—	45,000
Total property, plant, and equipment	$830,000	$365,000	465,000

Exercise 10–28

Ratio of fixed assets to long-term liabilities

Objective 10

The following data were taken from recent annual reports of **Intuit Inc.**, a developer and distributor of computer software:

	Current Year	Preceding Year
Property and equipment (net)	$69,413,000	$83,404,000
Long-term notes payable	35,566,000	36,444,000

a. Compute the ratio of fixed assets to long-term liabilities for the current and preceding years. Round to one decimal place.
b. What conclusions can you draw?

Exercise 10–29

Ratio of fixed assets to long-term liabilities

Objective 10

The financial statements of **Cisco Systems, Inc.**, presented in Appendix G at the end of the text, indicate that Cisco Systems has no long-term liabilities.
    What conclusions can you draw?

Appendix
Exercise 10–30
Sum-of-the-years-digits depreciation

✓ First year: $28,000

Based on the data in Exercise 10–9, determine the depreciation for the backhoe for each of the first two years, using the sum-of-the-years-digits depreciation method.

Appendix
Exercise 10–31
Sum-of-the-years-digits depreciation

✓ First year: $14,400

Based on the data in Exercise 10–10, determine the depreciation for the dairy storage tank for each of the first two years, using the sum-of-the-years-digits depreciation method.

Appendix
Exercise 10–32
Partial-year depreciation

✓ First year: $12,600

Based on the data in Exercise 10–11, determine the depreciation for the sandblasting equipment for each of the first two years, using the sum-of-the-years-digits depreciation method.

PROBLEMS SERIES A

Problem 10–1A
Allocate payments and receipts to fixed asset accounts

Objective 1

SPREADSHEET

The following payments and receipts are related to land, land improvements, and buildings acquired for use in a wholesale ceramic business. The receipts are identified by an asterisk.

a.	Fee paid to attorney for title search	$ 3,500
b.	Cost of real estate acquired as a plant site: Land	200,000
	Building	55,000
c.	Delinquent real estate taxes on property, assumed by purchaser	18,750
d.	Cost of razing and removing building	4,800
e.	Proceeds from sale of salvage materials from old building	3,100
f.	Special assessment paid to city for extension of water main to the property	5,000
g.	Premium on 1-year insurance policy during construction	6,600
h.	Cost of filling and grading land	29,700
i.	Cost of repairing windstorm damage during construction	1,500
j.	Cost of paving parking lot to be used by customers	12,500
k.	Cost of trees and shrubbery planted	15,000
l.	Architect's and engineer's fees for plans and supervision	40,000
m.	Cost of repairing vandalism damage during construction	1,500
n.	Interest incurred on building loan during construction	48,000
o.	Cost of floodlights installed on parking lot	13,500
p.	Money borrowed to pay building contractor	500,000*
q.	Payment to building contractor for new building	750,000
r.	Proceeds from insurance company for windstorm and vandalism damage	3,000*
s.	Refund of premium on insurance policy (g) canceled after 11 months	750*

Instructions

1. Assign each payment and receipt to Land (unlimited life), Land Improvements (limited life), Building, or Other Accounts. Indicate receipts by an asterisk. Identify each item by letter and list the amounts in columnar form, as follows:

Item	Land	Land Improvements	Building	Other Accounts

2. Determine the amount debited to Land, Land Improvements, and Building.
3. ◖━━▶ The costs assigned to the land, which is used as a plant site, will not be depreciated, while the costs assigned to land improvements will be depreciated. Explain this seemingly contradictory application of the concept of depreciation.

Problem 10–2A
Compare three depreciation methods

Objective 2

✓ 2002: straight-line depreciation, $105,000

Diamondback Company purchased packaging equipment on January 3, 2002, for $340,000. The equipment was expected to have a useful life of 3 years, or 18,000 operating hours, and a residual value of $25,000. The equipment was used for 7,500 hours during 2002, 6,000 hours in 2003, and 4,500 hours in 2004.

Instructions
Determine the amount of depreciation expense for the years ended December 31, 2002, 2003, and 2004, by (a) the straight-line method, (b) the units-of-production method, and (c) the declining-balance method, using twice the straight-line rate. Also determine the total depreciation expense for the three years by each method. The following columnar headings are suggested for recording the depreciation expense amounts:

	Depreciation Expense		
Year	Straight-Line Method	Units-of-Production Method	Declining-Balance Method

Problem 10–3A
Depreciation by three methods; partial years

Objective 2

SPREADSHEET

✓ a. 2002: $17,000

Newbauer Company purchased plastic laminating equipment on July 1, 2002, for $108,000. The equipment was expected to have a useful life of 3 years, or 13,600 operating hours, and a residual value of $6,000. The equipment was used for 2,400 hours during 2002, 4,500 hours in 2003, 5,000 hours in 2004, and 1,700 hours in 2005.

Instructions
Determine the amount of depreciation expense for the years ended December 31, 2002, 2003, 2004, and 2005, by (a) the straight-line method, (b) the units-of-production method, and (c) the declining-balance method, using twice the straight-line rate.

Problem 10–4A
Depreciation by two methods; trade of fixed asset

Objectives 2, 4

GENERAL LEDGER

✓ 1. b. Year 1: $50,000 depreciation expense
✓ 2. $146,200

New lithographic equipment, acquired at a cost of $125,000 at the beginning of a fiscal year, has an estimated useful life of 5 years and an estimated residual value of $10,000. The manager requested information regarding the effect of alternative methods on the amount of depreciation expense each year. On the basis of the data presented to the manager, the declining-balance method was selected.

In the first week of the fifth year, the equipment was traded in for similar equipment priced at $150,000. The trade-in allowance on the old equipment was $20,000, cash of $30,000 was paid, and a note payable was issued for the balance.

Instructions
1. Determine the annual depreciation expense for each of the estimated 5 years of use, the accumulated depreciation at the end of each year, and the book value of the equipment at the end of each year by (a) the straight-line method and (b) the declining-balance method (at twice the straight-line rate). The following columnar headings are suggested for each schedule:

Year	Depreciation Expense	Accumulated Depreciation, End of Year	Book Value, End of Year

2. For financial reporting purposes, determine the cost of the new equipment acquired in the exchange.
3. Journalize the entry to record the exchange.
4. Journalize the entry to record the exchange, assuming that the trade-in allowance was $15,000 instead of $20,000.

Problem 10–5A
Transactions for fixed assets, including trade

Objectives 1, 3, 4

SPREADSHEET

GENERAL
LEDGER

The following transactions, adjusting entries, and closing entries were completed by Trail-ways Furniture Co. during a 3-year period. All are related to the use of delivery equipment. The declining-balance method (at twice the straight-line rate) of depreciation is used.

2002
Jan. 3. Purchased a used delivery truck for $26,750, paying cash.
5. Paid $1,250 for a new transmission for the truck. (Debit Delivery Equipment.)
Aug. 16. Paid garage $285 for miscellaneous repairs to the truck.
Dec. 31. Recorded depreciation on the truck for the fiscal year. The estimated useful life of the truck is 4 years, with a residual value of $6,000.
31. Closed the appropriate accounts to the income summary account.

2003
June 30. Traded in the used truck for a new truck priced at $41,000, receiving a trade-in allowance of $11,500 and paying the balance in cash. (Record depreciation to date in 2003.)
Aug. 10. Paid garage $175 for miscellaneous repairs to the truck.
Dec. 31. Recorded depreciation on the truck. It has an estimated residual value of $7,500 and an estimated life of 5 years.
31. Closed the appropriate accounts to the income summary account.

2004
Oct. 1. Purchased a new truck for $42,000, paying cash.
2. Sold the truck purchased June 30, 2003, for $26,750. (Record depreciation for the year.)
Dec. 31. Recorded depreciation on the remaining truck. It has an estimated residual value of $5,000 and an estimated useful life of 8 years.
31. Closed the appropriate accounts to the income summary account.

Instructions

Journalize the transactions and the adjusting and closing entries. Post to the following accounts in the ledger and determine the balances after each posting:

122 Delivery Equipment
123 Accumulated Depreciation—Delivery Equipment
616 Depreciation Expense—Delivery Equipment
617 Truck Repair Expense
812 Gain on Disposal of Fixed Assets

Problem 10–6A
Amortization and depletion entries

Objectives 7, 8

✓ 1. (a) $121,600

Data related to the acquisition of timber rights and intangible assets during the current year ended December 31 are as follows:

a. Timber rights on a tract of land were purchased for $480,000 on July 12. The stand of timber is estimated at 1,500,000 board feet. During the current year, 380,000 board feet of timber were cut.
b. Goodwill in the amount of $5,000,000 was purchased on January 3. It is decided to amortize over the maximum period allowable.
c. Governmental and legal costs of $80,000 were incurred on October 2 in obtaining a patent with an estimated economic life of 10 years. Amortization is to be for one-fourth year.

Instructions

1. Determine the amount of the amortization or depletion expense for the current year for each of the foregoing items.
2. Journalize the adjusting entries required to record the amortization or depletion for each item.

PROBLEMS SERIES B

Problem 10–1B

Allocate payments and receipts to fixed asset accounts

Objective 1

SPREADSHEET

The following payments and receipts are related to land, land improvements, and buildings acquired for use in a wholesale apparel business. The receipts are identified by an asterisk.

a.	Finder's fee paid to real estate agency	$ 10,000
b.	Cost of real estate acquired as a plant site: Land	250,000
	Building	50,000
c.	Fee paid to attorney for title search	2,500
d.	Delinquent real estate taxes on property, assumed by purchaser	18,500
e.	Cost of razing and removing building	11,250
f.	Proceeds from sale of salvage materials from old building	3,500
g.	Cost of filling and grading land	15,500
h.	Special assessment paid to city for extension of water main to the property	9,000
i.	Architect's and engineer's fees for plans and supervision	50,000
j.	Premium on 1-year insurance policy during construction	5,700
k.	Cost of repairing windstorm damage during construction	3,500
l.	Cost of repairing vandalism damage during construction	800
m.	Cost of paving parking lot to be used by customers	17,500
n.	Cost of trees and shrubbery planted	20,000
o.	Proceeds from insurance company for windstorm and vandalism damage	4,300*
p.	Interest incurred on building loan during construction	65,000
q.	Money borrowed to pay building contractor	1,000,000*
r.	Payment to building contractor for new building	1,250,000
s.	Refund of premium on insurance policy (j) canceled after 10 months	1,050*

Instructions

1. Assign each payment and receipt to Land (unlimited life), Land Improvements (limited life), Building, or Other Accounts. Indicate receipts by an asterisk. Identify each item by letter and list the amounts in columnar form, as follows:

Item	Land	Land Improvements	Building	Other Accounts

2. Determine the amount debited to Land, Land Improvements, and Building.
3. The costs assigned to the land, which is used as a plant site, will not be depreciated, while the costs assigned to land improvements will be depreciated. Explain this seemingly contradictory application of the concept of depreciation.

Problem 10–2B

Compare three depreciation methods

Objective 2

✓ 2002: straight-line depreciation, $57,500

Sunlight Company purchased waterproofing equipment on January 2, 2002, for $255,000. The equipment was expected to have a useful life of 4 years, or 28,750 operating hours, and a residual value of $25,000. The equipment was used for 8,500 hours during 2002, 8,100 hours in 2003, 7,800 hours in 2004, and 4,350 hours in 2005.

Instructions

Determine the amount of depreciation expense for the years ended December 31, 2002, 2003, 2004, and 2005, by (a) the straight-line method, (b) the units-of-production method, and (c) the declining-balance method, using twice the straight-line rate. Also determine the total depreciation expense for the four years by each method. The following columnar headings are suggested for recording the depreciation expense amounts:

	Depreciation Expense		
Year	Straight-Line Method	Units-of-Production Method	Declining-Balance Method

Problem 10–3B

Depreciation by three methods; partial years

Objective 2

SPREADSHEET

✓ a. 2002, $10,200

Autostock Company purchased tool sharpening equipment on July 1, 2002, for $64,800. The equipment was expected to have a useful life of 3 years, or 15,300 operating hours, and a residual value of $3,600. The equipment was used for 3,100 hours during 2002, 5,000 hours in 2003, 4,900 hours in 2004, and 2,300 hours in 2005.

Instructions

Determine the amount of depreciation expense for the years ended December 31, 2002, 2003, 2004, and 2005, by (a) the straight-line method, (b) the units-of-production method, and (c) the declining-balance method, using twice the straight-line rate.

Problem 10–4B

Depreciation by two methods; trade of fixed asset

Objectives 2, 4

GENERAL LEDGER

✓ 1. b. Year 1, $50,000 depreciation expense

✓ 2. $122,500

New tire retreading equipment, acquired at a cost of $100,000 at the beginning of a fiscal year, has an estimated useful life of 4 years and an estimated residual value of $10,000. The manager requested information regarding the effect of alternative methods on the amount of depreciation expense each year. On the basis of the data presented to the manager, the declining-balance method was selected.

In the first week of the fourth year, the equipment was traded in for similar equipment priced at $125,000. The trade-in allowance on the old equipment was $15,000, cash of $10,000 was paid, and a note payable was issued for the balance.

Instructions

1. Determine the annual depreciation expense for each of the estimated 4 years of use, the accumulated depreciation at the end of each year, and the book value of the equipment at the end of each year by (a) the straight-line method and (b) the declining-balance method (at twice the straight-line rate). The following columnar headings are suggested for each schedule:

Year	Depreciation Expense	Accumulated Depreciation, End of Year	Book Value, End of Year

2. For financial reporting purposes, determine the cost of the new equipment acquired in the exchange.
3. Journalize the entry to record the exchange.
4. Journalize the entry to record the exchange, assuming that the trade-in allowance was $8,000 instead of $15,000.

Problem 10–5B

Transactions for fixed assets, including trade

Objectives 1, 3, 4

SPREADSHEET

GENERAL LEDGER

The following transactions, adjusting entries, and closing entries were completed by Heritage Furniture Co. during a 3-year period. All are related to the use of delivery equipment. The declining-balance method (at twice the straight-line rate) of depreciation is used.

2001

Jan. 2. Purchased a used delivery truck for $18,000, paying cash.

    5. Paid $2,000 to replace the automatic transmission and install new brakes on the truck. (Debit Delivery Equipment.)

April 7. Paid garage $125 for changing the oil, replacing the oil filter, and tuning the engine on the delivery truck.

Dec. 31. Recorded depreciation on the truck for the fiscal year. The estimated useful life of the truck is 8 years, with a residual value of $3,000.

    31. Closed the appropriate accounts to the income summary account.

2002

Mar. 13. Paid garage $180 to tune the engine and make other minor repairs on the truck.

Apr. 30. Traded in the used truck for a new truck priced at $40,000, receiving a trade-in allowance of $15,500 and paying the balance in cash. (Record depreciation to date in 2002.)

Dec. 31. Recorded depreciation on the truck. It has an estimated trade-in value of $4,000 and an estimated life of 10 years.

    31. Closed the appropriate accounts to the income summary account.

2003

Sept. 1. Purchased a new truck for $45,000, paying cash.

2. Sold the truck purchased April 30, 2002, for $30,500. (Record depreciation for the year.)

Dec. 31. Recorded depreciation on the remaining truck. It has an estimated residual value of $4,500 and an estimated useful life of 10 years.

31. Closed the appropriate accounts to the income summary account.

Instructions

Journalize the transactions and the adjusting and closing entries. Post to the following accounts in the ledger and determine the balances after each posting:

122	Delivery Equipment
123	Accumulated Depreciation—Delivery Equipment
616	Depreciation Expense—Delivery Equipment
617	Truck Repair Expense
812	Gain on Disposal of Fixed Assets

Problem 10–6B

Amortization and depletion entries

Objectives 7, 8

✓ 1. (a) $46,875

Data related to the acquisition of timber rights and intangible assets during the current year ended December 31 are as follows:

a. Goodwill in the amount of $1,875,000 was purchased on January 4. It is decided to amortize over the maximum period allowable.

b. Governmental and legal costs of $75,200 were incurred on July 2 in obtaining a patent with an estimated economic life of 8 years. Amortization is to be for one-half year.

c. Timber rights on a tract of land were purchased for $520,000 on April 2. The stand of timber is estimated at 2,000,000 board feet. During the current year, 250,000 board feet of timber were cut.

Instructions

1. Determine the amount of the amortization or depletion expense for the current year for each of the foregoing items.

2. Journalize the adjusting entries to record the amortization or depletion expense for each item.

SPECIAL ACTIVITIES

Activity 10–1
Tri-State Co.

Ethics and professional conduct in business

Stuart Madden, CPA, is an assistant to the controller of Tri-State Co. In his spare time, Stuart also prepares tax returns and performs general accounting services for clients. Frequently, Stuart performs these services after his normal working hours, using Tri-State Co.'s computers and laser printers. Occasionally, Stuart's clients will call him at the office during regular working hours.

◆■■■■▶ Discuss whether Stuart is performing in a professional manner.

Activity 10–2
Stanza Co.

Financial vs. tax depreciation

The following is an excerpt from a conversation between two employees of Stanza Co., Geoff Haines and Allison Foster. Geoff is the accounts payable clerk, and Allison is the cashier.

Geoff: Allison, could I get your opinion on something?

Allison: Sure, Geoff.

Geoff: Do you know Kris, the fixed assets clerk?

Allison: I know who she is, but I don't know her real well. Why?

Geoff: Well, I was talking to her at lunch last Monday about how she liked her job, etc. You know, the usual . . . and she mentioned something about having to keep two sets of books . . . one for taxes and one for the financial statements. That can't be good accounting, can it? What do you think?

Allison: Two sets of books? It doesn't sound right.

Geoff: It doesn't seem right to me either. I was always taught that you had to use generally accepted accounting principles. How can there be two sets of books? What can be the difference between the two?

➤ How would you respond to Allison and Geoff if you were Kris?

Activity 10–3
Heimlich Construction Co.
Effect of depreciation on net income

Heimlich Construction Co. specializes in building replicas of historic houses. Ami Lamb, president of Heimlich, is considering the purchase of various items of equipment on July 1, 2001, for $150,000. The equipment would have a useful life of 5 years and no residual value. In the past, all equipment has been leased. For tax purposes, Ami is considering depreciating the equipment by the straight-line method. She discussed the matter with her CPA and learned that, although the straight-line method could be elected, it was to her advantage to use the modified accelerated cost recovery system (MACRS) for tax purposes. She asked for your advice as to which method to use for tax purposes.

1. Compute depreciation for each of the years (2001, 2002, 2003, 2004, 2005, and 2006) of useful life by (a) the straight-line method and (b) MACRS. In using the straight-line method, one-half year's depreciation should be computed for 2001 and 2006. Use the MACRS rates presented in the chapter.
2. Assuming that income before depreciation and income tax is estimated to be $150,000 uniformly per year and that the income tax rate is 30%, compute the net income for each of the years 2001, 2002, 2003, 2004, 2005, and 2006, if (a) the straight-line method is used and (b) MACRS is used.
3. ➤ What factors would you present for Ami's consideration in the selection of a depreciation method?

Activity 10–4
Into the Real World
Shopping for a delivery truck

You are planning to acquire a delivery truck for use in your business for three years. In groups of three or four, explore a local dealer's purchase and leasing options for the truck. Summarize the costs of purchasing versus leasing, and list other factors that might help you decide whether to buy or lease the truck.

Group Activity

Activity 10–5
Into the Real World
Applying for patents, copyrights, and trademarks

Go to the Internet and review the procedures for applying for a patent, a copyright, and a trademark. One Internet site that is useful for this purpose is:

www.idresearch.com

Prepare a written summary of these procedures.

ANSWERS TO SELF-EXAMINATION QUESTIONS

Matching

1.	M	5.	Y	9.	F	13.	W	17.	J	21.	Q
2.	K	6.	I	10.	U	14.	E	18.	O	22.	H
3.	T	7.	D	11.	C	15.	G	19.	B	23.	X
4.	V	8.	A	12.	L	16.	P	20.	N	24.	R

Multiple Choice

1. **C** All amounts spent to get a fixed asset (such as machinery) in place and ready for use are proper charges to the asset account. In the case of machinery acquired, the freight (answer A) and the installation costs (answer B) are both (answer C) proper charges to the machinery account.

2. **C** The periodic charge for depreciation under the declining-balance method (twice the straight-line rate) for the second year is determined by first computing the depreciation charge for the first year. The depreciation for the first year of $6,000 (answer A) is computed by multiplying the cost of the equipment, $9,000, by 2/3 (the straight-line rate of 1/3 multiplied by 2). The depreciation for the second year of $2,000 (answer C) is then determined by multiplying the book value at the end of the first year, $3,000 (the cost of $9,000 minus the first-year depreciation of $6,000), by 2/3. The third year's depreciation is $400 (answer D). It is determined by multiplying the book value at the end of the second year, $1,000, by 2/3, thus yielding $667. However, the equipment cannot be depreciated below its residual value of $600; thus, the third-year depreciation is $400 ($1,000 − $600).

3. **B** A depreciation method that provides for a higher depreciation amount in the first year of the use of an asset and a gradually declining periodic amount thereafter is called an accelerated depreciation method. The declining-balance method (answer B) is an example of such a method.

4. **B** The acceptable method of accounting for an exchange of similar assets in which the trade-in allowance ($30,000) exceeds the book value of the old asset ($25,000) requires that the cost of the new asset be determined by adding the amount of cash given ($70,000) to the book value of the old asset ($25,000), which totals $95,000. Alternatively, the unrecognized gain ($5,000) can be subtracted from the list price ($100,000).

5. **D** Long-lived assets that are useful in operations, not held for sale, and without physical qualities are called intangible assets. Patents, goodwill, and copyrights are examples of intangible assets (answer D).

Current Liabilities

1   Define and give examples of current liabilities.

2   Journalize entries for short-term notes payable.

3   Describe the accounting treatment for contingent liabilities and journalize entries for product warranties.

4   Determine employer liabilities for payroll, including liabilities arising from employee earnings and deductions from earnings.

5   Describe payroll accounting systems that use a payroll register, employee earnings records, and a general journal.

6   Journalize entries for employee fringe benefits, including vacation pay and pensions.

7   Use the quick ratio to analyze the ability of a business to pay its current liabilities.

I f you are employed, you know that your paycheck is normally less than the total amount you earned because your employer deducted amounts for such items as federal income tax and social security tax. For example, if you worked 20 hours last week at $10 per hour and you are paid weekly, your payroll check could appear as follows:

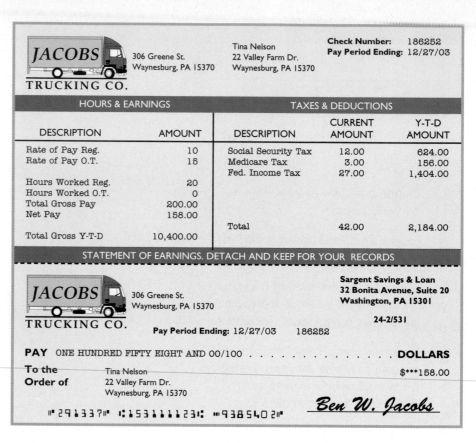

Your employer has a liability to you for your earnings until you are paid. Your employer also has a liability to deposit the taxes withheld. In this chapter, we will discuss liabilities for amounts that must be paid within a short period of time. In addition to liabilities related to payroll and payroll taxes, we will discuss liabilities from notes payable and product warranties.

The Nature of Current Liabilities

objective 1

Define and give examples of current liabilities.

Your credit card balance is probably due within a short time, such as 30 days. Such liabilities that are to be paid out of current assets and are due within a short time, usually within one year, are called **current liabilities**. Most current liabilities arise from two basic transactions:

1. Receiving goods or services prior to making payment.
2. Receiving payment prior to delivering goods or services.

An example of the first type of transaction is **accounts payable** arising from purchases of merchandise for resale. An example of the second type of transaction is **unearned rent** arising from the receipt of rent in advance. Some additional examples of current liabilities that we discussed in previous chapters are:

- Taxes payable—the amount of taxes owed to governmental units
- Interest payable—the amount of interest owed on borrowed funds
- Wages payable—the amount owed to employees

In this chapter, we will introduce some other common current liabilities. These include short-term notes payable, contingencies, payroll liabilities, and employee fringe benefits.

Short-Term Notes Payable

objective 2

Journalize entries for short-term notes payable.

Notes may be issued when merchandise or other assets are purchased. They may also be issued to creditors to temporarily satisfy an account payable created earlier. For example, assume that a business issues a 90-day, 12% note for $1,000, dated August 1, 2003, to Murray Co. for a $1,000 overdue account. The entry to record the issuance of the note is as follows:

Aug.	1	Accounts Payable—Murray Co.	1 0 0 0 00	
		Notes Payable		1 0 0 0 00
		Issued a 90-day, 12% note on account.		

When the note matures, the entry to record the payment of $1,000 principal plus $30 interest ($1,000 × 12% × 90/360) is as follows:

Oct.	30	Notes Payable	1 0 0 0 00	
		Interest Expense	3 0 00	
		Cash		1 0 3 0 00
		Paid principal and interest due on note.		

The interest expense is reported in the Other Expense section of the income statement for the year ended December 31, 2003. The interest expense account is closed at December 31.

The preceding entries for notes payable are similar to those we discussed in an earlier chapter for notes receivable. Notes payable entries are presented from the viewpoint of the borrower, while notes receivable entries are presented from the viewpoint of the creditor or lender. To illustrate, the following entries are journalized for a borrower (Bowden Co.), who issues a note payable to a creditor (Coker Co.):

	Bowden Co. (Borrower)		Coker Co. (Creditor)	

May 1. Bowden Co. purchased merchandise on account from Coker Co., $10,000, 2/10, n/30. The merchandise cost Coker Co. $7,500.	Merchandise Inventory
	  Accounts Payable
		10,000
		10,000
			Accounts Receivable
			  Sales
			
			Cost of Merchandise Sold
			  Merchandise Inventory
				10,000
				10,000
				
				7,500
				7,500

May 31. Bowden Co. issued a 60-day, 12% note for $10,000 to Coker Co. on account.	Accounts Payable
	  Notes Payable
		10,000
		10,000
			Notes Receivable
			  Accounts Receivable
				10,000
				10,000

July 30. Bowden Co. paid Coker Co. the amount due on the note of May 31. Interest: $10,000 × 12% × 60/360.	Notes Payable
	Interest Expense
	  Cash
		10,000
		200
		10,200
			Cash
			  Interest Revenue
			  Notes Receivable
				10,200
				200
				10,000

Notes may also be issued when money is borrowed from banks. Although the terms may vary, many banks would accept from the borrower an interest-bearing note for the amount of the loan. For example, assume that on September 19 a firm borrows $4,000 from First National Bank by giving the bank a 90-day, 15% note. The entry to record the receipt of cash and the issuance of the note is as follows:

Sep.	19	Cash	4 0 0 0 00	
		Notes Payable		4 0 0 0 00
		Issued a 90-day, 15% note to the bank.		

On the due date of the note (December 18), the borrower owes $4,000, the principal of the note, plus interest of $150 ($4,000 × 15% × 90/360). The entry to record the payment of the note is as follows:

Dec.	18	Notes Payable	4 0 0 0 00	
		Interest Expense	1 5 0 00	
		Cash		4 1 5 0 00
		Paid principal and interest due on note.		

The U.S. Treasury issues short-term treasury bills to investors at a discount.

Sometimes a borrower will issue to a creditor a discounted note rather than an interest-bearing note. Although such a note does not specify an interest rate, the creditor sets a rate of interest and deducts the interest from the face amount of the note. This interest is called the **discount**. The rate used in computing the discount is called the **discount rate**. The borrower is given the remainder, called the **proceeds**.

To illustrate, assume that on August 10, Cary Company issues a $20,000, 90-day note to Seinfeld Company in exchange for inventory. Seinfeld discounts the note at a rate of 15%. The amount of the discount, $750, is debited to *Interest Expense*. The proceeds, $19,250, are debited to *Merchandise Inventory. Notes Payable* is credited for the face amount of the note, which is also its maturity value. This entry is shown on the following page.

In buying a used delivery truck, a business issues an $8,000, 60-day note dated July 15, which the truck's seller discounts at 12%. What is the cost of the truck (the proceeds)?

···

$7,840 [$8,000 − ($8,000 × 12% × 60/360)]

Aug.	10	Merchandise Inventory	19 2 5 0 00		
		Interest Expense	7 5 0 00		
		Notes Payable		20 0 0 0 00	
		Issued a 90-day note to Seinfeld Co.,			
		discounted at 15%.			

When the note is paid, the following entry is recorded:[1]

Nov.	8	Notes Payable	20 0 0 0 00		
		Cash		20 0 0 0 00	
		Paid note due.			

Contingent Liabilities

objective 3

Describe the accounting treatment for contingent liabilities and journalize entries for product warranties.

Some past transactions will result in liabilities if certain events occur in the future. These potential obligations are called **contingent liabilities**. For example, **Ford Motor Company** would have a contingent liability for the estimated costs associated with warranty work on new car sales. The obligation is contingent upon a *future event*, namely, a customer requiring warranty work on a vehicle. The obligation is the result of a *past transaction*, which is the original sale of the vehicle.

If a contingent liability is *probable* and the amount of the liability can be *reasonably estimated*, it should be recorded in the accounts. **Ford Motor Company's** vehicle warranty costs are an example of a *recordable* contingent liability. The warranty costs are *probable* because it is known that warranty repairs will be required on some vehicles. In addition, the costs can be *estimated* from past warranty experience.

To illustrate, assume that during June a company sells a product for $60,000 on which there is a 36-month warranty for repairing defects. Past experience indicates that the average cost to repair defects is 5% of the sales price over the warranty period. The entry to record the estimated product warranty expense for June is as follows:

A business sells to a customer $120,000 of commercial audio equipment with a one-year repair and replacement warranty. Historically, the average cost to repair or replace is 2% of sales. How is this contingent liability recorded?

···

Product Warranty Expense   2,400
   Product Warranty Payable   2,400

June	30	Product Warranty Expense	3 0 0 0 00		
		Product Warranty Payable		3 0 0 0 00	
		Warranty expense for June, 5% × $60,000.			

This transaction matches revenues and expenses properly by recording warranty costs in the same period in which the sale is recorded. When the defective product is repaired, the repair costs are recorded by debiting *Product Warranty Payable* and crediting *Cash*, *Supplies*, or other appropriate accounts. Thus, if a customer required a $200 part replacement on August 16, the entry would be:

---

[1] If the accounting period ends before a discounted note is paid, an adjusting entry should record the prepaid (deferred) interest that is not yet an expense. This deferred interest would be deducted from Notes Payable in the Current Liabilities section of the balance sheet.

Aug.	16	Product Warranty Payable		2 0 0 00	
		Supplies			2 0 0 00
		Replaced defective part under warranty.			

If a contingent liability is probable but cannot be *reasonably estimated* or is only *possible*, then the nature of the contingent liability should be disclosed in the footnotes to the financial statements. Professional judgment is required in distinguishing between contingent liabilities that are probable versus those that are only possible.

Common examples of contingent liabilities disclosed in notes to the financial statements are litigation, environmental matters, guarantees, and sale of receivables. The following example of a contingency disclosure, related to patent infringement litigation, was taken from a recent annual report of **priceline.com**: *A third party patent applicant . . . , Thomas Woolston, . . . had filed . . . a request to declare an interference between (his) patent application . . . describing an electronic market for used and collectible goods and priceline.com's core buyer-driven commerce patent. . . . If an interference is declared and thereafter resolved in favor of Woolston, such resolution could result in an award of some or all of the disputed patent claims to Woolston. If, following such award, Woolston were successful in a patent infringement action against priceline.com, . . . this could require priceline.com to obtain licenses from Woolston at a cost which could significantly adversely affect priceline.com's business.*

The accounting treatment of contingent liabilities is summarized in Exhibit 1.

Exhibit 1 Accounting Treatment of Contingent Liabilities

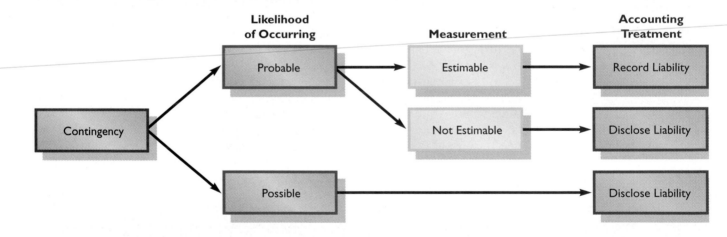

Payroll and Payroll Taxes

objective 4

Determine employer liabilities for payroll, including liabilities arising from employee earnings and deductions from earnings.

We are all familiar with the term payroll. In accounting, the term **payroll** refers to the amount paid to employees for the services they provide during a period. A business's payroll is usually significant for several reasons. First, employees are sensitive to payroll errors and irregularities. Maintaining good employee morale requires that the payroll be paid on a timely, accurate basis. Second, the payroll is subject to various federal and state regulations. Finally, the payroll and related payroll taxes have a significant effect on the net income of most businesses. Although the amount of such expenses varies widely, it is not unusual for a business's payroll and payroll-related expenses to equal nearly one-third of its revenue.

Liability for Employee Earnings

Salaries and wages paid to employees are an employer's labor expenses. The term **salary** usually refers to payment for managerial, administrative, or similar services. The rate of salary is normally expressed in terms of a month or a year. The term **wages** usually refers to payment for manual labor, both skilled and unskilled. The rate of wages is normally stated on an hourly or weekly basis. In practice, the terms salary and wages are often used interchangeably.

Employee salaries and wages are expenses to an employer.

The basic salary or wage of an employee may be increased by commissions, profit sharing, or cost-of-living adjustments. Many businesses pay managers an annual bonus in addition to a basic salary. The amount of the bonus is often based on some measure of productivity, such as income or profit of the business. Although payment is usually made by check or in cash, it may be in the form of securities, notes, lodging, or other property or services. Generally, the form of payment has no effect on how salaries and wages are treated by either the employer or the employee.

Salary and wage rates are determined by agreement between the employer and the employees. Businesses engaged in interstate commerce must follow the requirements of the Fair Labor Standards Act. Employers covered by this legislation, which is commonly called the Federal Wage and Hour Law, are required to pay a minimum rate of 1½ times the regular rate for all hours worked in excess of 40 hours per week. Exemptions are provided for executive, administrative, and certain supervisory positions. Premium rates for overtime or for working at night, holidays, or other less desirable times are fairly common, even when not required by law. In some cases, the premium rates may be as much as twice the base rate.

Point of Interest

Information on average salaries for a variety of professions can be found at the *Economic Research Institute's* Web site at **www.erieri.com**.

To illustrate computing an employee's earnings, assume that John T. McGrath is employed by McDermott Supply Co. at the rate of $28 per hour. Any hours in excess of 40 hours per week are paid at a rate of 1½ times the normal rate, or $42 ($28 + $14) per hour. For the week ended December 27, McGrath's time card indicates that he worked 42 hours. His earnings for that week are computed as follows:

Earnings at base rate (40 × $28)	$1,120
Earnings at overtime rate (2 × $42)	84
Total earnings	$1,204

Deductions from Employee Earnings

The total earnings of an employee for a payroll period, including bonuses and overtime pay, are called **gross pay**. From this amount is subtracted one or more **deductions** to arrive at the net pay. **Net pay** is the amount the employer must pay the employee. The deductions for federal taxes are usually the largest deduction. Deductions may also be required for state or local income taxes. Other deductions may be made for medical insurance, contributions to pensions, and for items authorized by individual employees.

Income Taxes

Professional athletes must pay local taxes in each location in which they play their sport.

Except for certain types of employment, all employers must withhold a portion of employee earnings for payment of the employees' federal income tax. As a basis for determining the amount to be withheld, each employee completes and submits to the employer an "Employee's Withholding Allowance Certificate," often called a W-4. Exhibit 2 is an example of a completed W-4 form.

You may recall filling out a W-4 form. On the W-4, an employee indicates marital status, the number of withholding allowances, and whether any additional withholdings are authorized. A single employee may claim one withholding allowance. A married employee may claim an additional allowance for a spouse. An employee may also claim an allowance for each dependent other than a spouse. Each allowance claimed reduces the amount of federal income tax withheld from the employee's check.

Exhibit 2 Employee's Withholding Allowance Certificate (W-4 Form)

------------------------------- Cut here and give Form W-4 to your employer. Keep the top part for your records. -------------------------------

| Form **W-4** Department of the Treasury Internal Revenue Service | **Employee's Withholding Allowance Certificate** ▶ For Privacy Act and Paperwork Reduction Act Notice, see page 2. | OMB No. 1545-0010 **2002** |

1 Type or print your first name and middle initial	Last name	2 Your social security number
John T.	McGrath	381 48 9120

| Home address (number and street or rural route) 1830 4ᵗʰ Street | 3 ☒ Single ☐ Married ☐ Married, but withhold at higher Single rate. Note: If married, but legally separated, or spouse is a nonresident alien, check the Single box. |
| City or town, state, and ZIP code Clinton, Iowa 52732-6142 | 4 If your last name differs from that on your social security card, check here. You must call 1-800-772-1213 for a new card . . . ▶ ☐ |

5 Total number of allowances you are claiming (from line H above **OR** from the applicable worksheet on page 2) . . **5** | 1
6 Additional amount, if any, you want withheld from each paycheck . . . . **6** $
7 I claim exemption from withholding for 2002, and I certify that I meet **BOTH** of the following conditions for exemption:
 • Last year I had a right to a refund of **ALL** Federal income tax withheld because I had **NO** tax liability **AND**
 • This year I expect a refund of **ALL** Federal income tax withheld because I expect to have **NO** tax liability.
 If you meet both conditions, write "EXEMPT" here . . . . ▶ | **7**

Under penalties of perjury, I certify that I am entitled to the number of withholding allowances claimed on this certificate, or I am entitled to claim exempt status.

Employee's signature (Form is not valid unless you sign it) ▶ *John T. McGrath*   Date ▶ June 2, 2002

| 8 Employer's name and address (Employer: Complete lines 8 and 10 only if sending to the IRS.) | 9 Office code (optional) | 10 Employer identification number |

Federal income tax withholding tables are available from the Internal Revenue Service as part of *Circular E*, "Employer's Tax Guide."

The amount that must be withheld for income tax differs, depending upon each employee's gross pay and completed W-4. Most employers use wage bracket withholding tables furnished by the Internal Revenue Service to determine the amount to be withheld.

Exhibit 3 is an example of a wage bracket withholding table. This table is for a single employee who is paid weekly. Other tables are used for employees who are married or who are paid biweekly, semimonthly, monthly, or at other time periods. Unlike social security tax, there is no ceiling on the amount of employee earnings subject to federal income tax withholding.

In using the withholding table, the amount of federal income tax withheld each pay period is indicated where the row showing the employee's wage bracket intersects the column showing the employee's withholding allowances. For example,

Exhibit 3 Wage Bracket Withholding Table

SINGLE Persons—WEEKLY Payroll Period

If the wages are—		And the number of withholding allowances claimed is—										
At least	But less than	0	1	2	3	4	5	6	7	8	9	10
		The amount of income tax to be withheld is—										
900	910	178	163	148	133	118	103	89	74	65	57	49
910	920	180	165	151	136	121	106	91	77	66	58	50
920	930	183	168	153	139	124	109	94	79	68	60	52
930	940	186	171	156	141	127	112	97	82	69	61	53
940	950	189	174	159	144	129	115	100	85	71	63	55
950	960	192	177	162	147	132	117	103	88	73	64	56
960	970	194	179	165	150	135	120	105	91	76	66	58
970	980	197	182	167	153	138	123	108	93	79	67	59
980	990	200	185	170	155	141	126	111	96	81	69	61
990	1,000	203	188	173	158	143	129	114	99	84	70	62
1,000	1,010	206	191	176	161	146	131	117	102	87	72	64
1,010	1,020	208	193	179	164	149	134	119	105	90	75	65
1,020	1,030	211	196	181	167	152	137	122	107	93	78	67
1,030	1,040	214	199	184	169	155	140	125	110	95	81	68
1,040	1,050	217	202	187	172	157	143	128	113	98	83	70
1,050	1,060	220	205	190	175	160	145	131	116	101	86	71
1,060	1,070	222	207	193	178	163	148	133	119	104	89	74
1,070	1,080	225	210	195	181	166	151	136	121	107	92	77
1,080	1,090	228	213	198	183	169	154	139	124	109	95	80
1,090	1,100	231	216	201	186	171	157	142	127	112	97	83
1,100	1,110	234	219	204	189	174	159	145	130	115	100	85
1,110	1,120	236	221	207	192	177	162	147	133	118	103	88
1,120	1,130	239	224	209	195	180	165	150	135	121	106	91
1,130	1,140	242	227	212	197	183	168	153	138	123	109	94
1,140	1,150	245	230	215	200	185	171	156	141	126	111	97
1,150	1,160	248	233	218	203	188	173	159	144	129	114	99
1,160	1,170	252	235	221	206	191	176	161	147	132	117	102
1,170	1,180	255	238	223	209	194	179	164	149	135	120	105
1,180	1,190	258	241	226	211	197	182	167	152	137	123	108
1,190	1,200	261	244	229	214	199	185	170	155	140	125	111
1,200	1,210	264	248	232	217	202	187	173	158	143	128	113
1,210	1,220	267	251	235	220	205	190	175	161	146	131	116
1,220	1,230	270	254	237	223	208	193	178	163	149	134	119
1,230	1,240	273	257	240	225	211	196	181	166	151	137	122
1,240	1,250	276	260	244	228	213	199	184	169	154	139	125

assume that John T. McGrath, who is single and has declared one withholding allowance, made $1,204 for the week ended December 27. Using the withholding table in Exhibit 3, the amount of federal income tax withheld is $248.

In addition to the federal income tax, employees may also be required to pay a state income tax and a city income tax. State and city taxes are withheld from employees' earnings and paid to state and city governments.

FICA Tax

Most of us have FICA tax withheld from our payroll checks by our employers. Employers are required by the Federal Insurance Contributions Act (FICA) to withhold a portion of the earnings of each of the employees. The amount of **FICA tax** withheld is the employees' contribution to two federal programs. Tax is withheld separately under each program. The first program, called **social security**, is for old age, survivors, and disability insurance (OASDI). The second program, called **Medicare**, is health insurance for senior citizens.

The amount of tax that employers are required to withhold from each employee is normally based on the amount of earnings paid in the *calendar* year. Although both the schedule of future tax rates and the maximum amount subject to tax are revised often by Congress, such changes have little effect on the basic payroll system. In this text, we will use a social security rate of 6% on the first $80,000 of annual earnings and a Medicare rate of 1.5% on all annual earnings.

To illustrate, assume that John T. McGrath's annual earnings prior to the current payroll period total $79,296. Assume also that the current period earnings are $1,204. The total FICA tax of $60.30 is determined as follows:

Earnings subject to 6% social security tax		
($80,000 − $79,296)	$ 704	
Social security tax rate	× 6%	
Social security tax		$42.24
Earnings subject to 1.5% Medicare tax	$1,204	
Medicare tax rate	× 1.5%	
Medicare tax		18.06
Total FICA tax		$60.30

Point of Interest

In 1936, the Social Security Board described how the tax was expected to affect a worker's pay, as follows:

The taxes called for in this law will be paid both by your employer and by you. For the next 3 years you will pay maybe 15 cents a week, maybe 25 cents a week, maybe 30 cents or more, according to what you earn. That is to say, during the next 3 years, beginning January 1, 1937, you will pay 1 cent for every dollar you earn, and at the same time your employer will pay 1 cent for every dollar you earn, up to $3,000 a year.…

… Beginning in 1940 you will pay, and your employer will pay, 1½ cents for each dollar you earn, up to $3,000 a year … and then beginning in 1943, you will pay 2 cents, and so will your employer, for every dollar you earn for the next three years. After that, you and your employer will each pay half a cent more for 3 years, and finally, beginning in 1949, … you and your employer will each pay 3 cents on each dollar you earn, up to $3,000 a year. That is the most you will ever pay.

The rate on January 1, 2001, was 7.65 cents per dollar earned (7.65%). The social security portion was 6.20% on the first $80,400 of earnings. The Medicare portion was 1.45% on all earnings.

Source: Arthur Lodge, "That Is the Most You Will Ever Pay," *Journal of Accountancy,* October 1985, p. 44.

Other Deductions

Neither the employer nor the employee has any choice in deducting taxes from gross earnings. However, employees may choose to have additional amounts deducted for other purposes. For example, you as an employee may authorize deductions for retirement savings, for contributions to charitable organizations, or for premiums on employee insurance. A union contract may also require the deduction of union dues.

Computing Employee Net Pay

Gross earnings less payroll deductions equals the amount to be paid to an employee for the payroll period. This amount is the *net pay*, which is often called the *take-home pay.* Assuming that John T. McGrath authorized deductions for retirement savings and for a United Way contribution, the amount to be paid McGrath for the week ended December 27 is $870.70, as shown at the top of the following page.

Gross earnings for the week		$1,204.00
Deductions:		
Social security tax	$ 42.24	
Medicare tax	18.06	
Federal income tax	248.00	
Retirement savings	20.00	
United Way	5.00	
Total deductions		333.30
Net pay		$ 870.70

Liability for Employer's Payroll Taxes

So far, we have discussed the payroll taxes that are withheld from the employees' earnings. Most employers are also subject to federal and state payroll taxes based on the amount paid their employees. Such taxes are an operating expense of the business. Exhibit 4 summarizes the responsibility for employee and employer payroll taxes.

Exhibit 4 Responsibility for Tax Payments

The U.S. Government receives income from various taxes, which are spent on a variety of government services. The relative sizes of these incomes and outlays for a recent fiscal year are:

FEDERAL INCOME

Corporate income tax

Estate, gift and other

11%

8%

FICA and FUTA

33%

48%

Personal income tax

FICA Tax

Employers are required to contribute to the social security and Medicare programs for each employee. The employer must match the employee's contribution to each program.

Federal Unemployment Compensation Tax

The Federal Unemployment Tax Act (FUTA) provides for temporary payments to those who become unemployed as a result of layoffs due to economic causes beyond their control. Types of employment subject to this program are similar to those covered by FICA taxes. A tax of 6.2% is levied on employers only, rather than on both employers and employees.[2]

[2] This rate may be reduced to 0.8% for credits for state unemployment compensation tax.

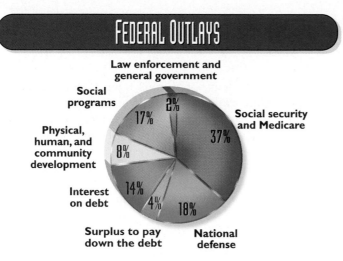

FEDERAL OUTLAYS

Law enforcement and general government 2%

Social programs 17%

Physical, human, and community development 8%

Interest on debt 14%

Surplus to pay down the debt 4%

National defense 18%

Social security and Medicare 37%

Source: Internal Revenue Service

It is applied to only the first $7,000 of the earnings of each covered employee during a calendar year. Congress often revises the rate and maximum earnings subject to federal unemployment compensation tax. The funds collected by the federal government are not paid directly to the unemployed but are allocated among the states for use in state programs.

State Unemployment Compensation Tax

State Unemployment Tax Acts (SUTA) also provide for payments to unemployed workers. The amounts paid as benefits are obtained, for the most part, from a tax levied upon employers only. A few states require employee contributions also. The rates of tax and the tax bases vary. In most states, employers who provide stable employment for their employees are granted reduced rates. The employment experience and the status of each employer's tax account are reviewed annually, and the tax rates are adjusted accordingly.[3]

[3] As of January 1, 2001, the maximum state rate credited against the federal unemployment rate was 5.4% of the first $7,000 of each employee's earnings during a calendar year.

BUSINESS ON STAGE

Teaming up for High Performance

Picture a factory in your mind. Do you see employees working alone, performing mind-numbing repetitive work? Fortunately, this picture is fast disappearing from the employment landscape. Many companies, such as **Procter & Gamble, Hewlett-Packard,** and **Federal Express,** are using teams. Teams typically consist of between 8 to 15 full-time employees. Often team members represent different functions, such as marketing, manufacturing, and finance.

Why are companies using teams? Teams have the following advantages over individual employees:

- Teams are able to put employees' skills together to solve problems, complete projects, and combine tasks that form a process.

- Teams perform the coordination and communication tasks formerly performed by middle management.
- Empowered teams are more creative and more satisfied in their work.
- Teams take on expanded responsibilities, such as ordering materials, conducting quality checks, making team hiring and firing decisions, developing work schedules, and jointly establishing performance targets with management.

One area of challenge is in the area of team compensation and rewards. Popular plans develop individual base pay rates on the basis of skills obtained, rather than just seniority. A recent survey noted that 85% of companies using teams set base pay

rates above the industry average. Additional bonuses are available based on achieving team goals. The same survey noted such bonuses averaged around 10% of base pay.

Team-based management assigns responsibility and authority to the team members and provides rewards for this added work. As one team member put it, "It's a real mind shift. You're used to the expectation that it's your job to have the best idea. But no individual is going to have the best idea. That's not how it works—the best ideas come from the collective intelligence of the team. If you accept that, you're in for a big change in how you think about yourself." ■

Accounting Systems for Payroll and Payroll Taxes

objective 5

Describe payroll accounting systems that use a payroll register, employee earnings records, and a general journal.

In designing payroll systems, the requirements of various federal, state, and local agencies for payroll data are considered. Payroll data must also be maintained accurately for each payroll period and for each employee. Periodic reports using payroll data must be submitted to government agencies. The payroll data itself must be retained for possible inspection by the various agencies.

Payroll systems must be designed to pay employees on a timely basis. Payroll systems should also be designed to provide useful data for management decision-making needs. Such needs might include settling employee grievances and negotiating retirement or other benefits with employees.

Although payroll systems differ among businesses, the major elements common to most payroll systems are the payroll register, employee's earnings record, and payroll checks. We discuss and illustrate each of these elements next. We have kept the illustrations relatively simple, and they may be modified in practice to meet the needs of each individual business.

Payroll Register

The **payroll register** is a multicolumn form used in assembling and summarizing the data needed for each payroll period. Its design varies according to the number and classes of employees and the extent to which computers are used. Exhibit 5 shows a form suitable for a small number of employees.

The nature of the data appearing in the payroll register is evident from the column headings. The number of hours worked and the earnings and deduction data are inserted in their proper columns. The sum of the deductions for each employee is then subtracted from the total earnings to yield the amount to be paid. The check numbers are recorded in the payroll register as evidence of payment.

The last two columns of the payroll register are used to accumulate the total wages or salaries to be debited to the various expense accounts. This process is usually called **payroll distribution**.

The format of the payroll register in Exhibit 5 aids in determining the mathematical accuracy of the payroll before checks are issued to employees. All column totals should be verified, as shown at the top of the following page.

Exhibit 5 Payroll Register

	Employee Name	Total Hours	Earnings			
			Regular	Overtime	Total	
1	Abrams, Julie S.	40	500.00		500.00	1
2	Elrod, Fred G.	44	392.00	58.80	450.80	2
3	Gomez, Jose C.	40	840.00		840.00	3
4	**McGrath, John T.**	42	1,120.00	84.00	1,204.00	4
25	Wilkes, Glenn K.	40	480.00		480.00	25
26	Zumpano, Michael W.	40	600.00		600.00	26
27	Total		13,328.00	574.00	13,902.00	27
28						28

Earnings:

Regular	$13,328.00	
Overtime	574.00	
Total		$13,902.00

Deductions:

Social security tax	$ 643.07	
Medicare tax	208.53	
Federal income tax	3,332.00	
Retirement savings	680.00	
United Way	470.00	
Accounts receivable	50.00	
Total		5,383.60

Paid—net amount	$ 8,518.40

Accounts debited:

Sales Salaries Expense	$11,122.00
Office Salaries Expense	2,780.00
Total (as above)	$13,902.00

Recording Employees' Earnings

Amounts in the payroll register may be posted directly to the accounts. An alternative is to use the payroll register as a supporting record for a journal entry. The entry based on the payroll register in Exhibit 5 follows.

Dec.	27	Sales Salaries Expense	11 122 00	
		Office Salaries Expense	2 780 00	
		Social Security Tax Payable		6 43 07
		Medicare Tax Payable		2 08 53
		Employees Federal Income Tax Payable		3 332 00
		Retirement Savings Deductions Payable		6 80 00
		United Way Deductions Payable		4 70 00
		Accounts Receivable—Fred G. Elrod (emp.)		5 0 00
		Salaries Payable		8 518 40
		Payroll for week ended December 27.		

Exhibit 5 (concluded)

	Deductions							Paid		Accounts Debited		
	Social Security Tax	Medicare Tax	Federal Income Tax	Retirement Savings	Misc.		Total	Net Amount	Check No.	Sales Salaries Expense	Office Salaries Expense	
1	30.00	7.50	74.00	20.00	UW	10.00	141.50	358.50	6857	500.00		1
2	27.05	6.76	62.00		AR	50.00	145.81	304.99	6858		450.80	2
3	50.40	12.60	131.00	25.00	UW	10.00	229.00	611.00	6859	840.00		3
4	42.24	18.06	248.00	20.00	UW	5.00	333.30	870.70	6860	1,204.00		4
25	28.80	7.20	69.00	10.00			115.00	365.00	6880	480.00		25
26	36.00	9.00	79.00	5.00	UW	2.00	131.00	469.00	6881		600.00	26
27	643.07	208.53	3,332.00	680.00	UW	470.00	5,383.60	8,518.40		11,122.00	2,780.00	27
28					AR	50.00						28

Miscellaneous Deductions: UW—United Way; AR—Accounts Receivable

Recording and Paying Payroll Taxes

The employer's payroll taxes become liabilities when the related payroll is *paid* to employees. In addition, employers are required to compute and report payroll taxes on a *calendar-year* basis, even if a different fiscal year is used for financial reporting and income tax purposes.

To illustrate, assume that Everson Company's fiscal year ends on April 30. Also, assume that Everson Company owes its employees $26,000 of wages on December 31. The following portions of the $26,000 of wages are subject to payroll taxes on December 31:

	Earnings Subject to Payroll Taxes
Social Security Tax (6.0%)	$18,000
Medicare Tax (1.5%)	26,000
State and Federal Unemployment Compensation Tax	1,000

If the payroll is paid on December 31, the payroll taxes will be based on the preceding amounts. If the payroll is paid on January 2, however, the *entire* $26,000 will be subject to *all* payroll taxes. This is because the maximum earnings limitation for determining social security and unemployment taxes will not be exceeded at the beginning of the calendar year.

The payroll register for McDermott Supply Co. in Exhibit 5 indicates that the amount of social security tax withheld is $643.07 and Medicare tax withheld is $208.53. Since the employer must match the employees' FICA contributions, the employer's social security payroll tax will also be $643.07, and the Medicare tax will be $208.53. Further, assume that the earnings subject to state and federal unemployment compensation taxes are $2,710. Multiplying this amount by the state (5.4%) and federal (0.8%) rates yields the unemployment compensation taxes shown in the following payroll tax computation:

Social security tax	$ 643.07
Medicare tax	208.53
State unemployment compensation tax (5.4% × $2,710)	146.34
Federal unemployment compensation tax (0.8% × $2,710)	21.68
Total payroll tax expense	$1,019.62

The entry to journalize the payroll tax expense for the week and the liability for the taxes accrued is shown below.

Social security contributions (both the employees' and employer's amounts) and federal income taxes must be deposited quarterly in a federal depository bank. An "Employer's Quarterly Federal Tax Return" (Form 941) must also be filed. Unemployment compensation tax returns and payments are required annually by the federal government and most state governments.

Dec.	27	Payroll Tax Expense	1 0 1 9 62		
		Social Security Tax Payable		6 4 3 07
		Medicare Tax Payable		2 0 8 53
		State Unemployment Tax Payable		1 4 6 34
		Federal Unemployment Tax Payable		2 1 68
		Payroll taxes for week ended		
		December 27.		

Employee's Earnings Record

The amount of each employee's earnings to date must be available at the end of each payroll period. This cumulative amount is required in order to compute each employee's social security and Medicare tax withholding and the employer's payroll taxes. It is essential, therefore, that a detailed payroll record be maintained for each employee. This record is called an **employee's earnings record**.

Exhibit 6 shows a portion of the employee's earnings record for John T. McGrath. The relationship between this record and the payroll register can be seen by tracing the amounts entered on McGrath's earnings record for December 27 back to its source—the fourth line of the payroll register in Exhibit 5.

In addition to spaces for recording data for each payroll period and the cumulative total of earnings, the employee's earnings record has spaces for quarterly totals and the yearly total. These totals are used in various reports for tax, insurance, and other purposes. One such report is the Wage and Tax Statement, commonly called a **Form W-2**. You may recall receiving a W-2 form for use in preparing your individual tax return. This form must be provided annually to each employee as well as to the Social Security Administration. The amounts reported in the Form W-2 shown below were taken from McGrath's employee's earnings record.

a Control number 22222 Void ☐	For Official Use Only ▶ OMB No. 1545-0008		
b Employer's identification number 61-8436524	**1** Wages, tips, other compensation 80,500.00	**2** Federal income tax withheld 17,710.00	
c Employer's name, address, and ZIP code McDermott Supply Co. 415 5th Ave. So. Dubuque, IA 52736-0142	**3** Social security wages 80,000.00	**4** Social security tax withheld 4,800.00	
	5 Medicare wages and tips 80,500.00	**6** Medicare tax withheld 1,207.50	
	7 Social security tips	**8** Allocated tips	
d Employee's social security number 381-48-9120	**9** Advance EIC payment	**10** Dependent care benefits	
e Employee's name (first, middle initial, last) John T. McGrath 1830 4th St. Clinton, IA 52732-6142	**11** Nonqualified plans	**12** Benefits included in box 1	
	13 See Instrs. for box 13	**14** Other	
f Employee's address and ZIP code	**15** Statutory employee ☐ Deceased ☐ Pension plan ☐ Legal rep. ☐ Hshld. emp. ☐ Subtotal ☐ Deferred compensation ☐		
16 State Employer's state I.D. No. IA	**17** State wages, tips, etc.	**18** State income tax	**19** Locality name Dubuque	**20** Local wages, tips, etc.	**21** Local income tax

Cat. No. 10134D   Department of the Treasury—Internal Revenue Service

Form **W-2** Wage and Tax Statement   For Paperwork Reduction Act Notice, see separate instructions.
Copy A For Social Security Administration

Payroll Checks

At the end of each pay period, **payroll checks** are prepared. Each check includes a detachable statement showing the details of how the net pay was computed. Exhibit 7 on page 448 is a payroll check for John T. McGrath.

The amount paid to employees is normally recorded as a single amount, regardless of the number of employees. There is no need to record each payroll check separately in the journal, since all of the details are available in the payroll register.

For paying their payroll, most employers use payroll checks drawn on a special bank account. After the data for the payroll period have been recorded and summarized in the payroll register, a single check for the total amount to be paid is written on the firm's regular bank account. This check is then deposited in the special payroll bank account. Individual payroll checks are written from the payroll account, and the numbers of the payroll checks are inserted in the payroll register.

An advantage of using a separate payroll bank account is that the task of reconciling the bank statements is simplified. In addition, a payroll bank account establishes control over payroll checks by preventing the theft or misuse of uncashed payroll checks.

Exhibit 6 Employee's
Earnings Record

John T. McGrath
1830 4th Street
Clinton, IA 52732-6142   PHONE: 555-3148

SINGLE	NUMBER OF WITHHOLDING ALLOWANCES: 1	PAY RATE: $1,120.00 Per Week
OCCUPATION:	Salesperson	EQUIVALENT HOURLY RATE: $28

			Earnings			
	Period Ending	Total Hours	Regular Earnings	Overtime Earnings	Total Earnings	Cumulative Total
42	SEP. 27	50	1,120.00	420.00	1,540.00	60,540.00
43	THIRD QUARTER		14,560.00	5,650.00	20,210.00	
44	OCT. 4	49	1,120.00	378.00	1,498.00	62,038.00
50	NOV. 15	48	1,120.00	336.00	1,456.00	71,848.00
51	NOV. 22	52	1,120.00	504.00	1,624.00	73,472.00
52	NOV. 29	51	1,120.00	462.00	1,582.00	75,054.00
53	DEC. 6	50	1,120.00	420.00	1,540.00	76,594.00
54	DEC. 13	48	1,120.00	336.00	1,456.00	78,050.00
55	DEC. 20	43	1,120.00	126.00	1,246.00	79,296.00
56	DEC. 27	42	1,120.00	84.00	1,204.00	80,500.00
57	FOURTH QUARTER		14,560.00	5,400.00	19,960.00	
58	YEARLY TOTAL		58,240.00	22,260.00	80,500.00	

Currency may be used to pay payroll. However, many employees have their net pay deposited directly in a bank. In these cases, funds are transferred electronically.

Payroll System Diagram

You may find Exhibit 8 useful in following the flow of data within the payroll segment of an accounting system. The diagram indicates the relationships among the primary components of the payroll system we described in this chapter.

Our focus in the preceding discussion has been on the outputs of a payroll system: the payroll register, payroll checks, the employees' earnings records, and tax and other reports. As shown in the diagram in Exhibit 8, the inputs into a payroll system may be classified as either constants or variables.

Constants are data that remain unchanged from payroll to payroll and thus do not need to be entered into the system each pay period. Examples of constants include such data as each employee's name and social security number, marital status, number of income tax withholding allowances, rate of pay, payroll category (office, sales, etc.), and department where employed. The FICA tax rates and various tax tables are also constants that apply to all employees. In a computerized accounting system, constants are stored within a payroll file.

Variables are data that change from payroll to payroll and thus must be entered into the system each pay period. Examples of variables include such data as the

| SOC. SEC. NO.: 381-48-9120 | | | | | | | EMPLOYEE NO.: 814 | |

DATE OF BIRTH: February 15, 1977

DATE EMPLOYMENT TERMINATED:

	Deductions						Paid		
	Social Security Tax	Medicare Tax	Federal Income Tax	Retirement Savings	Other		Total	Net Amount	Check No.
42	92.40	23.10	338.80	20.00			474.30	1,065.70	6175
43	1,212.60	303.15	4,446.20	260.00	UW	40.00	6,261.95	13,948.05	
44	89.88	22.47	329.56	20.00			461.91	1,036.09	6225
50	87.36	21.84	320.32	20.00			449.52	1,006.48	6530
51	97.44	24.36	357.28	20.00			499.08	1,124.92	6582
52	94.92	23.73	348.04	20.00			486.69	1,095.31	6640
53	92.40	23.10	338.80	20.00	UW	5.00	479.30	1,060.70	6688
54	87.36	21.84	320.32	20.00			449.52	1,006.48	6743
55	74.76	18.69	260.00	20.00			373.45	872.55	6801
56	42.24	18.06	248.00	20.00	UW	5.00	333.30	870.70	6860
57	1,167.60	299.40	4,391.20	260.00	UW	15.00	6,133.20	13,826.80	
58	4,800.00	1,207.50	17,710.00	1,040.00	UW	100.00	24,857.50	55,642.50	

Exhibit 6 (concluded)

Point of Interest

In the movie *Superman III*, Gus Gorman embezzled payroll funds by programming the computer to round down each employee's payroll amount to the nearest penny. He then added the amount "rounded out" to his own payroll check. For example, if an employee's total pay was $458.533, the payroll program would pay the employee $458.53 and add the $0.003 to a special account. The total in this special account would be transferred to Gus's paycheck at the end of the processing of the payroll. In this way, Gus's check increased from $143.80 to $85,000 in one pay period!

number of hours or days worked for each employee during the payroll period, days of sick leave with pay, vacation credits, and cumulative earnings and taxes withheld. If salespersons are paid commissions, the amount of their sales would also vary from period to period.

Internal Controls for Payroll Systems

Payroll processing, as we discussed above, requires the input of a large amount of data, along with numerous and sometimes complex computations. These factors, combined with the large dollar amounts involved, require controls to ensure that payroll payments are timely and accurate. In addition, the system must also provide adequate safeguards against theft or other misuse of funds.

The cash payment controls we discussed in the cash chapter also apply to payrolls. Thus, it is normally desirable to use a system that includes procedures for proper authorization and approval of payroll. When a check-signing machine is used, it is important that blank payroll checks and access to the machine be carefully controlled to prevent the theft or misuse of payroll funds.

It is especially important to authorize and approve in writing employee additions and deletions and changes in pay rates. For example, numerous

Exhibit 7 Payroll Check

	McDermott Supply Co. 415 5th Ave. So. Dubuque, IA 52736-0142	John T. McGrath 1830 4th St. Clinton, IA 52732-6142	Check Number: 6860 Pay Period Ending: 12/27/02

HOURS & EARNINGS		TAXES & DEDUCTIONS		
DESCRIPTION	AMOUNT	DESCRIPTION	CURRENT AMOUNT	Y-T-D AMOUNT
Rate of Pay Reg.	28	Social Security Tax	42.24	4,800.00
Rate of Pay O.T.	42	Medicare Tax	18.06	1,207.50
Hours Worked Reg.	40	Fed. Income Tax	248.00	17,710.00
Hours Worked O.T.	2	U.S. Savings Bonds	20.00	1,040.00
		United Fund	5.00	100.00
Net Pay	870.70			
Total Gross Pay	1,204.00	Total	333.30	24,857.50
Total Gross Y-T-D	80,500.00			

STATEMENT OF EARNINGS. DETACH AND KEEP FOR YOUR RECORDS

- -

	McDermott Supply Co. 415 5th Ave. So. Dubuque, IA 52736-0142	LaGesse Savings & Loan 33 Katie Avenue, Suite 33 Clinton, IA 52736-3581 24-2/531

Pay Period Ending: 12/27/02   6860

PAY EIGHT HUNDRED SEVENTY AND 70/100 . . . . **DOLLARS**

To the Order of   JOHN T. MCGRATH
1830 4TH ST.
CLINTON, IA 52732-6142 $***870.70

Franklin D. McDermott

⑆6860⑆ ⑇153111123⑇ ⑈938540 2⑈

Exhibit 8 Flow of Data in a Payroll System

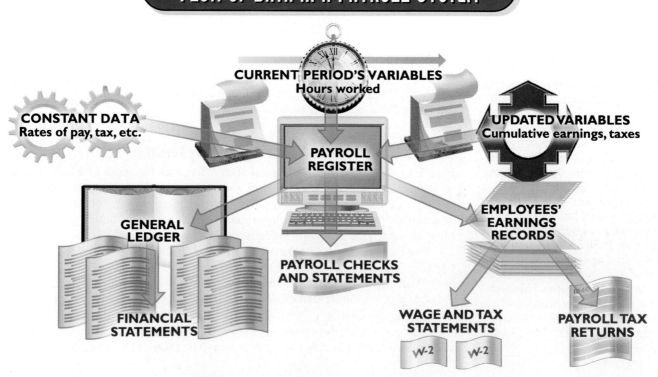

payroll frauds have involved a supervisor adding fictitious employees to the payroll. The supervisor then cashes the fictitious employees' checks. Similar frauds have occurred where employees have been fired but the Payroll Department is not notified. As a result, payroll checks to the fired employees are prepared and cashed by a supervisor.

To prevent or detect frauds such as those we described above, employees' attendance records should be controlled. For example, you may have used an "In and Out" card on which your time of arrival to and departure from work was recorded when you inserted the card into a time clock. A Payroll Department employee may be stationed near the time clock during normal arrival and departure times in order to verify that employees "clock in" only once and only for themselves. Employee identification cards or badges may also be used to verify that only authorized employees are clocking in and are permitted to enter work areas. When payroll checks are distributed, employee identification cards may be used to deter one employee from picking up another's check.

Other controls include verifying and approving all payroll rate changes. In addition, in a computerized system, all program changes should be properly approved and tested by employees who are independent of the payroll system. The use of a special payroll bank account, as we discussed earlier in this chapter, also enhances control over payroll.

Employees' Fringe Benefits

objective 6

Journalize entries for employee fringe benefits, including vacation pay and pensions.

Many companies provide their employees a variety of benefits in addition to salary and wages earned. Such **fringe benefits** may take many forms, including vacations, pension plans, and health, life, and disability insurance. When the employer pays part or all of the cost of the fringe benefits, these costs must be recognized as expenses. To properly match revenues and expenses, the estimated cost of these benefits should be recorded as an expense during the period in which the employee earns the benefit.

Exhibit 9 shows benefit dollars as a percent of total benefits for 864 companies surveyed by the U.S. Chamber of Commerce.

Exhibit 9 Benefit Dollars as a Percent of Total

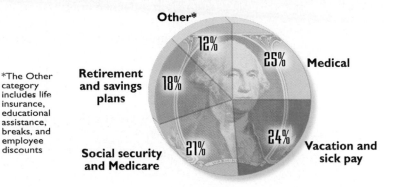

*The Other category includes life insurance, educational assistance, breaks, and employee discounts

Source: U.S. Chamber of Commerce.

Vacation Pay

Most employers grant vacation rights, sometimes called **compensated absences**, to their employees. Such rights give rise to a recordable contingent liability. The liability for employees' vacation pay should be accrued as a liability as the vacation rights are earned. The entry to accrue vacation pay may be recorded in total at the end of each fiscal year, or it may be recorded at the end of each pay period. To illustrate this latter case, assume that employees earn one day of vacation for each month worked during the year. Assume also that the estimated vacation pay for the payroll period ending May 5 is $2,000. The entry to record the accrued vacation pay for this pay period is shown as follows.

May	5	Vacation Pay Expense		2 0 0 0 00	
		Vacation Pay Payable			2 0 0 0 00
		Vacation pay for week ended May 5.			

If employees are required to take all their vacation time within one year, the vacation pay payable is reported on the balance sheet as a current liability. If employees are allowed to accumulate their vacation time, the estimated vacation pay liability that is applicable to time that will *not* be taken within one year is a long-term liability.

When payroll is prepared for the period in which employees have taken vacations, the vacation pay payable is reduced. The entry debits *Vacation Pay Payable* and credits *Salaries Payable* and the other related accounts for taxes and withholdings.

Pensions

A **pension** represents a cash payment to retired employees. Rights to pension payments are earned by employees during their working years, based on the pension plan established by the employer. One of the fundamental characteristics of such a plan is whether it is a defined contribution plan or a defined benefit plan.

Defined Contribution Plan

A **defined contribution plan** requires that a fixed amount of money be invested for the employee's behalf during the employee's working years. In a defined contribution plan, the employer is required to make annual pension contributions. There is no promise of future pension payments, however, so the employee bears the investment risk in a defined contribution plan. The employer's cost is debited to *Pension Expense*. To illustrate, assume that the pension plan of Flossmoor Industries requires a contribution equal to 10% of employee annual salaries. The entry to record the transaction, assuming $500,000 of annual salaries, is as follows:

Dec.	31	Pension Expense		50 0 0 0 00	
		Cash			50 0 0 0 00
		Contributed 10% of annual salaries to			
		pension plan.			

One of the more popular defined contribution pension plans is the *401K plan*. Under this plan, employees may contribute a limited part of their income to investments, such as mutual funds. A 401K plan offers employees two advantages: (1) the tax on the contribution is deferred (within limits), and (2) future investment earnings are tax deferred until withdrawn at retirement. In addition, for approximately 90% of the 401K plans, the employer matches some portion of the employee's contribution. For example, if the plan has a 50% matching feature, then each $1 contributed by the employee will be matched with a $0.50 contribution by the employer. Many financial planners advise employees to contribute to a 401K plan because of these benefits.

While 42 million American workers are covered by defined benefit plans, the number of defined contribution plans has been increasing. Over 75% of all new plans are structured as defined contribution plans.

Once Flossmoor makes the annual contribution to the pension fund, its obligation is completed. The employee's final pension will depend on the investment results earned by the pension fund on the contributed balances.

Defined Benefit Plan

Employers may choose to promise employees a fixed annual pension benefit at retirement, based on years of service and compensation levels. An example would be a promise to pay an annual pension based on a formula, such as the following:

1.5% × years of service × average salary for most recent 3 years prior to retirement

Pension benefits based on a formula are termed a **defined benefit plan**. Unlike a defined contribution plan, the employer bears the investment risk in funding a future retirement income benefit. As a result, many companies are replacing their defined benefit plans with defined contribution plans.

The accounting for defined benefit plans is usually very complex due to the uncertainties of projecting future pension obligations. These obligations depend upon such factors as employee life expectancies, employee turnover, expected employee compensation levels, and investment income on pension contributions.

The pension cost of a defined benefit plan is debited to *Pension Expense*. The amount funded is credited to *Cash*. Any unfunded amount is credited to *Unfunded Pension Liability*. For example, assume that the pension plan of Hinkle Co. requires an annual pension cost of $80,000, based on an estimate of the future benefit obligation. Further assume that Hinkle Co. pays $60,000 to the pension fund. The entry to record this transaction is as follows:

Dec.	31	Pension Expense		80 0 0 0 00	
		Cash			60 0 0 0 00
		Unfunded Pension Liability			20 0 0 0 00
		To record annual pension cost and			
		contribution to pension plan.			

If the unfunded pension liability is to be paid within one year, it will be classified as a current liability. That portion of the liability to be paid beyond one year is a long-term liability.

Postretirement Benefits Other than Pensions

In addition to the pension benefits described above, employees may earn rights to other **postretirement benefits** from their employer. Such benefits may include dental care, eye care, medical care, life insurance, tuition assistance, tax services, and legal services for employees or their dependents. The amount of the annual benefits expense is based upon health statistics of the workforce. This amount is recorded by debiting *Postretirement Benefits Expense*. *Cash* is credited for the same amount if the benefits are fully funded. If the benefits are not fully funded, a postretirement benefits plan liability account is credited. Thus, the accounting for postretirement health benefits is very similar to that of defined benefit pension plans.

A business's financial statements should fully disclose the nature of its postretirement benefit obligations. These disclosures are usually included as footnotes to the financial statements. The complex nature of accounting for postretirement benefits is described in more advanced accounting courses.

FINANCIAL ANALYSIS AND INTERPRETATION

objective 7

Use the quick ratio to analyze the ability of a business to pay its current liabilities.

A business must be able to pay its current liabilities within a short period of time, usually one year. One measure of its ability to make these payments is the **quick ratio** or **acid-test ratio**. The quick ratio is computed as follows:

$$\text{Quick Ratio} = \frac{\text{Quick Assets}}{\text{Current Liabilities}}$$

The quick ratio measures the "instant" debt-paying ability of a company, using quick assets. Quick assets are cash, cash equivalents, and receivables that can quickly be converted into cash. It is often considered desirable to have a quick ratio exceeding 1. A ratio less than 1 would indicate that current liabilities cannot be covered by cash and "near cash" assets.

To illustrate, assume that Noble Co. and Hart Co. have the following quick assets, current liabilities, and quick ratios:

	Noble Co.	Hart Co.
Quick assets:		
Cash	$100,000	$ 55,000
Cash equivalents	47,000	65,000
Accounts receivable (net)	84,000	472,000
Total	$231,000	$592,000
Current liabilities:		
Accounts payable	$125,000	$427,000
Wages payable	65,000	120,000
Employees federal income tax payable	18,000	36,000
Social security tax payable	3,025	7,200
Medicare tax payable	975	1,800
Notes payable	8,000	148,000
Total	$220,000	$740,000
Quick ratio	1.05	0.8

As you can see, Noble Co. has quick assets in excess of current liabilities, or a quick ratio of 1.05. The ratio exceeds 1, indicating that the quick assets should be sufficient to meet current liabilities. Hart Co., however, has a quick ratio of 0.8. Its quick assets will not be sufficient to cover the current liabilities. Hart could solve this problem by working with a bank to convert its short-term debt of $148,000 into a long-term obligation. This would remove the notes payable from current liabilities. If Hart did this, then its quick ratio would improve to 1 ($592,000 ÷ $592,000), which would be just sufficient for quick assets to cover current liabilities.

ENCORE

Do You Want to Be a Millionaire?

A recent survey found that 66% of individuals believe that their standard of living at retirement will be the same or higher than during their current working years. Yet, a third of these respondents don't have a formal savings plan for retirement. One-fourth of these respondents believe that they will need to save only $100,000 in order to maintain their lifestyle in retirement. However, experts believe that today's 25-year-old will need savings of $750,000 to $1 million to support a basic retirement, given increased life expectancies and inflation. How do you save this much money? The two keys to savings success are (1) save regularly, such as monthly or quarterly, even if it's a small amount, and (2) start early. For example, to have the same retirement income as a 25-year-old saving $100 per month, a 30-year-old would need to save $200 per month. Waiting until you are 35 years old would require saving $400 per month. Every five years of delay requires doubling the necessary contribution. This is the power of compound interest. Therefore, the worst strategy is to begin retirement saving at middle age. Unfortunately, according to one survey, 41% of workers age 25 to 34 who are eligible for defined contribution pension plans, such as a 401K, do not take advantage of them.

So how much would a 25-year-old need to save monthly to reach the $1 million mark? There are many assumptions that go into such a calculation. Let's assume that an individual begins saving $150 per month at the age of 25, earns 8% on these savings, increases the amount contributed by 5% per year (to match salary increases), and retires at the age of 65. Under these assumptions, the individual would accumulate $975,000 by age 65. What would be the retirement savings if the assumptions were changed so that the savings plan began at age 35, 45, or 55? The graph at the right shows what happens to the savings amount. As you can see, time is money. Beginning just 10 years later at age 35 reduces the accumulated savings by over 60%, to approximately $374,000.

Retirement planning work sheets are available from a number of mutual fund companies on the Internet. One easy-to-use work sheet is provided at the Web site of **T. Rowe Price, www.troweprice.com.** ■

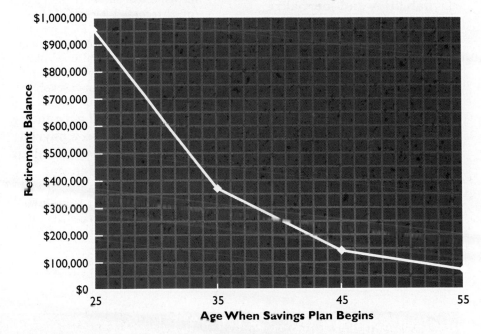

Retirement Balance Under Different Savings Scenarios

KEY POINTS

1 Define and give examples of current liabilities.

Current liabilities are obligations that are to be paid out of current assets and are due within a short time, usually within one year. Current liabilities arise from either (1) receiving goods or services prior to making payment or (2) receiving payment prior to delivering goods or services.

2 Journalize entries for short-term notes payable.

A note issued to a creditor to temporarily satisfy an account payable is recorded as a debit to *Accounts Payable* and a credit to *Notes Payable*. At the time the note is paid, *Notes Payable* and *Interest Expense* are debited and *Cash* is credited. Notes may also be issued to purchase merchandise or other assets or to borrow money from a bank. When a discounted note is issued, *Interest Expense* is debited for the interest deduction at the time of issuance, an asset account is debited for the proceeds, and *Notes Payable* is credited for the face value of the note. The face value and the maturity value of a discounted note are equal.

3 Describe the accounting treatment for contingent liabilities and journalize entries for product warranties.

A contingent liability is a potential obligation that results from a past transaction but depends on a future event. If the contingent liability is both probable and estimable, the liability should be recorded. If the contingent liability is reasonably possible or is not estimable, it should be disclosed in the footnotes to the financial statements. An example of a recordable contingent liability is

product warranties. If a company grants a warranty on a product, an estimated warranty expense and liability should be recorded in the period of the sale. The expense and the liability are recorded by debiting *Product Warranty Expense* and crediting *Product Warranty Payable*.

4 Determine employer liabilities for payroll, including liabilities arising from employee earnings and deductions from earnings.

An employer's liability for payroll is calculated by determining employees' total earnings for a payroll period, including overtime pay. From this amount, employee deductions are subtracted to arrive at the net pay to be paid each employee. The employer's liabilities for employee deductions are recognized at the time the payroll is recorded. Most employers also incur liabilities for payroll taxes, such as social security tax, Medicare tax, federal unemployment compensation tax, and state unemployment compensation tax.

5 Describe payroll accounting systems that use a payroll register, employee earnings records, and a general journal.

The payroll register is used in assembling and summarizing the

data needed for each payroll period. The data recorded in the payroll register include the number of hours worked and the earnings and deduction data for each employee. The payroll register also includes columns for accumulating total wages or salaries to be debited to the various expense accounts. It is supported by a detailed payroll record for each employee, called an employee's earnings record.

6 Journalize entries for employee fringe benefits, including vacation pay and pensions.

Fringe benefits are expenses of the period in which the employees earn the benefits. Fringe benefits are recorded by debiting an expense account and crediting a liability account. For example, the entry to record accrued vacation pay debits *Vacation Pay Expense* and credits *Vacation Pay Payable*.

7 Use the quick ratio to analyze the ability of a business to pay its current liabilities.

The quick ratio or acid-test ratio is a measure of a business's ability to pay current liabilities within a short period of time. The quick ratio is quick assets divided by current liabilities. A quick ratio exceeding 1 is usually desirable.

ILLUSTRATIVE PROBLEM

Selected transactions of Taylor Company, completed during the fiscal year ended December 31, are as follows:

Mar. 1. Purchased merchandise on account from Kelvin Co., $20,000.
Apr. 10. Issued a 60-day, 12% note for $20,000 to Kelvin Co. on account.
June 9. Paid Kelvin Co. the amount owed on the note of April 10.
Aug. 1. Issued a $50,000, 90-day note to Harold Co. in exchange for a building. Harold Co. discounted the note at 15%.
Oct. 30. Paid Harold Co. the amount due on the note of August 1.
Dec. 27. Journalized the entry to record the biweekly payroll. A summary of the payroll record follows:

Salary distribution:

Sales	$63,400	
Officers	36,600	
Office	10,000	$110,000

Deductions:

Social security tax	$ 5,050	
Medicare tax	1,650	
Federal income tax withheld	17,600	
State income tax withheld	4,950	
Savings bond deductions	850	
Medical insurance deductions	1,120	31,220
Net amount		$ 78,780

Dec. 30. Issued a check in payment of liabilities for employees' federal income tax of $17,600, social security tax of $10,100, and Medicare tax of $3,300.

31. Issued a check for $9,500 to the pension fund trustee to fully fund the pension cost for December.

31. Journalized an entry to record the employees' accrued vacation pay, $36,100.

31. Journalized an entry to record the estimated accrued product warranty liability, $37,240.

Instructions

Journalize the preceding transactions.

Solution

Mar.	1	Merchandise Inventory		20 0 0 0 00	
		Accounts Payable—Kelvin Co.			20 0 0 0 00
Apr.	10	Accounts Payable—Kelvin Co.		20 0 0 0 00	
		Notes Payable			20 0 0 0 00
June	9	Notes Payable		20 0 0 0 00	
		Interest Expense		4 0 0 00	
		Cash			20 4 0 0 00
Aug.	1	Building		48 1 2 5 00	
		Interest Expense		1 8 7 5 00	
		Notes Payable			50 0 0 0 00
Oct.	30	Notes Payable		50 0 0 0 00	
		Cash			50 0 0 0 00
Dec.	27	Sales Salaries Expense		63 4 0 0 00	
		Officers Salaries Expense		36 6 0 0 00	
		Office Salaries Expense		10 0 0 0 00	
		Social Security Tax Payable			5 0 5 0 00
		Medicare Tax Payable			1 6 5 0 00
		Employees Federal Income Tax Payable			17 6 0 0 00
		Employees State Income Tax Payable			4 9 5 0 00
		Bond Deductions Payable			8 5 0 00
		Medical Insurance Payable			1 1 2 0 00
		Salaries Payable			78 7 8 0 00

Dec.	30	Employees Federal Income Tax Payable	17 6 0 0 00	
		Social Security Tax Payable	10 1 0 0 00	
		Medicare Tax Payable	3 3 0 0 00	
		Cash		31 0 0 0 00
	31	Pension Expense	9 5 0 0 00	
		Cash		9 5 0 0 00
	31	Vacation Pay Expense	36 1 0 0 00	
		Vacation Pay Payable		36 1 0 0 00
	31	Product Warranty Expense	37 2 4 0 00	
		Product Warranty Payable		37 2 4 0 00

SELF-EXAMINATION QUESTIONS

Answers at End of Chapter

Matching

Match each of the following statements with its proper term. Some terms may not be used.

A. defined benefit plan	___ 1. A detailed record of each employee's earnings.
B. defined contribution plan	___ 2. A multicolumn form used to assemble and summarize payroll data at the end of each payroll period.
C. discount	___ 3. A pension plan that promises employees a fixed annual pension benefit at retirement, based on years of service and compensation levels.
D. discount rate	
E. employee's earnings record	___ 4. Gross pay less payroll deductions; the amount the employer is obligated to pay the employee.
F. FICA tax	___ 5. The net amount available from discounting a note payable.
G. fringe benefits	___ 6. A pension plan that requires a fixed amount of money to be invested for the employee's behalf during the employee's working years.
H. gross pay	
I. net pay	___ 7. Benefits provided to employees in addition to wages and salaries.
J. payroll	___ 8. The rate used in computing the interest to be deducted from the maturity value of a note.
K. payroll register	
L. postretirement benefits	___ 9. The total earnings of an employee for a payroll period.
	___ 10. Rights to benefits that employees earn during their term of employment, for themselves and their dependents, after they retire.
M. proceeds	
N. quick ratio	___ 11. The total amount paid to employees for a certain period.
	___ 12. Federal Insurance Contributions Act tax used to finance federal programs for old-age and disability benefits (social security) and health insurance for the aged (Medicare).
	___ 13. A financial ratio that measures the ability to pay current liabilities within a short period of time.
	___ 14. The interest deducted from the maturity value of a note.

Multiple Choice

1. A business issued a $5,000, 60-day, 12% note to the bank. The amount due at maturity is:
   A. $4,900   C. $5,100
   B. $5,000   D. $5,600

2. A business issued a $5,000, 60-day note to a supplier, which discounted the note at 12%. The proceeds are:
   A. $4,400   C. $5,000
   B. $4,900   D. $5,100

3. Which of the following taxes are employers usually not required to withhold from employees?
   A. Federal income tax
   B. Federal unemployment compensation tax
   C. Medicare tax
   D. State and local income tax

4. An employee's rate of pay is $20 per hour, with time and a half for all hours worked in excess of 40 during a week. The social security rate is 6.0% on the first $80,000 of annual earnings, and the Medicare rate is 1.5% on all earnings. The following additional data are available:

Hours worked during current week	45
Year's cumulative earnings prior to current week	$79,400
Federal income tax withheld	$212

Based on these data, the amount of the employee's net pay for the current week is:
   A. $620.50
   B. $641.50
   C. $666.75
   D. $687.75

5. Within limitations on the maximum earnings subject to the tax, employers do not incur an expense for which of the following payroll taxes?
   A. Social security tax
   B. Federal unemployment compensation tax
   C. State unemployment compensation tax
   D. Employees' federal income tax

CLASS DISCUSSION QUESTIONS

1. What two types of transactions cause most current liabilities?
2. When are short-term notes payable issued?
3. When should the liability associated with a product warranty be recorded? Discuss.
4. **Compaq Computer Corporation** reported $752 million of product warranties in the current liabilities section of a recent balance sheet. How would costs of repairing a defective product be recorded?
5. The "Questions and Answers Technical Hotline" in the *Journal of Accountancy* included the following question:

   Several years ago, Company B instituted legal action against Company A. Under a memorandum of settlement and agreement, Company A agreed to pay Company B a total of $17,500 in three installments—$5,000 on March 1, $7,500 on July 1, and the remaining $5,000 on December 31. Company A paid the first two installments during its fiscal year ended September 30. Should the unpaid amount of $5,000 be presented as a current liability at September 30?

   How would you answer this question?
6. What programs are funded by the FICA (Federal Insurance Contributions Act) tax?
7. a. Identify the federal taxes that most employers are required to withhold from employees.
   b. Give the titles of the accounts to which the amounts withheld are credited.
8. For each of the following payroll-related taxes, indicate whether there is a ceiling on the annual earnings subject to the tax: (a) social security tax, (b) Medicare tax, (c) federal income tax, (d) federal unemployment compensation tax.
9. Why are deductions from employees' earnings classified as liabilities for the employer?
10. Do payroll taxes levied against employers become liabilities at the time the liabilities for wages are incurred or at the time the wages are paid?
11. Taylor Company, with 20 employees, is expanding operations. It is trying to decide whether to hire one employee full-time for $25,000 or two employees part-time for a total of $25,000. Would any of the employer's payroll taxes discussed in this chapter have a bearing on this decision? Explain.
12. For each of the following payroll-related taxes, indicate whether they generally apply to (a) employees only, (b) employers only, (c) both employees and employers:
    1. Social security tax
    2. Medicare tax
    3. Federal income tax
    4. Federal unemployment compensation tax
    5. State unemployment compensation tax
13. What are the principal reasons for using a special payroll checking account?
14. In a payroll system, what type of input data are referred to as (a) constants, (b) variables?

15. To strengthen internal controls, what department should provide written authorizations for the addition of names to the payroll?

16. Explain how a payroll system that is properly designed and operated tends to ensure that (a) wages paid are based on hours actually worked and (b) payroll checks are not issued to fictitious employees.

17. To match revenues and expenses properly, should the expense for employee vacation pay be recorded in the period during which the vacation privilege is earned or during the period in which the vacation is taken? Discuss.

18. Identify several factors that influence the future pension obligation of an employer under a defined benefit pension plan.

19. Where should the unfunded pension liability from a defined benefit pension plan be reported on the balance sheet?

20. What are some examples of postretirement benefits other than pensions that employees may earn for themselves and their dependents?

RESOURCES FOR YOUR SUCCESS ONLINE AT

http://warren.swcollege.com

Remember! If you need additional help, visit South-Western's Web site.
See page 26 for a description of the online and printed materials that are available.

EXERCISES

Exercise 11–1
Current liabilities

Objective 1

✓ Total current liabilities, $218,000

Net World Magazine Inc. sold 4,800 annual subscriptions of *Net World* for $45 during December 2003. These new subscribers will receive monthly issues, beginning in January 2004. In addition, the business had taxable income of $160,000 during the first calendar quarter of 2004. The federal tax rate is 35%. A quarterly tax payment will be made on April 7, 2004.

Prepare the current liabilities section of the balance sheet for Net World Magazine Inc. on March 31, 2004.

Exercise 11–2
Entries for discounting notes payable

Objective 2

National Electric Lighting Co. issues a 90-day note for $500,000 to Home Products Supply Co. for merchandise inventory. Home Products discounts the note at 10%.

a. Journalize National Electric's entries to record:
   1. the issuance of the note.
   2. the payment of the note at maturity.
b. Journalize Home Products' entries to record:
   1. the receipt of the note.
   2. the receipt of the payment of the note at maturity.

Exercise 11–3
Evaluate alternative notes

Objective 2

A borrower has two alternatives for a loan: (1) issue a $60,000, 90-day, 8% note or (2) issue a $60,000, 90-day note that the creditor discounts at 8%.

a. Calculate the amount of the interest expense for each option.
b. Determine the proceeds received by the borrower in each situation.
c. Which alternative is more favorable to the borrower? Explain.

Exercise 11–4
Entries for notes payable

Objective 2

A business issued a 60-day, 9% note for $20,000 to a creditor on account. Journalize the entries to record (a) the issuance of the note and (b) the payment of the note at maturity, including interest.

Exercise 11–5
Fixed asset purchases with note
Objective 2

On June 30, Zelda Game Company purchased land for $250,000 and a building for $730,000, paying $380,000 cash and issuing an 8% note for the balance, secured by a mortgage on the property. The terms of the note provide for 20 semiannual payments of $30,000 on the principal plus the interest accrued from the date of the preceding payment. Journalize the entry to record (a) the transaction on June 30, (b) the payment of the first installment on December 31, and (c) the payment of the second installment the following June 30.

Exercise 11–6
Accrued product warranty
Objective 3

Precision Audio Company warrants its products for one year. The estimated product warranty is 3% of sales. Assume that sales were $600,000 for January. In February, a customer received warranty repairs requiring $310 of parts and $460 of labor.

a. Journalize the adjusting entry required at January 31, the end of the first month of the current year, to record the accrued product warranty.
b. Journalize the entry to record the warranty work provided in February.

Exercise 11–7
Accrued product warranty
Objective 2

✓ a. 0.77%

During a recent year, **Motorola, Inc.**, had sales of $29,398,000,000. An analysis of Motorola's product warranty payable account for the year was as follows:

Product warranty payable, January 1	$337,000,000
Product warranty expense	226,000,000
Warranty claims paid	(230,000,000)
Product warranty payable, December 31	$333,000,000

a. Determine the product warranty expense as a percent of sales.
b. Record the adjusting entry for the product warranty expense for the year.

Exercise 11–8
Contingent liabilities
Objective 3

Several months ago, Endurance Battery Company experienced a hazardous materials spill at one of its plants. As a result, the Environmental Protection Agency (EPA) fined the company $170,000. The company is contesting the fine. In addition, an employee is seeking $500,000 damages related to the spill. Lastly, a homeowner has sued the company for $120,000. The homeowner lives 20 miles from the plant, but believes that the incident has reduced the home's resale value by $120,000.

  Endurance Battery's legal counsel believes that it is probable that the EPA fine will stand. In addition, counsel indicates that an out-of-court settlement of $250,000 has recently been reached with the employee. The final papers will be signed next week. Counsel believes that the homeowner's case is much weaker and will be decided in favor of Endurance. Other litigation related to the spill is possible, but the damage amounts are uncertain.

a. Journalize the contingent liabilities associated with the hazardous materials spill.
b. ✏ Prepare a footnote disclosure relating to this incident.

Exercise 11–9
Contingent liabilities
Objective 3

The following footnote accompanied recent financial statements for **eBAY, Inc.**:

> *. . . The Company was sued by Network Engineering Software, Inc. . . . for the Company's alleged willful and deliberate violation of a patent. The suit seeks unspecified monetary damages as well as an injunction against the Company's operations. It also seeks treble damages and attorneys' fees and costs. The Company believes that it has meritorious defenses against this suit and intends to vigorously defend itself. The Company could be forced to incur material expenses during this defense and in the event it were to lose this suit, its business would be harmed.*

Was a liability recorded by eBAY, Inc., for this contingent liability? Why or why not?

Exercise 11–10
Calculate payroll
Objective 4

✓ b. Net pay, $989.75

An employee earns $26 per hour and 1½ times that rate for all hours in excess of 40 hours per week. Assume that the employee worked 50 hours during the week, and that the gross pay prior to the current week totaled $62,140. Assume further that the social security tax rate was 6.0% (on earnings up to $80,000), the Medicare tax rate was 1.5%, and federal income tax to be withheld was $333.

a. Determine the gross pay for the week.
b. Determine the net pay for the week.

Exercise 11–11
Calculate payroll

Objective 4

✓ Administrator net pay, $854.50

Prism Business Consultants has three employees—a consultant, a computer programmer, and an administrator. The following payroll information is available for each employee:

	Consultant	Computer Programmer	Administrator
Regular earnings rate	$2,500 per week	$30 per hour	$24 per hour
Overtime earnings rate	Not applicable	1½ times hourly rate	1½ times hourly rate
Gross pay prior to current pay period	$120,000	$79,200	$53,200
Number of withholding allowances	1	0	3

For the current pay period, the computer programmer worked 41 hours and the administrator worked 45 hours. For the current pay period, the federal income tax withheld for the consultant was $670. The federal income tax withheld for the computer programmer and the administrator can be determined from the wage bracket withholding table in Exhibit 3 in the chapter. Assume further that the social security tax rate was 6.0% on the first $80,000 of annual earnings, and the Medicare tax rate was 1.5%.

Determine the gross pay and the net pay for each of the three employees for the current pay period.

Exercise 11–12
Summary payroll data

Objectives 4, 5

✓ a. (3) Total earnings, $211,000

In the following summary of data for a payroll period, some amounts have been intentionally omitted:

Earnings:
1.	At regular rate	?
2.	At overtime rate	$ 32,500
3.	Total earnings	?

Deductions:
4.	Social security tax	12,000
5.	Medicare tax	3,165
6.	Income tax withheld	29,500
7.	Medical insurance	3,150
8.	Union dues	?
9.	Total deductions	50,000
10.	Net amount paid	161,000

Accounts debited:
11.	Factory Wages	121,600
12.	Sales Salaries	?
13.	Office Salaries	34,300

a. Calculate the amounts omitted in lines (1), (3), (8), and (12).
b. Journalize the entry to record the payroll accrual.
c. Journalize the entry to record the payment of the payroll.
d. ✏️ From the data given in this exercise and your answer to (a), would you conclude that this payroll was paid sometime during the first few weeks of the calendar year? Explain.

Exercise 11–13
Payroll internal control procedures

Objective 5

Memphis Sounds is a retail store specializing in the sale of jazz compact discs and cassettes. The store employs 3 full-time and 10 part-time workers. The store's weekly payroll averages $2,200 for all 13 workers.

Memphis Sounds uses a personal computer to assist in preparing paychecks. Each week, the store's accountant collects employee time cards and enters the hours worked into the payroll program. The payroll program calculates each employee's pay and prints a paycheck. The accountant uses a check-signing machine to sign the paychecks. Next, the store's owner authorizes the transfer of funds from the store's regular bank account to the payroll account.

For the week of May 10, the accountant accidentally recorded 400 hours worked instead of 40 hours for one of the full-time employees.

◄ ▬ ► Does Memphis Sounds have internal controls in place to catch this error? If so, how will this error be detected?

Exercise 11–14
Internal control procedures
Objective 5

Sure-Grip Tools is a small manufacturer of home workshop power tools. The company employs 30 production workers and 10 administrative persons. The following procedures are used to process the company's weekly payroll:

a. All employees are required to record their hours worked by clocking in and out on a time clock. Employees must clock out for lunch break. Due to congestion around the time clock area at lunch time, management has not objected to having one employee clock in and out for an entire department.
b. Whenever a salaried employee is terminated, Personnel authorizes Payroll to remove the employee from the payroll system. However, this procedure is not required when an hourly worker is terminated. Hourly employees only receive a paycheck if their time cards show hours worked. The computer automatically drops an employee from the payroll system when that employee has six consecutive weeks with no hours worked.
c. Whenever an employee receives a pay raise, the supervisor must fill out a wage adjustment form, which is signed by the company president. This form is used to change the employee's wage rate in the payroll system.
d. Sure-Grip maintains a separate checking account for payroll checks. Each week, the total net pay for all employees is transferred from the company's regular bank account to the payroll account.
e. Paychecks are signed by using a check-signing machine. This machine is located in the main office so that it can be easily accessed by anyone needing a check signed.

◄ ▬ ► State whether each of the procedures is appropriate or inappropriate after considering the principles of internal control. If a procedure is inappropriate, describe the appropriate procedure.

Exercise 11–15
Payroll tax entries
Objective 5

According to a summary of the payroll of All Sport Publishing Co., $630,000 was subject to the 6.0% social security tax and $700,000 was subject to the 1.5% Medicare tax. Also, $15,000 was subject to state and federal unemployment taxes.

a. Calculate the employer's payroll taxes, using the following rates: state unemployment, 4.3%; federal unemployment, 0.8%.
b. Journalize the entry to record the accrual of payroll taxes.

Exercise 11–16
Payroll procedures
Objective 5

The fiscal year for Country Road Stores Inc. ends on June 30. In addition, the company computes and reports payroll taxes on a fiscal-year basis. Thus, social security and FUTA maximum earnings limitations apply to the fiscal-year payroll.

◄ ▬ ► What is wrong with these procedures for accounting for payroll taxes?

Exercise 11–17
Accrued vacation pay
Objective 6

A business provides its employees with varying amounts of vacation per year, depending on the length of employment. The estimated amount of the current year's vacation pay is $224,400. Journalize the adjusting entry required on January 31, the end of the first month of the current year, to record the accrued vacation pay.

Exercise 11–18
Pension plan entries
Objective 6

Perpetual Images Inc. operates a chain of photography stores. The company maintains a defined contribution pension plan for its employees. The plan requires quarterly installments to be paid to the funding agent, Interstate Insurance Company, by the fifteenth of the month following the end of each quarter. Assuming that the pension cost is $225,000 for the quarter ended December 31, journalize entries to record (a) the accrued pension liability on December 31 and (b) the payment to the funding agent on January 15.

Exercise 11–19
Defined benefit pension plan terms

Objective 6

In a recent year's financial statements, **Procter & Gamble Co.** showed an unfunded pension liability of $815 million and a periodic pension cost of $173 million.

Explain the meaning of the $815 million unfunded pension liability and the $173 million periodic pension cost.

Exercise 11–20
Quick ratio

Objective 7

The financial statements for **Cisco Systems, Inc.**, are presented in Appendix G at the end of the text.

a. Compute the quick ratio as of July 29, 2000 and July 31, 1999.
b. What conclusions can be drawn from these data as to Cisco Systems' ability to meet its current liabilities?

PROBLEMS SERIES A

Problem 11–1A
Liability transactions

Objectives 2, 3

SPREADSHEET
GENERAL
LEDGER

The following items were selected from among the transactions completed by Pride Polymers during the current year:

Apr. 7. Borrowed $15,000 from First Financial Corporation, issuing a 60-day, 12% note for that amount.
May 10. Purchased equipment by issuing a $120,000, 120-day note to Milford Equipment Co., which discounted the note at the rate of 10%.
June 6. Paid First Financial Corporation the interest due on the note of April 7 and renewed the loan by issuing a new 30-day, 16% note for $15,000. (Record both the debit and credit to the notes payable account.)
July 6. Paid First Financial Corporation the amount due on the note of June 6.
Aug. 3. Purchased merchandise on account from Hamilton Co., $36,000, terms, n/30.
Sept. 2. Issued a 60-day, 15% note for $36,000 to Hamilton Co., on account.
     7. Paid Milford Equipment Co. the amount due on the note of May 10.
Nov. 1. Paid Hamilton Co. the amount owed on the note of September 2.
    15. Purchased store equipment from Shingo Equipment Co. for $100,000, paying $23,000 and issuing a series of seven 12% notes for $11,000 each, coming due at 30-day intervals.
Dec. 15. Paid the amount due Shingo Equipment Co. on the first note in the series issued on November 15.
    21. Settled a product liability lawsuit with a customer for $65,000, to be paid in January. Pride Polymers accrued the loss in a litigation claims payable account.

Instructions

1. Journalize the transactions.
2. Journalize the adjusting entry for each of the following accrued expenses at the end of the current year:
   a. Product warranty cost, $11,200.
   b. Interest on the six remaining notes owed to Shingo Equipment Co.

Problem 11–2A
Entries for payroll and payroll taxes

Objectives 4, 5

The following information about the payroll for the week ended December 30 was obtained from the records of Hannah Co.:

✓ 1. (b) Dr. Payroll Taxes
Expense, $41,990

Salaries:			Deductions:	
Sales salaries	$327,000		Income tax withheld	$104,500
Warehouse salaries	87,400		Social security tax withheld	32,600
Office salaries	165,600		Medicare tax withheld	8,700
	$580,000		U.S. savings bonds	24,400
			Group insurance	32,800

Tax rates assumed:
Social security, 6% on first $80,000 of employee annual earnings
Medicare, 1.5%
State unemployment (employer only), 3.8%
Federal unemployment (employer only), 0.8%

Instructions

1. Assuming that the payroll for the last week of the year is to be paid on December 31, journalize the following entries:
   a. December 30, to record the payroll.
   b. December 30, to record the employer's payroll taxes on the payroll to be paid on December 31. Of the total payroll for the last week of the year, $15,000 is subject to unemployment compensation taxes.
2. Assuming that the payroll for the last week of the year is to be paid on January 4 of the following fiscal year, journalize the following entries:
   a. December 30, to record the payroll.
   b. January 4, to record the employer's payroll taxes on the payroll to be paid on January 4.

Problem 11–3A
Wage and tax statement data and employer FICA tax

Objectives 4, 5

✓ 2. (e) $26,348.25

Safety-Haul Distribution Company began business on January 2, 2002. Salaries were paid to employees on the last day of each month, and social security tax, Medicare tax, and federal income tax were withheld in the required amounts. An employee who is hired in the middle of the month receives half the monthly salary for that month. All required payroll tax reports were filed, and the correct amount of payroll taxes was remitted by the company for the calendar year. Early in 2003, before the Wage and Tax Statements (Form W-2) could be prepared for distribution to employees and for filing with the Social Security Administration, the employees' earnings records were inadvertently destroyed.

None of the employees resigned or were discharged during the year, and there were no changes in salary rates. The social security tax was withheld at the rate of 6.0% on the first $80,000 of salary and Medicare tax at the rate of 1.5% on salary. Data on dates of employment, salary rates, and employees' income taxes withheld, which are summarized as follows, were obtained from personnel records and payroll records.

Employee	Date First Employed	Monthly Salary	Monthly Income Tax Withheld
Albright	June 2	$6,200	$1,305.10
Charles	Jan. 2	6,800	1,492.60
Given	Mar. 1	4,100	764.65
Nelson	Jan. 2	3,700	682.65
Quinn	Nov. 15	4,000	740.00
Ramirez	Apr. 15	3,000	535.50
Wu	Jan. 16	7,500	1,676.25

Instructions

1. Calculate the amounts to be reported on each employee's Wage and Tax Statement (Form W-2) for 2002, arranging the data in the following form:

Employee	Gross Earnings	Federal Income Tax Withheld	Social Security Tax Withheld	Medicare Tax Withheld

(continued)

2. Calculate the following employer payroll taxes for the year: (a) social security; (b) Medicare; (c) state unemployment compensation at 3.8% on the first $7,000 of each employee's earnings; (d) federal unemployment compensation at 0.8% on the first $7,000 of each employee's earnings; (e) total.

If the working papers correlating with this textbook are not used, omit Problem 11–4A.

Problem 11–4A
Payroll register

Objectives 4, 5

✓ 3. Dr. Payroll Taxes Expense, $667.58

The payroll register for Chopin Piano Co. for the week ended December 12, 2003, is presented in the working papers.

Instructions

1. Journalize the entry to record the payroll for the week.
2. Journalize the entry to record the issuance of the checks to employees.
3. Journalize the entry to record the employer's payroll taxes for the week. Assume the following tax rates: state unemployment, 3.2%; federal unemployment, 0.8%. Of the earnings, $750 is subject to unemployment taxes.
4. Journalize the entry to record a check issued on December 15 to Second National Bank in payment of employees' income taxes, $1,540.81, social security taxes, $1,020.12, and Medicare taxes, $255.04.

Problem 11–5A
Payroll register

Objectives 4, 5

SPREADSHEET

✓ I. Total net amount payable, $6,297.25

The following data for Rainbow Paint Co. relate to the payroll for the week ended December 7, 2003:

Employee	Hours Worked	Hourly Rate	Weekly Salary	Federal Income Tax	U.S. Savings Bonds	Accumulated Earnings, Nov. 30
A	48.00	$28.00		$334.88	$15.00	$70,800.00
B	40.00	22.00		176.00		41,500.00
C			$2,100.00	525.00	70.00	100,800.00
D	45.00	18.00		171.00	10.00	43,200.00
E	40.00	15.00		108.00		28,800.00
F	42.00	22.50		203.18	20.00	47,400.00
G	40.00	16.00		108.80	25.00	30,700.00
H			1,100.00	242.00		4,400.00
I	25.00	12.00		36.00	15.00	14,400.00

Employees C and H are office staff, and all of the other employees are sales personnel. All sales personnel are paid 1½ times the regular rate for all hours in excess of 40 hours per week. The social security tax rate is 6.0% on the first $80,000 of each employee's annual earnings, and Medicare tax is 1.5% of each employee's annual earnings. The next payroll check to be used is No. 981.

Instructions

1. Prepare a payroll register for Rainbow Paint Co. for the week ended December 7, 2003.
2. Journalize the entry to record the payroll for the week.

Problem 11–6A
Payroll accounts and year-end entries

Objectives 4, 5, 6

GENERAL LEDGER

The following accounts, with the balances indicated, appear in the ledger of Yellowstone Outdoor Equipment Company on December 1 of the current year:

211	Salaries Payable	—
212	Social Security Tax Payable	$5,278
213	Medicare Tax Payable	1,389
214	Employees Federal Income Tax Payable	8,566
215	Employees State Income Tax Payable	8,334
216	State Unemployment Tax Payable	840
217	Federal Unemployment Tax Payable	210

218	Bond Deductions Payable	$ 1,400
219	Medical Insurance Payable	3,600
611	Sales Salaries Expense	640,200
711	Officers Salaries Expense	283,800
712	Office Salaries Expense	94,600
719	Payroll Taxes Expense	79,114

The following transactions relating to payroll, payroll deductions, and payroll taxes occurred during December:

Dec. 1. Issued Check No. 728 to Pico Insurance Company for $3,600, in payment of the semiannual premium on the group medical insurance policy.

2. Issued Check No. 729 to First National Bank for $15,233, in payment for $5,278 of social security tax, $1,389 of Medicare tax, and $8,566 of employees' federal income tax due.

3. Issued Check No. 730 for $1,400 to First National Bank to purchase U.S. savings bonds for employees.

14. Journalized the entry to record the biweekly payroll. A summary of the payroll record follows:

Salary distribution:		
Sales	$29,000	
Officers	13,200	
Office	4,500	$46,700
Deductions:		
Social security tax	$ 2,569	
Medicare tax	701	
Federal income tax withheld	8,313	
State income tax withheld	2,102	
Savings bond deductions	700	
Medical insurance deductions	600	14,985
Net amount		$31,715

14. Issued Check No. 738 in payment of the net amount of the biweekly payroll.

14. Journalized the entry to record payroll taxes on employees' earnings of December 14: social security tax, $2,569; Medicare tax, $701; state unemployment tax, $180; federal unemployment tax, $45.

17. Issued Check No. 744 to First National Bank for $14,853, in payment for $5,138 of social security tax, $1,402 of Medicare tax, and $8,313 of employees' federal income tax due.

28. Journalized the entry to record the biweekly payroll. A summary of the payroll record follows:

Salary distribution:		
Sales	$29,500	
Officers	13,100	
Office	4,400	$47,000
Deductions:		
Social security tax	$ 2,538	
Medicare tax	705	
Federal income tax withheld	8,366	
State income tax withheld	2,115	
Savings bond deductions	700	14,424
Net amount		$32,576

28. Issued Check No. 782 for the net amount of the biweekly payroll.

Dec. 28. Journalized the entry to record payroll taxes on employees' earnings of December 28: social security tax, $2,538; Medicare tax, $705; state unemployment tax, $110; federal unemployment tax, $28.
   30. Issued Check No. 791 for $12,551 to First National Bank, in payment of employees' state income tax due on December 31.
   30. Issued Check No. 792 to First National Bank for $1,400 to purchase U.S. savings bonds for employees.
   31. Paid $61,700 to the employee pension plan. The annual pension cost is $65,000. (Record both the payment and the unfunded pension liability.)

Instructions

1. Journalize the transactions.
2. Journalize the following adjusting entries on December 31:
   a. Salaries accrued: sales salaries, $2,950; officers salaries, $1,310; office salaries, $440. The payroll taxes are immaterial and are not accrued.
   b. Vacation pay, $12,900.

PROBLEMS SERIES B

Problem 11–1B

Liability transactions

Objectives 2, 3

SPREADSHEET

GENERAL LEDGER

The following items were selected from among the transactions completed by Renaissance Products Co. during the current year:

Feb. 15. Purchased merchandise on account from Ranier Co., $24,000, terms n/30.
Mar. 17. Issued a 30-day, 8% note for $24,000 to Ranier Co., on account.
Apr. 16. Paid Ranier Co. the amount owed on the note of March 17.
July 15. Borrowed $20,000 from Security Bank, issuing a 90-day, 8% note.
   25. Purchased tools by issuing a $90,000, 120-day note to Sun Supply Co., which discounted the note at the rate of 7%.
Oct. 13. Paid Security Bank the interest due on the note of July 15 and renewed the loan by issuing a new 30-day, 9% note for $20,000. (Journalize both the debit and credit to the notes payable account.)
Nov. 12. Paid Security Bank the amount due on the note of October 13.
   22. Paid Sun Supply Co. the amount due on the note of July 25.
Dec. 1. Purchased office equipment from Valley Equipment Co. for $95,000, paying $15,000 and issuing a series of ten 12% notes for $8,000 each, coming due at 30-day intervals.
   17. Settled a product liability lawsuit with a customer for $46,000, payable in January. Renaissance accrued the loss in a litigation claims payable account.
   31. Paid the amount due Valley Equipment Co. on the first note in the series issued on December 1.

Instructions

1. Journalize the transactions.
2. Journalize the adjusting entry for each of the following accrued expenses at the end of the current year: (a) product warranty cost, $18,250; (b) interest on the nine remaining notes owed to Valley Equipment Co.

Problem 11–2B

Entries for payroll and payroll taxes

Objectives 4, 5

GENERAL LEDGER

The following information about the payroll for the week ended December 30 was obtained from the records of Wong Co.:

Salaries:		Deductions:	
Sales salaries	$205,000	Income tax withheld	$66,000
Warehouse salaries	36,800	Social security tax withheld	19,900
Office salaries	108,200	Medicare tax withheld	5,250
	$350,000	U.S. savings bonds	19,300
		Group insurance	28,700

Tax rates assumed:

Social security, 6% on first $80,000 of employee annual earnings

Medicare, 1.5%

State unemployment (employer only), 4.2%

Federal unemployment (employer only), 0.8%

Instructions

1. Assuming that the payroll for the last week of the year is to be paid on December 31, journalize the following entries:
   a. December 30, to record the payroll.
   b. December 30, to record the employer's payroll taxes on the payroll to be paid on December 31. Of the total payroll for the last week of the year, $12,000 is subject to unemployment compensation taxes.
2. Assuming that the payroll for the last week of the year is to be paid on January 5 of the following fiscal year, journalize the following entries:
   a. December 30, to record the payroll.
   b. January 5, to record the employer's payroll taxes on the payroll to be paid on January 5.

Problem 11–3B
Wage and tax statement data on employer FICA tax

Objectives 4, 5

✓ 2. (e) $26,105.25

Sunrise Bakery Inc. began business on January 2, 2002. Salaries were paid to employees on the last day of each month, and social security tax, Medicare tax, and federal income tax were withheld in the required amounts. An employee who is hired in the middle of the month receives half the monthly salary for that month. All required payroll tax reports were filed, and the correct amount of payroll taxes was remitted by the company for the calendar year. Early in 2003, before the Wage and Tax Statements (Form W-2) could be prepared for distribution to employees and for filing with the Social Security Administration, the employees' earnings records were inadvertently destroyed.

None of the employees resigned or were discharged during the year, and there were no changes in salary rates. The social security tax was withheld at the rate of 6.0% on the first $80,000 of salary and Medicare tax at the rate of 1.5% on salary. Data on dates of employment, salary rates, and employees' income taxes withheld, which are summarized as follows, were obtained from personnel records and payroll records.

Employee	Date First Employed	Monthly Salary	Monthly Income Tax Withheld
Alvarez	Jan. 16	$7,200	$1,548.00
Carver	Nov. 1	3,000	544.20
Felix	Jan. 2	2,600	465.14
Lydall	July 16	3,900	727.35
Porter	Jan. 2	8,400	1,877.40
Song	May 1	4,500	744.75
Walker	Feb. 16	5,400	1,109.16

Instructions

1. Calculate the amounts to be reported on each employee's Wage and Tax Statement (Form W-2) for 2002, arranging the data in the following form:

Employee	Gross Earnings	Federal Income Tax Withheld	Social Security Tax Withheld	Medicare Tax Withheld

2. Calculate the following employer payroll taxes for the year: (a) social security; (b) Medicare; (c) state unemployment compensation at 4.2% on the first $7,000 of each employee's earnings; (d) federal unemployment compensation at 0.8% on the first $7,000 of each employee's earnings; (e) total.

If the working papers correlating with this textbook are not used, omit Problem 11–4B.

Problem 11–4B
Payroll register
Objectives 4, 5

✓ 3. Dr. Payroll Taxes Expense,
$692.58

The payroll register for Argentina Leather Goods Co. for the week ended December 12, 2003, is presented in the working papers.

Instructions

1. Journalize the entry to record the payroll for the week.
2. Journalize the entry to record the issuance of the checks to employees.
3. Journalize the entry to record the employer's payroll taxes for the week. Assume the following tax rates: state unemployment, 3.6%; federal unemployment, 0.8%. Of the earnings, $1,250 is subject to unemployment taxes.
4. Journalize the entry to record a check issued on December 15 to Second National Bank in payment of employees' income taxes, $1,540.81, social security taxes, $1,020.12, and Medicare taxes, $255.04.

Problem 11–5B
Payroll register
Objectives 4, 5

SPREADSHEET

✓ 1. Total net amount payable,
$6,897.88

The following data for Forever Ready Products Inc. relate to the payroll for the week ended December 7, 2003:

Employee	Hours Worked	Hourly Rate	Weekly Salary	Federal Income Tax	U.S. Savings Bonds	Accumulated Earnings, Nov. 30
M	46.00	$28.00		$301.84	$35.00	$64,200.00
N	20.00	22.00		66.00		12,600.00
O			$1,900.00	456.00	50.00	91,200.00
P	40.00	18.00		144.00	15.00	35,600.00
Q	42.00	20.00		180.60	10.00	40,500.00
R	44.00	18.50		178.71		38,700.00
S	40.00	16.00		121.60	15.00	30,720.00
T			1,000.00	215.00		48,000.00
U	48.00	36.00		430.56	40.00	82,600.00

Employees O and T are office staff, and all of the other employees are sales personnel. All sales personnel are paid 1½ times the regular rate for all hours in excess of 40 hours per week. The social security tax rate is 6.0% on the first $80,000 of each employee's annual earnings, and Medicare tax is 1.5% of each employee's annual earnings. The next payroll check to be used is No. 818.

Instructions

1. Prepare a payroll register for Forever Ready Products Inc. for the week ended December 7, 2003.
2. Journalize the entry to record the payroll for the week.

Problem 11–6B
Payroll accounts and year-end entries
Objectives 4, 5, 6

GENERAL
LEDGER

The following accounts, with the balances indicated, appear in the ledger of Mid States CableView Co. on December 1 of the current year:

211	Salaries Payable	—
212	Social Security Tax Payable	$ 7,659
213	Medicare Tax Payable	1,998
214	Employees Federal Income Tax Payable	12,321
215	Employees State Income Tax Payable	11,988
216	State Unemployment Tax Payable	1,180
217	Federal Unemployment Tax Payable	310
218	Bond Deductions Payable	1,200
219	Medical Insurance Payable	6,000
611	Operations Salaries Expense	847,000
711	Officers Salaries Expense	376,200
712	Office Salaries Expense	242,000
719	Payroll Taxes Expense	113,689

The following transactions relating to payroll, payroll deductions, and payroll taxes occurred during December:

Dec. 2. Issued Check No. 728 for $1,200 to First National Bank to purchase U.S. savings bonds for employees.

3. Issued Check No. 729 to First National Bank for $21,978, in payment of $7,659 of social security tax, $1,998 of Medicare tax, and $12,321 of employees' federal income tax due.

14. Journalized the entry to record the biweekly payroll. A summary of the payroll record follows:

Salary distribution:		
Operations	$38,000	
Officers	17,400	
Office	10,800	$66,200
Deductions:		
Social security tax	$ 3,641	
Medicare tax	993	
Federal income tax withheld	11,784	
State income tax withheld	2,979	
Savings bond deductions	600	
Medical insurance deductions	1,000	20,997
Net amount		$45,203

14. Issued Check No. 738 in payment of the net amount of the biweekly payroll.

14. Journalized the entry to record payroll taxes on employees' earnings of December 14: social security tax, $3,641; Medicare tax, $993; state unemployment tax, $285; federal unemployment tax, $75.

17. Issued Check No. 744 to First National Bank for $21,052, in payment of $7,282 of social security tax, $1,986 of Medicare tax, and $11,784 of employees' federal income tax due.

18. Issued Check No. 750 to Pico Insurance Company for $6,000, in payment of the semiannual premium on the group medical insurance policy.

28. Journalized the entry to record the biweekly payroll. A summary of the payroll record follows:

Salary distribution:		
Operations	$39,000	
Officers	17,500	
Office	11,000	$67,500
Deductions:		
Social security tax	$ 3,645	
Medicare tax	1,013	
Federal income tax withheld	12,015	
State income tax withheld	3,038	
Savings bond deductions	600	20,311
Net amount		$47,189

28. Issued Check No. 782 in payment of the net amount of the biweekly payroll.

28. Journalized the entry to record payroll taxes on employees' earnings of December 28: social security tax, $3,645; Medicare tax, $1,013; state unemployment tax, $171; federal unemployment tax, $43.

30. Issued Check No. 791 to First National Bank for $1,200 to purchase U.S. savings bonds for employees.

30. Issued Check No. 792 for $18,005 to First National Bank in payment of employees' state income tax due on December 31.

31. Paid $48,000 to the employee pension plan. The annual pension cost is $50,000. (Record both the payment and unfunded pension liability.)

Instructions

1. Journalize the transactions.
2. Journalize the following adjusting entries on December 31:
   a. Salaries accrued: operations salaries, $3,900; officers salaries, $1,750; office salaries, $1,100. The payroll taxes are immaterial and are not accrued.
   b. Vacation pay, $11,000.

COMPREHENSIVE PROBLEM 3

GENERAL LEDGER

✓ 5. Total assets, $994,290

Selected transactions completed by Fore-Most Co. during its first fiscal year ending December 31 were as follows:

Jan. 2. Issued a check to establish a petty cash fund of $600.

Mar. 1. Replenished the petty cash fund, based on the following summary of petty cash receipts: office supplies, $189; miscellaneous selling expense, $125; miscellaneous administrative expense, $205.

Apr. 5. Purchased $9,000 of merchandise on account, terms 1/10, n/30. The perpetual inventory system is used to account for inventory.

May 5. Paid the invoice of April 5 after the discount period had passed.

     10. Received cash from daily cash sales for $8,920. The amount indicated by the cash register was $8,960.

June 2. Received a 60-day, 12% note for $60,000 on account.

Aug. 1. Received amount owed on June 2 note, plus interest at the maturity date.

    3. Received $900 on account and wrote off the remainder owed on a $1,300 accounts receivable balance. (The allowance method is used in accounting for uncollectible receivables.)

    28. Reinstated the account written off on August 3 and received $400 cash in full payment.

Sept. 2. Purchased land by issuing a $90,000, 90-day note to Ace Development Co., which discounted it at 12%.

Oct. 1. Traded office equipment for new equipment with a list price of $160,000. A trade-in allowance of $30,000 was received on the old equipment that had cost $90,000 and had accumulated depreciation of $50,000 as of October 1. A 120-day, 12% note was issued for the balance owed.

Nov. 30. Journalized the monthly payroll for November, based on the following data:

Salaries:		Deductions:	
Sales salaries	$18,500	Income tax withheld	$4,625
Office salaries	6,500	Social security tax	
	$25,000	withheld	1,500
		Medicare tax withheld	375

Unemployment tax rates:	
State unemployment	3.8%
Federal unemployment	0.8%

Amount subject to unemployment taxes:	
State unemployment	$500
Federal unemployment	500

    30. Journalized the employer's payroll taxes on the payroll.

Dec. 1. Journalized the payment of the September 2 note at maturity.

    30. The pension cost for the year was $45,000, of which $42,800 was paid to the pension plan trustee.

Instructions

1. Journalize the selected transactions.
2. Based on the following data, prepare a bank reconciliation for December of the current year:
   a. Balance according to the bank statement at December 31, $102,610.
   b. Balance according to the ledger at December 31, $85,910.
   c. Checks outstanding at December 31, $29,570.
   d. Deposit in transit, not recorded by bank, $12,600.
   e. Bank debit memorandum for service charges, $70.
   f. A check for $220 in payment of an invoice was incorrectly recorded in the accounts as $20.
3. Based on the bank reconciliation prepared in (2), journalize the entry or entries to be made by Fore-Most Co.
4. Based on the following selected data, journalize the adjusting entries as of December 31 of the current year:
   a. Estimated uncollectible accounts at December 31, $4,760. The balance of Allowance for Doubtful Accounts at December 31 was $800 (debit).
   b. The physical inventory on December 31 indicated an inventory shrinkage of $1,050.
   c. Prepaid insurance expired during the year, $12,200.
   d. Office supplies used during the year, $4,150.
   e. Depreciation is computed as follows:

Asset	Cost	Residual Value	Acquisition Date	Useful Life in Years	Depreciation Method Used
Buildings	$270,000	$ 0	January 2	50	Straight-line
Office Equip.	84,500	12,000	July 1	5	Straight-line
Store Equip.	36,000	10,000	January 3	8	Declining-balance (at twice the straight-line rate)

   f. A patent costing $51,000 when acquired on January 2 has a remaining legal life of 9 years and is expected to have value for 6 years.
   g. The cost of mineral rights was $128,000. Of the estimated deposit of 25,000 tons of ore, 5,000 tons were mined during the year.
   h. Total vacation pay expense for the year, $6,000.
   i. A product warranty was granted beginning December 1 and covering a one-year period. The estimated cost is 3% of sales, which totaled $476,000 in December.
5. Based on the following information and the post-closing trial balance on the next page, prepare a balance sheet in report form at December 31 of the current year.

Notes receivable is a current asset.

The merchandise inventory is stated at cost by the LIFO method.

The product warranty payable is a current liability.

Vacation pay payable:

Current liability	$ 5,000
Long-term liability	1,000

The unfunded pension liability is a long-term liability.

Notes payable:

Current liability	$115,000
Long-term liability	335,000

Fore-Most Co.
Post-Closing Trial Balance
December 31, 2003

Petty Cash	600	
Cash	69,450	
Notes Receivable	50,000	
Accounts Receivable	194,300	
Allowance for Doubtful Accounts		4,760
Merchandise Inventory	40,250	
Prepaid Insurance	24,400	
Office Supplies	6,300	
Land	100,000	
Buildings	270,000	
Accumulated Depreciation—Buildings		5,400
Office Equipment	84,500	
Accumulated Depreciation—Office Equipment		7,250
Store Equipment	36,000	
Accumulated Depreciation—Store Equipment		9,000
Mineral Rights	128,000	
Accumulated Depletion		25,600
Patents	42,500	
Social Security Tax Payable		3,100
Medicare Tax Payable		780
Employees Federal Income Tax Payable		4,700
State Unemployment Tax Payable		45
Federal Unemployment Tax Payable		20
Salaries Payable		26,000
Accounts Payable		94,000
Product Warranty Payable		14,280
Vacation Pay Payable		6,000
Unfunded Pension Liability		2,200
Notes Payable		450,000
B. Joiner, Capital		393,165
	1,046,300	1,046,300

6. On February 7 of the following year, the merchandise inventory was destroyed by fire. Based on the following data obtained from the accounting records, estimate the cost of the merchandise destroyed:

Jan. 1 Merchandise inventory	$ 40,250
Jan. 1—Feb. 7 Purchases (net)	246,720
Jan. 1—Feb. 7 Sales (net)	430,000
Estimated gross profit rate	40%

SPECIAL ACTIVITIES

Activity 11–1
Tester and Morris, CPAs
Ethics and professional conduct in business

Marge McMaster is a certified public accountant (CPA) and staff assistant for Tester and Morris, a local CPA firm. It had been the policy of the firm to provide a holiday bonus equal to two weeks' salary to all employees. The firm's new management team announced on November 25 that a bonus equal to only one week's salary would be made available to employees this year. Marge thought that this policy was unfair because she and her co-workers planned on the full two-week bonus. The two-week bonus had been given for ten straight years, so it seemed as though the firm had breached an implied commitment. Thus, Marge decided that she would make up the lost bonus week by working an extra six hours of overtime per week over the next five weeks until the end of the year. Tester and Morris' policy is to pay overtime at 150% of straight time.

Marge's supervisor was surprised to see overtime being reported, since there is generally very little additional or unusual client service demands at the end of the calendar year. However, the overtime was not questioned, since firm employees are on the "honor system" in reporting their overtime.

Discuss whether the firm is acting in an ethical manner by changing the bonus. Is Marge behaving in an ethical manner?

Activity 11–2
ProMatic Company
Recognizing pension expense

The annual examination of ProMatic Company's financial statements by its external public accounting firm (auditors) is nearing completion. The following conversation took place between the controller of ProMatic Company (Peter) and the audit manager from the public accounting firm (Mary).

Mary: You know, Peter, we are about to wrap up our audit for this fiscal year. Yet, there is one item still to be resolved.
Peter: What's that?
Mary: Well, as you know, at the beginning of the year, ProMatic began a defined benefit pension plan. This plan promises your employees an annual payment when they retire, using a formula based on their salaries at retirement and their years of service. I believe that a pension expense should be recognized this year, equal to the amount of pension earned by your employees.
Peter: Wait a minute. I think you have it all wrong. The company doesn't have a pension expense until it actually pays the pension in cash when the employee retires. After all, some of these employees may not reach retirement, and if they don't, the company doesn't owe them anything.
Mary: You're not really seeing this the right way. The pension is earned by your employees during their working years. You actually make the payment much later—when they retire. It's like one long accrual—much like incurring wages in one period and paying them in the next. Thus, I think that you should recognize the expense in the period the pension is earned by the employees.
Peter: Let me see if I've got this straight. I should recognize an expense this period for something that may or may not be paid to the employees in 20 or 30 years, when they finally retire. How am I supposed to determine what the expense is for the current year? The amount of the final retirement depends on many uncertainties: salary levels, employee longevity, mortality rates, and interest earned on investments to fund the pension. I don't think that an amount can be determined, even if I accepted your arguments.

Evaluate Mary's position. Is she right or is Peter correct?

Activity 11–3
Camden Trucking Company
Executive bonuses and accounting methods

Mark Camden, the owner of Camden Trucking Company, initiated an executive bonus plan for his chief executive officer (CEO). The new plan provides a bonus to the CEO equal to 3% of the income before taxes. Upon learning of the new bonus arrangement, the CEO issued instructions to change the company's accounting for trucks. The CEO has asked the controller to make the following two changes:

a. Change from the double-declining-balance method to the straight-line method of depreciation.
b. Add 50% to the useful lives of all trucks.

Why did the CEO ask for these changes? How would you respond to the CEO's request?

Activity 11–4
Into the Real World
Salary survey

Several Internet services provide career guidance, classified employment ads, placement services, resumé posting, career questionnaires, and salary surveys. Select one of the following Internet sites to determine current average salary levels for one of your career options:

Activity 11–5
Into the Real World
Payroll forms

Payroll accounting involves the use of government-supplied forms to account for payroll taxes. Three common forms are the W-2, Form 940, and Form 941. Form a team with three of your classmates and retrieve copies of each of these forms. They may be obtained from a local IRS office, a library, or downloaded from the Internet at **www.irs.treas.gov** (go to forms and publications).

a. Briefly describe the purpose of each of the three forms.
b. Fill in the forms using the information provided (leaving blanks where there is no information provided). Assume that your group began a business, called Audit-Proof Tax Services, on November 1 of the current year. Each of you makes a salary of $2,000 per month and claims a single exemption. Salaries were paid on November 30 and December 31. Assume that the withholding tax, social security tax, and Medicare tax are $234, $124, and $29, respectively, per month for each person in the group. Assume further that the federal unemployment tax was $744.

ANSWERS TO SELF-EXAMINATION QUESTIONS

Matching

| 1. E | 3. A | 5. M | 7. G | 9. H | 11. J | 13. N |
| 2. K | 4. I | 6. B | 8. D | 10. L | 12. F | 14. C |

Multiple Choice

1. **C** The maturity value is $5,100, determined as follows:

Face amount of note	$5,000
Plus interest ($5,000 × 12% × 60/360)	100
Maturity value	$5,100

2. **B** The net amount available to a borrower from discounting a note payable is called the proceeds. The proceeds of $4,900 (answer B) is determined as follows:

Face amount of note	$5,000
Less discount ($5,000 × 12% × 60/360)	100
Proceeds	$4,900

3. **B** Employers are usually required to withhold a portion of their employees' earnings for payment of federal income taxes (answer A), Medicare tax (answer C), and state and local income taxes (answer D). Generally, federal unemployment compensation taxes (answer B) are levied against the employer only and thus are not deducted from employee earnings.

4. **D** The amount of net pay of $687.75 (answer D) is determined as follows:

Gross pay:		
40 hours at $20		$800.00
5 hours at $30		150.00 $950.00
Deductions:		
Federal income tax withheld		$212.00
FICA:		
Social security tax ($600 × 0.06)	$36.00	
Medicare tax ($950 × 0.015)	14.25	50.25 262.25
		$687.75

5. **D** The employer incurs an expense for social security tax (answer A), federal unemployment compensation tax (answer B), and state unemployment compensation tax (answer C). The employees' federal income tax (answer D) is not an expense of the employer. It is withheld from the employees' earnings.

Corporations: Organization, Capital Stock Transactions, and Dividends

objectives

After studying this chapter, you should be able to:

1 Describe the nature of the corporate form of organization.

2 List the two main sources of stockholders' equity.

3 List the major sources of paid-in capital, including the various classes of stock.

4 Journalize the entries for issuing stock.

5 Journalize the entries for treasury stock transactions.

6 State the effect of stock splits on corporate financial statements.

7 Journalize the entries for cash dividends and stock dividends.

8 Compute and interpret the dividend yield on common stock.

I f you own stock in a corporation, you are interested in how the stock is doing in the market. If you are considering buying stocks, you are interested in your rights as a stockholder and returns that you can expect from the stock. In either case, you should be able to interpret stock market quotations, such as the following:

34^{69}	22^{06}	Walgreen	WAG	.14	.4	50	13406	35^{44}	33^{75}	35^{31}	$+\ 0^{13}$
23^{13}	8^{56}	WallaceCS	WCS	.66	6.9	13	1738	9^{81}	9^{25}	9^{63}	$-\ 0^{13}$
70^{25}	43^{44}	WalMart	WMT	.24	.5	36	49020	50^{13}	49	49^{06}	$-\ 0^{44}$
13^{69}	7^{25}	WaterInd	WLT	.12	1.5	dd	557	8^{19}	8^{06}	8^{19}	$-\ 0^{13}$
23^{69}	3^{94}	Warnaco	WAC	.36	7.0	26	733	5^{13}	5	5^{13}	$+\ 0^{06}$
29^{44}	21^{75}	WA GasLt	WGL	1.24	4.9	14	422	25^{63}	25	25^{56}	$-\ 0^{06}$
7^{50}	4^{69}	WA Homes	WHI		...	4	32	7^{19}	7	7^{19}	$+\ 0^{13}$

Although you may not own any stocks, you probably buy services or products from corporations, and you may work for a corporation. Understanding the corporate form of organization will help you in your role as a stockholder, a consumer, or an employee. In this chapter, we discuss the characteristics of corporations, as well as how corporations account for stocks.

Nature of a Corporation

In the preceding chapters, we used the proprietorship in illustrations. As we mentioned in a previous chapter, more than 70% of all businesses are proprietorships and 10% are partnerships. Most of these businesses are small businesses. The remaining 20% of businesses are corporations. Many corporations are large and, as a result, they generate more than 90% of the total business dollars in the United States.

Characteristics of a Corporation

A **corporation** is a legal entity, distinct and separate from the individuals who create and operate it. As a legal entity, a corporation may acquire, own, and dispose of property in its own name. It may also incur liabilities and enter into contracts.

Because a corporation is a legal entity, it can sell shares of ownership, called stock, without affecting its operations or continued existence. The stockholders or **shareholders** who own the stock own the corporation. Corporations whose shares of stock are traded in public markets are called **public corporations**. Corporations whose shares are not traded publicly are usually owned by a small group of investors and are called **nonpublic** or **private corporations**.

Corporations can be large because they have the ability to raise large amounts of capital by selling stock. In contrast, a proprietorship's ability to raise capital is limited because it has only one owner. A **partnership** is similar to a proprietorship, except that it has more than one owner. Like a proprietorship, a partnership's ability to raise capital is limited because ownership is not easily transferred.[1]

Stockholders can buy and sell stock without affecting the corporation. In contrast, a proprietorship or a partnership ceases to exist whenever the owner or a partner leaves the business. Likewise, if a new partner is admitted, a new partnership must be formed.

---

[1] The accounting for partnerships is discussed in Appendix F.

Point of Interest

If you invest in a public corporation, the most you can lose is the amount of your investment, regardless of actions of the corporation.

Point of Interest

If you start a business as a proprietorship or as a partnership with others, your personal assets are at risk for any debts incurred by the business. For example, you could be personally liable for damages awarded in a lawsuit against the business.

Corporations have a separate legal existence, transferable units of ownership, and limited stockholder liability.

The stockholders of a corporation have **limited liability**. This means that a corporation's creditors usually may not go beyond the assets of the corporation to satisfy their claims. Thus, the financial loss that a stockholder may suffer is limited to the amount invested. This feature has contributed to the rapid growth of the corporate form of business.

In contrast, the owner of a proprietorship and the partners of a partnership have **unlimited liability**. They are individually liable to creditors for debts incurred by the business. Thus, if a proprietorship or a partnership is not able to pay its debts, the owner or the partners must contribute personal assets to settle the business debts. This characteristic is significant for partnerships because partners are **mutual agents**, which means that the actions of one partner bind the entire partnership.[2]

A proprietorship is controlled directly by its owner. A partnership is controlled by the partners according to a contract, called the *articles of partnership* or *partnership agreement*. In contrast, the stockholders control a corporation by electing a **board of directors**. This board meets periodically to establish corporate policies. It also selects the chief executive officer (CEO) and other major officers to manage the corporation's day-to-day affairs. Exhibit 1 shows the organizational structure of a corporation.

Exhibit 1 Organizational Structure of a Corporation

As a separate entity, a corporation is subject to taxes. For example, corporations must pay federal income taxes on their income.[3] Thus, corporate income that is distributed to stockholders in the form of **dividends** has already been taxed. In turn, stockholders must pay income taxes on the dividends they receive. This *double taxation* of corporate earnings is a major disadvantage of the corporate form.[4] In contrast, proprietorships and partnerships are not required to pay federal income taxes. Instead, the owner or partners report their share of the business's income on their personal tax returns.

Forming a Corporation

The first step in forming a corporation is to file an **application of incorporation** with the state. State incorporation laws differ, and corporations often organize in

---

[2] Some states permit limited partnerships, in which the liability of some partners is limited to the amount of their capital investment. However, a limited partnership must have at least one partner who has unlimited liability.

[3] Some states also require corporations to pay income taxes.

[4] Under the *Internal Revenue Code*, a corporation with a few stockholders may elect to be treated like a partnership for income tax purposes. Such corporations are known as Subchapter S corporations.

Corporations may be organized for non-profit reasons, such as recreational, educational, charitable, or humanitarian purposes. Such corporations are not required to pay federal taxes. Examples of nonprofit corporations include the **Sierra Club** and the **National Audubon Society**. However, most corporations are organized to earn a profit and a fair rate of return for their stockholders. Examples of for-profit corporations include **PepsiCo**, **General Motors**, and **Microsoft**.

those states with the more favorable laws. For this reason, more than half of the largest companies are incorporated in Delaware. Exhibit 2 lists some corporations that you may be familiar with, their states of incorporation, and the location of their headquarters.

Exhibit 2 Examples of Corporations and Their States of Incorporation

Corporation	State of Incorporation	Headquarters
Borden, Inc.	New Jersey	New York, N.Y.
Caterpillar, Inc.	Delaware	Peoria, Ill.
Delta Air Lines, Inc.	Delaware	Atlanta, Ga.
Dow Chemical Company	Delaware	Midland, Mich.
General Electric Company	New York	Fairfield, Conn.
The Home Depot	Delaware	Atlanta, Ga.
Kellogg Company	Delaware	Battle Creek, Mich.
3M	Delaware	St. Paul, Minn.
May Department Stores	New York	St. Louis, Mo.
RJR Nabisco	Delaware	New York, N.Y.
Tandy Corporation	Delaware	Ft. Worth, Tex.
The Washington Post Company	Delaware	Washington, D.C.
Whirlpool Corporation	Delaware	Benton Harbor, Mich.

After the application of incorporation has been approved, the state grants a **charter** or **articles of incorporation**. The articles of incorporation formally create the corporation.[5] The corporate management and board of directors then prepare a set of **bylaws**, which are the rules and procedures for conducting the corporation's affairs.

Significant costs may be incurred in organizing a corporation. These costs include legal fees, taxes, state incorporation fees, license fees, and promotional costs. Such costs, referred to as organizational costs or startup costs, should be expensed when they are incurred.

The following entries illustrate the recording of a corporation's organization costs of $8,500 on January 5.

Jan.	5	Organization Costs		8 5 0 0 00			
		Cash				8 5 0 0 00	
		Paid costs of organizing the corporation.					

---

[5] The articles of incorporation may also restrict a corporation's activities in certain areas, such as owning certain types of real estate, conducting certain types of business activities, or purchasing its own stock.

BUSINESS ON STAGE

Stock Exchanges

Stocks are bought and sold through stock exchanges. The New York Stock Exchange and the American Stock Exchange are the two national exchanges. In addition, regional exchanges and the over-the-counter market serve important roles in the trading of stocks.

New York Stock Exchange (**nyse.com**). This exchange, founded in 1792, is located on Wall Street in New York City. It consists of over 1,366 members who own "seats" on the exchange and who are allowed to trade securities. Only stocks listed on the exchange (the "Big Board") can be traded. Currently, stocks of over 3,000 generally older, well-established, larger companies are listed. To qualify for listing, a company must have over 1 million shares outstanding and $2.5 million of pretax profits. Examples of

such companies include **General Motors** and **Alcoa**.

American Stock Exchange (**amex.com**). This exchange is similar to the New York Stock Exchange, except that the companies are generally small to medium-size companies. To qualify for listing, a company must have over 500,000 shares outstanding and $750,000 of pretax profits. Currently, about 800 stocks are listed on the American Stock Exchange. As a company grows, it may move from the American Stock Exchange to the New York Stock Exchange. Examples of American Stock Exchange companies include **El Paso Electric** and **TWA**.

Regional Exchanges. There are several regional exchanges, including Chicago, Boston, Cincinnati, Philadelphia, and San Francisco. Initially, such exchanges traded mostly in stocks of

local firms. Today, many firms, such as **Sears**, are traded on both regional and national exchanges.

Nasdaq (**nasdaq.com**). This market refers to a network of brokers who communicate with each other to set prices and trade securities. This system is referred to as the *National Association of Securities Dealers Automated Quotation* system, or more simply by its abbreviation, *Nasdaq*. Larger, actively traded issues are referred to as Nasdaq National Market issues, while less active issues are referred to as Nasdaq Small-Cap issues. Many Internet companies are initially listed on Nasdaq. Examples of Nasdaq companies include **Apple Computer**, **Intel**, **Cisco Systems**, and **Amazon.com**. ■

Stockholders' Equity

objective 2

List the two main sources of stockholders' equity.

The owners' equity in a corporation is commonly called **stockholders' equity**, **shareholders' equity**, **shareholders' investment**, or **capital**. In a corporation balance sheet, the Stockholders' Equity section reports the amount of each of the two main sources of stockholders' equity. The first source is capital contributed to the corporation by the stockholders and others, called **paid-in capital** or **contributed capital**. The second source is net income retained in the business, called **retained earnings**.

An example of a Stockholders' Equity section of a corporation balance sheet is shown below.

Stockholders' Equity		
Paid-in capital:		
Common stock	$330,000	
Retained earnings	80,000	
Total stockholders' equity		$410,000

The paid-in capital contributed by the stockholders is recorded in separate accounts for each class of stock. If there is only one class of stock, the account is entitled *Common Stock* or *Capital Stock*.

STOCKHOLDERS' EQUITY

PAID-IN CAPITAL

Stockholder investments

RETAINED EARNINGS

Reinvested earnings

Retained earnings are generated from operations. Net income increases retained earnings while dividends decrease retained earnings. Thus, retained earnings represents a corporation's accumulated net income that has not been distributed to stockholders as dividends.

The balance of the retained earnings account at the end of the fiscal year is created by closing entries. First, the balance in the income summary account (the net income or net loss) is transferred to Retained Earnings. Second, the balance of the dividends account, which is similar to the drawing account for a proprietorship, is transferred to Retained Earnings.

Other terms that may be used to identify retained earnings in the financial statements include *earnings retained for use in the business* and *earnings reinvested in the business*. A debit balance in Retained Earnings is called a **deficit**. Such a balance results from accumulated net losses. In the Stockholders' Equity section, a deficit is deducted from paid-in capital in determining total stockholders' equity.

The balance of retained earnings should not be interpreted as representing surplus cash or cash left over for dividends. The reason for this is that earnings retained in the business and the related cash generated from these earnings are normally used by management to improve or expand operations. As cash is used to expand or improve operations, its balance decreases. However, the balance of the retained earnings account is unaffected. As a result, over time the balance of the retained earnings account normally becomes less and less related to the balance of the cash account.

Sources of Paid-In Capital

objective 3

List the major sources of paid-in capital, including the various classes of stock.

As we mentioned in the preceding section, the two main sources of stockholders' equity are paid-in capital (or contributed capital) and retained earnings. The main source of paid-in capital is from issuing stock. In the following paragraphs, we discuss the characteristics of the various classes of stock. We conclude this section with a brief discussion of other sources of paid-in capital.

Stock

The number of shares of stock that a corporation is *authorized* to issue is stated in its charter. The term *issued* refers to the shares issued to the stockholders. A corporation may, under circumstances we discuss later in this chapter, reacquire some of the stock that it has issued. The stock remaining in the hands of stockholders is then called **outstanding stock**. The relationship between authorized, issued, and outstanding stock is shown in the graphic at the left.

Shares of stock are often assigned a monetary amount, called **par**. Corporations may issue **stock certificates** to stockholders to document their ownership. Printed on a stock certificate is the par value of the stock, the name of the stockholder, and the number of shares owned. Stock may also be issued without par, in which case it is called **no-par stock**. Some states require the board of directors to assign a **stated value** to no-par stock.

AUTHORIZED

ISSUED

OUTSTANDING

Number of shares authorized, issued, and outstanding

Real World

Some corporations have stopped issuing stock certificates except on special request. In these cases, the corporation maintains records of ownership by using electronic media.

On its balance sheet, a corporation reports the following three numbers related to its common stock: 200,000 shares; 150,000 shares; and 138,000 shares. What is the number of shares authorized, issued, outstanding, and reacquired?

200,000 shares authorized; 150,000 shares issued; 138,000 shares outstanding; 12,000 (150,000 − 138,000) shares reacquired.

> The two primary classes of paid-in capital are common stock and preferred stock.

Because corporations have limited liability, creditors have no claim against the personal assets of stockholders. However, some state laws require that corporations maintain a minimum **stockholder** contribution to protect creditors. This minimum amount is called *legal capital.* The amount of required legal capital varies among the states, but it usually includes the amount of par or stated value of the shares of stock issued.

The major rights that accompany ownership of a share of stock are as follows:

1. The right to vote in matters concerning the corporation.
2. The right to share in distributions of earnings.
3. The right to share in assets on liquidation.

When only one class of stock is issued, it is called **common stock**. In this case, each share of common stock has equal rights. To appeal to a broader investment market, a corporation may issue one or more classes of stock with various preference rights. A common example of such a right is the preference to dividends. Such a stock is generally called a **preferred stock**.

The dividend rights of preferred stock are usually stated in monetary terms or as a percent of par. For example, *$4 preferred stock* has a right to an annual $4 per share dividend. If the par value of the preferred stock were $50, the same right to dividends could be stated as *8% ($4/$50) preferred stock.*

The board of directors of a corporation has the sole authority to distribute dividends to the stockholders. When such action is taken, the directors are said to *declare* a dividend. Since dividends are normally based on earnings, a corporation cannot guarantee dividends even to preferred stockholders. However, because they have first rights to any dividends, the preferred stockholders have a greater chance of receiving regular dividends than do the common stockholders.

Nonparticipating Preferred Stock

Preferred stockholders' dividend rights are usually limited to a certain amount. Such stock is said to be **nonparticipating preferred stock.**[6] To continue our preceding example, assume that a corporation has 1,000 shares of $4 nonparticipating preferred stock and 4,000 shares of common stock outstanding. Also assume that the net income, amount of earnings retained, and the amount of earnings distributed by the board of directors for the first three years of operations are as follows:

	2002	2003	2004
Net income	$20,000	$55,000	$62,000
Amount retained	10,000	20,000	40,000
Amount distributed	$10,000	$35,000	$22,000

Exhibit 3 shows the earnings distributed each year to the preferred stock and the common stock. In this example, the preferred stockholders received an annual dividend of $4 per share, compared to the common stockholders' dividends of $1.50, $7.75, and $4.50 per share. You should note that although preferred stockholders have a greater chance of receiving a regular dividend, common stockholders have a greater chance of receiving larger dividends than do the preferred stockholders.

---

[6] In some cases, preferred stock may receive additional dividends if certain conditions are met. Such stock is called *participating preferred stock.* It is rarely used in today's financial markets.

Exhibit 3 Dividends to Nonparticipating Preferred Stock

	2002	2003	2004
Amount distributed	$10,000	$35,000	$22,000
Preferred dividend (1,000 shares)	4,000	4,000	4,000
Common dividend (4,000 shares)	$ 6,000	$31,000	$18,000
Dividends per share:			
Preferred	$ 4.00	$ 4.00	$ 4.00
Common	$ 1.50	$ 7.75	$ 4.50

Q&A

Romer Corporation has 50,000 shares of $2, $100 par cumulative preferred stock outstanding. Preferred dividends are three years in arrears (not including the current year). What amount of preferred dividends must be paid before any dividends on common shares can be paid?

$400,000 [3 years in arrears (50,000 × $2 × 3) plus the current year's dividend of $100,000]

Cumulative Preferred Stock

Cumulative preferred stock has a right to receive regular dividends that have been passed (not declared) before any common stock dividends are paid. Noncumulative preferred stock does not have this right.

Dividends that have been passed are said to be **in arrears**. Such dividends should be disclosed, normally in a footnote to the financial statements.

To illustrate how dividends on cumulative preferred stock are calculated, assume that the preferred stock in Exhibit 3 is cumulative, and that no dividends were paid in 2002 and 2003. In 2004, the board of directors declares dividends of $22,000. Exhibit 4 shows how the dividends paid in 2004 are distributed between the preferred and common stockholders.

Exhibit 4 Dividends to Cumulative Preferred Stock

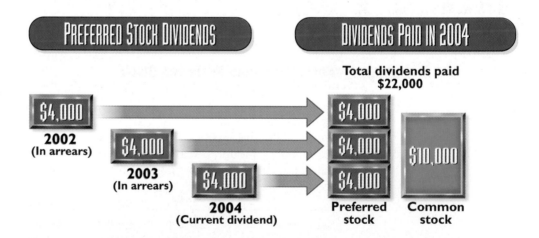

Amount distributed		$22,000
Preferred dividend (1,000 shares):		
2002 dividend in arrears	$4,000	
2003 dividend in arrears	4,000	
2004 dividend	4,000	12,000
Common dividend (4,000 shares)		$10,000
Dividends per share:		
Preferred		$ 12.00
Common		$ 2.50

The gains [from purchasing preferred stock with dividends in arrears] can be impressive. **Bethlehem Steel** announced in April that it would pay $22.5 million in arrears and resume the regular quarterly dividend on its two classes of preferred stock. Because Bethlehem had missed four payments, investors receive an extra year's worth of dividends: One class that usually pays $1.25 quarterly will return $6.25—not bad on a stock that traded in the low 30s just a few months ago.

Source: Troy Segal, "Preferred Stock: The Risky Hunt for Hidden Rewards," *Business Week,* June 13, 1988, p. 114.

Other Preferential Rights

In addition to dividend preference, preferred stock may be given preferences to assets if the corporation goes out of business and is liquidated. However, claims of creditors must be satisfied first. Preferred stockholders are next in line to receive any remaining assets, followed by the common stockholders.

Other Sources of Paid-In Capital

In addition to arising from the issuance of stock, paid-in capital may arise from receiving donations of real estate or other assets. Civic groups and municipalities sometimes give land or buildings to a corporation as an incentive to locate or remain in a community. In such cases, the corporation debits the assets for their fair market value and credits *Donated Capital.*

To illustrate, assume that on April 20 the city of Moraine donated land to Merrick Corporation as an incentive for it to relocate its headquarters to Moraine. The land was valued at $500,000. Merrick Corporation would record the land as follows:

Apr.	20	Land	500 0 0 0 00	
		Donated Capital		500 0 0 0 00
		Recorded land donated by the city		
		of Moraine.		

Paid-in capital may also arise when a corporation buys and sells its own stock in the marketplace. Later in this chapter, we will discuss the recording of such transactions.

Issuing Stock

objective 4

Journalize the entries for issuing stock.

A separate account is used for recording the amount of each class of stock issued to investors in a corporation. For example, assume that a corporation is authorized to issue 10,000 shares of preferred stock, $100 par, and 100,000 shares of common stock, $20 par. One-half of each class of authorized shares is issued at par for cash. The corporation's entry to record the stock issue is as follows:[7]

	Cash	1,500 0 0 0 00		
	Preferred Stock		500 0 0 0 00	
	Common Stock		1,000 0 0 0 00	
	Issued preferred stock and common			
	stock at par for cash.			

Stock is often issued by a corporation at a price other than its par. This is because the par value of a stock is simply its legal capital. The price at which stock can be sold by a corporation depends on a variety of factors, such as:

1. The financial condition, earnings record, and dividend record of the corporation.
2. Investor expectations of the corporation's potential earning power.
3. General business and economic conditions and prospects.

[7] The accounting for investments in stocks from the point of view of the investor is discussed in a later chapter.

When stock is issued for a price that is more than its par, the stock has sold at a **premium**. When stock is issued for a price that is less than its par, the stock has sold at a **discount**. Thus, if stock with a par of $50 is issued for a price of $60, the stock has sold at a premium of $10. If the same stock is issued for a price of $45, the stock has sold at a discount of $5. Many states do not permit stock to be issued at a discount. In others, it may be done only under unusual conditions. Since issuing stock at a discount is rare, we will not illustrate it.

A corporation issuing stock must maintain records of the stockholders in order to issue dividend checks and distribute financial statements and other reports. Large public corporations normally use a financial institution, such as a bank, for this purpose.[8] In such cases, the financial institution is referred to as a *transfer agent* or *registrar*. For example, the transfer agent and registrar for **Coca-Cola Enterprises** is **First Chicago Trust Company of New York**.

Premium on Stock

When stock is issued at a premium, Cash or other asset accounts are debited for the amount received. Common Stock or Preferred Stock is then credited for the par amount. The excess of the amount paid over par is a part of the total investment of the stockholders in the corporation. Therefore, such an amount in excess of par should be classified as a part of the paid-in capital. An account entitled *Paid-In Capital in Excess of Par* is usually credited for this amount.

To illustrate, assume that Caldwell Company issues 2,000 shares of $50 par preferred stock for cash at $55. The entry to record this transaction is as follows:

The following stock quotation for **Wal-Mart Corporation** is taken from *The Wall Street Journal*:

Cash	110000 00	
Preferred Stock		100000 00
Paid-In Capital in Excess of		
Par—Preferred Stock		10000 00
Issued $50 par preferred stock at $55.		

NEW YORK STOCK EXCHANGE

52 Weeks Hi	Lo	Stock	Sym	Div	Yld %	PE	Vol 100s	Hi	Lo	Close	Net Chg
70²⁵	43⁴⁴	WalMart	WMT	.24	.5	36	49020	50¹³	49	49⁰⁶	− 0⁴⁴

The preceding quotation is interpreted as follows:

Hi	Highest price during the past 52 weeks
Lo	Lowest price during the past 52 weeks
Stock	Name of the company
Sym	Stock exchange symbol (WMT for Wal-Mart)
Div	Dividends paid per share during the past year
Yld %	Annual dividend yield per share based on the closing price (Wal-Mart's 0.5% yield on common stock is computed as $0.24/$49.06)
PE	Price-earnings ratio on common stock (price ÷ earnings per share)
Vol	The volume of stock traded in 100s
Hi	Highest price for the day
Lo	Lowest price for the day
Close	Closing price for the day
Net Chg	The net change in price from the previous day

When stock is issued in exchange for assets other than cash, such as land, buildings, and equipment, the assets acquired should be recorded at their fair market value. If this value cannot be objectively determined, the fair market price of the stock issued may be used.

To illustrate, assume that a corporation acquired land for which the fair market value cannot be determined. In exchange, the corporation issued 10,000 shares of its $10 par common. Assuming that the stock has a current market price of $12 per share, this transaction is recorded as follows:

Land	120000 00	
Common Stock		100000 00
Paid-In Capital in Excess of Par		20000 00
Issued $10 par common stock, valued		
at $12 per share, for land.		

[8] Small corporations may use a subsidiary ledger, called a *stockholders ledger*. In this case, the stock accounts (Preferred Stock and Common Stock) are controlling accounts for the subsidiary ledger.

No-Par Stock

In most states, both preferred and common stock may be issued without a par value. When no-par stock is issued, the entire proceeds are credited to the stock account. This is true even though the issue price varies from time to time. For example, assume that a corporation issues 10,000 shares of no-par common stock at $40 a share and at a later date issues 1,000 additional shares at $36. The entries to record the no-par stock are as follows:

Cash		400 0 0 0 00	
Common Stock			400 0 0 0 00
Issued 10,000 shares of no-par			
common at $40.			
Cash		36 0 0 0 00	
Common Stock			36 0 0 0 00
Issued 1,000 shares of no-par			
common at $36.			

Some states require that the entire proceeds from the issue of no-par stock be recorded as legal capital. In this case, the preceding entries would be proper. In other states, no-par stock may be assigned a *stated value per share*. The stated value is recorded like a par value, and the excess of the proceeds over the stated value is recorded as follows:

Cash		400 0 0 0 00	
Common Stock			250 0 0 0 00
Paid-In Capital in Excess of Stated Value			150 0 0 0 00
Issued 10,000 shares of no-par common			
at $40; stated value, $25.			
Cash		36 0 0 0 00	
Common Stock			25 0 0 0 00
Paid-In Capital in Excess of Stated Value			11 0 0 0 00
Issued 1,000 shares of no-par common			
at $36; stated value, $25.			

Treasury Stock Transactions

objective 5

Journalize the entries for treasury stock transactions.

A corporation may buy its own stock to provide shares for resale to employees, for reissuing as a bonus to employees, or for supporting the market price of the stock. For example, **General Motors** bought back its common stock and stated that two primary uses of this stock would be for incentive compensation plans and employee savings plans. Such stock that a corporation has once issued and then reacquires is called **treasury stock**.

A commonly used method of accounting for the purchase and resale of treasury stock is the **cost method**.[9] When the stock is purchased by the corporation, the account *Treasury Stock* is debited for its cost (the price paid for it). The par value and the price at which the stock was originally issued are ignored. When the stock is resold, Treasury Stock is credited for its cost, and any difference between the cost and the selling price is normally debited or credited to *Paid-In Capital from Sale of Treasury Stock.*

To illustrate, assume that the paid-in capital of a corporation is as follows:

Common stock, $25 par (20,000 shares authorized and issued)	$500,000	
Excess of issue price over par	150,000	$650,000

The purchase and sale of the treasury stock are recorded as follows:

Treasury Stock	45 000 00	
Cash		45 000 00
Purchased 1,000 shares of treasury stock at $45.		
Cash	12 000 00	
Treasury Stock		9 000 00
Paid-In Capital from Sale of Treasury Stock		3 000 00
Sold 200 shares of treasury stock at $60.		
Cash	8 000 00	
Paid-In Capital from Sale of Treasury Stock	1 000 00	
Treasury Stock		9 000 00
Sold 200 shares of treasury stock at $40.		

As shown above, a sale of treasury stock may result in a decrease in paid-in capital. To the extent that Paid-In Capital from Sale of Treasury Stock has a credit balance, it should be debited for any decrease. Any remaining decrease should then be debited to the retained earnings account.

At the end of the period, the balance in the treasury stock account is reported as a deduction from the total of the paid-in capital and retained earnings. The balance of Paid-In Capital from Sale of Treasury Stock is reported as part of the paid-in capital, as shown in Exhibit 5.

Exhibit 5 Stockholders' Equity Section with Treasury Stock

Stockholders' Equity		
Paid-in capital:		
Common stock, $25 par (20,000 shares authorized and issued)	$500,000	
Excess of issue price over par	150,000	
From sale of treasury stock	2,000	
Total paid-in capital		$652,000
Retained earnings		130,000
Total		$782,000
Deduct treasury stock (600 shares at cost)		27,000
Total stockholders' equity		$755,000

[9] Another method that is infrequently used, called the *par value method*, is discussed in advanced accounting texts.

Stock Splits

objective 6

State the effect of stock splits on corporate financial statements.

Corporations sometimes reduce the par or stated value of their common stock and issue a proportionate number of additional shares. When this is done, a corporation is said to have *split* its stock, and the process is called a **stock split**.

When stock is split, the reduction in par or stated value applies to all shares, including the unissued, issued, and treasury shares. A major objective of a stock split is to reduce the market price per share of the stock. This, in turn, should attract more investors to enter the market for the stock and broaden the types and numbers of stockholders.

 When **Nature's Sunshine Products Inc.** declared a two-for-one stock split, the company president said:

We believe the split will place our stock price in a range attractive to both individual and institutional investors, broadening the market for the stock.

To illustrate a stock split, assume that Rojek Corporation has 10,000 shares of $100 par common stock outstanding with a current market price of $150 per share. The board of directors declares a 5-for-1 stock split, reduces the par to $20, and increases the number of shares to 50,000. The amount of common stock outstanding is $1,000,000 both before and after the stock split. Only the number of shares and the par per share are changed. Each Rojek Corporation shareholder owns the same total par amount of stock before and after the stock split.

For example, a stockholder who owned 4 shares of $100 par stock before the split (total par of $400) would own 20 shares of $20 par stock after the split (total par of $400).

Since there are more shares outstanding after the stock split, we would expect that the market price of the stock would fall. For example, in the preceding example, there would be 5 times as many shares outstanding after the split. Thus, we would expect the market price of the stock to fall from $150 to approximately $30 ($150/5).

Since a stock split changes only the par or stated value and the number of shares outstanding, it is not recorded by a journal entry. Although the accounts are not affected, the details of stock splits are normally disclosed in the notes to the financial statements.

A stock split does not change the balance of any corporation accounts.

LTM Corporation announced a 4-for-1 stock split of its $50 par value common stock, which is currently trading for $120 per share. What is the new par value and the estimated market price of the stock after the split?

$12.50 ($50/4) par value; $30 ($120/4) estimated market price.

Accounting for Dividends

objective 7

Journalize the entries for cash dividends and stock dividends.

When a board of directors declares a cash dividend, it authorizes the distribution of a portion of the corporation's cash to stockholders. When a board of directors declares a stock dividend, it authorizes the distribution of a portion of its stock. In both cases, the declaration of a dividend reduces the retained earnings of the corporation.[10]

---

[10] In rare cases, when a corporation is reducing its operations or going out of business, a dividend may be a distribution of paid-in capital. Such a dividend is called a *liquidating dividend*.

Cash Dividends

A cash distribution of earnings by a corporation to its shareholders is called a **cash dividend**. Although dividends may be paid in the form of other assets, cash dividends are the most common form.

There are usually three conditions that a corporation must meet to pay a cash dividend:

1. Sufficient retained earnings
2. Sufficient cash
3. Formal action by the board of directors

A large amount of retained earnings does not always mean that a corporation is able to pay dividends. As we indicated earlier in the chapter, the balance of the cash and retained earnings account are often unrelated. Thus, a large retained earnings account does not mean that there is cash available to pay dividends.

A corporation's board of directors is not required by law to declare dividends. This is true even if both retained earnings and cash are large enough to justify a dividend. However, most corporations try to maintain a stable dividend record in order to make their stock attractive to investors. Although dividends may be paid once a year or semiannually, most corporations pay dividends quarterly. In years of high profits, a corporation may declare a *special* or *extra* dividend.

You may have seen announcements of dividend declarations in financial newspapers or investor services. An example of such an announcement is shown below.

*On June 26, the board of directors of **Campbell Soup Co.** declared a quarterly cash dividend of $0.225 per common share to stockholders of record as of the close of business on July 8, payable on July 31.*

Board of Directors takes action to declare dividends.

ENTRY:
Debit *Cash Dividends*

Credit *Cash Dividends Payable*

Ownership of shares determines who receives dividend (no entry required).

Dividend is paid.

ENTRY:
Debit *Cash Dividends Payable*

Credit *Cash*

This announcement includes three important dates: the *date of declaration* (June 26), the *date of record* (July 8), and the *date of payment* (July 31). During the period of time between the record date and the payment date, the stock price is usually quoted as selling *ex-dividends*. This means that since the date of record has passed, a new investor will not receive the dividend.

To illustrate, assume that on *December 1* the board of directors of Hiber Corporation declares the following quarterly cash dividends. The date of record is *December 10*, and the date of payment is *January 2.*

	Dividend per Share	Total Dividends
Preferred stock, $100 par, 5,000 shares outstanding	$2.50	$12,500
Common stock, $10 par, 100,000 shares outstanding	$0.30	30,000
Total		$42,500

Hiber Corporation records the $42,500 liability for the dividends on December 1, the declaration date, as follows:

Dec.	1	Cash Dividends	42 5 0 0 00	
		Cash Dividends Payable		42 5 0 0 00
		Declared cash dividend.		

No entry is required on the date of record, December 10, since this date merely determines which stockholders will receive the dividend. On the date of payment, January 2, the corporation records the $42,500 payment of the dividends as follows:

Jan.	2	Cash Dividends Payable	42 5 0 0 00	
		Cash		42 5 0 0 00
		Paid cash dividend.		

If Hiber Corporation's fiscal year ends December 31, the balance in Cash Dividends will be transferred to Retained Earnings as a part of the closing process by debiting Retained Earnings and crediting Cash Dividends. Cash Dividends Payable will be listed on the December 31 balance sheet as a current liability.

If a corporation that holds treasury stock declares a cash dividend, the dividends are not paid on the treasury shares. To do so would place the corporation in the position of earning income through dealing with itself. For example, if Hiber Corporation in the preceding illustration had held 5,000 shares of its own common stock, the cash dividends on the common stock would have been $28,500 [(100,000 − 5,000) × $0.30] instead of $30,000.

Stock Dividends

A distribution of shares of stock to stockholders is called a **stock dividend**. Usually, such distributions are in common stock and are issued to holders of common stock. Stock dividends are different from cash dividends in that there is no distribution of cash or other assets to stockholders.

The effect of a stock dividend on the stockholders' equity of the issuing corporation is to transfer retained earnings to paid-in capital. For public corporations, the amount transferred from retained earnings to paid-in capital is normally the *fair value* (market price) of the shares issued in the stock dividend.[11] To illustrate, assume that the stockholders' equity accounts of Hendrix Corporation as of December 15 are as follows:

Common Stock, $20 par (2,000,000 shares issued)	$40,000,000
Paid-In Capital in Excess of Par—Common Stock	9,000,000
Retained Earnings	26,600,000

On December 15, the board of directors declares a stock dividend of 5% or 100,000 shares (2,000,000 shares × 5%) to be issued on January 10 to stockholders of record on December 31. The market price of the stock on the declaration date is $31 a share. The entry to record the declaration is as follows:

Dec.	15	Stock Dividends (100,000 × $31 market price)	3,100 0 0 0 00	
		Stock Dividends Distributable		
		(100,000 × $20 Par)		2,000 0 0 0 00
		Paid-In Capital in Excess of		
		Par—Common Stock		1,100 0 0 0 00
		Declared stock dividend.		

[11] The use of fair market value is justified as long as the number of shares issued for the stock dividend is small (less than 25% of the shares outstanding).

The $3,100,000 balance in Stock Dividends is closed to Retained Earnings on December 31. The stock dividends distributable account is listed in the Paid-In Capital section of the balance sheet. Thus, the effect of the stock dividend is to transfer $3,100,000 of retained earnings to paid-in capital.

On January 10, the number of shares outstanding is increased by 100,000 by the following entry to record the issue of the stock:

Jan.	10	Stock Dividends Distributable	2,000 0 0 0 00	
		Common Stock		2,000 0 0 0 00
		Issued stock for the stock dividend.		

A stock dividend does not change the assets, liabilities, or total stockholders' equity of the corporation. Likewise, it does not change a stockholder's proportionate interest (equity) in the corporation. For example, if a stockholder owned 1,000 of a corporation's 10,000 shares outstanding, the stockholder owns 10% (1,000/10,000) of the corporation. After declaring a 6% stock dividend, the corporation will issue 600 additional shares (10,000 shares × 6%), and the total shares outstanding will be 10,600. The stockholder of 1,000 shares will receive 60 additional shares and will now own 1,060 shares, which is still a 10% equity.

FINANCIAL ANALYSIS AND INTERPRETATION

objective 8

Compute and interpret the dividend yield on common stock.

The **dividend yield** indicates the rate of return to stockholders in terms of cash dividend distributions. Although the dividend yield can be computed for both preferred and common stock, it is most often computed for common stock. This is because most preferred stock has a stated dividend rate or amount. In contrast, the amount of common stock dividends normally varies with the profitability of the corporation.

The dividend yield is computed by dividing the annual dividends paid per share of common stock by the market price per share at a specific date, as shown below.

$$\text{Dividend Yield} = \frac{\textbf{Dividends per Share of Common Stock}}{\textbf{Market Price per Share of Common Stock}}$$

To illustrate, the market price of **Coca-Cola's** common stock was $58.88 as of the close of business, August 23, 2000. During the past year, Coca-Cola had paid dividends of $0.68 per share. Thus, the dividend yield of Coca-Cola's common stock is 1.2% ($0.68/$58.88). Because the market price of a corporation's stock will vary from day to day, its dividend yield will also vary from day to day.

The dividend yield on common stock is of special interest to investors whose main objective is to receive a current dividend return on their investment. This is in contrast to investors whose main objective is a rapid increase in the market price of their investments. For example, technology companies often do not pay dividends but reinvest their earnings in research and development. The main attraction of such stocks, such as **Microsoft's** common stock, is the expectation of the market price of the stock rising. Since many factors affect stock prices, an investment strategy relying solely on market price increases is more risky than a strategy based on dividend yields.

ENCORE

Would You Like to Own a Sports Team?

The **Florida Panthers**, a National League Hockey team based in Fort Lauderdale, sold its common stock to the public. At an initial offering price of $10 per share, the stock appeared to be a bargain compared to some of the Panthers' official merchandise. For example, a classic Panthers' cap is $20, a home jersey is $159, and a tire cover is $39.

Like many sports teams, the Panthers are facing some difficult financial issues. For example, the team's margins are being squeezed by players' salaries, which more than doubled in two years. In addition, the Panthers must share equally the franchise fees as well as broadcasting revenues with other NHL clubs. Also, the Panthers must pay $10 million to the NHL's collective bargaining fund by April 2003. The prospectus distributed to potential investors indicates that

the Panthers expected losses and have no plans to pay a dividend "in the foreseeable future."

But what about the thrill of owning a team and voting on draft picks, hiring and firing coaches, and attending games in the owner's box? Not likely. The stock offering was structured so that the current owner, H. Wayne Huizenga, received shares of Class B common stock that entitle him to 10,000 votes for each share of Class A common stock outstanding.

So, are you interested? With no dividend, projected losses, and no voting power, do you think that buying a share of Panthers stock would be a good investment or just end up being a piece of sports memorabilia? In November 1996, the Panthers issued their stock at $10 per share. The stock traded on the NYSE under the symbol *PAW* until September

1999, when the company changed its name to **Boca Resorts, Inc.** Boca Resorts, Inc., also owns **National Car Rental** and such luxury resorts as the **Arizona Biltmore Hotel**. At the end of trading on August 25, 2000, the stock was trading on the NYSE, under the symbol *RST*, at $10.88. ■

Source: Tim Carvell, "So You Want to Own a Team?" *Fortune*, November 11, 1996, pp. 46–48.

KEY POINTS

1 Describe the nature of the corporate form of organization.

Corporations have a separate legal existence, transferable units of stock, and limited stockholders' liability. Corporations may be either public or private corporations, and they are subject to federal income taxes.

The documents included in forming a corporation include an application of incorporation, articles of incorporation, and bylaws. Costs often incurred in organizing

a corporation include legal fees, taxes, state incorporation fees, and promotional costs. Such costs are debited to an expense account entitled Organization Costs.

2 List the two main sources of stockholders' equity.

The two main sources of stockholders' equity are (1) capital contributed by the stockholders and others, called paid-in capital, and (2) net income retained in the business, called retained earnings. Stockholders' equity is reported

in a corporation balance sheet according to these two sources.

3 List the major sources of paid-in capital, including the various classes of stock.

The main source of paid-in capital is from issuing stock. The two primary classes of stock are common stock and preferred stock. Preferred stock is normally nonparticipating and may be cumulative or noncumulative. In addition to the issuance of stock, paid-in capital may arise from donations of assets and from treasury stock transactions.

4 Journalize the entries for issuing stock.

When a corporation issues stock at par for cash, the cash account is debited and the class of stock issued is credited for its par amount. When a corporation issues stock at more than par, Paid-In Capital in Excess of Par is credited for the difference between the cash received and the par value of the stock. When stock is issued in exchange for assets other than cash, the assets acquired should be recorded at their fair market value.

When no-par stock is issued, the entire proceeds are credited to the stock account. No-par stock may be assigned a stated value per share, and the excess of the proceeds over the stated value may be credited to Paid-In Capital in Excess of Stated Value.

5 Journalize the entries for treasury stock transactions.

When a corporation buys its own stock, the cost method of account-ing is normally used. Treasury Stock is debited for its cost, and Cash is credited. If the stock is resold, Treasury Stock is credited for its cost and any difference between the cost and the selling price is normally debited or credited to Paid-In Capital from Sale of Treasury Stock.

6 State the effect of stock splits on corporate financial statements.

When a corporation reduces the par or stated value of its common stock and issues a proportionate number of additional shares, a stock split has occurred. There are no changes in the balances of any corporation accounts, and no entry is required for a stock split.

7 Journalize the entries for cash dividends and stock dividends.

The entry to record a declaration of cash dividends debits Dividends and credits Dividends Payable for each class of stock. The payment of dividends is recorded in the normal manner. When a stock dividend is declared, Stock Divi-dends is debited for the fair value of the stock to be issued. Stock Dividends Distributable is credited for the par or stated value of the common stock to be issued. The difference between the fair value of the stock and its par or stated value is credited to Paid-In Capital in Excess of Par—Common Stock. When the stock is issued on the date of payment, Stock Dividends Distributable is debited and Common Stock is credited for the par or stated value of the stock issued.

8 Compute and interpret the dividend yield on common stock.

The dividend yield indicates the rate of return to stockholders in terms of cash dividend distributions. It is computed by dividing the annual dividends paid per share of common stock by the market price per share at a specific date. This ratio is of special interest to investors whose main objective is to receive a current dividend return on their investment.

ILLUSTRATIVE PROBLEM

Altenburg Inc. is a lighting fixture wholesaler located in Arizona. During its current fiscal year, ended December 31, 2003, Altenburg Inc. completed the following selected transactions:

Feb.   3. Purchased 2,500 shares of its own common stock at $26, recording the stock at cost. (Prior to the purchase, there were 40,000 shares of $20 par common stock outstanding.)

May   1. Declared a semiannual dividend of $1 on the 10,000 shares of preferred stock and a 30¢ dividend on the common stock to stockholders of record on May 31, payable on June 15.

June 15. Paid the cash dividends.

Sept. 23. Sold 1,000 shares of treasury stock at $28, receiving cash.

Nov.   1. Declared semiannual dividends of $1 on the preferred stock and 30¢ on the common stock. In addition, a 5% common stock dividend was declared on the common stock outstanding, to be capitalized at the fair market value of the common stock, which is estimated at $30.

Dec.   1. Paid the cash dividends and issued the certificates for the common stock dividend.

Instructions
Journalize the entries to record the transactions for Altenburg Inc.

Solution

2003 Feb.	3	Treasury Stock		65 0 0 0 00		
		Cash			65 0 0 0 00	
May	1	Cash Dividends		21 2 5 0 00		
		Cash Dividends Payable			21 2 5 0 00*	
		*(10,000 × $1) + [(40,000 − 2,500)				
		× $0.30]				
June	15	Cash Dividends Payable		21 2 5 0 00		
		Cash			21 2 5 0 00	
Sept.	23	Cash		28 0 0 0 00		
		Treasury Stock			26 0 0 0 00	
		Paid-In Capital from Sale of Treasury Stock			2 0 0 0 00	
Nov.	1	Cash Dividends		21 5 5 0 00*		
		Cash Dividends Payable			21 5 5 0 00	
		*(10,000 × $1) + [(40,000 − 1,500)				
		× $0.30]				
	1	Stock Dividends		57 7 5 0 00*		
		Stock Dividends Distributable			38 5 0 0 00	
		Paid-In Capital in Excess of				
		Par—Common Stock			19 2 5 0 00	
		*(40,000 − 1,500) × 5% × $30				
Dec.	1	Cash Dividends Payable		21 5 5 0 00		
		Stock Dividends Distributable		38 5 0 0 00		
		Cash			21 5 5 0 00	
		Common Stock			38 5 0 0 00	

SELF-EXAMINATION QUESTIONS   Answers at End of Chapter

Matching
Match each of the following statements with its proper term. Some terms may not be used.

A. cash dividend	___ 1. Shares of ownership of a corporation.
B. common stock	___ 2. The owners of a corporation.
C. cumulative preferred stock	___ 3. The owners' equity in a corporation.
D. deficit	___ 4. Capital contributed to a corporation by the stockholders and others.
E. discount	___ 5. Net income retained in a corporation.
F. dividend yield	___ 6. A debit balance in the retained earnings account.
	___ 7. The stock in the hands of stockholders.

G. nonparticipating preferred stock

H. outstanding stock

I. paid-in capital

J. par

K. preferred stock

L. premium

M. retained earnings

N. stated value

O. stock

P. stock dividend

Q. stock split

R. stockholders

S. stockholders' equity

T. treasury stock

___ 8. A value, similar to par value, approved by the board of directors of a corporation for no-par stock.

___ 9. The stock outstanding when a corporation has issued only one class of stock.

___ 10. A class of stock with preferential rights over common stock.

___ 11. A class of preferred stock whose dividend rights are usually limited to a certain amount.

___ 12. A class of preferred stock that has a right to receive regular dividends that have been passed (not declared) before any common stock dividends are paid.

___ 13. The excess of the issue price of a stock over its par value.

___ 14. The excess of the par value of a stock over its issue price.

___ 15. Stock that a corporation has once issued and then reacquires.

___ 16. A reduction in the par or stated value of a common stock and the issuance of a proportionate number of additional shares.

___ 17. A cash distribution of earnings by a corporation to its shareholders.

___ 18. A distribution of shares of stock to its stockholders.

___ 19. A ratio, computed by dividing the annual dividends paid per share of common stock by the market price per share at a specific date, that indicates the rate of return to stockholders in terms of cash dividend distributions.

___ 20. The monetary amount printed on a stock certificate.

Multiple Choice

1. If a corporation has outstanding 1,000 shares of $9 cumulative preferred stock of $100 par and dividends have been passed for the preceding three years, what is the amount of preferred dividends that must be declared in the current year before a dividend can be declared on common stock?
   A. $ 9,000   C. $36,000
   B. $27,000   D. $45,000

2. Paid-in capital for a corporation may arise from which of the following sources?
   A. Issuing cumulative preferred stock
   B. Receiving donations of real estate
   C. Selling the corporation's treasury stock
   D. All of the above

3. The Stockholders' Equity section of the balance sheet may include:

     A. Common Stock   C. Preferred Stock
     B. Donated Capital   D. All of the above

4. If a corporation reacquires its own stock, the stock is listed on the balance sheet in the:
   A. Current Assets section.
   B. Long-Term Liabilities section.
   C. Stockholders' Equity section.
   D. Investments section.

5. A corporation has issued 25,000 shares of $100 par common stock and holds 3,000 of these shares as treasury stock. If the corporation declares a $2 per share cash dividend, what amount will be recorded as cash dividends?
   A. $22,000   C. $44,000
   B. $25,000   D. $50,000

CLASS DISCUSSION QUESTIONS

1. Contrast the owners' liability to creditors of (a) a partnership (partners) and (b) a corporation (stockholders).
2. Why is it said that the earnings of a corporation are subject to *double taxation*? Discuss.
3. Why are most large businesses organized as corporations?
4. a. What type of expenditure is charged to the organization costs account?
   b. Give examples of such expenditures.
5. Distinguish between paid-in capital and retained earnings of a corporation.

6. The retained earnings account of a corporation at the beginning of the year had a credit balance of $65,000. The only other entry in the account during the year was a debit of $150,000 transferred from the income summary account at the end of the year. (a) What is the term applied to the $150,000 debit? (b) What is the term applied to the debit balance of retained earnings at the end of the year, after all closing entries have been posted?

7. Of two corporations organized at approximately the same time and engaged in competing businesses, one issued $50 par common stock, and the other issued $1 par common stock. Do the par designations provide any indication as to which stock is preferable as an investment? Explain.

8. What are the three basic rights that accompany ownership of a share of common stock?

9. a. Differentiate between common stock and preferred stock.
   b. Describe briefly (1) nonparticipating preferred stock and (2) cumulative preferred stock.

10. A stockbroker advises a client to "buy cumulative preferred stock. . . . With that type of stock, . . . [you] will never have to worry about losing the dividends." Is the broker right?

11. What are some sources of paid-in capital other than the issuance of stock?

12. If a corporation is given land as an inducement to locate in a particular community, (a) how should the amount of the debit to the land account be determined, and (b) what is the title of the account that should be credited for the same amount?

13. If common stock of $100 par is sold for $130, what is the $30 difference between the issue price and par called?

14. What are some of the factors that influence the market price of a corporation's stock?

15. When a corporation issues stock at a premium, is the premium income? Explain.

16. Land is acquired by a corporation for 15,000 shares of its $25 par common stock, which is currently selling for $70 per share on a national stock exchange. What accounts should be credited to record the transaction?

17. Indicate which of the following accounts would be reported as part of paid-in capital on the balance sheet:
    a. Retained Earnings
    b. Common Stock
    c. Donated Capital
    d. Preferred Stock

18. a. In what respect does treasury stock differ from unissued stock?
    b. How should treasury stock be presented on the balance sheet?

19. A corporation reacquires 5,000 shares of its own $40 par common stock for $370,000, recording it at cost. (a) What effect does this transaction have on revenue or expense of the period? (b) What effect does it have on stockholders' equity?

20. The treasury stock in Question 19 is resold for $400,000. (a) What is the effect on the corporation's revenue of the period? (b) What is the effect on stockholders' equity?

21. What is the primary purpose of a stock split?

22. What are the three conditions for the declaration and the payment of a cash dividend?

23. The dates in connection with the declaration of a cash dividend are October 1, November 15, and December 30. Identify each date.

24. A corporation with both cumulative preferred stock and common stock outstanding has a substantial credit balance in its retained earnings account at the beginning of the current fiscal year. Although net income for the current year is sufficient to pay the preferred dividend of $100,000 each quarter and a common dividend of $300,000 each quarter, the board of directors declares dividends only on the preferred stock. Suggest possible reasons for passing the dividends on the common stock.

25. An owner of 200 shares of Dunston Company common stock receives a stock dividend of 4 shares. (a) What is the effect of the stock dividend on the stockholder's proportionate interest (equity) in the corporation? (b) How does the total equity of 204 shares compare with the total equity of 200 shares before the stock dividend?

26. a. Where should a declared but unpaid cash dividend be reported on the balance sheet?
    b. Where should a declared but unissued stock dividend be reported on the balance sheet?

RESOURCES FOR YOUR SUCCESS ONLINE AT

http://warren.swcollege.com

Remember! If you need additional help, visit South-Western's Web site.
See page 26 for a description of the online and printed materials that are available.

EXERCISES

Exercise 12–1
Dividends per share
Objective 3

✓ Preferred stock, 3rd year: $2.00

Masini Inc., a developer of radiology equipment, has stock outstanding as follows: 20,000 shares of $2 nonparticipating, noncumulative preferred stock of $100 par, and 250,000 shares of $50 par common. During its first five years of operations, the following amounts were distributed as dividends: first year, none; second year, $30,000; third year, $90,000; fourth year, $200,000; fifth year, $240,000. Calculate the dividends per share on each class of stock for each of the five years.

Exercise 12–2
Dividends per share
Objective 3

✓ Preferred stock, 3rd year: $2.50

Mystic.com, a computer software development firm, has stock outstanding as follows: 10,000 shares of $1.50 cumulative, nonparticipating preferred stock of $50 par, and 50,000 shares of $100 par common. During its first five years of operations, the following amounts were distributed as dividends: first year, none; second year, $5,000; third year, $80,000; fourth year, $180,000; fifth year, $75,000. Calculate the dividends per share on each class of stock for each of the five years.

Exercise 12–3
Entries for issuing par stock
Objective 4

On March 10, Candler Inc., a marble contractor, issued for cash 30,000 shares of $20 par common stock at $30, and on August 9, it issued for cash 5,000 shares of $100 par preferred stock at $105.

a.   Journalize the entries for March 10 and August 9.
b.   What is the total amount invested (total paid-in capital) by all stockholders as of August 9?

Exercise 12–4
Entries for issuing no-par stock
Objective 4

On November 2, Catalpa Corp., a carpet wholesaler, issued for cash 5,000 shares of no-par common stock (with a stated value of $25) at $75, and on December 3, it issued for cash 1,000 shares of $50 par preferred stock at $65.

a.   Journalize the entries for November 2 and December 3, assuming that the common stock is to be credited with the stated value.
b.   What is the total amount invested (total paid-in capital) by all stockholders as of December 3?

Exercise 12–5
Issuing stock for assets other than cash
Objective 4

On February 27, Sims Corporation, a wholesaler of hydraulic lifts, acquired land in exchange for 4,000 shares of $10 par common stock with a current market price of $73. Journalize the entry to record the transaction.

Exercise 12–6
Selected stock transactions
Objective 4

Koala Corp., an electric guitar retailer, was organized by Nicole West, Shawn Rainey, and Ginger Macke. The charter authorized 100,000 shares of common stock with a par of $20. The following transactions affecting stockholders' equity were completed during the first year of operations:

a.   Issued 1,000 shares of stock at par to Rainey for cash.
b.   Issued 50 shares of stock at par to West for promotional services provided in connection with the organization of the corporation, and issued 950 shares of stock at par to West for cash.

c.   Purchased land and a building from Macke. The building is mortgaged for $125,000 for 25 years at 8%, and there is accrued interest of $1,000 on the mortgage note at the time of the purchase. It is agreed that the land is to be priced at $45,000 and the building at $150,000, and that Macke's equity will be exchanged for stock at par. The corporation agreed to assume responsibility for paying the mortgage note and the accrued interest.

Journalize the entries to record the transactions.

Exercise 12–7

Issuing stock

Objective 4

Gyro.com, with an authorization of 25,000 shares of preferred stock and 100,000 shares of common stock, completed several transactions involving its stock on October 1, the first day of operations. The trial balance at the close of the day follows:

Cash	565,000	
Land	40,000	
Buildings	95,000	
Preferred $5 Stock, $100 par		100,000
Paid-In Capital in Excess of Par—Preferred Stock		35,000
Common Stock, $75 par		450,000
Paid-In Capital in Excess of Par—Common Stock		115,000
	700,000	700,000

All shares within each class of stock were sold at the same price. The preferred stock was issued in exchange for the land and buildings.

Journalize the two entries to record the transactions summarized in the trial balance.

Exercise 12–8

Issuing stock

Objective 4

Fourier Products Inc., a wholesaler of office products, was organized on January 6 of the current year, with an authorization of 50,000 shares of $2 noncumulative preferred stock, $100 par and 250,000 shares of $10 par common stock. The following selected transactions were completed during the first year of operations:

Jan.   6. Issued 25,000 shares of common stock at par for cash.
      11. Issued 150 shares of common stock at par to an attorney in payment of legal fees for organizing the corporation.
Feb. 28. Issued 11,500 shares of common stock in exchange for land, buildings, and equipment with fair market prices of $20,000, $100,000, and $18,000, respectively.
Mar. 15. Issued 5,000 shares of preferred stock at $102 for cash.

Journalize the transactions.

Exercise 12–9

Treasury stock transactions

Objective 5

✓ b. $8,500 credit

Chico Springs Inc. bottles and distributes spring water. On March 1 of the current year, Chico reacquired 5,500 shares of its common stock at $40 per share. On July 8, Chico sold 3,500 of the reacquired shares at $43 per share. The remaining 2,000 shares were sold at $39 per share on December 19.

a.   Journalize the transactions of March 1, July 8, and December 19.
b.   What is the balance in Paid-In Capital from Sale of Treasury Stock on December 31 of the current year?
c.   Where will the balance in Paid-In Capital from Sale of Treasury Stock be reported on the balance sheet?
d.   ✏️ ➤ For what reasons might Chico Springs have purchased the treasury stock?

Exercise 12–10

Treasury stock transactions

Objective 5

✓ b. $9,000 credit

Aorta Inc. develops and produces spraying equipment for lawn maintenance and industrial uses. On September 6 of the current year, Aorta Inc. reacquired 6,000 shares of its common stock at $90 per share. On November 15, 2,000 of the reacquired shares were sold at $93 per share, and on December 21, 3,000 of the reacquired shares were sold at $91.

a.   Journalize the transactions of September 6, November 15, and December 21.

(continued)

b. What is the balance in Paid-In Capital from Sale of Treasury Stock on December 31 of the current year?
c. What is the balance in Treasury Stock on December 31 of the current year?
d. How will the balance in Treasury Stock be reported on the balance sheet?

Exercise 12–11
Treasury stock transactions

Objective 5

✓ b. $3,000 credit

Heavenly Inc. bottles and distributes spring water. On July 1 of the current year, Heavenly Inc. reacquired 3,000 shares of its common stock at $40 per share. On August 10, Heavenly Inc. sold 1,500 of the reacquired shares at $43 per share. The remaining 1,500 shares were sold at $39 per share on December 19.

a. Journalize the transactions of July 1, August 10, and December 19.
b. What is the balance in Paid-In Capital from Sale of Treasury Stock on December 31 of the current year?
c. Where will the balance in Paid-In Capital from Sale of Treasury Stock be reported on the balance sheet?
d. ✏️ For what reasons might Heavenly Inc. have purchased the treasury stock?

Exercise 12–12
Effect of stock split

Objective 6

Headwaters Corporation wholesales ovens and ranges to restaurants throughout the Northwest. Headwaters Corporation, which had 30,000 shares of common stock outstanding, declared a 3-for-1 stock split (2 additional shares for each share issued).

a. What will be the number of shares outstanding after the split?
b. If the common stock had a market price of $120 per share before the stock split, what would be an approximate market price per share after the split?

Exercise 12–13
Effect of cash dividend and stock split

Objectives 6, 7

Indicate whether the following actions would (+) increase, (−) decrease, or (0) not affect Collier Inc.'s total assets, liabilities, and stockholders' equity:

		Assets	Liabilities	Stockholders' Equity
(1)	Declaring a stock dividend	_____	_____	_____
(2)	Issuing stock certificates for the stock dividend declared in (1)	_____	_____	_____
(3)	Declaring a cash dividend	_____	_____	_____
(4)	Paying the cash dividend declared in (3)	_____	_____	_____
(5)	Authorizing and issuing stock certificates in a stock split	_____	_____	_____

Exercise 12–14
Entries for cash dividends

Objective 7

The dates of importance in connection with a cash dividend of $75,000 on a corporation's common stock are January 4, February 3, and March 5. Journalize the entries required on each date.

Exercise 12–15
Entries for stock dividends

Objective 7

✓ b. (1) $362,500
(3) $833,500

Heartwood Inc. is an HMO for twelve businesses in the Cleveland area. The following account balances appear on the balance sheet of Heartwood: Common stock (100,000 shares authorized), $50 par, $300,000; Paid-in capital in excess of par—common stock, $62,500; and Retained earnings, $471,000. The board of directors declared a 1% stock dividend when the market price of the stock was $76 a share. Heartwood reported no income or loss for the current year.

a. Journalize the entries to record (1) the declaration of the dividend, capitalizing an amount equal to market value, and (2) the issuance of the stock certificates.
b. Determine the following amounts before the stock dividend was declared: (1) total paid-in capital, (2) total retained earnings, and (3) total stockholders' equity.
c. Determine the following amounts after the stock dividend was declared and closing entries were recorded at the end of the year: (1) total paid-in capital, (2) total retained earnings, and (3) total stockholders' equity.

Exercise 12–16

Selected stock and dividend transactions

Objectives 6, 7

Selected transactions completed by Aft Boating Supply Corporation during the current fiscal year are as follows:

Jan. 7. Split the common stock 4 for 1 and reduced the par from $100 to $25 per share. After the split, there were 200,000 common shares outstanding.

Mar. 1. Declared semiannual dividends of $2 on 8,000 shares of preferred stock and $0.10 on the common stock to stockholders of record on March 31, payable on April 15.

Apr. 15. Paid the cash dividends.

Nov. 1. Declared semiannual dividends of $2 on the preferred stock and $0.25 on the common stock (before the stock dividend). In addition, a 1% common stock dividend was declared on the common stock outstanding. The fair market value of the common stock is estimated at $30.

Dec. 15. Paid the cash dividends and issued the certificates for the common stock dividend.

Journalize the transactions.

Exercise 12–17

Dividend yield

Objective 8

The financial statements for **Cisco Systems, Inc.**, are presented in Appendix G at the end of this text.

a. What was the amount of the dividends declared and paid by Cisco Systems, Inc., in 2000 and 1999?

b. Given Cisco Systems' dividend policy, why would an investor be attracted to this company?

Exercise 12–18

Dividend yield

Objective 8

In 1999, **Hershey Foods Corporation** paid dividends of $1.00 per share to its common stockholders (excluding its Class B Common Stock). The market price of Hershey's common stock on December 31, 1999, was $47.44.

a. Determine Hershey's dividend yield on its common stock as of December 31, 1999.

b. What conclusions can you draw from an analysis of Hershey's dividend yield?

PROBLEMS SERIES A

Problem 12–1A

Dividends on preferred and common stock

Objective 3

SPREADSHEET

✓ 1. Common dividends in 2001: $31,000

Magnifico Inc. owns and operates movie theaters throughout Georgia and Mississippi. Magnifico has declared the following annual dividends over a six-year period: 1999, $32,000; 2000, $65,000; 2001, $84,000; 2002, $60,000; 2003, $72,000; and 2004, $95,000. During the entire period, the outstanding stock of the company was composed of 25,000 shares of cumulative, nonparticipating, $2 preferred stock, $100 par, and 50,000 shares of common stock, $7 par.

Instructions

1. Calculate the total dividends and the per-share dividends declared on each class of stock for each of the six years. There were no dividends in arrears on January 1, 1999. Summarize the data in tabular form, using the following column headings:

Year	Total Dividends	Preferred Dividends		Common Dividends	
		Total	Per Share	Total	Per Share
1999	$32,000				
2000	65,000				
2001	84,000				

(continued)

Year	Total Dividends	Preferred Dividends		Common Dividends	
		Total	Per Share	Total	Per Share
2002	$60,000				
2003	72,000				
2004	95,000				

2. Calculate the average annual dividend per share for each class of stock for the six-year period.
3. Assuming that the preferred stock was sold at par and common stock was sold at $8 at the beginning of the six-year period, calculate the percentage return on initial shareholders' investment, based on the average annual dividend per share (a) for preferred stock and (b) for common stock.

Problem 12–2A
Stock transactions for corporate expansion

Objective 4

GENERAL LEDGER

On January 1 of the current year, the following accounts and their balances appear in the ledger of Osaka Corp., a meat processor:

Preferred $4 Stock, $100 par (20,000 shares authorized, 7,500 shares issued)	$ 750,000
Paid-In Capital in Excess of Par—Preferred Stock	150,000
Common Stock, $50 par (100,000 shares authorized, 40,000 shares issued)	2,000,000
Paid-In Capital in Excess of Par—Common Stock	300,000
Retained Earnings	805,000

At the annual stockholders' meeting on February 20, the board of directors presented a plan for modernizing and expanding plant operations at a cost of approximately $1,200,000. The plan provided (a) that a building, valued at $375,000, and the land on which it is located, valued at $75,000, be acquired in accordance with preliminary negotiations by the issuance of 8,000 shares of common stock, (b) that 5,000 shares of the unissued preferred stock be issued through an underwriter, and (c) that the corporation borrow $200,000. The plan was approved by the stockholders and accomplished by the following transactions:

Mar. 7. Issued 8,000 shares of common stock in exchange for land and a building, according to the plan.
21. Issued 5,000 shares of preferred stock, receiving $125 per share in cash from the underwriter.
29. Borrowed $200,000 from US East National Bank, giving a 7% mortgage note.

No other transactions occurred during March.

Instructions
Journalize the entries to record the foregoing transactions.

Problem 12–3A
Selected stock transactions

Objectives 4, 5, 7

GENERAL LEDGER

The following selected accounts appear in the ledger of Cyma Environmental Corporation on July 1, 2003, the beginning of the current fiscal year:

Preferred 3% Stock, $75 par (10,000 shares authorized, 7,000 shares issued)	$525,000
Paid-In Capital in Excess of Par—Preferred Stock	60,000
Common Stock, $10 par (50,000 shares authorized, 30,000 shares issued)	300,000
Paid-In Capital in Excess of Par—Common Stock	100,000
Retained Earnings	937,000

During the year, the corporation completed a number of transactions affecting the stockholders' equity. They are summarized as follows:

a. Issued 10,000 shares of common stock at $20, receiving cash.
b. Sold 1,000 shares of preferred 3% stock at $90.

c. Purchased 5,000 shares of treasury common for $105,000.
d. Sold 3,000 shares of treasury common for $75,000.
e. Sold 1,000 shares of treasury common for $20,000.
f. Declared cash dividends of $2.25 per share on preferred stock and $0.50 per share on common stock.
g. Paid the cash dividends.

Instructions

Journalize the entries to record the transactions. Identify each entry by letter.

Problem 12–4A

Entries for selected corporate transactions

Objectives 4, 5, 7

SPREADSHEET
GENERAL
LEDGER

✓ 3. $3,001,100

Sasquatch Enterprises Inc. manufactures bathroom fixtures. The stockholders' equity accounts of Sasquatch Enterprises Inc., with balances on January 1 of the current fiscal year, are as follows:

Common Stock, $20 stated value (100,000 shares authorized, 80,000 shares issued)	$1,600,000
Paid-In Capital in Excess of Stated Value	300,000
Retained Earnings	625,000
Treasury Stock (4,000 shares, at cost)	120,000

The following selected transactions occurred during the year:

Jan. 10. Received land from the Wilsall City Council as a donation. The land had an estimated fair market value of $100,000.
       30. Paid cash dividends of $1 per share on the common stock. The dividend had been properly recorded when declared on December 30 of the preceding fiscal year for $76,000.
Feb. 19. Issued 10,000 shares of common stock for $350,000.
Apr.   1. Sold all of the treasury stock for $140,000.
July   1. Declared a 5% stock dividend on common stock, to be capitalized at the market price of the stock, which is $42 a share.
Aug. 11. Issued the certificates for the dividend declared on July 1.
Oct. 20. Purchased 7,500 shares of treasury stock for $285,000.
Dec. 27. Declared a $0.90-per-share dividend on common stock.
       31. Closed the credit balance of the income summary account, $369,400.
       31. Closed the two dividends accounts to Retained Earnings.

Instructions

1. Enter the January 1 balances in T accounts for the stockholders' equity accounts listed. Also prepare T accounts for the following: Paid-In Capital from Sale of Treasury Stock; Donated Capital; Stock Dividends Distributable; Stock Dividends; Cash Dividends.
2. Journalize the entries to record the transactions, and post to the nine selected accounts.
3. Determine the total stockholders' equity on December 31.

Problem 12–5A

Entries for selected corporate transactions

Objectives 4, 5, 6, 7

SPREADSHEET
GENERAL
LEDGER

Selected transactions completed by Silver Gate Boating Supply Corporation during the current fiscal year are as follows:

Jan.   6. Split the common stock 4 for 1 and reduced the par from $100 to $25 per share. After the split, there were 150,000 common shares outstanding.
Mar. 13. Purchased 7,500 shares of the corporation's own common stock at $35, recording the stock at cost.
May   1. Declared semiannual dividends of $2 on 18,000 shares of preferred stock and $0.60 on the common stock to stockholders of record on May 20, payable on June 1.
June   1. Paid the cash dividends.
Sept. 17. Sold 2,500 shares of treasury stock at $40, receiving cash.
Nov.   2. Declared semiannual dividends of $2 on the preferred stock and $0.60 on the common stock (before the stock dividend). In addition, a 2% common stock

dividend was declared on the common stock outstanding. The fair market value of the common stock is estimated at $38.

Dec. 3. Paid the cash dividends and issued the certificates for the common stock dividend.

Instructions

Journalize the transactions.

PROBLEMS SERIES B

Problem 12–1B
Dividends on preferred and common stock

Objective 3

SPREADSHEET

✓ 1. Common dividends in 1999: $10,000

LaMancha Corp. manufactures mountain bikes and distributes them through retail outlets in Idaho and Montana. LaMancha Corp. has declared the following annual dividends over a six-year period: 1999, $25,000; 2000, $8,000; 2001, $10,000; 2002, $4,000; 2003, $50,000; and 2004, $75,500. During the entire period, the outstanding stock of the company was composed of 5,000 shares of cumulative, nonparticipating, $3 preferred stock, $50 par, and 50,000 shares of common stock, $5 par.

Instructions

1. Calculate the total dividends and the per-share dividends declared on each class of stock for each of the six years. There were no dividends in arrears on January 1, 1999. Summarize the data in tabular form, using the following column headings:

Year	Total Dividends	Preferred Dividends		Common Dividends	
		Total	**Per Share**	**Total**	**Per Share**
1999	$25,000				
2000	8,000				
2001	10,000				
2002	4,000				
2003	50,000				
2004	75,500				

2. Calculate the average annual dividend per share for each class of stock for the six-year period.
3. Assuming that the preferred stock was sold at par and common stock was sold at $11 at the beginning of the six-year period, calculate the percentage return on initial shareholders' investment, based on the average annual dividend per share (a) for preferred stock and (b) for common stock.

Problem 12–2B
Stock transaction for corporate expansion

Objective 4

GENERAL LEDGER

Neural Corp. produces medical lasers for use in hospitals. The following accounts and their balances appear in the ledger of Neural Corp. on June 30 of the current year:

Preferred $5 Stock, $100 par (20,000 shares authorized, 10,000 shares issued)	$1,000,000
Paid-In Capital in Excess of Par—Preferred Stock	150,000
Common Stock, $25 par (100,000 shares authorized, 60,000 shares issued)	1,500,000
Paid-In Capital in Excess of Par—Common Stock	200,000
Retained Earnings	915,000

At the annual stockholders' meeting on July 21, the board of directors presented a plan for modernizing and expanding plant operations at a cost of approximately $2,000,000. The plan provided (a) that the corporation borrow $650,000, (b) that 5,000 shares of the unissued preferred stock be issued through an underwriter, and (c) that a building, valued at $750,000, and the land on which it is located, valued at $100,000, be acquired in accordance with preliminary negotiations by the issuance of 20,000 shares of common stock. The plan was approved by the stockholders and accomplished by the following transactions:

Aug. 3. Borrowed $650,000 from First National Bank, giving an 8% mortgage note.

12. Issued 5,000 shares of preferred stock, receiving $120 per share in cash from the underwriter.

30. Issued 20,000 shares of common stock in exchange for land and a building, according to the plan.

No other transactions occurred during June.

Instructions

Journalize the entries to record the foregoing transactions.

Problem 12–3B

Selected stock transactions

Objectives 4, 5, 7

GENERAL LEDGER

Cutthroat Corporation sells and services pipe welding equipment in Montana. The following selected accounts appear in the ledger of Cutthroat Corporation on January 1, 2003, the beginning of the current fiscal year:

Preferred 2% Stock, $100 par (40,000 shares authorized, 15,000 shares issued)	$1,500,000
Paid-In Capital in Excess of Par—Preferred Stock	112,500
Common Stock, $10 par (800,000 shares authorized, 400,000 shares issued)	4,000,000
Paid-In Capital in Excess of Par—Common Stock	600,000
Retained Earnings	3,450,000

During the year, the corporation completed a number of transactions affecting the stockholders' equity. They are summarized as follows:

a. Purchased 25,000 shares of treasury common for $550,000.
b. Sold 8,000 shares of treasury common for $192,000.
c. Sold 6,000 shares of preferred 2% stock at $110.
d. Issued 50,000 shares of common stock at $20, receiving cash.
e. Sold 7,000 shares of treasury common for $140,000.
f. Declared cash dividends of $2 per share on preferred stock and $0.25 per share on common stock.
g. Paid the cash dividends.

Instructions

Journalize the entries to record the transactions. Identify each entry by letter.

Problem 12–4B

Entries for selected corporate transactions

Objectives 4, 5, 7

SPREADSHEET
GENERAL LEDGER

✓ 3. $2,232,410

Loran Enterprises Inc. produces aeronautical navigation equipment. The stockholders' equity accounts of Loran Enterprises Inc., with balances on January 1 of the current fiscal year, are as follows:

Common Stock, $10 stated value (100,000 shares authorized, 75,000 shares issued)	$750,000
Paid-In Capital in Excess of Stated Value	150,000
Retained Earnings	597,750
Treasury Stock (5,000 shares, at cost)	90,000

The following selected transactions occurred during the year:

Jan. 15. Paid cash dividends of $0.80 per share on the common stock. The dividend had been properly recorded when declared on December 28 of the preceding fiscal year for $56,000.

Feb. 28. Sold all of the treasury stock for $125,000.

Apr. 5. Issued 10,000 shares of common stock for $300,000.

May 19. Received land from the Lyndon City Council as a donation. The land had an estimated fair market value of $200,000.

July 30. Declared a 3% stock dividend on common stock, to be capitalized at the market price of the stock, which is $28 a share.

Aug. 30. Issued the certificates for the dividend declared on July 30.

Sept. 3. Purchased 4,000 shares of treasury stock for $116,000.

Dec. 30. Declared an $0.80-per-share dividend on common stock.

      31. Closed the credit balance of the income summary account, $382,500.

      31. Closed the two dividends accounts to Retained Earnings.

Instructions

1. Enter the January 1 balances in T accounts for the stockholders' equity accounts listed. Also prepare T accounts for the following: Paid-In Capital from Sale of Treasury Stock; Donated Capital; Stock Dividends Distributable; Stock Dividends; Cash Dividends.
2. Journalize the entries to record the transactions, and post to the nine selected accounts.
3. Determine the total stockholders' equity on December 31.

Problem 12–5B
Entries for selected corporate transactions

Objectives 4, 5, 6, 7

SPREADSHEET

GENERAL LEDGER

Ocean Atlantic Corporation manufactures and distributes leisure clothing. Selected transactions completed by Ocean Atlantic during the current fiscal year are as follows:

Jan.   3. Split the common stock 5 for 1 and reduced the par from $50 to $10 per share. After the split, there were 125,000 common shares outstanding.

Mar. 15. Declared semiannual dividends of $3 on 10,000 shares of preferred stock and $0.40 on the 125,000 shares of $10 par common stock to stockholders of record on March 31, payable on April 15.

Apr. 15. Paid the cash dividends.

May   8. Purchased 15,000 shares of the corporation's own common stock at $20, recording the stock at cost.

June 10. Sold 5,000 shares of treasury stock at $23, receiving cash.

Sept. 15. Declared semiannual dividends of $3 on the preferred stock and $0.40 on the common stock (before the stock dividend). In addition, a 2% common stock dividend was declared on the common stock outstanding, to be capitalized at the fair market value of the common stock, which is estimated at $25.

Oct. 15. Paid the cash dividends and issued the certificates for the common stock dividend.

Instructions
Journalize the transactions.

SPECIAL ACTIVITIES

Activity 12–1
Derby Unlimited Inc.
Ethics and professional conduct in business

Holly Abernathy and Garreth Scott are organizing Derby Unlimited Inc. to undertake a high-risk gold-mining venture in Canada. Holly and Garreth tentatively plan to request authorization for 100,000,000 shares of common stock to be sold to the general public. Holly and Garreth have decided to establish par of $1 per share in order to appeal to a wide variety of potential investors. Holly and Garreth feel that investors would be more willing to invest in the company if they received a large quantity of shares for what might appear to be a "bargain" price.

      ► Discuss whether Holly and Garreth are behaving in a professional manner.

Activity 12–2
Omen Inc.
Issuing stock

What do you think?

Omen Inc. began operations on January 8, 2003, with the issuance of 500,000 shares of $100 par common stock. The sole stockholders of Omen Inc. are Fay Barnes and Dr. Joseph Cawley, who organized Omen Inc. with the objective of developing a new flu vaccine. Dr. Cawley claims that the flu vaccine, which is nearing the final development stage, will protect individuals against 99% of the flu types that have been medically identified. To complete the project, Omen Inc. needs $10,000,000 of additional funds. The local banks have been unwilling to loan the funds because of the lack of sufficient collateral and the riskiness of the business.

The following is a conversation between Fay Barnes, the chief executive officer of Omen Inc., and Dr. Joseph Cawley, the leading researcher.

Barnes: What are we going to do? The banks won't loan us any more money, and we've got to have $10 million to complete the project. We are so close! It would be a disaster to quit now. The only thing I can think of is to issue additional stock. Do you have any suggestions?

Cawley: I guess you're right. But if the banks won't loan us any more money, how do you think we can find any investors to buy stock?

Barnes: I've been thinking about that. What if we promise the investors that we will pay them 2% of net sales until they have received an amount equal to what they paid for the stock?

Cawley: What happens when we pay back the $10 million? Do the investors get to keep the stock? If they do, it'll dilute our ownership.

Barnes: How about, if after we pay back the $10 million, we make them turn in their stock for $200 per share? That's twice what they paid for it, plus they would have already gotten all their money back. That's a $200 profit per share for the investors.

Cawley: It could work. We get our money, but don't have to pay any interest, dividends, or the $200 until we start generating net sales. At the same time, the investors could get their money back plus $200 per share.

Barnes: We'll need current financial statements for the new investors. I'll get our accountant working on them and contact our attorney to draw up a legally binding contract for the new investors. Yes, this could work.

In late 2003, the attorney and the various regulatory authorities approved the new stock offering, and 100,000 shares of common stock were privately sold to new investors at the stock's par of $100.

In preparing financial statements for 2003, Fay Barnes and Tanya Kuchar, the controller for Omen Inc., have the following conversation.

Kuchar: Fay, I've got a problem.

Barnes: What's that, Tanya?

Kuchar: Issuing common stock to raise that additional $10 million was a great idea. But . . .

Barnes: But what?

Kuchar: I've got to prepare the 2003 annual financial statements, and I am not sure how to classify the common stock.

Barnes: What do you mean? It's common stock.

Kuchar: I'm not so sure. I called the auditor and explained how we are contractually obligated to pay the new stockholders 2% of net sales until $100 per share is paid. Then, we may be obligated to pay them $200 per share.

Barnes: So . . .

Kuchar: So the auditor thinks that we should classify the additional issuance of $10 million as debt, not stock! And, if we put the $10 million on the balance sheet as debt, we will violate our other loan agreements with the banks. And, if these agreements are violated, the banks may call in all our debt immediately. If they do that, we are in deep trouble. We'll probably have to file for bankruptcy. We just don't have the cash to pay off the banks.

1. ◖▬▬➤ Discuss the arguments for and against classifying the issuance of the $10 million of stock as debt.

2. ◖▬▬➤ What do you think might be a practical solution to this classification problem?

Activity 12–3
Ball-Peen Inc.
Dividends

Ball-Peen Inc. has paid quarterly cash dividends since 1990. These dividends have steadily increased from $0.05 per share to the latest dividend declaration of $0.40 per share. The board of directors would like to continue this trend and is hesitant to suspend or decrease the amount of quarterly dividends. Unfortunately, sales dropped sharply in the fourth quarter of 2003 because of worsening economic conditions and increased competition. As a result, the board is uncertain as to whether it should declare a dividend for the last quarter of 2003.

On November 1, 2003, Ball-Peen Inc. borrowed $500,000 from City National Bank to use in modernizing its retail stores and to expand its product line in reaction to its competition. The terms of the 10-year, 12% loan require Ball-Peen Inc. to:

a. Pay monthly interest on the last day of month.
b. Pay $50,000 of the principal each November 1, beginning in 2004.
c. Maintain a current ratio (current assets ÷ current liabilities) of 2.
d. Maintain a minimum balance (a compensating balance) of $25,000 in its City National Bank account.

On December 31, 2003, $125,000 of the $500,000 loan had been disbursed in modernization of the retail stores and in expansion of the product line. Ball-Peen Inc.'s balance sheet as of December 31, 2003, is as follows:

Ball-Peen Inc.
Balance Sheet
December 31, 2003

Assets

Current assets:			
Cash		$ 40,000	
Marketable securities		375,000	
Accounts receivable	$ 91,500		
Less allowance for doubtful accounts	6,500	85,000	
Merchandise inventory		125,000	
Prepaid expenses		4,500	
Total current assets			$ 629,500
Property, plant, and equipment:			
Land		$150,000	
Buildings	$950,000		
Less accumulated depreciation	215,000	735,000	
Equipment	$460,000		
Less accumulated depreciation	110,000	350,000	
Total property, plant, and equipment			1,235,000
Total assets			$1,864,500

Liabilities

Current liabilities:			
Accounts payable	$ 71,800		
Notes payable (City National Bank)	50,000		
Salaries payable	3,200		
Total current liabilities		$125,000	
Long-term liabilities:			
Notes payable (City National Bank)		450,000	
Total liabilities			$ 575,000

Stockholders' Equity

Paid-in capital:			
Common stock, $20 par (50,000 shares authorized,			
25,000 shares issued)	$500,000		
Excess of issue price over par	40,000		
Total paid-in capital		$540,000	
Retained earnings		749,500	
Total stockholders' equity			1,289,500
Total liabilities and stockholders' equity			$1,864,500

The board of directors is scheduled to meet January 6, 2004, to discuss the results of operations for 2003 and to consider the declaration of dividends for the fourth quarter of 2003. The chairman of the board has asked for your advice on the declaration of dividends.

1. ◖▬▶ What factors should the board consider in deciding whether to declare a cash dividend?
2. ◖▬▶ The board is considering the declaration of a stock dividend instead of a cash dividend. Discuss the issuance of a stock dividend from the point of view of (a) a stockholder and (b) the board of directors.

Activity 12–4
Into the Real World
Profiling a corporation

Select a public corporation you are familiar with or which interests you. Using the Internet, your school library, and other sources, develop a short (2 to 5 pages) profile of the corporation. Include in your profile the following information:

1. Name of the corporation.
2. State of incorporation.
3. Nature of its operations.
4. Total assets for the most recent balance sheet.
5. Total revenues for the most recent income statement.
6. Net income for the most recent income statement.
7. Classes of stock outstanding.
8. Market price of the stock outstanding.
9. High and low price of the stock for the past year.
10. Dividends paid for each share of stock during the past year.

In groups of three or four, discuss each corporate profile. Select one of the corporations, assuming that your group has $100,000 to invest in its stock. Summarize why your group selected the corporation it did and how financial accounting information may have affected your decision. Keep track of the performance of your corporation's stock for the remainder of the term.

Note: Most major corporations maintain "home pages" on the Internet. This home page provides a variety of information on the corporation and often includes the corporation's financial statements. In addition, the New York Stock Exchange Web site (**www.nyse.com**) includes links to the home pages of many listed companies. Financial statements can also be accessed using EDGAR, the electronic archives of financial statements filed with the Securities and Exchange Commission (SEC).

SEC documents can also be retrieved using the EdgarScan™ service from **Pricewater-houseCoopers** at **edgarscan.pwcglobal.com**. To obtain annual report information, key in a company name in the appropriate space. EdgarScan will list the reports, available to you for the company you've selected. Select the most recent annual report filing, identified as a 10-K or 10-K405. EdgarScan provides an outline of the report, including the separate financial statements, which can also be selected in an Excel® spreadsheet.

ANSWERS TO SELF-EXAMINATION QUESTIONS

Matching

1. O	4. I	7. H	10. K	13. L	16. Q	19. F
2. R	5. M	8. N	11. G	14. E	17. A	20. J
3. S	6. D	9. B	12. C	15. T	18. P	

Multiple Choice

1. **C** If a corporation has cumulative preferred stock outstanding, dividends that have been passed for prior years plus the dividend for the current year must be paid before dividends may be declared on common stock. In this case, dividends of $27,000 ($9,000 × 3) have been passed for the preceding three years, and the current year's dividends are $9,000, making a total of $36,000 (answer C) that must be paid to preferred stockholders before dividends can be declared on common stock.

2. **D** Paid-in capital is one of the two major subdivisions of the stockholders' equity of a corporation. It may result from many sources, including the issuance of cumulative preferred stock (answer A), the receipt of donated real estate (answer B), or the sale of a corporation's treasury stock (answer C).

3. **D** The Stockholders' Equity section of corporate balance sheets is divided into two principal subsections: (1) investments contributed by the stockholders and others and (2) net income retained in the business. Included as part of the investments by stockholders and others is the par of common stock (answer A), donated capital (answer B), and the par of preferred stock (answer C).

4. **C** Reacquired stock, known as treasury stock, should be listed in the Stockholders' Equity section (answer C) of the balance sheet. The price paid for the treasury stock is deducted from the total of all the stockholders' equity accounts.

5. **C** If a corporation that holds treasury stock declares a cash dividend, the dividends are not paid on the treasury shares. To do so would place the corporation in the position of earning income through dealing with itself. Thus, the corporation will record $44,000 (answer C) as cash dividends [(25,000 shares issued less 3,000 shares held as treasury stock) × $2 per share dividend].

Corporations: Income and Taxes, Stockholders' Equity, and Investments in Stocks

13

objectives

After studying this chapter, you should be able to:

1. Journalize the entries for corporate income taxes, including deferred income taxes.

2. Prepare an income statement reporting the following unusual items: discontinued operations, extraordinary items, and changes in accounting principles.

3. Prepare an income statement reporting earnings per share data.

4. Prepare financial statement presentations of stockholders' equity.

5. Describe the concept and the reporting of comprehensive income.

6. Describe the accounting for investments in stocks.

7. Describe alternative methods of combining businesses and how consolidated financial statements are prepared

8. Compute and interpret the price-earnings ratio.

I f you apply for a bank loan, you will be required to list your assets and liabilities on a loan application. In addition, you will be asked to indicate your monthly income. Assume that the day you were filling out the application, you won $3,000 in the state lottery. The $3,000 lottery winnings increase your assets by $3,000. Should you also show your lottery winnings as part of your monthly income?

The answer, of course, is no. Winning the lottery is an unusual event and, for most of us, a nonrecurring event. In determining whether to grant the loan, the bank is interested in your ability to make monthly loan payments. Such payments depend upon your recurring monthly income.

Businesses also experience unusual and nonrecurring events that affect their financial statements. Such events should be clearly disclosed in the financial statements so that stakeholders in the business will not misinterpret the financial effects of the events. In this chapter, we discuss unusual items that affect corporate income statements and illustrate how such items should be reported.

Corporate Income Taxes

objective 1

Journalize the entries for corporate income taxes, including deferred income taxes.

Under the United States tax code, corporations are taxable entities that must pay federal income taxes. Depending upon where it is located, a corporation may also be required to pay state and local income taxes. Although we limit our discussion to federal income taxes, the basic concepts also apply to other income taxes.

Payment of Income Taxes

Most corporations are required to pay estimated federal income taxes in four installments throughout the year. For example, assume that a corporation with a calendar-year accounting period estimates its income tax expense for the year as $84,000. The entry to record the first of the four estimated tax payments of $21,000 (1/4 of $84,000) is as follows:

Point of Interest

Individuals must pay estimated taxes (on the 15th of January, April, June, and September) if the amount of tax withholding is not sufficient to pay their taxes at the end of the year. This usually occurs when a significant portion of an individual's income is from rent, dividends, or interest.

April	15	Income Tax Expense	21 0 0 0 00	
		Cash		21 0 0 0 00
		To record quarterly payment of		
		estimated income tax.		

At year end, the actual taxable income and the related tax are determined.[1] If additional taxes are owed, the additional liability is recorded. If the total estimated tax payments are greater than the tax liability based on actual taxable income, the overpayment should be debited to a receivable account and credited to *Income Tax Expense*.

[1] A corporation's income tax returns and supporting records are subject to audits by taxing authorities, who may assess additional taxes. Because of this possibility, the liability for income taxes is sometimes described in the balance sheet as *Estimated income tax payable*.

Because income taxes are often a significant amount, they are normally reported on the income statement as a special deduction, as shown below in an excerpt from an income statement for **The Procter & Gamble Company**.

Year Ended June 30, 2000	(Amounts in millions)
Net Sales	$39,951
Cost of products sold	21,514
Marketing, research, and administrative expenses	12,483
Operating Income	5,954
Interest expense	722
Other income, net	304
Earnings Before Income Taxes	5,536
Income taxes	1,994
Net Earnings	$ 3,542

Allocation of Income Taxes

The **taxable income** of a corporation is determined according to the tax laws. It is often different from the income before income taxes reported in the income statement according to generally accepted accounting principles. As a result, the *income tax based on taxable income* usually differs from the *income tax based on income before taxes*. This difference may need to be allocated between various financial statement periods, depending on the nature of the items causing the differences.

Some differences between taxable income and income before income taxes are created because items are recognized in one period for tax purposes and in another period for income statement purposes. Such differences, called **temporary differences**, reverse or turn around in later years. Some examples of items that create temporary differences are listed below.

1. *Revenues or gains are taxed **after** they are reported in the income statement.* Example: In some cases, companies who make sales under an installment plan recognize revenue for financial reporting purposes when a sale is made but defer recognizing revenue for tax purposes until cash is collected.
2. *Expenses or losses are deducted in determining taxable income **after** they are reported in the income statement.* Example: Product warranty expense estimated and reported in the year of the sale for financial statement reporting is deducted for tax reporting when paid.
3. *Revenues or gains are taxed **before** they are reported in the income statement.* Example: Cash received in advance for magazine subscriptions is included in taxable income when received, but included in the income statement only when earned in a future period.
4. *Expenses or losses are deducted in determining taxable income **before** they are reported in the income statement.* Example: MACRS depreciation is used for tax purposes, and the straight-line method is used for financial reporting purposes.

Since temporary differences reverse in later years, they do not change or reduce the total amount of taxable income over the life of a business. Exhibit 1 illustrates the reversing nature of temporary differences in which a business uses MACRS depreciation for tax purposes and straight-line depreciation for financial statement purposes. MACRS recognizes more depreciation in the early years, but less depreciation in the later years. The total depreciation expense is the same for both methods over the life of the asset.

Exhibit 1 Temporary
Differences

As Exhibit 1 illustrates, temporary differences affect only the timing of when revenues and expenses are recognized for tax purposes. As a result, the total amount of taxes paid does not change. Only the timing of the payment of taxes is affected. In most cases, managers use tax-planning techniques so that temporary differences delay or defer the payment of taxes to later years. As a result, at the end of each year the amount of the current tax liability and the postponed (deferred) liability must be recorded.

To illustrate, assume that at the end of the first year of operations a corporation reports $300,000 income before income taxes on its income statement. If we assume an income tax rate of 40%, the income tax expense reported on the income statement is $120,000 ($300,000 × 40%).[2] However, to reduce the amount owed for current income taxes, the corporation uses tax planning to reduce the taxable income to $100,000. Thus, the income tax actually due for the year is only $40,000 ($100,000 × 40%). The $80,000 ($120,000 − $40,000) difference between the two tax amounts is created by timing differences in recognizing revenue. This amount is deferred to future years. The example is summarized below.

Income tax based on $300,000 reported income at 40%	$120,000
Income tax based on $100,000 taxable income at 40%	40,000
Income tax deferred to future years	$ 80,000

To match the current year's expenses (including income tax) against the current year's revenue on the income statement, income tax is allocated between periods, using the following journal entry:

Income Tax Expense		120 0 0 0 00	
Income Tax Payable			40 0 0 0 00
Deferred Income Tax Payable			80 0 0 0 00
To record income tax for the year.			

Q&A

A corporation has $300,000 income before income taxes, a 40% tax rate, and $130,000 taxable income. What is the amount of deferred income tax?

$68,000 [($300,000 × 40%) − ($130,000 × 40%)]

[2] For purposes of illustration, the 40% rate is assumed to include all federal, state, and local income taxes.

The income tax expense reported on the income statement is the total tax, $120,000, expected to be paid on the income for the year. In future years, the $80,000 in *Deferred Income Tax Payable* will be transferred to *Income Tax Payable* as the timing differences reverse and the taxes become due. For example, if $48,000 of the deferred tax reverses and becomes due in the second year, the following journal entry would be made in the second year:

Deferred Income Tax Payable	48 0 0 0 00	
Income Tax Payable		48 0 0 0 00
To record current liability for		
deferred tax.		

Point of Interest
Interest from investments in municipal bonds is also tax exempt for individual tax purposes.

The balance of *Deferred Income Tax Payable* at the end of a year is reported as a liability. The amount due within one year is classified as a current liability. The remainder is classified as a long-term liability or reported in a Deferred Credits section following the Long-Term Liabilities section.[3]

Differences between taxable income and income (before taxes) reported on the income statement may also arise because certain revenues are exempt from tax and certain expenses are not deductible in determining taxable income.[4] For example, interest income on municipal bonds may be exempt from taxation. Such differences create no special financial reporting problems, since the amount of income tax determined according to the tax laws is the *same* amount reported on the income statement.

Unusual Items that Affect the Income Statement

objective 2

Prepare an income statement reporting the following unusual items: discontinued operations, extraordinary items, and changes in accounting principles.

Three types of unusual items that may affect the current year's net income are:

1. The results of discontinued operations.
2. Extraordinary items that result in a gain or loss.
3. A change from one generally accepted accounting principle to another.

These items are reported separately in the income statement, as shown in the income statement for Jones Corporation in Exhibit 2. Many different terms and formats may be used. For example, the related tax effects of unusual items may be reported with the item with which they are associated or in the notes to the statement.

In the following paragraphs, we briefly discuss each of the three types of unusual items. We assume that these items are material to the financial statements. Immaterial items would not affect the normal financial statement presentation.

Discontinued Operations

A gain or loss from disposing of a business segment is reported on the income statement as a gain or loss from discontinued operations. The term **business segment** refers to a major line of business for a company, such as a division or a department or a certain class of customer. For example, assume that Jones Corporation

---

[3] In some cases, a deferred tax asset may arise for tax benefits to be received in the future. Such deferred tax assets are reported as either a current or a long-term asset, depending on when the benefits are expected to be realized.

[4] Such differences, which will not reverse with the passage of time, are sometimes called *permanent differences*.

Exhibit 2 Unusual Items in Income Statement

Jones Corporation
Income Statement
For the Year Ended December 31, 2003

Net sales	$9,600,000
Cost of merchandise sold	5,800,000
Gross profit	$3,800,000
Operating expenses	2,490,000
Income from continuing operations before income tax	$1,310,000
Income tax expense	620,000
Income from continuing operations	$ 690,000
Loss on discontinued operations (Note A)	100,000
Income before extraordinary items and cumulative effect	
of a change in accounting principle	$ 590,000
Extraordinary item:	
Gain on condemnation of land, net of applicable income	
tax of $65,000	150,000
Cumulative effect on prior years of changing to a different	
depreciation method (Note B)	92,000
Net income	$ 832,000

Note A.

On July 1 of the current year, the electrical products division of the corporation was sold at a loss of $100,000, net of applicable income tax of $50,000. The net sales of the division for the current year were $2,900,000. The assets sold were composed of inventories, equipment, and plant totaling $2,100,000. The purchaser assumed liabilities of $600,000.

Note B.

Depreciation of all property, plant, and equipment has been computed by the straight-line method in 2003. Prior to 2003, depreciation of equipment for one of the divisions had been computed on the double-declining-balance method. In 2003, the straight-line method was adopted for this division in order to achieve uniformity and to better match depreciation charges with the estimated economic utility of such assets. Consistent with APB Opinion No. 20, this change in depreciation has been applied to prior years. The effect of the change was to increase income by $30,000 before extraordinary items for 2003. The adjustment of $92,000 (after reduction for income tax of $88,000) to apply the new method to prior years is also included in income for 2003.

has separate divisions that produce electrical products, hardware supplies, and lawn equipment. Jones sells its electrical products division at a loss. As shown in Exhibit 2, this loss is deducted from Jones's income from continuing operations (income from its hardware and lawn equipment divisions). In addition, Note A discloses the identity of the segment sold, the disposal date, a description of the segment's assets and liabilities, and the manner of disposal.

Extraordinary Items

Extraordinary items result from events and transactions that (1) are significantly different (unusual) from the typical or the normal operating activities of the business and (2) occur infrequently. The gains and losses that result from natural disasters which occur infrequently, such as floods, earthquakes, and fires, are extraordinary

Events that are both unusual and infrequent are uncommon. For example, a recent edition of *Accounting Trends & Techniques* indicated that only 74 of 600 companies surveyed reported extraordinary items.

During 1999, **Ascent Entertainment Group, Inc.,** reported a combined loss of over $26 million from discontinued operations related to Ascent's sale of its sports-related businesses. Ascent's sports-related businesses included the **Denver Nuggets** and the **Colorado Avalanche.**

items. Gains or losses from condemning land or buildings for public use are also extraordinary. Such gains and losses, other than those from disposing of a business segment, should be reported in the income statement as extraordinary items, as shown in Exhibit 2.

Sometimes extraordinary items result in unusual financial results. For example, **Delta Air Lines** once reported an extraordinary gain of over $5.5 million as the result of the crash of one of its 727s. The plane that crashed was insured for $6.5 million, but its book value in Delta's accounting records was $962,000.

Gains and losses on the disposal of fixed assets are *not* extraordinary items. This is because (1) they are not unusual and (2) they recur from time to time in the normal operations of a business. Likewise, gains and losses from the sale of investments are usual and recurring for most businesses.

Changes in Accounting Principles

A recent edition of *Accounting Trends & Techniques* indicated that the majority of accounting changes were due to adopting a new accounting standard issued by the Financial Accounting Standards Board.

Businesses are often required to change their accounting principles when the Financial Accounting Standards Board (FASB) issues a new accounting standard. In addition, a business may voluntarily change from one generally accepted accounting principle to another. For example, a corporation may change from the fifo to the lifo method of costing inventory to better match revenues and expenses. Changes in generally accepted accounting principles should be disclosed in the financial statements (or in notes to the statements) of the period in which they occur. This disclosure should include the following:

1. The nature of the change.
2. The justification for the change.
3. The effect on the current year's net income.
4. The cumulative effect of the change on the net income of prior periods.

To illustrate, assume that one of Jones Corporation's divisions changes from the double-declining-balance method to the straight-line method of depreciation. As shown in Exhibit 2, the cumulative effect of this change is reported after the extraordinary items. The effect on the prior period is explained in Note B. If financial statements for prior periods are also presented, they should be restated as if the change had been made in the prior periods, and the effect of the restatement should be reported either on the face of the statements or in a note.

Reporting unusual items separately on the income statement allows investors to isolate the effects of these items on income and cash flows. By reporting such items, investors and other users of the financial statements can consider such factors in assessing a business's future income and cash flows.

Earnings per Common Share

objective 3

Prepare an income statement reporting earnings per share data.

The amount of net income is often used by investors and creditors in evaluating a company's profitability. However, net income by itself is difficult to use in comparing companies of different sizes. Also, trends in net income may be difficult to evaluate, using only net income, if there have been significant changes in a company's stockholders' equity. Thus, the profitability of companies is often expressed as earnings per share. **Earnings per common share (EPS)**, sometimes called **basic earnings per share**, is the net income per share of common stock outstanding during a period.

Because of its importance, earnings per share is reported in the financial press and by various investor services, such as **Moody's** and **Standard & Poor's**. Changes in earnings per share can lead to significant changes in the price of a corporation's stock in the marketplace. For example, the stock of **Scientific-Atlanta Inc.** surged by over 13 percent to $39 per share after the company announced earnings per share of 53 cents as compared to 25 cents per share a year earlier. Wall Street analysts had been expecting earnings per share of 41 cents.

Corporations whose stock is traded in a public market must report earnings per common share on their income statements.[5] If no preferred stock is outstanding, the earnings per common share is calculated as follows:

$$\text{Earnings per common share} = \frac{\text{Net income}}{\text{Number of common shares outstanding}}$$

When the number of common shares outstanding has changed during the period, a weighted average number of shares outstanding is used. If a company has preferred stock outstanding, the net income must be reduced by the amount of any preferred dividends, as shown below.

$$\text{Earnings per common share} = \frac{\text{Net income} - \text{Preferred stock dividends}}{\text{Number of common shares outstanding}}$$

Comparing the earnings per share of two or more years, based on only the net incomes of those years, could be misleading. For example, assume that Jones Corporation, whose partial income statement was presented in Exhibit 2, reported $700,000 net income for 2002. Also assume that no extraordinary or other unusual items were reported in 2002. Jones has no preferred stock outstanding and has 200,000 common shares outstanding in 2002 and 2003. The earnings per common share is $3.50 ($700,000/200,000 shares) for 2002 and $4.16 ($832,000/200,000 shares) for 2003. Comparing the two earnings per share amounts suggests that operations have improved. However, the 2003 earnings per share comparable to the $3.50 is $3.45, which is the income from continuing operations of $690,000 divided by 200,000 shares. The latter amount indicates a slight downturn in normal earnings.

When unusual items exist, earnings per common share should be reported for those items. To illustrate, a partial income statement for Jones Corporation, showing earnings per common share, is shown in Exhibit 3. In this income statement, Jones reports all the earnings per common share amounts on the face of the income statement. However, only earnings per share amounts for income from continuing operations and net income are required to be presented on the face of the statement. The other per share amounts may be presented in the notes to the financial statements.[6]

Exhibit 3 Income Statement with Earnings per Share

Jones Corporation
Income Statement
For the Year Ended December 31, 2003

Earnings per common share:	
Income from continuing operations	$3.45
Loss on discontinued operations (Note A)	0.50
Income before extraordinary items and cumulative effect of a change in accounting principle	$2.95
Extraordinary item:	
Gain on condemnation of land, net of applicable income tax of $65,000	0.75
Cumulative effect on prior years of changing to a different depreciation method (Note B)	0.46
Net income	$4.16

[5] *Statement of Financial Accounting Standards No. 128,* "Earnings per Share," Financial Accounting Standards Board (Norwalk, Connecticut: 1997).
[6] Ibid., pars. 36 & 37.

In the preceding paragraphs, we have assumed a simple capital structure with only common stock or common stock and preferred stock outstanding. Often, however, corporations have complex capital structures with various types of securities outstanding, such as convertible preferred stock, options, warrants, and contingently issuable shares. In such cases, the possible effects of converting such securities to common stock must be calculated and reported as *earnings per common share assuming dilution* or *diluted earnings per share*.[7] This topic is discussed further in advanced accounting texts.

Reporting Stockholders' Equity

objective 4

Prepare financial statement presentations of stockholders' equity.

As with other sections of the balance sheet, alternative terms and formats may be used in reporting stockholders' equity. In addition, the significant changes in the sources of stockholders' equity—paid-in capital and retained earnings—may be reported in separate statements or notes that support the balance sheet presentation.

Reporting Paid-In Capital

Two alternatives for reporting paid-in capital in the balance sheet are shown in Exhibit 4. In the first example, each class of stock is listed first, followed by its related paid-in capital accounts. In the second example, the stock accounts are listed first. The other paid-in capital accounts are listed as a single item described as *Additional paid-in capital*. These combined accounts could also be described as *Capital in excess of par (or stated value) of shares* or a similar title.

Exhibit 4 Paid-In Capital Section of Stockholders' Equity

Stockholders' Equity		
Paid-in capital:		
Preferred $5 stock, cumulative, $50 par (2,000 shares authorized and issued)	$100,000	
Excess of issue price over par	10,000	$ 110,000
Common stock, $20 par (50,000 shares authorized, 45,000 shares issued)	$900,000	
Excess of issue price over par	132,000	1,032,000
From donated land		60,000
Total paid-in capital		$1,202,000

Shareholders' Equity	
Contributed capital:	
Preferred 10% stock, cumulative, $50 par (2,000 shares authorized and issued)	$100,000
Common stock, $20 par (50,000 shares authorized, 45,000 shares issued)	900,000
Additional paid-in capital	202,000
Total contributed capital	$1,202,000

---

[7] Ibid., pars. 11–39.

The 1999 edition of *Accounting Trends & Techniques* reported that over 90% of the companies surveyed presented a statement of stockholders' equity.

The 1999 edition of *Accounting Trends & Techniques* indicated that 2.5% of the companies surveyed presented a separate statement of retained earnings, 1% presented a combined income and retained earnings statement, and 2.6% presented changes in retained earnings in the notes to the financial statements. The other 94% of the companies presented changes in retained earnings in a statement of stockholders' equity.

Significant changes in paid-in capital during a period may be presented either in a *statement of stockholders' equity* or in notes to the financial statements. We describe and illustrate the statement of stockholders' equity later in this section. In addition, relevant rights and privileges of the various classes of stock outstanding must be disclosed.[8] Examples of types of information that must be disclosed include dividend and liquidation preferences, rights to participate in earnings, conversion rights, and redemption rights. Such information may be disclosed on the face of the balance sheet or in the accompanying notes.

Reporting Retained Earnings

A corporation may report changes in retained earnings by preparing a separate retained earnings statement, a combined income and retained earnings statement, or a statement of stockholders' equity.

When a separate retained earnings statement is prepared, the beginning balance of retained earnings is reported. The net income is then added (or net loss is subtracted) and any dividends are subtracted to arrive at the ending retained earnings for the period. An example of a such a statement for Adang Corporation is shown in Exhibit 5.

Exhibit 5 Retained Earnings Statement

Adang Corporation Retained Earnings Statement For the Year Ended June 30, 2003		
Retained earnings, July 1, 2002		$350,000
Net income	$280,000	
Less dividends declared	75,000	
Increase in retained earnings		205,000
Retained earnings, June 30, 2003		$555,000

An alternative format for presenting the retained earnings statement is to combine it with the income statement. An advantage of the combined format is that it emphasizes net income as the connecting link between the income statement and the retained earnings portion of stockholders' equity. Since the combined form is not often used, we do not illustrate it.

Appropriations

The retained earnings available for use as dividends may be restricted by action of a corporation's board of directors. The amount restricted, called an **appropriation**, remains part of the retained earnings. However, it must be disclosed, usually in the notes to the financial statements.

Appropriations may be classified as either legal, contractual, or discretionary. The board of directors may be legally required to restrict retained earnings because of state laws. For example, some state laws require that retained earnings be restricted by the amount of treasury stock purchased, so that legal capital will not be used for dividends. The board may also be required to restrict retained earnings because of contractual requirements. For example, the terms of a bank loan may require restrictions, so that money for repaying the loan will not be used for dividends. Finally, the board

The 1999 edition of *Accounting Trends & Techniques* reported that 329 of the 600 companies surveyed disclosed dividend restrictions in notes to their financial statements.

[8] *Statement of Financial Accounting Standards No. 129,* "Disclosure Information about Capital Structure," Financial Accounting Standards Board (Norwalk, Connecticut: 1997).

may restrict retained earnings voluntarily. For example, the board may limit dividend distributions so that more money is available for expanding the business.

Prior Period Adjustments

Material errors in a prior period's net income may arise from mathematical mistakes and from mistakes in applying accounting principles. The effect of material errors that are not discovered within the same fiscal period in which they occurred should not be included in determining net income for the current period. Instead, corrections of such errors, called **prior period adjustments**, are reported in the retained earnings statement. These adjustments are reported as an adjustment to the retained earnings balance at the beginning of the period in which the error is discovered and corrected. Because prior period adjustments are rare, we do not illustrate their reporting.

Statement of Stockholders' Equity

Significant changes in stockholders' equity should be reported for the period in which they occur. These changes may be reported in a **statement of stockholders' equity**. This statement is often prepared in a columnar format, where each column represents a major stockholders' equity classification. Changes in each classification are then described in the left-hand column. Exhibit 6 is a statement of stockholders' equity for Telex Inc.

Exhibit 6 Statement of Stockholders' Equity

Telex Inc.
Statement of Stockholders' Equity
For the Year Ended December 31, 2003

	Preferred Stock	Common Stock	Paid-In Capital in Excess of Par— Common Stock	Retained Earnings	Treasury (Common) Stock	Total
Balance, January 1	$5,000,000	$10,000,000	$3,000,000	$2,000,000	$(500,000)	$19,500,000
Net income				850,000		850,000
Dividends on preferred stock				(250,000)		(250,000)
Dividends on common stock				(400,000)		(400,000)
Issuance of additional common stock		500,000	50,000			550,000
Purchase of treasury stock					(30,000)	(30,000)
Balance, December 31	$5,000,000	$10,500,000	$3,050,000	$2,200,000	$(530,000)	$20,220,000

Comprehensive Income

In 1997, the Financial Accounting Standards Board issued an accounting standard that required the reporting concept referred to as *comprehensive income*.[9] This standard defines **comprehensive income** as all changes in stockholders' equity during

[9] *Statement of Financial Accounting Standards No. 130,* "Reporting Comprehensive Income," Financial Accounting Standards Board (Norwalk, Connecticut: 1997).

a period except those resulting from dividends and stockholders' investments. Under this standard, companies must report traditional net income plus or minus other comprehensive income items to arrive at comprehensive income. *Other comprehensive income items* include foreign currency items, pension liability adjustments, and unrealized gains and losses on investments.

To the extent that other comprehensive income items give rise to tax effects, the taxes should be allocated to these items as we illustrated earlier in this chapter. The cumulative effects of other comprehensive income items must be reported separately from retained earnings and paid-in capital on the balance sheet. When other comprehensive income items are not present, the income statement and balance sheet formats are similar to those we have illustrated in this and preceding chapters.

Companies may report comprehensive income on the income statement, in a separate statement of comprehensive income, or in the statement of stockholders' equity. In addition, companies may use terms other than comprehensive income, such as *total nonowner changes in equity.*

You should note that comprehensive income does not affect the determination of net income or retained earnings as we have discussed and illustrated. In the next section, we will illustrate the reporting of unrealized gains and losses on investments as part of other comprehensive income.

Accounting for Investments in Stocks

objective 6

Describe the accounting for investments in stocks.

Real World

Warren Buffett became one of the wealthiest men in the world through wise and patient investing. Buffett invests through a public company called **Berkshire Hathaway Inc.**, of which he owns 40%. Berkshire Hathaway started as an old-line textile company. Today, however, it has over $34 billion of equity investment holdings, listed on its balance sheet as "available-for-sale" securities. Some of these investments include **Coca-Cola Company, Gillette Company,** and **American Express.**

Corporations not only issue stock, but they also purchase stocks of other companies for investment purposes. Like individuals, businesses have a variety of reasons for investing in stocks, called **equity securities**. A business may purchase stocks as a means of earning a return (income) on excess cash that it does not need for its normal operations. Such investments are usually for a short period of time. In other cases, a business may purchase the stock of another company as a means of developing or maintaining business relationships with the other company. A business may also purchase common stock as a means of gaining control of another company's operations. In these two latter cases, the business usually intends to hold the investment for a long period of time.

The equity securities in which a business invests may be classified as trading securities or available-for-sale securities. **Trading securities** are securities that management intends to actively trade for profit. Businesses holding trading securities are those whose normal operations involve buying and selling securities. Examples of such businesses include banks and insurance companies. **Available-for-sale securities** are securities that management expects to sell in the future, but which are not actively traded for profit. In this section, we describe and illustrate the accounting for available-for-sale equity securities. The accounting for trading securities is described and illustrated in advanced accounting texts.

Short-Term Investments in Stocks

Rather than allow excess cash to be idle until it is needed, a business may invest all or part of it in income-yielding securities. Since these investments can be quickly sold and converted to cash as needed, they are called **temporary investments** or **marketable securities**. Although such investments may be retained for several years, they continue to be classified as temporary, provided they meet two conditions. First, the securities are readily marketable and can be sold for cash at any time. Second, management intends to sell the securities when the business needs cash for operations.

Temporary investments are recorded in a current asset account, *Marketable Securities*, at their cost. This cost includes all amounts spent to acquire the securities, such as broker's commissions. Any dividends received on the investment are recorded as a debit to *Cash* and a credit to *Dividend Revenue*.[10]

To illustrate, assume that on June 1 Crabtree Co. purchased 2,000 shares of Inis Corporation common stock at $89.75 per share plus a brokerage fee of $500. On October 1, Inis declared a $0.90 per share cash dividend payable on November 30. Crabtree's entries to record the stock purchase and the receipt of the dividend are as follows:

June	1	Marketable Securities	180 0 0 0 00	
		Cash		180 0 0 0 00
		Purchased 2,000 shares of Inis		
		Corporation common stock		
		($89.75 × 2,000 shares = $179,500;		
		$179,500 + $500 = $180,000).		
Nov.	30	Cash	1 8 0 0 00	
		Dividend Revenue		1 8 0 0 00
		Received dividend on Inis Corporation		
		common stock		
		(2,000 shares × $0.90 = $1,800).		

On the balance sheet, temporary investments are reported at their fair market value. Market values are normally available from stock quotations in financial newspapers, such as *The Wall Street Journal*. Any difference between the fair market values of the securities and their cost is an **unrealized holding gain or loss**. This gain or loss is termed "unrealized" because a transaction (the sale of the securities) is necessary before a gain or loss becomes real (realized).

To illustrate, assume that Crabtree Co.'s portfolio of temporary investments has the following fair market values and unrealized gains and losses on December 31, 2003:

Common Stock	Cost	Market	Unrealized Gain (Loss)
Edwards Inc.	$150,000	$190,000	$40,000
SWS Corp.	200,000	200,000	—
Inis Corporation	180,000	210,000	30,000
Bass Co.	160,000	150,000	(10,000)
Total	$690,000	$750,000	$60,000

If income taxes of $18,000 are allocated to the unrealized gain, Crabtree's temporary investments should be reported at their total cost of $690,000, plus the unrealized gain (net of applicable income tax) of $42,000 ($60,000 − $18,000), as shown in Exhibit 7.

The unrealized gain (net of applicable taxes) of $42,000 should also be reported as an *other comprehensive income item*, as we mentioned in the preceding section. For example, assume that Crabtree Co. has net income of $720,000 for the year ended December 31, 2003. Crabtree elects to report net income and comprehensive income on one financial statement, *Statement of Income and Comprehensive Income*, as shown in Exhibit 8.

---

[10] Stock dividends received on an investment are not journalized, since they have no effect on the investor's assets and revenues.

Exhibit 7 Temporary Investments on the Balance Sheet

Crabtree Co. Balance Sheet December 31, 2003		
Assets		
Current assets:		
Cash		$119,500
Temporary investments in marketable securities at cost	$690,000	
Plus unrealized gain (net of applicable income tax of $18,000)	42,000	732,000

Exhibit 8 Statement of Income and Comprehensive Income

Crabtree Co. Statement of Income and Comprehensive Income For the Year Ended December 31, 2003	
Net income	$720,000
Other comprehensive income:	
Unrealized gain on temporary investments in marketable securities (net of applicable income tax of $18,000)	42,000
Comprehensive income	$762,000

Unrealized losses are reported in a similar manner. Unrealized gains and losses are reported as other comprehensive income items until the related securities are sold. When temporary securities are sold, the unrealized gains or losses become realized and are included in determining net income.[11]

Long-Term Investments in Stocks

Long-term investments in stocks are not intended as a source of cash in the normal operations of the business. They are reported in the balance sheet under the caption **Investments**, which usually follows the Current Assets section.

There are two methods of accounting for long-term investments in stock: (1) the cost method and (2) the equity method. The method used depends on whether the investor (the buyer of the stock) has a significant influence over the operating and financing activities of the company (the investee) whose stock is owned. If the investor does not have a significant influence, the cost method is used. If the investor has a significant influence, the equity method is used. Evidence of such influence includes the percentage of ownership, the existence of intercompany transactions, and the interchange of managerial personnel. Generally, if the investor owns 20% or more of the voting stock of the investee, it is assumed that the investor has significant influence over the investee.

---

[11]To avoid double-counting, realized gains and losses must be removed from comprehensive income. These adjustments are discussed in advanced accounting texts.

Cost Method

Under the **cost method**, the accounting for long-term investments in stocks is similar to that for short-term investments in stocks, which we illustrated in the preceding section. The cost of the stocks is debited to an investment (asset) account. Cash dividends received on the stock are recorded as a debit to *Cash* and a credit to *Dividend Revenue*. On the balance sheet, the stocks are reported at their fair market value net of any applicable income tax effects. In addition, the unrealized gains and losses are reported as part of the comprehensive income.[12]

To illustrate the purchase of stock and the receipt of dividends under the cost method, assume that on March 1, Makowski Corporation purchases 100 shares of Compton Corporation common stock at 59 plus a brokerage fee of $40. On April 30, Compton Corporation declares a $2-per-share dividend, payable on June 15. Makowski's entries to record the investment and the dividend are as follows:

The 1999 edition of *Accounting Trends & Techniques* indicated that 15% of the companies surveyed used the cost method to account for investments.

Mar.	1	Investment in Compton Corp. Stock	5 9 4 0 00	
		Cash		5 9 4 0 00
		Purchased 100 shares of Compton		
		Corp. common stock at 59 plus		
		brokerage fee of $40.		
June	15	Cash	2 0 0 00	
		Dividend Revenue		2 0 0 00
		Received dividend of $2 per share on		
		Compton Corp. common stock.		

Equity Method

Under the **equity method**, a stock purchase is recorded in the same manner as if the cost method were used. The equity method, however, is different from the cost method in the way in which net income and cash dividends of the investee are recorded. The equity method of recording these items is summarized as follows:

The 1999 edition of *Accounting Trends & Techniques* indicated that over 47% of the companies surveyed used the equity method to account for investments.

1. The investor's share of the periodic net income of the investee is recorded as an *increase in the investment account* and as *revenue for the period*. Likewise, the investor's share of an investee's net loss is recorded as a *decrease in the investment account* and as a *loss for the period*.
2. The investor's share of cash dividends from the investee is recorded as an *increase in the cash account* and a *decrease in the investment account*.

To illustrate, assume that on January 2, Hally Inc. pays cash of $350,000 for 40% of the common stock and net assets of Brock Corporation. Assume also that, for the year ending December 31, Brock Corporation reports net income of $105,000 and declares and pays $45,000 in dividends. Using the equity method, Hally Inc. (the investor) records these transactions as follows:

Jan.	2	Investment in Brock Corp. Stock	350 0 0 0 00	
		Cash		350 0 0 0 00
		Purchased 40% of Brock Corp.		
		common stock.		

[12]An exception to reporting unrealized gains and losses as part of comprehensive income is made if the decrease in the market value for a stock is considered permanent. In this case, the cost of the individual stock is written down (decreased), and the amount of the write-down is included in net income.

Dec.	31	Investment in Brock Corp. Stock	42 0 0 0 00		
		Income of Brock Corp.		42 0 0 0 00	
		Recorded share (40%) of Brock Corp.			
		net income of $105,000.			
	31	Cash	18 0 0 0 00		
		Investment in Brock Corp. Stock		18 0 0 0 00	
		Recorded share (40%) of dividends of			
		$45,000 paid by Brock Corp.			

The combined effect of recording 40% of Brock Corporation's net income and dividends is to increase Hally's interest in the net assets of Brock by $24,000 ($42,000 − $18,000), as shown below.

Q&A

Assume that Hally Inc. increased its ownership in Brock Corporation to 60% at the beginning of the next year. If Brock Corporation reported net income of $80,000 and declared dividends of $50,000, how much would Hally Inc. debit Investment in Brock Corp. Stock?

$18,000 [($80,000 × 60%) − ($50,000 × 60%)]

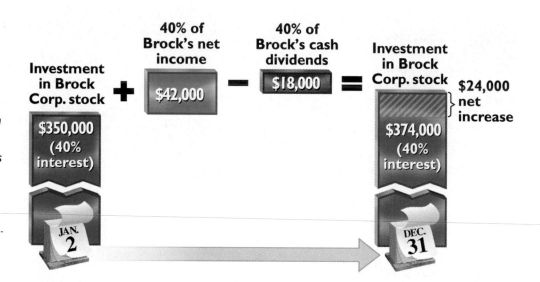

Sale of Investments in Stocks

The accounting for the sale of stock is the same for both short-term and long-term investments. When shares of stock are sold, the investment account is credited for the carrying amount (book value) of the shares sold. The cash or receivables account is debited for the proceeds (sales price less commission and other selling costs). Any difference between the proceeds and the carrying amount is recorded as a gain or loss on the sale and is included in the determination of net income.

To illustrate, assume that an investment in Drey Inc. stock has a carrying amount of $15,700 when it is sold on March 1. If the proceeds from the sale of the stock are $17,500, the entry to record the transaction is as follows:

Mar.	1	Cash	17 5 0 0 00		
		Investment in Drey Inc. Stock		15 7 0 0 00	
		Gain on Sale of Investments		1 8 0 0 00	
		Sold investment in Drey Inc. stock.			

BUSINESS ON STAGE

Buying and Selling Stocks

After you have evaluated a business and identified companies in which you would like to make an investment, how would you go about making the purchase? The most common method is to purchase common stock through a stockbroker, or account representative. A *stockbroker* is a person who executes trades on the major stock exchanges on your behalf. Stockbrokers can be associated with large "full-service" firms, such as **Merrill Lynch**; "discount" brokerage firms, such as **OLDE Discount Brokers**; or regional and local firms.

Once you've selected your stockbroker, you begin by opening an account. This usually involves placing money in the account. After your account is opened, you can place an order for the purchase of your selected stocks. There are two basic types of purchase orders—a market order and a limit order.

A *market order* instructs the broker to buy the stock at the best possible price. If the stock is actively traded, the buy price will usually be close to the last traded price prior to the order. Stockbrokers usually execute trades within minutes of taking an order. A *limit order* instructs the broker to buy the stock at a specified price or lower. An example of a limit order would be to buy 50 shares of **Coca-Cola** common stock at $60 or lower. The limit order prohibits the broker from purchasing the stock at a price higher than $60.

When you decide to sell, you can place a stop-loss order. With a *stop-loss order*, you set a selling market price below the current price. If the market price drops to your limit, then the sale is executed, thus limiting your loss. After your trade is executed, you will receive a statement confirming your trade, which shows your investment, the number of shares bought or sold, the dollar value, and the stockbroker's commission. These statements should be kept for tax purposes.

Internet trading is an alternative to using a stockbroker. For more information, see E*TRADE's home page at **www.etrade.com**. ■

Business Combinations

objective 7

Describe alternative methods of combining businesses and how consolidated financial statements are prepared.

Each year, many businesses combine in order to produce more efficiently or to diversify product lines. Business combinations often involve complex accounting principles and terminology. Our objective in this section is to introduce you to some of the unique terminology and concepts related to business combinations. We also briefly describe the use and preparation of consolidated financial statements.

Mergers and Consolidations

One corporation may acquire all the assets and liabilities of another corporation, which is then dissolved. This joining of two corporations is called a **merger**. The acquiring company may use cash, debt, or its own stock as the payment. Whatever the form of payment, the amount received by the dissolving corporation is distributed to its stockholders in final liquidation.

A new corporation may be created, and the assets and liabilities of two or more existing corporations transferred to it. This type of combination is called a **consolidation**. The new corporation usually issues its own stock in exchange for the net assets acquired. The original corporations are then dissolved. For example, **Exxon-Mobil Corporation** became the new consolidated company that resulted from the combining of the individual corporations—Exxon and Mobil.

Boeing Co. acquired **McDonnell Douglas Corporation** for $15 billion in mid-1997. The merged company became the United States' biggest aerospace company, with projected sales of more than $38 billion. As a result of the merger, McDonnell Douglas no longer exists as a separate company.

The 1999 edition of *Accounting Trends & Techniques* reported that 92% of the business combinations surveyed were accounted for by the purchase method.

Parent and Subsidiary Corporations

Business combinations may also occur when one corporation buys a controlling share of the outstanding voting stock of one or more other corporations. In this case, none of the corporations dissolve. The corporations continue as separate legal entities in a parent-subsidiary relationship. The corporation owning all or a majority of the voting stock of the other corporation is called the **parent company**. The corporation that is controlled is called the **subsidiary company**. Two or more corporations closely related through stock ownership are sometimes called **affiliated** companies. An example of an affiliated company is **Waldenbooks**, a subsidiary of **Kmart**.

A corporation may acquire the controlling share of the voting common stock of another corporation by paying cash, exchanging other assets, issuing debt, or using some combination of these methods. The stockholders of the acquired company, in turn, transfer their stock to the parent corporation. In such cases, the transaction is recorded like a normal purchase of assets, and the combination is accounted for by the **purchase method**.

A parent-subsidiary relationship may be created by exchanging the voting common stock of the acquiring corporation (the parent) for the common stock of the acquired corporation (the subsidiary). If at least 90% of the stock of the subsidiary is acquired in this way, the transaction is a pooling of interests, and the combination is accounted for by the **pooling-of-interests method**. In a pooling of interests, the stockholders of the acquired company (the subsidiary) become stockholders of the acquiring company (the parent).

The accounting for a purchase and a pooling of interests are significantly different. A purchase is accounted for as a *sale-purchase transaction*, whereas a pooling of interests is accounted for as a *joining of ownership interests*. Because businesses must meet very strict criteria to use the pooling-of-interests method, the vast majority of business combinations are accounted for by using the purchase method.[13]

Consolidated Financial Statements

Although parent and subsidiary corporations may operate as a single economic unit, they continue to maintain separate accounting records and prepare their own periodic financial statements. At the end of the year, the financial statements of the parent and subsidiary are combined and reported as a single company. These combined financial statements are called **consolidated financial statements**. Such statements are usually identified by adding "and subsidiary(ies)" to the name of the parent corporation or by adding "consolidated" to the statement title.

To the stockholders of the parent company, consolidated financial statements are more meaningful than separate statements for each corporation. This is because the parent company, in substance, controls the subsidiaries, even though the parent and its subsidiaries are separate entities.

When a business combination is accounted for as a purchase, the subsidiary's net assets are reported in the consolidated balance sheet at their fair market value at the time of the purchase. In some cases, a parent may pay more than the fair market value of a subsidiary's net assets because the subsidiary has prospects for high future earnings. The difference between the amount paid by the parent and the fair market value of the subsidiary's net assets is reported on the consolidated balance sheet as an intangible asset. This asset is identified as **Goodwill** or **Excess of cost of business acquired over related net assets**.

When a consolidated balance sheet is prepared, the ownership interest of the parent in the subsidiary's stock, which is the balance in the parent's investment in subsidiary account, must be eliminated. This is done by eliminating the parent's investment in subsidiary account against the balances of the subsidiary's stockholders' equity accounts.

---

[13]The FASB has proposed a standard that would eliminate the pooling-of-interests method.

A recent edition of *Accounting Trends & Techniques* indicates that most of the companies surveyed reported minority interest in the long-term liabilities (noncurrent) section of the consolidated balance sheet.

If the parent owns less than 100% of the subsidiary stock, the subsidiary stock owned by outsiders is *not* eliminated but is normally reported immediately preceding the consolidated stockholders' equity. This amount is described as the **minority interest**.

When the data on the financial statements of the parent and its subsidiaries are combined to form the consolidated statements, intercompany transactions are given special attention. An example of such a transaction is the parent purchasing goods from the subsidiary or the subsidiary loaning money to the parent. These transactions affect the individual accounts of the parent and subsidiary and thus the financial statements of both companies.[14] To illustrate, assume that P Inc. (the parent) sold merchandise to S Inc. (the subsidiary) for $90,000. The merchandise cost P Inc. $50,000. In turn, S Inc. sold the merchandise to a customer for $120,000.

The individual income statements for P Inc. and S Inc. are shown in Exhibit 9. The consolidated (combined) income statement is shown in Exhibit 10. The consolidated income statement presents the income statements for P Inc. and S Inc. as if they were one operating entity. Thus, the $90,000 sale (P Inc.) and the $90,000 cost of merchandise sold (S Inc.) are eliminated. This is because the consolidated entity cannot sell to itself or buy from itself.

Exhibit 9 Income Statements for P Inc. and S Inc.

	P Inc.		S Inc.	
Sales		$950,000		$400,000
Cost of merchandise sold		625,000		240,000
Gross profit		$325,000		$160,000
Operating expenses:				
Selling expenses	$155,000		$55,000	
Administrative expenses	85,000	240,000	35,000	90,000
Net income		$ 85,000		$ 70,000

Exhibit 10 Consolidated Income Statement for P Inc. and S Inc.

Sales		$1,260,000*
Cost of merchandise sold		775,000**
Gross profit		$ 485,000
Operating expenses:		
Selling expenses	$210,000	
Administrative expenses	120,000	330,000
Net income		$ 155,000

*$950,000 − $90,000 + $400,000
**$625,000 + $240,000 − $90,000

General Motors Corporation is a multinational company that consolidates its foreign subsidiaries, such as the European *Opel* division, into U.S. dollars.

Many U.S. corporations own subsidiaries in foreign countries. Such corporations are often called *multinational corporations*. The financial statements of the foreign subsidiary are usually prepared in the foreign currency. Before the financial statements of foreign subsidiaries are consolidated with their domestic parent's financial statements, the amounts shown on the statements for the foreign companies must be converted to U.S. dollars.

---

[14] Examples of accounts often affected by intercompany transactions include *Accounts Receivable* and *Accounts Payable*, *Interest Receivable* and *Interest Payable*, and *Interest Expense* and *Interest Revenue*.

FINANCIAL ANALYSIS AND INTERPRETATION

objective 8

Compute and interpret the
price-earnings ratio.

The assessment of a firm's growth potential and future earnings prospects is indicated by how much the market is willing to pay per dollar of a company's earnings. This ratio, called the price-earnings ratio, or **P/E ratio**, is commonly included in stock market quotations reported by the financial press. A high P/E ratio indicates that the market expects high growth and earnings in the future. Likewise, a low P/E ratio indicates lower growth and earnings expectations.

The price-earnings ratio on common stock is computed by dividing the stock's market price per share at a specific date by the company's annual earnings per share, as shown below.

$$\text{Price-earnings ratio} = \frac{\textbf{Market price per share of common stock}}{\textbf{Earnings per share of common stock}}$$

To illustrate, assume that Harper Inc. reported earnings per share of $1.64 in 2003 and $1.35 in 2002. The market prices per common share are $20.50 at the end of 2003 and $13.50 at the end of 2002. The price-earnings ratio on this stock is computed as follows:

	Price-Earnings Ratio
Year 2003	12.5 ($20.50/$1.64)
Year 2002	10.0 ($13.50/$1.35)

The price-earnings ratio indicates that a share of Harper Inc.'s common stock was selling for 10 times the amount of earnings per share at the end of 2002. At the end of 2003, the common stock was selling for 12.5 times the amount of earnings per share. These results would indicate a generally improving expectation of growth and earnings for Harper Inc. However, a prospective investor should also consider the price-earnings ratios for competing firms in the same industry.

ENCORE

Monster Eats into Mattell's Profits

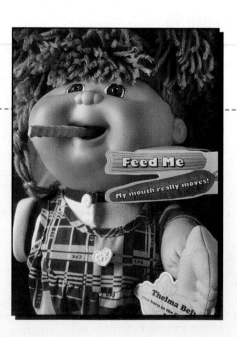

Mattell Inc., one of the largest toy makers in the world, is best known for its Barbie dolls, Fisher-Price infant and preschool toys, Hot Wheels die-cast cars, and its Cabbage Patch dolls. It is estimated that over 80 million Cabbage Patch dolls have been sold since they were introduced in 1983.

In the late 1990s, Mattell decided to introduce a new version of the Cabbage Patch dolls, called Snacktime Kids. The Snacktime Kids came with pieces of plastic shaped carrots, pretzels, biscuits, and licorice that could be put into the doll's mechanical mouth. Once in the doll's mouth, a battery-driven motor "chewed" them and ejected them into a pack on the doll's back.

Unfortunately, the dolls could not discern between the plastic snacks and other small objects provided by its owner, such as hair and fingers. One young father demonstrated how he was forced to decapitate a Snacktime Kid after it "attacked" his daughter. Evidently, the doll began devouring the little girl's hair as if it were spaghetti. Fearing the worst, the father terminated the ravenous toy *with extreme*

prejudice. Similar hair-gobbling incidents were reported across the country.

Mattell announced a refund program for the dolls, offering to buy back Snacktime Kids from parents for $40 a doll. Mattell estimated that 500,000 Snacktime Kids had been sold and another 200,000 dolls were still on the shelves. The buyback of the monster dolls cost Mattell $10 million in sales and $8 million in after-tax

earnings. In addition, at least one lawsuit claiming grievous psychological trauma was filed against Mattell. The lawsuit asked for $25 million in punitive damages.

Although Mattell hoped that the buyback program would have a non-recurring impact on its profits, it wasn't the first time that Mattell had

had to pull a toy from the market. In the early 1990s, Mattell pulled Teacher Barbie from stores after the talking doll was criticized by educators, who said it set a bad example with comments like, "Math class is tough." Teacher Barbie was "reeducated," however, and put back on the market. ■

KEY POINTS

1 Journalize the entries for corporate income taxes, including deferred income taxes.

Corporations are subject to federal income tax and are required to make estimated payments throughout the year. To record the payment of estimated tax, Income Tax is debited and Cash is credited. If additional taxes are owed at the end of the year, Income Tax is debited and Income Tax Payable is credited for the amount owed. If the estimated tax payments are greater than the actual tax liability, a receivable account is debited and Income Tax is credited.

The tax effects of temporary differences between taxable income and income before income taxes must be allocated between periods. The journal entry for such allocations normally debits Income Tax and credits Income Tax Payable and Deferred Income Tax Payable.

2 Prepare an income statement reporting the following unusual items: discontinued operations, extraordinary items, and changes in accounting principles.

A gain or loss resulting from the disposal of a business segment should be identified on the income statement, net of related income tax. The results of continuing operations should also be identified.

Gains and losses may result from events and transactions that are unusual and occur infrequently. Such extraordinary items, net of related income tax, should be identified on the income statement.

A change in an accounting principle results from the adoption of a generally accepted accounting principle different from the one used previously for reporting purposes. The effect of the change in principle on net income in the current period, as well as the cumulative effect on income of prior periods, should be disclosed in the financial statements. The effects of a change in an accounting principle should be reported net of related income tax.

3 Prepare an income statement reporting earnings per share data.

Earnings per share is reported on the income statements of public corporations. If there are unusual items on the income statement, the per share amount should be presented for each of these items as well as net income.

4 Prepare financial statement presentations of stockholders' equity.

Significant changes in the sources of stockholders' equity—paid-in capital and retained earnings—may be reported in separate statements or notes that support the balance sheet presentation. Changes in retained earnings

may be reported by preparing a separate retained earnings statement, a combined income and retained earnings statement, or a statement of stockholders' equity. Restrictions to retained earnings, called appropriations, must be disclosed, usually in the notes to the financial statements. Material errors in a prior period's net income, called prior-period adjustments, are reported in the retained earnings statement. Significant changes in stockholders' equity may also be reported in a statement of stockholders' equity.

5 Describe the concept and the reporting of comprehensive income.

Comprehensive income is all changes in stockholders' equity during a period except those resulting from dividends and stockholders' investments. Companies must report traditional net income plus or minus other comprehensive income items to arrive at comprehensive income. Other comprehensive income items include transactions and events that are excluded from net income, such as unrealized gains and losses on certain investments in debt and equity securities.

6 Describe the accounting for investments in stocks.

A business may purchase stocks as a means of earning a return (income) on excess cash that it does not need for its normal operations. Such investments are recorded in a marketable securities account. Their cost includes all amounts spent to acquire the securities. Any dividends received on an investment are recorded as a debit to Cash and a credit to Dividend Revenue. On the balance sheet, temporary investments are reported at their fair market values. Any difference between the fair market values of the securities and their cost is an unrealized holding gain or loss (net of applicable taxes) that is reported as an other comprehensive income item.

Long-term investments in stocks are not intended as a source of cash in the normal operations of the business. They are reported in the balance sheet under the caption Investments. Two methods of accounting for long-term investments in stock are (1) the cost method and (2) the equity method.

The accounting for the sale of stock is the same for both short-term and long-term investments. The investment account is credited for the carrying amount (book value) of the shares sold, the cash

or receivables account is debited for the proceeds, and any difference between the proceeds and the carrying amount is recorded as a gain or loss on the sale.

7 Describe alternative methods of combining businesses and how consolidated financial statements are prepared.

Businesses may combine in a merger or a consolidation. Business combinations may also occur when one corporation acquires a controlling share of the outstanding voting stock of another corporation. In this case, a parent-subsidiary relationship exists, and the companies are called affiliated or associated companies.

Although the corporations that make up a parent-subsidiary affiliation may operate as a single economic unit, they usually continue to maintain separate accounting records and prepare their own periodic financial statements. The financial statements prepared by combining the parent

and subsidiary statements are called consolidated financial statements.

When a parent corporation purchases less than 100% of the subsidiary's stock, the remaining stockholders' equity is identified as minority interest. The minority interest is reported on the consolidated balance sheet, usually preceding stockholders' equity.

In preparing consolidated income statements for a parent and its subsidiary, all amounts from intercompany transactions, such as intercompany sales of merchandise and cost of merchandise sold, are eliminated.

8 Compute and interpret the price-earnings ratio.

The assessment of a firm's growth potential and future earnings prospects is indicated by the price-earnings ratio, or P/E ratio. It is computed by dividing the stock's market price per share at a specific date by the company's annual earnings per share.

ILLUSTRATIVE PROBLEM

The following data were selected from the records of Botanica Greenhouses Inc. for the current fiscal year ended August 31:

Administrative expenses	$ 82,200
Cost of merchandise sold	750,000
Gain on condemnation of land	25,000
Income tax:	
Applicable to continuing operations	27,200
Applicable to gain on condemnation of land	10,000
Applicable to loss from disposal of a segment	
of the business (reduction)	24,000
Interest expense	15,200
Loss from disposal of a segment of the business	60,200
Sales	1,097,500
Selling expenses	182,100

Instructions

Prepare a multiple-step income statement, concluding with a section for earnings per share in the form illustrated in this chapter. There were 10,000 shares of common stock (no preferred) outstanding throughout the year. Assume that the gain on condemnation of land is an extraordinary item.

Solution

Botanica Greenhouses Inc.
Income Statement
For the Year Ended August 31, 2003

Sales		$1,097,500
Cost of merchandise sold		750,000
Gross profit		$ 347,500
Operating expenses:		
Selling expenses	$182,100	
Administrative expenses	82,200	
Total operating expenses		264,300
Income from operations		$ 83,200
Other expense:		
Interest expense		15,200
Income from continuing operations before		
income tax		$ 68,000
Income tax expense		27,200
Income from continuing operations		$ 40,800
Loss from disposal of a segment of the		
business	$ 60,200	
Less applicable income tax	24,000	36,200
Income before extraordinary item		$ 4,600
Extraordinary item:		
Gain on condemnation of land	$ 25,000	
Less applicable income tax	10,000	15,000
Net income		$ 19,600
Earnings per share:		
Income from continuing operations		$4.08
Loss on discontinued operations		3.62
Income before extraordinary item		$0.46
Extraordinary item		1.50
Net income		$1.96

SELF-EXAMINATION QUESTIONS
Answers at End of Chapter

Matching

Match each of the following statements with its proper term. Some terms may not be used.

A.	**appropriation**
B.	**available-for-sale securities**
C.	**balance sheet**
D.	**comprehensive income**

___ 1. The income according to the tax laws that is used as a base for determining the amount of taxes owed.

___ 2. Differences between taxable income and income before income taxes, created because items are recognized in one period for tax purposes and in another period for income statement purposes. Such differences reverse or turn around in later years.

___ 3. Operations of a major line of business for a company, such as a division, a department, or a certain class of customer, that have been disposed of.

E. consolidated financial statements

F. consolidation

G. cost method

H. discontinued operations

I. earnings per common share (EPS)

J. equity method

K. equity per share

L. equity security

M. extraordinary items

N. investments

O. merger

P. minority interest

Q. parent company

R. permanent differences

S. pooling-of-interests method

T. price-earnings ratio

U. prior period adjustments

V. purchase method

W. statement of cash flows

X. statement of stockholders' equity

Y. subsidiary company

Z. taxable income

AA. temporary differences

BB. temporary investments

CC. trading securities

DD. unrealized holding gain or loss

___ 4. Events and transactions that (1) are significantly different (unusual) from the typical or the normal operating activities of a business and (2) occur infrequently.

___ 5. Net income per share of common stock outstanding during a period.

___ 6. The amount of retained earnings that has been restricted and therefore is unavailable for use as dividends.

___ 7. Errors in a prior period's net income that arise from mathematical mistakes or from mistakes in applying accounting principles.

___ 8. A statement summarizing significant changes in stockholders' equity that have occurred during a period.

___ 9. All changes in stockholders' equity during a period except those resulting from dividends and stockholders' investments.

___ 10. Preferred or common stock.

___ 11. Securities that management intends to actively trade for profit.

___ 12. Securities that management expects to sell in the future but which are not actively traded for profit.

___ 13. The balance sheet caption used to report investments in income-yielding securities that can be quickly sold and converted to cash as needed.

___ 14. The difference between the fair market values of the securities and their cost.

___ 15. The balance sheet caption used to report long-term investments in stocks not intended as a source of cash in the normal operations of the business.

___ 16. A method of accounting for an investment in common stock by which the investor recognizes as income its share of cash dividends of the investee.

___ 17. A method of accounting for an investment in common stock by which the investment account is adjusted for the investor's share of periodic net income and cash dividends of the investee.

___ 18. The joining of two corporations in which one company acquires all the assets and liabilities of another corporation, which is then dissolved.

___ 19. The creation of a new corporation by the transfer of assets and liabilities of two or more existing corporations, which are then dissolved.

___ 20. The corporation owning all or a majority of the voting stock of the other corporation.

___ 21. The corporation that is controlled by a parent company.

___ 22. The accounting method used when a corporation acquires the controlling share of the voting common stock of another corporation by paying cash, exchanging other assets, issuing debt, or some combination of these methods.

___ 23. The accounting method used when a corporation acquires the controlling share of the voting common stock of another corporation by exchanging the voting common stock of the acquiring corporation for the common stock of the acquired corporation.

___ 24. Financial statements resulting from combining parent and subsidiary statements.

___ 25. The portion of a subsidiary corporation's stock owned by outsiders.

___ 26. The ratio computed by dividing a corporation's stock market price per share at a specific date by the company's annual earnings per share.

Multiple Choice

1. During its first year of operations, a corporation elected to use the straight-line method of depreciation for financial reporting purposes and MACRS in determining taxable income. If the income tax is 40% and the amount of depreciation expense is $60,000 under the straight-line method and $100,000 under MACRS, what is the amount of income tax deferred to future years?

A. $16,000   C. $40,000

B. $24,000   D. $60,000

2. A material gain resulting from condemning land for public use would be reported on the income statement as:
   A. an extraordinary item
   B. an other income item
   C. revenue from sales
   D. a change in estimate

3. Gwinnett Corporation's temporary investments cost $100,000 and have a market value of $120,000 at the end of the accounting period. Assuming a tax rate of 40%, the difference between the cost and market value would be reported as a:
   A. $12,000 realized gain
   B. $12,000 unrealized gain
   C. $20,000 realized gain
   D. $20,000 unrealized gain

4. Parker Corporation, which owns 100% of Sweeney Company, sold merchandise costing $50,000 to Sweeney Company for $75,000. Sweeney then sold the merchandise to a customer for $100,000. Before consolidation, Parker and Sweeney reported the following sales, cost of merchandise sold, and gross profit:

	Parker Corporation	Sweeney Company
Sales	$980,000	$600,000
Cost of merchandise sold	500,000	360,000
Gross profit	$480,000	$240,000

What is the total sales and cost of merchandise sold that should be reported on the consolidated income statement?
   A. Sales: $1,505,000; cost of merchandise sold: $785,000
   B. Sales: $1,505,000; cost of merchandise sold: $860,000
   C. Sales: $1,580,000; cost of merchandise sold: $785,000
   D. Sales: $1,580,000; cost of merchandise sold: $860,000

5. Cisneros Corporation owns 75% of Harrell Inc. During the current year, Harrell Inc. reported net income of $150,000 and declared dividends of $40,000. How much would Cisneros Corporation increase Investment in Harrell Inc. Stock for the current year?
   A. $0   C. $82,500
   B. $30,000   D. $112,500

CLASS DISCUSSION QUESTIONS

1. A corporation has paid estimated federal income tax during the year on the basis of its estimated income. Indicate the accounts that would be debited and credited at the end of the year if the corporation (a) owes an additional tax; (b) overpaid its tax.

2. How would the amount of deferred income tax payable be reported in the balance sheet if (a) it is payable within one year and (b) it is payable beyond one year?

3. What two criteria must be met to classify an item as an extraordinary item on the income statement?

4. During the current year, 40 acres of land that cost $200,000 were condemned for construction of an interstate highway. Assuming that an award of $350,000 in cash was received and that the applicable income tax on this transaction is 40%, how would this information be presented in the income statement?

5. Corporation X realized a material gain when its facilities at a designated floodway were acquired by the urban renewal agency. How should the gain be reported in the income statement?

   Source: "Technical Hotline," Journal of Accountancy, June 1989, p. 32.

6. An annual report of **Sears, Roebuck and Co.** disclosed the discontinuance of several business segments, including **Coldwell Banker Residential Services**. The estimated loss on disposal of these operations was $64 million, including $22 million of tax expense. Indicate how the loss from discontinued operations should be reported by Sears, Roebuck and Co. on its income statement.

7. If significant changes are made in the accounting principles applied from one period to the next, why should the effect of these changes be disclosed in the financial statements?

8. A corporation reports earnings per share of $1.38 for the most recent year and $1.10 for the preceding year. The $1.38 includes a $0.45-per-share gain from insurance proceeds related to a fully depreciated asset that was destroyed by fire. (a) Should the composition of the $1.38 be disclosed in the financial reports? (b) On the basis of the limited information presented, would you conclude that operations had improved or declined?

9. What is the primary advantage of combining the retained earnings statement with the income statement?

10. What are the three classifications of appropriations and how are appropriations normally reported in the financial statements?

11. Indicate how prior period adjustments would be reported on the financial statements presented only for the current period.

12. Describe the format of the statement of stockholders' equity.

13. How is comprehensive income determined?

14. a. List some examples of other comprehensive income items.
    b. Does the reporting of comprehensive income affect the determination of net income and retained earnings?

15. Why might a business invest in another company's stock?

16. How are temporary investments in marketable securities reported on the balance sheet?

17. How are unrealized gains and losses on temporary investments in marketable securities reported on the statement of income and comprehensive income?

18. a. What are two methods of accounting for long-term investments in stock?
    b. Under what caption are long-term investments in stock reported on the balance sheet?

19. Plaster Inc. received a $0.15-per-share cash dividend on 50,000 shares of Gestalt Corporation common stock, which Plaster Inc. carries as a long-term investment. (a) Assuming that Plaster Inc. uses the cost method of accounting for its investment in Gestalt Corporation, what account would be credited for the receipt of the $7,500 dividend? (b) Assuming that Plaster Inc. uses the equity method of accounting for its investment in Gestalt Corporation, what account would be credited for the receipt of the $7,500 dividend?

20. Which method of accounting for long-term investments in stock (cost or equity) should be used by the parent company in accounting for its investments in stock of subsidiaries?

21. What are the two methods of accounting for the creation of a parent-subsidiary relationship?

22. Polska Company purchases the entire common stock of Strabo Corporation for $30,000,000. What accounts are eliminated on Strabo's balance sheet and Polska's balance sheet upon consolidation?

23. Parent Corporation owns 90% of the outstanding common stock of Subsidiary Corporation, which has no preferred stock. (a) What is the term applied to the remaining 10% interest? (b) On the consolidated balance sheet, where is the amount of Subsidiary's book equity allocable to outsiders reported?

24. An annual report of **The Campbell Soup Company** reported on its income statement $2.4 million as "equity in earnings of affiliates." Journalize the entry that Campbell would have made to record this equity in earnings of affiliates.

 RESOURCES FOR YOUR SUCCESS ONLINE AT

http://warren.swcollege.com

Remember! If you need additional help, visit South-Western's Web site.
See page 26 for a description of the online and printed materials that are available.

Warren
Reeve
Fess

EXERCISES

Exercise 13–1

Income tax entries

Objective 1

Journalize the entries to record the following selected transactions of Supernal Grave Markers Inc.:

Apr. 15. Paid the first installment of the estimated income tax for the current fiscal year ending December 31, $80,000. No entry had been made to record the liability.

June 15. Paid the second installment of $80,000.

Sept. 15. Paid the third installment of $80,000.

Dec. 31. Recorded the estimated income tax liability for the year just ended and the deferred income tax liability, based on the transactions above and the following data:

Income tax rate	40%
Income before income tax	$1,200,000
Taxable income according to tax return	850,000

Jan. 15. Paid the fourth installment of $100,000.

Exercise 13–2

Extraordinary item

Objective 2

A company received life insurance proceeds on the death of its president before the end of its fiscal year. It intends to report the amount in its income statement as an extraordinary item.

➤ Would this be in conformity with generally accepted accounting principles? Discuss.

Source: "Technical Hotline," *Journal of Accountancy*, June 1989, p. 31.

Exercise 13–3

Extraordinary item

Objective 2

On May 11, 1996, **ValuJet** tragically lost its Flight 592 en route from Miami to Atlanta. One hundred and ten people lost their lives. The crash cost ValuJet millions of dollars, including $2 million the company paid to the Federal Aviation Administration (FAA) to compensate it for the costs of the special inspections that were conducted. Do you believe that the costs related to this crash should be reported as an extraordinary item on the 1996 income statement of ValuJet?

Exercise 13–4

Identifying extraordinary items

Objective 2

Assume that the amount of each of the following items is material to the financial statements. Classify each item as either normally recurring (NR) or extraordinary (E).

a. Interest revenue on notes receivable.
b. Uninsured flood loss. (Flood insurance is unavailable because of periodic flooding in the area.)
c. Loss on sale of fixed assets.
d. Salaries of corporate officers.
e. Gain on sale of land condemned for public use.
f. Uncollectible accounts expense.
g. Uninsured loss on building due to hurricane damage. The firm was organized in 1920 and had not previously incurred hurricane damage.
h. Loss on disposal of equipment considered to be obsolete because of development of new technology.

Exercise 13–5

Income statement

Objectives 2, 3

✓ Net income, $77,000

Trafalgar Inc. produces and distributes equipment for sailboats. On the basis of the following data for the current fiscal year ended June 30, 2003, prepare a multiple-step income statement for Trafalgar Inc., including an analysis of earnings per share in the form illustrated in this chapter. There were 10,000 shares of $150 par common stock outstanding throughout the year.

Administrative expenses	$ 26,750
Cost of merchandise sold	684,500
Cumulative effect on prior years of changing to a different depreciation method (decrease in income)	60,000
Gain on condemnation of land (extraordinary item)	37,750
Income tax reduction applicable to change in depreciation method	18,200
Income tax applicable to gain on condemnation of land	7,750
Income tax reduction applicable to loss from discontinued operations	56,000
Income tax applicable to ordinary income	105,200
Loss on discontinued operations	125,000
Sales	1,050,000
Selling expenses	75,750

Exercise 13–6
Income statement

Objectives 2, 3

✓ Correct EPS for net income, $8.55

Boss Sound Inc. sells automotive and home stereo equipment. It has 50,000 shares of $100 par common stock and 10,000 shares of $2, $100 par cumulative preferred stock outstanding as of December 31, 2003. It also holds 10,000 shares of common stock as treasury stock as of December 31, 2003. How many errors can you find in the following income statement for the year ended December 31, 2003?

Boss Sound Inc.
Income Statement
For the Year Ended December 31, 2003

Net sales		$9,450,000
Cost of merchandise sold		7,100,000
Gross profit		$2,350,000
Operating expenses:		
Selling expenses	$920,000	
Administrative expenses	380,000	1,300,000
Income from continuing operations before income tax		$1,050,000
Income tax expense		420,000
Income from continuing operations		$ 730,000
Cumulative effect on prior years' income (decrease) of changing to a different depreciation method (net of applicable income tax of $86,000)		(204,000)
Correction of error (understatement) in December 31, 2002 physical inventory (net of applicable income tax of $20,000)		30,000
Income before condemnation of land and discontinued operations		$ 556,000
Extraordinary item:		
Gain on condemnation of land, net of applicable income tax of $80,000		120,000
Loss on discontinued operations (net of applicable income tax of $76,000)		(184,000)
Net income		$ 492,000
Earnings per common share:		
Income from continuing operations		$14.60
Cumulative effect on prior years' income (decrease) of changing to a different depreciation method		(4.08)
Correction of error (understatement) in December 31, 2002 physical inventory		0.60
Income before extraordinary item and discontinued operations		$11.12
Extraordinary item		2.40
Loss on discontinued operations		(3.68)
Net income		$ 9.84

Exercise 13–7
Reporting paid-in capital

Objective 4

The following accounts and their balances were selected from the unadjusted trial balance of Vintage Inc., a freight forwarder, at December 31, the end of the current fiscal year:

Preferred $2 Stock, $100 par	$1,000,000
Paid-In Capital in Excess of Par—Preferred Stock	120,000
Common Stock, no par, $5 stated value	750,000
Paid-In Capital in Excess of Stated Value—Common Stock	100,000
Paid-In Capital from Sale of Treasury Stock	85,000
Donated Capital	270,000
Retained Earnings	2,230,000

Prepare the Paid-In Capital portion of the Stockholders' Equity section of the balance sheet. There are 300,000 shares of common stock authorized and 70,000 shares of preferred stock authorized.

Exercise 13–8
Stockholders' equity section of balance sheet

Objective 4

✓ Total stockholders' equity, $1,082,500

The following accounts and their balances appear in the ledger of Siphon Inc. on April 30 of the current year:

Common Stock, $10 par	$375,000
Paid-In Capital in Excess of Par	60,000
Paid-In Capital from Sale of Treasury Stock	12,500
Retained Earnings	675,000
Treasury Stock	40,000

Prepare the Stockholders' Equity section of the balance sheet as of April 30. Fifty thousand shares of common stock are authorized, and 1,000 shares have been reacquired.

Exercise 13–9
Stockholders' equity section of balance sheet

Objective 4

✓ Total stockholders' equity, $4,327,500

Motor Toys Inc. retails racing products for BMWs, Porsches, and Ferraris. The following accounts and their balances appear in the ledger of Motor Toys Inc. on December 31, the end of the current year:

Common Stock, $5 par	$ 500,000
Paid-In Capital in Excess of Par—Common Stock	175,000
Paid-In Capital in Excess of Par—Preferred Stock	65,000
Paid-In Capital from Sale of Treasury Stock—Common	35,000
Preferred $2 Stock, $100 par	400,000
Retained Earnings	3,252,500
Treasury Stock—Common	100,000

Ten thousand shares of preferred and 350,000 shares of common stock are authorized. There are 4,000 shares of common stock held as treasury stock.

Prepare the Stockholders' Equity section of the balance sheet as of December 31, the end of the current year.

Exercise 13–10
Retained earnings statement

Objective 4

✓ Retained earnings, Aug. 31, $1,627,600

Mohawk Corporation, a manufacturer of industrial pumps, reports the following results for the year ending August 31, 2003:

Retained earnings, September 1, 2002	$1,475,600
Net income	372,000
Cash dividends declared	120,000
Stock dividends declared	100,000

Prepare a retained earnings statement for the fiscal year ended August 31, 2003.

Exercise 13–11
Stockholders' equity section of balance sheet

Objective 4

✓ Corrected total stockholders' equity, $2,228,000

How many errors can you find in the following Stockholders' Equity section of the balance sheet prepared as of the end of the current year?

Stockholders' Equity

Paid-in capital:		
Preferred $2 stock, cumulative, $100 par		
(3,500 shares authorized and issued)	$ 350,000	
Excess of issue price over par	60,000	$ 410,000
Retained earnings		540,000
Treasury stock (4,000 shares at cost)		75,000
Dividends payable		100,000
Total paid-in capital		$1,125,000
Common stock, $25 par (50,000 shares		
authorized, 40,000 shares issued)	$1,278,000	
Donated capital	75,000	
Organization costs	80,000	1,433,000
Total stockholders' equity		$2,558,000

Exercise 13–12
Statement of stockholders' equity

Objective 4

✓ Total stockholders' equity, Dec. 31, $2,270,000

The stockholders' equity accounts of Galapagos Corporation for the current fiscal year ended December 31, 2003, are as follows:

ACCOUNT *Common Stock, $2 Par*

Date		Item	Debit	Credit	Balance Debit	Balance Credit
2003						
Jan.	1	Balance				500,000
March	13	Issued 50,000 shares		100,000		600,000

ACCOUNT *Paid-In Capital in Excess of Par*

Date		Item	Debit	Credit	Balance Debit	Balance Credit
2003						
Jan.	1	Balance				400,000
March	13	Issued 50,000 shares		45,000		445,000

ACCOUNT *Treasury Stock*

Date		Item	Debit	Credit	Balance Debit	Balance Credit
2003						
April	30	Purchased 10,000 shares	25,000		25,000	

ACCOUNT *Retained Earnings*

Date		Item	Debit	Credit	Balance Debit	Balance Credit
2003						
Jan.	1	Balance				1,075,000
Dec.	31	Income summary		220,000		1,295,000
	31	Cash dividends	45,000			1,250,000

ACCOUNT *Cash Dividends*

Date		Item	Debit	Credit	Balance Debit	Balance Credit
2003						
June	30		22,500		22,500	
Dec.	30		22,500		45,000	
	31	Closing		45,000	—	—

Prepare a statement of stockholders' equity for the fiscal year ended December 31, 2003.

Exercise 13–13
Temporary investments in marketable securities

Objective 6

During its first year of operations, Genotype Corporation purchased the following securities as a temporary investment:

Security	Shares Purchased	Cost	Cash Dividends Received
Research Inc.	1,000	$25,000	$ 800
Crisp Corp.	2,500	36,000	1,200

a. Journalize the purchase of the temporary investments for cash.
b. Journalize the receipt of the dividends.

Exercise 13–14
*Financial statement
reporting of temporary
investments*

Objectives 5, 6

✓ b. Comprehensive income,
$81,200

Using the data for Genotype Corporation in Exercise 13–13, assume that as of December 31, 2003, the Research Inc. stock had a market value of $28 per share and the Crisp Corp. stock had a market value of $14 per share. For the year ending December 31, 2003, Genotype Corporation had net income of $80,000. Its tax rate is 40%.

a. Prepare the balance sheet presentation for the temporary investments.
b. Prepare a statement of income and comprehensive income presentation for the temporary investments.

Exercise 13–15
*Entries for investment in
stock, receipt of dividends,
and sale of shares*

Objective 6

On February 27, Gourmet Corporation acquired 3,000 shares of the 50,000 outstanding shares of Goulash Co. common stock at 58 plus commission charges of $420. On July 8, a cash dividend of $1 per share and a 2% stock dividend were received. On December 7, 1,000 shares were sold at 62, less commission charges of $375. Journalize the entries to record (a) the purchase of the stock, (b) the receipt of dividends, and (c) the sale of the 1,000 shares.

Exercise 13–16
Equity method

Objective 6

Real World

The following note to the consolidated financial statements for **The Goodyear Tire and Rubber Co.** relates to the principles of consolidation used in preparing the financial statements:

The Company's investments in 20% to 50% owned companies in which it has the ability to exercise significant influence over operating and financial policies are accounted for by the equity method. Accordingly, the Company's share of the earnings of these companies is included in consolidated net income.

Is it a requirement that Goodyear use the equity method in this situation? Explain.

Exercise 13–17
*Entries using equity method
for stock investment*

Objective 6

At a total cost of $13,500,000, Southern Corporation acquired 150,000 shares of Northern Corp. common stock as a long-term investment. Southern Corporation uses the equity method of accounting for this investment. Northern Corp. has 500,000 shares of common stock outstanding, including the shares acquired by Southern Corporation. Journalize the entries by Southern Corporation to record the following information:

a. Northern Corp. reports net income of $8,500,000 for the current period.
b. A cash dividend of $1.25 per common share is paid by Northern Corp. during the current period.

Exercise 13–18
*Eliminations for
consolidated income
statement*

Objective 7

✓ a. (1) $80,000
✓ b. $1,950,000

For the current year ended June 30, the results of operations of Iowa Corporation and its wholly owned subsidiary, Hawkee Enterprises, are as follows:

	Iowa Corporation		Hawkee Enterprises	
Sales		$8,150,000		$750,000
Cost of merchandise sold	$5,000,000		$440,000	
Selling expenses	800,000		75,000	
Administrative expenses	600,000		35,000	
Interest expense (revenue)	(30,000)	6,370,000	30,000	580,000
Net income		$1,780,000		$170,000

During the year, Iowa sold merchandise to Hawkee for $80,000. The merchandise was sold by Hawkee to nonaffiliated companies for $120,000. Iowa's interest revenue was realized from a long-term loan to Hawkee.

a. Determine the amounts to be eliminated from the following items in preparing a consolidated income statement for the current year: (1) sales and (2) cost of merchandise sold.
b. Determine the consolidated net income.

Exercise 13–19
Price-earnings ratio

Objective 8

The financial statements for **Cisco Systems, Inc.**, are presented in Appendix G at the end of the text.

a. Determine the price-earnings ratio for Cisco Systems for 2000 and 1999. The high market price of Cisco Systems' common stock was $33.53 in the fourth quarter of fiscal year 1999 and $71.44 in the fourth quarter of fiscal year 2000.

b. ▬▬▶ What conclusions can you reach by considering the price-earnings ratio?

PROBLEMS SERIES A

Problem 13–1A
Income tax allocation

Objective 1

SPREADSHEET

✓ 1. Year-end balance, 3rd year, $72,000

Differences between the accounting methods applied to accounts and financial reports and those used in determining taxable income yielded the following amounts for the first four years of a corporation's operations:

	First Year	Second Year	Third Year	Fourth Year
Income before income taxes	$300,000	$450,000	$400,000	$500,000
Taxable income	250,000	300,000	420,000	510,000

The income tax rate for each of the four years was 40% of taxable income, and each year's taxes were promptly paid.

Instructions

1. Determine for each year the amounts described by the following captions, presenting the information in the form indicated:

Year	Income Tax Deducted on Income Statement	Income Tax Payments for the Year	Deferred Income Tax Payable	
			Year's Addition (Deduction)	Year-End Balance

2. Total the first three amount columns.

Problem 13–2A
Income tax; income statement

Objectives 1, 2, 3

✓ Net income, $57,000

The following data were selected from the records of Mantra Greenhouses Inc. for the current fiscal year ended June 30, 2003:

Advertising expense	$ 40,000
Cost of merchandise sold	266,000
Depreciation expense—office equipment	5,000
Depreciation expense—store equipment	29,000
Gain from disposal of a segment of the business	37,500
Income tax:	
Applicable to continuing operations	32,000
Applicable to gain from disposal of a segment of the business	15,000
Applicable to loss on condemnation of land (reduction)	9,000
Insurance expense	8,000
Interest expense	15,000
Loss on condemnation of land	22,500
Miscellaneous administrative expense	6,000
Miscellaneous selling expense	5,000

Office salaries expense	$ 50,000
Rent expense	21,000
Sales	665,000
Sales commissions expense	140,000

Instructions

Prepare a multiple-step income statement, concluding with a section for earnings per share in the form illustrated in this chapter. There were 75,000 shares of common stock (no preferred) outstanding throughout the year. Assume that the loss on condemnation of land is an extraordinary item.

Problem 13–3A
Income statement, retained earnings statement, balance sheet

Objectives 1, 2, 3, 4

SPREADSHEET

✓ Net income, $313,500

The following data were taken from the records of Pushkin Corporation for the year ended October 31, 2003:

Income statement data:

Administrative expenses	$ 100,000
Cost of merchandise sold	732,000
Gain on condemnation of land	30,000
Income tax:	
Applicable to continuing operations	234,000
Applicable to loss from disposal of a segment of the business	37,000
Applicable to gain on condemnation of land	12,000
Interest expense	8,000
Interest revenue	5,000
Loss from disposal of a segment of the business	92,500
Sales	1,820,000
Selling expenses	400,000

Retained earnings and balance sheet data:

Accounts payable	$ 149,500
Accounts receivable	309,050
Accumulated depreciation	3,050,000
Allowance for doubtful accounts	21,500
Cash	145,500
Common stock, $15 par (400,000 shares authorized; 152,000 shares issued)	2,280,000
Deferred income taxes payable (current portion, $4,700)	25,700
Dividends:	
Cash dividends for common stock	120,000
Cash dividends for preferred stock	75,000
Stock dividends for common stock	60,000
Dividends payable	30,000
Equipment	9,541,050
Income tax payable	55,900
Interest receivable	2,500
Merchandise inventory (October 31, 2003), at lower of cost (fifo) or market	425,000
Notes receivable	77,500
Organization costs	55,000
Paid-in capital from sale of treasury stock	16,000
Paid-in capital in excess of par—common stock	666,250
Paid-in capital in excess of par—preferred stock	240,000
Preferred 5% stock, $100 par (30,000 shares authorized; 15,000 shares issued)	1,500,000
Prepaid expenses	15,900
Retained earnings, November 1, 2002	2,548,150
Treasury stock (2,000 shares of common stock at cost of $35 per share)	70,000

Instructions

1. Prepare a multiple-step income statement for the year ended October 31, 2003, concluding with earnings per share. In computing earnings per share, assume that the average number of common shares outstanding was 150,000 and preferred dividends were $75,000. Assume that the gain on condemnation of land is an extraordinary item.
2. Prepare a retained earnings statement for the year ended October 31, 2003.
3. Prepare a balance sheet in report form as of October 31, 2003.

Problem 13–4A

Entries for investments in stock

Objective 6

SPREADSHEET

Thematic Company is a wholesaler of men's hair products. The following transactions relate to certain securities acquired by Thematic Company, whose fiscal year ends on December 31:

2001
Jan. 3. Purchased 3,000 shares of the 40,000 outstanding common shares of Perch Corporation at 89 plus commission and other costs of $594.
July 2. Received the regular cash dividend of $1 a share on Perch Corporation stock.
Dec. 5. Received the regular cash dividend of $1 a share plus an extra dividend of $0.10 a share on Perch Corporation stock.
        (Assume that all intervening transactions have been recorded properly and that the number of shares of stock owned have not changed from December 31, 2001, to December 31, 2003.)
2004
Jan. 2. Purchased controlling interest in Villard Inc. for $890,000 by purchasing 60,000 shares directly from the estate of the founder of Villard. There are 80,000 shares of Villard Inc. stock outstanding.
July 6. Received the regular cash dividend of $1 a share and a 3% stock dividend on the Perch Corporation stock.
Oct. 23. Sold 750 shares of Perch Corporation stock at 90. The broker deducted commission and other costs of $140, remitting the balance.
Dec. 10. Received a cash dividend at the new rate of $1.10 a share on the Perch Corporation stock.
     31. Received $24,000 of cash dividends on Villard Inc. stock. Villard Inc. reported net income of $315,000 in 2004. Thematic uses the equity method of accounting for its investment in Villard Inc.

Instructions

Journalize the entries for the preceding transactions.

PROBLEMS SERIES B

Problem 13–1B

Income tax allocation

Objective 1

SPREADSHEET

✓ 1. Year-end balance, 3rd year,
$56,000

Differences between the accounting methods applied to accounts and financial reports and those used in determining taxable income yielded the following amounts for the first four years of a corporation's operations:

	First Year	Second Year	Third Year	Fourth Year
Income before income taxes	$350,000	$440,000	$520,000	$695,000
Taxable income	270,000	350,000	550,000	710,000

The income tax rate for each of the four years was 40% of taxable income, and each year's taxes were promptly paid.

Instructions

1. Determine for each year the amounts described by the following captions, presenting the information in the form indicated:

Year	Income Tax Deducted on Income Statement	Income Tax Payments for the Year	Deferred Income Tax Payable	
			Year's Addition (Deduction)	Year-End Balance

2. Total the first three amount columns.

Problem 13–2B
Income tax; income statement

Objectives 1, 2, 3

✓ Net income, $51,500

SUV Inc. produces and sells off-road motorcycles and jeeps. The following data were selected from the records of SUV Inc. for the current fiscal year ended October 31, 2003:

Advertising expense	$ 60,000
Cost of merchandise sold	553,500
Depreciation expense—office equipment	6,000
Depreciation expense—store equipment	21,500
Gain on condemnation of land	31,250
Income tax:	
Applicable to continuing operations	36,250
Applicable to loss from disposal of a segment	
of the business (reduction)	5,000
Applicable to gain on condemnation of land	12,500
Interest revenue	7,500
Loss from disposal of a segment of the business	26,000
Miscellaneous administrative expense	10,000
Miscellaneous selling expense	4,500
Office salaries expense	68,000
Rent expense	20,000
Sales	950,000
Sales salaries expense	120,000
Store supplies expense	4,000

Instructions
Prepare a multiple-step income statement, concluding with a section for earnings per share (rounded to the nearest cent) in the form illustrated in this chapter. There were 25,000 shares of common stock (no preferred) outstanding throughout the year. Assume that the gain on condemnation of land is an extraordinary item.

Problem 13–3B
Income statement, retained earnings statement, balance sheet

Objectives 1, 2, 3, 4

SPREADSHEET

✓ Net income, $255,000

The following data were taken from the records of Onyx Corporation for the year ended July 31, 2003:

Income statement data:

Administrative expenses	$ 130,000
Cost of merchandise sold	884,000
Gain on condemnation of land	25,000
Income tax:	
Applicable to continuing operations	220,000
Applicable to loss from disposal of a	
segment of the business	54,000
Applicable to gain on condemnation of land	10,000
Interest expense	7,500
Interest revenue	1,500
Loss from disposal of a segment of the business	134,000
Sales	2,100,000
Selling expenses	540,000

Retained earnings and balance sheet data:

Accounts payable	$ 149,500
Accounts receivable	276,050

Accumulated depreciation	$ 3,050,000
Allowance for doubtful accounts	11,500
Cash	125,500
Common stock, $10 par (500,000 shares authorized; 251,000 shares issued)	2,510,000
Deferred income taxes payable (current portion, $4,700)	25,700
Dividends:	
Cash dividends for common stock	80,000
Cash dividends for preferred stock	120,000
Stock dividends for common stock	40,000
Dividends payable	25,000
Equipment	11,064,050
Income tax payable	55,900
Interest receivable	2,500
Merchandise inventory (July 31, 2003), at lower of cost (fifo) or market	522,500
Organization costs	55,000
Paid-in capital from sale of treasury stock	5,000
Paid-in capital in excess of par—common stock	437,500
Paid-in capital in excess of par—preferred stock	240,000
Preferred 8% stock, $100 par (30,000 shares authorized; 15,000 shares issued)	1,500,000
Prepaid expenses	15,900
Retained earnings, August 1, 2002	4,076,400
Treasury stock (1,000 shares of common stock at cost of $40 per share)	40,000

Instructions

1. Prepare a multiple-step income statement for the year ended July 31, 2003, concluding with earnings per share. In computing earnings per share, assume that the average number of common shares outstanding was 250,000 and preferred dividends were $120,000. Assume that the gain on condemnation of land is an extraordinary item.
2. Prepare a retained earnings statement for the year ended July 31, 2003.
3. Prepare a balance sheet in report form as of July 31, 2003.

Problem 13–4B

Entries for investments in stock

Objective 6

SPREADSHEET

Wilhelm Company produces and sells theater costumes. The following transactions relate to certain securities acquired by Wilhelm Company, whose fiscal year ends on December 31:

2001

Feb. 10. Purchased 4,000 shares of the 150,000 outstanding common shares of Moore Corporation at 42 plus commission and other costs of $300.

June 15. Received the regular cash dividend of $0.80 a share on Moore Corporation stock.

Dec. 15. Received the regular cash dividend of $0.80 a share plus an extra dividend of $0.05 a share on Moore Corporation stock.

    (Assume that all intervening transactions have been recorded properly and that the number of shares of stock owned have not changed from December 31, 2001, to December 31, 2003.)

2004

Jan. 3. Purchased controlling interest in Sirloin Inc. for $750,000 by purchasing 40,000 shares directly from the estate of the founder of Sirloin. There are 50,000 shares of Sirloin Inc. stock outstanding.

Apr. 1. Received the regular cash dividend of $0.80 a share and a 2% stock dividend on the Moore Corporation stock.

July 20. Sold 1,000 shares of Moore Corporation stock at 43. The broker deducted commission and other costs of $150, remitting the balance.

Dec. 15. Received a cash dividend at the new rate of $0.90 a share on the Moore Corporation stock.

    31. Received $30,000 of cash dividends on Sirloin Inc. stock. Sirloin Inc. reported net income of $245,000 in 2004. Wilhelm uses the equity method of accounting for its investment in Sirloin Inc.

Instructions

Journalize the entries for the preceding transactions.

SPECIAL ACTIVITIES

Activity 13–1
Mojave Inc.
Ethics and professional conduct in business

At a recent dinner party, you met Steph Melick, the controller for Mojave Inc. Steph has worked for Mojave for the past seven years. During your conversation, you complained about having to pay your third-quarter estimated taxes on Monday, September 15. In response, Steph indicated that she always *underpays* her estimated taxes. That way, she can use her money as long as possible. Is it appropriate to deliberately underpay your estimated taxes?

Activity 13–2
Ratchet Corporation
Ethics and professional conduct in business

Reed Osborn is the president and chief operating officer of Ratchet Corporation, a developer of personal financial planning software. During the past year, Ratchet Corporation was forced to sell ten acres of land to the city of Houston for expansion of a freeway exit. The corporation fought the sale, but after condemnation hearings, a judge ordered it to sell the land. Because of the location of the land and the fact that Ratchet Corporation had purchased the land over 15 years ago, the corporation recorded a $0.20-per-share gain on the sale. Always looking to turn a negative into a positive, Reed Osborn has decided to announce the corporation's earnings per share of $1.05, without identifying the $0.20 impact of selling the land. Although he will retain majority ownership, Reed plans on selling 20,000 of his shares in the corporation sometime within the next month. Are Reed's plans to announce earnings per share of $1.05 without mentioning the $0.20 impact of selling the land ethical and professional?

Activity 13–3
Ulster Inc.
Reporting extraordinary item

Ulster Inc. is in the process of preparing its annual financial statements. Ulster Inc. is a large citrus grower located in central Florida. The following is a discussion between Jason Kirk, the controller, and April Gwinn, the chief executive officer and president of Ulster Inc.

April: Jason, I've got a question about your rough draft of this year's income statement.
Jason: Sure, April. What's your question?
April: Well, your draft shows a net loss of $750,000.
Jason: That's right. We'd have had a profit, except for this year's frost damage. I figured that the frost destroyed over 30 percent of our crop. We had a good year otherwise.
April: That's my concern. I estimated that if we eliminate the frost damage, we'd show a profit of . . . let's see . . . about $250,000.
Jason: That sounds about right.
April: This income statement seems misleading. Why can't we show the loss on the frost damage separately? That way the bank and our outside investors will be able to see that this year's loss is just temporary. I'd hate to get them upset over nothing.
Jason: Maybe we can do something. I recall from my accounting courses something about showing unusual items separately. Let's see . . . yes, I remember. They're called extraordinary items.
April: Well, we haven't had any frost damage in over five years. This year's damage is certainly extraordinary. Let's do it!

    Discuss the appropriateness of revising Ulster Inc.'s income statement to report the frost damage separately as an extraordinary item.

Activity 13–4
Charlene Seymour
*Consolidated financial
statements*

Charlene Seymour, your grandmother, recently retired, sold her condominium in New York City, and moved to a retirement community in Florida. With some of the proceeds from the sale of her condominium, she is considering investing $800,000 in the stock market.

In the process of selecting among alternative stock investments, your grandmother collected annual reports from fifteen different companies. In reviewing these reports, however, she has become confused and has questions concerning several items that appear in the financial reports. She has asked for your help and has written down the following questions for you to answer:

a. *In reviewing the annual reports, I noticed many references to "consolidated financial statements." What are consolidated financial statements?*
b. *"Excess of cost of business acquired over related net assets" appears on the consolidated balance sheets in several annual reports. What does this mean? Is it an asset (it appears with other assets)?*
c. *What is minority interest?*
d. *A footnote to one of the consolidated statements indicated interest and the amount of a loan from one company to another had been eliminated. Is this good accounting? A loan is a loan. How can a company just eliminate a loan that hasn't been paid off?*
e. *How can financial statements for an American company (in dollars) be combined with a German subsidiary (in marks)?*

1. ➤ Briefly respond to each of your grandmother's questions.
2. ➤ While discussing the items in (1) with your grandmother, she asked for your advice on whether she should limit her investment to one stock. What would you advise?

Activity 13–5
Into the Real World
*Extraordinary items and
discontinued operations*

In groups of three or four students, search company annual reports, news releases, or the Internet for extraordinary items and announcements of discontinued operations. Identify the most unusual extraordinary item in your group. Also, select a discontinued operation of a well-known company that might be familiar to other students or might interest them.

Prepare a brief analysis of the earnings per share impact of both the extraordinary item and the discontinued operation. Estimate the *potential* impact on the company's market price by multiplying the current price-earnings ratio by the earnings per share amount of each item.

One Internet site that has annual reports is EDGAR (Electronic Data Gathering, Analysis, and Retrieval), the electronic archives of financial statements filed with the Securities and Exchange Commission. SEC documents can be retrieved using the EdgarScan service from **PricewaterhouseCoopers** at **edgarscan.pwcglobal.com**.

To obtain annual report information, type in a company name in the appropriate space. EdgarScan will list the reports available to you for the company you've selected. Select the most recent annual report filing, identified as a 10-K or 10-K405. EdgarScan provides an outline of the report, including the separate financial statements. You can double click the income statement and balance sheet for the selected company into an Excel™ spreadsheet for further analysis.

ANSWERS TO SELF-EXAMINATION QUESTIONS

Matching

1.	Z	5.	I	9.	D	13.	BB	17.	J	21.	Y	25.	P
2.	AA	6.	A	10.	L	14.	DD	18.	O	22.	V	26.	T
3.	H	7.	U	11.	CC	15.	N	19.	F	23.	S		
4.	M	8.	X	12.	B	16.	G	20.	Q	24.	E		

Multiple Choice

1. **A** The amount of income tax deferred to future years is $16,000 (answer A), determined as follows:

Depreciation expense, MACRS	$100,000
Depreciation expense, straight-line method	60,000
Excess expense in determining taxable income . .	$ 40,000
Income tax rate	× 40%
Income tax deferred to future years	$ 16,000

2. **A** Events and transactions that are distinguished by their unusual nature and by the infrequency of their occurrence, such as a gain on condemning land for public use, are reported in the income statement as extraordinary items (answer A).

3. **B** The difference between the cost of temporary investments held as available-for-sale securities and their market value is reported as an unrealized gain, net of applicable income taxes, as shown below:

Market value of investments	$120,000
Cost of investments	100,000
	$ 20,000
Applicable taxes (40%)	8,000
Unrealized gain, net of taxes	$ 12,000

The unrealized gain of $12,000 (answer B) is reported on the balance sheet as an addition to the cost of the investments and as part of other comprehensive income.

4. **A** The consolidated income statement should report the incomes of Parker and Sweeney as if they were one operating entity. Because an entity cannot sell to itself or buy from itself, the $75,000 sale from Parker to Sweeney must be eliminated. In addition, the $75,000 purchase by Sweeney must be eliminated from Sweeney's cost of merchandise sold. Thus, sales of $1,505,000 ($980,000 − $75,000 + $600,000) and cost of merchandise sold of $785,000 ($500,000 + $360,000 − $75,000) would be reported on the consolidated income statement (answer A).

5. **C** Under the equity method of accounting for investments in stocks, Cisneros Corporation records its share of both net income and dividends of Harrell Inc. in Investment in Harrell Inc. Stock. Thus, Investment in Harrell Inc. Stock would increase by $82,500 [($150,000 × 75%) − ($40,000 × 75%)] for the current year. $30,000 (answer B) is only Cisneros Corporation's share of Harrell's dividends for the current year. $112,500 (answer D) is only Cisneros Corporation's share of Harrell's net income for the year.

Bonds Payable and Investments in Bonds

1 Compute the potential impact of long-term borrowing on the earnings per share of a corporation.

2 Describe the characteristics of bonds.

3 Compute the present value of bonds payable.

4 Journalize entries for bonds payable.

5 Describe bond sinking funds.

6 Journalize entries for bond redemptions.

7 Journalize entries for the purchase, interest, discount and premium amortization, and sale of bond investments.

8 Prepare a corporation balance sheet.

9 Compute and interpret the number of times interest charges are earned.

Y ou have just inherited $50,000 from a distant relative, and you are considering some options for investing the money. Some of your friends have suggested that you invest it in long-term bonds. As a result, you have scanned *The Wall Street Journal's* September 7, 2000 listing of New York Exchange Bonds. You've identified the following two listings as possible bond investments, both of which mature in the year 2007:

- AT&T (American Telephone & Telegraph) 7¾% Bonds
- Honywll (Honeywell) Zero

The AT&T bonds are selling for 102, while the Honeywell bonds are selling for only 59¾. The AT&T bonds are selling for over one and one-half times the price of the Honeywell bonds. Does this mean that the Honeywell bonds are a better buy? Does the 7¾% mean that if you buy the AT&T bonds you can actually earn 7¾% interest? What does the "zero" mean? Does it have anything to do with the fact that the Honeywell bonds are only selling for 59¾?

In this chapter, we will answer each of these questions. We first discuss the advantages and disadvantages of financing a corporation's operations by issuing debt rather than equity. We then discuss the accounting principles related to issuing long-term debt. Finally, we discuss the accounting for investments in bonds.

Financing Corporations

objective 1

Compute the potential impact of long-term borrowing on the earnings per share of a corporation.

Most of you have financed (purchased on credit) an automobile, a home, or a computer. Similarly, corporations often finance their operations by purchasing on credit and issuing notes or bonds. We have discussed accounts payable and notes payable in earlier chapters. A **bond** is simply a form of an interest-bearing note. Like a note, a bond requires periodic interest payments, and the face amount must be repaid at the maturity date. Bondholders are creditors of the issuing corporation, and their claims on the assets of the corporation rank ahead of stockholders.

One of the many factors that influence the decision to issue debt or equity is the effect of each alternative on earnings per share. To illustrate the possible effects, assume that a corporation's board of directors is considering the following alternative plans for financing a $4,000,000 company:

Plan 1: 100% financing from issuing common stock, $10 par

Plan 2: 50% financing from issuing preferred 9% stock, $50 par
50% financing from issuing common stock, $10 par

Plan 3: 50% financing from issuing 12% bonds
25% financing from issuing preferred 9% stock, $50 par
25% financing from issuing common stock, $10 par

In each case, we assume that the stocks or bonds are issued at their par or face amount. The corporation is expecting to earn $800,000 annually, before deducting interest on the bonds and income taxes estimated at 40% of income. Exhibit 1 shows the effect of the three plans on the income of the corporation and the earnings per share on common stock.

Exhibit 1 indicates that Plan 3 yields the highest earnings per share on common stock and is thus the most attractive for common stockholders. If the estimated earnings are more than $800,000, the difference between the earnings per share to com-

Point of Interest
Bonds of major corporations are actively traded on bond exchanges. You can purchase bonds through a financial services firm, such as **Merrill Lynch** or **A. G. Edwards & Sons**.

Exhibit 1 Effect of Alternative Financing Plans—$800,000 Earnings

	Plan 1	Plan 2	Plan 3
12% bonds	—	—	$2,000,000
Preferred 9% stock, $50 par	—	$2,000,000	1,000,000
Common stock, $10 par	$4,000,000	2,000,000	1,000,000
Total	$4,000,000	$4,000,000	$4,000,000
Earnings before interest and income tax	$ 800,000	$ 800,000	$ 800,000
Deduct interest on bonds	—	—	240,000
Income before income tax	$ 800,000	$ 800,000	$ 560,000
Deduct income tax	320,000	320,000	224,000
Net income	$ 480,000	$ 480,000	$ 336,000
Dividends on preferred stock	—	180,000	90,000
Available for dividends on common stock	$ 480,000	$ 300,000	$ 246,000
Shares of common stock outstanding	÷ 400,000	÷ 200,000	÷ 100,000
Earnings per share on common stock	$ 1.20	$ 1.50	$ 2.46

mon stockholders under Plan 1 and Plan 3 is even greater.[1] However, if smaller earnings occur, Plans 2 and 3 become less attractive to common stockholders. To illustrate, the effect of earnings of $440,000 rather than $800,000 is shown in Exhibit 2.

Exhibit 2 Effect of Alternative Financing Plans—$440,000 Earnings

	Plan 1	Plan 2	Plan 3
12% bonds	—	—	$2,000,000
Preferred 9% stock, $50 par	—	$2,000,000	1,000,000
Common stock, $10 par	$4,000,000	2,000,000	1,000,000
Total	$4,000,000	$4,000,000	$4,000,000
Earnings before interest and income tax	$ 440,000	$ 440,000	$ 440,000
Deduct interest on bonds	—	—	240,000
Income before income tax	$ 440,000	$ 440,000	$ 200,000
Deduct income tax	176,000	176,000	80,000
Net income	$ 264,000	$ 264,000	$ 120,000
Dividends on preferred stock	—	180,000	90,000
Available for dividends on common stock	$ 264,000	$ 84,000	$ 30,000
Shares of common stock outstanding	÷ 400,000	÷ 200,000	÷ 100,000
Earnings per share on common stock	$ 0.66	$ 0.42	$ 0.30

Real World

When interest rates are low, corporations usually finance their operations with debt. For example, as interest rates fell in the early 1990s, corporations rushed to issue new debt. In one day alone, more than $4.5 billion of debt was issued.

In addition to the effect on earnings per share, the board of directors should consider other factors in deciding whether to issue debt or equity. For example, once bonds are issued, periodic interest payments and repayment of the face value of the bonds are beyond the control of the corporation. That is, if these payments are not made, the bondholders could seek court action and could force the company into bankruptcy. In contrast, a corporation is not legally obligated to pay dividends.

---

[1] The higher earnings per share under Plan 1 is due to a finance concept known as **leverage**. This concept is discussed further in a later chapter.

Characteristics of Bonds Payable

objective 2

Describe the characteristics of bonds.

Real World

AT&T 7½% bonds maturing in 2006 were listed as selling for 100½ on September 7, 2000.

A corporation that issues bonds enters into a contract, called a **bond indenture** or **trust indenture**, with the bondholders. A bond issue is normally divided into a number of individual bonds. Usually the face value of each bond, called the **principal**, is $1,000 or a multiple of $1,000. The interest on bonds may be payable annually, semiannually, or quarterly. Most bonds pay interest semiannually.

The prices of bonds are quoted as a percentage of the bonds' face value. Thus, investors could purchase or sell **TimeWarner** bonds quoted at 109⅞ for $1,098.75. Likewise, bonds quoted at 109 could be purchased or sold for $1,090.

When all bonds of an issue mature at the same time, they are called **term bonds**. If the maturities are spread over several dates, they are called **serial bonds**. For example, one-tenth of an issue of $1,000,000 bonds, or $100,000, may mature 16 years from the issue date, another $100,000 in the 17th year, and so on until the final $100,000 matures in the 25th year.

Bonds that may be exchanged for other securities, such as common stock, are called **convertible bonds**. Bonds that a corporation reserves the right to redeem before their maturity are called **callable bonds**. Bonds issued on the basis of the general credit of the corporation are called **debenture bonds**.

BUSINESS ON STAGE

Bond Ratings

Bonds are rated as to their riskiness as investments by such independent financial reporting services as Moody's (www.moodys.com) and Standard and Poor's (www.standardandpoors.com). These services rely heavily on analysis of the financial statements and the terms of the bond indenture in setting the credit rating. This credit rating, in turn, influences how much the bonds will sell for in the marketplace. Moody's and Standard and Poor's rate bonds slightly differently. The following table shows all but the lowest ratings and their accompanying interpretation.

Moody's will use a "+" sign or "−" sign to indicate the relative strength of a bond within a general rating category. For example, AAA+ indicates that a bond is at the high end of the AAA category.

Instead of using a "+" or "−" sign to indicate relative strength within a rating category, Standard & Poor's uses 1, 2, and 3. For example, Aaa1 indicates that a bond is in the upper third of the Aaa category, while Aaa3 indicates that a bond is in the bottom third. ■

Moody's Rating	Standard and Poor's Rating	Interpretation
AAA	Aaa	Highest rating; ability to pay interest and principal is very secure.
AA	Aa	High quality; differs from highest-rated bonds only to a small degree.
A	A	Upper-medium quality; interest and principal may be in jeopardy if a long, deep economic downturn (recession) occurs.
BBB	Baa	Medium grade; adequate ability to pay interest and principal in normal economic conditions.
BB	Ba	Quite risky; modest ability to pay interest and principal.
B	B	Poor investment; highly speculative; ability to pay interest and principal over a long period is small.

The Present-Value Concept and Bonds Payable

objective 3

Compute the present value of bonds payable.

MARKET RATE=CONTRACT RATE

Selling price of bond = $1,000

$1,000 BOND

MARKET RATE > CONTRACT RATE

Selling price of bond < $1,000

$1,000 BOND −

Discount

MARKET RATE < CONTRACT RATE

Selling price of bond > $1,000

$1,000 BOND +

Premium

When a corporation issues bonds, the price that buyers are willing to pay for the bonds depends upon the following three factors:

1. The face amount of the bonds, which is the amount due at the maturity date.
2. The periodic interest to be paid on the bonds.
3. The market rate of interest.

The face amount and the periodic interest to be paid on the bonds are identified in the bond indenture. The periodic interest is expressed as a percentage of the face amount of the bond. This percentage or rate of interest is called the **contract rate** or **coupon rate**.

The **market** or **effective rate of interest** is determined by transactions between buyers and sellers of similar bonds. The market rate of interest is affected by a variety of factors, including investors' assessment of current economic conditions as well as future expectations.

If the contract rate of interest equals the market rate of interest, the bonds will sell at their face amount. If the market rate is higher than the contract rate, the bonds will sell at a **discount**, or less than their face amount. Why is this the case? Buyers are not willing to pay the face amount for bonds whose contract rate is lower than the market rate. The discount, in effect, represents the amount necessary to make up for the difference in the market and the contract interest rates. In contrast, if the market rate is lower than the contract rate, the bonds will sell at a **premium**, or more than their face amount. In this case, buyers are willing to pay more than the face amount for bonds whose contract rate is higher than the market rate.

The face amount of the bonds and the periodic interest on the bonds represent cash to be received by the buyer in the future. The buyer determines how much to pay for the bonds by computing the present value of these future cash receipts, using the market rate of interest. The concept of present value is based on the time value of money.

The time value of money concept recognizes that an amount of cash to be received today is worth more than the same amount of cash to be received in the future. For example, what would you rather have: $100 today or $100 one year from now? You would rather have the $100 today because it could be invested to earn income. For example, if the $100 could be invested to earn 10% per year, the $100 will accumulate to $110 ($100 plus $10 earnings) in one year. In this sense, you can think of the $100 in hand today as the **present value** of $110 to be received a year from today. This present value is illustrated in the following time line:

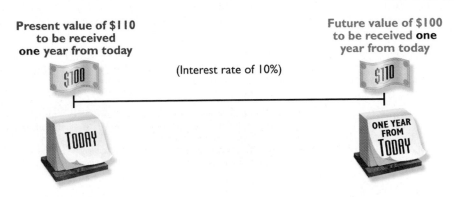

**Present value of $110
to be received
one year from today**

$100

TODAY

(Interest rate of 10%)

**Future value of $100
to be received one
year from today**

$110

ONE YEAR
FROM
TODAY

*If IBM 7¼%
bonds maturing in
2005 are listed as
selling for 104⅜, is the market
rate of interest higher or lower
than that for similar bonds?*

Lower

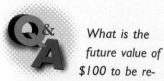

What is the future value of $100 to be received in two years, assuming an interest rate of 10%?

$121 ($100 × 1.10 × 1.10)

A related concept to present value is **future value**. In the preceding illustration, the $110 to be received a year from today is the future value of $100 today, assuming an interest rate of 10%.

Present Value of the Face Amount of Bonds

The present value of the face amount of bonds is the value today of the amount to be received at a future maturity date. For example, assume that you are to receive the face value of a $1,000 bond in one year. If the market rate of interest is 10%, the present value of the face value of the $1,000 bond is $909.09 ($1,000/1.10). This present value is illustrated in the following time line:

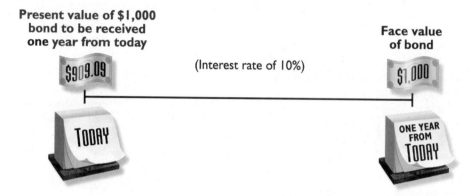

If you are to receive the face value of a $1,000 bond in two years, with interest of 10% compounded at the end of the first year, the present value is $826.45 ($909.09/1.10).[2] We illustrate this present value in the following time line:

What is the present value of $1,000 to be received in three years, assuming an interest rate of 10%?

$751.32 ($826.45/1.10)

Point of Interest
Spreadsheet software with built-in present value functions can be used to calculate present values.

You can determine the present value of the face amount of bonds to be received in the future by a time line and a series of divisions. In practice, however, it is easier to use a table of present values. The *present value of $1 table* can be used to find the present-value factor for $1 to be received after a number of periods in the future. The face amount of the bonds is then multiplied by this factor to determine its present value. Exhibit 3 is a partial table of the present value of $1.[3]

[2] Note that the future value of $826.45 in two years, at an interest rate of 10% compounded annually, is $1,000.
[3] To simplify the illustrations and homework assignments, the tables presented in this chapter are limited to 10 periods for a small number of interest rates, and the amounts are carried to only five decimal places. Computer programs are available for determining present value factors for any number of interest rates, decimal places, or periods. More complete interest tables, including future value tables, are presented in Appendix A.

Exhibit 3 Present Value of $1 at Compound Interest

Periods	5%	5½%	6%	6½%	7%	10%	11%	12%	13%	14%
1	0.95238	0.94787	0.94340	0.93897	0.93458	0.90909	0.90090	0.89286	0.88496	0.87719
2	0.90703	0.89845	0.89000	0.88166	0.87344	0.82645	0.81162	0.79719	0.78315	0.76947
3	0.86384	0.85161	0.83962	0.82785	0.81630	0.75132	0.73119	0.71178	0.69305	0.67497
4	0.82270	0.80722	0.79209	0.77732	0.76290	0.68301	0.65873	0.63552	0.61332	0.59208
5	0.78353	0.76513	0.74726	0.72988	0.71299	0.62092	0.59345	0.56743	0.54276	0.51937
6	0.74622	0.72525	0.70496	0.68533	0.66634	0.56447	0.53464	0.50663	0.48032	0.45559
7	0.71068	0.68744	0.66506	0.64351	0.62275	0.51316	0.48166	0.45235	0.42506	0.39964
8	0.67684	0.65160	0.62741	0.60423	0.58201	0.46651	0.43393	0.40388	0.37616	0.35056
9	0.64461	0.61763	0.59190	0.56735	0.54393	0.42410	0.39092	0.36061	0.33288	0.30751
10	0.61391	0.58543	0.55840	0.53273	0.50835	0.38554	0.35218	0.32197	0.29459	0.26974

What is the present value of $3,000 to be received in 5 years at a market rate of interest of 14% compounded annually?

$1,558.11 ($3,000 × 0.51937)

Exhibit 3 indicates that the present value of $1 to be received in two years with a market rate of interest of 10% a year is 0.82645. Multiplying the $1,000 face amount of the bond in the preceding example by 0.82645 yields $826.45.

In Exhibit 3, the Periods column represents the number of compounding periods, and the percentage columns represent the compound interest rate per period. For example, 10% for two years compounded *annually*, as in the preceding example, is 10% for two periods. Likewise, 10% for two years compounded *semiannually* would be 5% (10% per year/2 semiannual periods) for four periods (2 years × 2 semiannual periods). Similarly, 10% for three years compounded semiannually would be 5% (10%/2) for six periods (3 years × 2 semiannual periods).

Present Value of the Periodic Bond Interest Payments

The present value of the periodic bond interest payments is the value today of the amount of interest to be received at the end of each interest period. Such a series of equal cash payments at fixed intervals is called an **annuity**.

The **present value of an annuity** is the sum of the present values of each cash flow. To illustrate, assume that the $1,000 bond in the preceding example pays interest of 10% annually and that the market rate of interest is also 10%. In addition, assume that the bond matures at the end of two years. The present value of the two interest payments of $100 ($1,000 × 10%) is $173.56, as shown in the time line at the left. It can be determined by using the present value table shown in Exhibit 3.

Instead of using present value of amount tables, such as Exhibit 3, separate present value tables are normally used for annuities. Exhibit 4 is a partial table of the *present value of an annuity of $1* at compound interest. It shows the present value of $1 to be received at the end of each period for various compound rates of interest. For example, the present

Interest payment $100   Interest payment $100

TODAY   END OF YEAR 1   END OF YEAR 2

$90.91 ← $100 x 0.90909

$82.65 ← $100 x 0.82645

$173.56

Present value of $100 interest payments to be received each year for 2 years (rounded to the nearest cent)

value of $100 to be received at the end of each of the next two years at 10% compound interest per period is $173.55 ($100 × 1.73554). This amount is the same amount that we computed previously, except for rounding.

Exhibit 4 Present Value of Annuity of $1 at Compound Interest

Periods	5%	5½%	6%	6½%	7%	10%	11%	12%	13%	14%
1	0.95238	0.94787	0.94340	0.93897	0.93458	0.90909	0.90090	0.89286	0.88496	0.87719
2	1.85941	1.84632	1.83339	1.82063	1.80802	1.73554	1.71252	1.69005	1.66810	1.64666
3	2.72325	2.69793	2.67301	2.64848	2.62432	2.48685	2.44371	2.40183	2.36115	2.32163
4	3.54595	3.50515	3.46511	3.42580	3.38721	3.16987	3.10245	3.03735	2.97447	2.91371
5	4.32948	4.27028	4.21236	4.15568	4.10020	3.79079	3.69590	3.60478	3.51723	3.43308
6	5.07569	4.99553	4.91732	4.84101	4.76654	4.35526	4.23054	4.11141	3.99755	3.88867
7	5.78637	5.68297	5.58238	5.48452	5.38929	4.86842	4.71220	4.56376	4.42261	4.28830
8	6.46321	6.33457	6.20979	6.08875	5.97130	5.33493	5.14612	4.96764	4.79677	4.63886
9	7.10782	6.95220	6.80169	6.65610	6.51523	5.75902	5.53705	5.32825	5.13166	4.94637
10	7.72174	7.53763	7.36009	7.18883	7.02358	6.14457	5.88923	5.65022	5.42624	5.21612

What is the present value of a $10,000, 7%, 5-year bond that pays interest annually, assuming a market rate of interest of 7%?

$10,000 [($10,000 × 0.71299) + ($700 × 4.10020)]

As we stated earlier, the amount buyers are willing to pay for a bond is the sum of the present value of the face value and the periodic interest payments, calculated by using the market rate of interest. In our example, this calculation is as follows:

Present value of face value of $1,000 due in 2 years at 10% compounded annually: $1,000 × 0.82645 (present value factor of $1 for 2 periods at 10%)	$ 826.45
Present value of 2 annual interest payments of $100 at 10% compounded annually: $100 × 1.73554 (present value of annuity of $1 for 2 periods at 10%)	173.55
Total present value of bonds	$1,000.00

In this example, the market rate and the contract rate of interest are the same. Thus, the present value is the same as the face value.

Accounting for Bonds Payable

objective 4

Journalize entries for bonds payable.

In the preceding section, we described and illustrated how present value concepts are used in determining how much buyers are willing to pay for bonds. In this section, we describe and illustrate how corporations record the issuance of bonds and the payment of bond interest.

Bonds Issued at Face Amount

To illustrate the journal entries for issuing bonds, assume that on January 1, 2002, a corporation issues for cash $100,000 of 12%, five-year bonds, with interest of $6,000 payable *semiannually*. The market rate of interest at the time the bonds are issued is 12%. Since the contract rate and the market rate of interest are the same, the bonds will sell at their face amount. This amount is the sum of (1) the present value of the face amount of $100,000 to be repaid in five years and (2) the present value of ten *semiannual* interest payments of $6,000 each. This computation and a time line are shown below.

Present value of face amount of $100,000 due in 5 years,
  at 12% compounded semiannually: $100,000 × 0.55840
  (present value of $1 for 10 periods at 6%) .... $ 55,840
Present value of 10 semiannual interest payments of $6,000,
  at 12% compounded semiannually: $6,000 × 7.36009
  (present value of annuity of $1 for 10 periods at 6%) 44,160*
Total present value of bonds $100,000

*Because the present-value tables are rounded to five decimal places, minor rounding differences may appear in the illustrations.

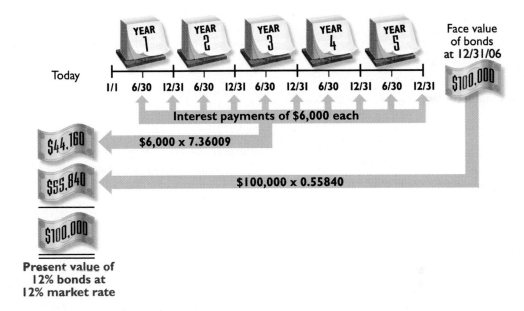

Present value of 12% bonds at 12% market rate

The following entry records the issuing of the $100,000 bonds at their face amount:

2002 Jan.	1	Cash		100 0 0 0 00		
		Bonds Payable			100 0 0 0 00
		Issued $100,000 bonds payable at			
		face amount.			

Every six months after the bonds have been issued, interest payments of $6,000 are made. The first interest payment is recorded as shown below.

June	30	Interest Expense		6 0 0 0 00		
		Cash			6 0 0 0 00
		Paid six months' interest on bonds.			

At the maturity date, the payment of the principal of $100,000 is recorded as follows:

	2006														
	Dec.	31	Bonds Payable		100 0 0 0 00								
			Cash					100 0 0 0 00				
			Paid bond principal at maturity									
			date.									

Bonds Issued at a Discount

What if the market rate of interest is higher than the contract rate of interest? If the market rate of interest is 13% and the contract rate is 12% on the five-year, $100,000 bonds, the bonds will sell at a discount. The present value of these bonds is calculated as follows:

Bonds will sell at a discount when the market rate of interest is higher than the contract rate.

Present value of face amount of $100,000 due in
  5 years, at 13% compounded semiannually: $100,000
  × 0.53273 (present value of $1 for 10 periods at 6½%) $53,273

Present value of 10 semiannual interest payments of $6,000,
  at 13% compounded semiannually: $6,000 × 7.18883
  (present value of an annuity of $1 for 10 periods at 6½%)   43,133

Total present value of bonds $96,406

The two present values that make up the total are both less than the related amounts in the preceding example. This is because the market rate of interest was 12% in the first example, while the market rate of interest is 13% in this example. The present value of a future amount becomes less and less as the interest rate used to compute the present value increases.

The entry to record the issuing of the $100,000 bonds at a discount is shown below.

Q&A *What is the present value of a $100,000, 6%, 5-year bond paying semiannual interest if the market rate of interest is 10%?*

$84,556 [($100,000 × 0.61391) + ($3,000 × 7.72174)]

	2002														
	Jan.	1	Cash		96 4 0 6 00								
			Discount on Bonds Payable		3 5 9 4 00								
			Bonds Payable					100 0 0 0 00				
			Issued $100,000 bonds at discount.									

The $3,594 discount may be viewed as the amount that is needed to entice investors to accept a contract rate of interest that is below the market rate. You may think of the discount as the market's way of adjusting a bond's contract rate of interest to the higher market rate of interest. Using this logic, generally accepted accounting principles require that bond discounts be amortized as interest expense over the life of the bond.

Amortizing a Bond Discount

There are two methods of amortizing a bond discount: (1) the **straight-line method** and (2) the effective interest rate method, often called the **interest method**. Both methods amortize the same total amount of discount over the life of the bonds. The interest method is required by generally accepted accounting principles. However, the straight-line method is acceptable if the results obtained do not materially differ from the results that would be obtained by using the interest method. Because the straight-line method illustrates the basic concept of amortizing discounts and is simpler, we will use it in this chapter. We illustrate the interest method in an appendix to this chapter.

The straight-line method of amortizing a bond discount provides for amortization in equal periodic amounts. Applying this method to the preceding example yields amortization of $\frac{1}{10}$ of $3,594, or $359.40, each half year. The amount of the interest expense on the bonds is the same, $6,359.40 ($6,000 + $359.40) for each half year. The entry to record the first interest payment and the amortization of the related discount is shown below.

2002						
June	30	Interest Expense		6 3 5 9 40		
		Discount on Bonds Payable			3 5 9 40	
		Cash			6 0 0 0 00	
		Paid semiannual interest and				
		amortized $\frac{1}{10}$ of bond discount.				

Bonds Issued at a Premium

If the market rate of interest is 11% and the contract rate is 12% on the five-year, $100,000 bonds, the bonds will sell at a premium. The present value of these bonds is computed as follows:

> **Bonds will sell at a premium when the market rate of interest is less than the contract rate.**

Present value of face amount of $100,000 due in 5 years,
    at 11% compounded semiannually: $100,000 × 0.58543
    (present value of $1 for 10 periods at 5½%) .... $ 58,543
Present value of 10 semiannual interest payments of $6,000,
    at 11% compounded semiannually: $6,000 × 7.53763
    (present value of an annuity of $1 for 10 periods at 5½%) 45,226
Total present value of bonds $103,769

The entry to record the issuing of the bonds is as follows:

2002						
Jan.	1	Cash		103 7 6 9 00		
		Bonds Payable			100 0 0 0 00	
		Premium on Bonds Payable			3 7 6 9 00	
		Issued $100,000 bonds at a				
		premium.				

Amortizing a Bond Premium

The amortization of bond premiums is basically the same as that for bond discounts, except that interest expense is decreased. In the above example, the straight-line method yields amortization of $\frac{1}{10}$ of $3,769, or $376.90, each half year. The entry to record the first interest payment and the amortization of the related premium is as follows:

2002						
June	30	Interest Expense		5 6 2 3 10		
		Premium on Bonds Payable		3 7 6 90		
		Cash			6 0 0 0 00	
		Paid semiannual interest and				
		amortized $\frac{1}{10}$ of bond premium.				

Zero-Coupon Bonds

Some corporations issue bonds that provide for only the payment of the face amount at the maturity date. Such bonds are called **zero-coupon bonds**. Because they do not provide for interest payments, these bonds sell at a large discount. For example, **Honeywell's** zero-coupon bonds maturing in 2007 were selling for 59¼ on September 7, 2000.

Some bonds with high contract rates, as well as some zero-coupon bonds, are issued by weak companies. Because such bonds are high-risk bonds, they are called **junk bonds**.

The issuing price of zero-coupon bonds is the present value of their face amount. To illustrate, if the market rate of interest is 13%, the present value of $100,000 zero-coupon, five-year bonds is calculated as follows:

Present value of $100,000 due in 5 years, at 13%
  compounded semiannually: $100,000 × 0.53273
  (present value of $1 for 10 periods at 6½%) $53,273

The accounting for zero-coupon bonds is similar to that for interest-bearing bonds that have been sold at a discount. The discount is amortized as interest expense over the life of the bonds. The entry to record the issuing of the bonds is as follows:

2002					
Jan.	1	Cash		53 2 7 3 00	
		Discount on Bonds Payable		46 7 2 7 00	
		Bonds Payable			100 0 0 0 00
		Issued $100,000 zero-coupon			
		bonds.			

Bond Sinking Funds

objective 5

Describe bond sinking funds.

A bond indenture may restrict dividend payments to stockholders as a means of increasing the likelihood that the bonds will be paid at maturity. In addition to or instead of this restriction, the bond indenture may require that funds for the payment of the face value of the bonds at maturity be set aside over the life of the bond issue. The amounts set aside are kept separate from other assets in a special fund called a **sinking fund**.

When cash is transferred to the sinking fund, it is recorded in an account called *Sinking Fund Cash*. When investments are purchased with the sinking fund cash, they are recorded in an account called *Sinking Fund Investments*. As income (interest or dividends) is received, it is recorded in an account called *Sinking Fund Revenue*.

Sinking fund revenue represents earnings of the corporation and is reported in the income statement as Other Income. The cash and the securities making up the sinking fund are reported in the balance sheet as Investments, immediately below the Current Assets section.

Bond Redemption

objective 6

Journalize entries for bond redemptions.

Indo Rayon issued 5-year, 10% bonds, callable after 3 years.

A corporation may call or redeem bonds before they mature. This is often done if the market rate of interest declines significantly after the bonds have been issued. In this situation, the corporation may sell new bonds at a lower interest rate and use the funds to redeem the original bond issue. The corporation can thus save on future interest expenses.

A corporation often issues callable bonds to protect itself against significant declines in future interest rates. However, callable bonds are more risky for investors, who may not be able to replace the called bonds with investments paying an equal amount of interest.

Callable bonds can be redeemed by the issuing corporation within the period of time and at the price stated in the bond indenture. Normally, the call price is above the face value. A corporation may also redeem its bonds by purchasing them on the open market.

A corporation usually redeems its bonds at a price different from that of the carrying amount (or book value) of the bonds. The **carrying amount** of bonds payable is the balance of the bonds payable account (face amount of the bonds) less any unamortized discount or plus any unamortized premium. If the price paid for redemption is below the bond carrying amount, the difference in these two amounts is recorded as a gain. If the price paid for the redemption is above the carrying amount, a loss is recorded. Gains and losses on the redemption of bonds are reported as an extraordinary item on the income statement.

To illustrate, assume that on June 30 a corporation has a bond issue of $100,000 outstanding, on which there is an unamortized premium of $4,000. Assuming that the corporation purchases one-fourth ($25,000) of the bonds for $24,000 on June 30, the entry to record the redemption is as follows:

	2002				
	June	30	Bonds Payable	25 0 0 0 00	
			Premium on Bonds Payable	1 0 0 0 00	
			Cash		24 0 0 0 00
			Gain on Redemption of Bonds		2 0 0 0 00
			Redeemed $25,000 bonds for		
			$24,000.		

In the preceding entry, only a portion of the premium relating to the redeemed bonds is written off. The difference between the carrying amount of the bonds purchased, $26,000 ($25,000 + $1,000), and the price paid for the redemption, $24,000, is recorded as a gain.

If the corporation calls the entire bond issue for $105,000 on June 30, the entry to record the redemption is as follows:

Q&A A $250,000 bond issue on which there is an unamortized discount of $20,000 is redeemed for $235,000. What is the gain or loss on the redemption of the bonds?

$5,000 loss ($250,000 − $20,000 − $235,000)

	2002				
	June	30	Bonds Payable	100 0 0 0 00	
			Premium on Bonds Payable	4 0 0 0 00	
			Loss on Redemption of Bonds	1 0 0 0 00	
			Cash		105 0 0 0 00
			Redeemed $100,000 bonds for		
			$105,000.		

Investments in Bonds

Loews' 3⅛% bonds maturing in 2007 were listed as selling for 92¾ on September 7, 2000.

Throughout this chapter, we have discussed bonds and the related transactions of the issuing corporation (the debtor). However, these transactions also affect investors. In this section, we discuss the accounting for bonds from the point of view of investors.

Accounting for Bond Investments—Purchase, Interest, and Amortization

Bonds may be purchased either directly from the issuing corporation or through an organized bond exchange. Bond exchanges publish daily bond quotations. These quotations normally include the bond interest rate, maturity date, volume of sales, and the high, low, and closing prices for each corporation's bonds traded during the day. Prices for bonds are quoted as a percentage of the face amount. Thus, the price of a $1,000 bond quoted at 99½ would be $995, while the price of a bond quoted at 104¼ would be $1,042.50.

As with other assets, the cost of a bond investment includes all costs related to the purchase. For example, for bonds purchased through an exchange, the amount paid as a broker's commission should be included as part of the cost of the investment.

When bonds are purchased between interest dates, the buyer normally pays the seller the interest accrued from the last interest payment date to the date of purchase. The amount of the interest paid is normally debited to *Interest Revenue*, since it is an offset against the amount that will be received at the next interest date.

To illustrate, assume that an investor purchases a $1,000 bond at 102 plus a brokerage fee of $5.30 and accrued interest of $10.20. The investor records the transaction as follows:

2002 Apr.	2	Investment in Lewis Co. Bonds		1 0 2 5 30		
		Interest Revenue		1 0 20		
		Cash			1 0 3 5 50	

The cost of the bond is recorded in a single investment account. The face amount of the bond and the premium (or discount) are normally not recorded in separate accounts. This is different from the accounting for bonds payable. Separate premium and discount accounts are usually not used by investors, because they usually do not hold bond investments until the bonds mature.

When bonds held as long-term investments are purchased at a price other than the face amount, the premium or discount should be amortized over the remaining life of the bonds. The amortization of premiums and discounts affects the investment and interest accounts as shown below.

Premium Amortization:			Discount Amortization:		
Interest Revenue	XXX		Investment in Bonds	XXX	
Investment in Bonds		XXX	Interest Revenue		XXX

The amount of the amortization can be determined by using either the straight-line or interest methods. Unlike bonds payable, the amortization of premiums and discounts on bond investments is usually recorded at the end of the period, rather than when interest is received.

To illustrate the accounting for bond investments, assume that on July 1, 2002, Crenshaw Inc. purchases $50,000 of 8% bonds of Deitz Corporation, due in 8¾ years. Crenshaw Inc. purchases the bonds directly from Deitz Corporation to yield an effective interest rate of 11%. The purchase price is $41,706 plus interest of $1,000 ($50,000 × 8% × $^3/_{12}$) accrued from April 1, 2002, the date of the last semiannual interest payment. Entries in the accounts of Crenshaw Inc. at the time of purchase and for the remainder of the fiscal period ending December 31, 2002, are as follows:

2002					
July	1	Investment in Deitz Corp. Bonds		41 7 0 6 00	
		Interest Revenue		1 0 0 0 00	
		Cash			42 7 0 6 00
		Purchased investment in bonds,			
		plus accrued interest:			
		Cost of $50,000 of Deitz			
		Corp. bonds $41,706			
		Interest accrued ($50,000			
		× 8% × $^3/_{12}$) 1,000			
		Total $42,706			
Oct.	1	Cash		2 0 0 0 00	
		Interest Revenue			2 0 0 0 00
		Received semiannual interest for			
		April 1 to October 1 ($50,000 ×			
		8% × $^6/_{12}$).			
Dec.	31	Interest Receivable		1 0 0 0 00	
		Interest Revenue			1 0 0 0 00
		Adjusting entry for interest			
		accrued from October 1 to			
		December 31 ($50,000 ×			
		8% × $^3/_{12}$).			
	31	Investment in Deitz Corp. Bonds		4 7 4 00	
		Interest Revenue			4 7 4 00
		Adjusting entry for amortization of			
		discount for July 1 to December 31:			
		Face value of bonds $50,000			
		Cost of bond			
		investment 41,706			
		Discount on bond			
		investment $ 8,294			
		Number of months to			
		maturity (8 ¾ years			
		× 12) 105 months			
		Monthly amortization			
		($8,294/105 months,			
		rounded to nearest			
		dollar) $79 per mo.			
		Amortization for 6			
		months ($79 × 6) $474			

The effect of these entries on the interest revenue account is shown below.

Interest Revenue

July 1	1,000	Oct. 1	2,000	
		Dec. 31	1,000	
		31	474	
		Bal. 2,474	3,474	

Accounting for Bond Investments—Sale

Many long-term investments in bonds are sold before their maturity date. When this occurs, the seller receives the sales price (less commissions and other selling costs) plus any accrued interest since the last interest payment date. Before recording the cash proceeds, the seller should amortize any discount or premium for the current period up to the date of sale. Any gain or loss on the sale is then recorded when the cash proceeds are recorded. Such gains and losses are normally reported in the Other Income section of the income statement.

To illustrate, assume that the Deitz Corporation bonds in the preceding example are sold for $47,350 plus accrued interest on June 30, 2009. The *carrying amount* of the bonds (cost plus amortized discount) as of January 1, 2009 (78 months after their purchase) is $47,868 [$41,706 + ($79 per month × 78 months)]. The entries to amortize the discount for the current year and to record the sale of the bonds are as follows:

2009 June	30	Investment in Deitz Corp. Bonds		4 7 4 00	
		Interest Revenue			4 7 4 00
		Amortized discount for current			
		year ($79 × 6 months).			
	30	Cash		48 3 5 0 00	
		Loss on Sale of Investments		9 9 2 00	
		Interest Revenue			1 0 0 0 00
		Investment in Deitz Corp. Bonds			48 3 4 2 00
		Received interest and proceeds			
		from sale of bonds.			
		Interest for April 1 to June 30 =			
		$50,000 × 8% × $^3/_{12}$ = $1,000			
		Carrying amount of			
		bonds on Jan. 1, 2009 $47,868			
		Discount amortized,			
		Jan. 1 to June 30, 2009 474			
		Carrying amount of			
		bonds on June 30, 2009 $48,342			
		Proceeds of sale 47,350			
		Loss on sale $ 992			

 If the Deitz Corporation bonds had been sold on September 30 instead of June 30, what would have been the amount of the loss?

$1,229 {$47,350 − [$48,342 + ($79 × 3 months)]}

Corporation Balance Sheet

objective 8

Prepare a corporation balance sheet.

In previous chapters, we illustrated the income statement and retained earnings statement for a corporation. The consolidated balance sheet in Exhibit 5 illustrates the presentation of many of the items discussed in this and preceding chapters. These items include bond sinking funds, investments in bonds, goodwill, deferred income taxes, bonds payable and unamortized discount, and minority interest in subsidiaries.

Exhibit 5 Balance Sheet of a Corporation

Escoe Corporation and Subsidiaries
Consolidated Balance Sheet
December 31, 2003

Assets

Current assets:

Cash and cash equivalents			$ 407,500
Accounts and notes receivable	$ 722,000		
Less allowance for doubtful receivables	37,000		685,000
Inventories, at lower of cost (first-in, first-out) or market			917,500
Prepaid expenses			70,000
Total current assets				$2,080,000

Investments:

Bond sinking fund (market value, $473,000)		$ 422,500
Investment in bonds of Dalton Company (market value, $231,000)		240,000
Total investments		662,500

	Cost	Accumulated Depreciation	Book Value	
Property, plant, and equipment (depreciated by the straight-line method):				
Land	$ 250,000	—	$ 250,000	
Buildings	920,000	$ 379,955	540,045	
Machinery and equipment	2,764,400	766,200	1,998,200	
Total property, plant, and equipment	$3,934,400	$1,146,155		2,788,245
Intangible assets:				
Goodwill			$ 300,000	
Organization costs			50,000	
Total intangible assets				350,000
Total assets				$5,880,745

Liabilities

Current liabilities:

Accounts payable		$ 508,810
Income tax payable		120,500
Dividends payable		94,000
Accrued liabilities		81,400
Deferred income tax payable		10,000
Total current liabilities		$ 814,710

Long-term liabilities:

Debenture 8% bonds payable, due December 31, 2018 (market value, $950,000)	$1,000,000		
Less unamortized discount	60,000	$ 940,000	
Minority interest in subsidiaries		115,000	
Total long-term liabilities			1,055,000

Deferred credits:

Deferred income tax payable		85,500
Total liabilities		$1,955,210

Stockholders' Equity

Paid-in capital:

Common stock, $20 par (250,000 shares authorized, 100,000 shares issued)	$2,000,000		
Excess of issue price over par	320,000		
Total paid-in capital		$2,320,000	
Retained earnings		1,605,535	
Total stockholders' equity			3,925,535
Total liabilities and stockholders' equity			$5,880,745

Balance Sheet Presentation of Bonds Payable

In Exhibit 5, Escoe Corporation's bonds payable are reported as long-term liabilities. If there were two or more bond issues, the details of each would be reported on the balance sheet or in a supporting schedule or note. Separate accounts are normally maintained for each bond issue.

When the balance sheet date is within one year of the maturity date of the bonds, the bonds may be classified as a current liability. This would be the case if the bonds are to be paid out of current assets. If the bonds are to be paid from a sinking fund or if they are to be refinanced with another bond issue, they should remain in the noncurrent category. In this case, the details of the retirement of the bonds are normally disclosed in a note to the financial statements.

The balance in Escoe's discount on bonds payable account is reported as a *deduction* from the bonds payable. Conversely, the balance in a bond premium account would be reported as an *addition* to the related bonds payable. Either on the face of the financial statements or in accompanying notes, a description of the bonds (terms, due date, and effective interest rate) and other relevant information such as sinking fund requirements should be disclosed.[4] Finally, the market (fair) value of the bonds payable should also be disclosed.

Balance Sheet Presentation of Bond Investments

Investments in bonds or other debt securities that management intends to hold to their maturity are called **held-to-maturity securities**. Such securities are classified as long-term investments under the caption Investments. These investments are reported at their cost less any amortized premium or plus any amortized discount. In addition, the market (fair) value of the bond investments should be disclosed, either on the face of the balance sheet or in an accompanying note.

FINANCIAL ANALYSIS AND INTERPRETATION

objective 9

Compute and interpret the number of times interest charges are earned.

Some corporations, such as railroads and public utilities, have a high ratio of debt to stockholders' equity. For such corporations, analysts often assess the relative risk of the debtholders in terms of the **number of times the interest charges are earned** during the year. The higher the ratio, the greater the chance that interest payments will continue to be made if earnings decrease.[5]

The amount available to make interest payments is not affected by taxes on income. This is because interest is deductible in determining taxable income. To illustrate, the following data were taken from the 1999 annual report of **Briggs & Stratton Corporation**:

Interest expense	$17,024,000
Income before income tax	$169,771,000

The number of times interest charges are earned, 10.97, is calculated below.

$$\text{Number of times interest charges earned} = \frac{\text{Income before income tax} + \text{Interest expense}}{\text{Interest expense}}$$

---

[4] *Statement of Financial Accounting Standards No. 129*, "Disclosure Information About Capital Structure," Financial Accounting Standards Board (Norwalk, Connecticut: 1997).

[5] A similar analysis can also be applied to dividends on preferred stock. In such cases, net income would be divided by the amount of preferred dividends to yield the number of times preferred dividends were earned. This measure gives an indication of the relative assurance of continued dividend payments to preferred stockholders.

$$\text{Number of times interest charges earned} = \frac{\$169{,}771{,}000 + \$17{,}024{,}000}{\$17{,}024{,}000} = 10.97$$

The number of times interest charges are earned indicates that the debtholders of Briggs & Stratton have adequate protection against a potential drop in earnings jeopardizing their receipt of interest payments. However, a final assessment should include a review of trends of past years and a comparison with industry averages.

ENCORE

Let's Dance—A Bond with a Tune

How would you like to tune into some of the royalties from David Bowie's hit song, *Let's Dance*? The British rock star has offered bonds backed by future royalties from his hit songs and albums recorded prior to 1990. In addition to *Let's Dance*, other songs include *Jean Genie*, *A Space Oddity*, *Changes*, *Diamond Dogs*, and *Rebel*.

Bowie's bonds, which have an average maturity of 10 years, pay 7.9% annual interest. Such asset-backed bonds have grown in popularity. However, this is the first time that a popular artist has made use of future royalties as asset backing. The Bowie Bonds, which are officially called Class-A royalty-backed securities, were rated AAA—the highest rating—by **Moody's Investors Service.**

Bowie is one of the most financially savvy rock stars in the world, with a well-chosen art collection and

an appreciation for market trends. Bowie's principal residence is a $3.4 million, 640-acre estate in County Wicklow, Ireland, a noted tax haven. He lives there with his second wife, the supermodel and actress Iman. Still, Bowie's business manager said that when he approached him with the bond idea, "he [Bowie] kind of looked at me cross-eyed and said, 'What?'"

Potential investors were reassured by the fact that Bowie never sells fewer than a million albums a year. At the time of the offering, Bowie's album, "Earthling," was near the top of the European charts. In addition, the month before the offering, he performed for a sold-out concert at New York's Madison Square Garden.

Prudential Insurance Co. isn't kidding when it says you can own a piece of the *rock*. In a private placement, Prudential purchased all of

David Bowie's $55 million bonds for its general investment fund, where the money of life insurance policyholders is invested.

In addition to Bowie, other musicians who have issued royalty-backed bonds include James Brown and the heavy-metal band Iron Maiden. The Iron Maiden bonds were successfully sold for $30 million. ∎

APPENDIX—EFFECTIVE INTEREST RATE METHOD OF AMORTIZATION

The effective interest rate method of amortizing discounts and premiums provides for a constant rate of interest on the carrying amount of the bonds at the beginning of each period. This is in contrast to the straight-line method, which provides for a constant amount of interest expense.

The interest rate used in the interest method of amortization is the market rate on the date the bonds are issued. The carrying amount of the bonds to which the interest rate is applied is the face amount of the bonds minus any unamortized discount or plus any unamortized premium. Under the interest method, the interest expense to be reported on the income statement is computed by multiplying the effective interest rate by the carrying amount of the bonds. The difference between the interest expense computed in this way and the periodic interest payment is the amount of discount or premium to be amortized for the period.

Amortization of Discount by the Interest Method

To illustrate the interest method for amortizing bond discounts, we assume the following data from the chapter illustration of issuing $100,000 bonds at a discount:

Face value of 12%, 5-year bonds, interest compounded semiannually	$100,000
Present value of bonds at effective (market) rate of interest of 13%	96,406
Discount on bonds payable	$ 3,594

Applying the interest method to these data yields the amortization table in Exhibit 6. You should note the following items in this table:

1. The interest paid (Column A) remains constant at 6% of $100,000, the face amount of the bonds.
2. The interest expense (Column B) is computed at 6½% of the bond carrying amount at the beginning of each period. This results in an increasing interest expense each period.
3. The excess of the interest expense over the interest payment of $6,000 is the amount of discount to be amortized (Column C).
4. The unamortized discount (Column D) decreases from the initial balance, $3,594, to a zero balance at the maturity date of the bonds.
5. The carrying amount (Column E) increases from $96,406, the amount received for the bonds, to $100,000 at maturity.

Exhibit 6 Amortization of Discount on Bonds Payable

Interest Payment	A Interest Paid (6% of Face Amount)	B Interest Expense (6½% of Bond Carrying Amount)	C Discount Amortization (B − A)	D Unamortized Discount (D − C)	E Bond Carrying Amount ($100,000 − D)
				$3,594	$ 96,406
1	$6,000	$6,266 (6½% of $96,406)	$266	3,328	96,672
2	6,000	6,284 (6½% of $96,672)	284	3,044	96,956
3	6,000	6,302 (6½% of $96,956)	302	2,742	97,258
4	6,000	6,322 (6½% of $97,258)	322	2,420	97,580
5	6,000	6,343 (6½% of $97,580)	343	2,077	97,923
6	6,000	6,365 (6½% of $97,923)	365	1,712	98,288
7	6,000	6,389 (6½% of $98,288)	389	1,323	98,677
8	6,000	6,414 (6½% of $98,677)	414	909	99,091
9	6,000	6,441 (6½% of $99,091)	441	468	99,532
10	6,000	6,470 (6½% of $99,532)	468*	—	100,000

*Cannot exceed unamortized discount.

The entry to record the first interest payment on June 30, 2002, and the related discount amortization is as follows:

2002 June	30	Interest Expense		6 2 6 6 00		
		Discount on Bonds Payable			2 6 6 00	
		Cash			6 0 0 0 00	
		Paid semiannual interest and				
		amortized bond discount for				
		one-half year.				

If the amortization is recorded only at the end of the year, the amount of the discount amortized on December 31 would be $550. This is the sum of the first two semiannual amortization amounts ($266 and $284) from Exhibit 6.

Amortization of Premium by the Interest Method

To illustrate the interest method for amortizing bond premiums, we assume the following data from the chapter illustration of issuing $100,000 bonds at a premium:

Present value of bonds at effective (market) rate of interest of 11%	$103,769
Face value of 12%, 5-year bonds, interest compounded semiannually	100,000
Premium on bonds payable	$ 3,769

Using the interest method to amortize the above premium yields the amortization table in Exhibit 7.

Exhibit 7 Amortization of Premium on Bonds Payable

Interest Payment	A Interest Paid (6% of Face Amount)	B Interest Expense (5½% of Bond Carrying Amount)	C Premium Amortization (A – B)	D Unamortized Premium (D – C)	E Bond Carrying Amount ($100,000 + D)
				$3,769	$103,769
1	$6,000	$5,707 (5½% of $103,769)	$293	3,476	103,476
2	6,000	5,691 (5½% of $103,476)	309	3,167	103,167
3	6,000	5,674 (5½% of $103,167)	326	2,841	102,841
4	6,000	5,656 (5½% of $102,841)	344	2,497	102,497
5	6,000	5,637 (5½% of $102,497)	363	2,134	102,134
6	6,000	5,617 (5½% of $102,134)	383	1,751	101,751
7	6,000	5,596 (5½% of $101,751)	404	1,347	101,347
8	6,000	5,574 (5½% of $101,347)	426	921	100,921
9	6,000	5,551 (5½% of $100,921)	449	472	100,472
10	6,000	5,526 (5½% of $100,472)	472*	—	100,000

*Cannot exceed unamortized premium.

You should note the following items in this table:

1. The interest paid (Column A) remains constant at 6% of $100,000, the face amount of the bonds.
2. The interest expense (Column B) is computed at 5½% of the bond carrying amount at the beginning of each period. This results in a decreasing interest expense each period.
3. The excess of the periodic interest payment of $6,000 over the interest expense is the amount of premium to be amortized (Column C).

4. The unamortized premium (Column D) decreases from the initial balance, $3,769, to a zero balance at the maturity date of the bonds.
5. The carrying amount (Column E) decreases from $103,769, the amount received for the bonds, to $100,000 at maturity.

The entry to record the first interest payment on June 30, 2002, and the related premium amortization is as follows:

2002 June	30	Interest Expense		5 7 0 7 00	
		Premium on Bonds Payable		2 9 3 00	
		Cash			6 0 0 0 00
		Paid semiannual interest and			
		amortized bond premium for			
		one-half year.			

If the amortization is recorded only at the end of the year, the amount of the premium amortized on December 31, 2002, would be $602. This is the sum of the first two semiannual amortization amounts ($293 and $309) from Exhibit 7.

HEY POINTS

1 Compute the potential impact of long-term borrowing on the earnings per share of a corporation.
Three alternative plans for financing a corporation by issuing common stock, preferred stock, or bonds are illustrated in Exhibits 1 and 2. The effects of alternative financing on the earnings per share vary significantly, depending upon the level of earnings.

2 Describe the characteristics of bonds.
The characteristics of bonds depend upon the type of bonds issued by a corporation. Bonds that may be issued include term bonds, serial bonds, convertible bonds, callable bonds, and debenture bonds.

3 Compute the present value of bonds payable.
The concept of present value is based on the time value of money. That is, an amount of cash to be received at some date in the future is worth less than

the same amount of cash held today. For example, if $100 cash today can be invested to earn 10% per year, the $100 today is referred to as the present value amount that is equal to $110 to be received a year from today.

A price that a buyer is willing to pay for a bond is the sum of (1) the present value of the face amount of the bonds at the maturity date and (2) the present value of the periodic interest payments.

4 Journalize entries for bonds payable.
The journal entry for issuing bonds payable debits Cash for the proceeds received and credits Bonds Payable for the face amount of the bonds. Any difference between the face amount of the bonds and the proceeds is debited to Discount on Bonds Payable or credited to Premium on Bonds Payable.

A discount or premium on bonds payable is amortized to interest expense over the life of

the bonds. The entry to amortize a discount debits Interest Expense and credits Discount on Bonds Payable. The entry to amortize a premium debits Premium on Bonds Payable and credits Interest Expense.

5 Describe bond sinking funds.
A bond indenture may require that funds for the payment of the bonds at maturity be set aside over the life of the bonds. The amounts set aside are kept separate from other assets in a special fund called a sinking fund. A sinking fund is reported as an Investment on the balance sheet. Income from a sinking fund is reported as Other Income on the income statement.

6 Journalize entries for bond redemptions.
When a corporation redeems bonds, Bonds Payable is debited for the face amount of the bonds, the premium (discount) on bonds account is debited (credited) for

its balance, Cash is credited, and any gain or loss on the redemption is recorded.

7 Journalize entries for the purchase, interest, discount and premium amortization, and sale of bond investments.

A long-term investment in bonds is recorded by debiting Investment in Bonds. When bonds are purchased between interest dates, the amount of the interest paid should be debited to Interest Revenue. Any discount or premium on bond investments should be amortized, using the straight-line or effective interest rate methods. The amortization of a discount is recorded by debiting Investment in Bonds and crediting Interest Revenue. The amortization of a premium is recorded by debiting Interest Revenue and crediting Investment in Bonds.

When bonds held as long-term investments are sold, any discount or premium for the current period should first be amortized. Cash is then debited for the proceeds of the sale, Investment in Bonds is credited for its balance, and any gain or loss is recorded.

8 Prepare a corporation balance sheet.

The corporation balance sheet may include bond sinking funds, investments in bonds, goodwill, deferred income taxes, bonds payable and unamortized premium or discount, and minority interest in subsidiaries.

Bonds payable are usually reported as long-term liabilities.

A discount on bonds should be reported as a deduction from the related bonds payable. A premium on bonds should be reported as an addition to the related bonds payable. Investments in bonds that are held-to-maturity securities are reported as Investments at cost less any amortized premium or plus any amortized discount.

9 Compute and interpret the number of times interest charges are earned.

The number of times interest charges are earned during the year is a measure of the risk that interest payments to debtholders will continue to be made if earnings decrease. It is computed by dividing income before income tax plus interest expense by interest expense.

ILLUSTRATIVE PROBLEM

The fiscal year of Russell Inc., a manufacturer of acoustical supplies, ends December 31. Selected transactions for the period 2002 through 2009, involving bonds payable issued by Russell Inc., are as follows:

2002
June 30. Issued $2,000,000 of 25-year, 7% callable bonds dated June 30, 2002, for cash of $1,920,000. Interest is payable semiannually on June 30 and December 31.
Dec. 31. Paid the semiannual interest on the bonds.
    31. Recorded straight-line amortization of $1,600 of discount on the bonds.
    31. Closed the interest expense account.

2003
June 30. Paid the semiannual interest on the bonds.
Dec. 31. Paid the semiannual interest on the bonds.
    31. Recorded straight-line amortization of $3,200 of discount on the bonds.
    31. Closed the interest expense account.

2009
June 30. Recorded the redemption of the bonds, which were called at 101½. The balance in the bond discount account is $57,600 after the payment of interest and amortization of discount have been recorded. (Record the redemption only.)

Instructions

1. Journalize entries to record the preceding transactions.
2. Determine the amount of interest expense for 2002 and 2003.
3. Estimate the effective annual interest rate by dividing the interest expense for 2002 by the bond carrying amount at the time of issuance and multiplying by 2.
4. Determine the carrying amount of the bonds as of December 31, 2003.

Solution

1.

2002						
June	30	Cash	1,920 0 0 0 00			
		Discount on Bonds Payable	80 0 0 0 00			
		Bonds Payable			2,000 0 0 0 00	
Dec.	31	Interest Expense	70 0 0 0 00			
		Cash			70 0 0 0 00	
	31	Interest Expense	1 6 0 0 00			
		Discount on Bonds Payable			1 6 0 0 00	
	31	Income Summary	71 6 0 0 00			
		Interest Expense			71 6 0 0 00	
2003						
June	30	Interest Expense	70 0 0 0 00			
		Cash			70 0 0 0 00	
Dec.	31	Interest Expense	70 0 0 0 00			
		Cash			70 0 0 0 00	
	31	Interest Expense	3 2 0 0 00			
		Discount on Bonds Payable			3 2 0 0 00	
	31	Income Summary	143 2 0 0 00			
		Interest Expense			143 2 0 0 00	
2009						
June	30	Bonds Payable	2,000 0 0 0 00			
		Loss on Redemption of Bonds Payable	87 6 0 0 00			
		Discount on Bonds Payable			57 6 0 0 00	
		Cash			2,030 0 0 0 00	

2. a.   2002—$71,600
    b.   2003—$143,200

3. $71,600 ÷ $1,920,000 = 3.73% rate for six months of a year
    3.73% × 2 = 7.46% annual rate

4. | Initial carrying amount of bonds | $1,920,000 |
    |---|---|
    | Discount amortized on December 31, 2002 | 1,600 |
    | Discount amortized on December 31, 2003 | 3,200 |
    | Carrying amount of bonds, December 31, 2003 | $1,924,800 |

SELF-EXAMINATION QUESTIONS   Answers at End of Chapter

Matching
Match each of the following statements with its proper term. Some terms may not be used.

A.	**annuity**
B.	**available-for-sale securities**

___ 1. A form of an interest-bearing note used by corporations to borrow on a long-term basis.

___ 2. The contract between a corporation issuing bonds and the bondholders.

C. bond

D. bond fund

E. bond indenture

F. carrying amount

G. contract rate

H. discount

I. dividend yield

J. effective interest rate method

K. effective rate of interest

L. future value

M. held-to-maturity securities

N. number of times interest charges earned

O. premium

P. present value

Q. present value of an annuity

R. sinking fund

___ 3. The periodic interest to be paid on the bonds that is identified in the bond indenture; expressed as a percentage of the face amount of the bond.

___ 4. A series of equal cash flows at fixed intervals.

___ 5. The sum of the present values of a series of equal cash flows to be received at fixed intervals.

___ 6. The estimated worth today of an amount of cash to be received (or paid) in the future.

___ 7. The estimated worth in the future of an amount of cash on hand today invested at a fixed rate of interest.

___ 8. The excess of the face amount of bonds over their issue price.

___ 9. The excess of the issue price of bonds over their face amount.

___ 10. A fund in which cash or assets are set aside for the purpose of paying the face amount of the bonds at maturity.

___ 11. The balance of the bonds payable account (face amount of the bonds) less any unamortized discount or plus any unamortized premium.

___ 12. Investments in bonds or other debt securities that management intends to hold to their maturity.

___ 13. A ratio that measures the risk that interest payments to debtholders will continue to be made if earnings decrease.

___ 14. The market rate of interest at the time bonds are issued.

Multiple Choice

1. If a corporation plans to issue $1,000,000 of 12% bonds at a time when the market rate for similar bonds is 10%, the bonds can be expected to sell at:
   A. their face amount
   B. a premium
   C. a discount
   D. a price below their face amount

2. If the bonds payable account has a balance of $500,000 and the discount on bonds payable account has a balance of $40,000, what is the carrying amount of the bonds?
   A. $460,000
   B. $500,000
   C. $540,000
   D. $580,000

3. The cash and securities that make up the sinking fund established for the payment of bonds at maturity are classified on the balance sheet as:

   A. current assets
   B. investments
   C. long-term liabilities
   D. current liabilities

4. If a firm purchases $100,000 of bonds of X Company at 101 plus accrued interest of $2,000 and pays broker's commissions of $50, the amount debited to Investment in X Company Bonds would be:
   A. $100,000
   B. $101,050
   C. $103,000
   D. $103,050

5. The balance in the discount on bonds payable account would usually be reported in the balance sheet in the:
   A. Current Assets section
   B. Current Liabilities section
   C. Long-Term Liabilities section
   D. Investments section

CLASS DISCUSSION QUESTIONS

1. Describe the two distinct obligations incurred by a corporation when issuing bonds.
2. Explain the meaning of each of the following terms as they relate to a bond issue: (a) convertible, (b) callable, and (c) debenture.
3. What is meant by the "time value of money"?
4. What has the higher present value: (a) $5,000 to be received at the end of two years, or (b) $2,500 to be received at the end of each of the next two years?

5. If you asked your broker to purchase for you a 6% bond when the market interest rate for such bonds was 7%, would you expect to pay more or less than the face amount for the bond? Explain.

6. A corporation issues $10,000,000 of 6% bonds to yield interest at the rate of 5%. (a) Was the amount of cash received from the sale of the bonds greater or less than $10,000,000? (b) Identify the following terms related to the bond issue: (1) face amount, (2) market or effective rate of interest, (3) contract rate of interest, and (4) maturity amount.

7. If bonds issued by a corporation are sold at a premium, is the market rate of interest greater or less than the contract rate?

8. The following data relate to a $1,000,000, 6% bond issue for a selected semiannual interest period:

Bond carrying amount at beginning of period	$1,150,000
Interest paid at end of period	30,000
Interest expense allocable to the period	28,750

(a) Were the bonds issued at a discount or at a premium? (b) What is the unamortized amount of the discount or premium account at the beginning of the period? (c) What account was debited to amortize the discount or premium?

9. Assume that Abacus Co. amortizes premiums and discounts on bonds payable at the end of the year rather than when interest is paid. What accounts would be debited and credited to record (a) the amortization of a discount on bonds payable and (b) the amortization of a premium on bonds payable?

10. Would a zero-coupon bond ever sell for its face amount?

11. What is the purpose of a bond sinking fund?

12. How are earnings from investments in a sinking fund reported on the income statement?

13. How are cash and securities comprising a sinking fund classified on the balance sheet?

14. Assume that two 15-year, 7% bond issues are identical, except that one bond issue is callable at its face amount at the end of 10 years. Which of the two bond issues do you think will sell for a lower value?

15. Bonds Payable has a balance of $750,000, and Discount on Bonds Payable has a balance of $12,500. If the issuing corporation redeems the bonds at 99, is there a gain or loss on the bond redemption?

16. How are gains or losses on bond redemptions reported on the income statement?

17. Assume that a company purchases bonds between interest dates. What accounts would normally be debited?

18. Indicate how the following accounts should be reported on the balance sheet: (a) Premium on Bonds Payable and (b) Discount on Bonds Payable.

19. Where are investments in bonds that are classified as held-to-maturity securities reported on the balance sheet?

20. At what amount are held-to-maturity investments in bonds reported on the balance sheet?

 RESOURCES FOR YOUR SUCCESS ONLINE AT

http://warren.swcollege.com

Remember! If you need additional help, visit South-Western's Web site.
See page 26 for a description of the online and printed materials that are available.

EXERCISES

Exercise 14–1
Effect of financing on earnings per share

Objective 1

✓ a. $0.30

Compatriot Co., which produces and sells skiing equipment, is financed as follows:

Bonds payable, 8% (issued at face amount)	$5,000,000
Preferred $3 stock (nonparticipating), $50 par	5,000,000
Common stock, $25 par	5,000,000

Income tax is estimated at 40% of income.

Determine the earnings per share of common stock, assuming that the income before bond interest and income tax is (a) $1,000,000, (b) $1,500,000, and (c) $2,500,000.

Exercise 14–2
Evaluate alternative financing plans

Objective 1

◖▬▬▶ Based upon the data in Exercise 14–1, discuss factors other than earnings per share that should be considered in evaluating such financing plans.

Exercise 14–3
Corporate financing

Objective 1

Real World

The financial statements for **Cisco Systems, Inc.** are presented in Appendix G at the end of the text.

a. What is the major source of financing for Cisco Systems?
b. Why would you expect that Cisco Systems has not used any long-term debt in its financing?

Exercise 14–4
Present value of amounts due

Objective 3

Determine the present value of $10,000 to be received in three years, using an interest rate of 6%, compounded annually, as follows:

a. By successive divisions. (Round to the nearest dollar.)
b. By using the present value table in Exhibit 3.

Exercise 14–5
Present value of annuity

Objective 3

Determine the present value of $6,000 to be received at the end of each of four years, using an interest rate of 5%, compounded annually, as follows:

a. By successive computations, using the present value table in Exhibit 3.
b. By using the present value table in Exhibit 4.

Exercise 14 6
Present value of an annuity

Objective 3

On January 1, 2003, you win $10,000,000 in the state lottery. The $10,000,000 prize will be paid in equal installments of $400,000 over 25 years. The payments will be made on December 31 of each year, beginning on December 31, 2003. If the current interest rate is 7%, determine the present value of your winnings. Use the present value tables in Appendix A.

Exercise 14–7
Present value of an annuity

Objective 3

Assume the same data as in Exercise 14–6, except that the current interest rate is 14%.
◖▬▬▶ Will the present value of your winnings using an interest rate of 14% be one-half the present value of your winnings using an interest rate of 7%? Why or why not?

Exercise 14–8
Present value of bonds payable; discount
Objectives 3, 4

Czerny Co. produces and sells bottle capping equipment for soft drink and spring water bottlers. To finance its operations, Czerny Co. issued $8,000,000 of five-year, 9% bonds with interest payable semiannually at an effective interest rate of 10%. Determine the present value of the bonds payable, using the present value tables in Exhibits 3 and 4. Round to the nearest dollar.

Exercise 14–9
Present value of bonds payable; premium
Objectives 3, 4

Descartes Alarms Co. issued $10,000,000 of five-year, 12% bonds with interest payable semiannually, at an effective interest rate of 11%. Determine the present value of the bonds payable, using the present value tables in Exhibits 3 and 4. Round to the nearest dollar.

Exercise 14–10
Bond price
Objectives 3, 4

IBM Corporation 7½% bonds due in 2013 were reported in *The Wall Street Journal* as selling for 102⅜ on September 7, 2000.

➤ Were the bonds selling at a premium or at a discount on September 7, 2000? Explain.

Exercise 14–11
Entries for issuing bonds
Objective 4

Elba Co. produces and distributes fiber optic cable for use by telecommunications companies. Elba Co. issued $12,000,000 of 15-year, 9% bonds on April 1 of the current year, with interest payable on April 1 and October 1. The fiscal year of the company is the calendar year. Journalize the entries to record the following selected transactions for the current year:

Apr.   1. Issued the bonds for cash at their face amount.
Oct.   1. Paid the interest on the bonds.
Dec. 31. Recorded accrued interest for three months.

Exercise 14–12
Entries for issuing bonds and amortizing discount by straight-line method
Objective 4

✓ b. $513,065

On the first day of its fiscal year, Electrokinetics Company issued $5,000,000 of five-year, 8% bonds to finance its operations of producing and selling home electronics equipment. Interest is payable semiannually. The bonds were issued at an effective interest rate of 11%, resulting in Electrokinetics Company receiving cash of $4,434,676.

a.   Journalize the entries to record the following:
    1.   Sale of the bonds.
    2.   First semiannual interest payment. (Amortization of discount is to be recorded annually.)
    3.   Second semiannual interest payment.
    4.   Amortization of discount at the end of the first year, using the straight-line method. (Round to the nearest dollar.)
b.   Determine the amount of the bond interest expense for the first year.

Exercise 14–13
Computing bond proceeds, entries for bond issuing, and amortizing premium by straight-line method
Objectives 3, 4

Fajitas Corporation wholesales oil and grease products to equipment manufacturers. On March 1, 2003, Fajitas Corporation issued $10,000,000 of five-year, 11% bonds at an effective interest rate of 10%. Interest is payable semiannually on March 1 and September 1. Journalize the entries to record the following:

a.   Sale of bonds on March 1, 2003. (Use the tables of present values in Exhibits 3 and 4 to determine the bond proceeds.)
b.   First interest payment on September 1, 2003, and amortization of bond premium for six months, using the straight-line method. (Round to the nearest dollar.)

Exercise 14–14
Entries for issuing and calling bonds; loss

Objectives 4, 6

Farouk Corp., a wholesaler of office furniture, issued $15,000,000 of 30-year, 8% callable bonds on March 1, 2003, with interest payable on March 1 and September 1. The fiscal year of the company is the calendar year. Journalize the entries to record the following selected transactions:

2003
Mar. 1. Issued the bonds for cash at their face amount.
Sept. 1. Paid the interest on the bonds.
2007
Sept. 1. Called the bond issue at 101, the rate provided in the bond indenture. (Omit entry for payment of interest.)

Exercise 14–15
Entries for issuing and calling bonds; gain

Objectives 4, 6

Gehrig Corp. produces and sells automotive and aircraft safety belts. To finance its operations, Gehrig Corp. issued $20,000,000 of 25-year, 9% callable bonds on June 1, 2003, with interest payable on June 1 and December 1. The fiscal year of the company is the calendar year. Journalize the entries to record the following selected transactions:

2003
June 1. Issued the bonds for cash at their face amount.
Dec. 1. Paid the interest on the bonds.
2008
Dec. 1. Called the bond issue at 99, the rate provided in the bond indenture. (Omit entry for payment of interest.)

Exercise 14–16
Reporting bonds

Objectives 5, 6, 8

At the beginning of the current year, two bond issues (A and B) were outstanding. During the year, bond issue A was redeemed and a significant loss on the redemption of bonds was reported as Other Expense on the income statement. At the end of the year, bond issue B was reported as a current liability because its maturity date was early in the following year. A sinking fund of cash and securities sufficient to pay the series B bonds was reported in the balance sheet as *Investments.*

Can you find any flaws in the reporting practices related to the two bond issues?

Exercise 14–17
Amortizing discount on bond investment

Objective 7

A company purchased a $1,000, 20-year zero coupon bond for $189 to yield 8.5% to maturity. How is the interest revenue computed?

Source: "Technical Hotline," *Journal of Accountancy,* January 1989, p. 100.

Exercise 14–18
Entries for purchase and sale of investment in bonds; loss

Objective 7

Gloucester Co. sells optical supplies to opticians and ophthalmologists. Journalize the entries to record the following selected transactions of Gloucester Co.:

a. Purchased for cash $300,000 of Glitz Co. 8% bonds at 102½ plus accrued interest of $6,000.
b. Received first semiannual interest.
c. At the end of the first year, amortized $250 of the bond premium.
d. Sold the bonds at 98½ plus accrued interest of $2,000. The bonds were carried at $302,500 at the time of the sale.

Exercise 14–19
Entries for purchase and sale of investment in bonds; gain

Objective 7

Nelson Company develops and sells graphics software for use by architects. Journalize the entries to record the following selected transactions of Nelson Company:

a. Purchased for cash $180,000 of Sequoyah Co. 5% bonds at 96 plus accrued interest of $1,500.
b. Received first semiannual interest.
c. Amortized $1,440 on the bond investment at the end of the first year.
d. Sold the bonds at 99 plus accrued interest of $3,000. The bonds were carried at $176,300 at the time of the sale.

Exercise 14–20
Number of times interest charges earned

Objective 9

The following data were taken from recent annual reports of **Mirage Resorts, Inc.**, which owns and operates casino-based entertainment resorts in Las Vegas and Laughlin, Nevada.

	Current Year	Preceding Year
Interest expense	$130,598,000	$ 70,350,000
Income before income tax	135,178,000	329,079,000

a. Determine the number of times interest charges were earned for the current and preceding years. Round to one decimal place.
b. What conclusions can you draw?

Appendix
Exercise 14–21
Amortize discount by interest method

✓ b. $490,229

On the first day of its fiscal year, Electrokinetics Company issued $5,000,000 of five-year, 8% bonds to finance its operations of producing and selling home electronics equipment. Interest is payable semiannually. The bonds were issued at an effective interest rate of 11%, resulting in Electrokinetics Company receiving cash of $4,434,676.

a. Journalize the entries to record the following:
    1. Sale of the bonds.
    2. First semiannual interest payment. (Amortization of discount is to be recorded annually.)
    3. Second semiannual interest payment.
    4. Amortization of discount at the end of the first year, using the interest method. (Round to the nearest dollar.)
b. Compute the amount of the bond interest expense for the first year.

Appendix
Exercise 14–22
Amortize premium by interest method

✓ b. $1,037,071

Fajitas Corporation wholesales oil and grease products to equipment manufacturers. On March 1, 2003, Fajitas Corporation issued $10,000,000 of five-year, 11% bonds at an effective interest rate of 10%, receiving cash of $10,386,057. Interest is payable semiannually on March 1 and September 1. Fajitas Corporation's fiscal year begins on March 1.

a. Journalize the entries to record the following:
    1. First interest payment on September 1, 2003. (Amortization of premium is to be recorded annually.)
    2. Second interest payment on March 1, 2004.
    3. Amortization of premium at the end of the first year, using the interest method. (Round to the nearest dollar.)
b. Determine the bond interest expense for the first year.

Appendix
Exercise 14–23
Compute bond proceeds, amortizing premium by interest method, and interest expense

✓ a. $25,942,195
✓ b. $73,179

Pyrite Co. produces and sells spray painting equipment for construction contractors. On the first day of its fiscal year, Pyrite Co. issued $25,000,000 of five-year, 12% bonds at an effective interest rate of 11%, with interest payable semiannually. Compute the following, presenting figures used in your computations.

a. The amount of cash proceeds from the sale of the bonds. (Use the tables of present values in Exhibits 3 and 4.)
b. The amount of premium to be amortized for the first semiannual interest payment period, using the interest method. (Round to the nearest dollar.)
c. The amount of premium to be amortized for the second semiannual interest payment period, using the interest method. (Round to the nearest dollar.)
d. The amount of the bond interest expense for the first year.

Appendix
Exercise 14–24
Compute bond proceeds, amortizing discount by interest method, and interest expense

Viceroy Co. produces and sells concrete mixing equipment. On the first day of its fiscal year, Viceroy Co. issued $14,000,000 of five-year, 10% bonds at an effective interest rate of 12%, with interest payable semiannually. Compute the following, presenting figures used in your computations.

a. The amount of cash proceeds from the sale of the bonds. (Use the tables of present values in Exhibits 3 and 4.)
b. The amount of discount to be amortized for the first semiannual interest payment period, using the interest method. (Round to the nearest dollar.)

✓ a. $12,969,663

✓ b. $78,180

c. The amount of discount to be amortized for the second semiannual interest payment period, using the interest method. (Round to the nearest dollar.)

d. The amount of the bond interest expense for the first year.

PROBLEMS SERIES A

Problem 14–1A

Effect of financing on earnings per share

Objective 1

SPREADSHEET

✓ 1. Plan 3: $5.20

Three different plans for financing a $15,000,000 corporation are under consideration by its organizers. Under each of the following plans, the securities will be issued at their par or face amount, and the income tax rate is estimated at 40% of income.

	Plan 1	Plan 2	Plan 3
12% bonds			$ 6,250,000
Preferred $4 stock, $50 par		$ 7,500,000	5,000,000
Common stock, $30 par	$15,000,000	7,500,000	3,750,000
Total	$15,000,000	$15,000,000	$15,000,000

Instructions

1. Determine for each plan the earnings per share of common stock, assuming that the income before bond interest and income tax is $2,500,000.
2. Determine for each plan the earnings per share of common stock, assuming that the income before bond interest and income tax is $1,500,000.
3. Discuss the advantages and disadvantages of each plan.

Problem 14–2A

Present value; bond premium; entries for bonds payable transactions

Objectives 3, 4

GENERAL LEDGER

✓ 3. $415,075

Moresby Inc. produces and sells voltage regulators. On July 1, 2002, Moresby Inc. issued $8,000,000 of ten-year, 11% bonds at an effective interest rate of 10%. Interest on the bonds is payable semiannually on December 31 and June 30. The fiscal year of the company is the calendar year.

Instructions

1. Journalize the entry to record the amount of the cash proceeds from the sale of the bonds. Use the tables of present values in Appendix A to compute the cash proceeds, rounding to the nearest dollar.
2. Journalize the entries to record the following:
   a. The first semiannual interest payment on December 31, 2002, including the amortization of the bond premium, using the straight-line method.
   b. The interest payment on June 30, 2003, and the amortization of the bond premium, using the straight-line method.
3. Determine the total interest expense for 2002.
4. Will the bond proceeds always be greater than the face amount of the bonds when the contract rate is greater than the market rate of interest? Explain.

Problem 14–3A

Present value; bond discount; entries for bonds payable transactions

Objectives 3, 4

GENERAL LEDGER

On July 1, 2002, Cucumber Communications Equipment Inc. issued $10,000,000 of ten-year, 9% bonds at an effective interest rate of 10%. Interest on the bonds is payable semiannually on December 31 and June 30. The fiscal year of the company is the calendar year.

Instructions

1. Journalize the entry to record the amount of the cash proceeds from the sale of the bonds. Use the tables of present values in Appendix A to compute the cash proceeds, rounding to the nearest dollar. *(continued)*

✓ 3. $481,155

2. Journalize the entries to record the following:
   a. The first semiannual interest payment on December 31, 2002, and the amortization of the bond discount, using the straight-line method. (Round to the nearest dollar.)
   b. The interest payment on June 30, 2003, and the amortization of the bond discount, using the straight-line method.
3. Determine the total interest expense for 2002.
4. ███████ ► Will the bond proceeds always be less than the face amount of the bonds when the contract rate is less than the market rate of interest? Explain.

Problem 14–4A
Entries for bonds payable transactions

Objectives 4, 6

SPREADSHEET
GENERAL LEDGER

✓ 2. a. $1,252,787

Downing Co. produces and sells synthetic string for tennis rackets. The following transactions were completed by Downing Co., whose fiscal year is the calendar year:

2002
July 1. Issued $20,000,000 of 5-year, 14% callable bonds dated July 1, 2002, at an effective rate of 12%, receiving cash of $21,472,126. Interest is payable semiannually on December 31 and June 30.
Dec. 31. Paid the semiannual interest on the bonds.
     31. Recorded bond premium amortization of $147,213, which was determined by using the straight-line method.
     31. Closed the interest expense account.

2003
June 30. Paid the semiannual interest on the bonds.
Dec. 31. Paid the semiannual interest on the bonds.
     31. Recorded bond premium amortization of $294,425, which was determined by using the straight-line method.
     31. Closed the interest expense account.

2004
July 1. Recorded the redemption of the bonds, which were called at 102. The balance in the bond premium account is $883,275 after the payment of interest and amortization of premium have been recorded. (Record the redemption only.)

Instructions

1. Journalize the entries to record the foregoing transactions.
2. Indicate the amount of the interest expense in (a) 2002 and (b) 2003.
3. Determine the carrying amount of the bonds as of December 31, 2003.

Problem 14–5A
Entries for bond investments

Objective 7

SPREADSHEET
GENERAL LEDGER

The following selected transactions relate to certain securities acquired by Custom Blueprints Inc., whose fiscal year ends on December 31:

2002
Sept. 1. Purchased $500,000 of Donner Company 20-year, 9% bonds dated July 1, 2002, directly from the issuing company, for $482,150 plus accrued interest of $7,500.
Dec. 31. Received the semiannual interest on the Donner Company bonds.
     31. Recorded bond discount amortization of $300 on the Donner Company bonds. The amortization amount was determined by using the straight-line method.

(Assume that all intervening transactions and adjustments have been properly recorded and that the number of bonds owned has not changed from December 31, 2002, to December 31, 2006.)

2007
June 30. Received the semiannual interest on the Donner Company bonds.
Oct. 31. Sold one-half of the Donner Company bonds at 96½ plus accrued interest. The broker deducted $400 for commission, etc., remitting the balance. Prior to the sale, $375 of discount on one-half of the bonds was amortized, reducing the carrying amount of those bonds to $243,400.
Dec. 31. Received the semiannual interest on the Donner Company bonds.
     31. Recorded bond discount amortization of $450 on the Donner Company bonds.

Instructions

Journalize the entries to record the foregoing transactions.

Appendix
Problem 14–6A

Entries for bonds payable transactions; interest method of amortizing bond premium

✓ 2. $424,925

Moresby Inc. produces and sells voltage regulators. On July 1, 2002, Moresby Inc. issued $8,000,000 of ten-year, 11% bonds at an effective interest rate of 10%, receiving proceeds of $8,498,492. Interest on the bonds is payable semiannually on December 31 and June 30. The fiscal year of the company is the calendar year.

Instructions

1. Journalize the entries to record the following:
   a. The first semiannual interest payment on December 31, 2002, and the amortization of the bond premium, using the interest method. (Round to nearest dollar.)
   b. The interest payment on June 30, 2003, and the amortization of the bond premium, using the interest method. (Round to nearest dollar.)
2. Determine the total interest expense for 2002.

Appendix
Problem 14–7A

Entries for bonds payable transactions; interest method of amortizing bond discount

✓ 2. $468,845

On July 1, 2002, Cucumber Communications Equipment Inc. issued $10,000,000 of ten-year, 9% bonds at an effective interest rate of 10%, receiving proceeds of $9,376,895. Interest on the bonds is payable semiannually on December 31 and June 30. The fiscal year of the company is the calendar year.

Instructions

1. Journalize the entries to record the following:
   a. The first semiannual interest payment on December 31, 2002, and the amortization of the bond discount, using the interest method.
   b. The interest payment on June 30, 2003, and the amortization of the bond discount, using the interest method.
2. Determine the total interest expense for 2002.

PROBLEMS SERIES B

Problem 14–1B

Effect of financing on earnings per share

Objective 1

SPREADSHEET

✓ 1. Plan 3: $10.30

Three different plans for financing a $10,000,000 corporation are under consideration by its organizers. Under each of the following plans, the securities will be issued at their par or face amount, and the income tax rate is estimated at 40% of income.

	Plan 1	Plan 2	Plan 3
10% bonds			$ 5,000,000
Preferred 5% stock, $100 par		$ 5,000,000	2,500,000
Common stock, $10 par	$10,000,000	5,000,000	2,500,000
Total	$10,000,000	$10,000,000	$10,000,000

Instructions

1. Determine for each plan the earnings per share of common stock, assuming that the income before bond interest and income tax is $5,000,000.
2. Determine for each plan the earnings per share of common stock, assuming that the income before bond interest and income tax is $800,000.
3. ━━━ Discuss the advantages and disadvantages of each plan.

Problem 14–2B

Present value; bond premium; entries for bonds payable transactions

Objectives 3, 4

GENERAL LEDGER

Parnell Corporation produces and sells burial vaults. On July 1, 2003, Parnell Corporation issued $12,000,000 of ten-year, 12% bonds at an effective interest rate of 10%. Interest on the bonds is payable semiannually on December 31 and June 30. The fiscal year of the company is the calendar year.

Instructions

1. Journalize the entry to record the amount of the cash proceeds from the sale of the bonds. Use the tables of present values in Appendix A to compute the cash proceeds, rounding to the nearest dollar.
(continued)

✓ 3. $645,226

2. Journalize the entries to record the following:
   a. The first semiannual interest payment on December 31, 2003, and the amortization of the bond premium, using the straight-line method. (Round to the nearest dollar.)
   b. The interest payment on June 30, 2004, and the amortization of the bond premium, using the straight-line method.
3. Determine the total interest expense for 2003.
4. Will the bond proceeds always be greater than the face amount of the bonds when the contract rate is greater than the market rate of interest? Explain.

Problem 14–3B
Present value; bond discount; entries for bonds payable transactions

Objectives 3, 4

GENERAL LEDGER

✓ 3. $418,010

On July 1, 2002, Raptor Corporation, a wholesaler of used robotic equipment, issued $7,500,000 of ten-year, 10% bonds at an effective interest rate of 12%. Interest on the bonds is payable semiannually on December 31 and June 30. The fiscal year of the company is the calendar year.

Instructions

1. Journalize the entry to record the amount of the cash proceeds from the sale of the bonds. Use the tables of present values in Appendix A to compute the cash proceeds, rounding to the nearest dollar.
2. Journalize the entries to record the following:
   a. The first semiannual interest payment on December 31, 2002, and the amortization of the bond discount, using the straight-line method. (Round to the nearest dollar.)
   b. The interest payment on June 30, 2003, and the amortization of the bond discount, using the straight-line method.
3. Determine the total interest expense for 2002.
4. Will the bond proceeds always be less than the face amount of the bonds when the contract rate is less than the market rate of interest? Explain.

Problem 14–4B
Entries for bonds payable transactions

Objectives 4, 6

SPREADSHEET
GENERAL LEDGER

✓ 2. a. $477,220

The following transactions were completed by Shadwell Inc., whose fiscal year is the calendar year:

2002
July   1. Issued $10,000,000 of 5-year, 8% callable bonds dated July 1, 2002, at an effective rate of 10%, receiving cash of $9,227,796. Interest is payable semiannually on December 31 and June 30.
Dec. 31. Paid the semiannual interest on the bonds.
     31. Recorded bond discount amortization of $77,220, which was determined by using the straight-line method.
     31. Closed the interest expense account.

2003
June 30. Paid the semiannual interest on the bonds.
Dec. 31. Paid the semiannual interest on the bonds.
     31. Recorded bond discount amortization of $154,440, which was determined by using the straight-line method.
     31. Closed the interest expense account.

2004
June 30. Recorded the redemption of the bonds, which were called at 98½. The balance in the bond discount account is $463,324 after payment of interest and amortization of discount have been recorded. (Record the redemption only.)

Instructions

1. Journalize the entries to record the foregoing transactions.
2. Indicate the amount of the interest expense in (a) 2002 and (b) 2003.
3. Determine the carrying amount of the bonds as of December 31, 2003.

Problem 14–5B
Entries for bond investments

Objective 7

Genesis Inc. develops and leases databases of publicly available information. The following selected transactions relate to certain securities acquired as a long-term investment by Genesis Inc., whose fiscal year ends on December 31:

SPREADSHEET

GENERAL
LEDGER

2002
Sept. 1. Purchased $240,000 of Joshua Company 10-year, 8% bonds dated July 1, 2002, directly from the issuing company, for $247,375 plus accrued interest of $3,200.
Dec. 31. Received the semiannual interest on the Joshua Company bonds.
      31. Recorded bond premium amortization of $250 on the Joshua Company bonds. The amortization amount was determined by using the straight-line method.

(Assume that all intervening transactions and adjustments have been properly recorded and that the number of bonds owned has not changed from Dec. 31, 2002, to Dec. 31, 2007.)

2008
June 30. Received the semiannual interest on the Joshua Company bonds.
Aug. 31. Sold one-half of the Joshua Company bonds at 102 plus accrued interest. The broker deducted $500 for commission, etc., remitting the balance. Prior to the sale, $250 of premium on one-half of the bonds is to be amortized, reducing the carrying amount of those bonds to $121,438.
Dec. 31. Received the semiannual interest on the Joshua Company bonds.
      31. Recorded bond premium amortization of $375 on the Joshua Company bonds.

Instructions
Journalize the entries to record the foregoing transactions.

Appendix
Problem 14–6B

Entries for bonds payable transactions; interest method of amortizing bond premium

✓ 2. $674,774

Parnell Corporation produces and sells burial vaults. On July 1, 2003, Parnell Corporation issued $12,000,000 of ten-year, 12% bonds at an effective interest rate of 10%, receiving proceeds of $13,495,471. Interest on the bonds is payable semiannually on December 31 and June 30. The fiscal year of the company is the calendar year.

Instructions

1. Journalize the entries to record the following:
   a. The first semiannual interest payment on December 31, 2003, and the amortization of the bond premium, using the interest method. (Round to nearest dollar.)
   b. The interest payment on June 30, 2004, and the amortization of the bond premium, using the interest method. (Round to nearest dollar.)
2. Determine the total interest expense for 2003.

Appendix
Problem 14–7B

Entries for bonds payable transactions; interest method of amortizing bond discount

✓ 2. $398,388

On July 1, 2002, Raptor Corporation, a wholesaler of used robotic equipment, issued $7,500,000 of ten-year, 10% bonds at an effective interest rate of 12%, receiving proceeds of $6,639,795. Interest on the bonds is payable semiannually on December 31 and June 30. The fiscal year of the company is the calendar year.

Instructions

1. Journalize the entries to record the following:
   a. The first semiannual interest payment on December 31, 2002, and the amortization of the bond discount, using the interest method. (Round to nearest dollar.)
   b. The interest payment on June 30, 2003, and the amortization of the bond discount, using the interest method. (Round to nearest dollar.)
2. Determine the total interest expense for 2002.

COMPREHENSIVE PROBLEM 4

GENERAL
LEDGER

Selected transactions completed by Heywood Products Inc. during the fiscal year ending July 31, 2003, were as follows:

a. Issued 12,000 shares of $25 par common stock at $45, receiving cash.
b. Issued 7,500 shares of $100 par preferred 8% stock at $120, receiving cash.

✓ 2.a. Net income, $163,000

c. Issued $6,000,000 of 10-year, 11% bonds at an effective interest rate of 10%, with interest payable semiannually. Use the present value tables in Appendix A to determine the bond proceeds. Round to the nearest dollar.

d. Declared a dividend of $0.25 per share on common stock and $2 per share on preferred stock. On the date of record, 100,000 shares of common stock were outstanding, no treasury shares were held, and 15,000 shares of preferred stock were outstanding.

e. Paid the cash dividends declared in (d).

f. Redeemed $500,000 of 8-year, 12% bonds at 101. The balance in the bond premium account is $6,150 after the payment of interest and amortization of premium have been recorded. (Record only the redemption of the bonds payable.)

g. Purchased 5,000 shares of treasury common stock at $42 per share.

h. Declared a 2% stock dividend on common stock and a $2 cash dividend per share on preferred stock. On the date of declaration, the market value of the common stock was $41 per share. On the date of record, 100,000 shares of common stock had been issued, 5,000 shares of treasury common stock were held, and 15,000 shares of preferred stock had been issued.

i. Issued the stock certificates for the stock dividends declared in (h) and paid the cash dividends to the preferred stockholders.

j. Purchased $100,000 of Key West Sports Inc. 10-year, 15% bonds, directly from the issuing company, for $97,000 plus accrued interest of $3,750.

k. Sold, at $48 per share, 3,000 shares of treasury common stock purchased in (g).

l. Recorded the payment of semiannual interest on the bonds issued in (c) and the amortization of the premium for six months. The amortization was determined using the straight-line method. (Round the amortization to the nearest dollar.)

m. Accrued interest for four months on the Key West Sports Inc. bonds purchased in (j). Also recorded amortization of $100.

Instructions

1. Journalize the selected transactions.
2. After all of the transactions for the year ended July 31, 2003, had been posted (including the transactions recorded in (1) and all adjusting entries), the following data were taken from the records of Heywood Products Inc.:

Income statement data:

Advertising expense	$ 75,000
Cost of merchandise sold	1,890,000
Delivery expense	17,000
Depreciation expense—office buildings and equipment	13,100
Depreciation expense—store buildings and equipment	45,000
Gain on redemption of bonds	1,150
Income tax:	
Applicable to continuing operations	156,043
Applicable to loss from disposal of a segment of the business	48,000
Applicable to gain from redemption of bonds	150
Interest expense	311,307
Interest revenue	1,350
Loss from disposal of a segment of the business	120,000
Miscellaneous administrative expenses	1,600
Miscellaneous selling expenses	5,000
Office rent expense	25,000
Office salaries expense	85,000
Office supplies expense	5,300
Sales	3,150,000
Sales commissions	98,000
Sales salaries expense	180,000
Store supplies expense	10,000

Retained earnings and balance sheet data:

Accounts payable	$ 149,500
Accounts receivable	280,500
Accumulated depreciation—office buildings and equipment	835,250
Accumulated depreciation—store buildings and equipment	2,214,750
Allowance for doubtful accounts	21,500
Bonds payable, 11%, due 2013	6,000,000
Cash	125,500
Common stock, $25 par (400,000 shares authorized; 101,900 shares outstanding)	2,547,500
Deferred income tax payable (current portion, $4,700)	25,700
Dividends:	
Cash dividends for common stock	55,000
Cash dividends for preferred stock	105,000
Stock dividends for common stock	77,900
Dividends payable	30,000
Income tax payable	55,900
Interest receivable	5,000
Investment in Key West Sports Inc. bonds (long-term)	97,100
Merchandise inventory (July 31, 2003), at lower of cost (fifo) or market	425,000
Notes receivable	77,500
Office buildings and equipment	3,762,329
Paid-in capital from sale of treasury stock	18,000
Paid-in capital in excess of par—common stock	560,000
Paid-in capital in excess of par—preferred stock	240,000
Preferred 8% stock, $100 par (30,000 shares authorized; 15,000 shares issued)	1,500,000
Premium on bonds payable	355,176
Prepaid expenses	15,900
Retained earnings, August 1, 2002	677,124
Store buildings and equipment	10,282,671
Treasury stock (2,000 shares of common stock at cost of $42 per share)	84,000

a. Prepare a multiple-step income statement for the year ended July 31, 2003, concluding with earnings per share. In computing earnings per share, assume that the average number of common shares outstanding was 100,000 and preferred dividends were $105,000.

b. Prepare a retained earnings statement for the year ended July 31, 2003.

c. Prepare a balance sheet in report form as of July 31, 2003.

SPECIAL ACTIVITIES

Activity 14–1
Fun Inc.
Ethics and professional conduct in business

Fun Inc. produces and sells water slides for theme parks. Fun Inc. has outstanding a $50,000,000, 25-year, 10% debenture bond issue dated July 1, 1998. The bond issue is due June 30, 2023. The bond indenture requires a sinking fund, which has a balance of $6,000,000 as of July 1, 2003. Fun Inc. is currently experiencing a shortage of funds due to a recent plant expansion. Lee Noel, treasurer of Fun Inc., has suggested using the sinking fund cash to temporarily relieve the shortage of funds. Noel's brother-in-law, who is trustee of the sinking fund, is willing to loan Fun Inc. the necessary funds from the sinking fund.

    Discuss whether Lee Noel is behaving in a professional manner.

Activity 14–2
Carlisle Distributors Inc.
Present values

Carlisle Distributors Inc. is a wholesaler of oriental rugs. The following is a luncheon conversation between Jenny Wilder, the assistant controller, and Peter Isaacs, an assistant financial analyst for Carlisle.

Peter: Jenny, do you mind if I spoil your lunch and ask you an accounting question?
Jenny: No, go ahead. This chicken salad sandwich is pretty bad. It smells like it's three days old, and I've already picked three bones out of it.
Peter: Well, as you know, in finance we use present values for capital budgeting analysis, assessing financing alternatives, etc. It's probably the most important concept that I learned in school that I actually use.
Jenny: So . . . ?
Peter: I was just wondering why accountants don't use present values more.
Jenny: What do you mean?
Peter: Well, it seems to me that you ought to value all the balance sheet liabilities at their present values.

➤ How would you respond if you were Jenny?

Activity 14–3
Daffodil Inc.
Preferred stock vs. bonds

Daffodil Inc. has decided to expand its operations to owning and operating theme parks. The following is an excerpt from a conversation between the chief executive officer, JoAnn Hanson, and the vice-president of finance, Chris Fowler.

JoAnn: Chris, have you given any thought to how we're going to finance the acquisition of WaterWave Corporation?
Chris: Well, the two basic options, as I see it, are to issue either preferred stock or bonds. The equity market is a little depressed right now. The rumor is that the Federal Reserve Bank's going to increase the interest rates either this month or next.
JoAnn: Yes, I've heard the rumor. The problem is that we can't wait around to see what's going to happen. We'll have to move on this next week if we want any chance to complete the acquisition of WaterWave.
Chris: Well, the bond market is strong right now. Maybe we should issue debt this time around.
JoAnn: That's what I would have guessed as well. WaterWave's financial statements look pretty good, except for the volatility of their income and cash flows. But that's characteristic of their industry.

➤ Discuss the advantages and disadvantages of issuing preferred stock versus bonds.

Activity 14–4
Into the Real World
Investing in bonds

Select a bond from listings that appear daily in *The Wall Street Journal*, and summarize the information related to the bond you select. Include the following information in your summary:

1. Contract rate of interest
2. Year when the bond matures
3. Current yield (effective rate of interest)
4. Closing price of bond (indicate date)
5. Other information noted about the bond, such as whether it is a zero-coupon bond (see the Explanatory Notes to the listings)

In groups of three or four, share the information you developed about the bond you selected. As a group, select one bond to invest $100,000 in and prepare a justification for your choice for presentation to the class. For example, your justification should include a consideration of risk and return.

Activity 14–5
Inman Bottling Co.
Financing business expansion

You hold a 25% common stock interest in the family-owned business, a soft drink bottling distributorship. Your sister, who is the manager, has proposed an expansion of plant facilities at an expected cost of $5,000,000. Two alternative plans have been suggested as methods of financing the expansion. Each plan is briefly described as follows:

Plan 1. Issue $5,000,000 of 20-year, 8% notes at face amount.
Plan 2. Issue an additional 70,000 shares of $20 par common stock at $25 per share, and $3,250,000 of 20-year, 8% notes at face amount.

The balance sheet as of the end of the previous fiscal year is as follows:

Inman Bottling Co.
Balance Sheet
December 31, 2003

Assets

Current assets	$2,350,000
Property, plant, and equipment	5,150,000
Total assets	$7,500,000

Liabilities and Stockholders' Equity

Liabilities	$2,000,000
Common stock, $20	800,000
Paid-in capital in excess of par	80,000
Retained earnings	4,620,000
Total liabilities and stockholders' equity	$7,500,000

Net income has remained relatively constant over the past several years. The expansion program is expected to increase yearly income before bond interest and income tax from $500,000 in the previous year to $700,000 for this year. Your sister has asked you, as the company treasurer, to prepare an analysis of each financing plan.

1. Prepare a table indicating the expected earnings per share on the common stock under each plan. Assume an income tax rate of 40%.
2. a. ✐ Discuss the factors that should be considered in evaluating the two plans.
   b. ✐ Which plan offers the greater benefit to the present stockholders? Give reasons for your opinion.

Activity 14–6
Into the Real World
Bond ratings

Moody's Investors Service maintains a Web site at **www.Moodys.com**. One of the services offered at this site is a listing of announcements of recent bond rating changes. Visit this site and read over some of these announcements. Write down several of the reasons provided for rating downgrades and upgrades. If you were a bond investor or bond issuer, would you care if Moody's changed the rating on your bonds? Why or why not?

ANSWERS TO SELF-EXAMINATION QUESTIONS

Matching

1. C	3. G	5. Q	7. L	9. O	11. F	13. N
2. E	4. A	6. P	8. II	10. R	12. M	14 K

Multiple Choice

1. **B** Since the contract rate on the bonds is higher than the prevailing market rate, a rational investor would be willing to pay more than the face amount, or a premium (answer B), for the bonds. If the contract rate and the market rate were equal, the bonds could be expected to sell at their face amount (answer A). Likewise, if the market rate is higher than the contract rate, the bonds would sell at a price below their face amount (answer D) or at a discount (answer C).

2. **A** The bond carrying amount is the face amount plus unamortized premium or less unamortized discount. For this question, the carrying amount is $500,000 less $40,000, or $460,000 (answer A).

3. **B** Although the sinking fund may consist of cash as well as securities, the fund is listed on the balance sheet as an investment (answer B) because it is to be used to pay the long-term liability at maturity.

4. **B** The amount debited to the investment account is the cost of the bonds, which includes the amount paid to the seller for the bonds (101% × $100,000) plus broker's commissions ($50), or $101,050 (answer B). The $2,000 of accrued interest that is paid to the seller should be debited to Interest Revenue, since it is an offset against the amount that will be received as interest at the next interest date.

5. **C** The balance of Discount on Bonds Payable is usually reported as a deduction from Bonds Payable in the Long-Term Liabilities section (answer C) of the balance sheet. Likewise, a balance in a premium on bonds payable account would usually be reported as an addition to Bonds Payable in the Long-Term Liabilities section of the balance sheet.

Statement of Cash Flows

15

objectives

After studying this chapter, you should be able to:

1 Explain why the statement of cash flows is one of the basic financial statements.

2 Summarize the types of cash flow activities reported in the statement of cash flows.

3 Prepare a statement of cash flows, using the indirect method.

4 Prepare a statement of cash flows, using the direct method.

5 Calculate and interpret the free cash flow.

H ow much cash do you have in the bank or in your wallet or purse? How much cash did you have at the beginning of the month? The difference between these two amounts is the net change in your cash during the month. Knowing the reasons for the change in cash may be useful in evaluating whether your financial position has improved and whether you will be able to pay your bills in the future.

For example, assume that you had $200 at the beginning of the month and $550 at the end of the month. The net change in cash is $350. Based on this net change, it appears that your financial position has improved. However, this conclusion may or may not be valid, depending upon how the change of $350 was created. If you borrowed $1,000 during the month and spent $650 on living expenses, your cash would have increased by $350 by living off borrowed funds. On the other hand, if you earned $1,000 and spent $650 on living expenses, your cash would have also increased by $350, but your financial position is improved compared to the first scenario.

In previous chapters, we have used the income statement, balance sheet, and retained earnings statement and other information to analyze the effects of management decisions on a business's financial position and operating performance. In this chapter, we present how to prepare and use the statement of cash flows.

Purpose of the Statement of Cash Flows

objective 1

Explain why the statement of cash flows is one of the basic financial statements.

The **statement of cash flows** reports a firm's major cash inflows and outflows for a period.[1] It provides useful information about a firm's ability to generate cash from operations, maintain and expand its operating capacity, meet its financial obligations, and pay dividends.

The statement of cash flows is one of the basic financial statements. It is useful to managers in evaluating past operations and in planning future investing and financing activities. It is useful to investors, creditors, and others in assessing a firm's profit potential. In addition, it is a basis for assessing the firm's ability to pay its maturing debt.

Reporting Cash Flows

objective 2

Summarize the types of cash flow activities reported in the statement of cash flows.

The statement of cash flows reports cash flows by three types of activities:

1. **Cash flows from operating activities** are cash flows from transactions that affect net income. Examples of such transactions include the purchase and sale of merchandise by a retailer.
2. **Cash flows from investing activities** are cash flows from transactions that affect the investments in noncurrent assets. Examples of such transactions include the sale and purchase of fixed assets, such as equipment and buildings.

---

[1] As used in this chapter, cash refers to cash and cash equivalents. Examples of cash equivalents include marketable securities, certificates of deposit, U.S. Treasury bills, and money market funds.

3. **Cash flows from financing activities** are cash flows from transactions that affect the equity and debt of the business. Examples of such transactions include issuing or retiring equity and debt securities.

> The statement of cash flows reports cash flows from operating, investing, and financing activities.

The cash flows from operating activities is normally presented first, followed by the cash flows from investing activities and financing activities. The total of the net cash flow from these activities is the net increase or decrease in cash for the period. The cash balance at the beginning of the period is added to the net increase or decrease in cash, resulting in the cash balance at the end of the period. The ending cash balance on the statement of cash flows equals the cash reported on the balance sheet.

Exhibit 1 shows common cash flow transactions reported in each of the three sections of the statement of cash flows. By reporting cash flows by operating, investing, and financing activities, significant relationships within and among the activities can be evaluated. For example, the cash receipts from issuing bonds can be related to repayments of borrowings when both are reported as financing activities. Also, the impact of each of the three activities (operating, investing, and financing) on cash flows can be identified. This allows investors and creditors to evaluate the effects of cash flows on a firm's profits and ability to pay debt.

Exhibit 1 Cash Flows

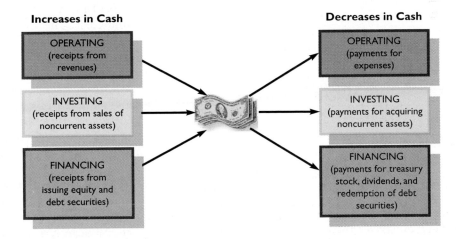

BUSINESS ON STAGE

Focus on Cash Flow

In the past, investors and creditors have relied heavily on a company's earnings information in judging the company's performance. Now, more and more investors and creditors are also focusing on cash flows for providing additional information, as described below.

As the term suggests, cash flow is basically a measure of the money flowing into—or out of—a business. If large companies were run, like lemonade stands, on a cash basis, earnings and cash flow would be identical.

Every major corporation, however, keeps its books on an accrual basis.... [This] can give a truer picture of corporate profitability, but sometimes it obscures important developments.

Take a company that spent $140 million on new machinery last year. If it depreciates the equipment over a seven-year period, it will be subtracting $20 million from reported profits each year.

But if the machines will stay up to date and useful for 25 years, the company's reported earnings may understate its true strength....

Sometimes the reverse is true. If a company has been neglecting capital spending, its earnings may look good. But on a cash-flow basis, it will look no better...than its competitors. ■

Source: John R. Dorfman, "Stock Analysts Increase Focus on Cash Flow," The Wall Street Journal, February 17, 1987, Section 2, p. 1.

Cash Flows from Operating Activities

The most important cash flows of a business often relate to operating activities. There are two alternative methods for reporting cash flows from operating activities in the statement of cash flows. These methods are (1) the direct method and (2) the indirect method.

The **direct method** reports the sources of operating cash and the uses of operating cash. The major source of operating cash is cash received from customers. The major uses of operating cash include cash paid to suppliers for merchandise and services and cash paid to employees for wages. The difference between these operating cash receipts and cash payments is the net cash flow from operating activities.

The primary advantage of the direct method is that it reports the sources and uses of cash in the statement of cash flows. Its primary disadvantage is that the necessary data may not be readily available and may be costly to gather.

The **indirect method** reports the operating cash flows by beginning with net income and adjusting it for revenues and expenses that do not involve the receipt or payment of cash. In other words, accrual net income is adjusted to determine the net amount of cash flows from operating activities.

A major advantage of the indirect method is that it focuses on the differences between net income and cash flows from operations. In this sense, it shows the relationship between the income statement, the balance sheet, and the statement of cash flows. Because the data are readily available, the indirect method is normally less costly to use than the direct method. Because of these advantages, most firms use the indirect method to report cash flows from operations.

Exhibit 2 illustrates the cash flow from operating activities section of the statement of cash flows under the direct and indirect methods. Both statements are for NetSolutions for the month ended November 2002. Both methods show the same amount of net cash flow from operating activities, regardless of the method. We will illustrate both methods in detail later in this chapter.

Which U.S. industrial companies have the largest cash balances? A recent list is as follows:

	In millions
Ford Motor Co.	$24,773
General Motors	20,024
Microsoft	13,927
Intel	7,626
IBM	5,768

These companies have had substantial cash flows from operations over the past 3–5 years, and as a result, have been able to build large cash balances (in the billions!). These balances can be used to cushion future business downturns, as would be the case for businesses subject to boom and bust cycles, such as Ford and GM. Alternatively, the cash can be used to expand the business or move into new markets, as would be the case for technology companies, such as Microsoft, Intel, and IBM.

Cash Flows from Investing Activities

Cash inflows from investing activities normally arise from selling fixed assets, investments, and intangible assets. Cash outflows normally include payments to acquire fixed assets, investments, and intangible assets.

Cash flows from investing activities are reported on the statement of cash flows by first listing the cash inflows. The cash outflows are then presented. If the inflows

Exhibit 2 Cash Flow from Operations: Direct and Indirect Methods

Direct Method	
Cash flows from operating activities:	
Cash received from customers	$7,500
Deduct cash payments for expenses	
and payments to creditors	4,600
Net cash flow from operating activities	$2,900

Indirect Method	
Cash flows from operating activities:	
Net income, per income statement	$3,050
Add increase in accounts payable	400
	$3,450
Deduct increase in supplies	550
Net cash flow from operating activities	$2,900

The **Walt Disney Company** recently invested $3.3 billion to develop new action and animated films and $2.3 billion to design and develop new theme park attractions and resort properties, such as Disney's California Adventure and the Disney Cruise Line.

are greater than the outflows, **net cash flow provided by investing activities** is reported. If the inflows are less than the outflows, **net cash flow used for investing activities** is reported.

The cash flows from investing activities section in the statement of cash flows for NetSolutions is shown below.

Cash flows from investing activities:
   Cash payments for acquiring land .... $(20,000)

Cash Flows from Financing Activities

Cash inflows from financing activities normally arise from issuing debt or equity securities. Examples of such inflows include issuing bonds, notes payable, and preferred and common stocks. Cash outflows from financing activities include paying cash dividends, repaying debt, and acquiring treasury stock.

Cash flows from financing activities are reported on the statement of cash flows by first listing the cash inflows. The cash outflows are then presented. If the inflows are greater than the outflows, **net cash flow provided by financing activities** is reported. If the inflows are less than the outflows, **net cash flow used for financing activities** is reported.

The cash flows from financing activities section in the statement of cash flows for NetSolutions is shown below.

Intel Corp. plans to keep enough cash on hand to build two computer chip factories and to repurchase common stock (treasury stock).

Cash flows from financing activities:
   Cash received as owner's investment $25,000
   Deduct cash withdrawal by owner 2,000
   Net cash flow from financing activities $23,000

Noncash Investing and Financing Activities

A business may enter into investing and financing activities that do not directly involve cash. For example, it may issue common stock to retire long-term debt. Such a transaction does not have a direct effect on cash. However, the transaction does eliminate the need for future cash payments to pay interest and retire the bonds. Thus, because of their future effect on cash flows, such transactions should be reported to readers of the financial statements.

When noncash investing and financing transactions occur during a period, their effect is reported in a separate schedule. This schedule usually appears at the bottom of the statement of cash flows. For example, in such a schedule, **Amazon.com** disclosed the issuance of $217 million in common stock for Internet acquisitions. Other examples of noncash investing and financing transactions include acquiring fixed assets by issuing bonds or capital stock and issuing common stock in exchange for convertible preferred stock.

BUSINESS ON STAGE

Seasonal Cash Management

A business must manage its cash position so that there is enough cash on hand to pay bills and other liabilities. Cash management is particularly important for seasonal businesses, which use cash in one part of the year and generate it in another. For example, consider this assumed cash position from operations for Smart Toys, Inc., a toy retailer:

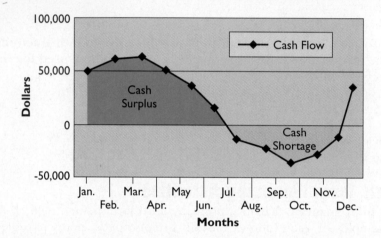

Smart Toys uses cash to purchase inventory prior to the winter holiday season. It is able to generate surplus cash by selling its inventory through-out the holiday season and into the early part of the calendar year.

If the cash required to purchase inventory exceeds Smart Toys' ability to generate operating cash flow, it may experience a cash shortage. In such a case, it must obtain short-term credit, which may be structured as a line of credit from a bank. A line of credit is an agreement that allows the business to borrow an unsecured amount of money up to some stated limit. For example, Smart Toys has a line of credit of $60,000, of which $40,000 was used during the year. Amounts drawn on a line of credit must usually be paid back within a year.

Seasonal businesses must be careful to avoid overextending their cash position during the "down cycle." For example, if Smart Toys purchases items that do not sell, a cash surplus will not be generated during the selling season. ■

No Cash Flow per Share

The term *cash flow per share* is sometimes reported in the financial press. Often, the term is used to mean "cash flow from operations per share." Such reporting may be misleading to users of the financial statements. For example, users might interpret cash flow per share as the amount available for dividends. This would not be the case if most of the cash generated by operations is required for repaying loans or for reinvesting in the business. Users might also think that cash flow per share is equivalent or perhaps superior to earnings per share. For these reasons, the financial statements, including the statement of cash flows, should not report cash flow per share.

Statement of Cash Flows—The Indirect Method

objective 3

Prepare a statement of cash flows, using the indirect method.

The indirect method of reporting cash flows from operating activities is normally less costly and more efficient than the direct method. In addition, when the direct method is used, the indirect method must also be used in preparing a supplemental reconciliation of net income with cash flows from operations. The 1999 edition of *Accounting Trends & Techniques* reported that 99% of the companies surveyed used the indirect method. For these reasons, we will discuss first the indirect method of preparing the statement of cash flows.

To collect the data for the statement of cash flows, all the cash receipts and cash payments for a period could be analyzed. However, this procedure is expensive and time-consuming. A more efficient approach is to analyze the changes in the noncash balance sheet accounts. The logic of this approach is that a change in any balance sheet account (including cash) can be analyzed in terms of changes in the other balance sheet accounts. To illustrate, the accounting equation is rewritten below to focus on the cash account:

$$\textbf{Assets} = \textbf{Liabilities} + \textbf{Stockholders' Equity}$$
$$\textbf{Cash} + \textbf{Noncash Assets} = \textbf{Liabilities} + \textbf{Stockholders' Equity}$$
$$\textbf{Cash} = \textbf{Liabilities} + \textbf{Stockholders' Equity} - \textbf{Noncash Assets}$$

Any change in the cash account results in a change in one or more noncash balance sheet accounts. That is, if the cash account changes, then a liability, stockholders' equity, or noncash asset account must also change.

Additional data are also obtained by analyzing the income statement accounts and supporting records. For example, since the net income or net loss for the period is closed to *Retained Earnings*, a change in the retained earnings account can be partially explained by the net income or net loss reported on the income statement.

There is no order in which the noncash balance sheet accounts must be analyzed. However, it is usually more efficient to analyze the accounts in the reverse order in which they appear on the balance sheet. Thus, the analysis of retained earnings provides the starting point for determining the cash flows from operating activities, which is the first section of the statement of cash flows.

The comparative balance sheet for Rundell Inc. on December 31, 2003 and 2002, is used to illustrate the indirect method. This balance sheet is shown in Exhibit 3. Selected ledger accounts and other data are presented as needed.[2]

Retained Earnings

The comparative balance sheet for Rundell Inc. shows that retained earnings increased $80,000 during the year. Analyzing the entries posted to the retained earnings account indicates how this change occurred. The retained earnings account for Rundell Inc. is shown below.

ACCOUNT *Retained Earnings*					ACCOUNT NO.		
						Balance	
Date		**Item**	**Debit**	**Credit**	**Debit**	**Credit**	
2003 Jan.	1	Balance				202,300	
Dec.	31	Net income		108,000		310,300	
	31	Cash dividends	28,000			282,300	

The retained earnings account must be carefully analyzed because some of the entries to retained earnings may not affect cash. For example, a decrease in retained earnings resulting from issuing a stock dividend does not affect cash. Such transactions are not reported on the statement of cash flows.

---

[2] An appendix that discusses using a work sheet as an aid in assembling data for the statement of cash flows is presented at the end of this chapter. This appendix illustrates a work sheet that can be used with the indirect method and a work sheet that can be used with the direct method of reporting cash flows from operating activities.

Exhibit 3 Comparative
Balance Sheet

Rundell Inc.
Comparative Balance Sheet
December 31, 2003 and 2002

Assets	2003	2002	Increase Decrease*
Cash	$ 97,500	$ 26,000	$ 71,500
Accounts receivable (net)	74,000	65,000	9,000
Inventories	172,000	180,000	8,000*
Land	80,000	125,000	45,000*
Building	260,000	200,000	60,000
Accumulated depreciation—building	(65,300)	(58,300)	(7,000)
Total assets	$618,200	$537,700	$ 80,500
Liabilities			
Accounts payable (merchandise creditors)	$ 43,500	$ 46,700	$ 3,200*
Accrued expenses payable (operating expenses)	26,500	24,300	2,200
Income taxes payable	7,900	8,400	,500*
Dividends payable	14,000	10,000	4,000
Bonds payable	100,000	150,000	50,000*
Total liabilities	$191,900	$239,400	$ 47,500*
Stockholders' Equity			
Common stock ($2 par)	$ 24,000	$ 16,000	$ 8,000
Paid-in capital in excess of par	120,000	80,000	40,000
Retained earnings	282,300	202,300	80,000
Total stockholders' equity	$426,300	$298,300	$128,000
Total liabilities and stockholders' equity	$618,200	$537,700	$ 80,500

For Rundell Inc., the retained earnings account indicates that the $80,000 change resulted from net income of $108,000 and cash dividends declared of $28,000. The effect of each of these items on cash flows is discussed in the following sections.

Cash Flows from Operating Activities

The net income of $108,000 reported by Rundell Inc. normally is not equal to the amount of cash generated from operations during the period. This is because net income is determined using the accrual method of accounting.

Under the accrual method of accounting, revenues and expenses are recorded at different times from when cash is received or paid. For example, merchandise may be sold on account and the cash received at a later date.

Likewise, insurance expense represents the amount of insurance expired during the period. The premiums for the insurance may have been paid in a prior period. Thus, the net income reported on the income statement must be adjusted in determining cash flows from operating activities. The typical adjustments to net income are summarized in Exhibit 4.[3]

---

[3] Other items that also require adjustments to net income to obtain cash flow from operating activities include amortization of bonds payable discounts (add), losses on debt retirement (add), amortization of bonds payable premium (deduct), and gains on retirement of debt (deduct).

Exhibit 4 Adjustments to Net Income—Indirect Method

Net income, per income statement		$XX
Add: Depreciation of fixed assets and amortization of intangible assets ..	$XX	
Decreases in current assets (receivables, inventories, prepaid expenses)	XX	
Increases in current liabilities (accounts and notes payable, accrued liabilities)	XX	
Losses on disposal of assets	XX	XX
Deduct: Increases in current assets (receivables, inventories, prepaid expenses)	$XX	
Decreases in current liabilities (accounts and notes payable, accrued liabilities)	XX	
Gains on disposal of assets	XX	XX
Net cash flow from operating activities		$XX

Some of the adjustment items in Exhibit 4 are for expenses that affect noncurrent accounts but not cash. For example, depreciation of fixed assets and amortization of intangible assets are deducted from revenue but do not affect cash.

Some of the adjustment items in Exhibit 4 are for revenues and expenses that affect current assets and current liabilities but not cash flows. For example, a sale of $10,000 on account increases accounts receivable by $10,000. However, cash is not affected. Thus, the increase in accounts receivable of $10,000 between two balance sheet dates is deducted from net income in arriving at cash flows from operating activities.

Cash flows from operating activities should not include investing or financing transactions. For example, assume that land costing $50,000 was sold for $90,000 (a gain of $40,000). The sale should be reported as an investing activity: "Cash receipts from the sale of land, $90,000." However, the $40,000 gain on the sale of the land is included in net income on the income statement. Thus, the $40,000 gain is deducted from net income in determining cash flows from operations in order to avoid "double counting" the cash flow from the gain. Losses from the sale of fixed assets are added to net income in determining cash flows from operations.

The effect of dividends payable on cash flows from operating activities is omitted from Exhibit 4. Dividends payable is omitted because dividends do not affect net income. Later in the chapter, we will discuss how dividends are reported in the statement of cash flows. In the following paragraphs, we will discuss each of the adjustments that change Rundell Inc.'s net income to "Cash flows from operating activities."

Depreciation

The comparative balance sheet in Exhibit 3 indicates that Accumulated Depreciation —Building increased by $7,000. As shown below, this account indicates that depreciation for the year was $7,000 for the building.

ACCOUNT *Accumulated Depreciation—Building*					ACCOUNT NO.	
					Balance	
Date		**Item**	**Debit**	**Credit**	**Debit**	**Credit**
2003 Jan.	1	Balance				58,300
Dec.	31	Depreciation for year		7,000		65,300

The $7,000 of depreciation expense reduced net income but did not require an outflow of cash. Thus, the $7,000 is added to net income in determining cash flows from operating activities, as follows:

Cash flows from operating activities:		
Net income	$108,000	
Add depreciation	7,000	$115,000

Current Assets and Current Liabilities

As shown in Exhibit 4, decreases in noncash current assets and increases in current liabilities are added to net income. In contrast, increases in noncash current assets and decreases in current liabilities are deducted from net income. The current asset and current liability accounts of Rundell Inc. are as follows:

	December 31		Increase
Accounts	2003	2002	Decrease*
Accounts receivable (net)	$ 74,000	$ 65,000	$9,000
Inventories	172,000	180,000	8,000*
Accounts payable (merchandise creditors)	43,500	46,700	3,200*
Accrued expenses payable (operating expenses)	26,500	24,300	2,200
Income taxes payable	7,900	8,400	500*

The $9,000 increase in **accounts receivable** indicates that the sales on account during the year are $9,000 more than collections from customers on account. The amount reported as sales on the income statement therefore includes $9,000 that did not result in a cash inflow during the year. Thus, $9,000 is deducted from net income.

The $8,000 decrease in **inventories** indicates that the merchandise sold exceeds the cost of the merchandise purchased by $8,000. The amount deducted as cost of merchandise sold on the income statement therefore includes $8,000 that did not require a cash outflow during the year. Thus, $8,000 is added to net income.

The $3,200 decrease in **accounts payable** indicates that the amount of cash payments for merchandise exceeds the merchandise purchased on account by $3,200. The amount reported on the income statement for cost of merchandise sold therefore excludes $3,200 that required a cash outflow during the year. Thus, $3,200 is deducted from net income.

The $2,200 increase in **accrued expenses payable** indicates that the amount incurred during the year for operating expenses exceeds the cash payments by $2,200. The amount reported on the income statement for operating expenses therefore includes $2,200 that did not require a cash outflow during the year. Thus, $2,200 is added to net income.

The $500 decrease in **income taxes payable** indicates that the amount paid for taxes exceeds the amount incurred during the year by $500. The amount reported on the income statement for income tax therefore is less than the amount paid by $500. Thus, $500 is deducted from net income.

Gain on Sale of Land

The ledger or income statement of Rundell Inc. indicates that the sale of land resulted in a gain of $12,000. As we discussed previously, the sale proceeds, which include the gain and the carrying value of the land, are included in cash flows from investing activities.[4] The gain is also included in net income. Thus, to avoid double

---

[4] The reporting of the proceeds (cash flows) from the sale of land as part of investing activities is discussed later in this chapter.

reporting, the gain of $12,000 is deducted from net income in determining cash flows from operating activities, as shown below.

Cash flows from operating activities:
Net income $108,000
Deduct gain on sale of land   12,000

Reporting Cash Flows from Operating Activities

We have now presented all the necessary adjustments to convert the net income to cash flows from operating activities for Rundell Inc. These adjustments are summarized in Exhibit 5 in a format suitable for the statement of cash flows.

Exhibit 5 Cash Flows from Operating Activities—Indirect Method

Cash flows from operating activities:		
Net income		$108,000
Add: Depreciation	$ 7,000	
Decrease in inventories	8,000	
Increase in accrued expenses	2,200	17,200
		$125,200
Deduct: Increase in accounts receivable	$ 9,000	
Decrease in accounts payable	3,200	
Decrease in income taxes payable	500	
Gain on sale of land	12,000	24,700
Net cash flow from operating activities		$100,500

Cash Flows Used for Payment of Dividends

According to the retained earnings account of Rundell Inc., shown earlier in the chapter, cash dividends of $28,000 were declared during the year. However, the dividends payable account, shown below, indicates that dividends of only $24,000 were paid during the year.

ACCOUNT *Dividends Payable*					ACCOUNT NO.	
					Balance	
Date		**Item**	**Debit**	**Credit**	**Debit**	**Credit**
2003 Jan.	1	Balance				10,000
	10	Cash paid	10,000		—	
June	20	Dividends declared		14,000	—	14,000
July	10	Cash paid	14,000		—	—
Dec.	20	Dividends declared		14,000		14,000

The $24,000 of dividend payments represents a cash outflow that is reported in the financing activities section as follows:

Cash flows from financing activities:
Cash paid for dividends $24,000

eToys, Inc. has had a negative cumulative cash flow from operations from its inception until recently. However, eToys has been able to grow by obtaining cash from the sale of common stock. Investors are willing to purchase the common stock on the belief that eToys will have a very profitable future as e-commerce matures.

Common Stock

The common stock account increased by $8,000, and the paid-in capital in excess of par—common stock account increased by $40,000, as shown below. These increases result from issuing 4,000 shares of common stock for $12 per share.

ACCOUNT Common Stock					ACCOUNT NO.		
						Balance	
Date		Item	Debit	Credit	Debit	Credit	
2003 Jan.	1	Balance				16,000	
Nov.	1	4,000 shares issued for cash		8,000		24,000	

ACCOUNT Paid-In Capital in Excess of Par—Common Stock					ACCOUNT NO.		
						Balance	
Date		Item	Debit	Credit	Debit	Credit	
2003 Jan.	1	Balance				80,000	
Nov.	1	4,000 shares issued for cash		40,000		120,000	

This cash inflow is reported in the financing activities section as follows:

Cash flows from financing activities:
  Cash received from sale of common stock $48,000

Bonds Payable

The bonds payable account decreased by $50,000, as shown below. This decrease results from retiring the bonds by a cash payment for their face amount.

ACCOUNT Bonds Payable					ACCOUNT NO.		
						Balance	
Date		Item	Debit	Credit	Debit	Credit	
2003 Jan.	1	Balance				150,000	
June	30	Retired by payment of cash at face amount	50,000			100,000	

This cash outflow is reported in the financing activities section as follows:

Cash flows from financing activities:
  Cash paid to retire bonds payable $50,000

Building

The building account increased by $60,000, and the accumulated depreciation—building account increased by $7,000, as shown below.

ACCOUNT *Building*				ACCOUNT NO.		
					Balance	
Date		Item	Debit	Credit	Debit	Credit
2003 Jan.	1	Balance			200,000	
Dec.	27	Purchased for cash	60,000		260,000	

ACCOUNT *Accumulated Depreciation—Building*				ACCOUNT NO.		
					Balance	
Date		Item	Debit	Credit	Debit	Credit
2003 Jan.	1	Balance				58,300
Dec.	31	Depreciation for the year		7,000		65,300

A building with a cost of $145,000 and accumulated depreciation of $35,000 was sold for a $10,000 gain. How much cash was generated from this investing activity?

$120,000 ($145,000 − $35,000 + $10,000)

The purchase of a building for cash of $60,000 is reported as an outflow of cash in the investing activities section, as follows:

Cash flows from investing activities:
Cash paid for purchase of building $60,000

The credit in the accumulated depreciation—building account, shown earlier, represents depreciation expense for the year. This depreciation expense of $7,000 on the building has already been considered as an addition to net income in determining cash flows from operating activities, as reported in Exhibit 5.

Land

The $45,000 decline in the land account resulted from two separate transactions, as shown below.

ACCOUNT *Land*				ACCOUNT NO.		
					Balance	
Date		Item	Debit	Credit	Debit	Credit
2003 Jan.	1	Balance			125,000	
June	8	Sold for $72,000 cash		60,000	65,000	
Oct.	12	Purchased for $15,000 cash	15,000		80,000	

The first transaction is the sale of land with a cost of $60,000 for $72,000 in cash. The $72,000 proceeds from the sale are reported in the investing activities section, as follows:

Cash flows from investing activities:
Cash received from sale of land (includes $12,000 gain reported
in net income) $72,000

The proceeds of $72,000 include the $12,000 gain on the sale of land and the $60,000 cost (book value) of the land. As shown in Exhibit 5, the $12,000 gain is also deducted from net income in the cash flows from operating activities section. This is necessary so that the $12,000 cash inflow related to the gain is not included twice as a cash inflow.

The second transaction is the purchase of land for cash of $15,000. This transaction is reported as an outflow of cash in the investing activities section, as follows:

Cash flows from investing activities:
    Cash paid for purchase of land $15,000

Preparing the Statement of Cash Flows

The statement of cash flows for Rundell Inc. is prepared from the data assembled and analyzed above, using the indirect method. Exhibit 6 shows the statement of cash flows prepared by Rundell Inc. The statement indicates that the cash position increased by $71,500 during the year. The most significant increase in net cash flows, $100,500, was from operating activities. The most significant use of cash, $26,000, was for financing activities.

Exhibit 6 Statement of Cash Flows—Indirect Method

Rundell Inc.
Statement of Cash Flows
For the Year Ended December 31, 2003

Cash flows from operating activities:			
Net income		$108,000	
Add: Depreciation	$ 7,000		
Decrease in inventories	8,000		
Increase in accrued expenses	2,200	17,200	
		$125,200	
Deduct: Increase in accounts receivable	$ 9,000		
Decrease in accounts payable	3,200		
Decrease in income taxes payable	500		
Gain on sale of land	12,000	24,700	
Net cash flow from operating activities			$100,500
Cash flows from investing activities:			
Cash from sale of land		$ 72,000	
Less: Cash paid to purchase land	$15,000		
Cash paid for purchase of building	60,000	75,000	
Net cash flow used for investing activities			(3,000)
Cash flows from financing activities:			
Cash received from sale of common stock		$ 48,000	
Less: Cash paid to retire bonds payable	$50,000		
Cash paid for dividends	24,000	74,000	
Net cash flow used for financing activities			(26,000)
Increase in cash			$ 71,500
Cash at the beginning of the year			26,000
Cash at the end of the year			$ 97,500

Statement of Cash Flows—The Direct Method

Prepare a statement of cash flows, using the direct method.

As we discussed previously, the manner of reporting cash flows from investing and financing activities is the same under the direct and indirect methods. In addition, the direct method and the indirect method will report the same amount of cash flows from operating activities. However, the methods differ in how the cash flows from operating activities data are obtained, analyzed, and reported.

To illustrate the direct method, we will use the comparative balance sheet and the income statement for Rundell Inc. In this way, we can compare the statement of cash flows under the direct method and the indirect method.

Exhibit 7 shows the changes in the current asset and liability account balances for Rundell Inc. The income statement in Exhibit 7 shows additional data for Rundell Inc.

Exhibit 7 Balance Sheet and Income Statement Data for Direct Method

Rundell Inc.
Schedule of Changes in Current Accounts

Accounts	December 31 2003	December 31 2002	Increase Decrease*
Cash	$ 97,500	$ 26,000	$71,500
Accounts receivable (net)	74,000	65,000	9,000
Inventories	172,000	180,000	8,000*
Accounts payable (merchandise creditors)	43,500	46,700	3,200*
Accrued expenses payable (operating expenses)	26,500	24,300	2,200
Income taxes payable	7,900	8,400	500*
Dividends payable	14,000	10,000	4,000

Rundell Inc.
Income Statement
For the Year Ended December 31, 2003

Sales		$1,180,000
Cost of merchandise sold		790,000
Gross profit		$ 390,000
Operating expenses:		
Depreciation expense	$ 7,000	
Other operating expenses	196,000	
Total operating expenses		203,000
Income from operations		$ 187,000
Other income:		
Gain on sale of land	$ 12,000	
Other expense:		
Interest expense	8,000	4,000
Income before income tax		$ 191,000
Income tax expense		83,000
Net income		$ 108,000

The direct method reports cash flows from operating activities by major classes of operating cash receipts and operating cash payments. The difference between the major classes of total operating cash receipts and total operating cash payments is the net cash flow from operating activities.

Cash Received from Customers

The $1,180,000 of sales for Rundell Inc. is reported by using the accrual method. To determine the cash received from sales to customers, the $1,180,000 must be adjusted. The adjustment necessary to convert the sales reported on the income statement to the cash received from customers is summarized below.

For Rundell Inc., the cash received from customers is $1,171,000, as shown below.

Sales	$1,180,000
Less increase in accounts receivable	9,000
Cash received from customers	$1,171,000

The additions to **accounts receivable** for sales on account during the year were $9,000 more than the amounts collected from customers on account. Sales reported on the income statement therefore included $9,000 that did not result in a cash inflow during the year. In other words, the increase of $9,000 in accounts receivable during 2003 indicates that sales on account exceeded cash received from customers by $9,000. Thus, $9,000 is deducted from sales to determine the cash received from customers. The $1,171,000 of cash received from customers is reported in the cash flows from operating activities section of the cash flow statement.

Cash Payments for Merchandise

The $790,000 of cost of merchandise sold is reported on the income statement for Rundell Inc., using the accrual method. The adjustments necessary to convert the cost of merchandise sold to cash payments for merchandise during 2003 are summarized below.

Sales reported on the income statement were $350,000. The accounts receivable balance declined $8,000 over the year. What was the amount of cash received from customers?

$358,000 ($350,000 + $8,000)

For Rundell Inc., the amount of cash payments for merchandise is $785,200, as determined below.

Cost of merchandise sold	$790,000
Deduct decrease in inventories	(8,000)
Add decrease in accounts payable	3,200
Cash payments for merchandise	$785,200

The $8,000 decrease in **inventories** indicates that the merchandise sold exceeded the cost of the merchandise purchased by $8,000. The amount reported on the income statement for cost of merchandise sold therefore includes $8,000 that did not require a cash outflow during the year. Thus, $8,000 is deducted from the cost of merchandise sold in determining the cash payments for merchandise.

The $3,200 decrease in **accounts payable** (merchandise creditors) indicates a cash outflow that is excluded from cost of merchandise sold. In other words, the decrease in accounts payable indicates that cash payments for merchandise were $3,200 more than the purchases on account during 2003. Thus, $3,200 is added to the cost of merchandise sold in determining the cash payments for merchandise.

Cash Payments for Operating Expenses

The $7,000 of depreciation expense reported on the income statement did not require a cash outflow. Thus, under the direct method, it is not reported on the statement of cash flows. The $196,000 reported for other operating expenses is adjusted to reflect the cash payments for operating expenses, as summarized below.

For Rundell Inc., the amount of cash payments for operating expenses is $193,800, determined as follows:

Operating expenses other than depreciation	$196,000
Deduct increase in accrued expenses	2,200
Cash payments for operating expenses	$193,800

The increase in **accrued expenses** (operating expenses) indicates that operating expenses include $2,200 for which there was no cash outflow (payment) during the year. In other words, the increase in accrued expenses indicates that the cash payments for operating expenses were $2,200 less than the amount reported as an expense during the year. Thus, $2,200 is deducted from the operating expenses on the income statement in determining the cash payments for operating expenses.

Gain on Sale of Land

The income statement for Rundell Inc. in Exhibit 7 reports a gain of $12,000 on the sale of land. As we discussed previously, the gain is included in the proceeds from the sale of land, which is reported as part of the cash flows from investing activities.

Interest Expense

The income statement for Rundell Inc. in Exhibit 7 reports interest expense of $8,000. The interest expense is related to the bonds payable that were outstanding during the year. We assume that interest on the bonds is paid on June 30 and December 31. Thus, $8,000 cash outflow for interest expense is reported on the statement of cash flows as an operating activity.

If interest payable had existed at the end of the year, the interest expense would be adjusted for any increase or decrease in interest payable from the beginning to the end of the year. That is, a decrease in interest payable would be added to interest expense and an increase in interest payable would be subtracted from interest expense. This is similar to the adjustment for changes in income taxes payable, which we will illustrate in the following paragraphs.

Cash Payments for Income Taxes

The adjustment to convert the income tax reported on the income statement to the cash basis is summarized below.

For Rundell Inc., cash payments for income tax are $83,500, determined as follows:

Income tax	$83,000
Add decrease in income taxes payable	500
Cash payments for income tax	$83,500

The cash outflow for income taxes exceeded the income tax deducted as an expense during the period by $500. Thus, $500 is added to the amount of income tax reported on the income statement in determining the cash payments for income tax.

Reporting Cash Flows from Operating Activities—Direct Method

Exhibit 8 is a complete statement of cash flows for Rundell Inc., using the direct method for reporting cash flows from operating activities. The portions of this statement that differ from the indirect method are highlighted in color. Exhibit 8 also includes the separate schedule reconciling net income and net cash flow from operating activities. This schedule must accompany the statement of cash flows when the direct method is used. This schedule is similar to the cash flows from operating activities section of the statement of cash flows prepared using the indirect method.

Dell Computer Corporation is one of the few companies that has a *negative cash conversion cycle*. This means that Dell receives payment for a computer before it pays for the parts that went into that computer. This can only be done by collecting the sale with a credit card, maintaining very little inventory, and holding accounts payable open for 30 days.

Exhibit 8 Statement of Cash Flows—Direct Method

Rundell Inc.
Statement of Cash Flows
For the Year Ended December 31, 2003

Cash flows from operating activities:			
Cash received from customers		$1,171,000	
Deduct: Cash payments for merchandise	$785,200		
Cash payments for operating expenses	193,800		
Cash payments for interest	8,000		
Cash payments for income taxes	83,500	1,070,500	
Net cash flow from operating activities			$100,500
Cash flows from investing activities:			
Cash from sale of land		$ 72,000	
Less: Cash paid to purchase land	$ 15,000		
Cash paid for purchase of building	60,000	75,000	
Net cash flow used for investing activities			(3,000)
Cash flows from financing activities:			
Cash received from sale of common stock		$ 48,000	
Less: Cash paid to retire bonds payable	$ 50,000		
Cash paid for dividends	24,000	74,000	
Net cash flow used for financing activities			(26,000)
Increase in cash			$ 71,500
Cash at the beginning of the year			26,000
Cash at the end of the year			$ 97,500

Schedule Reconciling Net Income with Cash Flows from Operating Activities:

Net income, per income statement		$108,000	
Add: Depreciation	$ 7,000		
Decrease in inventories	8,000		
Increase in accrued expenses	2,200	17,200	
		$125,200	
Deduct: Increase in accounts receivable	$ 9,000		
Decrease in accounts payable	3,200		
Decrease in income taxes payable	500		
Gain on sale of land	12,000	24,700	
Net cash flow from operating activities		$100,500	

FINANCIAL ANALYSIS AND INTERPRETATION

objective 5

Calculate and interpret the free cash flow.

A valuable tool for evaluating the cash position of a business is free cash flow. **Free cash flow** is a measure of operating cash flow available for corporate purposes after providing sufficient fixed asset additions to maintain current productive capacity and dividends. Thus, free cash flow can be calculated as follows:

	Cash flow from operating activities
Less:	Cash used to purchase fixed assets to maintain productive capacity used up in producing income during the period
Less:	Cash used for dividends
	Free cash flow

Real World

Many high technology firms must aggressively reinvest in new technology to remain competitive. This can reduce free cash flow. For example, **Motorola's** free cash flow is less than 10% of the cash flow from operating activities. In contrast, **Coca-Cola's** free cash flow is approximately 75% of the cash flow from operating activities.

To illustrate, assume that O'Brien Company had cash flow from operating activities of $1,400,000. O'Brien Company invested $450,000 in fixed assets to maintain productive capacity, and another $300,000 to expand capacity. Dividends were $100,000. Thus, free cash flow is as follows:

Cash flow from operating activities		$1,400,000
Less: Cash invested in fixed assets to		
maintain productive capacity	$450,000	
Cash for dividends	100,000	550,000
Free cash flow		$ 850,000

A company that has free cash flow is able to fund internal growth, retire debt, and enjoy financial flexibility. A company with no free cash flow is unable to maintain current productive capacity or dividend payouts to stockholders. Lack of free cash flow can be an early indicator of liquidity problems. Indeed, as stated by one analyst, "Free cash flow gives the company firepower to reduce debt and ultimately generate consistent, actual income."[5]

ENCORE

Cash Is King for the Pack

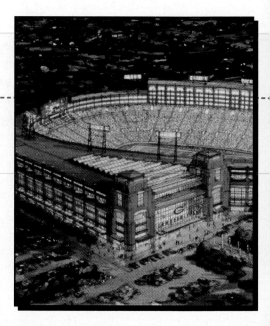

The **Green Bay Packers** is the only team in the NFL to be owned by the fans (over 109,000 of them). Indeed, over 10,000 fans show up in early July at Lambeau Field for the shareholders' meeting, the largest shareholders' meeting in corporate America. Unfortunately, the recent financial news has not been good. Although the club had a profit of $1 million, it had a negative cash flow of $10.7 million (excluding a one-time expansion team payment). Why did the cash decline in the face of positive earnings? The answer is simple. The Packers have paid over $32 million in player-signing bonuses, while continuing to make improvements to Lambeau Field. John Underwood, treasurer, stated, "We really need to focus our attention on generating higher levels of cash. In the business we're in, cash is king. And every dollar we make in

this franchise goes to only one of two purposes: the football team or the facilities." While the Packers place 15th out of 31 teams in total revenue, the president predicts that they will fall to last place by 2003 if Lambeau Field is not renovated. A stadium renovation will allow the Packers to:

• expand the concourse for additional retail shops and concession space.
• build a stadium club that can be used for banquets and events.
• expand Lambeau's rather small 61,000-seat capacity by 8,000 seats.
• rebuild the luxury boxes.

The added cash flow from stadium improvements is the key to financial success in professional football. The question is how to come up with $150

million for stadium renovations. The team is presently considering a one-time, $1,000 per-seat user fee to be assessed to the season ticket holders to cover part of it. Apparently, if you're a stockholder who also holds season tickets, the news is doubly bad. ∎

[5] Jill Krutick, *Fortune*, March 30, 1998, p. 106.

APPENDIX: WORK SHEET FOR STATEMENT OF CASH FLOWS

A work sheet may be useful in assembling data for the statement of cash flows. Whether or not a work sheet is used, the concepts of cash flow and the statements of cash flows presented in this chapter are not affected. In this appendix, we will describe and illustrate the use of work sheets for the indirect method and the direct method.

Work Sheet—Indirect Method

We will use the data for Rundell Inc., presented in Exhibit 3, as a basis for illustrating the work sheet for the indirect method. The procedures used in preparing this work sheet, shown in Exhibit 9, are outlined at the top of the next page.

Exhibit 9 Work Sheet for Statement of Cash Flows—Indirect Method

Rundell Inc.
Work Sheet for Statement of Cash Flows
For the Year Ended December 31, 2003

	Accounts	Balance Dec. 31, 2002	Transactions Debit	Transactions Credit	Balance Dec. 31, 2003	
1	Cash	26,000	(o) 71,500		97,500	1
2	Accounts receivable (net)	65,000	(n) 9,000		74,000	2
3	Inventories	180,000		(m) 8,000	172,000	3
4	Land	125,000	(k) 15,000	(l) 60,000	80,000	4
5	Building	200,000	(j) 60,000		260,000	5
6	Accumulated depreciation—building	(58,300)		(i) 7,000	(65,300)	6
7	Accounts payable (merchandise creditors)	(46,700)	(h) 3,200		(43,500)	7
8	Accrued expenses payable (operating expenses)	(24,300)		(g) 2,200	(26,500)	8
9	Income taxes payable	(8,400)	(f) 500		(7,900)	9
10	Dividends payable	(10,000)		(e) 4,000	(14,000)	10
11	Bonds payable	(150,000)	(d) 50,000		(100,000)	11
12	Common stock	(16,000)		(c) 8,000	(24,000)	12
13	Paid-in capital in excess of par	(80,000)		(c) 40,000	(120,000)	13
14	Retained earnings	(202,300)	(b) 28,000	(a) 108,000	(282,300)	14
15	Totals	0	237,200	237,200	0	15
16	Operating activities:					16
17	Net income		(a) 108,000			17
18	Depreciation of building		(i) 7,000			18
19	Decrease in inventories		(m) 8,000			19
20	Increase in accrued expenses		(g) 2,200			20
21	Increase in accounts receivable			(n) 9,000		21
22	Decrease in accounts payable			(h) 3,200		22
23	Decrease in income taxes payable			(f) 500		23
24	Gain on sale of land			(l) 12,000		24
25	Investing activities:					25
26	Sale of land		(l) 72,000			26
27	Purchase of land			(k) 15,000		27
28	Purchase of building			(j) 60,000		28
29	Financing activities:					29
30	Issued common stock		(c) 48,000			30
31	Retired bonds payable			(d) 50,000		31
32	Declared cash dividends			(b) 28,000		32
33	Increase in dividends payable		(e) 4,000			33
34	Net increase in cash			(o) 71,500		34
35	Totals		249,200	249,200		35

1. List the title of each balance sheet account in the Accounts column. For each account, enter its balance as of December 31, 2002, in the first column and its balance as of December 31, 2003, in the last column. Place the credit balances in parentheses. The column totals should equal zero, since the total of the debits in a column should equal the total of the credits in a column.
2. Analyze the change during the year in each account to determine the net increase (decrease) in cash and the cash flows from operating activities, investing activities, financing activities, and the noncash investing and financing activities. Show the effect of the change on cash flows by making entries in the Transactions columns.

Analyzing Accounts

An efficient method of analyzing cash flows is to determine the type of cash flow activity that led to changes in balance sheet accounts during the period. As we analyze each noncash account, we will make entries on the work sheet for specific types of cash flow activities related to the noncash accounts. After we have analyzed all the noncash accounts, we will make an entry for the increase (decrease) in cash during the period. These entries, however, are not posted to the ledger. They only aid in assembling the data on the work sheet.

The order in which the accounts are analyzed is unimportant. However, it is more efficient to begin with the retained earnings account and proceed upward in the account listing.

Retained Earnings. The work sheet shows a Retained Earnings balance of $202,300 at December 31, 2002, and $282,300 at December 31, 2003. Thus, Retained Earnings increased $80,000 during the year. This increase resulted from two factors: (1) net income of $108,000 and (2) declaring cash dividends of $28,000. To identify the cash flows by activity, we will make two entries on the work sheet. These entries also serve to account for or explain, in terms of cash flows, the increase of $80,000.

In closing the accounts at the end of the year, the retained earnings account was credited for the net income of $108,000. The $108,000 is reported on the statement of cash flows as "cash flows from operating activities." The following entry is made in the Transactions columns on the work sheet. This entry (1) accounts for the credit portion of the closing entry (to Retained Earnings) and (2) identifies the cash flow in the bottom portion of the work sheet.

| (a) | Operating Activities—Net Income | 108,000 | |
| | Retained Earnings | | 108,000 |

In closing the accounts at the end of the year, the retained earnings account was debited for dividends declared of $28,000. The $28,000 is reported as a financing activity on the statement of cash flows. The following entry on the work sheet (1) accounts for the debit portion of the closing entry (to Retained Earnings) and (2) identifies the cash flow in the bottom portion of the work sheet.

| (b) | Retained Earnings | 28,000 | |
| | Financing Activities—Declared Cash Dividends | | 28,000 |

The $28,000 of declared dividends will be adjusted later for the actual amount of cash dividends paid during the year.

Other Accounts. The entries for the other accounts are made in the work sheet in a manner similar to entries (a) and (b). A summary of these entries is as follows:

(c)	Financing Activities—Issued Common Stock	48,000	
	Common Stock		8,000
	Paid-In Capital in Excess of Par—Common Stock		40,000

(d)	Bonds Payable		50,000	
	Financing Activities—Retired Bonds Payable			50,000
(e)	Financing Activities—Increase in Dividends Payable		4,000	
	Dividends Payable			4,000
(f)	Income Taxes Payable		500	
	Operating Activities—Decrease in Income Taxes Payable			500
(g)	Operating Activities—Increase in Accrued Expenses		2,200	
	Accrued Expenses Payable			2,200
(h)	Accounts Payable		3,200	
	Operating Activities—Decrease in Accounts Payable			3,200
(i)	Operating Activities—Depreciation of Building		7,000	
	Accumulated Depreciation—Building			7,000
(j)	Building		60,000	
	Investing Activities—Purchase of Building			60,000
(k)	Land		15,000	
	Investing Activities—Purchase of Land			15,000
(l)	Investing Activities—Sale of Land		72,000	
	Operating Activities—Gain on Sale of Land			12,000
	Land			60,000
(m)	Operating Activities—Decrease in Inventories		8,000	
	Inventories			8,000
(n)	Accounts Receivable		9,000	
	Operating Activities—Increase in Accounts Receivable			9,000
(o)	Cash		71,500	
	Net Increase in Cash			71,500

Completing the Work Sheet

After we have analyzed all the balance sheet accounts and made the entries on the work sheet, all the operating, investing, and financing activities are identified in the bottom portion of the work sheet. The accuracy of the work sheet entries is verified by the equality of each pair of the totals of the debit and credit Transactions columns.

Preparing the Statement of Cash Flows

The statement of cash flows prepared from the work sheet is identical to the statement in Exhibit 6. The data for the three sections of the statement are obtained from the bottom portion of the work sheet.

In the cash flows from operating activities section, the effect of depreciation is normally presented first. The effects of increases and decreases in current assets and current liabilities are then presented. The effects of any gains and losses on operating activities are normally reported last. The cash paid for dividends is reported as $24,000 instead of the amount of dividends declared ($28,000) less the increase in dividends payable ($4,000). Any noncash investing and financing activities are usually reported in a separate schedule at the bottom of the statement.

Work Sheet—Direct Method

As a basis for illustrating the direct method work sheet, we will use the balance sheet data for Rundell Inc. in Exhibit 3 and the income statement data in Exhibit 7. The procedures used in preparing the work sheet are outlined following Exhibit 10.

1. List the title of each balance sheet account in the Accounts column. For each account, enter its balance as of December 31, 2002, in the first column and its balance as of December 31, 2003, in the last column. Place the credit balances in parentheses. The column totals should equal zero, since the total of the debits in a column should equal the total of the credits in a column.

Exhibit 10 Work Sheet for Statement of Cash Flows—Direct Method

Rundell Inc.
Work Sheet for Statement of Cash Flows
For the Year Ended December 31, 2003

#	Accounts	Balance Dec. 31, 2002	Transactions Debit	Transactions Credit	Balance Dec. 31, 2003	
1	**Balance Sheet**					1
2	Cash	26,000	(t) 71,500		97,500	2
3	Accounts receivable (net)	65,000	(s) 9,000		74,000	3
4	Inventories	180,000		(r) 8,000	172,000	4
5	Land	125,000	(q) 15,000	(e) 60,000	80,000	5
6	Building	200,000	(p) 60,000		260,000	6
7	Accumulated depreciation—building	(58,300)		(c) 7,000	(65,300)	7
8	Accounts payable (merchandise creditors)	(46,700)	(o) 3,200		(43,500)	8
9	Accrued expenses payable (operating expenses)	(24,300)		(n) 2,200	(26,500)	9
10	Income taxes payable	(8,400)	(m) 500		(7,900)	10
11	Dividends payable	(10,000)		(l) 4,000	(14,000)	11
12	Bonds payable	(150,000)	(k) 50,000		(100,000)	12
13	Common stock	(16,000)		(j) 8,000	(24,000)	13
14	Paid-in capital in excess of par	(80,000)		(j) 40,000	(120,000)	14
15	Retained earnings	(202,300)	(i) 28,000	(h) 108,000	(282,300)	15
16	Totals	0	237,200	237,200	0	16
17	**Income Statement**					17
18	Sales			(a) 1,180,000		18
19	Cost of merchandise sold		(b) 790,000			19
20	Depreciation expense		(c) 7,000			20
21	Other operating expenses		(d) 196,000			21
22	Gain on sale of land			(e) 12,000		22
23	Interest expense		(f) 8,000			23
24	Income taxes		(g) 83,000			24
25	Net income		(h) 108,000			25
26	**Cash Flows**					26
27	Operating activities:					27
28	Cash received from customers		(a) 1,180,000	(s) 9,000		28
29	Cash payments:					29
30	Merchandise		(r) 8,000	(b) 790,000		30
31				(o) 3,200		31
32	Operating expenses		(n) 2,200	(d) 196,000		32
33	Interest			(f) 8,000		33
34	Income taxes			(g) 83,000		34
35				(m) 500		35
36	Investing activities:					36
37	Sale of land		(e) 72,000			37
38	Purchase of land			(q) 15,000		38
39	Purchase of building			(p) 60,000		39
40	Financing activities:					40
41	Issued common stock		(j) 48,000			41
42	Retired bonds payable			(k) 50,000		42
43	Declared cash dividends			(i) 28,000		43
44	Increase in dividends payable		(l) 4,000			44
45	Net increase in cash			(t) 71,500		45
46	Totals		2,506,200	2,506,200		46

2. List the title of each income statement account and "Net income" on the work sheet.
3. Analyze the effect of each income statement item on cash flows from operating activities. Beginning with sales, enter the balance of each item in the proper Transactions column. Complete the entry in the Transactions columns to show the effect on cash flows.
4. Analyze the change during the year in each balance sheet account to determine the net increase (decrease) in cash and the cash flows from operating activities, investing activities, financing activities, and the noncash investing and financing activities. Show the effect of the change on cash flows by making entries in the Transactions columns.

Analyzing Accounts

Under the direct method of reporting cash flows from operating activities, analyzing accounts begins with the income statement. As we analyze each income statement account, we will make entries on the work sheet that show the effect on cash flows from operating activities. After we have analyzed the income statement accounts, we will analyze changes in the balance sheet accounts.

The order in which the balance sheet accounts are analyzed is unimportant. However, it is more efficient to begin with the retained earnings account and proceed upward in the account listing. As each noncash balance sheet account is analyzed, we will make entries on the work sheet for the related cash flow activities. After we have analyzed all the noncash accounts, we will make an entry for the increase (decrease) in cash during the period.

Sales. The income statement for Rundell Inc. shows sales of $1,180,000 for the year. Sales for cash provide cash when the sale is made. Sales on account provide cash when customers pay their bills. The entry on the work sheet is as follows:

(a)	Operating Activities—Receipts from Customers	1,180,000	
	Sales		1,180,000

Cost of Merchandise Sold. The income statement for Rundell Inc. shows cost of merchandise sold of $790,000 for the year. The cost of merchandise sold requires cash payments for cash purchases of merchandise. For purchases on account, cash payments are made when the invoices are due. The entry on the work sheet is as follows:

(b)	Cost of Merchandise Sold	790,000	
	Operating Activities—Payments for Merchandise		790,000

Depreciation Expense. The income statement for Rundell Inc. shows depreciation expense of $7,000. Depreciation expense does not require a cash outflow and thus is not reported on the statement of cash flows. The entry on the work sheet to fully account for the depreciation expense is as follows:

(c)	Depreciation Expense	7,000	
	Accumulated Depreciation—Building		7,000

Other Accounts. The entries for the other accounts are made on the work sheet in a manner similar to entries (a), (b), and (c). A summary of these entries is as follows:

(d)	Other Operating Expenses	196,000	
	Operating Activities—Paid Operating Expenses		196,000

(e)	Investing Activities—Sale of Land	72,000	
	Land		60,000
	Gain on Sale of Land		12,000
(f)	Interest Expense	8,000	
	Operating Activities—Paid Interest		8,000
(g)	Income Taxes	83,000	
	Operating Activities—Paid Income Taxes		83,000
(h)	Net Income	108,000	
	Retained Earnings		108,000
(i)	Retained Earnings	28,000	
	Financing Activities—Declared Cash Dividends		28,000
(j)	Financing Activities—Issued Common Stock	48,000	
	Common Stock		8,000
	Paid-In Capital in Excess of Par—Common Stock		40,000
(k)	Bonds Payable	50,000	
	Financing Activities—Retired Bonds Payable		50,000
(l)	Financing Activities—Increase in Dividends Payable	4,000	
	Dividends Payable		4,000
(m)	Income Taxes Payable	500	
	Operating Activities—Cash Paid for Income Taxes		500
(n)	Operating Activities—Cash Paid for Operating Expenses	2,200	
	Accrued Expenses Payable		2,200
(o)	Accounts Payable	3,200	
	Operating Activities—Cash Paid for Merchandise		3,200
(p)	Building	60,000	
	Investing Activities—Purchase of Building		60,000
(q)	Land	15,000	
	Investing Activities—Purchase of Land		15,000
(r)	Operating Activities—Cash Paid for Merchandise	8,000	
	Inventories		8,000
(s)	Accounts Receivable	9,000	
	Operating Activities—Cash Received from Customers		9,000
(t)	Cash	71,500	
	Net Increase in Cash		71,500

Completing the Work Sheet

After we have analyzed all the income statement and balance sheet accounts and have made the entries on the work sheet, all the operating, investing, and financing activities are identified in the bottom portion of the work sheet. The mathematical accuracy of the work sheet entries is verified by the equality of each pair of the totals of the debit and credit Transactions columns.

Preparing the Statement of Cash Flows

The statement of cash flows prepared from the work sheet is identical to the statement in Exhibit 8. The data for the three sections of the statement are obtained from the bottom portion of the work sheet. Some of these data may not be reported exactly as they appear on the work sheet. The cash paid for dividends is reported as $24,000 instead of the amount of dividends declared ($28,000) less the increase in the dividends payable ($4,000).

KEY POINTS

1 Explain why the statement of cash flows is one of the basic financial statements.

The statement of cash flows reports useful information about a firm's ability to generate cash from operations, maintain and expand its operating capacity, meet its financial obligations, and pay dividends. This information assists investors, creditors, and others in assessing the firm's profit potential and its ability to pay its maturing debt. The statement of cash flows is also useful to managers in evaluating past operations and in planning future operating, investing, and financing activities.

2 Summarize the types of cash flow activities reported in the statement of cash flows.

The statement of cash flows reports cash receipts and cash payments by three types of activities: operating activities, investing activities, and financing activities.

Cash flows from operating activities are cash flows from transactions that affect net income. There are two methods of reporting cash flows from operating activities: (1) the direct method and (2) the indirect method.

Cash inflows from investing activities are cash flows from the sale of investments, fixed assets, and intangible assets. Cash outflows generally include payments to acquire investments, fixed assets, and intangible assets.

Cash inflows from financing activities include proceeds from issuing equity securities, such as preferred and common stock. Cash inflows also arise from issuing bonds, mortgage notes payable, and other long-term debt. Cash outflows from financing activities arise from paying cash dividends, purchasing treasury stock, and repaying amounts borrowed.

Investing and financing for a business may be affected by transactions that do not involve cash. The effect of such transactions should be reported in a separate schedule accompanying the statement of cash flows.

Because it may be misleading, cash flow per share is not reported in the statement of cash flows.

3 Prepare a statement of cash flows, using the indirect method.

To prepare the statement of cash flows, changes in the noncash balance sheet accounts are analyzed. This logic relies on the fact that a change in any balance sheet account can be analyzed in terms of changes in the other balance sheet accounts. Thus, by analyzing the noncash balance sheet accounts, those activities that resulted in cash flows can be identified. Although the noncash balance sheet accounts may be analyzed in any order, it is usually more efficient to begin with retained earnings. Additional data are obtained by analyzing the income statement accounts and supporting records.

4 Prepare a statement of cash flows, using the direct method.

The direct method and the indirect method will report the same amount of cash flows from operating activities. Also, the manner of reporting cash flows from investing and financing activities is the same under both methods. The methods differ in how the cash flows from operating activities data are obtained, analyzed, and reported. The direct method reports cash flows from operating activities by major classes of operating cash receipts and cash payments. The difference between the major classes of total operating cash receipts and total operating cash payments is the net cash flow from operating activities.

The data for reporting cash flows from operating activities by the direct method can be obtained by analyzing the cash flows related to the revenues and expenses reported on the income statement. The revenues and expenses are adjusted from the accrual basis of accounting to the cash basis for purposes of preparing the statement of cash flows.

When the direct method is used, a reconciliation of net income and net cash flow from operating activities is reported in a separate schedule. This schedule is similar to the cash flows from operating activities section of the statement of cash flows prepared using the indirect method.

5 Calculate and interpret the free cash flow.

Free cash flow is the amount of operating cash flow remaining after replacing current productive capacity and maintaining current dividends. Free cash flow is the amount of cash available to reduce debt, expand the business, or return to shareholders through increased dividends or treasury stock purchases.

ILLUSTRATIVE PROBLEM

The comparative balance sheet of Dowling Company for December 31, 2004 and 2003, is as follows:

Dowling Company
Comparative Balance Sheet
December 31, 2004 and 2003

	2004	2003
Assets		
Cash	$ 140,350	$ 95,900
Accounts receivable (net)	95,300	102,300
Inventories	165,200	157,900
Prepaid expenses	6,240	5,860
Investments (long-term)	35,700	84,700
Land	75,000	90,000
Buildings	375,000	260,000
Accumulated depreciation—buildings	(71,300)	(58,300)
Machinery and equipment	428,300	428,300
Accumulated depreciation—machinery and equipment	(148,500)	(138,000)
Patents	58,000	65,000
Total assets	$1,159,290	$1,093,660
Liabilities and Stockholders' Equity		
Accounts payable (merchandise creditors)	$ 43,500	$ 46,700
Accrued expenses (operating expenses)	14,000	12,500
Income taxes payable	7,900	8,400
Dividends payable	14,000	10,000
Mortgage note payable, due 2004	40,000	0
Bonds payable	150,000	250,000
Common stock, $30 par	450,000	375,000
Excess of issue price over par—common stock	66,250	41,250
Retained earnings	373,640	349,810
Total liabilities and stockholders' equity	$1,159,290	$1,093,660

The income statement for Dowling Company is shown below.

Dowling Company
Income Statement
For the Year Ended December 31, 2004

Sales		$1,100,000
Cost of merchandise sold		710,000
Gross profit		$ 390,000
Operating expenses:		
Depreciation expense	$ 23,500	
Patent amortization	7,000	
Other operating expenses	196,000	
Total operating expenses		226,500
Income from operations		$ 163,500
Other income:		
Gain on sale of investments	$ 11,000	
Other expense:		
Interest expense	26,000	(15,000)
Income before income tax		$ 148,500
Income tax expense		50,000
Net income		$ 98,500

An examination of the accounting records revealed the following additional information applicable to 2004:

a. Land costing $15,000 was sold for $15,000.
b. A mortgage note was issued for $40,000.
c. A building costing $115,000 was constructed.
d. 2,500 shares of common stock were issued at 40 in exchange for the bonds payable.
e. Cash dividends declared were $74,670.

Instructions

1. Prepare a statement of cash flows, using the indirect method of reporting cash flows from operating activities.
2. Prepare a statement of cash flows, using the direct method of reporting cash flows from operating activities.

Solution

1.

Dowling Company
Statement of Cash Flows—Indirect Method
For the Year Ended December 31, 2004

Cash flows from operating activities:			
Net income, per income statement		$ 98,500	
Add: Depreciation	$23,500		
Amortization of patents	7,000		
Decrease in accounts receivable	7,000		
Increase in accrued expenses	1,500	39,000	
		$137,500	
Deduct: Increase in inventories	$ 7,300		
Increase in prepaid expenses	380		
Decrease in accounts payable	3,200		
Decrease in income taxes payable	500		
Gain on sale of investments	11,000	22,380	
Net cash flow from operating activities			$115,120
Cash flows from investing activities:			
Cash received from sale of:			
Investments	$60,000		
Land	15,000	$ 75,000	
Less: Cash paid for construction of building		115,000	
Net cash flow used for investing activities			(40,000)
Cash flows from financing activities:			
Cash received from issuing mortgage note payable		$ 40,000	
Less: Cash paid for dividends		70,670	
Net cash flow used for financing activities			(30,670)
Increase in cash			$ 44,450
Cash at the beginning of the year			95,900
Cash at the end of the year			$140,350

Schedule of Noncash Investing and
Financing Activities:

Issued common stock to retire bonds payable	$100,000

2.

Dowling Company
Statement of Cash Flows—Direct Method
For the Year Ended December 31, 2004

Cash flows from operating activities:			
Cash received from customers[1]			$1,107,000
Deduct: Cash paid for merchandise[2]	$720,500		
Cash paid for operating expenses[3]	194,880		
Cash paid for interest expense	26,000		
Cash paid for income tax[4]	50,500	991,880	
Net cash flow from operating activities			$115,120
Cash flows from investing activities:			
Cash received from sale of:			
Investments	$ 60,000		
Land	15,000	$ 75,000	
Less: Cash paid for construction of building		115,000	
Net cash flow used for investing activities			(40,000)
Cash flows from financing activities:			
Cash received from issuing mortgage note payable		$ 40,000	
Less: Cash paid for dividends[5]		70,670	
Net cash flow used for financing activities			(30,670)
Increase in cash			$ 44,450
Cash at the beginning of the year			95,900
Cash at the end of the year			$140,350

Schedule of Noncash Investing and Financing Activities:

Issued common stock to retire bonds payable	$100,000

Computations:

^{1}$1,100,000 + $7,000 = $1,107,000
^{2}$710,000 + $3,200 + $7,300 = $720,500
^{3}$196,000 + $380 - $1,500 = $194,880
^{4}$50,000 + $500 = $50,500
^{5}$74,670 + $10,000 - $14,000 = $70,670

SELF-EXAMINATION QUESTIONS   **Answers at End of Chapter**

Matching

Match each of the following statements with its proper term. Some terms may not be used.

A.	**cash flows from financing activities**	___ 1. An addition to sales under the direct method for determining cash flows from operating activities.
B.	**cash flows from investing activities**	___ 2. A statement of cash flows disclosure item.
C.	**cash flows from operating activities**	___ 3. The section of the statement of cash flows that reports cash flows from transactions affecting the equity and debt of the business.
D.	**decrease in accounts payable**	___ 4. A financing activity that increases cash.
		___ 5. An addition to net income under the indirect method for determining cash flows from operating activities.
E.	**decrease in accounts receivable**	___ 6. The section of the statement of cash flows that reports cash flows from transactions affecting investments in noncurrent assets.

F. direct method	___ 7. A summary of the major cash receipts and cash payments for a period.
G. dividends declared	___ 8. A deduction from net income under the indirect method for determining cash flows from operating activities.
H. free cash flow	___ 9. A method of reporting the cash flows from operating activities as the difference between the operating cash receipts and the operating cash payments.
I. loss on sale of land	
J. indirect method	___ 10. The section of the statement of cash flows that reports the cash transactions affecting the determination of net income.
K. issuance of common stock	___ 11. A method of reporting the cash flows from operating activities as the net income from operations adjusted for all deferrals of past cash receipts and payments and all accruals of expected future cash receipts and payments.
L. purchase of land with common stock	
M. sale of land	___ 12. An investing activity.
N. statement of cash flows	___ 13. The amount of operating cash flow remaining after replacing current productive capacity and maintaining current dividends.

Multiple Choice

1. An example of a cash flow from an operating activity is:
   A. receipt of cash from the sale of stock
   B. receipt of cash from the sale of bonds
   C. payment of cash for dividends
   D. receipt of cash from customers on account

2. An example of a cash flow from an investing activity is:
   A. receipt of cash from the sale of equipment
   B. receipt of cash from the sale of stock
   C. payment of cash for dividends
   D. payment of cash to acquire treasury stock

3. An example of a cash flow from a financing activity is:
   A. receipt of cash from customers on account
   B. receipt of cash from the sale of equipment
   C. payment of cash for dividends
   D. payment of cash to acquire land

4. Which of the following methods of reporting cash flows from operating activities adjusts net income for revenues and expenses not involving the receipt or payment of cash?

    A. Direct method   C. Reciprocal method
    B. Purchase method   D. Indirect method

5. The net income reported on the income statement for the year was $55,000, and depreciation of fixed assets for the year was $22,000. The balances of the current asset and current liability accounts at the beginning and end of the year are as follows:

	End	Beginning
Cash	$ 65,000	$ 70,000
Accounts receivable	100,000	90,000
Inventories	145,000	150,000
Prepaid expenses	7,500	8,000
Accounts payable (merchandise creditors)	51,000	58,000

The total amount reported for cash flows from operating activities in the statement of cash flows, using the indirect method, is:
A. $33,000   C. $65,500
B. $55,000   D. $77,000

CLASS DISCUSSION QUESTIONS

1. What is the principal disadvantage of the direct method of reporting cash flows from operating activities?
2. What are the major advantages of the indirect method of reporting cash flows from operating activities?
3. A corporation issued $200,000 of common stock in exchange for $200,000 of fixed assets. Where would this transaction be reported on the statement of cash flows?
4. a. What is the effect on cash flows of declaring and issuing a stock dividend?
   b. Is the stock dividend reported on the statement of cash flows?
5. A retail business, using the accrual method of accounting, owed merchandise creditors (accounts payable) $290,000 at the beginning of the year and $315,000 at the end of the year. How would the $25,000 increase be used to adjust net income in

determining the amount of cash flows from operating activities by the indirect method? Explain.

6. If salaries payable was $75,000 at the beginning of the year and $65,000 at the end of the year, should $10,000 be added to or deducted from income to determine the amount of cash flows from operating activities by the indirect method? Explain.

7. A long-term investment in bonds with a cost of $75,000 was sold for $80,000 cash. (a) What was the gain or loss on the sale? (b) What was the effect of the transaction on cash flows? (c) How should the transaction be reported in the statement of cash flows if cash flows from operating activities are reported by the indirect method?

8. A corporation issued $5,000,000 of 20-year bonds for cash at 105. How would the transaction be reported on the statement of cash flows?

9. Fully depreciated equipment costing $55,000 was discarded. What was the effect of the transaction on cash flows if (a) $5,000 cash is received, (b) no cash is received?

10. For the current year, Accord Company decided to switch from the indirect method to the direct method for reporting cash flows from operating activities on the statement of cash flows. Will the change cause the amount of net cash flow from operating activities to be (a) larger, (b) smaller, or (c) the same as if the indirect method had been used? Explain.

11. Name five common major classes of operating cash receipts or operating cash payments presented on the statement of cash flows when the cash flows from operating activities are reported by the direct method.

12. In a recent annual report, **PepsiCo, Inc.**, reported that during the year it issued stock of $438 million for acquisitions. How would this be reported on the statement of cash flows?

RESOURCES FOR YOUR SUCCESS ONLINE AT

http://warren.swcollege.com

Remember! If you need additional help, visit South-Western's Web site.
See page 26 for a description of the online and printed materials that are available.

EXERCISES

Exercise 15–1
Cash flows from operating activities—net loss

Objective 2

On its income statement for a recent year, **Amazon.com, Inc.** reported a net loss of $124 million from operations. On its statement of cash flows, it reported $31 million of cash flows from operating activities.

✏️➤ Explain this apparent contradiction between the loss and the positive cash flows.

Exercise 15–2
Effect of transactions on cash flows

Objective 2

✓ b. Cash payment, $501,000

State the effect (cash receipt or payment and amount) of each of the following transactions, considered individually, on cash flows:

a. Purchased a building by paying $30,000 cash and issuing a $90,000 mortgage note payable.

b. Retired $500,000 of bonds, on which there was $2,500 of unamortized discount, for $501,000.

c.   Paid dividends of $1.50 per share. There were 30,000 shares issued and 5,000 shares of treasury stock.
d.   Sold a new issue of $100,000 of bonds at 101.
e.   Purchased 5,000 shares of $30 par common stock as treasury stock at $50 per share.
f.   Purchased land for $120,000 cash.
g.   Sold equipment with a book value of $42,500 for $41,000.
h.   Sold 5,000 shares of $30 par common stock for $45 per share.

Exercise 15–3
Classifying cash flows

Objective 2

Identify the type of cash flow activity for each of the following events (operating, investing, or financing):

a.   Issued bonds.
b.   Issued common stock.
c.   Sold long-term investments.
d.   Paid cash dividends.
e.   Redeemed bonds.
f.   Issued preferred stock.
g.   Net income.
h.   Sold equipment.
i.   Purchased treasury stock.
j.   Purchased buildings.
k.   Purchased patents.

Exercise 15–4
Cash flows from operating activities—indirect method

Objective 3

Indicate whether each of the following would be added to or deducted from net income in determining net cash flow from operating activities by the indirect method:

a.   Loss on disposal of fixed assets
b.   Decrease in accounts payable
c.   Decrease in salaries payable
d.   Depreciation of fixed assets
e.   Amortization of patent
f.   Decrease in accounts receivable
g.   Gain on retirement of long-term debt
h.   Increase in merchandise inventory
i.   Decrease in prepaid expenses
j.   Increase in notes receivable due in 90 days from customers
k.   Amortization of goodwill
l.   Increase in notes payable due in 90 days to vendors

Exercise 15–5
Cash flows from operating activities—indirect method

Objectives 2, 3

✓ a. Cash flows from operating activities, $196,150

The net income reported on the income statement for the current year was $167,900. Depreciation recorded on equipment and a building amounted to $41,300 for the year. Balances of the current asset and current liability accounts at the beginning and end of the year are as follows:

	End of Year	Beginning of Year
Cash	$ 27,900	$ 30,900
Accounts receivable (net)	75,100	70,250
Inventories	120,400	110,900
Prepaid expenses	5,800	6,000
Accounts payable (merchandise creditors)	67,200	65,300
Salaries payable	7,150	7,950

a.   Prepare the cash flows from operating activities section of the statement of cash flows, using the indirect method.
b.   If the direct method had been used, would the net cash flow from operating activities have been the same? Explain.

Exercise 15–6
Cash flows from operating activities—indirect method

Objective 3

The net income reported on the income statement for the current year was $489,000. Depreciation recorded on store equipment for the year amounted to $135,700. Balances of the current asset and current liability accounts at the beginning and end of the year are as follows:

	End of Year	Beginning of Year
Cash	$420,400	$509,000
Accounts receivable (net)	625,100	693,200
Merchandise inventory	724,600	704,700
Prepaid expenses	32,000	30,500
Accounts payable (merchandise creditors)	432,700	452,500
Wages payable	40,600	35,000

Prepare the cash flows from operating activities section of the statement of cash flows, using the indirect method.

Exercise 15–7

Determining cash payments to stockholders

Objective 3

The board of directors declared cash dividends totaling $280,000 during the current year. The comparative balance sheet indicates dividends payable of $60,000 at the beginning of the year and $70,000 at the end of the year. What was the amount of cash payments to stockholders during the year?

Exercise 15–8

Reporting changes in equipment on statement of cash flows

Objective 3

An analysis of the general ledger accounts indicates that office equipment, which had cost $200,000 and on which accumulated depreciation totaled $95,000 on the date of sale, was sold for $125,000 during the year. Using this information, indicate the items to be reported on the statement of cash flows.

Exercise 15–9

Reporting changes in equipment on statement of cash flows

Objective 3

An analysis of the general ledger accounts indicates that delivery equipment, which had cost $50,000 and on which accumulated depreciation totaled $23,000 on the date of sale, was sold for $24,000 during the year. Using this information, indicate the items to be reported on the statement of cash flows.

Exercise 15–10

Reporting land transactions on statement of cash flows

Objective 3

On the basis of the details of the following fixed asset account, indicate the items to be reported on the statement of cash flows:

ACCOUNT Land   **ACCOUNT NO.**

Date		Item	Debit	Credit	Balance Debit	Balance Credit
2003						
Jan.	1	Balance			400,000	
Feb.	5	Purchased for cash	200,000		600,000	
Oct.	30	Sold for $105,000		80,000	520,000	

Exercise 15–11

Reporting stockholders' equity items on statement of cash flows

Objective 3

On the basis of the following stockholders' equity accounts, indicate the items, exclusive of net income, to be reported on the statement of cash flows. There were no unpaid dividends at either the beginning or the end of the year.

ACCOUNT Common Stock, $10 Par   **ACCOUNT NO.**

Date		Item	Debit	Credit	Balance Debit	Balance Credit
2003						
Jan.	1	Balance, 50,000 shares				500,000
Feb.	11	6,000 shares issued for cash		60,000		560,000
June	30	2,750-share stock dividend		27,500		587,500

ACCOUNT *Paid-In Capital in Excess of Par—Common Stock*   **ACCOUNT NO.**

Date		Item	Debit	Credit	Balance Debit	Balance Credit
2003						
Jan.	1	Balance				90,000
Feb.	11	6,000 shares issued for cash		240,000		330,000
June	30	Stock dividend		137,500		467,500

ACCOUNT *Retained Earnings*   **ACCOUNT NO.**

Date		Item	Debit	Credit	Balance Debit	Balance Credit
2003						
Jan.	1	Balance				475,000
June	30	Stock dividend	165,000			310,000
Dec.	30	Cash dividend	180,000			130,000
	31	Net income		450,000		580,000

Exercise 15–12

Reporting land acquisition for cash and mortgage note on statement of cash flows

Objective 3

On the basis of the details of the following fixed asset account, indicate the items to be reported on the statement of cash flows:

ACCOUNT *Land*   **ACCOUNT NO.**

Date		Item	Debit	Credit	Balance Debit	Balance Credit
2003						
Jan.	1	Balance			450,000	
Feb.	10	Purchased for cash	210,000		660,000	
Nov.	20	Purchased with long-term mortgage note	250,000		910,000	

Exercise 15–13

Determining net income from net cash flow from operating activities

Objective 3

Tiger Golf Inc. reported a net cash flow from operating activities of $93,200 on its statement of cash flows for the year ended December 31, 2003. The following information was reported in the cash flows from operating activities section of the statement of cash flows, using the indirect method:

Decrease in income taxes payable	$ 1,600
Decrease in inventories	7,400
Depreciation	12,500
Gain on sale of investments	2,350
Increase in accounts payable	3,200
Increase in prepaid expenses	1,500
Increase in accounts receivable	4,850

Determine the net income reported by Tiger Golf Inc. for the year ended December 31, 2003.

Exercise 15–14

Cash flows from operating activities

Objective 3

Selected data derived from the income statement and balance sheet of **Intel Corp.** for a recent year are as follows:

Income Statement Data (dollars in millions)

Net earnings	$6,068
Depreciation	2,807
Loss on sale of property, plant, and equipment	282
Other noncash expenses	242

✓ Cash flows from operating activities, $9,191

Balance Sheet Data (dollars in millions)

Increase in accounts receivable	$ 38
Decrease in inventories	167
Decrease in other operating assets	37
Decrease in accounts payable and accrued expenses	163
Decrease in income tax payable	211

Prepare the cash flows from operating activities section of the statement of cash flows (using the indirect method) for Intel Corp., for the year.

Exercise 15–15
Cash flows from operating activities—direct method

Objective 4

✓ a. $723,000

The cash flows from operating activities are reported by the direct method on the statement of cash flows. Determine the following:

a. If sales for the current year were $685,000 and accounts receivable decreased by $38,000 during the year, what was the amount of cash received from customers?
b. If income tax expense for the current year was $72,000 and income tax payable decreased by $4,500 during the year, what was the amount of cash payments for income tax?

Exercise 15–16
Cash paid for merchandise purchases

Objective 4

The cost of merchandise sold for **Toys 'R' Us, Inc.**, for a recent year was $8,191 million. The balance sheet showed the following current account balances (in millions):

	Balance, End of Year	Balance, Beginning of Year
Merchandise inventories	$1,902	$2,464
Accounts payable	1,415	1,280

Determine the amount of cash payments for merchandise.

Exercise 15–17
Determining selected amounts for cash flows from operating activities—direct method

Objective 4

✓ b. $87,500

Selected data taken from the accounting records of Zippy Electronics Company for the current year ended December 31 are as follows:

	Balance December 31	Balance January 1
Accrued expenses (operating expenses)	$ 5,800	$ 6,200
Accounts payable (merchandise creditors)	35,700	39,100
Inventories	25,000	27,400
Prepaid expenses	3,000	3,500

During the current year, the cost of merchandise sold was $315,000 and the operating expenses other than depreciation were $87,600. The direct method is used for presenting the cash flows from operating activities on the statement of cash flows.

Determine the amount reported on the statement of cash flows for (a) cash payments for merchandise and (b) cash payments for operating expenses.

Exercise 15–18
Cash flows from operating activities—direct method

Objective 4

✓ Cash flows from operating activities, $51,800

The income statement of Tender Memories Greeting Card Company for the current year ended June 30 is as follows:

Sales		$358,000
Cost of merchandise sold		163,400
Gross profit		$194,600
Operating expenses:		
Depreciation expense	$ 32,500	
Other operating expenses	142,600	
Total operating expenses		175,100
Income before income tax		$ 19,500
Income tax expense		7,300
Net income		$ 12,200

Changes in the balances of selected accounts from the beginning to the end of the current year are as follows:

	Increase Decrease*
Accounts receivable (net)	$17,000*
Inventories	5,300
Prepaid expenses	3,100*
Accounts payable (merchandise creditors)	13,600*
Accrued expenses (operating expenses)	8,300
Income tax payable	2,400*

Prepare the cash flows from operating activities section of the statement of cash flows, using the direct method.

Exercise 15–19
Cash flows from operating activities—direct method

Objective 4

✓ Cash flows from operating activities, $130,100

The income statement for Wholly Donut Company for the current year ended June 30 and balances of selected accounts at the beginning and the end of the year are as follows:

Sales		$935,600
Cost of merchandise sold		534,200
Gross profit		$401,400
Operating expenses:		
Depreciation expense	$ 54,200	
Other operating expenses	195,700	
Total operating expenses		249,900
Income before income tax		$151,500
Income tax expense		65,300
Net income		$ 86,200

	End of Year	Beginning of Year
Accounts receivable (net)	$ 96,500	$ 93,000
Inventories	143,200	132,700
Prepaid expenses	7,500	8,900
Accounts payable (merchandise creditors)	102,300	98,400
Accrued expenses (operating expenses)	12,400	14,000
Income tax payable	2,000	2,000

Prepare the cash flows from operating activities section of the statement of cash flows, using the direct method.

Exercise 15–20
Analysis of statement of cash flows

Objectives 3, 5

The financial statements for **Cisco Systems, Inc.**, are presented in Appendix G at the end of the text.

a. From Cisco Systems' statement of cash flows, determine the free cash flow for 1999 and 2000. Assume that 40% of the acquisition of property and equipment and 20% of the acquisition of technology licenses are used to maintain productive capacity. The remaining 60% and 80%, respectively, add to productive capacity.

b. ✏ What conclusions can you draw from your analysis?

Exercise 15–21
Statement of cash flows

Objective 3

The comparative balance sheet of Maria's Memories Inc. for December 31, 2003 and 2002, is as follows:

✓ Net cash flow from operating
activities, $22

	Dec. 31, 2003	Dec. 31, 2002
Assets		
Cash	$ 54	$ 34
Accounts receivable (net)	23	27
Inventories	16	14
Land	20	30
Equipment	26	12
Accumulated depreciation—equipment	(8)	(5)
Total	$131	$112
Liabilities and Stockholders' Equity		
Accounts payable (merchandise creditors)	$ 17	$ 18
Dividends payable	8	6
Common stock, $1 par	3	2
Paid-in capital in excess of par—common stock	15	10
Retained earnings	88	76
Total	$131	$112

The following additional information is taken from the records:

a. Land was sold for $17.
b. Equipment was acquired for cash.
c. There were no disposals of equipment during the year.
d. The common stock was issued for cash.
e. There was a $25 credit to Retained Earnings for net income.
f. There was a $13 debit to Retained Earnings for cash dividends declared.

Prepare a statement of cash flows, using the indirect method of presenting cash flows from operating activities.

Exercise 15–22
Statement of cash flows

Objective 3

List the errors you find in the following statement of cash flows. The cash balance at the beginning of the year was $70,700. All other figures are correct, except the cash balance at the end of the year.

Cyber-Master Games Inc.
Statement of Cash Flows
For the Year Ended December 31, 2003

Cash flows from operating activities:			
Net income, per income statement		$100,500	
Add: Depreciation	$ 49,000		
Increase in accounts receivable	11,500		
Gain on sale of investments	7,000	67,500	
		$168,000	
Deduct: Increase in accounts payable	$ 4,400		
Increase in inventories	18,300		
Decrease in accrued expenses	1,600	24,300	
Net cash flow from operating activities			$143,700
Cash flows from investing activities:			
Cash received from sale of investments		$ 85,000	
Less: Cash paid for purchase of land	$ 90,000		
Cash paid for purchase of equipment	150,100	240,100	
Net cash flow used for investing activities			(155,100)
Cash flows from financing activities:			
Cash received from sale of common stock		$107,000	
Cash paid for dividends		36,800	
Net cash flow provided by financing activities			143,800
Increase in cash			$132,400
Cash at the end of the year			105,300
Cash at the beginning of the year			$237,700

PROBLEMS SERIES A

Problem 15–1A
Statement of cash flows—indirect method

Objective 3

✓ Net cash flow from operating activities, $139,800

The comparative balance sheet of Everlast Flooring Co. for June 30, 2003 and 2002, is as follows:

	June 30, 2003	June 30, 2002
Assets		
Cash	$124,200	$ 67,900
Accounts receivable (net)	102,400	97,600
Inventories	142,700	123,500
Investments	0	58,000
Land	124,000	0
Equipment	373,400	201,400
Accumulated depreciation	(79,400)	(58,900)
	$787,300	$489,500
Liabilities and Stockholders' Equity		
Accounts payable (merchandise creditors)	$ 93,200	$ 84,600
Accrued expenses (operating expenses)	13,000	12,300
Dividends payable	15,000	12,500
Common stock, $10 par	120,000	80,000
Paid-in capital in excess of par—common stock	310,000	130,000
Retained earnings	236,100	170,100
	$787,300	$489,500

The following additional information was taken from the records of Everlast Flooring Co.:

a. Equipment and land were acquired for cash.
b. There were no disposals of equipment during the year.
c. The investments were sold for $50,000 cash.
d. The common stock was issued for cash.
e. There was a $126,000 credit to Retained Earnings for net income.
f. There was a $60,000 debit to Retained Earnings for cash dividends declared.

Instructions
Prepare a statement of cash flows, using the indirect method of presenting cash flows from operating activities.

Problem 15–2A
Statement of cash flows—indirect method

Objective 3

SPREADSHEET

✓ Net cash flow from operating activities, $151,800

The comparative balance sheet of Bon Voyage Luggage Company at December 31, 2003 and 2002, is as follows:

	Dec. 31, 2003	Dec. 31, 2002
Assets		
Cash	$ 155,400	$ 134,600
Accounts receivable (net)	192,400	176,400
Inventories	287,500	312,300
Prepaid expenses	8,500	6,000
Land	100,000	100,000
Buildings	550,000	415,000
Accumulated depreciation—buildings	(201,500)	(176,000)
Machinery and equipment	295,700	295,700
Accumulated depreciation—machinery & equipment	(119,800)	(84,600)
Patents	37,400	40,000
	$1,305,600	$1,219,400

(continued)

	Dec. 31, 2003	Dec. 31, 2002
Liabilities and Stockholders' Equity		
Accounts payable (merchandise creditors)	$ 131,400	$ 146,700
Dividends payable	12,000	10,000
Salaries payable	10,500	12,800
Mortgage note payable, due 2004	50,000	—
Bonds payable	—	164,000
Common stock, $1 par	19,000	15,000
Paid-in capital in excess of par—common stock	210,000	50,000
Retained earnings	872,700	820,900
	$1,305,600	$1,219,400

An examination of the income statement and the accounting records revealed the following additional information applicable to 2003:

a. Net income, $99,800.
b. Depreciation expense reported on the income statement: buildings, $25,500; machinery and equipment, $35,200.
c. Patent amortization reported on the income statement, $2,600.
d. A building was constructed for $135,000.
e. A mortgage note for $50,000 was issued for cash.
f. 4,000 shares of common stock were issued at $41 in exchange for the bonds payable.
g. Cash dividends declared, $48,000.

Instructions

Prepare a statement of cash flows, using the indirect method of presenting cash flows from operating activities.

Problem 15–3A

Statement of cash flows—indirect method

Objective 3

✓ Net cash flow from operating activities, ($1,500)

The comparative balance sheet of Union Wholesale Supply Co. at December 31, 2003 and 2002, is as follows:

	Dec. 31, 2003	Dec. 31, 2002
Assets		
Cash	$ 24,900	$ 27,400
Accounts receivable (net)	113,100	94,600
Inventories	194,000	176,500
Prepaid expenses	3,400	4,000
Land	60,000	80,000
Buildings	265,000	155,000
Accumulated depreciation—buildings	(55,800)	(43,500)
Equipment	195,600	185,600
Accumulated depreciation—equipment	(71,500)	(74,500)
	$728,700	$605,100
Liabilities and Stockholders' Equity		
Accounts payable (merchandise creditors)	$140,000	$143,700
Income tax payable	4,000	3,800
Bonds payable	50,000	—
Common stock, $1 par	26,000	25,000
Paid-in capital in excess of par—common stock	350,000	280,000
Retained earnings	158,700	152,600
	$728,700	$605,100

The noncurrent asset, the noncurrent liability, and the stockholders' equity accounts for 2003 are as follows:

ACCOUNT *Land*   **ACCOUNT NO.**

Date		Item	Debit	Credit	Balance Debit	Balance Credit
2003						
Jan.	1	Balance			80,000	
April	20	Realized $34,000 cash				
		from sale		20,000	60,000	

ACCOUNT *Buildings*   **ACCOUNT NO.**

Date		Item	Debit	Credit	Balance Debit	Balance Credit
2003						
Jan.	1	Balance			155,000	
April	20	Acquired for cash	110,000		265,000	

ACCOUNT *Accumulated Depreciation—Buildings*   **ACCOUNT NO.**

Date		Item	Debit	Credit	Balance Debit	Balance Credit
2003						
Jan.	1	Balance				43,500
Dec.	31	Depreciation for year		12,300		55,800

ACCOUNT *Equipment*   **ACCOUNT NO.**

Date		Item	Debit	Credit	Balance Debit	Balance Credit
2003						
Jan.	1	Balance			185,600	
	26	Discarded, no salvage		30,000	155,600	
Aug.	11	Purchased for cash	40,000		195,600	

ACCOUNT *Accumulated Depreciation—Equipment*   **ACCOUNT NO.**

Date		Item	Debit	Credit	Balance Debit	Balance Credit
2003						
Jan.	1	Balance				74,500
	26	Equipment discarded	30,000			44,500
Dec.	31	Depreciation for year		27,000		71,500

ACCOUNT *Bonds Payable*   **ACCOUNT NO.**

Date		Item	Debit	Credit	Balance Debit	Balance Credit
2003						
May	1	Issued 20-year bonds		50,000		50,000

ACCOUNT *Common Stock, $1 Par*   **ACCOUNT NO.**

Date		Item	Debit	Credit	Balance Debit	Balance Credit
2003						
Jan.	1	Balance				25,000
Dec.	7	Issued 1,000 shares of common				
		stock for $71 per share		1,000		26,000

ACCOUNT *Paid-In Capital in Excess of Par—Common Stock*   **ACCOUNT NO.**

Date		Item	Debit	Credit	Balance Debit	Balance Credit
2003						
Jan.	1	Balance				280,000
Dec.	7	Issued 1,000 shares of common				
		stock for $71 per share		70,000		350,000

ACCOUNT *Retained Earnings*   **ACCOUNT NO.**

Date		Item	Debit	Credit	Balance Debit	Balance Credit
2003						
Jan.	1	Balance				152,600
Dec.	31	Net income		12,100		164,700
	31	Cash dividends	6,000			158,700

Instructions

Prepare a statement of cash flows, using the indirect method of presenting cash flows from operating activities.

Problem 15–4A

*Statement of cash flows—
direct method*

Objective 4

GENERAL
LEDGER

SPREADSHEET

✓ Net cash flow from operating
activities, $99,900

The comparative balance sheet of Green Thumb Nursery Inc. for December 31, 2003 and 2004, is as follows:

	Dec. 31, 2004	Dec. 31, 2003
Assets		
Cash	$ 154,700	$176,500
Accounts receivable (net)	261,300	243,200
Inventories	317,800	303,300
Investments	—	65,000
Land	95,000	—
Equipment	365,000	275,000
Accumulated depreciation	(123,700)	(103,200)
	$1,070,100	$959,800
Liabilities and Stockholders' Equity		
Accounts payable (merchandise creditors)	$ 248,300	$235,700
Accrued expenses (operating expenses)	10,900	12,500
Dividends payable	24,000	20,000
Common stock, $1 par	15,000	12,000
Paid-in capital in excess of par—common stock	185,000	110,000
Retained earnings	586,900	569,600
	$1,070,100	$959,800

The income statement for the year ended December 31, 2004, is as follows:

Sales		$1,250,000
Cost of merchandise sold		759,000
Gross profit		$ 491,000
Operating expenses:		
Depreciation expense	$ 20,500	
Other operating expenses	284,500	
Total operating expenses		305,000
Operating income		$ 186,000
Other income:		
Gain on sale of investments		14,000
Income before income tax		$ 200,000
Income tax expense		85,000
Net income		$ 115,000

The following additional information was taken from the records:

a. Equipment and land were acquired for cash.
b. There were no disposals of equipment during the year.
c. The investments were sold for $79,000 cash.
d. The common stock was issued for cash.
e. There was a $97,700 debit to Retained Earnings for cash dividends declared.

Instructions

Prepare a statement of cash flows, using the direct method of presenting cash flows from operating activities.

Problem 15–5A

Statement of cash flows—direct method applied to Problem 15–1A

Objective 4

✓ Net cash flow from operating activities, $139,800

The comparative balance sheet of Everlast Flooring Co. for June 30, 2003 and 2002, is as follows:

	June 30, 2003	June 30, 2002
Assets		
Cash	$124,200	$ 67,900
Accounts receivable (net)	102,400	97,600
Inventories	142,700	123,500
Investments	0	58,000
Land	124,000	0
Equipment	373,400	201,400
Accumulated depreciation	(79,400)	(58,900)
	$787,300	$489,500
Liabilities and Stockholders' Equity		
Accounts payable (merchandise creditors)	$ 93,200	$ 84,600
Accrued expenses (operating expenses)	13,000	12,300
Dividends payable	15,000	12,500
Common stock, $10 par	120,000	80,000
Paid-in capital in excess of par—common stock	310,000	130,000
Retained earnings	236,100	170,100
	$787,300	$489,500

The income statement for the year ended June 30, 2003, is as follows:

Sales		$543,800
Cost of merchandise sold		198,200
Gross profit		$345,600
Operating expenses:		
Depreciation expense	$ 20,500	
Other operating expenses	110,300	
Total operating expenses		130,800
Operating income		$214,800
Other expenses:		
Loss on sale of investments		8,000
Income before income tax		$206,800
Income tax expense		80,800
Net income		$126,000

The following additional information was taken from the records:

a. Equipment and land were acquired for cash.
b. There were no disposals of equipment during the year.
c. The investments were sold for $50,000 cash.
d. The common stock was issued for cash.
e. There was a $60,000 debit to Retained Earnings for cash dividends declared.

Instructions

Prepare a statement of cash flows, using the direct method of presenting cash flows from operating activities.

Problem 15–1B
Statement of cash flows—indirect method
Objective 3

✓ Net cash flow from operating activities, $368,900

The comparative balance sheet of Idaho Al's Golf Shops Co. for December 31, 2003 and 2002, is as follows:

	Dec. 31, 2003	Dec. 31, 2002
Assets		
Cash	$ 524,300	$ 313,400
Accounts receivable (net)	132,500	126,700
Inventories	342,600	332,100
Investments	0	90,000
Land	125,000	0
Equipment	755,000	535,000
Accumulated depreciation—equipment	(189,000)	(158,000)
	$1,690,400	$1,239,200
Liabilities and Stockholders' Equity		
Accounts payable (merchandise creditors)	$ 85,200	$ 80,300
Accrued expenses (operating expenses)	4,300	7,400
Dividends payable	24,000	20,000
Common stock, $10 par	80,000	50,000
Paid-in capital in excess of par—common stock	335,000	200,000
Retained earnings	1,161,900	881,500
	$1,690,400	$1,239,200

The following additional information was taken from the records:

a. The investments were sold for $114,000 cash.
b. Equipment and land were acquired for cash.
c. There were no disposals of equipment during the year.
d. The common stock was issued for cash.
e. There was a $376,400 credit to Retained Earnings for net income.
f. There was a $96,000 debit to Retained Earnings for cash dividends declared.

Instructions
Prepare a statement of cash flows, using the indirect method of presenting cash flows from operating activities.

Problem 15–2B
Statement of cash flows—indirect method
Objective 3

SPREADSHEET

✓ Net cash flow from operating activities, $262,100

The comparative balance sheet of Gold Medal Athletic Apparel Co. at December 31, 2003 and 2002, is as follows:

	Dec. 31, 2003	Dec. 31, 2002
Assets		
Cash	$ 232,500	$ 257,900
Accounts receivable (net)	497,800	532,500
Merchandise inventory	635,200	621,300
Prepaid expenses	17,000	15,000
Equipment	720,000	600,000
Accumulated depreciation—equipment	(265,000)	(297,500)
	$1,837,500	$1,729,200
Liabilities and Stockholders' Equity		
Accounts payable (merchandise creditors)	$ 423,100	$ 397,600
Mortgage note payable	0	205,000
Common stock, $10 par	120,000	70,000
Paid-in capital in excess of par—common stock	820,000	620,000
Retained earnings	474,400	436,600
	$1,837,500	$1,729,200

Additional data obtained from the income statement and from an examination of the accounts in the ledger for 2003 are as follows:

a. Net income, $125,800.
b. Depreciation reported on the income statement, $92,000.
c. Equipment was purchased at a cost of $244,500, and fully depreciated equipment costing $124,500 was discarded, with no salvage realized.
d. The mortgage note payable was not due until 2006, but the terms permitted earlier payment without penalty.
e. 5,000 shares of common stock were issued at $50 for cash.
f. Cash dividends declared and paid, $88,000.

Instructions

Prepare a statement of cash flows, using the indirect method of presenting cash flows from operating activities.

Problem 15–3B

Statement of cash flows— indirect method

Objective 3

✓ Net cash flow from operating activities, ($131,800)

The comparative balance sheet of Handyman's Helper Hardware Company at December 31, 2003 and 2002, is as follows:

	Dec. 31, 2003	Dec. 31, 2002
Assets		
Cash	$ 263,400	$ 275,400
Accounts receivable (net)	375,200	356,800
Inventories	543,200	512,400
Prepaid expenses	8,500	9,000
Land	95,000	120,000
Buildings	470,000	350,000
Accumulated depreciation—buildings	(182,300)	(170,000)
Equipment	198,700	185,500
Accumulated depreciation—equipment	(44,000)	(48,000)
	$1,727,700	$1,591,100
Liabilities and Stockholders' Equity		
Accounts payable (merchandise creditors)	$ 367,900	$ 377,100
Bonds payable	60,000	0
Common stock, $1 par	90,000	70,000
Paid-in capital in excess of par—common stock	450,000	250,000
Retained earnings	759,800	894,000
	$1,727,700	$1,591,100

The noncurrent asset, the noncurrent liability, and the stockholders' equity accounts for 2003 are as follows:

ACCOUNT *Land* **ACCOUNT NO.**

Date		Item	Debit	Credit	Balance Debit	Balance Credit
2003						
Jan.	1	Balance			120,000	
April	20	Realized $38,000 cash from sale		25,000	95,000	

ACCOUNT *Buildings* **ACCOUNT NO.**

Date		Item	Debit	Credit	Balance Debit	Balance Credit
2003						
Jan.	1	Balance			350,000	
April	20	Acquired for cash	120,000		470,000	

ACCOUNT *Accumulated Depreciation—Buildings*   **ACCOUNT NO.**

Date		Item	Debit	Credit	Balance Debit	Balance Credit
2003						
Jan.	1	Balance				170,000
Dec.	31	Depreciation for year		12,300		182,300

ACCOUNT *Equipment*   **ACCOUNT NO.**

Date		Item	Debit	Credit	Balance Debit	Balance Credit
2003						
Jan.	1	Balance			185,500	
	26	Discarded, no salvage		45,000	140,500	
Aug.	11	Purchased for cash	58,200		198,700	

ACCOUNT *Accumulated Depreciation—Equipment*   **ACCOUNT NO.**

Date		Item	Debit	Credit	Balance Debit	Balance Credit
2003						
Jan.	1	Balance				48,000
	26	Equipment discarded	45,000			3,000
Dec.	31	Depreciation for year		41,000		44,000

ACCOUNT *Bonds Payable*   **ACCOUNT NO.**

Date		Item	Debit	Credit	Balance Debit	Balance Credit
2003						
May	1	Issued 20-year bonds		60,000		60,000

ACCOUNT *Common Stock, $1 Par*   **ACCOUNT NO.**

Date		Item	Debit	Credit	Balance Debit	Balance Credit
2003						
Jan.	1	Balance				70,000
Dec.	7	Issued 20,000 shares of common stock for $11 per share		20,000		90,000

ACCOUNT *Paid-In Capital in Excess of Par—Common Stock*   **ACCOUNT NO.**

Date		Item	Debit	Credit	Balance Debit	Balance Credit
2003						
Jan.	1	Balance				250,000
Dec.	7	Issued 20,000 shares of common stock for $11 per share		200,000		450,000

ACCOUNT *Retained Earnings*   **ACCOUNT NO.**

Date		Item	Debit	Credit	Balance Debit	Balance Credit
2003						
Jan.	1	Balance				894,000
Dec.	31	Net loss	114,200			779,800
	31	Cash dividends	20,000			759,800

Instructions

Prepare a statement of cash flows, using the indirect method of presenting cash flows from operating activities.

Problem 15–4B
Statement of cash flows—direct method

Objective 4

The comparative balance sheet of Nature's Bounty Markets, Inc., for December 31, 2004 and 2003, is as follows:

✓ Net cash flow from operating
activities, $70,900

	Dec. 31, 2004	Dec. 31, 2003
Assets		
Cash	$ 65,800	$ 83,500
Accounts receivable (net)	101,200	95,800
Inventories	132,400	125,700
Investments	—	45,000
Land	70,500	—
Equipment	300,500	210,500
Accumulated depreciation	(65,900)	(45,600)
	$604,500	$514,900
Liabilities and Stockholders' Equity		
Accounts payable (merchandise creditors)	$ 93,500	$ 86,700
Accrued expenses (operating expenses)	10,200	12,000
Dividends payable	6,000	4,000
Common stock, $1 par	17,000	15,000
Paid-in capital in excess of par—common stock	200,000	150,000
Retained earnings	277,800	247,200
	$604,500	$514,900

The income statement for the year ended December 31, 2004, is as follows:

Sales		$545,000
Cost of merchandise sold		294,000
Gross profit		$251,000
Operating expenses:		
Depreciation expense	$ 20,300	
Other operating expenses	152,500	
Total operating expenses		172,800
Operating income		$ 78,200
Other expense:		
Loss on sale of Investments		4,000
Income before income tax		$ 74,200
Income tax expense		20,500
Net income		$ 53,700

The following additional information was taken from the records:

a. Equipment and land were acquired for cash.
b. There were no disposals of equipment during the year.
c. The investments were sold for $41,000 cash.
d. The common stock was issued for cash.
e. There was a $23,100 debit to Retained Earnings for cash dividends declared.

Instructions
Prepare a statement of cash flows, using the direct method of presenting cash flows from operating activities.

Problem 15–5B
*Statement of cash flows—
direct method applied to
Problem 15–1B*

Objective 4

The comparative balance sheet of Idaho Al's Golf Shops Co. for December 31, 2003 and
2002, is as follows:

	Dec. 31, 2003	Dec. 31, 2002
Assets		
Cash	$ 524,300	$ 313,400
Accounts receivable (net)	132,500	126,700
Inventories	342,600	332,100
Investments	0	90,000
Land	125,000	0
Equipment	755,000	535,000
Accumulated depreciation—equipment	(189,000)	(158,000)
	$1,690,400	$1,239,200
Liabilities and Stockholders' Equity		
Accounts payable (merchandise creditors)	$ 85,200	$ 80,300
Accrued expenses (operating expenses)	4,300	7,400
Dividends payable	24,000	20,000
Common stock, $10 par	80,000	50,000
Paid-in capital in excess of par—common stock	335,000	200,000
Retained earnings	1,161,900	881,500
	$1,690,400	$1,239,200

The income statement for the year ended December 31, 2003, is as follows:

Sales		$1,096,500
Cost of merchandise sold		401,200
Gross profit		$ 695,300
Operating expenses:		
Depreciation expense	$ 31,000	
Other operating expenses	163,400	
Total operating expenses		194,400
Operating income		$ 500,900
Other income:		
Gain on sale of investments		24,000
Income before income tax		$ 524,900
Income tax expense		148,500
Net income		$ 376,400

The following additional information was taken from the records:

a. The investments were sold for $114,000 cash.
b. Equipment and land were acquired for cash.
c. There were no disposals of equipment during the year.
d. The common stock was issued for cash.
e. There was a $96,000 debit to Retained Earnings for cash dividends declared.

Instructions

Prepare a statement of cash flows, using the direct method of presenting cash flows from operating activities.

SPECIAL ACTIVITIES

Activity 15–1
Fine Fashions Inc.
Ethics and professional conduct in business

Toni Lance, president of Fine Fashions Inc., believes that reporting operating cash flow per share on the income statement would be a useful addition to the company's just completed financial statements. The following discussion took place between Toni Lance and Fine Fashions' controller, Tom Kee, in January, after the close of the fiscal year.

Toni: I have been reviewing our financial statements for the last year. I am disappointed that our net income per share has dropped by 10% from last year. This is not going to look good to our shareholders. Isn't there anything we can do about this?

Tom: What do you mean? The past is the past, and the numbers are in. There isn't much that can be done about it. Our financial statements were prepared according to generally accepted accounting principles, and I don't see much leeway for significant change at this point.

Toni: No, no. I'm not suggesting that we "cook the books." But look at the cash flow from operating activities on the statement of cash flows. The cash flow from operating activities has increased by 20%. This is very good news—and, I might add, useful information. The higher cash flow from operating activities will give our creditors comfort.

Tom: Well, the cash flow from operating activities is on the statement of cash flows, so I guess users will be able to see the improved cash flow figures there.

Toni: This is true, but somehow I feel that this information should be given a much higher profile. I don't like this information being "buried" in the statement of cash flows. You know as well as I do that many users will focus on the income statement. Therefore, I think we ought to include an operating cash flow per share number on the face of the income statement—someplace under the earnings per share number. In this way users will get the complete picture of our operating performance. Yes, our earnings per share dropped this year, but our cash flow from operating activities improved! And all the information is in one place where users can see and compare the figures. What do you think?

Tom: I've never really thought about it like that before. I guess we could put the operating cash flow per share on the income statement, under the earnings per share. Users would really benefit from this disclosure. Thanks for the idea—I'll start working on it.

Toni: Glad to be of service.

✎➤ How would you interpret this situation? Is Tom behaving in an ethical and professional manner?

Activity 15–2
VideoToGo.com Inc.
Using the statement of cash flows

You are considering an investment in a new start-up Internet company, VideoToGo.com Inc. A review of the company's financial statements reveals a negative retained earnings. In addition, it appears as though the company has been running a negative cash flow from operating activities since the company's inception.

✎➤ How is the company staying in business under these circumstances? Could this be a good investment?

Activity 15–3
Biltmore Company
Analysis of cash flow from operations

The Retailing Division of Biltmore Company provided the following information on its cash flow from operations:

Net income	$ 450,000
Increase in accounts receivable	(340,000)
Increase in inventory	(300,000)
Decrease in accounts payable	(90,000)
Depreciation	100,000
Cash flow from operating activities	$(180,000)

The manager of the Retailing Division provided the accompanying memo with this report:

From: Senior Vice President, Retailing Division

I am pleased to report that we had earnings of $450,000 over the last period. This resulted in a return on invested capital of 10%, which is near our targets for this division. I have been aggressive in building the revenue volume in the division. As a result, I am happy to report that we have increased the number of new credit card customers as a result of an aggressive marketing campaign. In addition, we have found some excellent merchandise opportunities. Some of our suppliers have made some of their apparel merchandise available at a deep discount. We have purchased as much of these goods as possible in order to improve profitability. I'm also happy to report that our vendor payment problems have improved. We are nearly caught up on our overdue payables balances.

▰▬▶ Comment on the senior vice president's memo in light of the cash flow information.

Activity 15–4
Elite Cabinets, Inc.
Analysis of statement of cash flows

Alan Hart is the president and majority shareholder of Elite Cabinets, Inc., a small retail store chain. Recently, Hart submitted a loan application for Elite Cabinets, Inc., to Montvale National Bank. It called for a $200,000, 11%, ten-year loan to help finance the construction of a building and the purchase of store equipment, costing a total of $250,000, to enable Elite Cabinets, Inc., to open a store in Montvale. Land for this purpose was acquired last year. The bank's loan officer requested a statement of cash flows in addition to the most recent income statement, balance sheet, and retained earnings statement that Hart had submitted with the loan application.

As a close family friend, Hart asked you to prepare a statement of cash flows. From the records provided, you prepared the following statement.

Elite Cabinets, Inc.
Statement of Cash Flows
For the Year Ended December 31, 2003

Cash flows from operating activities:			
Net income, per income statement		$ 86,400	
Add: Depreciation	$31,000		
Decrease in accounts receivable	11,500	42,500	
		$128,900	
Deduct: Increase in inventory	$12,000		
Increase in prepaid expenses	1,500		
Decrease in accounts payable	3,000		
Gain on sale of investments	7,500	24,000	
Net cash flow from operating activities			$104,900
Cash flows from investing activities:			
Cash received from investments sold	$ 42,500		
Less: Cash paid for purchase of store equipment	31,000		
Net cash flow from investing activities			11,500
Cash flows from financing activities:			
Cash paid for dividends	$ 40,000		
Net cash flow used for financing activities			(40,000)
Increase in cash			$ 76,400
Cash at the beginning of the year			27,500
Cash at the end of the year			$103,900

Schedule of Noncash Financing and Investing Activities:

Issued common stock at par for land	$ 40,000

After reviewing the statement, Hart telephoned you and commented, "Are you sure this statement is right?" Hart then raised the following questions:

1. "How can depreciation be a cash flow?"
2. "Issuing common stock for the land is listed in a separate schedule. This transaction has nothing to do with cash! Shouldn't this transaction be eliminated from the statement?"
3. "How can the gain on sale of investments be a deduction from net income in determining the cash flow from operating activities?"
4. "Why does the bank need this statement anyway? They can compute the increase in cash from the balance sheets for the last two years."

After jotting down Hart's questions, you assured him that this statement was "right." However, to alleviate Hart's concern, you arranged a meeting for the following day.

a. ➤ How would you respond to each of Hart's questions?
b. ➤ Do you think that the statement of cash flows enhances the chances of Elite Cabinets, Inc., receiving the loan? Discuss.

Activity 15–5
Into the Real World
Statement of cash flows

This activity will require two teams to retrieve cash flow statement information from the Internet. One team is to obtain the most recent year's statement of cash flows for **Philip Morris Companies**, and the other team the most recent year's statement of cash flows for **Loral Space & Communications, LTD.**, a satellite-based mobile phone company.

The statement of cash flows is included as part of the annual report information that is a required disclosure to the Securities and Exchange Commission (SEC). The SEC, in turn, provides this information online through its EDGAR service. EDGAR (Electronic Data Gathering, Analysis, and Retrieval) is the electronic archive of financial statements filed with the Securities and Exchange Commission (SEC). SEC documents can be retrieved using the EdgarScan service from **PricewaterhouseCoopers** at **edgarscan.pwcglobal.com**.

To obtain annual report information, type in a company name in the appropriate space. EdgarScan will list the reports available to you for the company you've selected. Select the most recent annual report filing, identified as a 10-K or 10-K405. EdgarScan provides an outline of the report, including the separate financial statements. You can double-click the income statement and balance sheet for the selected company into an Excel™ spreadsheet for further analysis.

As a group, compare the two statements of cash flows. How are Philip Morris and Loral Space & Communications similar or different regarding cash flows?

ANSWERS TO SELF-EXAMINATION QUESTIONS

Matching

1. E	3. A	5. I	7. N	9. F	11. J	13. H
2. L	4. K	6. B	8. D	10. C	12. M	

Multiple Choice

1. **D** Cash flows from operating activities affect transactions that enter into the determination of net income, such as the receipt of cash from customers on account (answer D). Receipts of cash from the sale of stock (answer A) and the sale of bonds (answer B) and payments of cash for dividends (answer C) are cash flows from financing activities.

2. **A** Cash flows from investing activities include receipts from the sale of noncurrent assets, such as equipment (answer A), and payments to acquire noncurrent assets. Receipts of cash from the sale of stock (answer B) and payments of cash for dividends (answer C) and to acquire treasury stock (answer D) are cash flows from financing activities.

3. **C** Payment of cash dividends (answer C) is an example of a financing activity. The receipt of cash from customers on account (answer A) is an operating activity. The receipt of cash from the sale of equipment (answer B) is an investing activity. The payment of cash to acquire land (answer D) is an example of an investing activity.

4. **D**   The indirect method (answer D) reports cash flows from operating activities by beginning with net income and adjusting it for revenues and expenses not involving the receipt or payment of cash.

5. **C**   The cash flows from operating activities section of the statement of cash flows would report net cash flow from operating activities of $65,500, determined as follows:

Net income		$55,000
Add: Depreciation	$22,000	
Decrease in inventories	5,000	
Decrease in prepaid expenses	500	27,500
		$82,500
Deduct: Increase in accounts receivable	$10,000	
Decrease in accounts payable	7,000	17,000
Net cash flow from operating activities		$65,500

Financial Statement Analysis

16

objectives

After studying this chapter, you should be able to:

1 List basic financial statement analytical procedures.

2 Apply financial statement analysis to assess the solvency of a business.

3 Apply financial statement analysis to assess the profitability of a business.

4 Summarize the uses and limitations of analytical measures.

5 Describe the contents of corporate annual reports.

T he *Wall Street Journal* (September 18, 2000) reported that the common stock of **Microsoft Corporation** was selling for $64.19 per share. If you had funds to invest, would you invest in Microsoft common stock?

Microsoft is a well-known, international company. However, **Eastern Airlines**, **Pan Am**, **Montgomery Ward**, **Woolworth's**, and **Planet Hollywood** were also well-known companies. These latter companies share the common characteristic of having declared bankruptcy!

Obviously, being well-known is not necessarily a good basis for investing. Knowledge that a company has a good product, by itself, may also be an inadequate basis for investing in the company. Even with a good product, a company may go bankrupt for a variety of reasons, such as inadequate financing. For example, Planet Hollywood sought bankruptcy protection, even though it was owned and promoted by such prominent Hollywood stars as Bruce Willis, Whoopi Goldberg, and Arnold Schwarzenegger.

How, then, does one decide on the companies in which to invest? This chapter describes and illustrates common financial data that can be analyzed to assist you in making investment decisions. In addition, the contents of corporate annual reports are also discussed.

Basic Analytical Procedures

objective 1

List basic financial statement analytical procedures.

The basic financial statements provide much of the information users need to make economic decisions about businesses. In this chapter, we illustrate how to perform a complete analysis of these statements by integrating individual analytical measures.

Analytical procedures may be used to compare items on a current statement with related items on earlier statements. For example, cash of $150,000 on the current balance sheet may be compared with cash of $100,000 on the balance sheet of a year earlier. The current year's cash may be expressed as 1.5 or 150% of the earlier amount, or as an increase of 50% or $50,000.

Analytical procedures are also widely used to examine relationships within a financial statement. To illustrate, assume that cash of $50,000 and inventories of $250,000 are included in the total assets of $1,000,000 on a balance sheet. In relative terms, the cash balance is 5% of the total assets, and the inventories are 25% of the total assets.

In this chapter, we will illustrate a number of common analytical measures. The measures are not ends in themselves. They are only guides in evaluating financial and operating data. Many other factors, such as trends in the industry and general economic conditions, should also be considered.

Horizontal Analysis

The percentage analysis of increases and decreases in related items in comparative financial statements is called **horizontal analysis**. The amount of each item on the most recent statement is compared with the related item on one or more earlier statements. The amount of increase or decrease in the item is listed, along with the percent of increase or decrease.

Horizontal analysis may compare two statements. In this case, the earlier statement is used as the base. Horizontal analysis may also compare three or more statements. In this case, the earliest date or period may be used as the base for comparing all later dates or periods. Alternatively, each statement may be compared to the immediately preceding statement. Exhibit 1 is a condensed comparative balance sheet for two years for Lincoln Company, with horizontal analysis.

We cannot fully evaluate the significance of the various increases and decreases in the items shown in Exhibit 1 without additional information. Although total assets at the end of 2003 were $91,000 (7.4%) less than at the beginning of the year, liabilities were reduced by $133,000 (30%), and stockholders' equity increased $42,000 (5.3%). It appears that the reduction of $100,000 in long-term liabilities was achieved mostly through the sale of long-term investments.

Exhibit 1 Comparative Balance Sheet—Horizontal Analysis

Lincoln Company
Comparative Balance Sheet
December 31, 2003 and 2002

	2003	2002	Increase (Decrease) Amount	Percent
Assets				
Current assets	$ 550,000	$ 533,000	$ 17,000	3.2%
Long-term investments	95,000	177,500	(82,500)	(46.5%)
Property, plant, and				
equipment (net)	444,500	470,000	(25,500)	(5.4%)
Intangible assets	50,000	50,000	—	
Total assets	$1,139,500	$1,230,500	$ (91,000)	(7.4%)
Liabilities				
Current liabilities	$ 210,000	$ 243,000	$ (33,000)	(13.6%)
Long-term liabilities	100,000	200,000	(100,000)	(50.0%)
Total liabilities	$ 310,000	$ 443,000	$(133,000)	(30.0%)
Stockholders' Equity				
Preferred 6% stock, $100 par	$ 150,000	$ 150,000	—	—
Common stock, $10 par	500,000	500,000	—	—
Retained earnings	179,500	137,500	$ 42,000	30.5%
Total stockholders' equity	$ 829,500	$ 787,500	$ 42,000	5.3%
Total liabilities and				
stockholders' equity	$1,139,500	$1,230,500	$ (91,000)	(7.4%)

Q&A

Accounts Payable was $600,000 in the current year and $500,000 in the preceding year. What is the amount and the percentage of increase or decrease that would be shown in a balance sheet with horizontal analysis?

$100,000 or 20% ($100,000/ $500,000) increase

The balance sheet in Exhibit 1 may be expanded to include the details of the various categories of assets and liabilities. An alternative is to present the details in separate schedules. Exhibit 2 is a supporting schedule with horizontal analysis.

The decrease in accounts receivable may be due to changes in credit terms or improved collection policies. Likewise, a decrease in inventories during a period of increased sales may indicate an improvement in the management of inventories.

The changes in the current assets in Exhibit 2 appear favorable. This assessment is supported by the 24.8% increase in net sales shown in Exhibit 3.

An increase in net sales may not have a favorable effect on operating performance. The percentage increase in Lincoln Company's net sales is accompanied by a greater percentage increase in the cost of goods (merchandise) sold.[1] This has the

---

[1] The term *cost of goods sold* is often used in practice in place of *cost of merchandise sold*. Such usage is followed in this chapter.

Exhibit 2 Comparative
Schedule of Current Assets
—Horizontal Analysis

Lincoln Company
Comparative Schedule of Current Assets
December 31, 2003 and 2002

	2003	2002	Increase (Decrease) Amount	Increase (Decrease) Percent
Cash	$ 90,500	$ 64,700	$ 25,800	39.9%
Marketable securities	75,000	60,000	15,000	25.0%
Accounts receivable (net)	115,000	120,000	(5,000)	(4.2%)
Inventories........................	264,000	283,000	(19,000)	(6.7%)
Prepaid expenses	5,500	5,300	200	3.8%
Total current assets	$550,000	$533,000	$ 17,000	3.2%

Exhibit 3 Comparative
Income Statement—
Horizontal Analysis

Lincoln Company
Comparative Income Statement
For the Years Ended December 31, 2003 and 2002

	2003	2002	Increase (Decrease) Amount	Increase (Decrease) Percent
Sales	$1,530,500	$1,234,000	$296,500	24.0%
Sales returns and allowances	32,500	34,000	(1,500)	(4.4%)
Net sales	$1,498,000	$1,200,000	$298,000	24.8%
Cost of goods sold	1,043,000	820,000	223,000	27.2%
Gross profit	$ 455,000	$ 380,000	$ 75,000	19.7%
Selling expenses	$ 191,000	$ 147,000	$ 44,000	29.9%
Administrative expenses	104,000	97,400	6,600	6.8%
Total operating expenses	$ 295,000	$ 244,400	$ 50,600	20.7%
Income from operations	$ 160,000	$ 135,600	$ 24,400	18.0%
Other income	8,500	11,000	(2,500)	(22.7%)
	$ 168,500	$ 146,600	$ 21,900	14.9%
Other expense	6,000	12,000	(6,000)	(50.0%)
Income before income tax	$ 162,500	$ 134,600	$ 27,900	20.7%
Income tax expense	71,500	58,100	13,400	23.1%
Net income	$ 91,000	$ 76,500	$ 14,500	19.0%

effect of reducing gross profit. Selling expenses increased significantly, and administrative expenses increased slightly. Overall, operating expenses increased by 20.7%, whereas gross profit increased by only 19.7%.

The increase in income from operations and in net income is favorable. However, a study of the expenses and additional analyses and comparisons should be made before reaching a conclusion as to the cause.

Exhibit 4 illustrates a comparative retained earnings statement with horizontal analysis. It reveals that retained earnings increased 30.5% for the year. The increase is due to net income of $91,000 for the year, less dividends of $49,000.

Exhibit 4 Comparative Retained Earnings Statement —Horizontal Analysis

Lincoln Company
Comparative Retained Earnings Statement
December 31, 2003 and 2002

	2003	2002	Increase (Decrease) Amount	Increase (Decrease) Percent
Retained earnings, January 1	$137,500	$100,000	$37,500	37.5%
Net income for the year	91,000	76,500	14,500	19.0%
Total	$228,500	$176,500	$52,000	29.5%
Dividends:				
On preferred stock	$ 9,000	$ 9,000	—	—
On common stock	40,000	30,000	$10,000	33.3%
Total	$ 49,000	$ 39,000	$10,000	25.6%
Retained earnings, December 31	$179,500	$137,500	$42,000	30.5%

Vertical Analysis

A percentage analysis may also be used to show the relationship of each component to the total within a single statement. This type of analysis is called **vertical analysis**. Like horizontal analysis, the statements may be prepared in either detailed or condensed form. In the latter case, additional details of the changes in individual items may be presented in supporting schedules. In such schedules, the percentage analysis may be based on either the total of the schedule or the statement total. Although vertical analysis is limited to an individual statement, its significance may be improved by preparing comparative statements.

In vertical analysis of the balance sheet, each asset item is stated as a percent of the total assets. Each liability and stockholders' equity item is stated as a percent of the total liabilities and stockholders' equity. Exhibit 5 is a condensed comparative balance sheet with vertical analysis for Lincoln Company.

The major percentage changes in Lincoln Company's assets are in the current asset and long-term investment categories. In the Liabilities and Stockholders' Equity sections of the balance sheet, the greatest percentage changes are in long-term liabilities and retained earnings. Stockholders' equity increased from 64% to 72.8% of total liabilities and stockholders' equity in 2003. There is a comparable decrease in liabilities.

In a vertical analysis of the income statement, each item is stated as a percent of net sales. Exhibit 6 is a condensed comparative income statement with vertical analysis for Lincoln Company.

We must be careful when judging the significance of differences between percentages for the two years. For example, the decline of the gross profit rate from 31.7% in 2002 to 30.4% in 2003 is only 1.3 percentage points. In terms of dollars of potential gross profit, however, it represents a decline of approximately $19,500 (1.3% × $1,498,000).

At the end of the current year, Accounts Payable was $600,000 and total liabilities and stockholders' equity was $1,200,000. What percent would be shown for Accounts Payable in a balance sheet with vertical analysis?

50% ($600,000/$1,200,000)

Common-Size Statements

Horizontal and vertical analyses with both dollar and percentage amounts are useful in assessing relationships and trends in financial conditions and operations of a business. Vertical analysis with both dollar and percentage amounts is also useful in comparing one company with another or with industry averages. Such comparisons are easier to make with the use of common-size statements. In a **common-size statement**, all items are expressed in percentages.

Exhibit 5 Comparative Balance Sheet—Vertical Analysis

Lincoln Company
Comparative Balance Sheet
December 31, 2003 and 2002

	2003		2002	
	Amount	Percent	Amount	Percent
Assets				
Current assets	$ 550,000	48.3%	$ 533,000	43.3%
Long-term investments	95,000	8.3	177,500	14.4
Property, plant, and equipment (net)	444,500	39.0	470,000	38.2
Intangible assets	50,000	4.4	50,000	4.1
Total assets	$1,139,500	100.0%	$1,230,500	100.0%
Liabilities				
Current liabilities	$ 210,000	18.4%	$ 243,000	19.7%
Long-term liabilities	100,000	8.8	200,000	16.3
Total liabilities	$ 310,000	27.2%	$ 443,000	36.0%
Stockholders' Equity				
Preferred 6% stock, $100 par	$ 150,000	13.2%	$ 150,000	12.2%
Common stock, $10 par	500,000	43.9	500,000	40.6
Retained earnings	179,500	15.7	137,500	11.2
Total stockholders' equity	$ 829,500	72.8%	$ 787,500	64.0%
Total liabilities and stockholders' equity	$1,139,500	100.0%	$1,230,500	100.0%

Exhibit 6 Comparative Income Statement—Vertical Analysis

Lincoln Company
Comparative Income Statement
For the Years Ended December 31, 2003 and 2002

	2003		2002	
	Amount	Percent	Amount	Percent
Sales	$1,530,500	102.2%	$1,234,000	102.8%
Sales returns and allowances	32,500	2.2	34,000	2.8
Net sales	$1,498,000	100.0%	$1,200,000	100.0%
Cost of goods sold	1,043,000	69.6	820,000	68.3
Gross profit	$ 455,000	30.4%	$ 380,000	31.7%
Selling expenses	$ 191,000	12.8%	$ 147,000	12.3%
Administrative expenses	104,000	6.9	97,400	8.1
Total operating expenses	$ 295,000	19.7%	$ 244,400	20.4%
Income from operations	$ 160,000	10.7%	$ 135,600	11.3%
Other income	8,500	0.6	11,000	0.9
	$ 168,500	11.3%	$ 146,600	12.2%
Other expense	6,000	0.4	12,000	1.0
Income before income tax	$ 162,500	10.9%	$ 134,600	11.2%
Income tax expense	71,500	4.8	58,100	4.8
Net income	$ 91,000	6.1%	$ 76,500	6.4%

The percentages of gross profit and net income to sales for fiscal year-end 1999 for **Kmart Corp.** and **Wal-Mart Stores Inc.** are shown below.

	Kmart Corp.	Wal-Mart Stores Inc.
Gross profit to sales	21.8%	21.0%
Net income to sales	1.5%	3.3%

Wal-Mart has a slightly lower gross profit margin than Kmart, which is likely due to lower prices. However, Wal-Mart has a much leaner operating expense structure, so it is able to earn an overall higher percentage of net income to sales.

Common-size statements are useful in comparing the current period with prior periods, individual businesses, or one business with industry percentages. Industry data are often available from trade associations and financial information services. Exhibit 7 is a comparative common-size income statement for two businesses.

Exhibit 7 indicates that Lincoln Company has a slightly higher rate of gross profit than Madison Corporation. However, this advantage is more than offset by Lincoln Company's higher percentage of selling and administrative expenses. As a result, the income from operations of Lincoln Company is 10.7% of net sales, compared with 14.4% for Madison Corporation—an unfavorable difference of 3.7 percentage points.

Other Analytical Measures

In addition to the preceding analyses, other relationships may be expressed in ratios and percentages. Often, these items are taken from the financial statements and thus are a type of vertical analysis. Comparing these items with items from earlier periods is a type of horizontal analysis.

Exhibit 7 Common-Size Income Statement

Lincoln Company and Madison Corporation
Condensed Common-Size Income Statement
For the Year Ended December 31, 2003

	Lincoln Company	Madison Corporation
Sales	102.2%	102.3%
Sales returns and allowances	2.2	2.3
Net sales	100.0%	100.0%
Cost of goods sold	69.6	70.0
Gross profit	30.4%	30.0%
Selling expenses	12.8%	11.5%
Administrative expenses	6.9	4.1
Total operating expenses	19.7%	15.6%
Income from operations	10.7%	14.4%
Other income	0.6	0.6
	11.3%	15.0%
Other expense	0.4	0.5
Income before income tax	10.9%	14.5%
Income tax expense	4.8	5.5
Net income	6.1%	9.0%

Solvency Analysis

objective 2

Apply financial statement analysis to assess the solvency of a business.

Some aspects of a business's financial condition and operations are of greater importance to some users than others. However, all users are interested in the ability of a business to pay its debts as they are due and to earn income. The ability of a business to meet its financial obligations (debts) is called **solvency**. The ability of a business to earn income is called **profitability**.

The factors of solvency and profitability are interrelated. A business that cannot pay its debts on a timely basis may experience difficulty in obtaining credit. A lack of available credit may, in turn, lead to a decline in the business's profitability. Eventually, the business may be forced into bankruptcy. Likewise, a business that is less profitable than its competitors is likely to be at a disadvantage in obtaining credit or new capital from stockholders.

In the following paragraphs, we discuss various types of financial analyses that are useful in evaluating the solvency of a business. In the next section, we discuss various types of profitability analyses. The examples in both sections are based on Lincoln Company's financial statements presented earlier. In some cases, data from Lincoln Company's financial statements of the preceding year and from other sources are also used. These historical data are useful in assessing the past performance of a business and in forecasting its future performance. The results of financial analyses may be even more useful when they are compared with those of competing businesses and with industry averages.

Solvency analysis focuses on the ability of a business to pay or otherwise satisfy its current and noncurrent liabilities. It is normally assessed by examining balance sheet relationships, using the following major analyses:

1. Current position analysis
2. Accounts receivable analysis
3. Inventory analysis
4. The ratio of fixed assets to long-term liabilities
5. The ratio of liabilities to stockholders' equity
6. The number of times interest charges are earned

> **Solvency analysis focuses on the ability of a business to pay or otherwise satisfy its current and noncurrent liabilities.**

Current Position Analysis

To be useful in assessing solvency, a ratio or other financial measure must relate to a business's ability to pay or otherwise satisfy its liabilities. Using measures to assess a business's ability to pay its current liabilities is called **current position analysis**. Such analysis is of special interest to short-term creditors.

An analysis of a firm's current position normally includes determining the working capital, the current ratio, and the acid-test ratio. The current and acid-test ratios are most useful when analyzed together and compared to previous periods and other firms in the industry.

Working Capital

The excess of the current assets of a business over its current liabilities is called working capital. The working capital is often used in evaluating a company's ability to meet currently maturing debts. It is especially useful in making monthly or other period-to-period comparisons for a company. However, amounts of working capital are difficult to assess when comparing companies of different sizes or in comparing such amounts with industry figures. For example, working capital of $250,000 may be adequate for a small local hardware store, but it would be inadequate for all of **Home Depot**.

Current Ratio

Another means of expressing the relationship between current assets and current liabilities is the current ratio. This ratio is sometimes called the **working capital ratio** or **bankers' ratio**. The ratio is computed by dividing the total current assets by the total current liabilities. For Lincoln Company, working capital and the current ratio for 2003 and 2002 are as follows:

	2003	2002
Current assets	$550,000	$533,000
Current liabilities	210,000	243,000
Working capital	$340,000	$290,000
Current ratio	2.6	2.2

The Wm. Wrigley Company maintains a high current ratio—3.9 for a recent year. Wrigley's stable and profitable chewing gum business has allowed it to develop a strong cash position coupled with no short-term notes payable.

The current ratio is a more reliable indicator of solvency than is working capital. To illustrate, assume that as of December 31, 2003, the working capital of a competitor is much greater than $340,000, but its current ratio is only 1.3. Considering these facts alone, Lincoln Company, with its current ratio of 2.6, is in a more favorable position to obtain short-term credit than the competitor, which has the greater amount of working capital.

Acid-Test Ratio

The working capital and the current ratio do not consider the makeup of the current assets. To illustrate the importance of this consideration, the current position data for Lincoln Company and Jefferson Corporation as of December 31, 2003, are as follows:

	Lincoln Company	Jefferson Corporation
Current assets:		
Cash	$ 90,500	$ 45,500
Marketable securities	75,000	25,000
Accounts receivable (net)	115,000	90,000
Inventories	264,000	380,000
Prepaid expenses	5,500	9,500
Total current assets	$550,000	$550,000
Current liabilities	210,000	210,000
Working capital	$340,000	$340,000
Current ratio	2.6	2.6

Both companies have a working capital of $340,000 and a current ratio of 2.6. But the ability of each company to pay its current debts is significantly different. Jefferson Corporation has more of its current assets in inventories. Some of these inventories must be sold and the receivables collected before the current liabilities can be paid in full. Thus, a large amount of time may be necessary to convert these inventories into cash. Declines in market prices and a reduction in demand could also impair its ability to pay current liabilities. In contrast, Lincoln Company has cash and current assets (marketable securities and accounts receivable) that can generally be converted to cash rather quickly to meet its current liabilities.

A ratio that measures the "instant" debt-paying ability of a company is called the **acid-test ratio** or **quick ratio**. It is the ratio of the total quick assets to the total current liabilities. Quick assets are cash and other current assets that can be quickly converted to cash. Quick assets normally include cash, marketable securities, and receivables. The acid-test ratio data for Lincoln Company are as follows:

A balance sheet shows $300,000 of cash, marketable securities, and receivables, and $250,000 of inventories. Current liabilities are $200,000. What are (a) the current ratio and (b) the acid-test ratio?

(a) 2.75 ($550,000/$200,000);
(b) 1.5 ($300,000/$200,000)

	2003	2002
Quick assets:		
Cash	$ 90,500	$ 64,700
Marketable equity securities	75,000	60,000
Accounts receivable (net)	115,000	120,000
Total quick assets	$280,500	$244,700
Current liabilities	$210,000	$243,000
Acid-test ratio	1.3	1.0

Accounts Receivable Analysis

The size and makeup of accounts receivable change constantly during business operations. Sales on account increase accounts receivable, whereas collections from customers decrease accounts receivable. Firms that grant long credit terms usually have larger accounts receivable balances than those granting short credit terms. Increases or decreases in the volume of sales also affect the balance of accounts receivable.

It is desirable to collect receivables as promptly as possible. The cash collected from receivables improves solvency. In addition, the cash generated by prompt collections from customers may be used in operations for such purposes as purchasing merchandise in large quantities at lower prices. The cash may also be used for payment of dividends to stockholders or for other investing or financing purposes. Prompt collection also lessens the risk of loss from uncollectible accounts.

Accounts Receivable Turnover

The relationship between credit sales and accounts receivable may be stated as the **accounts receivable turnover**. This ratio is computed by dividing net sales on account by the average net accounts receivable. It is desirable to base the average on monthly balances, which allows for seasonal changes in sales. When such data are not available, it may be necessary to use the average of the accounts receivable balance at the beginning and end of the year. If there are trade notes receivable as well as accounts, the two may be combined. The accounts receivable turnover data for Lincoln Company are as follows. All sales were made on account.

	2003	2002
Net sales on account	$1,498,000	$1,200,000
Accounts receivable (net):		
Beginning of year	$ 120,000	$ 140,000
End of year	115,000	120,000
Total	$ 235,000	$ 260,000
Average (Total ÷ 2)	$ 117,500	$ 130,000
Accounts receivable turnover	12.7	9.2

The increase in the accounts receivable turnover for 2003 indicates that there has been an improvement in the collection of receivables. This may be due to a change in the granting of credit or in collection practices or both.

Number of Days' Sales in Receivables

Another measure of the relationship between credit sales and accounts receivable is the **number of days' sales in receivables**. This ratio is computed by dividing the net accounts receivable at the end of the year by the average daily sales on account. Average daily sales on account is determined by dividing net sales on account by 365 days. The number of days' sales in receivables is computed for Lincoln Company as follows:

	2003	2002
Accounts receivable (net), end of year	$115,000	$120,000
Net sales on account	$1,498,000	$1,200,000
Average daily sales on account (sales ÷ 365)	$4,104	$3,288
Number of days' sales in receivables	28.0*	36.5*

*Accounts receivable ÷ Average daily sales on account

The number of days' sales in receivables is an estimate of the length of time (in days) the accounts receivable have been outstanding. Comparing this measure with

Q&A

Sales were $1,200,000, of which 80% were on account. The accounts receivable balance at the beginning of the year was $56,000, and at the end of the year it was $40,000. What are (a) the accounts receivable turnover and (b) the number of days' sales in receivables?

(a) 20 [(0.80 × $1,200,000)/($56,000 + $40,000)/2]; (b) 15.2 days [$40,000/ ($960,000/365)]

the credit terms provides information on the efficiency in collecting receivables. For example, assume that the number of days' sales in receivables for Grant Inc. is 40. If Grant Inc.'s credit terms are n/45, then its collection process appears to be efficient. On the other hand, if Grant Inc.'s credit terms are n/30, its collection process does not appear to be efficient. A comparison with other firms in the same industry and with prior years also provides useful information. Such comparisons may indicate efficiency of collection procedures and trends in credit management.

Inventory Analysis

A business should keep enough inventory on hand to meet the needs of its customers and its operations. At the same time, however, an excessive amount of inventory reduces solvency by tying up funds. Excess inventories also increase insurance expense, property taxes, storage costs, and other related expenses. These expenses further reduce funds that could be used elsewhere to improve operations. Finally, excess inventory also increases the risk of losses because of price declines or obsolescence of the inventory. Two measures that are useful for evaluating the management of inventory are the inventory turnover and the number of days' sales in inventory.

Inventory Turnover

The relationship between the volume of goods (merchandise) sold and inventory may be stated as the **inventory turnover**. It is computed by dividing the cost of goods sold by the average inventory. If monthly data are not available, the average of the inventories at the beginning and the end of the year may be used. The inventory turnover for Lincoln Company is computed as follows:

	2003	2002
Cost of goods sold	$1,043,000	$820,000
Inventories:		
Beginning of year	$ 283,000	$311,000
End of year	264,000	283,000
Total	$ 547,000	$594,000
Average (Total ÷ 2)	$ 273,500	$297,000
Inventory turnover	3.8	2.8

Real World The inventory turnover of **McDonald's Corporation** for a recent year was 39, while for **Toys "R" Us Inc.**, it was 4.3. McDonald's inventory turnover is higher because It sells perishable food products, while toys can sit on the shelf longer without "spoiling."

The inventory turnover improved for Lincoln Company because of an increase in the cost of goods sold and a decrease in the average inventories. Differences across inventories, companies, and industries are too great to allow a general statement on what is a good inventory turnover. For example, a firm selling food should have a higher turnover than a firm selling furniture or jewelry. Likewise, the perishable foods department of a supermarket should have a higher turnover than the soaps and cleansers department. However, for each business or each department within a business, there is a reasonable turnover rate. A turnover lower than this rate could mean that inventory is not being managed properly.

Number of Days' Sales in Inventory

Another measure of the relationship between the cost of goods sold and inventory is the **number of days' sales in inventory**. This measure is computed by dividing the inventory at the end of the year by the average daily cost of goods sold (cost of goods sold divided by 365). The number of days' sales in inventory for Lincoln Company is computed as follows:

	2003	2002
Inventories, end of year	$264,000	$283,000
Cost of goods sold	$1,043,000	$820,000
Average daily cost of goods sold (COGS ÷ 365 days)	$2,858	$2,247
Number of days' sales in inventory	92.4	125.9

The number of days' sales in inventory is a rough measure of the length of time it takes to acquire, sell, and replace the inventory. For Lincoln Company, there is a major improvement in the number of days' sales in inventory during 2003. However, a comparison with earlier years and similar firms would be useful in assessing Lincoln Company's overall inventory management.

Ratio of Fixed Assets to Long-Term Liabilities

Long-term notes and bonds are often secured by mortgages on fixed assets. The ratio of fixed assets to long-term liabilities is a solvency measure that indicates the margin of safety of the noteholders or bondholders. It also indicates the ability of the business to borrow additional funds on a long-term basis. The ratio of fixed assets to long-term liabilities for Lincoln Company is as follows:

	2003	2002
Fixed assets (net)	$444,500	$470,000
Long-term liabilities	$100,000	$200,000
Ratio of fixed assets to long-term liabilities	4.4	2.4

The major increase in this ratio at the end of 2003 is mainly due to liquidating one-half of Lincoln Company's long-term liabilities. If the company needs to borrow additional funds on a long-term basis in the future, it is in a strong position to do so.

Ratio of Liabilities to Stockholders' Equity

Claims against the total assets of a business are divided into two groups: (1) claims of creditors and (2) claims of owners. The relationship between the total claims of the creditors and owners—the ratio of liabilities to stockholders' equity—is a solvency measure that indicates the margin of safety for creditors. It also indicates the ability of the business to withstand adverse business conditions. When the claims of creditors are large in relation to the equity of the stockholders, there are usually significant interest payments. If earnings decline to the point where the company is unable to meet its interest payments, the business may be taken over by the creditors.

The relationship between creditor and stockholder equity is shown in the vertical analysis of the balance sheet. For example, the balance sheet of Lincoln Company in Exhibit 5 indicates that on December 31, 2003, liabilities represented 27.2% and stockholders' equity represented 72.8% of the total liabilities and stockholders' equity (100.0%). Instead of expressing each item as a percent of the total, this relationship may be expressed as a ratio of one to the other, as follows:

	2003	2002
Total liabilities	$310,000	$443,000
Total stockholders' equity	$829,500	$787,500
Ratio of liabilities to stockholders' equity	0.37	0.56

The balance sheet of Lincoln Company shows that the major factor affecting the change in the ratio was the $100,000 decrease in long-term liabilities during 2003. The ratio at the end of both years shows a large margin of safety for the creditors.

Real World The ratio of liabilities to stockholders' equity varies across industries. For example, recent annual reports of some selected companies showed the following ratio of liabilities to stockholders' equity:

Continental Airlines	4.31
Procter & Gamble	1.85
Circuit City Stores	0.93

The airline industry generally uses more debt financing than the consumer product or retail industries. Thus, the airline industry is generally considered more risky.

Number of Times Interest Charges Earned

Corporations in some industries, such as airlines, normally have high ratios of debt to stockholders' equity. For such corporations, the relative risk of the debtholders is normally measured as the **number of times interest charges are earned** during the year. The higher the ratio, the lower the risk that interest payments will not be made if earnings decrease. In other words, the higher the ratio, the greater the assurance that interest payments will be made on a continuing basis. This measure also indicates the general financial strength of the business, which is of interest to stockholders and employees as well as creditors.

The amount available to meet interest charges is not affected by taxes on income. This is because interest is deductible in determining taxable income. Thus, the number of times interest charges are earned is computed as shown below.

What would be the number of times interest charges are earned for a company with $1,500,000, 10% debt; net income of $120,000; and a corporate tax rate of 40%?

$$\frac{[\$120,000/(1.0 - 0.4)] + \$150,000}{\$150,000} = 2.33$$

	2003	2002
Income before income tax	$ 900,000	$ 800,000
Add interest expense	300,000	250,000
Amount available to meet interest charges	$1,200,000	$1,050,000
Number of times interest charges earned	4	4.2

Analysis such as this can also be applied to dividends on preferred stock. In such a case, net income is divided by the amount of preferred dividends to yield the **number of times preferred dividends are earned**. This measure indicates the risk that dividends to preferred stockholders may not be paid.

Profitability Analysis

objective 3

Apply financial statement analysis to assess the profitability of a business.

The ability of a business to earn profits depends on the effectiveness and efficiency of its operations as well as the resources available to it. Profitability analysis, therefore, focuses primarily on the relationship between operating results as reported in the income statement and resources available to the business as reported in the balance sheet. Major analyses used in assessing profitability include the following:

1. Ratio of net sales to assets
2. Rate earned on total assets
3. Rate earned on stockholders' equity
4. Rate earned on common stockholders' equity
5. Earnings per share on common stock
6. Price-earnings ratio
7. Dividends per share
8. Dividend yield

> **Profitability analysis focuses on the relationship between operating results and the resources available to a business.**

Ratio of Net Sales to Assets

The **ratio of net sales to assets** is a profitability measure that shows how effectively a firm utilizes its assets. For example, two competing businesses have equal amounts of assets. If the sales of one are twice the sales of the other, the business with the higher sales is making better use of its assets.

In computing the ratio of net sales to assets, any long-term investments are excluded from total assets, because such investments are unrelated to normal operations involving the sale of goods or services. Assets may be measured as the total at the end of the year, the average at the beginning and end of the year, or the average of monthly totals. The basic data and the computation of this ratio for Lincoln Company are as follows:

	2003	2002
Net sales	$1,498,000	$1,200,000
Total assets (excluding long-term investments):		
Beginning of year	$1,053,000	$1,010,000
End of year	1,044,500	1,053,000
Total	$2,097,500	$2,063,000
Average (Total ÷ 2)	$1,048,750	$1,031,500
Ratio of net sales to assets	1.4	1.2

This ratio improved during 2003, primarily due to an increase in sales volume. A comparison with similar companies or industry averages would be helpful in assessing the effectiveness of Lincoln Company's use of its assets.

Rate Earned on Total Assets

The **rate earned on total assets** measures the profitability of total assets, without considering how the assets are financed. This rate is therefore not affected by whether the assets are financed primarily by creditors or stockholders.

The rate earned on total assets is computed by adding interest expense to net income and dividing this sum by the average total assets. Adding interest expense to net income eliminates the effect of whether the assets are financed by debt or equity. The rate earned by Lincoln Company on total assets is computed as follows:

	2003	2002
Net income	$ 91,000	$ 76,500
Plus interest expense	6,000	12,000
Total	$ 97,000	$ 88,500
Total assets:		
Beginning of year	$1,230,500	$1,187,500
End of year	1,139,500	1,230,500
Total	$2,370,000	$2,418,000
Average (Total ÷ 2)	$1,185,000	$1,209,000
Rate earned on total assets	8.2%	7.3%

The rate earned on total assets of Lincoln Company during 2003 improved over that of 2002. A comparison with similar companies and industry averages would be useful in evaluating Lincoln Company's profitability on total assets.

Sometimes it may be desirable to compute the **rate of income from operations to total assets**. This is especially true if significant amounts of nonoperating income and expense are reported on the income statement. In this case, any assets related to the nonoperating income and expense items should be excluded from total assets in computing the rate. In addition, using income from operations (which is before tax) has the advantage of eliminating the effects of any changes in the tax structure on the rate of earnings. When evaluating published data on rates earned on assets, you should be careful to determine the exact nature of the measure that is reported.

Rate Earned on Stockholders' Equity

Another measure of profitability is the **rate earned on stockholders' equity**. It is computed by dividing net income by average total stockholders' equity. In contrast to the rate earned on total assets, this measure emphasizes the rate of income earned on the amount invested by the stockholders.

The total stockholders' equity may vary throughout a period. For example, a business may issue or retire stock, pay dividends, and earn net income. If monthly amounts are not available, the average of the stockholders' equity at the beginning and the end of the year is normally used to compute this rate. For Lincoln Company, the rate earned on stockholders' equity is computed as follows:

	2003	2002
Net income	$ 91,000	$ 76,500
Stockholders' equity:		
Beginning of year	$ 787,500	$ 750,000
End of year	829,500	787,500
Total	$1,617,000	$1,537,500
Average (Total ÷ 2)	$ 808,500	$ 768,750
Rate earned on stockholders' equity	11.3%	10.0%

The rate earned by a business on the equity of its stockholders is usually higher than the rate earned on total assets. This occurs when the amount earned on assets acquired with creditors' funds is more than the interest paid to creditors. This difference in the rate on stockholders' equity and the rate on total assets is called **leverage**.

Lincoln Company's rate earned on stockholders' equity for 2003, 11.3%, is greater than the rate of 8.2% earned on total assets. The leverage of 3.1% (11.3% − 8.2%) for 2003 compares favorably with the 2.7% (10.0% − 7.3%) leverage for 2002. Exhibit 8 shows the 2003 and 2002 leverages for Lincoln Company.

Exhibit 8 Leverage

Rate Earned on Common Stockholders' Equity

A corporation may have both preferred and common stock outstanding. In this case, the common stockholders have the residual claim on earnings. The **rate earned on common stockholders' equity** focuses only on the rate of profits earned on the amount invested by the common stockholders. It is computed by subtracting preferred dividend requirements from the net income and dividing by the average common stockholders' equity.

The approximate rates earned on assets and stockholders' equity for **Adolph Coors Company** and **Anheuser-Busch Companies** for a recent fiscal year are shown below.

	Adolph Coors	Anheuser-Busch
Rate earned on assets	5%	13%
Rate earned on stockholders' equity	9%	30%

Anheuser-Busch has been more profitable and has benefited from a greater use of leverage than has Adolph Coors.

Lincoln Company has $150,000 of 6% nonparticipating preferred stock outstanding on December 31, 2003 and 2002. Thus, the annual preferred dividend requirement is $9,000 ($150,000 × 6%). The common stockholders' equity equals the total stockholders' equity, including retained earnings, less the par of the preferred stock ($150,000). The basic data and the rate earned on common stockholders' equity for Lincoln Company are as follows:

	2003	2002
Net income	$ 91,000	$ 76,500
Preferred dividends	9,000	9,000
Remainder—identified with common stock	$ 82,000	$ 67,500
Common stockholders' equity:		
Beginning of year	$ 637,500	$ 600,000
End of year	679,500	637,500
Total	$1,317,000	$1,237,500
Average (Total ÷ 2)	$ 658,500	$ 618,750
Rate earned on common stockholders' equity	12.5%	10.9%

The rate earned on common stockholders' equity differs from the rates earned by Lincoln Company on total assets and total stockholders' equity. This occurs if there are borrowed funds and also preferred stock outstanding, which rank ahead of the common shares in their claim on earnings. Thus, the concept of leverage, as we discussed in the preceding section, can also be applied to the use of funds from the sale of preferred stock as well as borrowing. Funds from both sources can be used in an attempt to increase the return on common stockholders' equity.

BUSINESS ON STAGE

Analysis and Red Flags

An additional source of information about a corporation is the independent auditor's report, which must accompany the financial statements of a public corporation. The purpose of this report is to provide assurance to investors that the financial statements are fairly presented in conformity with generally accepted accounting principles.

The auditor's report may raise "red flags" indicating that profitability and solvency measures should be analyzed further. In such cases, an investor should read the auditor's report carefully to see if the "reliability" of these measures has been affected

by one or more of the following factors:

1. There may be substantial doubt as to the ability of the company to continue as a going concern beyond one year.
2. An unusual accounting practice is being followed.
3. The company changed accounting principles from prior years.
4. The auditor wants to call your attention to a specific matter of importance.
5. The financial statements do not conform to generally accepted accounting principles.

The date of the auditor's report is also significant. It represents the last date that the auditor searched for events occurring subsequent to the date of the financial statements— events that might be significant to the interpretation of those statements. For example, the company may have sold a subsidiary after year-end or suffered a substantial loss as a result of some disaster. Such events should be disclosed in notes to the financial statements. ■

Earnings per Share on Common Stock

One of the profitability measures often quoted by the financial press is **earnings per share (EPS) on common stock**. It is also normally reported in the income statement in corporate annual reports. If a company has issued only one class of stock, the earnings per share is computed by dividing net income by the number of shares of stock outstanding. If preferred and common stock are outstanding, the net income is first reduced by the amount of preferred dividend requirements.[2]

The data on the earnings per share of common stock for Lincoln Company are as follows:

	2003	2002
Net income	$91,000	$76,500
Preferred dividends	9,000	9,000
Remainder—identified with common stock	$82,000	$67,500
Shares of common stock outstanding	50,000	50,000
Earnings per share on common stock	$1.64	$1.35

Price-Earnings Ratio

Another profitability measure quoted by the financial press is the **price-earnings (P/E) ratio** on common stock. The price-earnings ratio is an indicator of a firm's future earnings prospects. It is computed by dividing the market price per share of common stock at a specific date by the annual earnings per share. To illustrate, assume that the market prices per common share are 41 at the end of 2003 and 27 at the end of 2002. The price-earnings ratio on common stock of Lincoln Company is computed as follows:

	2003	2002
Market price per share of common stock	$41.00	$27.00
Earnings per share on common stock	÷ 1.64	÷ 1.35
Price-earnings ratio on common stock	25	20

The price-earnings ratio indicates that a share of common stock of Lincoln Company was selling for 20 times the amount of earnings per share at the end of 2002. At the end of 2003, the common stock was selling for 25 times the amount of earnings per share.

Dividends per Share and Dividend Yield

Since the primary basis for dividends is earnings, **dividends per share** and earnings per share on common stock are commonly used by investors in assessing alternative stock investments. The dividends per share for Lincoln Company were $0.80 ($40,000 ÷ 50,000 shares) for 2003 and $0.60 ($30,000 ÷ 50,000 shares) for 2002.

Dividends per share can be reported with earnings per share to indicate the relationship between dividends and earnings. Comparing these two per share amounts indicates the extent to which the corporation is retaining its earnings for use in operations. Exhibit 9 shows these relationships for Lincoln Company:

The **dividend yield** on common stock is a profitability measure that shows the rate of return to common stockholders in terms of cash dividends. It is of special interest to investors whose main investment objective is to receive current returns

---

[2] Additional details related to earnings per share were discussed in a previous chapter.

Exhibit 9 Dividends and Earnings per Share of Common Stock

DIVIDENDS AND EARNINGS PER SHARE

The dividend per share, dividend yield, and P/E ratio of a common stock are normally quoted on the daily listing of stock prices in *The Wall Street Journal* and other financial publications.

(dividends) on an investment rather than an increase in the market price of the investment. The dividend yield is computed by dividing the annual dividends paid per share of common stock by the market price per share on a specific date. To illustrate, assume that the market price was 41 at the end of 2003 and 27 at the end of 2002. The dividend yield on common stock of Lincoln Company is as follows:

	2003	2002
Dividends per share of common stock	$ 0.80	$ 0.60
Market price per share of common stock	÷ 41.00	÷ 27.00
Dividend yield on common stock	1.95%	2.22%

Summary of Analytical Measures

objective 4

Summarize the uses and limitations of analytical measures.

Exhibit 10 presents a summary of the analytical measures that we have discussed. These measures can be computed for most medium-size businesses. Depending on the specific business being analyzed, some measures might be omitted or additional measures could be developed. The type of industry, the capital structure, and the diversity of the business's operations usually affect the measures used. For example, analysis for an airline might include revenue per passenger mile and cost per available seat as measures. Likewise, analysis for a hotel might focus on occupancy rates.

Percentage analyses, ratios, turnovers, and other measures of financial position and operating results are useful analytical measures. They are helpful in assessing a business's past performance and predicting its future. They are not, however, a substitute for sound judgment. In selecting and interpreting analytical measures, conditions peculiar to a business or its industry should be considered. In addition, the influence of the general economic and business environment should be considered.

In determining trends, the interrelationship of the measures used in assessing a business should be carefully studied. Comparable indexes of earlier periods should also be studied. Data from competing businesses may be useful in assessing the efficiency of operations for the firm under analysis. In making such comparisons, however, the effects of differences in the accounting methods used by the businesses should be considered.

Exhibit 10 Summary of Analytical Measures

	Method of Computation	Use
Solvency measures:		
Working capital	Current assets − Current liabilities	To indicate the ability to meet currently maturing obligations
Current ratio	$\dfrac{\text{Current assets}}{\text{Current liabilities}}$	
Acid-test ratio	$\dfrac{\text{Quick assets}}{\text{Current liabilities}}$	To indicate instant debt-paying ability
Accounts receivable turnover	$\dfrac{\text{Net sales on account}}{\text{Average accounts receivable}}$	To assess the efficiency in collecting receivables and in the management of credit
Numbers of days' sales in receivables	$\dfrac{\text{Accounts receivable, end of year}}{\text{Average daily sales on account}}$	
Inventory turnover	$\dfrac{\text{Cost of goods sold}}{\text{Average inventory}}$	To assess the efficiency in the management of inventory
Number of days' sales in inventory	$\dfrac{\text{Inventory, end of year}}{\text{Average daily cost of goods sold}}$	
Ratio of fixed assets to long-term liabilities	$\dfrac{\text{Fixed assets (net)}}{\text{Long-term liabilities}}$	To indicate the margin of safety to long-term creditors
Ratio of liabilities to stockholders' equity	$\dfrac{\text{Total liabilities}}{\text{Total stockholders' equity}}$	To indicate the margin of safety to creditors
Number of times interest charges earned	$\dfrac{\text{Income before income tax + Interest expense}}{\text{Interest expense}}$	To assess the risk to debtholders in terms of number of times interest charges were earned
Profitability measures:		
Ratio of net sales to assets	$\dfrac{\text{Net sales}}{\text{Average total assets (excluding long-term investments)}}$	To assess the effectiveness in the use of assets
Rate earned on total assets	$\dfrac{\text{Net income + Interest expense}}{\text{Average total assets}}$	To assess the profitability of the assets
Rate earned on stockholders' equity	$\dfrac{\text{Net income}}{\text{Average total stockholders' equity}}$	To assess the profitability of the investment by stockholders
Rate earned on common stockholders' equity	$\dfrac{\text{Net income − Preferred dividends}}{\text{Average common stockholders' equity}}$	To assess the profitability of the investment by common stockholders
Earnings per share on common stock	$\dfrac{\text{Net income − Preferred dividends}}{\text{Shares of common stock outstanding}}$	
Price-earnings ratio	$\dfrac{\text{Market price per share of common stock}}{\text{Earnings per share of common stock}}$	To indicate future earnings prospects, based on the relationship between market value of common stock and earnings
Dividends per share of common stock	$\dfrac{\text{Dividends}}{\text{Shares of common stock outstanding}}$	To indicate the extent to which earnings are being distributed to common stockholders
Dividend yield	$\dfrac{\text{Dividends per share of common stock}}{\text{Market price per share of common stock}}$	To indicate the rate of return to common stockholders in terms of dividends

Corporate Annual Reports

Describe the contents of
corporate annual reports.

Corporations normally issue annual reports to their stockholders and other interested parties. Such reports summarize the corporation's operating activities for the past year and plans for the future. There are many variations in the order and form for presenting the major sections of annual reports. However, one section of the annual report is devoted to the financial statements, including the accompanying notes. In addition, annual reports usually include the following sections:

1. Financial Highlights
2. President's Letter to the Stockholders
3. Management Discussion and Analysis
4. Independent Auditors' Report
5. Historical Summary

In the following paragraphs, we describe these sections. Each section, as well as the financial statements, is illustrated in the 2000 annual report for **Cisco Systems, Inc.**, in Appendix G.

Financial Highlights

The Financial Highlights section summarizes the operating results for the last year or two. It is sometimes called *Results in Brief*. It is usually presented on the first one or two pages of the annual report.

There are many variations in the format and content of the Financial Highlights section. Such items as sales, net income, net income per common share, cash dividends paid, cash dividends per common share, and the amount of capital expenditures are typically presented. In addition to these data, information about the financial position at the end of the year may be presented. The Financial Highlights section for Cisco Systems, Inc., includes the year-end amounts of stockholders' equity, common shares outstanding, net income, and working capital.

President's Letter to the Stockholders

A letter from the company president to the stockholders is also presented in most annual reports. These letters usually discuss such items as reasons for an increase or decrease in net income, changes in existing plants, purchase or construction of new plants, significant new financing commitments, social responsibility issues, and future plans.

Management Discussion and Analysis

A required disclosure in the annual report filed with the Securities and Exchange Commission is the **Management Discussion and Analysis (MDA)**. The MDA provides critical information in interpreting the financial statements and assessing the future of the company.

The MDA includes an analysis of the results of operations and discusses management's opinion about future performance. It compares the prior year's income statement with the current year's to explain changes in sales, significant expenses, gross profit, and income from operations. For example, an increase in sales may be explained by referring to higher shipment volume or stronger prices.

The MDA also includes an analysis of the company's financial condition. It compares significant balance sheet items between successive years to explain changes in liquidity and capital resources. In addition, the MDA discusses significant risk exposure. For example, Cisco Systems has identified fluctuations in foreign currencies, credit risk, and worldwide economic conditions among its risk factors.

The largest companies in the U.S. and in most parts of the world are audited by one of five large international accounting firms: **Arthur Andersen, Pricewater-houseCoopers, Deloitte & Touche, Ernst & Young,** and **KPMG Peat Marwick.**

Independent Auditors' Report

Before issuing annual statements, all publicly held corporations are required to have an independent audit (examination) of their financial statements. For the financial statements of most companies, the CPAs who conduct the audit render an opinion on the fairness of the statements, as shown in the Independent Auditors' Report for Cisco Systems, Inc.

Historical Summary

The Historical Summary section reports selected financial and operating data of past periods, usually for five or ten years. It is usually presented near the financial statements for the current year. There are wide variations in the types of data reported and the title of this section. In the annual report for Cisco Systems, Inc., this section is called "Selected Financial Data" and includes data for five years.

ENCORE

Bricks vs. Clicks

Online retailing has surged as consumers have begun purchasing items on the Internet. One of the largest online retailers is **Amazon.com, Inc.,** which began as an online bookseller. Amazon competes with such traditional retailers as **Borders** and **Barnes & Noble.** Amazon promises to provide cheaper products than the traditional retailer, because they are able to replace expensive "bricks" with less expensive "clicks." The financial statements can give us some clues as to how this business strategy is working. The charts shown were prepared from recent (1998) annual reports for Amazon.com and Barnes & Noble.

First, notice the chart labeled "Asset Efficiency." Here we see that Amazon generates over $5 of sales for each dollar of assets. This compares to Barnes & Noble, which generates only around $1.70 for each dollar of assets. This means that Amazon does not require the same amount of assets to generate sales. This makes sense, because Amazon doesn't have real estate and stores (bricks), as does Barnes & Noble. Amazon has computers (clicks), but they are not as costly as the traditional retail infrastructure. As further evidence, consider the inventory turnover. The inventory turnover for Amazon is over 15,

while for Barnes & Noble it's around 2. Barnes & Noble must stock its stores with inventory, while Amazon just passes electronic orders to publishers and thus avoids holding much inventory.

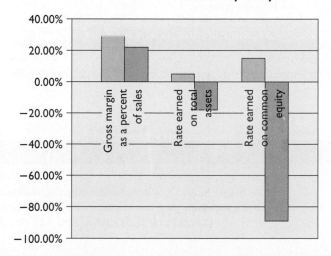

Now let's look at the profitability of the two companies in the chart labeled "Profitability Analysis." First, a vertical analysis of the income statement indicates that the gross margin as a percent of sales for Barnes & Noble is nearly 29%, while for Amazon, it is only 22%. This means that Amazon is selling its products at a lower price than Barnes & Noble, since we assume that the two companies pay the same amount for their sold goods. This is consistent with Amazon's business strategy to undercut the traditional "bricks and mortar" competition. Unfortunately, at the time of this writing, Amazon has not been able to earn an operating profit. Both the rate earned on total assets and common equity are negative, while Barnes & Noble is profitable. Indeed, comparing Amazon's rate earned on total assets to the rate earned on common equity indicates that Amazon is also highly leveraged. The reason for Amazon's losses is the high operating expenses incurred to grow the business. Amazon's revenue grew over 4,000% over the three-year reporting period. Eventually, however, Amazon will need to earn a profit. This may require improving the gross margin percentage or reducing expenditures for growth. Either way, Amazon has a fundamentally different business model than does the traditional retailer. It remains to be seen if this model can become profitable. ∎

KEY POINTS

1 List basic financial statement analytical procedures.

The analysis of percentage increases and decreases in related items in comparative financial statements is called horizontal analysis. The analysis of percentages of component parts to the total in a single statement is called vertical analysis. Financial statements in which all amounts are expressed in percentages for purposes of analysis are called common-size statements.

2 Apply financial statement analysis to assess the solvency of a business.

The primary focus of financial statement analysis is the assessment of solvency and profitability. All users are interested in the ability of a business to pay its debts as they come due (solvency) and to earn income (profitability). Solvency analysis is normally assessed by examining the following balance sheet relationships: (1) current position analysis, (2) accounts receivable analysis, (3) inventory analysis, (4) the ratio of fixed assets to long-term liabilities, (5) the ratio of liabilities to stockholders' equity, and (6) the number of times interest charges are earned.

3 Apply financial statement analysis to assess the profitability of a business.

Profitability analysis focuses mainly on the relationship between operating results (income statement) and resources available (balance sheet). Major analyses used in assessing profitability include (1) the ratio of net sales to assets, (2) the rate earned on total assets, (3) the rate earned on stockholders' equity, (4) the rate earned on common stockholders' equity, (5) earnings per share on common stock, (6) the price-earnings ratio, (7) dividends per share, and (8) dividend yield.

4 Summarize the uses and limitations of analytical measures.

In selecting and interpreting analytical measures, conditions peculiar to a business or its industry should be considered. For example, the type of industry, capital structure, and diversity of the business's operations affect the measures used. In addition, the influence of the general economic and business environment should be considered.

5 Describe the contents of corporate annual reports.

Corporate annual reports normally include financial statements and the following sections: Financial Highlights, President's Letter to the Stockholders, Management Discussion and Analysis, Independent Auditors' Report, and Historical Summary.

ILLUSTRATIVE PROBLEM

Rainbow Paint Co.'s comparative financial statements for the years ending December 31, 2003 and 2002, are as follows. The market price of Rainbow Paint Co.'s common stock was $30 on December 31, 2002, and $25 on December 31, 2003.

Rainbow Paint Co.
Comparative Income Statement
For the Years Ended December 31, 2003 and 2002

	2003	2002
Sales (all on account)	$5,125,000	$3,257,600
Sales returns and allowances	125,000	57,600
Net sales	$5,000,000	$3,200,000
Cost of goods sold	3,400,000	2,080,000
Gross profit	$1,600,000	$1,120,000
Selling expenses	$ 650,000	$ 464,000
Administrative expenses	325,000	224,000
Total operating expenses	$ 975,000	$ 688,000
Income from operations	$ 625,000	$ 432,000
Other income	25,000	19,200
	$ 650,000	$ 451,200
Other expense (interest)	105,000	64,000
Income before income tax	$ 545,000	$ 387,200
Income tax expense	300,000	176,000
Net income	$ 245,000	$ 211,200

Rainbow Paint Co.
Comparative Retained Earnings Statement
For the Years Ended December 31, 2003 and 2002

	2003	2002
Retained earnings, January 1	$723,000	$581,800
Add net income for year	245,000	211,200
Total	$968,000	$793,000
Deduct dividends:		
On preferred stock	$ 40,000	$ 40,000
On common stock	45,000	30,000
Total	$ 85,000	$ 70,000
Retained earnings, December 31	$883,000	$723,000

Rainbow Paint Co.
Comparative Balance Sheet
December 31, 2003 and 2002

	2003	2002
Assets		
Current assets:		
Cash	$ 175,000	$ 125,000
Marketable securities	150,000	50,000
Accounts receivable (net)	425,000	325,000
Inventories	720,000	480,000
Prepaid expenses	30,000	20,000
Total current assets	$1,500,000	$1,000,000
Long-term investments	250,000	225,000
Property, plant, and equipment (net)	2,093,000	1,948,000
Total assets	$3,843,000	$3,173,000

(continued)

Liabilities

Current liabilities	$ 750,000	$ 650,000
Long-term liabilities:		
Mortgage note payable, 10%, due 2006	$ 410,000	—
Bonds payable, 8%, due 2009	800,000	$ 800,000
Total long-term liabilities	$1,210,000	$ 800,000
Total liabilities	$1,960,000	$1,450,000

Stockholders' Equity

Preferred 8% stock, $100 par	$ 500,000	$ 500,000
Common stock, $10 par	500,000	500,000
Retained earnings	883,000	723,000
Total stockholders' equity	$1,883,000	$1,723,000
Total liabilities and stockholders' equity	$3,843,000	$3,173,000

Instructions

Determine the following measures for 2003:

1. Working capital
2. Current ratio
3. Acid-test ratio
4. Accounts receivable turnover
5. Number of days' sales in receivables
6. Inventory turnover
7. Number of days' sales in inventory
8. Ratio of fixed assets to long-term liabilities
9. Ratio of liabilities to stockholders' equity
10. Number of times interest charges earned
11. Number of times preferred dividends earned
12. Ratio of net sales to assets
13. Rate earned on total assets
14. Rate earned on stockholders' equity
15. Rate earned on common stockholders' equity
16. Earnings per share on common stock
17. Price-earnings ratio
18. Dividends per share of common stock
19. Dividend yield

Solution

(Ratios are rounded to the nearest single digit after the decimal point.)

1. Working capital: $750,000
    $1,500,000 − $750,000
2. Current ratio: 2.0
    $1,500,000 ÷ $750,000
3. Acid-test ratio: 1.0
    $750,000 ÷ $750,000
4. Accounts receivable turnover: 13.3
    $5,000,000 ÷ [($425,000 + $325,000) ÷ 2]
5. Number of days' sales in receivables: 31 days
    $5,000,000 ÷ 365 = $13,699
    $425,000 ÷ $13,699
6. Inventory turnover: 5.7
    $3,400,000 ÷ [($720,000 + $480,000) ÷ 2]
7. Number of days' sales in inventory: 77.3 days
    $3,400,000 ÷ 365 = $9,315
    $720,000 ÷ $9,315
8. Ratio of fixed assets to long-term liabilities: 1.7
    $2,093,000 ÷ $1,210,000
9. Ratio of liabilities to stockholders' equity: 1.0
    $1,960,000 ÷ $1,883,000

10. Number of times interest charges earned: 6.2
    ($545,000 + $105,000) ÷ $105,000
11. Number of times preferred dividends earned: 6.1
    $245,000 ÷ $40,000
12. Ratio of net sales to assets: 1.5
    $5,000,000 ÷ [($3,593,000 + $2,948,000) ÷ 2]
13. Rate earned on total assets: 10.0%
    ($245,000 + $105,000) ÷ [($3,843,000 + $3,173,000) ÷ 2]
14. Rate earned on stockholders' equity: 13.6%
    $245,000 ÷ [($1,883,000 + $1,723,000) ÷ 2]
15. Rate earned on common stockholders' equity: 15.7%
    ($245,000 − $40,000) ÷ [($1,383,000 + $1,223,000) ÷ 2]
16. Earnings per share on common stock: $4.10
    ($245,000 − $40,000) ÷ 50,000
17. Price-earnings ratio: 6.1
    $25 ÷ $4.10
18. Dividends per share of common stock: $0.90
    $45,000 ÷ 50,000 shares
19. Dividend yield: 3.6%
    $0.90 ÷ $25

SELF-EXAMINATION QUESTIONS

Answers at End of Chapter

Matching

Match each of the following statements with its proper term. Some terms may not be used.

A. **accounts receivable turnover**

B. **acid-test ratio**

C. **common-size statement**

D. **current ratio**

E. **dividend yield**

F. **dividends per share**

G. **earnings per share (EPS) on common stock**

H. **horizontal analysis**

I. **inventory turnover**

J. **leverage**

K. **Management Discussion and Analysis**

L. **number of days' sales in inventory**

M. **number of days' sales in receivables**

N. **number of times interest charges earned**

O. **price-earnings (P/E) ratio**

P. **profitability**

Q. **quick assets**

R. **rate earned on common stockholders' equity**

S. **rate earned on stockholders' equity**

____ 1. The percentage of increases and decreases in corresponding items in comparative financial statements.

____ 2. The sum of cash, receivables, and marketable securities.

____ 3. The relationship between the volume of sales and inventory, computed by dividing the inventory at the end of the year by the average daily cost of goods sold.

____ 4. The ability of a firm to pay its debts as they come due.

____ 5. The relationship between credit sales and accounts receivable, computed by dividing the net accounts receivable at the end of the year by the average daily sales on account.

____ 6. The relationship between credit sales and accounts receivable, computed by dividing net sales on account by the average net accounts receivable.

____ 7. The tendency of the rate earned on stockholders' equity to vary from the rate earned on total assets because the amount earned on assets acquired through the use of funds provided by creditors varies from the interest paid to these creditors.

____ 8. A financial statement in which all items are expressed only in relative terms.

____ 9. A measure of profitability computed by dividing net income by total stockholders' equity.

____ 10. The excess of total current assets over total current liabilities at some point in time.

____ 11. The ratio of the market price per share of common stock, at a specific date, to the annual earnings per share.

____ 12. A measure of the profitability of assets, without regard to the equity of creditors and stockholders in the assets.

____ 13. The profitability ratio of net income available to common shareholders to the number of common shares outstanding.

____ 14. The ratio of the sum of cash, receivables, and marketable securities to current liabilities.

T.	**rate earned on total assets**
U.	**ratio of fixed assets to long-term liabilities**
V.	**ratio of liabilities to stockholders' equity**
W.	**ratio of net sales to assets**
X.	**solvency**
Y.	**vertical analysis**
Z.	**working capital**

___ 15. The percentage analysis of component parts in relation to the total of the parts in a single financial statement.

___ 16. A measure of profitability computed by dividing net income, reduced by preferred dividend requirements, by common stockholders' equity.

___ 17. The ratio of current assets to current liabilities.

___ 18. The relationship between the volume of goods sold and inventory, computed by dividing the cost of goods sold by the average inventory.

___ 19. The ability of a firm to earn income.

___ 20. An annual report disclosure that provides an analysis of the results of operations and financial condition.

Multiple Choice

1. What type of analysis is indicated by the following?

	Amount	Percent
Current assets	$100,000	20%
Property, plant, and equipment	400,000	80
Total assets	$500,000	100%

    A. Vertical analysis
    B. Horizontal analysis
    C. Profitability analysis
    D. Contribution margin analysis

2. Which of the following measures indicates the ability of a firm to pay its current liabilities?
    A. Working capital
    B. Current ratio
    C. Acid-test ratio
    D. All of the above

3. The ratio determined by dividing total current assets by total current liabilities is:
    A. current ratio
    B. working capital ratio
    C. bankers' ratio
    D. all of the above

4. The ratio of the quick assets to current liabilities, which indicates the "instant" debt-paying ability of a firm, is:
    A. current ratio
    B. working capital ratio
    C. acid-test ratio
    D. bankers' ratio

5. A measure useful in evaluating the efficiency in the management of inventories is:
    A. working capital ratio
    B. acid-test ratio
    C. number of days' sales in inventory
    D. ratio of fixed assets to long-term liabilities

CLASS DISCUSSION QUESTIONS

1. What is the difference between horizontal and vertical analysis of financial statements?
2. What is the advantage of using comparative statements for financial analysis rather than statements for a single date or period?
3. The current year's amount of net income (after income tax) is 15% larger than that of the preceding year. Does this indicate an improved operating performance? Discuss.
4. How would you respond to a horizontal analysis that showed an expense increasing by over 100%?
5. a. Name the major ratios useful in assessing solvency and profitability.
    b. Why is it important not to rely on only one ratio or measure in assessing the solvency or profitability of a business?
6. How would the current and acid-test ratios of a service business compare?
7. For Lindsay Corporation, the working capital at the end of the current year is $5,000 greater than the working capital at the end of the preceding year, reported as follows:

	Current Year	Preceding Year
Current assets:		
Cash, marketable securities, and receivables	$34,000	$30,000
Inventories	51,000	32,500
Total current assets	$85,000	$62,500
Current liabilities	42,500	25,000
Working capital	$42,500	$37,500

Has the current position improved? Explain.

8. A company that grants terms of n/30 on all sales has a yearly accounts receivable turnover, based on monthly averages, of 6. Is this a satisfactory turnover? Discuss.
9. What does an increase in the number of days' sales in receivables ordinarily indicate about the credit and collection policy of the firm?
10. a. Why is it advantageous to have a high inventory turnover?
    b. Is it possible for the inventory turnover to be too high? Discuss.
    c. Is it possible to have a high inventory turnover and a high number of days' sales in inventory? Discuss.
11. What do the following data taken from a comparative balance sheet indicate about the company's ability to borrow additional funds on a long-term basis in the current year as compared to the preceding year?

	Current Year	Preceding Year
Fixed assets (net)	$175,000	$170,000
Total long-term liabilities	70,000	85,000

12. What does a decrease in the ratio of liabilities to stockholders' equity indicate about the margin of safety for a firm's creditors and the ability of the firm to withstand adverse business conditions?
13. In computing the ratio of net sales to assets, why are long-term investments excluded in determining the amount of the total assets?
14. In determining the number of times interest charges are earned, why are interest charges added to income before income tax?
15. In determining the rate earned on total assets, why is interest expense added to net income before dividing by total assets?
16. a. Why is the rate earned on stockholders' equity by a thriving business ordinarily higher than the rate earned on total assets?
    b. Should the rate earned on common stockholders' equity normally be higher or lower than the rate earned on total stockholders' equity? Explain.
17. The net income (after income tax) of A. L. Gibson Inc. was $25 per common share in the latest year and $40 per common share for the preceding year. At the beginning of the latest year, the number of shares outstanding was doubled by a stock split. There were no other changes in the amount of stock outstanding. What were the earnings per share in the preceding year, adjusted for comparison with the latest year?
18. The price-earnings ratio for the common stock of Essian Company was 10 at December 31, the end of the current fiscal year. What does the ratio indicate about the selling price of the common stock in relation to current earnings?
19. Why would the dividend yield differ significantly from the rate earned on common stockholders' equity?
20. Favorable business conditions may bring about certain seemingly unfavorable ratios, and unfavorable business operations may result in apparently favorable ratios. For example, Sanchez Company increased its sales and net income substantially for the current year, yet the current ratio at the end of the year is lower than at the beginning of the year. Discuss some possible causes of the apparent weakening of the current position, while sales and net income have increased substantially.
21. a. What are the major components of an annual report?
    b. Indicate the purpose of the Financial Highlights section and the Management Discussion and Analysis.

EXERCISES

Exercise 16–1
Vertical analysis of income statement

Objective 1

✓ 2003 net income: $77,000; 10% of sales

Revenue and expense data for Murry Cabinet Co. are as follows:

	2003	2002
Sales	$770,000	$700,000
Cost of goods sold	415,800	350,000
Selling expenses	138,600	140,000
Administrative expenses	84,700	105,000
Income tax expense	53,900	49,000

a. Prepare an income statement in comparative form, stating each item for both 2003 and 2002 as a percent of sales.
b. Comment on the significant changes disclosed by the comparative income statement.

Exercise 16–2
Vertical analysis of income statement

Objective 1

✓ a. Fiscal year 1998 income from operations, 11.2% of revenues

The following comparative income statement (in thousands of dollars) for the fiscal years 1999 and 1998 was adapted from the annual report of **Dell Computer Corporation**:

	Fiscal Year 1999	Fiscal Year 1998
Revenues	$25,265	$18,243
Costs and expenses:		
Cost of sales	20,047	14,137
Gross profit	$ 5,218	$ 4,106
Operating expenses	2,955	2,060
Income from operations	$ 2,263	$ 2,046

a. Prepare a comparative income statement for fiscal years 1999 (ended January 28, 2000) and 1998 (ended January 29, 1999) in vertical form, stating each item as a percent of revenues. Round to one digit after the decimal place.
b. Comment on the significant changes.

Exercise 16–3
Common-size income statement

Objective 1

✓ a. Keystone net income: $218,500; 9.1% of sales

Revenue and expense data for the current calendar year for Keystone Publishing Company and for the publishing industry are as follows. The Keystone Publishing Company data are expressed in dollars. The publishing industry averages are expressed in percentages.

	Keystone Publishing Company	Publishing Industry Average
Sales	$2,450,000	101.0%
Sales returns and allowances	24,500	1.0
Cost of goods sold	850,000	40.0
Selling expenses	970,000	39.0
Administrative expenses	280,000	10.5
Other income	30,000	1.2
Other expense	40,000	1.7
Income tax expense	97,000	4.0

a. Prepare a common-size income statement comparing the results of operations for Keystone Publishing Company with the industry average. Round to one digit after the decimal place.
b. As far as the data permit, comment on significant relationships revealed by the comparisons.

Exercise 16–4
Vertical analysis of balance sheet

Objective 1

✓ Retained earnings, Dec. 31, 2003, 37.27%

Balance sheet data for Atlas Fitness Equipment Company on December 31, the end of the fiscal year, are as follows:

	2003	2002
Current assets	$180,000	$150,000
Property, plant, and equipment	340,000	330,000
Intangible assets	30,000	35,000
Current liabilities	120,000	125,000
Long-term liabilities	175,000	150,000
Common stock	50,000	40,000
Retained earnings	205,000	200,000

Prepare a comparative balance sheet for 2003 and 2002, stating each asset as a percent of total assets and each liability and stockholders' equity item as a percent of the total liabilities and stockholders' equity. Round to two digits after the decimal place.

Exercise 16–5
Horizontal analysis of the income statement

Objective 1

✓ a. Net income decrease, 31.67%

Income statement data for Neon Flashlight Company for the year ended December 31, 2003 and 2002, are as follows:

	2003	2002
Sales	$400,000	$460,000
Cost of goods sold	170,000	200,000
Gross profit	$230,000	$260,000
Selling expenses	$ 70,000	$ 60,000
Administrative expenses	50,000	40,000
Total operating expenses	$120,000	$100,000
Income before income tax	$110,000	$160,000
Income tax expense	28,000	40,000
Net income	$ 82,000	$120,000

a. Prepare a comparative income statement with horizontal analysis, indicating the increase (decrease) for 2003 when compared with 2002. Round to two digits after the decimal place.
b. What conclusions can be drawn from the horizontal analysis?

Exercise 16–6
Current position analysis

Objective 2

✓ Current year working capital, $1,085,000

The following data were taken from the balance sheet of Precision Gears Company:

	Current Year	Preceding Year
Cash	$280,000	$265,000
Marketable securities	131,000	121,000
Accounts and notes receivable (net)	395,000	384,000
Inventories	570,000	555,000
Prepaid expenses	19,000	40,000
Accounts and notes payable (short-term)	250,000	285,700
Accrued liabilities	60,000	64,300

a. Determine for each year (1) the working capital, (2) the current ratio, and (3) the acid-test ratio.
b. What conclusions can be drawn from these data as to the company's ability to meet its currently maturing debts?

Exercise 16–7
Current position analysis

Objective 2

PepsiCo, the parent company of Frito-Lay snack foods and Pepsi beverages, had the following current assets and current liabilities at the end of two recent years:

	Current Year (in millions)	Preceding Year (in millions)
Cash	$ 311	$1,928
Marketable securities	83	955
Accounts and notes receivable (net)	2,453	2,150
Inventories	1,016	732
Prepaid expenses	499	486
Short-term borrowings	3,921	—
Accounts and notes payable (short-term)	3,870	3,617
Income taxes payable	123	640

✓ a. (1) Current year's current ratio, 0.55

a. Determine the (1) current ratio and (2) acid-test ratio for both years. Round to two digits after the decimal place.
b. What conclusions can you draw from these data?

Exercise 16–8
Current position analysis
Objective 2

The bond indenture for the 10-year, 9½% debenture bonds dated January 2, 2002, required working capital of $350,000, a current ratio of 1.5, and an acid-test ratio of 1 at the end of each calendar year until the bonds mature. At December 31, 2003, the three measures were computed as follows:

1. Current assets:

Cash	$245,000	
Marketable securities	123,000	
Accounts and notes receivable (net)	172,000	
Inventories	295,000	
Prepaid expenses	35,000	
Goodwill	150,000	
Total current assets		$1,020,000
Current liabilities:		
Accounts and short-term notes payable	$350,000	
Accrued liabilities	250,000	
Total current liabilities		600,000
Working capital		$ 420,000

2. Current ratio = 1.7 ($1,020,000 ÷ $600,000)
3. Acid-test ratio = 1.54 ($540,000 ÷ $350,000), rounded

a. Can you find any errors in the determination of the three measures of current position analysis?
b. Is the company satisfying the terms of the bond indenture?

Exercise 16–9
Accounts receivable analysis
Objective 2

The following data are taken from the financial statements of Northern Expressions Company. Terms of all sales are 1/10, n/60.

	Current Year	Preceding Year
Accounts receivable, end of year	$ 222,466	$ 235,068
Monthly average accounts receivable (net)	207,143	216,667
Net sales on account	1,450,000	1,300,000

✓ a. Accounts receivable turnover, current year, 7.0

a. Determine for each year (1) the accounts receivable turnover and (2) the number of days' sales in receivables. Round to one digit after the decimal place.
b. What conclusions can be drawn from these data concerning accounts receivable and credit policies?

Exercise 16–10
Accounts receivable analysis
Objective 2

Sears and **JCPenney** are two of the largest department store chains in the United States. Both companies offer credit to their customers through their own credit card operations. Information from the financial statements for both companies for two recent years is as follows (all numbers are in millions):

	Sears	JCPenney
Sales—recent year	$41,332	$30,678
Credit card receivables—recent year balance	18,946	4,415
Credit card receivables—previous year balance	20,956	3,819

✓ a. (1) Sears' accounts receivable turnover, 2.1

a. Determine the (1) accounts receivable turnover and (2) the number of days' sales in receivables for both companies. Round to one digit after the decimal place.

b. Compare the two companies with regard to their credit card policies.

Exercise 16–11
Inventory analysis

Objective 2

✓ a. Inventory turnover, current year, 6.0

The following data were extracted from the income statement of Sierra Instruments Inc.:

	Current Year	Preceding Year
Sales	$3,600,000	$3,900,000
Beginning inventories	310,000	290,000
Cost of goods sold	2,010,000	2,400,000
Ending inventories	360,000	310,000

a. Determine for each year (1) the inventory turnover and (2) the number of days' sales in inventory. Round to two digits after the decimal place.

b. What conclusions can be drawn from these data concerning the inventories?

Exercise 16–12
Inventory analysis

Objective 2

✓ a. (1) Dell inventory turnover, 55.9

Dell Computer Corporation and **Compaq Computer Corporation** compete with each other in the personal computer market. Dell's strategy is to assemble computers to customer orders, rather than for inventory. Thus, for example, Dell will build and deliver a computer within four days of a customer entering an order on a Web page. Compaq, on the other hand, builds some computers prior to receiving an order, then sells from this inventory once an order is received. Below is selected financial information for both companies from a recent year's financial statements (in millions):

	Dell Computer Corporation	Compaq Computer Corporation
Sales	$18,243	$31,169
Cost of goods sold	14,137	23,980
Inventory, beginning of period	233	1,570
Inventory, end of period	273	2,005

a. Determine for both companies (1) the inventory turnover and (2) the number of days' sales in inventory. Round to one digit after the decimal place.

b. Interpret the inventory ratios by considering Dell's and Compaq's operating strategies.

Exercise 16–13
Ratio of liabilities to stockholders' equity and number of times interest charges earned

Objective 2

✓ a. Ratio of liabilities to stockholders' equity, Dec. 31, 2003, 0.63

The following data were taken from the financial statements of Clear Spring Water Co. for December 31, 2003 and 2002:

	December 31, 2003	December 31, 2002
Accounts payable	$ 150,000	$ 204,000
Current maturities of serial bonds payable	300,000	300,000
Serial bonds payable, 8%, issued 1998, due 2008	1,800,000	2,100,000
Common stock, $1 par value	100,000	100,000
Paid-in capital in excess of par	800,000	800,000
Retained earnings	2,700,000	2,200,000

The income before income tax was $252,000 and $216,000 for the years 2003 and 2002, respectively.

a. Determine the ratio of liabilities to stockholders' equity at the end of each year. Round to two digits after the decimal place. *(continued)*

b.   Determine the number of times the bond interest charges are earned during the year
for both years.
c.   What conclusions can be drawn from these data as to the company's ability to meet
its currently maturing debts?

Exercise 16–14
Profitability ratios

Objective 3

✓ a. Rate earned on total assets,
2004, 18.7%

The following selected data were taken from the financial statements of Central States
Transportation Co. for December 31, 2004, 2003, and 2002:

	December 31, 2004	December 31, 2003	December 31, 2002
Total assets	$3,200,000	$2,800,000	$2,200,000
Notes payable (10% interest)	400,000	400,000	400,000
Common stock	900,000	900,000	900,000
Preferred $12 stock, $100 par, cumulative, nonparticipating (no change during year)	500,000	500,000	500,000
Retained earnings	1,330,000	870,000	330,000

The 2004 net income was $520,000, and the 2003 net income was $600,000. No dividends
on common stock were declared between 2002 and 2004.

a.   Determine the rate earned on total assets, the rate earned on stockholders' equity,
and the rate earned on common stockholders' equity for the years 2003 and 2004.
Round to one digit after the decimal place.
b.   What conclusions can be drawn from these data as to the company's profitability?

Exercise 16–15
Profitability ratios

Objective 3

✓ a. 1999 rate earned on total
assets, 7.87%

Ann Taylor Stores Corporation sells professional women's apparel through company-
owned retail stores. Recent financial information for Ann Taylor is provided below (all
numbers in thousands):

	Fiscal Year Ended	
	Jan. 31, 1999	Jan. 31, 1998
Net income	$39,324	$11,824
Interest expense	18,117	19,989

	Jan. 31, 1999	Jan. 31, 1998	Jan. 31, 1997
Total assets	$775,417	$683,661	$688,139
Total stockholders' equity	432,699	384,107	370,582

An analysis of 50 apparel retail companies indicates an industry average rate earned on
total assets of 24.4% and an average rate earned on stockholders' equity of 53.03%.

a.   Determine the rate earned on total assets for Ann Taylor for the fiscal years ended
January 31, 1999, and January 31, 1998. Round to two digits after the decimal place.
b.   Determine the rate earned on stockholders' equity for Ann Taylor for the fiscal years
ended January 31, 1999, and January 31, 1998. Round to two digits after the decimal
place.
c.   Evaluate the two-year trend for the profitability ratios determined in (a) and (b).
d.   Evaluate Ann Taylor's profit performance relative to the industry.

Exercise 16–16
*Six measures of solvency or
profitability*

Objectives 2, 3

✓ c. Ratio of net sales to assets, 1.14

The following data were taken from the financial statements of Austin Labs Inc. for the
current fiscal year:

Property, plant, and equipment (net)	$2,500,000
Liabilities:	
Current liabilities	$ 100,000
Mortgage note payable, 7.5%, issued 1993, due 2008	1,200,000
Total liabilities	$1,300,000

(continued)

Stockholders' equity:

Preferred $8 stock, $100 par, cumulative, nonparticipating (no change during year)			$ 600,000
Common stock, $10 par (no change during year)			1,600,000
Retained earnings:			
Balance, beginning of year	$900,000		
Net income	500,000	$1,400,000	
Preferred dividends	$ 48,000		
Common dividends	52,000	100,000	
Balance, end of year			1,300,000
Total stockholders' equity			$3,500,000
Net sales			$5,000,000
Interest expense			$ 90,000

Assuming that long-term investments totaled $200,000 throughout the year and that total assets were $4,400,000 at the beginning of the year, determine the following: (a) ratio of fixed assets to long-term liabilities, (b) ratio of liabilities to stockholders' equity, (c) ratio of net sales to assets, (d) rate earned on total assets, (e) rate earned on stockholders' equity, and (f) rate earned on common stockholders' equity. Round to two digits after the decimal place.

Exercise 16–17
Five measures of solvency or profitability

Objectives 2, 3

✓ d. Price-earnings ratio, 20

The balance sheet for Aspen Properties Inc. at the end of the current fiscal year indicated the following:

Bonds payable, 12% (issued in 1993, due in 2013)	$3,000,000
Preferred $10 stock, $100 par	500,000
Common stock, $20 par	5,000,000

Income before income tax was $800,000, and income taxes were $200,000 for the current year. Cash dividends paid on common stock during the current year totaled $220,000. The common stock was selling for $44 per share at the end of the year. Determine each of the following: (a) number of times bond interest charges were earned, (b) number of times preferred dividends were earned, (c) earnings per share on common stock, (d) price-earnings ratio, (e) dividends per share of common stock, and (f) dividend yield. Round to two digits after the decimal place.

Exercise 16–18
Earnings per share, price-earnings ratio, dividend yield

Objective 3

✓ b. Price-earnings ratio, 30

The following information was taken from the financial statements of Arctic Air Conditioners Inc. for December 31 of the current fiscal year:

Common stock, $12 par value (no change during the year)	$4,800,000
Preferred $9 stock, $100 par, cumulative, nonparticipating (no change during year) ...	1,200,000

The net income was $588,000 and the declared dividends on the common stock were $500,000 for the current year. The market price of the common stock is $36 per share.

For the common stock, determine the (a) earnings per share, (b) price-earnings ratio, (c) dividends per share, and (d) dividend yield. Round to two digits after the decimal place.

Exercise 16–19
Earnings per share

Objective 3

✓ b. Earnings per share on common stock, $8.64

The net income reported on the income statement of Southern Pulp and Paper Co. was $2,800,000. There were 250,000 shares of $20 par common stock and 80,000 shares of $8 cumulative preferred stock outstanding throughout the current year. The income statement included two extraordinary items: a $400,000 gain from condemnation of land and a $600,000 loss arising from flood damage, both after applicable income tax. Determine the per share figures for common stock for (a) income before extraordinary items and (b) net income.

PROBLEMS SERIES A

Problem 16–1A
Horizontal analysis for income statement
Objective 1

GENERAL LEDGER

✓ 1. Sales, 30% increase

For 2003, Better Biscuit Company reported its most significant increase in net income in years. At the end of the year, John Newton, the president, is presented with the following condensed comparative income statement:

Better Biscuit Company
Comparative Income Statement
For the Years Ended December 31, 2003 and 2002

	2003	2002
Sales	$715,000	$550,000
Sales returns and allowances	5,000	5,000
Net sales	$710,000	$545,000
Cost of goods sold	281,250	225,000
Gross profit	$428,750	$320,000
Selling expenses	$136,400	$110,000
Administrative expenses	42,350	35,000
Total operating expenses	$178,750	$145,000
Income from operations	$250,000	$175,000
Other income	3,500	3,000
Income before income tax	$253,500	$178,000
Income tax expense	85,000	60,000
Net income	$168,500	$118,000

Instructions

1. Prepare a comparative income statement with horizontal analysis for the two-year period, using 2002 as the base year. Round to two digits after the decimal place.
2. To the extent the data permit, comment on the significant relationships revealed by the horizontal analysis prepared in (1).

Problem 16–2A
Vertical analysis for income statement
Objective 1

GENERAL LEDGER
SPREADSHEET

✓ 1. Net income, 2003, 8.55%

For 2003, Stainless Flow Systems Inc. initiated a sales promotion campaign that included the expenditure of an additional $50,000 for advertising. At the end of the year, Edwardo Gonzalez, the president, is presented with the following condensed comparative income statement:

Stainless Flow Systems Inc.
Comparative Income Statement
For the Years Ended December 31, 2003 and 2002

	2003	2002
Sales	$810,000	$775,000
Sales returns and allowances	5,000	5,000
Net sales	$805,000	$770,000
Cost of goods sold	438,700	416,000
Gross profit	$366,300	$354,000
Selling expenses	$165,800	$115,800
Administrative expenses	96,600	93,400
Total operating expenses	$262,400	$209,200
Income from operations	$103,900	$144,800
Other income	2,000	1,800
Income before income tax	$105,900	$146,600
Income tax expense	37,000	51,000
Net income	$ 68,900	$ 95,600

Instructions

1. Prepare a comparative income statement for the two-year period, presenting an analysis of each item in relationship to net sales for each of the years. Round to two digits after the decimal place.
2. To the extent the data permit, comment on the significant relationships revealed by the vertical analysis prepared in (1).

Problem 16–3A
Effect of transactions on current position analysis
Objective 2

✓ 1. Acid-test ratio, 1.45

Data pertaining to the current position of Flintstone Aggregates Inc. are as follows:

Cash	$150,000
Marketable securities	64,000
Accounts and notes receivable (net)	221,000
Inventories	294,000
Prepaid expenses	11,000
Accounts payable	204,000
Notes payable (short-term)	66,000
Accrued expenses	30,000

Instructions

1. Compute (a) the working capital, (b) the current ratio, and (c) the acid-test ratio. Round to two digits after the decimal place.
2. List the following captions on a sheet of paper:

Transaction	Working Capital	Current Ratio	Acid-Test Ratio

Compute the working capital, the current ratio, and the acid-test ratio after each of the following transactions, and record the results in the appropriate columns. Consider each transaction separately and assume that only that transaction affects the data given above. Round to two digits after the decimal point.
a. Sold marketable securities at no gain or loss, $34,000.
b. Paid accounts payable, $60,000.
c. Purchased goods on account, $40,000.
d. Paid notes payable, $20,000.
e. Declared a cash dividend, $25,000.
f. Declared a common stock dividend on common stock, $16,500.
g. Borrowed cash from bank on a long-term note, $120,000.
h. Received cash on account, $86,000.
i. Issued additional shares of stock for cash, $100,000.
j. Paid cash for prepaid expenses, $9,000.

Problem 16–4A
Nineteen measures of solvency and profitability
Objectives 2, 3

 SPREADSHEET

✓ 9. Ratio of liabilities to stockholders' equity, 0.7

The comparative financial statements of Integrity Technologies Inc. are as follows. The market price of Integrity Technologies Inc. common stock was $80 on December 31, 2003.

Integrity Technologies Inc.
Comparative Retained Earnings Statement
For the Years Ended December 31, 2003 and 2002

	Dec. 31, 2003	Dec. 31, 2002
Retained earnings, January 1	$ 964,000	$ 689,000
Add net income for year	503,000	435,000
Total	$1,467,000	$1,124,000
Deduct dividends:		
On preferred stock	$ 48,000	$ 40,000
On common stock	120,000	120,000
Total	$ 168,000	$ 160,000
Retained earnings, December 31	$1,299,000	$ 964,000

Integrity Technologies Inc.
Comparative Income Statement
For the Years Ended December 31, 2003 and 2002

	2003	2002
Sales (all on account)	$6,130,000	$5,640,000
Sales returns and allowances	30,000	40,000
Net sales	$6,100,000	$5,600,000
Cost of goods sold	2,800,000	2,550,000
Gross profit	$3,300,000	$3,050,000
Selling expenses	$1,450,000	$1,440,000
Administrative expenses..............................	1,000,000	910,000
Total operating expenses	$2,450,000	$2,350,000
Income from operations	$ 850,000	$ 700,000
Other income	40,000	30,000
	$ 890,000	$ 730,000
Other expense (interest)	157,000	85,000
Income before income tax	$ 733,000	$ 645,000
Income tax expense	230,000	210,000
Net income	$ 503,000	$ 435,000

Integrity Technologies Inc.
Comparative Balance Sheet
December 31, 2003 and 2002

	Dec. 31, 2003	Dec. 31, 2002
Assets		
Current assets:		
Cash	$ 200,000	$ 180,000
Marketable securities	923,000	215,000
Accounts receivable (net)	350,000	365,000
Inventories..............................	500,000	480,000
Prepaid expenses	26,000	24,000
Total current assets	$1,999,000	$1,264,000
Long-term investments	700,000	500,000
Property, plant, and equipment (net)	3,100,000	2,600,000
Total assets	$5,799,000	$4,364,000
Liabilities		
Current liabilities	$ 600,000	$ 400,000
Long-term liabilities:		
Mortgage note payable, 9%, due 2008	$ 800,000	—
Bonds payable, 8.5%, due 2012	1,000,000	$1,000,000
Total long-term liabilities	$1,800,000	$1,000,000
Total liabilities	$2,400,000	$1,400,000
Stockholders' Equity		
Preferred $8 stock, $100 par	$ 600,000	$ 500,000
Common stock, $10 par	1,500,000	1,500,000
Retained earnings........................	1,299,000	964,000
Total stockholders' equity	$3,399,000	$2,964,000
Total liabilities and stockholders' equity	$5,799,000	$4,364,000

Instructions
Determine the following measures for 2003, rounding to nearest single digit after the decimal point:

1. Working capital
2. Current ratio
3. Acid-test ratio
4. Accounts receivable turnover
5. Number of days' sales in receivables
6. Inventory turnover
7. Number of days' sales in inventory
8. Ratio of fixed assets to long-term liabilities
9. Ratio of liabilities to stockholders' equity
10. Number of times interest charges earned
11. Number of times preferred dividends earned
12. Ratio of net sales to assets
13. Rate earned on total assets
14. Rate earned on stockholders' equity
15. Rate earned on common stockholders' equity
16. Earnings per share on common stock
17. Price-earnings ratio
18. Dividends per share of common stock
19. Dividend yield

Problem 16–5A

Solvency and profitability trend analysis

Objectives 2, 3

Jupiter Company has provided the following comparative information:

	2003	2002	2001	2000	1999
Net income	$ 100,000	$ 150,000	$ 150,000	$ 200,000	$ 250,000
Income tax expense	30,000	45,000	45,000	60,000	75,000
Interest	144,000	138,000	138,000	126,000	120,000
Average total assets	2,300,000	2,150,000	2,000,000	1,750,000	1,500,000
Average total stockholders' equity	1,100,000	1,000,000	850,000	700,000	500,000

You have been asked to evaluate the historical performance of the company over the last five years.

Selected industry ratios have remained relatively steady for the last five years at the following levels:

	1999–2003
Rate earned on total assets	12%
Rate earned on stockholders' equity	15%
Number of times interest charges earned	3.0
Ratio of liabilities to stockholders' equity	1.5

Instructions

1. Prepare four line graphs, with the ratio on the vertical axis and the years on the horizontal axis for the following four ratios (round to two digits after the decimal place):
   a. Rate earned on total assets
   b. Rate earned on stockholders' equity
   c. Number of times interest charges earned
   d. Ratio of liabilities to stockholders' equity (using average balances)
   Display both the company ratio and the industry benchmark on each graph (each graph should have two lines).
2. Prepare an analysis of the graphs in (1).

PROBLEMS SERIES B

Problem 16–1B
Horizontal analysis for income statement

Objective 1

GENERAL LEDGER

✓ 1. Sales, 15% increase

For 2003, Chow Company reported its most significant decline in net income in years. At the end of the year, Hai Chow, the president, is presented with the following condensed comparative income statement:

Chow Company
Comparative Income Statement
For the Years Ended December 31, 2003 and 2002

	2003	2002
Sales	$690,000	$600,000
Sales returns and allowances	5,000	2,000
Net sales	$685,000	$598,000
Cost of goods sold	341,600	280,000
Gross profit	$343,400	$318,000
Selling expenses	$147,000	$105,000
Administrative expenses	81,250	65,000
Total operating expenses	$228,250	$170,000
Income from operations	$115,150	$148,000
Other income	2,500	2,000
Income before income tax	$117,650	$150,000
Income tax expense	32,000	40,000
Net income	$ 85,650	$110,000

Instructions

1. Prepare a comparative income statement with horizontal analysis for the two-year period, using 2002 as the base year. Round to two digits after the decimal place.
2. To the extent the data permit, comment on the significant relationships revealed by the horizontal analysis prepared in (1).

Problem 16–2B
Vertical analysis for income statement

Objective 1

GENERAL LEDGER

SPREADSHEET

✓ 1. Net income, 2003, 13.58%

For 2003, Guardian Home Security Company initiated a sales promotion campaign that included the expenditure of an additional $10,000 for advertising. At the end of the year, Gordon Kincaid, the president, is presented with the following condensed comparative income statement:

Guardian Home Security Company
Comparative Income Statement
For the Years Ended December 31, 2003 and 2002

	2003	2002
Sales	$595,000	$485,000
Sales returns and allowances	6,000	5,000
Net sales	$589,000	$480,000
Cost of goods sold	253,000	216,000
Gross profit	$336,000	$264,000
Selling expenses	$153,000	$136,500
Administrative expenses	71,000	64,500
Total operating expenses	$224,000	$201,000
Income from operations	$112,000	$ 63,000
Other income	2,500	2,000
Income before income tax	$114,500	$ 65,000
Income tax expense	34,500	20,000
Net income	$ 80,000	$ 45,000

Instructions

1. Prepare a comparative income statement for the two-year period, presenting an analysis of each item in relationship to net sales for each of the years. Round to two digits after the decimal place.
2. To the extent the data permit, comment on the significant relationships revealed by the vertical analysis prepared in (1).

Problem 16–3B

Effect of transactions on current position analysis

Objective 2

✓ 1. Current ratio, 1.96

Data pertaining to the current position of Porter Glass Company are as follows:

Cash	$221,000
Marketable securities	95,000
Accounts and notes receivable (net)	345,000
Inventories	410,000
Prepaid expenses	22,000
Accounts payable	412,000
Notes payable (short-term)	100,000
Accrued expenses	45,000

Instructions

1. Compute (a) the working capital, (b) the current ratio, and (c) the acid-test ratio. Round to two digits after the decimal place.
2. List the following captions on a sheet of paper:

Transaction	Working Capital	Current Ratio	Acid-Test Ratio

Compute the working capital, the current ratio, and the acid-test ratio after each of the following transactions, and record the results in the appropriate columns. Consider each transaction separately and assume that only that transaction affects the data given above. Round to two digits after the decimal point.
   a. Sold marketable securities at no gain or loss, $56,000.
   b. Paid accounts payable, $60,000.
   c. Purchased goods on account, $80,000.
   d. Paid notes payable, $40,000.
   e. Declared a cash dividend, $25,000.
   f. Declared a common stock dividend on common stock, $28,500.
   g. Borrowed cash from bank on a long-term note, $120,000.
   h. Received cash on account, $164,000.
   i. Issued additional shares of stock for cash, $250,000.
   j. Paid cash for prepaid expenses, $10,000.

Problem 16–4B

Nineteen measures of solvency and profitability

Objectives 2, 3

SPREADSHEET

✓ 5. Number of days' sales in receivables, 45.4

The comparative financial statements of Victor Audio Company are as follows. The market price of Victor Audio Company common stock was $105 on December 31, 2003.

Victor Audio Company
Comparative Retained Earnings Statement
For the Years Ended December 31, 2003 and 2002

	Dec. 31, 2003	Dec. 31, 2002
Retained earnings, January 1	$394,000	$ 50,000
Add net income for year	420,000	378,000
Total	$814,000	$428,000
Deduct dividends:		
On preferred stock	$ 30,000	$ 18,000
On common stock	16,000	16,000
Total	$ 46,000	$ 34,000
Retained earnings, December 31	$768,000	$394,000

Victor Audio Company
Comparative Income Statement
For the Years Ended December 31, 2003 and 2002

	2003	2002
Sales (all on account)	$2,170,000	$1,960,000
Sales returns and allowances	70,000	60,000
Net sales	$2,100,000	$1,900,000
Cost of goods sold	840,000	770,000
Gross profit	$1,260,000	$1,130,000
Selling expenses	$ 410,000	$ 370,000
Administrative expenses	305,000	290,000
Total operating expenses	$ 715,000	$ 660,000
Income from operations	$ 545,000	$ 470,000
Other income	20,000	15,000
	$ 565,000	$ 485,000
Other expense (interest)	104,000	72,000
Income before income tax	$ 461,000	$ 413,000
Income tax expense	41,000	35,000
Net income	$ 420,000	$ 378,000

Victor Audio Company
Comparative Balance Sheet
December 31, 2003 and 2002

	Dec. 31, 2003	Dec. 31, 2002
Assets		
Current assets:		
Cash	$ 87,000	$ 176,000
Marketable securities	258,000	335,000
Accounts receivable (net)	261,000	235,000
Inventories	212,000	190,000
Prepaid expenses	25,000	18,000
Total current assets	$ 843,000	$ 954,000
Long-term investments	1,000,000	400,000
Property, plant, and equipment (net)	1,675,000	1,050,000
Total assets	$3,518,000	$2,404,000
Liabilities		
Current liabilities	$ 450,000	$ 310,000
Long-term liabilities:		
Mortgage note payable, 8%, due 2008	$ 400,000	—
Bonds payable, 12%, due 2012	600,000	$ 600,000
Total long-term liabilities	$1,000,000	$ 600,000
Total liabilities	$1,450,000	$ 910,000
Stockholders' Equity		
Preferred $6 stock, $100 par	$ 500,000	$ 300,000
Common stock, $10 par	800,000	800,000
Retained earnings	768,000	394,000
Total stockholders' equity	$2,068,000	$1,494,000
Total liabilities and stockholders' equity	$3,518,000	$2,404,000

Instructions

Determine the following measures for 2003, rounding to the nearest single digit after the decimal point:

1. Working capital
2. Current ratio
3. Acid-test ratio
4. Accounts receivable turnover
5. Number of days' sales in receivables
6. Inventory turnover
7. Number of days' sales in inventory
8. Ratio of fixed assets to long-term liabilities
9. Ratio of liabilities to stockholders' equity
10. Number of times interest charges earned
11. Number of times preferred dividends earned
12. Ratio of net sales to assets
13. Rate earned on total assets
14. Rate earned on stockholders' equity
15. Rate earned on common stockholders' equity
16. Earnings per share on common stock
17. Price-earnings ratio
18. Dividends per share of common stock
19. Dividend yield

Problem 16–5B
Solvency and profitability trend analysis

Objectives 2, 3

Nova Company has provided the following comparative information:

	2003	2002	2001	2000	1999
Net income	$ 400,000	$ 300,000	$ 200,000	$ 100,000	$ 50,000
Income tax expense	100,000	75,000	50,000	25,000	12,500
Interest	88,000	72,000	56,000	48,000	40,000
Average total assets	2,600,000	2,000,000	1,500,000	1,200,000	1,000,000
Average total stockholders' equity	1,500,000	1,100,000	800,000	600,000	500,000

You have been asked to evaluate the historical performance of the company over the last five years. Selected industry ratios have remained relatively steady for the last five years at the following levels:

	1999–2003
Rate earned on total assets	14%
Rate earned on stockholders' equity	18%
Number of times interest charges earned	5.0
Ratio of liabilities to stockholders' equity	0.9

Instructions

1. Prepare four line graphs, with the ratio on the vertical axis and the years on the horizontal axis for the following four ratios (rounded to two digits after the decimal place):
   a. Rate earned on total assets
   b. Rate earned on stockholders' equity
   c. Number of times interest charges earned
   d. Ratio of liabilities to stockholders' equity (using average balances)
   Display both the company ratio and the industry benchmark on each graph (each graph should have two lines).
2. Prepare an analysis of the graphs in (1).

CISCO SYSTEMS, INC. PROBLEM

Financial Statement Analysis

The financial statements for **Cisco Systems, Inc.**, are presented in Appendix G at the end of the text. The following additional information is available:

Accounts receivable at July 25, 1998	$1,303,000,000
Inventories at July 25, 1998	362,000,000
Total assets at July 25, 1998	9,043,000,000
Stockholders' equity at July 25, 1998	7,197,000,000

Assume that all sales are credit sales.

Instructions

1. Determine the following measures for 2000 and 1999, rounding to two digits after the decimal place.
   a. Working capital
   b. Current ratio
   c. Acid-test ratio
   d. Accounts receivable turnover
   e. Number of days' sales in receivables
   f. Inventory turnover
   g. Number of days' sales in inventory
   h. Ratio of liabilities to stockholders' equity
   i. Ratio of net sales to average total assets
   j. Rate earned on average total assets
   k. Rate earned on average common stockholders' equity
   l. Price-earnings ratio, assuming that the market price was $30.00 per share on July 31, 1999 and $62.75 on July 29, 2000.
   m. Percentage relationship of net income to net sales
2. What conclusions can be drawn from these analyses?

SPECIAL ACTIVITIES

**Activity 16–1
Camden Equipment Co.**
Ethics and professional conduct in business

Lee Camden, president of Camden Equipment Co., prepared a draft of the President's Letter to be included with Camden Equipment Co.'s 2003 annual report. The letter mentions a 10% increase in sales and a recent expansion of plant facilities but fails to mention the net loss of $180,000 for the year. You have been asked to review the letter for inclusion in the annual report.

How would you respond to the omission of the net loss of $180,000? Specifically, is such an action ethical?

**Activity 16–2
Crest Brewery**
Analysis of financing corporate growth

Assume that the president of Crest Brewery made the following statement in the President's Letter to Shareholders:

"The founding family and majority shareholders of the company do not believe in using debt to finance future growth. The founding family learned from hard experience during Prohibition and the Great Depression that debt can cause loss of flexibility and eventual loss of corporate control. The company will not place itself at such risk. As such, all future growth will be financed either by stock sales to the public or by internally generated resources."

As a public shareholder of this company, how would you respond to this policy?

Activity 16–3
Imex Computer
Company
Receivables and inventory turnover

Imex Computer Company has completed its fiscal year on December 31, 2003. The auditor, Sandra Blake, has approached the CFO, Travis Williams, regarding the year-end receivables and inventory levels of Imex. The following conversation takes place:

Sandra: We are beginning our audit of Imex and have prepared ratio analyses to determine if there have been significant changes in operations or financial position. This helps us guide the audit process. This analysis indicates that the inventory turnover has decreased from 5 to 2.8, while the accounts receivable turnover has decreased from 12 to 8. I was wondering if you could explain this change in operations.

Travis: There is little need for concern. The inventory represents computers that we were unable to sell during the holiday buying season. We are confident, however, that we will be able to sell these computers as we move into the next fiscal year.

Sandra: What gives you this confidence?

Travis: We will increase our advertising and provide some very attractive price concessions to move these machines. We have no choice. Newer technology is already out there, and we have to unload this inventory.

Sandra: . . . and the receivables?

Travis: As you may be aware, the company is under tremendous pressure to expand sales and profits. As a result, we lowered our credit standards to our commercial customers so that we would be able to sell products to a broader customer base. As a result of this policy change, we have been able to expand sales by 35%.

Sandra: Your responses have not been reassuring to me.

Travis: I'm a little confused. Assets are good, right? Why don't you look at our current ratio? It has improved, hasn't it? I would think that you would view that very favorably.

➤ Why is Sandra concerned about the inventory and accounts receivable turnover ratios and Travis' responses to them? What action may Sandra need to take? How would you respond to Travis' last comment?

Activity 16–4
Apple Computer and
Dell Computer
Vertical analysis

The condensed income statements through income from operations for **Apple Computer Co.** and **Dell Computer Corporation** are reproduced below for recent fiscal years (numbers in millions):

	Dell Computer Corporation For the Year Ended January 29, 1999	Apple Computer Co. For the Year Ended September 25, 1999
Sales (net)	$18,243	$6,134
Cost of sales	14,137	4,438
Gross profit	$ 4,106	$1,696
Selling, general, and administrative expense	$ 1,788	$ 314
Research and development	272	1,023
Operating expenses	$ 2,060	$1,337
Income from operations	$ 2,046	$ 359

Prepare comparative vertical analyses, rounding to two digits after the decimal point. Interpret the analyses.

Activity 16–5
Into the Real World
Horizontal analysis and profitability analysis

Go to the **Microsoft** Web site at **www.microsoft.com** and download Microsoft's comparative income statements for the last two fiscal years as an Excel® file. The most recent downloadable annual report can be found in the "Investor Relations" area of Microsoft's Web environment. Next, go to *The Wall Street Journal* and look up Microsoft in the NASDAQ National Market pages. Under this listing, report the price-earnings ratio and dividend yield for Microsoft.

Use the comparative income statement Excel file to prepare a horizontal analysis for the last two fiscal years. Use Microsoft's balance sheet and income statement information to determine the rate earned on stockholders' equity for the latest fiscal year. How do these analyses reconcile with Microsoft's price-earnings ratio and dividend yield?

Activity 16–6
Into the Real World
Solvency and profitability
analysis

One team should obtain the latest annual report for **Wal-Mart Stores Inc.**, and the other team should obtain the latest **Kmart Corp.** annual report. These annual reports can be obtained from a library or the SEC's EDGAR service.

EDGAR (Electronic Data Gathering, Analysis, and Retrieval) is the electronic archive of financial statements filed with the Securities and Exchange Commission (SEC). SEC documents can be retrieved using the EdgarScan service from **PricewaterhouseCoopers** at **edgarscan.pwcglobal.com**. To obtain annual report information, type in a company name in the appropriate space. EdgarScan will list the reports available to you for the company you've selected. Select the most recent annual report filing, identified as a 10-K or 10-K405. EdgarScan provides an outline of the report, including the separate financial statements. You can double-click the income statement and balance sheet for the selected company into an Excel spreadsheet for further analysis.

Each team should compute the following for their company:

a. Current ratio
b. Inventory turnover
c. Rate earned on stockholders' equity
d. Rate earned on total assets
e. Net income as a percentage of sales
f. Ratio of liabilities to stockholders' equity

As a class, prepare a report comparing the two companies for the latest fiscal period.

ANSWERS TO SELF-EXAMINATION QUESTIONS

Matching

1. H	4. X	7. J	10. Z	13. G	16. R	19. P
2. Q	5. M	8. C	11. O	14. B	17. D	20. K
3. L	6. A	9. S	12. T	15. Y	18. I	

Multiple Choice

1. **A** Percentage analysis indicating the relationship of the component parts to the total in a financial statement, such as the relationship of current assets to total assets (20% to 100%) in the question, is called vertical analysis (answer A). Percentage analysis of increases and decreases in corresponding items in comparative financial statements is called horizontal analysis (answer B). An example of horizontal analysis would be the presentation of the amount of current assets in the preceding balance sheet, along with the amount of current assets at the end of the current year, with the increase or decrease in current assets between the periods expressed as a percentage. Profitability analysis (answer C) is the analysis of a firm's ability to earn income. Contribution margin analysis (answer D) is discussed in a later managerial accounting chapter.

2. **D** Various solvency measures, categorized as current position analysis, indicate a firm's ability to meet currently maturing obligations. Each measure contributes in the analysis of a firm's current position and is most useful when viewed with other measures and when compared with similar measures for other periods and for other firms. Working capital (answer A) is the excess of current assets over current liabilities; the current ratio (answer B) is the ratio of current assets to current liabilities; and the acid-test ratio (answer C) is the ratio of the sum of cash, receivables, and marketable securities to current liabilities.

3. **D** The ratio of current assets to current liabilities is usually called the current ratio (answer A). It is sometimes called the working capital ratio (answer B) or bankers' ratio (answer C).

4. **C** The ratio of the sum of cash, receivables, and marketable securities (sometimes called quick assets) to current liabilities is called the acid-test ratio (answer C) or quick ratio. The current ratio (answer A), working capital ratio (answer B), and bankers' ratio (answer D) are terms that describe the ratio of current assets to current liabilities.

5. **C** The number of days' sales in inventory (answer C), which is determined by dividing the inventories at the end of the year by the average daily cost of goods sold, expresses the relationship between the cost of goods sold and inventory. It indicates the efficiency in the management of inventory. The working capital ratio (answer A) indicates the ability of the business to meet currently maturing obligations (debt). The acid-test ratio (answer B) indicates the "instant" debt-paying ability of the business. The ratio of fixed assets to long-term liabilities (answer D) indicates the margin of safety for long-term creditors.

Appendices

Appendix A: Interest Tables

Present Value of $1 at Compound Interest Due in n Periods: $p_{\overline{n}|i} = \dfrac{1}{(1 + i)^n}$						
n / i	5%	5.5%	6%	6.5%	7%	8%
1	0.95238	0.94787	0.94334	0.93897	0.93458	0.92593
2	0.90703	0.89845	0.89000	0.88166	0.87344	0.85734
3	0.86384	0.85161	0.83962	0.82785	0.81630	0.79383
4	0.82270	0.80722	0.79209	0.77732	0.76290	0.73503
5	0.78353	0.76513	0.74726	0.72988	0.71290	0.68058
6	0.74622	0.72525	0.70496	0.68533	0.66634	0.63017
7	0.71068	0.68744	0.66506	0.64351	0.62275	0.58349
8	0.67684	0.65160	0.62741	0.60423	0.58201	0.54027
9	0.64461	0.61763	0.59190	0.56735	0.54393	0.50025
10	0.61391	0.58543	0.55840	0.53273	0.50835	0.46319
11	0.58468	0.55491	0.52679	0.50021	0.47509	0.42888
12	0.55684	0.52598	0.49697	0.46968	0.44401	0.39711
13	0.53032	0.49856	0.46884	0.44102	0.41496	0.36770
14	0.50507	0.47257	0.44230	0.41410	0.38782	0.34046
15	0.48102	0.44793	0.41726	0.38883	0.36245	0.31524
16	0.45811	0.42458	0.39365	0.36510	0.33874	0.29189
17	0.43630	0.40245	0.37136	0.34281	0.31657	0.27027
18	0.41552	0.38147	0.35034	0.32189	0.29586	0.25025
19	0.39573	0.36158	0.33051	0.30224	0.27651	0.23171
20	0.37689	0.34273	0.31180	0.28380	0.25842	0.21455
21	0.35894	0.32486	0.29416	0.26648	0.24151	0.19866
22	0.34185	0.30793	0.27750	0.25021	0.22571	0.18394
23	0.32557	0.29187	0.26180	0.23494	0.21095	0.17032
24	0.31007	0.27666	0.24698	0.22060	0.19715	0.15770
25	0.29530	0.26223	0.23300	0.20714	0.18425	0.14602
26	0.28124	0.24856	0.21981	0.19450	0.17211	0.13520
27	0.26785	0.23560	0.20737	0.18263	0.16093	0.12519
28	0.25509	0.22332	0.19563	0.17148	0.15040	0.11591
29	0.24295	0.21168	0.18456	0.16101	0.14056	0.10733
30	0.23138	0.20064	0.17411	0.15119	0.13137	0.09938
31	0.22036	0.19018	0.16426	0.14196	0.12277	0.09202
32	0.20987	0.18027	0.15496	0.13329	0.11474	0.08520
33	0.19987	0.17087	0.14619	0.12516	0.10724	0.07889
34	0.19036	0.16196	0.13791	0.11752	0.10022	0.07304
35	0.18129	0.15352	0.13010	0.11035	0.09366	0.06764
40	0.14205	0.11746	0.09722	0.08054	0.06678	0.04603
45	0.11130	0.08988	0.07265	0.05879	0.04761	0.03133
50	0.08720	0.06877	0.05429	0.04291	0.03395	0.02132

Present Value of \$1 at Compound Interest Due in *n* Periods: $p_{\overline{n}|i} = \dfrac{1}{(1 + i)^n}$

n \ i	9%	10%	11%	12%	13%	14%
1	0.91743	0.90909	0.90090	0.89286	0.88496	0.87719
2	0.84168	0.82645	0.81162	0.79719	0.78315	0.76947
3	0.77218	0.75132	0.73119	0.71178	0.69305	0.67497
4	0.70842	0.68301	0.65873	0.63552	0.61332	0.59208
5	0.64993	0.62092	0.59345	0.56743	0.54276	0.51937
6	0.59627	0.56447	0.53464	0.50663	0.48032	0.45559
7	0.54703	0.51316	0.48166	0.45235	0.42506	0.39964
8	0.50187	0.46651	0.43393	0.40388	0.37616	0.35056
9	0.46043	0.42410	0.39092	0.36061	0.33288	0.30751
10	0.42241	0.38554	0.35218	0.32197	0.29459	0.26974
11	0.38753	0.35049	0.31728	0.28748	0.26070	0.23662
12	0.35554	0.31863	0.28584	0.25668	0.23071	0.20756
13	0.32618	0.28966	0.25751	0.22917	0.20416	0.18207
14	0.29925	0.26333	0.23199	0.20462	0.18068	0.15971
15	0.27454	0.23939	0.20900	0.18270	0.15989	0.14010
16	0.25187	0.21763	0.18829	0.16312	0.14150	0.12289
17	0.23107	0.19784	0.16963	0.14564	0.12522	0.10780
18	0.21199	0.17986	0.15282	0.13004	0.11081	0.09456
19	0.19449	0.16351	0.13768	0.11611	0.09806	0.08295
20	0.17843	0.14864	0.12403	0.10367	0.08678	0.07276
21	0.16370	0.13513	0.11174	0.09256	0.07680	0.06383
22	0.15018	0.12285	0.10067	0.08264	0.06796	0.05599
23	0.13778	0.11168	0.09069	0.07379	0.06014	0.04911
24	0.12640	0.10153	0.08170	0.06588	0.05323	0.04308
25	0.11597	0.09230	0.07361	0.05882	0.04710	0.03779
26	0.10639	0.08390	0.06631	0.05252	0.04168	0.03315
27	0.09761	0.07628	0.05974	0.04689	0.03689	0.02908
28	0.08955	0.06934	0.05382	0.04187	0.03264	0.02551
29	0.08216	0.06304	0.04849	0.03738	0.02889	0.02237
30	0.07537	0.05731	0.04368	0.03338	0.02557	0.01963
31	0.06915	0.05210	0.03935	0.02980	0.02262	0.01722
32	0.06344	0.04736	0.03545	0.02661	0.02002	0.01510
33	0.05820	0.04306	0.03194	0.02376	0.01772	0.01325
34	0.05331	0.03914	0.02878	0.02121	0.01568	0.01162
35	0.04899	0.03558	0.02592	0.01894	0.01388	0.01019
40	0.03184	0.02210	0.01538	0.01075	0.00753	0.00529
45	0.02069	0.01372	0.00913	0.00610	0.00409	0.00275
50	0.01345	0.00852	0.00542	0.00346	0.00222	0.00143

Present Value of Ordinary Annuity of $1 per Period: $p_{\overline{n}|i} = \dfrac{1 - \dfrac{1}{(1 + i)^n}}{i}$

n \ i	5%	5.5%	6%	6.5%	7%	8%
1	0.95238	0.94787	0.94340	0.93897	0.93458	0.92593
2	1.85941	1.84632	1.83339	1.82063	1.80802	1.78326
3	2.72325	2.69793	2.67301	2.64848	2.62432	2.57710
4	3.54595	3.50515	3.46511	3.42580	3.38721	3.31213
5	4.32948	4.27028	4.21236	4.15568	4.10020	3.99271
6	5.07569	4.99553	4.91732	4.84101	4.76654	4.62288
7	5.78637	5.68297	5.58238	5.48452	5.38923	5.20637
8	6.46321	6.33457	6.20979	6.08875	5.97130	5.74664
9	7.10782	6.95220	6.80169	6.65610	6.51523	6.24689
10	7.72174	7.53763	7.36009	7.18883	7.02358	6.71008
11	8.30641	8.09254	7.88688	7.68904	7.49867	7.13896
12	8.86325	8.61852	8.38384	8.15873	7.94269	7.53608
13	9.39357	9.11708	8.85268	8.59974	8.35765	7.90378
14	9.89864	9.58965	9.29498	9.01384	8.74547	8.22424
15	10.37966	10.03758	9.71225	9.40267	9.10791	8.55948
16	10.83777	10.46216	10.10590	9.76776	9.44665	8.85137
17	11.27407	10.86461	10.47726	10.11058	9.76322	9.12164
18	11.68959	11.24607	10.82760	10.43247	10.05909	9.37189
19	12.08532	11.60765	11.15812	10.73471	10.33560	9.60360
20	12.46221	11.95038	11.46992	11.01851	10.59401	9.81815
21	12.82115	12.27524	11.76408	11.28498	10.83553	10.01680
22	13.16300	12.58317	12.04158	11.53520	11.06124	10.20074
23	13.48857	12.87504	12.30338	11.77014	11.27219	10.37106
24	13.79864	13.15170	12.55036	11.99074	11.46933	10.52876
25	14.09394	13.41393	12.78336	12.19788	11.65358	10.67478
26	14.37518	13.66250	13.00317	12.39237	11.82578	10.80998
27	14.64303	13.89810	13.21053	12.57500	11.98671	10.93516
28	14.89813	14.12142	13.40616	12.74648	12.13711	11.05108
29	15.14107	14.33310	13.59072	12.90749	12.27767	11.15841
30	15.37245	14.53375	13.76483	13.05868	12.40904	11.25778
31	15.59281	14.72393	13.92909	13.20063	12.53181	11.34980
32	15.80268	14.90420	14.08404	13.33393	12.64656	11.43500
33	16.00255	15.07507	14.23023	13.45909	12.75379	11.51389
34	16.19290	15.23703	14.36814	13.57661	12.85401	11.58693
35	16.37420	15.39055	14.49825	13.68696	12.94767	11.65457
40	17.15909	16.04612	15.04630	14.14553	13.33171	11.92461
45	17.77407	16.54773	15.45583	14.48023	13.60552	12.10840
50	18.25592	16.93152	15.76186	14.72452	13.80075	12.23348

Present Value of Ordinary Annuity of $1 per Period: $p_{\overline{n}|i} = \dfrac{1 - \dfrac{1}{(1 + i)^n}}{i}$

n \ i	9%	10%	11%	12%	13%	14%
1	0.91743	0.90909	0.90090	0.89286	0.88496	0.87719
2	1.75911	1.73554	1.71252	1.69005	1.66810	1.64666
3	2.53130	2.48685	2.44371	2.40183	2.36115	2.32163
4	3.23972	3.16986	3.10245	3.03735	2.97447	2.91371
5	3.88965	3.79079	3.69590	3.60478	3.51723	3.43308
6	4.48592	4.35526	4.23054	4.11141	3.99755	3.88867
7	5.03295	4.86842	4.71220	4.56376	4.42261	4.28830
8	5.53482	5.33493	5.14612	4.96764	4.79677	4.63886
9	5.99525	5.75902	5.53705	5.32825	5.13166	4.94637
10	6.41766	6.14457	5.88923	5.65022	5.42624	5.21612
11	6.80519	6.49506	6.20652	5.93770	5.68694	5.45273
12	7.16072	6.81369	6.49236	6.19437	5.91765	5.66029
13	7.48690	7.10336	6.74987	6.42355	6.12181	5.84236
14	7.78615	7.36669	6.96187	6.62817	6.30249	6.00207
15	8.06069	7.60608	7.19087	6.81086	6.46238	6.14217
16	8.31256	7.82371	7.37916	6.97399	6.60388	6.26506
17	8.54363	8.02155	7.54879	7.11963	6.72909	6.37286
18	8.75562	8.20141	7.70162	7.24967	6.83991	6.46742
19	8.95012	8.36492	7.83929	7.36578	6.93797	6.55037
20	9.12855	8.51356	7.96333	7.46944	7.02475	6.62313
21	9.29224	8.64869	8.07507	7.56200	7.10155	6.68696
22	9.44242	8.77154	8.17574	7.64465	7.16951	6.74294
23	9.58021	8.88322	8.26643	7.71843	7.22966	6.79206
24	9.70661	8.98474	8.34814	7.78432	7.28288	6.83514
25	9.82258	9.07704	8.42174	7.84314	7.32998	6.87293
26	9.92897	9.16094	8.48806	7.89566	7.37167	6.90608
27	10.02658	9.23722	8.54780	7.94255	7.40856	6.93515
28	10.11613	9.30657	8.60162	7.98442	7.44120	6.96066
29	10.19828	9.36961	8.65011	8.02181	7.47009	6.98304
30	10.27365	9.42691	8.69379	8.05518	7.49565	7.00266
31	10.34280	9.47901	8.73315	8.08499	7.51828	7.01988
32	10.40624	9.52638	8.76860	8.11159	7.53830	7.03498
33	10.46444	9.56943	8.80054	8.13535	7.55602	7.04823
34	10.51784	9.60858	8.82932	8.15656	7.57170	7.05985
35	10.56682	9.64416	8.85524	8.17550	7.58557	7.07005
40	10.75736	9.77905	8.95105	8.24378	7.63438	7.10504
45	10.88118	9.86281	9.00791	8.28252	7.66086	7.12322
50	10.96168	9.91481	9.04165	8.30450	7.67524	7.13266

Future Amount of $1 at Compound Interest Due in n Periods: $A_{\overline{n}|i} = (1 + i)^n$

n \ i	5%	5.5%	6%	6.5%	7%	8%
1	1.05000	1.05500	1.06000	1.06500	1.07000	1.08000
2	1.10250	1.11303	1.12360	1.13423	1.14490	1.16640
3	1.15762	1.17424	1.19102	1.20795	1.22504	1.25971
4	1.21551	1.23882	1.26248	1.28647	1.31080	1.36049
5	1.27628	1.30696	1.33823	1.37009	1.40255	1.46933
6	1.34100	1.37884	1.41852	1.45914	1.50073	1.58687
7	1.40710	1.45468	1.50363	1.55399	1.60578	1.71382
8	1.54347	1.53469	1.59385	1.65500	1.71819	1.85093
9	1.55133	1.61909	1.68948	1.76257	1.83846	1.99900
10	1.62890	1.70814	1.79085	1.87714	1.96715	2.15892
11	1.71034	1.80209	1.89830	1.99915	2.10485	2.33164
12	1.79586	1.90121	2.01220	2.12910	2.25219	2.51817
13	1.88565	2.00577	2.13293	2.26749	2.40984	2.71962
14	1.97993	2.11609	2.26091	2.41487	2.57853	2.93719
15	2.07893	2.23248	2.39656	2.57184	2.75903	3.17217
16	2.18288	2.35526	2.54035	2.73901	2.95216	3.42594
17	2.29202	2.48480	2.69277	2.91705	3.15882	3.70002
18	2.40662	2.62147	2.85434	3.10665	3.37993	3.99602
19	2.52695	2.76565	3.02560	3.30859	3.61653	4.31570
20	2.65330	2.91776	3.20714	3.52365	3.86968	4.66096
21	2.78596	3.07823	3.39956	3.75268	4.14056	5.03383
22	2.92526	3.24754	3.60354	3.99661	4.43040	5.43654
23	3.07152	3.42615	3.81975	4.25639	4.74053	5.87146
24	3.22510	3.61459	4.04894	4.53305	5.07237	6.34118
25	3.38636	3.81339	4.29187	4.82770	5.42743	6.84848
26	3.55567	4.02313	4.54938	5.14150	5.80735	7.39635
27	3.73346	4.24440	4.82235	5.47570	6.21387	7.98806
28	3.92013	4.47784	5.11169	5.83162	6.64884	8.62711
29	4.11614	4.72412	5.41839	6.21067	7.11426	9.31728
30	4.32194	4.98395	5.74349	6.61437	7.61226	10.06266
31	4.53804	5.25807	6.08810	7.04430	8.14511	10.86767
32	4.76494	5.54726	6.45339	7.50218	8.71527	11.73708
33	5.00319	5.85236	6.84059	7.98982	9.32534	12.67605
34	5.25335	6.17424	7.25102	8.50916	9.97811	13.69013
35	5.51602	6.51383	7.68609	9.06225	10.67658	14.78534
40	7.03999	8.51331	10.28572	12.41607	14.97446	21.72452
45	8.98501	11.12655	13.76461	17.01110	21.00245	31.92045
50	11.46740	14.54196	18.42015	23.30668	29.45702	46.90161

Future Amount of $1 at Compound Interest Due in n Periods: $A_{\overline{n}\backslash i} = (1 + i)^n$

n \ i	9%	10%	11%	12%	13%	14%
1	1.09000	1.10000	1.11000	1.12000	1.13000	1.14000
2	1.18810	1.21000	1.23210	1.25440	1.27690	1.29960
3	1.29503	1.33100	1.36763	1.40493	1.44290	1.48154
4	1.41158	1.46410	1.51807	1.57352	1.63047	1.68896
5	1.53862	1.61051	1.68506	1.76234	1.84244	1.92541
6	1.67710	1.77156	1.87041	1.97382	2.08195	2.19497
7	1.82804	1.94872	2.07616	2.21068	2.35261	2.50227
8	1.99256	2.14359	2.30454	2.47596	2.65844	2.85259
9	2.17189	2.35795	2.55804	2.77308	3.00404	3.25195
10	2.36736	2.59374	2.83942	3.10585	3.39457	3.70722
11	2.58043	2.85312	3.15176	3.47855	3.83586	4.22623
12	2.81266	3.13843	3.49845	3.89598	4.33452	4.81790
13	3.06580	3.45227	3.88328	4.36349	4.89801	5.49241
14	3.34173	3.79750	4.31044	4.88711	5.53475	6.26135
15	3.64248	4.17725	4.78459	5.47357	6.25427	7.13794
16	3.97031	4.59497	5.31089	6.13039	7.06733	8.13725
17	4.32763	5.05447	5.89509	6.86604	7.98608	9.27646
18	4.71712	5.55992	6.54355	7.68997	9.02427	10.57517
19	5.14166	6.11591	7.26334	8.61276	10.19742	12.05569
20	5.60441	6.72750	8.06231	9.64629	11.52309	13.74349
21	6.10881	7.40025	8.94917	10.80385	13.02109	15.66758
22	6.65860	8.14028	9.93357	12.10031	14.71383	17.86104
23	7.25787	8.95430	11.02627	13.55235	16.62663	20.36158
24	7.91108	9.84973	12.23916	15.17863	18.78809	23.21221
25	8.62308	10.83471	13.58546	17.00006	21.23054	26.46192
26	9.39916	11.91818	15.07986	19.04007	23.99051	30.16658
27	10.24508	13.10999	16.73865	21.32488	27.10928	34.38991
28	11.16714	14.42099	18.57990	23.88387	30.63349	39.20449
29	12.17218	15.86309	20.62369	26.74993	34.61584	44.69312
30	13.26768	17.44940	22.89230	29.95992	39.11590	50.95016
31	14.46177	19.19434	25.41045	33.55511	44.20096	58.08318
32	15.76333	21.11378	28.20560	37.58173	49.94709	66.21483
33	17.18203	23.22515	31.30821	42.09153	56.44021	75.48490
34	18.72841	25.54767	34.75212	47.14252	63.77744	86.05279
35	20.41397	28.10244	38.57485	52.79962	72.06851	98.10018
40	31.40942	45.25926	65.00087	93.05097	132.78155	188.88351
45	48.32729	72.89048	109.53024	163.98760	244.64140	363.67907
50	74.35752	117.39085	184.56483	289.00219	450.73593	700.23299

Future Amount of Ordinary Annuity of $1 per Period: $A_{\overline{n}|i} = (1 + i)^n - 1/i$

n \ i	5%	5.5%	6%	6.5%	7%	8%
1	1.00000	1.00000	1.00000	1.00000	1.00000	1.00000
2	2.05000	2.05500	2.06000	2.06500	2.07000	2.08000
3	3.15250	3.16802	3.18360	3.19922	3.21490	3.24640
4	4.31012	4.34227	4.37462	4.40717	4.43994	4.50611
5	5.52563	5.58109	5.63709	5.69364	5.75074	5.86660
6	6.80191	6.88805	6.97532	7.06373	7.15329	7.33593
7	8.14201	8.26689	8.39384	8.52287	8.65402	8.92280
8	9.54911	9.72157	9.89747	10.07688	10.25980	10.63663
9	11.02656	11.25626	11.49132	11.73185	11.97799	12.48756
10	12.57789	12.87535	13.18080	13.49442	13.81645	14.48656
11	14.20679	14.58350	14.97184	15.37156	15.78360	16.64549
12	15.91713	16.38559	16.86994	17.37071	17.88845	18.97713
13	17.71298	18.28680	18.88214	19.49981	20.14064	21.49530
14	19.59863	20.29257	21.01505	21.76730	22.55049	24.21492
15	21.57856	22.40866	23.27597	24.18217	25.12902	27.15211
16	23.65749	24.64114	25.67253	26.75401	27.88805	30.32428
17	25.84037	28.99640	28.21288	29.49302	30.84022	33.75023
18	28.13238	29.48120	30.90565	32.41007	33.99903	37.45024
19	30.53900	32.10267	33.75999	35.51672	37.37896	41.44626
20	33.06595	34.86832	36.78559	38.82531	40.99549	45.76196
21	35.71925	37.78608	39.99273	42.34895	44.86518	50.42292
22	38.50521	40.86431	43.39229	46.10164	49.00574	55.45676
23	41.43048	44.11185	46.99583	50.09824	53.43614	60.89330
24	44.50200	47.53800	50.81558	54.35463	58.17667	66.76476
25	47.72710	51.15259	54.86451	58.88768	63.24904	73.10594
26	51.11345	54.96598	59.15638	63.71538	68.67647	79.95442
27	54.66913	58.98911	63.70577	68.85688	74.48382	87.35077
28	58.40258	63.23351	68.52811	74.33257	80.69769	95.33883
29	62.32271	67.71135	73.62980	80.16419	87.34653	103.96594
30	66.43885	72.43548	79.05819	86.37486	94.46079	113.28321
31	70.76079	77.41943	84.80168	92.98923	102.07304	123.34587
32	75.29883	82.67750	90.88978	100.03353	110.21815	134.21354
33	80.06377	88.22476	97.34316	107.53571	118.93342	145.95062
34	85.06696	94.07712	104.18376	115.52553	128.25876	158.62667
35	90.32031	100.25136	111.43478	124.03469	138.23688	172.31680
40	120.79977	136.60561	154.76197	175.63192	199.63511	259.05652
45	159.70016	184.11917	212.74351	246.32459	285.74931	386.50562
50	209.34800	246.21748	290.33591	343.17967	406.52893	573.77016

Future Amount of Ordinary Annuity of $1 per Period: $A_{\overline{n}|i} = (1 + i)^n - 1/i$

n \ i	9%	10%	11%	12%	13%	14%
1	1.00000	1.00000	1.00000	1.00000	1.00000	1.00000
2	2.09000	2.10000	2.11000	2.12000	2.13000	2.14000
3	3.27810	3.31000	3.34210	3.37440	3.40690	3.43960
4	4.57313	4.64100	4.70973	4.77933	4.84980	4.92114
5	5.98471	6.10510	6.22780	6.35285	6.48027	6.61010
6	7.52334	7.71561	7.91286	8.11519	8.32271	8.53552
7	9.20044	9.48717	9.78327	10.08901	10.40466	10.73049
8	11.02847	11.43589	11.85943	12.29969	12.75726	13.23276
9	13.02104	13.57948	14.16397	14.77566	15.41571	16.08535
10	15.19293	15.93742	16.72201	17.54874	18.41975	19.33730
11	17.56029	18.53117	19.56143	20.65458	21.81432	23.04452
12	20.14072	21.38428	22.71319	24.13313	25.65018	27.27075
13	22.95338	24.52271	26.21164	28.02911	29.98470	32.08865
14	26.01919	27.97498	30.09492	32.39260	34.88271	37.58107
15	29.36092	31.77248	34.40536	37.27972	40.41746	43.84241
16	33.00340	35.94973	39.18995	42.75328	46.67173	50.98035
17	36.97370	40.54470	44.50084	48.88367	53.73906	59.11760
18	41.30134	45.59917	50.39594	55.74972	61.72514	68.39407
19	46.01846	51.15909	56.93949	63.43968	70.74941	78.96923
20	51.16012	57.27500	64.20283	72.05244	80.94683	91.02493
21	56.76453	64.00250	72.26514	81.69874	92.46992	104.76842
22	62.87334	71.40275	81.21431	92.50258	105.49101	120.43600
23	69.53194	79.54302	91.14788	104.60289	120.20484	138.29704
24	76.78981	88.49733	102.17415	118.15524	136.83147	158.65862
25	84.70090	98.34706	114.41331	133.33387	155.61956	181.87083
26	93.32398	109.18176	127.99877	150.33393	176.85010	208.33274
27	102.72314	121.09994	143.07864	169.37401	200.84061	238.49933
28	112.96822	134.20994	159.81729	190.69889	227.94989	272.88923
29	124.13536	148.63093	178.39719	214.58275	258.58338	312.09373
30	136.30754	164.49402	199.02088	241.33268	293.19922	356.78683
31	149.57522	181.94342	221.91317	271.29261	332.31511	407.73701
32	164.03699	201.13777	247.32362	304.84772	376.51608	465.82019
33	179.80032	222.25154	275.52922	342.42945	426.46317	532.03501
34	196.98234	245.47670	306.83744	384.52098	482.90338	607.51991
35	215.71076	271.02437	341.58955	431.66350	546.68082	693.57270
40	337.88244	442.59256	581.82607	767.09142	1013.70424	1342.02510
45	525.85873	718.90484	986.63856	1358.23003	1874.16463	2590.56480
50	815.08356	1163.90853	1668.77115	2400.01825	3459.50712	4994.52135

Appendix B: Codes of Professional Ethics for Accountants

In recent years, governments, businesses, and the public have given increased attention to ethical conduct. They have insisted upon a level of human behavior that goes beyond that required by laws and regulations. Thus many businesses, as well as professional groups (such as accountants) and governmental organizations, have established standards of ethical conduct. This text emphasizes the ethical conduct of accountants, who serve various business interests as well as the public.

This appendix sets forth the standards of professional conduct expected of accountants in public accounting and private accounting. For accountants employed in public accounting, the American Institute of Certified Public Accountants' *Code of Professional Conduct* is presented.[1] For accountants employed in private accounting, the Institute of Management Accountants' *Standards of Ethical Conduct for Practitioners of Management Accounting and Financial Management* is presented as a guide to professional conduct.[2]

Supplementing the codes of professional ethics are ethics discussion cases that appear at the end of each chapter. These cases represent "real world" examples of ethical issues facing accountants. It should be noted that codes of professional ethics are general guides to good behavior and their application to specific situations often requires the exercise of professional judgment. In some cases, the line between right and wrong may be quite fine, and reasonable people may disagree. In addition, business is dynamic and everchanging, and what society considers to be acceptable behavior changes from time to time.

Code of Professional Conduct

Composition, Applicability, and Compliance

The Code of Professional Conduct of the American Institute of Certified Public Accountants consists of two sections—(1) the Principles and (2) the Rules. The Principles provide the framework for the Rules, which govern the performance of professional services by members. The Council of the American Institute of Certified Public Accountants is authorized to designate bodies to promulgate technical standards under the Rules, and the bylaws require adherence to those Rules and standards.

The Code of Professional Conduct was adopted by the membership to provide guidance and rules to all members—those in public practice, in industry, in government, and in education—in the performance of their professional responsibilities.

Compliance with the Code of Professional Conduct, as with all standards in an open society, depends primarily on members' understanding and voluntary actions, secondarily on reinforcement by peers and public opinion, and ultimately on disciplinary proceedings, when necessary, against members who fail to comply with the Rules.

Other Guidance

The Principles and Rules as set forth herein are further amplified by interpretations and rulings contained in *AICPA Professional Standards* (Volume 2).

Interpretations of Rules of Conduct consists of interpretations which have been adopted, after exposure to state societies, state boards, practice units, and other interested parties, by the professional ethics division's executive committee to provide guidelines as to the scope and application of the Rules but are not intended to limit such scope or application. A member who departs from such guidelines shall have the burden of justifying such departure in any disciplinary hearing.

---

[1] *Code of Professional Conduct* (New York: American Institute of Certified Public Accountants, 2000), pp. 3–8.
[2] *Standards of Ethical Conduct for Practitioners of Management Accounting and Financial Management,* Institute of Management Accountants, Montvale, New Jersey, 1997, pp. 1–2.

Ethics Rulings consist of formal rulings made by the professional ethics division's executive committee after exposure to state societies, state boards, practice units, and other interested parties. These rulings summarize the application of Rules of Conduct and interpretations to a particular set of factual circumstances. Members who depart from such rulings in similar circumstances will be requested to justify such departures.

Publication of an interpretation or ethics ruling in the *Journal of Accountancy* constitutes notice to members. Hence, the effective date of the pronouncement is the last day of the month in which the pronouncement is published in the *Journal of Accountancy*. The professional ethics division will take into consideration the time that would have been reasonable for the member to comply with the pronouncement.

Members should also consult, if applicable, the ethical standards of their state CPA society, state board of accountancy, the Securities and Exchange Commission, and any other governmental agency which may regulate their client's business or use their reports to evaluate the client's compliance with applicable laws and related regulations.

Section I—Principles

Preamble

Membership in the American Institute of Certified Public Accountants is voluntary. By accepting membership, a certified public accountant assumes an obligation of self-discipline above and beyond the requirements of laws and regulations.

These Principles of the Code of Professional Conduct of the American Institute of Certified Public Accountants express the profession's recognition of its responsibilities to the public, to clients, and to colleagues. They guide members in the performance of their professional responsibilities and express the basic tenets of ethical and professional conduct. The Principles call for an unswerving commitment to honorable behavior, even at the sacrifice of personal advantage.

Article I—Responsibilities

In carrying out their responsibilities as professionals, members should exercise sensitive professional and moral judgments in all their activities.

As professionals, certified public accountants perform an essential role in society. Consistent with that role, members of the American Institute of Certified Public Accountants have responsibilities to all those who use their professional services. Members also have a continuing responsibility to cooperate with each other to improve the art of accounting, maintain the public's confidence, and carry out the profession's special responsibilities for self-governance. The collective efforts of all members are required to maintain and enhance the traditions of the profession.

Article II—The Public Interest

Members should accept the obligation to act in a way that will serve the public interest, honor the public trust, and demonstrate commitment to professionalism.

A distinguishing mark of a profession is acceptance of its responsibility to the public. The accounting profession's public consists of clients, credit grantors, governments, employers, investors, the business and financial community, and others who rely on the objectivity and integrity of certified public accountants to maintain the orderly functioning of commerce. This reliance imposes a public interest responsibility on certified public accountants. The public interest is defined as the collective well-being of the community of people and institutions the profession serves.

In discharging their professional responsibilities, members may encounter conflicting pressures from among each of those groups. In resolving those conflicts, members should act with integrity, guided by the precept that when members fulfill their responsibility to the public, clients' and employers' interests are best served.

Those who rely on certified public accountants expect them to discharge their responsibilities with integrity, objectivity, due professional care, and a genuine interest in serving the public. They are expected to provide quality services, enter into fee arrangements, and offer a range of services—all in a manner that demonstrates a level of professionalism consistent with these Principles of the Code of Professional Conduct.

All who accept membership in the American Institute of Certified Public Accountants commit themselves to honor the public trust. In return for the faith that the public reposes in them, members should seek continually to demonstrate their dedication to professional excellence.

Article III—Integrity

To maintain and broaden public confidence, members should perform all professional responsibilities with the highest sense of integrity.

Integrity is an element of character fundamental to professional recognition. It is the quality from which the public trust derives and the benchmark against which a member must ultimately test all decisions.

Integrity requires a member to be, among other things, honest and candid within the constraints of client confidentiality. Service and the public trust should not be subordinated to personal gain and advantage. Integrity can accommodate the inadvertent error and the honest difference of opinion; it cannot accommodate deceit or subordination of principle.

Integrity is measured in terms of what is right and just. In the absence of specific rules, standards, or guidance, or in the face of conflicting opinions, a member should test decisions and deeds by asking: "Am I doing what a person of integrity would do? Have I retained my integrity?" Integrity requires a member to observe both the form and the spirit of technical and ethical standards; circumvention of those standards constitutes subordination of judgment.

Integrity also requires a member to observe the principles of objectivity and independence and of due care.

Article IV—Objectivity and Independence

A member should maintain objectivity and be free of conflicts of interest in discharging professional responsibilities. A member in public practice should be independent in fact and appearance when providing auditing and other attestation services.

Objectivity is a state of mind, a quality that lends value to a member's services. It is a distinguishing feature of the profession. The principle of objectivity imposes the obligation to be impartial, intellectually honest, and free of conflicts of interest. Independence precludes relationships that may appear to impair a member's objectivity in rendering attestation services.

Members often serve multiple interests in many different capacities and must demonstrate their objectivity in varying circumstances. Members in public practice render attest, tax, and management advisory services. Other members prepare financial statements in the employment of others, perform internal auditing services, and serve in financial and management capacities in industry, education, and government. They also educate and train those who aspire to admission into the profession. Regardless of service or capacity, members should protect the integrity of their work, maintain objectivity, and avoid any subordination of their judgment.

For a member in public practice, the maintenance of objectivity and independence requires a continuing assessment of client relationships and public responsibility. Such a member who provides auditing and other attestation services should be independent in fact and appearance. In providing all other services, a member should maintain objectivity and avoid conflicts of interest.

Although members not in public practice cannot maintain the appearance of independence, they nevertheless have the responsibility to maintain objectivity in rendering professional services. Members employed by others to prepare financial statements or to perform auditing, tax, or consulting services are charged with the same responsibility for objectivity as members in public practice and must be scrupulous in their application of generally accepted accounting principles and candid in all their dealings with members in public practice.

Activity V—Due Care

A member should observe the profession's technical and ethical standards, strive continually to improve competence and the quality of services, and discharge professional responsibility to the best of the member's ability.

The quest for excellence is the essence of due care. Due care requires a member to discharge professional responsibilities with competence and diligence. It imposes the obligation to perform professional services to the best of a member's ability with concern for the best interest of those for whom the services are performed and consistent with the profession's responsibility to the public.

Competence is derived from a synthesis of education and experience. It begins with a mastery of the common body of knowledge required for designation as a certified public accountant. The maintenance of competence requires a commitment to learning and professional improvement that must continue throughout a member's professional life. It is a member's individual responsibility. In all engagements and in all responsibilities, each member should undertake to achieve a level of competence that will assure that the quality of the member's services meets the high level of professionalism required by these Principles.

Competence represents the attainment and maintenance of a level of understanding and knowledge that enables a member to render services with facility and acumen. It also establishes the limitations of a member's capabilities by dictating that consultation or referral may be required when a professional engagement exceeds the personal competence of a member or a member's firm. Each member is responsible for assessing his or her own competence—of evaluating whether education, experience, and judgment are adequate for the responsibility to be assumed.

Members should be diligent in discharging responsibilities to clients, employers, and the public. Diligence imposes the responsibility to render services promptly and carefully, to be thorough, and to observe applicable technical and ethical standards.

Due care requires a member to plan and supervise adequately any professional activity for which he or she is responsible.

Article VI—Scope and Nature of Services

A member in public practice should observe the Principles of the Code of Professional Conduct in determining the scope and nature of services to be provided.

The public interest aspect of certified public accountants' services requires that such services be consistent with acceptable professional behavior for certified public accountants. Integrity requires that service and the public trust not be subordinated to personal gain and advantage. Objectivity and independence require that members be free from conflicts of interest in discharging professional responsibilities. Due care requires that services be provided with competence and diligence.

Each of these Principles should be considered by members in determining whether or not to provide specific services in individual circumstances. In some instances, they may represent an overall constraint on the nonaudit services that might be offered to a specific client. No hard-and-fast rules can be developed to help members reach these judgments, but they must be satisfied that they are meeting the spirit of the Principles in this regard.

In order to accomplish this, members should:

- Practice in firms that have in place internal quality-control procedures to ensure that services are competently delivered and adequately supervised.

- Determine, in their individual judgments, whether the scope and nature of other services provided to an audit client would create a conflict of interest in the performance of the audit function for that client.
- Assess, in their individual judgments, whether an activity is consistent with their role as professionals (for example, Is such activity a reasonable extension or variation of existing services offered by the member or others in the profession?).

Standards of Ethical Conduct for Practitioners of Management Accounting and Financial Management

Practitioners of management accounting and financial management have an obligation to the public, their profession, the organization they serve, and themselves to maintain the highest standards of ethical conduct. In recognition of this obligation, the Institute of Management Accountants has promulgated the following standards of ethical conduct for management accounting and financial management. Adherence to these standards, both domestically and internationally, is integral to achieving the *Objectives of Management Accounting*.[3] Practitioners of management accounting and financial management shall not commit acts contrary to these standards nor shall they condone the commission of such acts by others within their organizations.

Competence

Practitioners of management accounting and financial management have a responsibility to:

- Maintain an appropriate level of professional competence by ongoing development of their knowledge and skills.
- Perform their professional duties in accordance with relevant laws, regulations, and technical standards.
- Prepare complete and clear reports and recommendations after appropriate analyses of relevant and reliable information.

Confidentiality

Practitioners of management accounting and financial management have a responsibility to:

- Refrain from disclosing confidential information acquired in the course of their work except when authorized, unless legally obligated to do so.
- Inform subordinates as appropriate regarding the confidentiality of information acquired in the course of their work and monitor their activities to assure the maintenance of that confidentiality.
- Refrain from using or appearing to use confidential information acquired in the course of their work for unethical or illegal advantage either personally or through third parties.

Integrity

Practitioners of management accounting and financial management have a responsibility to:

- Avoid actual or apparent conflicts of interest and advise all appropriate parties of any potential conflict.
- Refrain from engaging in any activity that would prejudice their ability to carry out their duties ethically.
- Refuse any gift, favor, or hospitality that would influence or would appear to influence their actions.

---

[3] National Association of Accountants, *Statements on Management Accounting: Objectives of Management Accounting*, Statement No. 1B, New York, N.Y., June 17, 1982.

- Refrain from either actively or passively subverting the attainment of the organization's legitimate and ethical objectives.
- Recognize and communicate professional limitations or other constraints that would preclude responsible judgment or successful performance of an activity.
- Communicate unfavorable as well as favorable information and professional judgments or opinions.
- Refrain from engaging in or supporting any activity that would discredit the profession.

Objectivity

Practitioners of management accounting and financial management have a responsibility to:

- Communicate information fairly and objectively.
- Disclose fully all relevant information that could reasonably be expected to influence an intended user's understanding of the reports, comments, and recommendations presented.

Appendix C: Alternative Methods of Recording Deferrals

As discussed in Chapter 3, deferrals are created by recording a transaction in a way that delays or defers the recognition of an expense or a revenue. Deferrals may be either deferred expenses (prepaid expenses) or deferred revenues (unearned revenues).

In Chapter 2, deferred expenses (prepaid expenses) were debited to an *asset* account at the time of payment. As an alternative, deferred expenses may be debited to an *expense* account at the time of payment. In Chapter 2, deferred revenues (unearned revenues) were credited to a *liability* account at the time of receipt. As an alternative, deferred revenues may be credited to a *revenue* account at the time of receipt. This appendix describes and illustrates these alternative methods of recording deferred expenses and deferred revenues.

Deferred Expenses (Prepaid Expenses)

As a basis for illustrating the alternative methods of recording deferred expenses, the insurance premium paid by NetSolutions in Chapter 2 is used. The amounts related to this insurance are as follows:

Prepayment of insurance for 24 months, starting December 1	$2,400
Insurance premium expired during December	100
Unexpired insurance premium at the end of December	$2,300

Based on the above data, the entries to account for the deferred expense (prepaid insurance) recorded initially as an *asset* are shown in the journal and T accounts in Exhibit 1. The adjusting entry in Exhibit 1 was shown in Chapter 3. The entries to account for the prepaid insurance recorded initially as an *expense* are shown in the journal and T accounts in Exhibit 2.

EXHIBIT 1

Prepaid Expense Recorded Initially as Asset

Initial entry (to record initial payment):

Dec. 1	Prepaid Insurance	2,400	
	Cash		2,400

Adjusting entry (to transfer amount *used* to the proper *expense* account):

Dec. 31	Insurance Expense	100	
	Prepaid Insurance		100

Closing entry (to close income statement accounts with debit balances):

Income Summary		XXXX	
Supplies Expense			XXXX
~~			
Insurance Expense			100

Prepaid Insurance

Dec. 1		2,400	Dec. 31	Adjusting	100

Insurance Expense

Dec. 31	Adjusting	100	Dec. 31	Closing	100

EXHIBIT 2

Prepaid Expense Recorded Initially as Expense

Initial entry (to record initial payment):

Dec. 1	Insurance Expense	2,400	
	Cash		2,400

Adjusting entry (to transfer amount *unused* to the proper *asset* account):

Dec. 31	Prepaid Insurance	2,300	
	Insurance Expense		2,300

Closing entry (to close income statement accounts with debit balances):

Income Summary		XXXX	
Supplies Expense			XXXX
~~			
Insurance Expense			100

Prepaid Insurance

Dec. 31	Adjusting	2,300	

Insurance Expense

Dec. 1		2,400	Dec. 31	Adjusting	2,300
			31	Closing	100

Either of the two methods of recording deferred expenses (prepaid expenses) may be used. As illustrated in Exhibits 1 and 2, both methods result in the same account balances after the adjusting entries have been recorded. Therefore, the amounts reported as expenses in the income statement and as assets on the balance sheet will not be affected by the method used. To avoid confusion, the method used by a business for each kind of prepaid expense should be followed consistently from year to year.

Some businesses record all deferred expenses using one method. Other businesses use one method to record the prepayment of some expenses and the other method for other expenses. Initial debits to the asset account are logical for prepayments of insurance, which are usually for periods of one to three years. On the other hand, rent on a building may be prepaid on the first of each month. The prepaid rent will expire by the end of the month. In this case, it is logical to record the payment of rent by initially debiting an expense account rather than an asset account.

Deferred Revenues (Unearned Revenues)

To illustrate the alternative methods of recording deferred revenues, we will use the rent received by NetSolutions in Chapter 2. NetSolutions rented land on December 1 to a local retailer for use as a parking lot for three months and received $360 for the entire three months. On December 31, $120 (1/3 × $360) of the rent has been earned, and $240 (2/3 × $360) of the rent is still unearned.

Based on the above data, the entries to account for the deferred revenue (unearned rent) recorded initially as a liability are shown in the journal and ledger in Exhibit 3. The adjusting entry in Exhibit 3 was shown in Chapter 3. The entries to account for the unearned rent recorded initially as revenue are shown in the journal and ledger in Exhibit 4.

As illustrated in Exhibits 3 and 4, both methods result in the same account balances after the adjusting entries have been recorded. Therefore, the amounts reported as revenues in the income statement and as liabilities on the balance sheet

EXHIBIT 3 — Unearned Revenue Recorded Initially as Liability / **EXHIBIT 4** — Unearned Revenue Recorded Initially as Revenue

will not be affected by the method used. Either of the methods may be used for all revenues received in advance. Alternatively, the first method may be used for advance receipts of some kinds of revenue and the second method for other kinds. To avoid confusion, the method used by a business for each kind of unearned revenue should be followed consistently from year to year.

Reversing Entries for Deferrals

As discussed in the appendix at the end of Chapter 4, the use of reversing entries is optional. However, the use of reversing entries generally simplifies the analysis of transactions and reduces the likelihood of errors in the subsequent recording of transactions. Normally, reversing entries are prepared for deferrals in the following two cases:

1. When a deferred expense (prepaid expense) is initially recorded as an expense.
2. When a deferred revenue (unearned revenue) is initially recorded as a revenue.

The entry to reverse the adjustment to record the prepaid insurance in Exhibit 2 is as follows:

Jan.	1	Insurance Expense	2,300	
		Prepaid Insurance		2,300

The entry to reverse the adjustment to record the unearned rent in Exhibit 4 is as follows:

Jan.	1	Unearned Rent	240	
		Rent Revenue		240

EXERCISES

Exercise C–1
Adjusting entries for office supplies

The office supplies purchased during the year total $3,570, and the amount of office supplies on hand at the end of the year is $415.

a. Record the following transactions directly in T accounts for Office Supplies and Office Supplies Expense, using the system of initially recording supplies as an asset: (1) purchases for the period; (2) adjusting entry at the end of the period. Identify each entry by number.

b. Record the following transactions directly in T accounts for Office Supplies and Office Supplies Expense, using the system of initially recording supplies as an expense: (1) purchases for the period; (2) adjusting entry at the end of the period. Identify each entry by number.

Exercise C–2
Adjusting entries for prepaid insurance

During the first year of operations, insurance premiums of $9,135 were paid. At the end of the year, unexpired premiums totaled $3,478. Journalize the adjusting entry at the end of the year, assuming that (a) prepaid expenses were initially recorded as assets and (b) prepaid expenses were initially recorded as expenses.

Exercise C–3
Adjusting entries for advertising revenue

The advertising revenues received during the year total $351,200, and the unearned advertising revenue at the end of the year is $48,500.

a. Record the following transactions directly in T accounts for Unearned Advertising Revenue and Advertising Revenue, using the system of initially recording advertising fees as a liability: (1) revenues received during the period; (2) adjusting entry at the end of the period. Identify each entry by number.

b. Record the following transactions directly in T accounts for Unearned Advertising Revenue and Advertising Revenue, using the system of initially recording advertising fees as revenue: (1) revenues received during the period; (2) adjusting entry at the end of the period. Identify each entry by number.

Exercise C-4
Year-end entries for deferred revenues

In its first year of operation, Magna Publishing Co. received $2,275,000 from advertising contracts and $6,195,000 from magazine subscriptions, crediting the two amounts to Unearned Advertising Revenue and Circulation Revenue, respectively. At the end of the year, the unearned advertising revenue amounts to $196,000, and the circulation revenue amounts to $1,150,000. Journalize the adjusting entries that should be made at the end of the year.

Appendix D: Periodic Inventory Systems for Merchandising Businesses

In this text, we emphasize the perpetual inventory system of accounting for purchases and sales of merchandise. Not all merchandise businesses, however, use perpetual inventory systems. For example, some managers/owners of small merchandise businesses, such as locally owned hardware stores, may feel more comfortable using manually kept records. Because a manual perpetual inventory system is time-consuming and costly to maintain, the periodic inventory system is often used in these cases.

Merchandise Transactions in a Periodic Inventory System

In a periodic inventory system, the revenues from sales are recorded when sales are made in the same manner as in a perpetual inventory system. However, no attempt is made on the date of sale to record the cost of the merchandise sold. Instead, the merchandise inventory on hand at the end of the period is counted. This physical inventory is then used to determine (1) the cost of merchandise sold during the period and (2) the cost of merchandise on hand at the end of the period.

In a periodic inventory system, purchases of inventory are recorded in a purchases account rather than in a merchandise inventory account. No attempt is made to keep a detailed record of the amount of inventory on hand at any given time.

The purchases account is normally debited for the amount of the invoice before considering any purchases discounts. Purchases discounts are normally recorded in a separate purchases discounts account.[1] The balance of this account is reported as a deduction from the amount initially recorded in Purchases for the period. Thus, the purchases discounts account is viewed as a contra (or offsetting) account to Purchases.

Purchases returns and allowances are recorded in a similar manner as purchases discounts. A separate account is used to keep a record of the amount of purchases returns and allowances during a period. Purchases returns and allowances are reported as a deduction from the amount initially recorded as Purchases. Like Purchases Discounts, the purchases returns and allowances account is a contra (or offsetting) account to Purchases.

When merchandise is purchased FOB shipping point, the buyer is responsible for paying the freight charges. In a periodic inventory system, freight charges paid when purchasing merchandise FOB shipping point are debited to Transportation In, Freight In, or a similarly titled account.

To illustrate the recording of merchandise transactions in a periodic system, we will use the following selected transactions for Taylor Co. We will also explain how the transaction would have been recorded under a perpetual system.

June 5 Purchased $30,000 of merchandise on account from Owen Clothing, terms 2/10, n/30.

Purchases	30,000	
Accounts Payable—Owen Clothing		30,000

Under the perpetual inventory system, such purchases would be recorded in the merchandise inventory account at their cost, $30,000.

June 8. Returned merchandise purchased on account from Owen Clothing on June 5, $500.

Accounts Payable—Owen Clothing	500	
Purchases Returns and Allowances		500

---

[1] Some businesses prefer to credit the purchases account. If this alternative is used, the balance of the purchases account will be a net amount—the total purchases less the total purchases discounts for the period.

Under the perpetual inventory system, returns would be recorded as a credit to the merchandise inventory account at their cost of $500.

June 15.   Paid Owen Clothing for purchase of June 5, less return of $500 and discount of $590 [($30,000 − $500) × 2%].

Accounts Payable—Owen Clothing	29,500	
Cash		28,910
Purchases Discounts		590

Under a perpetual inventory system, a purchases discount account is not used. Instead the merchandise inventory account is credited for the amount of the discount, $590.

June 18.   Sold merchandise on account to Jones Co., $12,500, 1/10, n/30. The cost of the merchandise sold was $9,000.

Accounts Receivable—Jones Co.	12,500	
Sales		12,500

The entry to record the sale is the same under both systems. Under the perpetual inventory system, the cost of merchandise sold and the reduction in merchandise inventory would also be recorded on the date of sale.

June 21.   Received merchandise returned on account from Jones Co., $4,000. The cost of the merchandise returned was $2,800.

Sales Returns and Allowances	4,000	
Accounts Receivable—Jones Co.		4,000

The entry to record the sales return is the same under both systems. In addition, the cost of the merchandise returned would be debited to the merchandise inventory account and credited to the cost of merchandise sold account under the perpetual inventory system.

June 22.   Purchased merchandise from Norcross Clothiers, $15,000, terms FOB shipping point, 2/15, n/30, with prepaid transportation charges of $750 added to the invoice.

Purchases	15,000	
Transportation In	750	
Accounts Payable—Norcross Clothiers		15,750

This entry is similar to the June 5 entry for the purchase of merchandise. Since the transportation terms were FOB shipping point, the prepaid freight charges of $750 must be added to the invoice cost of $15,000. Under the perpetual inventory system, the purchase is recorded in the merchandise inventory account at the cost of $15,750 (invoice price plus transportation).

June 28.   Received $8,415 as payment on account from Jones Co., less return of June 21 and less discount of $85 [($12,500 − $4,000) × 1%].

Cash	8,415	
Sales Discounts	85	
Accounts Receivable—Jones Co.		8,500

This entry is the same under the perpetual inventory system.

June 29.   Received $19,600 from cash sales. The cost of the merchandise sold was $13,800.

Cash	19,600	
Sales		19,600

The entry to record the sale is the same under both systems. Under the perpetual inventory system, the cost of merchandise sold and the reduction in merchandise inventory would also be recorded on the date of sale.

Cost of Merchandise Sold

Under the periodic inventory system, the cost of merchandise sold during a period is reported in a separate section in the income statement. To illustrate, assume that on January 3, 2003, NetSolutions began operations as an Internet-based retailer of software and hardware. During 2003, NetSolutions purchased $340,000 of merchandise. The inventory on December 31, 2003, is $59,700. The cost of merchandise sold during 2003 is reported as follows:

Cost of merchandise sold:	
Purchases	$340,000
Less merchandise inventory, December 31, 2003	59,700
Cost of merchandise sold	$280,300

To continue the example, assume that during 2004 NetSolutions purchased additional merchandise of $521,980. NetSolutions also received credit for purchases returns and allowances of $9,100, took purchases discounts of $2,525, and paid transportation costs of $17,400. The purchases returns and allowances and the purchases discounts are deducted from the total purchases to yield the net purchases. The transportation costs are then added to the net purchases to yield the cost of merchandise purchased. These amounts are reported in the cost of merchandise sold section of the NetSolutions income statement for 2004 as follows:

Purchases			$521,980
Less: Purchases returns and allowances	$9,100		
Purchases discounts	2,525	11,625	
Net purchases		$510,355	
Add transportation in		17,400	
Cost of merchandise purchased			$527,755

The ending inventory of NetSolutions on December 31, 2003, $59,700, becomes the beginning inventory for 2004. In the cost of merchandise sold section of the income statement for 2004, this beginning inventory is added to the cost of merchandise purchased to yield the merchandise available for sale. The ending inventory on December 31, 2004, $62,150, is then subtracted from the merchandise available for sale to yield the cost of merchandise sold. Exhibit 1 shows the cost of merchandise sold during 2004.

Exhibit 1 Cost of Merchandise Sold—Periodic Inventory System

Cost of merchandise sold:			
Merchandise inventory, January 1, 2004 ..			$ 59,700
Purchases		$521,980	
Less: Purchases returns and allowances ..	$9,100		
Purchases discounts	2,525	11,625	
Net purchases		$510,355	
Add transportation in		17,400	
Cost of merchandise purchased			527,755
Merchandise available for sale			$587,455
Less merchandise inventory,			
December 31, 2004			62,150
Cost of merchandise sold			$525,305

The multiple-step income statement under the periodic inventory system is illustrated in Exhibit 2. The multiple-step income statement under a perpetual inventory system is similar, except that the cost of merchandise sold is reported as a single amount.

Exhibit 2 Multiple-Step Income Statement—Periodic Inventory System

NetSolutions Income Statement For the Year Ended December 31, 2004			
Revenue from sales:			
Sales		$720,185	
Less: Sales returns and allowances	$ 6,140		
Sales discounts	5,790	11,930	
Net sales			$708,255
Cost of merchandise sold:			
Merchandise inventory, January 1, 2004		$ 59,700	
Purchases	$521,980		
Less: Purchases returns and allowances $9,100			
Purchases discounts 2,525	11,625		
Net purchases	$510,355		
Add transportation in	17,400		
Cost of merchandise purchased		527,755	
Merchandise available for sale		$587,455	
Less merchandise inventory,			
December 31, 2004		62,150	
Cost of merchandise sold			525,305
Gross profit			$182,950
Operating expenses:			
Selling expenses:			
Sales salaries expense	$ 60,030		
Advertising expense	10,860		
Depreciation expense—store equipment ..	3,100		
Miscellaneous selling expense	630		
Total selling expenses		$ 74,620	
Administrative expenses:			
Office salaries expense	$ 21,020		
Rent expense	8,100		
Depreciation expense—office equipment ..	2,490		
Insurance expense	1,910		
Office supplies expense	610		
Miscellaneous administrative expense	760		
Total administrative expenses		34,890	
Total operating expenses			109,510
Income from operations			$ 73,440
Other income:			
Interest revenue	$ 3,800		
Rent revenue	600		
Total other income		$ 4,400	
Other expense:			
Interest expense		2,440	1,960
Net income			$ 75,400

Chart of Accounts for a Periodic Inventory System

Exhibit 3 is the chart of accounts for NetSolutions when a periodic inventory system is used. The periodic inventory accounts related to merchandising transactions are shown in color.

Exhibit 3 Chart of Accounts
—Periodic Inventory System

Balance Sheet Accounts		Income Statement Accounts	
	100 Assets		400 Revenues
110	Cash	410	Sales
111	Notes Receivable	411	Sales Returns and Allowances
112	Accounts Receivable	412	Sales Discounts
113	Interest Receivable		500 Costs and Expenses
115	Merchandise Inventory	510	Purchases
116	Office Supplies	511	Purchases Returns and
117	Prepaid Insurance		Allowances
120	Land	512	Purchases Discounts
123	Store Equipment	513	Transportation In
124	Accumulated Depreciation—	520	Sales Salaries Expenses
	Store Equipment	521	Advertising Expense
125	Office Equipment	522	Depreciation Expense—Store
126	Accumulated Depreciation—		Equipment
	Office Equipment	523	Transportation Out
	200 Liabilities	529	Miscellaneous Selling Expense
210	Accounts Payable	530	Office Salaries Expense
211	Salaries Payable	531	Rent Expense
212	Unearned Rent	532	Depreciation Expense—Office
215	Notes Payable		Equipment
	300 Owner's Equity	533	Insurance Expense
310	Chris Clark, Capital	534	Office Supplies Expense
311	Chris Clark, Drawing	539	Misc. Administrative Expense
312	Income Summary		600 Other Income
		610	Rent Revenue
		611	Interest Revenue
			700 Other Expense
		710	Interest Expense

End-of-Period Procedures in a Periodic Inventory System

The end-of-period procedures are generally the same for the periodic and perpetual inventory systems. In the remainder of this appendix, we will discuss the differences in procedures for the two systems that affect the work sheet, the adjusting entries, and the closing entries. As the basis for illustrations, we will use the data for NetSolutions, presented in Chapter 6.

Work Sheet

The differences in the work sheet for a merchandising business that uses the periodic inventory system are highlighted in the work sheet for NetSolutions in Exhibit 4. As we illustrated earlier, accounts for purchases, purchases returns and allowances, purchases discounts, and transportation in are used in a periodic inventory system.

Under the periodic inventory system, the merchandise inventory account, throughout the accounting period, shows the inventory at the beginning of the period. As shown in Exhibit 1, the merchandise inventory on January 1, 2004, $59,700, is a part of the merchandise available for sale. At the end of the period, the beginning inventory amount in the ledger is replaced with the ending inventory amount. To update the inventory account, two adjusting entries are used.[2] The first adjusting entry

---

[2] Another method of updating the merchandise inventory account at the end of the period is called the *closing method*. This method adjusts the merchandise inventory through the use of closing entries. This method may not be appropriate for use in computerized accounting systems. Since the financial statements are the same under both methods and since computerized accounting systems are used by most businesses, the closing method is not illustrated.

Exhibit 4 Work Sheet—Periodic Inventory System

NetSolutions
Work Sheet
For the Year Ended December 31, 2004

Account Title	Trial Balance Dr.	Trial Balance Cr.	Adjustments Dr.	Adjustments Cr.	Adjusted Trial Balance Dr.	Adjusted Trial Balance Cr.	Income Statement Dr.	Income Statement Cr.	Balance Sheet Dr.	Balance Sheet Cr.
Cash	52,950				52,950				52,950	
Notes Receivable	35,000				35,000				35,000	
Accounts Receivable	55,880				55,880				55,880	
Interest Receivable			(a) 200		200				200	
Merchandise Inventory	59,700		(c)62,150	(b)59,700	62,150				62,150	
Office Supplies	1,090			(d) 610	480				480	
Prepaid Insurance	4,560			(e) 1,910	2,650				2,650	
Land	20,000				20,000				20,000	
Store Equipment	27,100				27,100				27,100	
Accum. Depr.—Store Equipment		2,600		(f) 3,100		5,700				5,700
Office Equipment	15,570				15,570				15,570	
Accum. Depr.—Office Equipment		2,230		(g) 2,490		4,720				4,720
Accounts Payable		22,420				22,420				22,420
Salaries Payable				(h) 1,140		1,140				1,140
Unearned Rent		2,400	(i) 600			1,800				1,800
Notes Payable (final payment, 2014)		25,000				25,000				25,000
Chris Clark, Capital		153,800				153,800				153,800
Chris Clark, Drawing	18,000				18,000				18,000	
Income Summary			(b)59,700	(c)62,150	59,700	62,150	59,700	62,150		
Sales		720,185				720,185		720,185		
Sales Returns and Allowances	6,140				6,140		6,140			
Sales Discounts	5,790				5,790		5,790			
Purchases	521,980				521,980		521,980			
Purchases Returns & Allowances		9,100				9,100		9,100		
Purchases Discounts		2,525				2,525		2,525		
Transportation In	17,400				17,400		17,400			
Sales Salaries Expense	59,250		(h) 780		60,030		60,030			
Advertising Expense	10,860				10,860		10,860			
Depr. Expense—Store Equipment			(f) 3,100		3,100		3,100			
Miscellaneous Selling Expense	630				630		630			
Office Salaries Expense	20,660		(h) 360		21,020		21,020			
Rent Expense	8,100				8,100		8,100			
Depr. Expense—Office Equipment			(g) 2,490		2,490		2,490			
Insurance Expense			(e) 1,910		1,910		1,910			
Office Supplies Expense			(d) 610		610		610			
Misc. Administrative Expense	760				760		760			
Rent Revenue				(i) 600		600		600		
Interest Revenue		3,600		(a) 200		3,800		3,800		
Interest Expense	2,440				2,440		2,440			
	943,860	943,860	131,900	131,900	1,012,940	1,012,940	722,960	798,360	289,980	214,580
Net income							75,400			75,400
							798,360	798,360	289,980	289,980

(a) Interest earned but not received on notes receivable, $200.

(b) Beginning merchandise inventory, $59,700.

(c) Ending merchandise inventory, $62,150.

(d) Office supplies used, $610 ($1,090 − $480).

(e) Insurance expired, $1,910.

(f) Depreciation of store equipment, $3,100.

(g) Depreciation of office equipment, $2,490.

(h) Salaries accrued but not paid (sales salaries, $780; office salaries, $360), $1,140.

(i) Rent earned from amount received in advance, $600.

transfers the beginning inventory balance to Income Summary. This entry, shown below, has the effect of increasing the cost of merchandise sold and decreasing net income.

Dec. 31	Income Summary	59,700	
	Merchandise Inventory		59,700

After the first adjusting entry has been recorded and posted, the balance of the merchandise inventory account is zero. The second adjusting entry records the cost of the merchandise on hand at the end of the period by debiting Merchandise Inventory. Since the merchandise inventory at December 31, 2004, $62,150, is subtracted from the cost of merchandise available for sale in determining the cost of merchandise sold, Income Summary is credited. This credit has the effect of decreasing the cost of merchandise available for sale during the period, $587,455, by the cost of the unsold merchandise. The second adjusting entry is shown below.

Dec. 31	Merchandise Inventory	62,150	
	Income Summary		62,150

After the second adjusting entry has been recorded and posted, the balance of the merchandise inventory account is the amount of the ending inventory. The accounts for Merchandise Inventory and Income Summary after both entries have been posted would appear in T account form as follows:

Merchandise Inventory

2004						
Jan. 1	Beginning inventory	59,700	Dec. 31	Beginning inventory		59,700
Dec. 31	Ending inventory	62,150				

Income Summary

Dec. 31	Beginning inventory	59,700	Dec. 31	Ending inventory		62,150

No separate adjusting entry can be made for merchandise inventory shrinkage in a periodic inventory system. This is because no perpetual inventory records are available to show what inventory should be on hand at the end of the period. One disadvantage of the periodic inventory system is that inventory shrinkage cannot be measured.[3]

Completing the Work Sheet

After all of the necessary adjustments have been entered on the work sheet, the work sheet is completed in the normal manner. An exception to the usual practice of extending only account balances is Income Summary. Both the debit and credit amounts for Income Summary are extended to the Adjusted Trial Balance columns. Extending both amounts aids in the preparation of the income statement because the debit adjustment (the beginning inventory of $59,700) and the credit adjustment (the ending inventory of $62,150) are reported as part of the cost of merchandise sold.

The purchases, purchases discounts, purchases returns and allowances, and transportation in accounts are extended to the Income Statement Columns of the work sheet, since they are used in computing the cost of merchandise sold. You should note that the two merchandise inventory amounts in Income Summary are extended to the Income Statement columns. After all of the items have been extended to the statement columns, the four columns are totaled and the net income or net loss is determined.

---

[3] Any inventory shrinkage that does exist is part of the cost of merchandise sold and is reported on the income statement, since a smaller ending inventory is deducted from other merchandise available for sale.

Financial Statements

The financial statements for NetSolutions are essentially the same under both the perpetual and periodic inventory systems. The main difference is that the cost of goods is reported as a single amount under the perpetual system. Exhibit 2 illustrates the manner in which cost of merchandise sold is reported in a multiple-step income statement when the periodic inventory system is used.[4]

Adjusting and Closing Entries

The adjusting entries are the same under both inventory systems, except for merchandise inventory. As indicated previously, two adjusting entries for beginning and ending merchandise inventory are necessary in a periodic inventory system.

The closing entries differ in the periodic inventory system in that there is no cost of merchandise sold account to be closed to Income Summary. Instead, the purchases, purchases discounts, purchases returns and allowances, and transportation in accounts are closed to Income Summary.[5] To illustrate, the adjusting and closing entries under a periodic inventory system for NetSolutions are shown below.

	Date		Description	Post. Ref.	Debit	Credit	
1			Adjusting Entries				1
2	2004 Dec.	31	Interest Receivable	113	2 0 0 00		2
3			Interest Revenue	611		2 0 0 00	3
4							4
5		31	Income Summary	312	59 7 0 0 00		5
6			Merchandise Inventory	115		59 7 0 0 00	6
7							7
8		31	Merchandise Inventory	115	62 1 5 0 00		8
9			Income Summary	312		62 1 5 0 00	9
10							10
11		31	Office Supplies Expense	534	6 1 0 00		11
12			Office Supplies	116		6 1 0 00	12
13							13
14		31	Insurance Expense	533	1 9 1 0 00		14
15			Prepaid Insurance	117		1 9 1 0 00	15
16							16
17		31	Depreciation Expense—Store Equip.	522	3 1 0 0 00		17
18			Accumulated Depr.—Store Equip.	124		3 1 0 0 00	18
19							19
20		31	Depreciation Expense—Office Equip.	532	2 4 9 0 00		20
21			Accumulated Depr.—Office Equip.	126		2 4 9 0 00	21
22							22
23		31	Sales Salaries Expense	520	7 8 0 00		23
24			Office Salaries Expense	530	3 6 0 00		24
25			Salaries Payable	211		1 1 4 0 00	25
26							26
27		31	Unearned Rent	212	6 0 0 00		27
28			Rent Revenue	610		6 0 0 00	28

JOURNAL   PAGE 16

---

[4] The single-step income statement would be the same for both the perpetual and the periodic inventory systems.
[5] The balance of Income Summary, after the merchandise inventory adjustments and the first two closing entries have been posted, is the net income or net loss for the period.

	Date		Description	Post. Ref.	Debit	Credit	
			Closing Entries				1
2	2004 Dec.	31	Sales	410	720 1 8 5 00		2
3			Purchases Returns and Allowances	511	9 1 0 0 00		3
4			Purchases Discounts	512	2 5 2 5 00		4
5			Rent Revenue	610	6 0 0 00		5
6			Interest Revenue	611	3 8 0 0 00		6
7			Income Summary	312		736 2 1 0 00	7
8							8
9		31	Income Summary	312	663 2 6 0 00		9
10			Sales Returns and Allowances	411		6 1 4 0 00	10
11			Sales Discounts	412		5 7 9 0 00	11
12			Purchases	510		521 9 8 0 00	12
13			Transportation In	513		17 4 0 0 00	13
14			Sales Salaries Expense	520		60 0 3 0 00	14
15			Advertising Expense	521		10 8 6 0 00	15
16			Depreciation Exp.—Store Equip.	522		3 1 0 0 00	16
17			Miscellaneous Selling Expense	529		6 3 0 00	17
18			Office Salaries Expense	530		21 0 2 0 00	18
19			Rent Expense	531		8 1 0 0 00	19
20			Depreciation Exp.—Office Equip.	532		2 4 9 0 00	20
21			Insurance Expense	533		1 9 1 0 00	21
22			Office Supplies Expense	534		6 1 0 00	22
23			Miscellaneous Administrative Exp.	539		7 6 0 00	23
24			Interest Expense	710		2 4 4 0 00	24
25							25
26		31	Income Summary	312	75 4 0 0 00		26
27			Chris Clark, Capital	310		75 4 0 0 00	27
28							28
29		31	Chris Clark, Capital	310	18 0 0 0 00		29
30			Chris Clark, Drawing	311		18 0 0 0 00	30

JOURNAL   **PAGE 17**

EXERCISES

Exercise D–1
Purchases-related transactions—periodic inventory system

Journalize entries for the following related transactions, assuming that Fairways 'N Greens, Inc. uses the periodic inventory system.

a. Purchased $7,000 of merchandise from Bertha Co. on account, terms 2/10, n/30.
b. Discovered that some of the merchandise was defective and returned items with an invoice price of $1,000, receiving credit.
c. Paid the amount owed on the invoice within the discount period.
d. Purchased $4,000 of merchandise from Precision Golf, Inc. on account, terms 1/10, n/30.
e. Paid the amount owed on the invoice within the discount period.

Exercise D–2
Sales-related transactions—periodic inventory system

Journalize entries for the following related transactions, assuming that Triad Company uses the periodic inventory system.

Mar. 8 Sold merchandise to a customer for $8,300, terms FOB shipping point, 2/10, n/30.
     8 Paid the transportation charges of $250, debiting the amount to Accounts Receivable.

Mar. 12 Issued a credit memorandum for $1,600 to the customer for merchandise returned.
18 Received a check for the amount due from the sale.

Exercise D–3
Adjusting entries for merchandise inventory—periodic inventory system

Data assembled for preparing the work sheet for Lancaster Co. for the fiscal year ended December 31, 2003, included the following:

Merchandise inventory as of January 1, 2003	$273,000
Merchandise inventory as of December 31, 2003	$309,600

Journalize the two adjusting entries for merchandise inventory that would appear on the work sheet, assuming that the periodic inventory system is used.

Exercise D–4
Identification of missing items from income statement—periodic inventory system

For (a) through (i), identify the items designated by "X".

a. Purchases − (X + X) = Net purchases
b. Sales − (X + X) = Net sales
c. Merchandise inventory (beginning) + Cost of merchandise purchased = X
d. Net purchases + X = Cost of merchandise purchased
e. Net sales − Cost of merchandise sold = X
f. Merchandise available for sale − X = Cost of merchandise sold
g. Gross profit − Operating expenses = X
h. X + X = Operating expenses
i. Income from operations + X − X = Net income

Exercise D–5
Multiple-step income statement—periodic inventory system

✓ Gross profit: $144,100

Selected data for Tower Stores Company for the year ended December 31, 2003, are as follows:

Merchandise inventory, January 1	$ 53,600
Merchandise inventory, December 31	63,900
Purchases	657,000
Purchases discounts	8,000
Purchases returns and allowances	15,500
Sales	805,000
Sales discounts	6,500
Sales returns and allowances	8,700
Transportation in	22,500

Prepare a multiple-step income statement through gross profit for Tower Stores Company for the current year ended December 31.

Exercise D–6
Adjusting and closing entries—periodic inventory system

Selected account titles and related amounts appearing in the Income Statement and Balance Sheet columns of the work sheet of Field of Dreams Company for the year ended December 31 are listed in alphabetical order as follows:

Administrative Expenses	$ 69,500
Building	312,500
Cash	58,500
Ted Kostner, Capital	472,580
Ted Kostner, Drawing	36,000
Interest Expense	2,500
Merchandise Inventory (1/1)	285,000
Merchandise Inventory (12/31)	247,000
Notes Payable	25,000
Office Supplies	10,600
Purchases	760,000
Purchases Discounts	6,000
Purchases Returns and Allowances	7,000
Salaries Payable	4,220
Sales	1,315,000
Sales Discounts	10,200
Sales Returns and Allowances	44,300
Selling Expenses	232,700
Store Supplies	7,700
Transportation In	21,300

All selling expenses have been recorded in the account entitled Selling Expenses, and all administrative expenses have been recorded in the account entitled Administrative Expenses. Assuming that Field of Dreams Company uses the periodic inventory system, journalize (a) the adjusting entries for merchandise inventory and (b) the closing entries.

PROBLEMS

Problem D–1
Sales-related and purchase-related transactions—periodic inventory system

The following were selected from among the transactions completed by Cargo Shops, Inc., during April of the current year:

Apr. 4. Purchased merchandise on account from Turner Co., list price $18,000, trade discount 40%, terms FOB destination, 2/10, n/30.
  5. Sold merchandise for cash, $4,100.
  7. Purchased merchandise on account from Summit Co., $6,800, terms FOB shipping point, 2/10, n/30, with prepaid transportation costs of $200 added to the invoice.
  7. Returned $2,200 of merchandise purchased on April 4 from Turner Co.
  11. Sold merchandise on account to Fawcett Co., list price $2,500, trade discount 20%, terms 1/10, n/30.
  14. Paid Turner Co. on account for purchase of April 4, less return of April 7 and discount.
  15. Sold merchandise on nonbank credit cards and reported accounts to the card company, American Express, $5,850.
  17. Paid Summit Co. on account for purchase of April 7, less discount.
  21. Received cash on account from sale of April 11 to Fawcett Co., less discount.
  25. Sold merchandise on account to Clemons Co., $3,000, terms 1/10, n/30.
  28. Received cash from American Express for nonbank credit card sales of April 15, less $280 service fee.
  30. Received merchandise returned by Clemons Co. from sale on April 25, $1,700.

Instructions
Journalize the transactions for Cargo Shops, Inc., in a two-column general journal.

Problem D–2
Sales-related and purchase-related transactions—periodic inventory system

The following were selected from among the transactions completed by Home Sentry Company during March of the current year:

Mar 2. Purchased merchandise on account from Diane Co., list price $32,000, trade discount 30%, terms FOB shipping point, 2/10, n/30, with prepaid transportation costs of $720 added to the invoice.
  4. Purchased merchandise on account from Lambert Co., $8,000, terms FOB destination, 1/10, n/30.
  6. Sold merchandise on account to C. F. Howell Co., list price $7,500, trade discount 40%, terms 2/10, n/30.
  9. Returned merchandise purchased on March 4 from Lambert Co., $1,300.
  12. Paid Diane Co. on account for purchase of March 2, less discount.
  14. Paid Lambert Co. on account for purchase of March 4, less return of March 9 and discount.
  16. Received cash on account from sale of March 6 to C. F. Howell Co., less discount.
  19. Sold merchandise on nonbank credit cards and reported accounts to the card company, American Express, $4,450.
  22. Sold merchandise on account to Wu Co., $4,420, terms 2/10, n/30.
  24. Sold merchandise for cash, $4,350.
  25. Received merchandise returned by Wu Co. from sale on March 22, $1,610.
  31. Received cash from American Express for nonbank credit card sales of March 19, less $290 service fee.

Instructions
Journalize the transactions for Home Sentry Co. in a two-column general journal.

Problem D–3

Sales-related and purchase-related transactions for seller and buyer—periodic inventory system

GENERAL LEDGER

The following selected transactions were completed during July between Tramley Company and Simpson Co.:

July 3. Tramley Company sold merchandise on account to Simpson Co., $12,400, terms FOB destination, 2/15, n/eom.

3. Tramley Company paid transportation costs of $450 for delivery of merchandise sold to Simpson Co. on July 3.

10. Tramley Company sold merchandise on account to Simpson Co., $9,600, terms FOB shipping point, n/eom.

11. Simpson Co. returned merchandise purchased on account on July 3 from Tramley Company, $2,000.

14. Simpson Co. paid transportation charges of $200 on July 10 purchase from Tramley Company.

17. Tramley Company sold merchandise on account to Simpson Co., $30,000, terms FOB shipping point, 1/10, n/30. Tramley prepaid transportation costs of $1,750, which were added to the invoice.

18. Simpson Co. paid Tramley Company for purchase of July 3, less discount and less return of July 11.

27. Simpson Co. paid Tramley Company on account for purchase of July 17, less discount.

31. Simpson Co. paid Tramley Company on account for purchase of July 10.

Instructions

Journalize the July transactions for (1) Tramley Company and for (2) Simpson Co.

Problem D–4

Preparation of work sheet, financial statements, and adjusting and closing entries—periodic inventory system

GENERAL LEDGER

✓ 1. Net income: $174,350

The accounts and their balances in the ledger of Bait and Tackle Co. on December 31, 2003, are as follows:

Cash	$ 38,000
Accounts Receivable	112,500
Merchandise Inventory	180,000
Prepaid Insurance	9,700
Store Supplies	4,250
Office Supplies	2,100
Store Equipment	132,000
Accumulated Depreciation—Store Equipment	40,300
Office Equipment	50,000
Accumulated Depreciation—Office Equipment	17,200
Accounts Payable	66,700
Salaries Payable	—
Unearned Rent	1,200
Note Payable (final payment, 2010)	105,000
J. Milner, Capital	154,600
J. Milner, Drawing	40,000
Income Summary	—
Sales	915,000
Sales Returns and Allowances	11,900
Sales Discounts	7,100
Purchases	540,000
Purchases Returns and Allowances	10,100
Purchases Discounts	4,900
Transportation In	6,200
Sales Salaries Expense	71,400
Advertising Expense	25,000
Depreciation Expense—Store Equipment	—
Store Supplies Expense	—
Miscellaneous Selling Expense	1,600
Office Salaries Expense	44,000
Rent Expense	26,000

Insurance Expense	—
Depreciation Expense—Office Equipment	—
Office Supplies Expense	—
Miscellaneous Administrative Expense	$ 1,650
Rent Revenue	—
Interest Expense	11,600

The data needed for year-end adjustments on December 31 are as follows:

Merchandise inventory on December 31		$196,000
Insurance expired during the year		5,400
Supplies on hand on December 31:		
Store supplies		1,300
Office supplies		750
Depreciation for the year:		
Store equipment		7,500
Office equipment		3,800
Salaries payable on December 31:		
Sales salaries	$3,850	
Office salaries	1,150	5,000
Unearned rent on December 31		400

Instructions

1. Prepare a work sheet for the fiscal year ended December 31, listing all accounts in the order given.
2. Prepare a multiple-step income statement.
3. Prepare a statement of owner's equity.
4. Prepare a report form of balance sheet, assuming that the current portion of the note payable is $15,000.
5. Journalize the adjusting entries.
6. Journalize the closing entries.

Appendix E: Foreign Currency Transactions

In this appendix, we describe and illustrate the accounting for transactions in which a U.S. company sells products or services to foreign companies or buys foreign products or services. If transactions with foreign companies require payment or receipt in U.S. dollars, no special accounting problems arise.[1] Such transactions are recorded as we described and illustrated earlier in this text. For example, the sale of merchandise to a Japanese company that is billed in and paid for in dollars would be recorded by the U.S. company in the normal manner. However, if the transaction is billed and payment is to be received in Japanese yen, the U.S. company may incur an exchange gain or loss. Some foreign manufacturers have begun building manufacturing plants in the United States, which avoids such gains and losses. For example, **BMW** has constructed its first U.S. plant.

Realized Currency Exchange Gains and Losses

When a U.S. company receives foreign currency, the amount must be converted to its equivalent in U.S. dollars for recording in the accounts. When payment is to be made in a foreign currency, U.S. dollars must be exchanged for the foreign currency for payment. To illustrate, assume that a U.S. company purchases merchandise from a British company that requires payment in British pounds. In this case, U.S. dollars ($) must be exchanged for British pounds (£) to pay for the merchandise. This exchange of one currency for another involves using an exchange rate. The **exchange rate** is the rate at which one unit of currency (the dollar, for example) can be converted into another currency (the British pound, for example).

To continue the example, assume that the U.S. company had purchased merchandise for £1,000 from a British company on June 1, when the exchange rate was $1.40 per British pound. Thus, $1,400 must be exchanged for £1,000 to make the purchase.[2] The U.S. company records the transaction in dollars, as follows:

June	1	Merchandise Inventory		1 4 0 0 00	
		Cash			1 4 0 0 00
		Payment of Invoice No. 1725 from			
		W. A. Sterling Co., £1,000; exchange			
		rate, $1.40 per British pound.			

Instead of a cash purchase, the purchase may be made on account. In this case, the exchange rate may change between the date of purchase and the date of payment of the account payable in the foreign currency. In practice, exchange rates vary daily.

To illustrate, assume that the preceding purchase was made on account. The entry to record it is as follows:

June	1	Merchandise Inventory		1 4 0 0 00	
		Accounts Payable—W. A. Sterling Co.			1 4 0 0 00
		Purchase on account; Invoice			
		No. 1725 from W. A. Sterling Co.,			
		£1,000; exchange rate, $1.40 per			
		British pound.			

[1] This discussion is from the point of view of a U.S. company. Unless otherwise indicated, the reference to the dollar refers to the U.S. dollar rather than a dollar of another country, such as Canada.

[2] Foreign exchange rates are quoted in major financial reporting services. Because the exchange rates are quite volatile, those used in this chapter are assumed rates.

Assume that on the date of payment, June 15, the exchange rate was $1.45 per pound. The £1,000 account payable must be settled by exchanging $1,450 (£1,000 × $1.45) for £1,000. In this case, the U.S. company incurs an exchange loss of $50 because $1,450 was needed to settle a $1,400 account payable. The cash payment is recorded as follows:

June	15	Accounts Payable—W. A. Sterling Co.	1 4 0 0 00	
		Exchange Loss	5 0 00	
		Cash		1 4 5 0 00
		Cash paid on Invoice No. 1725, for		
		£1,000, or $1,400, when exchange		
		rate was $1.45 per pound.		

We can analyze all transactions with foreign companies in the manner described. For example, assume that a sale on account for $1,000 to a Swiss company on May 1 was billed in Swiss francs. The cost of the merchandise sold was $600, and the selling company uses a perpetual inventory system. If the exchange rate was $0.25 per Swiss franc (F) on May 1, the transaction is recorded as follows:

May	1	Accounts Receivable—D. W. Robinson Co.	1 0 0 0 00	
		Sales		1 0 0 0 00
		Invoice No. 9772, F4,000; exchange		
		rate, $0.25 per Swiss franc.		
	1	Cost of Merchandise Sold	6 0 0 00	
		Merchandise Inventory		6 0 0 00

Assume that the exchange rate increases to $0.30 per Swiss franc on May 31 when cash is received. In this case, the U.S. company realizes an exchange gain of $200. This gain is realized because the F4,000, which had a value of $1,000 on the date of sale, has increased in value to $1,200 (F4,000 × $0.30) on May 31 when the payment is received. The receipt of the cash is recorded as follows:

May	31	Cash	1 2 0 0 00	
		Accounts Receivable—D. W. Robinson Co.		1 0 0 0 00
		Exchange Gain		2 0 0 00
		Cash received on Invoice No. 9772,		
		for F4,000, $1,000, when exchange		
		rate was $0.30 per Swiss franc.		

Unrealized Currency Exchange Gains and Losses

In the previous examples, the transactions were completed by either the receipt or the payment of cash. On the date the cash was received or paid, any related exchange gain or loss was realized and was recorded in the accounts. However, financial statements may be prepared between the date of the sale or purchase on account and the date the cash is received or paid. In this case, any exchange gain or loss created by a change in exchange rates between the date of the original transaction and the balance sheet date must be recorded. Such an exchange gain or loss is reported in the financial statements as an unrealized exchange gain or loss.

To illustrate, assume that a sale on account for $1,000 had been made to a German company on December 20 and had been billed in deutsche marks (DM). The cost of merchandise sold was $700. On this date, the exchange rate was $0.50 per deutsche mark. The transaction is recorded as follows:

Dec.	20	Accounts Receivable—T. A. Mueller Inc.	1 0 0 0 00	
		Sales		1 0 0 0 00
		Invoice No. 1793, DM2,000; exchange		
		rate, $0.50 per deutsche mark.		
	20	Cost of Merchandise Sold	7 0 0 00	
		Merchandise Inventory		7 0 0 00

Assume that the exchange rate decreases to $0.45 per deutsche mark on December 31, the date of the balance sheet. Thus, the $1,000 account receivable on December 31 has a value of only $900 (DM2,000 × $0.45). This unrealized loss of $100 ($1,000 − $900) is recorded as follows:

Dec.	31	Exchange Loss	1 0 0 00	
		Accounts Receivable—T. A. Mueller Inc.		1 0 0 00
		Invoice No. 1793, DM2,000 × $0.05		
		decrease in exchange rate.		

Any additional change in the exchange rate during the following period is recorded when the cash is received. To continue the illustration, assume that the exchange rate declines from $0.45 to $0.42 per deutsche mark by January 19, when the DM2,000 is received. The receipt of the cash on January 19 is recorded as follows:

Jan.	19	Cash (DM2,000 × $0.42)	8 4 0 00	
		Exchange Loss (DM2,000 × $0.03)	6 0 00	
		Accounts Receivable—T. A. Mueller Inc.		9 0 0 00
		Cash received on Invoice No. 1793,		
		for DM2,000, or $900, when exchange		
		rate was $0.42 per deutsche mark.		

In contrast, assume that in the preceding example the exchange rate increases between December 31 and January 19. In this case, an exchange gain would be recorded on January 19. For example, if the exchange rate increases from $0.45 to $0.47 per deutsche mark during this period, Exchange Gain would be credited for $40 (DM2,000 × $0.02).

A balance in the exchange loss account at the end of the fiscal period is reported in the Other Expense section of the income statement. A balance in the exchange gain account is reported in the Other Income section.

EXERCISES

Exercise E–1
Entries for sales made in foreign currency

The Cuddly Toy Company makes sales on account to several Swedish companies that it bills in kronas. Journalize the entries for the following selected transactions completed during the current year, assuming that Cuddly uses the perpetual inventory system:

Aug. 2. Sold merchandise on account, 20,000 kronas; exchange rate, $0.14 per krona. The cost of merchandise sold was $1,600.

Sept. 1. Received cash from sale of August 2, 20,000 kronas; exchange rate, $0.15 per krona.
Oct. 30. Sold merchandise on account, 18,000 kronas; exchange rate, $0.15 per krona. The cost of merchandise sold was $1,550.
Nov. 29. Received cash from sale of October 30, 18,000 kronas; exchange rate, $0.13 per krona.

Exercise E–2
Entries for purchases made in foreign currency

Synthetic Care Inc. sells artificial arms and legs to hospitals and physicians. It purchases merchandise from a German company that requires payment in deutsche marks. Journalize the entries for the following selected transactions completed during the current year, assuming that Synthetic Care Inc. uses the perpetual inventory system:

Mar. 1. Purchased merchandise on account, net 30, 10,000 deutsche marks; exchange rate, $0.57 per deutsche mark.
      31. Paid invoice of March 1; exchange rate, $0.60 per deutsche mark.
June 5. Purchased merchandise on account, net 30, 7,500 deutsche marks; exchange rate, $0.60 per deutsche mark.
July 5. Paid invoice of June 5; exchange rate, $0.55 per deutsche mark.

PROBLEMS

Problem E–1
Foreign currency transactions

GENERAL
LEDGER

Universal Sports is a wholesaler of sports equipment, including golf clubs and gym sets. It sells to and purchases from companies in Canada and the Philippines. These transactions are settled in the foreign currency. The following selected transactions were completed during the current fiscal year:

April 8. Sold merchandise on account to Islands Company, net 30, 300,000 pesos; exchange rate, $0.030 per Philippines peso. The cost of merchandise sold was $5,500.
May 8. Received cash from Islands Company; exchange rate, $0.028 per Philippines peso.
      15. Purchased merchandise on account from LeMan Inc., net 30, $10,000 Canadian; exchange rate, $0.65 per Canadian dollar.
June 14. Issued check for amount owed to LeMan Inc.; exchange rate, $0.60 per Canadian dollar.
      30. Sold merchandise on account to Ella Company, net 30, 150,000 pesos; exchange rate, $0.031 per Philippines peso. The cost of merchandise sold was $2,200.
July 30. Received cash from Ella Company; exchange rate, $0.032 per Phillipines peso.
Oct. 8. Purchased merchandise on account from Chevalier Company, net 30, $50,000 Canadian; exchange rate, $0.73 per Canadian dollar.
Nov. 7. Issued check for amount owed to Chevalier Company; exchange rate, $0.74 per Canadian dollar.
Dec. 15. Sold merchandise on account to Cassandra Company, net 30, $120,000 Canadian; exchange rate, $0.75 per Canadian dollar. The cost of merchandise sold was $50,000.
      16. Purchased merchandise on account from Juan Company, net 30, 500,000 pesos; exchange rate, $0.033 per Philippines peso.
      31. Recorded unrealized currency exchange gain and/or loss on transactions of December 15 and 16. Exchange rates on December 31: $0.76 per Canadian dollar; $0.034 per Philippines peso.

Instructions

1. Journalize the entries to record the transactions and adjusting entries for the year, assuming that Universal Sports uses the perpetual inventory system.
2. Journalize the entries to record the payment of the December 16 purchase, on January 15, when the exchange rate was $0.031 per Philippines peso, and the receipt of cash from the December 15 sale, on January 17, when the exchange rate was $0.77 per Canadian dollar.

Appendix F: Partnerships

The partnership form of business organization allows two or more persons to combine capital, managerial talent, and experience with a minimum of effort. This form is widely used by small businesses. In many cases, the only alternative form of organization for multiple owners is the corporate form. Some states, however, do not permit the corporate form for certain types of businesses. For example, physicians, attorneys, and certified public accountants often organize as partnerships.

Characteristics of Partnerships

A **partnership** is "an association of two or more persons to carry on as co-owners a business for profit."[1] Partnerships have several characteristics with accounting implications.

A partnership has a **limited life**. A partnership dissolves whenever a partner ceases to be a member of the firm. For example, a partnership is dissolved if a partner withdraws due to bankruptcy, incapacity, or death. Likewise, admitting a new partner dissolves the old partnership. When a partnership is dissolved, a new partnership must be formed if operations of the business are to continue.

In most partnerships, the partners have **unlimited liability**. Each partner is individually liable to creditors for debts incurred by the partnership. Thus, if a partnership becomes insolvent, the partners must contribute sufficient personal assets to settle the debts of the partnership.

Partners have **co-ownership of partnership property**. The property invested in a partnership by a partner becomes the property of all the partners jointly. When a partnership is dissolved, the partners' claims against the assets are measured by the amount of the balances in their capital accounts.

Another characteristic of a partnership is **mutual agency**. This means that each partner is an agent of the partnership. Thus, each partner has the authority to enter into contracts for the partnership. The acts of each partner bind the entire partnership and become the obligations of all partners.

An important right of partners is **participation in income** of the partnership. Net income and net loss are distributed among the partners according to their agreement.

A partnership, like a sole proprietorship, is a **nontaxable entity** and thus does not pay federal income taxes. However, revenue and expense and other results of partnership operations must be reported annually to the Internal Revenue Service. The partners must, in turn, report their share of partnership income on their personal tax returns.

A partnership is created by a contract, known as the **partnership agreement** or **articles of partnership**. It should include statements regarding such matters as amounts to be invested, limits on withdrawals, distributions of income and losses, and admission and withdrawal of partners.

Advantages and Disadvantages of Partnerships

The partnership form of business organization is less widely used than are the proprietorship and corporate forms. For many business purposes, however, the advantages of the partnership form are greater than its disadvantages.

A partnership is relatively easy and inexpensive to organize, requiring only an agreement between two or more persons. A partnership has the advantage of bringing together more capital, managerial skills, and experience than does a proprietorship. Since a partnership is a nontaxable entity, the combined income taxes paid by

---

[1] This definition of a partnership is included in the Uniform Partnership Act, which has been adopted by over ninety percent of the states.

the individual partners may be lower than the income taxes that would be paid by a corporation, which is a taxable entity.

A major disadvantage of the partnership form of business organization is the unlimited liability feature for partners. Other disadvantages of a partnership are that its life is limited, and one partner can bind the partnership to contracts. Also, raising large amounts of capital is more difficult for a partnership than for a corporation. To overcome these limitations, other hybrid forms of organization, such as Subchapter S Corporations and Limited Liability Corporations (LLC), have been replacing partnerships as preferred legal methods of organization.

Accounting for Partnerships

Most of the day-to-day accounting for a partnership is the same as the accounting for any other form of business organization. The accounting system described in this text may, with little change, be used by a partnership. However, the formation, income distribution, dissolution, and liquidation of partnerships give rise to unique transactions. In the remainder of this appendix, we discuss accounting principles related to these areas.

Forming a Partnership

A separate entry is made for the investment of each partner in a partnership. The assets contributed by a partner are debited to the partnership asset accounts. If liabilities are assumed by the partnership, the partnership liability accounts are credited. The partner's capital account is credited for the net amount.

To illustrate, assume that Joseph A. Stevens and Earl S. Foster, sole owners of competing hardware stores, agree to combine their businesses in a partnership. Each is to contribute certain amounts of cash and other assets. It is also agreed that the partnership is to assume the liabilities of the separate businesses. The entry to record the assets contributed and the liabilities transferred by Stevens is as follows:

Apr.	1	Cash	7 2 0 0 00	
		Accounts Receivable	16 3 0 0 00	
		Merchandise Inventory	28 7 0 0 00	
		Store Equipment	5 4 0 0 00	
		Office Equipment	1 5 0 0 00	
		Allowance for Doubtful Accounts		1 5 0 0 00
		Accounts Payable		2 6 0 0 00
		Joseph A. Stevens, Capital		55 0 0 0 00

A similar entry would record the assets contributed and the liabilities transferred by Foster. In each entry, the noncash assets are recorded at values agreed upon by the partners. These values normally represent current market values and therefore usually differ from the book values of the assets in the records of the separate businesses. For example, the store equipment recorded at $5,400 in the preceding entry may have had a book value of $3,500 in Stevens's ledger (cost of $10,000 less accumulated depreciation of $6,500).

Dividing Net Income or Net Loss

Many partnerships have been dissolved because partners could not agree on an equitable distribution of income. Therefore, the method of dividing partnership income should be stated in the partnership agreement. In the absence of an agreement or if the agreement is silent on dividing net income or net losses, all partners share equally. However, if one partner contributes a larger portion of capital than the others, then net income should be divided to reflect the unequal capital contributions. Likewise, if the services rendered by one partner are more important than those of the others, net income should be divided to reflect the unequal service contributions. In the following paragraphs, we illustrate partnership agreements that recognize these differences.

Income Division—Services of Partners

One method of recognizing differences in partners' abilities and in amount of time devoted to the business provides for salary allowances to partners. Since partners are legally not employees of the partnership, such allowances are treated as divisions of the net income and are credited to the partners' capital accounts.

To illustrate, assume that the partnership agreement of Jennifer L. Stone and Crystal R. Mills provides for monthly salary allowances. Jennifer Stone is to receive a monthly allowance of $2,500 ($30,000 annually), and Crystal Mills is to receive $2,000 a month ($24,000 annually). Any net income remaining after the salary allowances is to be divided equally. Assume also that the net income for the year is $75,000.

A report of the division of net income may be presented as a separate statement to accompany the balance sheet and the income statement. Another format is to add the division to the bottom of the income statement. If the latter format is used, the lower part of the income statement would appear as follows:

Net income $75,000

Division of net income:

	J. L. Stone	C. R. Mills	Total
Annual salary allowance	$30,000	$24,000	$54,000
Remaining income	10,500	10,500	21,000
Net income	$40,500	$34,500	$75,000

Net income division is recorded as a closing entry, even if the partners do not actually withdraw the amounts of their salary allowances. The entry for dividing net income is as follows:

Dec.	31	Income Summary	75 0 0 0 00		
		Jennifer L. Stone, Capital			40 5 0 0 00
		Crystal R. Mills, Capital			34 5 0 0 00

If Stone and Mills had withdrawn their salary allowances monthly, the withdrawals would have been debited to their drawing accounts during the year. At the end of the year, the debit balances of $30,000 and $24,000 in their drawing accounts would be transferred as reductions to their capital accounts.

Accountants should be careful to distinguish between salary allowances and partner withdrawals. The amount of net income distributed to each partner's capital account at the end of the year may differ from the amount the partner withdraws during the year. In some cases, the partnership agreement may limit the amount of withdrawals a partner may make during a period.

Income Division—Services of Partners and Investment

Partners may agree that the most equitable plan of dividing income is to provide for (1) salary allowances and (2) interest on capital investments. Any remaining net income is then divided as agreed. For example, assume that the partnership agreement for Stone and Mills divides income as follows:

1. Monthly salary allowances of $2,500 for Stone and $2,000 for Mills.
2. Interest of 12% on each partner's capital balance on January 1.
3. Any remaining net income divided equally between the partners.

Stone had a credit balance of $80,000 in her capital account on January 1 of the current fiscal year, and Mills had a credit balance of $60,000 in her capital account. The $75,000 net income for the year is divided in the following schedule:

Net income $75,000

Division of net income:

	J. L. Stone	C. R. Mills	Total
Annual salary allowance	$30,000	$24,000	$54,000
Interest allowance	9,600[1]	7,200[2]	16,800
Remaining income	2,100	2,100	4,200
Net income	$41,700	$33,300	$75,000

[1]0.12 × $80,000   [2]0.12 × $60,000

For the above example, the entry to close the income summary account is shown below.

Dec.	31	Income Summary		75 0 0 0 00	
		Jennifer L. Stone, Capital			41 7 0 0 00
		Crystal R. Mills, Capital			33 3 0 0 00

Income Division—Allowances Exceed Net Income

In the examples so far, the net income has exceeded the total of the salary and interest allowances. If the net income is less than the total of the allowances, the **remaining balance** will be a negative amount. This amount must be divided among the partners as though it were a net loss.

To illustrate, assume the same salary and interest allowances as in the above example, but assume that the net income is $50,000. The salary and interest allowances total $39,600 for Stone and $31,200 for Mills. The sum of these amounts, $70,800, exceeds the net income of $50,000 by $20,800. It is necessary to divide the $20,800 excess between Stone and Mills. Under the partnership agreement, any net income or net loss remaining after deducting the allowances is divided equally between Stone and Mills. Thus, each partner is allocated one-half of the $20,800, and $10,400 is deducted from each partner's share of the allowances. The final division of net income between Stone and Mills is shown below.

Net income $50,000

Division of net income:

	J. L. Stone	C. R. Mills	Total
Annual salary allowance	$30,000	$24,000	$54,000
Interest allowance	9,600	7,200	16,800
Total	$39,600	$31,200	$70,800
Deduct: excess of allowances over income	10,400	10,400	20,800
Net income	$29,200	$20,800	$50,000

In closing Income Summary at the end of the year, $29,200 would be credited to Jennifer L. Stone, Capital, and $20,800 would be credited to Crystal R. Mills, Capital.

Partnership Dissolution

When a partnership dissolves, its affairs are not necessarily wound up. For example, a partnership of two partners may admit a third partner. Or if one of the partners in a business withdraws, the remaining partners may continue to operate the business. In such cases a new partnership is formed and a new partnership agreement should be prepared. Many partnerships provide for the admission of new partners and partner withdrawals in the partnership agreement so that the partnership may continue operations without executing a new agreement.

Admission of a Partner

A person may be admitted to a partnership only with the consent of all the current partners, through either of two methods:[2]

1. Purchasing an interest from one or more of the current partners.
2. Contributing assets to the partnership.

When the first method is used, the capital interest of the incoming partner is obtained from current partners, and *neither the total assets nor the total owner's equity of the business is affected.* When the second method is used, *both the total assets and the total owner's equity of the business are increased.* In the following paragraphs, we discuss each of these methods.

Purchasing an Interest in a Partnership. A person may be admitted to a partnership by buying an interest from one or more of the existing partners. The purchase and sale of the partnership interest occurs between the new partner and the existing partners acting as individuals. The only entry needed is to transfer owner's equity amounts from the capital accounts of the selling partners to the capital account established for the incoming partner.

As an example, assume that partners Tom Andrews and Nathan Bell have capital balances of $50,000 each. On June 1, each sells one-fifth of his equity to Joe Canter for $10,000 in cash. The exchange of cash is not a partnership transaction and thus is not recorded by the partnership. The only entry required in the partnership accounts is as follows:

June	1	Tom Andrews, Capital	10 0 0 0 00	
		Nathan Bell, Capital	10 0 0 0 00	
		Joe Canter, Capital		20 0 0 0 00

The effect of the transaction on the partnership accounts is presented in the following diagram:

Partnership Accounts

---

[2] Although an individual cannot become a partner without the consent of the other partners, the rights of a partner, such as the right to share in the income of a partnership, may be assigned to others without the consent of the other partners. Such issues are discussed in business law textbooks.

The preceding entry is not affected by the amount paid by Canter for the one-fifth interest. Any gain or loss on the sale of the partnership interest accrues to the selling partners as individuals, and not to the partnership. Thus, in either case, the entry to transfer the capital interests is the same as shown above.

After Canter is admitted to the partnership, the total owner's equity of the firm is still $100,000. Canter now has a one-fifth interest, or a $20,000 capital balance. However, Canter may not be entitled to a one-fifth share of the partnership net income. Division of net income or net loss will be made according to the new partnership agreement.

Contributing Assets to a Partnership. Instead of buying an interest from the current partners, the incoming partner may contribute assets to the partnership. In this case, both the assets and the owner's equity of the firm increase. For example, assume that Donald Lewis and Gerald Morton are partners with capital accounts of $35,000 and $25,000. On June 1, Sharon Nelson invests $20,000 cash in the business for an ownership equity of $20,000. The entry to record this transaction is as follows:

June	1	Cash		20 0 0 0 00	
		Sharon Nelson, Capital			20 0 0 0 00

The major difference between the admission of Nelson and the admission of Canter in the preceding example may be observed by comparing the following diagram with the preceding diagram.

Partnership Accounts

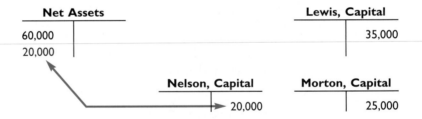

By admitting Nelson, the total owners' equity of the new partnership becomes $80,000, of which Nelson has a one-fourth interest, or $20,000. The extent of Nelson's share in partnership net income will be determined by the partnership agreement.

Revaluation of Assets. A partnership's asset account balances should be stated at current values when a new partner is admitted. If the accounts do not approximate current market values, the accounts should be adjusted. The net adjustment (increase or decrease) in asset values is divided among the capital accounts of the existing partners according to their income-sharing ratio. Failure to adjust the accounts for current values may result in the new partner sharing in asset gains or losses that arose in prior periods.

To illustrate, assume that in the preceding example for the Lewis and Morton partnership, the balance of the merchandise inventory account is $14,000 and the current replacement value is $17,000. Assuming that Lewis and Morton share net income equally, the revaluation is recorded as follows:

June	1	Merchandise Inventory		3 0 0 0 00	
		Donald Lewis, Capital			1 5 0 0 00
		Gerald Morton, Capital			1 5 0 0 00

Partner Bonuses. When a new partner is admitted to a partnership, the incoming partner may pay a bonus to the existing partners for the privilege of joining the partnership. Such a bonus is usually paid in expectation of high partnership profits in the future due to the contributions of the existing partners. Alternatively, the existing partners may pay the incoming partner a bonus to join the partnership. In this case, the bonus is usually paid in recognition of special qualities or skills that the incoming partner is bringing to the partnership. For example, celebrities such as actors, musicians, or sports figures often provide name recognition that is expected to increase partnership profits in the future. The amount of any bonus paid to the partnership is distributed among the partner capital accounts.[3]

To illustrate, assume that on March 1 the partnership of Marsha Jenkins and Helen Kramer is considering admitting a new partner, William Larson. After the assets of the partnership have been adjusted to current market values, the capital balance of Jenkins is $20,000 and the capital balance of Kramer is $24,000. Jenkins and Kramer agree to admit Larson to the partnership for $31,000. In return, Larson will receive a one-third equity in the partnership and will share equally with Jenkins and Kramer in partnership income or losses.

In this case Larson is paying Jenkins and Kramer a $6,000 bonus to join the partnership. This bonus is computed as follows:

Equity of Jenkins	$20,000
Equity of Kramer	24,000
Contribution of Larson	31,000
Total equity after admission of Larson	$75,000
Larson's equity interest after admission	× 1/3
Larson's equity after admission	$25,000
Contribution of Larson	$31,000
Larson's equity after admission	25,000
Bonus paid to Jenkins and Kramer	$ 6,000

The bonus is distributed to Jenkins and Kramer according to their income-sharing ratio. Assuming that Jenkins and Kramer share profits and losses equally, the entry to record the admission of Larson to the partnership is as follows:

Mar	1	Cash	31 0 0 0 00	
		William Larson, Capital		25 0 0 0 00
		Marsha Jenkins, Capital		3 0 0 0 00
		Helen Kramer, Capital		3 0 0 0 00

If a new partner possesses unique qualities or skills, the existing partners may agree to pay the new partner a bonus to join the partnership. To illustrate, assume that after adjusting assets to market values the capital balance of Janice Cowen is $80,000 and the capital balance of Steve Dodd is $40,000. Cowen and Dodd agree to admit Sandra Ellis to the partnership on June 1 for an investment of $30,000. In return, Ellis will receive a one-fourth equity interest in the partnership and will share in one-fourth of the profits and losses.

In this case Cowen and Dodd are paying Ellis a $7,500 bonus to join the partnership. This bonus is computed as follows:

---

[3] Another method is sometimes used to record the admission of partners in situations such as that described in this paragraph. This method attributes goodwill rather than a bonus to the partners. This method is discussed in advanced accounting textbooks.

Equity of Cowen	$ 80,000
Equity of Dodd	40,000
Contribution of Ellis	30,000
Total equity after admission of Ellis	$150,000
Ellis's equity interest after admission	× 25%
Ellis's equity after admission	$ 37,500
Contribution of Ellis	30,000
Bonus paid to Ellis	$ 7,500

Assuming that the income-sharing ratio of Cowen and Dodd was 2:1 before the admission of Ellis, the entry to record the bonus and admission of Ellis to the partnership is as follows:

June	1	Cash	30 0 0 0 00	
		Janice Cowen, Capital	5 0 0 0 00	
		Steve Dodd, Capital	2 5 0 0 00	
		Sandra Ellis, Capital		37 5 0 0 00

Withdrawal of a Partner

When a partner retires or withdraws from a partnership, one or more of the remaining partners may buy the withdrawing partner's interest. The firm may then continue its operations uninterrupted. In such cases the purchase and sale of the partnership interest is between the partners as individuals. The only entry on the partnership's records is to debit the capital account of the partner withdrawing and to credit the capital account of the partner or partners buying the additional interest.

If the withdrawing partner sells the interest directly to the partnership, both the assets and the owner's equity of the partnership are reduced. Before the sale, the asset accounts should be adjusted to current values, so that the withdrawing partner's equity may be accurately determined. The net amount of the adjustment should be divided among the capital accounts of the partners according to their income-sharing ratio. If not enough partnership cash or other assets are available to pay the withdrawing partner, a liability may be created (credited) for the amount owed the withdrawing partner.

Death of a Partner

When a partner dies, the accounts should be closed as of the date of death. The net income for the current year should be determined and divided among the partners' capital accounts. The balance in the capital account of the deceased partner is then transferred to a liability account with the deceased's estate. The remaining partner or partners may continue the business, or the affairs may be terminated. If the partnership continues in business, the procedures for settling with the estate are the same as those discussed for the withdrawal of a partner.

Liquidating Partnerships

When a partnership goes out of business, it usually sells the assets, pays the creditors, and distributes the remaining cash or other assets to the partners. This winding-up process is called the **liquidation** of the partnership. Although liquidating refers to the payment of liabilities, it is often used to include the entire winding-up process.

When the partnership goes out of business and the normal operations are discontinued, the accounts should be adjusted and closed. The only accounts remaining open will be the asset, contra asset, liability, and owner's equity accounts.

The sale of the assets is called **realization**. As cash is realized, it is used to pay the claims of creditors. After all liabilities have been paid, the remaining cash is distributed to the partners based on the balances in their capital accounts.

The liquidating process may extend over a long period of time as individual assets are sold. This delays the distribution of cash to partners but does not affect the amount each partner will receive.

To illustrate, assume that Farley, Greene, and Hall share income and losses in a ratio of 5:3:2 (5/10, 3/10, 2/10). On April 9, after discontinuing business operations of the partnership and closing the accounts, the following trial balance in summary form was prepared:

Cash	11,000	
Noncash Assets	64,000	
Liabilities		9,000
Jean Farley, Capital		22,000
Brad Greene, Capital		22,000
Alice Hall, Capital		22,000
Total	75,000	75,000

Based on these facts, we will show the accounting for liquidating the partnership by using three different selling prices for the noncash assets. To simplify, we assume that all noncash assets are sold in a single transaction and that all liabilities are paid at one time. In addition, Noncash Assets and Liabilities will be used as account titles in place of the various asset, contra asset, and liability accounts.

Gain on Realization

Between April 10 and April 30 of the current year, Farley, Greene, and Hall sell all noncash assets for $72,000. Thus, a gain of $8,000 ($72,000 − $64,000) is realized. The gain is divided among the capital accounts in the income-sharing ratio of 5:3:2. The liabilities are paid, and the remaining cash is distributed to the partners. *The cash is distributed to the partners based on the balances in their capital accounts.* A statement of partnership liquidation, which summarizes the liquidation process, is shown in Exhibit 1.

Exhibit 1 Gain on Realization

Farley, Greene, and Hall
Statement of Partnership Liquidation
For Period April 10–30, 2003

	Cash	+	Noncash Assets	=	Liabilities	+	Farley (50%)	+	Greene (30%)	+	Hall (20%)
Balances before realization	$11,000		$64,000		$9,000		$22,000		$22,000		$22,000
Sale of assets and division of gain	+72,000		−64,000		—		+ 4,000		+ 2,400		+ 1,600
Balances after realization	$83,000		$ 0		$9,000		$26,000		$24,400		$23,600
Payment of liabilities	− 9,000		—		−9,000		—		—		—
Balances after payment of liabilities	$74,000		$ 0		$ 0		$26,000		$24,400		$23,600
Cash distributed to partners	−74,000		—		—		−26,000		−24,400		−23,600
Final balances	$ 0		$ 0		$ 0		$ 0		$ 0		$ 0

The entries to record the steps in the liquidating process are as follows:

Cash		72 0 0 0 00		
Noncash Assets			64 0 0 0 00	
Gain on Realization			8 0 0 0 00	
Sold assets.				
Gain on Realization		8 0 0 0 00		
Jean Farley, Capital			4 0 0 0 00	
Brad Greene, Capital			2 4 0 0 00	
Alice Hall, Capital			1 6 0 0 00	
Divided gain from sale of assets.				
Liabilities		9 0 0 0 00		
Cash			9 0 0 0 00	
Paid liabilities.				
Jean Farley, Capital		26 0 0 0 00		
Brad Greene, Capital		24 4 0 0 00		
Alice Hall, Capital		23 6 0 0 00		
Cash			74 0 0 0 00	
Distributed cash to partners.				

As shown in Exhibit 1, the cash is distributed to the partners based on the balances of their capital accounts. These balances are determined after the gain on realization has been divided among the partners. *The income-sharing ratio should not be used as a basis for distributing the cash to partners.*

Loss on Realization

Assume that in the preceding example, Farley, Greene, and Hall dispose of all noncash assets for $44,000. A loss of $20,000 ($64,000 − $44,000) is realized. The steps in liquidating the partnership are summarized in Exhibit 2.

Exhibit 2 Loss on Realization

Farley, Greene, and Hall Statement of Partnership Liquidation For Period April 10–30, 2003											
							Capital				
	Cash	+	Noncash Assets	=	Liabilities	+	Farley (50%)	+	Greene (30%)	+	Hall (20%)
Balances before realization	$11,000		$64,000		$9,000		$22,000		$22,000		$22,000
Sale of assets and division of loss	+44,000		−64,000		—		−10,000		− 6,000		− 4,000
Balances after realization	$55,000		$ 0		$9,000		$12,000		$16,000		$18,000
Payment of liabilities	− 9,000		—		−9,000		—		—		—
Balances after payment of liabilities	$46,000		$ 0		$ 0		$12,000		$16,000		$18,000
Cash distributed to partners	−46,000		—		—		−12,000		−16,000		−18,000
Final balances	$ 0		$ 0		$ 0		$ 0		$ 0		$ 0

The entries to liquidate the partnership are as follows:

Cash		44 0 0 0 00		
Loss on Realization		20 0 0 0 00		
Noncash Assets			64 0 0 0 00	
Sold assets.				
Jean Farley, Capital		10 0 0 0 00		
Brad Greene, Capital		6 0 0 0 00		
Alice Hall, Capital		4 0 0 0 00		
Loss on Realization			20 0 0 0 00	
Divided loss from sale of assets.				
Liabilities		9 0 0 0 00		
Cash			9 0 0 0 00	
Paid liabilities.				
Jean Farley, Capital		12 0 0 0 00		
Brad Greene, Capital		16 0 0 0 00		
Alice Hall, Capital		18 0 0 0 00		
Cash			46 0 0 0 00	
Distributed cash to partners.				

Loss on Realization—Capital Deficiency

In the preceding example, the capital account of each partner was large enough to absorb the partner's share of the loss from realization. The partners received cash to the extent of the remaining balances in their capital accounts. The share of loss on realization may exceed, however, the balance in the partner's capital account. The resulting debit balance in the capital account is called a **deficiency**. It represents a claim of the partnership against the partner.

To illustrate, assume that Farley, Greene, and Hall sell all of the noncash assets for $10,000. A loss of $54,000 ($64,000 − $10,000) is realized. The share of the loss allocated to Farley, $27,000 (50% of $54,000), exceeds the $22,000 balance in her capital account. This $5,000 deficiency represents an amount that Farley owes the partnership. Assuming that Farley pays the entire deficiency to the partnership, sufficient cash is available to distribute to the remaining partners according to their capital balances.

The entries to record the liquidation are as follows:

Cash		10 0 0 0 00		
Loss on Realization		54 0 0 0 00		
Noncash Assets			64 0 0 0 00	
Sold assets.				
Jean Farley, Capital		27 0 0 0 00		
Brad Greene, Capital		16 2 0 0 00		
Alice Hall, Capital		10 8 0 0 00		
Loss on Realization			54 0 0 0 00	
Divided loss from sale of assets.				
Liabilities		9 0 0 0 00		
Cash			9 0 0 0 00	
Paid liabilities.				

	Cash		5 0 0 0 00		
	Jean Farley, Capital			5 0 0 0 00	
	Received cash from deficient partner.				
	Brad Greene, Capital		5 8 0 0 00		
	Alice Hall, Capital		11 2 0 0 00		
	Cash			17 0 0 0 00	
	Distributed cash to partners.				

The steps in liquidating the partnership in this case are summarized in Exhibit 3.

Exhibit 3 Loss on Realization—Capital Deficiency

<table>
<tr><td colspan="12" align="center">Farley, Greene, and Hall
Statement of Partnership Liquidation
For Period April 10–30, 2003</td></tr>
<tr><td></td><td></td><td></td><td></td><td></td><td></td><td colspan="5" align="center">Capital</td></tr>
<tr><td></td><td>Cash</td><td>+</td><td>Noncash Assets</td><td>=</td><td>Liabilities</td><td>+</td><td>Farley (50%)</td><td>+</td><td>Greene (30%)</td><td>+</td><td>Hall (20%)</td></tr>
<tr><td>Balances before realization</td><td>$11,000</td><td></td><td>$64,000</td><td></td><td>$9,000</td><td></td><td>$22,000</td><td></td><td>$22,000</td><td></td><td>$22,000</td></tr>
<tr><td>Sale of assets and division of loss</td><td>+10,000</td><td></td><td>−64,000</td><td></td><td>—</td><td></td><td>−27,000</td><td></td><td>−16,200</td><td></td><td>−10,800</td></tr>
<tr><td>Balances after realization</td><td>$21,000</td><td></td><td>$ 0</td><td></td><td>$9,000</td><td></td><td>$ 5,000(Dr.)</td><td></td><td>$ 5,800</td><td></td><td>$11,200</td></tr>
<tr><td>Payment of liabilities</td><td>− 9,000</td><td></td><td>—</td><td></td><td>−9,000</td><td></td><td>—</td><td></td><td>—</td><td></td><td>—</td></tr>
<tr><td>Balances after payment of liabilities</td><td>$12,000</td><td></td><td>$ 0</td><td></td><td>$ 0</td><td></td><td>$ 5,000(Dr.)</td><td></td><td>$ 5,800</td><td></td><td>$11,200</td></tr>
<tr><td>Receipt of deficiency</td><td>+ 5,000</td><td></td><td>—</td><td></td><td>—</td><td></td><td>+ 5,000</td><td></td><td>—</td><td></td><td>—</td></tr>
<tr><td>Balances</td><td>$17,000</td><td></td><td>$ 0</td><td></td><td>$ 0</td><td></td><td>$ 0</td><td></td><td>$ 5,800</td><td></td><td>$11,200</td></tr>
<tr><td>Cash distributed to partners</td><td>−17,000</td><td></td><td>—</td><td></td><td>—</td><td></td><td>—</td><td></td><td>− 5,800</td><td></td><td>−11,200</td></tr>
<tr><td>Final balances</td><td>$ 0</td><td></td><td>$ 0</td><td></td><td>$ 0</td><td></td><td>$ 0</td><td></td><td>$ 0</td><td></td><td>$ 0</td></tr>
</table>

If cash is not collected from a deficient partner, the partnership cash will not be large enough to pay the other partners in full. Any uncollected deficiency becomes a loss to the partnership and is divided among the remaining partners' capital balances, based on their income-sharing ratio. The cash balance will then equal the sum of the capital account balances. Cash is then distributed to the remaining partners, based on the balances of their capital accounts.[4]

EXERCISES

Exercise F–1

Entry for partner's original investment

Kim Taylor and S. Mondale decide to form a partnership by combining the assets of their separate businesses. Taylor contributes the following assets to the partnership: cash, $11,000; accounts receivable with a face amount of $99,000 and an allowance for doubtful accounts of $6,600; merchandise inventory with a cost of $85,000; and equipment with a cost of $140,000 and accumulated depreciation of $90,000.

The partners agree that $8,000 of the accounts receivable are completely worthless and are not to be accepted by the partnership, that $10,000 is a reasonable allowance

---

[4] The accounting for uncollectible deficiencies of partners is discussed and illustrated in advanced accounting texts.

for the uncollectibility of the remaining accounts, that the merchandise inventory is to be recorded at the current market price of $78,500, and that the equipment is to be valued at $73,400.

Journalize the partnership's entry to record Taylor's investment.

Exercise F–2
Dividing partnership income

✓ e. Still net income, $76,500

Ken Still and Duncan Leif formed a partnership, investing $300,000 and $150,000 respectively. Determine their participation in the year's net income of $150,000 under each of the following independent assumptions: (a) no agreement concerning division of net income; (b) divided in the ratio of original capital investment; (c) interest at the rate of 12% allowed on original investments and the remainder divided in the ratio of 2:3; (d) salary allowances of $60,000 and $75,000 respectively, and the balance divided equally; (e) allowance of interest at the rate of 12% on original investments, salary allowances of $60,000 and $75,000 respectively, and the remainder divided equally.

Exercise F–3
Dividing partnership income

✓ d. Leif net income, $148,500

Determine the participation of Still and Leif in the year's net income of $282,000, according to each of the five assumptions as to income division listed in Exercise F–2.

Exercise F–4
Admitting new partners

Jenny Kirk and Harold Spock are partners who share in the income equally and have capital balances of $90,000 and $62,500, respectively. Kirk, with the consent of Spock, sells one-third of her interest to Benjamin McCoy. What entry is required by the partnership if the sale price is (a) $25,000? (b) $40,000?

Exercise F–5
Admitting new partners who buy an interest and contribute assets

✓ b. Mayer, Capital, $51,000

The capital accounts of Chase Conners and Cindy Wong have balances of $116,000 and $110,000, respectively. Don Mayer and Eric Rodriguez are to be admitted to the partnership. Mayer buys one-fourth of Conner's interest for $32,000 and one-fifth of Wong's interest for $24,000. Rodriguez contributes $110,000 cash to the partnership, for which he is to receive an ownership equity of $90,000. All partners share equally in income.

a. Journalize the entries to record the admission of (1) Mayer and (2) Rodriguez. Mayer is not credited with any of Rodriguez's bonus.
b. What are the capital balances of each partner after the admission of the new partners?

Exercise F–6
Withdrawal of partner

Debbie Jenkins is to retire from the partnership of Jenkins and Associates as of March 31, the end of the current fiscal year. After closing the accounts, the capital balances of the partners are as follows: Debbie Jenkins, $220,000; Jenny Watson, $125,000; and Pierre Periot, $140,000. They have shared net income and net losses in the ratio of 4:3:3. The partners agree that the merchandise inventory should be increased by $36,000, and the allowance for doubtful accounts should be increased by $2,000. Jenkins agrees to accept a note for $120,000 in partial settlement of her ownership equity. The remainder of her claim is to be paid in cash. Watson and Periot are to share equally in the net income or net loss of the new partnership.

Journalize the entries to record (a) the adjustment of the assets to bring them into agreement with current market prices and (b) the withdrawal of Jenkins from the partnership.

Exercise F–7
Distribution of cash upon liquidation

✓ a. $16,000 loss

Ashton and Grant are partners, sharing gains and losses equally. At the time they decide to terminate their partnership, their capital balances are $16,000 and $50,000, respectively. After all noncash assets are sold and all liabilities are paid, there is a cash balance of $50,000.

a. What is the amount of a gain or loss on realization?
b. How should the gain or loss be divided between Ashton and Grant?
c. How should the cash be divided between Ashton and Grant?

Exercise F–8
Liquidating partnerships— capital deficiency

✓ b. $53,500

Parker, Owens, and Dodd share equally in net income and net losses. After the partnership sells all assets for cash, divides the losses on realization, and pays the liabilities, the balances in the capital accounts are as follows: Parker, $20,000 Cr.; Owens, $45,500 Cr.; and Dodd, $12,000 Dr.

a. What term is applied to the debit balance in Dodd's capital account?
b. What is the amount of cash on hand?
c. Journalize the transaction that must take place for Parker and Owens to receive cash in the liquidation process equal to their capital account balances.

Exercise F–9
Distribution of cash upon liquidation

SPREADSHEET

✓ a. Feld net income, $70

D. Martin, K. Chow, and L. E. Feld arranged to import and sell orchid corsages for a university dance. They agreed to share equally the net income or net loss of the venture. Martin and Chow advanced $260 and $140 of their own respective funds to pay for advertising and other expenses. After collecting for all sales and paying creditors, the partnership has $610 in cash.

a. How should the money be distributed?
b. Assuming that the partnership has only $250 cash instead of $610, do any of the three partners have a capital deficiency? If so, how much?

Exercise F–10
Statement of partnership liquidation

✓ Cash distributed to Garcia, $17,500

After closing the accounts on July 1, prior to liquidating the partnership, the capital account balances of Woods, Els, and Garcia are $50,000, $35,000, and $20,000, respectively. Cash, noncash assets, and liabilities total $40,000, $105,000, and $40,000, respectively. Between July 1 and July 29, the noncash assets are sold for $90,000, the liabilities are paid, and the remaining cash is distributed to the partners. The partners share net income and loss in the ratio of 3:2:1. Prepare a statement of partnership liquidation for the period July 1–29, 2003.

PROBLEMS

Problem F–1
Dividing partnership income

✓ 1. f. Norman, $172,100 at $276,000 level

Dawn Norman and Phil Dryer have decided to form a partnership. They have agreed that Norman is to invest $140,000 and that Dryer is to invest $210,000. Norman is to devote full time to the business, and Dryer is to devote one-half time. The following plans for the division of income are being considered:

a. Equal division.
b. In the ratio of original investments.
c. In the ratio of time devoted to the business.
d. Interest of 10% on original investments and the remainder in the ratio of 5:3.
e. Interest of 10% on original investments, salary allowances of $100,000 to Norman and $50,000 to Dryer, and the remainder equally.
f. Plan (e), except that Norman is also to be allowed a bonus equal to 20% of the amount by which net income exceeds the salary allowances.

Instructions
For each plan, determine the division of the net income under each of the following assumptions: (1) net income of $276,000 and (2) net income of $162,000. Present the data in tabular form, using the following columnar headings:

	$276,000		$162,000	
Plan	Norman	Dryer	Norman	Dryer

Problem F–2
Statement of partnership liquidation

SPREADSHEET

✓ 1. d. O'Brien, $13,750

After the accounts are closed on May 10, 2003, prior to liquidating the partnership, the capital accounts of Chris Wendell, Sarah Lawson, and May O'Brien are $56,800, $15,400, and $35,600, respectively. Cash and noncash assets total $21,900 and $142,400, respectively. Amounts owed to creditors total $56,500. The partners share income and losses in the ratio of 2:1:1. Between May 10 and May 30, the noncash assets are sold for $55,000, the partner with the capital deficiency pays his or her deficiency to the partnership, and the liabilities are paid.

Instructions

1. Prepare a statement of partnership liquidation, indicating (a) the sale of assets and division of loss, (b) the receipt of the deficiency (from the appropriate partner), (c) the payment of liabilities, and (d) the cash distributed to the partners.

2. ━━▶ If the partner with the capital deficiency declares bankruptcy and is unable to pay the deficiency, explain how the deficiency would be divided between the partners.

Appendix G

Cisco Systems Inc., Excerpts from 2000 Annual Report

PROFILE

CISCO SYSTEMS, INC. is the worldwide leader in networking for the Internet. Cisco hardware, software, and service offerings are used to create Internet solutions so that individuals, companies, and countries have seamless access to information—regardless of differences in time and place. Cisco solutions provide competitive advantage to our customers through more efficient and timely exchange of information, which in turn leads to cost savings, process efficiencies, and closer relationships with their customers, prospects, business partners, suppliers, and employees. These solutions form the networking foundation for companies, universities, utilities, and government agencies worldwide.

The company was founded in 1984 by a small group of computer scientists from Stanford University seeking an easier way to connect different types of computer systems. Cisco Systems shipped its first product in 1986. Since then, Cisco has grown into a multinational corporation with more than 34,000 employees around the world. We invite you to learn more about Cisco Systems at www.cisco.com.

TABLE OF CONTENTS

This report may contain projections or other forward-looking statements regarding future events or the future financial performance of the Company that involve risks and uncertainties. Readers are cautioned that these forward-looking statements are only predictions and may differ materially from actual future events or results. Readers are referred to the documents filed by Cisco with the Securities and Exchange Commission, specifically the most recent reports on Forms 10-K, 8-K, and 10-Q, including amendments thereto, which identify important risk factors that could cause actual results to differ from those contained in the forward-looking statements, including risks associated with acquisition strategy, dependence on new product offerings, competition, patents, intellectual property and licensing, future growth, rapid technological and market change, manufacturing and sourcing risks, Internet infrastructure and regulation, international operations, volatility of stock price, financial risk management, and potential volatility in operating results, among others.

FINANCIAL HIGHLIGHTS[1]

NET SALES
(Dollars in billions)

NET INCOME
(Dollars in billions)

DILUTED NET INCOME PER SHARE
(In dollars)

CONSOLIDATED STATEMENTS OF OPERATIONS DATA[1]
(In millions, except per-share amounts)

Years Ended	July 29, 2000	July 31, 1999	July 25, 1998
Net sales	$18,928	$12,173	$8,489
Income before provision for income taxes	$ 4,343	$ 3,203	$2,271
Net income	$ 2,668[a]	$ 2,023[b]	$1,331[c]
Net income per common share—diluted*	$ 0.36[a]	$ 0.29[b]	$ 0.20[c]
Shares used in per-common share calculation—diluted*	7,438	7,062	6,658

* Reflects the two-for-one stock split effective March 2000.

[a] Net income and net income per common share include in-process research and development expenses of $1.37 billion, amortization of goodwill and purchased intangible assets of $291 million, acquisition-related costs of $62 million, payroll tax on stock option exercises of $51 million, and net gains realized on minority investments of $531 million. Pro forma net income and diluted net income per common share, excluding these items net of tax of $0, were $3.91 billion and $0.53, respectively.

[b] Net income and net income per common share include in-process research and development expenses of $471 million, amortization of goodwill and purchased intangible assets of $61 million, and acquisition-related costs of $16 million. Pro forma net income and diluted net income per common share, excluding these items net of related tax benefits of $54 million, were $2.52 billion and $0.36, respectively.

[c] Net income and net income per common share include in-process research and development expenses of $594 million, amortization of goodwill and purchased intangible assets of $23 million, and net gains realized on minority investments of $5 million. Pro forma net income and diluted net income per common share, excluding these items net of related tax benefits of $67 million, were $1.88 billion and $0.28, respectively.

CONSOLIDATED BALANCE SHEETS DATA[1]
(In millions)

	July 29, 2000	July 31, 1999	July 25, 1998
Working capital	$ 5,914	$ 1,723	$2,057
Total assets	$32,870	$14,893	$9,043
Shareholders' equity	$26,497	$11,811	$7,197

[1] All historical financial information has been restated to reflect the acquisitions of StratumOne Communications, Inc. and TransMedia Communications, Inc. in the first quarter of fiscal 2000, Cerent Corporation and WebLine Communications Corporation in the second quarter of fiscal 2000, and ArrowPoint Communications, Inc., InfoGear Technology Corporation, and SightPath, Inc. in the fourth quarter of fiscal 2000, which were accounted for as poolings of interests. In addition, the historical financial information has been restated to reflect the acquisition of Fibex Systems, which was completed in the fourth quarter of fiscal 1999 and accounted for as a pooling of interests.

TO OUR SHAREHOLDERS

Over the next two decades, the Internet economy will bring about more dramatic changes in the way we work, live, play, and learn than we witnessed during the last 200 years of the Industrial Revolution. Cisco is well-positioned to help our customers survive the Internet Revolution by turning these changes into competitive advantage. We provide the Internet solutions that will help our customers generate new revenue, reduce costs, increase productivity, and empower their employees.

For the past two years, Cisco has been asking business and government leaders around the world, "Are you ready?" Using our company as an example, our focus has been on educating customers about how effective use of the Internet can increase productivity and revolutionize their business models. Today, our customers are not only ready, but are turning to Cisco to show them how to capture the power of the Internet by implementing open standards-based Internet business models.

During the last decade, our passion has been to increase customer satisfaction and to achieve our stretch goal of maintaining the number-one or -two market share position in every market in which we compete. Today, Cisco holds a leadership position in 16 of our 17 key markets. Cisco's success is the result of our solutions that provide data, voice, and video over a single network and our ability to blend internal development, acquisitions, and partnerships.

Cisco benefited from exceptional returns this past year because we successfully increased our customers' satisfaction. For fiscal 2000, Cisco reported revenue of $18.93 billion, a 55-percent increase when compared with revenue of $12.17 billion in fiscal 1999. Pro forma net income was $3.91 billion or $0.53 per share for fiscal 2000, compared with pro forma net income of $2.52 billion or $0.36 per share for fiscal 1999, increases of 56 percent and 47 percent, respectively. Actual net income for the year was $2.67 billion or $0.36 per share, compared with fiscal 1999 net income of $2.02 billion or $0.29 per share.

Cisco has been one of the fastest-growing and most profitable companies in the history of the computer industry. We are widely accepted as the Internet expert and the Internet company, which is an obvious advantage when we talk to customers about their futures. Our success has been rewarded with one of the highest market capitalizations in the world. This achievement is the result of our commitment to help customers become successful in today's ever-changing, competitive landscape.

The Internet economy has grown more rapidly than even our most optimistic predictions and fuels the strongest period of economic prosperity in history. In the United States alone, this economy added 650,000 jobs and generated revenue in excess of half a trillion dollars in 1999. To put this in perspective, the Internet economy's workforce now surpasses the entire active U.S. military, insurance, communications, and public utilities industries and is twice the size of the airline, chemical and allied products, legal, and real-estate industries.

There is a direct correlation between the strength of this economy and the unprecedented productivity gains we are witnessing today. We refer to this phenomenon as the "Network Effect," which is the result of information technology becoming networked and Internet applications being used to re-engineer business processes. Companies that understand the Network Effect can gain competitive advantage by quickly detecting and responding to situations such as real-time changes in customer demand.

Cisco has become a trusted technology partner and business advisor to many of the largest companies in the world. We are not only a technology advisor, but also an advanced user of Internet technology to run our own business. The adoption of Internet applications in each of Cisco's functional areas is an integral part of our business-planning process and results in tremendous productivity benefits and cost savings. During this past fiscal year, for example, 90 percent of our customer orders were transacted over the Internet. We have created world-class e-commerce, customer support, and workforce optimization applications and are the leader in virtual manufacturing, virtual close, and e-learning solutions.

Our goal is to help customers develop similar, Internet-centric business models so that they can benefit from productivity improvements. For example, our Internet Business Solutions Group has consulted with executives in more than 50 percent of the Fortune 250 companies, 45 percent of the top companies in Europe, the Middle East, Africa, and Asia, and 65 percent of the leading service providers. This group provides business-strategy consulting and helps move our relationships with customers from that of a vendor to a strategic partner.

Successful companies in the 1980s achieved their leadership positions with a vertical business model and an internal focus. In the 1990s, Cisco changed the dynamics of market leadership by focusing on a combination of internal development and acquisitions. This decade, leading companies will develop internally, acquire effectively, and form an "ecosystem" of partnerships in a horizontal, rather than a vertical, business model.

Companies participating in an ecosystem—an open standards-based community that works toward a common goal—will emerge as the market and industry leaders of the future. Customers are the real beneficiaries of our ecosystem model because it allows us to remain agile, quickly enter new markets, and provide both breadth and depth of solutions through the ecosystem community.

In addition to expanding our ecosystem, we also increased our investment in internal product development by 61 percent and continued to grow through acquisitions. Since 1993, we have acquired or announced our intent to acquire 65 companies. Moving forward, our technology strategy will continue to be driven by internal development complemented by acquisitions and strategic alliances.

> **INSIDE CISCO**
>
> Five years ago it took Cisco 14 days to close its books each quarter. Now, with the "virtual close," using powerful Internet technology, Cisco executives have real-time, daily access to company financial information, empowering them and their employees to instantly react to market shifts and changing business requirements.

Following the lead of business, we saw governments from around the world begin to recognize the strong correlation between the Internet and economic success. This past year, we met with government leaders from many countries, including Argentina, Chile, China, France, Germany, Italy, Japan, Jordan, Korea, South Africa, Taiwan, and the United Kingdom. They all realized the Internet's potential impact on their country's future and were eager to learn how to use the Internet more effectively.

The Industrial Revolution of 200 years ago divided society by creating a gap between the "haves" and "have-nots." Today's Internet Revolution has the potential to unite everyone by combining the strength of the Internet and education, the two great equalizers in life. By applying what we've learned in business to all aspects of society, we have the power to use technology to create an Internet gateway that has the potential to positively change people's lives.

Cisco is in a unique position to be a pioneer in embracing this digital opportunity and closing the gap. As such, our philanthropy strategy focuses on education, workforce development, and basic human needs. We continue to invest and grow the Cisco Networking Academy Program, which has enrolled more than 81,000 students in 83 countries. These academies provide networking skills to a broad range of students, including those in high school, community colleges, homeless shelters, and juvenile centers and outgoing military personnel.

In addition, our employees contributed more than $1 million to the Second Harvest Food Bank this past year. Cisco gave more than $2.5 million in grants to our global community and committed another $5 million to Habitat for Humanity over the next five years. We also launched the Netaid.org Web site and movement, a joint initiative with the United Nations Development Program, a number of talented musicians, and several technology companies, to help end the cycle of extreme poverty. Our employees supported additional programs such as the Special Olympics, InnVision, the National Teacher Training Institute, and a variety of global relief efforts. These efforts are Cisco's way of preparing future generations and less-developed nations to participate in the Internet economy.

In our opinion, the radical business transformations taking place around the world will accelerate, making the opportunities ahead of Cisco far greater than ever before. We believe that Cisco has the potential to be the most influential and generous company in history. We are in the fortunate position to be at the center of the Internet economy, and we recognize that although this position gives us confidence, we must balance this confidence with healthy paranoia.

We are proud of our accomplishments and want to thank our shareholders, customers, employees, partners, and suppliers for their continued commitment and confidence in our ability to execute. Together, we are only beginning to explore all that's possible on the Internet.

JOHN T. CHAMBERS
PRESIDENT AND
CHIEF EXECUTIVE OFFICER

JOHN P. MORGRIDGE
CHAIRMAN OF THE BOARD

DONALD T. VALENTINE
VICE CHAIRMAN OF THE BOARD

FINANCIAL REVIEW

SELECTED FINANCIAL DATA[1]

Five Years Ended July 29, 2000 (In millions, except per-share amounts)

	July 29, 2000	July 31, 1999	July 25, 1998	July 26, 1997	July 28, 1996
Net sales	$18,928	$12,173	$8,489	$6,452	$4,101
Net income	$ 2,668[2]	$ 2,023[3]	$1,331[4]	$1,047[5]	$ 915[6]
Net income per common share—basic	$ 0.39	$ 0.30	$ 0.21	$ 0.17	$ 0.16
Net income per common share—diluted	$ 0.36[2]	$ 0.29[3]	$ 0.20[4]	$ 0.17[5]	$ 0.15[6]
Shares used in per-common share calculation—basic*	6,917	6,646	6,312	6,007	5,758
Shares used in per-common share calculation—diluted*	7,438	7,062	6,658	6,287	6,008
Total assets	$32,870	$14,893	$9,043	$5,504	$3,647

* Reflects the two-for-one stock split effective March 2000.

(1) All historical financial information has been restated to reflect the acquisitions that were accounted for as poolings of interests (see Note 3 to the Consolidated Financial Statements).

(2) Net income and net income per common share include in-process research and development expenses of $1.37 billion, amortization of goodwill and purchased intangible assets of $291 million, acquisition-related costs of $62 million, payroll tax on stock option exercises of $51 million, and net gains realized on minority investments of $531 million. Pro forma net income and diluted net income per common share, excluding these items net of tax of $0, were $3.91 billion and $0.53, respectively.

(3) Net income and net income per common share include in-process research and development expenses of $471 million, amortization of goodwill and purchased intangible assets of $61 million, and acquisition-related costs of $16 million. Pro forma net income and diluted net income per common share, excluding these items net of tax benefits of $54 million, were $2.52 billion and $0.36, respectively.

(4) Net income and net income per common share include in-process research and development expenses of $594 million, amortization of goodwill and purchased intangible assets of $23 million, and net gains realized on minority investments of $5 million. Pro forma net income and diluted net income per common share, excluding these items net of tax benefits of $67 million, were $1.88 billion and $0.28, respectively.

(5) Net income and net income per common share include in-process research and development expenses of $508 million, amortization of goodwill and purchased intangible assets of $11 million, and net gains realized on minority investments of $152 million. Pro forma net income and diluted net income per common share, excluding these items net of tax benefits of $7 million, were $1.42 billion and $0.23, respectively.

(6) Net income and net income per common share include amortization of goodwill and purchased intangible assets of $14 million. Pro forma net income and diluted net income per common share, excluding this item net of a tax benefit of $2 million, were $927 million and $0.15, respectively.

MANAGEMENT'S DISCUSSION AND ANALYSIS OF FINANCIAL CONDITION AND RESULTS OF OPERATIONS

All historical financial information has been restated to reflect the acquisitions that were accounted for as poolings of interests (see Note 3 to the Consolidated Financial Statements).

FORWARD-LOOKING STATEMENTS

Certain statements contained in this Annual Report, including, without limitation, statements containing the words "believes," "anticipates," "estimates," "expects," "projections," and words of similar import, constitute "forward-looking statements." You should not place undue reliance on these forward-looking statements. Our actual results could differ materially from those anticipated in these forward-looking statements for many reasons, including risks faced by us described in the Risk Factors sections, among others, included in the documents we file with the Securities and Exchange Commission ("SEC"), including our most recent reports on Form 10-K, Form 8-K, and Form 10-Q, and amendments thereto.

COMPARISON OF FISCAL 2000 AND FISCAL 1999

Net sales in fiscal 2000 were $18.93 billion, compared with $12.17 billion in fiscal 1999, an increase of 55.5%. The increase in net sales was primarily a result of increased unit sales of switch, router, and access products; growth in the sales of add-on boards that provide increased functionality; optical transport products; and maintenance, service, and support sales (see Note 12 to the Consolidated Financial Statements).

We manage our business on four geographic theaters: the Americas; Europe, the Middle East, and Africa ("EMEA"); Asia Pacific; and Japan. Summarized financial information by theater for fiscal 2000 and 1999 is presented in the following table (in millions):

	Amount		Percentage of Net Sales	
Years Ended	July 29, 2000	July 31, 1999	July 29, 2000	July 31, 1999
Net sales:				
Americas	$12,924	$ 8,088	68.3%	66.4%
EMEA	4,770	3,216	25.2	26.4
Asia Pacific	1,705	825	9.0	6.8
Japan	935	566	4.9	4.7
Sales adjustments	(1,406)	(522)	(7.4)	(4.3)
Total	$18,928	$12,173	100.0%	100.0%

The revenue growth for each theater was primarily driven by market demand and the deployment of Internet technologies and business solutions.

Gross margin in fiscal 2000 was 64.4%, compared with 65.0% in fiscal 1999. The following table shows the standard margins for each theater:

Years Ended	July 29, 2000	July 31, 1999
Standard margins:		
Americas	72.8%	72.2%
EMEA	75.1%	74.0%
Asia Pacific	71.3%	71.0%
Japan	78.8%	77.0%

The net sales and standard margins by geographic theater differ from the amounts recognized under generally accepted accounting principles because we do not allocate certain sales adjustments, production overhead, and manufacturing variances and other related costs to the theaters. Sales adjustments relate to revenue deferrals and reserves, credit memos, returns, and other timing differences.

Standard margins increased for all geographic theaters as compared with fiscal 1999. The decrease in the overall gross margin was primarily due to shifts in product mix, introduction of new products, which generally have lower margins when first released, higher production-related costs, the continued pricing pressure seen from competitors in certain product areas, and the above-mentioned sales adjustments, which were not included in the standard margins.

We expect gross margin may be adversely affected by increases in material or labor costs, heightened price competition, increasing levels of services, higher inventory balances, introduction of new products for new high-growth markets, and changes in channels of distribution or in the mix of products sold. We believe gross margin may additionally be impacted due to constraints relating to certain component shortages that currently exist in the supply chain. We may also experience a lower gross margin as the product mix for access and optical product volume grows.

We have recently introduced several new products, with additional new products scheduled to be released in the future. Increase in demand would result in increased manufacturing capacity, which in turn would result in higher inventory balances. In addition, our vendor base is capacity-constrained, and this could result in increased cost pressure on certain components. If product or related warranty costs associated with these new products are greater than we have experienced, gross margin may be adversely affected. Our gross margin may also be impacted by geographic mix, as well as the mix of configurations within each product group. We continue to expand into third-party or indirect-distribution channels, which generally results in a lower gross margin. In addition, increasing third-party and indirect-distribution channels generally results in greater difficulty in forecasting the mix of our product, and to a certain degree, the timing of orders from our customers. Downward pressures on our gross margin may be further impacted by other factors, such as increased percentage of revenue from service provider markets, which may have lower margins or an increase in product costs, which could adversely affect our future operating results.

Research and development ("R&D") expenses in fiscal 2000 were $2.70 billion, compared with $1.66 billion in fiscal 1999, an increase of 62.6%. R&D expenses, as a percentage of net sales, increased to 14.3% in fiscal 2000, compared with 13.7% in fiscal 1999. The increase reflected our ongoing R&D efforts in a wide variety of areas such as data, voice, and video integration, digital subscriber line ("DSL") technologies, cable modem technology, wireless access, dial access, enterprise switching, optical transport, security, network management, and high-end routing technologies, among others. A significant portion of the increase was due to the addition of new personnel, partly through acquisitions, as well as higher expenditures on prototypes and depreciation on additional lab equipment. We also continued to purchase technology in order to bring a broad range of products to the market in a timely fashion. If we believe that we are unable to enter a particular market in a timely manner with internally developed products, we may license technology from other businesses or acquire businesses as an alternative to internal R&D. All of our R&D costs are expensed as incurred. We currently expect that R&D expenses will continue to increase in absolute dollars as we continue to invest in technology to address potential market opportunities.

Sales and marketing expenses in fiscal 2000 were $3.95 billion, compared with $2.46 billion in fiscal 1999, an increase of 60.1%. Sales and marketing expenses, as a percentage of net sales, increased to 20.8% in fiscal 2000, compared with 20.2% in fiscal 1999. The increase was principally due to an increase in the size of our direct sales force and related commissions, additional marketing and advertising investments associated with the introduction of new products, the expansion of distribution channels, and general corporate branding. The increase also reflected our efforts to invest in certain key areas, such as expansion of our end-to-end networking strategy and service provider coverage, in order to be positioned to take advantage of future market opportunities. We currently expect that sales and marketing expenses will continue to increase in absolute dollars.

General and administrative ("G&A") expenses in fiscal 2000 were $633 million, compared with $381 million in fiscal 1999, an increase of 66.1%. G&A expenses, as a percentage of net sales, increased to 3.3% in fiscal 2000, compared with 3.1% in fiscal 1999. G&A expenses for fiscal 2000 and 1999 included acquisition-related costs of approximately $62 million and $16 million, respectively. Excluding the acquisition-related costs, the increase in G&A expenses was primarily related to the addition of new personnel and investments in infrastructure. We intend to keep G&A expenses relatively constant as a percentage of net sales; however, this depends on the level of acquisition activity and our growth, among other factors.

Amortization of goodwill and purchased intangible assets included in operating expenses was $291 million in fiscal 2000, compared with $61 million in fiscal 1999. Amortization of goodwill and purchased intangible assets primarily relates to various purchase acquisitions (see Note 3 and Note 4 to the Consolidated Financial Statements). Amortization of goodwill and purchased intangible assets will continue to increase as we acquire companies and technologies.

MANAGEMENT'S DISCUSSION AND ANALYSIS OF FINANCIAL CONDITION AND RESULTS OF OPERATIONS

The amount expensed to in-process research and development ("in-process R&D") arose from the purchase acquisitions completed in fiscal 2000 (see Note 3 to the Consolidated Financial Statements).

The fair values of the existing products and patents, as well as the technology currently under development, were determined using the income approach, which discounts expected future cash flows to present value. The discount rates used in the present value calculations were typically derived from a weighted-average cost of capital analysis and venture capital surveys, adjusted upward to reflect additional risks inherent in the development life cycle. These risk factors have increased the overall discount rate for acquisitions in the current year. We consider the pricing model for products related to these acquisitions to be standard within the high-technology communications equipment industry. However, we do not expect to achieve a material amount of expense reductions or synergies as a result of integrating the acquired in-process technology. Therefore, the valuation assumptions do not include significant anticipated cost savings.

The development of these technologies remains a significant risk due to the remaining effort to achieve technical viability, rapidly changing customer markets, uncertain standards for new products, and significant competitive threats from numerous companies. The nature of the efforts to develop the acquired technologies into commercially viable products consists principally of planning, designing, and testing activities necessary to determine that the products can meet market expectations, including functionality and technical requirements. Failure to bring these products to market in a timely manner could result in a loss of market share or a lost opportunity to capitalize on emerging markets and could have a material adverse impact on our business and operating results.

The following table summarizes the significant assumptions underlying the valuations for our significant purchase acquisitions completed in fiscal 2000 and 1999 (in millions, except percentages):

| | Acquisition Assumptions | |
Acquired Company	Estimated Cost to Complete Technology at Time of Acquisition	Risk-Adjusted Discount Rate for In-Process R&D
FISCAL 2000		
Monterey Networks, Inc.	$ 4	30.0%
The optical systems business of Pirelli S.p.A.	$ 5	20.0%
Aironet Wireless Communications, Inc.	$ 3	23.5%
Atlantech Technologies	$ 6	37.5%
JetCell, Inc.	$ 7	30.5%
PentaCom, Ltd.	$13	30.0%
Qeyton Systems	$ 6	35.0%
FISCAL 1999		
Summa Four, Inc.	$ 5	25.0%
Clarity Wireless, Inc.	$42	32.0%
Selsius Systems, Inc.	$15	31.0%
PipeLinks, Inc.	$ 5	31.0%
Amteva Technologies	$ 4	35.0%

Regarding our purchase acquisitions completed in fiscal 2000 and 1999, actual results to date have been consistent, in all material respects, with our assumptions at the time of the acquisitions. The assumptions primarily consist of an expected completion date for the in-process projects, estimated costs to complete the projects, and revenue and expense projections once the products have entered the market. Shipment volumes of products from the above-acquired technologies are not material to our overall financial results at the present time. Therefore, it is difficult to determine the accuracy of overall revenue projections early in the technology or product life cycle. Failure to achieve the expected levels of revenue and net income from these products will negatively impact the return on investment expected at the time that the acquisitions were completed and potentially result in impairment of any other assets related to the development activities.

Interest and other income, net, was $577 million in fiscal 2000, compared with $330 million in fiscal 1999. The increase was primarily due to interest income related to the general increase in cash and investments, which was generated from our operations. Net gains realized on minority investments were $531 million in fiscal 2000. The net gains realized on minority investments were not material in fiscal 1999.

Our pro forma effective tax rate for fiscal 2000 was 30.0%. The actual effective tax rate was 38.6%, which included the impact of nondeductible in-process R&D and acquisition-related costs. Our future effective tax rates could be adversely affected if earnings are lower than anticipated in countries where we have lower effective rates or by unfavorable changes in tax laws and regulations. Additionally, we have provided a valuation allowance on certain of our deferred tax assets because of uncertainty regarding their realizability due to expectation of future employee stock option exercises (see Note 11 to the Consolidated Financial Statements).

COMPARISON OF FISCAL 1999 AND FISCAL 1998

Net sales in fiscal 1999 were $12.17 billion, compared with $8.49 billion in fiscal 1998, an increase of 43.4%. The increase in net sales was primarily a result of increased unit sales of LAN switching products, access servers, high-performance WAN switching and routing products, and maintenance service contracts.

Gross margin in fiscal 1999 was 65.0%, compared with 65.6% in fiscal 1998. The decrease in the overall gross margin was primarily due to our continued shift in revenue mix toward our lower-margin products and the continued pricing pressure seen from competitors in certain product areas.

R&D expenses in fiscal 1999 were $1.66 billion, compared with $1.05 billion in fiscal 1998, an increase of 58.1%. R&D expenses, as a percentage of net sales, increased to 13.7% in fiscal 1999, compared with 12.4% in fiscal 1998. The increase reflected our ongoing R&D efforts in a wide variety of areas such as data, voice, and video integration, DSL technologies, cable modem technology, wireless access, dial access, enterprise switching, security, network management, and high-end routing technologies, among others. A significant portion of the increase was due to the addition of new personnel, partly through acquisitions, as well as higher expenditures on prototypes and depreciation on additional lab equipment.

Sales and marketing expenses in fiscal 1999 were $2.46 billion, compared with $1.58 billion in fiscal 1998, an increase of 56.1%. Sales and marketing expenses, as a percentage of net sales, increased to 20.2% in fiscal 1999, compared with 18.6% in fiscal 1998. The increase was principally due to an increase in the size of our direct sales force and related commissions, television advertising campaigns to build brand awareness, additional marketing and advertising costs associated with the introduction of new products, and the expansion of distribution channels. The increase also reflected our efforts to invest in certain key areas, such as expansion of our end-to-end networking strategy and service provider coverage, in order to be positioned to take advantage of future market opportunities.

G&A expenses in fiscal 1999 were $381 million, compared with $247 million in fiscal 1998, an increase of 54.3%. G&A expenses, as a percentage of net sales, increased to 3.1% in fiscal 1999, compared with 2.9% in fiscal 1998. The increase was primarily related to additional personnel and acquisition-related costs of $16 million.

Amortization of goodwill and purchased intangible assets included in operating expenses was $61 million in fiscal 1999, compared with $23 million in fiscal 1998. Amortization of goodwill and purchased intangible assets increased as we acquired companies and technologies.

Interest and other income, net, in fiscal 1999 was $330 million, compared with $196 million in fiscal 1998. Interest income rose primarily as a result of additional investment income on our increased investment balances.

MANAGEMENT'S DISCUSSION AND ANALYSIS OF FINANCIAL CONDITION AND RESULTS OF OPERATIONS

RECENT ACCOUNTING PRONOUNCEMENTS

In June 1998, the Financial Accounting Standards Board ("FASB") issued Statement of Financial Accounting Standards No. 133, "Accounting for Derivative Instruments and Hedging Activities" ("SFAS 133"). SFAS 133, as amended, establishes accounting and reporting standards for derivative instruments and hedging activities. It requires an entity to recognize all derivatives as either assets or liabilities on the balance sheet and measure those instruments at fair value. We do not expect the initial adoption of SFAS 133 to have a material effect on our operations or financial position. We are required to adopt SFAS 133 in the first quarter of fiscal 2001.

In September 1999, the FASB issued Emerging Issues Task Force Topic No. D-83, "Accounting for Payroll Taxes Associated with Stock Option Exercises" ("EITF D-83"). EITF D-83 requires that payroll tax paid on the difference between the exercise price and the fair value of acquired stock in association with an employee's exercise of stock options be recorded as operating expenses. Payroll tax on stock option exercises of $51 million was expensed in fiscal 2000.

In December 1999, the SEC issued Staff Accounting Bulletin No. 101, "Revenue Recognition in Financial Statements" ("SAB 101"). SAB 101, as amended, summarizes certain of the SEC's views in applying generally accepted accounting principles to revenue recognition in financial statements. At this time, we do not expect the adoption of SAB 101 to have a material effect on our operations or financial position; however, the SEC's final guidance for implementation has not been released to date. We are required to adopt SAB 101 in the fourth quarter of fiscal 2001.

LIQUIDITY AND CAPITAL RESOURCES

Cash and cash equivalents, short-term investments, and investments were $20.50 billion at July 29, 2000, an increase of $10.28 billion from July 31, 1999. The increase was primarily a result of $5.00 billion of net unrealized gains on publicly held investments and $7.70 billion of cash generated by operating and financing activities partially offset by investing activities, including net capital expenditures of $1.09 billion, purchases of technology licenses of $444 million, and investments in lease receivables of $535 million.

Accounts receivable increased 83.9% during fiscal 2000. Days sales outstanding in receivables increased to 37 days for fiscal 2000, from 32 days for fiscal 1999. The increase in accounts receivable and days sales outstanding was due, in part, to growth in total net sales combined with conditions in a number of markets, resulting in longer payment terms.

Inventories increased 87.2% during fiscal 2000; however, inventory turns remained constant at 7.8 times. The increase in inventory levels reflected new product introductions, continued growth in our two-tier distribution system, and increased purchases to secure the supply of certain components. Inventory management remains an area of focus as we balance the need to maintain strategic inventory levels to ensure competitive lead times with the risk of inventory obsolescence due to rapidly changing technology and customer requirements.

At July 29, 2000, we had a line of credit totaling $500 million, which expires in July 2002. There have been no borrowings under this agreement (see Note 7 to the Consolidated Financial Statements).

We have entered into several agreements to lease 448 acres of land located in San Jose, California, where our headquarters operations are established, and 759 acres of land located in Boxborough, Massachusetts; Salem, New Hampshire; Richardson, Texas; and Research Triangle Park, North Carolina, where we have expanded certain R&D and customer-support activities. In connection with these transactions, we have pledged $1.29 billion of our investments as collateral for certain obligations of the leases. We anticipate that we will occupy more leased property in the future that will require similar pledged securities, however, we do not expect the impact of this activity to be material to our liquidity position (see Note 8 to the Consolidated Financial Statements).

We believe that our current cash and cash equivalents, short-term investments, line of credit, and cash generated from operations will satisfy our expected working capital, capital expenditure, and investment requirements through at least the next 12 months.

QUANTITATIVE AND QUALITATIVE DISCLOSURES ABOUT MARKET RISK

We maintain an investment portfolio of various holdings, types, and maturities. These securities are generally classified as available for sale and, consequently, are recorded on the balance sheet at fair value with unrealized gains or losses reported as a separate component of accumulated other comprehensive income, net of tax. Part of this portfolio includes minority equity investments in several publicly traded companies, the values of which are subject to market price volatility. For example, as a result of recent market price volatility of our publicly traded equity investments, we experienced a $111 million after-tax unrealized loss during the third quarter of fiscal 2000 and a $1.83 billion after-tax unrealized gain during the fourth quarter of fiscal 2000 on these investments. We have also invested in numerous privately held companies, many of which can still be considered in the start-up or development stages. These investments are inherently risky as the market for the technologies or products they have under development are typically in the early stages and may never materialize. We could lose our entire initial investment in these companies. We also have certain real estate lease commitments with payments tied to short-term interest rates. At any time, a sharp rise in interest rates could have a material adverse impact on the fair value of our investment portfolio while increasing the costs associated with our lease commitments. Conversely, declines in interest rates could have a material impact on interest earnings for our investment portfolio. We do not currently hedge these interest rate exposures.

INVESTMENTS

The following table presents the hypothetical changes in fair values in the financial instruments held at July 29, 2000 that are sensitive to changes in interest rates. These instruments are not leveraged and are held for purposes other than trading. The modeling technique used measures the change in fair values arising from selected potential changes in interest rates. Market changes reflect immediate hypothetical parallel shifts in the yield curve of plus or minus 50 basis points ("BPS"), 100 BPS, and 150 BPS over a 12-month horizon. Beginning fair values represent the principal plus accrued interest and dividends of the interest rate-sensitive financial instruments at July 29, 2000. Ending fair values are the market principal plus accrued interest, dividends, and reinvestment income at a 12-month horizon. The following table estimates the fair value of the portfolio at a 12-month horizon (in millions):

Issuer	Valuation of Securities Given an Interest Rate Decrease of X Basis Points			Fair Value as of July 29, 2000	Valuation of Securities Given an Interest Rate Increase of X Basis Points		
	(150 BPS)	(100 BPS)	(50 BPS)		50 BPS	100 BPS	150 BPS
U.S. government notes and bonds	$2,350	$2,329	$2,307	$2,285	$2,262	$2,240	$2,218
State, municipal, and county government notes and bonds	3,666	3,632	3,598	3,564	3,529	3,494	3,459
Corporate notes and bonds	3,296	3,266	3,235	3,204	3,173	3,141	3,110
Total	$9,312	$9,227	$9,140	$9,053	$8,964	$8,875	$8,787

A 50 BPS move in the Federal Funds Rate has occurred in nine of the last 10 years; a 100 BPS move in the Federal Funds Rate has occurred in six of the last 10 years; and a 150 BPS move in the Federal Funds Rate has occurred in four of the last 10 years.

QUANTITATIVE AND QUALITATIVE DISCLOSURES ABOUT MARKET RISK

The following analysis presents the hypothetical changes in fair values of public equity investments that are sensitive to changes in the stock market. These equity securities are held for purposes other than trading. The modeling technique used measures the hypothetical change in fair values arising from selected hypothetical changes in each stock's price. Stock price fluctuations of plus or minus 15%, plus or minus 35%, and plus or minus 50% were selected based on the probability of their occurrence. The following table estimates the fair value of the publicly traded corporate equities at a 12-month horizon (in millions):

	Valuation of Securities Given X% Decrease in Each Stock's Price			Fair Value as of July 29, 2000	Valuation of Securities Given X% Increase in Each Stock's Price		
	(50%)	(35%)	(15%)		15%	35%	50%
Corporate equities	$3,112	$4,046	$5,291	$6,225	$7,159	$8,404	$9,337

Our equity portfolio consists of securities with characteristics that most closely match the S&P Index or companies traded on the NASDAQ National Market. The NASDAQ Composite Index has shown a 15% movement in each of the last three years and a 35% and 50% movement in at least one of the last three years.

We also have an investment in KPMG Consulting, Inc. in the principal amount of $1.05 billion of Series A Mandatorily Redeemable Convertible Preferred Stock, which carries a 6% dividend rate on the original issue price until converted to common stock. Conversion is at our option upon or after the completion of an initial public offering of KPMG Consulting, Inc. We have not included the investment in the above sensitivity analyses due to the nature of this investment.

LEASES
We are exposed to interest rate risk associated with leases on our facilities where payments are tied to the London Interbank Offered Rate ("LIBOR"). We have evaluated the hypothetical change in lease obligations held at July 29, 2000 due to changes in the LIBOR. The modeling technique used measures hypothetical changes in lease obligations arising from selected hypothetical changes in the LIBOR. The hypothetical market changes reflected immediate parallel shifts in the LIBOR curve of plus or minus 50 BPS, 100 BPS, and 150 BPS over a 12-month period. The results of this analysis were not material in comparison to our financial results.

FOREIGN EXCHANGE FORWARD AND OPTION CONTRACTS
We enter into foreign exchange forward contracts to offset the impact of currency fluctuations on certain nonfunctional currency assets and liabilities, primarily denominated in Australian, Canadian, Japanese, Korean, and several European currencies, primarily the euro and British pound. We also periodically hedge anticipated transactions with purchased currency options.

The foreign exchange forward and option contracts we enter into generally have original maturities ranging from one to three months. We do not enter into foreign exchange forward and option contracts for trading purposes. We do not expect gains or losses on these contracts to have a material impact on our financial results (see Note 8 to the Consolidated Financial Statements).

CONSOLIDATED STATEMENTS OF OPERATIONS
(In millions, except per-share amounts)

Years Ended	July 29, 2000	July 31, 1999	July 25, 1998
NET SALES	$18,928	$12,173	$8,489
Cost of sales	6,746	4,259	2,924
GROSS MARGIN	12,182	7,914	5,565
Operating expenses:			
Research and development	2,704	1,663	1,052
Sales and marketing	3,946	2,465	1,579
General and administrative	633	381	247
Amortization of goodwill and purchased intangible assets	291	61	23
In-process research and development	1,373	471	594
Total operating expenses	8,947	5,041	3,495
OPERATING INCOME	3,235	2,873	2,070
Net gains realized on minority investments	531	–	5
Interest and other income, net	577	330	196
INCOME BEFORE PROVISION FOR INCOME TAXES	4,343	3,203	2,271
Provision for income taxes	1,675	1,180	940
NET INCOME	$ 2,668	$ 2,023	$1,331
Net income per common share—basic	$ 0.39	$ 0.30	$ 0.21
Net income per common share—diluted	$ 0.36	$ 0.29	$ 0.20
Shares used in per-common share calculation—basic	6,917	6,646	6,312
Shares used in per-common share calculation—diluted	7,438	7,062	6,658

See Notes to Consolidated Financial Statements.

CONSOLIDATED BALANCE SHEETS
(In millions, except par value)

	July 29, 2000	July 31, 1999
ASSETS		
Current assets:		
Cash and cash equivalents	$ 4,234	$ 913
Short-term investments	1,291	1,189
Accounts receivable, net of allowances for doubtful accounts of $43 at 2000 and $27 at 1999	2,299	1,250
Inventories, net	1,232	658
Deferred tax assets	1,091	580
Prepaid expenses and other current assets	963	171
Total current assets	11,110	4,761
Investments	13,688	7,032
Restricted investments	1,286	1,080
Property and equipment, net	1,426	825
Goodwill and purchased intangible assets, net	4,087	460
Lease receivables	527	500
Other assets	746	235
TOTAL ASSETS	$32,870	$14,893
LIABILITIES AND SHAREHOLDERS' EQUITY		
Current liabilities:		
Accounts payable	$ 739	$ 374
Income taxes payable	233	630
Accrued compensation	1,317	679
Deferred revenue	1,386	724
Other accrued liabilities	1,521	631
Total current liabilities	5,196	3,038
Commitments and contingencies (Note 8)		
Deferred tax liabilities	1,132	–
Minority interest	45	44
Shareholders' equity:		
Preferred stock, no par value: 5 shares authorized; none issued and outstanding	–	–
Common stock and additional paid-in capital, $0.001 par value: 20,000 shares authorized; 7,138 and 6,821 shares issued and outstanding at 2000 and 1999, respectively	14,609	5,731
Retained earnings	8,358	5,782
Accumulated other comprehensive income	3,530	298
Total shareholders' equity	26,497	11,811
TOTAL LIABILITIES AND SHAREHOLDERS' EQUITY	$32,870	$14,893

See Notes to Consolidated Financial Statements.

CONSOLIDATED STATEMENTS OF CASH FLOWS
(In millions)

Years Ended	July 29, 2000	July 31, 1999	July 25, 1998
Cash flows from operating activities:			
Net income	$ 2,668	$ 2,023	$ 1,331
Adjustments to reconcile net income to net cash provided by operating activities:			
Depreciation and amortization	863	489	329
Provision for doubtful accounts	40	19	43
Provision for inventory allowances	339	151	161
Deferred income taxes	(782)	(247)	(76)
Tax benefits from employee stock option plans	2,495	837	422
Adjustment to conform fiscal year ends of pooled acquisitions	(18)	1	–
In-process research and development	1,279	379	436
Gains on minority investments	(92)	–	–
Change in operating assets and liabilities:			
Accounts receivable	(1,043)	45	(166)
Inventories	(887)	(443)	(267)
Prepaid expenses and other current assets	(249)	(101)	21
Accounts payable	286	111	32
Income taxes payable	(365)	217	155
Accrued compensation	576	285	123
Deferred revenue	662	385	156
Other accrued liabilities	369	174	165
Net cash provided by operating activities	6,141	4,325	2,865
Cash flows from investing activities:			
Purchases of short-term investments	(2,473)	(1,250)	(1,611)
Proceeds from sales and maturities of short-term investments	2,481	1,660	1,751
Purchases of investments	(14,778)	(5,632)	(3,561)
Proceeds from sales and maturities of investments	13,240	1,994	1,107
Purchases of restricted investments	(458)	(1,101)	(527)
Proceeds from sales and maturities of restricted investments	206	560	337
Acquisition of property and equipment	(1,086)	(602)	(429)
Purchases of technology licenses	(444)	(95)	–
Acquisition of businesses, net of cash and cash equivalents	24	(19)	–
Net investment in lease receivables	(535)	(310)	(171)
Other	(554)	(190)	1
Net cash used in investing activities	(4,377)	(4,985)	(3,103)
Cash flows from financing activities:			
Issuance of common stock	1,564	947	555
Other	(7)	7	(7)
Net cash provided by financing activities	1,557	954	548
Net increase in cash and cash equivalents	3,321	294	310
Cash and cash equivalents, beginning of fiscal year	913	619	309
Cash and cash equivalents, end of fiscal year	$ 4,234	$ 913	$ 619

See Notes to Consolidated Financial Statements.

CONSOLIDATED STATEMENTS OF SHAREHOLDERS' EQUITY

(In millions)

	Common Stock Number of Shares	Common Stock and Additional Paid-In Capital	Retained Earnings	Accumulated Other Comprehensive Income	Total Shareholders' Equity
BALANCE AT JULY 26, 1997	6,163	$ 1,814	$2,478	$ 40	$ 4,332
Net income	–	–	1,331	–	1,331
Change in net unrealized gains on investments	–	–	–	28	28
Translation adjustments	–	–	–	(10)	(10)
Comprehensive income	–	–	–	–	1,349
Issuance of common stock	280	555	–	–	555
Tax benefits from employee stock option plans	–	422	–	–	422
Pooling of interests acquisitions	6	12	(9)	–	3
Purchase acquisitions	42	536	–	–	536
BALANCE AT JULY 25, 1998	6,491	3,339	3,800	58	7,197
Net income	–	–	2,023	–	2,023
Change in net unrealized gains on investments	–	–	–	234	234
Translation adjustments	–	–	–	6	6
Comprehensive income	–	–	–	–	2,263
Issuance of common stock	300	947	–	–	947
Tax benefits from employee stock option plans	–	837	–	–	837
Pooling of interests acquisitions	4	38	(42)	–	(4)
Purchase acquisitions	26	570	–	–	570
Adjustment to conform fiscal year ends of pooled acquisitions	–	–	1	–	1
BALANCE AT JULY 31, 1999	6,821	5,731	5,782	298	11,811
Net income	–	–	2,668	–	2,668
Change in net unrealized gains on investments	–	–	–	3,240	3,240
Translation adjustments	–	–	–	(8)	(8)
Comprehensive income	–	–	–	–	5,900
Issuance of common stock	219	1,564	–	–	1,564
Tax benefits from employee stock option plans	–	3,077	–	–	3,077
Pooling of interests acquisitions	20	75	(74)	–	1
Purchase acquisitions	78	4,162	–	–	4,162
Adjustment to conform fiscal year ends of pooled acquisitions	–	–	(18)	–	(18)
BALANCE AT JULY 29, 2000	7,138	$14,609	$8,358	$3,530	$26,497

See Notes to Consolidated Financial Statements.

NOTES TO CONSOLIDATED FINANCIAL STATEMENTS

1. DESCRIPTION OF BUSINESS

Cisco Systems, Inc. and its subsidiaries ("Cisco" or the "Company") is the worldwide leader in networking for the Internet. Cisco hardware, software, and service offerings are used to create Internet solutions so that individuals, companies, and countries have seamless access to information—regardless of differences in time and place. Cisco solutions provide competitive advantage to our customers through more efficient and timely exchange of information, which in turn leads to cost savings, process efficiencies, and closer relationships with their customers, prospects, business partners, suppliers, and employees. These solutions form the networking foundation for companies, universities, utilities, and government agencies worldwide.

2. SUMMARY OF SIGNIFICANT ACCOUNTING POLICIES

Fiscal Year The Company's fiscal year is the 52 or 53 weeks ending on the last Saturday in July. Fiscal 2000, 1999, and 1998 were 52-week, 53-week, and 52-week fiscal years, respectively.

Principles of Consolidation The Consolidated Financial Statements include the accounts of Cisco Systems, Inc. and its subsidiaries. All significant intercompany accounts and transactions have been eliminated.

Cash and Cash Equivalents The Company considers all highly liquid investments purchased with an original or remaining maturity of less than three months at the date of purchase to be cash equivalents. Substantially all cash and cash equivalents are custodied with three major financial institutions.

Investments The Company's investments comprise U.S., state, and municipal government obligations; corporate debt securities; and public corporate equity securities. Investments with maturities of less than one year are considered short-term and are carried at fair value. All investments are primarily held in the Company's name and custodied with two major financial institutions. The specific identification method is used to determine the cost of securities disposed. At July 29, 2000 and July 31, 1999, substantially all of the Company's investments were classified as available for sale. Unrealized gains and losses on these investments are included as a separate component of shareholders' equity, net of any related tax effect.

The Company also has certain other minority investments in nonpublicly traded companies. These investments are included in other assets on the Company's balance sheet and are generally carried at cost. The Company monitors these investments for impairment and makes appropriate reductions in carrying values when necessary.

Inventories Inventories are stated at the lower of cost or market. Cost is computed using standard cost, which approximates actual cost on a first-in, first-out basis.

Restricted Investments Restricted investments consist of U.S. government obligations with maturities of more than one year. These investments are carried at fair value and are restricted as to withdrawal. Restricted investments are held in the Company's name and custodied with two major financial institutions.

Fair Value of Financial Instruments Carrying amounts of certain of the Company's financial instruments, including cash and cash equivalents, accrued compensation, and other accrued liabilities, approximate fair value because of their short maturities. The fair values of investments are determined using quoted market prices for those securities or similar financial instruments.

Concentrations Cash and cash equivalents are primarily maintained with three major financial institutions in the United States. Deposits held with banks may exceed the amount of insurance provided on such deposits. Generally, these deposits may be redeemed upon demand and, therefore, bear minimal risk.

The Company performs ongoing credit evaluations of its customers and, with the exception of certain financing transactions, does not require collateral from its customers.

The Company receives certain of its components from sole suppliers. Additionally, the Company relies on a limited number of hardware manufacturers. The inability of any supplier or manufacturer to fulfill supply requirements of the Company could materially impact future operating results.

NOTES TO CONSOLIDATED FINANCIAL STATEMENTS

Revenue Recognition   The Company generally recognizes product revenue when persuasive evidence of an arrangement exists, delivery has occurred, fee is fixed or determinable, and collectibility is probable. Revenue from service obligations is deferred and generally recognized ratably over the period of the obligation. The Company makes certain sales to partners in two-tier distribution channels. These partners are generally given privileges to return a portion of inventory and participate in various cooperative marketing programs. The Company recognizes revenue to two-tier distributors based on estimates which approximate the point products have been sold by the distributors and also maintains accruals and allowances for all cooperative marketing and other programs. The Company accrues for warranty costs, sales returns, and other allowances based on its experience.

Lease Receivables   Cisco provides a variety of lease financing services to its customers to build, maintain, and upgrade their networks. Lease receivables represent the principal balance remaining in sales-type and direct-financing leases under these programs. These leases typically have two to three year terms and are collateralized by a security interest in the underlying assets.

Advertising Costs   The Company expenses all advertising costs as incurred.

Software Development Costs   Software development costs, which are required to be capitalized pursuant to Statement of Financial Accounting Standards No. 86, "Accounting for the Costs of Computer Software to Be Sold, Leased, or Otherwise Marketed," have not been material to date.

Depreciation and Amortization   Property and equipment are stated at cost less accumulated depreciation and amortization. Depreciation and amortization is computed using the straight-line method over the estimated useful lives of the assets. Estimated useful lives of 24 to 30 months are used on computer equipment and related software and production and engineering equipment and five years for office equipment, furniture, and fixtures. Depreciation and amortization of leasehold improvements is computed using the shorter of the remaining lease term or five years.

Goodwill and Purchased Intangible Assets   Goodwill and purchased intangible assets are carried at cost less accumulated amortization. Amortization is computed using the straight-line method over the economic lives of the respective assets, generally three to five years.

Income Taxes   Income tax expense is based on pre-tax financial accounting income. Deferred tax assets and liabilities are recognized for the expected tax consequences of temporary differences between the tax bases of assets and liabilities and their reported amounts.

Computation of Net Income per Common Share   Basic net income per common share is computed using the weighted-average number of common shares outstanding during the period. Diluted net income per common share is computed using the weighted-average number of common and dilutive common equivalent shares outstanding during the period. Dilutive common equivalent shares consist of stock options. Share and per-common share data for all periods presented reflect the two-for-one stock split effective March 2000.

Foreign Currency Translation   Assets and liabilities of non-U.S. subsidiaries that operate in a local currency environment are translated to U.S. dollars at exchange rates in effect at the balance sheet date with the resulting translation adjustments recorded directly to a separate component of shareholders' equity. Income and expense accounts are translated at average exchange rates during the year. Where the U.S. dollar is the functional currency, translation adjustments are recorded in income.

Derivatives   The Company enters into foreign exchange forward contracts to minimize the short-term impact of foreign currency fluctuations on assets and liabilities denominated in currencies other than the functional currency of the reporting entity. All foreign exchange forward contracts are highly inversely correlated to the hedged items and are designated as, and considered effective as, hedges of the underlying assets or liabilities. Gains and losses on the contracts are included in interest and other income, net, and offset foreign exchange gains or losses from the revaluation of intercompany balances or other current assets and liabilities denominated in currencies other than the functional currency of the reporting entity. Fair values of foreign exchange forward contracts are determined using published rates. If a derivative contract terminates prior to maturity, the investment is shown at its fair value with the resulting gain or loss reflected in interest and other income, net. The Company periodically hedges anticipated transactions with purchased currency options. The premium paid is amortized over the life of the option while any intrinsic value is recognized in income during the same period as the hedged transaction.

Minority Interest   Minority interest represents the preferred stockholders' proportionate share of the equity of Cisco Systems, K.K. (Japan). At July 29, 2000, the Company owned all issued and outstanding common stock amounting to 73.2% of the voting rights. Each share of preferred stock is convertible into one share of common stock at any time at the option of the holder.

Use of Estimates The preparation of financial statements and related disclosures in conformity with accounting principles generally accepted in the United States requires management to make estimates and assumptions that affect the amounts reported in the Consolidated Financial Statements and accompanying notes. Estimates are used for, but not limited to, the accounting for the allowance for doubtful accounts, inventory allowances, depreciation and amortization, sales returns, warranty costs, taxes, and contingencies. Actual results could differ from these estimates.

Impairment of Long-Lived Assets Long-lived assets and certain identifiable intangible assets to be held and used are reviewed for impairment whenever events or changes in circumstances indicate that the carrying amount of such assets may not be recoverable. Determination of recoverability is based on an estimate of undiscounted future cash flows resulting from the use of the asset and its eventual disposition. Measurement of an impairment loss for long-lived assets and certain identifiable intangible assets that management expects to hold and use are based on the fair value of the asset. Long-lived assets and certain identifiable intangible assets to be disposed of are reported at the lower of carrying amount or fair value less costs to sell.

Recent Accounting Pronouncements In June 1998, the Financial Accounting Standards Board ("FASB") issued Statement of Financial Accounting Standards No. 133, "Accounting for Derivative Instruments and Hedging Activities" ("SFAS 133"). SFAS 133, as amended, establishes accounting and reporting standards for derivative instruments and hedging activities. It requires an entity to recognize all derivatives as either assets or liabilities on the balance sheet and measure those instruments at fair value. Management does not expect the initial adoption of SFAS 133 to have a material effect on the Company's operations or financial position. The Company is required to adopt SFAS 133 in the first quarter of fiscal 2001.

In September 1999, the FASB issued Emerging Issues Task Force Topic No. D-83, "Accounting for Payroll Taxes Associated with Stock Option Exercises" ("EITF D-83"). EITF D-83 requires that payroll tax paid on the difference between the exercise price and the fair value of acquired stock in association with an employee's exercise of stock options be recorded as operating expenses. Payroll tax on stock option exercises of $51 million was expensed in fiscal 2000.

In December 1999, the Securities and Exchange Commission ("SEC") issued Staff Accounting Bulletin No. 101, "Revenue Recognition in Financial Statements" ("SAB 101"). SAB 101, as amended, summarizes certain of the SEC's views in applying generally accepted accounting principles to revenue recognition in financial statements. At this time, management does not expect the adoption of SAB 101 to have a material effect on the Company's operations or financial position; however, the SEC's final guidance for implementation has not been released to date. The Company is required to adopt SAB 101 in the fourth quarter of fiscal 2001.

Reclassifications Certain reclassifications have been made to prior year balances in order to conform to the current year presentation.

3. BUSINESS COMBINATIONS

Pooling of Interests Combinations
In fiscal 2000, the Company acquired StratumOne Communications, Inc. ("StratumOne"); TransMedia Communications, Inc. ("TransMedia"); Cerent Corporation ("Cerent"); WebLine Communications Corporation ("WebLine"); SightPath, Inc. ("SightPath"); InfoGear Technology Corporation ("InfoGear"); and ArrowPoint Communications, Inc. ("ArrowPoint"), which were accounted for as poolings of interests. All historical financial information has been restated to reflect these acquisitions. In addition, the historical financial information has been restated to reflect the acquisition of Fibex Systems ("Fibex"), which was completed in the fourth quarter of fiscal 1999 and accounted for as a pooling of interests. These transactions are summarized as follows (in millions):

Acquisition Date	Acquired Company	Shares of Cisco Stock Issued, Including Options Assumed	Fair Value of Acquisition
May 1999	Fibex	11.5	$ 314
September 1999	StratumOne	13.3	$ 435
September 1999	TransMedia	13.9	$ 407
November 1999	Cerent	200.0	$6,900
November 1999	WebLine	8.6	$ 325
May 2000	SightPath	11.4	$ 800
June 2000	InfoGear	4.7	$ 301
June 2000	ArrowPoint	90.2	$5,700

NOTES TO CONSOLIDATED FINANCIAL STATEMENTS

All of these acquired companies used a calendar year end. In order for all companies to operate on the same fiscal year, operations for the one-month period ending July 31, 1999, which were not significant to the Company, have been reflected as an adjustment to retained earnings in fiscal 2000. No significant adjustments were necessary to conform accounting policies. However, the companies' historical results have been adjusted to reflect the elimination of previously provided valuation allowances on deferred tax assets. There were no intercompany transactions requiring elimination in any period presented. The following table shows the historical results for the periods prior to the mergers of these entities (in millions):

	Nine Months Ended April 29, 2000	Years Ended July 31, 1999	Years Ended July 25, 1998
Net sales:			
Cisco	$13,147	$12,154	$8,488
Fibex	–	3	–
StratumOne	–	–	–
TransMedia	–	–	–
Cerent	35	10	–
WebLine	1	3	1
SightPath	–	–	–
InfoGear	–	–	–
ArrowPoint	25	3	–
Total	$13,208	$12,173	$8,489
Net income (loss):			
Cisco	$ 1,932	$ 2,096	$1,355
Fibex	–	(13)	(3)
StratumOne	(3)	(6)	(1)
TransMedia	(4)	(7)	–
Cerent	(15)	(31)	(9)
WebLine	(3)	(4)	(2)
SightPath	(8)	(2)	–
InfoGear	(15)	(5)	(5)
ArrowPoint	(12)	(5)	(4)
Total	$ 1,872	$ 2,023	$1,331

In fiscal 1999, the Company acquired GeoTel Communications Corporation and approximately 68 million shares of common stock were exchanged and options were assumed for a fair value of $2 billion. The transaction was accounted for as a pooling of interests and all periods presented prior to fiscal 1999 were restated.

Other Pooling of Interests Combinations Completed as of July 29, 2000

The Company has also completed a number of other pooling transactions during the three years ended July 29, 2000. The historical operations of these entities were not material to the Company's consolidated operations on either an individual or aggregate basis; therefore, prior period financial statements have not been restated for these acquisitions. These transactions are summarized as follows (in millions):

Fiscal Year	Acquired Company	Shares of Cisco Stock Issued, Including Options Assumed	Fair Value of Acquisition
1998	Precept Software, Inc.	6.0	$ 84
1999	Sentient Networks, Inc.	4.0	$131
2000	Cocom A/S	1.9	$ 66
2000	V-Bits, Inc.	2.8	$128
2000	Growth Networks, Inc.	5.6	$355
2000	Altiga Networks, Inc.	6.3	$335
2000	Compatible Systems Corporation	3.8	$232

Purchase Combinations

During the three years ended July 29, 2000, the Company completed a number of purchase acquisitions. The Consolidated Financial Statements include the operating results of each business from the date of acquisition. Pro forma results of operations have not been presented because the effects of these acquisitions were not material on either an individual or an aggregate basis.

The amounts allocated to in-process research and development ("in-process R&D") were determined through established valuation techniques in the high-technology communications equipment industry and were expensed upon acquisition because technological feasibility had not been established and no future alternative uses existed. Amounts allocated to goodwill and purchased intangible assets are amortized on a straight-line basis over periods not exceeding five years. A summary of purchase transactions is outlined as follows (in millions):

Acquired Company	Consideration	In-Process R&D Expense	Form of Consideration and Other Notes to Acquisition
FISCAL 2000			
Monterey Networks, Inc.	$ 517	$354	Common stock and options assumed; $14 in liabilities assumed; goodwill and other intangibles recorded of $154
The optical systems business of Pirelli S.p.A.	$2,018	$245	Common stock; $362 in liabilities assumed; goodwill and other intangibles recorded of $1,717
Aironet Wireless Communications, Inc.	$ 835	$243	Common stock and options assumed; $34 in liabilities assumed; goodwill and other intangibles recorded of $589
Atlantech Technologies	$ 179	$ 63	Cash of $92; common stock and options assumed; $1 in liabilities assumed; goodwill and other intangibles recorded of $140
JetCell, Inc.	$ 203	$ 88	Cash of $5; common stock and options assumed; $2 in liabilities assumed; goodwill and other intangibles recorded of $137
PentaCom, Ltd.	$ 102	$ 49	Cash of $26; common stock and options assumed; goodwill and other intangibles recorded of $40
Qeyton Systems	$ 887	$260	Common stock; goodwill and other intangibles recorded of $567
Other	$ 228	$ 71	Cash of $31; common stock and options assumed; $5 in liabilities assumed; goodwill and other intangibles recorded of $155
FISCAL 1999			
Summa Four, Inc.	$ 129	$ 64	Common stock and options assumed; $16 in liabilities assumed; goodwill and other intangibles recorded of $29
Clarity Wireless, Inc.	$ 153	$ 94	Common stock and options assumed; goodwill and other intangibles recorded of $73
Selsius Systems, Inc.	$ 134	$ 92	Cash of $111; options assumed; goodwill and other intangibles recorded of $41
PipeLinks, Inc.	$ 118	$ 99	Common stock and options assumed; goodwill and other intangibles recorded of $11
Amteva Technologies, Inc.	$ 159	$ 81	Common stock and options assumed; $9 in liabilities assumed; goodwill and other intangibles recorded of $85
Other	$ 58	$ 41	Common stock and options assumed; goodwill and other intangibles recorded of $18
FISCAL 1998			
Dagaz Technologies, Inc.	$ 130	$127	Cash of $108; $18 in common stock; liabilities assumed of $4
LightSpeed International, Inc.	$ 161	$143	Common stock and options assumed; other intangibles recorded of $15
WheelGroup Corporation	$ 124	$ 97	Common stock and options assumed; goodwill and other intangibles recorded of $38
NetSpeed International, Inc.	$ 252	$179	Cash of $12; common stock and options assumed; liabilities assumed of $18; goodwill and other intangibles recorded of $76
Other	$ 51	$ 48	Cash of $38 and options assumed

NOTES TO CONSOLIDATED FINANCIAL STATEMENTS

Other Purchase Combinations Completed as of July 29, 2000

In fiscal 2000, the Company acquired Maxcomm Technologies, Inc.; Calista, Inc.; Tasmania Network Systems, Inc.; Internet Engineering Group, LLC; Worldwide Data Systems, Inc.; and Seagull Networks, Ltd. for a total purchase price of $228 million, paid in common stock and cash. Total in-process R&D related to these acquisitions amounted to $71 million.

Total in-process R&D expense in fiscal 2000, 1999, and 1998 was $1.37 billion, $471 million, and $594 million, respectively. The in-process R&D expense that was attributable to stock consideration for the same periods was $1.28 billion, $379 million, and $436 million, respectively.

4. BALANCE SHEET DETAIL

The following tables provide details of selected balance sheet items (in millions):

	July 29, 2000	July 31, 1999
INVENTORIES, NET:		
Raw materials	$ 145	$ 143
Work in process	472	198
Finished goods	496	282
Demonstration systems	119	35
Total	$1,232	$ 658
PROPERTY AND EQUIPMENT, NET:		
Leasehold improvements	$ 607	$ 289
Computer equipment and related software	908	639
Production and engineering equipment	407	238
Office equipment, furniture, and fixtures	1,083	685
	3,005	1,851
Less, accumulated depreciation and amortization	(1,579)	(1,026)
Total	$1,426	$ 825
GOODWILL AND PURCHASED INTANGIBLE ASSETS, NET:		
Goodwill	$2,937	$ 157
Purchased intangible assets	1,558	395
	4,495	552
Less, accumulated amortization	(408)	(92)
Total	$4,087	$ 460

The following table presents the details of the amortization of goodwill and purchased intangible assets as reported in the Consolidated Statements of Operations:

Years Ended	July 29, 2000	July 31, 1999	July 25, 1998
Reported as:			
Cost of sales	$ 25	$ 1	$ —
Operating expenses	291	61	23
Total	$316	$62	$23

5. LEASE RECEIVABLES

Lease receivables represent sales-type and direct-financing leases resulting from the sale of the Company's and complementary third-party products and services. These lease arrangements typically have terms from two to three years and are usually collateralized by a security interest in the underlying assets. The net lease receivables are summarized as follows (in millions):

	July 29, 2000	July 31, 1999
Gross lease receivables	$1,310	$663
Unearned income and other reserves	(195)	(83)
Total	1,115	580
Less, current portion	(588)	(80)
Long-term lease receivables, net	$ 527	$500

Contractual maturities of the gross lease receivables at July 29, 2000 were $588 million in fiscal 2001, $354 million in fiscal 2002, $337 million in fiscal 2003, $29 million in fiscal 2004, and $2 million in fiscal 2005. Actual cash collections may differ from the contractual maturities due to early customer buyouts or refinancings. The current portion of lease receivables is included in prepaid expenses and other current assets.

6. INVESTMENTS

The following tables summarize the Company's investments in securities (in millions):

JULY 29, 2000	Amortized Cost	Gross Unrealized Gains	Gross Unrealized Losses	Fair Value
U.S. government notes and bonds	$ 2,317	$ –	$ (32)	$ 2,285
State, municipal, and county government notes and bonds	3,592	13	(41)	3,564
Corporate notes and bonds	3,222	1	(19)	3,204
Corporate equity securities	641	5,621	(37)	6,225
Mandatorily redeemable convertible preferred stock	987	–	–	987
Total	$10,759	$5,635	$(129)	$16,265
Reported as:				
Short-term investments				$ 1,291
Investments				13,688
Restricted investments				1,286
Total				$16,265

JULY 31, 1999	Amortized Cost	Gross Unrealized Gains	Gross Unrealized Losses	Fair Value
U.S. government notes and bonds	$ 2,187	$ –	$ (29)	$ 2,158
State, municipal, and county government notes and bonds	5,177	5	(44)	5,138
Corporate notes and bonds	1,145	–	(17)	1,128
Corporate equity securities	288	615	(26)	877
Total	$ 8,797	$ 620	$(116)	$ 9,301
Reported as:				
Short-term investments				$ 1,189
Investments				7,032
Restricted investments				1,080
Total				$ 9,301

NOTES TO CONSOLIDATED FINANCIAL STATEMENTS

Net gains realized on minority investments were $531 million in fiscal 2000. The net gains realized on minority investments that were attributable to noncash activity were $92 million in fiscal 2000. The net gains realized on minority investments were not material in fiscal 1999 and were $5 million in fiscal 1998.

The following table summarizes debt investment and mandatorily redeemable convertible preferred stock maturities (including restricted investments) at July 29, 2000 (in millions):

	Amortized Cost	Fair Value
Less than one year	$ 1,753	$ 1,744
Due in 1–2 years	1,930	1,922
Due in 2–5 years	4,218	4,161
Due after 5 years	2,217	2,213
Total	$10,118	$10,040

7. LINE OF CREDIT

At July 29, 2000, the Company had a syndicated credit agreement under the terms of which a group of banks committed a maximum of $500 million on an unsecured, revolving basis for borrowings of various maturities. The commitments made under this agreement expire on July 1, 2002. Under the terms of the agreement, borrowings bear interest at a spread over the London Interbank Offered Rate based on certain financial criteria and third-party rating assessments. As of July 29, 2000, this spread was 17.5 basis points. From this spread, a commitment fee of 5.5 basis points is assessed against any undrawn amounts. The agreement includes a single financial covenant that places a variable floor on tangible net worth, as defined, if certain leverage ratios are exceeded. There have been no borrowings under this agreement to date.

8. COMMITMENTS AND CONTINGENCIES

Leases

The Company has entered into several agreements to lease 448 acres of land located in San Jose, California, where it has established its headquarters operations, and 759 acres of land located in Boxborough, Massachusetts; Salem, New Hampshire; Richardson, Texas; and Research Triangle Park, North Carolina, where it has expanded certain research and development and customer-support activities.

All of the leases have initial terms of five to seven years and options to renew for an additional three to five years, subject to certain conditions. At any time during the terms of these leases, the Company may purchase the land. If the Company elects not to purchase the land at the end of each of the leases, the Company has guaranteed a residual value of $624 million.

The Company has also entered into agreements to lease certain buildings standing or to be constructed on the land described above. The lessors of the buildings have committed to fund up to a maximum of $1.40 billion (subject to reductions based on certain conditions in the respective leases) for the construction of the buildings, with the portion of the committed amount actually used to be determined by the Company. Rent obligations for the buildings commenced on various dates and will expire at the same time as the land leases.

The Company has options to renew the building leases for an additional three to five years, subject to certain conditions. The Company may, at its option, purchase the buildings during or at the end of the terms of the leases at approximately the amount expended by the lessors to construct the buildings. If the Company does not exercise the purchase options by the end of the leases, the Company will guarantee a residual value of the buildings as determined at the lease inception date of each agreement (approximately $748 million at July 29, 2000).

As part of the above lease transactions, the Company restricted $1.29 billion of its investment securities as collateral for specified obligations of the lessors under the leases. These investment securities are restricted as to withdrawal and are managed by a third party subject to certain limitations under the Company's investment policy. In addition, the Company must maintain a minimum consolidated tangible net worth, as defined.

The Company also leases office space in Santa Clara, California; Chelmsford, Massachusetts; and for its various U.S. and international sales offices.

Future annual minimum lease payments under all noncancelable operating leases as of July 29, 2000 are as follows (in millions):

Fiscal Year	
2001	$ 302
2002	299
2003	310
2004	251
2005	237
Thereafter	1,506
Total	$2,905

Rent expense totaled $229 million, $123 million, and $90 million for fiscal 2000, 1999, and 1998, respectively.

Foreign Exchange Forward and Option Contracts

The Company conducts business on a global basis in several major currencies. As such, it is exposed to adverse movements in foreign currency exchange rates. The Company enters into foreign exchange forward contracts to reduce the impact of certain currency exposures. These contracts hedge exposures associated with nonfunctional currency assets and liabilities denominated in Australian, Canadian, Japanese, Korean, and several European currencies, primarily the euro and British pound.

The Company does not enter into foreign exchange forward contracts for trading purposes. Gains and losses on the contracts are included in interest and other income, net, and offset foreign exchange gains or losses from the revaluation of intercompany balances or other current assets and liabilities denominated in currencies other than the functional currency of the reporting entity. The Company's foreign exchange forward contracts generally range from one to three months in original maturity.

The Company periodically hedges anticipated transactions with purchased currency options. A purchased currency option's premium is amortized over the life of the option while any intrinsic value is recognized in income during the same period as the hedged transaction. The deferred premium and intrinsic value from hedging anticipated transactions were not material at July 29, 2000. In the unlikely event that the underlying transaction terminates or becomes improbable, the remaining premium or deferred intrinsic value will be recorded in the Consolidated Statements of Operations. The Company does not purchase currency options for trading purposes. Foreign exchange forward and option contracts as of July 29, 2000 are summarized as follows (in millions):

	Notional Amount	Carrying Value	Fair Value
Forward contracts:			
Assets	$1,377	$ (5)	$(15)
Liabilities	$1,500	$12	$ 37
Option contracts:			
Assets	$ 561	$12	$ 14

The Company's foreign exchange forward and option contracts contain credit risk to the extent that its bank counterparties may be unable to meet the terms of the agreements. The Company minimizes such risk by limiting its counterparties to major financial institutions. In addition, the potential risk of loss with any one party resulting from this type of credit risk is monitored. Management does not expect any material losses as a result of default by other parties.

Legal Proceedings

The Company is subject to legal proceedings, claims, and litigation arising in the ordinary course of business. While the outcome of these matters is currently not determinable, management does not expect that the ultimate costs to resolve these matters will have a material adverse effect on the Company's consolidated financial position, results of operations, or cash flows.

NOTES TO CONSOLIDATED FINANCIAL STATEMENTS

9. SHAREHOLDERS' EQUITY

Authorized Shares

On November 10, 1999, the shareholders of the Company approved an increase to the authorized number of shares of common stock from 5.40 billion to 10 billion shares. On March 20, 2000, the Board of Directors of the Company approved an increase to the authorized number of shares of common stock from 10 billion to 20 billion shares relating to the two-for-one stock split distributed on March 22, 2000.

Stock Split

The Board of Directors authorized the splitting of the Company's common stock on a two-for-one basis for shareholders of record on February 22, 2000 and the resulting shares from the split were distributed on March 22, 2000. All references to share and per-share data for all periods presented have been adjusted to give effect to this two-for-one stock split.

Shareholders' Rights Plan

In June 1998, the Board of Directors approved a Shareholders' Rights Plan ("Rights Plan"). The Rights Plan is intended to protect shareholders' rights in the event of an unsolicited takeover attempt. It is not intended to prevent a takeover of the Company on terms that are favorable and fair to all shareholders and will not interfere with a merger approved by the Board of Directors. Each right entitles shareholders to buy a unit equal to a portion of a new share of Series A Preferred Stock of the Company. The rights will be exercisable only if a person or a group acquires or announces a tender or exchange offer to acquire 15% or more of the Company's common stock.

In the event the rights become exercisable, the Rights Plan allows for Cisco shareholders to acquire, at an exercise price of $108 per right owned, stock of the surviving corporation having a market value of $217, whether or not Cisco is the surviving corporation. The rights, which expire in June 2008, are redeemable for $0.00017 per right at the approval of the Board of Directors.

Preferred Stock

Under the terms of the Company's Articles of Incorporation, the Board of Directors may determine the rights, preferences, and terms of the Company's authorized but unissued shares of preferred stock.

Comprehensive Income

The components of comprehensive income, net of tax, are as follows (in millions):

Years Ended	July 29, 2000	July 31, 1999	July 25, 1998
Net income	$2,668	$2,023	$1,331
Other comprehensive income (loss):			
Change in net unrealized gains on investments, net of tax of $1,762, $144, and $17 in fiscal 2000, 1999, and 1998, respectively	3,240	234	25
Reclassification for net unrealized gains previously included in net income, net of tax of $2 in fiscal 1998	—	—	3
Net unrealized gains	3,240	234	28
Change in accumulated translation adjustments	(8)	6	(10)
Total	$5,900	$2,263	$1,349

10. EMPLOYEE BENEFIT PLANS

Employee Stock Purchase Plan

The Company has an Employee Stock Purchase Plan (the "Purchase Plan") under which 222 million shares of common stock have been reserved for issuance. Eligible employees may purchase a limited number of shares of the Company's common stock at 85% of the market value at certain plan-defined dates. The Purchase Plan terminates on January 3, 2005. In fiscal 2000, 1999, and 1998, seven million, 10 million, and 14 million shares, respectively, were issued under the Purchase Plan. At July 29, 2000, 123 million shares were available for issuance under the Purchase Plan.

Employee Stock Option Plans

The Company has two main stock option plans: the 1987 Stock Option Plan (the "Predecessor Plan") and the 1996 Stock Incentive Plan (the "1996 Plan"). The Predecessor Plan was terminated in 1996. All outstanding options under the Predecessor Plan were transferred to the 1996 Plan. However, all outstanding options under the Predecessor Plan continue to be governed by the terms and conditions of the existing option agreements for those grants.

The maximum number of shares under the 1996 Plan was initially limited to the 620 million shares transferred from the Predecessor Plan. However, under the terms of the 1996 Plan, the share reserve increased each December for the three fiscal years beginning with fiscal 1997, by an amount equal to 4.75% of the outstanding shares on the last trading day of the immediately preceding November. In fiscal 1999, the Company's shareholders approved the extension of the automatic share increase provision of the 1996 Plan for an additional three-year period.

Although the Board of Directors has the authority to set other terms, the options are generally 20% or 25% exercisable one year from the date of grant and then ratably over the following 48 or 36 months, respectively. Options issued under the Predecessor Plan generally had terms of four years. New options granted under the 1996 Plan expire no later than nine years from the grant date. A summary of option activity follows (in millions, except per-share amounts):

		Options Outstanding	
	Options Available for Grant	Options	Weighted-Average Exercise Price per Share
BALANCE AT JULY 26, 1997	96	810	$ 4.05
Granted and assumed	(282)	282	10.00
Exercised	–	(168)	2.40
Canceled	48	(48)	4.59
Additional shares reserved	314	–	–
BALANCE AT JULY 25, 1998	176	876	6.25
Granted and assumed	(245)	245	22.22
Exercised	–	(210)	3.09
Canceled	22	(22)	10.85
Additional shares reserved	359	–	–
BALANCE AT JULY 31, 1999	312	889	11.22
Granted and assumed	(295)	295	52.10
Exercised	–	(176)	5.75
Canceled	37	(37)	22.70
Additional shares reserved	339	–	–
BALANCE AT JULY 29, 2000	**393**	**971**	**$24.19**

The Company has, in connection with the acquisitions of various companies, assumed the stock option plans of each acquired company. During fiscal 2000, a total of approximately 31 million shares of the Company's common stock have been reserved for issuance under the assumed plans and the related options are included in the preceding table.

In 1997, the Company adopted a Supplemental Stock Incentive Plan (the "Supplemental Plan") under which options can be granted or shares can be directly issued to eligible employees. Officers and members of the Company's Board of Directors are not eligible to participate in the Supplemental Plan. Nine million shares have been reserved for issuance under the Supplemental Plan, of which 9,000 shares are subject to outstanding options and 66,600 shares have been issued in fiscal 2000.

NOTES TO CONSOLIDATED FINANCIAL STATEMENTS

The following table summarizes information concerning outstanding and exercisable options at July 29, 2000 (in millions, except number of years and per-share amounts):

Range of Exercise Prices	Options Outstanding			Options Exercisable	
	Number Outstanding	Weighted-Average Remaining Contractual Life (in Years)	Weighted-Average Exercise Price per Share	Number Exercisable	Weighted-Average Exercise Price per Share
$ 0.01– 5.56	229	5.20	$ 5.23	188	$ 4.44
5.57–12.27	258	6.16	9.56	162	8.95
12.28–28.61	194	7.49	23.59	63	22.47
28.62–54.53	241	8.34	49.91	5	31.02
54.54–72.56	49	8.64	65.65	–	–
Total	971	6.87	$24.19	418	$ 9.22

At July 31, 1999 and July 25, 1998, approximately 370 million and 312 million outstanding options, respectively, were exercisable. The weighted-average exercise prices for outstanding options were $5.75 and $3.64 at July 31, 1999 and July 25, 1998, respectively.

The Company is required under Statement of Financial Accounting Standards No. 123, "Accounting for Stock-Based Compensation" ("SFAS 123"), to disclose pro forma information regarding option grants made to its employees based on specified valuation techniques that produce estimated compensation charges. These amounts have not been reflected in the Company's Consolidated Statements of Operations because no compensation charge arises when the price of the employees' stock options equals the market value of the underlying stock at the grant date, as in the case of options granted to the Company's employees. Pro forma information under SFAS 123 is as follows (in millions, except per-share amounts):

Years Ended	July 29, 2000	July 31, 1999	July 25, 1998
Net income—as reported	$2,668	$2,023	$1,331
Net income—pro forma	$1,549	$1,487	$1,074
Basic net income per common share—as reported	$ 0.39	$ 0.30	$ 0.21
Diluted net income per common share—as reported	$ 0.36	$ 0.29	$ 0.20
Basic net income per common share—pro forma	$ 0.22	$ 0.22	$ 0.17
Diluted net income per common share—pro forma	$ 0.21	$ 0.21	$ 0.16

The fair value of each option grant is estimated on the date of grant using the Black-Scholes option pricing model with the following weighted-average assumptions:

	Employee Stock Option Plans			Employee Stock Purchase Plan		
	July 29, 2000	July 31, 1999	July 25, 1998	July 29, 2000	July 31, 1999	July 25, 1998
Expected dividend yield	0.0%	0.0%	0.0%	0.0%	0.0%	0.0%
Risk-free interest rate	6.4%	5.1%	5.7%	5.3%	4.9%	5.4%
Expected volatility	33.9%	40.2%	35.6%	43.3%	47.2%	44.8%
Expected life (in years)	3.1	3.1	3.1	0.5	0.5	0.5

The Black-Scholes option pricing model was developed for use in estimating the fair value of traded options that have no vesting restrictions and are fully transferable. In addition, option pricing models require the input of highly subjective assumptions including the expected stock price volatility. The Company uses projected volatility rates which are based upon historical volatility rates trended into future years. Because the Company's employee stock options have characteristics significantly different from those of traded options, and because changes in the subjective input assumptions can materially affect the fair value estimate, in management's opinion, the existing models do not necessarily provide a reliable single measure of the fair value of the Company's options. The weighted-average estimated fair values of employee stock options granted during fiscal 2000, 1999, and 1998 were $19.44, $8.40, and $3.57 per share, respectively.

The above pro forma disclosures under SFAS 123 are also not likely to be representative of the effects on net income and net income per common share in future years, because they do not take into consideration pro forma compensation expense related to grants made prior to fiscal 1996.

Employee 401(k) Plans

The Company sponsors the Cisco Systems, Inc. 401(k) Plan (the "Plan") to provide retirement benefits for its employees. As allowed under Section 401(k) of the Internal Revenue Code, the Plan provides tax-deferred salary deductions for eligible employees. The Company also has other 401(k) plans that it sponsors. These plans arose from acquisitions of other companies and are not material to the Company on either an individual or aggregate basis.

Employees may contribute from 1% to 15% of their annual compensation to the Plan, limited to a maximum annual amount as set periodically by the Internal Revenue Service. The Company matches employee contributions dollar for dollar up to a maximum of $1,500 per year per person. All matching contributions vest immediately. In addition, the Plan provides for discretionary contributions as determined by the Board of Directors. Such contributions to the Plan are allocated among eligible participants in the proportion of their salaries to the total salaries of all participants. The Company's matching contributions to the Plan totaled $34 million, $20 million, and $15 million in fiscal 2000, 1999, and 1998, respectively. No discretionary contributions were made in fiscal 2000, 1999, or 1998.

11. INCOME TAXES

The provision for (benefit from) income taxes consisted of (in millions):

Years Ended	July 29, 2000	July 31, 1999	July 25, 1998
Federal:			
Current	$1,843	$ 1,164	$855
Deferred	(652)	(221)	(54)
	1,191	943	801
State:			
Current	282	112	87
Deferred	(118)	(24)	(8)
	164	88	79
Foreign:			
Current	332	151	74
Deferred	(12)	(2)	(14)
	320	149	60
Total provision for income taxes	$1,675	$ 1,180	$940

NOTES TO CONSOLIDATED FINANCIAL STATEMENTS

The Company paid income taxes of $327 million, $301 million, and $440 million in fiscal 2000, 1999, and 1998, respectively. Income before provision for income taxes consisted of (in millions):

Years Ended	July 29, 2000	July 31, 1999	July 25, 1998
United States	$2,544	$2,092	$1,950
International	1,799	1,111	321
	$4,343	$3,203	$2,271

The items accounting for the difference between income taxes computed at the federal statutory rate and the provision for income taxes consisted of:

Years Ended	July 29, 2000	July 31, 1999	July 25, 1998
Federal statutory rate	35.0%	35.0%	35.0%
Effect of:			
State taxes, net of federal tax benefit	1.9	2.2	2.2
Foreign sales corporation	(1.9)	(1.6)	(2.4)
Foreign income at other than U.S. rates	(1.6)	(1.0)	–
Nondeductible in-process R&D	8.1	3.9	6.4
Tax-exempt interest	(1.8)	(1.9)	(1.6)
Tax credits	(1.6)	(1.2)	(1.4)
Other, net	0.5	1.5	3.2
Total	38.6%	36.9%	41.4%

U.S. income taxes and foreign withholding taxes were not provided for on a cumulative total of approximately $411 million of undistributed earnings for certain non-U.S. subsidiaries. The Company intends to reinvest these earnings indefinitely in operations outside the United States. The components of the deferred tax assets (liabilities) follow (in millions):

	July 29, 2000	July 31, 1999
ASSETS		
Allowance for doubtful accounts and returns	$ 418	$ 185
In-process R&D	265	163
Inventory allowances and capitalization	94	57
Accrued state franchise tax	–	32
Depreciation	41	28
Deferred revenue	177	65
Credits and net operating loss carryforwards	1,023	–
Other	451	256
Gross deferred tax assets	2,469	786
Valuation allowance	(299)	–
Total deferred tax assets	2,170	786
LIABILITIES		
Purchased intangible assets	(257)	(88)
Unrealized gain on investments	(1,954)	(192)
Total deferred tax liabilities	(2,211)	(280)
Total	$ (41)	$ 506

The noncurrent portion of the deferred tax liabilities, which totaled $74 million at July 31, 1999, is included in other assets.

The Company has provided a valuation allowance on certain of its deferred tax assets because of uncertainty regarding their realizability due to expectation of future employee stock option exercises. Deferred tax assets of approximately $963 million at July 29, 2000 pertain to certain tax credits and net operating loss carryforwards resulting from the exercise of employee stock options. When recognized, the tax benefit of these credits and losses will be accounted for as a credit to shareholders' equity rather than as a reduction of the income tax provision.

As of July 29, 2000, the Company's federal and state net operating loss carryforwards for income tax purposes were approximately $496 million and $865 million, respectively. If not utilized, the federal net operating loss carryforwards will begin to expire in fiscal 2020, and the state net operating loss carryforwards will begin to expire in fiscal 2005. As of July 29, 2000, the Company's federal and state tax credit carryforwards for income tax purposes were approximately $678 million and $197 million, respectively. If not utilized, the federal and state tax credit carryforwards will begin to expire in fiscal 2005.

The Company's income taxes payable for federal, state, and foreign purposes have been reduced, and the deferred tax assets increased, by the tax benefits associated with dispositions of employee stock options. The Company receives an income tax benefit calculated as the difference between the fair market value of the stock issued at the time of exercise and the option price, tax effected. These benefits were credited directly to shareholders' equity and amounted to $3.08 billion, $837 million, and $422 million for fiscal 2000, 1999, and 1998, respectively. Benefits reducing taxes payable amounted to $2.49 billion, $837 million, and $422 million for fiscal 2000, 1999, and 1998, respectively. Benefits increasing gross deferred tax assets amounted to $582 million in fiscal 2000.

12. SEGMENT INFORMATION AND MAJOR CUSTOMERS

The Company's operations involve the design, development, manufacture, marketing, and technical support of networking products and services. The Company offers end-to-end networking solutions for its customers. Cisco products include routers, LAN and ATM switches, dial-up access servers, and network-management software. These products, integrated by the Cisco IOS® software, link geographically dispersed LANs, WANs, and IBM networks.

The Company conducts business globally and is managed geographically. The Company's management relies on an internal management system that provides sales and standard cost information by geographic theater. Sales are attributed to a theater based on the ordering location of the customer. The Company's management makes financial decisions and allocates resources based on the information it receives from this internal management system. The Company does not allocate research and development, sales and marketing, or general and administrative expenses to its geographic theaters as management does not use this information to measure the performance of the operating segments. Management does not believe that allocating these expenses is material in evaluating a geographic theater's performance. Information from this internal management system differs from the amounts reported under generally accepted accounting principles due to certain corporate level adjustments not included in the internal management system. These corporate level adjustments are primarily sales adjustments relating to revenue deferrals and reserves, credit memos, returns, and other timing differences. Based on established criteria, the Company has four reportable segments: the Americas; Europe, the Middle East, and Africa ("EMEA"); Asia Pacific; and Japan.

NOTES TO CONSOLIDATED FINANCIAL STATEMENTS

Summarized financial information by theater for fiscal 2000, 1999, and 1998, as taken from the internal management system discussed previously, is as follows (in millions):

Years Ended	July 29, 2000	July 31, 1999	July 25, 1998
Net sales:			
Americas	$12,924	$ 8,088	$5,732
EMEA	4,770	3,216	2,114
Asia Pacific	1,705	825	535
Japan	935	566	459
Sales adjustments	(1,406)	(522)	(351)
Total	$18,928	$12,173	$8,489
Gross margin:			
Americas	$ 9,412	$ 5,836	$4,261
EMEA	3,581	2,380	1,565
Asia Pacific	1,215	586	395
Japan	737	436	340
Standard margins	14,945	9,238	6,561
Sales adjustments	(1,406)	(522)	(351)
Production overhead	(455)	(255)	(207)
Manufacturing variances and other related costs	(902)	(547)	(438)
Total	$12,182	$ 7,914	$5,565

The standard margins by geographic theater differ from the amounts recognized under generally accepted accounting principles because the Company does not allocate certain sales adjustments, production overhead, and manufacturing variances and other related costs to the theaters. The above table reconciles the net sales and standard margins by geographic theater to net sales and gross margin as reported in the Consolidated Statements of Operations by including such adjustments.

Enterprise-wide information provided on geographic sales is based on the ordering location of the customer. Property and equipment information is based on the physical location of the assets. The following table presents net sales and property and equipment information for geographic areas (in millions):

	July 29, 2000	July 31, 1999	July 25,1998
Net sales:			
United States	$12,013	$ 7,454	$5,232
International	8,321	5,241	3,608
Sales adjustments	(1,406)	(522)	(351)
Total	$18,928	$12,173	$8,489
Property and equipment, net:			
United States	$ 1,242	$ 711	$ 537
International	184	114	72
Total	$ 1,426	$ 825	$ 609

The following table presents net sales for groups of similar products and services (in millions):

Years Ended	July 29, 2000	July 31, 1999	July 25, 1998
Net sales:			
Routers	$ 7,611	$ 5,196	$3,856
Switches	7,509	5,167	3,613
Access	2,396	1,127	630
Other	2,818	1,205	741
Sales adjustments	(1,406)	(522)	(351)
Total	$18,928	$12,173	$8,489

Substantially all of the Company's assets at July 29, 2000 and July 31, 1999 were attributable to U.S. operations. In fiscal 2000, 1999, and 1998, no single customer accounted for 10% or more of the Company's net sales.

13. NET INCOME PER COMMON SHARE

The following table presents the calculation of basic and diluted net income per common share (in millions, except per-share amounts):

Years Ended	July 29, 2000	July 31, 1999	July 25, 1998
Net income	$2,668	$2,023	$1,331
Weighted-average shares—basic	6,917	6,646	6,312
Effect of dilutive securities:			
Employee stock options	521	416	346
Weighted-average shares—diluted	7,438	7,062	6,658
Net income per common share—basic	$ 0.39	$ 0.30	$ 0.21
Net income per common share—diluted	$ 0.36	$ 0.29	$ 0.20

14. SUBSEQUENT EVENTS (UNAUDITED)

Pending Business Combinations

The Company announced definitive agreements to acquire HyNEX, Ltd.; Netiverse, Inc.; Komodo Technology, Inc.; NuSpeed Internet Systems, Inc.; IPmobile, Inc.; and PixStream Incorporated for a total purchase price of approximately $1.76 billion, payable in common stock and cash. These acquisitions will be accounted for as purchases and are expected to close in the first quarter of fiscal 2001.

REPORT OF INDEPENDENT ACCOUNTANTS

To the Board of Directors and Shareholders of Cisco Systems, Inc.
In our opinion, the accompanying consolidated balance sheets and the related consolidated statements of operations and of shareholders' equity and of cash flows present fairly, in all material respects, the financial position of Cisco Systems, Inc. and its subsidiaries at July 29, 2000 and July 31, 1999, and the results of their operations and their cash flows for each of the three years in the period ended July 29, 2000, in conformity with accounting principles generally accepted in the United States. These financial statements are the responsibility of the Company's management; our responsibility is to express an opinion on these financial statements based on our audits. We conducted our audits of these statements in accordance with auditing standards generally accepted in the United States, which require that we plan and perform the audit to obtain reasonable assurance about whether the financial statements are free of material misstatement. An audit includes examining, on a test basis, evidence supporting the amounts and disclosures in the financial statements, assessing the accounting principles used and significant estimates made by management, and evaluating the overall financial statement presentation. We believe that our audits provide a reasonable basis for the opinion expressed above.

PricewaterhouseCoopers LLP

San Jose, California
August 8, 2000

SUPPLEMENTARY FINANCIAL DATA[1] (Unaudited)
(In millions, except per-share amounts)

	July 29, 2000	April 29, 2000	Jan. 29, 2000	Oct. 30, 1999	July 31, 1999	May 1, 1999	Jan. 23, 1999	Oct. 24, 1998
Net sales	$5,720	$4,933	$4,357	$3,918	$3,558	$3,172	$2,845	$2,598
Gross margin	$3,662	$3,172	$2,818	$2,530	$2,297	$2,059	$1,857	$1,701
Net income	$ 796[2]	$ 641[3]	$ 816[4]	$ 415[5]	$ 605[6]	$ 632[7]	$ 279[8]	$ 507[9]
Net income per common share—basic*	$ 0.11	$ 0.09	$ 0.12	$ 0.06	$ 0.09	$ 0.09	$ 0.04	$ 0.08
Net income per common share—diluted*	$ 0.11[2]	$ 0.08[3]	$ 0.11[4]	$ 0.06[5]	$ 0.08[6]	$ 0.09[7]	$ 0.04[8]	$ 0.07[9]

* Reflects the two-for-one stock split effective March 2000.

(1) All historical financial information has been restated to reflect the acquisitions that were accounted for as poolings of interests (see Note 3 to the Consolidated Financial Statements).

(2) Net income and net income per common share include in-process research and development expenses of $461 million, payroll tax on stock option exercises of $26 million, amortization of goodwill and purchased intangible assets of $169 million, acquisition-related costs of $37 million, and net gains realized on minority investments of $344 million. Pro forma net income and diluted net income per common share, excluding these items net of tax of $53 million, were $1.20 billion and $0.16, respectively.

(3) Net income and net income per common share include in-process research and development expenses of $488 million, payroll tax on stock option exercises of $25 million, amortization of goodwill and purchased intangible assets of $51 million, and net gains realized on minority investments of $156 million. Pro forma net income and diluted net income per common share, excluding these items net of tax benefits of $44 million, were $1.01 billion and $0.13, respectively.

(4) Net income and net income per common share include in-process research and development expenses of $43 million, amortization of goodwill and purchased intangible assets of $47 million, acquisition-related costs of $25 million, and net gains realized on minority investments of $31 million. Pro forma net income and diluted net income per common share, excluding these items net of tax benefits of $3 million, were $897 million and $0.12, respectively.

(5) Net income and net income per common share include in-process research and development expenses of $381 million and amortization of goodwill and purchased intangible assets of $24 million. Pro forma net income and diluted net income per common share, excluding these items net of tax benefits of $6 million, were $814 million and $0.11, respectively.

(6) Net income and net income per common share include in-process research and development expenses of $81 million, amortization of goodwill and purchased intangible assets of $19 million, and acquisition-related costs of $16 million. Pro forma net income and diluted net income per common share, excluding these items net of tax benefits of $11 million, were $710 million and $0.10, respectively.

(7) Net income and net income per common share include amortization of goodwill and purchased intangible assets of $19 million. Pro forma net income and diluted net income per common share, excluding this item net of a tax benefit of $6 million, were $645 million and $0.09, respectively.

(8) Net income and net income per common share include in-process research and development expenses of $349 million and amortization of goodwill and purchased intangible assets of $12 million. Pro forma net income and diluted net income per common share, excluding these items net of tax benefits of $34 million, were $606 million and $0.09, respectively.

(9) Net income and net income per common share include in-process research and development expenses of $41 million and amortization of goodwill and purchased intangible assets of $11 million. Pro forma net income and diluted net income per common share, excluding these items net of tax benefits of $3 million, were $556 million and $0.08, respectively.

STOCK MARKET INFORMATION

Cisco common stock (NASDAQ symbol CSCO) is traded on the NASDAQ National Market. The following table sets forth the range of high and low closing prices for each period indicated, adjusted to reflect the two-for-one split effective March 2000:

	2000		1999		1998	
	High	Low	High	Low	High	Low
First quarter	$37.00	$29.38	$17.32	$10.97	$ 9.37	$ 7.75
Second quarter	$57.63	$35.00	$26.67	$15.19	$10.05	$ 8.10
Third quarter	$80.06	$54.75	$29.69	$23.78	$12.31	$ 9.44
Fourth quarter	$71.44	$50.55	$33.53	$26.09	$17.20	$11.74

The Company has never paid cash dividends on its common stock and has no present plans to do so. There were approximately 60,150 shareholders of record at July 29, 2000.

Glossary

A

Accelerated depreciation method. A depreciation method that provides for a high depreciation expense in the first year of use of an asset and a gradually declining expense thereafter. (396)

Account. The form used to record additions and deductions for each individual asset, liability, owner's equity, revenue, and expense. (46)

Account form. The form of balance sheet with the assets section presented on the left-hand side and the liabilities and owner's equity sections presented on the right-hand side. (18, 245)

Account payable. A liability created by a purchase made on credit. (13)

Account receivable. A claim against a customer for services rendered or goods sold on credit. (14, 314)

Accounting. The process of identifying, measuring, and communicating economic information to permit informed judgments and decisions by users of the information. (6)

Accounting cycle. The sequence of basic accounting procedures during a fiscal period. (149)

Accounting equation. The expression of the relationship between assets, liabilities, and owner's equity; it is most commonly stated as Assets = Liabilities + Owner's Equity. (11)

Accounting period concept. An accounting principle that requires accounting reports be prepared at periodic intervals. (100)

Accounting system. The methods and procedures used by a business to record and report financial data for use by management and external users. (180)

Accounts payable subsidiary ledger. The subsidiary ledger containing the individual accounts with suppliers (creditors). (187)

Accounts receivable subsidiary ledger. The subsidiary ledger containing the individual accounts with customers (debtors). (187)

Accounts receivable turnover. The relationship between credit sales and accounts receivable. This ratio is computed by dividing net sales on account by the average net accounts receivable. (327, 650)

Accrual basis. A basis of accounting in which revenues are recognized in the period earned, and expenses are recognized in the period incurred in the process of generating revenues. (100)

Accrued expenses. Expenses that have been incurred but not paid. Sometimes called accrued liabilities. (102)

Accrued revenues. Revenues that have been earned but not collected. Sometimes called accrued assets. (102)

Accumulated depreciation account. The contra asset account used to accumulate the depreciation recognized to date on plant assets. (109)

Acid-test ratio. A ratio that measures the "instant" debt-paying ability of a company. Also known as quick ratio. (649)

Adjusted trial balance. The trial balance which is prepared after all the adjusting entries have been posted. Used to verify the equality of the total debit balances and total credit balances before preparing the financial statements. (113)

Adjusting entries. Entries required at the end of an accounting period to bring the ledger up to date. (101)

Adjusting process. The process of updating the accounts at the end of a period. (101)

Administrative expenses (general expenses). Expenses incurred in the administration or general operations of a business. (242)

Aging the receivables. The process of analyzing the accounts receivable and classifying them according to various age groupings, with the due date being the base point for determining age. (320)

Allowance method. A method of accounting for uncollectible receivables, whereby advance provision for the uncollectibles is made. (317)

Amortization. The periodic expense attributed to the decline in usefulness of an intangible asset. (407)

Annuity. A series of equal cash flows at fixed intervals. (542)

Appropriation. The amount of a corporation's retained earnings that has been restricted and therefore is not available for distribution to shareholders as dividends. (518)

Assets. Physical items (tangible) or rights (intangible) that have value and that are owned by the business entity. (11, 46)

Available-for-sale security. A debt or equity security that is not classified as either a held-to-maturity or a trading security. (520)

Average cost method. The method of inventory costing that is based on the assumption that costs should be charged against revenue in accordance with the weighted average unit costs of the items sold. (361)

B

Balance of the account. The amount of difference between the debits and the credits that have been entered into an account. (49)

Balance sheet. A financial statement listing the assets, liabilities, and owner's equity of a business entity as of a specific date. (16)

Bank reconciliation. The analysis that details the items responsible for the difference between the cash balance reported in the bank statement and the balance of the cash account in the ledger. (289)

Betterment. An expenditure that increases operating efficiency or capacity for the remaining useful life of a plant asset. (398)

Bond. A form of interest-bearing note employed by corporations to borrow on a long-term basis. (550)

Bond indenture. The contract between a corporation issuing bonds and the bondholders. (552)

Book value. The amount at which an asset or liability is reported on the balance sheet. Also called basis or carrying value. (395)

Book value of a fixed asset. The difference between the balance of a fixed asset account and its related accumulated depreciation account. (110)

Boot. The cash balance owed the seller when an old asset is traded for a new asset. (402)

Business. An organization in which basic resources (inputs), such as materials and labor, are assembled and processed to provide goods or services (outputs) to customers. (2)

Business entity concept. The concept that accounting applies to individual economic units and that each unit is separate from the persons who supply its assets. (10)

Business stakeholder. A person or entity that has an interest in the economic performance of the business. (4)

Business transaction. The occurrence of an economic event or a condition that must be recorded in the accounting records. (13)

C

Capital expenditures. Costs that add to the usefulness of assets for more than one accounting period. (398)

Capital leases. Leases that treat the leased assets as purchased assets in the accounts. (404)

Carrying amount. The amount at which a long-term investment or a long-term liability is reported on the balance sheet. (561)

Cash. Coins, currency (paper money), checks, money orders, and money on deposit that is available for unrestricted withdrawal from banks or other financial institutions. (280)

Cash basis. A basis of accounting in which revenue is recognized in the period cash is received, and expenses are recognized in the period cash is paid. (100)

Cash dividend. A cash distribution of earnings by a corporation to its shareholders. (488)

Cash equivalents. Highly liquid investments that are usually reported on the balance sheet with cash. (293)

Cash flows from financing activities. The section of the statement of cash flows that reports cash flows from transactions affecting the equity and debt of the entity. (591)

Cash flows from investing activities. The section of the statement of cash flows that reports cash flows from transactions affecting investments in noncurrent assets. (590)

Cash flows from operating activities. The section of the statement of cash flows that reports the cash transactions affecting the determination of net income. (590)

Cash payments journal. The special journal in which all cash payments are recorded. (195)

Cash receipts journal. The special journal in which all cash receipts are recorded. (192)

Cash short and over account. An account which has recorded errors in cash sales or errors in making change causing the amount of actual cash on hand to differ from the beginning amount of cash plus the cash sales for the day. (282)

Chart of accounts. The system of accounts that make up the ledger for a business. (46)

Closing entries. Entries necessary to eliminate the balances of temporary accounts in preparation for the following accounting period. (141)

Common-size statement. A financial statement in which all items are expressed only in relative terms. (645)

Common stock. The basic ownership class of corporate stock. (481)

Comprehensive income. All changes in stockholders' equity during a period, except those resulting from dividends and stockholders' investments. (519)

Consolidated financial statements. Financial statements resulting from combining parent and subsidiary company statements. (526)

Consolidation. The creation of a new corporation by the transfer of assets and liabilities from two or more existing corporations. (525)

Contra accounts. Accounts that are offset against other accounts. (109)

Contra asset. An account that affects an asset account, such as the allowance for uncollectible accounts receivable or accumulated depreciation. (317)

Contract rate. The interest rate specified on a bond; sometimes called the coupon rate of interest. (553)

Controlling account. The account in the general ledger that summarizes the balances of the accounts in a subsidiary ledger. (187)

Copyright. The exclusive right to publish and sell a literary, artistic, or musical composition. (407)

Corporation. A separate legal entity that is organized in accordance with state or federal statutes and in which ownership is divided into shares of stock. (4)

Cost concept. The basis for entering the exchange price, or cost, into the accounting records. (11)

Cost method. A method of accounting for an investment in common stock, by which the investor recognizes as income its share of cash dividends of the investee. (523)

Cost of merchandise sold. The cost of merchandise purchased by a merchandise business and sold. (227)

Credit. (1) The right side of an account; (2) the amount entered on the right side of an account; (3) to enter an amount on the right side of an account. (48)

Credit memorandum. The form issued by a seller to inform a buyer that a credit has been posted to the buyer's account receivable. (234)

Cumulative preferred stock. Preferred stock that is entitled to current and past dividends before dividends may be paid on common stock. (482)

Current assets. Cash or other assets that are expected to be converted to cash or sold or used up, usually within a year or less, through the normal operations of a business. (140)

Current liabilities. Liabilities that will be due within a short time (usually one year or less) and that are to be paid out of current assets. (141)

Current ratio. A financial ratio that is computed by dividing current assets by current liabilities. (151, 648)

D

Debit. (1) The left side of an account; (2) the amount entered on the left side of an account; (3) to enter an amount on the left side of an account. (48)

Debit memorandum. The form issued by a buyer to inform a seller that a debit has been posted to the seller's account payable. (230)

Declining-balance depreciation method. A method of depreciation that provides declining periodic depreciation expense over the estimated life of an asset. (395)

Deferred expenses. Items that are initially recorded as assets but are expected to become expenses over time or through the normal operations of the business. Sometimes called prepaid expenses. (101)

Deferred revenues. Items that are initially recorded as liabilities but are expected to become revenues over

time or through the normal operations of the business. Sometimes called unearned revenues. (101)

Deficit. A debit balance in the retained earnings account. (480)

Defined benefit plan. A pension plan that promises employees a fixed annual pension benefit at retirement, based on years of service and compensation levels. (451)

Defined contribution plan. A pension plan that requires a fixed amount of money to be invested for the employee's behalf during the employee's working years. (450)

Depletion. The cost of metal ores and other minerals removed from the earth. (406)

Depreciation. In a general sense, the decrease in usefulness of fixed assets other than land. In accounting, refers to the systematic allocation of a fixed asset's cost to expense. (109, 391)

Depreciation expense. The portion of the cost of a fixed asset that is recorded as an expense each year of its useful life. (109)

Direct method. A method of reporting the cash flows from operating activities as the net income from operations adjusted for all deferrals of past cash receipts and payments and all accruals of expected future cash receipts and payments. (592)

Direct write-off method. A method of accounting for uncollectible receivables, whereby an expense is recognized only when specific accounts are judged to be uncollectible. (317)

Discontinued operations. The operations of a business segment that has been disposed of. (513)

Discount. The interest deducted from the maturity value of a note. (434); The excess of the face amount of bonds over their issue price. (553); The excess of par value of stock over its sales price. (484)

Discount rate. The rate used in computing the interest to be deducted from the maturity value of a note. (434)

Dishonored note receivable. A note that the maker fails to pay on its due date. (325)

Dividends per share. The cash dividends per common shares commonly used by investors in assessing alternative stock investments, computed by dividing dividends by the number of shares of stock outstanding. (657)

Dividend yield. The rate of return to stockholders in terms of cash dividend distributions. (490)

Doomsday ratio. The ratio of cash and cash equivalents to current liabilities. (294)

Double-entry accounting. A system for recording transactions, based on recording increases and decreases in accounts so that debits always equal credits. (52)

Drawing. The account used to record amounts withdrawn by an owner of a proprietorship. (47)

E

Earnings per share (EPS) on common stock. The profitability ratio of net income available to common shareholders to the number of common shares outstanding. (515, 657)

Effective interest rate method. One method of amortizing a bond discount. Also known as the interest method. (558)

Effective rate of interest. The market rate of interest when bonds are issued. (553)

Electronic funds transfer (EFT). A payment system that uses computerized information rather than paper (money, checks, etc.) to effect a cash transaction. (285)

Elements of internal control. The control environment, risk assessment, control activities, information and communication, and monitoring. (182)

Employee fraud. The intentional act of deceiving an employer for personal gain. (182)

Employee's earnings record. A detailed record of each employee's earnings. (445)

Equity method. A method of accounting for investments in common stock, by which the investment account is adjusted for the investor's share of periodic net income and dividends of the investee. (526)

Equity security. A security that represents ownership in a business, such as stock in a corporation. (520)

Ethics. The moral principles that guide the conduct of individuals. (7)

Expenses. Assets used up or services consumed in the process of generating revenues. (14, 47)

Extraordinary items. Events or transactions that are unusual and infrequent. (514)

Extraordinary repair. An expenditure that increases the useful life of an asset beyond the original estimate. (398)

F

FICA tax. Federal Insurance Contributions Act tax used to finance federal programs for old-age and disability benefits (social security) and health insurance for the aged (Medicare). (439)

Financial accounting. The branch of accounting that is concerned with the recording of transactions using generally accepted accounting principles (GAAP) for a business or other economic unit and with a periodic preparation of various statements from such records. (9)

Financial Accounting Standards Board (FASB). An authoritative body for the development of accounting principles. (10)

First-in, first-out (FIFO) method. A method of inventory costing based on the assumption that the costs of merchandise sold should be charged against revenue in the order in which the costs were incurred. (354)

Fiscal year. The annual accounting period adopted by a business. (149)

Fixed assets. Physical resources that are owned and used by a business and are permanent or have a long life. (109, 390)

FOB (free on board) destination. Terms of agreement between buyer and seller whereby ownership passes when merchandise is received by the buyer, and the seller pays the transportation costs. (236)

FOB (free on board) shipping point. Terms of agreement between buyer and seller whereby ownership passes when merchandise is delivered to the freight carrier, and the buyer pays the transportation costs. (236)

Free cash flow. The amount of operating cash flow remaining after replacing current productive capacity and maintaining current dividends. (587)

Fringe benefits. A variety of employee benefits that may take many forms, including vacations, pension plans, and health, life, and disability insurance. (449)

Future value. The estimated worth in the future of an amount of cash on hand today invested at a fixed rate of interest. (554)

G

General journal. The two-column form used for entries that are otherwise not recorded in special journals. (189)

General ledger. The primary ledger, when used in conjunction with subsidiary ledgers, that contains all of the balance sheet and income statement accounts. (187)

Generally accepted accounting principles (GAAP). Generally accepted guidelines for the preparation of financial statements. (10)

Goodwill. An intangible asset of a business due to such favorable factors as location, product superiority, reputation, and managerial skill. (408)

Gross pay. The total earnings of an employee for a payroll period. (437)

Gross profit. The excess of net sales over the cost of merchandise sold. (227)

Gross profit method. A means of estimating inventory based on the relationship of gross profit to sales. (367)

H

Held-to-maturity securities. Investments in bonds or other debt securities that management intends to hold to their maturity. (566)

Horizontal analysis. Financial analysis that compares an item in a current statement with the same item in prior statements. (71, 642)

I

Income from operations (operating income). The excess of gross profit over total operating expenses. (243)

Income statement. A summary of the revenues and expenses of a business entity for a specific period of time. (16)

Income Summary. The account used in the closing process for transferring the revenue and expense account balances to the retained earnings account at the end of the period. (141)

Indirect method. A method of reporting the cash flows from operating activities as the net income from operations adjusted for all deferrals of past cash receipts and payments and all accruals of expected future cash receipts and payments. (592)

Intangible assets. Long-lived assets that are useful in the operations of a business, are not held for sale, and are without physical qualities. (407)

Internal controls. The detailed policies and procedures used to direct operations, ensure accurate reports, and ensure compliance with laws and regulations. (181)

Inventory shrinkage. Loss of inventory due to shoplifting, employee theft, or errors in recording or counting inventory. (244)

Inventory turnover. A ratio that measures the relationship between the volume of goods (merchandise) sold and the amount of inventory carried during the period. (368, 651)

Investments. The balance sheet caption used to report long-term investments in stocks or bonds not intended as a source of cash in the normal operations of the business. (522)

Invoice. The bill provided by the seller (who refers to it as a sales invoice) to a buyer (who refers to it as a purchase invoice) for items purchased. (228)

J

Journal. The initial record in which the effects of a transaction on accounts are recorded. (49)

Journal entry. The form of recording a transaction in a journal. (50)

Journalizing. The process of recording a transaction in a journal. (50)

L

Last-in, first-out (LIFO) method. A method of inventory costing based on the assumption that the most recent merchandise costs incurred should be charged against revenue. (354)

Ledger. The group of accounts used by a business. (46)

Leverage. The tendency of the rate earned on stockholders' equity to vary from the rate earned on total assets because the amount earned on assets acquired through the use of funds provided by creditors varies from the interest paid to these creditors (655)

Liabilities. Debts owed to outsiders (creditors). (11, 47)

Long-term liabilities. Liabilities that are not due for a long time (usually more than one year). (141)

Loss from operations. The excess of operating expenses over gross profit. (243)

Lower-of-cost-or-market (LCM) method. A method of valuing inventory that reports the inventory at the lower of its cost or current market value (replacement cost). (364)

M

Managerial accounting. The branch of accounting that uses both historical and estimated data in providing information that management uses in conducting daily operations, in planning future operations, and in developing overall business strategies. (9)

Managers. Individuals who the owners have authorized to operate the business. (4)

Manufacturing businesses. A type of business that changes basic inputs into products that are sold to individual customers. (3)

Matching concept. The concept that expenses incurred in generating revenue should be matched against the revenue in determining the net income or net loss for the period. (18, 101)

Materiality concept. A concept of accounting that accounts for items that are deemed significant for a given size of operations. (68)

Maturity value. The amount due (face value plus interest) at the maturity or due date of a note. (324)

Merchandise inventory. Merchandise on hand and available for sale to customers. (227)

Merchandising businesses. A type of business that purchases products from other businesses and sells them to customers. (3)

Merger. The combining of two corporations by the acquisition of the properties of one corporation by another, with the dissolution of one of the corporations. (525)

Minority interest. The portion of a subsidiary corporation's stock that is not owned by the parent corporation. (527)

Multiple-step income statement. An income statement with several sections, subsections, and subtotals. (240)

N

Natural business year. A year that ends when a business's activities have reached the lowest point in its annual operating cycle. (149)

Net income. The amount by which revenues exceed expenses. (18)

Net loss. The amount by which expenses exceed revenues. (18)

Net pay. Gross pay less payroll deductions; the amount the employer is obligated to pay the employee. (437)

Net realizable value. The valuation of an asset at an amount equal to the estimated selling price less any direct cost of disposal. (365)

Nonparticipating preferred stock. Preferred stock with a limited dividend preference. (481)

Notes receivable. A written promise to pay by the maker, representing an amount to be received by the payee. (140, 314)

Number of days' sales in inventory. A measure of the length of time it takes to acquire, sell, and replace the inventory. (368, 651)

Number of days' sales in receivables. An estimate of the length of time the accounts receivable have been outstanding. (327, 650)

Number of times the interest charges are earned. A ratio that measures the risk that interest payments to debtholders will continue to be made if earnings decrease. (566, 653)

O

Objectivity concept. Requires that the accounting records and reports be based upon objective evidence. (11)

Operating leases. Leases that do not meet the criteria for capital leases and thus are accounted for as operating expenses. (404)

Other expense. An expense that cannot be traced directly to operations. (243)

Other income. Revenue from sources other than the primary operating activity of a business. (243)

Outstanding stock. The stock that is in the hands of stockholders. (480)

Owner's equity. The owner's right to the assets of the business after the total liabilities are deducted. (11, 47)

P

Paid-in capital. The capital acquired from stockholders. (479)

Par. The monetary amount printed on a stock certificate. (480)

Parent company. The company owning a majority of the voting stock of another corporation. (526)

Partnership. An unincorporated business owned by two or more individuals. (4)

Patents. Exclusive rights to produce and sell goods with one or more unique features. (407)

Payroll. The total amount earned by employees for a certain period. (436)

Payroll register. A multicolumn form used to assemble and summarize payroll data at the end of each payroll period. (442)

Periodic inventory system. A system of inventory accounting in which only the revenue from sales is recorded each time a sale is made. The cost of merchandise on hand at the end of a period is determined by a detailed listing (physical inventory) of the merchandise on hand. (227)

Perpetual inventory system. A system of inventory accounting in which both the revenue from sales and the cost of merchandise sold are recorded each time a sale is made, so that the records continually disclose the amount of the inventory on hand. (227)

Petty cash fund. A special cash fund used to pay relatively small amounts. (292)

Physical inventory. The detailed listing of merchandise on hand. (227, 351)

Pooling-of-interests method. A method of accounting for an affiliation of two corporations resulting from an exchange of voting stock of one corporation for substantially all the voting stock of the other corporation. (526)

Post-closing trial balance. A trial balance prepared after all of the temporary accounts have been closed. (148)

Posting. The process of transferring debits and credits from a journal to the accounts. (54)

Postretirement benefits. Rights to benefits that employees earn during their term of employment for themselves and their dependents after they retire. (451)

Preferred stock. A class of stock with preferential rights over common stock. (481)

Premium. The excess of the sales price of stock over its par amount. (484, 553)

Prepaid expenses. Purchased commodities or services that have not been used up at the end of an accounting period. (13)

Present value. The estimated worth today of an amount of cash to be received (or paid) in the future. (553)

Present value of an annuity. The sum of the present values of a series of equal cash flows to be received at fixed intervals. (555)

Price-earnings ratio. The ratio, often called the P/E ratio, computed by dividing the market price per share of common stock at a specific date by the company's earnings per share on common stock. (528, 657)

Prior-period adjustments. Corrections of material errors related to a prior period or periods, excluded from the determination of net income. (519)

Proceeds. The net amount available from discounting a note. (434)

Profitability. The ability of a firm to earn income. (647)

Promissory note. A written promise to pay a sum in money on demand or at a definite time. (322)

Property, plant, and equipment. Fixed, or plant, assets that include equipment, machinery, buildings, and land. (140)

Proprietorship. A business owned by one individual. (4)

Purchase method. The accounting method employed when a parent company acquires a controlling share of the voting stock of a subsidiary other than by the exchange of voting common stock. (526)

Purchases discounts. An available discount taken by a buyer for early payment of an invoice. (229)

Purchases journal. The special journal in which all items purchased on account are recorded. (193)

Purchases returns and allowances. Reductions in purchases, resulting from merchandise being returned to the seller or from the seller's reduction in the original purchase price. (230)

Q

Quick ratio. A financial ratio that measures the ability to pay current liabilities within a short period of time. (452)

Quick assets. The sum of cash, receivables, and marketable securities. (649)

R

Rate earned on common stockholders' equity. A measure of profitability computed by dividing net income, reduced by preferred dividend requirements, by common stockholders' equity. (655)

Rate earned on stockholders' equity. A measure of profitability computed by dividing net income by total stockholders' equity. (655)

Rate earned on total assets. A measure of the profitability of assets, computed as net income plus interest expense divided by total average assets. (654)

Ratio of fixed assets to long-term liabilities. A financial ratio that provides a measure indicating the margin of safety to creditors. (409, 652)

Ratio of liabilities to stockholders' equity. The relationship between the total claims of the creditors and owners. (652)

Ratio of net sales to assets. A profitability measure that shows how effectively a firm utilizes its assets. (653)

Receivables. All money claims against other entities, including people, business firms, and other organizations. (314)

Report form. The form of balance sheet with the liabilities and owner's equity sections presented below the assets section. (18, 245)

Residual value. The estimated recoverable cost of a depreciable asset as of the time of its removal from service. (393)

Retail inventory method. A means of estimating inventory based on the relationship of the cost and the retail price of merchandise. (366)

Retained earnings. Net income retained in a corporation. (479)

Revenue. The gross increase in owner's equity as a result of business and professional activities that earn income. (13, 47)

Revenue expenditures. Expenditures that benefit only the current period. (398)

Revenue journal. The special journal in which all sales of services on account are recorded. (189)

Revenue recognition concept. The principle by which revenues are recognized in the period in which they are earned. (100)

S

Sales discounts. An available discount granted by a seller for early payment of an invoice; a contra account to Sales. (233)

Sales returns and allowances. Reductions in sales, resulting from merchandise being returned by customers or from the seller's reduction in the original sales price; a contra account to Sales. (234)

Selling expenses. Expenses incurred directly in the sale of merchandise. (242)

Services businesses. A business providing services rather than products to customers. (3)

Single-step income statement. An income statement in which the total of all expenses is deducted in one step from the total of all revenues. (243)

Sinking fund. Assets set aside in a special fund to be used for a specific purpose. (560)

Slide. The erroneous movement of all digits in a number, one or more spaces to the right or the left, such as writing $542 as $5,420. (69)

Solvency. The ability of a business to pay its debts. (151, 647)

Special journals. Journals designed to be used for recording a single type of transaction. (188)

Stated value. A value approved by the board of directors of a corporation for no-par stock. Similar to par value. (480)

Statement of cash flows. A summary of the major cash receipts and cash payments for a period. (16, 590)

Statement of owner's equity. A summary of the changes in the owner's equity of a business that have occurred during a specific period of time. (16)

Statement of stockholders' equity. A summary of the changes in the stockholders' equity of a corporation that have occurred during a specific period of time. (519)

Stock. Shares of ownership of a corporation. (476)

Stock dividend. Distribution of a company's own stock to its shareholders. (489)

Stock split. A reduction in the par or stated value of a share of common stock and the issuance of a proportionate number of additional shares. (487)

Stockholders. The owners of a corporation. (476)

Stockholders' equity. The equity of the stockholders of a corporation. (479)

Straight-line depreciation method. A method of depreciation that provides for equal periodic depreciation expense over the estimated life of an asset. (394)

Subsidiary company. The corporation that is controlled by a parent company. (526)

Subsidiary ledger. A ledger containing individual accounts with a common characteristic. (187)

Sum-of-the-years-digits depreciation method. A method of depreciation that provides for declining periodic depreciation expense over the estimated life of an asset. (410)

T

T account. A form of account resembling the letter T, showing debits on the left and credits on the right. (48)

Taxable income. The base on which the amount of income tax is determined. (511)

Temporary accounts. Revenue, expense, or income summary accounts that are periodically closed; nominal accounts. (141)

Temporary differences. Differences between income before income tax and taxable income created by items that are recognized in one period for income statement purposes and in another period for tax purposes. Such differences reverse, or turn around, in later years. (511)

Temporary investments. Investments in securities that can be readily sold when cash is needed. (520)

Trade discounts. Special discounts from published list prices offered by sellers to certain classes of buyers. (235)

Trade-in allowance. The amount a seller grants a buyer for a fixed asset that is traded in for a similar asset. (402)

Trademark. A name, term, or symbol used to identify a business and its products. (408)

Trading security. A debt or equity security that management intends to actively trade for profit. (520)

Transposition. The erroneous arrangement of digits in a number, such as writing $542 as $524. (69)

Treasury stock. A corporation's issued stock that has been reacquired. (485)

Trial balance. A summary listing of the titles and balances of the accounts in the ledger. (67)

Two-column journal. An all-purpose general journal. (55)

U

Uncollectible accounts expense. The operating expense incurred because of the failure to collect receivables. (317)

Unearned revenue. The liability created by receiving cash in advance of providing goods or services. (47)

Unit of measure concept. A concept of accounting that requires that economic data be recorded in dollars. (11)

Units-of-production depreciation method. A method of depreciation that provides for depreciation expense based on the expected productive capacity of an asset. (395)

Unrealized holding gain or loss. The difference between the fair market values of the securities and their cost. (521)

V

Vertical analysis. An analysis that compares each item in a current statement witha total amount within the same statement. (114, 645)

Voucher. A document that serves as evidence of authority to pay cash. (283)

Voucher system. Records, methods, and procedures used in verifying and recording liabilities and paying and recording cash payments. (283)

W

Working capital. The excess of the current assets of a business over its current liabilities. (151, 648)

Work sheet. A working paper used to summarize adjusting entries and assist in the preparation of financial statements. (138)

Subject Index

Company Index